WORLD
CIVILIZATIONS

W · W · NORTON & COMPANY · NEW YORK · LONDON

PHILIP LEE RALPH

ROBERT E. LERNER

STANDISH MEACHAM

EDWARD MCNALL BURNS

WORLD CIVILIZATIONS

Their History and Their Culture

VOLUME I / EIGHTH EDITION

PRINTED IN THE UNITED STATES OF AMERICA.

Library of Congress Cataloging-in-Publication Data
Main entry under title:
World civilizations, their history and their culture / Philip Lee Ralph
... [et al.].—8th ed.
    p. cm.
  Includes index.
  1. Civilization—History.   I. Ralph, Philip Lee.
CB69.W67 1991
909—dc20   90-45337
                                              CIP

The text of this book is composed in Bembo
Composition and manufacturing by Kingsport Press

Book design by Antonina Krass
Layout by Ben Gamit

W. W. Norton & Company Inc., 500 Fifth Avenue, New York, N.Y. 10110
W. W. Norton & Company Ltd., 10 Coptic Street, London WC1A 1PU

ISBN   0-393-95915-5

2 3 4 5 6 7 8 9 0

CONTENTS

Part Four   THE EARLY-MODERN WORLD

X

MAPS

XII

ILLUSTRATIONS IN COLOR

(Illustrations appear facing or following the pages indicated)

PREFACE

Edward McNall Burns observed in an earlier preface: "The time has long since passed when modern man could think of the world as consisting of Europe and the United States. Western culture is, of course, primarily a product of European origins. But it has never been that exclusively. Its original foundations were in Southwestern Asia and North Africa. These were supplemented by influences seeping in from India and eventually from China. From India and the Far East the West derived its knowledge of the zero, the compass, gunpowder, silk, cotton, and probably a large number of religious and philosophical concepts."

During the early centuries of the modern era European nations, by virtue of unprecedented advances in science and technology, spread their influence over the entire globe, with revolutionary effects upon the people of Asia and Africa. Large portions of these continents passed under Western domination but the present century has witnessed the beginning of a reversal of this trend. The political and economic ascendence that Europeans and North Americans long maintained has been eroded by the depletion of natural resources, the devastating effect of two world wars, and a frustrating competition between two superpowers striving for global hegemony. Today, as major and even minor nations of Asia enthusiastically enter the mainstream of economic development and technological progress, the West can no longer dictate their destinies, nor can it keep its own destiny separate from that of the rest of the world. The closing years of the past decade were marked by the dissolution of long-standing European and American power structures, an unforeseen development that obscured the future course of international politics, while at the same time offering hope of removing divisive ideological barriers between nations.

The mutual indebtedness of all peoples to one another for whatever progress they have made toward civilization; their increasing political, economic, and cultural interdependence; and their common responsibility for ensuring the survival of the human and all other living species have made traditional parochial curricula obsolete. The scope of education must be broadened to give students a deeper and more realistic vision of the world in which they live. Nowhere is the need more imperative than in the United States, because our nation rose to a position of leadership in the twentieth century against a background of relative isolation and because the requisites for leadership are changing in an increasingly complex world. The complexities of the present age can be successfully dealt with only by examining their roots, and these roots extend in many directions. Almost a decade ago, the president of the Association for Asian Studies reminded its members: "As Asia becomes part of our future, so it also becomes part of our past.... What is needed is painful rethinking, as we assert that the histories of China and India are not an add-on in the curriculum, but a necessity." The same admonition is applicable for the histories of the countries of Latin America, Africa, and other areas too long unfamiliar. Attempts to bridge the differences that separate the world's organized communities must be based not only on a recognition of the distinctive characteristics of these communities but on an understanding of the historic forces that molded them. In the words of the late Canadian historian Herbert Norman, "History is the discipline that makes the whole world kin and is for humanity what memory is for the individual."

This work attempts to present a compact survey of the human race's struggle for civilization from early times to the present. No major area or country has been omitted. Europe, North, Central, and South America, the Commonwealth of Nations, the Middle East, Southeast Asia, Africa, India, China, and Japan have all received appropriate emphasis. Obviously, the history of none of them could be covered in full detail. The aim throughout has been to give the student both an appreciation of the distinctive achievements and limitations of the principal human societies and cultures, and an awareness of their relevance for contemporary problems. Political events are recognized as important, but the facts of political history are presented in relationship to cultural, social, and economic movements. The authors consider the effects of the Industrial Revolutions to be no less important than the Napoleonic Wars. They believe it is of greater value to understand the significance of Buddha, Confucius, Newton, Darwin, and Einstein than it is to be able to name the kings of France. In accordance with this broader conception of history, more space has been given to the teachings of John Locke, Karl Marx, and John Stuart Mill, of Mahatma Gandhi, Mao Zedong, and Leopold Senghor than to the military exploits of Gustavus Adolphus and the Duke of Wellington. If any philosophical bias underlies the narrative, it stems from the conviction that most of human progress thus far has resulted from the growth of intelligence and respect for the rights of man, and that therein lies the chief hope for a better world in the future.

The first edition of *World Civilizations* was published in 1955, the second in 1958, the third in 1964, the fourth in 1969, the fifth in 1974, the sixth in 1982, and the seventh in 1986. Each edition has included the whole of Edward McNall Burns's *Western Civilizations*, except for sections on the non-Western world, which are more fully covered in this work. The sixth, seventh, and eighth editions of *World Civilizations* incorporate *Western Civilizations* as revised for the ninth, tenth, and eleventh editions, respectively, by Robert E. Lerner of Northwestern University and Standish Meacham of University of Texas at Austin. While preserving the distinctive qualities of the Burns text, the authors of *World Civilizations*, utilizing the results of recent scholarship, have sharpened the focus on areas of greatest concern for today's students, including living conditions, the status of women, and the treatment of minority groups in human societies of the past and present. Organizational strategies and interpretive schemes have been revised where the progress of the discipline has dictated such steps. In recent editions this has resulted in dramatic reworkings of the material on the Western world in the Middle Ages and the early-modern era and in the nineteenth and early twentieth centuries. Notable features of the eighth edition are the incorporation in Part One of the exciting recent findings of paleoanthropoligists regarding the earliest human communities, a new treatment of Mesopotamia from a developmental perspective, and a fully rewritten consideration of the history of the Hebrews stressing the magnitude of their influence on subsequent thought and behavior; and, in Part Seven, a careful analysis of the complex changes within European societies and in international relations since the Second World War.

This edition of *World Civilizations* embodies extensive changes throughout. Like its three immediate predecessors it benefits substantially from the contributions of Professor Richard Hull of New York University. Updating and expanding the sections on Africa in Chapters 11, 17, 21, 30, 33 and 38, Professor Hull's narrative provides a concise and informative account of the peoples and major civilizations of the African continent and of their present state.

A fuller treatment of Latin American societies, which began with the seventh edition of *World Civilizations*, has been carried still further and includes a reinterpretation of the earliest civilizations of the New World based on recent discoveries. This edition also incorporates a thoroughly revised presentation of the civilizations of South Asia and the states of the Indian subcontinent. Chapter 5 and sections of Chapters 11, 16, 21, and 37 have been carefully reexamined, reorganized, and expanded in order to give consideration in greater depth to key topics. Current scholarship has also been drawn on to provide a fresh perspective on modern and contemporary China and the changing character of the Chinese Communist revolution. Tracing events to the Middle East crisis that began in August 1990, the text focuses on recent cataclysmic changes in Eastern Europe and the USSR. Chapters 41 and 42 analyze the implications of Mikhail Gorbachev's reversal of Soviet domestic and foreign policies, changing international power relationships, contemporary warmaking and peacemaking, the weakening of ideologies, the insistent problems of the Third World, the social and cultural impact of science and technology, and the challenge of ecology.

In conjunction with textual revisions, the maps and illustrations have received serious attention. Eight new maps have been added and the remaining maps have been amended as necessary. Fully 25 percent of the nearly 1,100 illustrations are new to this edition, having been culled from a wide range of American, Asian, and European archives. The text was the first to include color illustrations and continues to include far more color plates than any other book in the field. In this edition the text is accompanied by a thoroughly revised *Study Guide*, which includes numerous extracts from original and secondary sources, and an entirely new *Instructor's Manual*, with detailed chapter outlines, short-answer and essay questions, and extensive annotated film guides. Additional teaching aids include map transparencies and a computerized test-item file.

In preparing this edition the authors have profited from the assistance and counsel of many individuals, including not only specialists in various fields but also teachers and students who have used the text. Special acknowledgment is due to Loretta Smith (Northwestern University), Carl Petry (Northwestern University), Arelene Wolinski (San Diego Mesa College), Seymour Scheinberg (California State University at Fullerton), William Harris (Columbia University), Richard Saller (University of Chicago), James Stanely (Moody Bible College), Stephen Knoble (Moody Bible College), Richard T. Nolan (Mattatuck Community College), Stephen Ferruolo, Patricia B. Ebrey (University of Illinois), A. N. Galpern (University of Pittsburgh), Martin Katz (University of Alberta), Ronald Toby (University of Illinois), Gert Wendelborn (University of Rostock, Germany), Stephen F. Dale (Ohio State University), James J. Sheehan (Stanford Unversity), Allen Cronenberg (Auburn University), James Boyden (University of Texas), Peter Hayes (Northwestern University), George Robb (Northwestern University), and Deeana Copeland.

For this edition, as for the fifth, sixth, and seventh, Robert E. Kehoe of W. W. Norton & Company has been a scrupulous editor, indispensable adviser, and faithful co-worker. His unflagging and enthusiastic devotion to the project has contributed greatly to its realization. Photo researcher Deborah Malmud was most resourceful in securing elusive illustrations, and makeup artist Ben Gamit arranged the closely coordinated illustrations and text with panache. Last but not least, I am grateful to my wife, Louise Conkling Ralph, for constructive suggestions on style and for typing the manuscript.

Philp Lee Ralph

WORLD
CIVILIZATIONS

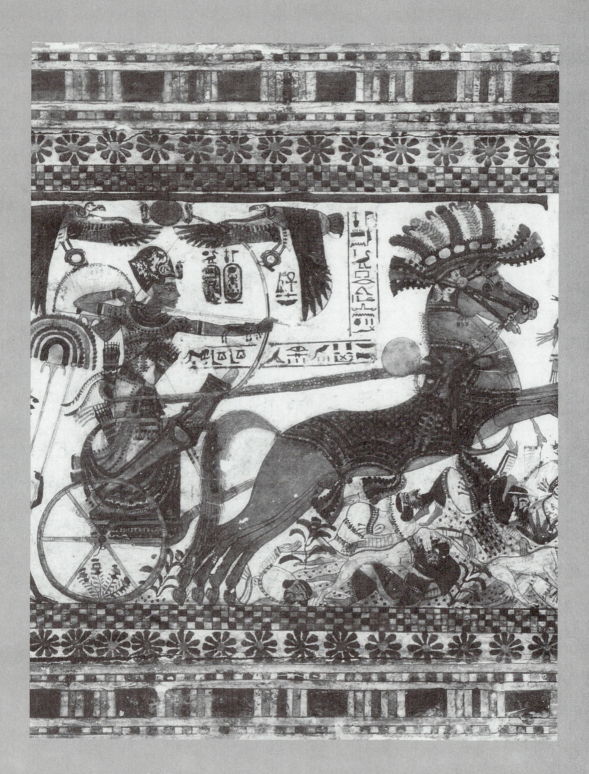

Part One

THE DAWN OF HISTORY

Our story—the human story—begins about two million years ago in Africa. Very recent field research has demonstrated that the earliest "humanlike" species was that of an upright, large-brained primate who foraged for food on the African savannahs some twenty thousand centuries before today. Four hundred thousand years later humanlike creatures began migrating out of Africa, and during the next million and a quarter years such creatures— spread throughout the Eastern Hemisphere—learned how to use fire and to communicate with each other by means of speech. "Neanderthal" peoples followed on the evolutionary chain, and then, around 40,000 years ago, peoples who were fully modern humans from the anatomical point of view. These earliest humans colonized America and Australia and also painted beautiful murals on the walls of western European caves. With the invention of agriculture in western Asia about 10,000 years ago came a dramatic change in the entire nature of human existence, for humans engaged in agriculture stopped being wanderers and settled instead in villages. Sedentary life led "rapidly" (over the course of about 5,000 years) to civilization— government, writing, arts, and sciences on the one hand; war, social inequalities, and oppression on the other. The earliest Western civilizations emerged in Mesopotamia around 3200 B.C. Thereafter, until about 600 B.C., the most prominent civilizations outside of eastern Asia and America were those of the Mesopotamians, Egyptians, Hebrews, Minoans, and Mycenaeans.

If we imagine the entire length of time when "humanlike" creatures and humans inhabited the earth as lasting one hour, then humans biologically like ourselves have been on earth only during the last minute. Seen in terms of the face of a clock the earliest humanlike creature (*Homo habilis*) appears at the beginning of the "hour," that is, 2 million years ago. *Homo erectus* follows "twelve minutes" later (1.6 million years ago) and endures until "nine minutes" before the end of the hour (300,000 years ago). During the last "nine minutes," archaic *Homo sapiens* predominates for the first five minutes (300,000 to 125,000 years ago), and Neanderthal humans for the following three minutes (125,000 to 40,000 years ago), leaving the "last minute" for anatomically modern humans.

Chapter 1

THE EARLIEST BEGINNINGS

What is particularly interesting about our species? For a start, we walk upright on our hindlegs at all times, which is an extremely unusual way of getting around for a mammal. There are also several unusual features about our head, not least of which is the very large brain it contains. . . . Our forelimbs, being freed from helping us to get about, possess a very high degree of manipulative skill. Part of this skill lies in the anatomical structure of the hands, but the crucial element is, of course, the power of the brain. . . . The most obvious product of our hands and brains is technology. No other animal manipulates the world in the extensive and arbitrary way that humans do. The termites are capable of constructing intricately structured mounds which create their own "air-conditioned" environment inside. But the termites cannot choose to build a cathedral instead. Humans are unique because they have the capacity to choose what they do.

—Richard E. Leakey, *The Making of Mankind*

1. THE NATURE OF HISTORY

Catherine Morland, the heroine of Jane Austen's novel *Northanger Abbey,* complained that history "tells me nothing that does not either vex or weary me. The quarrels of popes and kings, with wars or pestilences in every page; the men all so good for nothing, and hardly any women at all, it is very tiresome." Although Jane Austen's heroine said this around 1800, she might have lodged the same complaint until quite recently, for until deep into the twentieth century most historians considered history to be little more than "past politics"—and a dry chronicle of past politics at that. The content of history was restricted primarily to battles and treaties, the personalities and politics of statesmen, the laws and decrees of rulers. But important as such data are, they by no means constitute the whole substance of history. Especially within the last few decades historians have come to recognize that history comprises a record of past human activities in every sphere—not just political developments, but also social, economic, and intellectual ones. Women as well as men, the ruled as

History more than battles and treaties

well as the rulers, the poor as well as the rich, are part of history. So too are the social and economic institutions that men and women have created and that in turn have shaped their lives: family and social class; manorialism and city life; capitalism and industrialism. Ideas and attitudes too, not just of intellectuals but also of people whose lives may have been virtually untouched by "great books," are all part of the historian's concern. And most important, history includes an inquiry into the causes of events and patterns of human organization and ideas—a search for the forces that impelled humanity toward its great undertakings, and the reasons for its successes and failures.

New historical methods

As historians have extended the compass of their work, they have also equipped themselves with new methods and tools, the better to practice their craft. No longer do historians merely pore over the same old chronicles and documents to ask whether Charles the Fat was at Ingelheim or Lustnau on July 1, 887. To introduce the evidence of statistics they learn the methods of the computer scientist. To interpret the effect of a rise in the cost of living, they study economics. To deduce marriage patterns or evaluate the effect upon an entire population of wars and plagues, they master the skills of the demographer. To explore the phenomena of cave-dwelling or modern urbanization, they become archeologists, studying fossil remains, fragments of pots, or modern city landscapes. To understand the motives of the men and women who have acted in the past, they draw on the insights of social psychologists and cultural anthropologists. To illuminate the lives and thoughts of those who have left few or no written records, they look for other cultural remains such as folk songs, folk tales, and funerary monuments.

Limited evidence and the quest for valid reconstructions

Of course with all their ingenuity historians cannot create evidence. An almost infinite number of past events are not retrievable because they transpired without leaving any traces; many others are at best known imperfectly. Thus some of the most fundamental questions about "how things were" in the past cân either never be answered or answered only on the grounds of highly qualified inferences. Questions regarding motives and causes may not have definitive answers for other reasons. Since individual humans often hardly understand their own motives it is presumptuous to think that anyone can ever be entirely certain about establishing the motives of others. As for the causes of collective developments such as wars, economic growth trends, or changes in artistic styles, these are surely too complex to be reduced to a science. Nonetheless, the more evidence we have, the closer we come to providing valid reconstructions and explanations about what happened in the past. Moreover, the difficulties inherent in adducing and interpreting all sorts of data for the purposes of historical analysis should not be regarded with despair but looked upon as stimulating intellectual challenges.

Should we go to the past to celebrate one or another lost age or seek to learn how we got to be the way we are now? Obviously neither one of these extremes is satisfactory, for nostalgia almost invariably leads to distortion, and at any rate is useless, whereas extreme "present-mindedness" also leads to distortion, and at any rate is foolish in its assumption that everything we do now is better than whatever people did before. It seems best, then, to avoid either revering the past or condescending to it. Instead many historians seek to understand how people of a given era strove to solve their problems and live their lives fruitfully in terms appropriate to their particular environments and stages of development. Other historians alternatively look for change over time without postulating a march of progress to a current best of all possible worlds. Such historians believe (and let us hope they may be right) that identifying patterns and mechanisms of change will allow a better understanding of the present and a greater possibility of plotting prudent strategies for coping with the future.

Approaches to history

2. OUT OF AFRICA

The study of the earliest phases of human history, known as paleoanthropology, or human paleontology, has been revolutionized in the second half of the twentieth century by a series of momentous fossil discoveries made in East Africa. Before these finds paleoanthropologists assumed that humankind originated in Southeast Asia, whereas now they know the site of human origins was in Africa; and before then they thought that the earliest humanlike creatures originated about one million years ago, but now they double that figure.

Paleoanthropology transformed by fossil discoveries in East Africa

Many of the most sensational East African fossil discoveries were accomplished by a remarkable family of British paleoanthropologists, the Leakeys, and the others probably would have not been achieved without the Leakeys' initial impetus. Louis Leakey (1903–1972), the son of a British missionary in Kenya, decided early in life to search for fossil traces of early humanity in East Africa, a pursuit then considered by most experts to be foolhardy. (An individualist, Leakey continued to amaze many observers until shortly before his death by stalking African animals without any weapons in order to gain insights into how primeval human ancestors managed to survive.) In 1931 Leakey satisfied himself that he was on the right track in his fossil hunting by his discovery in Tanzania (then Tanganyika) of primitive handaxes fashioned by a species of early man approximately one million years ago. Impeded by other professional responsibilities and a lack of funds, he made little progress in his fossil research for more than a quarter-century thereafter. Then, in 1959, an enormous breakthrough was made not by Louis Leakey himself but by his wife and co-investigator Mary Leakey. Searching through a Tanzanian site in that year, Mary discovered some seemingly humanlike teeth and cranial bone fragments; when she put all her fragments in place and confirmed their

The work of the Leakey family

Mary, Louis, and Richard Leakey Hunting for Fossils. This photograph, taken in 1966, shows the three Leakeys (first, fourth, and fifth from the left) searching for fossil treasures in Kenya.

Homo Habilis Skull. A skull of our oldest known humanlike ancestor reconstructed from fossil remains dating from 1.8 million years ago.

The rapid pace of discovery in East Africa in the 1970s and 1980s

dating, it turned out that she had a nearly complete skull of a creature vaguely like a human who lived 1.8 million years ago. Because of the skull's huge jaw and large teeth the press quickly dubbed Mary's find "Nutcracker Man."

In fact Nutcracker Man was not a man but an advanced species of ape that walked erect. Recognizing this themselves, Louis and Mary Leakey wondered whether anything more human might be found in the vicinity, and sure enough, a mere two years later their eldest son, Jonathan, provided an answer by discovering the 1.8 million-year-old cranial remains of an erect primate with a much larger brain than Nutcracker Man's. Louis Leakey recognized that these fossils belonged to a different species that clearly was a direct ancestor of modern humans; therefore he placed it in the "manlike" rather than "apelike" genus and named it *Homo habilis,* or "man having ability."

Once it became clear that East African sites were the best places to look for evidence of human origins, other breathtaking finds occurred with bewildering rapidity. In 1972 a team led by the Leakeys' second son, Richard (currently the leading paleoanthropologist of the dynasty), discovered in Kenya pieces of a skull of *Homo habilis* that were more complete than those found by his brother, and that were about 200,000 years older. In 1974 a team headed by the American Donald Johanson discovered in Ethiopia 40 percent of the entire skeleton of an erect ape that lived about three and a quarter million years ago. (Johanson named this creature "Lucy" because as her bones were being assembled in the field camp someone was playing on a tape recorder the Beatles' song "Lucy in the Sky with Diamonds.") A year later Johanson and his team turned up numerous bones of at least thirteen of "Lucy's" contemporaries, and a year later Mary Leakey found in Tanzania footprints of an erect ape who walked there three and three-quarters million years ago. As of this writing, amazing discoveries continue: in 1984 Richard Leakey's team in Kenya found a skeleton of a 1.6 million-year-old human ancestor so complete that were it *Homo sapiens* it could almost be used for an anatomy-class lecture in a medical school.

Of course discovering skulls and skeletons is one thing and interpreting the evidence another. Not surprisingly, there is still much uncertainty and controversy concerning human origins, and theories are overhauled continually as better alternatives are proposed and new evidence adduced. Nonetheless, two fundamental propositions advanced within the last twenty years are now beyond the range of dispute. One is that the first "split off" between the chain of evolution that led to modern humans and the chain that includes all surviving apes did not relate to larger brain size, as was once thought, but rather concerned "bipedality," or upright walking. The proof for this is found in "Lucy" and the other erect apes like her whose fossils were found by the Johanson team, for the arm and leg bones of these creatures show that they walked upright, but the skulls show that their brains were small, indeed little more than the size of a chimp's. Since substantially larger brains are first present in fossils dating to a million and a quarter years after Lucy, there is no doubt that bipedality came first.

The Lucy evidence also shows that the advantage of moving on two feet did not immediately lie in freeing the hands for the fashioning and employment of tools and weapons because such could only come about with larger brain size. Instead it now seems likely that upright apes gained an advantage in the struggle for survival over other apes because they could grab their food, run with it, and then eat it in hiding. Since they did this in daytime they also needed to sweat more, which is why those survived best who had less fur. In fact some paleoanthropologists now think that larger brains first became a biological advantage because larger brain size could better regulate the body heat of upright apes. The genetic shift to bipedality because of advantageous feeding is thus a nice illustration of the fact that "Mother Nature" does not plan evolution with great foresight: free hands *could* have led to toolmaking, but for one or two million years they did not.

"Mother Nature," as the recent fossil discoveries in Africa have shown, is also sloppy since she created many apelike species such as Lucy that no longer survive. This is another way of saying that the second fundamental proposition about human evolution now beyond the range of dispute is that the second genetic "split off" leading to humans did indeed relate to brain size. *Homo habilis,* the first known species leading to modern man, existed at least as long ago as two million years and had a brain about 50 percent larger than coeval erect apes such as Nutcracker Man. Unquestionably it was this brain that allowed *Homo habilis* to replace the erect apes within 100,000 to 200,000 years, for it did enable him to employ tools. Self-evidently

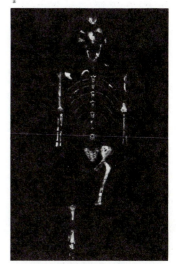

"Lucy"

Fossil Footprints Discovered by Mary Leakey. By studying these footprints she discovered in 1976, Mary Leakey could determine that the creatures who left them behind some three and three-quarters million years ago walked upright.

Homo habilis's tools were extremely crude—bones of animals, limbs from trees, and, most sophisticated, pieces of stone chipped to create sharp edges. It seems that, rather than being used for hunting, such tools helped the earliest humans increase their food supply by digging for tubers, cutting plants, cracking open nuts, and slicing scavenged meat. But gathering food with tools not only gave the earliest humans a greater and more varied food supply, it was also the first step toward civilization because it called for a degree of group cooperation hitherto unknown among the primates.

3. FROM *HOMO HABILIS* TO *HOMO SAPIENS*

Aside from his toolmaking abilities, we know very little about the activities of *Homo habilis,* who appears to have merged into his successor on the evolutionary chain, *Homo erectus* ("erect man"), in Africa around 1.6 million years ago. But we know a great deal more about this successor, who lived from about 1.6 million years ago to about 300,000 years ago. *Homo erectus* was the species that first migrated out of Africa and started peopling the earth; it was also this species that first engaged in collective hunting and learned how to use fire. So well was *Homo erectus* able to adapt himself to the extremely disparate environments in which he lived that he survived for more than five times as long as our own species, *Homo sapiens,* has existed so far.

From the physical point of view the differences between *Homo erectus* and his predecessor, *Homo habilis,* were dramatic. Whereas *Homo habilis* was probably about the size of a pygmy, *Homo erectus* was about as tall as most modern humans. The nearly complete skeleton that Richard Leakey's team discovered in 1984 was that of a *Homo erectus* boy of about twelve years old. Since this boy was already about five and a half feet tall he probably would have been a six-footer had he reached maturity; indeed, the boy was also so stocky that as Leakey observed, he "might have made a fine football player" on a prehistoric varsity team. Chances are the *Homo erectus* boy could also have executed a fairly complicated offensive play because of his intelligence. *Homo erectus* had on the average a cranial capacity more than 40 percent greater than that of *Homo habilis,* and there is some fossil evidence to show that the *shape* of his brain had changed in the direction of our own.

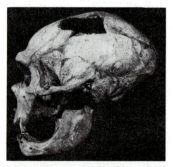

Homo Erectus Skull. This skull dates from "only" about half a million years ago.

Homo erectus's intelligence enabled him to migrate from Africa to Europe and Far Eastern Asia, and to adjust in the process to a wide variety of climates. Examples of *Homo erectus*'s distribution are the so-called Java man and Peking man, who by about 500,000 B.C. had reached the sites whose names they bear. Fragments of over forty skeletons of Peking man were found between 1926 and 1930 in a cave twenty-five miles southwest of Peking (Beijing). Specimens unearthed more recently near the same site, but dating from 200,000 years later, reveal significant anatomical differences: a diminution in the size of teeth and jaws and an increase in brain capacity by as much as 20 percent, suggesting a growth in intelligence as well as changes in dietary habits. Archeological research pursued vigorously since 1949 under the People's Republic of China has shown that much of Eastern Asia was continuously inhabited by human types since their first arrival half a million years ago. Evidence, still incomplete, suggests that modern *Homo sapiens* may have appeared in China as early as 65,000 B.C.

Apparently the most important single invention of *Homo erectus* was the use of language: very recent reconstructions of the *Homo erectus* larynx (accomplished in 1982) show that the species was able to make most of the sounds we do; moreover, although speech leaves no direct fossil remains, it is all but certain that *Homo erectus*'s tools were fashioned in adherence to complex rule systems that could only have been perpetuated by means of spoken languages. *Homo erectus* certainly knew how to cooperate in big-game hunting and in processing and distributing the food obtained from these activities. Prominent in such cooperation would have been the establishment of mutually beneficial male and female roles in food-gathering and food-processing. Finally, by at least 400,000 years ago *Homo erectus* learned how to use fire. Whether he knew how to *start* a fire is impossible to say, but he certainly could control fire for the purposes of keeping warm, protecting himself against marauding animals, and perhaps using fire to cook food. Evidence for the species' use of fire has been discovered in sites as far apart as China and Spain, showing that *Homo erectus* was intelligent enough to develop certain basic life-enhancing devices independently.

Intelligence and adaptability

About 300,000 years ago *Homo erectus* gradually began to evolve into *Homo sapiens*—indeed, so gradually that it is very difficult to tell from surviving remains where the one species left off and the other began. What is certain is that anatomically the physical changes

Transition from Homo erectus to Homo sapiens

An Artist's Reconstruction of Homo Erectus Hunters Returning from the Hunt

that took place over the course of several hundred centuries would have been most obvious above the neck, for although *Homo erectus* had something very roughly like a football player's physique, he still had an "ape-like" sloping forehead and a brain case on average about 70 percent the size of our own. Paleoanthropologists tend to agree that between *Homo erectus* and the fully modern human species there were two transitional stages of *Homo sapiens*—archaic *Homo sapiens,* living from about 300,000 to about 125,000 years ago, and "Neanderthal Man," living from then until about 40,000 years ago.

The Neanderthal phase

Owing to numerous archeological discoveries in Europe and the Near East (the first "Neanderthal" bones were found in the *Neanderthal* valley of the Neander River in Germany in 1856—hence the name), we are vastly better informed about the transitional phase of *Homo sapiens* known as Neanderthals than we are about any variety of early humans that came before them. Perhaps most in need of emphasis is the fact that although "Neanderthal" is often used as a synonym for primitive and dim-witted and although a Hollywood film about Neanderthal people makes then communicate in "uggah-muggah" talk, they were genetically as little different from one of the modern human races as any one of the modern races is different from another. Put another way, although Neanderthals were more barrel-chested than we are and had a somewhat differently shaped cranium, if a Neanderthal male were dressed in Western business clothes and placed on Wall Street or Madison Avenue he would fit right in.

The Neanderthal people were skilled toolmakers and crafty hunters. Whereas earlier humanlike species usually relied on one or two all-purpose tool/weapons, the Neanderthals created about sixty different specialized tools, including knives, scrapers, borers, and spearheads. Most of these they fashioned from stone, but they also employed bone for making more delicate tools in processes that called for very careful handling. Neanderthals also built shelters out of tree branches or bones, or, when caves were at hand, dwelled in them when shelter was needed and equipped them with great stone hearths. So successful were they in hunting that some Neanderthal bands limited themselves to hunting just one game species, such as bear or deer, rather than any animal they could kill. Some anthropologists have speculated that ritualistic reasons may have lain behind such hunting behavior—possibly the Neanderthals thought they were honoring the spirits of the game species they favored. Whether or not any Neanderthal people were ritualistic hunters, some were surely the earliest known humans to devote their time collectively to anything more than the quest for material survival. Some Neanderthals definitely buried their dead in distinctly reverential ways and provided them with food and goods apparently meant to aid them in their voyages to an afterlife.

How the Neanderthal variety of humanity evolved into the fully modern variety is a source of puzzlement to the experts since the process transpired within a more or less narrow range of time through-

Neanderthal Man

out the Eastern Hemisphere. (People like the Neanderthals inhabited Africa and eastern Asia around the time the Neanderthals lived in Europe and western Asia.) Suffice it to say that between 40,000 and 30,000 years ago the Neanderthals were gone, and the Eastern Hemisphere was populated by human beings anatomically just like us.[1] Concurrently the newly evolved human species migrated into the Western Hemisphere, needing no boats for this because there was then a land connection between Siberia and Alaska. Since Australia was colonized (in still mysterious ways) before 30,000 years ago, the entire globe then knew human habitation more or less as it does today.

*Modern humanity and
migration*

4. EARLY HUMAN ART AND EARLY HUMAN SURVIVAL

It is somehow gratifying to recognize that in addition to colonizing America one of the first things modern humans accomplished was the creation of some of the most stunning paintings known in the entire history of human art—the famous cave murals of southern France and northern Spain executed between 30,000 and 12,000 years ago. In over 200 caves so far discovered (the most famous of which is the cave of Lascaux in southern France and that of Altamira in Spain) the earliest known artists painted breathtaking murals of prancing animals—bison, bulls, horses, ponies, and stags. The emphasis in this cave art was unquestionably on movement. Almost all of the murals depict proud game species running, leaping, chewing their cud, or facing the hunter at bay. An ingenious device for giving the impression of motion was the drawing of additional outlines to indicate the areas in which the leg or the head of the animal had moved. The cave painters sometimes succeeded in achieving startling three-dimensional effects by profiting from the natural bumps and indentations of their cave surfaces. All in all, visitors today who are lucky enough to see the cave murals usually find them as evocative as any paintings hanging in the world's foremost art museums.

*Early human art: cave
murals*

What was the purpose of these prehistoric wonders? Aesthetic delight in being surrounded by beauty must be ruled out as an explanation because the peoples who painted in caves generally lived out of doors and when they did use caves for seasonal shelters they inhabited different parts of them (usually the entrances) rather than those where murals are found (usually the darkest and most inaccessible parts of the caves).

Cave Artist's Lamp. Found in a French cave site in 1960, this prehistoric receptacle was used for burning wood saturated with animal fat by underground artists as they went about their work.

---

[1] It is no longer customary to call the earliest anatomically modern humans "Cro-Magnon people." Since "Neanderthal" is a biological classification, all skeletons conforming to the Neanderthal type can be called Neanderthal regardless of where they were found. But if we were to call all anatomically modern humans "Cro-Magnons" simply because some remains of this type were found near the Cro-Magnon cave of southern France, we would have to call George Washington and Albert Einstein "Cro-Magnon people" too.

Cave Painting of Two Reindeer. From a cave in southern France, a painting executed by an extraordinarily gifted artist "of the French School," who worked about 15,000 years ago.

Furthermore, there is evidence that the peoples who created the murals were largely indifferent to them after they were finished, for numerous examples have been found of paintings superimposed upon earlier ones of the same type.

Abandoning one extreme of interpretation—pure aesthetic delight—some scholars have proposed another by maintaining that the cave paintings were sophisticated symbolic representations of human relationships. According to this theory, cave painters were early social philosophers who tried to interpret and thereby cope with the demands of their social structures by depicting them symbolically. On this understanding the cave bison were not really meant to be bison but rather the "female element," horses the "male element," and pictures of small animals gathered around larger ones were meant to show the gathering of less important people around leaders. Needless to say, such hypotheses can never be proven or disproven without written records, but they do appear to be farfetched. For example, there is nothing very obviously feminine about bison (indeed, some symbolic interpreters have seen bison as "male" and horses as "female"), and it is hard above all to understand why artists intent upon representing human reality would portray animals and not humans.

Cave Bison. Although not all the experts agree, it seems reasonably clear that this bison has been wounded with arrows or spears. If so, the representation from a cave wall in southern France supports the theory that cave artists were attempting to employ sympathetic magic.

Leaving aside the interpretative extremes of simplicity and sophistication, the view that cave art was an attempt at working *sympathetic magic* appears to be the most convincing explanation available. Sympathetic magic is founded on the belief that imitating a desired result will bring about that result. Regarding cave art, it seems reasonably clear that when prehistoric painters depicted bison with arrows piercing their flanks, the very act of representing such scenes was meant to ensure that arrows would pierce bison in reality. An objection lodged against the sympathetic magic theory is that only about 10 percent

Extreme interpretations of cave paintings

of all known cave murals show killing scenes. But since almost all cave paintings do depict game, it may be answered that the portrayal of plentiful cavorting game was meant to ensure that hunters would really find game in plenty. Moreover, further support for the view that cave artists worked as sympathetic magicians is found in the fact that archeologists have discovered traces of ritualistic practices in some of the cave areas where murals are located. From this it may be concluded that incantations and rites probably accompanied the acts of painting, and it may also be that all the magical practices were worked while the hunt itself was in progress.

The last inference assumes that the cave painters were not hunters. Although that is by no means an established fact, it is certain that the early human hunting society that produced the cave paintings was one that had arrived at extensive specialization and differentiation of labor. For example, strictly from the technical point of view cave painting could only have been accomplished by specialists since it entailed not only the use of charcoal sticks for drawing black outlines and lumps of clay-like ores (ochres) for coloring in tones of yellows, reds, and browns, but it also drew on the mixing of earthen pigments with fat (as in the later production of tempera paints) and the employment of feathers or bracken for "brushes." Handicraft workers in the same societies concurrently developed extraordinary facility in fashioning tools, not just from stones and bones but also from antlers and ivory. Examples of the implements they added to the ancient human tool kit include fishhooks, harpoons, bows and arrows, and needles for sewing together animal skins.

Hunting in the period between 30,000 and 12,000 years ago would also have called for specialized training since artful new techniques were being added to the hunting repertory. Specifically, with darts

Bison Carved from a Reindeer Horn. Perhaps the most graceful of all known European prehistoric carvings, this bison was carved from a piece of antler between 15,000 and 12,000 years ago. Whatever its use might have been no one quite knows.

Specialization and differentiation of labor

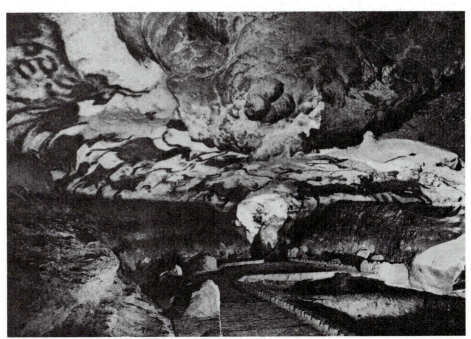

Interior View of "Hall of Bulls" in French Cave of Lascaux

and arrows hunters of that time learned how to bring down birds, with harpoons and fishhooks they learned how to catch fish, and by studying the instinctive movements of game animals they learned how to stampede and trap herds. Since they relied on game most of all, they migrated with game herds and there is some evidence that they followed preservation rules by not killing everything that they could. Nonetheless masses of charred bones found regularly at archeological sites dating from this period indicate that huge quantities of game were killed and then roasted in community feasts, proving that the peoples in question not only knew how to paint and how to hunt, but also how to share.

5. THE ORIGINS OF FOOD PRODUCTION

The "Ice Age" and its impact on hunting societies

Around 12,000 years ago (i.e., 10,000 B.C.) hunting feasts occurred ever more rarely or not at all for a simple reason—the herds were vanishing. The era between 35,000 and 12,000 years ago had been an "Ice Age": daytime temperatures in the Mediterranean regions of Europe and western Asia averaged about 60° F (16° C) in the summer and about 30° F (−1° C) in the winter. Accordingly, herds of cold-loving game species such as reindeer, elk, wild boar, European bison, and various kinds of mountain goats roamed the hills and valleys. But as the last glaciers receded northwards such species retreated with them. Some humans may have moved north with the game, but others stayed behind, creating an extremely different sort of world in comparatively short order.

Specifically, within about 3,000 to 4,000 years after the end of the Ice Age humans in western Asia had accomplished one of the

Eskimo Encampment in Greenland. This modern photo of an Eskimo camp may offer some idea of how humans provided shelter for themselves in "Ice-Age" times.

most momentous revolutions ever accomplished by any humans: a switch from subsistence by means of *food-gathering* to subsistence by means of *food producing*.[2] For roughly two million years humanlike species and humans had gained their sustenance by foraging, or by combined foraging and hunting. These modes of existence meant that such peoples could never stay very long in one place because they continually ate their way through local supplies of plant food, and, if they were hunters, they were forced to follow the movements of herds. But "suddenly" (that is in terms of the comparative time spans involved) substantial numbers of humans began to domesticate animals and raise crops, thereby "suddenly" settling down. As soon as this shift was accomplished villages were founded, trade developed, and populations in areas of sedentary habitation started increasing by leaps and bounds. Then, when villages began evolving into cities, *civilization* was born. "The rest is history" in a very literal sense, for human history—as opposed to prehistory—really began with the birth of civilization and written records.

To say that some humans became food producers all of a sudden is of course justifiable only in terms of the broadest chronological picture. Seen from the perspective of modern historical change, wherein technological revolutions transpire in a few decades and political ones in a few decades or years, the change in western Asia from food-gathering to food production was an extremely gradual one. Not only did the transition take place over the course of some 3,000 to 4,000 years (c. 10,000 to c. 7000/6000 B.C.), but it was so gradual that the peoples involved hardly knew themselves what was happening. It is essential to add that *had* they known what was happening they almost certainly would not have approved of the basic switch from gathering to raising food because Ice-Age hunting and gathering allowed its practitioners to live in health and comparative leisure, whereas early food-producing yielded poorer average diets (much less variety) and much harder everyday work. Yet the progression toward food production had its own internal step-by-step logic which did not allow individual humans much choice as step followed step.

The story of how humans became food producers is roughly as follows. (Details of this story are certain to be revised as research continues.) Around 10,000 B.C. most of the larger game herds had left western Asia. Yet people in coastal areas were not starving; on the contrary, they were surrounded by plenty because the melting glaciers had raised water levels and thereby had introduced huge quantities of fish, shellfish, and water fowl in newly created bays and swamps. Excavations near Mount Carmel and at the site of Jericho in modern-day Israel—locations not far from the Mediterranean Sea—prove that

[2] In earlier editions of this book this was called the "Neolithic Revolution." The term has been replaced because it suggests misleadingly that the innovation of food production was caused primarily by technological advances in stone tool-making.

Transition from food-gathering to food-producing economies

The "suddenness" of the progression toward food production

How humans became food producers

wildlife and vegetation in that area between about 10,000 and 9000 B.C. were so lush that people could sustain themselves in permanent settlements in an unprecedented fashion, easily catching fish and fowl, and picking fruits off trees as if they were in the Garden of Eden. But the plenty of Mount Carmel and Jericho had its costs in terms of population trends. Modern nomadic hunting peoples have low birthrates, and the same is presumed to have been true of prehistoric peoples. The given in this regard is that a woman can trek with one baby in her arms but hardly with two; hence nature finds ways to limit nomadic birthrates to one birth every three or four years. (The actual biological mechanisms may differ: frequent miscarriages might come from frequent trekking, or else longer periods of suckling—induced by the mother's carrying an infant in her arms longer—might delay fertility.) Once people became sedentary in Eden-like environments, however, their reproductive rates began to increase, until, over the course of centuries, there were too many people for the lush coastal terrains.

Domestication of animals

Accordingly, paleoanthropologists posit that around 9000 B.C. excess populations in western Asia started migrating inland to territories where wildlife and plant foods were less plentiful, and where they were forced to return to the nomadic ways of hunter-gatherers. What is certain is that between 9000 and 8000 B.C. some humans in Iran had taken the first known step toward food production by domesticating animals—in this case, sheep and goats. This would have been no more than the equivalent of taking out a small insurance policy. People seeking to avoid overreliance on one particular food source, and starvation if that source failed, captured live animals and gradually bred them so that they had meat on the hoof, available whenever the need arose. Owning a few sheep or goats did not inhibit the people who first domesticated them from continuing in their nomadic way of life (it is easier to travel with trained goats than with babies). But it did make them accustomed to the notion of actively manipulating their environments.

Plant food and human manipulation of the environment

Producing plant food came next. After the glaciers had receded, wild wheat and wild barley had begun to grow in scattered hilly parts of inland western Asia. Accustomed to gathering all sorts of seeds, hunter-gatherers between about 9000 and 8000 B.C. gladly drew on the wheat and barley because when these plants were ripe, gatherers could reap large amounts of seeds from them within as little as three weeks and then move on to other pursuits. Archeological discoveries reveal that the peoples in question developed flint sickles to accelerate their harvesting, mortars for grinding their harvested grain into flour, and—most significantly for future developments—lined storage pits for preserving their grain or flour. In other words, these peoples had not only begun to pay special attention to harvesting wild grain, but they were saving their harvests for use over time. Again, people were manipulating their environments instead of merely adjusting to them.

An Artist's Conception of Nomadic Hunter-Gatherers Reaping Grain with Flint Sickles. In 1966 an intrepid paleoanthropologist used a 9,000-year-old sickle to see how well it could deal with wild wheat in the hills of eastern Turkey. Sure enough, within an hour he had harvested six pounds of grain.

Still nomads, the same people most likely would have been content to gather their grain and other foods forever. But since grain could be stored particularly well, some groups of grain gatherers may have come gradually to rely on it more and more. In such cases they would have been adversely affected by a poor growing year or by gradual depletion caused by excessive harvesting. Then, paying more attention to keeping their wild grain growing profusely, they would have noticed that the grain would grow better if rival plants (weeds) were removed, still better if the soil were scratched so that falling seeds could take root more easily, and still better if they themselves sprinkled some seeds into sparser patches of soil. The people who did these things were more influential discoverers and explorers in terms of the origins of our own modern existence than Columbus or Copernicus, yet from their point of view they were merely adjusting some of the details of their ongoing hunting and gathering way of life.

Increasing reliance on grain among nomadic hunter-gatherers

Imperceptibly, however, they became "hooked" and surrendered their nomadic ways for sedentary ones. Already having small herds as "insurance policies," they must have decided at some point that it would be equally sensible to be able to count on having patches of planted grain awaiting them when they reached a given area on seasonal nomadic rounds. And then they would have learned that planting could be done better at a different time of year than harvesting, and then that their livestock might graze well on harvested stubble, and then that they might grow more than one crop a year in the same place. Meanwhile they would have become more and more accustomed to storing and would have seen less and less reason to move away from their fields and their stores. And so sedentary plant-food production, or *agriculture*, was invented.

Sedentary plant-food production, or agriculture

The earliest archeological evidence for fully sedentary agriculture comes from far eastern Anatolia (modern-day Turkey), Syria, Iraq, and Iran, and dates from roughly 7500 to roughly 7000 B.C. By 6000 B.C. the entire western-Asian region had adopted agriculture as the central mode of human survival. To be sure, agriculture was not the only means of survival. Livestock-raising supplemented it, and by 6000 B.C. the livestock raised included cattle and pigs as well as sheep and goats. Moreover, farming peoples continued to engage in some hunting and some gathering on the side. (Even today most farmers look forward to using their rifles from time to time and most farmers' wives to gathering wild berries or mushrooms.) Yet settled agriculture had not only become the dominant form of human existence in western Asia by 6000 B.C., but soon after it conquered the world. Agriculture arose independently in at least three areas in China and one or two sites in America around 5000 B.C. and fanned out in Far Eastern Asia and the Western Hemisphere from there. From western Asia it reached southeastern Europe (the Balkans) by about 5000 B.C. and spread from there over the entire European continent until by about 3500 B.C. it had reached its natural European limits in Scandinavia. "Amber waves of grain" have played a central role in European— and by extension, North American—history ever since.

6. THE EMERGENCE OF VILLAGES, TRADE, AND WARFARE

Focusing here on developments in western Asia after the switch from food-gathering to food production, the next steps in the region's accelerating evolution toward civilization were the emergence of villages, the rise of long-distance trade, and the onset of bitter warfare. Villages constituted the most advanced form of human organization in western Asia from about 6500 to about 3500/3000 B.C., when some villages gradually became cities. Village organization inevitably brought about long-distance trade, and it just as inevitably provoked the growth of war. No doubt warfare has been the bane of human existence, with famine and disease, at least since the appearance of agricultural villages, but since the growth of warfare in ancient times stimulated the growth of economic and social complexity it nonetheless must be counted as a step toward the emergence of civilization.

The progression in social organization that transpired in western Asia from wandering band to village to city was essentially a progression in function from gathering food to raising food to engaging in a variety of functions that presupposed the steady supply of food. At each stage the size of the organization typically became larger, but it must not be thought that villages were always larger than bands and smaller than cities. Rather, although the typical village numbered about 1,000, during the earliest part of what might be called the

Stone Foundation of a Sedentary Dwelling. Once people in western Asia became agriculturalists, they began to build homes for year-round habitation. This stone foundation for a prehistoric house was found at the site of the village of Jarmo (in Iraq) and dates from about 6000 B.C.

"age of villages" in western Asia some villages numbered as few as 200 inhabitants, making them smaller than the average bands, and at the height of the period some villages housed populations of more than 5,000, making them larger than the typical subsequent city.

Therefore it is wiser to put aside size and insist that a settlement cannot be considered a village if most of its inhabitants were not sedentary or if more than a very small percentage of its able-bodied inhabitants did not engage in fieldwork. To be sure, over the course of time handicrafts began to take an ever more prominent role in village activities after agriculture because village farmers were always seeking greater efficiencies and comforts. At first all the villagers would have engaged in a given new craft, but as the techniques of some crafts became more complicated specialists would arise who gradually would be allowed to become full-time artisans instead of going into the fields. Nonetheless, even toward the end of the western Asian age of villages such full-time artisans were very rare, probably comprising at most no more than one percent of the adult population.

The village based on a sedentary and overwhelmingly agricultural population

The most important village handicrafts were pottery, weaving, and tool- and weapon-making. Of these the emergence of the first two were immediate results of the shift to sedentary existence. Once humans became settled they obviously became particularly interested in storing, and just as obviously they no longer needed to worry about how well any storage receptacle might be suited for travel. Thus humans may have known how to make clay pots in much earlier periods, yet they did not bother to make them because such pots were too fragile to carry on treks. But when humans built villages they immediately built pots because they found them ideal for storing grain and other foods. Moreover, clay pots could also be used to haul and store water: with pottery people could thus keep drinking water in their

Handicrafts in village society: (1) pottery

Early Village Pottery. A shallow bowl from a western-Asian village site dating from about 5000 B.C.

homes, a step toward luxury perhaps comparable to the modern invention of indoor plumbing.

(2) weaving

Weaving also probably arose first because of the search for appropriate receptacles inasmuch as knowledge of basket-weaving seems to have preceded knowledge of cloth-weaving. Certainly twig baskets, which appear in the archeological record soon after settlement, were too bulky and fragile for incessant travel but more suitable than pots for certain kinds of storing and preferable to pots for bringing in harvests from the field because of their lightness. Once the weaving principle became widely known it could easily be put to use for manufacturing cloth, given that domesticated sheep were available to produce wool. And with woolen fabrics villagers had a more dependable and adaptable source of clothing than animal skins. (The weaving of cloth from plant fibers only arose with the domestication of a suitable plant, flax, the raw material for making linen, in Egypt around 3000 B.C.)

(3) tools and weapons

In contrast to pottery and weaving, the fashioning of tools and weapons was not new to humanity in the age of villages, but villagers did learn how to make tools and weapons out of new materials. The need for sharper and more durable tools became ever greater with the growth of agriculture: for example, early villagers sought the sharpest sickles and the most durable plows. And while weapons may have been used less for hunting, we will see that they were used more and more for war. At first Asian villagers seeking sharp edges recognized that some rocks could produce sharper cutting edges than others and used these whenever they could. Then they noticed that some "rocks" were particularly malleable and thus could be fashioned into pointed tips and resharpened when blunted. Such malleable "rocks" of course were not rocks at all but small pieces of copper standing free in nature, and because these were comparatively rare, between about 6500 and 4500 B.C. they were employed only for making tips and very small implements such as pins. But then someone, perhaps as the result of accidentally dropping a metallic rock into a pottery kiln, discovered that certain "rocks" (ore stones) would ooze forth copper under high heats. Whoever this person was, he or she discovered smelting, and thereafter, for roughly the next millennium, smelted copper was used in western Asia for manufacturing all sorts of containers, tools, and weapons.

Reference to the growing use of different rocks and copper inevitably introduces the subject of trade, for the sharp rocks and the copper early villagers desired were not found all over western Asia but had to be transported over long distances. Hunter-gatherers seldom, if ever, engaged in long-distance trade because they could not afford it—in other words, they produced no surpluses. Wandering from place to place such people kept their luggage to a minimum and hence were not at all oriented toward surplus production. Villagers, on the other hand, were natural storers, and not long after they started storing grain they came to realize that producing and storing more than they needed could serve as a hedge against famine and could provide goods for barter.

*Long-distance trade born of
surplus production*

Although we will never know for certain how step followed step, it seems most likely that short-distance gift-offering and exchange based on kin-group relations preceded long-distance trade in more recognizably mercantile forms. For example, a family group in a prosperous village might have sent some grain to hungry kin in a nearby village simply as a gift or in return for an implement or two; conceivably regular offerings of gifts or regular exchanges between kin in different villages may have arisen as ceremonial means of acknowledging family ties. As exchange and accumulation of goods continued, however, certain parties inevitably became richer than others until they had the wherewithal to send an emissary over a long distance to trade for, say, a good sharp cutting stone in a location where such stones were plentiful. At any rate, there is no doubt that as early as about 6500 B.C. trade in western Asia already extended over remarkably long distances. In particular, all the villages known to have existed in Iran and Iraq had found the means of acquiring steady supplies of obsidian (a volcanic glass particularly suited for making sharp cutting edges) from sources in what is now Armenia, 400 to 500 miles away, and the same villages were also acquiring small pieces of copper from central Anatolia, about twice as far. Thereafter trade in rocks, metals, foodstuffs, fabrics, hides, and trinkets became ever more brisk, and by the end of the age of villages, goods were being transported by boats as well as moving over land.

But trade was not the only means of acquiring goods, for successful pillaging could serve the acquisitive even better. No one knows exactly when human warfare began, but more and more experts are coming to doubt that aggressiveness is biologically "programmed" into us. Rather, it seems that humans have no strictly biological propensity for either peace or war and that before the switch to sedentary agriculture bands of roving humans were peaceable. At the very least it is certain that there are no depictions of humans fighting humans in

Flint Dagger. Discovered in Anatolia and dating from about 7000 B.C., this dagger made from flint-stone with an elaborately carved bone handle was a weapon worthy of a commander-in-chief.

the Ice-Age cave paintings and that the earliest known representations of warfare appear together with settled village life. Even more dramatic is the fact that many of the earliest known villages in western Asia were fortified villages. Evidently, whatever humanity's past had been, its future was to fight and kill.

Settled life would have inspired ongoing warfare for obvious reasons. Members of roving bands needed to cooperate with each other in hunting and gathering, and they seldom even saw members of other bands. Assuming that one band did occasionally run into another, there would have been little reason to fight since there was little or no loot to be gained. In contrast there was loot in a village, and villagers under attack would have tended to stand and fight rather than cut and run, not only to protect their belongings, but to preserve their fields which invariably had cost them great effort to clear and cultivate. Endemic fighting probably began during the period of transition between wandering and settlement when some bands of wanderers became bands of pillagers. Then, by the time there were many villages, one settlement definitely started fighting another to attain more property and wealth.

Warfare as a stimulus to technology and trade

Ironically, the onset of warfare stimulated the progress of technology and trade. Whether for defensive or offensive reasons, early villagers in western Asia achieved great technological advances in weaponry, experimenting in the manufacture of daggers, battle-axes, spears, slings, and maces. Moreover, an area-wide village "arms race" was probably what most stimulated the advance of metallurgy, since copper made better spear points and daggers than stone or bone, and bronze, an alloy of copper and tin, whose manufacture was perfected between 3500 and 3000 B.C., made vastly better weapons of all sorts than copper. Since metals had to be acquired by trade, villagers caught in

Early Representations of Warfare. On the left is a cave painting from Spain; on the right is a rock carving from Sweden. Although both representations are very difficult to date, it is almost certain that neither predated the establishment of settled agriculture in their respective regions.

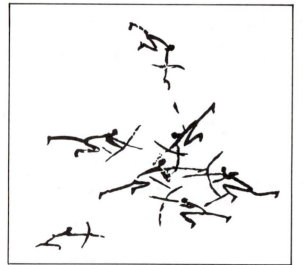

Links between village life and warfare

an arms race were forced to enhance their efficiency in producing surpluses of village products so that they could acquire metals. And so the search for the best weapons stimulated economic life even while causing death and destruction.

7. THE BIRTH OF CIVILIZATIONS

The last major development in western Asian prehistory was the emergence of cities, a phenomenon datable to the period between about 3500 and 3200 B.C. Since some villages imperceptibly turned into cities over the course of about five hundred years, it is easier to describe the difference between a city and a village on the basis of how the city appeared at the end of its development. Unlike the village, the city housed people from a wide variety of occupations. All early cities housed farmers, for the fields around a city needed to be tilled just like any others; cities additionally housed small numbers of artisans and merchants, since cities began to take shape at a time when some handicraft skills had become very specialized and when trading was also becoming a specialty. But the predominant personalities in cities, whose presence really determined the difference between the city and the village, were full-time warriors, administrators, and priests.

Distinctions between city and village

In a nutshell, cities existed to exploit villages. The foremost city dwellers themselves of course would not have put things that way. Since they were professional warriors, administrators, and priests, they would have said that their callings were to protect their regions by military means, to enhance regional productivity by good management, and to conciliate the gods with prayers. But since none of these people worked in the fields they surely could not have existed without the surpluses produced by those who did. Put another way, the leading city dwellers were *rulers* in their society, and the inhabitants of subordinated villages, as well as other city dwellers, were *the ruled*.

City versus village; ruler versus ruled

There is no doubt that the earliest western Asian cities arose in Mesopotamia, a region in modern-day Iraq lying between the Tigris and Euphrates rivers, and it is virtually certain that the ultimate cause for this lay in population pressure. We have already seen that settled peoples tend to reproduce more quickly than wanderers. Certainly, once people in western Asia became adept at settled agriculture food yields began to increase spectacularly, and so did human numbers. By a conservative estimate the population in the hilly area of western Iran, where settled agriculture had found one of its earliest homes, increased fiftyfold between 8000 and 4000 B.C. At a certain point excess populations needed to move on to new terrains in order to survive, and this was particularly true among early agriculturalists, who tended gradually to exhaust the fertility of their lands since they knew nothing of crop rotation or fertilizing techniques. In western Asia this point was reached around 4000 B.C. when excess peoples

The cities of Mesopotamia: the product of population pressure

The Earliest Beginnings

The trend toward government and coercion in Mesopotamia

Militarism reinforces government power

in Iran and Iraq began to move in considerable numbers into the previously uninhabited valley between the Tigris and the Euphrates.

Two requirements are necessary for successful agriculture: fertility and moisture. The earliest western Asian agricultural settlements were located in hilly regions where grain originally grew wild. These terrains were not particularly fertile, but at least they were fertile enough to support the beginnings of crop growing, and they did have abundant moisture from rainfall. The Mesopotamian valley, on the other hand, was extremely fertile but so lacking in moisture for long parts of the year that farming there was impossible without the introduction of artificial irrigation systems. Building and maintaining irrigation systems, however, called for a degree of planning and of intense, coordinated labor that was unprecedented in human societies until that time. The irrigation in question, initiated in the millennium between 4000 and 3000 B.C., had to be accomplished by means of leading canals and channels from the two big rivers in crisscrossing patterns over the dry lands, and the work was never completed because the canals and channels had constantly to be cleared when they began silting up. Such labors required that people be organized in force, that provisions be assembled to support them, that pots be mass-produced to serve as their food receptacles, and so forth. Obviously, therefore, planners were needed to determine how, when, and where to work, overseers were needed to direct and coerce laborers, and governors were needed to plan and oversee the overseers. Accordingly under such circumstances society became divided into the rulers and the ruled.

As population pressure entailing the necessity for irrigation systems created a trend toward government and coercion in Mesopotamia between 4000 and 3200 B.C., the trend was reinforced by the advance of militarism. How did some people manage to emerge as rulers?

Mesopotamian Archeological Mound. Several thousand years' worth of successive human building activities will often result in a mound of debris looking like this. Many decades of hard labor and intensive study by a team of archeologists would be necessary to recover all the historical information hidden in this mound, dating from about 5000 B.C. at the base and 500 A.D. at the top.

Surely the main explanation lay in brute force, the strongest in society being those who were the most skilled in fighting. During the millennium in question military power would have led to governmental power and ever more military power by a continual spiraling process: metal weapons were superior to stone ones but much more expensive, thus those who had acquired wealth from subduing and exploiting others were the only ones who could have afforded to acquire metal weapons with which to subdue and exploit still more people. It is particularly noteworthy that Mesopotamia has no natural supply of any metals or metallic ores, yet relatively large quantities of metal weaponry have been found there dating from between 3500 and 3000 B.C.; obviously the warrior-rulers of Mesopotamia were becoming ever more dominant and entrenched.

Given that dominant warriors needed trained administrators to help them govern and supervise the local irrigation works, the grouping together of these two classes in central locations might alone have created cities. But in fact there also emerged a full-time priesthood, which united with the first two groups in forming cities. Needless to say, religion was not invented in Mesopotamia. Belief in supernatural forces must have existed millennia earlier among the Neanderthals who buried their dead with provisions and among Ice-Age cave peoples whose art apparently was meant to work magic. What was new in Mesopotamia was the emergence of a full-time priesthood—people attached to centers of ritual practice, temples—whose performance of incantations and rites was supported by the agricultural labors of others.

Why a priestly caste first arose in Mesopotamia is a speculative question, but it seems likely that by about 3500 B.C. economic demands and social complexity there were becoming so great that people in effect needed priests. Wandering bands had no difficulty in maintaining social cohesiveness because there was little or no private property to fight over, because occupational functions were more or less equal, and because the bands were small enough in size—customarily numbering no more than 500 persons—for band members to feel united by mutual familiarity. But such conditions started changing in villages. There communal labor and distribution were still the rule, but inequalities in possessions would have become more pronounced over time, especially with the development of trade, and the growth of village populations from the hundreds to the thousands would have made it harder for people to recognize each other on, so to speak, a first-name basis. Attacks from the outside probably provided the basis for sufficient social cohesiveness among villagers to keep them from fighting each other intensively, but during the stressful beginnings of irrigation in Mesopotamia still more cohesiveness would have been needed. On this admittedly speculative reconstruction, religion inspired people in large groups to feel loyal to a common cause and to work hard in the belief that their labors were serving the local gods.

Cities as the manifestation of civilization

And religious dedication on this scale called for priests to propagate the faith and to preside over elaborate rituals in impressive temples.

Discussing the origins of cities is really the same as discussing the origins of *civilization,* which may be defined as the stage in human organization when governmental, social, and economic institutions have developed sufficiently to manage (however imperfectly) the problems of order, security, and efficiency in a complex society. Around 3200 B.C. Mesopotamia was "civilized." That is, at least five cities existed, which all included among their inhabitants warrior-rulers, administrators, and priests, which all encompassed several monumental temples, and which all boasted in addition elaborate private residences, communal workshops, public storage facilities, and large marketplaces. Rudimentary forms of record-keeping were being mastered, and writing was on its way. Herewith the story of civilizations in the West begins, and herewith we may begin following a story that is based on interpreting written evidence as well as archeological artifacts.

SELECTED READINGS

• *Items so designated are available in paperback editions.*

Binford, Lewis, *In Pursuit of the Past: Decoding the Archaeological Record,* London, 1983. One of the world's most influential archeologists offers this highly readable and personalized description of how archeologists analyze artifacts scientifically in order to describe past social behavior and processes of change.

De Waal Malefijt, Annemarie, *Religion and Culture: An Introduction to Anthropology of Religion,* New York, 1968. A straightforward account that reviews the ideas of leading modern social theorists in order to understand prehistoric and early religions and to locate common factors in religious practices and beliefs.

• Fagan, Brian, *Archaeology: A Brief Introduction,* 2nd ed., Boston, 1983. Defines the terminology and describes some of the basic methods of archeology. Clear and concise.

———, *People of the Earth,* 5th ed., Boston, 1986. The most accessible survey of all cultures without written records, ranging from the earliest humans to the Incas.

Harlan, Jack, J. M. DeWet, Ann Stemler, eds., *Origins of African Plant Domestication,* The Hague, 1976.

• Harris, Marvin, *Cannibals and Kings: The Origins of Cultures,* New York, 1977. A materialistic interpretation of the emergence of primitive societies as a process of interaction with environmental and economic determinants.

Lamberg-Karlovsky, C. C., and J. Sabloff, *Ancient Civilizations: The Near East and Mesoamerica,* Menlo Park, Calif., 1979. A lucid discussion of how the earliest states were formed and of how the earliest civilizations became increasingly complex over time.

Leakey, Richard E., *The Making of Mankind,* New York, 1981. The companion volume to a splendid BBC television series, lavishly illustrated. Leakey describes recent discoveries (including his own) concerning the earliest evolution of humanity and argues forcefully in favor of his belief that mankind is not innately aggressive.

Leroi-Gourhan, André, *The Art of Prehistoric Man in Western Europe,* London, 1968. Controversial in its symbolic interpretations of cave art, but rich in detailed information and abundantly illustrated with exquisite color photographs.

• Mauss, Marcel, *The Gift: Forms and Functions of Exchange in Archaic Societies,* New York, 1967. Originally written in 1927, this book offers enduring insights into the nature of social interaction between individuals and among groups.

• Pfeiffer, John, *The Emergence of Humankind,* 4th ed., New York, 1985. An up-to-date review of where the entire field of paleoanthropology stands, including dispassionate analyses of some of the field's thorniest problems and debates.

Phillips, Patricia, *The Prehistory of Europe,* Bloomington, Ind., 1980. Basically a reference work more addressed to presenting data than theories, yet crucial for understanding the evolution from Neanderthals to anatomically modern humans.

Phillipson, David W., *African Archeology,* Cambridge, 1984. A comprehensive and reliable survey of the continent's past from the appearance of hominids to the advent of written records.

• Sandars, Nancy K., *Prehistoric Art in Europe,* rev. ed., Baltimore, 1985. A short survey contrasting with Leroi-Gourhan in its emphasis on the techniques of early art rather than on its allegedly symbolic meanings.

Wertime, Theodore A., James D. Muhly, eds., *The Coming of the Age of Iron,* New Haven, 1980.

Ancient Civilizations of the East and West

	POLITICAL	ECONOMIC

3000
B.C.
	Supremacy of Sumerian cities in Mesopotamia,
	    c. 3200–c. 2340
	Archaic period in Egypt, c. 3100–c. 2770
	Old Kingdom in Egypt, c. 2770–c. 2200
	Indus valley civilization, c. 3200–c. 1600
	Dominance of Akkadian Empire in Mesopotamia,
	    2334–c. 2200
	Sumerian revival, c. 2200–c. 2000
	Middle Kingdom in Egypt, c. 2050–1786
	Old Babylonian Empire in Mesopotamia, c. 2000–
	    c. 1600
	Height of Minoan civilization under leadership of
	    Knosses, c. 2000–c. 1500
		Development of irrigation and large-scale farming
		    in Egypt and Mesopotamia, c. 3500–c. 2500
		
		Extended commerce in Egypt and Crete, c. 2000
		Horses introduced into western Asia, c. 2000

2000 B.C.		

1500
B.C.
	Shang Dynasty in China, c. 1766–1027
	Mycenaean civilization on mainland Greece,
	    c. 1600–c. 1200
	Hittite Empire in Asia Minor, c. 1600–c. 1200
	The New Kingdom in Egypt, c. 1560–1087
	Kassites overthrow Babylonians, c. 1550
	Mycenaean dominance on Crete, c. 1500–c. 1400
	Destruction of Knossos and end of Minoan
	    civilization, c. 1400	

1000
B.C.
	Trojan War, c. 1250
	Hebrew occupation of Canaan, c. 1200–c. 1025
	Collapse of Mycenaean civilization in Greece,
	    c. 1200–c. 1100
	Chou Dynasty in China, 1100–256
	Unified Hebrew monarchy under Saul, David, and
	    Solomon, c. 1025–933
	Kingdom of Israel, 933–722
	Kingdom of Judah, 933–586
	Feudalism in China, 800–250
	Height of Assyrian Empire, c. 750–612
	New Babylonian Empire, 612–539
	Nebuchadnezzar conquers Jerusalem, 586
	Persian Empire, 559–330
	Persian conquest of Babylon, 539
	Persian conquest of Egypt, 525
		Increasing use of iron throughout western Asia,
		    c. 1300–c. 1100

500 B.C.		

CULTURAL

Lunar calendar in Mesopotamia, c. 3200
Sumerian cunieform writing, c. 3200
Sumerian temple architecture, c. 3200–c. 2000
Egyptian hieroglyphic writing, c. 3100

Construction of first pyramid in Egypt, c. 2770

Development of Indus Valley writing, c. 2500
Solar calender in Egypt, c. 2000
Mathematical advances in Old Babylonia, c. 2000–
c. 1800
Minoan art on Crete, c. 2000–c. 1500
Gilgamesh epic, c. 1900
Code of Hammurabi, c. 1790
Development of ideographic writing in China,
c. 1700

Egyptian temple architecture, c. 1580–c. 1090

Development of alphabet by Phoenicians, c. 1400

Naturalistic art in Egypt under Akhenaton, c. 1375

Vedas in India, c. 1200–c. 800

Upanishads in India, c. 800–600
Astronomical observation and record-keeping by
New Babylonians, c. 750–c. 400

Deuteronomic code, c. 600

Hebrew Song of Songs, c. 450
Book of Job, c. 400

RELIGIOUS

Growth of anthropomorphic religion in
Mesopotamia, c. 3000–c. 2000

Minoan worship of mother goddess, c. 2000
Growth of personal religion in Mesopotamia,
c. 2000–c. 1600

Egyptian belief in personal immortality, c. 1800

Religious revolution of Akhenaton, c. 1375
Moses unites Hebrews in worship of Yahweh,
c. 1250

Hebrew prophetic revolution, c. 750–c. 600

Development of Buddhism as a religion in India,
c. 450–c. 300

3000
B.C.

2000
B.C.

1500
B.C.

1000
B.C.

500
B.C.

Chapter 2

MESOPOTAMIAN CIVILIZATION

In my school-days I learned the hidden treasure of writing. I solved complex mathematical reciprocals and products with no apparent solution. I read tables whose Sumerian is obscure and whose Akkadian is hard to construe. Then I advanced to the skills of archery and chariot-driving and mastered royal decorum.

—A tablet of Assurbanipal, King of Assyria, c. 650 B.C.

H istory begins in Sumer. Modern knowledge of the first 35,000 years of human life is based entirely on the archeological record, for until only a little more than 5,000 years ago humans left behind many things but no words. Around 3200 B.C., however, in a region of Mesopotamia known as Sumer, the earliest forms of writing were invented and "history began" in the sense that words were recorded that help current scholars understand what men and women were doing.

Obviously the invention of writing alone would earn the ancient Mesopotamians a prominent place among the most inventive and influential peoples who ever contributed to the forward movement of humankind. But amazingly the peoples who inhabited Mesopotamia in the centuries between roughly 3200 and roughly 500 B.C. contributed much more. We sometimes forget that somebody had to have invented the wheel, but somebody did, and he or she was a Mesopotamian who lived around 3000 B.C. Somebody had to invent the calendar too, and somebody had to invent the mathematical functions of multiplication and division, and those persons also were ancient Mesopotamians. Aside from arriving at such inventions, the Mesopotamians were profound thinkers who pioneered in the life of the mind to such an extent that their innovations in theology, jurisprudence, astronomy, and narrative literature all became fundamental for subsequent developments in these areas of thought and expression. Assuredly the ancient Mesopotamians had their unattractive qualities; for example, their rulers were usually ruthless militarists, and their art often seems frigid or fierce. Nevertheless, the "first chapter of history,"

"First chapter of history"

A rich and diverse record of achievement

which the Mesopotamians wrote by their exploits and their documents, was surely one of the most important chapters in the entire book of human events.

1. ANCIENT SUMER: THE WORLD OF THE FIRST CITIES

The Sumerian era

See color map facing page 39

Between 3500 and 3200 B.C., Mesopotamia, the land between the Tigris and Euphrates rivers, became the first civilized territory on the globe in the sense that its society and culture rested on the existence of cities. We may call the historical period that ensued, lasting from about 3200 B.C. to about 2000 B.C., the "Sumerian era" because the most advanced part of Mesopotamia was then its southernmost territory, Sumer, a region of mud-flats, which was roughly the size of Massachusetts. During the first nine centuries of the Sumerian era no unified government existed in Sumer; instead, the region was dotted with numerous independent city-states, the most important of which were Uruk, Ur, and Lagash. Then, around 2320 B.C., all Sumer was conquered by a mighty warrior from Akkad, the part of Mesopota-

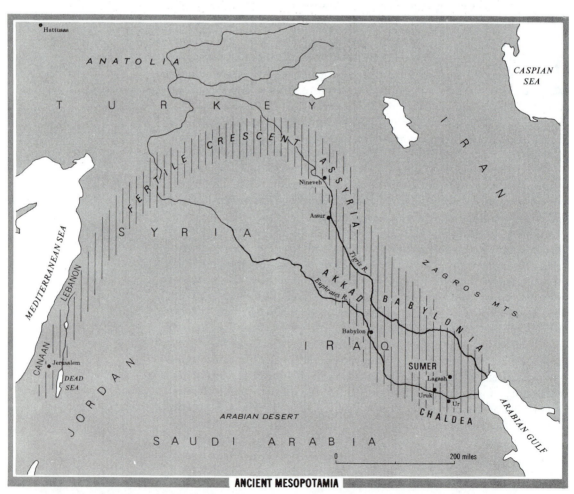

ANCIENT MESOPOTAMIA

mia lying directly to the north. This warrior's birth name does not survive, but we know that he took the title of "Sargon," which means "true king," and that contemporaries called him "Sargon the Great." Mesopotamian chronicles record that Sargon gained control of Sumer by winning thirty-four battles; when his victories finally brought him to "the lower sea" (the Arabian Gulf), he washed his weapons in its waters to signify the end of struggle. For almost two centuries thereafter Sargon the Great's dynasty ruled an empire composed of Akkad and Sumer. But around 2130 B.C. Sumer regained its independence and enjoyed a "revival" that lasted until roughly 2000 B.C., during which time most of the region was ruled by kings who resided in Ur.

Sumer's accomplishments were preponderantly influenced by its climate and geography. Although the soil between the southern Tigris and southern Euphrates was extremely fertile, irrigation was essential because there was almost no rainfall for eight months of each year and torrential spring showers came too late to water the main crops that had to be harvested in April. (The summer months were not productive in Sumer because temperatures then rose to a soil-parching 125°F.) As we have seen, collective work on irrigation projects demanded careful planning and assertive leadership, which in turn led to social stratification, professional specialization, and the emergence of cities. The situation in Sumer was further determined by the fact that southern Mesopotamia was entirely lacking in natural resources such as stone, minerals, and even trees. This meant that Sumer's inhabitants were forced to rely heavily on trade and to be very alert to any possible means of redressing economic imbalances to their advantage. In other words, the Sumerians had to subdue nature rather than live off its plenty.

One of the Sumerians' most remarkable inventions, which they perfected about the time the Sumerian era was opening (around 3200 B.C.), was wheeled transport. To appreciate how advanced this invention was from a comparative perspective it should be noted that wheeled transport was unknown in Egypt until about 1700 B.C. and that wheels were unknown in the Western Hemisphere (except for Peruvian children's toys) until they were introduced by Europeans. Probably the first Sumerian to think of employing a circular device turning on an axis for purposes of conveyance had seen a potter's wheel, for as early as about 4000 B.C., wheels were used in pottery-making in Iran, from whence they entered Sumer about 500 years later. The process of extending the principle of the wheel from pottery-making to transport was by no means obvious: the Egyptians knew the potter's wheel by at least 2700 B.C., but they did not use the wheel for transport until a millennium later, and even then they probably did not "reinvent the wheel" but learned of it from contacts with Mesopotamia. Thus the unknown Sumerian who first attached wheels to a sledge to make a better transportation vehicle really does have to be counted among the greatest technological geniuses of all time.

Sargon the Great. A bronze head thought to depict the mighty warrior who united Akkad and Sumer.

An Akkadian Soldier Leads Away Sumerian Captives. A fragment of a victory monument probably dating from the time of Sargon.

The invention of the wheel

Sumerian War Chariots. The earliest known representation of the wheel, dating from about 2600 B.C., shows how wheels were carpentered together from slabs of wood. (For a later Mesopotamian wheel with spokes, see the illustration on p. 48.) One can also observe that at the dawn of recorded history, military aims stimulated technological innovation as they have continued to do ever since.

Wheeled transport

The earliest Sumerian wheeled vehicles were two-wheeled chariots and four-wheeled carts. Both were drawn by oxen (horses were unknown in western Asia until they were introduced by Eastern invaders sometime between 2000 and 1700 B.C.), and both were mounted on wheels that were solid, not spoked: two or three slabs of wood were shaped into a circle and fastened together with studs or braces. Ox-drawn chariots obviously did not move very quickly, yet they appear to have contributed to an advance in phalanx warfare, for surviving illustrations dating from about 2600 B.C. depict them trampling the enemy. Carts meant for hauling freight had less need for speed and must have aided the Sumerians immeasurably in their numerous irrigation and urban building projects.

Lunar calendar

Along with the wheel, the Sumerians devised another of humanity's most crucial early inventions, the lunar (moon) calendar. In a perilous climate such as that of Mesopotamia it was absolutely essential to begin planting or harvesting at exactly the proper time; thus it was necessary to find some reliable way of marking the passage of days until the proper times for agricultural work came around. The simplest way of doing this was to utilize the cycles of the moon. Since the moon moves from the thinnest crescent back to the thinnest crescent over the course of twenty-nine and a half days, one could consider the completion of such a cycle to be a basic timekeeping unit (we would call it a month), and then count those units until the seasons themselves had made a complete revolution. Hence the Sumerians concluded that when the moon had passed through twelve such units (half assigned twenty-nine days and half thirty), a "year" had passed and it was time to start planting again. Unfortunately they did not know that a "year" is really determined by the completion of the earth's rotation around the sun and that twelve lunar cycles or months fall eleven days short of the solar year. Over the centuries they learned that they had to add a month to their calendars every few years in order to predict the recurrence of the seasons with sufficient accuracy. The Sumerian lunar reckonings were the first known human steps in the direction of what we now understand to be exact, predictive science (the measuring of nature toward the goal of fathoming its "rules of operation"). The fact that the lunar calendar itself is indeed usable if days are added from time to time is confirmed by the modern Jewish and Islamic calendars, both of which are based on lunar cycles that the Jews and Muslims inherited from ancient Mesopotamia.

Ranking together with the wheel and the calendar as one of Sumer's three most precious gifts to succeeding Western civilizations was the invention of writing. To say that writing was "invented" is slightly misleading inasmuch as the emergence of writing in Sumer was gradual, evolving over the course of a millennium (c. 3500 to c. 2500 B.C.) from the representation of ideas by means of pictorial conventions to writing (albeit not alphabetic writing) as we currently know it. Around 3500 B.C. Sumerians had begun to carve pictures in stone or to stamp them on clay as ownership marks: a picture might have stood for a person's nickname (perhaps a rock for "Rocky") or dwelling (a house by a tree). Some five centuries later the evolution toward writing had advanced vastly farther. By then Sumerian temple administrators were using many standardized schematic pictures in combination with each other to preserve records of temple property and business transactions. Although the script of this period was still pictographic, it had advanced beyond pictures standing for people and tangible things to pictures standing for abstractions: a bowl meant any kind of food and a head with a bowl conveyed the concept of eating. After five more centuries full-fledged writing had taken over, for by then the original pictures had become so schematized that they were no longer recognizable as pictures but had to be learned purely as signs, and many of these signs no longer represented specific words but had become symbols for syllables which turned into words when combined with other such signs.

Development of writing

Early Pictorial Writing. On the left, Mesopotamian carvings on a piece of shale, dating from about 3400 B.C., depict two men engaged in a commercial transaction, with pictographs around them telling what they were trading. On the right, a Sumerian clay tablet from about 3000 B.C. Here standardized pictures were beginning to represent abstractions.

The writing system that reached its fully developed form in Sumer around 2500 B.C. is known as *cuneiform* because it was based on wedge-shaped characters (*cuneus* is Latin for wedge) impressed on wet clay by a reed stylus with a triangular point. In total there were about 500 cuneiform characters, and many of these had multiple meanings (the "right one" could only be identified in context), making the system much more difficult to learn than subsequent writing systems based on alphabets. Nonetheless, cuneiform served well enough to be used as the sole writing system of Mesopotamia for two millennia and even to become the standard medium for commercial transactions throughout most of western Asia until about 500 B.C.

Cuneiform Writing. Carvings on limestone from around 2600 B.C., now in fully syllabic-phonetic cuneiform, announce that a certain king of Ur has built a temple.

All the cuneiform texts surviving from the Sumerian era were copied on clay tablets that have been excavated in modern times. Of these about 90 percent are business or administrative records, but the other 10 percent fall roughly into the category of literature—specifically, dialogues, proverbs, hymns, and fragments of mythic tales. The Sumerian dialogue was a genre in which two characters would argue opposing sides in debates—summer vs. winter, axe vs. plow, or farmer vs. shepherd. Since both sides had much to recommend them, there was usually no winner; rather, the genre seems to have been devised for teaching purposes, to help students in temple schools learn as much about a given subject as there was to know. The surviving proverbs, on the other hand, advanced firm opinions. A charming example of a worldly Sumerian proverb is "where servants are, there is quarrel; where cosmeticians are, there is slander"; from this we see that the gossipy hairdresser has been known to human civilization since the dawn of history.

Hymns and mythic tales surviving on Sumerian clay tablets (supplemented by Sumerian texts copied by later Mesopotamians) show that

Sumerian Praying Figures. The statues dating from about 2700 B.C. show Sumerians praying for divine aid to bring them prosperity.

assumptions concerning the gods underwent a process of steady evolution during the Sumerian era. For purposes of simplicity we may note two main phases: a shift from viewing the gods as being part of nature to imagining them acting like humans, and then a shift from assigning to the gods the attributes of humans to imagining them acting like omnipotent rulers. The oldest evidence reveals that the Sumerians originally worshiped disembodied natural forces. One "god" was the force that grew the grain, another the force of the rising sap, another the power that preserved food in storehouses. During the course of the third millennium (the time from 3000 to 2000 B.C.), however, it became easier for the Sumerians to interpret natural occurrences on the basis of anthropomorphic (human) analogies. Thus the torrid summer came to be understood as the annual "death" of the fertility god and the bringing of the harvest to the storehouse the "marriage" of the fertility god to the goddess of storage. Whether the gods were forces in nature or anthropomorphic entities, the purpose of worshiping them was to bring plenty and ward off natural disasters. But toward the end of the third millennium, after Sargon the Great's conquest of Sumer had introduced a period of national rivalries, some of Sumer's anthropomorphic gods inevitably began to assume political characteristics. Some gods were thought of as patron gods of cities, others as rulers of various spheres (such as the sky, the earth, or the underworld), and one, Enlil, was understood to be the ruler of all these rulers. These developments led ever more to notions of divine unity and divine omnipotence.

However the gods were conceived, Sumerian temples loomed mightily over Sumerian society throughout the period from 3200 to 2000 B.C. The temples literally dominated both the cities and the entire flat Sumerian skyline because they were built on huge platforms intended solely to lend them height. All were constructed out of slabs and bricks made from sun-dried clay because stone and wood were unavailable, and most were built in the form known as the *ziggurat,* a terraced (stepped) tower surmounted by a shrine. So massive was the typical Sumerian temple and so arduous the work necessary for building it, that according to modern estimates 1,500 laborers would have had to work on one for ten hours a day uninterruptedly for five years before it was finished. (Moreover, mud-brick edifices, once built, required constant large-scale repair, so building must have been nearly continuous.) Yet apparently such work was accomplished primarily in shifts by volunteers, as acts of devotion to the gods on whom all life was thought to depend.

Sumerian priests did not live in the temples themselves but rather in adjacent structures that were part of the temple precincts. Also dwelling within the precincts were temple administrators, craftsmen, and slaves. Since priests and administrators (the two terms may often have been synonymous) needed to learn cuneiform, temple precincts included schools for teaching it and for proferring other knowledge

Sumerian Ziggurat. This edifice, built in Ur around 2100 B.C., is the best-preserved surviving ziggurat. As can be seen from the diagram of its original form, a shrine, reached by climbing four stories and passing through a massive portal, was the goal of the worshiper's ascent and the most sacred part of the temple.

necessary for the priestly caste. These Sumerian schools were the earliest known schools in the history of human civilization.

The wide-ranging role of the temple

Invariably the temple complexes owned huge stretches of land outside the cities, for without the income provided by such agricultural holdings they could not have supported their vast enterprises. Usually the temple complexes also engaged in trade, selling the goods that were manufactured or stored within their precincts to buyers within their respective cities or shipping them for sale over long distances. Thus the temples were virtually "states within the state." Furthermore, before the time of Sargon they frequently were "the state" insofar as the priests of the Sumerian cities were often their cities' rulers. After the liberation from Sargon's dynasty secular kings customarily took over the rulership of Sumerian cities, but even then the king and his family would have intermarried with the families of the foremost priests.

Sumerian social structure

Aside from priests, kings, and prominent warriors (who would have been members of the families of priests and/or kings), Sumerian society knew three ranks: the "specialists" in the temple complexes, the free farmers, and the slaves. The specialists were administrators, merchants, and artisans, all of whom were reasonably well off but completely dependent on the priests. The free farmers seem to have been left with the worst land and often found it necessary to place themselves in financial debt to the temples in order to survive. As for the slaves, we know very little about them because their very existence was hardly noticed in the records, but it is virtually certain that their lives were supremely miserable.

2. OLD BABYLONIAN DEVELOPMENTS

Although the Sumerians achieved marvels in mastering their physical environment, an ecological problem that escaped their attention was the steady deterioration of their soil caused by mounting salt content,

Cave Paintings from Lascaux. Made with charcoal outlines and rich earth colors, these paintings have maintained their haunting vividness for some 15,000 years. (Ralph Morse/Life Picture Service)

Silver Figurine of a Kneeling Bull Holding a Vessel. Elamite, c. 3000 B.C.

Gold, Silver, Shell, and Lapis Lazuli Statuette of a Ram in a Thicket. Sumerian, 2500 B.C.

Gold and Lapis Lazuli Lyre with Bull's Head. Sumerian, c. 2500 B.C.

Stone Head of Ur-Ningirsu, Son of Gudea of Lagash. Sumerian, c. 2100 B.C.

Gold Plaque with Animals and Stylized Trees in Relief. Persian, VII cent. B.C.

Bronze Bull, Symbol of Strength. Arabian, VI cent. B.C.

Babylonian Lion. King Nebuchadnezzar's Ishtar Gate, erected around 575 B.C., was adorned with stately animals from brightly colored glazed brick. The Greeks counted the Ishtar Gate among the seven wonders of the world. (Museum of Modern Art)

Throne of "King Tut." Dating from about 1360 B.C., this relief in gold and
silver is part of the back of the young pharaoh's throne. The sun god Aton
shines down on Tutankhamen and his queen. The relaxed lounging position
of the pharaoh's right arm is typical of the stylistic informality of the period.
(Lee Boltin)

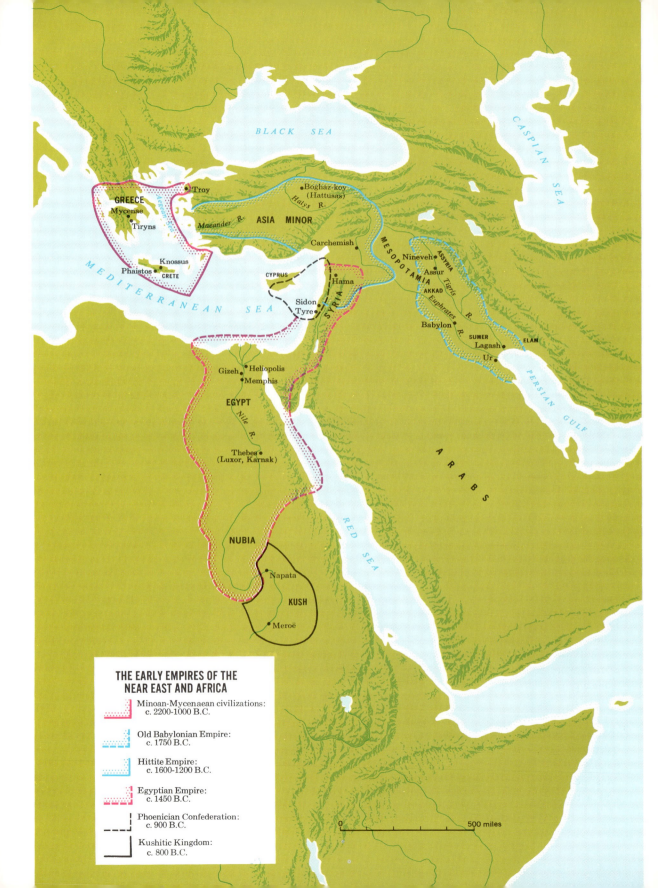

BLACK SEA

CASPIAN SEA

Troy

GREECE
Mycenae
Tiryns

Maeander R. ASIA MINOR

Boghaz-koy
(Hattusas)
Halys R.

MEDITERRANEAN SEA

Knossus
Phaistos
CRETE

Aegean Sea

Carchemish

MESOPOTAMIA

CYPRUS

Hama

Sidon
Tyre

SYRIA

Nineveh ASSYRIA
Assur
Tigris R.
AKKAD
Euphrates R.
Babylon
SUMER
Lagash ELAM
Ur

PERSIAN GULF

Gizeh Heliopolis
Memphis

EGYPT

Nile R.

Thebes
(Luxor, Karnak)

A R A B S

RED SEA

NUBIA

Napata

KUSH

Meroë

THE EARLY EMPIRES OF THE NEAR EAST AND AFRICA

Minoan-Mycenaean civilizations:
c. 2200-1000 B.C.

Old Babylonian Empire:
c. 1750 B.C.

Hittite Empire:
c. 1600-1200 B.C.

Egyptian Empire:
c. 1450 B.C.

Phoenician Confederation:
c. 900 B.C.

Kushitic Kingdom:
c. 800 B.C.

0   500 miles

a process technically known as salinization. The irrigation of the dry soil of Sumer from the nearby rivers brought moisture, but it also brought salt, and the salt remained when the river water evaporated. On a year by year basis the quantities of salt thus introduced into Sumer's soil were insignificant, but on a century by century basis they became deleterious to its fertility. Study of surviving cuneiform tablets has shown that arable lands were becoming less productive in parts of Sumer by as early as 2350 B.C., a fact that may help to account for Sargon of Akkad's ability to conquer the whole region. Sumer was not yet so weak that it could not rise up to overthrow the Akkadians two centuries later, but by around 2000 B.C. the region was sinking into permanent economic eclipse. Unable to produce agricultural surpluses, Sumer's cities could no longer support their priests, administrators, and armies, and the area gradually yielded primacy in Mesopotamia to territories lying farther north.

The Sumerian era of Mesopotamian history was followed by the Old Babylonian era, which lasted from about 2000 to about 1600 B.C. It must be emphasized that the first date is chosen arbitrarily, for nothing dramatic happened in the year 2000 to mark a break from one era to another. Indeed, not only was the transition from Sumerian to Old Babylonian dominance in Mesopotamia gradual, but even when the Old Babylonian era had come to its fullest flowering around 1770 B.C. its culture was not dramatically different from the Sumerian culture that had preceded it. Two criteria alone allow for drawing any sharp distinctions between Sumerians and Old Babylonians: geography and language. We have seen that the most prosperous and culturally advanced cities in Mesopotamia during the Sumerian era were those that lay farthest to the south; during the succeeding 400 years, on the other hand, the weight of civilization shifted northwards to Akkad, where for much of the time it became centered on the newly founded city of Babylon. In addition, unlike the Sumerians who had spoken a language unrelated to any other, the peoples who held sway in Mesopotamia during the Old Babylonian era spoke languages that belonged to the *Semitic* language group.

Semitic language peoples (today including Arabs, Israelis, and Ethiopians) trace their descent to a point of origin in the Arabian peninsula. Exactly why or when Semitic tribes headed toward Mesopotamia remains unknown. What is known is that Sargon the Great and his armies were Semites and that consequently Sumer had already undergone a period of Semitic dominance toward the end of the third millennium. The Sumerian revival occurring between 2130 and about 2000 B.C. had only been an interlude in this regard because even during that time other Semitic tribes were infiltrating Mesopotamia and taking over pockets of territory in Akkad and Sumer. Ultimately the most successful of these proved to be the Amorites, who advanced into Mesopotamia around 2000 B.C. and settled in parts of Akkad. Two and a half centuries later the Amorites conquered all of Sumer, at

Sumer's economic eclipse: salinization

Gradual transition to Old Babylonian dominance

Influx of Semitic language peoples

Hammurabi: King of Babylon and Law-Giver

"Code of Hammurabi"

The practical nature of Mesopotamian jurisprudence

which point the Semitic dialect they spoke replaced Sumerian as the spoken and written language of Mesopotamia. Yet the very same Amorites adopted all other aspects of the Sumerian cultural inheritance.

Because the Amorites made the city of Babylon in Akkad the capital of their empire, they are commonly called the Babylonians, or, more often, the Old Babylonians, to distinguish them from the Chaldeans, who ruled Mesopotamia more than a millennium later. The founder of the Old Babylonian empire and unquestionably the greatest Amorite ruler was Hammurabi (1792–1750 B.C.).[1] At the time of his accession the Amorites were still no more than one of several warring powers in southern Mesopotamia, but in 1763 B.C. Hammurabi conquered all of Sumer, and by 1755 B.C. he had subdued all the rest of Mesopotamia to its northern extremes at the borders of Syria. As his victories mounted, Hammurabi called himself "King of Akkad and Sumer," and then "King of the Four Quarters of the World." Despite this magniloquence his empire was short-lived (political events in Mesopotamia after the reign of Hammurabi will be treated in the next section), but another of his chosen titles, "King of Justice," refers to the source of his lasting fame, for Hammurabi was the promulgator of the earliest ordered collection of laws surviving in the human record.

Scholars agree that the "Code of Hammurabi," a stone document containing 282 laws, was based on Sumerian legal principles with an admixture of Semitic innovations, but since they seldom agree as to which principles were Sumerian and which Semitic it is wisest to consider the entire text as being simply the fullest-known document recording "Mesopotamian jurisprudence." Before considering some of the code's main premises it must be said that it was devoid of the modern notion of "equality before the law." In the Code of Hammurabi slaves have no rights whatsoever and are subject to frightful mutilations for trivial offenses. Otherwise, two legal classes appear: "men," clearly understood to be aristocrats; and all others neither "men" nor slaves, whom the law treated poorly but to whom it offered some rights. Crimes of "men" against their nonslave inferiors were punished less severely than crimes of "men" against "men," and crimes of "men" against slaves were punished only to the extent that they resulted in "property damage" to a slave owner.

The two most famous principles underlying Hammurabi's code are "an eye for an eye" and "let the buyer beware." At first both seem dreadfully primitive. In offering the recompense of exact retaliation ("if a man destroy the eye of another, his eye shall be destroyed"; "if a man breaks another's bone, his bone will be broken"), the code never considers whether the initial injury may have been accidental and is chillingly insistent on inflicting pain and humiliation. The "buyer beware" principle is less chilling but hardly seems like law. Why should the state announce in a legal code that the seller is free to get

[1] Here, and throughout, dates following a ruler's name refer to dates of reign.

away with trickeries? Hammurabi's code becomes more intelligible only if we recognize that it aimed at different ends than modern jurisprudence. The Mesopotamians promulgated laws primarily to stop fights. Thus they thought—and by no means without reason—that a person tempted to act violently might refrain from such behavior if he remembered that whatever wound he inflicted on another would probably be inflicted upon himself. They clearly also thought that punishments would exercise a deterrent effect only if they were executed swiftly and without hope of mercy, a point of view that made it necessary for them to dismiss motive as irrelevant because investigating circumstances and motives would have taken time and opened the possibility that truly willful crimes might have gone unpunished if the criminal knew how to defend himself. As for the "buyer beware" principle, that too was meant to stop fights because a buyer knew that he had no rights and would be swiftly punished if he tried to assert any.

Having considered these practical dimensions of Mesopotamian jurisprudence, it must be added that Hammurabi's code was not entirely indifferent to the notion of justice. Although the insistence on exact retaliation is surely cruel, it is not entirely lacking in a concept of fairness inasmuch as "an eye for an eye" is surely fairer than a head for an eye or an eye for a fingernail. Secondly, abstract ethical principles are embedded in Hammurabi's code in certain instances. For example, since the Mesopotamians believed that children should be deferential to their parents, law 195 of the code stated: "if a son has struck his father, his hand shall be cut off." Finally, the state is called upon occasionally to provide social well-being rather than merely to judge and punish. The most elevated aspect of this "welfare state" dimension to the code appears in law 23, wherein it is announced that if a man is robbed and the robber cannot be found, "the city . . . in whose territory the robbery was committed shall make good to the victim his lost property." We have seen that Hammurabi did wish to be known as "King of Justice," and by the measures of his time he was entirely that; moreover, although Western concepts of justice were to develop greatly thereafter, most of the principles inherent in the Code of Hammurabi were to become points of departure for much of that future development.

Equal in fame to Hammurabi's code as a monument of Old Babylonian civilization is the poem known as the epic of *Gilgamesh*. Like the code, this work was also a Sumerian-Babylonian hybrid. Its hero, Gilgamesh, was a real historical figure—a Sumerian king who ruled around 2600 B.C.—whose exploits so excited the imagination of contemporaries that they began to tell fanciful stories about him. Retold over the centuries in the Sumerian tongue, the stories grew ever more fanciful until they became almost pure fiction. So entertaining were these stories that late in the third millennium the various Semitic conquerors of Sumer began to translate them into their own dialects.

Code of Hammurabi. The entire code of Hammurabi survives on an eight-foot column made of basalt. The top quarter of the column depicts the Babylonian king paying homage to the seated god of justice. Directly below one can make out the cuneiform inscriptions that comprise the law code's text.

Concepts of justice and social welfare

Old Babylonian literature: epic of Gilgamesh

Old Babylonian Necklace, Earring, and Seal Caps Made of Gold. 1700 B.C.

The surviving epic of *Gilgamesh* represents a late stage in this evolutionary process. Sometime around 1900 B.C. a Semitic speaker wove four or five of the Gilgamesh stories into a loosely structured "epic," and this version is the marvelous poem we know today.

The most remarkable qualities of the epic of *Gilgamesh* are its sheer poetic forcefulness and its startling secularity, for it recounts nothing but the adventures and aspirations of a human hero in a world governed by the inevitability of death. After engaging in mighty battles and amorous encounters Gilgamesh seeks the secret of immortality from an old man and his wife who had been saved by taking refuge in an ark when the gods had decided to destroy the world by a flood. The aged couple assure him that immortality is unobtainable, but they do disclose the location of a plant that at least will restore his lost youth. Unfortunately, after gaining this plant by heroic effort from the floor of the sea, Gilgamesh leaves it unguarded while asleep and a snake eats it. (According to the poem, this is why snakes gain new life every year when they shed their skins.) Thus the aspirant to immortality is finally forced to acknowledge that he should enjoy each day as it comes without worrying about the morrow: "Gilgamesh, whither art thou wandering?/ Life, which thou seekest, thou wilt never find,/ For when the gods created man, they let death be his share./ . . . . Gilgamesh, put on clean clothes, and wash thine head and bathe./ Gaze at the child that holdeth thine hand, /and let thy wife delight in thine embrace./ These things alone are men's concerns."

Despite these secular teachings, it would be a mistake to think that Old Babylonian culture was at all irreligious, for all Old Babylonians (the *Gilgamesh* poet included) assumed that the gods held omnipotent sway over humans. In fact since temples were just as dominant in Old Babylonian cities as they had been in Sumerian ones it is clear that religion was just as dominant as well. Moreover, surviving prayers show that the Old Babylonians had arrived at a hitherto unprecedented variety of religious commitment: *personal religion*. Although the gods of Sumer had "arisen out of nature" to act ever more like supremely powerful rulers, they remained gods of cities or nations rather than gods whom individual humans could address personally. Then, during the Old Babylonian period, it came to be assumed that in addition to the "political gods" who looked over human collectivities there existed other deities who looked over the daily affairs of individual people, and that it was necessary to pray to these personal deities for personal success and forgiveness of misdeeds. For example, an Old Babylonian would plead to a goddess: "I have cried to thee as a suffering, distressed servant./ See me, O my lady; accept my prayers." The appearance of personal religion among the Old Babylonians is of particular interest to students of subsequent religious history because personal invocation to God and religious introspectiveness are basic features of the Judeo-Christian tradition. Additionally the fact that individual Old Babylonians were praying fervently to personal gods is noteworthy in its own terms because it shows that Old Babylonian culture was tolerating a certain degree of individualism within a society that was otherwise intent on conformism.

A final remarkable aspect of Old Babylonian culture lies in a very different area: mathematics. It is difficult to ascertain how far Old Babylonian accomplishments were indebted to Sumerian ones because the earliest records pertaining to the knowledge of mathematics in Mesopotamia are all Old Babylonian. Yet these display arithmetical and algebraic concepts that are so advanced that they must have been based on Sumerian foundations. As that may be, Old Babylonian temple scribes around 1800 B.C. were employing tables for multiplication and division, and also for calculating square roots, cube roots, reciprocals, and exponential functions. So impressive were these achievements that if only a single Old Babylonian mathematical tablet had survived it would still allow the conclusion that the Old Babylonians were the most accomplished arithmeticians in antiquity. (The Greeks were adept at geometry but not in mathematics of number.) A basic aspect of modern daily life that derives from Old Babylonian mathematical precedents ·is our division of the day into two sets of twelve hours, the hour into sixty minutes, and the minute into sixty seconds. When one stops to think of it, working with multiples of ten would be easier, but the Old Babylonians based their arithmetic on multiples of twelve (apparently because their most fundamental reckoning was that of twelve lunar cycles to a year), and all Western civilizations have adhered to Old Babylonian "duodecimal" time reckonings (those based on units of twelve) ever since.

3. THE KASSITE AND HITTITE INTERLUDE

Hammurabi's empire lasted only a century and a half after his death in 1750 B.C., and throughout that time the Old Babylonians continually faced local uprisings and foreign incursions until the rise of a second Mesopotamian-wide empire around 1300 B.C. One cause of Old Babylonian decline may have been the same process of salinization that earlier had ruined Sumer. This, however, was probably not a major influence because even though salinization might have injured the Old Babylonian economy to some degree, its effects would have been less pronounced than they had been earlier for three reasons: (1) the Old Babylonians had learned how to combat salt buildup by drainage techniques; (2) they had shifted to growing barley as their main crop rather than wheat, and barley was better able to grow in saline soil; and (3) they had learned how to conserve the fertility of their lands by leaving portions of them fallow in an annual rotation system. Thus it appears that lack of governing skills on the part of several of Hammurabi's successors, combined with some poor military judgments and inability to adjust to new fighting techniques, were the primary reasons for Old Babylon's rapid decline.

The major new means of warfare employed by the enemies of the Old Babylonian empire in the sixteenth century B.C. was swift chariot attack made possible by the use of horses rather than oxen and by spoked wheels rather than wheels made from attached slabs. The peoples who first put light-chariot warfare to its best effect were the Kassites and the Hittites, both non-Semitic peoples who arrived in western Asia from the steppe lands east of the Caspian Sea toward the end of the third millennium. By the time of Hammurabi the Kassites had settled peacefully within parts of Mesopotamia, but soon after they began to war with the Old Babylonians and to take ever-greater portions of Mesopotamian territory by force. This process was nearly complete by 1600 B.C., but the last nail on the Old Babylonian coffin was not driven in by the Kassites, for descendants of Hammurabi still ruled in Babylon itself. Instead it was the Hittites, who, by a lightning raid from the north in 1595 B.C., demolished Babylon and thereby destroyed the last remnants of the Old Babylonian empire.

Retiring northward as quickly as they came, the Hittites left the Mesopotamian field clear for Kassite domination, but the Kassites were unable to take full advantage of this opportunity, apparently because they lacked dynamic leadership as well as a binding sense of political or cultural identity. Consequently, Mesopotamia fell into a "dark age," lasting about three centuries, during which most of the south (Akkad and Sumer) was ruled by the Kassites, while the north was divided among warring Semitic and non-Semitic peoples. The period seems "dark" because it offered neither united rule nor cultural or intellectual advances. The Kassites were content to adopt the use of cuneiform and Sumerian/Babylonian administrative techniques, and even to worship the Sumerian/Babylonian gods, without introducing any noteworthy innovations, nor did their disunited neighbors in Mesopotamia's north make any noteworthy contributions to the history of civilization.

Consequently, historians' interest centers on the Hittites. Originating from the steppes of central Asia and speaking an Indo-European tongue (the Indo-European linguistic family includes Hindu, Persian, Greek, Latin, and all the Romance, Slavic, and Germanic languages of today), the Hittites had occupied most of Anatolia (modern-day Turkey) by 1600 B.C. and within the next two centuries extended their empire southward along the eastern Mediterranean to include Syria and Lebanon. Having destroyed Babylon in 1595 B.C. they immediately decided not to overextend their lines of communication by attempting to rule directly in Mesopotamia. (The Bible states accurately that Hittite rule extended "even unto the great river, the river Euphrates" [Joshua 1:4].) The Hittite empire reached its geographical and economic peak between about 1450 and 1300 B.C., but in the thirteenth century B.C. the Hittites were placed on the defensive by invasions arising separately out of Egypt and northern Mesopotamia. In 1286 B.C. they staved off a mighty Egyptian onslaught into Syria, and later in the century they still were able to defend themselves against incursions from northern Mesopotamia launched by Semitic Assyrians. But exhaustion finally overcame them. In the years around 1185 B.C. successive waves of maritime attacks from the west (the exact origin of the "Sea Peoples" who briefly appeared in western Asia has not yet been securely identified) resulted in the utter destruction of the Hittites' power.

Although the Bible refers to the Hittites frequently, it does so always in passing (for example, Bathsheba's husband was "Uriah the Hittite"). Otherwise, virtually nothing was known about them until their Anatolian capital, Hattusas (meaning Hittite City), was excavated in 1907, bringing to light an archive of 20,000 clay tablets. In 1915 a Czech scholar, Bedrich Hrozny, deciphered the language of these tablets, announcing that it was Indo-European, and thereupon a rush of scholarly interest in the Hittites ensued. Unfortunately some of this scholarship was racially biased or ill informed and hence introduced some misconceptions about the Hittites, including the notion that they were great because they were Indo-Europeans. This is a mistake on two counts, first because it assumes that all the Hittites belonged to an Indo-European race, and second because it assumes that all members of the Indo-European race possess superior intelligence. While a homogeneous tribe of Indo-European-speaking Hittites may once have migrated from central Asia into Anatolia, as soon as its members settled down they intermingled with native peoples so thoroughly that whatever "racial purity" they once may have had became completely lost. (The same would have been true of the Semitic tribes that settled in Mesopotamia.) In any case, biology demonstrates that there is no correspondence between intelligence and race. Another myth about the Hittites is that they owed their long-term success to monopolizing

Hittite Sculpture. Perhaps the most highly conventionalized sculpture of the ancient world is found in Hittite reliefs.

Assyrian Winged Human-Headed Bull. This relief was found in the palace of King Sargon II (722–705 B.C.). It measures 16 feet wide by 16 feet high and weighs approximately 40 tons.

a secret weapon, the manufacture of iron, which they zealously kept beyond the ken of foreigners for centuries. Strange as it may seem, this belief rests on the misreading of a single Hittite document. The truth of the matter is that the Hittites did start making and using iron in the fourteenth century B.C., but so did all their contemporaries; so far as is known the use of iron weaponry did not give any western Asian nation an advantage over any other.

If the Hittites were not supremely smart or supremely well armed, how can one explain their might? Part of the answer lies in the resources that lay at their disposal, for Anatolia, in contrast to Mesopotamia, was rich in metallic ores, especially those of copper, iron, and silver. Dwelling at the source of such metals, the Hittites could trade some of them advantageously in their raw state, and they also were well positioned to experiment in metallurgy, hence excelling first in bronze and then in iron manufacture. Although the manufacture of iron did not give the Hittites any exclusive military advantage, it did bring them wealth because iron was as useful in peace as in war (it was particularly useful for making or reinforcing agricultural implements), and because in the earliest years of iron production (from roughly 1400 to roughly 1200 B.C.) anything made from iron had great prestige value. Accordingly the Hittites grew rich from trade in a way that would have been impossible had they inhabited another region. To this must be added the fact that they devised an efficient governmental system, whereby a "Great King" theoretically ruled supreme but actually delegated much authority to regional representatives. Aside from their metallurgy and their law, the Hittites were not particularly given

Sources of Hittite strength

to experimentation; they adopted cuneiform from the Mesopotamians, their art was conventional, and they seem to have had no independent literature. Nonetheless, endowed with sufficient wealth and governmental skill, the Hittites were able to preserve their empire and their national identity longer than was typical in the ebb and flow of western Asian peoples and kingdoms.

4. THE MIGHT OF THE ASSYRIANS

Returning to the narrative of events in Mesopotamia, we find that the Kassite "dark age" was succeeded by the period of the Assyrian empire, which lasted from roughly 1300 B.C. until exactly 612 B.C. The Assyrians were a people of the Semitic language group, who around 3000 B.C. had settled on the Tigris in northernmost Mesopotamia, where they established a small state centered on their city of Assur. This state was never threatened by salinization problems because the northern Tigris region, being hilly and of a more temperate climate than southern Mesopotamia, needed no irrigation. Yet the Assyrians made no mark on history until the opening of the thirteenth century B.C. when they came to acquire skills in chariot warfare and began to conquer neighboring cities. By around 1250 B.C. they had become masters of the entire Mesopotamian north, and soon after they dedicated themselves to subduing the Kassites in Akkad and Sumer. Since the Kassite kingdom was moribund, they had no trouble making such conquests either. In 1225 B.C. the Assyrian monarch Tukulti-Ninurta took Babylon and ordered his scribes to record: "I captured Babylon's king and trod his proud neck as if it were a footstool. . . . Thus I became lord of all Sumer and Akkad and fixed the boundary of my realm at the Lower Sea."

The evolution of Assyrian supremacy

Direct Assyrian rule over Sumer and Akkad lasted for only eight years because the Assyrians did not have the resources to maintain a costly occupation of a region whose inhabitants resented their rule. Yet they did succeed in maintaining indirect overlordship over southern Mesopotamia for six centuries after Tukulti-Ninurta trod over his enemy, preserving their trading interests in the region and making sure that no political counterweights would rise to challenge them. Shortly after 900 B.C., moreover, the Assyrians began to expand in other directions, apparently seeking control over natural resources and access to trade routes. In the first half of the ninth century they conquered Syria and reached the Mediterranean, and around 840 B.C. they annexed southeastern Anatolia. Temporary internal political divisions kept them from advancing immediately any farther, but one hundred years later they were on the march again until conquests culminating in the reign of Sennacherib (705–681 B.C.) made them masters of almost all the inhabitable territory of western Asia.

Masters of western Asia under Sennacherib

Sennacherib's reign displays the Assyrians at their most magnificent

Assyrian Relief Sculptures. These panels, representative of Assyrian "frightfulness," depict the Emperor Assurbanipal on the hunt.

and their most frightful. To seal his military victories Sennacherib built a splendid new capital, Nineveh, on the banks of the upper Tigris. No city remotely so splendid had ever been seen in Mesopotamia before. Within walls whose circumference was seven and a half miles lay magnificent temples and a royal palace with at least seventy-one chambers. Outside the walls were orchards and zoos with rare trees and exotic animals that Sennacherib ordered to be brought from great distances. Dissatisfied with the quality of the local water supply, the mighty king supervised an extraordinary engineering project whereby water was led to Nineveh by channels and aqueducts from fresh mountain springs fifty miles distant. To commemorate the successful completion of the project, rock carvings at the source depicted the gods flanked by inscriptions listing all of Sennacherib's military victories.

The splendor of Nineveh

Among the chambers in Sennacherib's palace at Nineveh was a library of clay tablets amounting to a vast repository of practical knowledge and religious lore. This knowledge came from southern Mesopotamia, for the Assyrians were entirely in the debt of ancient Sumer and Old Babylonia when it came to the life of the mind. Intent on gaining whatever practical knowledge they could for the sake of administration and commerce, and willing to worship all of Old Babylonia's gods (along with "Assur" the Assyrians' own local deity), the Assyrians began carrying off cuneiform tablets from Babylon as early as their sack of that city in 1225 B.C. Hence when Sennacherib's learned successor Assurbanipal (668–627 B.C.) rounded out the holdings of the library at Nineveh it contained virtually the entire available store of Sumerian and Old Babylonian learning and literature.

Derivative nature of Assyrian culture

See color plates following page 38

A traveler through Nineveh in the seventh century B.C. would thus have concluded that the Assyrian empire's ruling class was not only mighty but technologically proficient and very cultivated in certain respects. On the other hand, he would have seen ample evidence of what history has taken to be the Assyrians' most distinctive trait, their "frightfulness." To be fair to the Assyrians, frightfulness was no more characteristic of their culture than it was of any other until the time of Sennacherib. Although frightfulness implies a culture's unrelenting emphasis on the virtues of brutal masculinity ("machismo"), it was the Assyrians, rather than any other Mesopotamian people, who once accepted the rule of a queen, Sammuramat (known to the Greeks and later Europeans as Semiramis). Indeed, her reign from 810 to 805 B.C. seemed so extraordinary to other peoples that it became the subject of legend.

Assyrian frightfulness

Beginning with the reign of Sennacherib, however, the Assyrians began to display traits of extraordinary brutality in both their art work and their actual policies. In the sculptured reliefs that adorned Nineveh they celebrated war and slaughter. Scenes of lion hunting were their favorites: men with the coolest bravery yet also the coolest cruelty are shown hunting leaping lions, with special attention being paid to the death agonies of wounded beasts. Meanwhile the Assyrians were slaughtering real humans just as pitilessly. One of Sennacherib's military exploits was the quelling in 689 B.C. of a revolt against Assyrian hegemony in Babylon. Once he accomplished this he commanded his troops to pillage and destroy with the utmost thoroughness, thereupon boasting in an inscription: "I made Babylon's destruction more complete than that by a flood. . . . I demolished it with torrents of water and made it like a meadow."

Brutality in art and policy

The Assyrian policy of frightfulness in military campaigns was meant above all to strike abject terror into the hearts of the nation's enemies. No doubt it did this, but it also succeeded in making the Assyrians more intensely hated than any western Asian conquerors had been until their time. Since the conquered peoples' hatred for the Assyrians often overcame their fear of them, uprisings against Assyrian domination flickered on and off throughout the seventh century B.C., with the most frequent center of resistance being the area around Babylon. Although Sennacherib had presided over Babylon's destruction in 689 B.C., his son undertook the city's rebuilding for motives of prestige, and by 650 B.C. the city had once more become the focal point of southern Mesopotamian revolt. In order to quell the unrest, Sennacherib's grandson Assurbanipal laid siege to Babylon in that year and forced its surrender in 648 B.C., once more unleashing Assyrian frightfulness. As he proclaimed in one of the most inhumane accounts of methodical carnage ever recorded, "I tore out the tongues of many who plotted against me and then had them murdered. The others I smashed to death with the statues of their local gods. . . . Then I fed their corpses, cut into small pieces, to the dogs, to the pigs, to the vultures, and to all the birds of the sky."

Repressive government

One might have thought that the southern Mesopotamians would

*The Babylonian-Median
vengeance*

have remained submissive for a long time after that, but in fact they continued to seek any possible opportunity to throw off the Assyrian yoke. In 614 B.C. this opportunity finally came in the form of an alliance with an Indo-European tribe, the Medes, who had recently consolidated their power in Iran, directly to the east. Two years of warfare then were all it took to destroy the Assyrian empire: in 612 B.C. Nineveh fell to a united Babylonian-Median force, was leveled, and unlike Babylon never rose again. The rejoicing of all the conquered nations is well reflected in the Old Testament Book of Nahum: "Woe to the bloody city! . . . There is no end of their corpses, they stumble upon their corpses. . . . Nineveh is laid waste, and who will bemoan her?"

5. THE NEW BABYLONIAN REVIVAL

*The Chaldeans as the New
Babylonians*

Throughout the century of southern Mesopotamian resistance to Assyrian domination, the peoples most prominently engaged in that resistance were Semitic speakers called Chaldeans (pronounced Kaldee-ans), who, with the Medes, laid waste to Nineveh. Since the Medes used their victory of 612 B.C. as a springboard for invading Anatolia, the Chaldeans were left as masters of all Mesopotamia, and since they located their capital in Babylon, they are usually referred to by historians as the New Babylonians. The most famous New Babylonian ruler was Nebuchadnezzar (604–562 B.C.), who conquered Jerusalem, transported large numbers of Judeans to Babylon, and made his empire the foremost power in western Asia. Soon after his death New Babylonian might was challenged by an Indo-European people from Iran, the Persians (closely allied and ultimately intermingled with the Medes, giving rise to the historians' joke that "one man's Mede is another man's Persian"). In 539 B.C. one of Nebuchadnezzar's successors, Belshazzar, failed to understand "the handwriting on the wall" (Daniel 5), and before he knew it the Persians had rushed into Mesopotamia so quickly that Babylon fell to them without a fight.

*Nebuchadnezzar's
Babylon*

The city of Babylon during the era of the New Babylonians is the Babylon best known to us today, partly because of familiarity brought by early twentieth-century excavations and partly because of surviving eyewitness Greek travelers' descriptions. Babylon's size alone during this period was astounding, for it extended to 2100 acres, in comparison to the 1850 acres of Sennacherib's Nineveh and the 135 acres of the typical Sumerian city. (One of western Europe's largest cities, Paris, had only about twice Babylon's acreage until the early twentieth century, when it began to succumb to modern "urban sprawl.") More astounding still was Babylon's *color,* for the New Babylonians had learned to build their major monuments in brightly colored glazed brick. The most famous example, so splendid that it was counted by the ancient Greeks as one of the "seven wonders of the world,"

Reconstruction of the Ishtar Gate. Visitors to the Near Eastern Museum in Berlin can see this awe-inspiring reconstruction of Nebuchadnezzar's master-work, rising to a height of about fifty feet.

was the city wall built by Nebuchadnezzar. Against a background of brilliant blue, lions, bulls, and dragons in shades of white and yellow promenaded the entire length of the wall and strutted in tiers along the entire height of the "Ishtar Gate" (so called because the gate was dedicated to the goddess Ishtar). German archeologists digging in the ruins of Babylon in 1902 were the first since ancient times to see this marvel, and they must have felt as thrilled as if they had discovered the Pacific. Had Nebuchadnezzar built no more than this, his fame as one of history's most magnificent builders would have been secure, but he also constructed another of the "seven ancient wonders": Babylon's "Hanging Gardens." This feat was so extraordinary that truth about it merges into legend. Apparently Nebuchadnezzar really did build ascending terraces of gardens from the Euphrates outward, each with splendid plants and trees, but it may be legendary that he did this to gratify his wife, a Median princess from Iran, who loathed southern Mesopotamia's flatness and longed for her homeland's rolling hills.

Aside from construction feats, New Babylonia's cultural accomplishments were greatest in the realm of astronomy. We have seen that in the earliest Sumerian times Mesopotamian peoples had observed the phases of the moon in order to make predictions about the recurrence of the seasons. Two thousand years later Mesopotamians were still carefully studying the night skies, but now they were concentrating on the movements of the planets and the stars because they had come to believe that some of their gods resided in the heavens and that by plotting and predicting the motions of the planets and stars they could predict which divinity was gaining power and how that might affect the course of human affairs. Such study of the heavens was brought to its perfection by the New Babylonians, who identified five "wander-

Discovery of the Ishtar Gate. Archeologists digging at a site they decided was Babylon in 1902 uncovered to their amazement part of the Ishtar Gate.

ing stars" (we would say planets) and linked them with the powers of five different gods. (If this sounds strange, we should remember that we still call the first five planets by the names of five Roman gods—Mercury, Venus, Mars, Jupiter, and Saturn—because the Greeks and Romans inherited this system.) Going further, the New Babylonians concluded that when a given planet appeared in a particular part of the night sky or in close proximity to another planet its movement would portend war or famine, or the victory of one nation over another. Fully developed, these systems amounted to what we would call *astrology,* although New Babylonian astrology concerned itself exclusively with predictions about cosmic events such as floods and famines and the fortunes of nations rather than the fortunes of individual people. (The Greeks and Romans took the next step of casting personal horoscopes dependent on the configuration of the skies at the time of a person's birth, yet they continued to call all astrologers *Chaldaei* because of astrology's Chaldean or New Babylonian origins.)

Efforts to measure and interpret the universe

Today it is recognized that all astrology is superstition, but the New Babylonians' search for correspondences between heavenly events and earthly ones was scientific in terms of their time. In other words, for humans to believe that they can measure and interpret their universe and thereby learn how to benefit from it is more scientific than cowering in ceaseless fear of inexplicable mysteries. Moreover, dedicated to this belief, the New Babylonians observed celestial phenomena more closely than any other ancient peoples before them, and recorded their observations so meticulously that they later could be used and supplemented by astronomers of other nations, particularly the Greeks. Most notably, starting in 747 B.C. Chaldean court astronomers kept "diaries" on a monthly basis in which they recorded all planetary movements and eclipses, together with reports of earthly affairs such as price changes, shifting river levels, storms, and temperature trends. Continued without interruption until the period around 400 B.C., when Greek scientists began to gain knowledge of New Babylonian accomplishments, these records became a direct point of departure for astronomical science in the Greco-Roman world.

6. THE MESOPOTAMIAN LEGACY

Babylon fades into obscurity

The hanging gardens of Babylon are no more. Although the city of Babylon was not damaged when it was taken by the Persians in 539 B.C., the Persian conquest marked the end of Mesopotamian civilization insofar as native peoples and dynasties would never rule in Mesopotamia again. Gradually, as Greeks replaced Persians, Romans replaced Greeks, and Arabs replaced Romans, cuneiform ceased to be used, foreign artistic and building styles were introduced, and the old cities fell into ruins, to be supplanted by new ones. (The most magnificent city to arise in the Tigris-Euphrates region after the decay of Babylon was Baghdad, founded by the Arabs.) Entirely abandoned two centuries after the birth of Christ, Babylon became so covered up by the nearby shifting waters and sands that nobody knew for sure where it was until excavations accomplished shortly after 1900.

Yet the Mesopotamian legacy endures in different ways. One is by means of the Hebrew Bible. Since the earliest Hebrew peoples dwelled somewhere in Mesopotamia before they migrated to Palestine and since they spoke a language closely related to that of the Old Babylonians, it is not surprising that the earliest chapters of the Bible often allude to Mesopotamia. According to the book of Genesis King Nimrod ruled "Babel (Babylon), Erech (Uruk), and Akkad," and Abraham came to Palestine from "Ur of the Chaldees"; the "Tower of Babel," built out of "brick for stone and slime for mortar" (Genesis 11:1–9), is surely a reference to an Old Babylonian ziggurat. Ancient Hebrew and Mesopotamian points of contact are further displayed by the appearance in the *Gilgamesh* epic of a flood story very similar to the ark narrative in Genesis: not only is a human couple saved in both by floating in an ark, but they learn in both of the waters' ebbing when a bird they send forth no longer returns. More noteworthy still is the fact that fundamental Hebrew religious concepts bear relationships to ancient Mesopotamian ones. This is to not say that the Hebrews were unoriginal in their theology. Quite to the contrary, the Hebrews were the most original religious thinkers in the ancient world. Yet Old Testament theological formulations emerged from an ancient Mesopotamian matrix, and specific Hebrew religious innovations may well have been adaptations of Mesopotamian precedents. By the time of Sennacherib and Nebuchadnezzar the Hebrews came to hate the Assyrians and Babylonians because those peoples were constantly attacking them, and thereafter the invectives of the Hebrew prophets were passed on so effectively to Christians that the name Babylon even today remains a term for the essence of sinfulness (for example: "Hollywood Babylon"). But the insults should not be allowed to obscure the kinships and the debts.

Influence on the Hebrews

There is also the technological and intellectual legacy of Mesopotamia. We have seen that the wheel was first used for transportation in ancient Sumer, that the earliest known writing appeared there, and that the Old Babylonians pioneered in mathematical functions such as square and cube roots. Scholars find it difficult to determine whether all of these early Mesopotamian inventions were transmitted to other peoples by diffusion or whether some (writing above all) were invented independently elsewhere. In either case, however, the Mesopotamian inventions led step by step to modern practices taken for granted in Europe and America today. Mesopotamian jurisprudence and natural science similarly stand behind much that we today customarily take for granted. The visual world around us looks entirely different from that of ancient Mesopotamia because we have borrowed next to nothing from ancient Mesopotamian art and architecture, yet

Technological and intellectual legacy

in fundamental aspects of technology and thought we owe a great debt to the ingenious people of five thousand years ago who resolved to wrest power and glory from a land of mud-flats.

SELECTED READINGS

• *Items so designated are available in paperback editions.*

   Cambridge Ancient History (3rd ed., vols. I–II), Cambridge, 1971–1975.
• Frankfort, H., *The Art and Architecture of the Ancient Orient,* rev. ed., Baltimore, 1970.
   Gurney, O. R., *The Hittites,* rev. ed., Baltimore, 1980. The standard survey in English.
• Jacobsen, T., *The Treasures of Darkness: A History of Mesopotamian Religion,* New Haven, 1976.
• Kramer, S. N., *Sumerian Mythology,* New York, 1961. Develops different point of view than that advanced by T. Jacobsen.
• ———, *The Sumerians: Their History, Culture and Character,* Chicago, 1963. The best general treatment of Sumerian civilization.
• Lloyd, Seton, *The Archaeology of Mesopotamia,* rev. ed., London, 1984. Technical, but clear and well illustrated.
   ———, *Foundations in the Dust,* rev. ed., London, 1980. Describes the development and accomplishments of Mesopotamian archeology.
   Macqueen, J. G., *The Hittites and Their Contemporaries in Asia Minor,* rev. ed., London, 1986. Topical coverage.
• Neugebauer, Otto, *The Exact Sciences in Antiquity,* 2nd. ed., New York, 1969. Includes the basic account of Mesopotamian mathematical accomplishments.
• Oates, Joan, *Babylon,* rev. ed., London, 1986. A well-illustrated narrative that concentrates on Akkad from Sargon to the Persians and Greeks.
• Oppenheim, A. Leo, *Ancient Mesopotamia,* 2nd ed., Chicago, 1977. Concentrates on Babylonian and Assyrian culture.
   Saggs, H. W. F., *The Encounter with the Divine in Mesopotamia and Israel,* London, 1978.
   Woolley, Sir Leonard, and P. R. S. Moorey, *Ur "of the Chaldees,"* London, 1982. A revised account of Woolley's excavations at Ur which took place between 1922 and 1934.

SOURCE MATERIALS

• *Epic of Gilgamesh,* tr. N. K. Sandars, Baltimore, 1960.
   Grayson, A. K., and D. B. Redford, *Papyrus and Tablet,* Englewood Cliffs, N.J., 1973.
   Kramer, S. N., *History Begins at Sumer,* 3rd ed., Philadelphia, 1981.
   Pritchard, James B., *Ancient Near Eastern Texts Relating to the Old Testament,* 3rd ed., Princeton, 1969.

Chapter 3

EGYPTIAN CIVILIZATION

Thou makest the Nile in the Nether World,
Thou bringest it as thou desirest,
To preserve alive the people of Egypt.
For thou hast made them for thyself,
Thou lord of them all. . . .
—Hymn to Aton, from reign of the Pharaoh Akhenaton

Modern crowds that flood museums to view fabled treasures of Egyptian art are still captivated by the spell of one of the oldest and most alluring civilizations in history. Almost as old as the civilization founded in Mesopotamia during the fourth millennium B.C., Egyptian civilization provides a fascinating comparison to that of Mesopotamia because it was characterized by stability and serenity in contrast to the turmoil and tension of Mesopotamia. Not only were the Egyptians very peaceful for long periods of their ancient history, but surviving Egyptian statuary and painted human figures often seem to smile and bask in the sun as if they were on summer vacation.

Egypt compared to Mesopotamia

Environmental factors best explain the striking differences. Since the Mesopotamian climate was harsh, and since the Tigris and Euphrates flooded irregularly, the Mesopotamians could not view nature as dependably life-enhancing. Furthermore, since Mesopotamia, located on an open plain, was not geographically protected from foreign incursions, its inhabitants were necessarily on continual military alert. Egyptian civilization, on the other hand, was centered on the dependably life-enhancing Nile. Not only did the richly fertile soil of the Nile valley provide great agricultural wealth, but the Nile flooded regularly year after year during the summer months and always receded in time for a bountiful growing season, offering Egyptians the feeling that nature was predictable and benign. In addition, since the Nile valley was surrounded by deserts and the Red Sea, Egypt was comparatively free from threats of foreign invasion. The centrality of the

Environmental basis of differences between Egypt and Mesopotamia

Nile in ancient Egyptian life is well illustrated by the fact that the Egyptians had two words for travel: either *khed,* which meant "to go downstream," or *khent,* which meant "to go upstream." All in all, the Greek historian Herodotus surely had warrant to designate Egypt as "the gift of the Nile."

1. POLITICAL HISTORY UNDER THE PHARAOHS

Foundation of Egypt's advanced civilization

The ancient history of Egypt is usually divided into six eras: the archaic period (c. 3100–c. 2770 B.C.), the Old Kingdom (c. 2770–c. 2200 B.C.), the first intermediate period (c. 2200–c. 2050 B.C.), the Middle Kingdom (c. 2050–1786 B.C.), the second intermediate period (c. 1786–c. 1560 B.C.), and the New Kingdom (c. 1560–1087 B.C.). Even before the beginning of the archaic period the Egyptians had taken some fundamental steps in the direction of creating an advanced civilization. Above all, they had begun to engage in settled farming; they had learned to use copper tools in addition to stone ones; and, shortly before 3100 B.C., they had developed a system of writing known as *hieroglyphic* (Greek for "priestly carving"). Experts are uncertain whether the Egyptians arrived at the idea of writing on their own, or whether the idea came to them from Mesopotamia. The strongest argument for the former position is that the hieroglyphic system is very different from Mesopotamian cuneiform, but the sudden appearance of hieroglyphic suggests that certain Egyptian administrator-priests decided to work out a record-keeping system on the basis of their knowledge of a foreign precedent. Whatever the case, writing surely allowed for greater governmental efficiency and apparently was a precondition for the greatest event in ancient Egyptian political history, the unification of the north and the south.

Egyptian unification, and therewith the beginning of the archaic period, occurred around 3100 B.C. Until then separate powers had ruled in Upper (or southern) Egypt, and Lower (or northern) Egypt, but unity was essential for Egypt's future because a single government was necessary to ensure the free flow of traffic along the entire length of the Nile, as well as to provide centralized direction of irrigation projects. Tradition attributes the unification of Egypt to a warrior from the south called Narmer, the first of the pharaohs (kings), who brought all of Egypt northward to the Mediterranean delta under his control. (Egyptian rulers are called "pharaohs" as the result of biblical usage, even though the ancient Egyptians themselves did not use this term.) It may be that the process was somewhat more gradual, but there is little doubt that for roughly four hundred years after about 3100 B.C. a succession of two ruling dynasties held sway over a united Egypt.

The first two Egyptian dynasties were succeeded around 2770 B.C. by the rule of the mighty Zoser, the first king of the Third Dynasty

Narmer Palette. Dating from about 3100 B.C., this stone carving shows a warrior-ruler from the south who was thought to be Narmer, subduing his counterpart from the north with a mace. The falcon probably represents the God Horus, who looks with approval on the birth of Egyptian unification in violence.

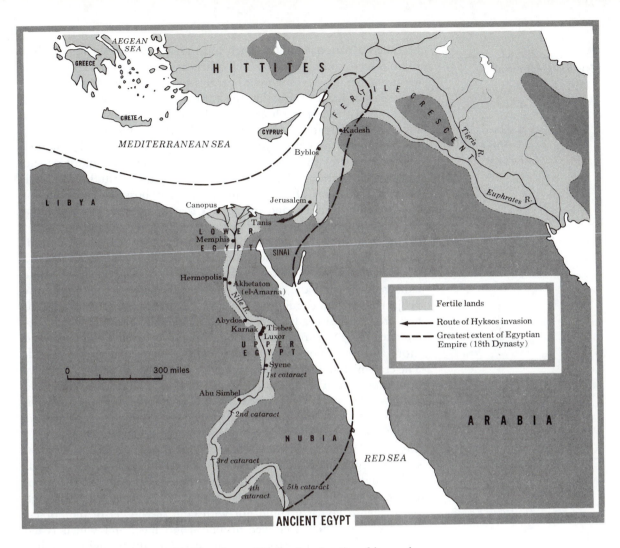

ANCIENT EGYPT

and the founder of the Old Kingdom. While the details of how the governmental system of the Old Kingdom differed from that of the archaic period will never be known, it is certain that Zoser's reign initiated a period of vastly greater state power and royal absolutism, best witnessed by the fact that Zoser presided over the building of the first pyramid. Under Zoser and his leading successors of the Old Kingdom the power of the pharaoh was virtually unlimited. The pharaoh was considered to be the child of the sun god, and by custom married one of his sisters to keep the divine blood from becoming contaminated. No separation of religious and political life existed. The pharaoh's chief subordinates were priests, and he himself was the chief priest.

The government of the Old Kingdom was founded upon a policy of peace. In this respect it was virtually unique among ancient states. The pharaoh had no standing army, nor was there anything that could

Zoser and the founding of the Old Kingdom

See color map facing page 39

The nonmilitaristic character of the Old Kingdom

End of the Old Kingdom

The Middle Kingdom

be called a national militia. Each local area had its own militia, but militias were commanded by civil officials, and when called into active service generally devoted their energies to labor on the public works. In case of a threat of invasion the various local units were assembled at the call of the pharaoh and placed under the command of one of his civil subordinates. At no other time did the head of the government have a military force at his disposal. The Egyptians of the Old Kingdom were content for the most part to work out their own destinies and to let other nations alone. The reasons for this attitude lie in the protected position of their country, in their possession of land of inexhaustible fertility, and in the fact that their state was a product of cooperative need instead of being grounded in exploitation.

After centuries of peace and relative prosperity the Old Kingdom came to an end with the downfall of the Sixth Dynasty about 2200 B.C. Several causes were responsible. Governmental revenues became exhausted because the pharaohs invested heavily in such grandiose projects as pyramid-building. To make matters worse, overall Egyptian prosperity was adversely affected by climatic disasters which precipitated crop failures. In the meantime provincial nobles usurped more and more power until central authority virtually disappeared. The era which followed is called the first intermediate period. Anarchy now prevailed. The nobles created their own rival principalities, and political chaos was aggravated by internal brigandage and invasion by desert tribes. The first intermediate period did not end until the rise of the Eleventh Dynasty, which restored centralized rule around 2050 B.C. from its base in Thebes (Upper Egypt). The next great stage of Egyptian history, known as the Middle Kingdom, ensued.

Throughout most of its life the government of the Middle Kingdom was more socially responsible than that of the Old Kingdom. Although the Eleventh Dynasty could not withstand the power of the nobles, the Twelfth, which followed around 1990 B.C., and which lasted until 1786 B.C., ruled strongly by means of an alliance with a middle class composed of officials, merchants, artisans, and farmers. This alliance kept the nobility in check and laid the foundations for unprecedented prosperity. During the rule of the Twelfth Dynasty there were advances in social justice and much intellectual achievement. Public works that benefited the whole population, such as extensive drainage and irrigation projects, replaced the building of pyramids, which had no practical use. There was also a democratization of religion which extended to common people a hope for salvation that they had not been granted before. Religion now emphasized proper moral conduct instead of ritual dependent on wealth. For all these reasons the reign of the Twelfth Dynasty is commonly considered to be Egypt's classical or golden age.

Immediately afterward, however, Egypt entered its second intermediate period. This was another era of internal chaos and foreign invasion

A Pharaoh of the New Kingdom. Ramses II (who reigned from 1295 to 1225 B.C.) brought Egyptian rule temporarily into Syria by means of lightning military campaigns with war chariots.

which lasted for more than two centuries, or from 1786 to about 1560 B.C. The contemporary records are scanty, but they seem to show that the internal disorder was the result of a counterrevolt of the nobles. The pharaohs were again reduced to impotence, and much of the social progress of the Twelfth Dynasty was destroyed. About 1750 B.C. the land was invaded by the Hyksos, or "Rulers of Foreign Lands," a mixed horde originating in western Asia. Their military prowess is commonly ascribed to the fact that they possessed horses and war chariots, but their victory was certainly made easier by the dissension among the Egyptians themselves. Their rule had profound effects upon Egyptian history. Not only did they introduce the Egyptians to new methods of warfare, but by providing them with a common grievance in the face of foreign tyranny they also enabled them to forget their differences and unite in a common cause.

The invasion of the Hyksos

Near the end of the seventeenth century B.C. the rulers of southern (Upper) Egypt launched a revolt against the Hyksos, a movement which was eventually joined by all of Egypt. By about 1560 B.C. the last conquerors who had not been killed or enslaved had been driven from the country. The hero of this victory, Ahmose, founder of the Eighteenth Dynasty, thereafter established a regime which was much more highly consolidated than any that had hitherto existed. In the great outpouring of patriotism which had accompanied the struggle against the Hyksos, local loyalties were reduced, and with them the power of the nobles.

The period that followed the accession of Ahmose is called the New Kingdom, and by some, the period of the Empire. It lasted from about 1560 to 1087 B.C., during which time Egypt was ruled by three dynasties of pharaohs in succession: the Eighteenth, Nineteenth, and Twentieth. No longer was the prevailing state policy pacific and isolationist; a spirit of aggressive imperialism pervaded the nation, for the military ardor generated by the successful war

Ramses II (19th Dynasty)

against the Hyksos whetted an appetite for further victories. Moreover, a vast military machine had been created to expel the invader, which proved to be too valuable an adjunct to the pharaoh's power to be discarded.

The first steps in the direction of the new policy were taken by the immediate successors of Ahmose in making extensive raids into Palestine and claiming sovereignty over Syria. With one of the most formidable armies of ancient times, the new pharaohs speedily eliminated all opposition in Syria and eventually made themselves masters of a vast domain extending from the Euphrates to the southern parts of the Nile. But they never succeeded in welding the conquered peoples into loyal subjects, and this weakness was the signal for widespread revolt in Syria. Although their successors suppressed the uprising and managed to hold the Empire together for some time, ultimate disaster could not be averted. More territory had been annexed than could be managed successfully. The influx of wealth into Egypt weakened the national fiber by fostering corruption, and the constant revolts of the vanquished eventually sapped the strength of the state beyond hope of recovery. By the twelfth century most of the conquered provinces had been permanently lost.

Failures of the Empire

The government of the New Kingdom or Empire resembled that of the Old Kingdom, but it was even more absolute. Military power now provided the basis of the pharaoh's rule. A professional army was always available with which to overawe his subjects. Most of the former nobles now became courtiers or members of the royal bureaucracy under the complete domination of the king.

The government of the Empire

The last of the great pharaohs was Ramses III, who ruled from 1182 to 1151 B.C. He was succeeded by a long line of nonentities who inherited his name but not his ability. By the end of the twelfth century Egypt had fallen prey to renewed barbarian invasions. About the same time the Egyptians appear to have lost most of their creative talents. To win immortality by magic devices was now the commanding interest of people of every class. The process of decline was hastened by the growing power of the priests, who usurped the royal prerogatives and dictated the pharaoh's decrees.

The last of the pharaohs

From the middle of the tenth century B.C. until the end of the eighth century B.C. a dynasty of Libyan barbarians held power. They were followed briefly by a line of Nubians, who overran Egypt from the deserts east of the Upper Nile. In 671 B.C. Egypt was conquered by the Assyrians, but the latter held their ascendancy for only eight years. After the collapse of Assyrian rule the Egyptians regained their independence, and a revival of traditionalism ensued. This was doomed to an untimely end, however, for in 525 B.C. Persian invaders defeated a defending Egyptian army in pitched battle. Egypt thence was absorbed into the Persian Empire and subsequently was ruled by Greeks and Romans.

The end of Egyptian independence

2. EGYPTIAN RELIGION

Religion played a very influential role in the life of the ancient Egyptians, leaving its impress on politics, literature, architecture, art, and the conduct of daily affairs. The evolution of Egyptian religion went through various stages: from simple polytheism to the earliest known expression of monotheism, and then back to polytheism. In the beginning each city or district appears to have had its local deities, who were guardian gods of the locality or personifications of nature powers. The unification of the country resulted not only in a consolidation of territory but in a fusion of divinities as well. All of the guardian deities were merged into the great sun god Re. Under the Theban rulers of the Middle Kingdom, this deity was called Amon or Amon-Re from the name of the chief god of Thebes. The gods who personified the vegetative powers of nature were fused into a deity called Osiris, who was also the god of the Nile. Thereafter these two great powers who ruled the universe, Amon and Osiris, vied with each other for supremacy. Other deities, as we shall see, were recognized also, but they occupied a distinctly subordinate place.

The early religious evolution

During the period of the Old Kingdom the solar faith, embodied in the worship of Re, was the dominant system of belief. It served as an official religion whose chief function was to give immortality to the state and to the people collectively. The pharaoh was the living representative of this faith on earth; through his rule the rule of the god was maintained. But Re was not only a guardian deity. He was in addition the god of righteousness, justice, and truth, and the upholder of the moral order of the universe. He offered no spiritual blessings or even material rewards to people as individuals. The solar faith was not a religion for the masses, except insofar as their welfare coincided with that of the state.

The solar faith

The cult of Osiris, as already observed, began its existence as a nature religion. The god personified the growth of vegetation and the life-giving powers of the Nile. The career of Osiris was marked by elaborate legend. In the remote past, according to belief, he had been a benevolent ruler, who taught his people agriculture and other practical arts and gave them laws. After a time he was treacherously slain by his wicked brother Set, and his body cut into pieces. His wife Isis, who was also his sister, went in search of the pieces, put them together, and miraculously restored his body to life. The risen god regained his kingdom and continued his beneficent rule for a time, but eventually descended to the underworld to serve as judge of the dead. Then his son Horus avenged his father's death by killing Set.

The Gods Isis, Osiris, and Horus

Originally this legend seems to have been little more than a nature myth. The death and resurrection of Osiris symbolized the drying of the Nile in the autumn and the coming of the flood in the spring.

Funerary Papyrus. The scene shows the heart of a princess of the Twenty-First Dynasty being weighed in a balance before the god Osiris. On the other side of the balance are the symbols for life and truth.

Significance of the Osiris legend

But in time the Osiris legend began to take on a deeper significance. The human qualities of the deities concerned—the paternal solicitude of Osiris for his subjects, the faithful devotion of his wife and son—appealed to the emotions of average Egyptians, who were now able to see their own tribulations and triumphs mirrored in the lives of the gods. More important still, the death and resurrection of Osiris came to be regarded as conveying a promise of personal immortality. As the god had triumphed over death, so might the individual who worshiped him inherit everlasting life. Finally, the victory of Horus over Set appeared to foreshadow the ultimate ascendancy of good over evil.

Egyptian ideas of the hereafter

Egyptian ideas of the hereafter attained their full development in the later history of the Middle Kingdom. For this reason elaborate preparations had to be made to prevent the loss of one's earthly remains. Not only were bodies mummified, but wealthy men left rich endowments to provide their mummies with food and other essentials. As the religion advanced toward maturity, however, a less naive conception of the afterlife was adopted. The dead were now believed to appear before Osiris to be judged according to their deeds on earth. All of the departed who met the tests entered a realm of physical delights. In marshes of lotus-flowers they would hunt geese and quail with never-ending success. Or they might build houses in the midst of orchards with luscious fruits of unfailing yield. They would find lily-lakes on which to sail, pools of sparkling water in which to bathe, and shady groves inhabited by singing birds. But the unfortunate victims whose hearts revealed their vicious lives were utterly destroyed.

Ethical synthesis

The Egyptian religion attained its fullest development about the end of the Middle Kingdom. By this time the solar faith and the cult of Osiris had been merged in such a way as to preserve the best features of both. The province of Amon as the god of the living, as the champion of good in this world, was accorded almost equal importance with the functions of Osiris as the judge of the dead and giver of immortality. The religion was now quite clearly an ethical one. People repeatedly avowed their desire to do justice because such conduct was pleasing to the great sun god.

Soon after the establishment of the Empire Egyptian religion underwent debasement. Its ethical significance was largely destroyed, and superstition and magic gained the ascendancy. The chief cause seems to have been that the bitter war to expel the Hyksos fostered the growth of irrational attitudes and correspondingly depreciated the intellect. The result was a marked increase in the power of the priests, who preyed upon the fears of the masses to promote their own advantage. They inaugurated the practice of selling magical charms, which were supposed to have the effect of preventing the heart of the deceased from betraying his or her real character. They also sold formulas which were alleged to be effective in facilitating the passage of the dead to the realm of the blessed. A collection of these formulas constituted what is referred to as the Book of the Dead.

This degradation of the religion into a system of magical practices finally resulted in a great religious upheaval. The leader of this movement was the Pharaoh Amenhotep IV, who began his reign about 1375 B.C. and died or was murdered about fifteen years later. After some fruitless attempts to correct the most flagrant abuses, he resolved to crush the system entirely. He drove the priests from the temples, hacked the names of the traditional deities from the public monuments, and initiated the worship of a new god whom he called "Aton," an ancient designation for the physical sun. He changed his own name from Amenhotep ("Amon rests") to Akhenaton, which meant "Aton is satisfied." His wife Nefertiti became Nefer-nefru-aton: "Beautiful is the beauty of Aton." In keeping with his desire to begin all over, Akhenaton built a new capital, El-Amarna, which he dedicated to the worship of the new deity.

More important than these physical changes was the set of doctrines enunciated by the reforming pharaoh. He taught first of all a religion of qualified monotheism. Aton and Akhenaton himself were the only gods in existence. Like none of the gods before him, Aton had no human or animal shape but was to be conceived in terms of the lifegiving, warming rays of the sun. He was the creator of all, and thus god not merely of Egypt but of the whole universe. Akhenaton deemed himself to be Aton's heir and co-regent; while the pharaoh and his wife worshiped Aton, others were to worship Akhenaton as a living deity. Aside from this important qualification, Akhenaton restored the ethical quality of Egyptian religion at its best by insisting that Aton was the author of the moral order of the world and the rewarder of humanity for integrity and purity of heart. He envisaged the new

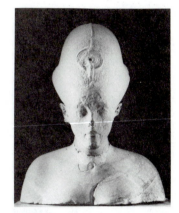

Akhenaton. A full-sized weathered bust.

Religion of Aton

Akhenaton, His Wife Nefertiti, and Their Children. The god Aton is depicted here as a sun-disk, raining down his power on the royal family.

Tutankhamen or "King Tut." This solid-gold coffin weighs 2,500 pounds.

god as the sustainer of all that is beneficial, and as a heavenly father who watches with benevolent care over all his creatures. Conceptions like these of the unity, righteousness, and benevolence of God were not attained again until the time of the Hebrew prophets some 600 years later.

Despite the energy with which Akhenaton pursued his religious revolution it was still a failure. The religion of Aton gained little popular following because the masses remained devoted to their old gods. The new religion was too strange for them and lacked the greatest attraction of the older faith: the promise of an afterlife. Moreover, the pharaohs who followed Akhenaton were allied with the priests of Amon and accordingly restored the older modes of worship. Akhenaton's successor, the pharaoh whom we refer to as "King Tut," changed his name from Tutankh*aton* to Tutankh*amen,* abandoned El-Amarna for the old capital of Thebes, and presided over a return to all the old ways. His own burial was a lavish demonstration of commitment to the old rituals and belief in life after death. Thereafter Egyptian religion was characterized by growing faith in ritualism and magic. Priests sold formulas and charms that were supposed to trick the gods into granting salvation: thus even the cult of Osiris lost most of its moral quality.

3. EGYPTIAN INTELLECTUAL ACHIEVEMENTS

Aside from the varied richness of their religious thought, the greatest intellectual accomplishments of the Egyptians lay in their system of writing and in the realm of certain practical sciences. We have seen that Egyptian writing, hieroglyphic, emerged after the appearance of cuneiform writing in Mesopotamia, perhaps even with an awareness of the Mesopotamian precedent. Thus it is not so much the idea of writing as the particular nature of Egyptian writing that is worth consideration here. Specifically, as early as the time of the Old Kingdom, Egyptian hieroglyphic was based on three types of characters: the pictographic, the syllabic, and the alphabetic. The first two were already components of cuneiform, but the last was a crucially significant innovation. Had the Egyptians taken the step of separating their alphabetic characters—twenty-four symbols, each representing a single consonant sound of the human voice—from their nonalphabetic ones and using the former exclusively in their written communication they would have developed a writing system that was fully modern. Since conservatism kept them from doing this, it was left for a Semitic people of the eastern Mediterranean shore, the Phoenicians, to devise the first exclusively alphabetical system around 1400 B.C. The Phoenician alphabet in turn became the model for the alphabets of the Hebrews, Arabs, Greeks, and Romans. Nevertheless, since the Phoeni-

Nature of Egyptian writing

cians definitely borrowed the idea of using single symbols for denoting single sounds from the Egyptians, and since they even modeled many of their letters on Egyptian exemplars, there is warrant for viewing the Egyptian alphabetical system as the parent of every alphabet that has been used in the Western world.

Blessed with a plant, the papyrus reed, that grew abundantly in the Nile delta region (papyrus in Lower Egypt was so plentiful that it was the pictographic symbol in hieroglyphic for "Lower Egypt"), the Egyptians possessed a cheap material on which to write. Strips of the papyrus reed, when flattened and dried, could be used for setting down hieroglyphic and then rolled up into scrolls for storage or transport. The advantage of writing on papyrus over writing on clay tablets was that papyrus rolls were less cumbersome and vastly lighter: hence they not only became the standard writing material in Egypt but their use spread from the Egyptians to the civilizations of ancient Greece and Rome. (Could the Roman Empire have established its vast administrative system on clay tablets? It is doubtful.)

Perhaps because it was so easy to write things down, the Egyptians experimented in several forms of literature. The Egyptians of the Middle Kingdom are considered by many literary historians to have been the fathers of the short story. Various kinds of short narratives were written at that time: a surviving papyrus roll from the nineteenth century B.C. contains a tall tale about a shipwrecked sailor; a somewhat later narrative describes the plight of a man who cannot sleep because of the bellowing of hippopotamuses on the Nile; and an ancient Egyptian bawdy tale tells of a lustful woman who says to the hero, "Come, let us spend an hour lying together, it will be good for you!" At the other extreme are collections of maxims similar to those of the Book of Proverbs in the Old Testament, offering practical wisdom and enjoining moderation and justice. Finally, there is at least one surviving Egyptian approximation of a political treatise, *The Plea of the Eloquent Peasant,* written around 2050 B.C. In this the author sets forth the ideal of a ruler committed to benevolence and justice for the good of his subjects. Although no single work of Egyptian literature approaches the Mesopotamian *Gilgamesh* epic, parts of the Hebrew Bible, or the Greek *Iliad* and *Odyssey* for enduring literary quality, Egyptian writing nonetheless has its entertaining features.

As for science, the Egyptians were most interested in those branches that aimed particularly at practical ends—astronomy, medicine, and mathematics. In the realm of astronomy the Egyptians' greatest achievement was their discovery of a way to avoid the imprecisions of a lunar calendar. We have seen that the peoples of ancient Mesopotamia remained limited in marking the passage of seasons and years to working with the cycles of the moon. In contrast, by around 2000 B.C. the Egyptians noticed that the brightest star in the sky, Sirius, rose in the morning once a year in direct alignment with the sun.

Practical nature of
Egyptian science: (1)
astronomy and the calendar

Constructing a calendar on this observation, wherein "New Year's Day" began with Sirius's solar alignment, they could foretell the coming of the Nile's floods and produced the best calendar in antiquity before that devised by Julius Caesar. Indeed, Caesar's calendar itself rested on the Egyptian precedent.

(2) Medicine and a nature-based view of disease

Ancient Egyptian medical practice was distinguished by the view that diseases came from natural rather than supernatural causes and hence that physicians should provide accurate diagnoses and predictably reliable treatments. Among diagnostic methods was the taking of the pulse and the listening to the heartbeat. As for therapeutics, surviving papyrus documents show that some treatments must have been predictably reliable and others not. For example, Egyptian doctors prescribed castor oil as a cathartic but offered whipped ostrich eggs mixed with tortoise shells and thorns to cure internal ulcers. Concerned with hygiene as well as health, they proposed the following remedy for sweaty feet: "take uadu-plant-of-the-Fields and eel-from-the-Canal, warm in oil, and smear both feet therewith." While it is easy to smile at such prescriptions, the Egyptian attempt to alleviate pain and enhance health by natural means deserves respect, not to mention the fact that some Egyptian medicinal remedies, carried to Europe by the Greeks, are still employed today.

(3) Mathematics and measurement

In mathematics the Egyptians excelled in methods of measurement. For example, they were the first to mark off 360 degrees to a circle and the first to notice that the ratio of the circumference of a circle to its diameter is the same for all circles (today this is known as the "pi" ratio). They also devised means for computing the areas of triangles and the volumes of pyramids, cylinders, and hemispheres. Such accomplishments obviously were interrelated with the Egyptians' spectacular building projects, to which we may now turn.

4. THE SPLENDOR OF EGYPTIAN ART

The pyramids

The most famous of all Egyptian visual monuments are of course the pyramids—vast constructions of towering simplicity, built at the dawn of recorded time to serve as tombs of the pharaohs. Awe for the pyramids must extend from amazement at their stark beauty to astonishment regarding the circumstances of their construction. The earliest pyramid, the step-pyramid of the pharaoh Zoser, was erected around 2770 B.C. at a time when nothing remotely resembling its scale had ever been attempted by humanity. Whereas contemporary Sumerians built solely with mud-bricks and prior Egyptians had gone no further than erecting edifices from a few tons of limestone, all of a sudden, under the guidance of Zoser's chief builder, Imhotep, one million tons of limestone were quarried, hauled without wheeled vehicles, and fitted precisely into place to a summit about 200 feet high. And that was just the beginning. Soon after, in the century from

The Pyramids of Gizeh with the Sphinx in the Foreground

roughly 2700 to roughly 2600 B.C., a total of some 25 million tons of limestone were hewn out of rock cliffs, dressed, hauled, and piled in the course of building a series of pyramids that are the most famous and beautiful of all. Of these the gem of gems is no doubt the pyramid of Khufu (a pharaoh known to the Greeks as Cheops), which rose to a height of 482 feet at the "perfect" angle of 52°, making its pinnacle stand in relation to its circumference as in the "pi" ratio of circles. When the Greeks decided to count the seven wonders of the world, they unhesitatingly ranked the pyramid of "Cheops" as the first.

While the great pyramids remain for us to see, many questions arise as to how and why they were built. By a conservative estimate some 70,000 laborers were needed to put up a pyramid. These were almost certainly seasonal laborers. During the summer months, when the Nile was at its flood stage, there was little or nothing for farmers to do, so they could be employed on massive building projects without detrimental effect to the Egyptian agricultural economy. But one summer does not make a pyramid. Rather, it has recently been concluded that pyramid laborers must have worked summer after summer, starting on a new pyramid after the last one was finished, without reference to whether a reigning pharaoh had died or not, because that is the only way to account for the transformation of 25 million tons of stone into several enormous pyramids during the course of one century. Thus for thousands of people, hewing and hauling limestone in the raging heat of an Egyptian summer was a yearly way of life without prospect of termination.

The perennial summer's work

The laborer's motivation: religious psychology and group dynamics

See color plates following page 38

Why did 70,000 laborers endure this? Brute coercion is surely not the answer, for Egypt at this time did not know slavery (aside from a small number of war captives); moreover, it is impossible to imagine that a handful of rulers could have forced tens of thousands of subjects to labor against their wills year after year without cowing them by any extraordinary weaponry. Religious psychology and group dynamics instead seem to provide the best explanations. The Egyptian laborers who built the pyramids apparently believed that their pharaohs were living gods who could ascend to eternal life upon their earthly exits solely by means of proper burial. Zoser's step-pyramid was thus in a literal sense a "stairway to heaven" and the later pyramids were simply straight-angle embodiments of the same ascent-to-heaven conception. The laborers who sweated to build these enormous monuments on the hot sands believed their own well-being was inextricably tied to that of their god-rulers: if the pharaohs journeyed well to their eternal glory, life on earth would flourish. In addition, collaborative labor must have given the individual toiler a sense of uplifting comradeship and team accomplishment. This point seems borne out by marks found on various pyramid stones reading "vigorous team," "enduring team," and so forth. Farmers who were relatively isolated during most of the year must have found teamwork on the most prestigious and exalted projects of the day to be a source of pride and emotional reward that made their heaving and sweating seem almost pleasurable.

Ultimately pyramid building was recognized by Egyptian leaders of state to be a wasteful occupation. Since concern for personal salvation

The Temple at Karnak. Most of this building has collapsed or been carried away, but the huge pylons give an idea of the massiveness of Egyptian temples.

became the major religious trend during the time of the Middle Kingdom, the temple, then and afterwards, replaced the pyramid as Egypt's leading architectural form. The most noted Egyptian temples are those of Karnak and Luxor, built during the period of the New Kingdom. Many of their gigantic, richly carved columns still stand as silent witness to a splendid architectural talent. Egyptian temples were characterized by massive size. The temple at Karnak, with a length of about 1,300 feet, covered the largest area of any religious edifice ever built. Its central hall alone could contain almost any of the cathedrals of Europe. The columns used in the temples had stupendous proportions. The largest were seventy feet high, with diameters in excess of twenty feet. It has been estimated that the capitals which surmounted them could furnish standing room for a hundred men.

Egyptian sculpture and painting served primarily as adjuncts to architecture. Sculpture was characterized by set conventions governing its style and meaning. Statues of pharaohs were commonly of colossal size. Those produced during the New Kingdom ranged in height from seventy-five to ninety feet. Some of them were colored to enhance the portrait, and the eyes were frequently inlaid with rock crystal. The figures were nearly always rigid, with the arms folded across the chest or fixed to the sides of the body, and with the eyes staring straight ahead. Countenances were generally represented as slightly smiling but otherwise devoid of emotional expression. Anatomical distortion was frequently practiced: the natural length of the thighs might be increased, the squareness of the shoulders accentuated, or all of the fingers of the hand made equal in length. A familiar example of nonnaturalistic sculpture was the Sphinx, of which there were thousands in Egypt; the best-known example was the Great Sphinx at Gizeh. This represented the head of a pharaoh on the body of a lion. The purpose was probably to symbolize the notion that the pharaoh possessed the lion's qualities of strength and courage. The figures of sculpture in relief were even less in conformity with nature. The head was presented in profile, with the eye full-face; the torso was shown in the frontal position, while the legs were rendered in profile.

The meaning of Egyptian sculpture is not hard to perceive. The colossal size of the statues of pharaohs was doubtless intended to symbolize their power and the power of the state they represented. It is significant that the size of these statues increased as the empire expanded and the government became more absolute. The conventions of rigidity and impassiveness were meant to express the timelessness and stability of the national life. Here was an empire that was not to be torn loose from its moorings by the uncertain mutations of fortune but was to remain fixed and imperturbable. The portraits of its chief men consequently must betray no anxiety, fear, or triumph, but an unvarying calmness throughout the ages. In similar fashion, the anatomical distortion can probably be interpreted as an attempt to express some national ideal.

Pharaoh Mycerinus and His Queen. Above: Sculpture from the Fourth Dynasty, c. 2590 B.C.—an example of the impassive, grandiloquent style. Below: A comparison of their profiles leaves little doubt that they were brother and sister as well as husband and wife.

The meaning of Egyptian sculpture

Akhenaton's artistic revolution

An intriguing exception to the mainstream of Egyptian artistic development is the art produced during the reign of Akhenaton. Because the pharaoh wished to break with all manifestations of the ancient Egyptian religion, including its artistic conventions, he presided over an artistic revolution. The new style he patronized was naturalistic because his new religion revered nature as the handiwork of Aton. Accordingly portrait busts of the pharaoh himself and his queen Nefertiti abandoned the earlier grandiloquent impassivity and distortion in favor of more realistic detail. A surviving bust of Nefertiti which reveals her slightly quizzical and haunting femininity is one of the greatest monuments in the history of art. For the same reasons painting under the patronage of Akhenaton also emerged as a highly expressive art form. Murals of this period display the world of experience above all in terms of movement. They catch the instant action of the wild bull leaping in the swamp, the headlong flight of the frightened stag, and the effortless swimming of ducks in a pond. But just as Akhenaton's religious reform was not lasting, neither was the more naturalistic art of his reign.

Nefertiti. The famous portrait bust executed in Akhenaton's studios at El-Amarna.

5. SOCIAL AND ECONOMIC LIFE

During the greater part of the history of Egypt the population was divided into five classes: the royal family; the priests; the nobles; the middle class of scribes, merchants, artisans, and wealthy farmers; and the peasants, who comprised by far the bulk of the population. During the New Kingdom a sixth class, the professional soldiers, was added, ranking immediately below the nobles. Thousands of slaves were also captured in this period, and for a time these formed a seventh class. Despised by all, they were forced to labor in the government quarries and on the temple estates. Gradually, however, they were allowed to enlist in the army and even in the personal service of the pharaoh. With these developments they ceased to constitute a separate class. The position of the various ranks of society shifted from time to time. In the Old Kingdom the nobles and priests among all of the pharaoh's subjects were supreme. During the Middle Kingdom the classes of commoners came into their own. Merchants, artisans, and farmers gained concessions from the government. Particularly impressive is the dominant role played by the merchants and artisans *The principal classes of Egyptian society* in this period. The establishment of the Empire, accompanied as it was by the extension of government functions, resulted in the ascendancy of a new nobility, primarily made up of officials. The priests also gained more power with the growth of magic and ritualism.

The gulf that separated the standards of living of the upper and lower classes of Egypt was perhaps even wider than it is today in Europe and America. The wealthy nobles lived in splendid villas that opened onto fragrant gardens and shady groves. Their food had all

Fishing and Fowling: Wall Painting, Thebes, Eighteenth Dynasty. Most of the women appear to belong to the prosperous classes, while the simple garb and insignificant size of the men indicates that they are probably slaves.

the richness and variety of sundry kinds of meat, poultry, cakes, fruit, wine, and sweets. They ate from vessels of alabaster, gold, and silver, and adorned themselves with expensive fabrics and costly jewels. By contrast, the life of the poor was wretched. The laborers in the towns inhabited congested quarters composed of mud-brick hovels whose only furnishings were stools, boxes, and a few crude pottery jars. The peasants on the great estates enjoyed a less crowded but no more abundant life.

The gulf between rich and poor

Although polygamy was permitted, normally the basic social unit was the monogamous family. Even the pharaoh, who could keep a harem of secondary wives and concubines, had a chief wife. Concubinage, however, was a socially reputable institution. Yet compared to women in most other ancient societies, Egyptian women were not entirely subordinated to men. Wives were not secluded; women could own and inherit property and engage in business. The Egyptians also permitted women to succeed to the throne: Queen Sobeknofru reigned during the Twelfth Dynasty and Queen Hatshepsut during the Eighteenth.

Egyptian women

The Egyptian economic system rested primarily upon an agrarian basis. Agriculture was diversified and highly developed, and the soil yielded excellent crops of wheat, barley, millet, vegetables, fruits, flax, and cotton. Theoretically the land was the property of the pharaoh, but in the earlier periods he granted most of it to his subjects, so that in actual practice it was largely in the possession of individuals. Commerce grew steadily after about 2000 B.C. to a position of first-rate importance. A flourishing trade was carried on with the island

Agriculture, trade, and industry

Egyptian Slaves at Work. Left: Sculptors at work in a tomb of the Sixth Dynasty, c. 2300 B.C. Right: A wall painting done around 1550 B.C. displays slave-laborers making bricks.

of Crete, and with territories on the eastern Mediterranean shore. Gold mines in Libya controlled by Egypt were an important source of wealth. The chief articles of export consisted of gold, wheat, and linen fabrics, with imports being confined primarily to silver, ivory, and lumber. Of no less significance than commerce was manufacturing. As early as 3000 B.C. large numbers of people were engaged in artisanal crafts. In later time factories were established, employing twenty or more persons under one roof, and with some degree of division of labor. The leading industries were shipbuilding and the manufacture of pottery, glass, and textiles.

The development of instruments of business

From an early date the Egyptians made progress in the development of instruments of business. They knew the elements of accounting and bookkeeping. Their merchants issued orders and receipts for goods. They invented deeds for property, written contracts, and wills. While they had no system of coinage, they had rings of copper or gold of set weight circulated as exchange, in effect the oldest known currency in the history of civilizations. The simple dealings of the peasants and poorer townsfolk, however, were doubtless based on barter.

Economic collectivism

The Egyptian economic system was primarily collective. From the very beginning the energies of the people had been drawn into socialized channels. The interests of the individual and the interests of society were conceived as identical. The productive activities of the entire nation revolved around huge state enterprises, and the government remained by far the largest employer of labor. But this collectivism was not all-inclusive; a considerable sphere was left for private initiative. Merchants conducted their own businesses; many of the craftsmen had their own shops; and as time went on, larger and larger numbers of peasants gained the status of independent farmers. The government continued to operate the quarries and mines, to build pyramids and temples, and to farm the royal estates.

6. THE EGYPTIAN ACHIEVEMENT

When a party of Greeks visited the Nile valley around 500 B.C. a dignified Egyptian priest supposedly told them, "You Greeks are always children; there is not an old man among you." The point of course is that members of a civilization that had outlasted two and a half millennia considered the Greeks to be mere whippersnappers: Egypt was into its Twenty-sixth Dynasty when the Greeks were just beginning to organize their thoughts. Seen from today's perspective, the relatively untroubled longevity of Egyptian civilization still commands respect. Apparently the ancient Egyptians had found a way to cooperate with nature and each other in order to live in peace and self-sufficiency for centuries at a stretch. The Greeks, who conquered the Egyptians in 332 B.C., were vastly more experimental and creative, but they also introduced continual upheaval into an Egyptian world that until then had been characterized by stability.

Peace and self-sufficiency

The ancient Egyptian success formula was so closely bound to the annual flooding of the Nile that it could not easily be transported. Hence, aside from a few specific accomplishments, such as the solar calendar or the reckoning of cubic space, the Egyptian achievement is not best estimated by the directness of its influence on subsequent thought or events. Rather, Egyptian patterns of living, thinking, sculpting, painting, and building are fascinating for their own sake. There is something in all of us that makes us wish we could go back in time to view Nefertiti, listen to King Tut's priests intone their timeless hymns, or float on a barge down the Nile past lotus-flowers while the pyramids are rising. This is understandable awe for a civilization that found its place in the sun when history's sun was still at its dawn.

Egypt's unique circumstances

7. KUSHITIC CIVILIZATION

Egyptian splendor rested in large measure on vast human and physical resources lying beyond its southern periphery. Successive Egyptian dynasties drew heavily on the area known today as the Sudan Republic for laborers and soldiers as well as for precious stones and exotic woods used in the crafting of jewelry and fine furniture. The contributions of these darker-skinned neighbors are vividly recorded in scenes etched on objets d'art found in the tombs of Egypt's pharaohs.

The origin of the Negroid southerners, long shrouded in mystery, is beginning to come to light through recent archeological discoveries. We are now fairly certain that from at least 2200 B.C. food-producing Neolithic groups from the ecologically-deteriorating southern Sahara were dispersing to more fertile parts of Africa. Some migrated to the Lower Nile where they joined peoples of Mediterranean and Asian stock in laying the foundations of the so-called New Kingdom of Egypt. Others wandered southward to the Upper Nile in a region later known to the Egyptians as "Kush." By 1500 B.C. these black-complexioned Kushites, showing remarkable cultural affinities to late predynastic Egypt, had established their own kingdom. Indeed, this Kingdom of Kush became the first highly advanced, essentially Negroid, civilization in Africa. Its vigorous inhabitants traded actively with Egypt and borrowed extensively from their culture. Within four centuries, the capital at Napata, just south of the Fourth Cataract, had flowered into a major religious center for the worship of the Egyptian god Amon-Re.

Foundation of the Kingdom of Kush

Under their king, Kashta, the Kushites began to take advantage of Egypt's decaying social fabric. In about 750 B.C. Kashta's armies swept into the temple city of Thebes, capital of Upper Egypt. Kashta's son, Piankhy, went on to capture Memphis and to extend Kushitic dominion over Lower Egypt as well. With the entire country in hand, Piankhy assumed the title of pharaoh and established Egypt's Twenty-fifth Dynasty

Kushitic invasion of Egypt

The rule of the Kushites was short-lived. Their genius at governance was no match for the Iron Age Assyrians who burst into Egypt in 670 B.C. The Kushites quickly retreated to their former homelands along the far reaches of the Upper Nile. A new Kushitic power base was established at Meroë, some 120 miles north of modern Khartoum, in the fertile pastures between the river Atbara and the Blue Nile. They may have acquired from the Assyrians the technique of

Meroë: black Africa's first industrial city

Egyptian Tomb Art. Egypt's Sundanic neighbors were frequently portrayed in Egyptian art.

iron-smelting, for Meroë soon became the major iron-working center of ancient Africa and the first black industrial city south of the Sahara.

The Kushites made an indelible imprint on numerous Mediterranean civilizations. By the fifth century B.C. their likeness appeared on vases, wall murals, and statues from Cyprus in the eastern Mediterranean to ancient Etruria on the Italian peninsula. They were variously depicted as athletes, dancers, court attendants, and warriors. Greek merchants, active in Egyptian markets, called the Kushites "Ethiopians" meaning "men with burnt faces."

In 322 B.C. Egypt was conquered by Alexander the Great and became a Greek-ruled kingdom. Thenceforth, via Hellenized Egypt, Kushitic exposure to Mediterranean civilizations increased. A brisk trade with the Greeks and Hellenized Egyptians brought prosperity to Kush and enabled its people to develop distinctive architectural and artistic traditions. Unique stone pyramids cast haunting shadows across the Nile at Meroë; and Meroitic pottery, decorated with incised geometric designs, could compare favorably to the finest produced in the ancient world at that time. Kush reached its zenith between 250 B.C. and 200 A.D. By that time Meroitic hieroglyphs had even begun to replace Egyptian as the literary language.

The Kushitic window on the non-African world opened still further between 13 A.D. and the third century, when Egypt was under Roman rule. After that, Nile valley trade quickly declined and with it Kushitic civilization. For centuries, the Nile's treacherous cataracts had shielded Kush from northern invasions and permitted its inhabitants to adopt only those aspects of Egyptian, Greek, and Roman culture they found desirable. But with the Nile valley connection weakened, Kush suffered economically and fell vulnerable to desert infiltrators from the west. This made it rather easy in the mid-fourth century for Meroë to be overrun by the armies of neighboring Axum, a rising kingdom in the southeast.

Tantalizing legends suggest that Meroë's royal family migrated to West Africa where they may have contributed to the evolution of new political and cultural institutions. West Africans were less advanced politically and economically even though their trans-Saharan links with North Africa and the Nile extend far into antiquity. Since at least 130 B.C. West Africans supplied the north with gold, slaves, precious stones, and wild animals for sports arenas. An ancient chariot route extended from the Punic settlements on the North African coast through the oases of the Fezzan to the Chad Basin. The Kushitic refugees may have followed an even more ancient trail connecting the Nile with the Niger river by way of Fezzan. Tragically, the middle Nile valley became a cul-de-sac rather than a corridor to the south. Indeed, comparatively little of the rich culture of the Nile valley radiated southward into East and Equatorial Africa.

Kushitic impact on Mediterranean civilizations

The flowering of Kushitic civilization 250 B.C.–200 A.D.

The downfall of Kush

Ancient trans-Saharan links

8. THE CHRISTIAN KINGDOM OF ETHIOPIA

In stark contrast to landlocked Kush, Axum to the southeast could profit from a fast-moving trade with Ptolemaic Egypt via the Red Sea. Axumite seaports were busy entrepôts for goods from the interior destined for the Mediterranean world, the Persian Gulf, India, and beyond. Egyptian Greek middlemen provided Axumites a window on the eastern Mediterranean while their Arabian counterparts exposed them to the outlets and cultures of the Orient.

The people of Axum were a product of peaceful mingling of African and Semitic Arabians. The latter had been migrating in small bands toward the rugged Ethiopian highlands since 1000 B.C. With intermarriage came cultural enrichment, so superbly reflected in giant religious obelisks, cut with incredible precision from single blocks of stone. Great strides were also made in agricultural productivity through the introduction of the plow and the art of stone terracing and irrigation.

In the mid-fourth century A.D. King Ezana converted to Christianity and declared it the official state religion. Christianity became an effective instrument for the cultural and political unification of the various Axumite chieftaincies into a centralized kingdom called Ethiopia. By the tenth century Christian Ethiopia had eradicated the last vestiges of the Axumite kingdom. Monasteries took root in Ethiopia and served as vital centers of learning and cultural transmission. Ethiopian monks translated the Bible into Ge'ez, the indigenous language. In time, the monasteries became economically powerful, as successive emperors endowed them with huge tracts of land. Monasticism as a way of life spread quickly to neighboring Nubian kingdoms, before it had appeared in Christian Western Europe.

Ethiopia, centered in mountainous and almost inaccessible highlands, became a natural citadel. In relative seclusion, its inhabitants forged

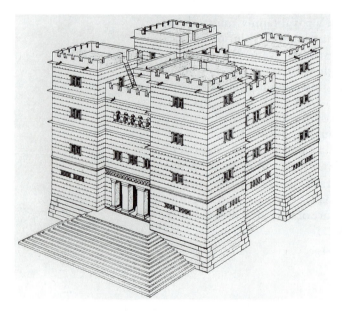

Axumite Residential Building on a Monumental Scale. This turn of the century reconstruction of the central portion of Enda Mika'el reveals a four-story-high castle-like structure anchored by four square towers.

a powerfully stable monarchy and a distinctive Christian culture. Representing one of the world's most stable and enduring civilizations, Ethiopia continued into the twentieth century under essentially the same time-honored institutions and the same royal family.

SELECTED READINGS

• *Items so designated are available in paperback editions.*

Aldred, Cyril, *Akhenaton, Pharaoh of Egypt: A New Study,* London, 1968. The standard treatment in English.

• ———, *The Egyptians,* rev. ed., London, 1984. A short but reliable treatment of political history and cultural accomplishments.

Bibby, Geoffrey, *Four Thousand Years Ago,* Baltimore, 1961. Egyptian developments from 2000 to 1000 B.C. seen from the perspective of contemporary events elsewhere in the ancient world.

Breasted, James H., *History of Egypt,* New York, 1912. By America's first great Egyptologist. A classic, although now regarded as out of date in its extreme claims for Egyptian originality and influence.

• Butzer, Karl W., and L. G. Freeman, eds. *Hydraulic Civilization in Egypt,* Chicago, 1976. A careful analysis of the Nile valley as an eco-system. Downplays grandeur in favor of examining the essential circumstances of daily existence.

Cambridge Ancient History (3rd ed., vols. I–II), Cambridge, 1971–1975.

Cottrell, Leonard, *Life under the Pharaohs,* New York, 1960. Fascinating recreation of life under the Empire.

Emery, Walter, *Archaic Egypt,* Baltimore, 1961. Controversial account of the earliest period.

• Frankfort, Henri, *Ancient Egyptian Religion: An Interpretation,* New York, 1948. A penetrating, profound study.

• Hayes, William C., *The Scepter of Egypt,* 2 vols., New York, 1953–1959. Written with special reference to the Egyptian holdings of the Metropolitan Museum of Art in New York.

• Mendelssohn, Kurt, *The Riddle of the Pyramids,* London, 1974. A lucid account of how the pyramids were built and a persuasive interpretation of why they were built.

• Mertz, B., *Temples, Tombs and Hieroglyphs,* rev. ed., New York, 1978. Intriguing approach by means of archeological discoveries.

Mokhtar, G., ed., *UNESCO General History of Africa,* II: *Ancient Civilizations of Africa,* London, 1981.

Redford, Donald B., *Akhenaten: The Heretic King,* Princeton, 1984. Reviews the most recent scholarship and takes a more negative view of the controversial pharaoh than that offered by Aldred.

• Smith, W. S., *The Art and Architecture of Ancient Egypt,* rev. ed., Baltimore, 1965.

• Steindorff, G., and K. C. Seele, *When Egypt Ruled the East,* rev. ed., Chicago, 1963. The political history of the Empire.

• Trigger, B. G., et al., *Ancient Egypt: A Social History,* London, 1983. A guide to current directions in Egyptology; exciting research, but unexciting prose.

• Wilson, John A., *The Burden of Egypt,* Chicago, 1951. (Paperback edition under title of *The Culture of Ancient Egypt.*) In a class by itself as the one book to read if the student wishes to read just one. Scintillating and masterful.

SOURCE MATERIALS

Grayson, A. Kirk, and D. B. Redford, *Papyrus and Tablet,* Englewood Cliffs, N.J., 1973. The best short collection.

• Lichtheim, M., *Ancient Egyptian Literature,* 3 vols., Berkeley, 1973–1980. The standard selection of representative works, many of which are highly entertaining.

• Pritchard, James B., ed., *The Ancient Near East: An Anthology of Texts and Pictures,* Princeton, 1965. Covers both Egypt and Mesopotamia.

Chapter 4

THE HEBREW AND EARLY GREEK CIVILIZATIONS

I am the Lord thy God, which brought thee out of the land of Egypt
   from the house of bondage.
Thou shalt have none other gods before me. . . .
Thou shalt not take the name of the Lord thy God in vain.

                                        —Deuteronomy 5:6–11

Then Agamemnon awoke from slumber . . . and put on a soft tunic,
fair and new, and he threw a great cloak about him; about his shining
feet he bound fair sandals. . . . Then he grasped his ancestral sceptre,
indestructible forever.

                                        —Homer, *The Iliad*

D warfed by the great empires of Mesopotamia and Egypt in
territory and military prowess, the civilizations of the Hebrews
and the early Greeks nonetheless merit full consideration.
The extraordinary historical significance of the Hebrews lies beyond
challenge, for despite their political insignificance, the Hebrews exerted
the greatest influence of any ancient western Asian peoples on the
thought and life of the modern world. As for the ancient Greek civilizations (as will be seen, there were two of them), they are memorable
for their grace and sophistication and for being the earliest civilizations
of Europe.

Importance of the Hebrew civilization

1. HEBREW BEGINNINGS

The first known appearance of the Hebrews, who were members of
the Semitic language family, was in Mesopotamia, for according to
the Bible the Hebrew patriarch Abraham's family was native to Sumer.
Since the Hebrews originally were a wandering pastoral people it is
not surprising that thereafter their exact whereabouts are often difficult

Hebrew migrations

to locate. Suffice it to say that between roughly 1900 and 1500 B.C. they gradually migrated from Mesopotamia to southern Syria (a land then known as Canaan) and thence into Egypt. During those centuries a tribe of Hebrews who claimed descent from Abraham's grandson Jacob began to call themselves "Israelites" after Jacob's alternative name. (According to the Book of Genesis, after Jacob wrestled with an angel for a whole night he received the name "Israel," which means "soldier of God.") After sojourning for about three centuries in Egypt the Hebrews were enslaved during the time when the pharaohs of the New Kingdom were attempting to create an Egyptian empire and seeking ever more slaves to keep their home economy running. It was then, around 1250 B.C., that the Hebrews found a leader in the heroic Moses, who led their exodus out of Egyptian bondage into the Sinai peninsula (a desert land located between Egypt and Canaan) and persuaded them to become worshipers of Yahweh, a god whose name was much later written as Jehovah. It was then too that all Hebrews became Israelites because Moses persuaded them that Yahweh had been the god of Abraham, Isaac, and Jacob, and that accordingly the god of Israel was the god now worshiped by them all.

After wandering for about a generation in the Sinai deserts the Hebrews resolved to move back into the much richer land of Canaan, a land indeed so much richer than the arid Sinai wastes that it seemed to them a land "flowing with milk and honey." Yet it was impossible simply to move in and settle down because Canaan was already occupied by the Canaanites, another Semitic language people, who did not care to share their land with the Hebrews. Hence the Hebrews had to fight their way into Canaan, and that proved to be a slow and difficult process, misrepresented by the famous line that "Joshua fit the battle of Jericho and the walls came a tumbling down." Moses' successor Joshua did indeed gain some territory in Canaan, but not very much because the pastoral Israelites were generally not well equipped to reduce the well-fortified Canaanite cities by siege warfare. Moreover, after Joshua's death the Israelites fared even less well because they lost their ability to pursue concerted military action as a result of the revival of tribal particularism. Thus after a century of fighting they had gained no more than some of Canaan's hills and a few of the less fertile valleys. Worse, just around that time they were forced to defend themselves, not only against the Canaanites, who hoped to recoup their losses, but against a mighty foreign invasion.

The invasion was that of the Philistines, a non-Semitic people from Asia Minor who quickly conquered so much of Canaan around 1050 B.C. that the region became known alternatively as Palestine, in effect meaning "the Philistine country." Faced with the threat of extinction, the Hebrews now intensified their struggle. Whereas hitherto they had preserved a tribal form of organization whereby wise men ("judges") in each tribe were chosen when need arose to resolve con-

The struggle for Canaan

A Canaanite Deity. Thought to be an image of Baal, a god of storms and fertility, this statuette was discovered in a thirteenth century B.C. temple in northern Palestine.

flicts, it now became clear that a tighter, "national," form of government was necessary to meet the Philistine challenge. Accordingly, around 1025 B.C., Samuel, a tribal judge with the force of personality to gain adherence from all the Israelite tribes, selected for all of them a king, Saul, who would make of them a united people.

2. THE RECORD OF POLITICAL HOPES AND FRUSTRATIONS

Although the reign of King Saul marked the beginning of Hebrew national unity, it was not in itself a happy one, either for the Hebrews or for the ruler himself. Only a few hints of the reasons are given in the Old Testament account. Evidently soon after he began acting assertively as king, Saul incurred the anger of Samuel, who had expected to remain the power behind the throne. So Samuel began to lend his support to an energetic young warrior, David, who carried on skillful maneuvers to draw popular support away from Saul. Waging his own military campaigns, David achieved one triumph over the Philistines after another. (His victory over "Goliath" would have been accomplished with more than a slingshot.) In contrast, the armies of Saul met frequent reverses. Finally the king, being critically wounded, ended the rivalry by slaying himself. The date would have been roughly 1005 B.C.—close enough to the millennium marker to make it easy to remember.

The reign of King Saul

With Saul in his grave, David now became king and initiated the most glorious period in Hebrew political history—at least until modern times. Advancing relentlessly against the Philistines, he reduced their territory to a narrow strip of coast in the south. He compelled the Canaanites to recognize his rule, with the effect that during the next few generations they lost their separate identity and became fully merged with the Hebrew people. As this process of amalgamation progressed, the Hebrews increasingly put aside pastoralism and took up either farming or urban occupations. Once David fully established his position as absolute monarch, he exacted forced labor from some of his subjects, instituted a census as a basis for collecting taxes, and then actually started to collect taxes. His ultimate goal was to build a splendid capital and religious center at Jerusalem, but although he made some progress in this enterprise he died before the work was completed.

David as absolute monarch

David was succeeded by his son Solomon, who ruled from 973 to 933 B.C., the last of the three kings of the united Hebrew monarchy. Solomon was determined to finish his father's work in building Jerusalem. The purpose, inherited from his father, was twofold. First, if the Israelites were to take their place among the great nations of western Asia, they had to have a magnificent capital as a visual manifestation of their greatness. And secondly, they also needed a splendid temple

Solomon, Jerusalem, and the Temple

Model of King Solomon's Temple. Significant details are: A, royal gates; B, treasury; C, royal palace; D, people's gate; E, western (wailing) wall; F, priests' quarters; G, courthouse; H, Solomon's porch.

to reaffirm their national religious commitment. Until then the "Ark of the Covenant," the biblical name for the chest containing the stone tablets supposedly given by Yahweh to Moses on Mount Sinai, had been carried by the Israelites in their wanderings in a "tabernacle," actually no more than a portable tent. To house an exalted shrine in a tent may have been barely satisfactory for a nomadic people, but not for settled agriculturalists of a great nation. Instead, the Ark, the physical token of Israel's special relationship with Yahweh, had to be located in a mighty capital and housed properly in the innermost precincts of a splendid temple. For these reasons Solomon spared no expense in building his capital, and especially in building the temple that would be the central monument of Hebrew national and religious life. In the long run this policy contributed fundamentally to the survival of the Hebrews, for Solomon indeed succeeded in erecting a splendid temple and Solomon's Temple thereafter served as an inspiring symbol whenever Israel was faced with the possibility of national and cultural obliteration. But in the short term the king's lavish building projects caused trouble because Palestine was poor in natural resources needed for basic building materials, not to mention lacking in the gold and gems needed to adorn these projects. When, despite mountingly oppressive taxation, Solomon found himself unable to pay his construction debts, he first ceded territory to his main supplier, the bordering country (to the north) of Phoenicia, and then he drafted and deported Hebrews to work in Phoenicia's forests and mines.

Northern antagonism and secession

Not surprisingly such tyrannical behavior provoked bitter antagonism among many of Solomon's subjects, especially those of the north. The northerners were the ones who saw their sons forcibly sent to Phoenicia, and they were least sympathetic to the building projects in Jerusalem, which lay more to the south of the Hebrew kingdom. (Apparently the northerners were also less ardent in exclusive dedication to Yahweh than the southerners, still another reason why they

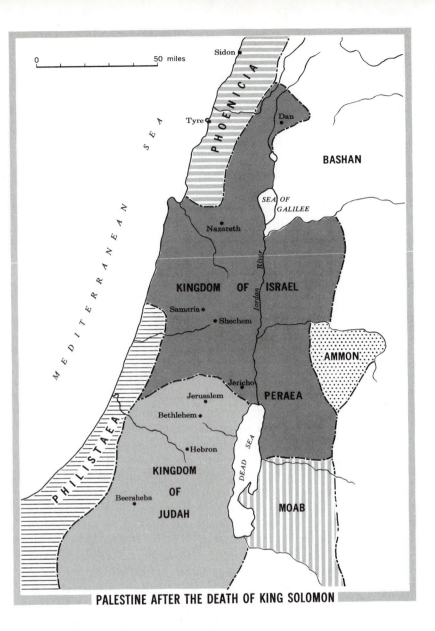

PALESTINE AFTER THE DEATH OF KING SOLOMON

would have been less enthusiastic about making personal sacrifices to import gold for the Ark of the Covenant.) While Solomon remained alive his northern subjects remained obedient to him, but his death was the signal for open revolt. Refusing to pay taxes to Solomon's son Rehoboam, the northerners quickly seceded from the united Hebrew state and set up their own kingdom.

The northern kingdom came to be known as the Kingdom of Israel, having its capital in Samaria, while the remnant in the south was the Kingdom of Judah, with its capital in Jerusalem. Even as a united state the Hebrew realm would not have been impressively strong, but split in half, the realm was pitifully weak. More by luck and the

The fragility and fate of the Kingdoms of Israel and Judah

forbearance of its neighbors than by intrinsic viability the Kingdom of Israel managed to survive (usually paying tribute) for two centuries until 722 B.C., when it was annihilated by the Assyrians. Since the Assyrians followed a policy of leveling all the important buildings of conquered nations and scattering their populations, the Kingdom of Israel was never heard from again. As for the Kingdom of Judah, it just barely eluded the Assyrian menace, partly because of its very insignificance, but in 586 B.C. it was conquered by the Babylonians under Nebuchadnezzar, who plundered and burned Jerusalem and its Temple, deporting Judah's leading citizens to Babylon. For a half-century thereafter the Judeans—from this point customarily called the Jews by historians—suffered their "Babylonian Captivity," fearing that they would never again see their homeland.

Palestine: from Persian overlordship to Roman annexation

As events would have it, they were mistaken, for upon conquering Babylon in 539 B.C. Cyrus the Persian magnanimously allowed the Jews to return to Palestine and to establish their rule there semi-independently under Persian overlordship. The returnees wasted no time in rebuilding the Jerusalem Temple (accomplished from 520 to 516 B.C.), and their heirs lived more or less peacefully within the Persian sphere of influence until 332 B.C., when Palestine was conquered by the Greek, Alexander the Great. Since Alexander died soon afterwards the Jews then passed under the rule of successive Greek-speaking overlords. In 168 B.C., one of them, Antiochus Epiphanes, attempted to destroy the Jewish faith by desecrating the Temple and prohibiting all worship in it, but this ruthlessness resulted in provoking a Jewish revolt led by the inspiring fighter Judas Maccabeus. After two decades of struggle the Jews of Palestine finally succeeded in gaining political independence under the rule of a native Maccabean dynasty, but that situation lasted only until 63 B.C., when the Roman general Pompey took advantage of the dynasty's internal feuding to turn Palestine into a Roman protectorate. Discontented under Roman rule, the Jews revolted in 66 A.D. in a desperate attempt to recreate the victory over Antiochus. But this time they faced the mightiest of all ancient empires and lost all they had. In 70 A.D. the Roman Emperor Titus put down the Jewish uprising mercilessly and razed the Temple, which has never been rebuilt since. Palestine then was annexed by the Romans outright, and the Jews gradually left for other parts of the vast Roman Empire. The *diaspora,* or migration of the Jews away from Palestine to country after country through the centuries, became the central fact of Jewish existence from then until the twentieth century.

Roman Coin Celebrating the Destruction of Jerusalem. The inscription IVDEAE CAPTA means "Judea Captured," and "S. C." is a standard abbreviation for "with consent of the Senate." A triumphant Roman soldier lords it over a female personification of the Jews shown in an attitude of dejection.

3. HEBREW RELIGIOUS DEVELOPMENT

Even during King David's time the ancient Hebrews were no more than a second-rate political power, and after Solomon's reign they were not even that. Hence the Hebrews would not be worth more

Menorah Mosaic from a Synagogue Pavement. After the Romans destroyed the Second Temple the seven-branched candelabrum *(menorah)* became the identifying emblem for Judaism because the candelabrum formerly had been placed next to the "Ark of the Covenant" in the Temple and now stood for the missing Temple itself. In this mosaic from a synagogue of Jericho (twenty-five miles east of Jerusalem), done around 500 A.D., the menorah is complemented by a branch associated with the Harvest Festival and a ram's horn *(shofar)* sounded at the New Year. The inscription reads "Peace upon Israel."

than passing consideration in this book were it not for their achievements in a different area, that of religion. Today Judaism, the religion of the Jews, is a coherent body of beliefs, customs, and liturgical practices, all of which are founded in passages from the Jewish Bible (known to Christians as the Old Testament). The student of history, however, must recognize that Judaism did not spring suddenly into place in one moment but was the product of a long process of change transpiring between the time of Moses and that of the Maccabees.

Evolution of Hebrew religion

Four stages can be distinguished in the growth of the Hebrew religion. The first, known to scholars solely by inference, was that in which the Hebrews were polytheists (worshipers of many gods), like all other contemporary western Asian peoples. Then came the stage of national *monolatry,* initiated by Moses around 1250 B.C. and lasting until about 750 B.C. Monolatry means the exclusive worship of one god, without denying that other gods exist. Due to the influence of Moses, the people of Israel adopted as their national deity a god whose name was written "Yhwh" and was probably pronounced as if spelled "Yahweh." The Hebrews agreed to worship no other gods aside from Yahweh, for Moses insisted "Hear, O Israel, the Lord our God is one Lord" (Deuteronomy 6:4).

Stage of national monolatry

During the time of national monolatry Yahweh was a rather peculiar figure. He was conceived almost exclusively in anthropomorphic terms. He possessed a physical body and the emotional qualities of men. He was capricious on occasions, and somewhat irascible—as capable of evil and wrathful judgments as he was of good. Sometimes he would punish someone who sinned unwittingly as readily as one whose guilt was real. By way of illustration, Yahweh reportedly struck Uzza dead merely because he placed his hand on the Ark of the Covenant to steady it while it was being transported to Jerusalem (I Chronicles 13:9–10). Yahweh was not omnipotent, for his power was limited

Anthropomorphic characteristics of Yahweh

*Moral precepts, rituals,
and tabus*

The prophetic revolution

to the territory occupied by the Hebrews. Nonetheless, some of the most important Hebrew contributions to subsequent Western thought were first formulated during this time. It was during this period that the Hebrews came to believe that God was not part of nature but entirely outside of it, and that humans, while part of nature, became the rulers of nature by divine will. This "transcendent" theology meant that God could gradually be understood in purely intellectual or abstract terms, and that humanity could be regarded as having the potential for altering nature as it pleased.

The Hebrews served and honored Yahweh during the period of monolatry by subscribing to a combination of moral precepts, rituals, and tabus. Although it is uncertain whether the exact form of the Ten Commandments, as they became known from the seventh century B.C. onwards (the form found in Exodus 20:3–17), existed before the Babylonian Captivity, there is little doubt that the Hebrews treasured some set of divine commandments and that these included certain ethical principles, such as injunctions against killing, committing adultery, bearing false witness, and "coveting anything that is thy neighbor's." In addition the Hebrews strictly observed ritualistic demands, such as celebrating feasts and offering sacrifices, and ritualistic prohibitions, such as refraining from labor on the seventh day or boiling a kid in its mother's milk. Although moral standards may have been observed rigorously within the Hebrew community, however, they were not always held to be applicable when dealing with outsiders. Thus even in regard to murder the Hebrews were no more averse to slaughtering innocent civilians in warfare than were the Assyrians. When Joshua conquered territories in Canaan the children of Israel "took for a prey unto themselves all the spoil of the cities, and every man they smote with the sword . . . until they had destroyed them, neither left they any to breathe" (Joshua 11:14). Rather than having any doubts about such a brutal policy, the Israelites believed it had been enjoined on them by their Lord himself—indeed that Yahweh had inspired the Canaanites to offer resistance so that there would be reason to slaughter them: "For it was of the Lord to harden their hearts, that they should come against Israel in battle, that he might destroy them utterly" (Joshua 11:20).

In comparison to such dubious ethics and notions of divine justice, the ideas advanced during the third stage of Hebrew religious development can be deemed revolutionary; in fact the stage is customarily called that of the *prophetic revolution*. The "prophets" who effected this revolution in religious thought were men who lived at the time of the threat to Hebrew nationhood coming from Assyria and Babylonia and during the period of the exile in Babylon, that is, from roughly 750 to roughly 550 B.C. Although the word "prophet" has come to mean someone who predicts the future, its original meaning, and the one that needs to be understood here, is closer to "preacher"—more exactly someone who has an urgent message to proclaim, in the belief that his message derives from divine inspiration. The foremost Hebrew prophets were Amos and Hosea, who "prophesied" (i.e., preached and exhorted) in the Kingdom of Israel shortly before its fall in 722 B.C.; Isaiah and Jeremiah, who prophesied in Judah before its fall in 586 B.C.; and Ezekiel and the second Isaiah,[1] who prophesied "by the waters of Babylon." Initially warning of imminent disaster to Israelites who worshiped and behaved improperly, and then announcing the justice of God's retribution, these men's messages were sufficiently similar to each other to warrant considering them as if they formed a single coherent body of religious thought.

Three basic doctrines made up the core of the prophets' teachings: (1) thoroughgoing monotheism—Yahweh is the ruler of the universe; He even makes use of nations other than the Hebrews to accomplish His purposes; the gods of others are false gods; (2) Yahweh is exclusively a god of righteousness; He wills only the good, and evil in the world comes from humanity, not from Him; (3) since Yahweh is righteous, he demands ethical behavior from his Israelite children more than anything else; He cares less for ritual and sacrifice than that His followers should "seek justice, relieve the oppressed, protect the fatherless, and plead for the widow." Merged with the Canaanites and practicing settled agriculture after the time of David, some Israelites had reverted to offering sacrifices to Canaanite fertility gods in the hope that such sacrifices would ensure rich harvests, while others who remained thoroughly loyal to Yahweh dedicated themselves ever more to ritualism as a demonstration of their loyalty. In fierce opposition to such practices, the prophet Amos summed up the prophetic revolution and marked one of the epoch-making moments in human cultural development when he expressed Yahweh's resounding warning:

The prophets' teachings

> I hate, I despise your feasts,
>   and I take no delight in your solemn assemblies.
> Even though you offer me your burnt offer-
>   ings and cereal offerings,
>   I will not accept them,
> and the peace offerings of your fatted beasts
>   I will not look upon.
> Take away from me the noise of your songs;
>   to the melody of your harps I will not listen.
> But let justice roll down like waters,
>   and righteousness like an ever-flowing
>   stream.   —Amos 5:21–24

---

[1] Most Old Testament authorities consider the Book of Isaiah to be the work of three different authors. They ascribe the first part to Isaiah, the second part (Chapters 40 to 55) to "the second Isaiah," and the last part to someone who wrote after the return to Jerusalem.

The post-exilic stage

The last stage in the shaping of Judaism took place during the four centuries after the return of the Jews from Babylon; thus it is called the post-exilic stage. The major contribution of post-exilic religious thinkers was a set of *eschatological* doctrines, writings on "last things" or what will happen at the end of time. Under the indirect or direct sway of Persians and Greeks, and during the years of the Maccabean revolt, Jewish thinkers in Palestine began to wonder ever more about what role their small and politically weak nation would play in the divine plan for the world, and hence began to fix upon messianic and millenarian expectations. In other words, they came to believe that God would soon send them a national savior or "messiah" (meaning "anointed one"), who would not only lift up the Jews to greatness but would spread the worship of Yahweh to the entire world during a millennium of peace and justice before the end of time. At first they assumed that the millennial kingdom of peace would be "this-worldly"—that humans would live to see and enjoy it, as in the words of the third Isaiah, "for as the earth bringeth forth her bud . . . so the Lord God will cause righteousness and praise to spring forth before nations" (Isaiah 61:11). But as time went on, the likelihood that the millennial kingdom would arise naturally "as the earth brings forth its bud" seemed for some ever more remote, with the alternative of otherworldly triumph seeming to them more inescapable. The fullest statement of otherworldly eschatology in the Old Testament appears in the Book of Daniel, written not by a Daniel who may have lived at the time of Nebuchadnezzar, but instead by someone who wrote under Daniel's name during the time of the revolt of the Maccabees. In the view of this seer the messiah, called by him "the Son of Man," would come "with the clouds of heaven," and would have an "everlasting dominion, which shall not pass away" (Daniel 7:13–14). Integral to this otherworldly view was the belief

Jewish Sarcophagus. A wealthy Jew commissioned this sarcophagus around 100 A.D. Today he would emblemize his religion with a Star of David, but then the standard emblem for Judaism was the menorah. Under the menorah are the three Hebrew children in the fiery furnace from the Book of Daniel, probably meant here to stand for the immortality of the soul and the patron's own hope for eternal life.

that the messiah would preside over a "last judgment"; in other words, that by supernatural means all the human dead would be resurrected to stand at judgment before the messiah for the quality of their lives, evil men and women being condemned to eternal suffering, "saints" remaining to serve in the "greatness of the kingdom under the whole heaven" (Daniel 7:26–28).

The Jewish expectation of a messiah has obvious bearing on the career of Jesus, a Jew who was considered to be the messiah by Jewish and Gentile followers, who thereafter became known as Christians. (Further treatment of the split-off of Christianity from Judaism will be found in Chapter 8). The Jews who denied that Jesus was the messiah continued to expect that the messiah would come. Some thought of him as coming in the clouds, as in Daniel, but most expected him to be an earthly savior who would exalt the nation of Israel and rebuild the Temple. Either way the expectation of the miraculous coming of the messiah motivated the Jewish people to maintain all their other beliefs and practices steadfastly even when they were forced to live thousands of miles away from the Holy Land. To a large degree it accounts for the real Jewish miracle—the capacity of an otherwise insignificant nation to endure until the present despite appalling adversity, enriching the world by its accomplishments in myriad ways.

Hopes for the coming of the messiah

4. HEBREW LAW AND LITERATURE

The ancient Hebrews were not great scientists, builders, or artists. So far as can be judged, even Solomon's Temple was not really a Hebrew building accomplishment, for it appears that Phoenician masons and artisans were called in to address the most challenging construction tasks involved in the project. Since the Hebrew religious code prohibited the making of any "graven image" or "likeness" of anything in heaven, earth, or water (Exodus 20:4), there was no sculpture and no painting. Instead it was in law and literature that ancient Hebrew culture found its most estimable expressions.

Hebrew culture: limitations and accomplishments

The major repository of Hebrew law is the Deuteronomic Code, which forms the core of the biblical Book of Deuteronomy. Although partly based on very ancient traditions that display kinship with the legal thought of the Old Babylonians, the Deuteronomic Code in its present form undoubtedly dates from the time of the prophetic revolution. In general its provisions are more altruistic and equitable than the laws found in the Old Babylonian Code of Hammurabi. As examples of altruism, it not only enjoins generosity to the poor and to the stranger, but it prescribes that the Hebrew slave who had served six years should be freed and given some provisions to start his own life, and it requires that every seven years all debtors be released from their debts. Fairness is found in principles dictating that children

Hebrew law: the Deuteronomic Code

Hebrew Inscription from a Synagogue Pavement. The Hebrew people created no statuary because of the biblical injunction against "graven images," and the same injunction apparently prohibited all figural art until roughly the time of Christ. Here, in a mosaic pavement from Palestine dating from about 400 A.D., a prayer takes the place of art. Note that Hebrew writing moves from right to left.

should not be held responsible for the guilt of their fathers and that judges under no circumstances should be allowed to accept gifts. Above all the Deuteronomic Code upholds the stringent ideal of what is "altogether just," for Yahweh demands no less, and only by living "altogether justly" could the Hebrews consider themselves worthy of inheriting the promised land.

Hebrew literature

Taken in total the literature of the Hebrews was the finest produced by any ancient civilization of western Asia. All of it that survives is found in the Old Testament and in the books of the Apocrypha (ancient Hebrew works not recognized as scriptural because of doubtful religious authority). Except for a few fragments like the Song of Deborah in Judges 5, the Old Testament is not really so old as is commonly supposed. Scholars now recognize that it was created from a series of collections and revisions in which old and new parts were merged and generally assigned to an ancient author—Moses, for example. But the oldest of these revisions was not prepared any earlier than 850 B.C. The majority of the books of the Old Testament were of still later origin, excepting some of the chronicles. Although the bulk of the Psalms were ascribed to King David, a good many of them refer to events of the Babylonian Captivity, and it is certain that the collection of Psalms as a whole was the work of several centuries.

Old Testament literary qualities

Granted that parts of the Old Testament consist of long lists of names or arcane ritual prohibitions, others, whether biographical or military narratives, thanksgiving prayers, battle hymns, prophetic exhortations, love lyrics, or dialogues, are rich in rhythm, evocative imagery, and emotional vigor. Few passages in any language can surpass the chaste beauty of the Twenty-third Psalm: "the Lord is my shepherd, I shall not want. He maketh me to lie down in green pastures, he leadeth me beside the still waters. He restoreth my soul . . ."; or the vision of peace in Isaiah: "and they shall beat their swords into plowshares, and their spears into pruninghooks; nation shall not lift up sword against nation, neither shall they learn war any more."

Among the most beautiful of all the world's love lyrics is the biblical Song of Songs. Although generations of readers have sought to find figurative spiritual meaning in it (and many modern critics tell us we are free to find any meaning in any text we like), the Song of Songs surely originated around the fifth century B.C. as a collection of purely secular wedding poems. The bridegroom praises his bride as his "dove," and she regards him as her "king." Together they rejoice in the prospect of sharing caresses and a loving life together in the orchards and the vineyards: "Rise up, my love, my fair one, and come away. For lo, the winter is past, the rain is over and gone; the flowers appear on the earth . . . and the vines with the tender grape give a good smell. . . . Behold, thou art fair, my love . . . thou hast doves' eyes . . . thy teeth are like a flock of sheep that are even shorn. . . . My beloved is gone down into his garden, to the beds of spices, to feed in the gardens and to gather lilies. I am my beloved's, and my beloved is mine."

An entirely different variety of Hebrew literary achievement is the Book of Job, written sometime between 500 to 300 B.C. In form the work is a drama of the tragic struggle between man and fate. Its central theme is the problem of evil: how it can be that the righteous suffer while the wicked prosper. The story was an old one, adapted very probably from an Old Babylonian writing of similar content. But the Hebrews introduced into it a much deeper realization of philosophical possibilities. The main character, Job, a man of virtue, is suddenly overtaken by a series of disasters: he is despoiled of his property, his children are killed, and his body is afflicted with disease. His attitude at first is one of stoic resignation; the evil must be accepted along with the good. But as his sufferings increase he is plunged into despair. He curses the day of his birth and praises death, where "the wicked cease from troubling and the weary be at rest."

Then follows a lengthy debate between Job and his friends over the meaning of evil. The latter take the view that all suffering is a punishment for sin, and that those who repent are forgiven and strengthened in character. But Job is not satisfied with any of their arguments. Torn between hope and despair, he strives to review the problem from every angle. He even considers the possibility that death may not be the end, that there may be some adjustment of the balance hereafter. But the mood of despair returns, and he decides that God is an omnipotent demon, destroying without mercy wherever His caprice or anger directs. Finally, in his anguish he appeals to the Almighty to reveal Himself and make known His ways to him. God answers him out of the whirlwind with a magnificent exposition of the tremendous works of nature. Convinced of his own insignificance and of the unutterable majesty of God, Job despises himself and repents in dust and ashes. In the end no solution for the problem of individual suffering is given. No promise is made of recompense in a life hereafter, nor does God make any effort to refute the hopeless pessimism of Job. Humans must take comfort in the philosophic reflection that the universe is greater than themselves, and that God in the pursuit of His sublime purposes cannot really be limited by human standards of equity and goodness.

Book of Ecclesiastes

As different as the lyric Song of Songs and the tragic Book of Job are from each other, the bleakly worldly-wise Book of Ecclesiastes is different from both. Unquestionably this book, attributed to Solomon but surely written no earlier than the third century B.C., contains some of the Bible's most pithy and forceful quotations. Yet its doctrine contradicts all the elevated presuppositions found in the rest of the Hebrew Bible, for the author of Ecclesiastes was a skeptic and a materialist. According to him humans die just like beasts, no afterlife being granted to either, and human history is no more than the successive passing away of generations. Everything is cyclical, and nothing adds up to lasting achievement, for "the sun also rises and the sun goeth down, and hasteth to the place where he arose . . . and there is nothing new under the sun." On top of all this purposeless repetition, in the realm of human affairs, blind fate rather than merit predominates, for "the race is not to the swift, nor the battle to the strong . . . nor yet riches to men of understanding, nor yet favor to men of skill, but time and chance happen to them all." In light of these circumstances the author proposes taking life as it comes without excess: "be not righteous overmuch, neither make thyself over wise . . . be not over much wicked, neither be thou foolish: why shouldest thou die before thy time?" Surprisingly in view of his bleakness he also "commends mirth," on the grounds that "a man hath no better thing under the sun than to eat, and drink, and to be merry."

Remains of an Ancient Synagogue at Capernaum. Capernaum was supposed to have been the scene of many of the miracles attributed to Jesus. Here also he called out Peter, Andrew, and Matthew to be his disciples.

How it came about that a text which offers the maxim "be not righteous overmuch" crept into the Hebrew Bible remains uncertain, but it cannot be stressed overmuch that it is exceptional. Therefore, rather than ending this survey of Hebrew literature with Ecclesiastes, it is best to point out that the last book of the Hebrew Bible, Malachi, ends on a highly characteristic note, both in terms of its prophetic-eschatological message and its vigorously affirmative expression, when it has Yahweh state: "unto you that fear my name shall the Sun of righteousness arise with healing in his wings . . . and ye shall tread down the wicked . . . Behold, I will send you Elijah the prophet before the coming of the great and dreadful day of the Lord."

5. THE MAGNITUDE OF THE HEBREW INFLUENCE

The history of Western existence during the past two thousand years has been profoundly influenced by the Hebrew heritage, partly because of the activities of the Jews and partly because Judaism was the matrix from whence sprang Christianity. (As will be seen in Chapter 9, a third great world religion, Islam, grew from both Judaism and Christianity.) Virtually all religious believers in the West today are monotheists—descendants in belief, therefore, from Moses and the Hebrew prophets. In addition Hebrew "transcendent theology" has given westerners the sense of assurance that they are masters of nature and need not waver in cutting down trees or changing the courses of rivers for fear of angering forest or water deities. Whether in its religious version or its secular adaptations, this worldview has surely contributed enormously to Western technological initiative. Hebrew morality, as shaped particularly by the great Hebrew prophets, essentially remains the morality all enlightened humans cherish: "Love thy neighbor as thyself" (Leviticus 19:18) speaks better than any paraphrase. And the vision of a world united in peace, when "the wolf shall dwell with the lamb, and the leopard shall lie down with the kid" (Isaiah 11:6), is a vision that we all know must be implemented soon or else no tradition will mean anything to anyone.

The Hebrew legacy

6. THE MINOAN AND MYCENAEAN CIVILIZATIONS

Before 1870 no one guessed that great civilizations flourished in the Greek archipelago many hundreds of years before the rise of Athens. Students of the Greek epic, Homer's *Iliad,* of course knew that a mighty Greek king, Agamemnon, was supposed to have led all the Greeks to victory in the "Trojan War" long before the eighth century B.C., when the *Iliad* was first set down in writing. But it was simply assumed that Homer's entire plot was fictional. Today, however, scholars are certain that Greek history—and thus European history—

*Long-forgotten
civilizations*

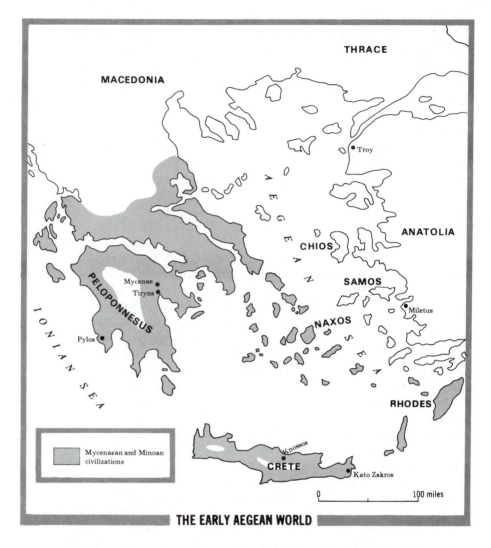

THE EARLY AEGEAN WORLD

began well over one thousand years before Socrates started discussing the nature of truth in the Athenian marketplace.

The breakthrough into certain knowledge of these ancient Greek civilizations came about as the result of the most famous "storybook triumph" in the annals of archeology. In the middle of the nineteenth century the German businessman, Heinrich Schliemann, fascinated from youth by the narrative in the *Iliad,* determined to prove his hunch that there was substantial truth in it as soon as he had gained sufficient income. Luckily Schliemann accumulated a fortune in his business ventures and thereupon retired to spend his time and his money in pursuit of Agamemnon. Although he had no archeological or scholarly training, in 1870 he began excavating in western Asia Minor at a site he felt confident was that of ancient Troy, and, amazingly enough, soon after he began digging he uncovered portions of nine different ancient cities, each built upon the ruins of its predecessor. Schliemann identified the second of these cities as the Troy of the

The discoveries of Schliemann

Iliad, but scholars now believe that Troy was probably the seventh city. Encouraged by his success, he started excavations in Greece in 1876, and, lo and behold, he struck gold again—this time literally as well as figuratively because he hit upon a grave site containing gold in staggering quantities. Since Schliemann's dig of 1876 was located at a deserted Greek site called Mycenae (pronounced Mysée-knee), he felt completely vindicated because the *Iliad* stated that Mycenae was Agamemnon's place of residence and termed it "Mycenae rich in gold." It is sad to report that Schliemann's excavations were not unqualifiedly beneficial to the study of the distant past because in his zealous enthusiasm and disregard of scientific procedures he destroyed evidence as he dug and scorned meticulous record-keeping. Yet all told his discoveries were so exciting and momentous that they themselves almost merit being memorialized in an epic.

Once Schliemann demonstrated that there was some truth in what formerly had been regarded as legend, others rushed to add to his discoveries. His most important successor in this regard was the Englishman Arthur Evans. In 1899 Evans began looking for "Minos" as Schliemann had been looking for Agamemnon—which meant that Evans began excavating on the Greek island of Crete because legend had identified the city of Knossos on Crete as the capital of a mighty empire ruled over by a ruler named Minos. Again, legend proved to have some kernel of fact, for Evans soon found remains as rich (and indeed more beautiful) than anything dug up by Schliemann. Although Evans's work (which earned him a knighthood) followed after Schliemann's, the civilization he found at Knossos dates back earlier than the Greek civilization uncovered by Schliemann. Hence we should look at the "world of Minos" before we see how it became drawn into the "world of Agamemnon."

Cretan Labyrinth Coin. According to legend, King Minos of Crete built a labyrinth to pen in the Minotaur, part man, part bull. This coin from about 300 B.C. shows the labyrinth as the emblem of Knossos.

Arthur Evans and the world of Minos

Central Staircase of the Palace at Knossos

A Linear B Tablet from Knossos

Flowering of Minoan civilization

The earliest traces of the *Minoan civilization,* so called by modern scholars after the legendary Cretan ruler Minos, date from the period around 2000 B.C. Around that time the Minoans, whose origins before they inhabited Crete are unknown, had begun to build cities and to develop a unique form of writing. The half-millennium from about 2000 to 1500 B.C. saw Minoan civilization at its peak. Rather than being the center of an empire, Knossos was one of several thriving cities on Crete that coexisted so harmoniously that none of them found it necessary to build protective walls. Only earthquakes, which periodically shook the island, interrupted the Minoans' serene existence. These natural disasters caused much devastation, but after each the Minoans set about rebuilding their cities and usually managed to found more splendid ones than those which had just been destroyed. At Knossos Sir Arthur Evans found not just beautiful stonework and paintings but humanity's first known flush-toilet. Later excavations at another Minoan site, Kato Zakros, unearthed a huge palace with 250 rooms, a swimming pool, and parquet floors.

Origins of the Mycenaean civilization

While the Minoan civilization was flourishing on Crete, potential rivals were gaining strength on the mainland of Greece. Around 2200 B.C. Indo-European peoples who spoke the earliest form of Greek invaded the Greek peninsula, and by 1600 B.C. they had begun to form small cities. Primarily owing to trading relations, these peoples gradually became influenced in their cultural development by Minoan Crete. The civilization that resulted from the fusion of Greek and Minoan elements is called *Mycenaean* after Mycenae, the leading city of Greece from about 1600 to 1200 B.C. It was this civilization that became dominant in the Aegean world (the Aegean Sea is that part of the Mediterranean lying between Greece and Asia Minor) after about 1500 B.C. and even gained predominance on Crete itself.

Linear B

One of the greatest scholarly accomplishments of the twentieth century radically altered our understanding of Cretan and Greek history in the century between 1500 and 1400 B.C. It was once thought that Greece throughout that time was still a semibarbarous economic colony of splendid Crete and that internal changes on Crete between 1500 and 1400 B.C. could be attributed to the rise of a "new dynasty." It was known that numerous specimens of the same linear script (called "Linear B") could be found on both Crete and the Greek mainland, but it was simply assumed that the script was Cretan in origin and spread from Crete to Greece. But in 1952 a brilliant young Englishman, Michael Ventris, who was then only thirty years old (and tragically died in an automobile accident four years later), succeeded in deciphering Linear B and demonstrating that it expressed an early form of Greek. Ventris's discovery revolutionized preclassical Greek studies by showing that the mainlanders dominated Crete in the late Minoan period and not vice versa.

Scholars now agree that the Mycenaeans supplanted the Minoans as rulers of the Aegean world sometime shortly after 1500 B.C., although they are uncertain exactly how that happened. Either a great earthquake on Crete resulted in sufficient local weakness to allow the mainlanders to take control of the island, or else the Mycenaeans had already become strong enough to conquer Crete swiftly. In either event, between about 1500 and 1400 B.C., the Mycenaeans presided over an era of prosperity and artistic accomplishment on Crete. Around 1400 B.C., however, another wave of Greek invaders crossed over to Crete, destroyed Knossos, and put a cataclysmic end to the Minoan civilization. Why this invasion was so destructive remains unknown, but it left mainland Greece unrivaled as the dominant power of the Aegean world for about another two hundred years. Around 1250 B.C., the Mycenaeans waged their successful war with the Trojans of western Asia Minor, but their own downfall was now on the horizon. In the course of the century between 1200 and 1100 B.C. the Mycenaeans succumbed to the Dorians—barbaric northern Greeks who had iron weapons. (Iron weapons may not at first have been much superior to the bronze ones used by the Mycenaeans, but since iron ore was found far more widely in western Asia and eastern Europe than the copper and tin needed for bronze, iron weapons were much cheaper, thereby allowing many more fighters to wield them.) Because the Dorians were primitive in all but their weaponry their ascendancy initiated a dark age in Greek history that lasted until about 800 B.C.

Rise and fall of the Mycenaeans

Mycenaean Warrior Vase, c. 1250 B.C. Found in the ruins of Mycenae, this vase displays the warlike aspects of Mycenaean culture: the men might be marching off to the Trojan War.

As can be seen from the foregoing account, the Minoan and Mycenaean civilizations were closely interrelated; even the greatest experts have difficulty in determining exactly where one left off and the other began. The problem is complicated by the fact that two forms of writing which predate Linear B and have been found on Crete alone have not yet been deciphered. (Anyone who wishes to become as famous as Schliemann, Evans, or Ventris may take the decipherment of Minoan writing as his or her goal.) Accordingly, discussions of Minoan civilization before about 1500 B.C. rely exclusively on visual and archeological evidence, leaving much to the realm of speculation. Such evidence, however, does suggest that Minoan civilization was one of the most progressive in all of early history.

Difficulty of distinguishing between early Minoan and Mycenaean characteristics

The Minoan ruler was not a bristling warlord like the Assyrian king. He does seem to have commanded a large navy, but this was

The Minoan king as economic overseer

A Minoan Vase, c. 1400 B.C.
Minoan potters glorified in creating a great variety of shapes.

not for war but for the maintenance of trade. In fact, the king was the chief entrepreneur in the country. The workshops located near his palace turned out great quantities of fine pottery, textiles, and metal goods. Although private enterprise apparently was not prohibited it seems to have been heavily taxed. Nevertheless there were some privately owned workshops, especially in smaller towns, and much agriculture was also in private hands.

The Minoan state is probably best described as a bureaucratic monarchy. The ruler of each leading city and its surrounding territory appears to have been absolute, and toward the end of Minoan history (exactly when is hard to say) the ruler of Knossos appears to have taken over the entire island. The absolute ruler governed by means of a large administrative class. Scribes, who seem to have had a monopoly on learning, kept close accounts of all aspects of economic life. All agricultural production and manufacturing were closely supervised for purposes of gathering or taxing whatever was owed to the king. Foreign trade too seems to have been closely supervised by the state; most likely the large Minoan ships that put into ports as far away as Syria and Egypt were owned or at least heavily taxed by the ruler and carefully watched over by the bureaucratic administration.

Despite such close supervision, the Minoan people of nearly all classes appear to have led fairly prosperous lives. Although there were great social and economic distinctions between the rulers and the ruled, there were apparently few gradations of wealth or status among the common people. If slavery existed at all, it certainly occupied an unimportant place. The dwellings in the poorest urban quarters were well built and commodious, often with as many as six or eight rooms, but we do not know how many families resided in them. Women seem to have enjoyed equality with men. Regardless of class there was no public activity from which they were debarred, and no occupation that they could not enter. In this the Minoans were the exception in the ancient world. Crete had female bullfighters and even female boxers. Women of the upper strata devoted much time to fashion and other leisure activities.

The love of sports and games

The natives of Crete delighted in games and sports of every description. Dancing, running matches, and boxing rivaled each other in their attraction for the people. The Minoans were the first to build stone theaters where processions and music entertained large audiences.

The matriarchal nature of Minoan religion

The religion of the Minoans was outstanding among those of the ancient world for being dominantly matriarchal. The chief deity was not a god but a goddess, who was the ruler of the entire universe—the sea and the sky as well as the earth. Originally no male deity seems to have been worshiped at all, but later a god emerged who was associated with the great goddess as her son and consort. Nonetheless this male figure was never regarded by the Minoans as having any independent importance. Although the mother goddess was considered to be the source of evil as well as of good, even her evil

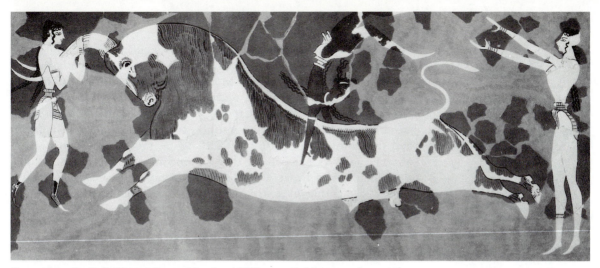

Scenes from the Bull Ring: Minoan Mural, c. 1500 B.C. Evident are the youth, skill, and agility of the Minoan athletes, the center one a male, the other two female. The body and horns of the bull are exaggerated, as are the slenderness of the athletes and their full-face eyes in profile heads. There is probably also some exaggeration in content: modern experts in bullfighting insist that it is impossible to somersault over the back of a charging bull.

powers were not morbid or terrifying: though she brought the storm and spread destruction, such acts served for the replenishment of nature as death served as the prerequisite for life. Mortals on earth were expected to make sacrifices to the goddess, as well as to her sacred animals, such as bulls and snakes. Minoan rites and rituals were administered by priestesses instead of priests in keeping with the female orientation of the entire belief system.

Since we cannot yet decipher the early Cretan scripts it is impossible to tell whether the Minoans had any literature, although the existence of such seems unlikely because there is none written in Linear B. The problem of scientific achievements is easier to solve, since we have material remains for our guidance. Archeological discoveries on the island of Crete indicate that the Minoans were gifted inventors and engineers. They built excellent stone roads about eleven feet wide. Nearly all the basic principles of modern sanitary engineering were known to the designers of the palace of Knossos, with the result that the royal family of Crete in the seventeenth century B.C. enjoyed comforts and conveniences, such as indoor running water, that were not even available to the rulers of France and England in the seventeenth century A.D.

The Minoans as inventors and engineers

If any achievement of the Minoans appears most to demonstrate the vitality of their civilization, it was their genius in painting. With the exception of the artistic attainments of the classical Greeks and Romans that evolved a millennium later, no art of the ancient world was its equal. The distinguishing features of Minoan painting were delicacy, spontaneity, and naturalism. It served, not to glorify the

The elegance of Minoan painting

"La Parisienne"

*Similarities between the
Minoan and Mycenaean
civilizations*

See color plates
following page 166

*Mycenaean departures from
the Minoan social model*

ambitions of an arrogant ruling class or to inculate the doctrines of a religion, but to express the delight of the individual in the beauty of the Minoan world. Most of Minoan painting consisted of murals done in fresco, but painted reliefs were occasionally to be found. The murals in the palaces of Crete are surely the best that have survived from ancient times, revealing instincts for the dramatic and rhythmic and the capturing of nature in its changing moods. So sophisticated and elegant was Minoan art that a Frenchman who was unearthing the remains of a fresco at Knossos could not help exclaiming when he saw a painting of a striking woman portrayed with curls, vivid eyes, and sensuous lips: "Mais, c'est la Parisienne!" ("Why, she's just like a woman from Paris!").

Not surprisingly for a people dedicated to elegance, artistic excellence among the Minoans extended from painting to sculpture and even to household objects of everyday use. Perhaps the most noteworthy fact about Minoan sculpture is that its scale is always reduced. One looks in vain among Minoan remains for equivalents of giant Mesopotamian kings smiting their puny enemies or colossal pharaohs of Egypt advancing toward the beholder like enormous zombies, for the ancient Minoans were averse to relying on size for creating stunning effects. Instead, Minoan statues of human figures are almost always smaller than life-size, and they rely on naturalism and delicacy to engage the imagination of the viewer. Similarly, carved gems, gold-work and bronze-work, and ceramics down to the humblest crockery utensils are invariably finely wrought and sometimes wryly humorous.

Mycenaean civilization appears to have been more warlike and less refined than the Minoan, but the most recent scholarship warns us to beware of exaggerating these differences. As on Crete, so on mainland Greece, the city was the center of civilization—the leading Mycenaean cities being Mycenae itself, Pylos, and Tiryns. Each city and its surrounding area was ruled over by a king called a *wanax*. As on Crete, the Mycenaean state was a bureaucratic monarchy. We know about some of the workings of this monarchy because of the decipherment of numerous Linear B tablets, all of which are records of a highly regulatory bureaucratic apparatus. Linear B tablets from Pylos report the minutest details of the economic lives of the king's subjects: the exact acreage of a given estate; the number of cooking utensils owned by so-and-so; the personal names given to somebody else's two oxen ("Glossy" and "Blackie"). Such detailed inventories show us that the state was highly centralized and that it was supreme in its control over the economic activities of its citizens.

Although the bureaucratic monarchies of the Minoans and the Mycenaeans were similar, there were still at least a few notable differences between the two related civilizations. One was that the Mycenaeans definitely had a slave system. Mycenaean society too was geared much more toward warfare. Because Mycenaean cities frequently fought with one another they were built on hilltops and were heavily fortified.

In keeping with a somewhat more rugged and barbaric style of life than that of Crete, Mycenaean kings built themselves ostentatious graves in which they buried their best inlaid bronze daggers and other signs of power and wealth.

It is also true that Mycenaean art is less elegant than Minoan. Without question the Mycenaeans never equaled the artistic delicacy and grace of their Minoan predecessors. Nevertheless, Myceanaean artwork done in Knossos between 1500 and 1400 B.C., while stiffer and more symmetrical in composition than earlier Minoan work, is by no means wholly different in kind. Moreover, the "Parisian woman" of Minoan Knossos has some very close stylistic relatives in a female procession fresco from about 1300 B.C. found in Mycenaean Tiryns. Nor should it be thought that all the best traits of Mycenaean art can merely be seen as debased borrowings from the Minoans: the superbly executed and exquisite Mycenaean inlaid daggers have no antecedents anywhere on Crete.

Detail from a Procession Fresco at Tiryns, c. 1300 B.C. Note the similarity of this Mycenaean female profile to the Minoan "La Parisienne" shown on p. 100.

The significance of the Minoan and the Mycenaean civilizations should not be estimated primarily in terms of subsequent influences. Minoan culture hardly influenced any peoples other than the Mycenaeans, and it was then destroyed more or less without a trace after about 1400 B.C. The Mycenaeans left behind a few more traces, but still not very many. Later Greeks retained some Mycenaean gods and goddesses like Zeus, Hera, Hermes, and Poseidon, but they completely altered their role in the religious pantheon. It may also be that the later Greeks gained from the Mycenaeans their devotion to athletics and their system of weights and measures, but these connections remain uncertain. Homer definitely remembered the successful Mycenaean siege of Troy, but it is just as important to realize how much Homer forgot: writing in the eighth century B.C. Homer (actually several different writers who have come down to us under that name) entirely forgot the whole pattern of Mycenaean bureaucratic monarchy which we know from the Linear B tablets. It may well be that the break between the Mycenaeans and the later Greeks was all for the good. Some historians maintain that the destruction of despotic Mycenae by the Dorians was a necessary prelude to the emergence of the freer and more enlightened later Greek outlook.

Influence of the Minoan and Mycenaean civilizations

Although the Minoan and Mycenaean civilizations had little subsequent influence, they are still noteworthy for at least four reasons. First of all, they were the earliest civilizations of Europe. Before the Minoan accomplishments all civilizations had existed farther east, but afterward Europe was to witness the development of one impressive civilization after another. Second, in some respects the Minoans and the Mycenaeans seem to have looked forward to certain later European values and accomplishments even if they did not directly influence them. Minoan and Mycenaean political organization was similar to that of many Asian states, but Minoan art in particular seems very different and more characteristic of later European patterns. Third,

Importance of the Minoan and Mycenaean civilizations

the Minoan civilization, and to a lesser degree also the Mycenaean one, is significant for its worldly and progressive outlook. This is exemplified in the devotion of the Aegean peoples to comfort and opulence, in their love of amusement, zest for life, and courage for experimentation. And finally, whereas ancient Assyria, ancient Babylon, and even ancient Egypt all breathed their last as "corpses in armor," ancient Crete breathed its last amid joyous festivals celebrated in cities without walls.

SELECTED READINGS

• *Items so designated are available in paperback editions.*

• Albright, W. F., *From the Stone Age to Christianity,* New York, 1957. Emphasizes the development of Hebrew monotheism.

Anderson, Bernard, *Understanding the Old Testament,* 4th ed., Englewood Cliffs, N.J., 1986.

Baron, Salo W., *A Social and Religious History of the Jews,* rev. ed., 18 vols., New York, 1952–1980. A modern classic: almost all work on Jewish history takes Baron as a point of departure.

Blegen, C. W., *Troy and the Trojans,* New York, 1963. The most reliable archeological appraisal.

Bright, John, *A History of Israel,* 3rd ed., Philadelphia, 1981. A standard account.

• Chadwick, John, *The Decipherment of Linear B,* 2nd ed., New York, 1968. Chadwick was a research colleague of Michael Ventris and here gives the most accessible account of Ventris's brilliant work.

———, *The Mycenaean World,* New York, 1976. A lively account of the society based on the evidence of the Linear B tablets.

• Finley, M. I., *Early Greece: The Bronze and Archaic Ages,* New York, 1970. An excellent survey that spans two different eras.

Hermann, Siegfried, *A History of Israel in Old Testament Times,* London, 1975. Iconoclastic and challenging.

• Higgins, Reynold, *Minoan and Mycenaean Art,* rev. ed., London, 1981.

Hood, Sinclair, *The Minoans,* London, 1971.

• Kaufmann, Yehezkel, *The Religion of Israel,* New York, 1972. Stresses the uniqueness of the Hebrew religious accomplishment.

• MacDonald, William A., *Progress into the Past: The Rediscovery of Mycenaean Civilization,* New York, 1967.

• McCullough, W. S., *The History and Literature of the Palestinian Jews from Cyrus to Herod, 550 B.C. to 4 B.C.,* Toronto, 1976.

• Orlinsky, H. M., *Ancient Israel,* 2nd ed., Ithaca, N.Y., 1960. A good brief overview of ancient Hebrew history.

• Schürer, E., *The History of the Jewish People in the Age of Jesus Christ (175 B.C.–A.D. 135),* rev. ed., 3 vols., Edinburgh, 1973–1983. A new edition of an irreplaceable nineteenth-century narrative.

Starr, C. G., *The Origins of Greek Civilization,* New York, 1961.

• Vaux, Roland de, *Ancient Israel: Its Life and Institutions,* New York, 1962. Especially valuable for archaeological data.

• Vermeule, Emily, *Greece in the Bronze Age,* Chicago, 1964. The best book on the subject.

Chapter 5

ANCIENT INDIAN CIVILIZATION

Hinduism does not distinguish ideas of God as true and false, adopting
one particular idea as the standard for the whole human race. It accepts
the obvious fact that mankind seeks its goal of God at various levels and
in various directions, and feels sympathy with every stage of the search.

—S. Radhakrishnan, *The Hindu View of Life*

The subcontinent of India (including Pakistan and Bangladesh)
has an area slightly more than half that of the United States
and is inhabited by more than three times as many people. Not
only is India a vast and densely populated region but it includes many
different levels of culture, different religions, languages, and economic conditions, and its history is extremely complex. Five or six
separate families of languages are represented among its people. The
population contains admixtures of all of the three main varieties of
mankind—black, yellow, and white—in various combinations and proportions. One of the most ancient peoples, a Negrito strain related to
the Pygmies of Africa, has almost disappeared from India but is still
found in the Andaman Islands to the east. In striking contrast to this
type are the fair-skinned Mediterraneans of the north and northwest,
descendants of the Indo-Aryans who invaded the country some 3,500
years ago. The most widespread group in southern India is that known
as Dravidian, but because the term is applied to all whose language
belongs to the Dravidian family, it no longer denotes a single ethnic
stock. Another type, perhaps more ancient than the Dravidians, is
called Australoid, because of its relationship with primitive peoples
extending over parts of southeastern Asia and as far east as Australia.
The Mongolian element is confined chiefly to the border region of the
north and northeast. Alpine types are found along the western coast,
sometimes with a slight Nordic admixture (evidenced by gray or blue
eyes). Thus the common practice of referring to the natives of India
as "colored" or "brown-skinned" is misleading. Their skins are indeed

The peoples of India

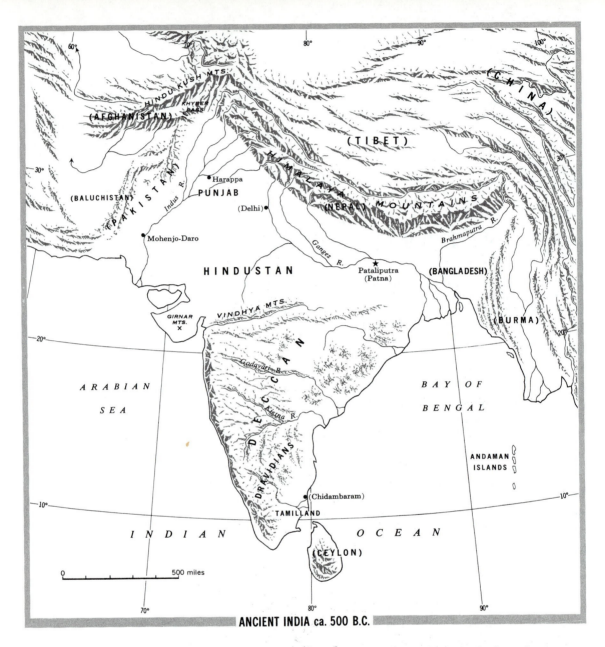

ANCIENT INDIA ca. 500 B.C.

of various shades, but since early times white stocks have been conspicuously present, especially in northern India. Even today some of the most typical examples of the tall variety of the Mediterranean white race can be seen in the Punjab and the northwest frontier. Yet they exist in close proximity to people who reveal Alpine, Australoid, Mongoloid, or Negrito features. Over the course of centuries, and in spite of the inexorable segregation of the caste system in historic times, India has been a human melting pot.

Geographically India falls into two main divisions. The southern triangle or peninsular portion, known as the Deccan, lies entirely within the tropics. The northern or continental half, also triangular in shape, is in the same latitudes as Mexico and the southern United States and has temperatures ranging from tropical heat to the intense cold of the northern mountain peaks. The northern Deccan is semi-mountainous and heavily forested, and shelters some of the primitive hill tribes whose ancestors were crowded into the wilderness by the pressure of expansion from more civilized communities. A mountain range known as the Western Ghats stretches along the western coast, but the greater part of the peninsula is a gently sloping plateau. The northern half of India, called Hindustan, is bounded on the north by the lofty Himalayan range and is separated from the Deccan by the low-lying Vindhya Mountains. Most of Hindustan is a level plain comprising an area about as large as France, Germany, and Italy combined, drained by the great river systems of the Indus and the Ganges. The rivers of Hindustan take their rise in the Himalayas or beyond and are fed by snows and glaciers. The Indus and the Brahmaputra each originate in Tibet and flow in opposite directions around the mountain ranges until they turn south into India, bringing with them virgin soil from the highlands which is deposited on the plain. The gently flowing Ganges, less subject to floods than the Indus, is the most beneficent of all. Referred to as "Mother Ganges," it has long been the sacred river of the Hindus. It is no wonder that its central valley, where every inch of soil is productive and no stone even the size of a pebble can be found, is one of the most densely populated spots in the world. The mouths of the Ganges are surrounded by forbidding jungle, and a desert separates the lower Indus valley from the Ganges and its tributaries; but the Indo–Gangetic region as a whole is lavishly endowed by nature. Here the most influential centers of Indian civilization have been located.

A climatic factor of overriding importance for India is the sharp distinction between its dry and rainy seasons. Normally between June and October of each year monsoon winds laden with moisture from the Arabian Sea and Indian Ocean sweep in a northeasterly direction across the subcontinent, bringing heavy but unevenly distributed precipitation. Rain falls abundantly along the western coast of the Deccan, on the Gangetic plain below the Himalayas, and with greatest intensity in the northeastern corner (now Bangladesh and West Bengal), where it may cause disastrous floods. The Indo-Gangetic river systems provide ample water for irrigation, but the peninsula of South India is almost totally dependent upon rainfall for cultivating its rich soil. The history of India is marked by recurring famines caused by seasons of drought.

1. THE FOUNDATIONS OF INDIAN CIVILIZATIONS

Northwestern India was the site of a great ancient civilization contemporary with those of Mesopotamia and the Nile valley. Forgotten

The earliest civilization of India

The culture of early Indian agricultural societies

Excavations at Mohenjo-Daro and Harappa

The Sewers of Mohenjo-Daro. This house drain was linked to mains under the city streets— a unique sewage system in this era.

for many centuries, its existence and extent were brought to light by archeological excavations begun in the 1920s. The Indus valley civilization, which reached its height in the third millenium B.C., differed in many respects from the Indian civilization of later historic times. Its origin as well as the cause of its decline was long a matter of speculation, but excavations during the 1970s produced convincing evidence that the Indus valley culture was indigenous, resting on foundations laid by food-producing, stone-tool–making peoples who inhabited the region as early as the sixth millennium B.C.

Excavations of farming villages on a five-hundred-acre site in northern Baluchistan (now part of Pakistan) reveal several successive levels of food-producing cultures, leading over a period of some three thousand years directly to the mature Indus valley civilization. As early as 4000 B.C. these villages produced wheel-turned pottery, had a diversified animal husbandry, and cultivated numerous crops, including cotton. Their decorated pottery and terra-cotta human and animal figurines show admirable artistic skill. Products from Baluchistan were traded over a wide area extending into Iran and Afghanistan.

The Indus valley civilization (c. 3200–1600 B.C.) covered an area of nearly half a million square miles, extending from the shores of the Arabian Sea northward through the Indus River system to Amu Darya (Oxus River) in northern Afghanistan. Although resting upon an agricultural foundation it was essentially an urban civilization, with a utilitarian, comfort-loving, cosmopolitan society and extensive trade connections with the outside world. Intercourse with Mesopotamia was especially active between 2300 and 2000 B.C. Among some seventy metropolitan centers thus far uncovered, the two principal sites are Mohenjo-Daro, about 300 miles from the seacoast, and Harappa, 400 miles farther up the river in the Punjab. It is estimated that each of these two cities held a population of 35,000 or more, and the contrasts in types of housing suggest a wide range of affluence and social status among classes. Both cities were fortified, durably constructed of brick, and laid out in accordance with ambitious and intelligent planning. Solidly built houses, some with three stories, were equipped with bathrooms that drained into sewer pipes running underneath the principal streets. Mohenjo-Daro housed a public bath with an area of 900 square feet, lined with watertight bricks and beautifully ornamented. A great granary in Harappa was supported by a raised platform to protect the several varieties of grain stored there from damage by floods. Domesticated animals included both humped and humpless cattle, the buffalo, goats, pigs, asses, and fowl. Only a small fraction of the Indus valley civilization's artifacts have been recovered, and many are unrecoverable because the water level has risen over the centuries. But the evidence obtained is sufficient to show that the civilization at its peak was highly advanced, comparing favorably with those of Egypt and Mesopotamia.

The Great Bath at Mohenjo-Daro, a Major Site of the Indus Valley Civilization.
Left: Note the brick walls of the bath (39 feet by 23 feet) on the fortified
citadel, crowned by a Buddhist stupa that was built more than two thousand
years later. Right: A reconstruction of the public bath and related structures.

The period of the Indus valley civilization was India's Bronze Age.
Admirable copper and bronze vessels and gold and silver ornaments
have been recovered. Craftsmanship was specialized and of excellent
quality. Although the Indus valley people did not leave imposing
monuments, they revealed their artistic talent in small objects of personal adornment and animal and human figurines of striking grace
and naturalness. Some of the symbols employed, including the swas-
tika, appear as decorative motifs in Indian art of later periods. Two
miniature male torsos, carved from stone and discovered at Harappa,
are anatomically perfect, appearing more lifelike than scuptured figures
of the Greek archaic period a thousand years later.

*Male Torso from Harappa, c.
2300–1750 B.C.* This three-and-
one-half-inch figure is suggestive of later Indian sculpture in
its anatomical realism and style.

A group of objects aesthetically significant but apparently intended
for utilitarian purposes consists of square or rectangular stone seals,
of which more than 2,000 have been found. Each seal—presumably
used to mark a personal signature as were the cylinder seals of Mesopotamia—typically bore the profile of an animal and a brief inscription,
providing the only examples of writing thus far discovered. The Indus
valley script, numbering some 270 pictographs or characters, appears
unrelated to any other system of writing. Because the script, unfortunately, has not yet been deciphered little can be said concerning the
intellectual life of those who used it.

Religious beliefs and practices of the early Indus valley inhabitants

Dancing Girl. Bronze statuette of a female dancer, from Mohenjo-Daro, a striking example of the art of the ancient Indus civilization. Bracelets and bangles have retained their popularity among the women of India to the present day.

Bull Seal. Impression of stone seal from Mohenjo-Daro, 2500 B.C., probably used as a signature. The animal figure (of a Brahmani bull or zebu) is assumed to have had religious significance.

are necessarily matters of surmise, but undoubtedly they contributed enduring elements to India's religious heritage. Carvings and figurines that have been found indicate the prominence of a fertility cult. Sacred objects included phallic symbols, a mother goddess, a male deity, a sacred tree, and a bull. A horned male figure depicted on three seals is believed to be a prototype of the widely popular Hindu god Shiva.

For reasons that remain in dispute the Indus valley civilization decayed during the first half of the second millennium B.C., and it seems to have ended about 1600 B.C. Probably an important disruptive factor was a series of floods and earthquakes that altered the course of the Indus River and inundated densely inhabited areas. During this same period northwestern India was invaded by semicivilized tribes whose warriors stormed the cities and occupied the land. It is no longer believed, however, that the Indus valley civilization fell in a sudden collapse or solely as the result of barbarian conquest. The invaders brought with them the seeds of a new Indian civilization, but they mingled their blood with that of the conquered population and absorbed and continued many aspects of their culture.

The invasion that coincided with the decline of India's earliest civilization was not an isolated event on the world scene. Shortly after 2000 B.C. some environmental factor—possibly a growing scarcity of grazing land in central and western Asia—induced a widespread migration of nomadic peoples. The migrants settled mainly in parts of southern and western Asia (an example is the occupation of Anatolia by the Hittites around 1600 B.C.), but this population movement produced cultural effects extending far beyond the regions physically affected. Although the migrating tribal societies were relatively primitive and lacked a system of writing, their spoken language was highly developed and tended to displace other tongues that it encountered. In modern times the term Indo-European was coined to denote a family of languages predominant over a wide area reaching from Hindustan to the western and northern fringes of Europe. It includes the ancient classical languages Greek and Latin, as well as the modern European tongues—Hellenic, Romance, Slavic, Celtic, and Teutonic (the principal exceptions are Hungarian, Finnish, and Estonian).

During the great migrations of the first half of the second millennium B.C. two closely related groups of tribes from the steppes of western Russia moved southward, one group into the Iranian plateau and the other through passes in the Hindu Kush mountains into northwestern India. Both of these peoples called themselves *Arya* (meaning "noble"), whence the geographical and political designation *Iran,* and several Indian variants of the same word. Strictly speaking, the name Aryan applies only to the Iranians (Persians) and the Indo-Aryans of the subcontinent, although it is sometimes used loosely to designate the whole Indo-European language group. There is no justification for applying it to any European nation or racial type.

Skeletons at Mohenjo-Daro. Although the downfall of this culture is a mystery, barbarian conquest was an important factor.

The early Indo-Aryans had a simple, largely pastoral, economy. Their domestic animals included sheep, goats, horses for pulling war chariots and for chariot racing, and they were avid cattle breeders. Although not worshiped, cattle were so highly prized that they served as currency. Barley and a few other grains were cultivated with the aid of a wooden plow drawn by bullocks. All the common handicrafts, including metalwork, were practiced. Music, both vocal and instrumental—with flutes, drums, cymbals, and stringed lutes or harps—was a popular source of entertainment, as was dancing. Gambling with dice was a national pastime and seems to have come close to being a national obsession. Early Indo-Aryan society resembled that of other semibarbarous, warlike peoples, as depicted in Homer's *Iliad,* the Anglo-Saxon *Beowolf,* and the Norse and Islandic sagas. The basic social unit was the patriarchal family, in rare cases polygamous, with women in a definitely subordinate position although not subject to the restraints and humiliations of later Hindu society.

Early Indo-Aryan economy and society

Legal and political institutions were rudimentary in early Indo-Aryan society. Each tribe had its chieftain or king (raja) whose main function was to lead its warriors in battle. Some tribes, in which the raja was selected by an assembly of warriors, resembled aristocratic republics rather than monarchies. Lacking populous cities from which to extract riches, the raja's powers were necessarily limited. The country villages within his territory managed their own internal affairs, paying part of their produce to the raja for "protection." The handling of crime and punishment followed patterns similar to those of the Germanic tribes that invaded the Roman Empire a thousand years later. An

Political and legal institutions

injured party or his family was expected to take the initiative in prosecuting an offender. Compensation for injuries was usually a payment to the plaintiff or, in the case of murder, to the victim's family. Another parallel to the early Germanic system of justice was the occasional resort to ordeal by fire or water to determine guilt or innocence. Theft was the most frequent complaint, especially cattle stealing, even though this crime was looked upon as especially reprehensible. An insolvent debtor—usually one who had gambled too recklessly—might be enslaved to his creditor.

Religion of the early Aryans

In every stage of civilization in India's long history, religion has been a factor of major importance. The relatively simple religion of the early Aryans was comparable to those of the early Greek, Roman, Norse, and Germanic societies. The Aryan gods—*deva,* or "shining ones"—were the forces of nature or personifications of these forces. No images or temples were erected, and worship consisted chiefly in performing sacrifices to the gods. Grain and milk were sacrificed, animal flesh was burned upon the altars (the worshipers themselves eating the flesh), but the choicest offering was *soma,* a psychedelic beverage fermented from the juice of a mountain plant. The gods were looked upon as splendid and powerful creatures, with human attributes but immortal as long as they drank the *soma* juice, and, on the whole, benevolent. It was assumed that they would reward men out of gratitude for the homage and gifts presented to them. Gradually, however, the notion took root that if the holy rites were conducted with unfailing accuracy they would compel the god to obedience.

The roster of gods

The roster of gods was a large one and tended to increase. While several deities can be identified with those of other Indo-European peoples, they did not have as clear-cut personalities as the Greek or Norse gods. The Aryan and later Hindu pantheon tended toward multiplicity and specialization. Dyaus, lord of the bright sky, was equivalent to the Greek Zeus (though less important). Varuna represented the sky or heaven in its capacity to encompass all things and hold the universe together. He was called Asura, a term which suggests close kinship with the supreme Persian deity, Ahura-Mazda. At least five different divinities were identified with the sun. One of them, Mitra, shared a common origin with the Persian Mithras, but this deity did not assume the prominence in India that Mithras attained in Persia and the West. Surya was the sun's golden disk, Pushan embodied its power to assist vegetation and animal growth, and Vishnu personified the swift-moving orb that traverses the sky in three strides.

Indra

The most popular deity of all in Vedic times was Indra, whose original significance is uncertain. He was alleged to have benefited mankind by slaying a malignant serpent, the demon of drought, thus releasing the pent-up waters to refresh the earth. Also, it was said, he discovered the light, made a path for the sun, and created lightning. He was chiefly honored as a mighty warrior and god of battle, the slayer of demons and the "black-skinned" enemies of the Aryans.

Indra was supposed to be particularly fond of *soma,* which fired his blood for combat, and he was reputed to be able to drink three lakes of this potent fluid at one draft while devouring the flesh of 300 buffaloes. *Soma,* the sacred liquor, was also deified, as was the sacrificial fire, Agni. Agni was conceived both as a god and as the mouth of the gods or as the servant who carried their savory food offerings up to the heavens for them.

The primitive Aryan religion—incorporating colorful nature myths and essentially mechanical and contractual in operation—changed gradually but markedly with the passage of time. Some deities, originally preeminent, declined in importance or disappeared, while others, probably from the cults of the pre-Aryan population, entered the pantheon. More significant changes, to be discussed in the next section, were the result of vigorous intellectual activity stimulated by social tensions and competition for authority among rival classes. An increasing sophistication in religion paralleled the growing complexity of a society in transition from a nomadic, pastoral economy to one of settled agricultural communities, ultimately with populous urban centers. From their base in northwestern India the Aryan tribes gradually pushed eastward into the Ganges valley, clearing by slash-and-burn technique tracts of jungle north of the river for agricultural use. Notoriously addicted to fighting, among themselves and against their non-Aryan neighbors, the Aryan warriors enhanced their military prowess around 800 B.C. by acquiring iron weapons. During the early centuries of the first millennium B.C. they conquered the eastern Ganges region and began penetration of the Deccan. Meanwhile, tribes and tribal confederations were transformed into kingdoms of considerable size with permanent courts and hierarchies of administrative officials.

Evolution of an increasingly complex Aryan society

The Aryan social structure, originally simply an association of heads of families who combined the functions of herdsman and warrior, gradually became stratified and complex. An early tradition postulates a divinely ordained division of society into four broad classes called *varna* (literally "covering," but designating a specific color assigned to each order). These were, respectively, the *brahman* (priest), *kshatriya* (warrior), *vaishya* (herdsman, artisan, merchant), and *shudra* (servant, menial laborer). The last named was looked upon as not only inferior but base, unfit for full membership in Aryan society. *Shudra* may have been the name of an aboriginal tribe—one of the *dasa* ("black-skinned people") who had occupied the fortified cities under attack by the Aryans and who were subsequently reduced to slavery. Slavery played a minor part in Aryan (and later Indian) society, but a type of dependency resembling serfdom appeared very early. The extreme isolation and humiliation implied in untouchability, however, was a phenomenon of post-Aryan times. In spite of taboos against intermarriage, large numbers of the "black-skinned" folk probably were assimilated into Aryan society, not only as *shudras* but as warriors and even priests. Although individual families sought to be identified with one

Four orders of Aryan society

of the upper three *varnas*—or were assigned against their will to the lowest one—the theory of the four orders was an artificial concept and had little to do with the social structure gradually evolving. As economic progress brought an increase in wealth and the centering of political authority, rivalry developed among various groups seeking a dominant position—rivalry most intense between the *brahmans* and the *kshatriyas*. Not before the third century B.C. was the preeminence of the *brahmans* generally recognized throughout India. At the other end of the scale, families allegedly of *shudra* descent became both prosperous and influential in some regions of India. Even *shudra* kings were not unknown.

The institution of caste

Not the theoretical four classes but the caste system became the dominant factor in shaping Indian society. Caste is difficult to define; exceptions can be found to every rigid definition. It is essentially a group of families actually or supposedly related by blood and governed internally by strict rules designed to control individual behavior, discharge collective responsibilities, and protect the membership from injury or disgrace. Its origins are obscure; its evolution extended over thousands of years; ultimately it became so firmly entrenched as to defy eradication. Kinship grouping has been important in every human society, but India is unique in retaining tightly closed kinship groups as key components of the overall social structure throughout sweeping changes in the level of civilization and shifting patterns of government.

The development of the caste system

Although Indo-Aryan society was not caste bound, the roots of caste can be traced back to this era, and even farther back to the Indus valley culture. Racial pride was certainly a contributing factor to the doctrine of social inequality and separation that is the rationale of caste. Degradation of the *shudras* reflected the conqueror's fear that intermingling with the aborigines would pollute Aryan blood. Economic specialization and the division of labor also played a part in the evolution of the caste system, but only partially and erratically. Brahmans, by definition priests and scholars, have engaged freely in many occupations, avoiding only those considered inherently polluting. Brahmans are divided into many castes, and only a minority of brahmans actually serve as priests. And while castes did become identified with particular crafts, trades, or services, their function and their niche in the social hierarchy differed from one locality to another. Caste arose from a great variety of circumstances, including deviation from accepted religious belief or conversion to a new one, commingling with an alien ethnic group, or migration to a distant region. The number of castes multiplied, eventually totaling more than 3,000. The word in northern India used to denote caste is *jati*—literally "species"—reflecting the belief that the institution is part of the natural order, sanctioned by divine decree and thus to be accepted as a religious duty. Typically, in a given locality each caste worships a particular deity or group of deities, and the ranking order of castes and the degree of their alleged inherent purity or impurity correspond to the ascending scale of divinities. Although varying in composition and arrangement, the caste system embodies a hierarchical view of reality, applying both to the cosmic order and to human society.

As the institution of caste evolved, it placed such restrictions on the individual as to seem—when contrasted with Western ideals of equality and freedom—almost unbearable. Marriage was typically restricted to within the caste though forbidden within the immediate circle of kin. Food could be eaten only if prepared by a member of one's own caste or of a higher caste. Occupation, dress codes, and the bounds of social intercourse were all prescribed. The caste system intensified the subjugation of women. In some cases a man was permitted to marry into a lower caste; for a woman to do so was considered utterly unacceptable. While a caste might rise in the social scale, the individual could neither escape from his caste nor rise within it, although he could, by breaking the rules, fall still lower.

In spite of its disadvantages the caste system, beyond illustrating the toughness of deeply ingrained social institutions, performed some useful functions in Indian society. If it denied the individual independence it offered him protection (not always enforceable) against injury from outside. It policed its own membership. A clearly delineated division of labor and services among castes enabled the community to accomplish its necessary work with a minimum of confusion. Separation was never absolute. Representatives of different castes participated jointly in the village councils which managed local affairs. All castes except the lowest (and the untouchables) participated in religious ceremonies and festivities. The instrument of caste facilitated the assimilation of intruders into India. Successful invaders of the subcontinent—sometimes accepted under the fiction that they were *kshatriyas* who had gone astray—found that they could neither dislodge caste nor prevent it from permeating their own society. Finally, because caste was grounded in the most basic of institutions—the family—it contributed to the durability of India's cultural and religious heritage.

2. INTELLECTUAL AND RELIGIOUS CONTRIBUTIONS OF THE VEDIC AGE

The major achievements of the Indo-Aryans were intangible rather than material, manifested primarily in products of verbal skill and poetic imagination. A huge body of hymns, prayers, and incantations composed over a long period of time and known collectively as the Four Vedas was passed on from generation to generation by oral tradition. The Vedas comprised the sacred books of the Indo-Aryan and later Hindu religion. Like the Hebrew, Christian, and Islamic scriptures they were regarded as divinely inspired, but because the Aryans were illiterate they believed their sacred texts had been "heard" rather than "revealed." In the absence of any contemporary written documents the Vedas (committed to writing centuries later) are the chief source of information for a vast period of Indian history occupying roughly the last two thousand years of the pre-Christian era and called accordingly the Vedic Age. One of the Vedas, the *Yajurveda,* is a manual of sacrifice for the officiating priest. The *Atharvaveda,* which probably drew heavily upon the folklore of the indigenous population, is a catalogue of charms and spells supposedly effective in curing illnesses, arousing passion in the object of one's desire, or destroying an enemy. The oldest and most important of the four is the *Rig Veda* ("verses of wisdom" or "knowledge"), a compilation of more than 1,000 poems composed between 1500 and 900 B.C., addressed to various Aryan deities. The poems range in content and mood from the heights of contemplation and reverence to the secular and mundane. Vivid and colorful phrases portray the earthshaking deeds of Indra, "wielder of the thunder" who "pierced the bellies of the mountains" to release the waters. A hymn of beautiful simplicity implores the protection of the goddess Night, whose radiance "drives out the dark." On a less exalted plane a gambler laments an unlucky throw of the dice, "too high by one," which has caused his wife to repel him and his mother-in-law to hate him. The best of the verses reflect poetic sensitivity of a high order.

Indo-European peoples have produced stirring epic poetry commemorating their early history, portrayed as a "heroic age" of individual prowess and bloody combat. About the same time that the Homeric epics were taking form among the ancient Greeks, Aryan bards were celebrating India's heroic age in two great epic poems, the *Mahabharata* and the *Ramayana*. Put into final form a few centuries later than the Vedas, they reflect the same general social and cultural milieu. The *Mahabharata,* the longer and presumably older of the two, is more than seven times the length of the *Iliad* and the *Odyssey* combined. A complex, rambling, and enigmatic tale of rivalry between two branches of the royal family in the kingdom of the Kurus, it is filled with exciting and bizarre episodes including a rare example of polyandry (a princess agrees to marry all four brothers of the noble warrior who won her in a bride contest), and the loss of a kingdom on a throw of the dice in a gambling match. An actual battle that was fought near Delhi, probably around 1400 B.C., provides the climax of the story. Allegedly kings from Greece and China as well as from all of India joined in the fight, which lasted eighteen days and ended with practically all the participants slain. The five brothers, having survived the slaughter and recovered their kingdom with the aid of the god Krishna, after a peaceful reign of several years renounced the world and, with their joint wife, climbed a Himalayan peak to enter the City of the Gods.

The locale of the *Ramayana* is east of the Kuru kingdom, and the poem reflects some knowledge of the Deccan as well. It relates the adventures of Prince Rama and his beautiful wife, Sita, who is exiled through the intrigue of a wicked stepmother, carried off by the demon king of Ceylon, and finally rescued by Rama with the help of a faithful ally, the monkey general Hanuman. The plot leaves Sita little peace. Suspected of having sullied her purity while in captivity, she attempts suicide by burning and is vindicated only when the fire god Agni refuses to harm her. Lacking the vivid realism and sharp characteriza-

The Indian epics: the Mahabharata

Bronze Figure of Hanuman, the monkey general and faithful ally of Rama in the *Ramayana,* eleventh century. He was given semidivine status for his selfless behavior.

Ravana, Rama, and Lakshmana. An Indian painting of the eighteenth century depicting an incident from the *Ramayana.* Rama, the epic hero, and his brother Lakshmana are fighting against Ravana, the demon king of Ceylon, who carried off Rama's faithful wife Sita.

tion of the *Mahabharata,* the *Ramayana* is more artfully contrived and contains beautiful descriptive passages. In contrast to the longer epic it is by tradition attributed to a single author, Valmiki. Originating in martial legends, the epics incorporated extraneous materials that reflect changing and increasingly sophisticated social and ethical standards. The *Ramayana* came to be regarded as an exemplar of the ideal man and woman, a definition hardly comforting to the female sex. A supplement to the epic, added probably after the beginning of the Christian era, relates that Sita, unable to remove the undeserved stain upon her character, retreated to the forest where she was swallowed up by Mother Earth. (This episode has been interpreted as an allegory of the advance of agriculture: the word *sita* means "furrow.") The *Mahabharata,* put into final form between 400 B.C. and 200 A.D., grew to resemble an encyclopedia of early Indian mythology and history. Chanted by priests performing sacrificial rites for royal courts, it acquired religious significance. Eventually the epics, rather than the Vedas, served as a bible for the common people, partly because the brahmans restricted study of the Vedas to the higher castes, whereas anyone could listen to a recitation of the epics

The language of the epics, derived from but differing from that of the Vedas, is known as Sanskrit. While many different dialects evolved, Sanskrit came to be accepted as the noblest form of discourse and was preserved as a standard for scholars, just as Latin became the classical language for Europe while Europeans were developing their own national tongues. Sanskrit is regarded by some linguistic scholars

The Ramayana

Sanskrit: the language of the epics

Scenes from the Mahabarata. This eighteenth-century cotton tapestry embroidered with colored silks and silver demonstrates the enduring impact of the *Mahabarata* on Indian culture.

as the most flexible and responsive to fine shades of meaning of all Indo-European languages. In contrast to the haphazard Western (Roman) alphabet, the Sanskrit alphabet is logically arranged and accommodates a wide gamut of sounds, with symbols for fourteen separate vowels and thirty-five consonants. Panini, a linguistic genius of the fourth century B.C., stabilized classical Sanskrit by devising a grammar with more than 4,000 rules. The only scientific grammar for any language before the nineteenth century, Panini's work deserves to rank among the greatest intellectual achievements of any ancient civilization.

The necessity of the oral tradition

An age accustomed to a constant flow of memoranda may find it incredible that great quantities of prose and poetry could be preserved for centuries without the aid of writing. Writing disappeared in India with the abandonment of the Indus valley script about 1550 B.C. Just when it reappeared is uncertain. The earliest extant inscriptions, on stone columns, date from the third century B.C., but these are executed in a script that had reached an advanced stage of development (see below, p. 128).

Ritual and the ascendancy of the priestly class

Religion during the Vedic Age evolved from the simple to the complex, embracing several levels of belief and practice and culminating in subtle philosophical speculation. Sacrifice to the gods, a central feature of the early Aryan cult, soon began to be interpreted as a cosmic principle. The gods for their continued existence were believed to be dependent upon the offerings they received, without which the universe would return to chaos. This assumption, making the rituals more powerful than the gods themselves, obviously exalted the importance of the human ministrants of the sacred rites. The ascendancy of the priestly caste is clearly reflected in the *Brahmanas,* a series of prose manuals composed between 800 and 600 B.C. and attached to the Vedas. These texts accord to the brahmans not only supreme religious authority but also special social, legal, and economic privileges as well. The claims of the brahmans, however, were challenged not only by competition from other social classes, especially those claiming *kshatriya* status, but by growing doubts as to the efficacy of sacrifice and the discovery of other paths to the fulfillment of religious needs. Following a tradition that has always been prominent in Indian religion and that may have originated in the Indus valley civilization, individuals sought holiness by renouncing the world and its rituals in favor of a life of asceticism and meditation. The ideal of self-sacrifice as the highest type of sacrifice was expressed in a late Vedic "Hymn of the Primeval Man." This creation myth attributes the origin of the universe to the sacrifice of a Great Being, who gave up the separate parts of his body to form the human race, other living creatures, and the earth and heavenly bodies as well. As in Judaism and other higher religions, a concept originating in an act of violence was later interpreted allegorically and endowed with spiritual significance.

Indian religion, while growing in intellectual content, continued to absorb local cults and traditions. The honoring of cattle as sacred animals and the adoption of taboos against their slaughter—unknown to the early Aryans—may represent the revival of a motif from Indus valley civilization, in which the bull was apparently an object of worship. The doctrines of rebirth and transmigration of souls began in the seventh century B.C. to displace the Aryan notion that souls of the just departed to a "World of the Fathers," while those of the unjust were consigned to a "House of Clay." Emphasis on ethical conduct as opposed to ritual characterized the worship of Varuna. Originally an Aryan sky god, Varuna was exalted as imperial guardian of the cosmic and the moral order. Conceived as omnipresent, hater of lies, and unwilling to accept sacrifice as appeasement for man's misdeeds, Varuna, like Babylonian deities or the Hebrew Yahweh, instilled in his worshipers fear and trembling.

Indian religion as shaped by local cults and traditions

A thirst for knowledge motivated the evolution of Indian religion, although opinions differed, as they do today, as to what constitutes knowledge and how best to reach it. Ascetics who fled to the wilderness hoped to sharpen their powers of perception through solitary meditation. Knowledge was the avowed objective of orgiastic practices in certain sects. The quest for knowledge found its noblest expression in the *Upanishads,* philosophical treatises in prose and verse which constitute the final portion of the Vedas. Cast in the form of dialogues between teacher and student (the term means "sitting down near"), the *Upanishads* probe searchingly into the nature of reality and the problem of man's place in the universe. Although varying in character

*The quest for knowledge:
the* Upanishads

and quality, these works reveal a genius for conceptual reasoning that has earned the admiration of intellectuals in Western and Eastern lands alike. Scorning conventional wisdom and perfunctory ritual, the authors of the *Upanishads*, like the Greek Socrates, affirmed that true knowledge could not only satisfy the intellect but also instill virtue. They taught that evil is the fruit of ignorance, that the pursuit of wisdom is pursuit of the highest possible good, and that its attainment bestows both power and virtue. Conflicting schools of thought have been traced to the *Upanishads*, but the main thrust of their teachings can be defined as a monistic idealism. Its tenets are: (1) the supreme reality of the World Soul or Absolute Being; (2) the impermanence and illusory character of the material world; (3) the cycle of rebirth of individual souls; (4) the possibility of attaining serenity through escape from this cycle by union with Absolute Being. Evil and suffering are explained as incidental to material beings. "Material beings" becomes a contradiction in terms because matter is held to be an illusion (*maya*) or, more precisely, a veil concealing true reality, which is soul or spirit. Hence if the soul can penetrate the veil to reach truth it escapes from discord and suffering. According to this philosophy, physical death does not provide a way of escape because the soul's transmigration in another body takes it back to the illusory world of sense.

The doctrine of transmigration and the caste system

The doctrine of transmigration as it gained popular acceptance reinforced the caste system. Members of a lowly caste were encouraged to believe that if they diligently performed their duties in this present life they would be born to higher status in the next; and that if they broke the rules their next birth would lower them in the scale of being, possibly to the animal or insect level. Deeds, it was affirmed, bear good or evil fruit, but with harvest deferred. The carrot-and-stick doctrine of *dharma* (faithful performance of one's assigned role) and *karma* (merits or demerits earned as a result of action) served to cement loyalty to the prescriptions of caste.

Serenity through union with Absolute Being

The philosophers of the *Upanishads*, while accepting the doctrine of *karma*, were little interested in the possibility of climbing upward in the monotonous cycle of rebirth. The goal they sought was a state of tranquil detachment that would create no *karma* whatsoever—"neither black nor white"—and thus dissolve the fetters binding them to the sensible world. Having broken with the cycle of births, the liberated soul could reach *nirvana*, which does not mean entrance into a heaven but union with *Brahman*, the undefinable Universal Soul or Absolute Being.[1]

---

[1] The concept of Brahman as Absolute Being or World Soul evolved through refinement of an earlier belief in a pervasive magical force. *Brahma* (masculine form of the noun) personified the concept as a deity that could be worshiped. *Brahman* as title of the priestly class is another derivative of the same word. *Nirvana*, though not appearing in the *Upanishads*, became the popular term for the ideal of spiritual liberation. Its literal meaning is "extinction."

The uncompromising idealism of the *Upanishads,* when viewed superficially, may appear to be hopelessly negative and pessimistic because it repudiates the world of immediate human experience. In intent, however, its message is positive and optimistic regarding human worth and destiny. It holds that *atman* (the individual soul) is actually a fragment of *Brahman* (the rational principle that pervades the universe), from which it has been separated and to which it longs to return. Every human, therefore, no matter how lowly or wretched, is a legitimate heir to all the grandeur of the cosmos. This doctrine combines the discipline of logical reasoning with the emotional appeal of mysticism.

The sixth century B.C. was a period of religious reform and innovation, initiated mainly by representatives of the upper classes, and breaking with Brahmanical tradition. The most enduring products of this religious ferment were Buddhism and Jainism, each of which became a distinct religion. The Jains today number something less than two million, located chiefly in southern and western India. Buddhism, after exerting profound influence on Indian society and culture for several centuries, largely disappeared from the land of its birth but played a role in other Asian countries somewhat parallel to that of Christianity in the West, and remains to this day one of the world's major faiths.

Little is known about the life of Gautama (c. 563–483 B.C.), who became known to his followers as the Buddha ("Enlightened One"). He was the son of the chief of a small tribe located on the slopes of the Himalayas in what is now Nepal. According to legend, after being reared with every comfort he suffered a profound shock when confronted with the phenomena of suffering and death. Finding his pampered existence no longer bearable, at the age of twenty-nine he left the palace in the middle of the night after a fond glance at his wife and infant son, cut off his hair, and sent back his jewels and fine clothes to his father. After studying philosophy with the brahmans without satisfaction, and after six years of extreme asceticism that led only to despair, he sat down one day discouraged under a large tree—henceforth called the Bohdi Tree ("Tree of Enlightenment"). Here a revelation or flash of insight enabled him to penetrate the mystery of evil and suffering. Henceforth he was free from doubts, but instead of retiring to enjoy his tranquillity of mind and spirit he determined to lead others along the path to enlightenment. For the next forty years, until his death at the age of eighty, he wandered through the Ganges valley, relying upon charity for his livelihood and instructing the disciples who gathered about him.

Gautama's teachings, as understood and elaborated by his disciples, are relatively clear and explicit. To judge both from their content and from their effect upon his followers, Gautama's unique personality combined a keen intellect and strong sense of dedication with sympathetic understanding of the problems of everyday life. Like Socrates and Confucius he was a stimulating teacher. His basic doctrines comprised a code of ethics grounded in philosophical materialism and a theory of human psychology that denied the reality of the self. In direct opposition to the absolute idealism of the *Upanishads,* he taught that only matter exists and denied the actuality of the soul. Because he regarded matter as in a state of flux, he recognized no Absolute Being or any fixed and universal principle other than constant change. Even the gods are subject to the laws of growth and decay; the universe is becoming, never being.

The Buddha's psychological principles

The Buddha's psychological principles derived logically from his materialist metaphysics. Lacking soul or permanent entity, distinct individual personality is an impossibility. What is mistaken for self is only a bundle of attributes (the senses and consciousness) held together temporarily as the spokes of a wheel are fastened around the hub. Oddly enough, while denying the existence of the soul, Gautama's teachings, at least as interpreted later, retained the doctrine of *karma,* affirming that a person's actions affect the condition of another person yet unborn—just as an expiring lamp can light another flame.

Gautama's doctrine of selflessness

Gautama's seemingly negative and deflating doctrines were intended to bring relief and encouragement. He believed that the root of suffering is desire: the pursuit of goals unattainable because the objects sought are fleeting and unreal. And because the concept of self is an illusion, the most frustrating of all desires is the craving for self-satisfaction and self-exaltation. The road to peace of mind and true happiness, in Gautama's view, directs one's energies outward, away from self. The egoist chases shadows; the altruist may find the light. Selflessness was presented not as an abstract ideal but as a positive injunction to render useful service and avoid injury to others. One of the innumerable legends surrounding the life of the Buddha is that he once stopped a

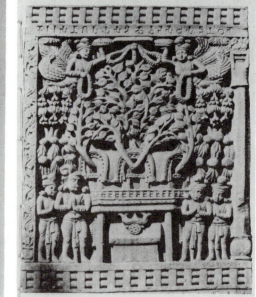

Symbols of Buddha. Left: Hindu divinities pay homage to Buddha, represented as the enthroned "wheel of law," in this second-century B.C. relief from Mathura. Right: The adoration of the Bodhi Tree under which Buddha experienced enlightenment is depicted on a first-century B.C. gateway pillar at Sanchi.

war by walking between two hostile armies poised for battle and persuading them not to fight.

Although Gautama approached the problem of human bondage from a direction opposite to that of the idealist philosophers of the *Upanishads,* his objective was similar: release from entanglement in a world of fleeting experience through the surrender of self. Relying on persuasion rather than coercion, he urged his followers to respect the brahmans and other truth seekers. Without repudiating caste he welcomed disciples from every stratum of society. Buddhism, while containing unique features, was basically a product of the intellectual milieu in which it arose. It has even been called the "Protestant form of Hinduism."

During the centuries following Gautama's death, his movement gradually acquired the character of an organized religion. The Buddhists in India became an order of monks. Candidates for admission to the order were required to undergo a long period of training, after which the novitiate shaved his head, put on the yellow robes, and took the monastic vows of poverty and chastity. In contrast to Christian monks, he did not take a vow of obedience because membership was considered a matter of free choice. The monks customarily remained in a monastery during the three months of the rainy season, which Gautama had devoted to instructing his disciples; for the rest of the year they lived as wandering mendicants dependent upon the alms they received in their beggars' bowls as they passed from village to village. Lay men or women who accepted the Buddhist teachings and contributed to the support of the monks were considered adherents of the faith and entitled to its benefits. While not adopting the sacrificial rites of Brahmanism, the Buddhists venerated sacred places, typically groves or individual trees. They raised mounds to contain ashes of the Buddha or of revered monks and ascetics. Commemorative pillars were also erected, but no temples were built before the beginning of the Christian era. The popularity of the religion is evidenced by the fact that during the period from 200 B.C. to 200 A.D. physical remains attributable to the Buddhists outnumber those of all other cults.

Some five hundred years after its beginning Buddhism split into two major divisions. *Hinayana,* the "Lesser Vehicle," was so called because it emphasized the goal of individual salvation, claiming that a diligent person could attain *nirvana* in the space of three lifetimes. The *Hinayana* school retained much of what was probably Gautama's original teaching, including denial of the soul. In theory at least, it honors the founder as a man, although prayers as well as gifts of flowers and incense are offered to his image. Carried to Ceylon in the third century B.C., *Hinayana* Buddhism spread farther to Burma, Siam, Cambodia, and Laos, and remains the dominant faith in these regions.

In India the *Hinayana* school soon lost ground to the *Mahayana* or "Great Vehicle," which, with broader ambition than its rival, set as

The Faces of Buddha. As Buddhism spread across Asia in the first century B.C., Buddha's portrait began to replace the symbols, such as the wheel, that his followers had respectfully employed. These three faces from Gandhara (left), Thailand (center), and Cambodia (right) suggest the diverse visions of Buddha.

The Mahayana *school*

its goal redemption of the entire human race. Nurturing a complex theology, the *Mahayana* school acquired some characteristics of a supernatural religion, including the worship of Buddha and associated deities. It shared with the *Hinayana* school the concept of the *Bodhisattva,* but with a differing interpretation. Viewed in the *Hinayana* tradition as successive incarnations of the Buddha, in the *Mahayana* the *Bodhisattva* came to represent the Buddha-elect, an individual who has won enlightenment but chooses to remain in the world for the liberation of others, agreeing "to suffer as a ransom for all beings, for the sake of all beings." Fundamentally optimistic, the Great Vehicle taught that everyone is a *Bodhisattva* and ultimately will become a Buddha. It embodied as cardinal virtues love, pity, joy, and serenity. As it spread within India and without, the Great Vehicle absorbed elements from local cults and traditions. In Tibet for example, fused with a type of magic, it acquired a character remarkably different from the original. But for several centuries *Mahayana* Buddhism in India not only stood as a highly ethical religion open to all classes but also contributed greatly to cultural and intellectual progress. It stimulated philosophical speculation and it produced a large body of beautiful and deeply emotional literature.

Mahavira: the founder of Jainism

The rise of Jainism (from *Jina,* "conqueror") was contemporary with and in some respects parallel to that of Buddhism. Its founder, believed to have lived from about 540 to 468 B.C., became known to his followers as Mahavira ("Great Hero"). Like Gautama he was a member of the oligarchic warrior class and like the founder of Buddhism he broke radically with traditional religions, rejecting both their deities and their scriptures. But while Gautama posited a radical materialism, Mahavira—though viewing the material universe as real—believed that it was filled with an infinite number of souls lodged not only in living creatures but even in inanimate objects.

However unconventional his metaphysical premises may appear, Mahavira's doctrines reflect themes prominent in the religious currents of his day. Rejecting the concept of an overriding World Soul, he taught that individual souls by entanglement with matter are held in bondage, a bondage perpetuated through successive births by the operation of *karma*. Because every action produces *karma* and *karma* adds weight to the chains, the only route to escape is to avoid action altogether. While *Mahayana* Buddhism envisions *nirvana* as a positive reality—conquering death and transcending thought and causality—in Mahavira's philosophy it represents a state of absolute passivity. Carrying the idea of the incompatibility of matter and spirit to its uttermost limit he prescribed a regime of extreme asceticism, culminating ideally in death through self-starvation—a feat Mahavira is alleged to have accomplished.

The doctrines of Mahavira

In spite of its avowed atheism, Jainism like Buddhism eventually came to resemble a religion, with prayers, scriptures, and sacred beings. Mahavira, though not deified is adored, and legends grew about his life similar to those surrounding the Buddha. The Jains became a monastic order comprising monks and an associated body of laity. During the first century of the Christian era a split occurred within the sect, resulting from the refusal of one zealous group, the "Space-Clad," to wear any clothing. In spite of ascetic traits, many Jains felt free to cultivate literature, and one of them during the medieval period attained distinction as a Sanskrit poet. Prominent in the Jain faith is the doctrine of *ahimsa* or noninjury to living beings. Imposing taboos upon the slaughter not only of animals but even of insects, *ahimsa* has also contributed ethical support to the ideal of pacifism. At the same time, since the doctrine of *ahimsa* ruled out the practice of agriculture, Jains turned to trade and moneylending as sources of livelihood. Ironically, a movement founded on the renunciation of all things material eventually produced some of the wealthiest members of Indian society.

Characteristics of Jainism

The evolution of religious thought during the Vedic Age stimulated intellectual activity in areas that would now be considered the domain of science. A late Vedic "Hymn of Creation" probes beyond myth, tradition, and sense experience to a time when "even nothingness was not." Hindu cosmology, though clothed in nature myths, was remarkably subtle. It included the concept of an eternally appearing and disappearing universe created each day out of his own being by an impersonal supreme deity (Brahma) and reabsorbed into himself every night. Contemplating enormous stretches of time, each cosmic "day of Brahma" was reckoned as exceeding four billion earthly years. Early Indian speculation on the nature and origin of the universe

Philosophical speculation

paralleled that of the naturalistic Milesian school in Greece during the sixth century B.C. The atomic theory of matter and the concept of a plurality of universes were entertained.

Along with astute philosophical speculation came scientific achievements in more practical fields. Medicine was highly developed in the Vedic Age. Not only were many specific remedies listed, but dissection was also practiced and delicate operations were performed. The knowledge of human anatomy was extensive, and a beginning had been made in the study of embryology. Medical science and the surgeon's vocation were held in high respect until inhibited by a fear of pollution through bodily contact with unclean persons. Astrologers, notwithstanding the fanciful premises underlying their research, acquired an appreciable knowledge of astronomy and tentatively entertained the suggestion that the earth revolves on its axis and that the sun only appears to rise and set. The most brilliant scientific attainments were those in mathematics. The Indians were able to handle extremely large numbers in their calculations and knew how to extract square and cube roots. Besides using the decimal system they invented the all-important principle of the zero, eventually adopted by the rest of the world. "Arabic numbers" now in universal use are of Indian origin. In geometry progress was not equal to that of the Greeks, but the Indians surpassed the Greeks in the development of algebra.

3. THE EARLIEST INDIAN EMPIRE

In the fourth century B.C. the kingdom of Magadha, located in the eastern Ganges valley where Gautama had taught his disciples two centuries earlier, became the center of a struggle that led to the unification of most of the states and tribal groups of northern India. The need for political consolidation and the means for achieving it had been demonstrated by India's inability to prevent foreign intrusions into its territory. As a result of the conquests of the Persian king, Darius I, about 500 B.C., the Indus valley had become a province (satrapy) of the Persian Empire, furnishing mercenary soldiers and an annual tribute in gold. After Alexander the Great, the famous Macedonian conqueror, overthrew the Persian Empire, he conducted his troops eastward through the passes of the Hindu Kush mountains into the upper Indus valley (327–326 B.C.). He spent less than two years in India but traversed most of the Punjab, fought and negotiated with local rajas, and installed Macedonian officials in the region. Although Alexander's invasion provides the first verifiable date in Indian history, it made so little impression upon the Hindus that their contemporary records do not even mention his name. However, the invasion promoted cultural exchange between the Hindus and the Greek-speaking world, and, more immediately, it paved the way for the erection of a powerful state in India.

In the revolts and confusion that followed the death of Alexander in 323 B.C., an Indian adventurer named Chandragupta Maurya seized the opportunity to found a dynasty. Chandragupta had profited from observing Greek military tactics and led in the movement to expel the Macedonian officials from India. Then he turned his army against the Magadha kingdom, which was the strongest state in Hindustan at this time. He defeated and killed the Magadhan king and established himself as ruler with his capital at Pataliputra (now Patna), a magnificent city eight miles long commanding the south bank of the Ganges. When Seleucus (Alexander's successor in Syria and Persia) tried to recover the lost Indian territory, Chandragupta defeated him soundly and forced him to cede Baluchistan and part of Afghanistan. Chandragupta extended his power over most of northern India and founded the first empire in Indian history. Although his dynasty, known as the Maurya, lasted less than a century and a half, its record is a distinguished one.

As a ruler Chandragupta Maurya was a far cry from the earlier Aryan rajas. Not only was his realm populous and wealthy but it also possessed features surprisingly like those of some modern states. Through a wide-ranging bureaucracy the government exerted paternalistic control over the lives and activities of its subjects, particularly in the economic sphere. The state controlled mines, forests, pearl fisheries, even the pans for salt manufacture. It operated farms, shipyards, and arsenals, and employed poor women workers for spinning and weaving. Besides a civil bureaucracy Chandragupta kept a formidable military establishment, reputed to number 600,000 infantry, 30,000 cavalry, and 9,000 elephants. The chief source of state revenue was a land tax, absorbing between one fourth and one half of the crops produced.

Chandragupta's rule was both efficient and harsh, meting out severe punishments for the infraction of royal decrees. The death penalty, sometimes by administering poison, was freely imposed. Maintaining an army of spies, informers, and secret police was typical of early Indian monarchies, but the Maurya emperor seems to have developed it to a fine art. Recruited from all social levels from brahmans to astrologers, outcastes, and prostitutes, spies were directed to gauge public opinion, check on officials, uncover crimes or conspiracies, and gather intelligence, combining the roles of a CIA and an FBI. The severity of the Maurya regime, as well as its sophistication, is illustrated by the *Arthashastra,* a treatise on polity put into final form five hundred years later but attributed to Chandragupta's prime minister. This manual, inviting comparison with Machiavelli's *The Prince,* urges the ruler to be firm, energetic, aggressive, and vigilant, guarding against collusion among his subordinates. On the assumption that two bordering states are always enemies, it advises the ruler to ally with his neighbor's more distant neighbor—the natural enemy of one's own enemy.

Capital improvements

King Ashoka: Buddhist conqueror

In addition to bringing stability to a large section of India, Chandragupta has to his credit the construction and improvement of public irrigation works and the building of roads, including a royal road reaching from his capital to the western frontier, a distance of 1,200 miles. In spite of his protective network of spies, fear of a possible assassination led him to change his sleeping quarters every night. According to tradition, after a warlike reign of twenty-two years Chandragupta abdicated his throne and ended his days as a Jain monk.

The most illustrious member of the Maurya dynasty, and one of the most remarkable rulers in the annals of any civilization, was Chandragupta's grandson Ashoka, royal patron of Buddhism, whose beneficent reign lasted forty-one years (c. 273–232 B.C.). Ashoka began his career in the tradition of his father and grandfather by making war, but after a bloody campaign that destroyed and enabled him to absorb a rival kingdom, in Orissa directly to the south, the character of his government changed abruptly. The victory—decisive but obtained at the price of wholesale slaughter—apparently made a profound impression both upon the conqueror and upon those who might oppose him in the future. King Ashoka publicly expressed his sorrow for the suffering his armies had caused and announced his decision to forswear violence, but at the same time he affirmed his determination to be accepted and obeyed as a legitimate sovereign. By successful diplomatic overtures he won submission from most of the remaining states of the subcontinent until his dominion extended from Afghanistan and Kashmir in the north to Mysore in the southern Deccan. Thus, for the first time, nearly all of India was brought under a central administration. Ashoka's conquests, however, were the aspect of his

Laughing Boy. Terracotta head of a laughing male, from Pataliputra (Patna). An example of the realistic sculpture of the Maurya period.

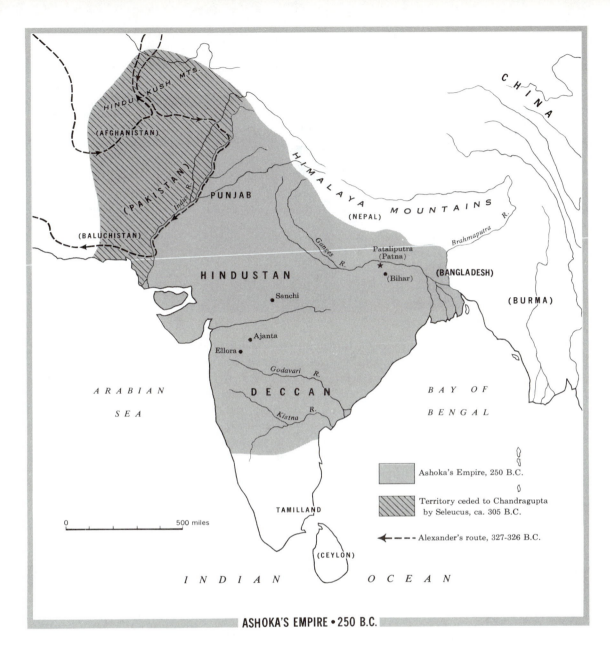

ASHOKA'S EMPIRE • 250 B.C.

Map labels:
CHINA
HINDU KUSH MTS.
(AFGHANISTAN)
(PAKISTAN)
Indus R.
PUNJAB
(BALUCHISTAN)
HIMALAYA MOUNTAINS
(NEPAL)
Ganges R.
Brahmaputra R.
Pataliputra (Patna)
(Bihar)
(BANGLADESH)
(BURMA)
HINDUSTAN
Sanchi
Ajanta
Ellora
Godavari R.
DECCAN
Kistna R.
ARABIAN SEA
BAY OF BENGAL
Ashoka's Empire, 250 B.C.
Territory ceded to Chandragupta by Seleucus, ca. 305 B.C.
Alexander's route, 327–326 B.C.
0   500 miles
TAMILLAND
(CEYLON)
INDIAN   OCEAN

reign that he considered least important. Attracted to the Buddhist
teachings, he at first became a lay adherent and later probably took
the formal vows of the order but without relinquishing his position
as king. He attempted, rather, to exemplify the precepts of Buddhism
in his personal life and to apply them to the administration of the
empire. Thus, without being a theocrat or divine-right ruler, he provides an almost unique example of the injection of religious idealism
into statecraft.

It is impossible to know how completely Ashoka's benign purposes
were carried out. He was particularly active in establishing rest houses

Ashokan Edict Pillar and Capital. These huge stone pillars stand as memorials to Ashoka's own authority and to the law of Buddha. This pillar (right) with a seated lion on the capital was erected in 243 B.C. at Lauriya Nandangarh, near the Nepal border. The bell-shaped Ashokan bull capital (left) from Rampurya, Bihar, shows the influence of contemporary Persian architecture.

The benevolent reign of King Ashoka

for travelers, in having trees planted, wells dug, and watering places built along the roads for the refreshment of man and beast, and in improving facilities for the treatment of the sick. He sent commissioners throughout the kingdom to inquire into the needs of the people, teach them religion, and report on their spiritual progress. In deference to the Buddhist injunction against taking life, Ashoka gave up hunting (replacing this sport by "pious tours" or pilgrimages) and gradually reduced the meat consumption in the royal household until—according to his announcement—only a vegetable diet was permitted. He reformed the harsh system of punishments which his grandfather had used, but he did not entirely abolish the death penalty. There is no evidence of any trend toward democracy in Ashoka's government. He adhered to the tradition of autocratic rule, but exercised it with conscience and benevolence. Although he was earnest in his support of Buddhism, Ashoka made religious toleration a state policy and urged that the brahmans of all the Hindu sects be treated with respect.

Patron of Buddhism

Ashoka's patronage during his long reign contributed markedly to the growth of the Buddhist religion. He sent missionaries of the faith to Ceylon, Burma, Kashmir, Nepal, and apparently even west to Macedonia, Syria, and Egypt. The king's own son was the missionary to Ceylon. Buddhist monks held a general council in 250 B.C. at Ashoka's capital, Pataliputra, where they agreed upon the basic texts that should be regarded as authentic. This "Council of Patna" established the canonical books of Buddhism, especially for the *Hinayana* school. The Buddhist scriptures are the oldest written literature of India—that is, they were the first to be committed to writing. However, although the texts were settled upon in 250 B.C., they were not actually written out in full until about 80 B.C. in Ceylon.

Ashoka raised a large number of reliquary mounds, several of which were made into elaborate monuments by Buddhists of later centuries. The pious emperor also had inscriptions carved on rocks and on thirty gigantic monolithic stone pillars erected in the fashion of Persian monarchs. The pillars, ten of which remain standing, are remarkable for their beautifully polished surfaces, and for the sculptures adorning some of their capitals. The rock-cut messages—exhortations to moral conduct—are, as previously noted, the earliest extant examples of writing in India of the historic period. Most of them were executed in the so-called Brahmi script, which is ancestral both to classical Sanskrit and to modern Hindi. Sculptured animal figures crown several of the pillars. A strikingly lifelike horse and bull appear to be in the same style as that found on stone seals of the ancient Indus valley civilization, suggesting that artistic traditions of that era were able to withstand the shock of the Aryan conquest and reappear a thousand years later.

The inscribed pillars of Ashoka

Ashoka's extraordinary administrative system did not long survive him. His successors seem to have been mediocrities who lacked both his reforming zeal and his organizing ability. In 184 B.C. the last Maurya ruler was assassinated by the army commander, an ambitious brahman who seated his own family on the throne. The efficiency of Ashoka's government was not duplicated until about 500 years after the end of his dynasty.

SELECTED READINGS

- *Items so designated are available in paperback editions.*
- Basham, A. L., *The Wonder That Was India: A Survey of the Culture of the Indian Sub-Continent before the Coming of the Muslims,* rev. ed., New York, 1963. A monumental work; illustrated.
- Brown, W. N., *The United States and India, Pakistan, Bangladesh,* Cambridge, Mass. 1972. An excellent general introduction.

  Cambridge History of India, Supplementary Volume: Wheeler, Mortimer, *The Indus Civilization,* 3d ed., Cambridge, 1968.

  Conze, Edward, *Buddhist Thought in India,* London, 1962.
- Coomaraswamy, A. K., *History of Indian and Indonesian Art,* New York, 1927.

  Eliot Charles, *Hinduism and Buddhism: An Historical Sketch,* 3 vols., New York, 1954. A standard work.

  Garratt, G. T., ed., *The Legacy of India,* Oxford, 1937.

  Hutton, J. S., *Caste in India,* 3rd ed., Oxford, 1961.

  Kabir, Humayun, *The Indian Heritage,* New York, 1955.

  Kramrisch, Stella, *The Art of India: Traditions of Indian Sculpture, Painting, and Architecture,* New York, 1954. Admirable photographs, with brief introduction.

  Kulke, H., and D. Rothermund, *A History of India,* Totowa, N.J., 1986. Scholarly, chiefly political history.

  Masefield, Peter, *Divine Revelation in Pali Buddhism,* London, 1986. Contends that the Buddha's teachings were more elitist and conservative than conventional interpretation acknowledges.

• Moore, C. A., ed., *The Indian Mind: Essentials of Indian Philosophy and Culture,* Honolulu, 1967.

• Piggott, Stuart, *Prehistoric India,* Baltimore, 1950.

• Prabhavananda, Swami, and F. Manchester, *The Upanishads, Breath of the Eternal,* New York, 1957.

Prebish, C. S., ed., *Buddhism: A Modern Perspective,* University Park, Pa., 1975. A useful account.

Raju, P. T., *Structural Depths of Indian Thought,* Albany, N.Y., 1985. Provides challenging interpretations and comparisons.

• Rawlinson, H. G., *India, a Short Cultural History,* rev. ed., New York, 1952. An excellent interpretive study.

——, *A Concise History of the Indian People,* 2d ed., New York, 1950.

Rowland, Benjamin, *The Art and Architecture of India: Buddhist, Hindu, Jain,* Baltimore, 1953. Informative and discriminating.

Snellgrove, David, *Indo-Tibetan Buddhism: Indian Buddhists and Their Tibetan Successors,* 2 vols., Boston, 1987. A scholarly and systematic exposition.

Spear, Percival, *India: A Modern History,* Ann Arbor, 1961.

Staal, Fritz, *Agni: The Vedic Ritual of the Fire Altar,* Berkeley, 1983. Describes the public performance in 1975 of an ancient rite.

• Wheeler, Mortimer, *Civilizations of the Indus Valley and Beyond,* London, 1966.

• Wolpert, Stanley, *A New History of India,* New York, 1977. An admirable survey, informative, and well written.

• Zimmer, Heinrich, *Philosophies of India,* (ed. Joseph Campbell), Princeton, 1969.

SOURCE MATERIALS

• de Bary, W. T., ed., *Sources of Indian Tradition,* "Brahmanism"; "Jainism and Buddhism"; "Hinduism," New York, 1958.

• Edgerton, Franklin, *The Beginnings of Indian Philosophy,* Cambridge, Mass., 1965. Carefully selected examples with a valuable introduction.

• Hamilton, C. H., ed., *Buddhism, a Religion of Infinite Compassion,* New York, 1952.

• Mueller, Max, tr., *The Upanishads,* 2 vols.

• Narayan, R. K., *Gods, Demons and Others,* London, 1964. Fine translation of ancient Indian stories.

The *Ramayana* and the *Mahabharata.*

Chapter 6

ANCIENT CHINESE CIVILIZATION

There have been many kings, emperors, and great men in history who enjoyed fame and honor while they lived and came to nothing at their death, while Confucius, who was but a common scholar clad in a plain gown, became the acknowledged Master of scholars for over ten generations. All people in China who discuss the six arts, from the emperors, kings, and princes down, regard the Master as the final authority. He may be called the Supreme Sage.

—*Historical Records* of Ssu-ma Ch'ien (145–c. 85 B.C.)

The beginning of a high civilization in China did not occur until about a thousand years after the flowering of the Indus-valley civilization in India. However, when once established the Far Eastern culture continued—not without changes and interruptions but with its essential features intact—into the twentieth century of our own era. The civilization of China, although it took form much later than that of Egypt, Mesopotamia, or the Indus valley, is one of the oldest in existence. Furthermore, its foundations rest upon a population that has retained its identity to a remarkable degree. Throughout successive cultural epochs, in spite of political upheavals and invasions, the Chinese have remained basically the same people since Neolithic times. In contrast to such regions as the Near East, the Mediterranean basin, and Europe, the area of China yielded a civilization that was both independent in origins and unmatched in durability. This does not mean that the Chinese were isolated from the rest of the world or that they did not benefit from foreign contacts. They fought defensively and offensively against neighboring peoples and succeeded in establishing their rule over large sections of Asia. But while they imposed their will upon conquered people by force, they considered it their mission to assimilate them and make them the beneficiaries of their superior culture.

Reasons for long survival of Chinese civilization

I. THE FORMATIVE STAGE

Early man in China: Peking man

In our study of preliterate cultures we have learned already that China was the home of one of the earliest human species, the so-called Peking man. His skeletal remains were found between 1926 and 1930 in a cave about 25 miles southwest of Peking. Fossilized fragments of over forty separate individuals were discovered, but, unfortunately, after being stored in a warehouse, most were lost during World War II. Anthropologists estimate that Peking man lived at least 500,000 years ago, and that he was probably a contemporary of Java man, one of the oldest human types. His culture was, of course, extremely primitive, but there is evidence that he used stone and bone tools, had a knowledge of fire, and buried his dead. Archeological research—interrupted by World War II but pursued vigorously since 1949 under the People's Republic—has yielded a wealth of information concerning early man in China. Recent excavations at the site where the bones of Peking man were first discovered have unearthed new specimens of the same human type but belonging to a period some 200,000 years later than that assigned to the first appearance of Peking man. Study of these recent finds reveals significant evolutionary changes in the course of 200 millennia. While the creature's teeth and jaws diminished in size, brain capacity increased by as much as 20 percent, indicating a growth in intelligence as well as changes in dietary habits. Contrary to what was formerly believed, it is now known that much of the area of China was continuously occupied by subhuman or human types throughout the Stone Ages. *Homo sapiens* appeared perhaps as early as 50,000 years ago. A later Paleolithic culture—the remains of which have not yet been fully excavated and classified—is identified with people who apparently were Mongoloid in race.

Neolithic cultures

The Neolithic Age in China can be dated from the sixth millennium B.C. Evidence of three Neolithic cultures has been discovered, one centered in the great highland plain that surrounds the Yellow River valley, a second in the valleys of the lower Yangtze and Huai rivers, and a third in the southeast coastal area, including the island of Taiwan. All were developed by communities of farmers, with millet the chief crop in the north, rice in the Yangtze region, and roots and tubers in the southeast. Each produced a distinctive type of pottery.

The loess highlands, cradle of Chinese civilization

There is still disagreement as to where and when Neolithic culture advanced to the level of civilization, characterized by metal working, city living, writing, and effective political organization. The first of the three areas mentioned above—the semiarid northern plain—is generally believed to have been the cradle of Chinese civilization. One contemporary scholar contends that, in contrast to the inhabitants of the well-watered Nile and Tigris-Euphrates valleys, the Chinese began as dry-land farmers and may have lacked irrigation facilities until the sixth century B.C. The highlands bordering the middle reaches of the

The Loess Highlands of Northern China

Yellow River are covered with a type of soil known as loess, composed of fine particles of loam and dust borne by northwest winds from the central plateaus of Asia and deposited in the valley and along the northeastern coast. This soil, which from its color has given rise to such geographical names as Yellow River and Yellow Sea, is pliable enough to be easily worked with primitive digging sticks, and also has the advantage of being free from a heavy growth of forest or grasses. In choosing farm sites close to the river or its tributaries but on high ground, the early inhabitants avoided the danger of floods. But they had to depend on plants capable of surviving with a minimum of rainfall. The principal crops of northern China in the Neolithic Age were several varieties of millet, hemp, and the mulberry (for raising silkworms). Rice, too was grown in the marsh areas of the northern plain, introduced from the Yangtze region to the south, where it was indigenous. In view of the wide extent of Neolithic communities in China, however, it is quite possible that an advance beyond this cultural level took place in more than one area. At any rate, contacts between regions were sufficient to promote the growth and spread of a homogeneous civilization.

Archeological finds in China have thrown light not only on preliterate epochs but on the early historical period as well. They have established that the Bronze Age—universally associated with the oldest civilizations—began in China somewhere around 2000 B.C. Excavations of Bronze Age remains in northern China supply concrete evidence concerning the Shang Dynasty, which according to tradition was the second of China's ruling houses (c. 1766–1123 B.C.). Long

The Bronze Age and the beginning of the Shang Dynasty

regarded by scholars as almost purely legendary, the Shang (or Yin) Dynasty has been verified and impressive examples of its workmanship recovered. Precise dates are not yet determined, but the civilization was flourishing by 1400 B.C. A study of objects that have been unearthed and especially the all-important deciphering of inscriptions make it possible to construct a fairly complete picture of this formative period of Chinese history.

Shang civilization

Shang culture was based upon that of the Neolithic farming communities. Presumably the dynasty was inaugurated by the conquest of a military chieftain, with no extensive displacement of population. Distinctive aspects of the civilization included the construction of fortified cities, the use of horse-drawn chariots in warfare, a highly developed bronze metallurgy, an elaborate system of writing, and a sharply stratified society composed of an aristocracy, craftsmen, and farmers. The last of these were obliged not only to labor but to render military service. The Shang kingdom evidently controlled only a small part of China—the plain surrounding the middle Yellow River valley—but its influence extended over a wide area. The Shang people carried on trade with other regions, including the Yangtze valley to the south, and they had to defend themselves against nomadic tribes from the north and west. The last capital of the dynasty was a city located at the northern tip of Honan Province, about 80 miles north of the Yellow River (the site of modern An yang).

The economy: agriculture

Though developing in close proximity to the wandering herdsmen of Mongolia, the Chinese were primarily a nation of farmers. Agriculture was the chief source of livelihood of the Shang people, although their tools for cultivating the soil were still quite primitive. Grains were the principal crop; wheat and barley were grown in addition to millet. Hunting and herding contributed to the food supply. Many animals had been domesticated, including not only the dog, pig, goat, sheep, ox, horse, and chicken, but also the water buffalo, monkey, and probably the elephant. Dog flesh as well as pork was a popular item of diet.

Shang housing

The houses the Shang people constructed show an intelligent adaptation to the environment. The Neolithic inhabitants of the region commonly lived in pits hollowed out of the loess. In Shang times rural villagers apparently also occupied pit dwellings, but the city residents built more comfortable houses above ground. For a foundation the firmly packed earth served admirably. Upon the rectangular foundation was erected a gabled-roof structure, with wooden poles holding up the central ridge of the roof and shorter posts supporting each of the two sides at the eaves. Thatching was used for the roof and packed earth for the outside walls of the house. This type of dwelling, which by coincidence is closer in design to the European style of home than to the tents of Mongolia or the mud-brick houses of Egypt and Mesopotamia, has been employed by the Chinese throughout their history.

The specimens of Shang craftsmanship that archeologists have recovered reveal a high degree of skill and versatility. In spite of familiarity with metal, Shang artisans still made many objects of stone—knives, axes, and even dishes—as well as of bone, shell, and horn. Bone implements inlaid with turquoise and exquisitely carved pieces of ivory were produced in abundance. Cowry shells were used for jewelry and probably also served as money. The bow and arrow was the most formidable weapon for the hunt or for combat. Bamboo arrows were feathered and tipped with bronze or bone points. The bow was of the composite or reflex type, formed of two separate arcs of wood held together with horn, and said to be almost twice as powerful as the famous English longbow. Two-horse chariots, of elaborate workmanship and with spoked wheels, were probably the exclusive property of the aristocracy. Armor was made of leather, sometimes reinforced with wooden slats. Evidently people of the royal court were fond of music. For musical instruments they employed drums, stone chimes, and a small pipe of hollow bone with five finger-holes.

The artistry of the Shang people is illustrated most strikingly by their sculpture and engraving. Shang metal work was truly remarkable, especially the superb bronze castings of intricate design. Bronze articles included weapons and chariot and harness fittings, but most impressive were the objects intended for religious and ceremonial functions—tripods, libation bowls, drinking cups, and grotesquely figured masks. The technique employed in their making was superlative. A leading American specialist in early Chinese culture asserts that it was more flawless than the technique employed for bronze sculpture at the height of the Italian Renaissance.

As has already been mentioned, this early civilization possessed a system of writing. The writing brush and an ink made of soot had been invented. Writing materials included silk cloth and wood, and it is quite possible that books were compiled from narrow strips of bamboo joined together by a thong. Fortunately, a great many specimens of writing have been preserved inscribed on pieces of animal bone, horn, and tortoise shells and pottery. These served in a process of divination by the king and priests; hence they are referred to as "oracle bones." After a question had been directed to the spirits, a flat piece of split cattle bone or a tortoise shell was heated until it cracked; then the shape of the crack was studied to ascertain the answer from the spirit world. The majority of the oracle bones contain no writing; but in about 10 percent of the cases the question was engraved upon the object after the divination rite had been performed. Although the inscriptions are brief, a careful study of them has thrown light upon many aspects of Shang society and activities.

While the Shang symbols are the earliest known examples of writing in the Far East, they were not primitive. They presuppose a long period of development, but the earlier stages have left no trace, except

Bronze Ritual Vessel. Shang Dynasty (1523–1027 B.C.). This piece shows the exaggerated use of decoration characteristic of the early Chou period.

Bronze Tripod Cup. Shang Dynasty. Used to heat wine at sacrificial ceremonies, the shape of the vessel is unique to the Shang period.

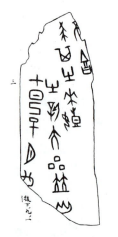

Oracle Bone. Dating from 1300 B.C., this artifact records the appearance of a new star. Note the pictographic characters.

Bronze Wine Vessel. Shang Dynasty. The human face trapped in the jaws of a devouring monster reflects the intimidating power of the social order. Human faces rarely appear on Shang dynasty bronzes but when they do they most likely represent the victim of human sacrifice.

perhaps for some enigmatic incisions on specimens of pottery. The Shang inscriptions embody practically all the principles employed by the fully developed Chinese literary language in character formation. The Shang characters—each of which represented an entire word as it does in classical and modern Chinese—were not only pictographs but sometimes ideographs, in which the meaning was conveyed by combining different symbols or concepts (the sun and moon joined together represent *bright* or *brightness;* the sun rising behind a tree stands for *east*). The phonetic principle was also applied. A character having one meaning might be used to indicate a word of different meaning but pronounced the same way. To avoid confusion, the phonetic symbol was combined with a conceptual symbol in the same character. Not surprisingly, fewer characters were employed in Shang times than later, although it is probable that the list compiled from the oracle bones is only partial. About 3,000 characters have been distinguished in the Shang records; the written language eventually came to include more than fifteen times that number.

Little definite information is available as to the political and social institutions of the Shang period. In addition to military activities, the king probably supervised public works and was important as the chief religious functionary. He was assisted by an educated class of priests, who served as astrologers, performed the divination rites, and supervised the calendar. Because the calendar was a lunar one, it frequently had to be adjusted to bring it into harmony with the solar year. There is some evidence from the oracle bones that the Shang priests had made considerable achievements in mathematics and astronomy. As early as the fourteenth century B.C. they recorded eclipses and perhaps had already conceived the decimal system.

Ample testimony exists for the religious practices of the Shang people. They worshiped many natural objects and forces—the earth, rivers, the winds, even the directions. To these gods they performed sacrifices in temples. Burnt offerings of animal flesh were common, and a kind of wine or beer made from millet was also considered acceptable. Although the Shang were in some ways highly civilized, there is gruesome evidence that, like several early Latin American societies, they practiced human sacrifice on a large scale. Apparently the victims were usually captives who had been taken in battle, and sometimes raiding expeditions were sent out for the express purpose of securing a batch of foreign tribesmen to be offered in sacrifice. The principal deity seems to have been a god concerned primarily with rainfall, the crops, and war. His name, Shang Ti, has persisted into later times. There is no evidence that Shang religion was essentially spiritual or ethical; it was directed toward the procuring of human prosperity, as among the Sumerians and Babylonians. The king was not a divinity like the Egyptian pharaoh, but he became an object of worship after his death, and sacrifices were performed to the departed spirits of both kings and queens. The royal tombs were sumptuous affairs. A large pit was excavated, provided with stairways, and a wooden tomb chamber was constructed at the bottom. The royal corpse was surrounded with magnificent furnishings, including figured bronzes and pottery, marble statuary, and richly adorned implements and jewels. After the funeral ceremonies the entire excavation was filled with firmly tamped earth.

It is noteworthy that the typical Chinese institution of ancestor worship was already in existence, at least in the circle of the court. Ancestral spirits were believed to possess the power of helping or hurting their descendants, and yet they depended upon their living representatives for nourishment in the form of food offerings. It was also customary, even among people of humble circumstance, to bury valuable objects with the deceased. Divination by means of the oracle bones—the practice which bequeathed so many valuable inscriptions—was a by-product of the cult of ancestor worship and the belief in the potency of departed spirits.

The Shang society represents the earliest genuine civilization of Eastern Asia for which historical records are available. In addition, it laid the foundation and provided materials for the distinctive Chinese culture pattern, as illustrated by methods of agriculture, handicrafts, artistic and architectural forms, emphasis upon the family as the basic social unit, religious concepts, and a system of writing. About 1027 B.C.[1] the city of Shang was captured and the dynasty overthrown, but the new rulers preserved basic institutions, encouraged cultural prog-

Bronze Ritual Vessel with Removable Top. Shang Dynasty. Vases cast in animal shapes (e.g., owl, rhinoceros, and tiger) were commonly used to hold sacrificial wine.

[1] The exact date is in dispute among scholars. Estimates range from 1122 to 1018 B.C.

Excavation of Royal Tombs of the Shang Dynasty. Charioteers have been found buried with their chariots and horses in the royal tombs at Anyang. Chariots were first introduced in China about 1300 B.C.

ress, and gave their name (Chou) to the longest dynasty in China's history.

2. THE CHOU DYNASTY, THE CLASSICAL AGE OF CHINA (c. 1100–256 B.C.)

Accession of the Chou Dynasty

While the civilization of the Vedic Age in India was still in its early stages, in the Yellow River valley of China the Shang Dynasty was succeeded by the Chou. However, the advent of a new ruling house brought no such profound change in the character of society as did the Indo-Aryan invasion of India. The Chou people, located west of the Shang frontier, were of the same basic ethnic stock and possessed a culture similar to that of the Shang, with whom they had had considerable contact. The demise of the Shang Dynasty was probably the result of an internal power struggle and bore little resemblance to a barbarian conquest.[2] Cultural developments continued uninterruptedly on foundations already laid and eventually completed the pattern of Chinese civilization for centuries to come.

Efforts of the Chou rulers to establish legitimacy

The new dynasty exerted zealous efforts to convince the people that it was a legitimate succession rather than a usurpation. Its spokesmen advanced the claim that the last Shang ruler had been incompetent and debauched, and that the divine powers had used the Chou as an instrument for his removal. The "Mandate of Heaven," they alleged, had been transferred from the Shang house to the Chou. There is no evidence that the Shang king was guilty of the faults ascribed to him, but the charge, even if a fabrication, shows the desire of the conquerors to fit their authority into accepted conventions rather than to break with the past. And the concept of governmental power as a commission from Heaven rather than an absolute and inalienable right—although possibly invented by the Chou for propaganda purposes—was to become a persistent element in Chinese political history.

The Chou government

The early Chou rulers maintained their capital near modern Sian (Shensi Province) in the Wei valley, where their power had already been established. The kings maintained large standing armies, which were used to suppress rebellions (including one by the deposed Shang) and to expand their authority, notably southward in the middle Yangtze valley. The king exercised direct rule over the region surrounding his capital but administered the outlying areas indirectly, through appointed officials, who were given almost complete jurisdiction within their own districts. The Chou administrative system was roughly similar to that which developed in Europe in the age of feudalism some 2,000 years later. The district governors, originally members of the royal

[2] K. C. Chang, *The Archaeology of Ancient China*, 3d ed., p. 383. Chang suggests that the traditional Three Dynasties—Hsia, Shang, and Chou—were actually contemporary and interrelated states, with political ascendancy passing from one to another during the second millennium B.C. Chang, *Shang Civilization*, pp. 347–48.

(MANCHURIA)

(MONGOLIA)

SEA OF
JAPAN

(JAPAN)

(Peking)

KOREAN
PENINSULA

YELLOW
SEA

(Anyang) ★
Yellow (Hwang) R.
SHANTUNG PENIN.

Wei R.
★ (Sian)   ★ (Loyang)
            (HONAN
            PROVINCE)

Huai River

Han R.

C H I N A

(SZECHWAN
PROVINCE)

(Shanghai)
Hangchow

Yangtze R.

EAST CHINA
SEA

Yangtze R.

(TAIWAN)

Hsi R.

SOUTH CHINA
SEA

0   500 miles

INDOCHINA

ANCIENT CHINA DURING THE CHOU DYNASTY · 1100-256 B.C.

family or generals of proved competence, were the king's vassals, but they were also great territorial lords, exercising wide military and judicial powers, and they gradually transformed their position from that of appointive official to hereditary ruler. Chou feudalism—like the later European variety—contained elements of danger for the central government, although for two or three centuries the Chou court was strong enough to remove overly ambitious officials and keep its own authority paramount.

By the eighth century B.C. the vigor of the ruling house had declined to the point where it was no longer able to protect the western frontier effectively against the attacks of barbarians. The fortunes of the dynasty seemed to reach their lowest point in 771 B.C., when a

*The end of the Western
Chou Period*

worthless king almost duplicated the villainies that had been unjustifiably attributed to the last of the Shang rulers. King Yu, particularly through his extravagant efforts to amuse his favorite concubine, angered the nobles beyond endurance. When he lit the beacon fires to summon aid in the face of a combined attack by barbarian tribes and one of the outraged nobles, his men refused to answer the summons. King Yu was killed and his palace looted. The dynasty might have been ended then and there, but the nobles of the realm found it expedient to install the king's son as nominal head, keeping in their own hands the actual authority over their respective dominions. This event marks the close of the "Western Chou" period. The royal seat of government was now moved about 100 miles east into safer territory (near the modern city of Loyang), and the ensuing period (771–c. 250 B.C.) is known accordingly as the "Eastern Chou."

Conditions under the Eastern Chou Dynasty

During the 500 years of the Eastern Chou Dynasty, China suffered from political disunity and internal strife. The king actually ruled over a domain much smaller than that of some of the great hereditary princes. For the kingdom as a whole his powers, while theoretically supreme (he was officially styled "Son of Heaven"), were limited to religious and ceremonial functions and to adjudicating disputes concerning precedence and the rights of succession in the various states. In spite of these conditions, however, it is not quite accurate to describe the Eastern Chou era as an age of feudalism. It is true that hereditary nobles enjoyed social prominence, wealth, and power, and acquired different degrees of rank, roughly equivalent to the European titles of duke, marquis, count, viscount, and baron. They became lords and vassals, held fiefs for which they owed military service, and were supported by the labor of the peasants on their lands. These warrior aristocrats not only raised armies and collected revenues from their dominions but also administered justice. Custom supplied the greater part of law, but severe penalties, including fines, mutilation, and death, were inflicted upon offenders. Nevertheless, a number of

Ceremonial Bronze Basin. Chou Dynasty (1100–256 B.C.). The inscription on this bronze piece, known as the *San P'an,* records the settlement of a territorial dispute between the feudal states of San and Nieh in Western Shensi Province.

factors prevented the complete ascendancy of a feudal regime. In the first place, a large proportion of the nobility failed to acquire estates of their own and remained jealous of the great territorial lords. The lesser aristocracy, generally well educated and frequently unemployed, constituted a sort of middle class that could not fit comfortably into a feudalized society. More important still, by the eighth century B.C., towns were growing and trade increasing throughout the Chou period, and the merchants (including part of the aristocracy) attained economic importance. Moreover, rulers of the larger states successfully pushed forward a program of centralization within their own dominions. They introduced regular systems of taxation based upon agriculture. To offset the entrenched position of the nobles they developed their own administrative bureaucracies and staffed them with trained officials, recruited largely from the ranks of the lesser aristocracy. In spite of the disorganized condition of China as a whole, the period provided valuable experience in the art of government which could eventually be drawn upon in the task of reuniting the country.

Although China was divided during the Eastern Chou period into many principalities with shifting boundaries and frequent wars, a few of the larger states held the balance of power, especially four which were located on the outer frontiers to the north, west, and south. Usually one state at a time was recognized as paramount and its ruler, designated as overlord or hegemon, took the lead in organizing the defense of the kingdom as a whole and even in collecting the revenues. The boundaries of Chinese civilization were extended by the aggressive initiative of the rulers of the frontier states. The Shantung peninsula, the seacoast as far south as modern Shanghai and Hangchow, and the rich Yangtze valley were all brought under Chinese jurisdiction. Thus the total area was much larger than the old Shang kingdom and included more than half of the eighteen provinces which have constituted the state of China during the greater portion of its history. The southern part of Manchuria was also occupied, and walls of earth—the first stages of the famous Great Wall of China—were constructed both south and north of the Yellow River for protection against the nomads of Mongolia.

During the 800 or 900 years of the Chou Dynasty, in spite of internal conflicts, cultural progress was almost continuous. The period is regarded as the classical age of Chinese civilization, and its contributions were fundamental to the whole subsequent history of the Far East. As has already been indicated, the culture of the Chou was based upon foundations that had been laid by their predecessors. Handicraft techniques improved under the Chou and the smelting of iron was introduced, although iron did not entirely displace bronze. While the great majority of the population lived in rural villages, there were some large towns and the merchant class assumed importance. Trade was by no means exclusively local. With the introduction of the donkey, and especially the camel (probably not before the third century

Expansion of the frontiers

Bronze Ceremonial Vessel. Chou Dynasty.

Cultural progress under the Chou

B.C.), it became possible to develop caravan trade routes across Central Asia for the transportation of grain, salt, silk, and other commodities. Coined copper money came into use before the close of the fifth century B.C. The manufacture of silk, already an old industry, was increased, and the fibers of several domestic plants were also employed in making textiles.

Class divisions of an aristocratic society

Society during the Chou period had a decidedly aristocratic character. By tradition society was believed to comprise five classes ranked in the order of their value to the commonwealth. These were, first, scholars; second, farmers; third, artisans; fourth, merchants; and last, soldiers, lumped together with beggars, thieves, and bandits.[3] The notable aspects of this classification are the high recognition granted to intellectual ability, the deprecation of violence and of nonproductive occupations, and the fact that the categories are based upon individual talents and capacities rather than upon birth. The five-class system was never fully realized or perfectly respected, but it was an ideal that tended to lessen the rigidity of Chinese institutions. Although there was a tremendous gulf between the great landowners and the peasants who comprised the vast majority of the people, Chinese society was never stratified by a caste system like that of India; and as civilization became more complex the nobility included contrasting interests and conditions rather than remaining a solidly united order. Because the numbers of the aristocracy tended to increase, many of them consequently possessed little or no landed property. They were forced to seek administrative employment with a powerful noble, to engage in trade, or even to undertake menial occupations, thereby undermining the fiction of the inherent superiority of the hereditary aristocracy. Unfortunately, very little is known about the condition of the lower classes. Evidently before the close of the Chou period a considerable number of peasants had become landowners. Others, however, were actually slaves, and most of the commoners were serfs, attached to the soil without having legal title to it and compelled to give the lord a large share of the produce.

Religious practice and the Shang past

Religion was fundamentally the same as it had been in Shang times. Many deities were worshiped, ranging from local spirits and nature gods with limited powers to such majestic divinities as Earth and Heaven. The practice of human sacrifice gradually disappeared, although there are records of the ears or heads of decapitated victims being sacrificed. Animals, agricultural produce, and liquor were offered upon the altars. Evidence of a "chariot sacrifice" was uncovered by archeologists north of the Yellow River when they excavated a deep pit about 30 feet square. In this instance seventy-two horses harnessed to twelve chariots, and eight dogs with bells fastened to their necks, had apparently been placed in the pit and buried alive. While worship did

[3] A famous ancient Chinese proverb is "Good iron is not used to make a nail; a good man is not used to make a soldier."

not necessarily include prayer, prayers were sometimes written out and burned with the sacrificial offering. A prominent deity from Chou times on was the one called T'ien, translated as "Heaven." Although of separate origin, this divinity was similar to and became practically identical with the earlier Shang Ti. T'ien was not conceived of primarily as a personal god but as representing the supreme spiritual powers collectively, the universal moral law, or an underlying impersonal cosmic force. It was by the "Mandate of Heaven" *(T'ien-ming)* that the king was supposed to rule, and he was referred to as "Son of Heaven," without, however, implying that he was divine. The worship of the earth as an agricultural deity came to be supplemented by the veneration of a specific locality with which the fortunes of the worshipers were associated. Every village had its sacred mound of earth; the lord of large territories had a mound to represent his domain; and the mound of the king was believed to have significance for the whole land of China. The most important rituals took place either at these mounds or in ancestral temples.

Among the Chinese at this time, as among the Hindus, there was no clear-cut religious system, no fixed creed, and no church. In contrast to Hindu society, however, the Chinese priests did not become a sacrosanct class in a position to dominate other groups. The priests, like those of the ancient Greeks, were merely assistants in the ritual. The indispensable religious functionaries were the heads of families, including, of course, the king, whose ancestral spirits were particularly formidable, and who propitiated the great deities of the rivers, earth, and sky. For most of the people religion was either a family affair, consisting of social functions invested with sentiment and emphasizing filial piety, or a matter of state, maintained by the proper authorities to ensure the general welfare. Sacrifices to the greatest gods were ordinarily performed only by the highest officials, to lesser deities by lower officials, and so on down to the ordinary folk who sacrificed to their own ancestors in the form of wooden tablets. They believed that the spirits of these ancestors could bring prosperity to the family and that dire consequences would follow any neglect of the rites. Aside from traditional ceremonies, everyday life was complicated by a medley of folklore and superstition hardly classifiable as religion but exerting a potent influence. This included the belief in witchcraft, in good and evil omens, in divination and spirit messages conveyed through mediums, and in the necessity of avoiding offense to numerous malignant beings. "Hungry ghosts," whose sacrifices had been neglected or cut off through the extinction of a family, were considered especially dangerous. In spite of the strong faith that the soul outlived the body, the notion of rewards and punishments in an afterlife was almost entirely lacking. The worst fate that could happen to a disembodied spirit, it was thought, was for it to be deprived of the nourishment supplied by sacrificial offerings.

By far the most significant contributions of the Chou period were

Large Bronze Bell. This bell, with bosses or nipples, decorative panels, and inscriptions, is typical of the Middle Chou style (ninth century B.C.). It was hung from the ring at the base of the shaft and was sounded by striking with a wooden mallet. The bell has a scooped mouth instead of being even at the bottom. (In the picture it is resting on a cushion.)

Extraordinary characteristics of Chinese religion

in the fields of literature and philosophy. The Shang system of writing, already highly advanced, was continued with slight modifications. Evidently the Chinese now considered written records as indispensable to the conduct of both public and private affairs. They sometimes recorded important transactions in lengthy inscriptions on bronze vessels, but they more frequently wrote with the brush upon wood or cloth of silk. Books composed of thin strips of bamboo were produced in abundance. Although only a minority of the population was literate, it must have been a large minority and included the feudal nobility as well as the merchants. In contrast to the feudal age of western Europe when writing was confined almost entirely to the clergy, the Chou aristocrats were versed in literature and kept full records of their properties, their dependents, and sometimes of their personal activities. Not only the king but the head of every feudal state maintained archives to preserve the luster of family traditions and to aid in settling disputes with rival princes. The Chinese, even in ancient times, were at the opposite pole from the Hindus in their attitude toward the importance of chronology and the recording of factual events (although this does not mean that Chinese documents were entirely accurate or free from fanciful elements). A young nobleman or prince, in the process of his education, was reminded by his tutors that later generations would study the annals of his administration and that he should, accordingly, choose his actions with care. Princes were regularly given instruction in history "to stimulate them to good conduct and warn them against evil"—apparently with no better results than have attended most modern efforts in this direction.

Of the tremendous output of Chou literature, only a few authentic portions have survived (aside from the imperishable bronze inscriptions). Some of them, however, are from a date earlier than 600 B.C. Probably the most ancient work is the *Book of Changes*. It contains a collection of hexagrams formed of straight and broken lines arranged in different combinations, with accompanying text. The figures, like the earlier Shang oracle bones, were used for divination. Thus the book was originally hardly more than a sorcerer's manual, but it came to be venerated as a work of mystic and occult wisdom.[4] Very different is the *Document Classic* (less accurately called *Book of History*), which is a collection of official documents, proclamations, and speeches purporting to be from the early Chou period. The *Book of Etiquette,* dealing with ceremonial behavior, formal occasions, and preparation for adult responsibilities, was intended to assist in the education of the lesser aristocracy. Most interesting of all is the *Book of Poetry,* an anthology of about 300 poems covering a wide range of subjects and moods. Some of the poems are religious, in the nature of

[4]For a contrary view see H. Wilhelm, *Change: Eight Lectures on the I Ching,* 1960. Wilhelm interprets the classic as an affirmation of man's ability to control his own destiny.

prayers or hymns to accompany the rites of sacrifice; others celebrate the exploits of heroes; still others are lyrical in quality, voicing the laments of a discharged official, a soldier's homesickness, delight in the beauties of nature, and the frustration or rapture of young lovers. Neither in quantity nor in profundity do these odes approach the *Vedas* of India, but they are graceful in expression and show vividly the practical down-to-earth temperament of the Chinese and their lively interest in and optimistic attitude toward the business of living—at least among the aristocracy. While the poems on the whole are neither philosophical nor spiritual, a few suggest the reforming fervor of the Hebrew prophets.

In view of the extent and the variety of writing during the Chou period, the literary collections which have survived are rather disappointing. But this deficiency is amply compensated for by achievements in the realm of philosophy, which reached a brilliant climax between the sixth and third centuries B.C. For some unexplained reason—perhaps by mere coincidence—philosophical activity of a high order was carried on at about the same time in three widely separated regions of the ancient world. While the Greeks were inquiring into the nature of the physical universe, and Indian thinkers were pondering the relationship of the soul to Absolute Being, Chinese sages were attempting to discover the basis of human society and the underlying principles of good government. The Chinese thinkers were not much interested in either physical science or metaphysics. They sought to define the principles underlying the natural material universe, not for the sake of abstract truth but to illuminate the problems of human existence. They attempted to prescribe rules for the stabilizing of society and the betterment of the individual. The leaders in this intellectual activity were largely from the lesser aristocracy, a scholarly group, fond of disputation, but also maintaining an interest in the practice of government and sometimes holding administrative posts or coaching pupils who aspired to such posts. It was a time of lively interchange of ideas, and a great variety of opinions was put forward. Out of this intellectual ferment and debate—one of the most productive in the annals of human thought—four main philosophic schools emerged, the most important being the Confucianist and the Taoist.

Confucius (c. 551–479 B.C.), who has proved to be one of the most influential men in all history, was largely a failure from the standpoint of what he hoped to accomplish. He spent his life advocating reforms that were not adopted; yet he left an indelible stamp upon the thought and political institutions of China and other lands that came under Chinese influence. He was a native of the state of Lu (in modern Shantung province) and was reputed to have been the child of an aged father, a gentleman soldier named K'ung (Confucius is the Latinized form of the name K'ung Fu-tzu, or "Master K'ung"). Probably his family was of the lesser aristocracy, respectable but poor. When he

Philosophy

Confucius in Royal Dress. A traditional representation in bronze.

was only about twenty-one he began to teach informally a group of young friends who were attracted by his alert mind and by his precocious knowledge of traditional forms and usages. Although his reputation spread rapidly, little is known concerning the incidents of his career. Possibly as a mature man he held office for a short time under the Duke of Lu. For more than ten years, until old age overtook him, he wandered from state to state, refusing to be employed as a time-serving flatterer but continually hoping that some ruler would give him a chance to apply his ideals and thus set in motion a tide of reform that might sweep the entire country. Although revered by his small band of disciples, some of whom became officeholders, Confucius received no offer of appointment that he could accept in good conscience. Finally he returned to his native country where he died, discouraged, at the age of seventy-two.

Frustrated as a statesman, Confucius made his real contribution as a teacher. The memoranda of his conversations with his disciples (the *Analects*)—which are considered on the whole authentic, even though not written down in the master's lifetime—convey the impression of a lively and untrammeled mind which challenged those with whom it came in contact. Like his contemporary Gautama Buddha, and like his near-contemporary Socrates, Confucius earnestly believed that knowledge was the key to happiness and successful conduct. He also believed that almost anyone was capable of acquiring knowledge, but only through unrelenting effort. He insisted that his student-disciples should think for themselves, saying that if he had demonstrated one corner of a subject it was up to them to work out the other three corners, and constantly pricking their complacency. While no ascetic, he frowned on indulgence and urged his associates to strive continually for improvement. Though he had moments of petulance and harshness, the nobility of his character is unmistakable, and he refused to let his disappointments make him cynical. His regret, he said, was not that he was misunderstood but that he did not understand others sufficiently.

The doctrines of Confucius centered upon the good life and the good community. He respected religious ceremonies as part of established custom, but he refused to speculate on religious or supernatural questions, saying, in substance: "We do not know life; how can we understand death? We do not fully understand our obligations to the living; what can we know of our obligations to the dead?" He was optimistic regarding the material world and regarding human nature, which he thought was essentially good; but he believed that the individual's worth would not be realized unless he was properly guided in the development of his faculties. For this reason he stressed propriety and the observance of ceremonial forms—which he thought were helpful in the acquisition of self-discipline—although he was really more concerned with sincerity and intelligence than with appearances. Impressed as he was by the evils of feudal contention, Confucius advocated the restoration of central authority in the kingdom, combined however, with a logical distribution of power. He visualized the ideal state as a benevolent paternalism, with the ruler not only commanding but also setting an example of conduct for the people to follow. He did not believe in equality and, rather than democracy, advocated an aristocracy of talent and high principles from whom officials would be selected to guide the ruler in his administration. The health of the entire state would depend upon the welfare of each village, and harmony would be achieved by the combined efforts of the common people from below and of the scholar-officials from above.

Confucius' teachings therefore embodied a political philosophy, which regarded the state as a natural institution but modifiable by man, and devoted to promoting the general well-being and the fullest growth of individual personalities. The state existed for man, not man for the state. On the ethical side he emphasized fellow feeling or reciprocity, the cultivation of sympathy and cooperation, which must begin in the family and then extend by degrees into the larger areas of association. He stressed the importance of the five cardinal human relationships which were already traditional among the Chinese: (1) ruler and subject, (2) father and son, (3) elder brother and younger brother, (4) husband and wife, and (5) friend and friend. These could be expanded indefinitely and were not bounded even by Chinese lines. The logic of this train of thought was summarized in the famous saying, "All men are brothers." But Confucius argued that a person must be a worthy member of his own community before he could think in terms of world citizenship. Laying no claim to originality, Confucius urged a return to an ideal order which he attributed to the ancients but which actually had never existed. Unknowingly, he was supplying guiding principles which could be utilized in the future.

The political and ethical philosophy of Confucius

Aside from its founder, the ablest exponent of the Confucianist school was Mencius (Meng-tzu), who lived about a century later (c. 373–288 B.C.). Like his master, Mencius affirmed the inherent goodness of human nature and the necessity of exemplary leadership to develop it. He looked upon government primarily as a moral enterprise, and he was more emphatic than Confucius in insisting that the material condition of the people should be improved. He wanted the government to take the initiative in lessening inequalities and in raising the living standards of the common folk. Perhaps because political confusion had increased since Confucius' day, he was outspoken in criticizing contemporary rulers. He taught that only a benevolent government, resting upon the tacit consent of the people, can possess the "Mandate of Heaven," and he defended the people's right to depose a corrupt or despotic sovereign. Hsün-tzu (c. 300–237 B.C.) is usually classified as a Confucianist, although his precepts diverged radically from those of Mencius. While both Confucius and Mencius had started with the assumption that man has a natural propensity for

Mencius and Hsün-tzu

Lao-tzu Atop a Water Buffalo.
Chou Dynasty.

good, Hsün-tzu regarded human nature as basically evil. However, like the earlier Confucianists he believed that man can be improved by proper education and rigorous discipline. He laid great stress upon observance of ritual, formal training in the classics and a strictly hierarchical ordering of society. In spite of his gloomy view of the natural man, he was far from a complete pessimist. He recommended vigorous action by the state to institute reforms and, like Mencius, favored the regulation of economic activities.

Lao-tzu and Taoism

The Taoist philosophical school was in many ways the opposite of the Confucianist. Its traditional founder was Lao-tzu ("Old Sage"), a shadowy figure of the sixth century B.C. Little is known about the facts of his life, and some scholars doubt that he was an actual historical person. According to tradition he served as an official at the Chou capital in charge of the archives until, becoming weary of the world, he set out for the western mountains in quest of peace and, at the request of a guard at the mountain pass, set down his words of wisdom in a little book before he disappeared. But the real authorship of the *Tao Teh Ching* (Classic of Nature and Virtue), from which the principles of Taoism are derived, is undetermined, and it may not have been written earlier than the third century B.C. The book is not only brief but enigmatical, paradoxical, and perhaps ironical. With its terse and cryptic style it seems almost like an intentional antidote to the Confucian glorification of scholarship, exhortation, and patient explanation. On the whole the Taoist book exalts nature (sometimes in the sense of impersonal cosmic force, "the Boundless" or Absolute) and deprecates human efforts. Its spirit is romantic, mystical, anti-intellectual. It not only lauds the perfection of nature but idealizes the primitive, suggesting that people would be better off without the arts of civilization, living in blissful ignorance and keeping records by means of knotted cords rather than writing. Wealth creates avarice and laws produce criminals, it asserts. It is useless to try to improve society by preachment, ritual, or elaborate regulations; the more virtue is talked about the less it is practiced. "Those who teach don't know anything; those who know don't teach." A person learns more by staying home than by traveling; the wise man sits and meditates instead of bustling about trying to reform the world.

As a political philosophy, Taoism advocates laissez faire. Unlike Confucius, Lao-tzu believed that governmental interference was the source of iniquity and that, if people were left to follow their intuition, they would live in harmony with nature and with one another. Nevertheless, Lao-tzu's ideal was not pure anarchism. Like Confucius he assumed the necessity of a wise and benevolent (although largely passive) ruler, and agreed that the only legitimate purpose of government was to promote human happiness. Perhaps his thought also reflects a rural protest against both the self-important aristocracy and the artificial society of the rapidly growing towns. In Lao-tzu's teachings there are strains of pacifism and the doctrine of nonretaliation for injury ("The virtuous man is for patching up; the vicious man is for fixing guilt"); of the efficacy of love in human relations ("Heaven arms with love those it would not see destroyed"); and of equalitarianism ("It is the way of Heaven to take away from those that have too much and give to those that have not enough"). The Taoist school produced several able thinkers in late Chou times and played a part in the shaping of Chinese philosophical traditions. However, in contrast to Confucianism, the Taoist doctrines were eventually transformed into a religious system, with a priesthood, temples, ritual, and emotional elements. But the Taoism that became one of the prominent religions of China had little connection with the principles expounded in the *Tao Teh Ching*.

A third school of political and ethical philosophy was associated with Mo Ti (or Mo-tzu), whose career is placed in the middle of the fifth century B.C. A man of decided originality, Mo Ti may have been of peasant stock; his sympathies lay with the downtrodden, and he regarded luxury and extravagance with aversion. The distinguishing feature of his thought is that he combined the doctrine of utilitarianism—insisting that everything should be judged by its usefulness—with a sweeping idealism that drew inspiration from religious faith. He condemned elaborate ceremonies dear to Confucianists, including the traditional three-year period of mourning, on the ground that they entailed needless expense. Sports, amusements, and even music met his disapproval because they were unproductive, absorbing energies which might be employed in useful labor. The pressing need, as he saw it, was to increase the supply of food and basic commodities to improve the health, longevity, and numbers of the population; and such a program called for hard work on the part of both common

Taoist political and ethical philosophy

Mo Ti

people and officials. His strong denunciation of offensive warfare was also rooted in utilitarianism.

Mo Ti's ethics were by far the boldest of any of the Chinese philosophers. In place of the Confucian system of an expanding series of loyalties beginning with the family and radiating outward, he proclaimed the universal and impartial love of all mankind and declared that there can be no satisfactory community until the distinction between "self" and "other" is completely transcended. Applying his utilitarian yardstick, he reasoned that, by cultivating sympathy and mutual helpfulness with everyone, the individual was ensuring his own welfare as well as contributing to the security of others. But while his doctrine of universal and impartial affection linked altruism to self-interest, it called for a rare degree of discipline and high-mindedness, and its similarity to the ethics of Christianity has often been remarked. Mo Ti believed that the state, like other human institutions, was created by divine ordinance and that it was the duty of the ruler to carry out the will of Heaven, which he interpreted to mean promoting the common welfare. Although the Mohist school, as it is called, was prominent for a while and attracted many adherents, it practically disappeared after the downfall of the Chou Dynasty—partly because of the enmity of the Confucianists—and the teachings of the utilitarian philosopher were almost entirely forgotten until modern times.

A fourth philosophical school, known as the "Legalist," stood far removed both from the bold idealism of Mo Ti and the optimistic humanism of Confucius. Formulated during the hectic period which witnessed the final collapse of the Chou Dynasty and the triumph of the Ch'in, it reflects Hsün-tzu's harsh view of human nature and his emphasis upon coercive discipline. At the same time the Legalists were indebted to Taoism in their contempt for scholarship, the intelligentsia, and conventional ethics; and in their preference for a simple agrarian society over a mobile, sophisticated, and economically diversified one. But, unlike the Taoists, they did not exalt nature or any supernatural agency, and they completely rejected laissez faire. Rather than mystics they were hardheaded realists, or even cynics. Asserting that man is by nature hopelessly selfish and incorrigible, they prescribed complete and unquestioning submission to the ruler. People's behavior, they argued, could be controlled only by carefully defined rewards and punishments, by a code of laws which was fundamentally punitive and which derived not from custom or natural instinct but from the will of the sovereign. Of all the schools of Chinese political thought, the Legalist was the most uncompromisingly authoritarian. Although its principles were systematically applied only during the short-lived Ch'in Dynasty, they exerted a continuing influence upon later dynasties also—tempered somewhat by the opposing Confucian tradition—and they find perhaps more than an echo in the present Chinese totalitarian regime.

Beginning about the middle of the fifth century B.C., internal conditions became extremely chaotic, inaugurating a bloody period known as that of "the Warring States." The relatively restrained competition which the feudal principalities had carried on with one another gave way to a struggle for supremacy in which proprieties and recognized codes were disregarded. The rulers of several of the states even assumed the title of "king" (*wang*), previously reserved for the prince of Chou. In the fourth and third centuries B.C. the state of Ch'in, seated in the Wei valley on the western frontier, gained ascendancy over the others. Not only were the Ch'in rulers aggressive, but within their own dominions they had developed the most effectively centralized government in China. After annexing the fertile plain lying south of the Wei valley (in modern Szechwan province), they constructed a splendid irrigation system which has lasted until the present day. Probably the Ch'in people had also mingled with and absorbed some of the barbarian tribesmen, but they were no less Chinese in culture than their rivals. In spite of alliances formed against them by other feudal princes, the Ch'in forces, employing ruthlessness, massacre, and treachery, annexed one region after another. Finally, in 256 B.C., they seized the tiny remaining portion of the royal domain and ended the Chou Dynasty. Within thirty-five years the Ch'in prince had brought all the Chinese territories under his control and, to indicate the extent of his triumph, assumed the title of Emperor. Although the Ch'in Dynasty hardly outlasted its founder, it did China the valuable service of abolishing the remnants of feudalism. The highly centralized government which the Ch'in emperor established did not prove to be permanent, but the feudal system never reappeared.

Although the later centuries of the Chou Dynasty were marked by strife and unrest and encumbered by the remnants of decaying feudal institutions, the material basis for a productive society had been laid and intellectual progress had reached a high point. An abundant and many-sided literature was in existence. Philosophers had come to grips in mature fashion with fundamental problems of individual and group behavior. Scholarship was an honorable profession, and scholars were considered indispensable to the business of government. There was a growing tradition—not yet very effective—that government entailed moral responsibilities as well as privileges, that those who exercised authority did so on sufferance and only so long as they conformed to the "Mandate of Heaven." Moreover, the Chinese had come to think of themselves as composing a unique society, not merely a political affiliation but the "Middle Kingdom"—the heart of civilization as contrasted with outlying "barbarian" areas. They had already mingled with and partially absorbed many non-Chinese tribes, and it is significant that the distinction between their civilization and the "barbarian" regions was not based upon race or nationality. The attitude of superiority which they adopted sometimes made them arrogant, but it gave them a toughness in resisting the shock of invasion and other adversities.

SELECTED READINGS

• *Items so designated are available in paperback editions.*

Blunden, C., and M. Elvin, *Cultural Atlas of China,* New York, 1983. One of the most valuable works on China available.

Chang Kwang-chih, *Early Chinese Civilization: Anthropological Perspectives,* Cambridge, Mass., 1972. Provocative essays on Shang and Chou civilizations.

• ———, *Shang Civilization,* New Haven, 1980.

• ———, *The Archaeology of Ancient China,* 3d ed., New Haven, 1977. The best account to date.

• Creel, H. G., *The Birth of China,* New York, 1937. A fascinating account of archeological exploration of Shang civilization, and an excellent introduction to the basic culture pattern of ancient China.

• ———, *Chinese Thought from Confucius to Mao Tse-tung,* Chicago, 1953.

• ———, *Confucius and the Chinese Way,* New York, 1960.

———, *The Origins of Statecraft in China,* Vol. I: *The Western Chou Empire,* Chicago, 1970. A valuable contribution.

• Eberhard, Wolfram, *A History of China,* 4th ed., Berkeley, 1977.

• Elvin, Mark, *The Pattern of the Chinese Past,* Stanford, 1975.

Fairbank, J. K., E. O. Reischauer, and A. M. Craig, *East Asia: Tradition and Transformation,* rev. ed., Boston, 1978. A shortened edition of a major text.

• Fitzgerald, C. P., *China, a Short Cultural History,* 3d ed., New York, 1961. Frequently unconventional in viewpoint.

• Fung Yu-lan, *A History of Chinese Philosophy,* I: *The Period of the Philosophers* [to about 100 B.C.]; II: *The Period of Classical Learning* [to 20th century], tr. Derk Bodde, Princeton, 1983.

Girardot, N. J., *Myth and Meaning in Early Taoism: The Theme of Chaos* (hun-tun), Berkeley, 1983.

Ho Ping-ti, *The Cradle of the East: An Enquiry into the Indigenous Origins of Techniques and Ideas of Neolithic and Early Historic China, 5000–1000 B.C.,* Chicago, 1976.

Hucker, C. O., *China's Imperial Past: An Introduction to Chinese History and Culture,* Stanford, 1975. Remarkably clear, comprehensive, and readable.

• ———, *China to 1850: A Short History,* Stanford, 1978.

Keightley, D. N., *Sources of Shang History: The Oracle Bone Inscriptions of Bronze Age China,* Berkeley, 1978. Synthesizes the research of earlier scholars.

• ———, ed., *The Origins of Chinese Civilization,* Berkeley, 1983. Essays by seventeen contributors.

• Goodrich, L. C., *Short History of the Chinese People,* 3d ed., New York, 1959. Brief but informative; fulfills the promise of its title.

Harrison, J. A., *The Chinese Empire: A Short History of China from Neolithic Times to the End of the Eighteenth Century,* New York, 1972. A good synthesis.

• Hsu, Cho-Yun, *Ancient China in Transition: An Analysis of Social Mobility, 722–222 B.C.,* Stanford, 1965.

King, F. H., *Farmers of Forty Centuries, or Permanent Agriculture in China, Korea and Japan,* Emmaus, Pa., 1948. A classic description.

• Moore, C. A., ed., *The Chinese Mind: Essentials of Chinese Philosophy and Culture,* Honolulu, 1967.

• Munro, D. J., *The Concept of Man in Early China,* Stanford, 1975.

Ronan, C. A., ed., *The Shorter Science and Civilization in China,* I, New York, 1978; II, 1981. Abridgement of the first four volumes of a monumental study by Joseph Needham.

Schwartz, Benjamin, *The World of Thought in Ancient China,* Cambridge, Mass., 1985.

Treistman, Judith, *The Prehistory of China: An Archaeological Exploration,* Garden City, N.Y., 1972.

• Watson, Burton, *Early Chinese Literature,* New York, 1962.

Wheatley, Paul, *The Pivot of the Four Quarters: A Preliminary Enquiry into the Origins of the Character of the Ancient Chinese City,* Chicago, 1971.

• Wilhelm, Hellmut, *Change: Eight Lectures on the I Ching,* tr. C. F. Baynes, New York, 1960 (Princeton, 1973).

SOURCE MATERIALS

• de Bary, W. T., ed., *Sources of Chinese Tradition,* "The Classical Period," New York, 1960.

Chai Ch'u, and Winberg Chai, *A Treasury of Chinese Literature,* New York, 1961.

Chan Wing-tsit, ed. and tr., *A Source Book in Chinese Philosophy,* Princeton, 1963. Traces the history of Chinese philosophy from Confucianism to Communism.

Soothill, W. E., tr., *The Analects of Confucius,* Yokohama, 1910.

Waley, Arthur, ed. and tr., *The Book of Songs,* London, 1937.

———, *The Way and Its Power,* London, 1934.

———, *Three Ways of Thought in Ancient China,* London, 1939.

• Watson, Burton, tr., *Mo Tzu: Basic Writings,* New York, 1967.

Wilhelm, Richard, and C. F. Baynes, trs., *The I Ching, or Book of Changes.* Princeton, 1967.

Part Two

THE WORLD IN THE
CLASSICAL ERA

*After about 600 B.C. the once mighty civilizations of Mesopotamia and
Egypt became overshadowed and then dominated by the classical civilizations
of Greece and Rome. The word* classical *comes from the Latin* classicus,
*meaning "of the first class," and is customarily used to denote the civilization
that flourished in Greece between about 600 B.C. and 300 B.C. and the
one centered in Rome between about 300 B.C. and 300 A.D. (There were
other civilizations located in Greece and Italy before and after the "classical"
ones, but they were not regarded by posterity as being "of the first class.")
Although the classical Roman civilization gradually began to take shape
around the time when the classical Greek civilization was losing its independent
identity, "Rome" did not directly supplant "Greece." Rather, transpiring
chronologically between the heyday of the Greek and Roman civilizations
was the time of the Hellenistic civilization, a hybrid composed of elements
derived from Greece and western Asia. Based territorially on conquests of
Alexander the Great completed in 323 B.C., the Hellenistic civilization
extended over all of Greece, all of Egypt, and most of Asia up to the
borders of India, and it maintained its separate identity from 323 B.C. until
shortly before the birth of Christ. The outstanding characteristic that
distinguishes the three civilizations in question from those that had gone
before was their secularism. No longer did religion absorb the interests and
expend the wealth of humans to the extent that it did in ancient Mesopotamia
and Egypt. The state now became much more independent of the priesthood,*

and intellectual endeavors became largely divorced from the dictates of organized belief-systems. In addition, ideals of human freedom and an emphasis on the welfare of the individual superseded the despotism and collectivism of the Tigris, Euphrates, and Nile. Only late in the development of Roman civilization did despotism begin to reassert itself. Around that time too, a new religion, Christianity, began to reshape the life of those who lived in the Roman world.

Developments in the Far East offer both parallels and contrasts to those of western Europe. Hindu civilization reached full flower during the first millennium A.D., India's classical era, marked by monumental achievements in sculpture, architecture, painting, and literature. In China a strong ruler ended a period of feudal warfare and established a centralized system of government, which was utilized by successive Chinese dynasties. The Chinese empire under the Han Dynasty was comparable in power and lasting influence to the contemporary Roman Empire. And just as the decay of the Roman Empire ushered in a period of confusion, so the fall of the Han in 220 A.D. was followed by barbarian invasions and internal discord that lasted some four centuries. However, the period of disunity ended earlier in China than in Europe; and when a strong government was re-established, it represented essentially a return to traditional ancient patterns. Under the T'ang Dynasty (618–907) the Chinese empire reached its greatest territorial extent under any native monarch, while nourishing a brilliant culture. Also, China was far ahead of western Europe at this time in urban growth and commercial contacts. Despite a late start, the inhabitants of Japan made rapid progress in state building, stimulated by political and cultural borrowings from China. In central and western Africa industrial and agricultural progress resulted from the introduction of superior iron-working techniques.

Eastern religious developments paralleled to some degree the spread of Christianity in the West. In India, Hinduism and the dominance of the Brahman caste were challenged by the ethical and nontheological system of Gautama Buddha. Buddhism also spread to China and Japan and became a major stimulus of cultural vitality in all three countries.

The World in the Classical Era

POLITICS	PHILOSOPHY AND SCIENCE	
Dark Ages of Greek history, 1500–800		**800**
Feudalism in China, c. 800–250		**B.C.**
Beginning of city-states in Greece, c. 800		
Rome founded, c. 750	Thales of Miletus, c. 640–546	
	Pythagoras, c. 582–c. 507	
Age of the tyrants in Greece, c. 650–c. 500	Confucius, c. 551–479	
Reforms of Solon in Athens, 594	Lao-tzu, c. 550	
Reforms of Cleisthenes in Athens, 508		**500**
Establishment of Roman Republic, c. 500	Protagoras, c. 490–c. 420	**B.C.**
Greco-Persian War, 490–479	Socrates, 469–399	
Delian League, 479–404	Hippocrates, 460–c. 377	
Perfection of Athenian democracy, 461–429	Democritus, c. 460–c. 362	
Law of the Twelve Tables, Rome, c. 450	The Sophists, c. 450–c. 400	
Peloponnesian War, 431–404	Plato, 427–347	**400**
	Aristotle, 384–322	**B.C.**
	Mencius, c. 373–288	
Macedonian conquest of Greece, 338	Epicurus, 342–270	
Conquests of Alexander the Great, 334–323	Zeno the Stoic, c. 320–c. 250	
Division of Alexander's empire, 323	Euclid, c. 323–285	
Reign of Emperor Ashoka in India, c. 273–232	Aristarchus, 310–230	**300**
Punic Wars between Rome and Carthage, 264–146	Archimedes, c. 287–212	**B.C.**
Ch'in Dynasty in China, 221–207	Eratosthenes, c. 276–c. 195	
Building of Great Wall in China, c. 220		
Han Dynasty in China, 206 B.C.	Herophilus, c. 220–c. 150	
–220 A.D.	Polybius, c. 205–118	**200**
Reforms of the Gracchi, 133–121	The Skeptics, c. 200–c. 100	**B.C.**
Beginning of Japanese state, c. 100		
	Introduction of Stoicism into Rome, c. 140	
	Cicero, 106–43	
		100
Dictatorship of Julius Caesar, 46–44		**B.C.**
Principate of Augustus Caesar, 27 B.C.–14 A.D.		
	Lucretius, 98–55	
	Seneca, 34 B.C.–65 A.D.	**100**
"Five Good Emperors," 96–180	Marcus Aurelius, 121–180	**A.D.**
Completion of Roman jurisprudence by great	Galen, 130–c. 200	**200**
jurists, c. 200	Plotinus, c. 204–270	**A.D.**
Civil war in Roman Empire, 235–284		
Diocletian, 284–305		
Constantine I, 306–337		**300**
Theodosius I, 379–395		**A.D.**
Visigoths sack Rome, 410		**400**
West African kingdom of Ghana, c. 450		**A.D.**
Deposition of last of Western Roman emperors, 476	Boethius, c. 480–524	**500**
Theodoric the Ostrogoth king of Italy, 493–526		**A.D.**
Justinian, 527–565		
Corpus of Roman law, c. 550		

The World in the Classical Era (continued)

	ECONOMICS	RELIGION	ARTS AND LETTERS
800 B.C.	Rise of caste system in India, 1000–500		*Vedas* in India, 1200–800 *Upanishads*, 800–600
	Concentration of landed wealth in Greece, c. 750–c. 600 Greek overseas expansion, c. 750–c. 600 Invention of coinage by Lydians, c. 600 Royal Road of Persians, c. 500	Zoroaster formulates Zoroastrian religion in Persia, c. 625 Gautama Buddha, c. 563–483	*Iliad* and *Odyssey*, c. 750 Doric architectural style, c. 650–c. 500
500 B.C.	Use of iron in China, c. 500	Orphic and Eleusinian mystery cults, c. 500–c. 100	Aeschylus, 525–456 Phidias, c. 500–c. 432 Ionic architectural style, c. 500–c. 400 Sophocles, 496–406 Herodotus, c. 484–c. 420 Euripides, 480–406 Thucydides, c. 471–c. 400 The Parthenon, c. 460 Aristophanes, c. 448–c. 380
400 B.C.	Development of coinage in China, c.400		Corinthian architectural style, c. 400–c. 300 Praxiteles, c. 370–c. 310
300 B.C.	Hellenistic international trade and growth of large cities, c. 300 B.C.–c. 100 A.D. Use of iron in sub-Saharan Africa, 200 Growth of slavery, decline of small farmer in Rome, c. 250–100	Emergence of Mithraism, c. 300 Oriental mystery cults in Rome, c. 250–50	Indian epics, c. 400 B.C.–200 A.D.
100 B.C.	Manufacture of paper in China, c. 100 Decline of slavery in Rome, c. 120–c. 476 Growth of serfdom in Rome, c. 200–500	Spread of Mithraism in Rome, 27 B.C.–270 A.D. The Crucifixion, c. 30 A.D. St. Paul's missionary work, c. 35–c. 67	Virgil, 70–19 Horace, 65–8 Livy, 59 B.C.–17 A.D. Ovid, c. 43 B.C.–17 A.D. Tacitus, c. 55 A.D.–c. 117 A.D. The Colosseum, c. 80 A.D.
100 A.D. **200 A.D.**	Sharp economic contraction in Rome, c. 200–c. 300 Expansion of Bantu speakers in Africa, 200–900	Development of Buddhism in China, 200–500 Beginning of toleration of Christians in the Roman Empire, 311	The Pantheon, c. 120 Height of Roman portrait statuary, c. 120–c. 250 Classical age of Hindu culture, c. 300–800
300 A.D. **400 A.D.**		St. Augustine, 354–430 Christianity made official Roman religion, 380	Adoption of Chinese system of writing in Japan, c. 405
500 A.D.	Manufacture of glass and invention of gunpowder and magnetic compass in China, c. 500	Benedictine monastic rule, c. 520 Spread of Buddhism in Japan, c. 552	

Chapter 7

GREEK CIVILIZATION

We love beauty without extravagance, and wisdom without weakness of
will. Wealth we regard not as a means for private display but rather for
public service; and poverty we consider no disgrace, although we think it
is a disgrace not to try to overcome it. We believe a man should be concerned about public as well as private affairs, for we regard the person
who takes no part in politics not as merely uninterested but as useless.

—Pericles, *Funeral Oration,* on the ideals of Athens

Now, what is characteristic of any nature is that which is best for it and
gives most joy. Such to man is the life according to reason, since it is this
that makes him man.

—Aristotle, *Nicomachean Ethics*

Among all the peoples of the ancient world, the one whose culture
most clearly exemplified the spirit of Western society was
the Greek or Hellenic. No one of these peoples had so strong
a devotion to liberty or so firm a belief in the nobility of human
achievement. The Greeks glorified humanity as the most important
creation in the universe and refused to submit to the dictation of
priests or despots. Their attitude was essentially secular and rationalistic; they exalted the spirit of free inquiry and made knowledge supreme
over faith. Largely for these reasons their culture advanced to the
highest stage that the ancient world was destined to reach.

*The character of Greek
civilization*

1. THE GREEK DARK AGES

The fall of the Mycenaean civilization was a major catastrophe for the
Greek world. It ushered in a period usually called by historians the
Dark Ages, which lasted from about 1150 to 800 B.C. Written records
disappeared, except where accidentally preserved, and culture reverted to simpler forms than had been known for centuries. Toward

The Dark Ages

Bronze Centaur and Man. These figures date from about 750 B.C. They are no more than about five inches high.

Political institutions

Bronze Statuette. Perhaps representing Apollo, this work dates from about 750 B.C.

the end of the period some decorated pottery and skillfully designed metal objects began to appear on the islands of the Aegean Sea, but essentially the period was a long night. Aside from the development of writing at the very end, intellectual accomplishment was limited to ballads, and short epics sung and embellished by bards as they wandered from one village to another. A large part of this material was finally woven into a great epic cycle by one or more poets in the eighth century B.C. Though not all the poems of this cycle have come down to us, the two most important, the *Iliad* and the *Odyssey,* the so-called Homeric epics, provide us with a rich store of information about many of the customs and institutions of the Dark Ages.

The political institutions of the Dark Ages were exceedingly primitive. Each little community of villages was independent of external control, but political authority was so tenuous that it would not be too much to say that the state scarcely existed at all. The *basileus* or ruler was not much more than a tribal leader. He could not make or enforce laws or administer justice. He received no remuneration of any kind, and had to cultivate his farm for a living the same as any other citizen. Practically his only functions were military and priestly. He commanded the army in time of war and offered sacrifices to keep the gods on the good side of the community. Although each little community had its council of nobles and assembly of warriors, neither of these bodies had any definite membership or status as an organ of government. Almost without exception custom took the place of law, and the administration of justice was private. Even willful murder was punishable only by the family of the victim. While it is true that disputes were sometimes submitted to the ruler for settlement, he acted in such cases merely as an arbitrator, not as a judge. As a matter of fact, the political consciousness of the Greeks of this time was so poorly developed that they had no conception of government as an indispensable agency for the preservation of social order. When Odysseus, ruler of Ithaca, was absent for twenty years, no regent governed in his place and no session of the council or assembly was held. No one seemed to think that the complete suspension of government, even for so long a time, was a matter of critical importance.

The pattern of social and economic life was simple. Though the general tone of the society portrayed in the epics is aristocratic, no rigid stratification of classes existed. Manual labor was not looked upon as degrading, and there were apparently no idle rich. There were dependent laborers who worked on the lands of the nobles and served them as faithful warriors. The slaves were chiefly women, employed as servants, wool-processors, or concubines. Many were war captives, but they do not appear to have been badly treated. Agriculture and herding were the basic occupations of free men. Except for a few skilled crafts like those of wagonmaker, swordsmith, goldsmith, and potter, there was no specialization of labor. For the most part every household made its own tools, wove its own clothing, and raised its own food. So far were the Greeks of this time from being a trading people that they had no word in their language for "merchant," for barter was the only method of exchange.

To the Greeks of the Dark Ages religion meant chiefly a system for: (1) explaining the physical world in such a way as to remove its awesome mysteries and give people a feeling of intimate relationship with it; (2) accounting for the tempestuous passions that seized human nature; and (3) obtaining such tangible benefits as good fortune, long life, skill in craftsmanship, and abundant harvests. The Greeks did not expect that their religion would save them from sin or endow them with spiritual blessings. As they conceived it, piety was neither a matter of conduct nor of faith. Their religion, accordingly, had no commandments, dogmas, or sacraments. All were at liberty to believe what they pleased and to conduct their own lives as they chose without fear of divine wrath.

Religious conceptions in the Dark Ages

As is commonly known, the deities of the early Greek religion were merely human beings writ large. It was really necessary that this should be so if the Greeks were to feel at home in the world over which they ruled. Remote, omnipotent beings like the gods of most Oriental religions would have inspired fear rather than a sense of security. What the Greeks wanted was not necessarily gods of great power, but deities who could be bargained with on equal terms. Consequently gods were endowed with attributes similar to human ones—with human bodies and human weaknesses and wants. The early Greeks imagined the divinities as frequently quarreling with one another, mingling freely with mortals, and even occasionally procreating children by mortal women. The gods differed from humans only in the fact that they were immortal. They dwelt not in the sky

Human qualities of the deities

Left: *Poseidon or Zeus*. Right: *Aphrodite*. Both works of sculpture date from about 470 B.C. The male god communicates masculine majesty. Aphrodite (her Roman name was Venus) is shown rising from the sea in one of the earliest Greek works of art to exhibit naturalistic attention to the female body.

or in the stars but on the summit of Mount Olympus, a peak in northern Greece.

The religion was polytheistic, with no one deity elevated very high above any of the others. Zeus, the sky god and wielder of the thunderbolt, who was sometimes referred to as the father of the gods and of men, frequently received less attention than did Poseidon, the sea god, Aphrodite, goddess of love, or Athena, variously considered goddess of wisdom and war and patroness of handicrafts. To account for evil all the deities were deemed capable of malevolence as well as good.

Indifference to life after death

The Greeks of the Dark Ages were almost completely indifferent to what happened to them after death. They did assume, however, that shades or ghosts survived for a time after the death of their bodies. All, with a few exceptions, went to the same abode—to the murky realm of Hades situated beneath the earth. This was neither a paradise nor a hell: no one was rewarded for good deeds, and no one was punished for sins. Each of the shades appeared to continue the same kind of life its human embodiment had lived on earth. The Homeric poems make casual mention of two other realms, the Elysian Plain and the realm of Tartarus, which seem at first glance to contradict the idea of no rewards and punishments in the hereafter. But the few individuals who enjoyed the ease and comfort of the Elysian Plain had done nothing to deserve such blessings: they were simply persons whom the gods had chosen to favor. The realm of Tartarus was not really an abode of the dead but a place of imprisonment for rebellious deities.

Worship in early Greek religion consisted primarily of sacrifice. The offerings were made, however, not as an atonement for sin, but chiefly in order to please the gods and induce them to grant favors. In other words, religious practice was external and mechanical and not far removed from magic. Reverence, humility, and purity of heart were not essentials in it. The worshiper just made the proper sacrifice and then hoped for the best. For a religion such as this no elaborate institutions were required. Even a professional priesthood was unnecessary. Since there were no mysteries and no sacraments, one man could perform the simple rites about as well as another. The Greek temple was not a church or place of religious assemblage, and no ceremonies were performed within it. Instead it was a shrine which the god might visit occasionally and use as a temporary house.

As intimated already, the morality of the Greeks in the Dark Ages had only the vaguest connection with their religion. While it is true that the gods were generally disposed to support the right, they did not consider it their duty to combat evil and make righteousness prevail. In meting out rewards to humans, they appear to have been influenced more by their own whims and by gratitude for sacrifices offered than by any consideration for moral character. The only crime they

Man Carrying a Calf for Sacrifice. A life-size Athenian sculpture from about 570 B.C.

punished was perjury, and that none too consistently. Nearly all the virtues extolled in the epics were those which would make the individual a better soldier—bravery, self-control, patriotism, wisdom (in the sense of cunning), love of one's friends, and hatred of one's enemies. There was no conception of sin in the Christian sense of wrongful acts to be repented of or atoned for.

At the end of the Dark Ages the Greeks already had started along the road of social ideals that they would follow in later centuries. They were optimists, convinced that life was worth living for its own sake, and could see no reason for looking forward to death as a glad release. They were egotists striving for the fulfillment of self. As a consequence, they rejected mortification of the flesh and all forms of denial which implied the frustration of life. They could see no merit in humility or in turning the other cheek. Finally, they were humanists, who worshiped the finite and the natural rather than the otherworldly or sublime. For this reason they refused to invest their gods with awe-inspiring qualities, or to invent any conception of humans as depraved and sinful creatures.

Greek social ideals

2. THE EVOLUTION OF THE CITY-STATES

About 800 B.C. the village communities, which had been founded mainly upon tribal or clan organization, began to give way to larger political units. As trade increased, cities grew up around marketplaces and defensive fortifications as seats of government for whole communities. Thus emerged the city-state, the most famous unit of political society developed by the Greeks. Examples could be found in almost every section of the Hellenic world: Athens, Thebes, and Megara on the mainland; Sparta and Corinth on the Peloponnesus; Miletus on the shore of Asia Minor; and Mitylene and Samos on the islands of the Aegean Sea. They varied enormously in both area and population. Sparta with more than 3,000 square miles and Athens with 1,060 had by far the greatest extent; the others averaged less than 100. At the peak of their power Athens and Sparta, each with a population of about 400,000, had approximately three times the numerical strength of most of their neighboring states.

The origin and nature of the city-states

More important is the fact that the Greek city-states varied widely in cultural evolution. From 800 to 500 B.C., commonly called the Archaic period, the Peloponnesian city of Corinth was a leader in the development of literature and the arts. In the seventh century Sparta outshone many of its rivals. Preeminent above all were the Greek-speaking cities on the coast of Asia Minor and the islands of the Aegean Sea. Foremost among them was Miletus, where a brilliant flowering of philosophy and science occurred as early as the sixth century. Athens lagged behind until at least one hundred years later.

Variations among the city-states

Political evolution

One of the Earliest Minted Greek Coins. Struck around 700 B.C. on the island of Aegina, near Athens, this coin shows a sea turtle, a symbol of the Greeks' ability to flourish by sea.

See color map facing page 167

Coin of the Gorgon Medusa. Viewing the face of Medusa supposedly turned men into stone. This Greek coin from around 400 B.C. may have been meant to ward off evil spirits as well as to serve as an instrument of trade.

With a few exceptions the Greek city-states went through a similar political evolution. They began their histories as monarchies. During the eighth century they were changed into oligarchies. About a hundred years later, on the average, most of the oligarchies were overthrown by dictators, or "tyrants," as the Greeks called them, meaning usurpers who ruled without legal right whether oppressively or not. Finally, in the sixth and fifth centuries, democracies were set up, or in some cases "timocracies," that is, governments based upon a property qualification for the exercise of political rights. The first change came about as a result of the concentration of landed wealth. As the owners of great estates gained ever-greater economic power, they determined to wrest political authority from the ruler, now commonly called king, and vest it in the council, which they generally controlled. In the end they abolished the kingship entirely. Then followed a period of sweeping economic changes and political turmoil.

These developments affected not only Greece itself but many other parts of the Mediterranean world. For they were accompanied and followed by a vast overseas expansion. The chief cause was an increasing scarcity of land. The Greeks rapidly learned of numerous areas, thinly populated, with climate and soil similar to those of the homelands. The parent states most active in the expansive movement were Corinth, Chalcis, and Miletus. Their citizens founded colonies along the Aegean shores and even in Italy and Sicily. Of the latter the best known were Taras (modern Taranto) and Syracuse. They also established trading centers on the coast of Egypt and as far east as Babylon. The results of this expansionist movement were momentous. Commerce and industry became leading pursuits and the urban population increased. Merchants and artisans now joined with dispossessed farmers in an attack upon the landholding oligarchy. The natural fruit of the bitter class conflicts that ensued was dictatorship. By encouraging extravagant hopes and promising relief from chaos, ambitious demagogues attracted enough popular support to ride into power in defiance of constitutions and laws. Ultimately, however, dissatisfaction with tyrannical rule and the increasing economic might and political consciousness of the common citizens led to the establishment of democracies or timocracies.

Unfortunately space does not permit an analysis of the political history of each of the Greek city-states. Except in the more backward sections of Thessaly and the Peloponnesus, it is safe to conclude that the internal development of all of them paralleled the account given above, although minor variations due to local conditions doubtless occurred. The two most important of the Hellenic states, Sparta and Athens, deserve more detailed study.

3. THE ARMED CAMP OF SPARTA

The history of Sparta[1] was the great exception to the political evolution of the city-states. Despite the fact that its citizens sprang from the same origins as most of the other Greeks, Sparta failed to make any progress in the direction of democratic rule. Instead, its government gradually evolved into a form more closely resembling a modern elite dictatorship. Culturally, also, the nation stagnated after the sixth century. The causes were due partly to isolation. Hemmed in by mountains on the northeast and west and lacking good harbors, the Spartan people had little opportunity to profit from the advances made in the outside world. Besides, no middle class arose to aid the masses in the struggle for freedom.

The peculiar development of Sparta

The major explanation is to be found, however, in militarism. The Spartans were originally Dorians who had come into the eastern Peloponnesus as an invading army. Though by the end of the ninth century they had gained dominion over all of Laconia, they were not satisfied. West of the Taygetus Mountains lay the fertile plain of Messenia. The Spartans determined to conquer it. The venture was successful, and the Messenian territory was annexed to Laconia. About 640 B.C. the Messenians enlisted the aid of Argos and launched a revolt. The war that followed was desperately fought, Laconia itself was invaded, and only the death of the Argive commander and the patriotic pleas of the fire-eating poet Tyrtaeus saved the day for the Spartans. This time the victors took no chances. They confiscated the lands of the Messenians, murdered or expelled their leaders, and turned the masses into serfs called *helots*. Thereafter Spartan foreign policy was defensive. Following the Messenian wars the Spartans feared that further foreign warfare would provide the opportunities for a helot uprising; consequently Sparta devoted itself to keeping what it had already gained.

The Spartan desire for conquest

Almost all the major features of Spartan life resulted from their wars with the Messenians. In subduing and despoiling their enemies they unwittingly enslaved themselves, for they lived through the remaining centuries of their history in deadly fear of insurrections. This fear explains their conservatism, their stubborn resistance to change, lest any innovation result in a fatal weakening of the system. Their provincialism can also be attributed to the same cause. Frightened by the prospect that dangerous ideas might be brought into the country, they discouraged travel and prohibited trade with the outside world. The necessity of maintaining the absolute supremacy of the citizen class

The results of Spartan militarism

[1] Sparta was the leading city of a district called Laconia or Lacedaemonia; sometimes the *state* was referred to by one or the other of these names. The people, also, were frequently called Laconians or Lacedaemonians. (The modern adjective "laconic" comes from the reputation of the ancient Spartans for being sparing with words.)

over an enormous population of serfs required an iron discipline and a strict subordination of the individual; hence the Spartan collectivism, which extended into every branch of the social and economic life. Finally, much of the cultural backwardness of Sparta grew out of the atmosphere of restraint which inevitably resulted from the bitter struggle to conquer the Messenians and hold them under stern repression.

The Spartan government

The Spartan constitution provided for a government preserving the forms of the old system of the Dark Ages. Instead of one king, however, there were two, representing separate families of exalted rank. The Spartan kings enjoyed but few powers and those were chiefly of a military and priestly character. A second branch of the government was the council, composed of the two kings and twenty-eight nobles sixty years of age and over. This body supervised the work of administration, prepared measures for submission to the assembly, and served as the highest court for criminal trials. The third organ of government, the assembly, composed of all adult male citizens, approved or rejected the proposals of the council and elected all public officials except the kings. But the highest authority under the Spartan constitution was vested in a board of five men known as the *ephorate*. The ephors virtually were the government. They presided over the council and the assembly, controlled the educational system and the distribution of property, censored the lives of the citizens, and exercised a veto power over all legislation. They had power also to determine the fate of newborn infants, to conduct prosecutions before the council, and even to depose the kings if the religious omens appeared unfavorable. The Spartan government dominated by the ephors was thus in effect an oligarchy.

The class system in Sparta

The population of Sparta was divided into three main classes. The ruling element was made up of the Spartiates, or descendants of the original conquerors. Though never exceeding one-twentieth of the total population, the Spartiates alone had political privileges. Next in order of rank were the *perioeci,* or "dwellers around." The origin of this class is uncertain, but it was probably composed of peoples that had at one time been allies of the Spartans or had submitted voluntarily to Spartan domination. In return for service as a buffer population between the ruling class and the helots, the perioeci were allowed to carry on trade and to engage in manufacturing. At the bottom of the scale were the helots, or serfs, bound to the soil.

Perioeci and helots

Among these classes only the perioeci enjoyed any appreciable measure of comfort and freedom. While it is true that the economic condition of the helots cannot be described in terms of absolute misery, since they were permitted to keep for themselves a good share of what they produced on the estates of their masters, they were personally subjected to such degrading treatment that they were constantly wretched and rebellious. To guard against rebellion young Spartiates were sometimes sent to live among the helots in disguise and act like a

Minoan Snake Goddess. A statuette in ivory and gold discovered near the palace of Knossus and dating from about 1550 B.C. (Lee Boltin)

Geometric Horse, VIII cent. B.C. Greek art of this early period was angular, formal, and conventionalized.

Geometric Jar, VIII cent. B.C. Another example of the stylized decorative patterns of early Greek art.

Sphinx, c. 540–530 B.C. Though doubtless of Oriental derivation, Greek sphinxes had a softer and more human aspect than the Oriental.

Statue of an Amazon, one of the fabled tribe of women warriors, V cent. B.C. (Roman copy)

Departure of a Warrior. Gravestone, *c. 530 B.C.*, a period when naturalism was the dominant note of Greek art.

Athena, c. 460 B.C. The young, graceful patron-goddess of Athens is about to send forth an owl as a sign of victory.

Jar, 500–490 B.C. The figures depicted in a fine black glaze on the natural red clay show athletes in the Panathenaic games.

Chorus of Satyrs, c. 420 B.C. The background is black with the figures in red clay. The satyrs, dressed in fleecy white, with flowing tails, are the chorus of a play.

Toilet Box, 465–460 B.C. This scene shows the judgment of Paris, an event which touched off the Trojan War.

Bronze Mirror Case, V cent. B.C. Greek articles of everyday use were commonly finished with the same delicacy and precision as major works of art.

Diadoumenos, after Polykleitos, V cent. B.C. An idealized statue of a Greek athlete tying the "diadem," or band of victory, around his head.

Bracelet Pendant, IV–III cent. B.C. This tiny figure of the god Pan is a masterpiece of detail and expression.

Woman Arranging Her Hair, 400–300 B.C. Sculptors of antiquity took pride in these statuettes of ordinary people in ordinary activities, which were usually made of terracotta painted soft blue, pink, or yellow.

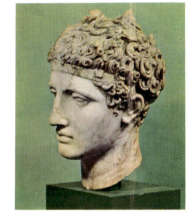

Head of an Athlete, c. 440–420 B.C. The sculptor aimed to express manly beauty in perfect harmony with physical and intellectual excellence.

Statuette of Hermarchos, III cent. B.C. An example of the realism of Hellenistic sculpture.

Sleeping Eros, 250–150 B.C. Along with a penchant for realism, Hellenistic sculptors were fond of portraying serenity or repose.

Comic Actor, 200–100 B.C. Hellenistic realism often included portrayal of ugly and even deformed individuals.

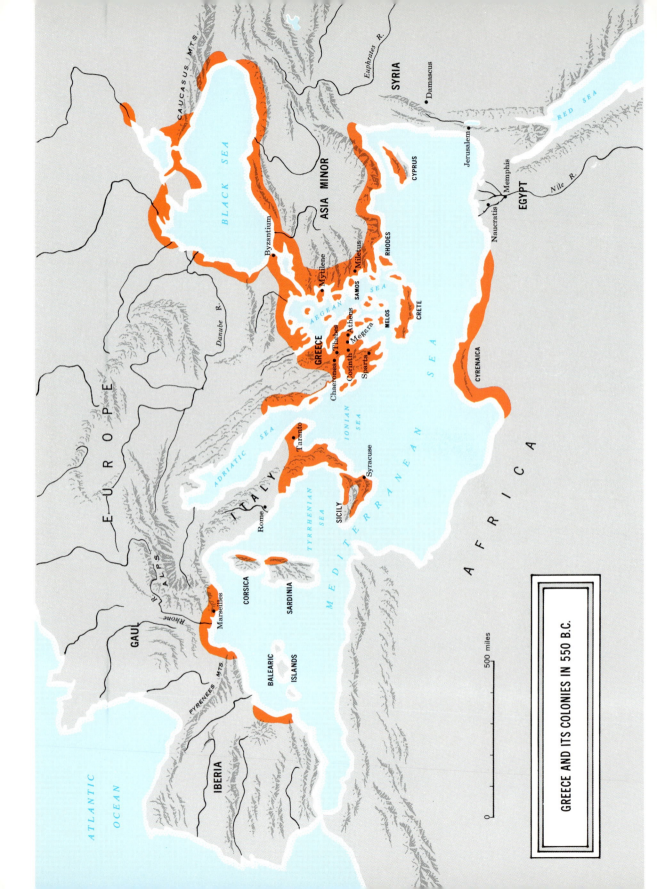

GREECE AND ITS COLONIES IN 550 B.C.

secret police with the power to murder whom they pleased. The brutalizing effects on both sides can be easily imagined.

Those who were born into the Spartiate class were doomed to a respectable slavery for the major part of their lives. Forced to submit to the severest discipline and to sacrifice individual interests, they were little more than cogs in a vast machine. Spartan babies were examined for hardiness at birth and those who were thought to be potential weaklings were carried off to the hills to die of neglect. The education of Spartan males was limited almost entirely to military training, which began at the age of seven, supplemented by merciless floggings to harden the boys for the duties of war. Between the ages of twenty and sixty the men gave almost all their time to state service. Although marriage was practically compulsory there was little family life: young men had to live in barracks, and after the age of thirty they still had to eat in military messes. The husbands carried off their wives on their wedding nights by a show of force. Because they saw so little of them afterwards it sometimes happened that men "had children before they ever saw their wives' faces in daylight."[2] The production of vigorous offspring was the wives' main duty, but mothers had to accept the fact that children were virtually the property of the state. It may be doubted that the Spartiates resented these hardships and deprivations. Pride in their status as the ruling class probably compensated in their minds for harsh discipline and denial of privileges.

Discipline for the benefit of the state

The economic organization of Sparta was designed almost solely for the ends of military efficiency and the supremacy of the citizen class. The best land was owned by the state and was originally divided into equal plots which were assigned to the Spartiate class as inalienable estates. Later these holdings as well as the inferior lands were permitted to be sold and exchanged, with the result that some of the citizens became richer than others. The helots, who did all the work of cultivating the soil, also belonged to the state and were assigned to their masters along with the land. Their masters were forbidden to emancipate them or to sell them outside of the country. The labor of the helots provided for the support of the whole citizen class, whose members were not allowed to be associated with any economic enterprise other than agriculture. The minimal trade and industry of the Spartan state were reserved exclusively for the perioeci. Thus the Spartan economy was as static as Sparta's government was repressive.

Economic regulations

4. THE ATHENIAN TRIUMPH AND TRAGEDY

Athens began its history under conditions quite different from those which prevailed in Sparta. The district of Attica in which Athens is situated had not been the scene of an armed invasion or of bitter conflict

Advantages enjoyed by the Athenians

[2] Plutarch, "Lycurgus," *Lives of Illustrious Men*, I, 81.

between opposing peoples. As a result, no military caste imposed its rule upon a vanquished nation. Furthermore, Attica's agricultural resources were complemented by ample mineral deposits and splendid harbors, making it possible for Athens to develop a prosperous trade and an essentially urban culture rather than remain a predominantly agrarian state as Sparta did.

From monarchy to oligarchy in Athens

Until the middle of the eighth century B.C. Athens, like the other Greek states, had a monarchical form of government. During the century that followed, the council of nobles, or Council of the Areopagus, as it came to be called, gradually stripped the king of his powers. The transition to rule by the few was both the cause and the result of an increasing concentration of wealth. The introduction of vine and olive culture about this time led to the growth of agriculture as a large-scale enterprise. Since vineyards and olive orchards require considerable time to become profitable, only those farmers with abundant resources were able to survive in the business. Their poorer and less thrifty neighbors sank rapidly into debt, especially since grain was now coming to be imported at ruinous prices. The small farmer had no alternative but to mortgage his land, and then his family and himself, in the vain hope that some day a way of escape would be found. Ultimately many of this class became serfs when the mortgages could not be paid; those without land to mortgage were sold into slavery.

Threats of revolution and the reforms of Solon

Bitter cries of distress now arose. The urban middle classes took up the cause of the peasants in demanding liberalization of the government. Finally, in 594 B.C., all parties agreed upon the appointment of the aristocrat Solon as chief magistrate with absolute power to carry out reforms. The measures Solon enacted provided for both political and economic adjustments. The former included: (1) the establishment of a new council, the Council of Four Hundred, and the admission of the middle classes to membership in it; (2) the enfranchisement of the lower classes by making them eligible for service in the assembly; and (3) the organization of a final court of appeals in criminal cases, open to all citizens and elected by universal manhood suffrage. The economic reforms benefited the poor farmers by cancelling existing mortgages, prohibiting enslavement for debt in the future, and limiting the amount of land any one individual could own.

The rise of tyranny

Significant though these reforms were, they did not allay the discontent. The nobles were disgruntled because some of their privileges had been taken away. The middle and lower classes were dissatisfied because they were still excluded from the offices of magistracy, and because the Council of the Areopagus was left with its powers intact. The chaos and disillusionment that followed paved the way in 546 B.C. for the triumph of Peisistratus, the first of the Athenian tyrants. Although he proved to be a benevolent despot who patronized culture, reduced the power of the aristocracy, and raised the standard of living of the average Athenian, his son Hippias, who succeeded him, was a ruthless and spiteful oppressor.

Greeks at War. A battle scene from the interior of a drinking cup, done in Athens between about 530 and 500 B.C.

In 510 B.C. Hippias's tyranny was overthrown by a group of nobles with aid from Sparta. Factional conflict raged for another two years until Cleisthenes, an intelligent aristocrat, enlisted the support of the masses to eliminate his rivals from the scene. Having promised concessions to the people as a reward for their help, he proceeded to reform the government in so sweeping a fashion that he has since been known as the father of Athenian democracy. Cleisthenes enlarged the citizen population by granting full rights to all free men who resided in the country at that time. He established a new council and made it the chief organ of government with power to prepare measures for submission to the assembly and with supreme control over executive and administrative functions. Members of this body were to be chosen by lot. Any male citizen over thirty years of age was eligible. Cleisthenes also expanded the authority of the assembly, giving it power to debate and pass or reject the measures submitted by the council, to declare war, to appropriate money, and to audit the accounts of retiring magistrates. Lastly, Cleisthenes instituted the Athenian device of ostracism, whereby any citizen considered dangerous to the state could be sent into honorable exile for a ten-year period. Ostracism was meant to eliminate men suspected of cherishing dictatorial ambitions, but sometimes its effect was to eliminate exceptional personalities.

The reforms of Cleisthenes

The Athenian democracy attained its full perfection in the Age of Pericles (461–429 B.C.). It was during this period that the assembly acquired the authority to initiate legislation in addition to its power to ratify or reject proposals of the council. During this time also the Board of Ten Generals rose to a position roughly comparable to that

The perfection of Athenian democracy

Bust of Pericles. A Roman copy of a Greek work possibly done from life.

of the British cabinet. The generals were chosen by the assembly for one-year terms and were eligible for reelection indefinitely. Pericles held the position of chief strategus or president of the Board of Generals for many years. The generals were not simply commanders of the army but the chief legislative and executive officials in the state. Though wielding enormous power, they could not become tyrants, for their policies were subject to review by the assembly, and they could easily be recalled at the end of their one-year terms or indicted for malfeasance at any time. Finally, in the Age of Pericles the Athenian system of courts reached its completion. No longer was there merely a supreme court to hear appeals from the decisions of magistrates, but an array of popular courts was formed to try all kinds of cases. At the beginning of each year a list of 6,000 citizens was chosen by lot from the various sections of the country. From this list separate juries, varying in size from 201 to 1,001, were made up for particular trials. Each of these juries constituted a court with power to decide by majority vote every question involved in the case. Although one of the magistrates presided, he had none of the prerogatives of a judge; the jury itself was the judge, and from its decision there was no appeal.

The Athenian democracy differed from the modern form in various ways. First of all, it entirely excluded women. Even taking that into account, it did not extend to the whole population, but only to the citizen class. While it is true that in the time of Cleisthenes the citizens probably included a majority of the inhabitants because of his enfranchisement of resident aliens, in the Age of Pericles the citizens were distinctly a minority. It may be well to observe, however, that within its limits Athenian democracy was more thoroughly applied than is the modern form. The choice by lot of nearly all magistrates except the Ten Generals, the restriction of all terms of public officials to one year, and the uncompromising adherence to the principle of majority rule even in judicial trials were examples of a confidence in the political capacity of the citizen which few modern nations would be willing to accept. The democracy of Athens differed from the contemporary ideal also in the fact that it was direct, not representative. Since the Athenians were not interested in being governed by a few men of reputation, the assembly of all male citizens met almost every week to vote on all major decisions.

In the century of its greatest expansion and creativity Athens fought two major wars. The first was a struggle with the Persian empire, which by then had replaced Babylonia as the mightiest power in western Asia. The Athenians resented Persia's rule over the Greek-speaking cities in Asia Minor and aided them in their struggle for freedom. (These cities shared with Athens a common Greek dialect—Ionian—a fact which made the Athenians feel a particularly close kinship with them.) The Persians retaliated by sending a powerful army and fleet to attack the Greeks. Although all Greece was in danger of conquest, Athens bore the chief burden of repelling the invader. The war, which began in 490 B.C. and lasted with interludes of peace until 479, B.C., is commonly regarded as one of the most significant in the history of the world. The heroic victories of the Greeks in such battles as Marathon (490) B.C.) and Salamis (480 B.C.) put an end to the menace of Persian conquest and prevented the destruction of Hellenic ideals of freedom by Persian despotism.

The other of the great struggles, the Peloponnesian War with Sparta, had results of a quite different character. Instead of being another milestone in the Athenian march to power, it ended in tragedy. The causes of this war are of particular interest to the student of the downfall of civilizations. First and most important was the growth of Athenian imperialism. In 478 B.C., Athens had joined with a number of other Greek states in the formation of an offensive and defensive alliance known as the Delian League. Despite the fact that Greece was no longer fighting Persia, the League was maintained year after year, for many of the Greeks feared that the Persians might come back. As time went on, Athens gradually transformed the league into a naval empire for the advancement of its own interests. It used some of the funds in the common treasury for its own purposes. It tried to reduce all the other members to a condition of subservience, and when one of them rebelled, Athens overwhelmed it by force, seized its navy, and imposed tribute upon it as if it were a conquered state. Such high-handed methods aroused the suspicions of the Spartans, who feared that an Athenian hegemony would soon be extended over all of Greece.

The Owl of Athens. An Athenian silver coin of around 470 B.C., showing the owl, thought to be sacred to Athens's protectress, the goddess Athena. The name Athens appears in the Greek letters AΘE.

A second major cause was to be found in the social and cultural differences between Athens and Sparta. Athens was democratic, progressive, urban, imperialist, and intellectually and artistically advanced. Sparta was aristocratic, conservative, agrarian, provincial, and culturally backward. Where such sharply contrasting systems exist side by side, conflicts are almost bound to occur. The attitude of the Athenians and Spartans had been hostile for some time. The former looked upon the latter as uncouth. The Spartans accused the Athenians of attempting to gain control over the northern Peloponnesian states and of encouraging the helots to rebel. Economic factors also played a large part in bringing the conflict to a head. Athens sought to dominate the Corinthian Gulf, the principal avenue of trade with Sicily and southern Italy. This made Athens the deadly enemy of Corinth, the chief ally of Sparta.

*Other causes of the
Peloponnesian War*

The war, which broke out in 431 B.C. and lasted until 404 B.C., was a record of frightful calamities for Athens. Athenian trade was destroyed, its democracy overthrown, and the population decimated by a terrible pestilence. Quite as bad was the moral degradation which followed in the wake of the military reverses. Treason, corruption, and brutality were among the hastening ills of the last few years of the conflict. On one occasion the Athenians even slaughtered the whole male population of the island of Melos, and enslaved the women

The defeat of Athens

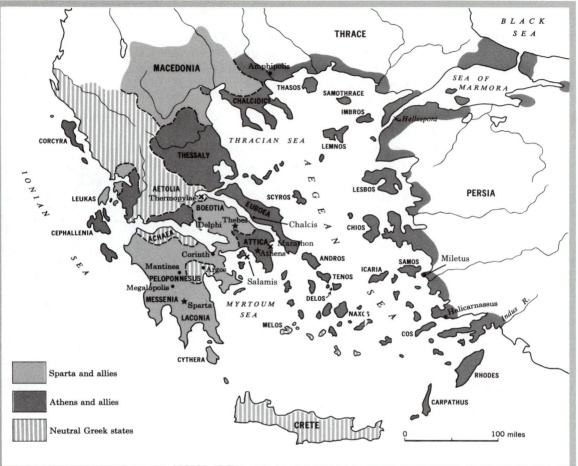

GREECE AT THE END OF THE AGE OF PERICLES

and children, for no other crime than refusing to abandon neutrality. Ultimately, deserted by all its allies except Samos and with its food supply cut off, Athens was left with no alternative but to surrender or starve. The terms imposed upon the Athenians were drastic: destruction of their fortifications, surrender of all foreign possessions and practically their entire navy, and submission to Sparta as a subject state.

Continuing conflict and chaos among the city-states

Worse than ending the political supremacy of Athens, the outcome of the Peloponnesian War led to political disaster for all Greece. Following the victory Sparta assumed supremacy in the Greek world, and oligarchies supported by Sparta replaced democracies in several Greek cities. Nonetheless, during the period between 404 and 371 B.C. it became increasingly clear that Sparta lacked the will and the governmental institutions to maintain firm control over the entire Greek world. The result was civil strife in several Greek cities in which anti-Spartan democrats rose up against Spartan-backed oligarchs, as well as attempts by Athens and Thebes—cities in which democrats had taken power—to wrest hegemony over Greece from Sparta. In 371 B.C. Thebes accomplished that goal by a victory over Spartan troops at the battle of Leuctra, yet Thebes soon proved no more able to rule Greece firmly than Sparta had been. Consequently from 371 until 338 B.C. shifting alliances between Greek cities led to interminable warfare and brought the combatants to the point of exhaustion. Although the splendor of Greek culture had hardly dimmed (Plato and Aristotle, the greatest of all Greek philosophers, were successively in their prime from about 390 to about 330 B.C.), all the leading cities of Greece had become prostrate and helpless from the military and political point of view.

5. GREEK THOUGHT AND CULTURE

In the realm of philosophy the Greeks attempted to find answers to every conceivable question about the nature of the universe, the problem of truth, and the meaning and purpose of life. The magnitude of their accomplishment is attested by the fact that philosophy ever since has been largely a debate over the validity of their conclusions.

The essence of Greek philosophy

Greek philosophy had its origins in the sixth century B.C. in the work of the so-called Milesian school, whose members were natives of the city of Miletus. Their philosophy was fundamentally scientific and materialistic. The problem which chiefly engaged them was to discover the nature of the physical world. They believed that all things could be reduced to some primary substance which was the source of worlds, stars, animals, plants, and humans, and to which all would ultimately return. Thales, the founder of the school, perceiving that all things contained moisture, taught that the primary substance is water. Anaximander insisted that it could not be any particular thing such as water or fire but something "uncreated and imperishable." He called this substance the Indefinite or the Boundless. A third Milesian, Anaximenes, declared that the original material of the universe is air. Air when rarefied becomes fire; when condensed it turns successively to wind, vapor, water, earth, and stone. Although seemingly naive in its conclusions, the philosophy of the Milesian school was of major significance because it broke through the mythological beliefs of the Greeks about the origin of the world and substituted purely rational explanations.

The philosophy of the Milesian school

Before the end of the sixth century B.C. Greek philosophy developed a metaphysical turn; it ceased to be occupied solely with problems of the physical world and shifted its attention to abstruse questions about the nature of being, the meaning of truth, and the position of the divine in the scheme of things. First to exemplify the new tendency were the Pythagoreans, who interpreted philosophy largely in terms of religion. Little is known about them except that their leader, Pythagoras, migrated from Greece to southern Italy, where he founded

The Pythagoreans

a religious community at Croton in 530 B.C. He and his followers taught that the speculative life is the highest good, but that in order to pursue it, the individual must be purified of the evil desires of the flesh. They held that the essence of things is not a material substance but an abstract principle, number. Their chief significance lies in the sharp distinctions they drew between spirit and matter, harmony and discord, good and evil, which made them the founders of dualism in Greek thought.

Renewal of the debate over the nature of the universe

A consequence of the work of the Pythagoreans was to intensify the debate over the nature of the universe. One of their contemporaries, Parmenides, argued that stability or permanence is the real nature of things; change and diversity are simply illusions of the senses. Directly opposed to this was the position taken by Heraclitus, who argued that permanence is an illusion, that change alone is real. The universe, he maintained, is in a condition of constant flux; therefore "it is impossible to step twice into the same stream." Creation and destruction, life and death, are but the obverse and reverse sides of the same picture. In other words, Heraclitus believed that the things we see, hear, and feel are all there is to reality. Evolution or constant change is the law of the universe. The tree or the stone that is here today is gone tomorrow; no underlying substance exists immutable through all eternity.

The atomists

A final alternative to the question of the underlying character of the universe was provided by the atomists. The philosopher chiefly responsible for the development of the atomic theory was Democritus, who lived in Abdera on the Thracian coast in the second half of the fifth century B.C. As their name implies, the atomists held that the ultimate constituents of the universe are atoms, infinite in number, indestructible, and indivisible. Although these differ in size and shape, they are exactly alike in composition. Because of the motion inherent in them, they are eternally uniting, separating, and reuniting in different arrangements. Every individual object or organism in the universe is thus the product of a fortuitous concourse of atoms. The only difference between a human and a tree is the difference in the number and arrangement of their atoms. This philosophy represented the final fruition of the materialistic tendencies of early Greek thought. Democritus denied the immortality of the soul and the existence of any spiritual world. Strange as it may appear to some people, he was a moral idealist, affirming that "good means not merely not to do wrong, but rather not to desire to do wrong."

The intellectual revolution begun by the Sophists

About the middle of the fifth century B.C. an intellectual revolution began in Greece. It accompanied the high point of democracy in Athens. The rise in the power of the citizen, the growth of individualism, and the demand for the solution of practical problems produced a reaction against the old ways of thinking. As a result some Greek philosophers abandoned the study of the physical universe and turned to consideration of subjects more intimately related to the individual.

The first exponents of the new intellectual trend were the Sophists. Originally the term meant "those who are wise," but later it came to be used in the derogatory sense of men who employ specious reasoning. Since most of our knowledge of the Sophists comes from Plato, one of their severest critics, they were commonly viewed as the enemies of all that was best in Hellenic culture. Modern research has rejected so extreme a conclusion, while conceding that some members of the group did lack a sense of social responsibility and were quite unscrupulous in "making the worse appear the better case."

One of the leading Sophists was Protagoras, a native of Abdera who did most of his teaching in Athens. His famous dictum, "Man is the measure of all things," contains the essence of the Sophist philosophy. By this he meant that goodness, truth, justice, and beauty are relative to the needs and interests of man. There are no absolute truths or eternal standards of right and justice. Since sense perception is the exclusive source of knowledge, there can be only particular truths valid for a given time and place. Morality likewise varies from one people to another, for there are no absolute canons of right and wrong eternally decreed in the heavens to fit all cases.

The doctrines of Protagoras

Some of the later Sophists went far beyond the teachings of Protagoras. The individualism implicit in the teachings of Protagoras was twisted by Thrasymachus into the doctrine that all laws and customs are merely expressions of the will of the strongest and shrewdest for their own advantage, and that therefore the wise man is the "perfectly unjust man" who is above the law and concerned with the gratification of his own desires. (It should also be mentioned that man, in the sense of the male, was the primary focus of this and all other Greek philosophy dealing with the individual.)

The extremist doctrines of the later Sophists

Yet there was much that was admirable in the teachings of the Sophists, even of those who were the most extreme. Some condemned slavery and the racial exclusiveness of the Greeks. Some were champions of liberty, the rights of the common man, and the practical and progressive point of view. Perhaps most important, the Sophists broadened philosophy to include not only physics and metaphysics, but ethics and politics. As the Roman Cicero expressed it, they "brought philosophy down from heaven to the dwellings of men."

The valuable contributions of the Sophists

Inevitably the relativism, skepticism, and individualism of the Sophists aroused strenuous opposition. In the judgment of the more conservative Greeks these doctrines appeared to lead straight to atheism and anarchy. If there is no final truth, and if goodness and justice are merely relative to the whims of the individual, then neither religion, morality, the state, nor society itself can long be maintained. The result of this conviction was the growth of a new philosophic movement grounded upon the theory that truth is real and that absolute standards do exist. The leaders of this movement were perhaps the three most famous individuals in the history of thought—Socrates, Plato, and Aristotle.

Socrates Gaining Wisdom from the Wise-Woman Diotima. In Plato's *Symposium* Socrates learns the philosophical meaning of love from Diotima, an ethereal female being, wiser than he. In this sculptural representation of the scene the winged figure between Diotima and Socrates is probably a personification of love itself.

Socrates

Socrates. According to Plato, Socrates looked like a goatman but spoke like a god.

Socrates was born in Athens in 469 B.C. of humble parentage; his father was a sculptor, his mother a midwife. How he obtained an education no one knows, but he was certainly familiar with the teachings of earlier Greek thinkers. The impression that he was a mere gabbler in the marketplace is quite unfounded. He became a philosopher on his own account chiefly to combat the doctrines of the Sophists. In 399 B.C. he was condemned to death on a charge of "corrupting the youth and introducing new gods." The real reason for the unjust sentence was the tragic outcome for Athens of the Peloponnesian War. Overwhelmed by resentment, the Athenian citizens turned against Socrates because of his associations with aristocrats, including the traitor Alcibiades, and because of his criticism of popular belief. There is also evidence that he disparaged democracy and contended that no government was worthy of the name except intellectual aristocracy.

Because Socrates wrote nothing himself, historians find it difficult to determine the exact scope of his teachings. He is generally regarded as primarily a teacher of ethics with no interest in abstract philosophy. Certain passages in Plato, however, raise the possibility that Plato's abstract doctrine of Ideas was ultimately of Socratic origin. At any rate we can be reasonably sure that Socrates believed in a stable and universally valid knowledge, which humans could possess if they pursued the right method. This would consist in the exchange and analysis of opinions, in the setting up and testing of provisional definitions, until finally an essence of truth recognizable by all could be distilled from them. Socrates argued that in similar fashion man could discover enduring principles of right and justice independent of the selfish desires of human beings. He believed, moreover, that the discovery of such rational principles of conduct would prove an infallible guide to virtuous living, for he denied that anyone who knows the good can choose the evil.

By far the most distinguished of Socrates's pupils was Plato, who was born in Athens around 429 B.C., the son of noble parents. At the age of twenty Plato joined the Socratic circle, remaining a member until the tragic death of his teacher. Unlike his great mentor, he was a prolific writer. The most noted of his works are such dialogues as the *Apology*, the *Phaedo*, the *Phaedrus*, the *Symposium*, and the *Republic*. He was engaged in the completion of the *Laws* when death overtook him in his eighty-first year.

Plato's objectives were similar to those of Socrates although somewhat broader: (1) to combat the theory of reality as a disordered flux and to substitute an interpretation of the universe as essentially spiritual and purposeful; (2) to refute the Sophist doctrines of relativism and skepticism; and (3) to provide a secure foundation for ethics. In order to realize these aims he developed his doctrine of Ideas. He admitted that relativity and change are characteristics of the world of physical things, of the world we perceive with our senses. But he denied that this world is the complete universe. A higher, spiritual realm exists, composed of eternal forms or Ideas which only the mind can conceive. These are not, however, mere abstractions invented by the mind, but spiritual things. Each is the pattern of some particular class of objects or relation between objects on earth. Thus there are Ideas of man, tree, shape, color, proportion, beauty, and justice. Highest of them all is the Idea of the Good, the active cause and guiding purpose of the universe. The things we perceive through our senses are merely imperfect copies of the supreme realities, Ideas.

Plato's ethical and religious philosophy was closely related to his doctrine of Ideas. Like Socrates he believed that true virtue has its basis in knowledge. But the knowledge derived from the senses is limited and variable; hence true virtue must consist in rational apprehension of the eternal Ideas of goodness and justice. By relegating the physical to an inferior place, he gave to his ethics an ascetic tinge. He regarded the body as a hindrance to the mind and taught that only the rational part of man's nature is noble and good. Yet in contrast with some of his later followers, he did not demand that appetites and emotions should be denied altogether, but urged that they should be strictly subordinated to reason. Plato never made his conception of God entirely clear, but it is certain that he conceived of the universe as spiritual in nature and governed by intelligent purpose. He rejected both materialism and mechanism. As for the soul, he regarded it not only as immortal but as preexisting through all eternity.

As a political philosopher Plato was motivated by the ideal of constructing a state which would be free from turbulence and self-seeking on the part of individuals and classes. Neither democracy nor liberty but harmony and efficiency were the ends he desired to achieve. Accordingly, he proposed in his *Republic* a plan for society which would

Plato's philosophy of Ideas

Plato

Plato's ethical and religious philosophy

Plato as a political philosopher

have divided the population into three principal classes corresponding to the functions of the soul. The lowest class, representing the appetitive function, would include the farmers, artisans, and merchants. The second class, representing the spirited element or will, would consist of the soldiers. The highest class, representing the function of reason, would be composed of the intellectual aristocracy. Each of these classes would perform those tasks for which it was best fitted. The function of the lowest class would be the production and distribution of goods for the benefit of the whole community; that of the soldiers, defense; the aristocracy, by reason of special aptitude for philosophy, would enjoy a monopoly of political power. The division of the people into these several ranks would not be made on the basis of birth or wealth, but through a sifting process that would take into account the ability of each individual to profit from education. Thus the farmers, artisans, and merchants would be those who had shown the least intellectual capacity, whereas the philosopher-kings would be those who had shown the greatest.

Aristotle

The last of the great champions of the Socratic tradition was Aristotle, a native of Stagira, born in 384 B.C. At the age of seventeen he entered Plato's Academy,[3] continuing as student and teacher there for twenty years. In 343 he was invited by Philip of Macedon to serve as tutor to the young Alexander the Great. Seven years later Aristotle returned to Athens, where he conducted a school of his own, known as the Lyceum, until his death in 322 B.C. Aristotle wrote even more voluminously than Plato and on a greater variety of subjects. His principal works include treatises on logic, metaphysics, rhetoric, ethics, natural sciences, and politics.

Aristotle compared with Plato and Socrates

Though Aristotle was as much interested as Plato and Socrates in absolute knowledge and eternal standards, his philosophy differed from theirs in several outstanding respects. To begin with, he had a higher regard for the concrete and the practical. In contrast with Plato, the aesthete, and Socrates, who declared he could learn nothing from trees and stones, Aristotle was an empirical scientist with a compelling interest in biology, physics, and astronomy. Moreover, he was less inclined than his predecessors to a spiritual outlook. And last, he did not share their strong aristocratic sympathies.

Aristotle's conception of the universe

Aristotle agreed with Plato that universals, Ideas (or forms as he called them), are real, and that knowledge derived from the senses is limited and inaccurate. But he refused to go along with his teacher in ascribing an independent existence to universals and in reducing material things to pale reflections of their spiritual patterns. On the contrary, he asserted that form and matter are of equal importance; both are eternal, and neither can exist without the other. The union of these two gives the universe its character. Forms are the causes of all things;

[3] So called from the grove of Academus, where Plato and his disciples met to discuss philosophic problems.

they are the purposive forces that shape the world of matter into the infinitely varied objects and organisms around us. All evolution, both cosmic and organic, results from the interaction of form and matter. Thus the presence of the form *man* in the human embryo molds and directs the development of the latter until it ultimately evolves as a human being. Aristotle's philosophy may be regarded as halfway between the spiritualism and transcendentalism of Plato on the one hand, and the mechanistic materialism of the atomists on the other. His conception of the universe was *teleological*—that is, governed by purpose; but he refused to regard the spiritual as overshadowing its material embodiment.

Aristotle's scientific attitude led him to conceive of God primarily as a First Cause. Aristotle's God was simply the Prime Mover, the original source of the purposive motion contained in the forms. In no sense was he a personal God, for his nature was pure intelligence, devoid of all feelings, will, or desire. Aristotle seems to have left no place for individual immortality: all the functions of the soul, except the creative reason which is not individual at all, depend upon the body and perish with it.

Aristotle's religious doctrines

Aristotle's ethical philosophy was less ascetic than Plato's. He did not regard the body as the prison of the soul, nor did he believe that physical appetites are necessarily evil in themselves. He taught that the highest good consists in self-realization, that is, in the exercise of that part of man's nature which most truly distinguishes him as a human being. Self-realization would therefore be identical with the life of reason. But the life of reason is dependent upon the proper combination of physical and mental conditions. The body must be kept in good health and the emotions under adequate control. The solution is to be found in the *golden mean,* in preserving a balance between excessive indulgence on the one hand and ascetic denial on the other. This was simply a reaffirmation of the characteristic Greek ideal of *sophrosyne,* "nothing too much."

Aristotle's ethical philosophy of the golden mean

Although Aristotle included in his *Politics* much descriptive and analytical material on the structure and functions of government, he dealt primarily with the broader aspects of political theory. He considered the state as the supreme institution for the promotion of the good life, and he was therefore vitally interested in its origin and development and in the best forms it could be made to assume. Declaring that man is by nature a political animal, he denied that the state is an artificial product of the ambitions of the few or of the desires of the many. On the contrary, he asserted that it is rooted in the instincts of man himself, and that civilized life outside of its limits is impossible. He considered the best state to be neither a monarchy, an aristocracy, nor a democracy, but a *polity*—which he defined as a commonwealth intermediate between oligarchy and democracy. Essentially it would be a state under the control of the middle class, but Aristotle intended to make sure that the members of that class would be fairly numerous,

The golden mean applied to politics

for he advocated measures to prevent the concentration of wealth. He defended the institution of private property, but he opposed the heaping up of riches beyond what is necessary for intelligent living. He recommended that the government provide the poor with money to buy small farms or to "make a beginning in trade and husbandry" and thus promote their prosperity and self-respect.

Greek thought not primarily scientific

Contrary to popular belief, the period of Greek civilization before the end of the fourth century B.C. was not a great age of science. The vast majority of the scientific achievements commonly thought of as Greek were made during the Hellenistic period, when the culture was no longer predominantly Greek but a mixture of Greek and western Asian. The interests of the Greeks in the Periclean Age and in the century that followed were chiefly speculative and artistic; they were not deeply concerned with material comforts or with mastery of the physical universe. Consequently, with the exception of some important developments in mathematics, biology, and medicine, scientific progress was relatively slight.

Pythagorean mathematics

The most significant Greek mathematical work was accomplished by the Pythagoreans. These followers of Pythagoras developed an elaborate theory of numbers, classifying them into various categories, such as odd, even, prime, composite, and perfect. They are also supposed to have discovered the theory of proportion and to have proved for the first time that the sum of the three angles of any triangle is equal to two right angles. But the most famous of their achievements was the discovery of the theorem attributed to Pythagoras himself: the square of the hypotenuse of any right-angled triangle is equal to the sum of the squares of the other two sides.

Biology

The first of the Greeks to manifest an interest in biology was the philosopher Anaximander, who developed a crude theory of organic evolution based upon the principle of survival through progressive adaptations to the environment. The earliest ancestral animals, he asserted, lived in the sea, which originally covered the whole face of the earth. As the waters receded, some organisms were able to adjust themselves to their new environment and became land animals. The final product of this evolutionary process was man himself. The real founder of the science of biology, however, was Aristotle. Devoting many years of his life to painstaking study of the structure, habits, and growth of animals, he made many remarkable observations. The metamorphoses of various insects, the reproductive habits of the eel, the embryological development of the dog-fish—these are only samples of the wide extent of his knowledge. Unfortunately, however, Aristotle's biology was also heavily laden with misconceptions: he denied the sexuality of plants, for example, and he believed in the spontaneous generation of certain species of worms and insects.

Greek medicine also had its origin with the philosophers. A pioneer was Empedocles, exponent of the theory of the four elements (earth, air, fire, and water). He discovered that blood flows to and from the heart, and that the pores of the skin supplement the work of the respiratory passages in breathing. More important was the work of Hippocrates of Cos in the fifth and fourth centuries B.C. By general consensus he is regarded as the father of medicine. He dinned into the ears of his pupils the doctrine that "every disease has a natural cause, and without natural causes, nothing ever happens." In addition, by his methods of careful study and comparison of symptoms he laid the foundations for clinical medicine. He discovered the phenomenon of crisis in disease and improved the practice of surgery. Though he had a wide knowledge of drugs, his chief reliances in treatment were diet and rest. The main fact to his discredit was his development of the theory of the four humors—the notion that illness is due to excessive amounts of yellow bile, black bile, blood, and phlegm in the system. The practice of bleeding the patient was the regrettable outgrowth of this theory.

Generally the most common medium of literary expression in the formative age of a people is the epic of heroic deeds. The most famous of the Greek epics, the *Iliad* and the *Odyssey,* were put into written form at the end of the eighth century B.C. and commonly attributed to Homer. The first, which deals with the Trojan War, has its theme in the wrath of Achilles; the second describes the wanderings and return of Odysseus. Both have supreme literary merit in their carefully woven plots, in the realism of their character portrayals, and in their mastery of the full range of emotional intensity. They exerted an almost incalculable influence upon later writers. Their style and language inspired the fervid emotional poetry of the sixth century B.C., and they were an unfailing source of plots and themes for the great tragedians of the Golden Age of the fifth century B.C.

The three centuries which followed the Dark Ages were distinguished, as we have already seen, by tremendous social changes. The rural pattern of life gave way to an urban society of steadily increasing complexity. The founding of colonies and the growth of commerce

Medicine

The Homeric epics

Development of the elegy

Interior of a Greek Cup. Depicted is the friendship of leading characters from the *Iliad:* Patroklus and Achilles. Here Achilles is bandaging Patroklus's wounds.

provided new interests and habits of living. Inevitably these changes were reflected in new forms of literature, especially of a more personal type. The first to be developed was the elegy, which was probably intended to be declaimed rather than sung to the accompaniment of music. Elegies varied in theme from individual reactions toward love to the idealism of patriots and reformers. Generally, however, they were devoted to melancholy reflection on the disillusionments of life or to bitter lament over the loss of prestige. Outstanding among the authors of elegiac verse was Solon the legislator.

Lyric poetry

In the sixth century B.C. and the early part of the fifth, the elegy found a rival in the lyric, which derives its name from the fact that it was sung to the music of the lyre. The new type of poetry was particularly well adapted to the expression of passionate feelings, the violent loves and hates engendered by the strife of classes. It was employed for other purposes also. Both Alcaeus and Sappho, the latter a woman poet from the island of Lesbos, used it to describe the poignant beauty of love, the delicate grace of spring, and the starlit splendor of a summer night. Meanwhile other poets developed the choral lyric, intended to express the feelings of the community rather than the sentiments of any one individual. Greatest of all the writers of this group was Pindar of Thebes, who wrote during the first half of the fifth century B.C. The lyrics of Pindar took the form of odes celebrating the victories of athletes and the glories of Greek civilization.

The origins of tragic drama

The supreme literary achievement of the Greeks was the tragic drama. Like so many of their other great works, it had its roots in religion. At the festivals dedicated to the worship of Dionysus, the god of spring and of wine, a chorus of men dressed as satyrs, or goat-men, sang and danced around an altar, enacting the various parts of a dithyramb or choral lyric that related the story of the god's career. In time a leader came to be separated from the chorus to recite the main parts of the story. The true drama was born about the beginning of the fifth century B.C. when Aeschylus introduced a second "actor" and relegated the chorus to the background. The name "tragedy," which came to be applied to this drama, was probably derived from the Greek word *tragos* meaning "goat."

Greek tragedy compared with modern tragedy

Greek tragedy stands out in marked contrast to the tragedies of Shakespeare or modern playwrights. There was, first of all, little action presented on the stage; the main business of the actors was to recite the incidents of a plot which was already familiar to the audience, for the story was drawn from popular legends. Second, Greek tragedy devoted little attention to the study of complicated individual personality. There was no development of character as shaped by the vicissitudes of a long career. Those involved in the plot were scarcely individuals at all, but types. On the stage they wore masks to disguise any characteristics which might serve to distinguish them too sharply from the rest of humanity. In addition, Greek tragedies differed from the modern variety in having as their theme the conflict between the individual and the universe, not the clash between personalities, or the internal conflicts of one person. The tragic fate that befell the main characters in these plays was external to individuals. It was brought on by the fact that someone had committed a crime against society, or against the gods, thereby violating the scheme of the universe. Punishment must follow in order to balance the scale of justice. Finally, the purpose of Greek tragedies was not merely to depict suffering and to interpret human actions, but to purify the emotions of the audience by representing the triumph of justice.

As already indicated, the first of the tragic dramatists was Aeschylus (525–456 B.C.). Though he is known to have written about eighty plays, only seven have survived in complete form, among them *Prometheus Bound* and a trilogy known as *The Oresteia*. Guilt and punishment is the recurrent theme of nearly all of them. The second of the leading tragedians, Sophocles (496–406 B.C.), is often considered the greatest. His style was more polished and his philosophy more profound than that of his predecessor. He was the author of over a hundred plays. More than any other Greek writer he expressed the ideal of "nothing too much." His attitude was distinguished by love of harmony and peace, intelligent respect for democracy, and profound sympathy for human weakness. The most famous of his plays are *Oedipus Rex* and *Antigone*.

The work of the last of the great tragedians, Euripides (480–406 B.C.), reflects a different spirit. He was a skeptic and individualist who took delight in ridiculing the ancient myths and the "sacred

Aeschylus and Sophocles

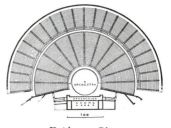

Epidauros Plan

Greek Theater in Epidauros. The construction, to take advantage of the slope of the hill, and the arrangement of the stage are of particular interest. Greek dramas were invariably presented in the open air.

cows" of his time. An embittered pessimist who suffered from the barbs of his conservative critics, he loved to humble the proud in his plays and exalt the lowly. He was the first to give the ordinary man, even the beggar and the peasant, a place in the drama. Euripides is also noted for his sympathy for the slave, for his condemnation of war, and for his protests against the exclusion of women from social and intellectual life. Because of his humanism, his tendency to portray men as they actually were (or even a little worse), and his introduction of the love motif into drama, he is often considered a modernist. It must be remembered, however, that in other respects his plays were perfectly consistent with the Greek model. They did not exhibit the evolution of individual character or the conflict of egos to any greater extent than did the works of Sophocles or Aeschylus. Nevertheless, he has been called the most tragic of the Greek dramatists because he dealt with situations having analogues in real life. Among the best-known tragedies of Euripides are *Alcestis, Medea,* and *The Trojan Women.*

Greek comedy, in common with tragedy, appears to have grown out of the Dionysian festivals, but it did not attain full development until late in the fifth century B.C. Its outstanding representative was Aristophanes (448?–380? B.C.), a somewhat coarse and belligerent aristocrat who lived in Athens. Most of his plays satirized the political and intellectual ideals of the radical democracy of his time. In *The Knights* he pilloried the incompetent and greedy politicians for their reckless adventures in imperialism. In *The Frogs* he lampooned Euripides's innovations in the drama. *The Clouds* he reserved for ridicule of the Sophists, ignorantly or maliciously classifying Socrates as one of them. While he was undoubtedly an imaginative and humorous writer, his thought tended toward caricature. He deserves much credit, however, for his sharp criticisms of the policies of the warhawks of Athens during the struggle with Sparta. Though written as a farce, his *Lysistrata* cleverly pointed a way—however infeasible—to the termination of any war: in this play wives refuse to have sexual relations with their husbands until the latter agree to make peace with their foreign enemies.

No account of Greek literature would be complete without some mention of the two great historians of the Golden Age. Herodotus, the "father of history" (c. 484–c. 420 B.C.), was a native of Halicarnassus in Asia Minor. He traveled extensively through the Persian empire, Egypt, Greece, and Italy, collecting a multitude of interesting data about various peoples. His famous account of the great war between the Greeks and the Persians included so much background that the work seems almost a history of the world. He regarded that war as an epic struggle between East and West, with Zeus giving victory to the Greeks against a mighty host of barbarians.

If Herodotus deserves to be called the father of history, much more does his younger contemporary, Thucydides (c. 460–c. 400 B.C.), deserve to be considered the founder of scientific history. Influenced by the skepticism and practicality of the Sophists, Thucydides chose to work on the basis of carefully sifted evidence, rejecting legends and hearsay. The subject of his *History* was the war between Sparta and Athens, which he described scientifically and dispassionately, emphasizing the complexity of causes which led to the clash. His aim was to present an accurate record which could be studied with profit by statesmen and generals of all time.

Thucydides

6. THE MEANING OF GREEK ART

Art as well as literature reflected the basic character of Hellenic civilization. The Greeks were essentially materialists who conceived of the world in physical terms. Plato and the followers of the mystic religions were exceptions, but few other Greeks believed in a universe of spiritual realities. It would be natural therefore to find that the material emblems of architecture and sculpture exemplified best the ideals the Greeks maintained.

Greek art as an expression of the Greek spirit

What did Greek art express? Above all, it symbolized humanism—the glorification of man as the most important creature in the universe. Though much of the sculpture depicted gods, and also goddesses, this did not detract in the slightest from its humanistic quality. The Greek deities existed for the benefit of man; in glorifying them he thus glorified himself. Both architecture and sculpture embodied the ideals of balance, harmony, order, and moderation. Anarchy and excess were abhorrent to the mind of the Greek, but so was absolute repression. Consequently, Greek art exhibited qualities of simplicity and dignified restraint—free from decorative extravagance on the one hand, and from restrictive conventions on the other. Moreover, Greek art was an expression of the national life. Its purpose was not merely aesthetic but political: to symbolize the pride of the people in their city and to enhance their consciousness of unity. The Parthenon at Athens, for example, was the temple of Athena, the protecting goddess who presided over the corporate life of the state. In providing her with a beautiful shrine which she might frequently visit, the Athenians were giving evidence of their love for their city and their hope for its continuing welfare.

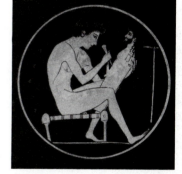

Greek Sculptor at Work. The Greeks were not prudish.

The art of the Greeks differed from that of nearly every people since their time in a variety of ways. Like the tragedies of Aeschylus and Sophocles, it was universal. It included few portraits either in sculpture or in painting. (Most of the portrait busts commonly considered Greek really belong to the Hellenistic Age.) The human beings depicted were generally types, not individuals. Again, Greek art differed from that of most later peoples in its ethical purpose. It was not art for the

Greek art compared with that of later peoples

See color plate facing page 166

sake of mere decoration or for the expression of the artist's own ideas, but a medium for the ennoblement of humanity. This does not mean that its merit depended upon the moral lesson it taught, but rather that it was supposed to exemplify qualities of living essentially artistic in themselves. The Athenian, at least, drew no sharp distinction between the ethical and aesthetic spheres; the beautiful and the good were really identical. True morality, therefore, consisted in rational living, in the avoidance of grossness, sensual excesses, and other forms of conduct aesthetically offensive. Finally, although the utmost attention was given to the depiction of beautiful bodies, this had little to do with fidelity to nature. The Greek was not interested in interpreting nature for its own sake, but in expressing *human* ideals.

The three periods of Greek art

The history of Greek art can be divided into three periods. The first covered the seventh and sixth centuries B.C. During the greater part of this so-called archaic period sculpture was dominated by Egyptian influence, as can be seen in the frontality and rigidity of the statues, with their square shoulders and one foot slightly advanced. Toward the end, however, these conventions were thrown aside. The chief architectural styles also had their origin in this period, and several crude temples were built. The second period, which occupied the fifth century B.C., witnessed the full perfection of both architecture and sculpture. The art of this time was completely idealistic. During the fourth century B.C., the last period of Greek art, architecture lost some of its balance and simplicity, and sculpture assumed new characteristics. It came to reflect more clearly the reactions of the individual artist, to incorporate more realism, and to lose some of its quality as an expression of civic pride.

Greek architecture

For all its artistic excellence, Greek temple architecture was extremely simple. Greek temples consisted of only five elements: (1) the cella or nucleus of the building, which was a rectangular chamber to house the statue of the god; (2) the columns, which formed the porch and surrounded the cella; (3) the entablature, which rested upon the columns and supported the roof; (4) the gabled roof itself; and (5) the pediment or triangular section under the gable of the roof. Two different architectural styles were developed, representing modifications of certain of these elements. The more common was the Doric, which

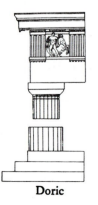

Doric

Ionic

Corinthian

Details of the Three Orders of Greek Architecture

The Parthenon. The largest and most famous of Athenian temples, the Parthenon is considered the classic example of Doric architecture. Its columns were made more graceful by tapering them in a slight curve toward the top. Its friezes and pediments were decorated with lifelike sculptures of prancing horses (see below), fighting giants, and benign and confident deities.

made use of a rather heavy, sharply fluted column surmounted by a plain capital. The other, the Ionic, had more slender and more graceful columns with flat flutings, a triple base, and a scroll or volute capital. The so-called Corinthian style, which was chiefly Hellenistic, differed from the Ionic primarily in being more ornate. The three styles differed also in their treatment of the entablature. In the Ionic style it was left almost plain. In the Doric and Corinthian styles it bore sculptured reliefs. The Parthenon, the best example of Greek architecture, was essentially a Doric building, but it reflected some of the grace and subtlety of Ionic influence.

According to the prevailing opinion among his contemporaries, Greek sculpture attained its height in the work of Phidias (c. 500–c. 432 B.C.). His masterpieces were the statue of Athena in the Parthenon and the statue of Zeus in the Temple of Olympian Zeus. In addition, he designed the Parthenon reliefs. The main qualities of his work are grandeur of conception, patriotism, proportion, dignity, and restraint. Nearly all of his figures are idealized representations of deities and mythological creatures in human form. The second most renowned fifth-century sculptor was Myron, noted for his statue of the discus thrower and for his glorification of other athletic types. The names of three great sculptors in the fourth century B.C. have come down to us. The most gifted was Praxiteles, renowned for his portrayal of humanized deities with slender, graceful bodies and countenances of

Parthenon Frieze

Greek sculpture

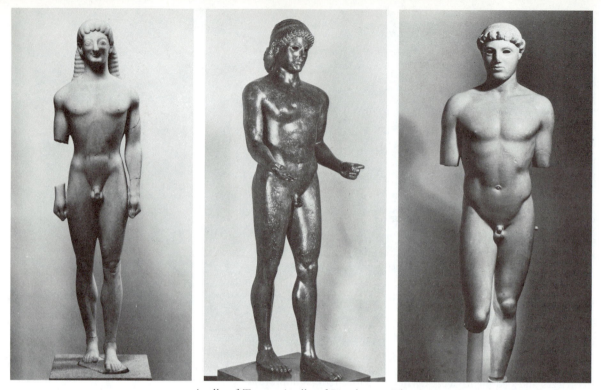

Apollo of Tenea; Apollo of Piombino; "The Critian Boy." These three statues, dating from about 560, 500, and 480 B.C. respectively, display the progressive "unfreezing" of Greek statuary art. The first stiff and symmetrical statue is imitative of Egyptian sculpture (see statue of the Pharoah Mycerinus, p. 69 above). Roughly half a century later it is succeeded by a figure which begins to display motion, as if awakening from a sleep of centuries in a fairy tale. The last figure introduces genuine naturalism in its delicate twists and depiction of the subject's weight resting on one leg.

philosophic repose. His older contemporary, Scopas, gained distinction as an emotional sculptor. One of his most successful creations was the statue of a religious ecstatic, a worshiper of Dionysus, in a condition of mystic frenzy. At the end of the century Lysippus pioneered in sculptural realism and individualism. He was the first great master of the realistic portrait as a study of personal character.

7. ATHENIAN LIFE IN THE GOLDEN AGE

The population of Athens in the fifth and fourth centuries B.C. comprised three groups: the citizens, the metics, and the slaves. The citizens, who numbered at the most about 40,000, included only those males born of citizen parents, except for the few who were occasionally enfranchised by special law. (Counting the families of citizens, there were roughly 200,000 Athenians of the citizen class.) The metics, who probably did not exceed a total of 35,000, were resident aliens, chiefly non-Athenian Greeks. Save for the fact that they had no political

Athenian classes

privileges and generally were not permitted to own land, male metics had equal opportunities with citizens. They could engage in any occupation they desired and participate in any social or intellectual activities. Contrary to a popular tradition, the slaves in Athens were never a majority of the population. Their maximum number did not exceed 100,000. Urban slaves, at least, were not shamefully treated and were sometimes rewarded for faithful service by being set free. The males could work for wages and own property. The treatment of slaves who worked in the mines, however, was often cruel.

Life in Athens stands out in sharp contrast to that in most other civilizations. One of its leading features was the great amount of social and economic equality that prevailed among most of the male citizens. Nearly all ate the same kind of food, wore the same kind of clothing, and participated in the same kind of amusement. This substantial equality was enforced in part by the system of *liturgies,* which were services to the state rendered by wealthy men, chiefly in the form of contributions to support the drama, equip the navy, or provide for the poor.

The large degree of social and economic equality

A second outstanding characteristic of Athenian life was its lack of comforts and luxuries. Part of this was a result of the low income of the mass of the people. Teachers, sculptors, masons, carpenters, and

Left: *The Discobolus or Discus Thrower of Myron.* The statue reflects the glorification of the human body characteristic of Athens in the Golden Age. Now in the Vatican Museum. Right: *Hermes with the Infant Dionysus, by Praxiteles, Fourth Century* B.C. Original in the Olympia Museum, Greece.

Men Weighing Goods on a Balance-Scale. From a pottery decoration of about 550 B.C.

The modesty of Athenian life

common laborers all received the same low standard wage. Part of it may have been a consequence also of the mild climate, which allowed for a life of simplicity. But whatever the cause, the fact remains that, in comparison with modern standards, the Athenians made do with the barest essentials. They knew nothing of such commodities as clocks, soap, newspapers, cotton cloth, sugar, tea, or coffee. Their beds had no springs, their houses had no drains, and their food consisted chiefly of barley cakes, onions, and fish, washed down with diluted wine. From the standpoint of clothing they were no better off. A rectangular piece of cloth wrapped around the body and fastened with pins at the shoulders and with a rope around the waist served as the main garment. A larger piece was draped around the body as an extra garment for outdoor wear. No one wore either stockings or socks, and few had any footgear except sandals.

Indifference toward material comforts and wealth

But lack of luxury was a matter of little consequence to the Athenian citizen. Instead his aim was to live as interestingly and contentedly as possible without spending all his days working for the sake of a little more comfort for his family or of piling up riches as a source of power or prestige. What each citizen really wanted was a small farm or business that would provide him with a reasonable income and at the same time allow him an abundance of leisure for politics, for gossip in the marketplace, and for intellectual or artistic activities if he had the talent to enjoy them.

The basic economic activities

In spite of the expansion of trade, Athenian economic organization never became very complex. Agriculture and commerce were by far the most important enterprises. Even in Pericles's day the majority of the citizens still lived in the country. Industry was not highly developed. Few examples of large-scale production are on record, and those chiefly in the manufacture of pottery and implements of war. The largest establishment that ever existed was apparently a shield factory owned by a metic and employing 120 slaves. No other was more than half as large. The enterprises which absorbed the most labor were the mines, but they were owned by the state and leased in sections to small contractors to be worked by slaves. The bulk of industry was carried on in shops owned by individual craftsmen who produced their wares directly to the order of the consumer.

Religion underwent some notable changes in the Golden Age of the fifth and fourth centuries B.C. The polytheism and anthropomorphism of earlier times were largely supplanted by a belief in one God as the creator and sustainer of the moral law. Other significant consequences flowed from the mystery cults. These new forms of religion first became popular in the sixth century B.C. because of the craving for an emotional faith to make up for the disappointments of life. One was the Orphic cult, which revolved around the myth of the death and resurrection of Dionysus. Another, the Eleusinian cult, had as its central theme the abduction of Persephone by Hades, god of the nether world, and her ultimate redemption by Demeter, the great Earth Mother. Both of these cults had as their original purpose worship of the life-giving powers of nature, but in time they came to express a much deeper significance. They communicated to their followers the ideas of vicarious atonement, salvation in an afterlife, and ecstatic union with the divine. Although entirely inconsistent with the spirit of the ancient religion, they made a powerful appeal to certain classes and were largely responsible for the spread of the belief in personal immortality. The more thoughtful Greeks, however, seem to have persisted in their adherence to the worldly, optimistic, and mechanical faith of their ancestors and to have shown little concern about sin or a desire for salvation in a life to come.

It remains to consider briefly the position of the family in Athens in the fifth and fourth centuries B.C. Though marriage was still an important institution for the procreation of children who would become citizens of the state, there is reason to believe that family life had declined. Men of the more prosperous classes, at least, now spent the greater part of their time away from their families. Wives were

Changes in religion

Head of Persephone. Obverse of a coin struck by the Greek city of Syracuse on the island of Sicily around 310 B.C.

The family in Athens in the Golden Age

Music and Poetry in Everyday Greek Life. The Greeks proudly used pottery design to depict their daily activities. Here a musician entertains a boy while a poet writes verses for another boy. The homoerotic implications of such scenes were intentional.

relegated to an inferior position and required to remain secluded in their homes. Their place as social and intellectual companions for their husbands was taken by alien women, the *hetaerae,* many of whom were highly cultured natives of the Ionian cities of Asia Minor. Marriage itself assumed the character of a political and economic arrangement devoid of romantic elements. Men married wives so as to ensure that at least some of their children would be legitimate and in order to obtain property in the form of a dowry. It was important also, of course, to have someone to care for the household. But husbands did not consider their wives as their equals and did not appear in public with them or encourage their participation in any form of social or intellectual activity.

8. THE GREEK ACHIEVEMENT AND ITS SIGNIFICANCE FOR US

The magnitude of the Greek achievement

No historian would deny that the achievement of the Greeks was one of the most remarkable in the history of the world. With no great expanse of fertile soil or abundance of mineral resources, they succeeded in developing a higher and more varied civilization than any that came before them. With only a limited cultural inheritance from the past to build upon, they produced intellectual and artistic achievements which have served ever since as models of attainment for the culture of the West. It may be argued as well that the Greeks achieved a more leisured and rational mode of living than most other peoples who took center stage upon this planet. The infrequency of brutal crimes and the contentment with simple amusements and modest wealth all point to a comparatively happy and satisfied existence.

Undesirable features of Greek life

It is necessary to be on guard, however, against uncritical adulation of the ancient Greeks. We must not assume that all were as cultured and free as the citizens of Athens and of the Ionian states across the Aegean. The Spartans, the Arcadians, the Thessalians, and the majority of the Boeotians remained much less culturally advanced. Further, Athenian civilization itself surely had its defects. It permitted some exploitation of the weak, especially of the slaves who toiled in the mines. It was based upon a principle of racial exclusiveness which reckoned every man a foreigner whose parents were not both Athenians, and consequently denied political rights to the majority of the inhabitants. It was also characterized by the overt repression of the female members of the society. Its statecraft was not sufficiently enlightened to avoid the pitfalls of imperialism and aggressive war. Finally, the attitude of its citizens was not always tolerant and just. Socrates was put to death for his opinions, and two other philosophers, Anaxagoras and Protagoras, were forced to leave the city. It must be conceded, however, that the record of the Athenians for tolerance was better than that of most other peoples, both ancient and modern.

There was probably more freedom of expression in Athens during the war with Sparta than there was in the United States during World War I.

Nor is it true that the Greek influence has been as great as is often supposed. No well-informed student could accept the sentimental verdict of Shelley: "We are all Greeks; our laws, our literature, our religion, our arts have their roots in Greece." Our laws do not really have their roots in Greece but chiefly in Roman sources. Much of our poetry is undoubtedly Greek in inspiration, but such is not the case with most of our prose literature. Our religion is no more than partly Greek; except as it was influenced by Plato and the Romans, it reflects primarily the spirit of the Hebrews. Even our arts derive from other sources almost as much as from Greece. Actually, modern civilization has been the result of the convergence of numerous influences coming from many different periods and places.

Nonetheless, the Greek adventure was of profound significance for the history of the world because the Greeks were the founders of numerous ideals commonly thought of as being central to the dignity and progress of humanity. This can be seen with particular clarity by a comparison of cultural traits characteristic of Mesopotamia and Egypt with those of the Greeks. The civilizations of Mesopotamia and Egypt were dominated by absolutism, supernaturalism, and the subjection of the individual to the group. It is noteworthy that the Greek word for freedom—*eleutheria*—cannot be translated into any ancient Near Eastern language, not even Hebrew. The typical political regime of western Asia was that of an absolute monarch supported by a powerful priesthood. Culture served mainly as an instrument to magnify the power of the state and to enhance the prestige of rulers and priests. In contrast, the civilization of Greece, notably in its Athenian form, was founded upon ideals of freedom, optimism, secularism, rationalism, the glorification of both body and mind, and

Greek influence sometimes exaggerated

Contrast of Greek and Near Eastern ideals

The Acropolis Today. Occupying the commanding position is the Parthenon. To the left is the Erechtheum with its Porch of the Maidens facing the Parthenon.

a high regard for the dignity and worth of the individual. Insofar as anyone other than a slave was repressed, his subjection was to the rule of the majority. As Herodotus made not an Athenian but a Spartan say to a Persian: "You understand how to be a slave, but you know nothing of freedom. . . . if you had but tasted it you would counsel us to fight for it not only with spears but with axes." The Greeks also had an extraordinary respect for the rule of law. In contrast to western Asian peoples, they kept their priests in the background, refusing to allow them to govern the realm of the intellect or to have any control over the sphere of morality. The culture of the Greeks was the first to be based upon the primacy of intellect—upon the supremacy of the spirit of free inquiry. There was no subject they feared to investigate, or any question they regarded as beyond the province of reason. To an extent never before realized, mind was supreme over faith, logic and science over superstition.

The tragedy of Greek history

The supreme tragedy of the Greeks was, of course, their failure to solve the problem of political conflict. To a large degree, this conflict was the product of social and cultural dissimilarities. Because of different geographic and economic conditions the Greek city-states developed at an uneven pace. Some went forward rapidly to high levels of cultural superiority, while others lagged behind and made little or no intellectual progress. The consequences were discord and suspicion, which gave rise eventually to hatred and fear. Though some of the more advanced thinkers attempted to propagate the notion that the Greeks were one people who should reserve their contempt for non-Greeks, or "barbarians," the conception never became part of a national ethos. Athenians hated Spartans, and vice versa, almost as vehemently as they hated Persians. Not even the danger of Asian conquest sufficed to dispel the distrust and antagonism of Greeks for one another. Thus the war that finally broke out between Athens and Sparta sealed the doom of Hellenic civilization even though Greece remained undefeated by foreigners.

SELECTED READINGS

• *Items so designated are available in paperback editions.*

• Andrewes, A., *The Greeks,* New York, 1967. An excellent, up-to-date account of archaic and classical Greek history from about 750 to 350 B.C.

• Austin, M., and P. Vidal-Naquet, *The Economic and Social History of Ancient Greece,* Berkeley, 1977.

• Boardman, J., *Greek Art,* New York, 1964.

• _____, *The Greeks Overseas,* rev. ed., London, 1982. The standard treatment of Greek colonization.

Burn, A. R., *The Lyric Age of Greece,* New York, 1961. A lively introduction to the seventh and sixth centuries B.C.

- Davies, J. K., *Democracy and Classical Greece,* Glasgow, 1978.
- Dodds, E. R., *The Greeks and the Irrational,* Berkeley, 1963. A novel approach to classical Greek culture.

  Dover, K. J., *Greek Homosexuality,* Cambridge, Mass., 1978. A serious analysis of a basic aspect of classical Greek life.
- _____, et al., *Ancient Greek Literature,* Oxford, 1980.
- Ehrenberg, V., *From Solon to Socrates,* New York, 1967. An excellent treatment of early Athenian history by one of the twentieth century's leading authorities.
- Finley, M. I., *The Ancient Greeks: An Introduction to Their Life and Thought,* New York, 1963. An expert brief introduction to the Greeks.
- _____, *The World of Odysseus,* rev. ed., New York, 1978. Attempts to use the Homeric poems as a guide to Dark Ages Greece.

  Foley, H. P., *Reflections of Women in Antiquity,* New York, 1981.

  Forrest, W. G., *The Emergence of Greek Democracy,* London, 1966. An engaging account of the origins of democratic ideas and practices.
- _____, *A History of Sparta, 950–192 B.C.,* London, 1969.
- Guthrie, W. K. C., *The Greeks and Their Gods,* Boston, 1965.
- Jones, A. H. M., *Athenian Democracy,* New York, 1957. Concentrates on actual political practice.
- Kitto, H. D. F., *The Greeks,* Baltimore, 1957. A delightfully written, highly personal interpretation.
- Lacey, W. K., *The Family in Classical Greece,* Ithaca, N.Y., 1968.
- Lloyd, G. E. R., *Early Greek Science: Thales to Aristotle,* London, 1970.
- Marrou, H. I., *A History of Education in Antiquity,* New York, 1964. A modern classic that covers the entire ancient world.
- Meiggs, R., *The Athenian Empire,* Oxford, 1972. The major study of fifth century Athenian imperialism; a monumental work.

  Michell, H., *The Economics of Ancient Greece,* rev. ed., Cambridge, 1956.
- Murray, O., *Early Greece,* Glasgow, 1980. An excellent analytical narrative of early Greek history before the fifth century B.C.

  Nilsson, M. P., *A History of Greek Religion,* New York, 1964.
- Pollitt, J. J., *Art and Experience in Classical Greece,* Cambridge, 1972. The best introduction to the social and intellectual forces behind Greek art.
- Pomeroy, Sarah B., *Goddesses, Whores, Wives, and Slaves: Women in Classical Antiquity,* New York, 1975. The best treatment of the role of women in Greece and Rome. Relies on a variety of source material and covers women of all classes.

  Rose, H. J., *A Handbook of Greek Literature,* New York, 1960.
- _____, *A Handbook of Greek Mythology,* New York, 1959.
- Sealey, R., *A History of the Greek City States, ca. 700–338 B.C.,* Berkeley, 1977. A provocative account that reconsiders older assumptions about Greek political life.

  Sinclair, T. A., *A History of Greek Political Thought,* London, 1951.

  Snell, Bruno, *The Discovery of the Mind: The Greek Origins of European Thought,* Cambridge, Mass., 1953. Stimulating essays.
- Snodgrass, A. M., *Archaic Greece,* London, 1980.
- Starr, C. G., *The Economic and Social Growth of Early Greece: 800–500 B.C.,* New York, 1978. An excellent study of this difficult but important topic.

  _____, *The Origins of Greek Civilization, 1100–650 B.C.,* New York, 1961. The best detailed treatment of the early periods.

SOURCE MATERIALS

Most Greek authors have been translated in the appropriate volumes of the
Loeb Classical Library, Harvard University Press.

In addition the following may be helpful:

- Barnstone, Willis, tr., *Greek Lyric Poetry,* New York, 1962.
  Kagan, Donald, *Sources in Greek Political Thought,* Glencoe, Ill., 1965.
- Lattimore, R., tr., *Greek Lyrics,* Chicago, 1960.
- _____, tr., *The Iliad,* Chicago, 1961.
- _____, tr., *The Odyssey,* New York, 1968.

Chapter 8

THE HELLENISTIC CIVILIZATION

Alexander wept when he heard from Anaxarchus that there was an infinite number of worlds. When his friends asked if any accident had befallen him, he answered: "Do you not think it a matter worthy of lamentation that when there is such a vast multitude of them, we have not yet conquered one?"

—Plutarch, *On the Tranquillity of the Mind*

G ravely weakened from the military and political point of view by the wars between cities that transpired virtually without interruption from 431 B.C. until 338 B.C., Greek civilization was simultaneously rescued and transformed by one of the most remarkable characters who ever trod on the world's stage, a young man known to posterity as Alexander the Great. In 338 B.C. Alexander's father, Philip of Macedon, a semibarbarian chieftain from the rocky wildernesses north of Greece, reduced all Greece to his will by decisively defeating a combined Athenian-Theban force in pitched battle. Two years later Philip was murdered as the result of a family feud, and his dashingly handsome and energetic son Alexander succeeded him at the age of twenty. Swiftly consolidating his own autocratic rule over all of Greece by putting to death all possible rivals, in 334 B.C. Alexander felt secure enough to leave behind a trusted deputy and cross with an army of 40,000 troops into Asia to carve out some additional territory. The Persians may at first have looked askance at this brash twenty-two-year-old advancing in their direction, but within four years, as the victor of three brilliantly fought battles— the Granicus (334), Issus (333), and Gaugamela (331)—Alexander had conquered the entire Persian Empire inclusive of Asia Minor, Egypt, Syria, Mesopotamia, and Persia itself. Rather than returning home or residing peacefully in the Persian capital of Persepolis after

The exploits of Alexander the Great

Marble Head of Alexander. Alexander the Great was understood to have been very handsome, but all surviving representations doubtless make him more handsome still. This one dates from about 180 B.C. and is typical in showing Alexander with "lion's-mane hair."

The hybrid nature of Hellenistic civilization

The rise of Cyrus

this whirlwind campaign, Alexander then marched farther east to conquer Bactria (modern Afghanistan) and cross the Indus River into India, spending two years (327–326 B.C.) trying to destroy Hindu armies equipped with war elephants. When Alexander's troops finally refused to fight any more in lands so distant from their native grounds, he toured them back to the Persian heartland and died of an infectious disease in 323 B.C. in Babylon while preparing for another expansionist campaign—this time to Arabia. Although Alexander supposedly wept because he had not conquered the world, between the ages of twenty-two and thirty-three he had traversed some 20,000 miles, fighting as he went, to become the ruler of the largest empire the world had ever seen.

As a by-product of his conquests, Alexander laid the foundations for the *Hellenistic civilization,* a civilization that endured from his own time until roughly the beginning of the Christian era in all the lands of the eastern Mediterranean and western Asia. The term "Hellenistic" means "Greek-like," and stands in contrast to "Hellenic," or purely Greek. Hellenistic civilization was "Greek-like" because it was a hybrid, composed of Greek and Asian elements. For example, Alexander himself spoke Greek and had been educated by none other than the great Greek philosopher Aristotle, yet he ignored the Greek precepts of modesty and living according to the "golden mean" by naming cities after himself (most notably Alexandria in Egypt, but also several other Alexandrias in Asia) and decking himself out in Oriental finery. Similarly, during the Hellenistic era Greek became the language of government in Mesopotamia, Syria, and Egypt, and Greek philosophy and literature were cultivated throughout western Asia, yet Greek-speaking rulers insisted upon being adored as divinities. We will presently see that Hellenistic culture was not just a hodgepodge but had its own distinctive traits. Before we examine the fascinating Hellenistic civilization itself, however, it is necessary to take account of its Persian background because just as the Hellenistic world could not have existed without Alexander the Great and the Greeks, so it could not have existed without the prior accomplishments of Cyrus the Great and the Persians.

1. THE PERSIAN EMPIRE

Almost nothing is known of the Persians before the middle of the sixth century B.C., other than that they lived on the eastern shore of the Persian Gulf, spoke an Indo-European language, and were subject to the Medes, a kindred people who inhabited territories east and north of the River Tigris. Out of this obscurity the Persians emerged suddenly into the spotlight of history owing to the extraordinary exploits of a prince named Cyrus, who succeeded to the rule of a southern Persian tribe in 559 B.C. Swiftly thereafter Cyrus made himself ruler of all the Persians, and around 549 B.C. he threw off the lordship of the Medes, taking over their domination of lands that stretched from the Persian Gulf to the Halys River in Asia Minor.

By occupying part of Asia Minor Cyrus became a neighbor of the kingdom of Lydia, which then comprised the western half of Asia Minor up to the Halys. The Indo-European Lydians had created one of the successor states of the Hittites and had attained great prosperity as a result of gold-prospecting and acting as intermediaries for overland commerce passing between Mesopotamia and the Aegean Sea. In connection with their commercial enterprises the Lydians invented the use of metallic coinage as a medium of exchange for goods and services—their single enduring contribution to the progress of humanity. When Cyrus reached their border, the reigning king of the Lydians was Croesus (pronounced Creesus), so rich that the simile "rich as Croesus" remains embedded in our language. Distrusting the newcomer, Croesus decided in 546 B.C. to wage a preventive war in order to preserve his kingdom from conquest. According to the Greek historian Herodotus, Croesus consulted the oracle at Delphi as to the advisability of an immediate attack and gained the reply that if he would cross the Halys he would destroy a great nation. He did, but the nation he destroyed was his own. His forces were completely overwhelmed, and his prosperous realm was annexed as a province of the Persian state.

As we have seen earlier, Cyrus invaded Mesopotamia in 539 B.C. and struck so quickly that he was able to take Babylon without a fight. Once in Babylon the entire New Babylonian Empire of Nebuchadnezzar was his. We have also seen that Cyrus allowed the Jews who had been held captive in Babylon to return to Palestine and set up a semi-independent vassal state; here it can be added that Cyrus allowed other conquered peoples considerable self-determination as well. Dying in 529 of wounds incurred in a minor skirmish with barbarian tribes to the north of his realms near the Aral Sea, Cyrus left behind him an empire vaster than any that had previously existed. Yet shortly afterward, in 525, the Persian Empire became vaster still when Cyrus's son Cambyses conquered all of Egypt.

Cambyses's successor, Darius I, who ruled Persia from 521 to 486 B.C., concentrated on consolidating his predecessors' military gains by improving the administration of the Persian state. Darius the Great, as he is usually called, presided over the division of the empire into provinces, known as *satrapies,* administered by governors called *satraps,* who were accorded extensive powers but who were obliged to send fixed annual tributes to the central government. (Vassal states such as the Jewish kingdom were obliged to send the Persian government annual tributes as well.) Adhering to the tolerant policy of Cyrus, Darius allowed the various non-Persian peoples of the Persian Empire to retain most of their local institutions while enforcing a standardized currency and system of weights and measures. For example, Darius's

The annexation of Lydia

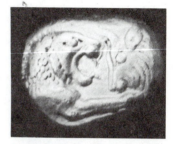

An Early Lydian Coin, Probably Struck during the Reign of Croesus

Cyrus's conquests and the policy of self-determination

Consolidation of the Persian Empire under Darius the Great

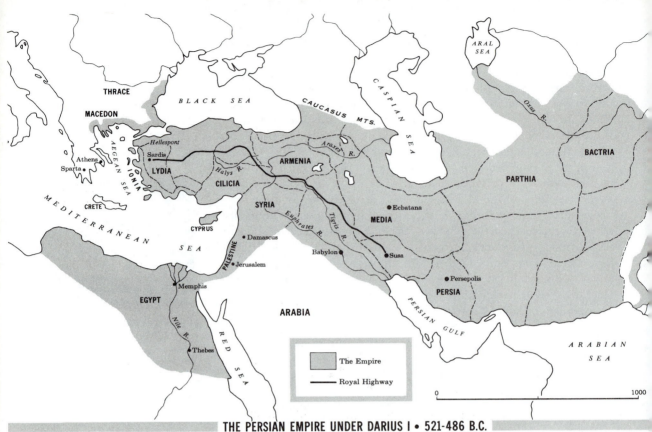

THE PERSIAN EMPIRE UNDER DARIUS I • 521-486 B.C.

satrap of Egypt restored ancient Egyptian temples and codified Egyptian laws in consultation with native priests.

Darius was also a great builder. He erected a new royal residence, called by the Greeks Persepolis ("Persian City"), which thereafter became the Persian ceremonial capital. Additionally he dug a canal from the Nile to the Red Sea and installed irrigation systems on the Persian plateau and on the fringe of the Syrian desert. Most impressive of Darius's public works was his system of roads, intended to enhance trade and communications in his far-flung realms. Justly the most famous was the "Royal Road" spanning 1,600 miles from Susa near the Persian Gulf to Sardis near the Aegean. Government couriers along this road comprised the first "postal system" because they passed messages and goods in relay stages from one *post* to another, with each post measured by the distance traversable in a day's horseback ride: a fresh horse and rider would be ready at each post to carry what had been brought by the "postman" before him. Few people today realize that the motto of the U.S. Post Office is borrowed from Herodotus's praise for the Persian messengers on the Royal Road: "neither snow nor rain nor heat nor gloom of night stays these couriers from the swift completion of their appointed rounds."

Darius as a builder

Extraordinarily gifted as an administrator, Darius the Great made one enormous mistake in geopolitical strategy: his attempt to extend Persian hegemony into Greece. After Cyrus's conquest of Lydia had made Persia the ruler of Greek-speaking cities on the western coast of Asia Minor, no matter how tolerant Persia's rule was, these cities wished to gain their freedom in view of the freedom of all other Greek city-states. Consequently, between 499 and 494 B.C. the Greeks on the Asian mainland waged a war for independence and briefly gained the support of troops from Athens, who joined the Asian Greeks in burning Sardis, the Persian regional administrative center. After Darius had quelled the uprising he decided to see to it that his Greek subjects would never again receive foreign Greek aid by sending a force across the Aegean in 490 to punish Athens and let all European Greeks know that henceforth he intended to be their overlord. Amazingly the Athenians defeated the Persian force in 490 at the battle of Marathon, dealing Darius the only major setback he had ever experienced. Although in 480 his son and successor, Xerxes I (486–465 B.C.), attempted to avenge the humiliation by crushing all Greece with a tremendous army, heroic resistance by both Athens and Sparta forced him a year later to retreat and abandon his plans. At that point the Persians must have realized that the limits of their expansionism had been reached, and, worse, that they now had to beware of the European Greeks as their implacable enemies.

In fact from 479 B.C. until Alexander the Great's invasion of Asia Minor in 334 B.C. the Greeks were usually too embroiled by internal rivalries to pose any aggressive challenge to Persia. From the Persian

Greek resistance to Persian overlordship

The Great Palace of Darius and Xerxes at Persepolis. Persian architecture made use of fluted columns, copied from the Greeks, and reliefs resembling those of the Assyrians.

perspective that was extremely fortunate, for during the period in question the Persian Empire was beset by mounting governmental instability caused by intrigues for the throne and rebellions in various provinces. Thus by the time of Alexander, although the empire had survived intact, it had become extremely rickety. Nonetheless, when Alexander gained the expanses won by Cyrus he also gained two intangible legacies—one religious, the other broadly cultural.

Persia's religious legacy was Zoroastrianism, which along with Buddhism and Judaism, was one of the three major *universal* and *personal* religions known to the world before Christianity and Islam. Although distant origins of Zoroastrianism can be traced back as far as the sixteenth century B.C., the religion's real founder, and the one who gave it its name, was Zoroaster (the Greek form of the Persian name Zarathustra), a Persian who seems to have lived shortly before 600 B.C. (There is scholarly disagreement on the latter point: some authorities argue for a date many centuries earlier.) Zoroaster was probably the first real theologian in history, the first known person to devise a fully developed system of religious belief. He seems to have conceived it as his mission to purify the traditional customs of the Persian tribes— to eradicate polytheism, animal sacrifice, and magic—and to establish their worship on a more coherent and ethical plane.

Zoroastrianism was a universal religion inasmuch as Zoroaster taught that there was one supreme god in the universe, whom he called Ahura-Mazda, meaning "the wise lord." Ahura-Mazda embodied the principles of light, truth, and righteousness—there was nothing wrathful, let alone evil, about him, and his light shone everywhere, not just upon one tribe or another. In view of the fact that sin or sorrow in the world could not be explained by reference to Ahura-Mazda, Zoroaster posited the existence of a counter-deity, Ahriman, treacherous and malignant, who presided over the forces of darkness and evil. Apparently in Zoroaster's own view Ahura-Mazda was vastly stronger than Ahriman, whom Ahura-Mazda allowed to exist almost by absent-mindedness, but the priests of Zoroastrianism, known as *magi,* gradually came to emphasize the dualistic aspect of the founder's thought by insisting that Ahura-Mazda and Ahriman were about evenly matched, and were engaged in a desperate struggle for supremacy. According to them, only on the last great day would "light" decisively triumph over "darkness," when Ahura-Mazda would overpower Ahriman and cast him down into the abyss.

In both its less dualistic and more dualistic forms Zoroastrianism was a thoroughly personal religion, by which is meant that it made private rather than public demands and offered private rewards. Specifically, Zoroastrianism assumed that Ahura-Mazda patronized neither tribes nor states but only individuals who served his cause of truth and justice. Humans possessed free will and were free to sin or not to sin. Of course Zoroastrianism urged them not to sin but to be truthful, to love and help one another to the best of their powers, to aid the poor, and to practice generous hospitality. Those who did so would be rewarded in an afterlife, for the religion assumed the resurrection of the dead on "judgment day" and their consignment either to a realm of bliss or a realm of flames. In the scriptures of the Zoroastrian faith known as the *Avesta* (a work compiled by accretion over the course of many centuries) the rewards for righteousness are made perfectly explicit: "Whosoever shall give meat to one of the faithful . . . he shall go to Paradise."

The brief recital of Zoroastrianism's tenets makes clear that the religion bore numerous similarities to Judaism and Christianity. Zoroastrianism's ethical content resembles the teachings of the Jewish prophets, its eschatology resembles aspects of post-exilic Judaism, and its heaven and hell resemble aspects of the afterlife teaching of Christianity. Even the existence of authoritative scriptures in Zoroastrianism is reminiscent of the weight accorded by Jews to the Old Testament and by Christians to the Old Testament and the New. Unfortunately it is not possible to determine with any precision in what direction influences may have flown because of nearly insuperable chronological complexities. Yet it is surely not coincidental that central aspects of Jewish religious thought took shape in an Asian world dominated by Cyrus and Darius—both convinced Zoroastrians—or that later Jewish beliefs about a judgment day, which themselves influenced Christianity, evolved in a Hellenistic world in which Zoroastrianism continued to exert influence. Furthermore, entirely aside from likely Zoroastrian influence on Judaism, the Persian faith exerted some influence on western Asia's Greek conquerors in encouraging them to think of religion in ever more universalistic and personal terms.

Universalism is also the expression that best characterizes Persia's cultural contribution to the Hellenistic synthesis. Unlike the Assyrians, the New Babylonians, and the Egyptians, all of whom tried to impose their own customs on conquered peoples (when they did not simply enslave them), the Persians adopted a tolerant "One World" policy, by which they conceived themselves to be the guiding force over an assemblage of united nations. Whereas Mesopotamian potentates characteristically called themselves "true king," the rulers of the Persian Empire took the title "King of Kings," thereby implying that they recognized the continued existence of various peoples with various rulers under the canopy of their rule. Moreover, the greatest Persian monarchs, Cyrus and Darius, continually sought to learn whatever they could from the customs and the science of the peoples they conquered. For example, they adopted and diffused the Lydian invention of metallic coinage, learned to chart the night skies from Babylonian astronomers, and commissioned Phoenician sailors to embark on exploratory voyages.

The Persian habit of borrowing ideas from others, known technically as eclecticism, can be observed particularly clearly in the evidence of architecture. The Persians copied the raised platform and the terraced

Persian Gold Drinking Cup. Persian fondness for lions probably derived from the art of the Assyrians.

Zoroastrianism's similarities to Judaism and Christianity

Persian Griffin. Typical Persian ornamentation dating from about 500 B.C.

Two Reliefs from the Staircase of the Great Palace at Persepolis

The eclectic character of Persian architecture

building style that had been standard in Babylonia, and they also imitated the winged bulls, the brilliantly colored glazed bricks, and other decorative motifs of Mesopotamian architecture. Yet in place of the Mesopotamian arch and vault they adopted the column and the colonnade from Egypt. In addition, interior arrangement and the use of palm and lotus designs at the base of columns also derived from Egyptian influence. Finally, the fluting of the columns and the scrolls beneath the capitals were not Egyptian, but Greek, adopted not from the mainland of Greece but from the Greek cities of Asia Minor. With Alexander's arrival the Persians would become directly subject to the mainland Greeks, but the Greeks would immediately begin borrowing from the Persians.

2. PHILIP OF MACEDON AND ALEXANDER THE GREAT

Political division in Greece

Throughout the first two-thirds of the fourth century B.C. many Greeks took to heart a verse from Euripides's play *Andromache*, "In Greece, alas! how ill things ordered are!" but none seemed able to do much about it. Greece's "ill order" was its political division: city fought city and faction fought faction. As Thebes warred with Sparta and Athens warred with Thebes, ever more Greeks began to long for a national "strong man" to quell all strife, however much imperialism and tyranny were at variance with pristine Greek ideals. Finally a strong man appeared in the person of Philip of Macedon.

Had Philip's fame not been overshadowed by that of his son Alexander, he surely would have been known as Philip the Great. Before he assumed rule in Macedon in 359 B.C. the Greek-speaking territory north of Greece had no cities, little agriculture, and no political stability, being little more than a warring-ground for rival clans. Yet by sheer force of will Philip transformed Macedon into a major power within two decades. First he eliminated all his rivals, then he introduced autocratic institutions of government, and then he began to expand his frontiers by a combination of military skill and "divide and conquer" diplomacy. Philip's fighting style led to a revolution in the art of warfare, as contemporaries themselves recognized. Hitherto the Greeks had formed their armies almost exclusively from citizen-volunteers and conscripts, all of whom could fight for only part of the year because they could not abandon their crops during farming seasons. With limited periods of training, almost all soldiers in such Greek armies fought the same way, as massed infantry with heavy arms. In contrast, drawing partly on mercenaries and partly on loyal Macedonians who had no farming commitments, Philip built a professional army.

The advantages of the Macedonian professional army, an army that later served Alexander the Great as well as Philip, were manifold. For one, the commander of such a force could count on a wide range of "specialists." Philip's army had an effective mobile cavalry and it had *skirmishers*—fighters whose goal was to demoralize and confuse the enemy at the onset of battle by distracting them with a rain of projectiles coming from the wrong part of the field. Not least among Philip's specialists were well-trained spies and counter-spies, adept at the art of spreading "disinformation." Another advantage of professionalism was that one could impose the strictest discipline. Free Greeks who volunteered for service might, from idealism, have imposed some discipline on themselves, yet it would have been difficult for a commander to address them peremptorily, and their idealism would have tended to diminish in inverse proportion to the length of campaigns. Philip's army, on the other hand, invariably took orders without flinching, having no doubts about the consequences of insubordination: supposedly Philip once murdered a sleeping sentry on the spot, stating coolly as he walked off, "I left him as I found him." Finally, professionalism allowed Philip to eliminate large numbers of noncombatant servants who carried provisions. Earlier Greek forces moved slowly

Macedon transformed under Philip

The Macedonian professional army

Macedonian Phalanx. Philip of Macedon's infantry—and Alexander the Great's thereafter—was armed with two-handed pikes and massed in squares sixteen rows deep and wide. Members of the phalanx were trained to wheel in step in any direction or to double their front by filing off in rows of eight.

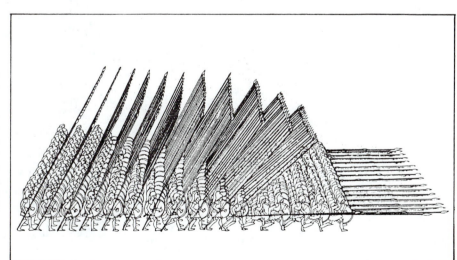

from site to site and were hampered by logistical problems because they were swelled with men who carried food and arms for other men, but Philip forced his fighters to carry their necessities for themselves as much as strength allowed. All of Philip's innovations were considered uncouth by the "gentlemanly" Greeks of the city-states, but his indifference to military "good manners" allowed him to engage in lightning strikes and ensured his total victory of 338 B.C. over combined Athenian and Theban forces at the battle of Chaeronea.

Despotism and conquest

That victory ended Greek city-state freedom once and for all because after Chaeronea Philip installed his despotic rule throughout Greece and his son Alexander thereafter maintained that despotism as the springboard for the conquest of half of Asia. Much irony resides in the fact that Alexander's tutor during his early teenage years had been Aristotle, the very Greek philosopher who insisted that humans are so designed by nature for life in city-states that "he who can live without one must be either a beast or a god," for Alexander proved indifferent to this teaching and proceeded to act as if his tutor had not been a Greek but a Persian. Some historians used to think that Alexander's amazing march through Asia Minor, Egypt, Mesopotamia, Persia, and Afghanistan, to the borders of India was motivated by an urgent sense of mission to bring Greek enlightenment to presumably benighted Asians, but it is now widely agreed upon that Alexander was driven forward solely by a quest for power and glory that verged on megalomania. In his own day the story was told that a sea pirate taken captive by the mighty conqueror told him that the only difference between them was one of scale. If we put aside motives, however,

Alexander in Battle. A scene from a sarcophagus of about 300 B.C. Alexander is shown on horseback at the left.

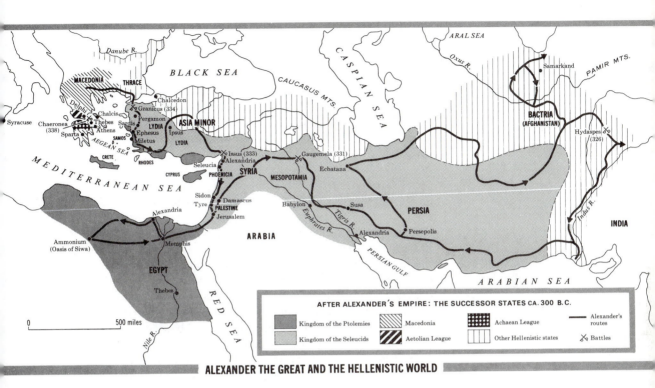

BLACK SEA · MACEDONIA · THRACE · Danube R. · CAUCASUS MTS. · CASPIAN SEA · ARAL SEA · Oxus R. · Samarkand · PAMIR MTS.

Delphi · Chalcedon · Chalcis · Granicus (334) · Pergamon · Sardis · ASIA MINOR · BACTRIA (AFGHANISTAN)

Syracuse · Chaeronea (338) · Thebes · Sparta · Athens · Ephesus · Miletus · LYDIA · Ipsus · LYDIA · Hydaspes (326)

SAMOS · AEGEAN SEA · CRETE · RHODES · CYPRUS · Seleucia · Alexandria · PHOENICIA · SYRIA · Issus (333) · Gaugemela (331) · Ecbatana · Echatana · INDIA · Indus R.

MEDITERRANEAN SEA · MESOPOTAMIA

Sidon · Tyre · Damascus · PALESTINE · Jerusalem · Babylon · Susa · PERSIA · Euphrates R. · Tigris R. · Persepolis · Alexandria

Alexandria · ARABIA · PERSIAN GULF · ARABIAN SEA

Ammonium (Oasis of Siwa) · Memphis

EGYPT · Thebes · RED SEA · Nile R.

0 — 500 miles

AFTER ALEXANDER'S EMPIRE: THE SUCCESSOR STATES CA. 300 B.C.

Kingdom of the Ptolemies · Macedonia · Achaean League · Alexander's routes
Kingdom of the Seleucids · Aetolian League · Other Hellenistic states · Battles

ALEXANDER THE GREAT AND THE HELLENISTIC WORLD

it was Alexander's conquests, and not the pirate's, that provided the foundations for the Hellenistic civilization.

Alexander's pattern of rule itself was Hellenistic in mixing Greek and Asiatic traits. For propaganda purposes the young Macedonian claimed to be punishing Persia for insults inflicted earlier on Greeks, and in fact he not only replaced Persian governors with Greek-speaking ones wherever he went, but he imported Greek settlers to inhabit newly founded cities as a means of keeping conquered populations in a state of subordination. Yet Alexander also recognized that he and his Greeks could never hope to rule a gigantic Asian empire as hated foreigners, and hence encouraged intermarriage. In keeping with this policy Alexander himself married a Bactrian princess, Roxane (his ultimate preferences were homosexual), and divided a loaf of bread with his bride at the wedding as a gesture of deference to local custom.

What inspired Alexander most about the ways of Asia were not princesses or loaves of bread, but any Asian customs that might enhance his autocracy and his glamour. The traditions of Greece, of course, were thoroughly at odds with flattery and ostentation. Well known is the story that when Alexander first assumed rule in Greece he met the philosopher Diogenes sitting in a wooden tub that served as his home and asked the sage if he would like a favor. "Yes," said

Alexander the Great. Hellenistic rulers depicted Alexander on their coins in order to stress their connection with the revered hero. This dramatic profile was struck by Lysimachus of Thrace around 300 B.C.

Diogenes, "move out of my sun." Determined not to be spoken to this way if he could possibly help it, Alexander adopted lavish Persian dress as he moved through Asia and commanded subjects to approach him, depending on their rank, on bended knee or fully prostrate. Most extreme was Alexander's decision to proclaim himself a god. Although he did this only in Egypt, where the pharaohs had been worshiped as offspring of the sun-god Amon for millennia, claiming divinity was an extraordinary measure for a Greek who was expected to move out of the sun when an unkempt philosopher told him to do so.

3. POLITICAL AND ECONOMIC TRENDS

When Alexander died in 323 B.C., he left no legitimate heir to succeed him save a feeble-minded half-brother. Tradition relates that when his friends requested him on his deathbed to designate a successor, he replied "To the strongest." After his death his highest-ranking generals proceeded to divide the empire among them. Some of the younger commanders contested this arrangement, and a series of wars followed which culminated in the decisive battle of Ipsus in 301 B.C. The result was a new division among the victors. Seleucus took possession of Persia, Mesopotamia, and Syria; Lysimachus assumed control over Asia Minor and Thrace; Cassander established himself in Macedonia; and Ptolemy added Phoenicia and Palestine to his original domain of Egypt. Twenty years later these four states were reduced to three when Seleucus defeated and killed Lysimachus in battle and appropriated his territory in Asia Minor. In the meantime most of the Greek cities had revolted against Macedonian rule. By banding together in defensive leagues several of them succeeded in maintaining some independence in federalist form for nearly a century. Finally, between 146 and 30 B.C. nearly all of the Hellenistic territory passed under Roman rule, except the easternmost part, which reverted to rule under native Persians.

The dominant form of government in the Hellenistic age throughout all the lands once conquered by Alexander, except for most of mainland Greece, was the despotism of rulers who represented themselves as at least semi-divine. Alexander's most powerful successors, the Seleucid kings in western Asia and the Ptolemies in Egypt, made systematic attempts to deify themselves. A Seleucid monarch, Antiochus IV, adopted the title "Epiphanes" or "God Manifest." The later members of the dynasty of the Ptolemies signed their decrees "Theos" (God) and revived the practice of sister marriage that had been followed by the pharaohs as a means of preserving the divine blood of the royal family from contamination. Needless to say, rulers such as these brooked no formal opposition, yet the inevitable consequence of un-

Antiochus I, "Soter." A Hellenistic ruler of Syria (281–261 B.C.), whose chosen title of *soter* meant "savior." The faraway stare connotes supernatural inspiration.

trammeled autocracy was frequent palace intrigue, leading to stabbings, poisonings, conspirings with foreign rivals, invasions, and wars. Following a policy of kill or be killed, Ptolemy IV of Egypt (221–204 B.C.) put to death his mother, his uncle, and his brother, and generations later his descendant, the beauteous Cleopatra (69–30 B.C.), intrigued with Romans in a vain hope to maintain some semblance of Hellenistic Egyptian independence.

Despotism of semi-divine rulers beyond Greece

The only viable alternative to Oriental despotism arrived at during the Hellenistic era was the city-state federalism developed in mainland Greece. After having gained independence from the Hellenistic state of Macedon, several Greek cities formed defensive alliances that rapidly evolved into two confederate leagues. The Aetolian League and the Achaean League, as they were known, thereupon dominated all of Greece between them until 146 B.C., when they were supplanted by the imperialism of Rome. The organization of both leagues was basically the same. Each had a federal council composed of representatives of the member cities with power to enact laws on subjects of general concern. An assembly that all of the citizens in the federated states could attend decided questions of war and peace and elected officials. Executive and military authority was vested in the hands of a general, elected for one year and eligible for reelection only in alternate years. Although these leagues are frequently described as federal states, they were scarcely more than confederacies, for the central authority depended upon the local governments for contributions of revenue and troops. Their primary significance lies in the fact that they constituted the nearest approach ever made in Greece to voluntary national union before modern times.

City-state federalism in mainland Greece

In regard to economics, the Hellenistic world was generally prosperous, owing to the growth of long-distance trade, the growth of finance, and the growth of cities. The growth of trade may be explained by reference to several factors, first among which was the opening up of a vast trading area as the result of Alexander's conquests. Long before the time of Alexander, Greeks had been energetic long-distance traders, but they were hampered in trading with Persian realms and with areas east of Persia because Persian emperors and satraps preferred to act in their own economic interests rather than in Greek ones. But when, suddenly, after 323 B.C. Greek rulers became ensconced throughout Egypt and western Asia, and when Greek-speaking communities dotted the terrain from Alexandria in Egypt, to another Alexandria in northern Syria, to yet another Alexandria at the head of the Persian Gulf, steady trading connections were facilitated from the eastern Mediterranean to central Asia. Moreover, with bases in Egypt, Asia Minor, Persia, and Bactria, Greek traders could fan out further, venturing into the hinterland of Africa, Russia, India, and China. Secondly, Alexander unwittingly stimulated an invigorating rise in prices, with a concomitant growth of intensive investment,

Dynamic aspects of Hellenistic economy: (1) the growth of trade

by sequestering hoards of Persian gold and silver and placing the bullion into circulation in the form of coins, jewelry, and luxury utensils. And thirdly, in addition to commerce, manufacturing industries aimed at providing items for trade were now more consciously promoted by autocratic rulers as a means of increasing their revenues.

The Ptolemies and Seleucids as patrons of trade

New trading ventures were particularly vigorous and lucrative in Ptolemaic Egypt and the area of western Asia ruled over by the Seleucid monarchs, the heartland of which was Syria. Every facility was provided by the Ptolemies and the Seleucids for the encouragement of trade. Harbors were improved, warships were sent out to police the seas, and roads and canals were built. Moreover, the Ptolemies employed geographers to discover new routes to distant lands and thereby open up valuable markets. As a result of such methods Egypt developed a flourishing commerce in the widest variety of products. Into the port of Alexandria came spices from Arabia, copper from Cyprus, gold from Ethiopia and India, tin from Britain, elephants and ivory from Nubia, silver from Spain, fine carpets from Asia Minor, and even silk from China. Profits for the government and for some of the merchants were often as high as 20 or 30 percent.

(2) the growth of finance

Further evidence of the significant economic development of the Hellenistic Age is to be found in the growth of finance. An international money economy, based upon gold and silver coins, now became general throughout the eastern Mediterranean and western Asia. Banks, usually owned by the government, developed as the chief institutions of credit for business ventures of every description. Speculation, cornering of markets, intense competition, the growth of large business houses, and the development of insurance were other phenomena of this remarkable age.

(3) the growth of cities

Finally, cities grew enormously during the Hellenistic age for a combination of noneconomic and economic reasons. Entirely aside from economic motives, Greek rulers imported Greek officials and especially Greek soldiers to maintain their control over non-Greek populations. Often this policy resulted in the creation of urban settlements from nothing. Alexander the Great himself had founded some seventy cities as outposts of Greek domination, and in the next two centuries his successors founded about two hundred more. Yet urbanization also increased because of the expansion of commerce and industry, as well as because of the proliferation of governmental bureaus responsible for economic oversight. Hence the growth of populations in some urban centers was truly explosive. The population of Antioch in Syria quadrupled during a single century. Seleucia on the Tigris grew from nothing to a metropolis of several hundred thousand in less than two centuries. The largest and most famous of all the Hellenistic cities was Alexandria in Egypt, with about 500,000 inhabitants. No other city in ancient times before imperial Rome surpassed it in size or in magnificence. Its streets were well paved and laid out in regular order. It had splendid public buildings and parks, a museum, and a library of 700,000 scrolls. The masses of its people, however, had no share in the brilliant and luxurious life around them, although it was paid for in part out of the fruits of their labor.

While the Hellenistic economy was basically a dynamic one, throughout the Hellenistic period agriculture remained in all the Hellenistic lands by far the major form of occupation and the primary source of wealth. (Only within the last century did trade and industry replace agriculture as the major source of wealth in western Europe and north America.) Furthermore, although industry advanced in Hellenistic Egypt and parts of western Asia, nowhere did a true "industrial revolution" based on any technological breakthrough occur. Rather, all industry was manual rather than power driven.

Despite the overall growth and prosperity of the Hellenistic economy, it must be emphasized that prosperity was by no means enjoyed by everyone. Quite to the contrary, for some people sudden wealth was followed by sudden penury, and for others poverty was a constant. Individual merchants and speculators were those most subject to drastic fluctuations in their fortunes, owing to the natural precariousness of mercantile endeavors. For example, a trader who did very well selling a luxury cloth might have decided to invest heavily in it, only to find that tastes had changed, or that a ship he had dispatched to convey his wares had sunk. Merchants were also particularly exposed to what economists now recognize as the "boom and bust" syndrome. A merchant, thinking he would make a fortune during an upward price spiral, might go into debt in order to take advantage of the upward trend, only to find that supply in the commodity he traded suddenly exceeded demand, leaving him nothing with which to pay back his creditors. Among those whose poverty remained unchanged were small-scale farmers growing for regional markets. (In Greece they may have become poorer because Greece suffered during the Hellenistic era from a negative balance of payments, having little to offer for long-distance trade except objects of art.) Recent immigrants to cities in most cases probably also did not improve their economic status, and many of them became subject to badly overcrowded living conditions. All told, therefore, it seems clear that the economic landscape of the Hellenistic world was one of contrasting extremes, an image worth remembering in moving to a consideration of Hellenistic thought and culture.

4. HELLENISTIC CULTURE: PHILOSOPHY AND RELIGION

Hellenistic philosophy exhibited two trends that ran almost parallel throughout the civilization. The major trend, exemplified by Stoicism and Epicureanism, showed a fundamental regard for reason as the key to the solution of human problems. This trend was a manifestation of Greek influence, though philosophy and science, as combined in Aristotle, had now come to a parting of the ways. The minor trend, exemplified by the Cynics, Skeptics, and various Asian cults, tended to reject reason, to deny the possibility of attaining truth, and in some cases to turn toward mysticism and reliance upon faith. Despite the differences in their teachings, the philosophers and religious enthusiasts of the Hellenistic age generally agreed upon one thing: the necessity of finding some release from the trials of human existence, for with the decline of free civic life as a means for the expression of human idealism, alternatives needed to be found to make life seem meaningful, or at least endurable.

The earliest of the new Hellenistic philosophical movements was that of the Cynics, who arose about 350 B.C. Their foremost leader, Diogenes, won fame by his ceaseless quest for an "honest" man. The Cynics argued for living a "natural" life and repudiating everything conventional and artificial. (The word "Cynic" comes from the Greek for "dog" and connoted the idea that people should live as naturally as beasts.) Their principal goal was self-sufficiency: everyone should cultivate within himself the ability to satisfy his own needs. Obviously the Cynics bore some resemblance to other movements that have cropped up through the ages—the hippie movement of the 1960s, for example. There were notable differences, however. The Cynics spurned music and art as manifestations of artificiality, and they were not representative of a youth generation. But all such movements seem to reflect a sense of frustration with the constraints and goals of society. According to one story, Alexander the Great once asked Diogenes's disciple Crates whether the city of Thebes, recently destroyed in war, should be rebuilt: "Why?" replied the Cynic, "Another Alexander will surely tear it down again."

Epicureanism and Stoicism both originated about 300 B.C. The founders were, respectively, Epicurus (c. 342–270) and Zeno (fl. after 300), who were residents of Athens. Epicureanism and Stoicism had several features in common. Both were individualistic, concerned not with the welfare of society but with the good of the individual. Both were materialistic, denying categorically the existence of any spiritual substances; even divine beings and the soul were declared to be formed of matter. Moreover, Stoicism and Epicureanism alike contained elements of universalism since both taught that people are the same the world over and recognized no distinctions between Greeks and non-Greeks.

But in many ways the two systems were quite different. The Stoics believed that the cosmos is an ordered whole in which all contradictions are resolved for ultimate good. Evil is, therefore, relative; the particular misfortunes that befall human beings are but necessary incidents to the final perfection of the universe. Everything that happens is rigidly determined in accordance with rational purpose. No individual is master of his fate; human destiny is a link in an unbroken chain. People are free only in the sense that they can accept their fate or rebel against it. But whether they accept or rebel, they cannot overcome it. Their supreme duty is to submit to the order of the universe in the knowledge that this order is good; in other words, to resign themselves as graciously as possible to their fate. Through such an act of resignation the highest happiness will be attained, which consists in tranquillity of mind. The individual who is most truly happy is therefore the one who by the assertion of his rational nature has accomplished a perfect adjustment of his life to the cosmic purpose and has purged his soul of all bitterness and whining protest against evil turns of fortune.

The Stoics developed an ethical and social theory that accorded well with their general philosophy. Believing that the highest good is serenity of mind, they naturally emphasized duty and self-discipline as cardinal virtues. Recognizing the prevalence of particular evil, they taught tolerance for and forgiveness of one another. Unlike the Cynics, they did not recommend withdrawal from society but urged participation in public affairs as a duty for those of rational mind. They condemned slavery and war, but it was far from their purpose to preach any crusade against these evils. They believed that the results that might arise from violent measures of social change would be worse than the diseases they were meant to cure. Besides, what difference did it make if the body were in bondage so long as the mind was free? Despite its partly negative character, the Stoic philosophy was one of the noblest products of the Hellenistic Age in teaching equalitarianism, pacifism, and humanitarianism.

The ethical and social teachings of the Stoics

Epicurus and the Epicureans based their philosophy on the materialistic "atomism" of the early Greek physicist Democritus. According to this theory the basic ingredients of all things are minute, indivisible atoms, and change and growth are the results of the combination and separation of these particles. Nevertheless, while accepting the materialism of the atomists, Epicurus rejected their absolute mechanism. He denied that an automatic, mechanical motion of the atoms can be the cause of all things in the universe. Though he taught that the atoms move downward in perpendicular lines because of their weight, he insisted upon endowing them with a spontaneous ability to swerve from the perpendicular and thereby to combine with one another. This modification of the atomic theory made possible a belief in human freedom. If the atoms were capable only of mechanical motion, then a human being, also made up of atoms, would be reduced to the status of an automaton, and fatalism would be the law of the universe. In this repudiation of the mechanistic interpretation of life, Epicurus was probably closer to the Hellenic spirit than either Democritus or the Stoics.

Epicurus and nonmechanistic atomism

The ethical philosophy of the Epicureans was based upon the doctrine that the highest good is pleasure. But they did not include all forms of indulgence in the category of genuine pleasure. The pleasures of the flesh should be avoided, since every excess of carnality is balanced by its portion of pain. On the other hand, a moderate satisfaction of bodily appetites is permissible and may be regarded as a good in itself. Better than this is mental pleasure, sober contemplation of the reasons for the choice of some things and the avoidance of others, and mature reflection upon satisfactions previously enjoyed. The highest of all pleasures, however, consists in serenity of soul, in the complete absence of both mental and physical pain. This end can be best achieved through the elimination of fear, especially fear of the supernatural, since that is the greatest source of mental pain. The individual must recognize from the study of philosophy that the soul is material and therefore cannot survive the body, that the universe operates of itself, and that the gods do not intervene in human affairs. The gods live remote from the world and are too intent upon their own concerns to bother about what takes place on earth. Since they do not reward or punish mortals either in this life or one to come there is no reason why they should be feared. The Epicureans thus came by a different route to the same general conclusion as the Stoics—there is nothing better than tranquillity of mind.

The practical moral teachings and the politics of the Epicureans rested upon utilitarianism. In contrast to the Stoics they did not insist upon virtue as an end in itself but taught that the only reason why one should be good is to increase his own happiness. In like manner, they denied that there is any such thing as absolute justice: laws and institutions are just only insofar as they contribute to the welfare of the individual. Certain rules have been found necessary in every complex society for the maintenance of security and order. These rules are obeyed solely because it is to each individual's advantage to do so. Epicurus held no high regard for either political or social life. He considered the state as a mere convenience and taught that the wise man should take no active part in politics. Unlike the Cynics, he did not propose that civilization should be abandoned; yet his conception of the happiest life was essentially passive and defeatist. Epicurus taught that the thinking person will recognize that evils in the world cannot be eradicated by human effort; the individual will therefore withdraw to study philosophy and enjoy the fellowship of a few congenial friends.

A more radically defeatist philosophy was that propounded by the Skeptics. Skepticism reached the zenith of its popularity about 200 B.C. under the influence of Carneades. The chief source of its inspiration was the Sophist teaching that all knowledge is derived from sense perception and therefore must be limited and relative. From this was deduced the conclusion that we cannot prove anything. Since the impressions of our senses deceive us, no truth can be certain. All we can say is that things *appear* to be such and such; we do not know what they really *are*. We have no definite knowledge of the supernatural, of the meaning of life, or even of right and wrong. It follows that the sensible course to pursue is suspension of judgment: this alone can lead to happiness. If we will abandon the fruitless quest for absolute truth and cease worrying about good and evil, we will attain that peace of mind which is the highest satisfaction that life affords. The Skeptics were even less concerned than the Epicureans with political and social problems. Their ideal was the typically Hellenistic one of escape for the individual from a world neither understandable nor capable of reform.

Hellenistic religion similarly tended to offer vehicles of individual escape from collective political commitments. The civic religion of the Greeks as it was in the age of the city-states had now lost its force. For the majority of society's leaders throughout the Hellenistic world its place was taken by the philosophies of Stoicism, Epicureanism, and Skepticism. On the other hand, those who were less philosophically inclined and the majority of the common people tended to embrace emotional personal religions offering intense ritual in this world and salvation in the next. In Greek-speaking communities the Orphic and Eleusinian mystery cults that stressed extreme ascetic atonement for sin, mystical union with divinity, and otherworldly salvation attracted more votaries than ever before. Correspondingly, among Persian speakers Zoroastrianism became ever more extreme in its dualism, with Zoroastrian priests, the *magi,* insisting that everything physical and material was evil and demanding that believers practice austerities in order to ready their immaterial souls for ethereal joy in the afterlife. Finally, among Greeks and non-Greeks alike an offshoot of Zoroastrianism known as Mithraism gained ever more popularity.

The appeal of emotional personal religions

Exactly when Mithraism became an independent religion is unknown, but it was certainly not later than the fourth century B.C. The cult gained its name from Mithras, a lieutenant of Zoroastrianism's omnipotent god Ahura-Mazda in the war against the forces of evil. At first only a minor deity in Zoroastrianism, Mithras gradually became recognized by many as the god most deserving of worship, probably because of the emotional appeal made by the incidents of his career. He was believed to have lived an earthly existence involving great suffering and sacrifice. He performed miracles giving bread and wine to humanity and ending a drought and also a disastrous flood. He proclaimed Sunday as the most sacred day of the week since the sun was the giver of light. He declared the twenty-fifth of December as the most sacred day of the year because as the approximate date of the winter solstice it marked the return of the sun from its long journey south of the Equator. It was in a sense the "birthday" of the sun since it connoted the revival of its life-giving powers for the benefit of humankind. Drawing its converts mostly from the lower classes of Hellenistic society, Mithraism offered them an elaborate ritual, a reason to harbor contempt for life in this world, and a clearly defined doctrine of redemption through Mithras, a personal savior. Not sur-

The spread and influence of Mithraism

prisingly it outlasted the Hellenistic period, becoming after about 100 A.D. one of the most popular religions in the Roman Empire and exerting a slight influence on Christianity.

5. HELLENISTIC CULTURE: LITERATURE AND ART

Both the literature and the art of the Hellenistic age was characterized by a tendency to take aspects of earlier Greek accomplishments to extremes. It is hard to be sure of the reasons for this, but apparently writers and artists wished to demonstrate their purely formal skills in order to please their autocratic patrons. Furthermore, the greater uncertainties of existence in Hellenistic times may have led consumers of art to seek gratification from more dramatic and less subtle forms of artistic expression. Whatever the case, rather than being an integral expression of civic activities, art definitely became ever more of a commodity, which meant that much of it was ephemeral or even trash: we know the names of at least 1,100 Hellenistic authors, yet hardly more than a handful of these possessed any true literary distinction. Nonetheless, rising above the numerous mediocre works of literature and art dating from the Hellenistic period, a few indubitably stand out as enduring masterpieces.

The two most prominent forms of Hellenistic literature were the drama and the pastoral, the one an established genre, the other a new one. The greatest Hellenistic dramatist was the Athenian comic playwright Menander (c.343–c.291 B.C.), who worked within a genre previously brought to perfection by Aristophanes. Menander learned much from Aristophanes, but in contrast to him Menander was no satirist and was indifferent to politics (something unimaginable for any Athenian writer until then). The exclusive subject of Menander's comedies was romantic love, with its pains and pleasures, its intrigues and seductions, and its culmination in happy marriage. Plots of this sort, set within the context of everyday life, succeeded well in engaging the attention of Menander's audiences. Yet Menander was more than a writer of mere "soap opera," for he was skilled in creating humorous situations and in portraying the foibles of human character.

Romance was also the subject of the pastoral, but rather than being set against a realistic backdrop the pastoral was located in a make-believe world of shepherds, nymphs, and pipes of Pan. The inventor of this genre was a Greek named Theocritus, who was born in Sicily yet lived and wrote in the big city of Alexandria. (His dates of activity were roughly 270 to roughly 250 B.C.) Theocritus was a model author of prototypically escapist literature. In the midst of urban bustle, faced with arrogant autocratic rulers demanding to be worshiped, and within sight of overcrowded living conditions for the poor verging on slums, he celebrated the charm of hazy or sun-drenched country vales and idealized the "simple pleasures" of rustic folk. "Begin my country

Cupid and Psyche. Hellenistic tastes often inclined toward "dainty" representations of eroticism. Cupid's right hand conveys a studied sensuality held in check only by his fig leaf.

Hellenistic literature: (1) the comedies of Menander

(2) the pastorals of Theocritus

song, sweet Muses, begin,/ I am Thrysis from Etna, this is Thrysis's lovely voice": so might one of his pastorals commence. The artificiality of such verse cannot be denied, but neither can its frequent lush effectiveness. Moreover, in creating the pastoral Theocritus was the founder of an enduring tradition taken up later by such poetic masters as Virgil and Milton, and one that also provided a wealth of themes for painters and sculptors. Even composers of modern concert music, such as Claude Debussy in his *Afternoon of a Faun,* bear a debt to the escapist poet from Alexandria.

The field of Hellenistic prose literature was dominated by the historians, the biographers, and the authors of utopias. By far the most profound of the writers of history was the mainland Greek Polybius, who lived during the second century B.C. According to Polybius, historical development proceeds in cycles, nations passing so inevitably through stages of growth and decay that it is possible to predict exactly where a nation is heading if one knows what has happened to it in the past. From the standpoint of his scientific approach, Polybius deserves to be ranked second only to Thucydides among all the historians of ancient times, and he even surpassed Thucydides in his grasp of the importance of social and economic forces.

(3) history

Although most of the biographies were of a light and gossipy character, their tremendous popularity bears eloquent testimony to the literary tastes of the time. Even more significant was the popularity of the utopias, or descriptive accounts of ideal states. Virtually all of them depicted a life of social and economic equality, free from greed, oppression, and strife, on an imaginary island or in some distant, unfamiliar region. Generally in these paradises money was considered to be unknown, trade was prohibited, all property was held in common, and all were required to work with their hands in producing the necessities of life. We are probably justified in assuming that the profusion of this utopian literature was a response to the economic and social tensions inherent in Hellenistic society, offering either escapism, similar to that of the pastorals, or perhaps a latent consciousness of the need for reform.

(4) biography and utopias

The Marble Streets of Ephesus. Taken from the Persians by Alexander in 334 B.C., this cosmopolitan city on the west coast of Asia Minor was noted for its splendor.

The very magniloquence implicitly criticized by the utopias is best observed in the main traits of Hellenistic architecture. In place of the balance and restraint that had distinguished Greek architecture of the fifth and early fourth centuries B.C., a stress on grandeur and luxuriance, partly derived from standards set by Egyptian pharaohs and Persian emperors, now became dominant. Two examples (both of which unfortunately no longer survive) are the great lighthouse of Alexandria, which rose to a height of nearly four hundred feet and had three diminishing stories and eight columns to support the light at the top, and the citadel of Alexandria dedicated to the god Serapis, which was built of stone covered with blue-tinted plaster and was said by a contemporary to have "risen into mid-air." In Pergamon, a Greek site in Asia Minor, an enormous altar to Zeus (transported in modern times to Berlin) and an enormous open-air theater looked out over a high hill, and in Ephesus, not far away, the streets were paved with marble. Of course not every building in the Hellenistic world was constructed on an enormous scale, yet the "signature" of Hellenistic architecture of whatever dimension was the Corinthian column, a form of column more ornate than the simple and dignified Doric and Ionic alternatives that had predominated in earlier Greek building.

In the final analysis, probably the most influential of all products of Hellenistic culture, and almost certainly the most congenial to modern tastes, were works of sculpture. Whereas earlier Greek sculpture had sought to idealize humanity and to express Greek ideals of modesty by understated restraint, Hellenistic sculpture emphasized extreme naturalism and unashamed extravagance. In practice this meant that sculptors went to great lengths to recreate facial furrows, muscular disten-

Hellenistic sculpture

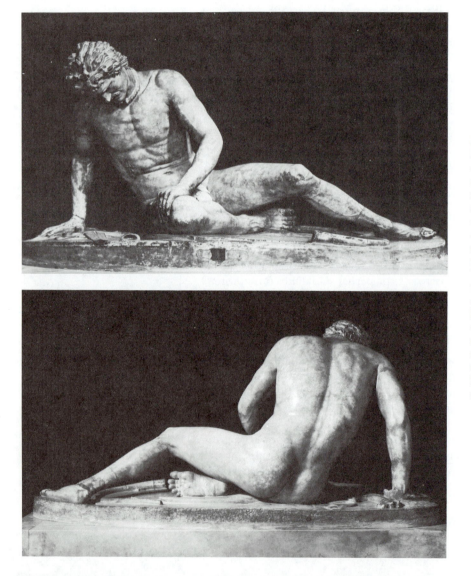

Dying Gaul Seen from Front and Back. A famous example of Hellenistic realism and pathos, this statue was executed around 230 B.C. in the court of Pergamon in Asia Minor. (The original is lost; shown here is a faithful Roman copy.) The sculptor clearly wished to exhibit skill in depicting an unusual human posture and succeeded remarkably in evoking the thin line that separates human dignity from unappeasable loneliness and physical suffering.

Left: *The Winged Victory of Samothrace*. In this figure, done around 200 B.C., a Hellenistic sculptor preserved some of the calmness and devotion to grace and proportion characteristic of Hellenic art in the Golden Age. Right: *Laocoön*. In sharp contrast to the serenity of the Winged Victory is this famous sculpture group from the late second century B.C., depicting the death of Laocoön. According to legend, Laocoön warned the Trojans not to touch the wooden horse sent by the Greeks and was punished by Poseidon, who sent two serpents to kill him and his sons. The intense emotionalism of this work later had a great influence on western European art from Michelangelo onward. See, for example, the painting by El Greco on page 729.

sions, and complex folds of drapery. Awkward human postures were considered to offer the greatest challenges to the artist in stone, to the degree that sculptors might prefer to show people stretching themselves or balancing themselves on one leg in ways that hardly ever occur in real life. Since most Hellenistic sculpture was executed for wealthy private patrons, it is clear that the goal was to create something unique in terms of its conception and craftsmanship—something a collector could show off as the only one of its type. Not surprisingly, therefore, complexity came to be admired for its own sake, and extreme naturalism sometimes teetered on the brink of distorted stylization. Yet when moderns see such works they frequently experience a shock of recognition, for the bizarre and exaggerated postures of Hellenistic sculptures later exerted an enormous influence on Michelangelo and his followers, and later inspired some of the most "modern" sculptors

See color plates following page 166

Top: *Hellenistic Aphrodite*. This figure, dating from the fourth century B.C., displays the Hellenistic fascination with ungainly, "unnatural," postures. Bottom: *French Bather*. This statuette done by Edgar Degas around 1890 shows some evident continuities between Hellenistic and modern art.

of the nineteenth and twentieth centuries. Three of the most famous examples of Hellenistic sculpture may be cited here which reveal different aspects of Hellenistic aesthetic ideals: the *Dying Gaul,* done in Pergamon around 220 B.C., shows consummate skill in portraying a distended human body; the *Winged Victory of Samothrace,* of about 200 B.C., displays flowing drapery as if it were not stone but real cloth; and the *Laocoön* group, of the first century B.C., offers one of the most intensely emotional as well as complex compositions known in the entire history of sculptural art.

6. THE FIRST GREAT AGE OF SCIENCE

The most brilliant age in the history of science prior to the seventeenth century A.D. was the period of the Hellenistic civilization. Indeed, some modern scientific achievements would not have been possible without the discoveries of the scientists of Alexandria, Pergamon, and other Hellenistic cities. There are two major reasons for the impressive development of science in the centuries after Alexander's conquest of the Persian Empire. One was the enormous stimulus given to intellectual inquiry by the fusion of Mesopotamian and Egyptian science with the learning and the curiosity of the Greeks. The other was that many Hellenistic rulers were generous patrons of scientific research, subsidizing scientists who belonged to their retinues just as they subsidized sculptors. It used to be thought that the motive for such patronage was purely practical—that rulers believed the progress of science would enhance the growth of industry in their territories and would also improve their own material comforts. Yet students of Hellenistic civilization now agree that it is anachronistic to think that any ruler was hoping for an "industrial revolution" in the sense of applying technology to save human labor. The reasons for this are that labor was cheap, and autocratic princes were completely indifferent to the pains and sufferings of the laboring classes. As for the supposed connection between science and the enhancement of material comfort, Hellenistic rulers in fact hardly thought along those lines because they had adequate numbers of slaves to fan them and were not inclined to introduce mechanical devices that would have lessened the public grandeur of being fanned by deferential subordinates. To be sure, practical aims motivated the patronage of science in some areas, above all in medicine and anything that might relate to military technology. Yet it has become clear that the autocrats who financed the scientific endeavors did so primarily for motives of prestige: sometimes a scientist might fashion a splendid gadget for a ruler that he could show off to visitors as he would show off his sculptures; and even if not, purely theoretical achievements were so much admired among the Greek-speaking leisured classes that a Hellenistic prince who subsidized a theoretical breakthrough would share the prestige for it in the way the mayor of an American city might bask in prestige today if his city's baseball team were to win the World Series.

The major Hellenistic sciences were astronomy, mathematics, geography, medicine, and physics. The most renowned of the earlier Hellenistic astronomers was Aristarchus of Samos (310–230 B.C.), sometimes called the "Hellenistic Copernicus." His primary accomplishment was his deduction that the earth and the other planets revolve around the sun. Unfortunately this view was not accepted by his successors because it conflicted with the teachings of Aristotle and with the conviction of the Greeks that man, and therefore the earth, must be at the center of the universe. Another important Hellenistic astronomer was Hipparchus, who flourished in Alexandria in the latter half of the second century B.C. His chief contributions were the invention of the astrolabe and the approximately correct calculation of the diameter of the moon and its distance from the earth. His fame was eventually overshadowed, however, by the reputation of Ptolemy of Alexandria (second century A.D.). Although Ptolemy made few original discoveries, he systematized the work of others. His principal writing, the *Almagest,* based upon the geocentric theory (the view that all heavenly bodies revolve around the earth), was handed down to medieval Europe as the classic summary of ancient astronomy.

Astronomy

Closely allied with astronomy were two other sciences, mathematics and geography. The Hellenistic mathematician of greatest renown was Euclid, the master of geometry. Until the middle of the nineteenth century his *Elements of Geometry* (written around 300 B.C.) remained the accepted basis for the study of that branch of mathematics. Much of the material in this work was not original but was a synthesis of the discoveries of others. The most original of the Hellenistic mathematicians were probably Hipparchus, who laid the foundations of both plane and spherical trigonometry, and Archimedes, who was primarily a physicist, but who also discovered the integral calculus. Hellenistic geography owed most of its development to Eratosthenes (c. 276–c. 196 B.C.), astronomer and librarian of Alexandria. By means of sundials placed some hundreds of miles apart, he calculated the circumference of the earth with an error of less than 200 miles. He propounded the theory that all of the oceans are really one, and he was the first to suggest the possibility of reaching eastern Asia by sailing west. One of his successors divided the earth into the five climatic zones which are still recognized, and explained the ebb and flow of the tides as due to the influence of the moon.

Mathematics and geography

Perhaps none of the Hellenistic advances in science surpassed in importance the progress in medicine. Especially significant was the work of Herophilus of Chalcedon, who conducted his researches in Alexandria about the beginning of the third century. Without question he was the greatest anatomist of antiquity and probably the first to

Medicine: the development of anatomy

practice human dissection. Among his most important achievements were a detailed description of the brain, with an insistence (against Aristotle) that the brain is the seat of human intelligence; the discovery of the significance of the pulse and its use in diagnosing illness; and the discovery that the arteries contain blood alone, not a mixture of blood and air as Aristotle had taught, and that their function is to carry blood from the heart to all parts of the body.

Physiology

The ablest of the colleagues of Herophilus was Erasistratus, who flourished in Alexandria about the middle of the third century. He is considered the founder of physiology as a separate science. Not only did he practice dissection, but he is believed to have gained much of his knowledge of bodily functions from vivisection. He discovered the valves of the heart, distinguished between motor and sensory nerves, and taught that the ultimate branches of the arteries and veins are connected. He was the first to reject Hippocrates's humoral theory of disease and to condemn excessive bloodletting as a method of cure. Unfortunately the humoral theory and the emphasis on bloodletting theory were revived by Galen, the great encyclopedist of medicine who lived in the Roman Empire in the second century A.D.

Physics

Prior to the third century B.C. physics had been a branch of philosophy. It was made a separate experimental science by Archimedes of Syracuse (c. 287–212 B.C.), who discovered the law of floating bodies, or specific gravity, and formulated with scientific exactness the principles of the lever, the pulley, and the screw. Among his memorable inventions were the compound pulley and the screw propeller for ships. Although he has been considered the greatest technical genius of antiquity, he really placed no emphasis on his mechanical contraptions and preferred to devote his time instead to pure scientific research. Tradition relates that he even discovered "Archimedes's principle" (specific gravity) while pondering possible theories in his bath: when he reached his stunning insight he dashed out naked into the street crying "Eureka" ("I have found it").

7. THE BALANCE SHEET

The Hellenistic contribution

Judged from the vantage of classical Greece, Hellenistic civilization may at first seem no more than a degenerate phase of Greek civilization. Doubtless the autocratic governments of the Hellenistic age appear debased and repugnant in contrast to Athenian democracy, and doubtless the Hellenistic penchant for extravagance appears debased in contrast to the earlier Greek taste for chaste beauty. It must also be admitted that the best Hellenistic literary works lack the inspired majesty of the great Greek tragedies and that none of the Hellenistic philosophers matched the profundity of Plato and Aristotle. Yet the Hellenistic civilization had its own accomplishments to offer. For example, most Hellenistic cities offered a greater range of public facilities, such as museums and libraries, than earlier Greek ones did, and we have seen that numerous Hellenistic thinkers, writers, and artists left to posterity important new ideas, impressive new genres, and imaginative new styles. Above all, the fact that Hellenistic science was the most advanced in the Western world until the seventeenth century demonstrates that the Hellenistic civilization was by no means retrograde on all fronts.

Probably the most important contribution of the Hellenistic era to subsequent historical development was the role it played as intermediary between Greece and Rome. In some cases the Hellenistic contribution was simply that of preservation. For example, most of the familiarity the ancient Romans had with classical Greek thought came to them by way of copies of Greek philosophical and literary texts preserved in Hellenistic libraries. In other areas, however, transfer involved transmutation. A case in point is architecture and art: as we have seen, Hellenistic art evolved from earlier Greek art into something related but quite different, and it was this "Greek-like" art that exerted the greatest influence on the tastes and artistic accomplishments of the Romans.

Intermediary between Greece and Rome

In conclusion, two particularly remarkable aspects of Hellenistic culture deserve special comment—Hellenistic cosmopolitanism and Hellenistic "modernity." Not only does the word "cosmopolitan" itself come from Greek *cosmopolis,* meaning "universal city," but it was the Greeks of the Hellenistic period who came the closest among westerners to turning this ideal of cosmopolitanism into reality. Specifically, around 250 B.C. a leisure-class Greek could have traveled from Sicily to the borders of India, always meeting people who "spoke his language," both literally and in terms of shared ideals. Moreover, this same Greek would not have been a nationalist in the sense of professing any deep loyalty to a city-state or kingdom. Rather, he would have considered himself a "citizen of the world." Hellenistic cosmopolitanism was partly a product of the cosmopolitanism of Persia, and it helped in turn to create the cosmopolitanism of Rome, but in contrast to both it was not imperial—that is, it was entirely divorced from constraints imposed by a supranational state. Unfortunately, however, it was achieved by means of Greek exploitation of subject peoples. Finally, although cosmopolitanism is surely not an obvious condition of the present, other aspects of Hellenistic civilization must seem very familiar to observers today. Authoritarian governments, ruler worship, economic instability, extreme skepticism existing side by side with intense religiosity, rational science existing side by side with irrational superstition, flamboyant art and ostentatious art collecting: all these traits might make the thoughtful student of history wonder whether the Hellenistic age is not one of the most "relevant" in the entire human record for comparison with our own.

Hellenistic cosmopolitanism and Hellenistic "modernity"

SELECTED READINGS

• *Items so designated are available in paperback editions.*

Boyce, Mary, *The History of Zoroastrianism,* Leiden, 1975.

Cambridge History of Iran, vol. II, Cambridge, 1985. The most up-to-date large-scale treatment of affairs relating to the Persian Empire during the centuries covered by this chapter.

• Cary, Max, *The Legacy of Alexander: A History of the Greek World from 323 to 146 B.C.,* New York, 1932. A firm guide to the complicated political history of the period.

Clagett, M., *Greek Science in Antiquity,* rev. ed., New York, 1971. A solid and dependable introduction.

Ferguson, John, *The Heritage of Hellenism: The Greek World From 323 to 31 B.C.,* New York, 1973. An engagingly written and lavishly illustrated exposition of typical characteristics of Hellenistic culture.

• Finley, M.I., *The Ancient Economy,* Berkeley, 1973. A fundamental topical treatment by a brilliant scholar. In contrast to Rostovtzeff, seeks to emphasize what was truly ancient about the ancient economy.

Frye, R. N., *The Heritage of Persia,* New York, 1963. A fascinating and authoritative history of Persia from earliest times to he triumph of Islam in the seventh century A.D.

• Grant, F. C., *Hellenistic Religions,* New York, 1953. A standard work.

• Grant, Michael, *From Alexander to Cleopatra: The Hellenistic World,* New York, 1982. A useful elementary introduction.

• Hamilton, J. R., *Alexander the Great,* London, 1973. The best concise scholarly biography currently available.

Lane Fox, R., *Alexander the Great,* London, 1973. Appearing in the same year as the biography by Hamilton, this is a startling contrast in length and goals. Very long, very interpretative, very good.

Larsen, J. A. O., *Greek Federal States,* Oxford, 1968.

Rostovtzeff, M., *The Social and Economic History of the Hellenistic World,* 3 vols., Oxford, 1941. A mine of information, yet anachronistic in its determination to stress the "modernity" of Hellenistic economic developments.

• Tarn, W. W., *Alexander the Great,* Cambridge, 1948. Tarn was the leading English expert on Hellenistic history of the earlier part of this century.

———, and G. T. Griffith, *Hellenistic Civilisation,* 3rd ed., London, 1952. Still indispensable.

• Walbank, F. W., *The Hellenistic World,* Cambridge, Mass., 1982. An excellent college-level survey by one of the world's prominent experts.

Zaehner, R. C., *The Dawn and Twilight of Zoroastrianism,* New York, 1961.

SOURCE MATERIALS

• Austin, M. M., *The Hellenistic World from Alexander to the Roman Conquest: A Selection of Ancient Sources in Translation,* Cambridge, 1981.

• Bagnall, R. S., and P. Derow, *Greek Historical Documents: The Hellenistic Period,* Chico, Calif., 1981.

Boyce, Mary, *Textual Sources for the Study of Zoroastrianism,* Totowa, N.J., 1984.

Chapter 9

ROMAN CIVILIZATION

My city and country, so far as I am Antoninus, is Rome, but so far as I am
a man, it is the world.

> —Marcus Aurelius Antoninus, *Meditations*

For the categories into which you divide the world are not Hellenes and
Barbarians. . . . The division which you substituted is one into Romans
and non-Romans. To such a degree have you expanded the name of your
city.

> —Aelius Aristides, *Oration to Rome*

Well before the glory that was Greece had begun to fade,
another civilization, ultimately much influenced by Greek
culture, had started its growth in the West on the banks of
the Tiber. Around the time of Alexander's conquests the emerging
power of Rome was already a dominant force on the Italian peninsula.
For five centuries thereafter Rome's power increased. By the end of
the first century B.C. it had imposed its rule over most of the Hellenistic
world as well as over most of western Europe. By conquering Hellenistic territory and destroying the North African civilization of Carthage,
Rome was able to make the Mediterranean a "Roman lake." In so
doing it brought Greek institutions and ideas to the western half of
the Mediterranean world. And by pushing northward to the Rhine
and Danube rivers it brought Mediterranean urban culture to lands
still sunk in the Iron Age. Rome, then, was the builder of a great
historical bridge between East and West.

Of course Rome would not have been able to play this role had it
not followed its own peculiar course of development. This was
marked by the tension between two different cultural outlooks. On
the one hand Romans throughout most of their history tended to be
conservative: they revered their old agricultural traditions, household
gods, and ruggedly warlike ways. But they also strove to be builders
and could not resist the attractions of Greek culture. For a few centu-

The Roman synthesis

ries their greatness was based on a synthesis of these different traits: respect for tradition, order, and military prowess, together with Greek urbanization and cultivation of the mind. The synthesis could not last forever, but as long as it did the glory that was Greece was replaced by the grandeur that was Rome.

1. EARLY ITALY AND THE ROMAN MONARCHY

The impact of geography on Roman history

The geographical character of the Italian peninsula contributed significantly to the course of Roman history. Except for some excellent marble and small quantities of tin, copper, iron, and gold, Italy has no mineral resources. The extensive coastline is broken by few good harbors. On the other hand, the amount of fertile land is greater than that of Greece. As a result, the Romans remained a predominantly agrarian people through the greater part of their history. They seldom enjoyed the intellectual stimulus which comes from extensive trading with other areas. In addition, the Italian peninsula was more open to invasion than was Greece. The Alps posed no effective barrier to the influx of peoples from central Europe, and the low-lying coast in many places invited conquest by sea. Domination of the territory by force was therefore more common than peaceful intermingling of immigrants

Left: *An Etruscan Musician.* Right: *Etruscan Winged Horses.* Both the well-coordinated flutist dating from about 480 B.C., and the proud horses (carved from wood) dating from about 300 B.C. reflect the Etruscans' delight in fluid movement.

Etruscan Sarcophagus. This work dating from around 520 B.C. shows a loving relationship between husband and wife meant to endure for eternity. As opposed to the Greeks, who usually created their statuary from stone, the Etruscans preferred to work with softer materials such as wood (see the horses on the previous page), or in this case, terra cotta.

with original settlers. The Romans became absorbed in military pursuits almost from the moment of their settlement on Italian soil, for they were forced to defend their own conquests against other invaders.

Archeological evidence indicates that between about 2000 and 1000 B.C. Italy was settled by waves of immigrants of the Indo-European language group, who arrived in the peninsula by way of the Alps. These people were herdsmen and farmers, and they brought with them the horse, the wheeled cart, and the ability to fashion bronze implements. Around 900 B.C. they appear to have acquired knowledge of iron-forging. A subgroup of these Indo-Europeans were ancestors of the Romans.

The rise of Rome

Probably during the eighth century B.C. two other nations of immigrants occupied different portions of the Italian peninsula: the Etruscans and the Greeks. Where the Etruscans came from is a question which has never been satisfactorily answered, although it is certain that they were not Indo-Europeans. Most authorities believe that they were natives of Asia Minor. Whatever their origins, by the sixth century B.C. they had established a confederation of cities that stretched over most of northern and central Italy. Although their writing has never been completely deciphered, enough materials survive to indicate the nature of their culture. They had an alphabet based upon the Greek, a high degree of skill in metalwork, great artistic talents, a flourishing trade with the East, and a religion based upon the worship of gods in human form. They bequeathed to the Romans a knowledge of the arch and the vault, the cruel amusement of gladiatorial combats, and the practice of foretelling the future by supernatural means such as studying the entrails of animals or the flight of birds. One of their most distinctive traits was the comparatively great respect they showed for women. Etruscan wives, unlike those in other contemporary societies, ate with their husbands, and some Etruscan families listed descent through the maternal line.

The Etruscans

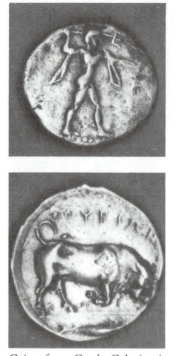

Coins from Greek Colonies in Southern Italy. The coin above showing the sea god Poseidon with his trident dates from c. 500 B.C., and the coin below with the bull from c. 400 B.C. In both cases the Greek artistic style is indistinguishable from anything found in Greece proper.

The Greeks settled mainly along the southern and southwestern shores of Italy and the island of Sicily, as well as along the southern coast of Gaul. Their most important settlements were Taranto, Naples, and Syracuse, each of which was an independent city-state. Greek civilization in Italy and Sicily was as advanced as in Greece itself. Such famous Greeks as Pythagoras, Archimedes, and even Plato for a time, lived in the Italian West. From the Greeks the Romans derived their alphabet, a number of their religious concepts, and much of their art and mythology.

The founders of Rome itself were Italic peoples who lived in the area south of the Tiber River. Though the exact year of the founding of the city is unknown, recent archeological research places the event quite near the traditional date of 753 B.C. By reason of its strategic location, Rome came to exercise an effective suzerainty over several of the most important neighboring cities. One conquest followed another until, by the sixth century B.C., Rome came to dominate most of the surrounding area.

At first Roman government aimed far more at establishing stability than at creating liberty. The original Roman state was essentially an application of the idea of the patriarchal family to the whole community, with the king exercising a jurisdiction over his subjects comparable to that of the head of the family over the members of his household. But just as the authority of the father was limited by custom and by the requirement that he respect the wishes of his adult sons, the authority of the king was limited by the ancient constitution, which he was powerless to change without the consent of the chief men of the realm. His prerogatives were not primarily legislative but executive, priestly, military, and judicial. Although his accession to office had to be confirmed by the people, he could not be deposed, and there was no one who could really challenge the exercise of his powers.

In addition to the kingship, the Roman government of this time included an assembly and a senate. The former was composed of all the male citizens of military age. As one of the chief sources of sovereign power, this body could veto any proposal for a change in the law which the king might make. Moreover, it determined whether aggressive war should be declared. But it was essentially a ratifying body with no right to initiate legislation or recommend changes of policy. The Senate, or council of elders, comprised in its membership the heads of the various clans which formed the community. Even more than the common citizens, the rulers of the clans embodied the sovereign power of the state. The king was only one of their number to whom they had delegated the active exercise of their authority. When the royal office became vacant, the powers of the king reverted to the Senate until the succession of a new monarch had been confirmed by the people. In ordinary times the chief function of the Senate was to examine royal proposals which had been ratified by the assembly

The Senate and the assembly

and to veto them if they violated rights established by ancient custom. It was thus almost impossible for fundamental changes to be made in the law even when the majority of the citizens were ready to sanction them. This extremely conservative attitude of the ruling classes persisted until the end of Roman history.

Toward the end of the sixth century (the date traditionally given is 509 B.C.) the monarchy was overthrown and replaced by a republic. Legend has it that this revolution was provoked by the crimes of the Tarquins, an Etruscan family that had taken over the kingship in Rome around the middle of the century. After suffering numerous indignities, the last and worst of which was the rape and subsequent suicide of a virtuous Roman matron, Lucretia, by a lustful Tarquin prince, the native Romans could stand no more and rose up to expel their alien oppressors. In fact the story of the rape of Lucretia is fictional but the change in government was probably in part a native uprising against foreigners, as well as a successful movement of the Roman senatorial aristocracy to gain full power for itself. The result was the beginning of Etruscan decline in Italy, as well as a lasting conviction among Romans that kingship was evil.

End of the monarchy

2. THE EARLY REPUBLIC

The history of the Roman Republic for more than two centuries after its establishment was one of almost constant warfare. Many of the most familiar Roman legends, such as that of the brave Horatio, who with only two friends held off an entire army in front of a bridge, date from this period. At first the Romans were on the defensive. The overthrow of the Tarquins resulted in acts of reprisal by their allies in neighboring regions, and other peoples on the borders took advantage of the confusion accompanying the change of regime to slice off portions of Roman territory. After Rome managed to ward off these attacks it began to expand in order to gain more land and satisfy a rapidly growing population. As time went on Rome steadily conquered all the Etruscan territories and then took over all the Greek cities in the southernmost portion of the Italian mainland. Not only did the latter add to the Roman domain, they also brought the Romans into fruitful contact with Greek culture. The Romans were then frequently confronted with revolts of peoples previously conquered. The suppression of these revolts awakened the suspicions of surrounding states and sharpened the appetite of the victors for further triumphs. New wars followed each other in what seemed an unending succession, until by 265 B.C. Rome had conquered the entire Italian peninsula.

Early Roman expansion

See color map facing page 230

This long series of military conflicts had profound social, economic, and cultural effects upon the subsequent history of Rome. It affected adversely the interests of the poorer citizens and furthered the concentration of land in the possession of wealthy proprietors. Long service

Roman Battle Sarcophagus. This relief displays the glories of war and expresses the Roman military ideal.

Effects of the early military conflicts

in the army forced the ordinary farmers to neglect the cultivation of the soil, with the result that they fell into debt and frequently lost their farms. Many took refuge in the city, until they were settled later as tenants on great estates in the conquered territories. The wars had the effect also of confirming the agrarian character of the Roman nation. The repeated acquisition of new lands made it possible to absorb the entire population into agricultural pursuits. As a consequence Romans saw no need for the development of industry and commerce. Last, the continual warfare of this formative period served to develop among the Romans a strong military ideal: along with Horatio, another of Rome's great early legendary heroes was Cincinnatus, who supposedly left his farm at a moment's notice for the battlefield.

During this same period of the early Republic, Rome underwent some significant political changes. These were not products so much of the revolution of the sixth century B.C. as of the developments of later years. The revolution which overthrew the monarchy was about as conservative as it is possible for a revolution to be. Its chief effect was to substitute two elected officials called consuls for the king and to exalt the position of the Senate by granting it control over the public funds and a veto on all actions of the assembly. The consuls themselves were usually senators and acted as the agents of their class. Each was supposed to possess the full executive and judicial authority which had previously been wielded by the king, limited by the right each possessed to veto the action of the other. If a conflict arose between them, the Senate might be called upon to decide; or, in time of grave emergency, a dictator might be appointed for a term not greater than six months. In other respects the government remained the same as in the days of the monarchy.

Political changes following the overthrow of the monarchy

Not long after the establishment of the Republic a struggle for power began among factions of the common citizens. Before the end

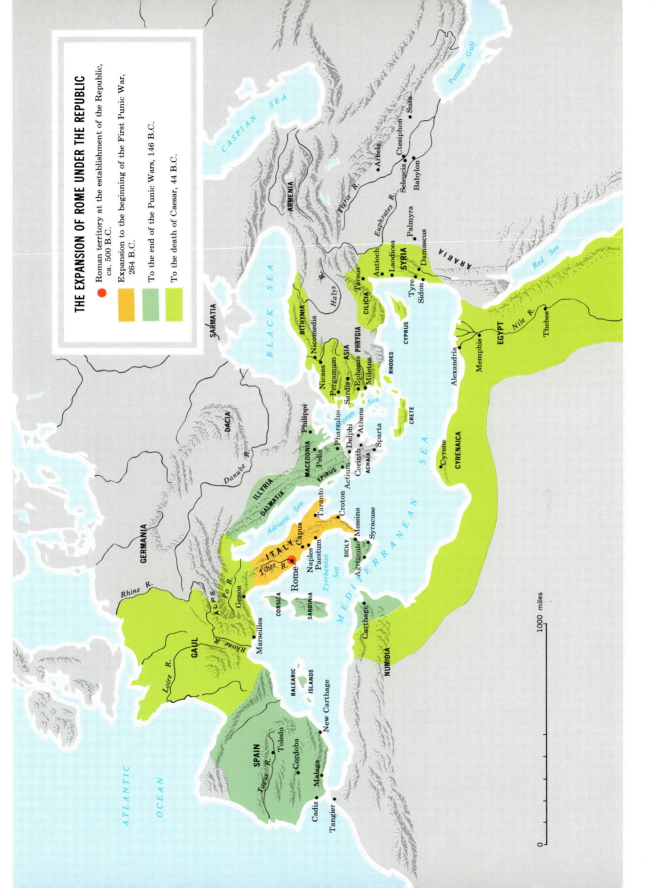

THE EXPANSION OF ROME UNDER THE REPUBLIC

- ● Roman territory at the establishment of the Republic, ca. 500 B.C.
- Expansion to the beginning of the First Punic War, 264 B.C.
- To the end of the Punic Wars, 146 B.C.
- To the death of Caesar, 44 B.C.

CASPIAN SEA

SARMATIA

ARMENIA

Susa

Arbela
Ctesiphon
Seleucia
Babylon

Tigris R.

Euphrates R.

Palmyra
Damascus
Antioch
Laodicea
SYRIA
Tyre
Sidon

ARABIA

Persian Gulf

Red Sea

Nile R.

EGYPT
Thebes

Memphis
Alexandria

CYRENAICA
Cyrene

CRETE

RHODES

CYPRUS

Tarsus
CILICIA

BLACK SEA

Halys

BITHYNIA
Nicomedia

Nicaea
Pergamum
ASIA
Sardis
PHRYGIA
Ephesus
Miletus

Aegean Sea

Philippi
MACEDONIA
Pella
Pharsalus
Delphi
Corinth
Athens
ACHAEA
Sparta
EPIRUS
Actium

DACIA

Danube R.

ILLYRIA
DALMATIA

GERMANIA

Rhine R.

Loire R.

GAUL

Rhône R.

ALPS

Po R.
Genoa

Marseilles

CORSICA

SARDINIA

Adriatic Sea

Taranto
Croton
ITALY
Capua
Naples Paestum
Tiber R.
Rome ●
Tyrrhenian Sea
Messina
SICILY
Agrigento
Syracuse

MEDITERRANEAN SEA

Carthage

NUMIDIA

BALEARIC
ISLANDS

New Carthage

SPAIN
Toledo
Tagus R.
Cordoba
Malaga
Cadiz
Tangier

ATLANTIC OCEAN

1000 miles

0

Etruscan Grotesques. These building ornaments of about 500 B.C. were meant to frighten away evil spirits. (Art Resource)

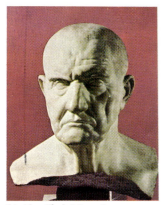

Unidentified Man, I cent. B.C.
The Romans excelled in portraits of sharp individuality.

*Augustus, Reigned 31 B.C.–A.D.
14.* This portrait suggests the
contradictory nature of the
genius who gave Rome peace
after years of strife.

*Constantine, Reigned A.D.
306–337.* The head is
from a statue sixteen feet
in height.

*Mummy Portrait, II
cent. A.D.* A Roman
woman buried in
Egypt.

Mosaic, I cent. A.D. A floor design
composed of small pieces of colored
marble fitted together to form a picture.

*Wall Painting of a
Satyr Mask, I cent.
B.C.* The belief in
satyrs, thought to
inhabit forests and
pastures, was tak-
en over from the
Greeks.

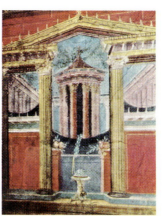

*Architectural Wall Paint-
ing from a Pompeiian Villa,
I cent. B.C.* Such paint-
ings suggest the Greek
origin of Roman forms
of architecture.

THE ROMAN EMPIRE AT ITS GREATEST EXTENT
98–117 A.D.

CASPIAN SEA

Persian Gulf

Cyrus R.
ARMENIA
Araxes R.
Tigris R.
Euphrates R.
MESOPOTAMIA

CAPPADOCIA
GALATIA
BITHYNIA
Nicomedia
Antioch
SYRIA

BLACK SEA

Red Sea

ASIA
Ephesus
EGYPT
Nile R.
Alexandria

THRACE
DACIA
MACEDONIA
Athens
CYRENAICA

MEDITERRANEAN SEA

ILLYRIA
PANNONIA
DALMATIA
Syracuse

Danube R.

GERMANIA
CONQUESTS TO ELBE
(ABANDONED, 17 A.D.)
Elbe R.
GERMANICUS
LIMES
GERMANICUS

RAETIA
ALPS
APPENINES
Tiber R.
Rome

TRIPOLIS
AFRICA

BALTIC SEA

HADRIAN'S WALL
NORTH
SEA
GAUL
NUMIDIA

HIBERNIA
(IRELAND)
NORTH BRITAIN
(ANNEXED, 84 A.D.)
BRITAIN
English Channel
Bay of
Biscay
MAURETANIA

ATLANTIC
OCEAN
SPAIN

1000 miles

0

of the monarchy the Roman population had come to be divided into two great classes—the patricians and the plebeians. The former were the aristocracy, wealthy landowners who monopolized the seats in the Senate and the offices of magistracy. Among the plebeians were some wealthy families who were barred from the patriciate because they were of recent foreign origin, but most plebeians were common people—small farmers, craftsmen, and tradesmen. Many were clients or dependents of the patricians, obliged to fight for them, to render them political support, and to cultivate their estates in return for protection. The grievances of the plebeians were numerous. Compelled to pay heavy taxes and forced to serve in the army in time of war, they were nevertheless excluded from all part in the government except membership in the assembly. Moreover, they felt themselves the victims of discriminatory decisions in judicial trials. They did not even know what legal rights they were supposed to enjoy, for the laws were unwritten, and the patricians alone had the power to interpret them. For default on debt the creditor was allowed to sell the debtor into slavery outside Rome.

In order to obtain a redress of these grievances the plebeians rebelled soon after the beginning of the fifth century B.C. They gained their first victory about 494 B.C., when they forced the patricians to agree to the election of a number of officers known as tribunes with power to protect the citizens by means of a veto over unlawful acts of the magistrates. This victory was followed by a successful demand for codification of the laws about 450 B.C. The result was the publication of the famous Law of the Twelve Tables, so called because it was written on tablets of wood. Although the Twelve Tables came to be revered by the Romans of later times as a kind of charter of the people's liberties, they were really nothing of the sort. For the most part they merely perpetuated ancient custom without even abolishing enslavement for unpaid debts. They did, however, enable the people to know where they stood in relation to the law. About a generation later the plebeians won eligibility to positions as lesser magistrates, and about 367 B.C. the first plebeian consul was elected. Since ancient custom provided that, upon completing their terms of office, consuls should automatically enter the Senate, the patrician monopoly of seats in that body was broken. The final plebeian victory came in 287 B.C. with the passage of a law which provided that measures enacted by the assembly should become binding upon the state whether the Senate approved them or not.

The significance of these changes must not be misinterpreted. They did not constitute a revolution to gain more liberty for the individual but merely to curb the power of the magistrates and to win for the plebeians a larger share in government. The state as a whole remained as despotic as ever, for its authority over the citizens was not even challenged. Indeed, the Romans of the early Republic "never really abandoned the principle that the people were not to govern but to be

The struggle between patricians and plebeians

The victories of the plebeians

Significance of the plebeian victories

governed."[1] Because of this attitude the grant of full legislative powers to the assembly seems to have meant little more than a formality; the Senate continued to rule as before. Nor did the admission of plebeians to membership in the Senate have any effect in liberalizing that body. So high was its prestige and so deep was the veneration of the Roman for authority, that the new members were soon swallowed up in the conservatism of the old. Moreover, the fact that the magistrates received no salaries prevented most of the poorer citizens from seeking public office.

Intellectually and culturally the Romans developed very slowly. Life in Rome was still harsh and crude. Though writing had been adopted as early as the sixth century B.C., little use was made of it except for the copying of laws, treaties, and funerary inscriptions. Inasmuch as education was limited to instruction imparted by the father in manly sports, practical arts, and soldierly virtues, the great majority of the people were still illiterate. War and agriculture continued as the chief occupations for the bulk of the citizens. A few craftsmen were to be found in the cities, and a minor development of trade had occurred. But the fact that the country had no standard system of coinage until 269 B.C. casts light on the comparative insignificance of Roman commerce at this time.

During the period of the early Republic Roman religion assumed the character it retained through the greater part of Roman history. In several ways this religion resembled that of the Greeks, partly for the reason that the Etruscan religion was deeply indebted to the Greek, and the Romans, in turn, were influenced by the Etruscans. Both the Greek and Roman religions emphasized the performances of rites in order to gain benefits from the gods or keep them from anger. The deities in both religions performed similar functions: Jupiter corresponded to Zeus as god of the sky, Minerva to Athena as goddess of wisdom and patroness of crafts, Venus to Aphrodite as goddess of love, Neptune to Poseidon as god of the sea, and so on. The Roman religion, like the Greek, had no dogmas or sacraments or belief in rewards and punishments in an afterlife.

But there were significant differences also. The Roman religion was distinctly more political. It served not to glorify humanity or establish a comfortable relationship between human beings and their world but to protect the state from its enemies and to augment its power and prosperity. The gods were less human; indeed, it was only as a result of Greek and Etruscan influences that they were made personal deities at all, having previously been worshiped as animistic spirits. The Romans never conceived of their deities as quarreling among themselves or mingling with human beings after the fashion of Homeric divinities. Finally, the Roman religion contained a stronger element of religious interaction with public political life than the Greek.

Roman society and culture still rather primitive

The religion of the Romans compared with that of the Greeks

Contrasts with Greek religion

[1] Theodor Mommsen, *The History of Rome*, I, 313.

Intervention of Jupiter. This scene from the first century A.D. depicts Jupiter, god of the sky, supporting the Romans in a battle against Germanic barbarians.

A committee of priests known as pontiffs formed a branch of the government, presiding over public sacrifices and serving as guardians of sacred traditions that they alone were allowed to interpret. It must be stressed, however, that these religious officials were by no means priests in a professional sense. Instead, they were aristocrats who served as pontiffs for limited terms of office before or after taking on other governmental duties and without having been trained in any specialized manner for a religious calling. Furthermore their role was strictly public, for they heard no confessions, forgave no sins, and administered no sacraments.

The morality of the Romans in this as in later periods had almost no connection with religion. The Romans did not ask their gods to make them good, but to bestow upon the community and upon their families material blessings. Morality was a matter of patriotism and of respect for authority and tradition. The chief virtues were bravery, honor, self-discipline, reverence for the gods and for one's ancestors, and duty to country and family. Loyalty to Rome took precedence over everything else. For the good of the state the citizen had to be ready to sacrifice not only his own life but, if necessary, the lives of his family and friends. The courage of certain consuls who dutifully put their sons to death for breaches of military discipline was a subject of profound admiration. Few peoples in European history, with the exception of the Spartans and modern totalitarians, have ever taken the problems of national interest so seriously or subordinated the individual so completely to the welfare of the state.

Morality in the Early Republic

3. THE FATEFUL WARS WITH CARTHAGE

The beginning of imperialism on a major scale

By 265 B.C. Rome had conquered and annexed almost the entire Italian mainland. Proud and confident of its strength, it was almost certain to strike out into new fields of empire. The prosperous island of Sicily was not yet within its grasp, nor could it regard with indifference the situation in other parts of the Mediterranean world. Rome was now prone to interpret almost any change in the status quo as a threat to its own power and security. It was for such reasons that Rome soon became involved in a series of wars with other great nations which decidedly altered the course of its history.

Carthage

The first and most important of these wars was the struggle with Carthage, a great maritime empire that stretched along the northern coast of Africa from modern-day Tunisia to the Strait of Gibraltar. Carthage had originally been founded about 800 B.C. as a Phoenician colony. In the sixth century B.C. it severed its ties with the homeland and gradually developed into a rich and powerful state. The prosperity of its upper classes was founded upon commerce and upon exploitation of the silver and tin resources of Spain and the tropical products of north central Africa. Carthaginian government was oligarchic. The real rulers were thirty merchant princes who constituted an inner council of the Senate. These men controlled elections and dominated every other branch of the government. The remaining 270 members of the Senate appear to have been summoned to meet only on special occasions. In spite of these political deficiencies and a cruel religion that demanded blood sacrifices, Carthage had a civilization superior in luxury and scientific attainment to that of Rome when the struggle between the two states began.

Causes of the First Punic War

The initial clash with Carthage started in 264 B.C.[2] The primary cause was Roman jealousy over Carthaginian expansion in Sicily. Carthage already controlled the western portion of the island and was threatening the Greek cities of Syracuse and Messina on the eastern coast. If these cities were captured, all chances of Roman occupation of Sicily would be lost. Faced with this danger, Rome declared war upon Carthage with the hope of forcing it back into its African domain. Twenty-three years of fighting finally brought victory to the Roman generals. Carthage was compelled to surrender its possessions in Sicily and to pay a very large indemnity.

The Second Punic War

But the Romans had exerted such heroic efforts to defeat Carthage that when victory was finally secured it made them more arrogant and acquisitive than ever. As a result, the struggle with Carthage was renewed on two subsequent occasions. In 218 B.C., the Romans interpreted the Carthaginian attempt to rebuild an empire in Spain as a

[2] The wars with Carthage are known as the Punic Wars. The Romans called the Carthaginians *Poeni*, i.e., Phoenicians, whence is derived the adjective "Punic."

threat to their interests and responded with a declaration of war. This struggle raged through a period of sixteen years. Italy was ravaged by the armies of Hannibal, the famous Carthaginian commander, who crossed the Alps with sixty elephants, and whose tactics have been copied by military experts to the present day. Rome escaped defeat by the narrowest of margins. Only the durability of its system of alliances in Italy saved the day. As long as these alliances held, Hannibal dared not besiege the city of Rome itself for fear of being attacked from the rear. In the end Carthage was more completely humbled than before, being compelled to abandon all its possessions except the capital city and its surrounding territory in Africa, and to pay an indemnity three times greater than that paid at the end of the First Punic War.

Roman vindictiveness reached its peak about the middle of the second century B.C. By this time Carthage had recovered a modicum of its former prosperity—enough to excite the displeasure of its conquerors. Nothing would now satisfy the senatorial magnates but the complete destruction of Carthage and the expropriation of its land. In 149 B.C. the Senate dispatched an ultimatum demanding that the Carthaginians abandon their city and settle at least ten miles from the coast. Since this demand was tantamount to a death sentence for a nation dependent upon commerce, it was refused—as the Romans probably hoped it would be. The result was the Third Punic War, a brutal conflict which was fought between 149 and 146 B.C. The final Roman assault upon the city was carried into the houses of the inhabitants and a frightful butchery took place. When the victorious Roman general saw Carthage going up in flames he said: "It is a glorious moment, but I have a strange feeling that some day the same fate will befall my own homeland." With the resistance of the Carthaginians finally broken, the few citizens left to surrender were sold into slavery, their once magnificent city was razed, and the ground was plowed over with salt. Carthaginian territory was then organized into a Roman province, with the best areas parceled out as senatorial estates.

The wars with Carthage had momentous effects on Rome. First, victory in the Second Punic War led to Roman occupation of Spain. This not only brought great new wealth—above all from Spanish silver—but was the beginning of a policy of westward expansion that proved to be one of the great formative influences on the history of Europe. Then too the wars brought Rome into conflict with eastern Mediterranean powers and thereby paved the way for still greater dominion. During the Second Punic War, Philip V of Macedon had entered into an alliance with Carthage and had plotted with the king of Syria to divide Egypt between them. Declaring a disinterested intention to forestall Philip's moves, Rome sent an army to the East, although the extension of Roman rule was evidently the real item on the Roman agenda. The result was the conquest of Greece and Asia Minor and the establishment of a protectorate over Egypt. Thus before the end of the second century B.C. virtually the entire Mediterranean area

Hannibal. A coin from Carthage representing Hannibal as a victorious general, with an elephant on the reverse.

The Third Punic War and the destruction of Carthage

Results of the wars with Carthage: (1) conquest of Spain and the Hellenistic East

See color map facing page 230

had been brought under Roman control. The conquest of the Hellenistic East led to the introduction of Greek ideas and customs into Rome. Despite formidable resistance, these novelties exerted considerable influence in changing some aspects of social and cultural life.

Still another effect of the Punic Wars was a great social and economic revolution that swept over Rome in the third and second centuries B.C. The changes wrought by this revolution may be enumerated as follows: (1) a marked increase in slavery due to the capture and sale of prisoners of war; (2) the decline of the small farmer as a result of the establishment of the plantation system in conquered areas and the influx of cheap grain from the provinces; (3) the growth of a disgruntled urban element composed of impoverished farmers and workers displaced by slave labor; (4) the appearance of a middle class comprising merchants, moneylenders, and men who held government contracts to operate mines, build roads, or collect taxes; and (5) an increase in luxury and vulgar display, particularly among the newly rich who fattened themselves on the profits of war.

*Cato's attempt to prevent
the transformation of
Roman society*

As a consequence of this social and economic revolution, Rome was changed from a republic of yeoman farmers into a complex society with new habits of luxury and indulgence. Though property had never been evenly distributed, the gulf which separated rich and poor now yawned more widely than before. The old-fashioned ideals of discipline and devotion to the service of the state were weakened, and people began to live more for pleasure. A few members of the senatorial aristocracy exerted efforts to check these tendencies and to restore the simple virtues of the past. The leader of this movement was the dour Cato the Elder, who inveighed against the new rich for their soft living and strove to set an example to his countrymen by performing hard labor on his farm and dwelling in a house with a dirt floor and no plaster on the walls. In addition he was a prude who showed contempt for women and boasted that his wife never came into his arms except during great thunder. Cato also strove, often cantankerously, to prevent the influx of Greek intellectual influences. But his efforts on all fronts had no lasting effect because the clock could not be turned back.

4. THE SOCIAL STRUGGLES OF THE LATE REPUBLIC

The period from the end of the Punic Wars in 146 B.C. to about 30 B.C. was one of the most turbulent in the history of Rome. It was between these years that the nation reaped the full harvest of the seeds of violence sown during the wars of conquest. Bitter class conflicts, assassinations, desperate struggles between rival dictators, wars, and insurrections were the all too common occurrences of this time. Even the slaves contributed to the general disorder: first, in 104 B.C. when they ravaged Sicily; and again in 73 B.C. when 70,000 of them under the leadership of a slave named Spartacus held the consuls at bay for more than a year. Spartacus was finally slain in battle and 6,000 of his followers were captured and left crucified along the length of a long road to provide a warning for others.

The first stage in the conflict between classes of citizens began with the ascendancy of the two Gracchi brothers. Though of aristocratic lineage themselves, the Gracchi strove for a program of reforms to alleviate the country's ills. They considered these to be a result of the decline of the free peasantry, and proposed the simple remedy of dividing state lands among the landless. The first of the brothers to take up the cause of reform was Tiberius. Elected tribune in 133 B.C., he proposed a law that restricted the current renters or holders of state lands to a maximum of 300 acres per citizen plus 150 acres for each child in the family. The excess was to be confiscated by the government and given to the poor in small plots. Conservative aristocrats bitterly opposed this proposal and brought about its veto by Tiberius's colleague in the tribunate, Octavius. Tiberius removed Octavius from office, and when his own term expired attempted to stand for reelection. Both of these moves seemed to threaten dictatorialism and gave the conservative senators an excuse for violence. Armed with clubs, they went on a rampage during the elections and murdered Tiberius and 300 of his followers.

The land program of Tiberius Gracchus

Nine years later Gaius Gracchus, the younger brother of Tiberius, renewed the struggle for reform. Though Tiberius's land law had finally been enacted by the Senate, Gaius believed that the campaign had to go further. Elected tribune in 123 B.C., and reelected in 122, he procured the enactment of various laws for the benefit of the less privileged. The first provided for stabilizing the price of grain in Rome. For this purpose great public granaries were built along the Tiber. A second law proposed to extend the franchise to Roman allies, giving them the rights of Latin citizens. Still a third gave the middle class the right to make up the juries that tried governors accused of exploiting the provinces. These and similar measures provoked so much anger and contention among the classes that riots broke out. Gaius was proclaimed an enemy of the state, and the Senate authorized the consuls to take all necessary steps for the defense of the Republic. In the ensuing conflict Gaius committed suicide and about 3,000 of his followers were killed.

Gaius Gracchus and the renewed fight for reform

The Gracchan turbulence had broad significance. It demonstrated, first of all, that the Roman Republic had outgrown its constitution. Over the years the assembly had gained powers almost equal to those of the Senate. Instead of working out a peaceful accommodation to these changes, both sides resorted to violence. By so doing they set a precedent for the unbridled use of force by any politician ambitious for supreme power and thereby paved the way for the destruction of the Republic. The Romans had shown a remarkable capacity for organizing an empire and for adapting the Greek idea of a city-state to a large territory, but the narrow conservatism of their upper classes

Significance of the Gracchan attempts at reform

Pompey

Julius Caesar

See color map facing
page 230

Caesar's achievements

was a fatal hindrance to the health of the state. Regarding all reform as evil, they failed to understand the reasons for internal discord and seemed to think that repression was its only remedy.

After the downfall of the Gracchi, two military leaders who had won fame in foreign wars successively made themselves rulers of the state. The first was Marius, who was elevated to the consulship by the masses in 107 B.C. and reelected six times thereafter. Unfortunately, Marius was no statesman and accomplished nothing for his followers beyond demonstrating the ease with which a general with an army at his back could override opposition. Following his death in 86 B.C. the aristocrats took a turn at government by force. Their champion was Sulla, another victorious commander. Appointed dictator in 82 B.C. for an unlimited term, Sulla ruthlessly proceeded to exterminate his opponents and to elevate the powers of the Senate. Even the senatorial veto over acts of the assembly was revived, and the authority of the tribunes was sharply curtailed. After three years of rule Sulla decided to exchange the pomp of power for the pleasures of the senses and retired to a life of luxury and ease on his country estate.

It was not to be expected that the actions of Sulla would stand unchallenged after he had relinquished his office, for the effect of his decrees was to give control to a selfish aristocracy. Several new leaders now emerged to espouse the cause of the people. The most famous of them were Pompey (106–48 B.C.) and Julius Caesar (100–44 B.C.). For a time they pooled their energies and resources in a plot to gain control of the government, but later they became rivals and sought to outdo each other in bids for popular support. Pompey won fame as the conqueror of Syria and Palestine, while Caesar devoted his talents to a series of brilliant forays against the Gauls, adding to the Roman state the territory of modern Belgium, Germany west of the Rhine, and France. In 52 B.C., after a series of mob disorders in Rome, the Senate turned to Pompey and caused his election as sole consul. Caesar, stationed in Gaul, was eventually branded an enemy of the state, and Pompey conspired with the senatorial faction to deprive him of political power. The result was a deadly war between the two men. In 49 B.C. Caesar crossed the Rubicon River into Italy (ever since then an image for a fateful decision) and marched on Rome. Pompey fled to the East in the hope of gathering an army large enough to regain control of Italy. In 48 B.C. the forces of the two rivals met at Pharsalus in Greece. Pompey was defeated and soon afterward was murdered by agents of the ruler of Egypt.

Caesar then intervened in Egyptian politics at the court of Cleopatra (whom he left pregnant). Then he conducted another military campaign in Asia Minor in which victory was so swift that he could report "I came, I saw, I conquered" (*veni, vidi, vici*). After that Caesar returned to Rome. There was now no one who dared to challenge his power. With the aid of his veterans he cowed the Senate into granting his every desire. In 46 B.C. he became dictator for ten years, and two years later for life. In addition, he assumed nearly every other title that could augment his power. He obtained from the Senate full authority to make war and peace and to control the revenues of the state. For all practical purposes he was above the law, and the other agents of the government were merely his servants. Unquestionably he had little respect for the constitution, and rumors spread that he intended to make himself king. At any rate, it was on such a charge that he was assassinated on the Ides of March in 44 B.C. by a group of conspirators, under the leadership of Brutus and Cassius, who hoped to rid Rome of the dictatorship.

Although Caesar used to be revered by historians as a superhuman hero, he is now often dismissed as insignificant. But both extremes of interpretation should be avoided. Certainly he did not "save Rome" and was not the greatest statesman of all time, for he treated the Republic with contempt and made the problem of governing more difficult for those who came after him. Yet some of the measures he took as dictator did have lasting effects. With the aid of a Greek astronomer he revised the calendar so as to make a year last for 365 days (with an extra day added every fourth year). This "Julian" calendar—subject to adjustments made by Pope Gregory XIII in 1582—is still with us. It is thus only proper that the seventh month is named after Julius as "July." By conferring citizenship upon thousands of Spaniards and Gauls, Caesar took an important step toward eliminating the distinction between Italians and provincials. He also helped relieve economic inequities by settling many of his veterans and some of the urban poor on unused lands. Vastly more important than these reforms, however, was Caesar's farsighted resolve, made before he seized power, to invest his efforts in the West. While Pompey, and before him Alexander, went to the East to gain fame and fortune, Caesar was the first great leader to recognize the potential significance of northwestern Europe. By incorporating Gaul into the Roman world he brought Rome great agricultural wealth and helped bring urban life and culture to what was then the wild West. Western European civilization, later to be anchored in just those regions that Caesar conquered, might not have been the same without him.

Ides of March Coin. This coin was struck by Brutus to commemorate the assassination of Julius Caesar. Brutus is depicted on the obverse; on the reverse is a liberty cap between two daggers and the Latin abbreviation for the Ides of March.

5. ROME BECOMES SOPHISTICATED

The culture that Rome brought to Gaul was itself taken from the Greek East. During the last two centuries of republican history Rome came under the influence of Hellenistic civilization. The result was a flowering of intellectual activity and a further impetus to social change beyond what the Punic Wars had produced. The fact must be noted, however, that several of the components of the Hellenistic pattern of culture were never adopted by the Romans. The science of the Hellenistic Age, for example, was largely ignored, and the same was true of some of its art.

One of the most notable effects of Hellenistic influence was the adoption of Epicureanism and, above all, Stoicism by numerous Romans of the upper classes. The most renowned of the Roman exponents of Epicureanism was Lucretius (98–55 B.C.), author of a booklength philosophical poem entitled *On the Nature of Things*. In writing this work Lucretius was moved to explain the universe in such a way as to remove all fear of the supernatural, which he regarded as the chief obstacle to peace of mind. Worlds and all things in them, he taught, are the results of fortuitous combinations of atoms. Though he admitted the existence of the gods, he conceived of them as living in eternal peace, neither creating nor governing the universe. Everything is a product of mechanical evolution, including human beings, and their habits, institutions, and beliefs. Since mind is indissolubly linked with matter, death means utter extinction; consequently, no part of the human personality can survive to be rewarded or punished in an afterlife. Lucretius's conception of the good life was simple: what one needs, he asserted, is not enjoyment but "peace and a pure heart." Whether one agrees with Lucretius's philosophy or not, there is no doubt that he was an extraordinarily fine poet. In fact his musical cadences, sustained majesty of expression, and infectious enthusiasm earn him a rank among the greatest poets who ever lived.

Stoicism was introduced into Rome about 140 B.C. and soon came to include among its converts numerous influential leaders of public life. The greatest of these was Cicero (106–43 B.C.), the "father of Roman eloquence." Although Cicero adopted doctrines from a number of philosophers, including both Plato and Aristotle, he derived more of his ideas from the Stoics than from any other source. Cicero's ethical philosophy was based on the Stoic premises that virtue is sufficient for happiness and that tranquillity of mind is the highest good. He conceived of the ideal human being as one who has been guided by reason to an indifference toward sorrow and pain. Where Cicero diverged from the Greek Stoics was in his greater approval of the active, political life. To this degree he still spoke for the older Roman tradition of service to the state. Cicero never claimed to be an original philosopher but rather conceived his goal to be that of bringing the best of Greek philosophy to the West. In this he was remarkably successful, for he wrote in a rich and elegant Latin prose style that has never been surpassed. Cicero's prose immediately became a standard for composition and has remained so until the present century. Thus even though not a truly great thinker Cicero was the most influential Latin transmitter of ancient thought to the medieval and modern western European worlds.

Lucretius and Cicero were the two leading exponents of Greek thought but not the only two fine writers of the later Roman Republic. It now became the fashion among the upper classes to learn Greek and to strive to reproduce in Latin some of the more popular forms of Greek literature. Some results of enduring literary merit were the ribald comedies of Plautus (257?–184 B.C.), the passionate love poems of Catullus (84?–54? B.C.), and the crisp military memoirs of Julius Caesar, the opening of which all beginning students of Latin used to know as well as the pledge of allegiance.

The conquest of the Hellenistic world accelerated the process of social change which the Punic Wars had begun. The effects were most clearly evident in the growth of luxury, in a widened cleavage between classes, and in a further increase in slavery. The Italian people, numbering about eight million at the end of the Republic, had come to be divided into four main social orders: the senatorial aristocracy, the equestrians, the common citizens, and the slaves. The senatorial aristocrats numbered 300 citizens and their families. The majority of them inherited their status, although occasionally a plebeian would gain admission to the Senate through serving a term as consul. Most of the senatorial aristocrats gained their living as officeholders and as owners of great landed estates. The equestrian order was made up of propertied aristocrats who were not in the Senate. Originally this class had been composed of those citizens with incomes sufficient to enable them to serve in the cavalry at their own expense, but the term equestrian came to be applied to all outside of the senatorial class who possessed property in substantial amount. The equestrians

Social conditions in the late Republic

Left: *Atrium of an Upper-class House in Pompeii, Seen from the Interior.* Around the atrium or central court were grouped suites of living rooms. The marble columns and decorated walls still give an idea of the luxury and refinement enjoyed by the privileged minority. Right: *Orpheus Floor Mosaic.* This luxurious adornment to an upper-class Roman dwelling, in what is today Arles in southern France, represents the inspired musician soothing lions and tigers as well as numerous other representatives of the animal kingdom.

were the chief offenders in the indulgence of vulgar tastes and in the exploitation of the poor and the provincials. As money-lenders they often charged exorbitant interest rates. By far the largest number of the citizens were mere commoners. Most of these were independent farmers, a few were industrial workers, and some were indigent city dwellers who lived by intermittent employment and public relief. When Julius Caesar became dictator, 320,000 citizens were receiving free grain from the state.

The status of the slaves

The Roman slaves were scarcely considered people at all but instruments of production like cattle or horses to be worked for the profit of their masters. Notwithstanding the fact that some of them were cultivated foreigners taken as prisoners of war, they had none of the privileges granted to slaves in Athens. The policy of many of their owners was to get as much work out of them as possible during their prime and then to turn them loose to be fed by the state when they became old and useless. Of course, there were exceptions. Cicero, for example, reported himself very fond of his slaves. It is, nevertheless, a sad commentary on Roman civilization that nearly all of the productive labor in the country was done by slaves. They produced practically all of the nation's food supply, for the amount contributed by the few surviving independent farmers was quite insignificant. At least 80 percent of the workers employed in shops were slaves or former slaves. But many of the members of the servile population were engaged in nonproductive activities. A lucrative form of investment for the business classes was ownership of slaves trained as gladiators, who could be rented to the government or to aspiring politicians for the amusement of the people. The growth of luxury also required the employment of thousands of slaves in domestic service. The man of great wealth insisted on having his doorkeepers, his litter-bearers, his couriers (for the government of the Republic had no postal service), his valets, and his tutors for his children. In some great households there were special servants with no other duties than to rub the master down after his bath or to care for his sandals.

Changes in religion

The religious beliefs of the Romans were altered in various ways in the last two centuries of the Republic—again mainly because of the extension of Roman power over most of the Hellenistic states. First of all, the upper classes tended to abandon the traditional religion for the philosophies of Stoicism and, to a lesser degree, Epicureanism. But many of the common people also found worship of the ancient gods no longer satisfying because it was too formal and mechanical and demanded too much in the way of duty and self-sacrifice to meet their needs. Furthermore, Italy had attracted a stream of immigrants from the East, most of whom had a religious background totally different from that of the Romans. The result was the spread of Eastern mystery cults, which satisfied the craving for a more emotional religion and offered the reward of immortality to the wretched and downtrodden of the earth. From Egypt came the cult of Osiris (or Serapis, as the god was now more commonly called), while from Phrygia in Asia Minor was introduced the worship of the Great Mother, with her eunuch priests and wild, symbolic orgies. So strong was the appeal of these cults that the decrees of the Senate against them proved almost impossible to enforce. In the last century B.C. the Persian cult of Mithraism, which came to surpass all the others in popularity, gained a foothold in Italy.

6. THE PRINCIPATE OR EARLY EMPIRE (27 B.C.–180 A.D.)

Shortly before his death in 44 B.C., Julius Caesar had adopted as his sole heir his grandnephew Octavian (63 B.C.–14 A.D.), then a young man of eighteen acting in his uncle's service in Illyria across the Adriatic Sea. Upon learning of Caesar's death, Octavian hastened to Rome to see if he could claim his inheritance. He soon found that he had to join forces with two of Caesar's powerful friends, Mark Antony and Lepidus. The following year the three formed an alliance for the purpose of crushing the power of the aristocratic group responsible for Caesar's murder. The methods employed were not to the new leaders' credit. Prominent members of the aristocracy were hunted down and slain and their property confiscated. The most noted of the victims was Cicero, brutally slain by Mark Antony's thugs though he had taken no part in the conspiracy against Caesar's life. The real murderers, Brutus and Cassius, escaped and organized an army, but were defeated by Octavian and his colleagues near Philippi in 42 B.C.

An alliance to avenge Caesar's death

Thereafter a quarrel developed between the members of the alliance, inspired primarily by Antony's jealousy of Octavian. The subsequent struggle became a contest between East and West. Antony went to the East and made an alliance with Cleopatra that was dedicated to introducing principles of Oriental despotism into Roman rule. Octavian consolidated the forces of the West and came forward as the champion of Greek cultural traditions. As in the earlier contest between Caesar and Pompey the victory again went to the West. In the naval battle of Actium (31 B.C.) Octavian's forces defeated those of Antony and Cleopatra, both of whom soon afterward committed suicide. It was now clear that Rome would not be swallowed up by the East. Actium guaranteed that there would be several more centuries for the consolidation of Greek ideals and urban life, a development important above all for the future of western Europe.

The victory of Octavian ushered in a new period in Roman history, the most glorious and the most prosperous that the nation experienced. Although problems of peace and order were still far from being completely solved, the deadly civil strife was over, and the people now had their first opportunity to show what their talents could achieve. Octavian was determined to preserve the forms if not the

The revival of constitutional government

Augustus's Daughter Julia. Hoping to accomplish moral as well as political reforms, Augustus ordered the minting of coins depicting either his wife, or in this case, his daughter, in order to propagandize for the virtues of family life. (Unfortunately Julia engaged in so many extramarital affairs that Augustus was ultimately forced to banish her to a distant island.)

Augustus

substance of constitutional government. He accepted the titles of Augustus and emperor (which then only meant "victorious general") conferred upon him by the Senate and the army. He held the authority of proconsul and tribune permanently; but he refused to make himself dictator or even consul for life, despite the pleas of the populace that he do so. Theoretically the Senate and the people were the supreme sovereigns, as they had been under the early Republic. The title by which he preferred to have his authority designated was princeps, or first citizen of the state. For this reason the period of his rule and that of his successors is properly called the Principate, or early Empire, to distinguish it from the periods of the Republic (sixth century B.C. to 27 B.C.), the time of upheavals (180 A.D. to 284 A.D.), and the period of the late Empire (284 A.D. to 610 A.D.).

Octavian, or Augustus as he was now more commonly called, ruled over Italy and the provinces for forty-four years (31 B.C.–14 A.D.). At the beginning of the period he governed by military power and by common consent, but in 27 B.C. the Senate bestowed upon him the series of offices and titles described above. His work as a statesman at least equaled in importance that of Julius Caesar. Among the reforms of Augustus were the establishment of a new coinage system for use throughout the entire Roman Empire and the introduction within Rome itself of a range of public services, including police and fire-fighting. Augustus also bestowed more self-government upon cities and provinces than they had enjoyed before, and he abolished the old system of farming out the collection of financial dues. Whereas previously tax collectors were remunerated solely by being allowed to keep a percentage of their intake, a system which led inevitably to graft and extortion, Augustus now appointed his own representatives as tax collectors at regular salaries whom he kept under strict control for corruption. Above all, Augustus instituted a program of incentives for colonization of the provinces in order to shift the excess free population out of Italy and thereby to remove a major source of social tensions and political upheaval. All told such measures in fact contributed to bringing about the enhancement of local peace.

After the death of Augustus in 14 A.D. until almost the end of the century Rome had no really capable rulers, with the single exception of Claudius (41–54). Several of Augustus's successors, most infamously Caligula (37–41) and Nero (54–68), were brutal tyrants who squandered the resources of the state and kept the city of Rome in an uproar by their deeds of bloody violence. But starting in 96 A.D., a period of strong and stable government returned with the advent of "five good emperors": Nerva (96–98), Trajan (98–117), Hadrian (117–138), Antoninus Pius (138–161), and Marcus Aurelius (161–180). These five ruled in harmony with the Senate, displayed great gifts as administrators, and, each in their turn, were able to bequeath a well-ordered and united realm to their designated successors.

From the time of Augustus until that of Trajan, the Roman Empire continued to expand. Augustus gained more land for Rome than did any other Roman ruler. His generals advanced into central Europe, conquering the territories known today as Switzerland, Austria, and Bulgaria. Only in modern-day central Germany did Roman troops meet defeat, a setback which convinced Augustus to hold the Roman borders at the Rhine and Danube. Subsequently, in 43 A.D., the Emperor Claudius began the conquest of Britain, and at the beginning of the next century Trajan pushed beyond the Danube to add Dacia (now Rumania) to the Roman realms. Trajan also conquered territories in Mesopotamia but thereby incurred the enmity of the Persians, causing his successor Hadrian to embark on a defensive policy. The Roman Empire had now reached its ultimate territorial limits; in the third century these limits would begin to recede.

Trajan

Rome's peaceful sway over a vast empire for about two centuries from the time of Augustus to that of Marcus Aurelius was certainly one of its most impressive accomplishments. As the historian Gibbon said, "the Empire of Rome comprehended the fairest part of the earth and the most civilized portion of mankind." The celebrated *Pax Romana,* or Roman peace, was unprecedented. The Mediterranean was now under the control of one power (as it has never been before or since) and experienced the passage of centuries without a single naval battle. On land one rule held without contention from the borders of Scotland to those of Persia. A contemporary orator justly boasted that "the whole civilized world lays down the arms which were its ancient load, as if on holiday . . . all places are full of gymnasia, fountains, monumental approaches, temples, workshops, schools; one can say that the civilized world, which had been sick from the beginning . . . , has been brought by the right knowledge to a state of health." But much of this health, as we will see, proved illusory.

The Pax Romana

See color map facing
page 231

7. CULTURE AND LIFE IN THE PERIOD OF THE PRINCIPATE

From the standpoint of variety of intellectual and artistic interests the period of the Principate outshone all other ages in the history of Rome. From 27 B.C. to about 200 A.D. Roman philosophy attained its most characteristic form. The same period also witnessed the production of outstanding literary works, the growth of a distinctive architecture and art, and the greatest triumphs of Roman engineering.

*Cultural progress under
the Principate*

The form of philosophy that appealed most strongly to the Romans was Stoicism. The reasons for Stoicism's popularity are easy to discover. With its emphasis upon duty, self-discipline, and subjection to the natural order of things, it accorded well with the ancient virtues of the Romans and with their habits of conservatism. Moreover, its insistence upon civic obligations and its doctrine of cosmopolitanism

Roman Stoicism

Marcus Aurelius. This equestrian statue is one of the few surviving from the ancient world: the Christians destroyed most Roman equestrian statues because they found them idolatrous, but they spared this one because they mistakenly believed that it represented Constantine, the first Christian Roman Emperor. The statue stood outdoors in Rome from the second century until 1980, when it was taken into storage to protect it from air pollution.

appealed to the Roman political-mindedness and pride in world empire. It is necessary to observe, however, that the Stoicism developed in the days of the Principate was somewhat different from that of Zeno and his school. The old physical theories borrowed from Heraclitus were now discarded and replaced by a broader interest in politics and ethics. Roman Stoicism also tended to assume a more distinctly religious tone than that which had characterized the original philosophy.

Seneca, Epictetus, and Marcus Aurelius

Three eminent apostles of Stoicism lived and taught in Rome in the two centuries that followed the rule of Augustus: Seneca (4 B.C.–65 A.D.), wealthy advisor for a time to Nero; Epictetus, the slave (60?–120 A.D.); and the Emperor Marcus Aurelius (121–180 A.D.). All of them agreed that inner serenity is the ultimate goal to be sought, that true happiness can be found only in surrender to the benevolent order of the universe. They preached the ideal of virtue for virtue's sake, deplored the sinfulness of human nature, and urged obedience to conscience as the voice of duty. Seneca and Epictetus adulterated their philosophy with such deep mystical yearnings as to make it almost a religion. They worshiped the cosmos as divine, governed by an all-powerful Providence who ordains all that happens for ultimate good. The last of the Roman Stoics, Marcus Aurelius, was more fatalistic and less hopeful. Although he did not reject the conception of an ordered and rational universe, he shared neither the faith nor the dogmatism of the earlier Stoics. He was confident of no blessed immortality to balance the sufferings of one's earthly career and was inclined to think of humans as creatures buffeted by evil fortune for which no distant perfection of the whole could fully atone. He urged, nevertheless, that people should continue to live nobly, that they should neither abandon themselves to gross indulgence nor break down in angry protest, but that they should derive what contentment they could from dignified resignation to suffering and tranquil submission to death.

The literary achievements of the Romans bore a definite relation to their philosophy. This was especially true of the works of the most distinguished writers of the Augustan Age. Horace (65–8 B.C.), for example, in his famous *Odes* drew copiously from the teachings of both Epicureans and Stoics. He confined his attention, however, to their doctrines of a way of life, for like most of the Romans he had little curiosity about the workings of the universe. He developed a philosophy which combined the Epicurean justification of pleasure with the Stoic bravery in the face of trouble. While he never reduced pleasure to the mere absence of pain, he was sophisticated enough to know that the highest enjoyment is possible only through the exercise of rational control.

Virgil (70–19 B.C.) likewise reflects a measure of the philosophical temper of his age. Though his *Eclogues* convey something of the Epicurean ideal of quiet pleasure, Virgil was much more of a Stoic. His utopian vision of an age of peace and abundance, his brooding sense of the tragedy of human fate, and his idealization of a life in harmony with nature indicate an intellectual heritage similar to that of Seneca and Epictetus. Virgil's most noted work, the *Aeneid,* like several of the *Odes* of Horace glorified Roman imperialism. The *Aeneid* in fact was an epic of empire recounting the toils and triumphs of the founding of the state, its glorious traditions, and its magnificent destiny. Other major writers of the Augustan Age were Ovid (43 B.C.?–17 A.D.) and Livy (59 B.C.–17 A.D.). The former was the chief representative of the cynical and individualist tendencies of his day. His brilliant and witty writings often reflected the dissolute tastes of the time. The chief claim of Livy to fame rests upon his skill as a prose stylist. As a historian he was woefully deficient. His main work, a history of Rome, is replete with dramatic and picturesque narrative, designed to appeal to the patriotic emotions rather than to present an accurate record of events.

The literature of the period which followed the death of Augustus also exemplified conflicting social and intellectual tendencies. The tales of Petronius and Apuleius and the epigrams of Martial describe the more exotic and sometimes sordid aspects of Roman life. The aim of the authors is not to instruct or uplift but chiefly to tell an entertaining story or turn a witty phrase. An entirely different viewpoint is presented in the works of the other most important writers of this age: Juvenal, the satirist (60?–140 A.D.), and Tacitus, the historian (55?–117? A.D.). Juvenal wrote under the influence of the Stoics but with narrow vision. Convinced that the troubles of the nation were due to moral degeneracy, he censured the vices of his countrymen with the fury of an evangelist. A somewhat similar attitude characterized the writing of his younger contemporary, Tacitus. The best-known of

Roman historians, Tacitus described the events of his age not with a view to dispassionate analysis but largely for the purpose of moral indictment. His description of the customs of the ancient Germans in his *Germania* served to heighten the contrast between the manly virtues of an unspoiled race and the effeminate vices of the decadent Romans. Whatever his failings as a historian, he was a master of ironic wit and brilliant aphorism. Referring to the boasted *Pax Romana,* he makes a barbarian chieftain say: "They create a wilderness and call it peace."

Achievements in art

Roman art first assumed its distinctive character during the period of the Principate. Before this time what passed for an art of Rome was really an importation from the Hellenistic East. Conquering armies brought back to Italy wagonloads of statues, reliefs, and marble columns as part of the plunder from Greece and Asia Minor. These became the property of wealthy businessmen and were used to embellish their sumptuous mansions. As the demand increased, hundreds of copies were made, with the result that Rome came to have by the end of the Republic a profusion of objects of art which had no more cul-

The Pantheon in Rome. Built by the Emperor Hadrian it boasted the largest dome without interior supports of the ancient world. The dome forms a perfect sphere, exactly as high as it is wide.

The Baths of Caracalla, Rome. The gigantic scale is typical of late empire buildings. Elaborate and luxurious public baths like these were often presented to the public by the emperor or rich citizens. The floor plan above indicates the separate chambers for hot tub baths.

tural significance than the Picassos in the home of some modern stockbroker. The aura of national glory which surrounded the early Principate stimulated the growth of an art that was more indigenous. Augustus himself boasted that he found Rome a city of brick and left it a city of marble. Nevertheless, much of the old Hellenistic influence remained until the talent of the Romans themselves was exhausted.

The arts most truly expressive of the Roman character were architecture and sculpture. Architecture was monumental, designed to symbolize power and grandeur. It contained as its leading elements the round arch, the vault, and the dome, although at times the Corinthian column was employed, especially in the construction of temples. The materials most commonly used were brick, squared stone blocks, and concrete, the last a Roman invention. As a further adornment of public buildings, sculptured entablatures and facades, built up of tiers of colonnades or arcades, were frequently added. Roman architecture was devoted primarily to utilitarian purposes. The foremost examples were government buildings, amphitheaters, baths, race courses, and private houses. Nearly all were of massive proportions and solid construction. Among the largest and most noted were the Pantheon, with its dome having a diameter of 142 feet, and the Colosseum, which could accommodate 65,000 spectators at the gladiatorial combats. Roman sculpture included as its main forms triumphal arches and columns, narrative reliefs, altars, and portrait busts and statues. Its distinguishing characteristics were individuality and naturalism. Sometimes Roman statues and busts served only to express the vanity of the aristocracy, but the best Roman sculptured portraiture succeeded in conveying qualities of simple human dignity similar to those espoused in the philosophy of the Stoics.

Closely related to their achievements in architecture were Roman triumphs in engineering and public services. The imperial Romans built marvelous roads and bridges, many of which still survive. In the

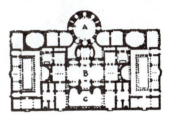

Floor Plan of the Baths of Caracalla

Architecture and sculpture

See color plates following page 230

Roman Aqueduct at Segovia, Spain. Aqueducts conveyed water from mountains to the larger cities.

time of Trajan eleven aqueducts brought water into Rome from the nearby hills and provided the city with 300 million gallons daily for drinking and bathing as well as for flushing a well-designed sewage system. Water was cleverly funneled into the homes of the rich for their private gardens, fountains, and pools. Romans also established the first hospitals in the Western world and the first system of state-supported medicine.

For all their achievements in engineering, the Romans accomplished little in science. They excelled, as has been jokingly but not inaccurately said, in drains, not brains. Scarcely an original discovery of fundamental importance was made by anyone of Latin nationality. This fact seems strange when we consider that the Romans had the advantage of Hellenistic science as a foundation upon which to build. But they neglected their opportunity almost completely because they had no vigorous curiosity about the natural world in which they lived. Roman writers on scientific subjects were hopelessly devoid of critical intelligence. The most renowned and typical of them was Pliny the Elder (23–79 A.D.), who completed about 77 A.D. a voluminous encyclopedia of "science" which he called *Natural History*. The subjects discussed varied from cosmology to economics. Despite the wealth of material it contains, Pliny's work is of limited value, for he was totally unable to distinguish between fact and fable.

The only real scientific advance made during the period of the Principate was the work of Greek scientists who lived in Italy or in the provinces. One of these was the astronomer Ptolemy, who flourished in Alexandria around the middle of the second century (see above p. 221). Another was the physician Galen, active in Rome at various times during the latter half of the second century. While Galen's fame rests primarily on his medical encyclopedia, systematizing the learning of others, he deserves more credit for his own experiments which brought him close to a discovery of the circulation of the blood. He not only taught but proved that the arteries carry blood, and that severance of even a small one is sufficient to drain away all of the blood of the body in little more than half an hour.

Galen

Roman society exhibited the same general tendencies under the Principate as in the last days of the Republic. One of the least attractive of its traits was the low status it accorded to women. The historian M. I. Finley has remarked that the two most famous women in Roman history were Cleopatra, who was not even a Roman, and the fictional Lucretia, who earned her fame by being raped and killing herself. Seldom have women been so confined to domesticity and obscurity. Roman women did not even really have their own names but were given family names with feminine endings—for example, Julia from Julius, Claudia from Claudius, and Livia from Livius. When there were two daughters in a family they would be distinguished only as "Julia the elder" and "Julia the younger," and when several as "Julia the first," "second," and "third." Women were expected to be subservient to their fathers and husbands, were valued to the degree they produced progeny, and were expected to stay at home. A typical tomb epitaph might say: "She loved her husband . . . she bore two sons . . . she was pleasant to talk with . . . she kept the house and worked in wool. That is all." During the Principate Roman women from imperial families not surprisingly tried to escape these limitations by taking a backstage and often literally murderous role in politics. Less highly placed women sought outlets in the excitement of gladiatorial shows—making gladiators the equivalent of modern rock-and-roll stars—or in the ceremonies of religious cults.

Roman women

Along with the confinement of women, the most serious indictment which can be brought against the age was the further growth of the passion for cruelty. Whereas the Greeks entertained themselves with theater, the Romans more and more preferred "circuses," which were really exhibitions of human slaughter. In the period of the Principate the great games and spectacles became bloodier than ever. The Romans could no longer obtain a sufficient thrill from mere exhibitions of athletic prowess: pugilists were now required to have their hands wrapped with thongs of leather loaded with iron or lead. The most popular amusement of all was watching the gladiatorial combats in the Colosseum or in other amphitheaters capable of accommodating thousands of spectators. Fights between gladiators were nothing new, but they were now presented on a much more elaborate scale. Not only the common people attended them, but wealthy aris-

Gladiatorial combat

The Colosseum. Built by the Roman emperors between 75 and 80 A.D. as a place of entertainment, it was the scene of gladiatorial combats. The most common form of Greek secular architecture was the theater (see p. 183), but the most common Roman form was the amphitheater.

tocrats also, and frequently the head of the government himself. The gladiators fought to the accompaniment of savage cries and curses from the audience. When one went down with a disabling wound, the crowd was asked to decide whether his life should be spared or whether the weapon of his opponent should be plunged into his heart. One contest after another, often featuring the sacrifice of men to wild animals, was staged in the course of a single exhibition. Should the arena become too sodden with blood, it was covered over with a fresh layer of sand, and the revolting performance went on. Most of the gladiators were condemned criminals or slaves, but some were volunteers even from the respectable classes. Commodus, the worthless son of Marcus Aurelius, entered the arena several times for the sake of the plaudits of the mob: this was his idea of a Roman holiday.

The spread of Mithraism and Christianity

Notwithstanding its low moral tone, the age of the Principate was characterized by an even deeper interest in salvationist religions than that which had prevailed under the Republic. Mithraism now gained adherents by the thousands, absorbing many of the followers of the cults of the Great Mother and of Serapis. About 40 A.D. the first Christians appeared in Rome. The new sect grew steadily and eventually succeeded in displacing Mithraism as the most popular of the salvationist faiths.

The establishment of stable government by Augustus ushered in a period of prosperity for Italy which lasted for more than two centuries. Trade was now extended to all parts of the known world, even to Arabia, India, and China. Manufacturing increased somewhat, especially in the production of pottery, textiles, and articles of metal and glass. In spite of all this, the economic order was far from healthy. Prosperity was not evenly distributed but was confined primarily to the upper classes. Since the stigma attached to manual labor persisted as strongly as ever, production was bound to decline as the supply of slaves diminished. Perhaps worse was the fact that Italy had a decidedly unfavorable balance of trade. The meager industrial development was by no means sufficient to provide enough articles of export to meet the demand for luxuries imported from the provinces and from the outside world. As a consequence, Italy was gradually drained of its supply of precious metals. By the third century the Western Roman economy began to collapse.

Portrait Bust of a Roman Lady. The ostentatiousness of upper-class culture during the period of the Principate is well displayed by this sculpture, done around 90 A.D.

8. ROMAN LAW

There is general agreement that one of the most important legacies which the Romans left to succeeding cultures was their system of law. This resulted from a gradual evolution which began roughly with the publication of the Twelve Tables about 450 B.C. In the later centuries of the Republic the law of the Twelve Tables was transformed by the growth of new precedents and principles. These emanated from different sources: from changes in custom, from the teachings of the Stoics, from the decisions of judges, but especially from the edicts of the *praetors,* magistrates who had authority to define and interpret the law in a particular suit and issue instructions to judges.

The early development of Roman law

Roman law attained its highest stage of development under the Principate. This was the result in part of the extension of the law over a wider field of jurisdiction, over the lives and properties of aliens in strange environments as well as over the citizens of Italy. But the major reason was the fact that Augustus and his successors gave to certain eminent jurists the right to deliver opinions on the legal issues of cases under trial in the courts. The most prominent of the men thus designated from time to time were Gaius, Ulpian, Papinian, and Paulus. Although most of them held high judicial office, they had gained their reputations primarily as lawyers and writers on legal subjects. The responses of these jurists came to embody a science and philosophy of law and were accepted as the basis of Roman jurisprudence.

Roman law under the Principate; the great jurists

The Roman law as it was developed under the influence of the jurists comprised three great branches or divisions: the civil law, the law of peoples, and the natural law. The civil law was the law of Rome and its citizens. As such it existed in both written and unwritten forms. It included the statutes of the Senate, the decrees of the princeps, the edicts of the praetors, and also certain ancient customs operating with the force of law. The law of peoples was the law held to be common to all people regardless of nationality. This law authorized the institutions of slavery and private ownership of property and defined the principles of purchase and sale, partnership, and contract. It was not superior to the civil law but supplemented it as especially applicable to the alien inhabitants of the Empire.

The most interesting and in many ways the most important branch of the Roman law was the natural law, a product not of judicial practice, but of philosophy. The Stoics had developed the idea of a rational order of nature which is the embodiment of justice and right. They had affirmed that all men are by nature equal, and that they are entitled to certain basic rights which governments have no authority to transgress. The father of the law of nature as a legal principle, however, was not one of the Hellenistic Stoics, but Cicero. "True law," he declared, "is right reason consonant with nature, diffused among all men, constant, eternal. To make enactments infringing this law, religion forbids, neither may it be repealed even in part, nor have we power through Senate or people to free ourselves from it." This law is prior to the state itself, and any ruler who defies it automatically becomes a tyrant. Most of the great jurists subscribed to conceptions of the law of nature very similar to those of the philosophers. Although the jurists did not regard this law as an automatic limitation upon the civil law, they thought of it as a great ideal to which the statutes and decrees of men ought to conform. This development of the concept of abstract justice as a legal principle was one of the noblest achievements of the Roman civilization.

Commodus. The self-deluded ruler encouraged artists to portray him as the equal of the superhuman Hercules.

9. THE CRISIS OF THE THIRD CENTURY (180–284 A.D.)

With the death of Marcus Aurelius in 180 A.D. the period of beneficent imperial rule came to an end. One reason for the success of the "five good emperors" was that the first four designated particularly promising young men, rather than sons or close relatives, for the succession. But Marcus Aurelius broke this pattern with results that were to prove fateful. Although he was one of the most philosophic and thoughtful rulers who ever reigned, he was not wise enough to recognize that his son Commodus was a vicious incompetent. Made emperor by his father's wishes, Commodus indulged his taste for perversities, showed open contempt for the Senate, and ruled so brutally that a palace clique finally had him murdered by strangling in 192. Matters thereafter became worse. With the lack of an obvious successor to Commodus, the armies of the provinces raised their own candidates and civil war ensued. Although a provincial general, Septimius Severus (193–211), emerged victorious, it now became clear that provincial armies could interfere in imperial politics at will. Severus and some of his successors aggravated the problem by eliminating even the theoretical rights of the Senate and ruling frankly as military dictators. Once the role of brute force was openly revealed any aspiring general could try his luck at seizing power. Hence civil war became endemic. From 235 to 284 there were no less than twenty-six "barracks emperors," of whom only one managed to escape a violent death.

The half-century between 235 and 284 was certainly the worst for Rome since its rise to world power. In addition to political chaos, a number of other factors combined to bring the Empire to the brink of ruin. One was that civil war had disastrous economic effects. Not only did constant warfare interfere with agriculture and trade, but the rivalry of aspirants to rule led them to drain the wealth of their territories in order to gain favor with their armies. Following the maxim of "enriching the soldiers and scorning the rest," they could only raise funds by debasing the coinage and by nearly confiscatory taxation of civilians. Landlords, small tenants, and manufacturers thus had little motive to produce at a time when production was most necessary. In human terms the poorest, as is usual in times of economic contraction, suffered the most. Often they were driven to the most abject destitution. In the wake of war and hunger, disease then became rampant. Already in the reign of Marcus Aurelius a terrible plague had swept through the Empire, decimating the army and the population at large. In the middle of the third century pestilence returned and struck at the population with its fearful scythe for fifteen years.

The resulting strain on human resources came at a time when Rome could least afford it, for still another threat to the Empire in the middle of the third century was the advance of Rome's external enemies. With Roman ranks thinned by disease and Roman armies fighting each other, Germans in the West and Persians in the East broke through the old Roman defense lines. In 251 the Goths defeated and slew the Emperor Decius, crossed the Danube, and marauded at will in the Balkans. A more humiliating disaster came in 260 when the Emperor Valerian was captured in battle by the Persians and made to kneel as a footstool for their ruler. When he died his body was stuffed and hung on exhibition. Clearly the days of Caesar and Augustus were very far off.

Understandably enough the culture of the third century was marked by pervasive anxiety. One can even see expressions of worry in the surviving statuary, as in the bust of the Emperor Philip (244–249) who appears almost to realize that he would soon be killed in battle. Suiting the spirit of the age, the Neoplatonic philosophy of

Consequences of civil war

The Emperor Decius. The extreme naturalism and furrowed brow is typical of the portraits of this period.

otherworldlyism came to the fore. Neoplatonism (meaning "New Platonism") drew the spiritualist tendency of Plato's thought to extremes. The first of its basic teachings was emanationism: everything that exists proceeds from God in a continuing stream of emanations. The initial stage in the process is the emanation of the world-soul. From this come the divine Ideas or spiritual patterns, and then the souls of particular things. The final emanation is matter. But matter has no form or quality of its own; it is simply the privation of spirit, the residue which is left after the spiritual rays from God have burned themselves out. It follows that matter is to be despised as the symbol of evil and darkness. The second major doctrine was mysticism. The human soul was originally a part of God, but it has become separated from its divine source through its union with matter. The highest goal of life should be mystic reunion with the divine, which can be accomplished through contemplation and through emancipation of the soul from bondage to matter. Human beings should be ashamed of the fact that they possess a physical body and should seek to subjugate it in every way possible. Asceticism was therefore the third main teaching of this philosophy.

The Emperor Philip the Arab. An artistic legacy of the Roman "age of anxiety."

The real founder of Neoplatonism was Plotinus, who was born in Egypt about 204 A.D. In the later years of his life he taught in Rome and won many followers among the upper classes before he died in 270. His principal successors diluted the philosophy with more and more bizarre superstitions. In spite of its antirational viewpoint and its utter indifference to the state, Neoplatonism became so popular in Rome in the third and fourth centuries A.D. that it almost completely supplanted Stoicism. No fact could have expressed more eloquently the turn of Rome away from the realities of the here and now.

Plotinus

10. CAUSES FOR ROME'S DECLINE

As Rome was not built in a day, so it was not lost in one. As we will see in the next chapter, strong rule returned in 284. Thereafter the Roman Empire endured in the West for two hundred years more and in the East for a millennium. But the restored Roman state differed greatly from the old one—so much so that it is proper to end the story of characteristically Roman civilization here and review the reasons for Rome's decline.

Turning point in 284

More has been written on the fall of Rome than on the death of any other civilization. The theories offered to account for the decline have been many and varied. A popular recent one is that Rome fell from the effects of lead poisoning, but this cannot be accepted for many reasons, one of which is that most Roman pipes were not made of lead but of terra-cotta. Moralists have found the explanation for Rome's fall in the descriptions of lechery and gluttony presented in the writings of such authors as Juvenal and Petronius. Such an approach, however,

Theories of decline

overlooks the facts that much of this evidence is patently overdrawn, and that nearly all of it comes from the period of the early Principate: in the later centuries, when the Empire was more obviously collapsing, morality became more austere through the influence of ascetic religions. One of the simplest explanations is that Rome fell only because of the severity of German attacks. But barbarians had always stood ready to attack Rome throughout its long history: German pressures indeed mounted at certain times but German invasions would never have succeeded had they not come at moments when Rome was already weakened internally.

It is best then, to concentrate on Rome's most serious internal problems. Some of these were political. The most obvious political failing of the Roman constitution under the Principate was the lack of a clear law of succession. Especially when a ruler died suddenly there was no certainty about who was to follow him. In modern America the deaths of a Lincoln or Kennedy might shock the nation, but people at least knew what would happen next; in imperial Rome no one knew and civil war was generally the result. From 235 to 284 such warfare fed upon itself. Civil war was also nurtured by the lack of constitutional means for reform. If regimes became unpopular, as most did after 180, the only means to alter them was to overthrow them. But the resort to violence always bred more violence. In addition to those problems, imperial Rome's greatest political weakness may ultimately have been that it did not involve enough people in the work of government. The vast majority of the Empire's inhabitants were subjects who did not participate in the government in any way. Hence they looked on the Empire at best with indifference and often with hostility, especially when tax collectors appeared. Loyalty to Rome was needed to keep the Empire going, but when the tests came such loyalty was lacking.

Internal causes of decline

Slaves Towing a Barge. This relief shows very graphically how heavily Roman civilizations relied on slave labor.

Economic causes

Even without political problems the Roman Empire would probably have been fated to extinction for economic reasons. Rome's worst economic problems derived from its slave system and from manpower shortages. Roman civilization was based on cities, and Roman cities existed largely by virtue of an agricultural surplus produced by slaves. Slaves were worked so hard that they did not normally reproduce to fill their own ranks. Until the time of Trajan Roman victories in war and fresh conquests provided fresh supplies of slaves to keep the system going, but thereafter the economy began to run out of human fuel. Landlords could no longer be so profligate of human life, barracks slavery came to an end, and the countryside produced less of a surplus to feed the towns. The fact that no technological advance took up the slack may also be attributed to slavery. Later in Western history agricultural surpluses were produced by technological revolutions, but Roman landlords were indifferent to technology because interest in it was thought to be demeaning. As long as slaves were present to do the work there was no interest in labor-saving devices, and attention to any sort of machinery was deemed a sign of slavishness. Landlords proved their nobility by their interest in "higher things," but while they were contemplating these heights their agricultural surpluses gradually became depleted.

Inadequate manpower

Manpower shortages greatly aggravated Rome's economic problems. With the end of foreign conquests and the decline of slavery there was a pressing need for people to stay on the farm, but because of constant barbarian pressures there was also a steady need for men to serve in the army. The plagues of the second and third centuries sharply reduced the population just at the worst time. It has been estimated that between the reign of Marcus Aurelius and the restoration of strong rule in 284 the population of the Roman Empire was reduced by one third. (Demoralization seems also to have lowered the birthrate.) The result was that there were neither sufficient forces to work the land nor men to fight Rome's enemies. No wonder Rome began to lose battles as it had seldom lost them before.

Lack of civic ideals

Enormous dedication and exertion on the part of large numbers might just possibly have saved Rome, but few were willing to work hard for the public good. For this cultural explanations may be posited. Most simply stated the Roman Empire of the third century could not draw upon commonly shared civic ideals. By then the old republican and senatorial traditions had been rendered manifestly obsolete. Worse, provincials could hardly be expected to fight or work hard for Roman ideals of any sort, especially when the Roman state no longer stood for beneficent peace but only brought recurrent war and oppressive taxation. Regional differences, the lack of public education, and social stratification were further barriers to the development of any unifying public spirit. As the Empire foundered new ideals indeed emerged, but these were religious, otherworldly ones. Ultimately, then, the decline of Rome was accompanied by disinterest, and the

Roman world slowly came to an end not so much with a bang as with a whimper.

11. THE ROMAN HERITAGE

It is tempting to believe that we today have many similarities to the Romans: first of all, because Rome is nearer to us in time than any of the other civilizations of antiquity; and second, because Rome seems to bear such a close kinship to the modern temper. The resemblances between Roman history and the history of Great Britain or the United States in the nineteenth and twentieth centuries have often been noted. The Roman economic evolution progressed all the way from a simple agrarianism to a complex urban system with problems of unemployment, gross disparities of wealth, and financial crises. The Roman Empire, in common with the British, was founded upon conquest. It must not be forgotten, however, that the heritage of Rome was an ancient heritage and that consequently, the similarities between the Roman and modern civilizations are not so important as they seem.

Comparison of Rome with the modern world

The Forum, the Civic Center of Ancient Rome. In addition to public squares, the Forum included triumphal arches, magnificent temples, and government buildings. In the foreground is the Temple of Saturn. Behind it is the Temple of Antoninus and Faustina. The three columns at the extreme right are what is left of the Temple of Castor and Pollux, and in the farthest background is the arch of Titus.

As noted already, the Romans disdained industrial activities, and they were not interested in science. Neither did they have any idea of the modern national state; the provinces were really colonies, not integral parts of a body politic. The Romans also never developed an adequate system of representative government. Finally, the Roman conception of religion was vastly different from our own. Their system of worship, like that of the Greeks, was external and mechanical, not inward or spiritual. What Christians consider the highest ideal of piety—an emotional attitude of love for the divine—the Romans regarded as gross superstition.

The influence of Roman civilization

Nevertheless, the civilization of Rome exerted a great influence upon later cultures. The form, if not the spirit, of Roman architecture was preserved in the ecclesiastical architecture of the Middle Ages and survives to this day in the design of many of our government buildings. The sculpture of the Augustan Age also lives on in the equestrian statues, the memorial arches and columns, and in the portraits in stone of statesmen and generals that adorn our streets and parks. Although subjected to new interpretations, the law of the great jurists became an important part of the Code of Justinian and was thus handed down to the Middle Ages and modern times. American judges frequently cite maxims originally invented by Gaius or Ulpian. Further, the legal systems of nearly all continental European countries today incorporate much of the Roman law. This law was one of the grandest of the Romans' achievements and reflected their genius for governing a vast and diverse empire. It should not be forgotten either that Roman literary achievements furnished much of the inspiration for the revival of learning that spread over Europe in the twelfth century and reached its zenith in the Renaissance. Perhaps not so well known is the fact that the organization of the Catholic Church, to say nothing of part of its ritual, was adapted from the structure of the Roman state and the complex of the Roman religion. For example, the pope still bears the title of supreme pontiff (*pontifex maximus*), which was used to designate the authority of the emperor as head of the civic religion.

Rome's role as conveyor of Greek civilization

Most important of all Rome's contributions to the future was the transmission of Greek civilization to the European West. The development in Italy of a culture that was highly suffused by Greek ideals from the second century B.C. onward was in itself an important counterweight to the earlier predominance of Greek-oriented civilization in the East. Then, following the path of Julius Caesar, this culture advanced still further West. Before the coming of Rome the culture of northwestern Europe (modern France, the Benelux countries, western and southern Germany, and England) was tribal. Rome brought cities and Greek ideas, above all conceptions of human freedom and individual autonomy that went along with the development of highly differentiated urban life. It is true that ideals of freedom were often ignored in practice—they did not temper Roman dependence on slavery and subjugation of women, or prevent Roman rule in conquered territories from being exploitive and sometimes oppressive. Nonetheless, Roman history is the real beginning of Western history as we now know it. Greek civilization brought to the East by Alexander was not enduring, but the same civilization brought West by the work of such men as Caesar, Cicero, and Augustus was the starting point for many of the subsequent accomplishments of western Europe. As we will see, the development was not continuous, and there were many other ingredients to later European success, but the influence of Rome was no less profound.

SELECTED READINGS

• *Items so designated are available in paperback editions.*

POLITICAL HISTORY

Bloch, Raymond, *The Origins of Rome,* New York, 1960.

Cary, M., and H. H. Scullard, *A History of Rome,* 3rd ed., New York, 1975. A basic college-level textbook.

• Chambers, M., ed., *The Fall of Rome,* 2nd ed., New York, 1970. A collection of readings on this perennially fascinating subject.

• Crawford, M. H., *The Roman Republic,* Atlantic Heights, N.J., 1978.

• Crook, J. A., *Law and Life of Rome, 90 B.C.–A.D. 212,* Ithaca, N.Y., 1977.

Grant, M., *The Etruscans,* New York, 1980.

Gruen, E. S., *The Last Generation of the Roman Republic,* Berkeley, 1964.

• Harris, William V., *War and Imperialism in Republican Rome,* Oxford, 1979. A searching and original examination of why the Romans became expansionists.

Haywood, R. M., *The Myth of Rome's Fall,* New York, 1958.

Millar, F., *The Emperor in the Roman World: 31 B.C.–A.D. 337,* Ithaca, N.Y., 1977.

Mommsen, Theodor, *The History of Rome,* Chicago, 1957. An abridged reissue of one of the greatest historical works of the nineteenth century. Emphasizes personalities, especially that of Julius Caesar.

Ogilvie, R. M., *Early Rome and the Etruscans,* Atlantic Heights, N.J., 1976. The best specialized review of the earliest period.

Pallottino, M., *The Etruscans,* rev. ed., Baltimore, 1978. The standard introduction.

• Scullard, H. H., *From the Gracchi to Nero,* New York, 1959. Good survey of events in this central period.

• Syme, Ronald, *The Roman Revolution,* New York, 1939. A pathfinding work on the late Republic and early Empire that stresses power politics and the role of factions rather than the clash of institutional principles. Also extremely well written.

• Taylor, Lily Ross, *Party Politics in the Age of Caesar,* Berkeley, 1949. Still the best introduction to society and politics in the late republican period.

Warmington, B. H., *Carthage,* Baltimore, 1965.

ECONOMIC, SOCIAL, AND CULTURAL HISTORY

Africa, T., *Rome of the Caesars,* New York, 1965. An entertaining approach to the history of imperial Rome by means of short biographies.

Arnold, E. V., *Roman Stoicism,* New York, 1911.

Balsdon, J. P. V. D., *Life and Leisure in Ancient Rome,* New York, 1969.

• Brunt, P. A., *Social Conflicts in the Roman Republic,* London, 1971.

• Carcopino, Jerome, *Daily Life in Ancient Rome,* New Haven, Conn., 1960.

Duff, J. W., *A Literary History of Rome in the Golden Age,* New York, 1964.

_____, *A Literary History of Rome in the Silver Age,* New York, 1960.

• Earl, Donald, *The Moral and Political Tradition of Rome,* Ithaca, N.Y., 1967.

Frank, T., *An Economic Survey of Ancient Rome,* 6 vols., Baltimore, 1933–1940. Remains the basic work of reference on its subject.

• Hopkins, K., *Conquerors and Slaves,* Cambridge, 1978. Interconnected essays that approach the world of the Roman Empire from an innovative sociological perspective.

Laistner, M. L. W., *The Greater Roman Historians,* Berkeley, 1947.

MacMullen, R., *Enemies of the Roman Order,* Cambridge, Mass., 1966.

• _____, *Paganism in the Roman Empire,* New Haven, Conn., 1981.

• _____, *Roman Social Relations: 50 B.C. to A.D. 284,* New Haven, Conn., 1974.

Rostovtzeff, M. I., *Social and Economic History of the Roman Empire,* 2nd ed., 2 vols., New York, 1957. By one of the greatest historians of the early twentieth century. Important both for its interpretations and the wealth of information it contains.

• Sandbach, F. H., *The Stoics,* London, 1975.

Scullard, H. H., *The Etruscan Cities and Rome,* Ithaca, N.Y., 1967.

• Starr, C. G., *Civilization and the Caesars,* Ithaca, N.Y., 1954. Surveys Roman intellectual developments in the four centuries after Cicero.

Toynbee, A. J., *Hannibal's Legacy,* 2 vols., London, 1965.

Westermann, W. L., *The Slave Systems of Greek and Roman Antiquity,* Philadelphia, 1955. The best overview of this basic subject.

• Wheeler, Mortimer, *The Art of Rome,* New York, 1964.

Yavetz, Z., *Plebs and Princeps,* London, 1969.

SOURCE MATERIALS

Translations of Roman authors are available in the appropriate volumes of the Loeb Classical Library, Harvard University Press.

See also:

Gruen, E. S., *The Image of Rome,* Englewood Cliffs, N.J., 1969.

• Lewis, Naphtali, and M. Reinhold, *Roman Civilization,* 2 vols., New York, 1955.

Chapter 10

CHRISTIANITY AND THE TRANSFORMATION OF THE ROMAN WORLD

Who will hereafter credit the fact . . . that Rome has to fight within her own borders not for glory but for bare life? . . . The poet Lucan describing the power of the city in a glowing passage says: "If Rome be weak, where shall we look for strength?" We may vary his words and say: "If Rome be lost, where shall we look for help?"

For mortals this life is a race: we run it on earth that we may receive our crown elsewhere. No man can walk secure amid serpents and scorpions.

—St. Jerome, *Letters*

The Roman Empire declined after 180 A.D., but it did not collapse. In 284 the vigorous soldier-emperor Diocletian began a reorganization of the empire which gave it a new lease on life. Thereafter, throughout the fourth century the Roman state continued to surround the Mediterranean. In the fifth century the western half of the empire did fall to invading Germans, but even then Roman institutions were not entirely destroyed, and in the sixth century the eastern half of the empire managed to reconquer a good part of the western Mediterranean shoreline. Only in the seventh century did it become fully evident that the Roman Empire could only hope to survive by turning away from the West and consolidating its strength in the East. When that happened antiquity clearly came to an end.

The protracted decline of the Roman Empire

Historians used to underestimate the longevity of Roman institutions and begin their discussions of medieval history in the third, fourth, or fifth century. Since historical periodization is always approximate and depends largely on which aspects of development a historian wishes to emphasize, this approach cannot be dismissed. Certainly the transition from the ancient to the medieval world was gradual and many "medieval" ways were slowly emerging in the West

The age of late antiquity (284–610)

264

*Christianity and the
Transformation of the Roman
World*

as early as the third century. But it is now more customary to conceive of ancient history as continuing after 284 and lasting until the Roman Empire lost control over the Mediterranean in the seventh century. The period from 284 to about 610, although transitional (as, of course, all ages are), has certain themes of its own and is perhaps best described as neither Roman nor medieval but as the age of late antiquity.

The major cultural trend of late-antique history was the spread and triumph of Christianity throughout the Roman world. At first Christianity was just one of several varieties of otherworldlyism which appealed to increasing numbers of persons during the later empire. But in the fourth century it was adopted as the Roman state religion and thereafter became one of the greatest shaping forces in the development of the West. While Christianity was spreading, the Roman Empire was indubitably declining. Central to this decline was a contraction of the urban life on which the empire had been based. As the empire began to experience severe pressures, urban contraction was most pronounced in the European northwest because city civilization there was least deeply rooted and most distant from the empire's major trade and communications lifelines on the Mediterranean. Contraction was also felt in parts of the West that were closer to the Mediterranean because western cities depended far more on declining agricultural production than eastern ones, which relied more on trade in luxury goods and industry. Consequently the entire period saw a steady shift in the weight of civilization and imperial government from West to East. The most visible manifestations of this shift were the German successes of the fifth century. These surely helped open a new chapter in Western political history, but their immediate impact should not be exaggerated. Even with the influx of Germans, Roman institutions continued to decline gradually. Particularly in areas that were on or close to the Mediterranean, Roman city life persisted, albeit with steadily declining vigor, until the Mediterranean was no longer a Roman lake.

1. THE REORGANIZED EMPIRE

Before we examine the emergence and triumph of Christianity, it is best to survey the nature of the government and society in which the new religion became a dominant force. The fifty years of chaos that threatened to destroy Rome in the third century were ended by the energetic work of a remarkable soldier named Diocletian, who ruled as emperor from 284 to 305. Conscious of some of the more obvious problems that had undone his predecessors, Diocletian embarked on a number of fundamental political and economic reforms. Recognizing that the dominance of the army in the life of the state had hitherto been too great, he introduced measures to separate military from civilian administrative chains of command. Aware that new pressures, both external and internal, had made it nearly impossible for one man to govern the entire Roman Empire, he divided his realm in half, granting the western part to a trusted colleague, Maximian, who recognized Diocletian as the senior ruler. The two then chose lieutenants, called *caesars,* to govern large subsections of their territories. This system was also meant to provide for an orderly succession, for the caesars were supposed to inherit the major rule of either East or West and then appoint new caesars in their stead. In the economic sphere Diocletian stabilized the badly debased currency, introduced a new system of taxation, and issued legislation designed to keep agricultural workers and town-dwellers at their jobs so that the basic work necessary to support the empire would continue to be done.

Although Diocletian's program of reorganization was remarkably successful in restoring an empire that had been on the verge of expiring, it also transformed the empire by "orientalizing" it in three primary and lasting ways. Most literally, Diocletian began a geographical orientalization of the empire by shifting its administrative weight toward the East. Since he was a "Roman" emperor we might assume that he ruled from Rome, but in fact between 284 and 303 he was never there, ruling instead from Nicomedia, a city in modern-day Turkey. This he did in tacit recognition of the fact that the wealthier and more vital part of the empire was clearly in the East. Second, as befitting one who turned his back on Rome, Diocletian adopted the titles and ceremonies of an Oriental potentate. Probably he did this less because he had Eastern tastes than because he wished to avoid the fate of his predecessors who were insufficiently respected. Most likely he thought that if he were feared and worshiped he would stand a greater chance of dying in bed. Accordingly, Diocletian completely abandoned Augustus's policy of appearing to be a constitutional ruler and came forward as an undisguised autocrat. He took the title not of *princeps,* or first citizen, but of *dominus,* or lord, and he introduced Oriental ceremony into his court. He wore a diadem and a purple gown of silk interwoven with gold. Those who gained an audience had to prostrate themselves before him; a privileged few were allowed to kiss his robe.

The third aspect of orientalization in Diocletian's policy was his growing reliance on an imperial bureaucracy. By separating civilian from military commands and legislating on a wide variety of economic and social matters, Diocletian created the need for many new officials. Not surprisingly, by the end of his reign subjects were complaining that "there were more tax-collectors than taxpayers." The officials did keep the empire going, but the new bureaucracy was prone—as all are—to graft and corruption; worse, the growth of officialdom called for reservoirs of manpower and wealth at a time when the Roman Empire no longer had large supplies of either. Taken together, the various aspects of Diocletian's easternizing made him

Diocletian. His short hair is in the Roman military style.

Diocletian's easternizing policy

The growth of imperial bureaucracy

The Emperor Honorius. An example of the impassive portrait sculpture brought in by the age of Diocletian. Compare the lack of individuality of this bust to the portraits of Decius and Philip the Arab, above, pp. 255, 256.

The reign of Constantine

seem more like a pharaoh than a Roman ruler: it was almost as if the defeat of Antony and Cleopatra at Actium was now being avenged.

The new coercive regime of Diocletian left no room for the cultivation of individual spontaneity or freedom. The results can be seen most clearly in the architecture and art of the age. Diocletian himself preferred a colossal bombastic style of building that was meant to emphasize his own power. The baths he had constructed in Rome, when he finally arrived there in 303, were the largest yet known, encompassing about thirty acres. When he retired in 305 Diocletian built a palace for himself in what is now Split (Yugoslavia) that was laid out along a rectilinear grid like an army camp. A plan of this palace shows clearly how Diocletian favored regimentation in everything.

Also in the age of Diocletian, Roman portrait statuary, which had hitherto featured striking naturalism and individuality, became impersonal. Human faces became impassive and symmetrical rather than reflecting a free play of emotions. Porphyry, a particularly hard and dark stone that had to be imported from Egypt—itself a sign of easternization—often replaced marble for imperial busts. Porphyry groups of Diocletian, Maximian, and their two caesars show the new hardness and symmetry at their fullest, for the figures were made to look so similar that they are indistinguishable from each other.

In 305 Diocletian decided to abdicate to raise cabbages—an unprecedented achievement for a late-Roman ruler. At the same time he obliged his colleague Maximian to retire as well, and their two caesars moved peacefully up the ladders of succession. Such concord, however, could not last. Soon civil war broke out among Diocletian's successors and continued until Constantine, the son of one of the original caesars, emerged victorious. From 312 until 324 Constantine ruled only in the West, but from the latter year until his death in 337 he did away with the sharing of powers and ruled over a reunited empire. Except for the fact that he favored Christianity, an epoch-making

Diocletian's Palace in Split. An artistic reconstruction.

Left: *Porphyry Sculptures of Diocletian and His Colleagues in Rule*. Every effort is made to make the two senior rulers and their two junior colleagues look identical by means of stylization. Note also the emphasis on military strength. Right: *Colossal Head of Constantine*. In the head of Constantine the eyes are enlarged as if to emphasize the ruler's spiritual vision. The head is approximately ten times larger than life.

decision to be examined in the next section, Constantine otherwise continued to govern along the lines laid down by Diocletian. Bureaucracy proliferated and the state became so vigilant in keeping town-dwellers and agricultural laborers at their posts that society began to harden into a caste system. Although Constantine was a Christian, he never thought for a moment of acting with any Christlike humility: on the contrary, he made court ceremonials more elaborate and generally behaved as if he were a god. In keeping with this he built a new capital in 330 and named it Constantinople, after himself. Although he declared that he moved his government from Rome to Constantinople in order to demonstrate his abandonment of paganism, self-esteem was no doubt a major factor, and the shift was the most visible manifestation of the continued move of Roman civilization to the East. Situated on the border of Europe and Asia, Constantinople had commanding advantages as a center for Eastern-oriented communications, trade, and defense. Surrounded on three sides by water and protected on land by walls, it was to prove nearly impregnable and would remain the center of "Roman" government for as long as the Roman Empire was to endure.

Constantine also made the succession hereditary. By so doing he

268

*Christianity and the
Transformation of the Roman
World*

Two Contemporary Representations of Theodosius. Above is a detail from a silver plate. Theodosius is shown here with an orb in his hand, symbolizing his worldly power, and a halo, symbolizing his supernatural strength. In both the plate and the coin shown below the emperor is depicted in military garb.

The origins and spread of Christianity

brought Rome back to the principle of dynastic monarchy that it had thrown off about eight hundred years earlier. But Constantine, who treated the empire as if it were his private property, did not pass on united rule to one son. Instead he divided his realm among three of them. Not surprisingly his three sons started fighting each other upon their father's death, a conflict exacerbated by religious differences. The warfare and succeeding dynastic squabbles that continued on and off for most of the fourth century need not detain us here. Suffice it to say that they were not as serious as the civil wars of the third century, and that from time to time one or another contestant was able to reunite the empire for a period of years. The last to do so was Theodosius I (379–395), who butchered thousands of innocent citizens of Thessalonica in retribution for the death of one of his officers, but whose energies in preserving the empire by holding off Germanic barbarians still gave him some claim to his surname "the Great."

The period between Constantine and Theodosius saw the steady development of earlier tendencies. With Constantinople now the leading city of the empire, the center of commerce and administration was located clearly in the East. Regionalism too grew more pronounced: the Latin-speaking West was losing a sense of rapport and contact with the Greek-speaking East, and in both West and East local differences were becoming accentuated. In economic life the hallmark of the age was the growing gap between rich and poor. In the West large landowners were able to consolidate their holdings, and in the East some individuals became prosperous by rising through the bureaucracy and enriching themselves with graft, or by trading in luxury goods. But the taxation system initiated by Diocletian and maintained throughout the fourth century weighed down heavily on the poor, forcing them to carry the burden of supporting the bureaucracy, the army, and the lavish imperial court or courts. The poor, moreover, had no chance to escape their poverty, for legislation demanded that they and their heirs stay at their unrewarding and heavily taxed jobs. Since most people in the fourth century were poor, most people lived in desperate and unrelenting poverty against a backdrop of ostentatious wealth. The Roman Empire may have been restored in the years from 284 to 395, but it was nonetheless a fertile breeding-ground for a new religion of otherworldly salvation.

2. THE EMERGENCE AND TRIUMPH OF CHRISTIANITY

Christian beginnings of course go back several centuries before Constantine to the time of Jesus. Christianity was formed primarily by Jesus and St. Paul and gained converts steadily thereafter. But the new religion only became widespread during the chaos of the third century and only triumphed in the Roman Empire during the demoralization of the fourth. At the time of its humble beginnings nobody could have known that Christianity would be decreed the sole religion of the Roman Empire by the year 380.

Jesus of Nazareth was born in Judea sometime near the beginning of the Christian era (but not exactly in the "year one"—we owe this mistake in our dating system to a sixth-century monk). While Jesus was growing up Judea was under Roman overlordship. The atmosphere of the region was charged with religious emotionalism and political discontent. Some of the people, notably the Pharisees, concentrated on preserving the Jewish law and looked forward to the coming of a political messiah who would rescue the Jews from Rome. Most extreme of those who sought hope in politics were the "Zealots," who wished to overthrow the Romans by means of armed force. Some groups, on the other hand, were not interested in politics at all. Typical of these were the Essenes, who hoped for spiritual deliverance through asceticism, repentance, and mystical union with God. The ministry of Jesus was clearly more allied to this pacific orientation.

In considering the story of Jesus's career as an historical event, it is important to recognize that the only surviving sources of information are the first four books of the New Testament, the four Gospels, the earliest of which (the Gospel of Mark) was written some thirty years after Jesus's death. Inevitably the Gospels are full of inaccuracies and legends, in part because they were not eyewitness accounts, and even more because they were never meant to be strictly factual reports but were intended as proclamations of supernatural faith. Bearing in mind that more or less anything in the Gospel record may not be true in the historical sense, so far as we know, when Jesus was about thirty years old he was acclaimed by a preacher of moral reform, John the Baptist, as one "mightier than I, whose shoes I am not worthy to stoop down and unloose." For about three years thereafter Jesus's career was a continuous course of preaching, healing the sick, "casting out devils," and teaching humility by precepts, parables, and by his own example.

Jesus Christ. An artist's conception from a sixth-century mosaic in Ravenna.

Believing he had a mission to save humanity from sin, Jesus denounced greed and licentiousness and urged love of God and neighbor. Additionally, it seems reasonably clear that he taught the following: (1) the fatherhood of God and the brotherhood of humanity; (2) the Golden Rule ("do unto others as you would have others do unto you"); (3) forgiveness and love of one's enemies; (4) repayment of evil with good; (5) shunning of hypocrisy; (6) opposition to religious ceremonialism; (7) the imminent approach of the end of the world; (8) the resurrection of the dead and the establishment of the kingdom of heaven.

The Gospel record is particularly controversial when it reaches the story of Jesus's death because aspects of it, which may or may not

The Gospel record and the death of Jesus

The crucifixion of Jesus and belief in the resurrection

be true, fueled Christian persecutions of Jews in subsequent eras. Purportedly when Jesus began to preach in Jerusalem, Judea's major city and religious center, the city's religious leaders quickly became antagonistic to him because of his contempt for form and ceremony. Moving swiftly to silence the troublemaker, they arrested him, tried him in their highest court for blasphemy, condemned him, and handed him over to Pontius Pilate, the Roman governor, for sentencing and execution of the sentence. Some scholars hold that this version of Jesus's last days is a fabrication, designed to shift blame for his death from the Romans, who were really responsible, to the Jews, who were not. Others believe that it is substantially correct. All that can be said here is that whoever arrested, tried, condemned, and executed Jesus, he did indeed die in agony by crucifixion.

The crucifixion of Jesus certainly marked a decisive moment in Christian history. At first Jesus's death was viewed by his followers as the end of their hopes. Yet after a few days their despair began to dissipate, for rumors began to spread that the Master was alive and had been seen by some of his faithful disciples. In short order Jesus's followers became convinced that Jesus not only had risen from the dead but that he had walked on earth thereafter for forty days and hence that he truly was a divine being. With their courage restored, they fanned out to preach the good news of Jesus's divinity and to testify in the name of their martyred leader. Soon belief in Jesus's godliness and resurrection became articles of faith for thousands: Jesus was the "Christ" (Greek for "the anointed one"), the divine Son of God who was sent to earth to suffer and die for the sins of humanity, and who, after three days in the tomb, had risen from the dead and ascended into heaven, whence he would come again to judge the world at the end of time.

Christianity was broadened and invested with a more elaborate theology by some of the successors of Jesus, above all the Apostle Paul, originally known as Saul of Tarsus (10?–67?A.D.). Paul was not a native of Palestine but a Jew born in the city of Tarsus in southeastern Asia Minor. Originally a persecutor of Christians, he later converted to Christianity and devoted his limitless energy to propagating that faith throughout the Near East. It would be almost impossible to overestimate the significance of his work. Denying that Jesus was sent merely as the redeemer of the Jews, Paul proclaimed Christianity to be a universal religion. Furthermore, he placed major emphasis on the idea of Jesus as the Christ, as the anointed God-man whose death on the cross was an atonement for the sins of humanity. Not only did he reject the works of the Law (i.e., Jewish ritualism) as of primary importance in religion, but he declared them to be utterly worthless in procuring salvation. Sinners by nature, human beings can be saved only by faith and by the grace of God "through the redemption that is in Christ Jesus." It follows, according to Paul, that human fate in the life to

St. Paul. From a Ravenna mosaic.

come is almost entirely dependent upon the will of God; for "Hath not the potter power over the clay, of the same lump to make one vessel unto honor, and another unto dishonor?" (Romans 9:21). God has mercy "on whom He will have mercy, and whom He will He hardeneth" (Romans 9:18).

Although it may be something of a simplification, it seems basically true to say that whereas Jesus proclaimed the imminent coming of the kingdom of God, Paul laid the basis for a religion of personal salvation through Christ and the ministry of the Church. Therefore, after Paul Christianity developed both ceremonies, or sacraments, to bring the believer closer to Christ and an organization of priests to administer those sacraments. In teaching that priests who administered sacraments were endowed with supernatural powers, Christianity gradually posited a distinction between clergy and laity much sharper than that which had existed in most earlier religions. This would become the basis of subsequent Western controversies and divisions between "Church" and "State." In the meantime, Christianity's emphasis on otherworldly salvation ministered by a priestly organization helped it greatly to grow and ultimately to flourish.

The beginnings of Church organization

Christianity grew steadily in the first two centuries after Christ but only really began to flourish in the third. To understand this we must recall that the third century in Roman history was an "age of anxiety." At a time of extreme political turbulence and economic hardship people understandably began to treat life on earth as an illusion and place their hopes in the beyond. The human body and the material world were more and more regarded as either evil or basically unreal. As the Neoplatonic philosopher and leading thinker of that age, Plotinus, wrote, "when I come to myself, I wonder how it is that I have a body . . . by what deterioration did this happen?" Plotinus devised a whole philosophical system to answer this question, but this system was far too abstruse to have much meaning for large numbers of people. Instead, several religions that emphasized the dominance of spiritual forces in this world and the absolute preeminence of otherworldly salvation gained hold as never before.

At first Christianity was just another of these religions; Mithraism and the Egyptian cults of Isis and Serapis were others. It is natural to ask, therefore, why Christianity gained converts in the third century at the expense of its rivals. A number of answers may be posited. One of the simplest, but not the least important, is that even though Christianity borrowed elements from older religions—above all Judaism—it was new and hence possessed a sense of dynamism lacking among the salvationist religions which had existed for centuries. Christianity's dynamism was also enhanced by its rigorous exclusiveness. Hitherto people had adopted religions as people today take on insurance policies, piling one on another in order to feel more secure. The fact that Christianity prohibited this, demanding that the Christian God

Altar of Mithras. Dating from the third century A.D., this altar used for Mithraic services in an underground chamber in the heart of Rome depicts Mithras slaying a bull. A century later, when Christianity triumphed in the Roman Empire, a Christian church was built over the Mithraic sanctuary.

be worshiped alone, made the new religion most appealing at a time when people were searching desperately for absolutes. Similarly, Christianity alone among its rivals had an all-embracing theory to explain evil on earth, namely as the work of demons governed by the devil. When Christian missionaries sought converts they successfully emphasized the new faith's ability to combat these demons by reputed miracles.

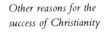

Other reasons for the success of Christianity

Although Christianity's novelty, exclusiveness, and theory of evil help greatly to explain its success, probably the greatest attractions of the religion had to do with three other traits: its view of salvation, its social dimensions, and its organizational structure. Exorcism of demons might help to make life more tolerable on earth, but ultimately people in the later Roman Empire were most concerned with otherworldly salvation. Rival religions also promised an afterlife, but Christianity's doctrine on this subject was the most far-reaching. Christian preachers who warned that nonbelievers would "liquefy in fierce fires" for eternity and that believers would enjoy eternal blessedness understandably made many converts in an age of fears. They made converts too among all classes because Christianity had from its origins been a religion of the humble—carpenters, fishermen, and tent-makers—which promised the exaltation of the lowly. As the religion grew it gained a few wealthy patrons, but it continued to find its greatest strength among the lower and middle classes who comprised the greatest numbers in the Roman Empire. Moreover, while Christianity forbade women to become priests or discuss the faith and, as we will see, adopted many attitudes hostile to women, it at least accorded women some rights of participation in worship and equal hope for salvation. This fact gave it an advantage over Mithraism, which excluded women from its cult entirely. In addition to all these considerations, a final reason for Christianity's success lay in its organization. Unlike the rival mystery religions, by the third century it had developed an organized hierarchy of priests to direct the life of the faith. More than that, Christian congregations were tightly knit communities that provided services to their members—such as nursing, support of the unprotected, and burial—that went beyond strictly religious concerns. Those who became Christians found human contacts and a sense of mission while the rest of the world seemed to be collapsing about them.

An Early-Christian Woman. A wall-painting from the catacomb of Priscilla, Rome, third century A.D.

Roman persecution of Christians relatively moderate

Christians were never as brutally persecuted by the Roman state as used to be thought. In fact the attitude of Rome was usually one of indifference: Christians were customarily tolerated unless certain magistrates decided to prosecute them for refusing to worship the official state gods. From time to time there were more concerted persecutions, but these were too intermittent and short-lived to do irreparable damage: on the contrary, they served to give Christianity some helpful publicity. To this degree the blood of martyrs really was the seed of the Church, but only because the blood did not flow too freely.

Jonah under the Gourd. A Christian marble statue done around the time of Constantine's conversion. Jonah resting after leaving the whale's belly was a symbol for the risen Christ.

One last great persecution took place toward the end of the reign of Diocletian and was continued by one of his immediate successors, a particularly bitter enemy of Christianity named Galerius. But by then the religion was far too strong to be wiped out by persecution, a fact that Galerius finally recognized by issuing an edict of toleration right before his death in 311. Thereafter Christianity was to be supported by the Roman state rather than persecuted by it.

The adoption of Christianity by the Roman Empire was initiated by Constantine and completed by Theodosius. Constantine did not yet make Christianity the official religion of the empire, but he clearly favored it. Probably he did so both because he associated his own conversion to the faith (around the year 312) with the rise of his political fortunes, and because he hoped that Christianity might bring a spiritual unity to an empire that had been badly demoralized and religiously divided. Some of his successors, who were brought up in the Christian religion, pursued this end by ordering the persecution of pagans even more ruthlessly than some pagan emperors had formerly persecuted Christians. Christianity probably would have triumphed merely with official support, however, because aspiring functionaries are usually quick to accept the religion of their rulers. The masses too were easily converted to the faith once it was supported by the state because, even though the fourth century was politically more stable than the third, the reorganization of the empire weighed most heavily on the lower classes and made them as desperate for otherworldly salvation as they had been in the century before. Substantial numbers, too, simply followed the lead of authority. Christians

The triumph of Christianity

274

*Christianity and the
Transformation of the Roman
World*

probably comprised no more than a fifth of the population of the Roman Empire at the time of the conversion of Constantine; with state support they quickly became an overwhelming majority. When Theodosius the Great decreed that all his subjects must adhere to Christianity by an edict of 380, paganism, already disappearing, was soon wiped out in all but the most rural backlands of the Roman realms.

3. THE NEW CONTOURS OF CHRISTIANITY

Once the new faith became dominant within the Roman Empire it underwent some major changes in forms of thought, organization, and conduct. These changes all bore relationships to earlier tendencies, but the triumph of the faith greatly accelerated certain trends and altered the course of others. The result was that in many respects the Christianity of the late fourth century was a very different religion from the one persecuted by Diocletian and Galerius.

Controversy over doctrinal matters

One consequence of Christianity's triumph was the flaring up of bitter doctrinal disputes. These brought great turmoil to the Church but resulted in the hammering out of dogma and discipline. Before the conversion of Constantine there had of course been disagreements among Christians about doctrinal matters, but as long as Christianity was a minority religion it managed to control its internal divisions in order to present a united front against hostile outsiders. Hardly had the new faith emerged victorious, however, than sharp splits developed within its own ranks. These were due partly to the fact that there had always been a tension between the intellectual and emotional tendencies within the religion which could now come more fully into the open, and partly to the fact that different regions of the empire tried to preserve a sense of their separate identities by preferring different theological formulas.

Division between the Arians and Athanasians

The first of the bitter disputes was between the Arians and Athanasians over the nature of the Trinity. The Arians—not to be confused with Aryans (a racial term)—were followers of a priest named Arius and were the more intellectual group. Under the influence of Greek philosophy they rejected the idea that Christ could be equal with God. Instead they maintained that the Son was created by the Father and therefore was not co-eternal with Him or formed of the same substance. The followers of St. Athanasius, indifferent to human logic, held that even though Christ was the Son he was fully God: that Father, Son, and Holy Ghost were all absolutely equal and composed of an identical substance. After protracted struggles Athanasius's side won out and the Athanasian doctrine became the Christian dogma of the Trinity, as it remains today.

The struggle between the Arians and Athanasians was followed by numerous other doctrinal quarrels during the next few centuries. The issues at stake were generally too abstruse to warrant explaining here, but the results were momentous. One was that the dogmas of the Catholic faith gradually became fixed. It should be emphasized that this was a slow development and that many basic tenets of Catholicism were only defined much later (for example, the theory of the Mass was not formally promulgated until 1215; the doctrine of the Immaculate Conception of the Virgin Mary until 1854; and that of the Bodily Assumption of the Virgin until 1950). Nonetheless, the faith was beginning to take on a sharply defined form unprecedented in the history of earlier religions. Above all, this meant that any who differed from a certain formulation would be excluded from the community and often persecuted as a heretic. In the subsequent history of Christianity this concern for doctrinal uniformity was to result in both strengths and weaknesses for the Church.

A second result of the doctrinal quarrels was that they aggravated regional hostilities. In the fourth century differences among Christians increased alienation between West and East and also aggravated hostilities among regions within the East. Although the Roman Empire was evolving toward regionalism for many different reasons, including economic and administrative ones, and although regionalism was partly a cause of religious differences, the sharper and more frequent doctrinal quarrels became, the more they served to intensify regional hostilities.

Finally, the doctrinal quarrels provoked the interference of the Roman state in the governance of the Church. The same Constantine who favored Christianity as a unifying force was horrified by the prompt emergence of the Arian conflict and intervened in it by calling the Council of Nicea (325), which condemned Arius. It is noteworthy that this council—the first general council of the Church—was con-

Consequences of successive doctrinal disputes

Regionalism

Imperial involvement in religious conflicts

Christ Separating the Sheep from the Goats as an Image for the Last Judgment. This early Christian sarcophagus (fourth century A.D.) illustrates a verse from the New Testament: "And before Him shall be gathered all nations: and He shall separate them one from another, as a shepherd divideth his sheep from his goats" (Matthew 25:31). The theme was obviously appropriate for a burial repository.

Christianity and the
Transformation of the Roman
World

vened by a Roman emperor and that Constantine served during its meetings as a presiding officer. Thereafter secular interference in Church matters continued, above all in the East. There were two major reasons for this. First, religious disputes were more prevalent in the East than the West and quarreling parties often appealed to the emperor for support. Second, the weight of imperial government was generally heavier in the East, and after 476 there were no Roman emperors in the West at all. When Eastern emperors were not appealed to by quarreling parties they interfered in religious disputes themselves, as Constantine had done before them, in order to preserve unity. The result was that in the East the emperor assumed great religious authority and control, while in the West the future of relations between State and Church was more open.

Even while emperors were interfering in religious matters, however, the Church's own internal organization was becoming more complex and articulated. We have seen that a clear distinction between clergy and laity was already a hallmark of the early Christian religion after the time of St. Paul. The next step was the development of a hierarchical organization within the ranks of the clergy. The superiority of bishops over priests was recognized before Christianity's triumph. Christian organization was centered in cities and one bishop in each important city became the authority to which all the clergy in the surrounding vicinity answered. This organization was sufficient for a minority religion, but as the number of congregations multiplied and as the influence of the Church increased due to the adoption of Christianity as the official religion of Rome, distinctions of rank among the bishops themselves began to appear. Those who had their headquarters in the larger cities came to be called metropolitans (today known in the West as archbishops), with authority over the clergy of an entire province. In the fourth century the still higher rank of patriarch was established to designate those bishops who ruled over the oldest and largest of Christian communities—such cities as Rome, Jerusalem, Constantinople, Antioch, and Alexandria, and their surrounding districts. Thus the Christian clergy by 400 A.D. had come to embrace a definite hierarchy of patriarchs, metropolitans, bishops, and priests.

The climax of all this development—still largely in the future—was the growth of the primacy of the bishop of Rome, or in other words the rise of the papacy. For several reasons the bishop of Rome enjoyed a preeminence over the other patriarchs of the Church. The city in which he ruled was venerated by the faithful as a scene of the missionary activities of the Apostles Peter and Paul. The tradition was widely accepted that Peter had founded the bishopric of Rome and that therefore all of his successors were heirs of his authority and prestige. This tradition was supplemented by the theory that Peter had been commissioned by Christ as his vicar on earth and had been

*The organization
of the clergy*

The rise of the papacy

given the keys of the kingdom of heaven with power to punish people for their sins and even to absolve them from guilt (Matthew 16:18–19). This theory, known as the doctrine of the Petrine Succession, has been used by popes ever since as a basis for their claims to authority over the Church. The bishops of Rome had an advantage also in the fact that after the transfer of the imperial capital to Constantinople there was seldom any emperor with effective sovereignty in the West. Finally, in 445 the Emperor Valentinian III issued a decree commanding all Western bishops to submit to the jurisdiction of the pope. It must not be supposed, however, that the Church was by any means yet under a monarchical form of government. The patriarchs in the East regarded the extreme assertions of papal claims as brazen effrontery, and even many bishops in the West continued to ignore them for some time. The clearest example of the papacy's early weakness is the fact that the popes did not even attend the first eight general councils of the Church (from 325 to 869), although later they were to convene and preside over all the others.

The growth of ecclesiastical organization helped the Church to conquer the Roman world in the fourth century and to minister to the needs of the faithful thereafter. The existence of an episcopal administrative structure was particularly influential in the West as the Roman Empire decayed and finally collapsed in the fifth century. Since every city had a bishop trained to some degree in the arts of administration, the Church in the West took over many of the functions of government and helped to preserve order amid the deepening chaos. But the new emphasis on administration also had its inevitably detrimental effects: as the Church developed its own rationalized administrative structure it inevitably became more worldly and distant in spirit from the simple faith of Jesus and the Apostles.

Effects of the rationalization of ecclesiastical administration

The clearest reaction to this trend was expressed in the spread of monasticism. Today we are accustomed to thinking of monks as groups of priests who live communally in order to dedicate themselves primarily to lives of contemplation and prayer. In their origins, however, monks were not priests but laymen who almost always lived alone and who sought extremes of self-torture rather than ordered lives of spirituality. Monasticism began to emerge in the third century as a response to the anxieties of that age, but it only became a dominant movement within Christianity in the fourth century. Two obvious reasons for this fact stand out. First of all, the choice of extreme hermitlike asceticism was a substitute for martyrdom. With the conversion of Constantine and the abandonment of persecution, most chances of winning a crown of glory in heaven by undergoing death for the faith were eliminated. But the desire to prove one's religious ardor by self-abasement and suffering was still present. Second, as the fourth century progressed the priesthood became more and more immersed in worldly concerns. Those who wished to avoid secular

The rise of monasticism

278

*Christianity and the
Transformation of the Roman
World*

temptations fled to the deserts and woods to practice an asceticism that priests and bishops were forgetting. (Monks customarily became priests only later during the Middle Ages.) In this way even while Christianity was accommodating itself to practical needs, monasticism satisfied the inclinations of ascetic extremists.

Monasticism first emerged in the East, where for about one hundred years after Constantine's conversion it spread like a mania Hermit monks of Egypt and Syria vied with each other in their pursuit of the most inhuman and humiliating excesses. Some grazed in the fields after the manner of cows, others penned themselves into small cages, and others hung heavy weights around their necks. A monk named Cyriacus stood for hours on one leg like a crane until he could bear it no more. The most extravagant of these monastic ascetics was St. Simeon Stylites, who performed self-punishing exercises—such as touching his feet with his head 1,244 times in succession—on top of a high pillar for thirty-seven years, while crowds gathered below to worship "the worms that dropped from his body."

In time such ascetic hysteria subsided and it became recognized that monasticism would be more enduring if monks lived in a community and did not concentrate on self-torture. The most successful architect of communal monasticism in the East was St. Basil (330?–379), who started his monastic career as a hermit and ascetic extremist but came to prefer communal and more moderate forms of life. Basil expressed this preference in writings for monks that laid down the basic guidelines for Eastern monasticism down to the present. Rather than encouraging extremes of self-torture, Basil encouraged monks to discipline themselves by useful labor. Although his teachings were still extremely severe by modern standards, he prohibited monks from

A Monastery of the Basilian Order on Mt. Athos. The asceticism of the Basilian monks caused them to build their monasteries in almost inaccessible places on lofty crags or on the steep sides of rugged mountains.

engaging in prolonged fasts or lacerating their flesh. Instead he urged them to submit to obligations of poverty and humility, and to spend many hours of the day in silent religious meditation. With the triumph of St. Basil's ideas, Eastern monasticism became more organized and subdued, but even so Basilian monks preferred to live as far away from the "world" as they could and never had the same civilizing influence on external society as did their brothers in western Europe.

Monasticism did not at first spread so quickly in the West as it did in the East because the appeal of asceticism was much weaker there. This situation changed only in the sixth century when St. Benedict (480?–547?) drafted his famous Latin rule which ultimately became the guide for nearly all the monks in the West. Recent research has shown that Benedict copied much of his rule from an earlier Latin text known as the "Rule of the Master," but he still produced a document notable for its brevity, flexibility, and moderation. The Benedictine rule imposed obligations similar to those laid down by St. Basil: poverty, obedience, labor, and religious devotion. Yet Benedict prescribed less austerity than Basil did: the monks were granted a sufficiency of simple food, clothing, and enough sleep; they were even allowed to drink a small amount of wine, although meat was only granted to the sick. The abbot's authority was absolute and the abbot was allowed to flog monks for disobedience, yet Benedict urged him to try "to be loved rather than feared," and ordained that the abbot gather advice before making decisions "because the Lord often reveals to a younger member what is best." For such reasons the Benedictine monastery became a home of religious enrichment rather than a school for punishment.

We will have occasion for continuing the story of Benedictine monasticism later on, but here we may point in advance to some of its greatest contributions to the development of Western civilization. One was that Benedictine monks were committed from an early date to missionary work: they were primarily responsible for the conversion of England and later most of Germany. Such activities not only helped to spread the faith but also served to create a sense of cultural unity for western Europe. Another positive contribution lay in the attitude of the Benedictines toward work. Whereas the highest goal for ancient philosophers and aristocrats was to have enough leisure time for unimpeded contemplation, St. Benedict wanted his monks always to keep busy, for he believed that "idleness is an enemy of the soul." Therefore he prescribed that they should be occupied at certain times in manual labor, a prescription that would have horrified most thinkers of earlier times. Accordingly, early Benedictines worked hard themselves and spread the idea of the dignity of labor to others. With Benedictine support, this idea would become one of the most distinctive traits of Western culture. We read of Benedictines who gladly milked cows, threshed, plowed, and hammered: in so doing

Monks Chopping Down Trees (above) *and Harvesting Grain* (below) From a twelfth-century French manuscript.

St. Benedict Offering His Rule to Grateful Monks. A late-medieval conception from an Austrian manuscript of about 1355.

The significance of Benedictine monasticism: (1) missionary activities; (2) attitude toward manual labor

they increased the prosperity of their own monasteries and provided good examples for others. Benedictine monasteries became particularly successful in farming and later in estate-managing. Thus they often helped to advance the level of the western European economy and sometimes even to provide wealth that could be drawn upon by emerging western European states.

The fact that Benedictine monasteries were often islands of culture when literacy and learning were all but forgotten in the secular world is better known. St. Benedict himself was no admirer of classical culture. Quite to the contrary, he wanted his monks to serve only Christ—not literature or philosophy. But he did assume that monks would have to read well enough to say their prayers. That meant that some teaching in the monasteries was necessary because it was seldom available outside, and because boys were often given over from birth to the monastic profession. Once there was teaching there would obviously be at least a few writing implements and books. This explains why Benedictines always maintained some literacy but not why some of them became devoted to perpetuating classical culture. The impetus behind the latter development was the work of a monastic thinker named Cassiodorus (477?–570?). Inspired by St. Augustine, whom we will treat in more detail later, Cassiodorus believed that some basic classical learning was necessary for the proper understanding of the Bible; this justified the study of the classics by monks. Furthermore, Cassiodorus recognized that copying manuscripts was in itself "manual labor" (literally work with the hands) and might be even more appropriate for monks than hard work in the fields. As Benedictines began to subscribe to these ideas, Benedictine monasteries became centers for learning and transcribing that were without rival for cen-

(3) the preservation of classical culture; Cassiodorus

turies. No work of classical Latin literature, including such "licentious" writings as the poems of Catullus and Ovid, would survive today had they not been copied and preserved during the early Middle Ages by Benedictine monks.

Carnal love of women was not, however, a Benedictine preference. Returning to our original subject—the changes that took place in Christian institutions and attitudes during the fourth century—a final fateful trend was the development of a negative attitude toward women. Compared to most other religions, Christianity was favorable to women. Female souls were regarded as equal to male souls in the eyes of God, and human nature was deemed to be complete only in both sexes. St. Paul even went so far as to say that after baptism "there is neither male nor female" (Galatians 3:28), a spiritual equalitarianism which meant that women could be saved as fully as men. But Christians from earliest times shared the view of their contemporaries that in everyday life and in marriage women were to be strictly subject to men. Not only did early Christians believe, with all male supremacists of the ancient world, that women should be excluded from positions of leadership or decision-making, meaning that they should be "silent in Church" (1 Corinthians 14:34–35) and could never be priests, but they added to this the view that women were more "fleshly" than men and therefore should be subjected to men as the flesh is subjected to the spirit (Ephesians 5:21–33).

With the growth of the ascetic movement in the third and fourth centuries, the denigration of women as dangerously "fleshly" creatures became more and more pronounced. Since sexual abstinence lay at the heart of asceticism, the most perfect men were expected to shun women. Monks, of course, shunned women the most. This was a primary reason why they fled to deserts and forests. One Eastern ascetic was struck by the need for virginity in the midst of his marriage ceremony, ran off to a hermit's cell, and blocked the entrance; another monk who was forced to carry his aged mother across a stream swaddled her up as thoroughly as he could so that he would not catch any "fire" and no thoughts of other women attack him. With monks taking such an uncompromising attitude, the call for continence was extended to the priesthood. Originally priests could be married; it seems that even some of the Apostles had wives (I Corinthians 9:5). But in the course of the fourth century the doctrine spread that priests could not be married after ordination, and that those already married were obliged to live continently with their wives afterward.

Once virginity was accepted as the highest standard, marriage was taken to be only second-best. St. Jerome expressed this view most earthily when he said that virginity was wheat, marriage barley, and fornication cow-dung: since people should not eat cow-dung he would permit them barley. The major purposes of marriage were to keep men from "burning" and to propagate the species. (St. Jerome

Christianity's negative attitiude toward women

Cassiodorus. This frontispiece of a Bible executed around 700 A.D. in an English Benedictine monastery depicts Cassiodorus as a copyist and as a preserver of books. (Since books were exceedingly rare until the invention of printing in the fifteenth century, they customarily were stored in cupboards, lying flat.)

Attitudes toward marriage

282

*Christianity and the
Transformation of the Roman
World*

went so far as to praise marriage above all because it brought more virgins into the world!) Thus Christianity reinforced the ancient view that woman's major earthly purpose was to serve as mother. Men and women were warned not to take pleasure even in marital intercourse but to indulge in it only for the purpose of procreation. Women were to be "saved in childbearing" (I Timothy 2:15). Since they could not become priests and only a very few could become nuns (female monasticism was regarded as a very expensive luxury in the premodern world), almost all women were expected to become submissive wives and mothers. As wives they were not expected to have their own careers and were not meant to be educated or even literate. Hence even though they had full hopes for salvation, they were treated as inferiors in the everyday affairs of the world, a treatment that would endure until modern times.

4. THE GERMANIC INVASIONS AND THE FALL OF THE ROMAN EMPIRE IN THE WEST

*The victories of the
Germanic barbarians*

While Christianity was conquering the Roman Empire from within, another force, that of the Germanic barbarians, was threatening it from without. The Germans, who had already almost brought Rome to its knees in the third century, were held off from the time of Diocletian until shortly before the reign of Theodosius the Great. But thereafter they demolished Western Roman resistance and, by the end of the fifth century, succeeded in conquering all of the Roman West. Germanic kingdoms then became the new form of government in territories once ruled over by Caesar and Augustus.

Character of the Germans

It was once customary to think that the Germans were fierce and thoroughly uncouth savages who wantonly destroyed the Western Roman Empire out of sheer hatred for civilization. But that is a misunderstanding. The Germans were barbarians in Roman eyes because they did not live in cities and were illiterate, but they were not therefore savages. On the contrary, they often practiced settled agriculture— although they preferred hunting and grazing—and were adept in making iron tools and weapons as well as lavish jewelry. Physically they looked enough like Romans to intermarry without causing much comment, and their Indo-European language was related to Latin and Greek. Prolonged interaction with the Romans had a decisive civilizing influence on the Germans before they started their final conquests. Germans and Romans who shared common borders along the Rhine and Danube had steady trading relations with each other. Even during times of war Romans were often allied with some German tribes while they fought others. By the fourth century, moreover, German tribes often served as auxiliaries of depleted Roman armies and were sometimes allowed to settle on borderlands of the empire where Roman farmers had given up trying to cultivate the land. Finally, many

283

*The Germanic Invasions and the
Fall of the Roman Empire
in the West*

German tribes had been converted to Christianity in the fourth century, although the Christianity they accepted was of the heretical Arian version. All these interactions made the "barbarians" very familiar with Roman civilization and substantially favorable to it.

The Germans began their final push not to destroy Rome but to find more and better land. The first breakthrough occurred in 378 when one tribe, the Visigoths, who had recently settled on some Roman lands in the Danube region, revolted against mistreatment by Roman officials and then decisively defeated a punitive Roman army in the Battle of Adrianople. The Visigoths did not immediately follow up this victory because they were cleverly bought off and made allies of the empire by Theodosius the Great. But when Theodosius died in 395 he divided his realm between his two sons, neither of whom was as competent as he, and both halves of the empire were weakened by political intrigues. The Visigoths under their leader Alaric took advantage of this situation to wander through Roman realms almost at will, looking for the best land and provisions. In 410 they sacked Rome itself—a great shock to some contemporaries—and in the following years marched into southern Gaul. Meanwhile, in December of 406, a group of allied Germanic tribes led by the Vandals crossed the frozen Rhine and capitalized on Roman preoccupation with the Visigoths by streaming through Gaul into Spain. Later they were able to cross the straits into northwest Africa, then one of the richest agricultural regions of the empire. From Africa they took control of the central Mediterranean, even sacking Rome from the sea in 455. By 476 the entirely ineffectual Western Roman emperor, a mere boy derisively nicknamed Augustulus ("little Augustus"), was easily deposed by a leader of a mixed band of Germans who then assumed the title of king of Rome. Accordingly, 476 is conventionally given as the date for the end of the Western Roman Empire. But it must be remembered that a Roman emperor, who maintained some claims to authority in the West, continued to rule in Constantinople.

Two questions that historians of the German invasions customarily ask are: How did the Germans manage to triumph so easily? Why was it that they were particularly successful in the West rather than the East? The ease of the German victories appears particularly striking when it is recognized that the German armies were remarkably small: the Goths who won at Adrianople numbered no more than 10,000 men, and the total number of the Vandal "hordes" (including women and children) was about 80,000—a population about the same as that of an average-sized American suburb. But the Roman armies themselves were depleted because of declining population and the need for manpower in other occupations, above all in the new bureaucracies. More than that, German armies often won by default (Adrianople was one of the few pitched battles in the history of their advance) because the Romans were no longer zealous about defending themselves. Ger-

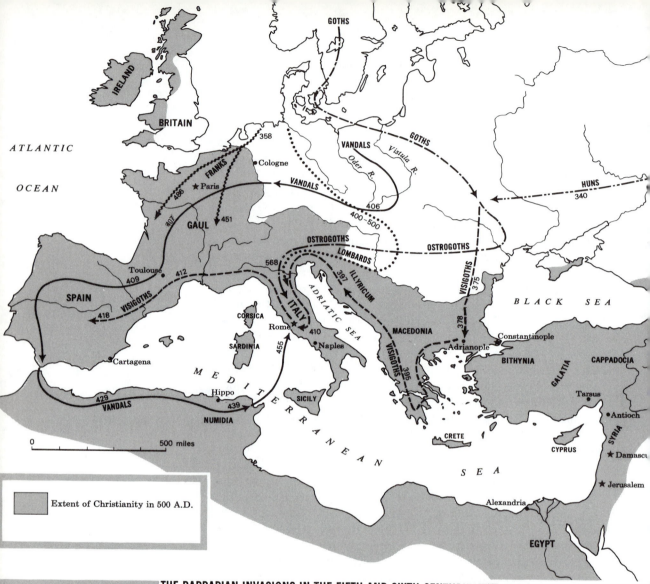

GOTHS

IRELAND

BRITAIN

ATLANTIC

OCEAN

358

FRANKS • Cologne

• Paris

GAUL

407

451

GOTHS

VANDALS

Vistula R.

Oder R.

VANDALS

406

400–500

HUNS
340

OSTROGOTHS

LOMBARDS

OSTROGOTHS

Toulouse
409

412

SPAIN

VISIGOTHS

568

ILLYRICUM

397

VISIGOTHS
375

418

CORSICA

ITALY

ADRIATIC SEA

MACEDONIA

BLACK SEA

Rome

410

Naples

455

VISIGOTHS
378

Adrianople

Constantinople

BITHYNIA

CAPPADOCIA

GALATIA

SARDINIA

Cartagena

395

MEDITERRANEAN

Tarsus

• Antioch

429

VANDALS

Hippo

439

SICILY

SYRIA

CYPRUS

★ Damascu

0

500 miles

NUMIDIA

SEA

CRETE

★ Jerusalem

Alexandria

Extent of Christianity in 500 A.D.

EGYPT

THE BARBARIAN INVASIONS IN THE FIFTH AND SIXTH CENTURIES

mans were seldom regarded with horror—many German soldiers had
even risen to positions of leadership within Roman ranks—and the coercive regime begun by Diocletian was not deemed to be worth fighting for.

The reasons why the Germans fared best in the West are complex—
some having to do with personalities and mistakes of the moment,
and others with geographical considerations. But the primary explanation why the Eastern Roman Empire survived while the Western
did not is that the East was simply richer. By the fifth century most
Western Roman cities had shrunk in terms of both population and
space to a small fraction of their earlier size and were often little more

*Why the Eastern Roman
Empire survived and the
Western collapsed*

than empty administrative shells or fortifications. The economy of the West was becoming more and more strictly agricultural, and agricultural produce served only to feed farm laborers and keep rich landlords in luxuries. In the East, on the other hand, cities like Constantinople, Antioch, and Alexandria were still teeming metropolises because of their trade and industry. Because the Eastern State had greater reserves of wealth to tax, it was more vigorous. It could also afford to buy off the barbarians with tribute money, which it did with increasing regularity. So Constantinople was able to stay afloat while Rome floundered and then sank.

The effects of the Germanic conquests in the West were not cataclysmic. The greatest difference between the Germans and the Romans had been that the former did not live in cities, but since the Western Roman cities were already in a state of decline, the invasions only served at most to accelerate the progress of urban decay. On the land Germans replaced Roman landlords without interrupting basic Roman agricultural patterns. Moreover, since the Germans never comprised very large numbers, they usually never took over more than a part of Roman lands. Germans also tried to avail themselves of Roman administrative apparatuses, but these tended to diminish gradually because of the diminishing of wealth and literacy. Thus the only major German innovation was to create separate tribal kingdoms in the West in place of a united empire.

The map of western Europe around the year 500 reveals the following major political divisions. Germanic tribes of Anglo-Saxons, who had crossed the English Channel in the middle of the fifth century, were extending their rule on the island of Britain. In the northern part of Gaul, around Paris and east to the Rhine, the growing kingdom of the Franks was ruled by a crafty warrior named Clovis. South of the Franks stood the Visigoths, who ruled the southern half of Gaul and most of Spain. South of them were the Vandals, who ruled throughout previously Roman northwest Africa. In all of Italy the Ostrogoths, eastern relatives of the Visigoths, held sway under their impressive King Theodoric. Of these kingdoms the Frankish would be the most promising for the future (for that reason it will be taken up in the next chapter) and the seemingly strongest for the present was that of the Ostrogoths.

Theodoric the Ostrogoth, who ruled in Italy from 493 to 526, was a great admirer of Roman civilization; this he tried to preserve as best he could. He fostered agriculture and commerce, repaired public buildings and roads, patronized learning, and maintained a policy of religious toleration. In short he gave Italy a more enlightened rule than it had known under most of its earlier emperors. But since Theodoric and his sparsely numbered Ostrogoths were Arian Christians while the local bishops and native population were Catholics, his rule, no matter how tolerant and benign, was viewed with some hostility. The

Theodoric the Ostrogoth. The barbarian ruler is shown here in Roman dress, with an ornate Roman hairstyle and a Roman symbol of victory in his hand. The inscription reads REX THEODERICVS PIVS PRINCIS, Latin for King Theodoric, pious prince.

Mosaic of Theodoric's Palace at Ravenna. At the right is a stylized conception of the ruler's palace, with the Latin inscription PALA TIVM; to the left of it is a row of saints, who would be indistinguishable were it not for the initials on their clothing: for early Christian artists, supernatural merits rather than individual personality traits were of the essence.

"Roman" rulers in Constantinople were also hostile to Theodoric because he was an Arian and because they had not given up hopes of reconquering Italy themselves. All these circumstances led to the demise of Theodoric's Ostrogothic kingdom not long after his death. In fact, none of the continental barbarian kingdoms would last long except for that of the Franks.

5. THE SHAPING OF WESTERN CHRISTIAN THOUGHT

The advance of Western Christian thought

The period of the decline and fall of the Roman Empire in the West was also the time when a few Western Christian thinkers formulated an approach to the world and to God that was to guide the thought of the West for roughly the next 800 years. This concurrence of political decline and theological advance was not coincidental. With the empire falling and being replaced by barbarian kingdoms, it seemed clearer than ever to thinking Christians both that the classical inheritance had to be reexamined and that God had not intended the world to be anything more than a transitory testing place. The consequences of these assumptions accordingly became urgent questions: Between about 380 and 525 answers were worked out by Western Christian thinkers whose accomplishments were intimately interrelated. The towering figure among them was St. Augustine, but some others had great influence as well.

Three contemporaries who knew and influenced each other—St.

Jerome (340?–420), St. Ambrose (340?–397), and St. Augustine (354–430)—count as three of the four greatest "fathers" of the Western, Latin Church. (The fourth, St. Gregory the Great, came later and will be discussed in the next chapter.) St. Jerome's greatest single contribution to the future was his translation of the Bible from Hebrew and Greek into Latin. His version, known as the "Vulgate" (or "common" version), became the standard Latin Bible used throughout the Middle Ages; with minor variations it continued to be used long afterward by the Roman Catholic Church. Fortunately Jerome was one of the best writers of his day, and he endowed his translation with vigorous, often colloquial prose and, occasionally, fine poetry. Since the Vulgate was the most widely read work in Latin for centuries, Jerome's writing had as much influence on Latin style and thought as the King James Bible has had on English literature. Jerome, who was the least original thinker of the great Latin fathers, also influenced the Western Christian future by his contentious but eloquent formulations of contemporary views. Among the most important of these were the beliefs that much of the Bible was to be understood allegorically rather than literally, that classical learning could be valid for Christians if it was thoroughly subordinated to Christian aims, and that the most perfect Christians were rigorous ascetics. In keeping with the last position Jerome avidly supported monasticism. He also taught that women should not take baths so that they would not see their own bodies naked.

St. Jerome

Unlike Jerome, who was primarily a scholar, St. Ambrose was most active in the concerns of the world. As archbishop of Milan, Ambrose was the most influential Church official in the West—more so even than the pope. Guided by practical concerns, he wrote an ethical work, *On the Duties of Ministers,* which followed closely upon Cicero's *On Duties* in title and form, and also drew heavily on Cicero's Stoic ethics. But Ambrose differed from Cicero and most of traditional classical thought on two major points. One was that the beginning and end of human conduct should be the reverence and search for God rather than any self-concern or interest in social adjustment. The other—Ambrose's most original contribution—was that God helps some Christians but not others in this pursuit by the gift of grace, a point that was to be greatly refined and amplified by St. Augustine. Ambrose put his concern for proper conduct into action by his most famous act, his confrontation with the Emperor Theodosius the Great for massacring innocent civilians. Ambrose argued that by violating divine commandments Theodosius had made himself subject to Church discipline. Remarkably the archbishop succeeded in forcing the sovereign emperor to do penance. This was the first time that a churchman had subordinated the Roman secular power in matters of morality. Consequently it symbolized the Church's claim to preeminence in this sphere, and particularly the *Western* Church's developing sense of autonomy and moral superiority that would sub-

St. Ambrose

sequently make it so much more independent and influential on the secular world than the Eastern Church.

St. Augustine

St. Ambrose's disciple, St. Augustine, was the greatest of all the Latin fathers; indeed he was one of the most powerful Christian intellects of all time. Augustine's influence on subsequent medieval thought was incalculable. Even after the Middle Ages his theology had a profound influence on the development of Protestantism; in the twentieth century many leading Christian thinkers have called themselves Neo-Augustinians. Augustine's Christianity may have been so searching because he began his career by searching for it. Nominally a Christian from birth, he hesitated until the age of thirty-three to be baptized, passing from one system of thought to another without being able to find intellectual or spiritual satisfaction in any. Only increasing doubts about all other alternatives, the appeals of St. Ambrose's teachings, and a mystical experience movingly described in his *Confessions* led Augustine to embrace the faith wholeheartedly in 387. Thereafter he advanced rapidly in ecclesiastical positions, becoming bishop of the North African city of Hippo in 395. Although he led a most active life in this office, he still found time to write a large number of profound, complex, and powerful treatises in which he set forth his convictions concerning the most fundamental problems of Christian thought and action.

Augustine's theology

St. Augustine's theology revolved around the principles of the profound sinfulness of humanity and divine omnipotence. Ever since Adam and Eve turned away from God in the Garden of Eden humans have remained basically sinful. One of Augustine's most vivid illustrations of human depravity appears in the *Confessions,* where he tells how he and some other boys once were driven to steal pears from a neighbor's garden, not because they were hungry or because the pears were beautiful, but for the sake of the evil itself. God would be purely just if He condemned all human beings to hell, but since He is also merciful He has elected to save a few. Ultimately human will has nothing to do with this choice: although one has the power to choose between good and evil, one does not have the power to decide whether he will be saved. God alone, from eternity, predestined a portion of the human race to be saved and sentenced the rest to be damned. In other words, God fixed for all time the number of human inhabitants of heaven. If any mere mortals were to respond that this seems unfair, the answer is first that strict "fairness" would confine all to perdition, and second that the basis for God's choice is a mystery shrouded in His omnipotence—far beyond the realm of human comprehension.

The doctrine of predestination

Even though it might seem to us that the practical consequences of this rigorous doctrine of predestination would be lethargy and fatalism, Augustine and subsequent medieval Christians did not see it that way at all. Humans themselves must do good, and if they are "chosen" they usually will do good; since no one knows who is chosen and who is not, all should try to do good in the hope that they are among the chosen. For Augustine the central guide to doing good was the doctrine of "charity," which meant leading a life devoted to loving God and loving one's neighbor for the sake of God. Seen from the opposite, humans should avoid "cupidity," or loving earthly things for their own sake. Put in other terms, Augustine taught that humans should behave on earth as if they were travelers or "pilgrims," keeping their eyes at all times on their heavenly home and avoiding all materialistic concerns.

Augustine built an interpretation of history on this view in one of his major works, *On the City of God.* In this, he argued that the entire human race from the Creation until the Last Judgment was and will be composed of two warring societies, those who "live according to man" and love themselves, and those who "live according to God." The former belong to the "City of Earth" and will be damned, while the blessed few who compose the "City of God" will on Judgment Day put on the garment of immortality. As for the time when the Last Judgment would come, Augustine argued vehemently that no human could know its exact date; nonetheless since the Judgment might come at any time, and since no other world-historical events were in store for humans that mattered, all mortals should devote their utmost efforts to preparing for it by leading lives of righteousness.

Although St. Augustine formulated major new aspects of Christian theology, he believed that he was doing no more than drawing out truths found in the Bible. Indeed, he was convinced that the Bible alone contained all the wisdom worth knowing. But he also believed that much of the Bible was expressed obscurely, and that it was therefore necessary to have a certain amount of education in order to understand it thoroughly. This conviction led him to a modified acceptance of classical learning. The ancient world had already worked out an educational system based on the "liberal arts," or those subjects necessary for the worldly success and intellectual growth of free men. Augustine argued that privileged Christians could learn the fundamentals of these subjects, but only in a limited way and for a completely different end—study of the Bible. Since nonreligious schools existed in his day which taught these subjects, he permitted a Christian elite to attend them; later, when such schools died out, their place was taken by schools in monasteries and cathedrals. Thus Augustine's teaching laid the groundwork for some continuity of educational practice as well as for the theory behind the preservation of some classical treatises. But we must qualify this by remarking that Augustine intended liberal education only for an elite; all others were simply to be catechized, or drilled, in the faith. He also thought it far worse that anyone should become engaged in classical thought for its own sake than that someone might not know any classical thought at all. The true wisdom of mortals, he insisted, was piety.

Augustine had many followers, of whom the most interesting and influential was Boethius, a Roman aristocrat who lived from about

On the City of God

Augustine's view of classical learning

Boethius

Boethius's intellectual contributions

Boethius. A twelfth-century artist's conception of Boethius as a musician, a reputation he earned because of his treatise on music.

The Consolation of Philosophy

480 to 524. To say that Boethius was a follower of St. Augustine might until recently have been regarded as controversial because some of his works make no explicit mention of Christianity. Indeed, since Boethius was indisputably interested in ancient philosophy, wrote in a polished, almost Ciceronian style, and came from a noble Roman family, it has been customary to view him as the "last of the Romans." But in fact he intended the classics to serve Christian purposes, just as Augustine had prescribed, and his own teachings were basically Augustinian.

Because Boethius lived a century after Augustine he could see far more clearly that the ancient world was coming to an end. Therefore he made it his first goal to preserve as much of the best ancient learning as possible by a series of handbooks, translations, and commentaries. Accepting a contemporary division of the liberal arts into seven subjects––grammar, rhetoric, logic, arithmetic, geometry, astronomy, and music—he wrote handbooks on two: arithmetic and music. These summaries were meant to convey all the basic aspects of the subject matter that a Christian might need to know. Had Boethius lived longer he probably would have written similar treatments of the other liberal arts, but as it was he concentrated his efforts on his favorite subject: logic. In order to preserve the best of classical logic, he translated from Greek into Latin some of Aristotle's logical treatises as well as an introductory work on logic by Porphyry (another ancient philosopher). He also wrote his own explanatory commentaries on these works in order to help beginners. Since Latin writers had never been interested in logic, even in the most flourishing periods of Roman culture, Boethius's translations and commentaries became a crucial link between the Greeks and the Middle Ages. Boethius helped endow the Latin language with a logical vocabulary, and when interest in logic was revived in the twelfth-century West it rested first on a Boethian basis.

Although Boethius was an exponent of Aristotle's logic, his worldview was not Aristotelian but Augustinian. This can be seen both in his several orthodox treatises on Christian theology and above all in his masterpiece, *The Consolation of Philosophy.* Boethius wrote the *Consolation* at the end of his life, after he had been condemned to death for treason by Theodoric the Ostrogoth, whom he had served as an official. (Historians are unsure about the justice of the charges.) In it Boethius asks the age-old question of what is human happiness and concludes that it is not found in earthly rewards such as riches or fame but only in the "highest good," which is God. Human life, then, should be spent in pursuit of God. Since Boethius speaks in the *Consolation* as a philosopher rather than a theologian, he does not refer to Christian revelation or to the role of divine grace in salvation. But his basically Augustinian message is unmistakable. *The Consolation of Philosophy* became one of the most popular books of the Middle Ages because it was extremely well written, because it showed how classical

Orpheus and Eurydice. Although dating from the later Middle Ages, this manuscript illumination may still intend to deliver Boethius's message that he who turns to look on the joys of earthly life is "turning toward hell" (note the devil standing at the far right).

expression and some classical ideas could be appropriated and subordinated into a clearly Christian framework, and most of all, because it seemed to offer a real meaning to life. In times when all earthly things really did seem crude or fleeting it was genuinely consoling to be told eloquently and "philosophically" that life has purpose if led for the sake of God.

At a climactic moment in the *Consolation* Boethius retold in verse the myth of Orpheus in a way that might stand for the common position of the four writers just discussed; i.e., how Christian thinkers were willing to accept and maintain some continuity with the classical tradition. But Boethius also made new sense of the story. According to Boethius Orpheus's wife, Eurydice, symbolized hell; since Orpheus could not refrain from looking at her he was forced to die and was condemned to hell himself. In other words, Orpheus was too worldly and material; he should not have loved a woman but should have sought God. True Christians, on the other hand, know that "happy is he who can look into the shining spring of good [i.e., the divine vision]; happy is he who can break the heavy chains of earth."

The myth of Orpheus as a symbol for Christian truths

6. EASTERN ROME AND THE WEST

Boethius's execution by Theodoric the Ostrogoth in 524 was in many ways an important historical turning point. For one, Boethius was

Boethius's execution a turning point

The Emperor Justinian

See color map facing page 294

both the last noteworthy philosopher and last writer of cultivated Latin prose the West was to have for many hundreds of years. Then too Boethius was a layman, and for hundreds of years afterward almost all western European writers would be priests or monks. In the political sphere Boethius's execution was symptomatic as well because it was the harbinger of the collapse of the Ostrogothic kingdom in Italy. Whether or not he was justly condemned, Boethius's execution showed that the Arian Ostrogoths could not live in perfect harmony with Catholic Christians such as himself. Soon afterward, therefore, the Ostrogoths were overthrown by the Eastern Roman Empire. That event in turn was to be a major factor in the ultimate divorce between East and West and the consequent final disintegration of the old Roman World.

The conquest of the Ostrogoths was part of a larger plan for Roman revival conceived and directed by the Eastern Roman Emperor Justinian (527–565). Eastern Rome, with its capital at Constantinople, had faced many external pressures from barbarians and internal religious dissensions since the time of Theodosius. But throughout the fifth century it had managed to weather these, and by the time of Justinian's accession had regained much of its strength. Although the Eastern Roman Empire—which then encompassed the modern-day territories of Greece, Turkey, most of the Middle East, and Egypt—

Justinian and Theodora. Sixth-century mosaics from the church of San Vitale, Ravenna. The emperor and empress are conceived here to have supernatural, almost priestly powers: they are advancing toward the altar, bringing the communion dish and chalice respectively. Both rulers are set off from their

was largely Greek- and Syriac-speaking, Justinian himself came from a westernmost province (modern-day Yugoslavia) and spoke Latin. Not surprisingly, therefore, he concentrated his interests on the West. He saw himself as the heir of imperial Rome, whose ancient power and western territory he was resolved to restore. Aided by his astute and determined wife Theodora, who, unlike earlier imperial Roman consorts, played an influential role in his reign, Justinian took great strides toward this goal. But ultimately his policy of recovering the West proved unrealistic.

One of Justinian's most impressive and lasting accomplishments was his codification of Roman law. This project was part of his attempt to emphasize continuities with earlier imperial Rome and was also meant to enhance his own prestige and absolute power. Codification of the law was necessary because between the third and sixth centuries the volume of statutes had continued to grow, with the result that the vast body of enactments contained many contradictory or obsolete elements. Moreover, conditions had changed so radically that many of the old legal principles could no longer be applied, due to the establishment of an Oriental despotism and the adoption of Christianity as the official religion. When Justinian came to the throne in 527, he immediately decided upon a revision and codification of the existing law to bring it into harmony with the new conditions and to

Codification and revision of Roman law; the Corpus Juris Civilis

retinues by their haloes. The observant viewer is also meant to note the representation of the "three wise kings from the East" at the hem of Theodora's gown: just as the "three magi" once had supernatural knowledge of Christ, so now do their counterparts, Justinian and Theodora.

establish it as an authoritative basis of his rule. To carry out the actual work he appointed a commission of lawyers under the supervision of his minister, Tribonian. Within two years the commission published the first result of its labors. This was the Code, a systematic revision of all of the statutory laws which had been issued from the reign of Hadrian to the reign of Justinian. The Code was later supplemented by the Novels, which contained the legislation of Justinian and his immediate successors. By 532 the commission had completed the Digest, a summary of all of the writings of the great jurists. The final product of the work of revision was the Institutes, a textbook of the legal principles reflected in both the Digest and the Code. The combination of all four of these results of the program of revision constitutes the *Corpus Juris Civilis,* or the body of the civil law.

General significance of Justinian's Corpus

Justinian's *Corpus* was a brilliant achievement in its own terms: the Digest alone has been justly called "the most remarkable and important lawbook that the world has ever seen." In addition, the *Corpus* had an extraordinarily great influence on subsequent legal and governmental history. Revived and restudied in western Europe from the eleventh century on, Justinian's *Corpus* became the basis of all the law and jurisprudence of European states, exclusive of England (which followed its own "common law"). The nineteenth-century Napoleonic Code, which provided the basis for the laws of modern European countries and also of Latin America, is fundamentally the Institutes of Justinian in modern dress.

Other influences

Only a few of the more specific influences of Justinian's legal work can be enumerated here. One is that in its basic governmental theory it was a bastion of absolutism. Starting from the maxim that "what pleases the prince has the force of law," it granted untrammeled powers to the imperial sovereign and therefore was adopted with alacrity by later European monarchs and autocrats. But the *Corpus* also provided some theoretical support for constitutionalism because it maintained that the sovereign originally obtained his powers from the people rather than from God. Since government came from the people it could in theory be given back to them. Perhaps most important and influential was the *Corpus*'s view of the state as an abstract public and secular entity. In the Middle Ages rival views of the state as the private property of the ruler or as a supernatural creation meant to control sin often predominated. The modern conception of the state as a public entity concerned not with the future life but with everyday affairs gained strength toward the end of the Middle Ages largely because of the revival of assumptions found in Justinian's legal compilations.

Justinian's policy of reconquest in the West

Justinian aimed to be a full Roman emperor in geographical practice as well as in legal theory. To this end he sent out armies to reconquer the West. At first they were quickly successful. In 533 Justinian's brilliant general Belisarius conquered the Vandal kingdom in northwest Africa, and in 536 Belisarius seemed to have won all Italy,

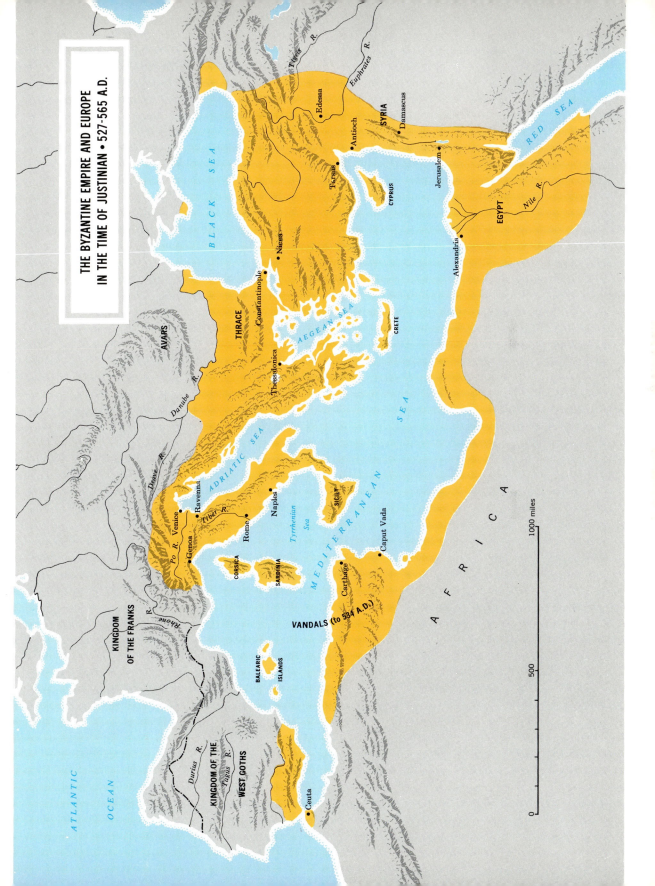

THE BYZANTINE EMPIRE AND EUROPE
IN THE TIME OF JUSTINIAN • 527-565 A.D.

ATLANTIC
OCEAN

KINGDOM
OF THE FRANKS

KINGDOM OF THE
WEST GOTHS

Durius R.
Tagus R.
Rhone R.

Ceuta

BALEARIC
ISLANDS

SARDINIA

CORSICA

Genoa
Venice
Po R.
Ravenna
Tiber R.
Rome
Naples

ADRIATIC SEA

Tyrrhenian
Sea

SICILY

Carthage

VANDALS (to 534 A.D.)

Caput Vada

MEDITERRANEAN
SEA

AFRICA

Drave R.
Danube R.

AVARS

THRACE

Thessalonica

Constantinople

Nicaea

BLACK SEA

AEGEAN
SEA

CRETE

Tigris R.
Euphrates R.

Edessa

Antioch
Tarsus

SYRIA
Damascus

CYPRUS

Jerusalem

EGYPT

Alexandria

Nile R.

RED SEA

1000 miles

500

0

Byzantine Gold Cup, VI–IX cent.
The relief shows Constantinople
personified as a queen holding the
sceptre of imperial rule. (MMA)

Merovingian Fibula or Brooch, VII cent. A
fabulous gold-plated animal set with
garnets and colored paste. (MMA)

*Sienese Madonna and Child, Byzantine School,
XIII cent.* The painters of Siena in Italy imitated the opulent style of Byzantine art. Their
madonnas were not earthly mothers, but
celestial queens reigning in dignified splendor. (National Gallery)

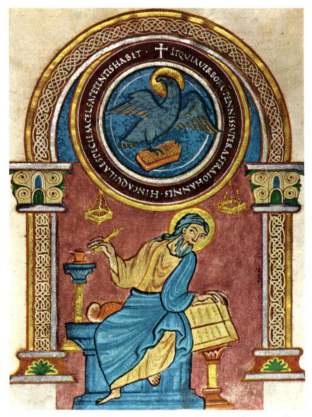

Saint John Writing His Gospel. From a Carolingian illuminated manuscript, c. 850. The monastic artist was
indifferent to perspective, but excelled in coloring and
conveying a sense of vitality and energy. (Morgan
Library)

where he was welcomed by the Catholic subjects of the Ostrogoths. But the first victories of the Italian campaign were illusory. After their initial defeats the Ostrogoths put up stubborn resistance and the war dragged on for decades until the exhausted Eastern Romans finally reduced the last Gothic outposts in 563. Shortly before he died Justinian became master of all Italy as well as northwest Africa and coastal parts of Spain that his troops had also managed to recapture. The Mediterranean was once more briefly a "Roman" lake. But the cost of the endeavor was soon going to call the very existence of the Eastern Roman Empire into question.

There were two major reasons why Justinian's Western campaigns were ill-advised. One was that his realm really could not afford them. Belisarius seldom had enough troops to do his job properly: he began his Italian campaign with only 8,000 men. Later, when Justinian did grant his generals enough troops, it was only at the cost of oppressive taxation. But additional troops would probably have been insufficient to hold the new lines in the West because the empire had greater interests, as well as enemies, to the East. While the Eastern Roman Empire was exhausting itself in Italy the Persians were gathering strength. Justinian's successors had to pull away from the West in order to meet the threat of a revived Persia, but even so, by the beginning of the seventh century, it seemed as if the Persians would be able to march all the way to the waters that faced Constantinople. Only a heroic reorganization of the empire after 610 saved the day, but it was one that helped withdraw Eastern Rome from the West and helped the West begin to lead a life of its own.

The Western campaigns unwise

In the meantime Justinian's wars had left most of Italy in a shambles. In the course of the protracted fighting much devastation had been wrought. Around Rome aqueducts were cut and parts of the countryside returned to marshes not drained until the twentieth century. In 568, only three years after Justinian's death, another Germanic tribe, the Lombards, invaded the country and took much of it away from the Eastern Romans. They met little resistance because the latter were now paying more attention to the East, but the Lombards were still too weak to conquer the whole Italian peninsula. Instead, Italy became divided between Lombard, Eastern Roman, and papal territories. At the same time Slavs took advantage of Eastern Roman weakness to sweep into the Balkans. Farther west the Franks in Gaul were fighting among themselves, and it would be only a matter of time before northwest Africa and most of Spain would fall to Arabs. So the Roman unity had finally come to an end. The future in this decentralized world may have looked bleak, but new forces in the separate areas would soon be gathering strength.

The end of Roman unity

SELECTED READINGS

• *Items so designated are available in paperback editions.*

Anderson, Hugh, *Jesus,* Englewood Cliffs, N.J., 1967. An excellent collection of readings displaying many different scholarly points of view.

Bonner, Gerald, *St. Augustine of Hippo,* London, 1963. The best biography for beginners.

• Brown, Peter, *Augustine of Hippo,* Berkeley, 1967. An extremely subtle study.

• ———, *The World of Late Antiquity,* New York, 1971. A survey that approaches the period in its own terms rather than as a prelude to the Middle Ages.

• Bultmann, Rudolf, *Primitive Christianity in Its Contemporary Setting,* New York, 1956. Summarizes the ideas of one of our century's most important biblical scholars.

Daniélou, J., and H. I. Marrou, *The Christian Centuries; I: The First Six Hundred Years,* London, 1964. A survey from the Roman Catholic perspective.

• Dodds, E. R., *Pagan and Christian in an Age of Anxiety,* Cambridge, 1965. A short but brilliant study of what pagans and Christians had in common as well as what made Christianity ultimately successful.

• Jones, A. H. M., *The Decline of the Ancient World,* New York, 1966. A survey that emphasizes economic and social factors.

• Katz, Solomon, *The Decline of Rome,* Ithaca, N.Y., 1955. The best brief introduction.

• Knowles, David, *Christian Monasticism,* New York, 1969.

Lane Fox, Robin, *Pagans and Christians,* New York, 1986. A highly acclaimed major new study of religion in the Late Roman world.

• Latourette, K. S., *A History of Christianity,* rev. ed., New York, 1975.

• L'Orange, H. P., *Art Forms and Civic Life in the Late Roman Empire,* Princeton, 1965. An imaginative and stimulating essay displaying how developments in art reflected developments in political and social life.

Lot, Ferdinand, *The End of the Ancient World,* New York, 1931. The best detailed treatment of the political history of the period.

MacMullen, Ramsay, *Constantine,* New York, 1969. A good popular biography.

Markus, R. A., *Christianity in the Roman World,* New York, 1974.

• Mattingly, Harold, *Christianity in the Roman Empire,* New York, 1967.

Pelikan, J., *The Christian Tradition; I: The Emergence of the Catholic Tradition,* Chicago, 1971. An advanced survey of doctrine.

• Rand, E. K., *Founders of the Middle Ages,* Cambridge, Mass., 1928. A thoroughly engaging account of the early Christian reactions to the classics.

• Riché, Pierre, *Education and Culture in the Barbarian West,* Columbia, S.C., 1976. A magisterial survey of learning in the Christian West from the fall of Rome to about 800.

• White, Lynn T., Jr., *The Transformation of the Roman World,* Berkeley, 1966. Stimulating essays.

Williams, Stephen, *Diocletian and the Roman Recovery,* New York, 1985. A well-informed "life and times."

Chapter 11

ASIA AND AFRICA IN TRANSITION (c. 200 B.C.– 900 A.D.)

If brave and ambitious men have sincere understanding and awareness; if they fear and heed the warnings of disaster and use transcendent vision and profound judgment; if they . . . rid themselves of the blind notion that the mandate of Heaven can be pursued like a deer in chase and realize that the sacred vessel of rule must be given from on high; . . . then will fortune and blessing flow to their sons and grandsons, and the rewards of Heaven will be with them to the end of their days.

—Pan Piao, *History of the Former Han Dynasty*

During the period when the Greco-Roman classical civilization was being extended throughout the Mediterranean world under the auspices of the Roman Empire, a high stage of cultural development had been reached in both India and China. The disturbances that characterized the downfall of the Roman Empire in the West had their parallels in Asia too. However, the invasions and political upheavals in East and South Asia did not produce the same drastic changes as those in the West. The structure of society continued without serious modification in India and China, and the cultures of these two countries attained a brilliant peak while Europe was experiencing its Dark Ages. In India a combination of commercial prosperity—which encouraged the growth of large cities—and the religious enthusiasm accompanying the spread of Buddhism stimulated an outpouring of artistic talent. During this period Indian influence extended far beyond the borders of the country. Buddhism was planted in Central Asia and from there carried to China, Korea, and Japan. Indian colonization led to the introduction of both Buddhism and Hinduism, together with their art and literature, in Southeast Asia and the Malay Archipelago (which is still called Indonesia). China, while importing a major religion from India, showed much greater success in achieving political unification and an effective administrative system. So great was the prestige of imperial China that its culture was studied and

Contrasts of East and West

eagerly assimilated by the Japanese in the sixth and succeeding centuries A.D. At the same time the West received some impact from the civilizations of Asia by way of the Hellenistic and imperial Roman commercial centers and, later, through the initiative of the Arabs. In sub-Saharan Africa civilization developed slowly. Geographic isolation limited cultural and commercial exchange to a far greater degree than it did in the case of Japan. Contact with the Romans was negligible and Arab incursions south of the Sahara were intermittent.

1. THE FLOWERING OF INDIAN CIVILIZATION

Conflict in post-Maurya India

The Maurya Dynasty, under the energetic and devout King Ashoka, had projected a common rule over the greater part of India. Upon the overthrow of this dynasty early in the second century B.C., the empire quickly fell apart, leaving India in a condition of political discord. For the next several hundred years the most powerful kingdoms were centered not in the Indo-Gangetic plain but in the Deccan, where a succession of dynasties contended with one another, and some of them emerged as major states with extensive territories and resources. It is clear that by this time the arts of civilization were well advanced in southern India, even though the most distinctive historic influences—Vedic literature and philosophy, the traditional religious and social concepts of Hinduism, and the creative force of Buddhism—had originated in the north. Moreover, the invasions which began to trouble northern India did not penetrate into the Deccan. The states of the Deccan carried on commercial intercourse with neighboring and even distant areas but were not seriously threatened with hostile assaults from foreign powers. On the contrary, their merchants and missionaries were ensuring the cultural ascendancy of India over Southeast Asia.

Chandra Gupta I and His Queen, Portrayed on a Gold Coin Dating from His Reign

After a period of domination by nomadic tribes from Turkestan northern India was reunited under the Gupta Dynasty, which ruled effectively during the fourth century A.D. and the first half of the fifth (320–c. 467). The dynasty's founder, Chandra Gupta I, was not descended from the Chandragupta who had instituted the Maurya Dynasty but he ruled from the same capital, Pataliputra (Patna), on the Ganges. Chandra's son Samudra, admonished by his dying father to "rule the whole world," is said to have overthrown nine northern rulers and eleven kings in the south while making others tributary. This report is doubtless an exaggeration, but after Samudra's son Chandra Gupta II seized ports on the Arabian seacoast to the west, the empire comprised all of Hindustan and exercized control over portions of the Deccan as well. Under the reign of Chandra Gupta II (375–415 A.D.), known as Vikramaditya ("Sun of Power"), the dynasty reached its height both in material opulence and in cultural achievements.

The Gupta Dynasty

The Gupta state resembled in some respects that of the Maurya 600 years earlier. The government controlled the working of gold and silver, the mining of salt and minerals, coinage and arms manufacture, employing a large bureaucracy together with a body of spies. Taxation included forced labor on public works and a fee for water use on irrigated lands as well as a share of the crops, but it was not so crushing as to prevent the flourishing of a large agricultural population. In spite of political disunity and almost continual interstate conflict, urban growth and prosperity among the upper classes was evident both in northern India and the Deccan. Besides providing luxury products such as spices, jewels, ivory, tortoise shells, and fine cloths for export, India had become the center of exchange between China and the West. Trade with the Roman Empire from which linens, copper, glass, and wines were imported produced a balance so heavily in India's favor that it weakened the Roman economy by draining it of specie, prompting the Roman emperor to order his subjects to give up the wearing of silks. East-West commerce was carried on both by land over the "Silk Route" from China and by sea. Indian merchants had from early days sailed across the Arabian Sea and up the Red Sea to Egypt. Not until the first century A.D. did Western traders discover the monsoon winds which enabled them to sail east to the Indian coast during the summer and then return when the wind direction changed in October. Traffic between the Near Eastern ports and southern India was probably even greater than with northern India. Pearls and beryls from the Deccan were especially prized, and Roman coins, testifying to a once flourishing trade, have been discovered along both the southwestern and southeastern coasts of the Indian peninsula. Apparently no obstacles were placed by the Indian rulers in the way of foreign intercourse or even against settlement by foreign traders, some of whom took up permanent residence in India. Southern India acquired small colonies of Romans, Jews, Nestorian Christians from Syria and Persia (a Syriac-speaking Christian church still exists in southwestern India), and Arabs.

Valuable information on conditions in northern India at this time has been preserved in the brief account written by a Chinese pilgrim, Fa-hsien, who spent six years in the realm of Vikramaditya. Buddhism had already spread into China, and the monk Fa-hsien undertook his hazardous journey to acquire sacred texts and firsthand knowledge of the religion in the land of its birth. The travels of Fa-hsien in themselves represent no mean undertaking. He made his way on foot across Sinkiang and the mountain passes, taking six years to reach India (399–405 A.D.). Here he taught himself the Sanskrit language, procured texts, drawings, and relics at the Gupta capital, and then returned to his native land by sea, spending two years in Ceylon en route and also visiting Java on the voyage. Altogether, during the fifteen years of his pilgrimage he traversed a distance of some 8,000 miles.

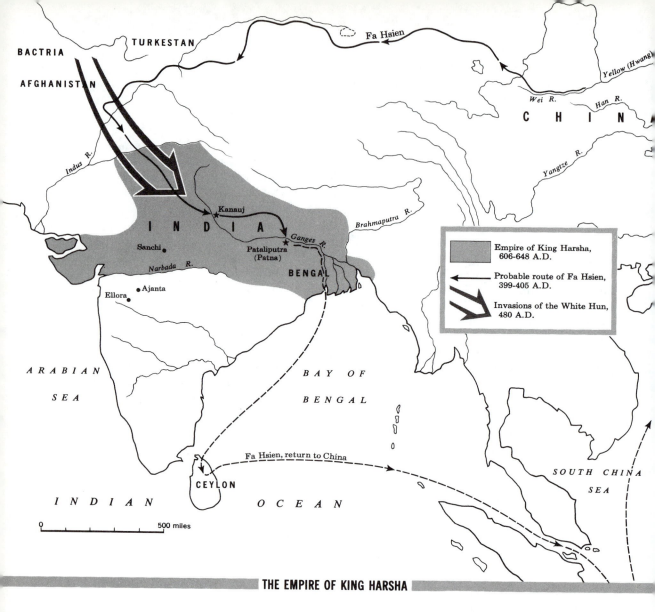

THE EMPIRE OF KING HARSHA

Legend:
- Empire of King Harsha, 606-648 A.D.
- Probable route of Fa Hsien, 399-405 A.D.
- Invasions of the White Hun, 480 A.D.

According to Fa-hsien's testimony, Buddhism was flourishing in the Gupta empire, but all the Hindu cults were tolerated and rivalry among the different religions was not embittered by persecution. Though he did not even mention the name of the great king Vikrama-ditya, Fa-hsien depicted his rule as just and beneficent. Roads he indicated were well maintained, brigandage rare, taxes relatively light, and capital punishment unknown. The tradition of state-supported charities, according to Fa-hsien's report, had been extended to provide free hospitalization to residents and visiting foreigners alike. Perhaps naiveté and piety colored his account: he asserted that all Indians were vegetarians and never used liquor, but he also witnessed the sight of poor unfortunates whose presence was considered so polluting that

they were required to sound gongs to warn of their approach—evidence
that untouchability had become an aspect of Indian society. On balance
it is reasonable to accept as valid Fa-hsien's testimony that the Gupta
empire was prosperous, relatively stable, and intellectually vital at a
time when the nations of western Europe were sinking into a state
of semibarbarism.

Another invasion of India destroyed the Gupta power and brought
a period of confusion lasting for more than a century. Almost simultaneously with the formal demise of the Roman Empire in the West,
a group of nomads called "White Huns" defeated the Gupta forces
and made themselves masters of northern India (480 A.D.). By the
early sixth century the White Huns had staked out an empire extending
from Bengal in the east into Afghanistan and Central Asia. It was
much more barbaric than its predecessors, and disrupted the splendid
administrative system of the Guptas. But after the Hunnish power
disintegrated in accordance with the usual cycle of hastily constructed
nomadic states, an able government was reestablished by one of the
most famous rulers in Indian history, King Harsha (606–648 A.D.).

Although Harsha's state was not literally a continuation of the Gupta,
it was so similar in important features that the term "Gupta" is often
used to designate the civilization of northern India from the fourth
to the seventh century, a period of cultural brilliance despite the devastating interlude of the Hunnish invasion. King Harsha, with a huge
army efficiently organized in divisions of infantry, cavalry, and elephants, reunited most of northern India. He was a capable administrator, an intelligent and prudent statesman, and a generous patron of
art, literature, and religion. His capital, Kanauj, extending four miles
along the river in the central Ganges valley, was a splendid city,
adorned with hundreds of temples and imposing public buildings,
and enlivened with festive pageantry. As in the reign of Vikramaditya,
the account of a Chinese Buddhist pilgrim throws revealing light
upon Harsha's administration.

According to the narrative of this foreign visitor, Hüan-tsang, and
other contemporary records, Harsha's administration was in the Gupta
tradition though somewhat less gentle. Punishments included mutilation and death through starvation. The state revenue was derived
chiefly from taxes on the royal domains, which amounted to one-
sixth of the produce of the villages and could hardly be regarded as
oppressive. Public expenditures for road and canal construction or
the improvement of agriculture may have been sacrificed to the king's
penchant for less practical objectives, but his deviation from the norms
of statecraft seems to have been in a benevolent direction: he allotted
only one-fourth of his revenue to administrative expenses and devoted
much of the remainder to education, religion, and the arts or to charity.
Hüan-tsang, received cordially at court, reported that Harsha was a
convert to Buddhism. Actually, he rendered homage to the Buddha,
Shiva, and a sun god, while adhering to a policy of religious toleration.

Hüan-tsang on His Pilgrimage.
Painting on silk from the Tun-
huang caves in western Kansu,
China. He carries a fly swatter
to drive away evil desires.

Indian religions and
cultural progress

The religions of India played a continuous and active role in cultural progress. Hinduism—based on the Indo-Aryan pantheon combined with vestiges of the ancient Indus valley rites—continued to absorb other indigenous cults, gradually acquiring the characteristics that have distinguished it down to the present. Several deities of the Vedic Age had lost their importance or faded from memory. Brahma, representing the universal World Soul of philosophers, was too impersonal to remain for long an object of popular worship. In western India a number of temples were dedicated to Surya, an early Aryan sun god. Two deities, Vishnu and Shiva, rose to such prominence as to overshadow all others in the Hindu pantheon. Vishnu, called "The Preserver" and viewed as essentially benevolent, was honored with offerings of flowers and sweets rather than bloody sacrifices. By attributing to Vishnu a whole series of reincarnations, local deities were added to his retinue. For example Krishna, originally a non-Aryan hero/god of northwestern India, was transformed into the most popular of Vishnu's reputed incarnations. Cherished as the playful and indefatigable youthful lover of dairymaids, he was also revered as Lord Krishna, purveyor of divine wisdom and Supreme Godhead. Commanding a following even surpassing Vishnu's was the awesome Shiva, whose complex nature—represented inconographically by a figure with four arms and five faces—derived from a minor Aryan storm god, Rudra, and the horned male deity of the ancient Indus valley fertility cult. Shiva "The Destroyer" inspired dread and terror. In his role as Lord of the Dance he would one day shatter the universe in a dance of cosmic frenzy. A recurring cycle in which all beings and matter are destroyed (by Shiva) and restored (by Vishnu) was accepted as an eternal principle. In another aspect Shiva appeared not only benevolent but as a peaceful ascetic, absorbed in meditation—the consummate yogi. Shiva's female consort was as ambivalent as he—Parvati, the beautiful daughter of the Himalayas and perfect bride, and bloodthirsty Kali wearing a necklace of skulls. By contrast, Vishnu's wife, Lakshmi, was adored as the goddess of good fortune.

Vishnu worship (Vaishnavism) and Shiva worship (Shaivism) were complementary rather than incompatible, and each developed different levels of belief and ritual. In isolated regions the sex-and-fertility aspects of Shaivism were celebrated with orgiastic rites, normally restricted to a specific time of year and defended as a spiritual catharsis. Hinduism as a whole had moved far from the early Aryan cult of sacrifice which treated religion as a mechanical and contractual arrangement between man and god. It was refining the concept of deity and converting ceremony into an act of adoration. A significant result of this shifting emphasis was the *bhakti* (devotional) movement, which invoked commitment to a personal god endowed with redemptive powers and readily accessible. Originating in South India, the *bhakti* movement was anti-Brahmanical, rejecting priests as intermediaries and, because it disregarded caste distinctions, appealed to broad segments of the

Vishnu. This tenth-century bronze from southeastern India depicts "the Preserver" in a characteristically rigid pose. The upper right hand holds a disk and the left hand holds a conch. His lower left hand rests on his thigh, while the lower right hand assumes a ritual pose symbolizing the realization of the absolute.

population. Among the Tamil-speaking peoples of southeastern India it produced a body of deeply emotional and morally uplifting sacred literature. Tamil poets exalted the peacemaker and denounced vengeance:

> They are great who fast and do penance,
> but they who forgive wrongs are even greater.

The *bhakti* ideal was given its noblest expression in the *Bhagavad Gita* ("Lord's Song"), one of the most famous religious poems in all literature. The *Gita,* which rather incongruously became attached to the ancient epic *Mahabharata,* is cast in the form of a dialogue between the noble warrior Arjuna and his charioteer Krishna, an incarnation of the god Vishnu. On the brink of a battle destined to annihilate the two opposing armies, Arjuna recoils from the prospect of slaughtering his own friends and relatives. Krishna assures him that as a warrior he must fight, with complete indifference to the consequences of his action. Because matter cannot control spirit, Krishna explains, physical life and death are merely incidental to the destiny of the soul: "It neither slays nor is it slain." At the same time, because every individual is through the body temporarily entangled in matter, he must deal with it on the material level. The categorical injunction addressed to everyone is the faithful performance of his or her assigned role (*dharma*), without valuing it or seeking any benefit in return. The ideal is action without attachment, "with unyoked soul."

Aspects of Shiva. Above: The Dance of Shiva within a ring of fire portrayed in this eleventh-century bronze is symbolic of the destructive forces in the world. Below: Shiva as beneficent teacher.

By sanctioning the doctrine of *dharma* with its rigid division of social responsibilities the *Gita* tacitly accepts the institution of caste. But it transcends the prejudices of the milieu from which it sprang by offering the prospect of spiritual fulfillment for all classes. In his dialogue with Arjuna, Krishna ranks knowledge above deeds, and understanding of the divine above all other levels of knowledge. In this the poem paraphrases a leading doctrine of the *Upanishads,* but it parts company with the philosophers in asking why anyone should attempt the difficult task of understanding an "unmanifested" impersonal Being when he could easily reach the desired goal by turning to a manifest and accessible god who in his own person is truth incarnate, the Supreme Godhead. Demanding only devotion from his followers, the god equates devotion with service, to be rendered unfailingly and without seeking reward. It transcends but does not exclude social action and service to the community and nation. The religion of the *Gita* is ethical, spiritual, and compassionate. Krishna is revealed as a loving god who takes upon himself the sins of humanity and offers salvation freely to all, even those classes considered of inferior intelligence (to which category women are unhesitatingly assigned). "For one who worships me . . . always meditating upon me . . . for him I am the swift deliverer from the ocean of birth and death." Because it distills the essence of Vedic thought into stirring poetry the *Bhagavad Gita* has become for Hindus what the New Testament's

The religious legacy of the Bhagavad Gita

Sermon on the Mount has for Christians. Freethinking nonconformists like Ralph Waldo Emerson and Henry David Thoreau have drawn inspiration from it. In the twentieth century Mahatma Ghandi acknowledged his indebtedness to the poem for its summons to unstinted disinterested service, while he rejected its endorsement of caste distinctions and its justification of warfare.

The manifold intellectual activity of this period of Indian history, reflecting the interests of a cosmopolitan society and the patronage of wealthy rulers, was consistently influenced by religious orders. High levels of scholarship were maintained both by the Brahmans and by Buddhist monks, and large libraries came into being. Particularly noteworthy were the educational foundations, for which the chief credit should be given to the Buddhists. The role of the Buddhist monks in education was comparable to that of the Christian monks of the West during the early Middle Ages, but the scope of their studies was broader because the general level of knowledge was far higher in India than in the West at this time. Some Buddhist monasteries were internationally famous centers of learning, unmatched in Europe until the rise of such universities as Paris, Montpellier, and Oxford in the late Middle Ages. One of the greatest Buddhist universities, at Nalanda in the Ganges valley (in modern Bihar), was functioning as early as the fourth or fifth century A.D. Endowed by the Gupta rulers with a substantial income, it maintained residence halls for students—with free tuition, board, lodging, and medical care for poor boys who were able to pass the entrance examinations—and had a library that occupied three buildings. Pilgrims visiting the university in the seventh century reported that 5,000 students were in attendance, including some from Tibet, China, and Korea. Although Nalanda

Ruins at Nalanda. The remains of the ancient university town, early seat of Buddhist learning.

was a Buddhist foundation and provided instruction in eighteen different schools of Buddhism, its faculty also offered courses in Hindu philosophy, grammar, medicine, mathematics, and in both Vedic and contemporary literature.

Between the fourth and eighth centuries of the Christian era Indian civilization attained its full maturity. What the Periclean Age and the Augustan Age were for the classical civilizations of the West the reigns of Vikramaditya and Harsha were for India. But India's classical age lasted far longer than its Greek or Roman equivalents. Sanskrit became the universally accepted literary vehicle both in North and South India, although the vernacular languages produced their own distinctive literature. The Buddhists felt constrained to translate their sacred texts from *Pali,* in which they had first been written, into Sanskrit, and the Sanskrit versions were carried by missionaries into Central Asia and China, Korea, and ultimately Japan. Literature of the Gupta Age in both prose and poetry ranged from scientific treatises and biographies to tales of popular entertainment. The latter included long romantic narratives suggestive of, and perhaps the prototype of, the *Arabian Nights;* and also "Beast Fables" comparable to those attributed to Aesop. Classical Sanskrit poetry though ornate is richly expressive. Adorned with such epithets as "sky-goer" (for *bird*), "frail" (for *woman*), and "mine of jewels" (for *the sea*), it reflects both love of nature and delight in the festivities and pageantry of royal courts. Kalidasa, poet-playwright in the court of Vikramaditya, is considered the greatest of all Sanskrit poets. His delicate short piece *The Cloud Messenger* portrays an earth spirit who, exiled from his wife, sends her a burning love message by a rain cloud traveling to the Himalayas.

As in Europe somewhat later, the drama in India evolved out of a type of popular religious instruction and entertainment. Combining dialogue in prose and poetry with gesture and dance, it was performed by troupes of men and women, not in public theaters but in private homes or temple courts. The plots, often diffuse, dealt with romantic love, drew heavily upon legendary themes from the epics, and resorted to magic or miracles to resolve a difficulty in the story. The plays were never tragedies, always ending happily. Also they employed the seemingly artificial device of having the principal characters speak in Sanskrit while women and lower-class figures used the less elegant dialect of ordinary conversation. Lacking the tight structure and sharp focus of either classical Greek or traditional Western theater, Sanskrit drama is enriched with beautiful and sensitive descriptions of nature and lyrical passages capturing human emotions of tenderness and anguish. Most famous of all Sanskrit dramas is Kalidasa's masterpiece *Shakuntala.* Built on a theme that in one form or another has frequently occurred in literature, it traces the vicissitudes of a woman deserted by her lover because an evildoer has robbed him of his memory. When the lover, a king, is shown a ring recovered from the belly of a fish, he recognizes it as the token he had given to his beloved, and

Great Stupa at Sanchi. Begun by Ashoka and completed under the Andhra Dynasty (72–25 B.C.), it was originally a burial mound containing relics of the Buddha. The fully developed stupa, designed with mathematical precision, became an architectural symbol of the cosmos. The tiered mast on top of the structure represents the earth's axis penetrating the dome of heaven.

after further misadventures the two are joyfully reunited. Characterizations are drawn with a skill comparable to Shakespeare's. A more realistic work is *The Little Clay Cart,* by one of Kalidasa's contemporaries. Rich in humor as well as pathos, the plot revolves around the troubled course of a poor *brahman's* love affair, political intrigue, and the protagonist's narrow escape from execution.

Buddhist monuments   The most superb expression of the Indian creative faculties during these centuries was in art, especially architecture and sculpture. By the Gupta era, architecture was nearing a point of perfection, as evidenced by imposing stone structures in all sections of India. The evolution of Buddhist monasteries and temples set the pattern for practically the whole of Hindu architecture and sculpture. The first typical Buddhist monument was the *stupa,* a simple burial mound in the shape of a dome or hemisphere crowned with an umbrella—the Indian symbol of sovereignty. Inside the brick- or rock-faced mound was buried a sacred relic, usually some object associated with Gautama or with a revered Buddhist saint. The most famous *stupa* is the large one at Sanchi in the very center of India, still in an excellent state of preservation although it was begun in Ashoka's reign and substantially completed during the first century B.C. More impressive than the stone-faced mound (which has a diameter at the base of 120 feet) are the four carved gateways surrounding the *stupa.* These massive fences of stone are supported by pillars 35 feet high and, in spite of their huge proportions, are adorned with intricate carvings, both pictorial and symbolic, of delicately formed human and animal figures. After the *stupa,* the next step in the evolution of religious architecture was the assembly hall, where monks and lay disciples gathered to honor the memory of Gautama, "Master of the Law." These halls were commonly tunneled out of solid rock in a mountain or the side of a cliff. Their general plan was similar to that of the Roman basilica and early Christian church, with a central passageway or nave separated from aisles on either side by round columns. Paralleling the evolution of the assembly hall was that of the Buddhist monastery. Like the assembly hall or temple, the monastery was often carved out of a single mass of rock, with successive stories of cells or cubicles so arranged that the structure as a whole appeared to be a terraced pyramid. Devotees of the Hindu cults soon began to construct temples in imitation of the Buddhist and eventually even more elaborate.

Although some free-standing temples were erected as early as the first century A.D., for several centuries the Indians seemed to prefer the more arduous method of hewing their edifices out of the solid rock of caves and cliffs. More than 1,200 rock-cut temples and monasteries were executed in various sections of India, the larger proportion being along the western coast. The two most remarkable groups of cliff excavations are located at Ajanta and Ellora, about 70 miles apart, in the northern part of what later became Hyderabad. The

Eastern Gateway of the Great Stupa at Sanchi. The relief carvings, depicting incidents from the life of the Buddha, are remarkable for their fine detail, vitality, and naturalism.

Ajanta. A section of the gorge from which more than thirty cave chambers of worship, assembly, and residence were cut and decorated over a period of 700 years, beginning in the second century B. C.

Entrance to the Ajanta Caves. The Gupta period (fourth to seventh centuries A.D.) constitutes the Golden Age of Indian art—in sculpture, architecture, and painting—as well as the climax of classical Sanskrit literature.

Ajanta caves were Buddhist sanctuaries, some of them dating from the second century B.C. and some from as late as the fifth century A.D. They include both assembly halls and monasteries, complete with stone beds, tables, water cisterns, and niches for oil reading lamps. The even more splendid caves at Ellora represent about 900 years of architectural and sculptural enterprise, extending from the fourth to the thirteenth century. The Buddhists were the first to utilize the site, but some of the caves were the work of Jains and the largest number were constructed as Hindu temples, of tremendous size and lavish design.

Temples composed of separate stone blocks, in contrast to the cave type, began to be more common in Gupta times and were typical of the most active period of Hindu temple building, between the sixth and the thirteenth centuries. The essential architectural features of these free-standing Hindu temples are (1) a base consisting of a square or rectangular chamber to house the image of the god, and (2) a lofty tower which rises from the roof of the chamber and dominates the entire edifice. The shape of the tower distinguishes the two main styles of Hindu temples. The "Dravidian" style, found only in the tropics, is identified by a terraced steeple divided into stories like a step pyramid and decidedly reminiscent of the early Buddhist rock-cut monasteries. The "Indo-Aryan" style, prevalent in northern India, has a curvilinear tower with vertical ribs which may possibly be derived from the Buddhist *stupa*.

Although sculpture in India seems to have ceased with the decline

The Shore Temple at Mamallapuram. This eighth-century shrine, executed in the "Dravidian" style, is the earliest known structured temple in southern India. It was built with granite blocks.

of the Indus valley civilization, traditions and techniques from that early culture very probably were preserved and passed on from one generation of craftsmen to another for more than a thousand years. When stone sculpture began to reappear—the earliest examples, already cited, are the animal figures on memorial columns of Emperor Ashoka—it bore stylistic features reminiscent of ancient Indus valley art. Shortly before the beginning of the Christian era both Jain and Buddhist monks began to add sculptured human figures to their places of worship. As the Roman Empire entered its most affluent period, brisk East-West trade facilitated exposure to Greco-Roman influences. Some statues of Buddha produced in northwestern India resemble a Greek Apollo or a Roman emperor draped in a toga rather than a monk's robe. Gradually Roman and Hellenistic characteristics receded as a distinctive Indian style of representation emerged. The Buddha was shown in a cross-legged position bearing an aspect of benign repose. The human form began to be treated with subtle delicacy, conveying a sense both of rhythmic movement and tranquillity. Garments became almost transparent or were suggested in faint outline so that the effect is that of nudity. The harmonious proportions and graceful curves of the limbs reflected a study of plant forms as well as human anatomy.

The richest creations of the Hindu artistic genius are to be found in the relief sculpture and fresco paintings executed in the rock-cut temples upon which so much energy was expended during the period corresponding to the Classical and Medieval ages of the West. The Buddhist caves at Ajanta contain the most important surviving collection of wall paintings. Religious in inspiration, they are at the same time spontaneous and unrestrained. Although long neglected and damaged by the ravages of bats, insects, smoke, and water seepage, they

Sculpture and the Indus valley legacy

Relief sculpture and painting

Left: *Yakshi or "Tree Spirit."* A female figure derived from an early fertility cult but here symbolizing the transition from the sensuous world of illusion to the world of the spirit. Right: *Cast Bronze Buddha from Sultanganj in Bengal.* This 7-foot 6-inch representation of Buddha, dating from the fifth century, is typical of Gupta art and metallurgy at its peak.

are still magnificent. (The Indian government is taking steps to clean and conserve this priceless heritage.) In the Hindu temples, which increased in number from the seventh century on as Buddhism began to decline, decoration was usually in sculpture rather than painting. Relief sculptures in the Ellora cave temples and in Hindu and Jain temples erected during the tenth and eleventh centuries at Khajuraho in east central India rank among masterpieces of the world's art. In these carvings not only the gods but a galaxy of figures and dramatic episodes out of India's historic and legendary past seem to come alive. Many scenes are boldly realistic, but the Hindu tendency toward abstraction is also evident in the practice of depicting gods with several pairs of arms or several faces to signify their separate attributes. The themes portrayed range from voluptuous ecstasy and heroic struggle to attitudes of piety and mystic contemplation. The magnificent sculptured forms of the high Gupta Age are distinctive and original, but in their treatment of the human body—giving it a soft, almost plantlike texture—they drew inspiration from a tradition dating back to the long-vanished Indus valley culture. Without idealizing the human form in the manner of a Phidias, sculptors and painters of the Gupta Age celebrated the natural man and woman with life-affirming vigor. Even the delicate figures chiseled on the gates of the great *stupa* at Sanchi in the first century B.C., while commemorating events of sacred legend, are invested with a freshness and spontaneity that suggests an uninhibited delight in the natural world.

The spread of Indian culture

While Indian communities were bringing their civilization to a point of refinement, they were also implanting it among various other peoples of Southeast Asia. Indian navigators and merchants were active in the eastern waters of the Indian Ocean as well as in the Arabian Sea to the west and apparently led the world in maritime enterprise during this period. Some of the Indian states maintained navies and had a Board of Shipping as a governmental department. They not only promoted commerce but chartered companies of merchants, giving them trade monopolies in certain areas and authority to establish colonies. During the early centuries A.D. Indian colonies were planted in the Malay Peninsula, Annam (eastern Indochina), Java, Sumatra, and many other islands of the Malay Archipelago. Between the fifth and tenth centuries an empire ruled by a Buddhist dynasty and possessing formidable naval strength was based on the island of Sumatra. It also controlled western Java, extended into the Malay Peninsula, sent colonists to Borneo and from thence to the Philippine Islands. It dominated the Strait of Malacca and effectively policed the waters of this area against piracy. Although weakened by a long struggle with one of the Hindu mainland states, the empire (known as the Srivijaya) remained intact until the fourteenth century. Indian influence was extensive in the peninsula of Indochina—in the Cham state on the southeastern coast (later absorbed into the Annamese empire), in the Cambodian kingdoms of the lower Mekong valley, and among the Thais (Siamese) to the northwest.

The Great Buddhist Stupa at Borobudur, Central Java. Originally constructed in the eighth century A.D., it has recently been restored under U.N. auspices.

The political vicissitudes of these various Eastern states were too complex to be enumerated here, but the entire region long remained an outpost of Indian culture. Sanskrit literature was introduced, along with Buddhism and the leading cults of Hinduism. Art and architecture, originating in Indian prototypes, were assiduously cultivated and attained considerable individuality. During the eighth and ninth centuries the Srivijaya empire in Sumatra and Java was perhaps the foremost center of Buddhist art. The colossal temple of Borobudur in central Java, one of the world's architectural marvels, is actually a stone-encased hill rising 150 feet high, with nine terraces, staircases, covered gateways, and four galleries containing 1,500 sculptured panels. This "great picture bible of the Mahayana creed," neglected for centuries, has been saved from the oblivion of decay by a $21-million reconstruction project funded by twenty-seven nations under UNESCO auspices, completed in the fall of 1982. In the ninth century, building on an ambitious scale was in progress in the Cambodian empire established by the Khmers, a native people who wielded dominion over a large part of Indochina between the ninth and the fourteenth centuries, and who responded energetically to the stimulus of Indian cultural contacts. Their capital city, Angkor (recovered from the jungle by French archeologists in the twentieth century), was of almost incredible magnificence in its heyday. Among several huge temples the most imposing was that of Angkor Wat, about a mile south of the capital, built during the twelfth century and said to be the largest work of its kind in the world, surpassing in mass even Luxor and Karnak of ancient

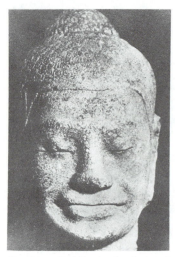

Gautama Buddha in the State of
Nirvana. A fragment from the
Early Khmer period.

Egypt. Angkor Wat was dedicated to the Hindu god Vishnu and was also designed as a tomb for the emperor, who was deified after his death and identified in some way with Vishnu. While Hindu influence was ascendant in Cambodia, Buddhism was also a potent force there. Khmer statues of Buddha are distinguished by the "smile of Angkor"—a countenance expressing the height of benevolence and the supreme peace associated with the attainment of an inner state of enlightenment or *nirvana*.

During the Middle Ages the whole region surrounding the Bay of Bengal, while comprising separate political units, was dominated by Indian culture, imparted through commercial contacts and manifest in the fields of religion, literature, and art. The creative activity in this "Greater India" was not inferior to that of the motherland, but decline eventually overtook the Buddhist and Hindu civilizations of Southeast Asia as the result of exhausting struggles among competing states, pressure from China to the north, and—more decisive—the impact of Arab and other adventurers who traded, proselytized, and conquered successfully in this area during the fourteenth, fifteenth, and sixteenth centuries.

Through commercial contacts India, during the centuries covered in this chapter, probably exerted more influence upon the West than has been generally recognized, although much of it came somewhat later and with the Arabs as intermediaries. The Indian numerals ("Arabic"), which were not adopted by Europeans until the late Middle Ages, were perhaps known in Alexandria as early as the second century A.D. In the eighth and ninth centuries important scientific and medical

Angkor Wat. Built in the twelfth century by Suryavarman II as a sepulcher and monument to the divinity of the monarch, this temple is one of the largest religious structures in the world. The architecture of Angkor Wat is derived from the Indian stupa form.

treatises were translated from Sanskrit into Arabic. In addition, it is quite possible that familiarity with Indian philosophy and religion contributed a stimulus to the growth of Christian monasticism. The earliest Christian hermit-ascetics appeared in Egypt, where there was considerable knowledge of Hinduism and Buddhism, both of which religions stressed the concepts of renunciation and mystic exaltation.

2. THE TERRITORIAL, POLITICAL, AND CULTURAL GROWTH OF CHINA

The Ch'in Dynasty, inaugurated after the Ch'in ruler overthrew the Chou, lasted only fourteen years (221–207 B.C.), but was one of the most important in Chinese history because it carried out a drastic reorganization of the government with permanent effects upon the character of the state. The founder of the dynasty, who posthumously was given the title of "First Emperor" (Shih Huang Ti), was a man of iron will and administrative genius. He did away with the rival kingdoms, divided the country into provinces, and instituted an elaborate bureaucracy directly responsible to himself. The centralized administration and effective military organization that had been carefully cultivated in the state of Ch'in now was applied to all of China, thus effecting a momentous break with the past. The feudal institutions of 500 years' standing were almost completely extinguished, and the government was brought into direct contact with the people. Determined to eliminate any competition for authority, the emperor's chief minister forbade the philosophic schools to continue their discussions and commanded their writings to be destroyed. His order for the burning of the books was a sweeping one, carrying the death penalty for disobedience, although copies of the forbidden works were locked up in the imperial library. Works on farming and medicine were spared, as well as some Taoist writings because the emperor was attracted by their reputed magic-working formulas. He was particularly anxious to root out the Confucianist and Mohist teachings because they emphasized moral restraints upon the ruler and his dependence upon the advice of learned counselors.

*The Ch'in Dynasty
(221–207 B.C.)*

The Ch'in Dynasty—brief, violent, but pivotal in China's history—commanded a high level of technological skill and artistic talent, as attested by the First Emperor's mausoleum, an enormous complex of underground chambers extending over an area of 21 square miles. To build it required the employment of 700,000 conscript laborers, whose lives were sacrificed to provide the emperor with companions for his journey to the spirit world. Although ancient writers left glowing accounts of the mausoleum, its treasures were not brought to light until the mausoleum was excavated in the 1970s. The findings, recently restored and arranged for display, almost surpass the imagination. The burial chambers housed an entire underground army of 8,000 terracotta figures— men, horses, chariots—arranged according to divisions

Artistic achievement
under the Ch'in
Dynasty

The Tomb of the First Emperor of the Ch'in Dynasty (221–210 B.C.). Discovered in 1974, this army of nearly 8,000 life-size terra cotta soldiers and horses equipped with bronze weapons was created to protect the First Emperor in the afterlife.

The First Emperor's Underground Army. These guardians of the tomb were individually modeled with the result that no two faces of this Ch'in army are alike.

and ranks, fully costumed, and equipped with weapons which are still bright and sharp. The startlingly realistic life-sized figures are individual likenesses rather than stylized forms. Seemingly the emperor commanded his troops to pose for their portraits (thus securing proper grave attendants while sparing the lives of their flesh-and-blood counterparts). Still awaiting excavation is the emperor's own burial chamber, reputed to have a ceiling studded with jewels and a floor watered by rivers of mercury but also booby-trapped to repel any intruder.

Every aspect of Shih Huang Ti's reign reveals tremendous force of personality and a ruthless determination. He carried out conquests in all directions. In the south he not only annexed regions but built canals, one of which linked the Yangtze to the West River (of which Canton is the principal port). While raising large armies by conscription he disarmed the bulk of the Chinese people as a precautionary measure. With forced labor he executed an ambitious building program that included a network of military roads radiating from his capital. His most impressive engineering project was to complete and join together the series of fortifications in the north, by which he created the Great Wall of China, reaching from the seacoast some 1,400 miles inland. At his capital (near Sian, the site of the old Western Chou capital) he had constructed a sumptuous palace measuring 2,500 by 500 feet and capable of accommodating 10,000 people. In addition to such undertakings he and his ministers found time to standardize weights, measures, and even the axle length of carts, and—still more important—to unify the Chinese system of writing, abolishing about half the old characters and restructuring many others. This radical reform facilitated communication among regions with differing spoken dialects. But because he required all books to be written or recopied in the new script, the original texts even of works he intended to preserve have been lost forever. That the First Emperor made a great impression not only upon the Chinese but upon foreign powers is illustrated by the fact that his country came to be known as "China"—after the name of his dynasty. This indomitable monarch's chief weaknesses were megalomania and addiction to superstitious fancies. He undertook several journeys in search of the elixir of immortality and died on one of these expeditions. Three years later his dynasty ended in a round of court conspiracies and assassinations, and his great palace was burned to the ground.

The Ch'in emperor had aimed at a social as well as political reconstruction, and although this was a more difficult undertaking it succeeded in part. On the whole his policy was to encourage and promote agriculture above commerce, assisting the farmers and holding the merchant class in check. Officially he abolished serfdom, decreeing that the peasants should be owners of the lands they worked. It is doubtful, however, that their lot was actually much better than before. Not only were there great differences between the small and the large proprietors, but the poor peasants became burdened with debts contracted with the merchants and moneylenders, the very group the government had intended to restrain. The Ch'in ruler exacted heavy taxes of various sorts, including a poll tax, and conscripted men for military and labor service with a callous disregard for human suffering. Thus, while the state was concerning itself more directly and actively than ever before with the welfare of the whole community, it reduced the dignity and freedom of the individual to a minimum. Large numbers of the population were forcibly moved from one region to another and many were made slaves of the state.

Social reforms and totalitarian methods of Shih Huang Ti

The Great Wall of China at Nankow Pass. The wall was erected about 221–207 B.C. for defense against northern invaders.

People's actions and, as far as possible, their thoughts also were controlled by the government. The Ch'in rule carried into practice the Legalist doctrines of coercion, punishment, and fear, and bore a striking resemblance to the European totalitarian regimes of the twentieth century

The overthrow of the Ch'in Dynasty was followed soon afterward by the establishment of the Han, which governed from 206 B.C. to 220 A.D. The Han government was a centralized bureaucracy but conducted with some regard for local differences and with deference to ancient tradition. Certain aspects of feudalism were reintroduced as the first Han emperor granted estates in the form of fiefs to his relatives and other prominent figures. However, the danger of feudal principalities becoming powerful and independent, as had happened in Chou times, was circumvented by a decree requiring the estates of nobles to be divided among the heirs instead of passing intact to the eldest son. Chinese society was still far from being equalitarian, but its aristocratic structure had been severely jolted. The imperial administration cut across class lines, and there was little danger that it would ever again be constituted on feudal principles. The power of the old Chou states was broken beyond recovery. Obviously, the Han rulers were profiting from and continuing the work begun by the hated house of Ch'in, although they softened the harshest features of the Ch'in regime. Whereas the Ch'in emperor had antagonized the class of scholars, the Han ruler sought their favor and support and instructed his officials to recommend to the public service young men of ability irrespective of birth. The Confucianists profited most from the government's policy of toleration toward the philosophical schools. Some of their books had escaped the flames, and the scholars had long memories. Under the patronage of the emperor, Confucianist teachings were reinterpreted, with more emphasis upon the supremacy of the central authority than Confucius had probably intended. Thus, instead of serving as a stumbling block, they assisted in the creation of an efficient imperial government.

The Han rule, while energetic, efficient, and relatively enlightened, was sufficiently severe. As under the Ch'in, ambitious public works of reclamation and canal- and road-building entailed enormous labor, much of which was performed by slaves. Taxes were high, the salt and iron industries were made state monopolies, and the currency was debased to yield a profit to the government at the expense of the people. At the same time, the emperor attempted to regulate prices, not merely for the protection of the poorer consumers but to divert the middleman's profit into the imperial coffers. The government also participated in the rapidly expanding foreign commerce of the empire.

From time immemorial the all-important Chinese enterprise has been farming. Methods of cultivation developed as early as the Shang and Chou periods continued essentially unchanged. These techniques were admirably adapted to the terrain and to the objectives of Chinese

The Han dynasty and centralized government

The severity of Han rule

China's vegetable civilization

society. While they were primitive in some ways, they embodied a great deal of experience and foresight. China has been said to possess a "vegetable civilization," because its people, while not socially or intellectually stagnant, adapted themselves so completely to the potentialities of their environment. The typical Chinese farming village—with fields of various sizes, often tiny but all carefully tended—appears almost as if it were part of the natural landscape instead of being an effort on man's part to manipulate nature for his own benefit. Although China is a large country, the relative scarcity of arable land made it difficult for food production to keep pace with an expanding population. Much of the country is hilly or mountainous, and the north and west portions are subject to drought which cannot be entirely overcome by irrigation. Consequently, attention was lavished upon every suitable plot that could be found. The bulk of labor was done by hand, with simple tools but in such a way as to produce the greatest possible yield. Wastes which had fertilizing value were collected and returned to the soil, as were ashes and even powdered sun-dried bricks when no longer serviceable for building purposes. Crops were rotated to avoid soil exhaustion, and hillsides were terraced to conserve moisture and prevent erosion.

Although draft animals had been known from early times and the ox-drawn plow was introduced about the sixth century B.C., their use was restricted because of the cheapness and—on small plots—greater efficiency of human labor. Besides, hayfields or grazing lands to provide animal fodder represented a curtailment of the area devoted to producing foodstuffs for human beings. The Chinese have subsisted largely on a vegetable diet, not because they had religious scruples against eating flesh as did the Hindus, but for practical reasons of economy. Instead of raising crops to feed cattle and then eating the cattle, they preferred to consume the crops directly themselves. For meats they chose animals that could be reared inexpensively—chickens, ducks, and especially pigs, which were also useful scavengers, and fish, with which even temporary ponds could be profitably stocked. Chinese methods of agriculture thus were intensive rather than extensive. As compared with modern Western countries, particularly the United States and Canada, the yield was low in proportion to the number of men employed and the hours of labor, but high in terms of acreage. While Chinese farming demanded exacting and arduous toil on the part of the cultivators, it made possible the growth of a large population.

As with most strong dynasties, efforts were directed to expanding the frontiers of the empire. Southern Manchuria and northern Korea were annexed, and Chinese settlers and culture penetrated this area. The provinces south of the Yangtze were secured, as was northeastern Indochina (Tonkin). Attempts to control Central Asia were checked by a confederacy of nomadic Huns (Hsiüng-nu) which had been formed at the very beginning of the Han rule and dominated the steppes for

Irrigation of a Rice Field. This eighteenth-century engraving reflects the timeless nature of rice cultivation. Note the manually operated sluice gate.

Labor intensive farming

Expansion of the empire

two and a half centuries. Although the emperors devoted much of their resources to fighting the Huns, they were unable to crush them and eventually negotiated pacts governing relations with them. Officially regarded as tributary, the Huns actually were paid subsidies of grain, wine, and silk and were granted trading privileges to dissuade them from raiding Chinese territory. In power and extent China under the Han was roughly equal to the contemporary Roman Empire. Nor was China isolated from other civilized areas. Her trade connections were far reaching, especially by the caravan routes which traversed Sinkiang and Turkestan. The Chinese had also begun to venture on the high seas, although ocean traffic was conducted chiefly by Indian navigators who sailed to the South China Sea and the Gulf of Tonkin. Chinese merchants exchanged products not only with India and Ceylon, but also with Japan, Persia, Arabia, Syria, and—indirectly—with Rome. The trade balance was generally favorable to China because of the high price commanded by her leading export, silk, frequently paid for in gold or precious stones.

The usurpation of Wang Mang

The Han Dynasty reached its climax in the latter half of the second century B.C., under the able leadership of an emperor who ruled for more than fifty years (Han Wu Ti, 140–87 B.C.). At the opening of the first century A.D. a court minister named Wang Mang, without military backing but with wide popular support, seized the imperial throne and proclaimed a new dynasty, which lasted only until the usurper's death fourteen years later (23 A.D.). During his brief and disastrous reign Wang Mang launched a radical reform program, sometimes described as an abortive attempt to establish a socialist society but which was actually inspired by Confucianist precepts as interpreted by Wang. He tried to re-establish early Chou institutions, including a semifeudal nobility, while at the same time alleviating the condition of slaves. Invoking the ancient doctrine that all land belongs to the ruler, he confiscated the property of great landowners to provide a farm plot for every family. However benevolent in intent, Wang's reforms were vitiated by his own inflexibility, inefficiency, and corruption through the exercise of power. He alienated almost all sections of the population, including those he was trying to help, and must go down as one of the supreme failures in the history of public administration. After he was murdered by rebels who broke into the palace, his program was scrapped. In 25 A.D. the Han family recovered the throne and retained it for two more centuries—a period known as the Later or Eastern Han because the capital was moved eastward to the site of Honan. The Later Han period exhibited the typical symptoms of decay at court and within the ruling house, although the administrative system remained intact and China's reputation in foreign parts was upheld by skillful diplomacy and force of arms. The dynasty crumbled as rebellions broke out and power passed into the hands of warlords, one of whom deposed the Han emperor in 220 A.D.

In the course of Chinese history many dynasties came and went, some very brief and some with only local jurisdiction. Several followed a path paralleling that of the Han, suggesting to historians of a generation ago that the major dynasties exhibited a common cyclical pattern: inauguration by force or usurpation, sometimes under an alien leader or one of lowly birth (the founder of the Han Dynasty was said to have come from a poor peasant family); and acceptance as legitimate if the new ruler were able to establish authority and maintain order. During the early years of a dynasty vigorous and efficient rule was accompanied by internal peace, prosperity, and an increase in population. When the imperial court and its officers became venal and corrupt, neglected administrative problems, and demanded exorbitant taxes, domestic upheaval ensued, frequently joined to the threat of attack from without. If the dynasty failed to resolve the crisis, it went down in bloodshed, and a new firm hand seized control, cleared away the debris, and began the process all over again under a new dynastic name. While this scenario of the rise and fall of dynasties is appealing because it equates political stability and social wellbeing with moral leadership on the part of the ruler (the "Mandate of Heaven" concept), it is no longer considered a valid formula for interpreting China's complex history. Regardless of its relevance for the cyclical theory, the Han Dynasty marks one of the most splendid periods in Chinese history, characterized by cultural progress and by the development of a form of government so satisfactory that its essential features remained unchanged—except for temporary interruptions—until the present century.

For almost four centuries after the collapse of the Han Dynasty, China was in a state of turbulence and upheaval. The country was divided, warfare was frequent, and it seemed that all the gains of the previous era were in jeopardy. Although the dates are not identical, this period of political disunity in China is comparable to the time of confusion which Europe experienced after the fall of the Roman Empire in the West. As in Europe during the early Middle Ages, the central government was weak or nonexistent; barbarian invasions affected a wide area; and, just as Christianity became rooted among the Latin and Germanic peoples of the West, a new otherworldly religion—Buddhism—made tremendous headway in China. Aside from these parallels, however, China's period of disunion was very different from the early Middle Ages in Europe. Although there was an appreciable decline in commerce and urban growth, it did not bring such a profound modification of culture and institutions as in Europe. The absence of a strong central authority was the only real disadvantage from which the country suffered, and this defect could be remedied by reviving the administrative machinery which had been temporarily disrupted. The Han state had been a practical and effective expression of Chinese experience, utilizing existing social and economic institutions and emphasizing ancient traditions. Consequently, even a long

Nomadic invaders from the north

Restoration of power and unity under the T'ang Dynasty (618–907)

The height of T'ang power

period of semianarchy could not destroy China's civilization. This period, dismal as it was, gave evidence of the toughness of Chinese society and culture, embodied in the patriarchal family, the village organization, and the sturdy enterprise of farmers.

As might be expected, the nomadic peoples on China's northern borders took advantage of her internal weakness to overrun the country. For about 250 years, from the fourth to the late sixth century A.D., practically all northern China including the Wei and Yellow River valleys was ruled by nomad dynasties of Hunnish, Turkish, and related stocks. It was not, however, successfully incorporated into any of the extensive but short-lived empires which arose in Central Asia and often impinged upon India as well as China. The dominance of non-Chinese rulers over the Yellow River valley—the historic center of Chinese culture—did not by any means destroy this culture. On the contrary, the rulers seemed eager to be accepted as custodians and defenders of civilization, and in the Far East civilization was synonymous with Chinese institutions. The nomads who settled south of the Great Wall assimilated the speech and customs of the older inhabitants. One of the few permanent changes in the habits of the Chinese people that can be attributed to their contact with the steppe nomads was in costume. During the fourth and fifth centuries they adopted trousers and boots similar to those worn by the northern horsemen, and this style of dress gradually supplanted the flowing tunic even in south China.

The contrast between China and western Europe during the medieval era is accentuated by the fact that four centuries of disunity in China were followed by another vigorous and highly successful dynasty, the T'ang (618–907), which re-established the imperial administration, again pushed back the territorial frontiers, and promoted brilliant cultural achievements. Thus, at the very time when feudalism was taking root in Europe and a new type of civilization was in process of formation there, China was resuming the course that had been marked out in Han times. Although it followed so closely upon the period of invasion and division, the T'ang Dynasty in many respects marked a high point in China's cultural evolution.[1]

The T'ang Dynasty was at its height during the first half of the eighth century, covered almost entirely by one distinguished reign, when the area under Chinese control was greater than it has been under any other native Chinese monarch. Furthermore, the empire was more consolidated than ever before, constituting a territorial state rather than an aggregate of semiautonomous regions surrounding a central authority. Wars in Mongolia broke the power of the Turks, who had been dominant there for about 150 years, and some of them became allies of the T'ang emperor. Parts of Manchuria were annexed,

---

[1] Actually the brief Sui Dynasty (589–618) had already reunited China and inaugurated the new era of progess.

The Grand Canal as Depicted in a Sui Dynasty Painting. Construction of the 1,000-mile-long Imperial Canal that linked the Yellow River and the Peking area to the Yangtze Basin was begun during the brief Sui Dynasty (580–618).

all Korea was tributary for a brief span, and control was again asserted over northern Indochina. The most redoubtable advances were in Central Asia. Chinese jurisdiction was recognized as far west as the Caspian Sea and the borders of Afghanistan and India, and some of the Indus valley princes accepted Chinese suzerainty. In carrying out their military exploits the T'ang rulers relied heavily upon the assistance of the non-Chinese peoples with whom their subjects were by this time familiar, either as friends or as foes. Now that the Chinese dragon was in the ascendancy, Mongols, Turks, and Huns were glad to be accepted as allies.

Imposing as was the T'ang hegemony over Central Asia, it could not be maintained indefinitely. When the rapid expansion of Islam began under Arab leadership in the seventh century, it seemed for a while that China, in spite of her remoteness from the West, was the only power to offer effective resistance. The last Sassanid king of Persia, fleeing from the Arabs, sought refuge at the T'ang court, and T'ang forces with the assistance of local princes checked the Muslim advance in Turkestan. The check was only temporary, however. When the T'ang administration passed its zenith (about 750), the Arabs gained control of Turkestan—bequeathing the religion of Islam as a permanent heritage—and for a time their influence extended as far east as the border of China's Kansu province. The T'ang rulers also encountered trouble with Tibet, which previously had remained in

Decline of the T'ang empire

The Emperor's Horse. This relief sculpture decorated the tomb of a T'ang emperor. The adoption of the long stirrup made the T'ang cavalry the most feared fighting force in all of Asia.

isolation from the turbulent politics of Central Asia. Early in the seventh century a kingdom was founded in the highland country by a leader who attained sufficient prestige to be given both a Chinese and an Indian princess in marriage. The Tibetans invaded Chinese territory several times, allied themselves alternately with the Turks and with the Arabs, and interrupted trade between China and Persia by blocking the passes through the Pamir Mountains. In 798 the T'ang court succeeded in obtaining a treaty of alliance with the famous Harun-al-Raschid, caliph of Baghdad, and the Tibetan power subsided in the ninth century. Meanwhile, a division of Turks had reoccupied Mongolia, and in spite of a long struggle the Chinese were unable to hold their northern and western frontiers inviolate. By the end of the ninth century internal rebellions, together with governmental corruption and decadence in the ruling house, had led again to a state of general disorder.

Development of the civil service

The T'ang administrative machinery, similar to the Han, was centralized under the emperor and staffed by a large bureaucracy. China proper was divided into fifteen provinces, which were subdivided into prefectures, and these again into smaller units or sub-prefectures, and each of the units was headed by an official appointed from the capital. The Han practice of recruiting talent for the imperial service had now developed into a rudimentary civil-service system in which written examinations were offered periodically throughout the provinces, and some officeholders were chosen from among the successful candidates.

Since the abolition of feudalism and the establishment of peasant proprietorship by the Ch'in emperor, the character of Chinese society had not greatly changed. Many peasants were tenants rather than independent owners, and slavery had not entirely disappeared.

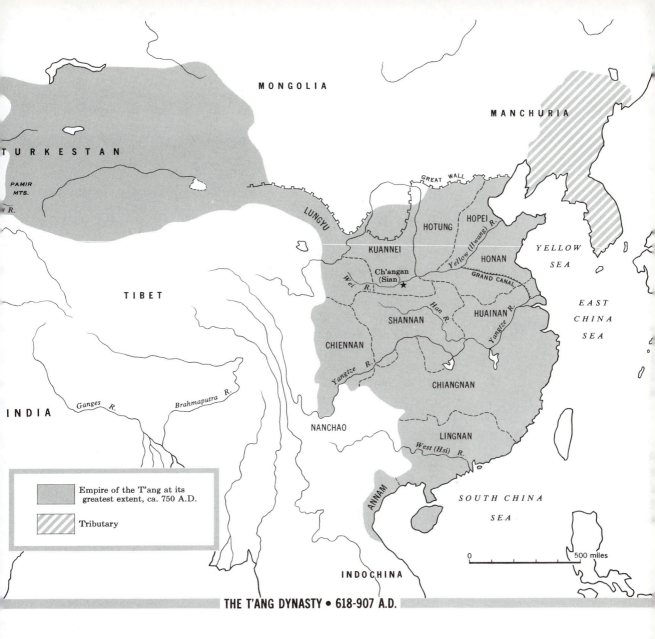

MONGOLIA

MANCHURIA

TURKESTAN

PAMIR
MTS.

R.

LUNGYU

GREAT WALL

HOTUNG   HOPEI

KUANNEI

Yellow (Hwang) R.

YELLOW
SEA

HONAN

Ch'angan
(Sian) ★

Wei R.

GRAND CANAL

TIBET

Han R.

HUAINAN

EAST
CHINA
SEA

SHANNAN

Yangtze R.

CHIENNAN

Yangtze R.

CHIANGNAN

INDIA

Ganges R.

Brahmaputra R.

NANCHAO

LINGNAN

West (Hsi) R.

ANNAM

SOUTH CHINA
SEA

Empire of the T'ang at its
greatest extent, ca. 750 A.D.

Tributary

0   500 miles

INDOCHINA

THE T'ANG DYNASTY • 618-907 A.D.

Inequalities in wealth and distinctions of rank were conspicuous. The T'ang emperors supported a titled nobility of several grades, but its prestige was based upon governmental favor rather than upon the possession of landed estates. Instead of hereditary titles carrying administrative power as in a feudal regime, the titles were bestowed upon eminent officials as a reward for their services. Ordinarily the emperor did not rule as a military despot but maintained a clear separation between the civil and military authority. It was only during periods of weakness and disorder that warlords usurped political functions. By T'ang times the Chinese had acquired a conviction that mil-

Chinese society under the T'ang

Buddhist Missionary. A sixth-century carving supposed to represent the first Indian Buddhist missionary to China. Buddhism had probably been introduced into China as early as the first century A.D.

itary regimes were incompatible with a normal, civilized state of affairs.

Continuing the policy of encouraging agriculture, every vigorous dynasty gave attention to irrigation works, usually maintained public granaries to provide food distribution in famine years, and sometimes attempted to relieve the farmers from their heavy burden of debt and taxes. Nevertheless, while China was already one of the world's leading agricultural countries, the poorer peasants undoubtedly suffered from a miserably low standard of living as has been the case throughout history. Furthermore, the farmer bore the chief burden of supporting the state. Theoretically the emperor reserved the right to redistribute holdings, but in practice he was usually content to break the power of overly ambitious wealthy houses that might challenge his own authority. Too often the interest of officials in the peasants centered upon the fact that they constituted the most lucrative and dependable source of taxation, collectible either in produce or labor, the latter including conscription for military service.

Curiously enough, in spite of the honored position of the farmer and the pro-agrarian policies of the government, the merchant class attained a prominence far superior to that of European merchants during this period, and the steady increase of trade induced the growth of thriving cities. During the eighth century the T'ang capital in the Wei valley (on the site of Sian, but known during this period as Ch'ang-an), the eastern terminus of the trans-Asiatic caravan routes, apparently had a population of close to 2 million, while the population of China as a whole was between 40 and 50 million—about 5 percent of the present number. Foreign commerce was greater under the T'ang than ever before, and an increasing proportion of it was oceanic, the leading ports of exchange being Canton and other cities along the southeast coast, where merchants of various nationalities from the Near and Middle East were to be found. In addition to silk and spices, porcelain ware was becoming a notable item in China's export trade.

During the period under consideration a religious development of overwhelming importance was the introduction of Buddhism, which brought the Chinese for the first time into contact with a complex religion with an elaborate theology, ecclesiastical organization, and emphasis upon personal salvation. For several centuries following the life of Gautama, the Buddhist faith gained such momentum in the regions surrounding India that it was bound to reach China. It was brought in over the northern trade routes as early as the first century A.D. and made rapid headway during the period of disunion that followed the collapse of the Han Dynasty. Buddhism met with a mixed reception in China, arousing both enthusiastic interest and repugnance. Mysticism, asceticism, contempt for the physical world, and the concept of transmigration of souls were quite alien to Chinese tradition; and the monastic life seemed to involve a repudiation of sacred family loyalties. On the other hand, Buddhism offered consolations not found in the native Chinese cults or philosophical disciplines. It was nonaristocratic, open to all classes, and—in contrast to the Confucian emphasis upon the inflexible will of Heaven—its *karma* doctrine affirmed that anyone could improve his chances in a future existence by diligent application. Converts were attracted by the rich symbolism of the new religion, and the voluminous scriptures which the Buddhist missionaries brought with them impressed the Chinese, who venerated scholarship. Buddhism's otherworldly orientation appealed particularly to the downtrodden and oppressed. In spite of violent opposition from some Chinese rulers, Buddhism continued to recruit adherents; congregations of women as well as of men were organized; pilgrims went to India to study and returned with copies of the Buddhist canons. By about 500 A.D. China had practically become a Buddhist country.

Buddhism in China

It might be supposed that after the restoration of a strong monarchy the interest in this imported salvationist faith would have subsided, but such was not the case. Although a few of the T'ang emperors tried to root out Buddhism (one emperor is reputed to have destroyed 40,000 temples), several of them encouraged it, and it was under the T'ang Dynasty that Chinese Buddhism reached its height as a creative influence. Many varieties of the religion had been brought into China—chiefly of the *Mahayana* school—and others were developed on Chinese soil, appealing to different temperaments and degrees of education. One of the most popular sects, called the "Pure Land" or "Lotus" school, promised an easy salvation in a western paradise to all who invoked the name of Amida (or Amitabha). Amida, theoretically an incarnation of Buddha, was actually visualized as a god, alleged to have been born of a lotus in the heavenly western realm of bliss. Several of the sects, however, encouraged a zeal for scholarship and also stimulated interest in the problems of government and society. The most vigorous philosophical speculation under the T'ang was found in Buddhist circles. But in spite of the great success of Buddhism its triumph was not comparable to the ascendancy of Christianity in western Europe during this same period. The Chinese Buddhists were not united in a common discipline, had no coercive power, and did not replace or challenge the authority of the state as did the Christian hierarchy in the West. And the fact that Buddhist monks and monasteries were found in almost all parts of the country did not mean that other religions had ceased to exist. The idea of an inclusive universal church was foreign to Chinese conceptions.

*Varieties of Chinese
Buddhism*

Head of Buddha. T'ang Dynasty (618–907). This stone head was found in the caves of Lung Men.

Paralleling the spread of Buddhism, Taoism, which had originated as a philosophical school, acquired the characteristic features of an otherworldly religion with wide popular appeal. Taoism developed not only a priesthood but an ecclesiastical hierarchy headed by a "Prince Celestial Master," who established pontifical headquarters in south central China. This Taoist hierarchy was given official recognition in the eighth century and was not formally abolished until

Taoism as a religion

Confucianism as a state cult

1927. The religion, incorporating many primitive beliefs, expounded the Way (*Tao*), which was interpreted to mean the road to individual happiness defined usually in material terms, although it offered elements to attract intellectuals and encouraged acts of charity. Taoism was greatly affected by Buddhism and borrowed ideas from the foreign faith, including the concepts of *karma* and transmigration and the belief in thirty-three heavens and eighteen hells. Its priesthood was modeled after the Buddhist monastic order, except that the Taoists did not practice celibacy; and the later Taoist scriptures show a strong resemblance to Buddhist texts. Inevitably rivalry sprang up between the two competing religions, but neither was able to eliminate the other and both received imperial as well as popular support. Some Taoist apologists claimed that their master, Lao-tzu, had actually been the Buddha or else had instructed him; while Buddhists countered with the assertion that Lao-tzu had rendered homage to Gautama.

In spite of the popularity of Taoism and the temporary ascendancy of Buddhism, Confucianism began to be revived in the later T'ang period and retained its hold upon the allegiance of the Chinese. Although usually described as one of the three great religions of China, Confucianism was not and never became a religion in the strict sense of the term. It was a body of ethical principles, of etiquette and formal ceremony, and also—as a result of the policies of Han and T'ang emperors—a code of government, strengthened by the practice of recruiting officials from scholars versed in the Confucian classics. Veneration for the great teacher finally became part of the state cult and was invested with formal religious observances. The later Han emperors had prescribed sacrifices to Confucius in every large city, and a T'ang ruler of the seventh century ordered temples to be built in his honor in each prefecture and subprefecture. Thus the sage, together with other famous men of antiquity, revered rulers, out-

The Ancestor of All Seismographs. Invented by a Chinese mathematician and geographer in 132 A.D., it was described in a contemporary document as an "earthquake weathercock." These conjectural reconstructions show the interior of the bronze, bell-shaped instrument. (A) The pendulum carries jointed arms radiating in eight directions, each arm ending in a crank connected with a dragon head. (B) When an earth tremor causes the pendulum to swing, one of the dragon heads is raised and releases a ball, which drops into the mouth of a toad below. After the swing of the pendulum, a catch mechanism immobilizes the instrument. Thus, by observing which ball has fallen, it is possible to determine the direction of the initial shock wave.

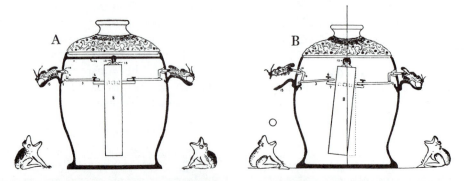

standing generals, etc., was ensured perpetual homage and respect, but he was not worshiped as were the Buddhist and Taoist deities. The Chinese idea of religion, it should be remembered, was different from that of most other peoples. The typical Chinese would be a Confucianist as a matter of course; but he might also be a Taoist, a Buddhist, or a combination of both.

Many economic and cultural changes took place during the thousand years between the Ch'in Dynasty and the end of the T'ang. Some items were borrowed from Western lands—grapes and alfalfa among the agricultural products, astrological concepts and the seven-day week. The Chinese began to use coal for fuel and for smelting iron in the fourth century A.D., far in advance of Europeans. Their astrologers had observed sunspots as early as 28 B.C.; a crude seismograph was constructed in 132 A.D. The magnetic compass, apparently developed by the Taoists around 500 A.D., was used chiefly to determine favorable locations for grave sites. The explosive properties of gunpowder had been discovered and were used in firecrackers to frighten away evil spirits. The highly important invention of paper (made of bark, hemp, and rags) was achieved by the beginning of the second century A.D., and printing from blocks was introduced about 500 years later. By the tenth century the printing of books was common not only in China but in Korea and Japan. The tradition of realistic sculpture, so vividly displayed in the Ch'in emperor's mausoleum, was continued in later dynasties. Han tombs were adorned with graceful and lifelike animal figures of stone and bronze, only a few of which have survived. Engravings on stone slabs and earthenware models found in the tombs shed light on architectural styles, popular customs, and religious concepts of the period. A polychrome painting on silk dating from about 168 B.C. suggests a definite belief not only in the spirit world but in a heaven.

A great deal of the intellectual and artistic progress of this era must be credited to the Buddhists, whose contributions were not confined to religion exclusively. Buddhism enriched Chinese music by the introduction of a liturgy of vocal chants and also with several new musical instruments, including the psaltery, guitar or mandolin and other stringed instruments, the reed organ, clarinet, and a type of flute. It was in the visual arts, however, that the impetus of Buddhism was most notable. The Buddhists of northern India, who had absorbed artistic motifs from the Greeks and Persians, spread them into Central Asia and thence into China. During the period of disunion and the early T'ang Dynasty, Chinese sculpture reached its climax, successfully blending together Indian, Iranian, and Hellenic characteristics into a distinctive Chinese style. Superbly beautiful examples of this sculpture have survived, the best of which were produced in the late sixth and early seventh centuries. The most impressive works of architecture were Buddhist temples or sacred grottoes in northwestern China, carved out of rock caves after the Indian man-

Two Carved Wood Bodhisattvas. T'ang Dynasty. The bodhisattva, or Buddha-to-be, represented a person eligible for enlightenment but who remained in the world to help others on the upward path. In Mahayana Buddhism a number of bodhisattvas came to be worshiped as deities.

*Porcelain Ewer or Pitcher, in the
Form of a Court Lady.* T'ang
Dynasty.

*The literary quality of
Chinese civilization*

*The retarded development
of civilization in Japan*

ner. Painting, too, reached a peak of realism and sensitivity which has rarely been surpassed. Skill in this medium was stimulated by the Chinese habit of writing with brush and ink, and pictorial figures or scenes were often combined with masterly specimens of calligraphy executed on scrolls of silk. Some paintings in fresco have been preserved from T'ang times and, like the sculpture, they show Buddhist influence. Outstanding among the minor arts was the production of pottery figurines representing human beings and animals with grace and naturalness, used chiefly as funeral presents to the departed. The manufacture of white porcelain—the beginning of the world-famous "china" ware—apparently began in the sixth or seventh century.

As early as Chou times, the Chinese civilization was highly literary, and by the T'ang period China had probably the most abundant collection of writings of any nation in the world. Philosophical activity did not equal the creative age of Confucius, Mo Ti, and Mencius, but a great variety of literary forms had come into existence, showing maturity of thought, sophistication, and aesthetic sensitivity. Writers of the T'ang period produced histories, essays, dictionaries, short stories and romances for popular entertainers, an embryonic form of the drama, and—outshining all the rest—poetry. Poetry had been developed prolifically during the centuries of disunion and civil strife. The influence of Buddhism and Taoism imparted emotional intensity and a quality of mysticism conducive to lyrical richness. The final result was a flowering in the eighth and ninth centuries which made the T'ang the supreme age of Chinese poetry. The verse forms were usually short, with words carefully chosen to evoke beauty of tone as well as to convey pithy thought and vivid imagery. While sometimes expressing philosophical ideas, they were frequently poignant in mood and romantic in theme, treating especially of nature, love, and friendship. A few of the best examples were tinged with a deep melancholy, expressing compassion for the miserable lot of the poor, distress over abuses in government, revulsion against the senseless brutality of war, and bewilderment at the apparent triumph of evil over good.

3. EARLY CIVILIZATION IN JAPAN

Of the great civilizations of East Asia, Japan's was the latest to develop. In origin it was derived from and was largely an adaptation of cultures from the mainland, especially from China. However, the fact that the Japanese lagged many centuries behind China and India and made their most rapid progress under the stimulus of borrowings from China does not prove that the island dwellers were lacking in ability or originality. Not only did the Japanese display remarkable ingenuity in assimilating foreign elements and in modifying them to meet their particular needs, but during some periods of history they seemed to possess more initiative than any of the other Far Eastern nations. The backwardness of Japan in early times is explained, at least in part, by the geographical circumstance of its isolation from the continent of Asia. Before oceanic commerce was well advanced, the Japanese islands could not be readily affected by political and cultural changes taking place on the mainland. These islands stand in the same relationship to Asia as do the British Isles to Europe. Just as European civilization was slowly extended from the Near Eastern centers westward to Italy and then to the northern countries, reaching Britain last of all, so Far Eastern civilization gradually radiated from the Yellow River valley to the south, west, and northeast, and necessarily reached Japan belatedly. Actually Japan is much more remote from the neighboring continent than is Britain from Continental Europe. At the narrowest point the Strait of Dover is only about 20 miles wide, while more than 100 miles separate the islands of Japan from the closest point on the Korean peninsula.

Japan's geographic setting is in some ways very favorable. Of the approximately 3,000 islands composing the group, only about 600 are inhabited, and the bulk of the population is concentrated on the four principal islands. The entire archipelago lies within the temperate zone, and the largest island, Honshu, holding about half of the Japanese people, lies between almost exactly the same latitudes as the state of California. The Black Current, drifting northward from tropical seas, moderates the severity of winter; and cyclonic storms, while sometimes destructive, bring fluctuations in temperature that are conducive to physical and mental vigor. Their proximity to the ocean encouraged the Japanese to develop navigation and to become hardy fishermen. With its expanse of seacoast, mountains, volcanoes and snow-capped peaks, the region is scenically one of the most beautiful in the world, a factor which has undoubtedly contributed to the keen aesthetic sensibilities of the Japanese people. At the same time Japan is by no means perfectly endowed by nature and suffers from several disadvantages. Except for having fair deposits of coal, the islands are poor in mineral resources. Even more serious has been the scarcity of good agricultural land, owing to the rocky or mountainous character of much of the country. Although throughout most of their history the Japanese have been a nation of farmers, only about 16 percent of their soil is cultivable. This sufficed when the population was small and generally stationary; it has posed a tremendous problem in modern times.

Geographic advantages and disadvantages

Small as is the land area of Japan (slightly less than that of California) and in spite of its relative isolation, it was inhabited even in early times by people of various stocks as the result of successive migrations from the continent. The earliest inhabitants, so far as is known, were a primitive people who possessed a Neolithic culture, crude in many respects but distinguished by pottery of striking design and skillfully fashioned weapons. They are represented today by the Ainu, a light-

Racial stocks in Japan

EARLY JAPAN

colored, flat-faced, and hairy people, who have largely disappeared except from Hokkaido and the Kuril Islands to the north. For the most part the Japanese nation is descended from Mongoloid invaders who crossed over to the islands at various times during the Neolithic Age and even later, chiefly by way of Korea. From the time of the Ch'in Dynasty on, the settlers in Japan possessed some knowledge of Chinese culture, which had already penetrated into Korea. Bronze mirrors, carved jewels, and swords of Chinese or Mongolian type appear in graves dating from the second and first centuries B.C. By the close of the first century B.C. the Japanese had begun to use iron as well as bronze.

Quite understandably, the leading centers of cultural evolution were in the south and west of Japan—the areas closest to Korea, from which the chief migrations came—and developments in this region gradually spread to the north and east. The real nucleus of the Japanese state was the peninsula of Yamato, on the southeastern side of the great island of Honshu, to which a group of families had migrated from Kyushu (opposite Korea) perhaps as early as the first century A.D. The Japanese communities at this time were very primitive. People wore clothing made from hemp or bark, although silk was not entirely unknown. They carried on trade by barter only and had no system of writing. The chief unit of society was the clan, a group of families claiming to be related by blood. Each clan venerated some particular deity, who was supposed to be the ancestor of the group; but the worship of human ancestors had not yet become an institution. The headship of the clan was vested hereditarily in a specific family, and the clan leader served both as a warrior chieftain and as priest. In primitive Japanese society women seem to have held a position of prominence, perhaps even of superiority. The clan head was sometimes a woman, and evidence points to the conclusion that originally the family was matriarchal, with descent traced through the mother—a remarkable circumstance in view of the rigid subordination of women in later times. The transition to a patriarchal system, however, was effected at an early date. According to Chinese accounts from the third century A.D., polygamy was a common practice, especially among men of the higher classes. Various crafts and skills were organized as occupational groups in the form of guilds with hereditary membership. Each guild was attached to a clan and tended to merge with it eventually, although a few guilds whose members performed distinctive services, such as administering religious rites, retained an independent existence and honorable status. Members of the agricultural and artisans' guilds, on the other hand, were practically serfs. Society was decidedly aristocratic, rank was generally hereditary, and slavery existed, although the number of slaves was relatively small.

The beginnings of Japanese society

Japanese religion, while comparable to that of other primitive peoples, was in some ways unique. It was basically animistic, a type of unreflecting and almost universal nature worship, with no well-defined conception of the nature of divine being. In a general way it was polytheistic, except that the term probably suggests too definite a catalogue of gods or too precise a theology. The Japanese later gave their religion the name of *Shinto* ("the way of the Gods"), simply because they needed to distinguish it from Buddhism when this articulate and mature faith began to compete with the native cult. Although the Japanese recognized some great deities, associated with the sun, moon, earth, crops, and storms, these were not endowed with distinct personalities and were not represented by images.

The foundations of Shintoism

Objects of worship were designated as *kami*, a term meaning "superior" but which was applied to almost anything having mysterious or interesting properties, ranging from heavenly phenomena to irregularly shaped stones and such lowly objects as sand, mud, and vermin. No sharp line was drawn between the natural and the supernatural or between magic and worship. The notion of life after death was extremely shadowy, and religion was largely devoid of ethical content. It involved taboos and scrupulous concern for ceremonial cleanness, with purification rites to remove contamination, but the requirements were not based on considerations of morality or even always of health. Uncleanness, for example, was associated with childbirth, with contact with the dead, and with wounds whether inflicted honorably or not. To placate the gods, respectful gestures, prayers, and sacrifices were employed. Offerings of food and drink gradually tended to be superseded by symbolic objects—of pottery, wood, and eventually paper.

*Attractive elements in
native Japanese religion*

In spite of its diffuse and elementary character, the native Japanese religion was not lacking in attractive elements. It reflected an attitude of cheerfulness and a rare sympathy for and appreciation of nature. The gods were not thought of as cruel and terrifying creatures; even the god of the storm was generally conceived as benign. On the whole, the religion of the Japanese was one "of love and gratitude rather than of fear, and the purpose of their religious rites was to praise and thank as much as to placate and mollify their divinities."[2] It was enlivened also with picturesque legends and poetic phrases that suggest a spontaneous delight in the natural world.

The clan which was dominant on the plain of Yamato, and gradually acquired an ascendancy over adjacent regions, probably came from Kyushu and claimed descent from the Sun Goddess. There was nothing remarkable in such a claim because all important families traced their ancestry to gods or goddesses. However, myths associated with the Sun Goddess assumed greater significance as the Yamato clan extended its political power and attempted to secure fuller recognition of its paramountcy over the other clans, for which purpose it was helpful to foster the legend that the Yamato chief had been divinely appointed to rule over Japan (even though most of it was still unconquered from the aborigines). According to this legend the Sun Goddess had sent down to earth her own grandson, Ninigino-Mikoto. Ninigi, "thrusting apart the many-piled clouds of Heaven, clove his way with an awful way-cleaving" to land on the western island of Kyushu, carrying with him the three symbols of Japanese royalty—a jewel, a sword, and a mirror. The grandson of this Ninigi, it was related, advanced along the coast of the larger island to Yamato, where he began to rule as Jimmu, the "first emperor." National tradition dates the empire from February 11, 660 B.C. Actually, it was at

Japanese Tomb Culture. Clay grave statues of ordinary people, such as this soldier, surrounded the tombs of more important people. This reflects the influence of Korean culture. Such statuary began to appear in the third and fourth centuries A.D.

[2] G. B. Sansom, *Japan, a Short Cultural History*, p. 47.

least 600 or 700 years later that the Yamato state was established, and then it was anything but imperial. The saga of the Sun Goddess and her descendants did not become a distinctive element in the national cult of Japan until the sixth century A.D., and not until the modern era was it deliberately exploited on a national scale for the purpose of instilling a fanatical and unquestioning patriotism among the people.

For many centuries the Japanese maintained contact with and continued to receive cultural impetus from Korea, which means that they were being influenced indirectly by the older and richer civilization of China of the Han and later dynasties. The Japanese invaded southern Korea in 369 A.D. and intervened in Korean politics to maintain a balance of power, siding with one and then another of the three kingdoms into which Korea was divided during this time. Of fundamental importance for the later history of Japan was the introduction, by way of Korea, of the Chinese system of writing (about 405 A.D.) and of Buddhism (about 552 A.D.).

Japanese writing

While the technique of writing was essential to the advance of civilization, it was unfortunate for the Japanese that they acquired it from China. If they had been able to devise or borrow a phonetic or alphabetic system, the problem of writing their language would have been comparatively simple. The Chinese characters—fundamentally pictographic or ideographic, with very little apparent relationship to pronunciation of the words for which they stand—had been developed to a state of complexity and utilized in producing masterpieces of Chinese literature; but they were ill suited to represent Japanese. The Japanese language is phonetically quite different from the Chinese, and the attempt to write it with Chinese characters was a feat as dif-

Japanese and Chinese Writing. The text on the right is a passage from Mencius in Chinese with kaeriten added on the left hand side of each column to indicate the sequence in which the characters should be read to transcribe the passage into Japanese. This adaptation of Chinese writing is called Kambun. The text on the left is the same passage in Japanese. The hiragana written between the characters indicate the appropriate verbal inflections and postpositions. The small hiragana beside each character indicate the correct Japanese pronunciation. Note the use of Chinese characters in the Japanese text.

JAPANESE TEXT

粟を以て械器に易ふる者は、陶冶を厲ましむと為さず。陶冶も亦其の械器を以て粟に易ふる者は、豈農夫を厲ましむと為んや。

KAMBUN TEXT

以粟易械器者、不為厲陶冶。陶冶亦以其械器、易粟者、豈為厲農夫哉。

Great Buddha, Todaiji Temple, Nara. This statue, cast in the middle of the eighth century A.D., is one of the two largest bronze statues in the world. The seated Buddha is 53 feet high.

ficult as it would be to try to write English in Chinese characters. Nevertheless, the Japanese struggled heroically with the task and eventually developed a script of their own, or, rather, two varieties of script. Although the original Chinese characters were abbreviated considerably and, during the ninth and tenth centuries, given phonetic value by identification with individual Japanese syllables, the resulting product was still cumbersome. Hence, the process of learning to write Japanese—in which 48 phonetic symbols plus 1,850 Chinese characters must be mastered—was and still is a laborious undertaking. The fact that the system of writing is alien to the structure, inflection, and idiosyncrasies of the spoken language hampered clarity of expression. To compensate for these disadvantages, however, along with the Chinese-derived script a great many Chinese words were adopted bodily by the Japanese, enriching their language in vocabulary and concepts. In view of the circumstances in which writing was introduced in Japan, a person who wished to become educated was almost bound to learn the Chinese language, especially since it was the vehicle of all literature considered worthy of the name. For several centuries Japanese scholars, officials, and men of letters wrote in classical Chinese, in somewhat the same manner that educated Europeans used Latin during the Middle Ages and later—except that while Latin was both written and spoken by educated Europeans, few Japanese scholars or literati learned to *speak* Chinese.[3]

In the middle of the sixth century Buddhism began to obtain a foothold in Japan. The first Buddhist missionary is said to have come from Korea; other evangelists of the new faith arrived not only from Korea

[3] For an illuminating discussion of the Japanese language, see E. O. Reischauer, *The Japanese,* chapter 37.

but from China and even from India. As in the case of China, the *Mahayana* school of Buddhism, with its elaborate theology and emphasis upon the soul's redemption, was most in evidence. And, just as had happened in China, a number of different sects arose in Japan from time to time. The appearance of Buddhism in Japan produced perhaps even greater agitation than had accompanied its introduction into China a few centuries earlier. The Chinese were at least familiar with mystical concepts through Taoism, but the Japanese had had no previous experience either with this type of otherworldly religion or with any analogous philosophy. Part of the appeal of Buddhism to the Japanese lay in its novelty. The Buddhist scriptures raised questions that had apparently never occurred to the Japanese before—as to the soul, the nature of the immaterial world, rewards and punishments after death—and then proceeded to answer them with impressive eloquence. For a while, sharp controversy raged over the acceptability of the foreign faith (the first statue of the Buddha sent from Korea was thrown into a canal when an epidemic of disease broke out). However, one prominent aristocratic family in Yamato, the Soga, adopted and championed the cause of Buddhism and prevailed upon the imperial clan to favor it, so that before the close of the sixth century the success of the religion was assured. To some extent its success was attributable to political maneuvers and expediency. In patronizing the scholarly faith the Soga family sought to enhance its own prestige and, through the benefit of whatever supernatural power the religion contained, to secure an advantage in the struggle against rival families. Buddhism rapidly acquired a wide following both among the common people and the aristocracy and became so firmly entrenched that it would survive any shift in equilibrium among the contending clans. Probably its popularity is largely explained by its being interpreted as a miraculous protector against disasters both in this world and the next rather than by its philosophical heritage. Nevertheless, the increasing familiarity with Buddhist doctrines stimulated intellectual activity and was conducive to the cultivation of attitudes of sympathy and humaneness.

One of the most significant aspects of the spread of Buddhism in Japan was that it proved to be a highly effective medium for disseminating Chinese culture, especially art, architecture, and literature. Temples and shrines were erected, paintings and images of the Buddha were produced, and libraries of the sacred texts were accumulated. Converts from the aristocratic class frequently went to China to study, returning with a broadened viewpoint and refined tastes. The native Japanese cult, now beginning to be called *Shinto,* was by no means extinguished, but it was influenced considerably by contact with Buddhism. There was very little antagonism between the two religions. Buddhism in Japan became tinged with national traditions, and frequently the same shrine was regarded as sacred to both faiths. The Japanese priests, whether Buddhist or Shinto, did not constitute

The establishment of Buddhism in Japan

Prince Shotoku. A leading patron of Buddhism is portrayed here with two of his sons in a seventh-century painting on paper.

Buddhism a medium for disseminating Chinese culture

Horyuji Temple, Nara. The Horyuji Temple, founded in 607 A.D. by Prince Shotoku, Regent of the Empress-Regnant Suiko, is a complex of about forty buildings and includes some of the oldest wooden structures in the world.

a hierarchy with coercive powers over the people any more than did the priests in China, although the Buddhist monasteries gained in economic importance as they were endowed with lands.

The Japanese turn to China for tutelage

During the most vigorous period of the T'ang Dynasty, the impact of Chinese civilization upon Japan reached such a climax that it marks a turning point in the evolution of Japanese institutions. It is not at all strange that the Japanese turned avidly to China for tutelage at this time. China under the early T'ang rulers was one of the most highly civilized states in the world, as well as the most powerful, and in the Far East had no close rivals for such a distinction. Throughout the seventh and eighth centuries the government in Yamato sent a succession of official embassies to the T'ang court, largely for the purpose of recruiting personnel trained in the sciences, arts, and letters. The result profoundly affected almost every aspect of Japanese life and society. Chinese medical practices, military tactics, and methods of road building were introduced; also styles of architecture, of household furniture, and even of dress. A system of weights and measures was adopted, and copper coins came into limited circulation, although a genuine money economy did not replace barter until centuries later. Many works of art had previously been imported and copied, but now Japanese painters and sculptors began to display both technical proficiency and originality. The Chinese classics, especially the Confucian writings, were studied intently, since every well-bred person was expected to be familiar with them. Along with these concrete and visible innovations came an attempt to fit the social structure into the Chinese pattern. A new emphasis was placed upon family solidarity and filial devotion, including the duty of sacrificing to ancestral spirits.[4] Japanese leaders and intellectuals seemed determined to remake their country in the image of China.

The most comprehensive project involved nothing less than reconstituting the government according to the T'ang model. It was announced by a decree known as the Taika Reform Edict, issued in 645 A.D. by the Yamato ruler at the instigation of a clique of scholar-reformers. This declaration, rather than the mythical events of 660 B.C., represents the founding of the Japanese imperial system. By the Taika Edict the ruler assumed the role not of a mere clan leader but of an emperor, with absolute power, although professedly honoring Confucian principles. All Japan was to be divided into provinces, prefectures, and subprefectures, which would be administered by a centrally appointed bureaucracy recruited from the populace. Faithful to the example of China, the reformers instituted a civil service, offering examinations to candidates for government posts, whose selection would be based not on familiarity with the problems of Japan but on proficiency in Chinese philosophy and classical literature. To give the new administration an economic foundation and to bring it to bear directly upon the people, the Reform Edict proclaimed that all the land belonged to the emperor, and that it would be divided equitably among the farmers and redistributed every six years. In return, every landholder would be required to pay taxes (in commodities, money, or labor) directly to the state.

Altogether, the reform program of the seventh century was one of the most ambitious that any government has ever attempted. It sought to graft upon a still fairly primitive society an administrative system that was the product of almost a thousand years of evolution among a people with cultural maturity and deeply entrenched traditions. Similarly, it involved an effort on the part of one corner of Japan to impose its regime on the entire area, much of which had hardly advanced beyond the Neolithic stage. In adopting the scheme of a centralized paternalism, one aspect of the Chinese prototype was studiously avoided: namely, the concept that imperial authority is conditional upon the promotion of public welfare and that it may be terminated—by rebellion as a last resort—if it fails in this objective. The Yamato group tried to attach a bureaucracy of scholar-officials to a government that called for perpetual rule by one family, whose head occupied a position of inviolable sanctity. To strengthen the prestige of the emperor, greater emphasis than ever before was placed upon his reputed descent from the Sun Goddess. He was represented as the embodiment of a "lineal succession unbroken for ages eternal" and as

Japanese Religious Sculpture. This wooden figure of Bishamon, revered as one of the Four Guardian Kings of the Budhist kingdom, dates from the twelfth century or earlier.

Consolidation of the Japanese government

---

[4] Some Japanese scholars deny that the custom of ancestor worship was an importation; but in any case it was intensified by contacts with the Chinese. An unfortunate consequence was the increasing subordination of women to male authority in the patriarchal family and in society at large.

divine in his own person—a significantly different concept from that of the "Mandate of Heaven," the conditional and temporary divinity that hedged the Chinese emperor. In addition to this fundamental contrast between the official Chinese and Japanese theories as to the ultimate basis and limits of political authority, there was a notable divergence in practice also. China knew many different dynasties, most of them begun through rebellion or usurpation; but when a vigorous emperor sat on the throne, he usually ruled effectively and sometimes autocratically, as is attested by the records of the first few rulers of every major dynasty. In Japan, on the other hand, while the imperial family was never dethroned in spite of violent or revolutionary changes within society and in foreign relations, and while the fiction of imperial sanctity was carefully preserved, the actual power for the most part was exercised by some other family, agency, or clique, using the sacred imperial office as a front. Indirect government, sometimes removed by several stages from the nominal sovereign, has been the rule rather than the exception in Japan ever since its attempt to incorporate the Chinese political machinery.

In view of the inherent difficulties, it is not surprising that the reform program of the seventh century was not entirely successful. The new administrative system existed on paper but not as an operating reality. The imperial clan, which had previously enjoyed only a limited and largely ceremonial authority over the others, could not compel absolute obedience from remote areas, and aristocratic traditions were too strong to be broken immediately. The emperor made it a practice to appoint clan heads as officials in their own territories instead of replacing them by loyal servants sent out from the capital. Thus the local magnates acquired new titles and kept much of their former power. Examinations were provided for candidates desiring posts in the government service, but important positions were almost always reserved for members of the aristocracy, while capable men of the lower class found themselves employed as underlings and clerks. The announced policy of land equalization, which was intended to serve as the basis for a uniform tax system, was the most dismal failure of all. It had been inspired by the Chinese ideal of community interest in the land, a sentiment which condemned the appropriation of land for the exclusive benefit of any individual and taught that it should be distributed equally among the cultivators. This was only a theory in China, and in Japan it was thoroughly unrealistic. Later large proprietors managed to evade taxation and so increased the burden upon the poorer farmers that some of them ran away from their homes in sheer desperation. In this manner the amount of taxable land diminished, and the emperors themselves contributed to the process by giving away estates to courtiers or to endow Buddhist monasteries. Furthermore, the decree regarding periodic redistribution of land applied only to the fields that had already been brought under rice cultivation, a relatively small area. As the frontier clans added to their domains

Partial failure of the reform program

either by conquest from the aborigines or by reclaiming waste lands for cultivation, these new territories were regarded as personal holdings not directly subject to imperial assessment. Consequently, economic progress lessened rather than increased the proportion of the land under effective control by the central government. Instead of securing large funds from taxation, the court became more and more dependent for revenue upon estates that were owned outright by the imperial family.

Although the central government failed in its political objectives, it succeeded in promoting cultural progress to an appreciable degree. Before the seventh century there had been no fixed Japanese capital even in Yamato, and in fact no cities at all. Impressed with the splendor of the T'ang capital, the great city of Ch'ang-an, the Japanese determined to build one like it to serve as the imperial headquarters. Their city, begun in 710 and located near the modern town of Nara, followed the Chinese model faithfully in its broad streets and carefully aligned squares of equal size, although it was unwalled and much smaller than Ch'ang-an. Even so, its plan was too large for the population that occupied it. In 794 a more imposing capital was built at Kyoto, which has been an important city ever since. The construction of these cities under imperial patronage, with palaces, temples, and other public buildings, provided a stimulus to all the arts. Scholarship, bent on the production of histories, treatises, and literary criticism, also flourished at the imperial court. If the bureaucracy had little real public responsibility, its members could find satisfaction and enhanced social prestige in polishing their classical Chinese, translating Buddhist sutras, painting, or composing poetry of a rather

Cultural progress under imperial patronage

Benten Playing on a Biwa. A Japanese painting on silk by an artist of the Heian (Fujiwara) period, 893–1185.

strained and artificial type. The refinement of ceremony and etiquette also received much attention. Life in court circles tended to become effete and frivolous, but it harbored some artistic and intellectual talent of high caliber. The best Japanese literature of this period was produced by women of the nobility and of the imperial household. Their contributions, outstanding in the tenth and eleventh centuries, were chiefly prose, typically in the form of diaries but including one justly famous romantic novel (*Tale of Genji*). In this instance it was fortunate that women, even of the court, were not held to the same educational standards as men. "While the men of the period were pompously writing bad Chinese, their ladies consoled themselves for their lack of education by writing good Japanese, and created, incidentally, Japan's first great prose literature."[5]

4. THE FOUNDATION OF CIVILIZATIONS IN AFRICA SOUTH OF THE SAHARA

The dilemmas of African development

Civilizations in much of sub-Saharan Africa did not develop as early, as rapidly, and as fully as their counterparts in Asia, Central and South America, and western Europe. (It is worth noting that the scholarly yardstick against which "development" has been measured in the West is firmly rooted in the European experience.) The fact that most of these civilizations did not develop their own systems of writing, did not evolve a body of law, did not articulate their own individualistic religious systems on the scale of Islam or Christianity, and did not place greater emphasis on the individual than on the collectivity has confounded scholars for years. There are no thoroughly satisfying explanations in sight. What they do know is that most of sub-Saharan Africa has suffered for more than a millennium from a devastating combination of developmental restraints.

Parasitic diseases and agriculture

Historically, no other continent has been so challenged by parasitic diseases that debilitate humans and livestock. Settled agriculture contributed to the spread of malaria, hookworm, sleeping sickness, and river blindness. The dreaded tsetse fly devastated cattle and human populations, limiting protein intake and precluding the use of draft animals and wheeled vehicles. High temperatures, erratic rainfall, and fragile, highly oxidized clay soils that made plows impractical combined to make farming extremely difficult and uncertain. Many hunter-gatherers stoutly resisted farming as a way of life because it was perceived as manifestly harder and in some ways more limiting than their own. Indigenous food plants were not well suited to the task of supporting a growing population in the face of serious ecological stresses. African populations generally remained thinly distributed be-

[5] E. O. Reischauer, *Japan, the Story of a Nation*, pp. 34–35.

fore the introduction from overseas of highly nutritious food staples that could sustain higher population densities.

In the absence of high population densities the need for centralized, coercive polities was not as acute as it was in western Europe and Asia, and monumental public-works projects were neither possible nor desirable. Writing on paper was not entirely feasible in humid sub-Saharan climates where the ravages of mold and termites made preservation problematic. In drier regions suitable wood and cotton fibers were generally unavailable until recent centuries. Knowledge, therefore, had to be committed to memory, which made data accumulation, processing, and accessibility difficult.

*Implications for politics and
the state of knowledge*

The vast expanses of the Atlantic and Indian oceans and the expanding Sahara Desert made contact with the outside world difficult, dangerous, and expensive. This meant that much of the continent, with the notable exception of northern and northeastern Africa, was spared massive invasions and systematic exploitation from without until the modern era. However, this relative isolation also limited cultural and technological exchange and other benefits of exposure to diverse civilizations. In some parts of the world the mining of salt and precious ores fueled rapid technological advancement. But in Africa a rudimentary technological base limited the expansion of salt, gold, and copper production in many areas. The constraints of transportation, scattered populations, and poverty circumscribed demand and impeded the easy expansion of exchange. Even the terrain of sub-Saharan Africa—the coastline boasts few natural harbors, and most of the rivers have irregular flows and are broken by cataracts—posed serious obstacles to the movement of populations, cultures, and commodities within the subcontinent.

*Geographical and cultural
isolation*

Much of sub-Saharan Africa was unaffected by the ancient Hebrew emphasis on the individual as opposed to the collective, and on the written word in contrast to the oral tradition. No single language existed to bind people together or to foster the spread of a universalistic religion. No systems of thought emerged to discourage veneration or divination of ancestors. The concept of private property was alien to the African experience and would not take root until modern times. As a result, the land and many material objects belonged not to the living but to the dead and, therefore, could not be radically transformed or even moderately reformed. In these remarkably conservative societies significantly more time was devoted to reenacting time-honored rituals than to questioning and reflection. Africans looked not so much to the perfection of the individual as to the protection and survival of the community—the extended family, the clan, and the lineage. In many African societies the emphasis was on cooperation rather than on competition. Nature was not to be challenged and conquered but to be revered. Notions of time were driven by the seasons and mattered little in the evaluation of labor productivity. Nonconformists were often banished or, later, sold into slavery in distant lands. When Africa

*Tradition and the African
world view*

finally came into sustained contact with the external world, the trade in slaves added a series of constraints; it slowed population growth and contributed to a general regression in social relationships; it deprived sub-Saharan Africa of substantial numbers of ablebodied people just at a time when its doors were opening on the world beyond. In many areas, private enterprise and capital accumulation were circumscribed not only by a lack of monetarization of the economy but by the dynamics of the extended family. Wealth was not to be reinvested or concentrated in the hands of individuals but to be distributed to less well endowed members of the extended family. Labor and loyalty were often obtained by manipulating structures of reciprocal obligations rather than from wages.

Uniquely African civilizations

Early African societies were not marked by a lack of originality, ability, or diversity. On the contrary, they responded to a harsh environment in a variety of imaginative, rational, and distinctive ways. Many of sub-Saharan Africa's institutions were probably created relatively free of external influences before the influx of Muslims from the north and east and, later, Europeans from the west. The resulting civilizations were uniquely African.

Metallurgy

From very early times, isolated groups of Africans developed exceptionally advanced skills in metallurgy. At least 1,500 years ago Africans on the western shore of Lake Victoria in East Africa produced medium carbon steel in forced-draft furnaces. Their sophisticated technique would not be matched by Europeans for centuries. Inexplicably, the African practice did not seem to have radiated beyond the ancestors of the present Haya people of modern Tanzania. Of greater conse-

The Iron Age in Africa. An iron smelter in Tanzania such as those that enabled th Bantu to create iron tools and weapons.

quence to Africa was the smelting of iron for the production of spears and hoes.

The Iron Age came to Africa quite early, with isolated sites dating to the sixth century B.C. in northern Ghana, Nigeria, northwestern Tanzania, and Ethiopia. Other sites along the Upper Nile and near East Africa's Great Lakes extend to the fourth and third centuries B.C. The East African sites owe nothing to south Arabian inspiration. But in West Africa, iron-smelting techniques may have filtered across the Sahara from Phoenician coastal settlements in North Africa. For unknown reasons, the African Iron Age did not diffuse widely or rapidly until the first century A.D., when it was carried southward by the intrepid Bantu-speakers. Before the end of the century these Bantu-speakers encountered high-yield food crops, including coco-yams, plantain, and the nutritious banana, in the watershed of the Congo-Zambezi River system. These plants apparently spread up the Zambezi River valley from Madagascar where they had been introduced by seagoing Southeast Asians of Javanese origins. Interestingly, this exchange worked both ways as African-derived sorghums became a major South Asian food crop in the first millennium B.C. Domesticated agriculture then took root with remarkable speed as the Bantu-speakers, equipped with sturdy iron hoes and machetes, were able to clear forests and to cultivate the new food crops.

Iron and the dispersion of the Bantu-speakers

Iron metallurgy, together with superior southeast Asian crops, greatly accelerated the transition from a food-gathering to a food-producing economy. By 200 A.D. agricultural surpluses had triggered a population explosion among the Bantu, propelling them in easterly and westerly directions across the breadth of equatorial Africa from coast to coast. Small, segmented Neolithic populations were either absorbed or eliminated by the Bantu, who enjoyed greater social cohesion and practiced efficient methods of farming and pastoralism. With plentiful food and meat, they could support many wives and large, extended families. Consequently, their numbers quickly multiplied.

Southeast Asian food crops trigger population explosions

Food-producing economies led to the emergence of village life. Trade became a necessary handmaiden to agriculture as metallurgists bartered their finished tools for iron ore, copper, salt, and other essential commodities. By the close of the tenth century, most Africans were using iron implements; and from the Cameroons to the South African veld they spoke Bantu-related languages. Bantu peoples had thus initiated an agricultural revolution and accelerated the development of new mechanisms for social organization and control in East, Central, and Southern Africa. In effect, they laid the necessary foundations for the civilizations which emerged in the millennium after 900 A.D.

The emergence of village life and trading activity

Iron technology brought forth similar changes in West Africa, even though the Bantu diaspora did not extend there. For centuries Nubians from the Upper Nile and Saharan Berbers, bearing iron tools and

Agriculture. A Ndebele granary in southern Zimbabwe. The ability to sustain sedentary village life depended on the community's ability to stockpile foodstuffs.

weapons, had infiltrated Negro cultures of the West African grasslands. Marrying local women, they quickly lost their ethnic identity. An excellent environment for fishing and cereal cultivation in the Niger River area and Chad basin had already stimulated a dramatic growth of the indigenous population.

The impact of iron in West Africa

While historians have paid considerable attention to the importance of trans-Saharan trade for the development of West Africa, recent archeological excavations in the area of the ancient city of Jenne on the Niger River clearly suggest that a wide regional network of trade routes existed in West Africa before the advent of the Arab trans-Saharan trade. Indeed, new evidence has revealed that a vigorous trade in gold, copper, and iron was keyed into an existing system of African-initiated sub-Saharan trade networks. Moreover, the establishment of towns and markets may have predated the dynamic growth of the trans-Saharan trade in the seventh and eighth centuries A.D. by as much as several centuries.

Regional trade networks

Before the introduction of the camel, Carthaginians and later Romans had conducted a minuscule Saharan trade by horse-drawn chariot. But few if any of them ever established direct commercial connections with West Africans. Their small purchases of gold, ivory, slaves, and pepper were made through the middlemen of Garamante in the Fezzan oases of central Sahara. The clever Garamantes received glass beads, fine cloth, and dates which they passed on to the West African producers. By 750 A.D. Arabian single-humped camels had come into wide use in the Sahara as transport vehicles. Camels possessed an exceptional capacity for carrying heavy loads over long distances without food or water and maneuvering effectively under

Introduction of the camel in the trans-Saharan trade

sandy conditions. They became, in effect, ships of the desert and greatly facilitated the movement of peoples and goods between North and West Africa. An ensuing revival and expansion of trans-Saharan trade also contributed to the eventual flowering of market centers and coherent civilizations in the grassland expanse between southern Mauretania and Lake Chad.

Roman departure from North Africa in the fourth century A.D. seems to have coincided with the organization by desert Berbers of the first West African kingdom, called Ghana, or Awkar. This Negro-Berber state, located in the southeastern corner of modern Mauretania, thrived on its middleman position between the gold miners of the southern forests and the Berber traders of North Africa. By the eighth century the "Ghana," or king, of Awkar was a Negro, and his people were known in North Africa and the Middle East as the world's major gold exporters.

Trans-Saharan traffic remained small and informally organized until the mid-seventh century when Muslim Arabs overran the strategic Fezzan oases. By 740 A.D. desert Berbers had begun to embrace Islam and to withdraw more deeply into the Sahara where they set up new trade centers. At Sijilmasa they exchanged Ghanaian gold with the Arabs for Saharan salt. The salt was resold in the south to perspiring miners while the Arabs carried their gold into North Africa and Europe. It was at this time that this great barren area acquired its present name. In Arabic *sahra* means "desert," and Sahara is plural. The Sahara is indeed many deserts.

The Arab presence in North Africa encouraged Berbers to probe more deeply into West Africa in search of gold or to seek refuge from Islamic persecution. Zaghawa Berbers established communities of highly cultured farmers and fishermen around Lake Chad. In 846 A.D. they founded a ruling dynasty, based on concepts of divine kingship. Like the Berbers in Ghana, they readily married into local families and were ethnically absorbed within a few generations.

Small chieftaincies were gradually coalescing into larger governing units from the upper Senegal eastward to the shores of Lake Chad. By about 800 A.D. trade routes had reached the upper Niger River, where caravan paths from Morocco, Algeria, Tunis, Tripoli, and Egypt converged at the emporium of Gao. The entire sub-Saharan region, from Mauritania to the Red Sea, was known in Arab and Berber commercial circles as the Bilad al-Sudan or "Land of the Blacks." Later, *sudan* became the generic term for the band of open savanna country immediately south of the Sahara.

Similar commercial and political trends were discernible along the coast of East Africa. The rise of Persian sea power in the late seventh century resulted in the eclipse of Ethiopian trade in the Red Sea and western Indian Ocean. Arabs from the Persian Shiraz swarmed along the Banadir coast of modern Somalia, where they established permanent trading settlements. Within a few generations they turned their

Foundation of Ghana, West Africa's first kingdom

The Arab invasion of North Africa

The Berbers in West Africa

The West African Sudan: Land of the Blacks

Indo-Shirazi encounters with the Bantu along the East African coast

Gateway to a Medieval City in the Sultanate of Morocco. Morocco was a major trading partner of the Western Sudanic cities and had a significant architectural impact on the area.

sailing boats, or dhows, southward along the coast of modern Kenya and Tanzania. There they encountered Bantu-speaking people who, centuries before, had reached the coast from the equatorial savanna. These Bantu peoples had already established distinct cultures and trading networks deep in the hinterlands of southern Africa. Thus, attempts to attribute the origins of interior African civilizations to Indo-Arabian stimuli seem increasingly unconvincing. Recent archeological findings contradict earlier theories that contact with the supposedly more advanced cultures of western Asia and India triggered the evolution of interior African civilizations.

The Indian Ocean trade

By 900 A.D. the Bantu were beginning to marry into Arab Shirazi and Indian families, who had only recently converted to Islam. Together they founded dynasties and organized a formal seaborne trade propelled by monsoon winds. As of old, turtle shells, ivory, rhinoceros horns, and small numbers of slaves were exported to Arabian ports and northwestern India. But by 900 A.D. increasing quantities of Central African copper had begun to arrive on the Mozambique coast. Growing Asian demands for copper led to trading operations through the Zambezi valley to reach the mines of Katanga. Indian Ocean trade, like that of the Sahara, acted as a powerful catalyst for the centralization of authority among groups engaged in mining and marketing activities.

The flowering of Nubian civilization

Meanwhile, in the sixth century along the upper reaches of the Nile, a number of Christian Nubian kingdoms appeared. The Nubians, though influenced by Byzantine Greece, developed their own language, laid out beautiful cities, constructed impressive brick monasteries and cathedrals, and adorned them with paintings. They also enjoyed a highly sophisticated tradition of ceramic art, with pottery of outstanding design. Their civilization reached its zenith during the ninth and tenth centuries. Powerful Nubian armies were strong enough to resist Muslim intrusions for nearly four centuries afterward.

SELECTED READINGS

• *Items so designated are available in paperback editions.*
• Binyon, Laurence, *Painting in the Far East*, 3d ed., New York, 1923.
• ———, *The Spirit of Man in Asian Art*, New York, 1935.
• Nakamura Hajime, *Ways of Thinking of Eastern Peoples: India, China, Tibet, Japan*, ed. P. P. Wiener, Honolulu, 1964.

INDIA—*See also Readings for Chapter* 5

Babb, L. A., *The Divine Hierarchy: Popular Hinduism in Central India*, New York, 1975. Examines the relationship between caste, social structure, and popular religion.
• Basham, A. L., *The Wonder That Was India*, rev. ed., New York, 1963.
Berkson, Carmel, *The Caves at Aurangabad: Early Buddhist Tantric Art in India*, Seattle, 1986. Illustrated description of recently excavated fifth- and sixth-century rock-cut temples.
Goyal, S. R. *Harsha and Buddhism*, Meerut, India, 1986. Disputes the claim that Harsha converted to Buddhism.
• Hiltebeitel, Alf, *The Cult of Draupadi*, vol. 1. Examines a southeast Indian cult typical of devotional Hinduism.
• O'Flaherty, W. D., et al., *Elephanta: The Cave of Shiva*, Princeton, 1983. Illustrated.
Sen, Gertrude E., *The Pageant of India's History*, Vol. I, New York. 1948.
Thapar, R., *A History of India*, part I, Harmondsworth, 1966.

CHINA—*See also Readings for Chapter* 6

Bagchi, P. C., *India and China, a Thousand Years of Cultural Relations*, rev. ed., New York, 1951.
Balazs, Etienne, *Chinese Civilization and Bureaucracy*, New Haven, 1964. An important interpretation of Chinese society.
Carter, T. F., and L. C. Goodrich, *The Invention of Printing in China and Its Spread Westward*, 2d ed., New York, 1955.
• Ch'en, Kenneth, *Buddhism in China, A Historical Survey*, Princeton, 1974. A solid and lucid study.
Ching, Julia, *Confucianism and Christianity: A Comparative Study*, New York, 1977.
• Lattimore, Owen, *The Inner Asian Frontiers of China*, 2d ed., New York, 1951.
• Levenson, J. R., and F. Schurmann, *China, an Interpretive History: From the Beginnings to the Fall of Han*, Berkeley, 1969.
Loewe, Michael, *Chinese Ideas of Life and Death: Faith, Myth, and Reason in the Han Period*, London, 1982. Incorporates evidence from tomb excavations.

Shryock, J. K., *The Origin and Development of the State Cult of Confucius*, New York, 1932.

Sickman, L., and A. Soper, *The Art and Architecture of China*, Baltimore, 1956. Reliable; richly illustrated.

• Sullivan, Michael, *The Arts of China*, rev. ed., Berkeley, 1978. Incorporates recent archeological discoveries.

• Wang Zhongshu, *Han Civilization*, tr. K. C. Chang, New Haven, 1982.

• Wittfogel, K. A., *Oriental Despotism: A Comparative Study of Total Power*, New Haven, 1957. Attempts to explain the despotic character of the Chinese imperial government by the necessities of a "hydraulic society," in which flood control and efficient irrigation systems were imperative.

Wright, Arthur F., *Buddhism in Chinese History*, Stanford, 1959. Brief but good.

Zurcher, E., *The Buddhist Conquest of China: The Spread and Adaptation of Buddhism in Early Medieval China*, 2 vols., Leiden, 1959. An illuminating study of the interaction between Chinese culture and Buddhism to the early fifth century A.D.

JAPAN

Anesaki, Masaharu, *Art, Life and Nature in Japan*, Boston, 1933.

Brower, R. H., and E. Miner, *Japanese Court Poetry*, Stanford, 1961. Covers the period from the sixth to the fourteenth centuries.

Cole, Wendell, *Kyoto in the Momoyama Period*, Norman, Okla., 1967.

Eliot, Charles, *Japanese Buddhism*, New York, 1959. A standard text.

• Fenollosa, E. F., *Epochs of Chinese and Japanese Art*, New York, 1927.

• Hall, J. W., *Japan: From Prehistory to Modern Times*, New York, 1971.

Langer, P. F., *Japan, Yesterday and Today*, New York, 1966. An excellent summary.

• Moore, C. A., ed., *The Japanese Mind: Essentials of Japanese Philosophy and Culture*, Honolulu, 1967.

• Morris, Ivan, *The World of the Shining Prince*, Baltimore, 1969.

• Munsterberg, Hugo, *The Arts of Japan: An Illustrated History*, Rutland, Vt., 1957.

• Reischauer, E. O., *Japan: The Story of a Nation*, New York, 1979. Lucid and well organized.

Sansom, George B., *A History of Japan to 1934*, Stanford, 1958. An outstanding work by an eminent British scholar.

———, *Japan: A Short Cultural History*, rev. ed., New York, 1962.

Swann, Peter C., *An Introduction to the Arts of Japan*, New York, 1958.

• Varley, H. P., *Japanese Culture*, 3rd ed., Honolulu, 1984.

• Warner, Langdon, *The Enduring Art of Japan*, Cambridge, Mass., 1952.

Wheatley, Paul, and Thomas See, *From Court to Capital: A Tentative Interpretation of the Origins of the Japanese Urban Tradition*, Chicago, 1978.

Whitney, J. H., and R. K. Beardsley, *Twelve Doors to Japan*, New York, 1965.

AFRICA

Adams, William Y., *Nubia—Corridor to Africa*, London, 1977.

• Bovill, E. W., *The Golden Trade of the Moors*. New York, 1958.

• Curtin, Philip D., *Cross-Cultural Trade in World History*, Cambridge, 1984.

Fage, J. D., ed., *The Cambridge History of Africa, c. 500 B.C. to A.D. 1050,* vol. 2, Cambridge, 1978.

Hall, Martin, *Settlement Patterns in the Iron Age of Zululand: An Ecological Interpretation,* Oxford, 1980.

Herbert, Eugenia, *Red Gold of Africa: Copper in Precolonial History and Culture,* Madison, Wis., 1984.

Lovejoy, Paul, *Salt of the Desert: A History of Salt Production and Trade in Central Sudan,* London, 1986.

Oliver, Roland, and Brian Fagan, eds., *Africa in the Iron Age c. 500 B.C. to A.D. 1400,* Cambridge, 1975.

Phillipson, D. W., *The Early Prehistory of Eastern and Southern Africa,* London, 1977.

• Posnansky, Merrick, ed., *Prelude to East African History,* London, 1966.

Shaw, Thurstan C., *Nigeria: Its Archaeology and Early History,* London, 1977.

SOURCE MATERIALS

Aston, W. G., tr., *Nihongi: Chronicles of Japan from the Earliest Times to* A.D. *697,* 2 vols., London, 1896.

Ayscough, Florence, ed., *Tu Fu, the Autobiography of a Chinese Poet,* London, 1934.

Beal, Samuel, tr., *Buddhist Records of the Western World,* 2 vols., London, 1884.

• *Bhagavad-Gita As It Is,* Los Angeles, 1968. Translation and explication by Bhaktivedanta Swami Prabhupada.

Bynner, Witter, and Kiang Kanghu, trs., *The Jade Mountain, a Chinese Anthology,* New York, 1929.

• de Bary, W. T., ed., *Sources of Chinese Tradition,* "The Imperial Age: Ch'in and Han"; "Neo-Taoism and Buddhism," New York, 1960.

• ———, ed., *Sources of Indian Tradition,* "Hinduism," New York, 1958.

• ———, ed., *Sources of Japanese Tradition,* "Ancient Japan"; "The Heian Period," New York, 1964.

• Fage, J. D., and R. A. Oliver, eds., *Papers in African Prehistory,* New York, 1970.

• Hueckstedt, R. A., *The Style of Bāna: An Introduction to Sanskrit Prose Poetry,* Lanham, Md., 1985.

Huntingford, G. W. B., tr., *The Periplus of the Erythraean Sea,* London, 1980.

• Keene, Donald, ed., *Anthology of Japanese Literature, from the Earliest Era to the Mid-Nineteenth Century,* New York, 1956.

Lu, David, ed., *Sources of Japanese History,* Vol. I, New York, 1973.

Morris, Ivan., tr., *As I Crossed the Bridge of Dreams: Recollections of a Woman in Eleventh-Century Japan.*

Oliver, Roland, ed., *The Cambridge Encyclopedia of Africa,* Cambridge, 1981.

Sanskrit Dramas: *Sakuntala, The Little Clay Cart.*

• van Buitenen, J. A. B., *Tales of Ancient India,* Chicago, 1959.

Waley, Arthur, tr., *Ballads and Stories from Tun-Huang, an Anthology* (T'ang era); *The Tale of Genji; Translations from the Chinese,* New York, 1960.

• Watson, Burton, tr., *Columbia Book of Chinese Poetry,* New York, 1984.

Part Three

THE WORLD IN
THE MIDDLE AGES

The term "Middle Ages" was coined by Europeans in the seventeenth century to express their view that a long and dismal period of interruption extended between the glorious accomplishments of classical Greece and Rome and their own "modern age." Because the term became so widespread, it is now an ineradicable part of our historical vocabulary; but no serious scholar uses it with the sense of contempt it once had. Between about 600 and 1500—the rough opening and closing dates of the Middle Ages—too many different things happened to be characterized in any single way. In the eastern parts of the old Roman Empire two new civilizations emerged, the Byzantine and the Islamic, which must rank among the most impressive civilizations of all time. Although the Byzantine civilization came to an end in 1453, the Islamic one has continued to exist without major interruption right up to the present. Seen from an Islamic perspective, therefore, the "Middle Ages" was not a middle period at all but a marvelous time of birth and vigorous early youth. The history of western Europe in the Middle Ages is conventionally divided into three parts: the early Middle Ages; the High Middle Ages; and the later Middle Ages. Throughout the early, High, and later Middle Ages the Christian religion played an extraordinarily important role in human life, but otherwise there are few common denominators. The early Middle Ages, from about 600 to about 1050, came closest to appearing like an interval of darkness, for the level of material and intellectual accomplishment was, in fact, very low.

Nonetheless, even during the early Middle Ages important foundations were being laid for the future: above all, western Europe was beginning to develop its own distinct sense of cultural identity. The High Middle Ages, from about 1050 to 1300, was one of the most creative epochs in the history of human endeavor. Europeans greatly improved their standard of living, established enduring national states, developed new institutions of learning and modes of thought, and created magnificent works of literature and art. During the later Middle Ages, from about 1300 to 1500, the survival of many high-medieval accomplishments was threatened by numerous disasters, particularly profound economic depression and lethal plague. But people in the later Middle Ages rose above adversity, tenaciously held on to what was most valuable in their inheritance, and, where necessary, created new institutions and thought-patterns to fit their altered circumstances. The Middle Ages thus were really many hundred years of enormous diversity. They may be studied profitably both for their own intrinsic interest and for the fundamental contributions they made to the development of the modern world.

During the 900-year period comprising Europe's Middle Ages, other parts of the world witnessed changes of various kinds, some of them highly dynamic. The great nations of southern and eastern Asia continued their cultural evolution along lines already established. Hindu culture and society suffered a rude shock when Muslim invaders from Afghanistan threw northern India into chaos, but gradually a degree of accommodation evolved between the two sharply contrasting faiths. Adherents of Islam were to be henceforth a significant minority in India, and for several centuries Muslim Turkish sultans ruled from Delhi as their capital. While India was experiencing convulsions, China maintained its political structure and enjoyed unprecedented prosperity, approaching the threshold of an industrial revolution. This progress was interrupted by the Mongol occupation of China during the thirteenth and fourteenth centuries. The Ming Dynasty, which ousted the Mongols, reverted to a policy of cautious conservatism. Chinese culture remained basically intact but henceforth showed little capacity for growth or innovation. Although not invaded like India and China, Japan had several centuries of internal turbulence, during which its society not only survived but in some respects gained new strength. A type of feudalism arose resembling the system which was to play a prominent role in the evolution of European society. But in contrast to western Europe during its feudal age, in Japan commerce and urban growth continued apace, peasants occupied a pivotal position, and great territorial lords developed efficient administrations which could eventually be utilized in unifying the country.

In Africa the religion of Islam spread rapidly, especially in the north and west of the continent. Muslim Arabs and Berbers promoted commerce, which in turn accelerated the process of state building. In the later Middle Ages the decadent Byzantine Empire fell to the Turks, a people of Central Asian origin who, after conversion to Islam, embarked on a program of vigorous expansion. The Ottoman Empire, which made Constantinople its capital in 1453, constituted a successor state both to Byzantium and to the Islamic kingdoms of northern Africa and the Near East. At the close of the Middle Ages it was stronger and more prosperous than any contemporary European state.

Without any discernible stimulus from the societies of Asia or Europe, in a few favored areas of the Americas civilizations had emerged, the most advanced of which were the Mayan in Central America and the Yucatán peninsula of Mexico, and the Inca civilization in the Andean region of South America. The Aztecs, most warlike of the Indian peoples, dominated the central valley of Mexico. None of these civilizations was able to survive the shock of European conquests of the sixteenth century.

The European Middle Ages

	POLITICS	PHILOSOPHY AND SCIENCE
600	Byzantine Emperor Heraclius, 610–641 Muhammad enters Mecca in triumph, 630 Muslims conquer Syria, Persia, and Egypt, 636–651	
	Muslims conquer Spain, 711	
700	Muslim attack on Constantinople repulsed, 717	
	Charles Martel defeats Muslims at Poitiers, 732	
	Abbasid dynasty in Islam, 750–1258 Pepin the Short anointed king of the Franks, 751	
800	Charlemagne, 768–814 Charlemagne crowned emperor, 800	
	Carolingian Empire disintegrates, c. 850–911	
	Alfred the Great of England, 871–899	
	High point of Viking raids in Europe, c. 880–911	Al-Farabi, d. 950
900	Otto the Great of Germany, 936–973	
1000	Foundation of Kievan state in Russia, c. 950 Norman Conquest of England, 1066 Seljuk Turks defeat Byzantines at Manzikert, 1071 Penance of Henry IV at Canossa, 1077	Avicenna, d. 1037 Peter Abelard, 1079–1142
1100	Henry I of England, 1100–1135	Origins of universities in the West, c. 1100–c. 1300
	Louis VI of France, 1108–1137	Translation of Aristotle's works into Latin, c. 1140–c. 1260
	Frederick I (Barbarossa) of Germany, 1152–1190	Peter Lombard's *Sentences,* c. 1155
	Henry II of England, 1154–1189	Robert Grosseteste, c. 1168–1253
	Philip Augustus of France, 1180–1223	Windmill invented, c. 1180
1200		Averroës, d. 1198 Maimonides, d. 1204
	Crusaders take Constantinople (Fourth Crusade), 1204	
	Spanish victory over Muslims at Las Navas de Tolosa, 1212	
	Frederick II of Germany and Sicily, 1212–1250	Roger Bacon, c. 1214–1294 St. Thomas Aquinas, 1225–1274
	Magna Carta, 1215 Louis IX (St. Louis) of France, 1226–1270	Height of Scholasticism, c. 1250–c. 1277 William of Ockham, c. 1285–1349 Mechanical clock invented, c. 1290
	Edward I of England, 1272–1307	
1300	Philip IV (the Fair) of France, 1285–1314	Master Eckhart, active c. 1300–c. 1327
	Hundred Years' War, 1337–1453 Political chaos in Germany, c. 1350–c. 1450	Height of nominalism, c. 1320–c. 1500
1400	Appearance of Joan of Arc, 1429–1431	
	Reassertion of royal power in France, c. 1143–c. 1513 Rise of princes in Germany, c. 1450–c. 1500	Printing with movable type, c. 1450 Heavy artillery helps Turks capture Constantinople and French end Hundred Years' War, 1453
	Capture of Constantinople by Ottoman Turks, 1453 Wars of the Roses in England, 1455–1485 Peace among northern Italian states, 1454–1485 Marriage of Ferdinand and Isabella, 1469 Ivan III lays groundwork for Russian Empire, 1462–1505 Strong Tudor dynasty in England, 1485–1603	

The European Middle Ages (continued)

ECONOMICS	RELIGION	ARTS AND LETTERS	
Decline of towns and trade in the West, c. 500–c. 700	Muhammad, c. 570–632 Pope Gregory I, 590–604 Muhammad's *Hijrah,* 622	Byzantine church of Santa Sophia, 532–537	*600*
Height of Islamic commerce and industry, c. 700–c. 1300 Predominantly agrarian economy in the West, c. 700–c. 1050	Split in Islam between Shiites and Sunnites, c. 656 Missionary work of St. Boniface in Germany, c. 715–754 Iconoclasm in Byzantine Empire, 726–843	The Venerable Bede, d. 735 *Beowulf,* c. 750 Irish "Book of Kells," c. 750 Carolingian Renaissance, c. 800–c. 850	*700*
Height of Byzantine commerce and industry, c. 800–c. 1000	Foundation of Cluny, 910 Byzantine conversion of Russia, c. 988 Beginning of Reform Papacy, 1046		*800*
Destruction of Byzantine free peasantry, c. 1025–c. 1100 Agricultural advance, revival of towns and trade in the West, c. 1050– c. 1300	Schism between Roman and Eastern Orthodox Churches, 1054 Pope Gregory VII, 1073–1085 St. Bernard of Clairvaux, 1090–1153 First Crusade, 1095–1099 Height of Cistercian monasticism, c. 1115–c. 1153 Concordat of Worms ends investiture struggle, 1122	Romanesque style in architecture and art, c. 1000–c. 1200 *Song of Roland,* c. 1095 Troubadour poetry, c. 1100–c. 1220	*900* *1000* *1100*
	Crusaders lose Jerusalem to Saladin, 1187 Pope Innocent III, 1198–1216 Albigensian Crusade, 1208–1213 Founding of Franciscan Order, 1210 Fourth Lateran Council, 1215 Founding of Dominican Order, 1216	*Rubaiyat* of Umar Khayyam, c. 1120 Anna Comnena's biography of Alexius, 1148 Gothic style in architecture and art, c. 1150–c. 1500 Poetry of Chretien de Troyes, c. 1165–c. 1190 Development of polyphony in Paris, c. 1170 Wolfram von Eschenbach, c. 1200 Gottfried von Strassburg, c. 1210	*1200*
	Fall of last Christian outposts in Holy Land, 1291 Pope Boniface VIII, 1294–1303	Persian poetry of Sadi, c. 1250 *Romance of the Rose,* c. 1270	
European economic depression, c. 1300–c. 1450 Floods through western Europe, 1315 Black Death, 1347–1350 Height of Hanseatic League, c. 1350–c. 1450 English Peasants' Revolt, 1381 Medici Bank, 1397–1494	Babylonian Captivity of papacy, 1305–1378 John Wyclif, c. 1330–1384 Great Schism of papacy, 1378–1417 John Hus preaches in Bohemia, c. 1408–1415 Council of Constance, 1414–1417 Hussite Revolt, 1420–1434 *Imitation of Christ,* c. 1427 Council of Basel, defeat of conciliarism, 1431–1449	Paintings of Giotto, c. 1305–1337 Dante's *Divine Comedy,* c. 1310 Boccaccio's *Decameron,* c. 1350 Persian poetry of Hafiz, c. 1370 Chaucer's *Canterbury Tales,* c. 1390 Paintings of Jan van Eyck, c. 1400–c. 1441	*1300* *1400*

The Non-European World, 600–1600

	AFRICA AND AMERICA	INDIA	EAST ASIA
	Teotihuacán culture in Mexico (c. 300 B.C.–700 A.D.)	Great stone temple architecture, c. 550–1250	
	Expansion of Bantu people, 200–900	Sanskrit drama, c. 600–1000	T'ang Dynasty in China, 618–907
	Mayan civilization in Central America (c. 300–1500)	King Harsha, 606–648	Taika Reform Edict, creating imperial government in Japan, 645
	Tiahuanaco culture in South America (c. 600–1000)		
700	Muslim conquest of Egypt, 641		
800			
900			Wood-block printing of books in China, Japan, and Korea, c. 900
			Sung Dynasty in China, 960–1279
1000	Expansion of Islam, 1000–1500	Muslim invasions, 1000–1500	
	Consolidation of states, 1000–1500		
	Inca civilization in South America (c. 1000–1500)		
1100	Bantu, Arab, and Indian cultures blend in Swahili civilization along eastern coast, c. 1100–1500		Neo-Confucianism, 1130–1200
			Highest development of landscape painting in China, 1141–1279
			Explosive powder used in weapons in China, c. 1150
			Genghis Khan, 1162?–1227
			Establishment of Shogunate in Japan, 1192
1200			Zen Buddhism in Japan, c. 1200
		Turkish Sultanate at Delhi, 1206–1526	Inoculation for smallpox in China, c. 1200
	Decline of Kingdom of Ghana, c. 1224		Development of Chinese drama, c. 1235
1300	Mali empire in middle Niger region, c. 1300–1500		Marco Polo in China, 1275–1292
	Tenochtitlán (Mexico City) founded by Aztecs, 1325		Mongol (Yüan) Dynasty in China, 1279–1368
	University of Timbuktu, c. 1330		Rise of daimyo in Japan, 1300–1500
			Ming Dynasty in China, 1368–1644
1400		Sack of Delhi by Timur, 1398	
	Expansion of Songhay, c. 1493–1582		

AFRICA AND AMERICA   INDIA   EAST ASIA

1500

Founding of Sikh religious
  sect, c. 1500

Introduction of Christianity
  into Japan, 1549–1551

Decline of Songhay after
  defeat by Moroccans, 1591

Chapter 12

ROME'S THREE HEIRS: THE BY-ZANTINE, ISLAMIC, AND EARLY-MEDIEVAL WESTERN WORLDS

Constantinople is a bustling city, and merchants come to it from all over, by sea or land, and there is none like it in the world except Baghdad, the great city of Islam. In Constantinople is the church of Santa Sophia, and the seat of the Pope of the Greeks, since the Greeks do not obey the Pope of Rome. There are also as many churches as there are days of the year. A quantity of wealth is brought to them from the islands, and the like of this wealth is not to be found in any other church in the world.

—Benjamin of Tudela, *Travels*

You have become the best community ever raised up for mankind, en-joining the right and forbidding the wrong, and having faith in God.

—The Koran, III, 110

He who ordains the fate of kingdoms and the march of events, the al-mighty Disposer, having destroyed one extraordinary image, that of the Romans, which had feet of iron, or even feet of clay, then raised up among the Franks the golden head of a second image, just as remarkable, in the person of the glorious Charlemagne.

—A monk of St. Gall

A new period in the history of Western civilizations began in the seventh century, when it became clear that there would no longer be a single empire ruling over all the territories border-ing on the Mediterranean. By about 700 A.D., in place of a united Rome, there were three successor civilizations that stood as rivals on different Mediterranean shores: the Byzantine, the Islamic, and the Western Christian. Each of these had its own language and distinctive forms of life. The Byzantine civilization, which descended directly from the Eastern Roman Empire, was Greek-speaking and dedicated to combining Roman governmental traditions with intense pursuit of

The successors of Rome

the Christian faith. The Islamic civilization was Arabic-speaking and inspired in government as well as culture by the idealism of a dynamic new religion. Western Christian civilization in comparison to the others was a laggard. It was the least economically advanced and faced organizational weaknesses in both government and religion. But it did have some base of unity in Christianity and the Latin language, and would soon begin to find greater political and religious cohesiveness.

*Reappraisal of the
Byzantine and Islamic
civilizations*

Because the Western Christian civilization ultimately outstripped its rivals, Western writers until recently have tended to denigrate the Byzantine and Islamic civilizations as backward and even irrational. Of the three, however, the Western Christian was certainly the most backward from about the seventh to the eleventh centuries. For some four or five hundred years the West lived in the shadow of Constantinople and Mecca. Scholars are only now beginning to recognize the full measure of Byzantine and Islamic accomplishments. These greatly merit our attention both for their own sakes and because they influenced western European development in many direct and indirect ways.

1. THE BYZANTINE EMPIRE AND ITS CULTURE

*The Byzantine
achievement impressive
despite weaknesses*

Once dismissed by the historian Gibbon as "a tedious and uniform tale of weakness and misery," the story of Byzantine civilization is today recognized as a most interesting and impressive one. It is true that the Byzantine Empire was in many respects not very innovative; it was also continually beset by grave external threats and internal weaknesses. Nonetheless it managed to survive for a millennium. In fact the empire did not just survive, it frequently prospered and greatly influenced the world around it. Among many other achievements, it helped preserve ancient Greek thought, created magnificent works of art, and brought Christian culture to pagan peoples, above all the Slavs. Simply stated it was one of the most enduring and influential empires the world has ever known.

*Problems of periodization
in Byzantine history*

It is impossible to date the beginning of Byzantine history with any precision because the Byzantine Empire was the uninterrupted successor of the Roman state. For this reason different historians prefer different beginnings. Some argue that "Byzantine" characteristics already emerged in Roman history as a result of the easternizing policy of Diocletian, and others that Byzantine history began when Constantine moved his capital from Rome to Constantinople, the city which subsequently became the center of the Byzantine world. (The old name for the site on which Constantinople was built was Byzantium, from which we get the adjective Byzantine; it would be more accurate but cumbersome to say Constantinopolitine.) Diocletian and Constantine, however, continued to rule a united Roman Empire. As we have seen, as late as the sixth century, after the western part of the empire had fallen to the Germans, the Eastern Roman Emperor Justinian thought of himself as an heir to Augustus and fought hard to win back the West. Justinian's reign was clearly an important turning point in the direction of Byzantine civilization because it saw the crystallization of new forms of thought and art that can be considered more "Byzantine" than "Roman." But this still remains a matter of subjective emphasis: some scholars emphasize these newer forms, while others respond that Justinian continued to speak Latin and dreamed of restoring old Rome. Only after 610 did a new dynasty emerge that came from the East, spoke Greek, and maintained a fully Eastern or properly "Byzantine" policy. Hence although good arguments can be made for beginning Byzantine history with Diocletian, Constantine, or Justinian, we will begin here with the accession in 610 of the Emperor Heraclius.

It is also convenient to begin in 610 because from then until 1071 the main lines of Byzantine military and political history were determined by resistance against successive waves of invasions from the East. When Heraclius came to the throne the very existence of the Byzantine Empire was being challenged by the Persians, who had conquered almost all of the empire's Asian territories. As a symbol of their triumph the Persians in 614 even carried off the relic believed to be part of the original cross from Jerusalem. By enormous effort Heraclius rallied Byzantine strength and turned the tide, routing the Persians and retrieving the cross in 627. Persia was then reduced to subordination and Heraclius reigned in glory until 641. But in his last years new armies began to invade Byzantine territory, swarming out of hitherto placid Arabia. Inspired by the new religion of Islam and profiting from Byzantine exhaustion after the struggle with Persia, the Arabs made astonishingly rapid gains. By 650 they had taken most of the Byzantine territories the Persians had occupied briefly in the early seventh century, had conquered all of Persia itself, and were making their way westward across North Africa. Having become a Mediterranean power, the Arabs also took to the sea. In 677 they tried to conquer Constantinople with a fleet. Failing that, they attempted to take the city again in 717 by means of a concerted land and sea operation.

The Arab threat to Constantinople in 717 was a new low in Byzantine fortunes, but the threat was countered by the Emperor Leo the Isaurian (717–741) with as much resolution as Heraclius had met the Persian threat a century before. With the help of a secret incendiary device known as "Greek fire"[1] and great military ability, Leo was able

---

[1] This is believed to have been a mixture of sulfur, naphtha, and quicklime. Bronze tubes placed on the prows of ships, and also on the walls of Constantinople, released this liquid fire at the enemy.

The reign of Heraclius; the rise of Islam

The Byzantine Emperor Heraclius, Shown Together with His Son. Comparison to coins of Trajan and Theodosius (above, pp. 245, 268) shows at a glance that a new style of civilization has emerged with much less attachment to naturalistic portraiture.

Greek Fire

Byzantine revival prior to the Battle of Manzikert

The Emperor John I (969–976) Being Crowned by Christ. Byzantine rulers characteristically used coins as objects of propaganda designed to show that their powers came to them supernaturally.

to defeat the Arab forces on sea and land. Leo's relief of Constantinople in 717 was one of the most significant battles in European history, not just because it allowed the Byzantine Empire to endure for centuries more, but also because it helped to save the West: had the Islamic armies taken Constantinople there would have been little to stop them from sweeping through the rest of Europe. Over the next few decades the Byzantines were able to reconquer most of Asia Minor. This territory, together with Greece, became the heartland of their empire for the next three hundred years. Thereafter the Byzantines achieved a stalemate with Islam until they were able to take the offensive against a decaying Islamic power in the second half of the tenth century. In that period—the greatest in Byzantine history—Byzantine troops reconquered most of Syria. But in the eleventh century a different Islamic people, the Seljuk Turks, cancelled out all the prior Byzantine gains. In 1071 the Seljuks annihilated a Byzantine army at Manzikert in Asia Minor, a stunning victory which allowed them to overrun the remaining Byzantine eastern provinces. Constantinople was now thrown back upon itself more or less as it had been in the days of Heraclius and Leo.

After Manzikert the Byzantine Empire managed to survive, but never regained its earlier vigor. One major reason for this was the fact that, from 1071 until the final destruction of the empire in 1453, Byzantine fortunes were greatly complicated by the rise of western Europe. Hitherto the West had been far too weak to present any major challenge to Byzantium, but that situation changed entirely in the course of the eleventh century. In 1071, the same year that saw the victory of the Seljuks over the Byzantines in Asia Minor, westerners known as Normans expelled the Byzantines from their last holdings in southern Italy. Despite this clear sign of Western enmity, in 1095 a Byzantine emperor named Alexius Comnenus issued a call for Western help against the Turks. He could hardly have made a worse mistake: his call helped inspire the Crusades, and the Crusades became a major cause for the fall of the Byzantine state. Westerners on the First Crusade did help the Byzantines win back Asia Minor but they also carved out territories for themselves in Syria, which the Byzantines considered to be their own. As time went on frictions mounted and the westerners, now militarily superior, looked more and more upon Constantinople as a fruit ripe for the picking. In 1204 they finally picked it: Crusaders who should have been intent on conquering Jerusalem conquered Constantinople instead and sacked the city with ruthless ferocity. A greatly reduced Byzantine government was able to survive nearby and return to Constantinople in 1261, but thereafter the Byzantine state was an "empire" in name and recollection of past glories only. After 1261 it eked out a reduced existence in parts of Greece until 1453, when powerful Turkish successors to the Seljuks, the Ottomans, completed the Crusaders' work of destruction by conquering the last vestiges of the empire and taking Constantinople. Turks rule in Constantinople—now Istanbul—even today.

That Constantinople was finally taken was no surprise. What *is* a cause for wonder is that the Byzantine state survived for so many centuries in the face of so many different hostile forces. This wonder becomes all the greater when it is recognized that the internal political history of the empire was exceedingly tumultuous. Because Byzantine rulers followed their late-Roman predecessors in claiming the powers of divinely appointed absolute monarchs, there was no way of opposing them other than by intrigue and violence. Hence Byzantine history was marked by repeated palace revolts; mutilations, murders, and blindings were almost commonplace. Byzantine politics became so famous for their behind-the-scenes complexity that we still use the word "Byzantine" to refer to highly complex and devious backstage machinations. Fortunately for the empire, some very able rulers did emerge from time to time to wield their untrammeled powers with efficiency, and, even more fortunately, a bureaucratic machinery continued to function during times of palace upheaval.

Factors contributing to the stability of the Byzantine Empire: (1) occasional able rulers

Efficient bureaucratic government indeed was one of the major elements of Byzantine success and longevity. The Byzantines could count on having an adequate supply of manpower for their bureaucracy because Byzantine civilization preserved and encouraged the practice of education for the laity. This was one of the major differences between the Byzantine East and the early Latin West: from about 600 to about 1200 there was practically no literate laity in Western Christendom, while lay literacy in the Byzantine East was the basis of governmental accomplishment. Byzantine officialdom regulated many aspects of life, far more than we would think proper

(2) efficient bureaucratic administration

today. Bureaucrats helped supervise education and religion and presided over all forms of economic endeavor. Urban officials in Constantinople, for example, regulated prices and wages, maintained systems of licensing, controlled exports, and enforced the observance of the Sabbath. What is more, they usually did this with comparative efficiency and did not stifle business initiative. Bureaucratic methods too helped regulate the army and navy, the courts, and the diplomatic service, endowing them with organizational strengths incomparable for their age.

(3) firm economic base

Another explanation for Byzantine endurance was the comparatively sound economic base of the state until the eleventh century. As the historian Sir Steven Runciman has said, "if Byzantium owed her strength and security to the efficiency of her Services, it was her trade that enabled her to pay for them." While long-distance trade and urban life all but disappeared in the West for hundreds of years, commerce and cities continued to flourish in the Byzantine East. Above all, in the ninth and tenth centuries Constantinople was a vital trade emporium for Far Eastern luxury goods and Western raw materials. The empire also nurtured and protected its own industries, most notably that of silk-making, and it was renowned until the eleventh century for its stable gold and silver coinage. Among its great urban centers was not only Constantinople, which at times may have had a population of close to a million, but also in certain periods Antioch, and up until the end of Byzantine history the bustling cities of Thessalonica and Trebizond.

The significance of Byzantine agricultural history

Historians emphasize Byzantine trade and industry because these were so advanced for the time and provided most of the surplus wealth which supported the state. But agriculture was really at the heart of the Byzantine economy as it was of all premodern ones. The story of Byzantine agricultural history is mainly one of a struggle of small peasants to stay free of the encroachments of large estates owned by wealthy aristocrats and monasteries. Until the eleventh century the free peasantry just managed to maintain its existence with the help of state legislation, but after 1025 the aristocracy gained power in the government and began to transform the peasants into impoverished tenants. This had many unfortunate results, not the least of which was that the peasants became less interested in resisting the enemy. The defeat at Manzikert was the inevitable result. The destruction of the free peasantry was accompanied and followed in the last centuries of Byzantine history by foreign domination of Byzantine trade. Primarily the Italian cities of Venice and Genoa established trading outposts and privileges within Byzantine realms after 1204, which channeled off much of the wealth on which the state had previously relied. In this way the empire was defeated by the Venetians from within before it was destroyed by the Turks from without.

So far we have spoken about military campaigns, government, and economics as if they were at the center of Byzantine survival. Seen from hindsight they were, but what the Byzantines themselves cared about most was usually religion. Remarkable as it might seem, Byzantines fought over abstruse religious questions as vehemently as we today might argue about politics and sports—indeed more vehemently because the Byzantines were often willing to fight and even die over some words in a religious creed. The intense preoccupation with questions of doctrine is well illustrated by the report of an early Byzantine writer who said that when he asked a baker for the price of bread, the answer came back, "the Father is greater than the Son," and when he asked whether his bath was ready, was told that "the Son proceeds from nothing." Understandably such zealousness could harm the state greatly during times of religious dissension but endow it with a powerful sense of confidence and mission during times of religious concord.

Byzantine religious dissensions were greatly complicated by the fact that the emperors took an active role in them. Because the emperors carried great power in the life of the Church—emperors were sometimes deemed by churchmen to be "similar to God"—they exerted great influence in religious debates. Nonetheless, especially in the face of provincial separatism, rulers could never force all their subjects to believe what they did. Only after the loss of many eastern provinces and the refinement of doctrinal formulae did religious peace seem near in the eighth century. But then it was shattered for still another century by what is known as the Iconoclastic Controversy.

The Iconoclasts were those who wished to prohibit the worship of icons—that is, images of Christ and the saints. Since the Iconoclastic movement was initiated by the Emperor Leo the Isaurian, and subsequently directed with even greater energy by his son Constantine V (740–775), historians have discerned in it different motives. One was certainly theological. The worship of images seemed to the Iconoclasts to smack of paganism. They believed that nothing made by human beings should be worshiped by them, that Christ was so divine that he could not be conceived of in terms of human art, and that the prohibition of worshiping "graven images" in the Ten Commandments (Exodus 20:4) placed the matter beyond dispute.

Iconoclasts' Cross. The Iconoclasts covered over beautiful apse mosaics with unadorned crosses. This example survives in St. Irene's church, Greece.

In addition to these theological points, there were probably other considerations. Since Leo the Isaurian was the emperor who saved Constantinople from the onslaught of Islam, and since Muslims zealously shunned images on the grounds that they were "the work of Satan" (Koran, V. 92), it has been argued that Leo's Iconoclastic policy was an attempt to answer one of Islam's greatest criticisms of Christianity and thereby deprive Islam of some of its appeal. There may also have been certain internal political and financial motives. By proclaiming a radical new religious movement the emperors may have wished to reassert their control over the Church and combat the

Christ as Ruler of the Universe. A twelfth-century Byzantine mosaic from the cathedral of Cefalù in Sicily. Although the Byzantines did not rule in Sicily in the twelfth century, the Norman rulers employed Byzantine workmen. Note the use of Greek—the Byzantine language—on the left-handed Bible page and Latin—the Norman language—on the right.

growing strength of monasteries. As events turned out, the monasteries did rally behind the cause of images, and as a result, they were bitterly persecuted by Constantine V, who took the opportunity to appropriate much monastic wealth.

Significance of the Iconoclastic Controversy

The Iconoclastic Controversy was resolved in the ninth century by a return to the status quo, namely the worship of images, but the century of turmoil over the issue had some profound results. One was the destruction by imperial order of a large amount of religious art. Pre–eighth-century Byzantine religious art that survives today comes mostly from places like Italy or Palestine, which were beyond the easy reach of the Iconoclastic emperors. When we see how great this art is we can only lament the destruction of the rest. A second consequence of the controversy was the opening of a serious religious breach between East and West. The pope, who until the eighth century had usually been a close ally of the Byzantines, could not accept Iconoclasm for many reasons. The most important of these was that extreme Iconoclasm tended to question the cult of saints, and the claims of papal primacy were based on an assumed descent from St. Peter. Accordingly, the eighth-century popes combated Byzantine Iconoclasm and turned to the Frankish kings for support. This "about-face of the papacy" was both a major step in the worsening of East-West relations and a landmark in the history of western Europe.

Other results: (1) reaffirmation of tradition

Those were some consequences of Iconoclasm's temporary victory; a major consequence of its defeat was the reassertion of some major traits of Byzantine religiosity, which from the ninth century until the end of Byzantine history remained predominant. One of these was the reemphasis of a faith in traditionalism. Even when Byzantines were experimenting in religious matters they consistently stated that they were only restating or developing the implications of tradition. Now, after centuries of turmoil, they abandoned experiment almost entirely and reaffirmed tradition more than ever. As one opponent of Iconoclasm said: "If an angel or an emperor announces to you a gospel other than the one you have received, close your ears." This view gave strength to Byzantine religion internally by ending controversy and heresy, and helped it gain new adherents in the ninth and tenth centuries. But it also inhibited free speculation not just in religion but also in related intellectual matters.

Allied to this development was the triumph of Byzantine contemplative piety. Supporters defended the use of icons not on the grounds that they were meant to be worshiped for themselves but because they helped lead the mind from the material to the immaterial. The emphasis on contemplation as a road to religious enlightenment thereafter became the hallmark of Byzantine spirituality. While westerners did not by any means reject such a path, the typical Western saint was an activist who saw sin as a vice and sought salvation through good works. Byzantine theologians on the other hand saw sin more as ignorance and believed that salvation was to be found in illumination. This led to a certain religious passivity and mysticism in Eastern Christianity which makes it seem different from Western varieties up to the present time.

(2) the triumph of Byzantine contemplative piety

Since religion was so dominant in Byzantine life, certain secular aspects of Byzantine civilization often go unnoticed, but there are good reasons why some of these should not be forgotten. One is Byzantine cultivation of the classics. Commitment to Christianity by no means inhibited the Byzantines from revering their ancient Greek heritage. Byzantine schools based their instruction on classical Greek literature to the degree that educated people could quote Homer more extensively than we today can quote Shakespeare. Byzantine scholars studied and commented on the philosophy of Plato and Aristotle, and Byzantine writers imitated the prose of Thucydides. Such dedicated classicism both enriched Byzantine intellectual and literary life, which is too often dismissed entirely by moderns because it generally lacked originality, and helped preserve the Greek classics for later ages. The bulk of classical Greek literature that we have today survives only because it was copied by Byzantine scribes.

Byzantine classicism

Byzantine classicism was a product of an educational system for the laity which extended to the education of women as well as men. Given attitudes and practices in the contemporary Christian West and Islam, Byzantine commitment to female education was truly unusual. Girls from aristocratic or prosperous families did not go to schools but were relatively well educated at home by private tutors. We are told, for example, of one Byzantine woman who could discourse like Plato or Pythagoras. The most famous Byzantine female intellectual was the Princess Anna Comnena, who described the deeds of her father

The education of women

Santa Sophia. The greatest monument of Byzantine architecture. The four minarets were added after the fall of the Byzantine Empire, when the Turks turned the church into a mosque. As the diagram shows, the central dome rests on four massive arches.

Byzantine architecture; the Church of Santa Sophia

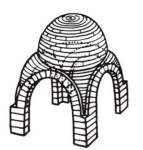

Diagram of Santa Sophia Dome

Novel structural design

Alexius in an urbane biography in which she copiously cited Homer and Euripides. In addition to such literary figures there were women doctors in the Byzantine Empire, a fact which may serve to remind us that there have hardly been any in America until recent times.

Byzantine achievements in the realms of architecture and art are more familiar. The finest example of Byzantine architecture was the Church of Santa Sophia (Holy Wisdom), built at enormous cost in the sixth century. Although built before the date taken here as the beginning of Byzantine history, it was typically Byzantine in both its style and subsequent influence. Though designed by architects of Hellenic descent, it was vastly different from any Greek temple. Its purpose was not to express human pride in the power of the individual, but to symbolize the inward and spiritual character of the Christian religion. For this reason the architects gave little attention to the external appearance of the building. Nothing but plain brick covered with plaster was used for the exterior walls; there were no marble facings, graceful columns, or sculptured entablatures. The interior, however, was decorated with richly colored mosaics, gold leaf, colored marble columns, and bits of tinted glass set on edge to refract the rays of sunlight after the fashion of sparkling gems. To emphasize a sense of the miraculous, the building was constructed in such a way that no light appeared to come from the outside at all but to be manufactured within.

The structural design of Santa Sophia was something altogether new in the history of architecture. Its central feature was the application of the principle of the dome to a building of square shape. The church was designed, first of all, in the form of a cross, and then over the central square was to be erected a magnificent dome, which would dominate the entire structure. The main problem was how to fit the round circumference of the dome to the square area it was supposed to cover. The solution consisted in having four great arches spring from pillars at the four corners of the central square. The rim of the dome was then made to rest on the keystones of the arches, with the curved triangular spaces between the arches filled in with masonry. The result was an architectural framework of marvelous strength, which at the same time made possible a style of imposing grandeur and even some delicacy of treatment. The great dome of Santa Sophia has a diameter of 107 feet and rises to a height of nearly 180 feet from the floor. So many windows are placed around its rim that the dome appears to have no support at all but to be suspended in midair.

As in architecture, so in art the Byzantines profoundly altered the earlier Greek classical style. Byzantines excelled in ivory-carving, manuscript illumination, jewelry-making, and, above all, the creation of mosaics—that is, designs of pictures produced by fitting together small pieces of colored glass or stone. Human figures in these mosaics were usually distorted and elongated in a very unclassical fashion to create the impression of intense piety or extreme majesty. Most Byzantine art is marked by highly abstract, formal, and jewel-like qualities. For this reason many consider Byzantine artistic culture to be a model of timeless perfection. The modern poet W. B. Yeats expressed this point of view most eloquently when he wrote in his "Sailing to Byzantium" of artificial birds made by Byzantine goldsmiths ". . . to sing / To lords and ladies of Byzantium / Of what is past, or passing, or to come."

Probably the single greatest testimony to the vitality of Byzantine civilization at its height was the conversion of many Slavic peoples, especially those of Russia. According to the legend, which has a basic kernel of fact, a Russian ruler named Vladimir decided around 988 to abandon the paganism of his ancestors. Accordingly, he sent emissaries to report on the religious practices of Islam, Roman Catholicism, and Byzantine Christianity. When they returned to tell him that only among the Byzantines did God seem to "dwell among men," he promptly agreed to be baptized by a Byzantine missionary. The event was momentous because Russia thereupon became a cultural province of Byzantium. From then until the twentieth century Russia remained a bastion of the Eastern Orthodox religion.

After Constantinople fell in 1453 Russians began to feel that they were chosen to carry on both the faith and the imperial mission of the fallen Byzantine Empire. Thus their ruler took the title of tsar—which simply means caesar—and Russians asserted that Moscow was "the third Rome": "Two Romes have fallen," said a Russian spokesman, "the third is still standing, and a fourth there shall not be." Such ideology helps explain in part the later growth of Russian imperialism. Byzantine traditions also may help explain the dominance of the ruler in the Russian state. Without question Byzantine stylistic principles

See color plates facing page 295

Byzantine Metalwork. **This dish,** from about 620, represents literally David and Goliath, and figuratively the New Dispensation (David was the ancestor of Christ) overcoming the Old. The New, Christian, Dispensation is also symbolized by the sun, and the Old by a crescent moon.

Russian Icon. This early–seventeenth-century Russian painting depicts an angel in a distinctly Byzantine style.

The Byzantine contribution to Western civilization

influenced Russian religious art, and Byzantine ideas influenced the thought of modern Russia's greatest writers, Dostoevsky and Tolstoy.

Unfortunately, just at the time when relations between Constantinople and Russia were solidifying, relations with the West were deteriorating to a point of no return. After the skirmishes of the Iconoclastic period relations between Eastern and Western Christians remained tense, partly because Constantinople resented Western claims (initiated by Charlemagne in 800) of creating a rival empire, but most of all because cultural and religious differences between the two were growing. From the Byzantine point of view westerners were uncouth and ignorant, while to western European eyes Byzantines were effeminate and prone to heresy. Once the West started to revive, it began to take the offensive against a weakened East in theory and practice. In 1054 extreme papal claims of primacy over the Eastern Church provoked a religious schism which since then has never been healed. Thereafter the Crusades drove home the dividing wedge.

After the sack of Constantinople in 1204 Byzantine hatred of westerners became understandably intense. "Between us and them," one Byzantine wrote, "there is now a deep chasm: we do not have a single thought in common." Westerners called easterners "the dregs of the dregs . . . unworthy of the sun's light," while easterners called westerners the children of darkness, alluding to the fact that the sun sets in the West. The beneficiaries of this hatred were the Turks, who not only conquered Constantinople in 1453, but soon after conquered most of southeastern Europe up to Vienna.

In view of this sad history of hostility it is best to end our treatment of Byzantine civilization by recalling how much we owe to it. In simple physical terms the Byzantine Empire acted as a bulwark against Islam from the seventh to the eleventh centuries, thus helping to preserve an independent West. If the Byzantines had not prospered and defended Europe, Western Christian civilization might well have been snuffed out. Then too we owe an enormous amount in cultural terms to Byzantine scholars who helped preserve classical Greek learning. The most famous moment of communication between Byzantine and western European scholars came during the Italian Renaissance, when Byzantines helped introduce Italian humanists to the works of Plato. But westerners were already learning from Byzantines before then, and they continued to gain riches from Byzantine manuscripts until the sixteenth century. Similarly, Byzantine art exerted a great influence on the art of western Europe over a long period of time. To take only some of the most famous examples, St. Mark's basilica in Venice was built in close imitation of the Byzantine style, and the art of such great Western painters as Giotto and El Greco owes much in different ways to Byzantine influences. Nor should we stop at listing influences because the great surviving monuments of Byzantine culture retain

St. Mark's Church, Venice. The most splendid example of Byzantine architecture in Italy.

their imposing appeal in and of themselves. Travelers who view Byzantine mosaics in such cities as Ravenna and Palermo are continually awe-struck; others who make their way to Istanbul still find Santa Sophia to be a marvel. In such jeweled beauty, then, the light from the Byzantine East, which once glowed so brightly, continues to shimmer.

2. THE FLOWERING OF ISLAM

In contrast to Byzantine history, which has no clearly datable beginning but a definite end in 1453, the history of Islamic civilization has a clear point of origin, beginning with the career of Muhammad in the seventh century, but no end since Islam, Muhammad's religion, is still a major force in the modern world. Believers in Islam, known as Muslims, currently comprise about one-seventh of the global population: in their greatest concentrations they extend from Africa through the Middle East and the Soviet Union to India, Bangladesh, and Indonesia. All these Muslims subscribe both to a common religion and a common way of life, for Islam has always demanded from its followers not just adherence to certain forms of worship but also adher-

The phenomenon of Islam

ence to set social and cultural norms. Indeed, more than Judaism or Christianity, Islam has been a great experiment in trying to build a worldwide society based on the fullest harmony between religious requirements and precepts for everyday existence. In practice, of course, that experiment has differed in its success and quality according to time and place, but it is still being tested, and it accounts for the fact that there remains an extraordinary sense of community between all Muslims regardless of race, language, and geographical distribution. In this section we will trace the early history of the Islamic experiment with primary emphasis on its orientation toward the West. But it must always be remembered that Islam expanded in many directions and that it ultimately had as much influence on the history of Africa and India as it did on that of Europe or western Asia.

Although Islam spread to many lands it was born in Arabia, so the story of its history must begin there. Arabia, a peninsula of deserts, had been so backward before the founding of Islam that the two dominant neighboring empires, the Roman and the Persian, had not deemed it worthwhile to extend their rule over Arabian territories.

Conditions in Arabia before the rise of Islam

Most Arabs were Bedouins, wandering camel herdsmen who lived off the milk of their animals and the produce, such as dates, that was grown in desert oases. In the second half of the sixth century there was a quickening of economic life owing to a shift in long-distance trade routes. The protracted wars between the Byzantine and Persian Empires made Arabia a safer transit route for caravans going between Africa and Asia than were other areas, and some towns grew to direct and take advantage of this growth of trade. Most prominent of these was Mecca, which not only lay on the junction of major trade routes, but also had long been a local religious center. In Mecca was located the Kabah, a pilgrimage shrine which served as a central place of worship for many different Arabian clans and tribes. (Within the Kabah was the Black Stone, a meteorite worshiped as a miraculous relic by adherents of many different divinities.) The men who controlled this shrine and also directed the economic life of the Meccan area belonged to the tribe of Quraish, an aristocracy of traders and entrepreneurs who provided the area with whatever little government it knew.

Muhammad

Muhammad, the founder of Islam, was born in Mecca to a family of the Quraish about 570. Orphaned early in life, he entered the service of a rich widow whom he later married, thereby attaining financial security. Until middle age he lived as a prosperous trader, behaving little differently from his fellow townsmen, but around 610 he underwent a religious experience which changed the course of his life and ultimately that of a good part of the world. Although most Arabs until then had been polytheists who recognized at most the vague superiority of a more powerful god they called Allah, Muhammad in 610 believed he heard a voice from heaven tell him that there was no god but Allah alone. In other words, as the result of a conversion experi-

The Kabah. It contains the black stone which was supposed to have been miraculously sent down from heaven, and rests in the courtyard of the great mosque in Mecca.

ence he became an uncompromising monotheist. Thereafter he received further messages which served as the basis for a new religion and which commanded him to accept the calling of "Prophet" to proclaim the monotheistic faith to the Quraish. At first he was not very successful in gaining converts beyond a limited circle, perhaps because the leading Quraish tribesmen believed that establishment of a new religion would deprive the Kabah, and therewith Mecca, of its central place in local worship. The town of Yathrib to the north, however, had no such concerns, and its representatives invited Muhammad to emigrate there so that he could serve as a neutral arbiter of local rivalries. In 622 Muhammad and his followers accepted the invitation. Because their migration—called in Arabic the *Hijrah* (or Hegira)—saw the beginning of an advance in Muhammad's fortunes, it is considered by Muslims to mark the beginning of their era: as Christians begin their era with the birth of Christ so Muslims begin their dating system with the *Hijrah* of 622.

Muhammad changed the name of Yathrib to Medina (the "city of the Prophet") and quickly succeeded in establishing himself as ruler of the town. In the course of doing this he consciously began to organize his converts into a political as well as religious community. But he still needed to find some means of support for his original Meccan followers, and he also desired to wreak vengeance on the Quraish for not heeding his calls for conversion. Accordingly, he started leading his followers in raids on Quraish caravans traveling beyond Mecca. The Quraish endeavored to defend themselves, but after a few years Mu-

The consolidation of Muhammad's religion

hammad's band, fired by religious enthusiasm, succeeded in defeating them. In 630, after several desert battles, Muhammad entered Mecca in triumph. The Quraish thereupon submitted to the new faith and the Kabah was not only preserved but made the main shrine of Islam, as it remains today. With the taking of Mecca other tribes throughout Arabia in turn accepted the new faith. Thus, although Muhammad died in 632, he lived long enough to see the religion he had founded become a success.

The doctrines of Islam

The doctrines of Islam are very simple. The word *islam* itself means submission, and the faith of Islam called for absolute submission to God. Although the Arabic name for the one God is Allah, it is mistaken to believe that Muslims worship a god like Zeus or Jupiter who is merely the first among many: Allah for Muslims means the Creator God Almighty—the same omnipotent deity worshiped by Christians and Jews. Instead of saying, then, that Muslims believe "there is no god but Allah," it is more correct to say they believe that "there is no divinity but God." In keeping with this, Muslims believe that Muhammad himself was God's last and greatest prophet, but not that he was God himself. In addition to strict monotheism Muhammad taught above all that men and women must surrender themselves entirely to God because divine judgment was imminent. Mortals must make a fundamental choice about whether to begin a new life of divine service: if they decide in favor of this, God will guide them to blessedness, but if they do not, God will turn away from them and they will become irredeemably wicked. On judgment day the pious will be granted eternal life in a fleshly paradise of delights, but the damned will be sent to a realm of eternal fire and torture. The practical steps the believer can take are found in the Koran, the compilation of the revelations purportedly sent by God to Muhammad, and hence the definitive Islamic scripture. These steps include thorough dedication to moral rectitude and compassion, and fidelity to set religious observances: i.e., a regimen of prayers and fasts, pilgrimage to Mecca, and frequent recitation of parts of the Koran.

*Judeo-Christian influence
on Islam*

The fact that much in the religion of Islam resembles Judaism and Christianity is not just coincidental; Muhammad was definitely influenced by the two earlier religions. (There were many Jews in Mecca and Medina; Christian thought was also known to Muhammad, although more indirectly.) Islam most resembles the two earlier religions in its strict monotheism, its stress on personal morality and compassion, and its reliance on written, revealed scripture. Muhammad proclaimed the Koran as the ultimate source of religious authority but accepted both the Old and New Testaments as divinely inspired. From Christianity Muhammad seems to have derived his doctrines of the last judgment, the resurrection of the body with subsequent rewards and punishments, and his belief in angels (he thought that God's first message to him had been sent by the angel Gabriel). But although Muhammad accepted Jesus Christ as one of the greatest of a long line

The Archangel Gabriel Brings Revelation to Muhammad. A much later Persian conception.

of prophets, he did not believe in Christ's divinity and laid claim to no miracles himself other than the writing of the Koran. He also ignored the Christian doctrine of sacrificial love, and most important, preached a religion without sacraments or priests. For Muslims every believer has direct responsibility for living the life of the faith without intermediaries; instead of priests there are only religious scholars who may comment on problems of Islamic faith and law. Muslims are expected to pray together in mosques, but there is nothing like a Muslim mass. The absence of clergy makes Islam more like Judaism, a similarity which is enhanced by Islamic stress on the inextricable connection between the religious and sociopolitical life of the divinely inspired community. But, unlike Judaism, Islam laid claim to universalism and a unique role in uniting the world as it started to spread far beyond the confines of Arabia.

This move toward world influence began immediately upon Muhammad's death. Since he had made no provision for the future, and since the Arabs had no clear concept of political succession, it was unclear whether Muhammad's community would survive at all. But his closest followers, led by his father-in-law Abu-Bakr and a zealous early convert named Umar, quickly took the initiative by naming Abu-Bakr *caliph* meaning "deputy of the Prophet." Thereafter, for about three hundred years, the caliph was to serve as the supreme religious and political leader of all Muslims. Immediately after becoming caliph Abu-Bakr began a military campaign to subdue various Arabian tribes that had followed Muhammad but were not willing to accept his successor's authority. In the course of this thoroughly successful military action Abu-Bakr's forces began to spill northward over the borders of Arabia. Probably to their surprise they found that they met minimal resistance from Byzantine and Persian forces.

The unification of Arabia after Muhammad: the caliphs

Two Views of the Dome of the Rock, Jerusalem. According to Muslim tradition, Muhammad made a miraculous journey to Jerusalem before his death and left a footprint in a rock. The mosque which was erected over the site in the seventh century is, after the Kabah, Islam's second-holiest shrine.

Arab expansion and conquests

Abu-Bakr died two years after his accession but was succeeded as caliph by Umar, who continued to direct the Arabian invasions of the neighboring empires. In the following years triumph was virtually uninterrupted. In 636 the Arabs routed a Byzantine army in Syria and then quickly swept over the entire area, occupying the leading cities of Antioch, Damascus, and Jerusalem; in 637 they destroyed the main army of the Persians and marched into the Persian capital of Ctesiphon. Once the Persian administrative center was taken, the Persian Empire offered scarcely any more resistance: by 651 the Arabian conquest of the entire Persian realm was complete. Since Byzantium was centered around distant Constantinople, the Arabs were not similarly able to stop its imperial heart from beating. But they did quickly manage to deprive the Byzantine Empire of Egypt by 646 and then swept west across North Africa. In 711 they crossed from there into Spain and quickly took almost all of that area too. Thus within less than a century Islam had conquered all of ancient Persia and much of the old Roman world.

How can we explain this prodigious expansion? The best approach is to see first what impelled the conquerors and then to see what circumstances helped to ease their way. Contrary to widespread belief the early spread of Islam was not achieved through a religious crusade.

At first the Arabs were not at all interested in converting other peoples: to the contrary, they hoped that conquered populations would not convert so that they could maintain their own identity as a community of rulers and tax-gatherers. But although their motives for expansion were not religious, religious enthusiasm played a crucial role in making the hitherto unruly Arabs take orders from the caliph and in instilling a sense that they were carrying out the will of God. What really moved the Arabs out of the desert was the search for richer territory and booty, and what kept them moving ever farther was the ease of acquiring new wealth as they progressed. Fortunately for the Arabs their inspiration by Islam came just at the right time in terms of the weakness of their enemies. The Byzantines and Persians had become so exhausted by their long wars that they could hardly rally for a new effort. Moreover, Persian and Byzantine local populations were hostile to the financial demands made by their bureaucratic empires; also, in the Byzantine lands of Syria and Egypt "heretical" Christians were at odds with the persecuting orthodoxy of Constantinople. Because the Arabs did not demand conversion and exacted fewer taxes than the Byzantines and Persians, they were often welcomed as preferable to the old rulers. One Christian writer in Syria went so far as to say "the God of vengeance delivered us out of the hands of the Romans [i.e., the Byzantine Empire] by means of the Arabs." For all these reasons Islam quickly spread over the vast extent of territory between Egypt and Iran, and has been rooted there ever since.

Reasons for the spread of Islam

While the Arabs were extending their conquests they ran into their first serious political divisions. In 644 the Caliph Umar died; he was replaced by one Uthman, a weak ruler who had the added drawback for many of belonging to the Umayyad family, a wealthy clan from Mecca which had not at first accepted Muhammad's call. Those dissatisfied with Uthman rallied around the Prophet's cousin and son-in-law Ali, whose blood, background, and warrior spirit made him seem a more appropriate leader of the cause. When Uthman was murdered in 656 by mutineers, Ali's partisans raised him up as caliph. But Uthman's powerful family and supporters were unwilling to accept Ali. In subsequent disturbances Ali was murdered and Uthman's party emerged triumphant. In 661 a member of the Umayyad family took over as caliph and that house ruled Islam until 750. Even then, however, Ali's followers did not accept defeat. As time went on they hardened into a minority religious party known as Shiites (*Shi'a* is Arabic for party, or faction); this group insisted that only descendants of Ali could be caliphs or have any authority over the Muslim community. Those who stood instead for the actual historical development of the caliphate and became committed to its customs were called Sunnites (*Sunna* is Arabic for religious custom). The cleft between the two parties has been a lasting one in Islamic history. Often persecuted, Shiites developed great militancy and a deep sense of being the only true preservers of the faith. From time to time they were able to

Division between Shiites and Sunnites

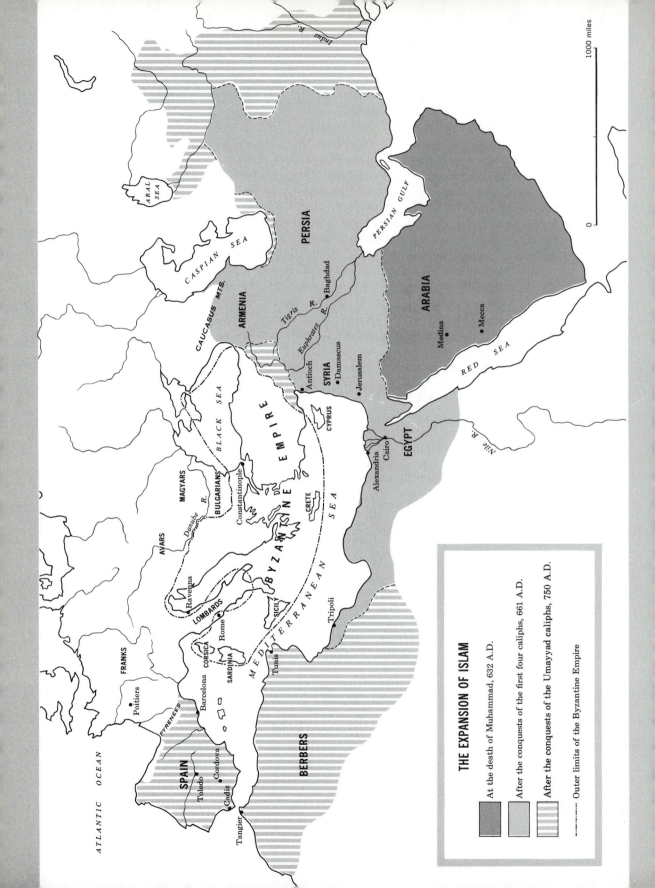

THE EXPANSION OF ISLAM

At the death of Muhammad, 632 A.D.

After the conquests of the first four caliphs, 661 A.D.

After the conquests of the Umayyad caliphs, 750 A.D.

—·—·— Outer limits of the Byzantine Empire

1000 miles

0

ATLANTIC OCEAN

ARAL SEA

CASPIAN SEA

BLACK SEA

MEDITERRANEAN SEA

RED SEA

PERSIAN GULF

Indus R.

Tigris R.

Euphrates R.

Nile R.

Danube R.

CAUCASUS MTS.

PYRENEES

PERSIA

ARABIA

ARMENIA

SYRIA

EGYPT

SPAIN

BYZANTINE EMPIRE

FRANKS

MAGYARS

AVARS

BULGARIANS

LOMBARDS

BERBERS

CORSICA

SARDINIA

SICILY

CRETE

CYPRUS

Mecca

Medina

Baghdad

Antioch

Damascus

Jerusalem

Alexandria

Cairo

Tripoli

Tunis

Rome

Ravenna

Constantinople

Poitiers

Barcelona

Toledo

Cordova

Cadiz

Tangier

seize power in one or another area, but they never succeeded in converting the majority of Muslims. Today they rule in Iran and are very numerous in Iraq but comprise only about one-tenth of the worldwide population of Islam.

The triumph of the Umayyads in 661 began a more settled period in the history of the caliphate, lasting until 945. During that time there were two major governing orientations: that represented by the rule of the Umayyads, and that represented by their successors, the Abbasids. The Umayyads centered their strength in the old Byzantine territories in Syria and continued to use local officials who were not Muslims for their administration. For these reasons the Umayyad caliphate appears to some extent like a Byzantine successor state. With their more Western orientation the Umayyads concentrated their energies on dominating the Mediterranean and conquering Constantinople. When their most massive attack on the Byzantine capital failed in 717, Umayyad strength was seriously weakened; it was only a matter of time before a new orientation would develop.

The Umayyads

This was represented by the takeover of a new family, the Abbasids, in 750. Their rule may be said to have stressed Persian more than Byzantine elements. Characteristic of this change was a shift in capitals, for the second Abbasid caliph built his new capital of Baghdad in Iraq near the ruins of the old Persian capital and even appropriated stones from the ruins. The Abbasids developed their own Muslim administration and imitated Persian absolutism. Abbasid caliphs ruthlessly cut down their enemies, surrounded themselves with elaborate court ceremonies, and lavishly patronized sophisticated literature. This is the world described in the *Arabian Nights,* a collection of stories of dazzling Oriental splendor written in Baghdad under the Abbasids. The dominating presence in those stories, Harun al-Rashid, actually reigned as caliph from 786 to 809 and behaved as extravagantly as he was described, tossing coins in the streets, passing out sumptuous gifts to his favorites and severe punishments to his enemies. From a Western point of view the Abbasid caliphate was of significance not just in creating legends and literature but also because its Eastern orientation took much pressure off the Mediterranean. The Byzantine state, accordingly, was able to revive, and the Franks in the far West began to develop some strength of their own. (The greatest Frankish ruler, Charlemagne, maintained diplomatic relations with the caliphate of Harun al-Rashid, who patronizingly sent the much poorer westerner a gift of an elephant.)

The Abbasids

When Abbasid power began to decline in the tenth century there followed an extended period of decentralization. The major cause for growing Abbasid weakness was the gradual impoverishment of their primary economic base, the agricultural wealth of the Tigris-Euphrates basin. Their decline was further accelerated by the later Abbasids' practice of surrounding themselves with Turkish soldiers, who

Islamic political history after the fall of the Abbasid Empire

soon realized that they could take over actual power in the state. In 945 the Abbasid Empire fell apart when a Shiite tribe seized Baghdad. Thereafter the Abbasids became powerless figureheads until their caliphate was completely destroyed with the destruction of Baghdad by the Mongols in 1258. From 945 until the sixteenth century Islamic political life was marked by localism, with different petty rulers, most often Turkish, taking command in different areas. It used to be thought that this decentralization also meant decay, but in fact Islamic civilization greatly prospered in the "middle period," above all from about 900 to about 1250, a time also when Islamic rule expanded into modern-day Turkey and India. Later, new Islamic empires developed, the leading one in the West being that of the Ottoman Turks, who controlled much of eastern Europe and the Near East from the fifteenth century until 1918. It is therefore entirely false to believe that Islamic history descended upon an ever-downward course sometime shortly after the reign of Harun al-Rashid.

The character of Islamic culture and society

For those who approach Islamic civilization with modern preconceptions, the greatest surprise is to realize that from the time of Muhammad until at least about 1500 Islamic culture and society was extraordinarily cosmopolitan and dynamic. Muhammad himself was not a desert Arab but a town-dweller and trader imbued with advanced ideals. Subsequently, Muslim culture became highly cosmopolitan for several reasons: it inherited the sophistication of Byzantium and Persia; it remained centered at the crossroads of long-distance trade between the Far East and West; and the prosperous town life in most Muslim territories counterbalanced agriculture. Because of the importance of trade there was much geographical mobility. Muhammad's teachings furthermore encouraged social mobility because the Koran stressed the equality of all Muslims. The result was that at the court of Baghdad, and later at those of the decentralized Muslim states, careers were open to those with talent. Since literacy was remarkably widespread—a rough estimate for around the year 1000 is 20 percent of all Muslim males—many could rise through education. Offices were seldom regarded as being hereditary and "new men" could arrive at the top by enterprise and skill. Muslims were also remarkably tolerant of other religions. As stated above, they rarely sought forced conversions, and they generally allowed a place within their own states for Jews and Christians, whom they accepted as "people of the book" because the Bible was seen as a precursor of the Koran. In keeping with this attitude of toleration an early caliph employed a Christian as his chief secretary, the Umayyads patronized a Christian who wrote poetry in Arabic, and Muslim Spain saw the greatest flowering of Jewish culture between ancient and modern times. The greatest fruit of this Jewish flowering was the work of Moses Maimonides (1135–1204), a profound religious thinker, sometimes called "the second Moses," who wrote both in Hebrew and Arabic.

There was one major exception to this rule of Muslim equalitarianism and tolerance: the treatment of women. Perhaps because social status was so fluid, successful men were extremely anxious to preserve and enhance their positions and their "honor." They could accomplish this by maintaining and/or expanding their worldly possessions, which category included women. For a man's females to be most "valuable" to his status, their inviolability had to be assured. The Koran allowed a man to marry four wives, so women were at a premium, and married ones were segregated from other males. A prominent man would also have a number of female servants and concubines, and he kept all these women in a part of his residence called the harem, where they were guarded by eunuchs, i.e., castrated men. Within these enclaves women vied with each other for preeminence and engaged in intrigues to advance the fortunes of their children. Although large harems could be kept only by the wealthy, the system was imitated as far as possible by all classes. Based on the principle that women were chattel, these practices did much to debase women and to emphasize attitudes of domination in sexual life. Male homosexual relations were tolerated in upper-class society, yet they too were based on patterns of domination, usually that of a powerful adult over an adolescent.

Women in Islam

There were two major Islamic avenues for devotion to the particularly religious life. One was that of the *ulama,* learned men who came closest to being like priests. Their job was to study and offer advice on all aspects of religion and religious law. Not surprisingly they usually stood for tradition and rigorous maintenance of the faith; most often they exerted great influence on the conduct of public life. But complementary to them were the *sufis,* religious mystics who might be equated with Christian monks were it not for the fact that they were not committed to celibacy and seldom withdrew from the life of the community. Sufis stressed contemplation and ecstasy as the ulama stressed religious law; they had no common program and in practice behaved very differently. Some sufis were "whirling dervishes," so known in the West because of their dances; others were *faqirs,* associated in the West with snake-charming in marketplaces; and others were quiet meditative men who practiced no exotic rites. Sufis were usually organized into "brotherhoods," which did much to convert outlying areas such as Africa and India. Throughout the Islamic world sufism provided a channel for the most intense religious impulses. The ability of the ulama and sufis to coexist is in itself a remarkable index of Islamic cultural pluralism.

Islamic religious life: the ulama *and the* sufis

More remarkable still is the fact that these two groups often coexisted with representatives of yet another worldview, students and practitioners of philosophy and science. Islamic philosophers were actually called *faylasufs* in Arabic because they were dedicated to the cultivation of what the Greeks had called *philosophia.* Islamic philosophy was based on the study of earlier Greek thought, above all the Aris-

Islamic philosophy

totelian and Neoplatonic strains. Around the time when the philosophical schools were closed in Athens by order of the Emperor Justinian, Greek philosophers migrated east, and the works of Aristotle and others were translated into Syriac, a Semitic dialect. From that point of transmission Greek philosophy gradually entered the life of Islam and became cultivated by the class of faylasufs, who believed that the universe is rational and that a philosophical approach to life was the highest god-given calling. The faylasufs' profound knowledge of Aristotle can be seen, for example, in the fact that Avicenna (d. 1037), one of the greatest of faylasufs, read practically all of Aristotle's works in the Far Eastern town of Bukhara before he reached the age of eighteen.

*The problem of
reconciling Greek ideas
with Islamic religion*

The most serious problem faced by the faylasufs was that of reconciling Greek philosophy with Islamic religion because they followed their Greek sources in believing—in opposition to Islamic doctrine—that the world is eternal and that there is no immortality for the individual soul. Different faylasufs reacted to this problem in different ways. Of the three greatest, Al-Farabi (d. 950), who lived mainly in Baghdad, was least concerned by it; he taught that an enlightened elite could philosophize without being distracted by the binding common beliefs of the masses. Even so, he never attacked these beliefs, considering them necessary to hold society together.

Avicenna and Averroës

Unlike Al-Farabi, Avicenna, who was active farther east, taught a less rationalistic philosophy that came close in many points to sufi mysticism. (A later story held that Avicenna said of a sufi "all I know, he sees," while the sufi replied "all I see, he knows.") Finally, Averroës (1126–98) of Cordova, in Spain, was a thoroughgoing Aristotelian who led two lives, one in private as an extreme rationalist and the other in public as a believer in the official faith, indeed even as an official censor. Averroës was the last really important Islamic philosopher: after him rationalism either blended into sufism, the direction pointed to by Avicenna, or became too constrained by religious orthodoxy to lead an independent existence. But in its heyday between about 850 and 1200 Islamic philosophy was far more advanced and sophisticated than anything found in either the Byzantine or Western Christian realms.

*Islamic science; the
practice of astrology*

Before their decline Islamic faylasufs were as distinguished in studying natural science as they were in philosophical speculation. Usually the same men were both philosophers and scientists because they could not make a living by commenting on Aristotle (there were no universities in which to teach) but could rise to positions of wealth and power by practicing astrology and medicine. Astrology sounds to us today less like science than superstition, but among the Muslims it was an "applied science" intimately related to accurate astronomical observation. After an Islamic astrologer carefully studied and foretold the courses of the heavenly bodies, he would endeavor to apply his knowledge to the course of human events, particularly the fortunes of

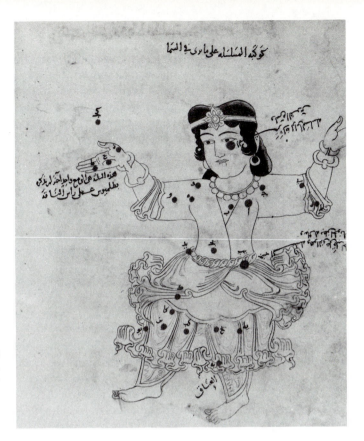

The Planetary Constellation of Andromeda as Visualized by the Muslims. This manuscript illumination executed in western Iran in 1009 A.D. shows clearly how Muslim culture reconceived Greek learning.

wealthy patrons. In order to account most simply for heavenly motions, some Muslims considered the possibilities that the earth rotates on its axis and revolves around the sun, but these theories were not accepted because they did not fit in with ancient preconceptions such as the assumption of circular planetary orbits. It was therefore not in these suggestions that Muslim astrologers later influenced the West, but rather in their extremely advanced observations and predictive tables that often went beyond the most careful work of the Greeks.

Islamic accomplishments in medicine were equally remarkable. Faylasufs serving as physicians appropriated the knowledge contained in the medical writings of the Hellenistic Age but were rarely content with that. Avicenna discovered the contagious nature of tuberculosis, described pleurisy and several varieties of nervous ailments, and pointed out that disease can be spread through contamination of water and soil. His chief medical writing, the *Canon,* was accepted in Europe as authoritative until late in the seventeenth century. Avicenna's older contemporary, Rhazes (865–925), was the greatest clinical physician of the medieval world. His major achievement was the discovery of the difference between measles and smallpox. Other Islamic physicians discovered the value of cauterization and of styptic agents, diagnosed cancer of the stomach, prescribed antidotes for cases of poisoning, and made notable progress in treating diseases of the eyes. In addition,

Islamic contributions to medicine

they recognized the infectious character of bubonic plague, pointing out that it could be transmitted by clothes. Finally, the Muslims excelled over all other medieval peoples in the organization of hospitals and in the control of medical practice. There were at least thirty-four great hospitals located in the principal cities of Persia, Syria, and Egypt, which appear to have been organized in a strikingly modern fashion. Each had wards for particular cases, a dispensary, and a library. The chief physicians and surgeons lectured to the students and graduates, examined them, and issued licenses to practice. Even the owners of leeches, who in most cases were also barbers, had to submit them for inspection at regular intervals.

Optics, chemistry, and mathematics

Other great Islamic scientific achievements were in optics, chemistry, and mathematics. Islamic physicists founded the science of optics and drew a number of significant conclusions regarding the theory of magnifying lenses and the velocity, transmission, and refraction of light. Islamic chemistry was an outgrowth of alchemy, an invention of the Hellenistic Greeks, the system of belief that was based upon the principle that all metals were the same in essence, and that baser metals could therefore be transmuted into gold if only the right instrument, the philosopher's stone, could be found. But the efforts of scientists in this field were by no means confined to this fruitless quest; some even denied the whole theory of transmutation of metals. As a result of experiments by Muslim scientists, various new substances and compounds were discovered, among them carbonate of soda, alum, borax, nitrate of silver, saltpeter, and nitric and sulphuric acids. In addition, Islamic scientists were the first to describe the chemical processes of distillation, filtration, and sublimation. In mathematics Islam's greatest accomplishment was to unite the geometry of the Greeks with the number science of the Hindus. Borrowing what westerners know as "Arabic numerals," including the zero, from the Hindus, Islamic mathematicians were able to develop an arithmetic based on the decimal system and also make advances in algebra (itself an Arabic word). Building upon Greek geometry with reference to heavenly motions, they made great progress in spherical trigonometry. Thus they brought together and advanced all the areas of mathematical knowledge which would later be further developed in the Christian West.

The Great Mosque, Qayrawan, Tunisia. This ninth-century minaret, from which the criers call the faithful to prayer, is a leading monument of the North African Islamic architectural style.

In addition to its philosophers and scientists Islam had its poets too. The primitive Arabs themselves had excelled in writing poetry, and literary accomplishment became recognized as a way to distinguish oneself at court. Probably the greatest of Islamic poets were the Persians (who wrote in their own language), the best known of whom in the West is Umar Khayyam (d. 1123) because his *Rubaiyat* was turned into a popular English poem by the Victorian Edward Fitzgerald. Although Fitzgerald's translation distorts much, Umar's hedonism ("a jug of wine, a loaf of bread—and thou") shows us that all Muslims were by no means dour puritans. Actually Umar's poetry was excelled by the works of Sadi (1193–1292) and Hafiz (d. 1389). And far

The Court of the Lions in the Alhambra, Granada, Spain. The palace-fortress of the Alhambra is one of the finest monuments of the Islamic architectural style. Notable are the graceful columns, the horseshoe arches, and the delicate tracery in stone that surmounts the arches.

from Persia lush poetry was cultivated as well in the courts of Muslim Spain. This poetry too was by no means inhibited, as can be seen from lines like "such was my kissing, such my sucking of his mouth / that he was almost made toothless."

In their artistic endeavors Muslims were highly eclectic. Their main source of inspiration came from the art of Byzantium and Persia. The former contributed many of the structural features of Islamic architecture, especially the dome, the column, and the arch. Persian influence was probably responsible for the intricate, nonnaturalistic designs which were used as decorative motifs in practically all of the arts. From both Persia and Byzantium came the tendency to subordinate form to rich and sensuous color. Architecture was the most important of the Islamic arts; the development of both painting and sculpture was inhibited by religious prejudice against representation of the human form. By no means all of the examples of this architecture were mosques; many were palaces, schools, libraries, private dwellings, and hospitals. Indeed, Islamic architecture had a much more decidedly secular character than any in medieval Europe. Among its principal elements were bulbous domes, minarets, horseshoe arches, and twisted columns, together with the use of tracery in stone, alternating stripes of black and white, mosaics, and Arabic script as decorative devices. As in the Byzantine style, comparatively little attention was given to exterior ornamentation. The so-called minor arts of the Muslims included the weaving of gorgeous pile carpets and rugs, magnificent leather tooling, and the making of brocaded silks and

The eclectic art of the Muslims

Interior of the Great Mosque at Cordova, Spain. This splendid specimen of Moorish architecture gives an excellent view of the cusped arches and alternating stripes of black and white so commonly used by Islamic architects.

tapestries, inlaid metalwork, enameled glassware, and painted pottery. Most of the products of these arts were embellished with complicated patterns of interlacing geometric designs, plants and fruits and flowers, Arabic script, and fantastic animal figures. In general, art laid particular emphasis on pure visual design. Separated from any role in religious teaching, it became highly abstract and nonrepresentational. For these reasons Islamic art often seems more secular and "modern" than any other art of premodern times.

The economic development of the Islamic Empire: (1) commerce

The economic life of the Islamic world varied greatly according to time and place, but underdevelopment was certainly not one of its primary characteristics. On the contrary, in the central areas of Islamic civilization from the first Arab conquests until about the fourteenth century mercantile life was extraordinarily advanced. The principal reason for this was that the Arabs inherited in Syria and Persia an area that was already marked by an enterprising urban culture and that was at the crossroads of the world, lying athwart the major trade routes between Africa, Europe, India, and China. Islamic traders and entrepreneurs built venturesomely on these earlier foundations. Muslim merchants penetrated into southern Russia and even into the equatorial regions of Africa, while caravans of thousands of camels traveled to the gates of India and China. (The Muslims used camels as pack animals instead of building roads and drawing wheeled carts.) Ships from Islam established new routes across the Indian Ocean, the Persian Gulf, and the Caspian Sea. For periods of time Islamic ships also dominated parts of the Mediterranean. Indeed, one reason for subsequent Islamic decline was that the Western Christians took hold of the Mediterranean in the eleventh and twelfth centuries and wrested control of the Indian Ocean in the sixteenth century.

The great Islamic expansion of commerce would scarcely have been possible without a corresponding development of industry. It was the ability of the people of one region to turn their natural resources into finished products for sale to other regions which provided a basis for a large part of the trade. Nearly every one of the great cities specialized in some particular variety of manufactures. Mosul, in Syria, was a center of the manufacture of cotton cloth; Baghdad specialized in glassware, jewelry, pottery, and silks; Damascus was famous for its fine steel and for its "damask" or woven figured silk; Morocco was noted for the manufacture of leather; and Toledo, in Spain, for its excellent swords. The products of these cities did not exhaust the list of manufactures. Drugs, perfumes, carpets, tapestries, brocades, woolens, satins, metal products, and a host of others were turned out by the craftsmen of many cities. From the Chinese the Muslims learned the art of papermaking, and the products of that industry were in great demand, not only within the empire itself but in Europe as well.

(2) industry

In all the areas we have reviewed Islamic civilization so overshadowed that of the Christian West until about the twelfth century that there can be no comparison. When the West did move forward it was able to do so partly because of what it learned from Islam. In the economic sphere westerners profited from absorbing many accomplishments of Islamic technology, such as irrigation techniques, the raising of new crops, papermaking, and the distillation of alcohol. The extent of our debt to Islamic economic influence is well mirrored in the large number of common English words which were originally of Arabic or Persian origin. Among these are traffic, tariff, magazine, alcohol, muslin, orange, lemon, alfalfa, saffron, sugar, syrup, and musk. (Our word admiral also comes from the Arabic—in this case deriving from the title of emir.)

Islamic economic influence on the West

The West was as much indebted to Islam in intellectual and scientific as in economic life. In those areas, too, borrowed words tell some of the story: algebra, cipher, zero, nadir, amalgam, alembic, alchemy, alkali, soda, almanac, and names of many stars such as Aldebaran and Betelgeuse. Islamic civilization both preserved and expanded Greek philosophical and scientific knowledge when such knowledge was almost entirely forgotten in the West. All the important Greek scientific works surviving from ancient times were translated into Arabic and most of these in turn were translated in the medieval West from Arabic into Latin. Above all, the preservation and interpretation of the works of Aristotle was one of Islam's most enduring accomplishments. Not only was Aristotle first reacquired in the West by means of the Arabic translations, but Aristotle was interpreted with Islamic help, above all that of Averroës, whose prestige was so great that he was simply called "the Commentator" by medieval Western writers. Of course Arabic numerals, too, rank as a tremendously important

Intellectual and scientific contributions

General significance of
Islamic civilization

intellectual legacy, as anyone will discover by trying to balance a checkbook with Roman ones.

Aside from all these specific contributions, the civilization of Islam probably had its greatest influence on the West merely by standing as a powerful rival and spur to the imagination. Byzantine civilization was at once too closely related to the Christian West and too weak to serve this function. Westerners usually, for right or wrong, looked down on the Byzantine Greeks, but they more often respected and feared the Muslims. And right they were as well, for Islamic civilization at its zenith (to use another Arabic word) was surely one of the world's greatest. Though loosely organized, it united peoples as diverse as Arabs, Persians, Turks, various African tribes, and Hindus by means of a great religion and common institutions. Unity within multiplicity was an Islamic hallmark, which created both a splendid diverse society and a splendid legacy of original discoveries and achievements.

3. WESTERN CHRISTIAN CIVILIZATION IN THE EARLY MIDDLE AGES

The shaping of a cultural
unity in the early-
medieval West

Western Europeans in the early Middle Ages (the period between about 600 and 1050) were so backward in comparison to their Byzantine and Islamic neighbors that a tenth-century Arabic geographer could write of them that "they have large bodies, gross natures, harsh manners, and dull intellects . . . those who live farthest north are particularly stupid, gross, and brutish." Material conditions throughout this period were so primitive that one can almost speak of five centuries of camping-out. Yet new and promising patterns were definitely taking shape. Above all, a new center of civilization was emerging in the North Atlantic regions. Around 800 the Frankish monarchy, based in agriculturally rich northwestern Europe, managed to create a western European empire in alliance with the Western Christian Church. Although this empire did not last long, it still managed to hew out a new Western cultural unity that was to be an important building block for the future.

The kingdom of the
Franks: the Merovingian
period

Once the Eastern Romans under Justinian had destroyed the Ostrogothic and Vandal kingdoms in Italy and Africa, and the Arabs had eliminated the Visigothic kingdom in Spain, the Frankish rulers in Gaul remained as the major surviving barbarian power in western Europe. But it took about two centuries before they began to exercise their full hegemony. The founder of the Frankish state was the brutal and wily chieftain Clovis, who conquered most of modern-day France and Belgium around 500 and cleverly converted to Western Catholic Christianity, the religion of the local bishops and indigenous population. Clovis founded the Merovingian dynasty (so called from Merovech, the founder of the family to which he belonged). He did not, however, pass on a united realm but followed the typical barbarian custom of dividing up his kingdom among his sons. More or less without interruption for the next two hundred years sons fought sons for a larger share of the Merovingian inheritance. Toward the end of that period the line also began to degenerate, and numerous so-called do-nothing kings left their government and fighting to their chief ministers, known as "mayors of the palace." Throughout this era, one of the darkest in the recorded history of Europe, trade contracted, towns declined, literacy was almost forgotten, and violence was endemic. Minimal agricultural self-sufficiency coexisted with the rule of the battle-axe.

Largely unnoticed, however, some hope for the future was coalescing around the institutions of the Roman papacy and Benedictine monasticism. The architect of a new western European religious policy that was based on an alliance between these two institutions was Pope Gregory I (reigned 590–604), known as St. Gregory the Great. Until his time the Roman popes were generally subordinate to the emperors in Constantinople and to the greater religious prestige of the Christian East, but Gregory sought to counteract this situation by creating a more autonomous Western-oriented Latin Church. This he tried to do in many ways. As a theologian—the fourth great "Latin father" of the Church—he built upon the work of his three predecessors, Jerome, Ambrose, and especially Augustine, in articulating a theology that had its own distinct characteristics. Among these were emphasis on the idea of penance and the concept of purgatory as a place for purification before admission into heaven. (Western belief in purgatory was thereafter to become one of the major differences in the dogmas of the Eastern and Western Churches.) In addition to his theological work, Gregory pioneered in the writing of a simplified unadorned Latin prose that corresponded to the actual spoken language of his contemporaries, and presided over the creation of a powerful Latin liturgy. If Gregory did not actually invent the "Gregorian chant," it was under his impetus that his new plainsong—forever after a central part of the Roman Catholic ritual—developed. All of these innovations helped to make the Christian West religiously and culturally more independent of the Greek-speaking East than it had ever been before.

Gregory the Great was as much a statesman as he was a theologian and shaper of Latin. Within Italy he assured the physical survival of the papacy in the face of the barbarian Lombard threat of his day by clever diplomacy and expert management of papal landed estates. He also began to reemphasize earlier claims of papal primacy, especially over Western bishops, that were in danger of being forgotten. Above all, he patronized the order of Benedictine monks and used them to help evangelize new Western territories. Gregory himself had been a Benedictine—perhaps the first Benedictine monk to become pope—and he wrote the standard life of St. Benedict. Because the Benedictine

Pope Gregory the Great. In this tenth-century German ivory panel the pope is receiving inspiration from the Holy Spirit in the form of a dove.

Gregory's religious policies

order was still very young and the times were turbulent, Gregory's patronage helped the order to survive and later to become for centuries the only monastic order in the West. In return the pope could profit from using the Benedictines to carry out special projects. The most significant of these was the conversion of Anglo-Saxon England to Christianity. This was a long-term project which took about a century to complete, but its great result was that it left a Christian outpost to the far northwest that was thoroughly loyal to the papacy and that would soon help to bring together the papacy and the Frankish state. Gregory the Great himself did not live to see that union, but it was his policy of invigorating the Western Church that most helped to bring it about.

Factors in the increasing stability of Frankish Gaul

Around 700, when the Benedictines were completing their conversion of England, the outlook for Frankish Gaul was becoming somewhat brighter. The most profound reason for this was that the long, troubled period of transition between the ancient and medieval worlds was finally coming to an end. The ancient Roman civilization of cities and Mediterranean trade was in its last gasps in Gaul in the time after Clovis. Then, when the Arabs conquered the southern Mediterranean shore and took to the sea in the seventh century, northwestern Europe was finally thrown back upon itself and forced to look away from the Mediterranean. In fact the lands of the north—modern-day northern France, the Low Countries, Germany, and England—were extremely fertile: with adequate farming implements they could yield great natural wealth. Given the proper circumstances, a new power could emerge in the north to make the most of a new pattern of life based predominantly on agrarianism instead of urban commerce and Mediterranean trade. Around 700 that is exactly what happened in Merovingian Gaul.

The alliance between Frankish rulers and the Church; Charles Martel and St. Boniface

The proper circumstances were the triumph of a succession of able rulers and their alliance with the Church. In 687 an energetic Merovingian mayor of the palace, Pepin of Heristal, managed to unite all the Frankish lands under his rule and build a new power base for his own family in the region of Belgium and the Rhine. He was succeeded by his aggressive son, Charles Martel ("the Hammer"), who is sometimes considered a second founder of the Frankish state. Charles's claim to this title is twofold. First, in 732 he turned back a Muslim force from Spain at the Battle of Tours, some 150 miles from Paris. Although the Muslim contingent was not a real army but merely a marauding band, the incursion was the high-water mark of their progress toward the northwest and Charles's victory won him great prestige. Equally important, around the end of his reign Charles began to develop an alliance with the Church, particularly with the Benedictines of England. Having finished most of their conversion work on their island, the Benedictines, under their idealistic leader St. Boniface, were moving across the English Channel in an attempt to convert central Germany. Charles Martel realized that he and they had common interests, for after he had guarded his southern flank against the Muslims he was seeking to direct Frankish expansion eastward in the direction of Germany. Missionary work and Frankish expansion could go hand in hand, so Charles offered St. Boniface and his Benedictines material aid in return for their support of his territorial aims.

Once allied with the Franks, St. Boniface provided further service in the next reign in helping to contribute to one of the most momentous events in Western history. Charles Martel had never assumed the royal title, but his son, Pepin the Short, wished to take it. Even though Pepin and not the reigning "do-nothing king" was the real power, Pepin needed the prestige of the Church for supporting a change in dynasties. Fortunately for him the times were highly propitious for obtaining Church support. St. Boniface supported Pepin because the young ruler continued his father's policy of collaborating with the Benedictines in Germany. And Boniface had great influence in Rome because the Anglo-Saxon Benedictines had remained in the closest touch with the papacy since the time of Gregory the Great.

The papacy was now fully prepared to cast its own lots with a strong Frankish ruler because it was in the midst of a bitter fight with the Byzantine emperors over Iconoclasm. The Byzantines until then had offered papal territories in Italy some protection against the Lombards, but the increasingly powerful Franks were now fully able to take over that role. The papacy accordingly made an epochal about-face, turning once and for all to the West. In 750 the pope encouraged Pepin to depose the Merovingian figurehead, and in 751 St. Boniface, acting as papal emissary, anointed Pepin as a divinely sanctioned king. Thus the Frankish monarchy attained a spiritual mandate and was fully integrated into the papal-Benedictine orbit. Shortly afterward Pepin paid his debt to the pope by conquering the Lombards in Italy. The West was now achieving its own unity based on the Frankish state and the Latin Church, not coincidentally just at the time when the Abbasid caliphate was being founded in the East and the Byzantines were going their own fully Greek way.

The ultimate consolidation of the new pattern took place in the reign of Pepin's son, Carolus Magnus or Charlemagne (768–814), from whom the new dynasty takes its name of "Carolingian." Without question Charlemagne ranks as one of the most important rulers of the whole medieval period. Had it been possible to ask him what his greatest accomplishment was, he almost certainly would have replied that it lay in greatly increasing the Frankish realm. Except for the English, there was scarcely a people of western Europe against whom he did not fight. Most of his campaigns were successful; he annexed the greater part of central Europe and northern and central Italy to the Frankish domain. To rule this vast area he bestowed all the powers of local government upon his own appointees, called counts, and tried to remain in control of them by sending representatives of the court to observe them. Among the counts' many duties were the administra-

Charlemagne. A silver penny struck between 804 and 814 in Mainz (as indicated by the letter M at the bottom) showing Charlemagne in a highly stylized fashion as emperor with Roman military cloak and laurel. The inscription reads KAROLVS IMP AVG (Charles, Emperor, Augustus). See p. 245, above, for the variety of late-Roman coin portraiture that must have served as the Carolingian minter's model.

The Carolingian Renaissance

tion of justice and the raising of armies. Although Charlemagne's system in practice was far from perfect, it led to the best government that Europe had seen since the Romans. Because of the military triumphs and internal peace of his reign, Charlemagne was long remembered and revered as a western European folk hero.

Primarily to aid his territorial expansion and help administer his realm Charlemagne presided over a revival of learning known as the "Carolingian Renaissance." Charlemagne extended his rule into Germany in the name of Christianity, but in order to proselytize he needed educated monks and priests. More than that, in order to administer his far-flung territories he needed at least a few people who could read and write. Amazing as it may seem to us, at first hardly any people in his entire realm were literate, so thoroughly had the rudiments of learning been forgotten since the decay of Roman city life. Only in Anglo-Saxon England had literacy been cultivated by the Benedictine monks. The reason for this was that the Anglo-Saxons spoke a form of German but the monks needed to learn Latin in order to say their offices and study the Bible. Since they knew no Latin to begin with they had to go about learning it by a very self-conscious program of studies. The greatest Anglo-Saxon Benedictine scholar before Charlemagne's time was the Venerable Bede (d. 735), whose *History of the English Church and People,* written in Latin, was one of the best historical writings of the early-medieval period and can still be read with pleasure. When Charlemagne came to the throne he invited the Anglo-Saxon Benedictine Alcuin—a student of one of Bede's students—to direct a revival of studies on the continent. With Charlemagne's active support Alcuin helped establish new schools to teach reading, directed the copying and correcting of important Latin works, including many Roman classics, and inspired the formulation of a new clear handwriting that is the ancestor of our modern "Roman"

Carolingian Handwriting. Even the untrained reader has little difficulty in reading this excerpt from a Carolingian manuscript.

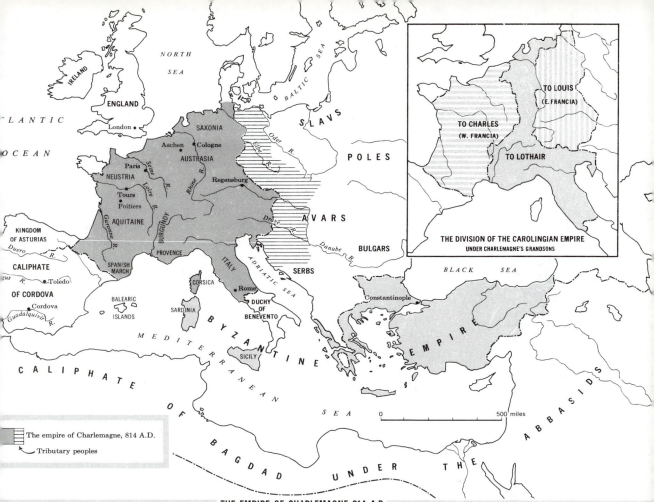

THE EMPIRE OF CHARLEMAGNE 814 A.D.

Within the map:
NORTH SEA
BALTIC SEA
IRELAND
ENGLAND
London
ATLANTIC OCEAN
SAXONIA
Aachen • Cologne
AUSTRASIA
Paris
NEUSTRIA
Seine R.
Rhine R.
Regensburg
Loire R.
Tours
Poitiers
AQUITAINE
Garonne R.
BURGUNDY
PROVENCE
KINGDOM OF ASTURIAS
Duero R.
CALIPHATE OF CORDOVA
Toledo
Cordova
Guadalquivir R.
SPANISH MARCH
BALEARIC ISLANDS
CORSICA
SARDINIA
ITALY
Rome
DUCHY OF BENEVENTO
SICILY
MEDITERRANEAN SEA
CALIPHATE OF BAGDAD UNDER THE ABBASIDS
SLAVS
POLES
Oder R.
Elbe R.
AVARS
Drave R.
Danube R.
BULGARS
SERBS
ADRIATIC SEA
BYZANTINE EMPIRE
Constantinople
BLACK SEA
0   500 miles

The empire of Charlemagne, 814 A.D.
Tributary peoples

Inset:
THE DIVISION OF THE CAROLINGIAN EMPIRE
UNDER CHARLEMAGNE'S GRANDSONS
TO LOUIS (E. FRANCIA)
TO CHARLES (W. FRANCIA)
TO LOTHAIR

print. These were the greatest achievements of the Carolingian Renaissance, which stressed practicality rather than original literary or intellectual endeavors. Thoroughly unpretentious as they were, they established a bridgehead for literacy on the Continent which thereafter would never be completely lost. They also helped to preserve Latin literature, and they made the Latin language the language of state and diplomacy for all of western Europe, as it remained until comparatively recent times.

The climax of Charlemagne's career came in the year 800 when he was crowned emperor on Christmas Day in Rome by the pope. Historians continue to debate whether this was Charlemagne's or the pope's idea, but there is no doubt that the pope did not gain any immediate power from it. Once the Franks ruled Italy they came to dominate the papacy, and indeed the whole Church, to such a degree that by 800 the pope was very close to being Charlemagne's puppet. Charlemagne did not gain any actual new power by taking the imperial title either, but the significance of the event is nonetheless great. Up until 800 the only emperor ruled in Constantinople and could lay

Charlemagne's coronation as emperor

claim to being the direct heir of Augustus. Although the Byzantines had lost most of their interest in the West, they still continued to regard it vaguely as an outlying province and were actively opposed to any westerner calling himself emperor. Charlemagne's assumption of the title was virtually a declaration of Western self-confidence and independence. Since Charlemagne's vast realm was fully as large as that of the Byzantines, had great reserves of agricultural wealth, and was defining its own culture based on Western Christianity and the Latin linguistic tradition, the claim to empire was largely justified. More than that, it was never forgotten. Both for its symbolism and for its contribution toward giving westerners a sense of unity and purpose it was a major landmark on the road to the making of a great western Europe.

Although the claim to empire was bold and memorable, Charlemagne's actual empire disintegrated quickly after his death for many reasons. The simplest was that hardly any of his successors were as competent and decisive as he was. In order to rule an empire in those still extremely primitive times, one had to have enormous reserves of strength and energy—one had to travel on horseback over enormous distances, fight and win battles at the head of unruly armies, and know how to delegate power to others yet guard against its abuse. Unfortunately for western Europe few of Charlemagne's heirs had such combinations of energy and talent. To make matters worse, Charlemagne's sole surviving son, Louis the Pious, who inherited the Frankish realm intact, divided his inheritance among his own three sons, thereby bringing civil war back to Frankish Europe. And to make matters worst of all, new waves of invasions began just as Charlemagne's grandsons and great-grandsons started fighting each other: from the north came the Scandinavian Vikings; from the east came the Asiatic Magyars (or Hungarians); and from the south came new attacks by marauding Muslims, attacking now from the sea. Under these pressures the Carolingian Empire completely fell apart and a new political map of Europe was drawn in the tenth century.

As the Carolingian period was crucial for marking the beginnings of a common North Atlantic western European civilization, so the tenth century was crucial for marking the beginnings of the major modern European political entities. England, which never had been part of Charlemagne's empire, and which hitherto had been divided among smaller warring Anglo-Saxon states, became unified in the late ninth and the tenth century owing to the work of King Alfred the Great (871–899) and his direct successors. Alfred and his heirs reorganized the army, infused new vigor into local government, and codified the English laws. In addition, Alfred founded schools and fostered an interest in Anglo-Saxon writing and other elements of a national culture.

Across the Channel, France (now the name for the main part of Roman Gaul because it was the original seat of the Frankish monar-

Viking Dragon Head. Wooden carvings like these on the stemposts of Viking ships were calculated to inspire terror.

England in the time of Alfred the Great

chy) was devastated by the invasions of Vikings, who had sailed up the French rivers. For that reason France broke up into small principalities rather than developing a strong national monarchy on the pattern of England. Nonetheless there was a king in France, who, however weak, was recognized as the ruler of the western part of Charlemagne's former territories. Directly to the east, the kings of Germany were the strongest continental monarchs of the tenth century, ruling over an essentially united realm. In addition to Germany, their lands encompassed most of the Low Countries and a good part of modern eastern France.

The most important German ruler of the period was Otto the Great. He became king in 936, resoundingly defeated the Hungarians in 955—thereby relieving Germany of its greatest foreign threat—and took the title of emperor in Rome in 962. By this last act Otto strengthened his claim to being the greatest continental monarch since Charlemagne. Otto and his successors, who continued to call themselves emperors, tried to rule over Italy but barely succeeded in doing so. Instead, Italy in the tenth century saw the greatest western European development of urban life, a pattern on which the Italians would subsequently build.

Although Italy did develop some city life in the tenth century, this was by no means typical of the early-medieval period in western Europe as a whole. Quite to the contrary, from the eighth to the eleventh century the European economy was based almost entirely on agriculture and very limited local trade. Roads deteriorated and barter widely replaced the use of money. Whatever cities survived from Roman days were usually empty shells that served at most as administrative centers for bishops and fortified places in case of common danger. The main economic unit throughout the period was the self-supporting large landed estate, usually owned by kings, warrior aristocrats, or large-scale monasteries. Although the northern European soil was rich, farming tools in most places were still too primitive to bring in a fully adequate return on the enormous investment of effort expended by the laboring masses. Agricultural yields in all but the most fertile Carolingian heartlands (and often even in them) were pitifully low, and Europeans, except the rulers and the higher clergy, lived on the edge of subsistence. It is true that some increase in agricultural income had underpinned the Carolingian successes and some progress in farming might have continued had the peace of Charlemagne's reign endured. But the subsequent invasions of the ninth and tenth centuries set agricultural life back and new beginnings would have to be made in the years thereafter.

*The economy of western
Europe in the early
Middle Ages*

Given the low level of early-medieval economic life, it is not surprising that the age was not a prosperous time for learning or the arts: with scarcely enough wealth to keep most people alive, there is not going to be much to support schools or major artistic projects. Throughout the period, even in the best of years, learning was a privilege for the few: the masses received no formal education, and even most members of the secular aristocracy were illiterate. Learning also consisted mostly of memorization, without regard for criticism or refutation. We have seen that there was some revival of learning under Charlemagne that may be called a "renaissance" but that it did not issue into any real intellectual creativity. Its major accomplishment was the founding of enough schools to educate the clergy in the rudiments of reading and the training of enough monastic scribes to re-copy and preserve some major works of Roman literature. Even this accomplishment was jeopardized in the period of invasions that accompanied the fall of the Carolingian Empire. Fortunately just enough schools and manuscripts survived to become the basis for another—far greater—revival of learning that began in the eleventh and twelfth centuries.

Literature

In the realm of literature the early Middle Ages had an extremely meager production. This was because few Christians could write and those who could were usually monks and priests, who were not supposed to engage in purely literary endeavors. There was some impressive writing of history in Latin, most notably that of Bede and Charlemagne's eloquent biographer, Einhard, but otherwise Latin composition was little cultivated. Toward the close of the period, however, the vernacular languages, which were either Germanic or based on different regional dialects of Latin (the "Romance" languages, so-called because they were based on "Roman" speech) began to be employed for crude poetic expression, usually first by oral transmission.

The best-known example of this literature in the vernacular is the Anglo-Saxon epic poem *Beowulf*. First put into written form about the eighth century, this poem incorporates ancient legends of the Germanic peoples of northwestern Europe. It is a story of fighting and seafaring and of heroic adventure against deadly dragons and the forces of nature. The background of the epic is pre-Christian, but the author of the work introduced into it some qualities of Christian idealism. *Beowulf* is important not only as one of the earliest specimens of Anglo-Saxon or Old English poetry, but also for the picture it gives of the society of the English and their ancestors in the early Middle Ages.

The artistic history of the early Middle Ages was a story of isolated and interrupted accomplishments because artistic life relied most of all on brief moments of local peace or royal patronage. The earliest enduring monuments of early-medieval art were those created by monks in Ireland—which had its own unique culture—between the sixth and the eighth centuries. Above all in manuscript illumination (i.e., painted illustrations) the Irish monks developed a thoroughly anticlassical and almost surrealistic style, whose origins are most difficult to account for. The greatest surviving product from this school is the stunning *Book of Kells,* an illuminated Gospel book that has been called "the most sophisticated work of decorative art in the history of

Irish Art. The opening of a gospel page that shows the Irish style at its most surrealistic.

Carolingian Art. The fountain of life: an illuminated manuscript page from Gottschalk's Evangeliary (book with four gospels), dating from 781.

painting." The Irish school declined without subsequent influence and was followed by artistic products of the Carolingian Renaissance.

For much of its inspiration, the art of Charlemagne's period returned to classical models, yet it also retained some of the spontaneous vitality of barbarian decoration. When Charlemagne's empire declined and disintegrated there was a corresponding decline and then interruption in the history of Western art. In the tenth century, however, new regional schools emerged. The greatest of these were the English, which emphasized restless fluency in manuscript illumination; the German, which was more grave but still managed to communicate extreme religious ecstasy; and the northern Spanish, which, though Christian, created a rather strange and independent style mostly influenced by the decorative style of Islamic art.

Regional variations in early-medieval art

Undoubtedly, there is no single, obvious terminal date for early-medieval history as a whole. The date 1000 is sometimes given because it is a convenient round number, but even as late as 1050 Europe had not changed on the surface very much from the way it had been since the end of the Carolingian period. Indeed, looking at Europe as late as 1050 it would at first seem that not much progress had been made over the entire course of the early-medieval centuries. Except for Germany, there was hardly any centralized government because by 1050 the Anglo-Saxon English state created by King Alfred and his successors was falling apart. Throughout Europe, all but the most privileged individuals continued to live on the brink of starvation, and cultural

A distinct western European civilization evident in 1050

See color plates facing page 295

Left: *Utrecht Psalter.* This Carolingian manuscript of the Psalms from about 820 later provided the basis for the "nervous expressiveness" of the tenth-century English regional school. Right: *Bamberg Apocalypse.* In this manuscript illumination from about 1000 A.D. the fall of Babylon in the Book of Revelation (18: 1–20) is displayed by depicting the city upside down. This is an example of the grave regional German style.

attainments were minimal and sparse. But actually much had been accomplished. By shifting its main weight to the Atlantic northwest, European civilization became centered in lands that would soon harvest great agricultural wealth. By preserving some of the traditions developed by Gregory the Great, St. Boniface, Pepin, and Charlemagne, European civilization had also developed an enduring sense of cultural unity based on Western Christianity and the Latin inheritance. And in the tenth century the beginnings of the future European kingdoms and city-states started to coalesce. Western European civilization was thus for the first time becoming autonomous and distinctive. From then on it would become a leading force in the history of the world.

SELECTED READINGS

• *Items so designated are available in paperback editions.*

BYZANTINE CIVILIZATION

Beckwith, John, *The Art of Constantinople,* 2nd ed., London, 1968. A standard account.

• Diehl, Charles, *Byzantium: Greatness and Decline,* New Brunswick, N.J., 1957. Evaluates strengths and weaknesses of Byzantine civilization.

Hussey, J. M., *The Byzantine World,* London, 1957. Half-narrative, half-topical; a useful short introduction.

• Krautheimer, R., *Early Christian and Byzantine Architecture,* Baltimore, 1970.

Magoulias, H. J., *Byzantine Christianity: Emperor, Church and the West,* Chicago, 1970. Limited to the three themes mentioned in the title.

• Ostrogorsky, George, *History of the Byzantine State,* New Brunswick, N.J., 1957. The most authoritative longer account of political developments; very scholarly.

• Pelikan, J., *The Christian Tradition; II: The Spirit of Eastern Christendom,* Chicago, 1974. An advanced treatment of religious doctrines.

Runciman, S., *Byzantine Civilization,* New York, 1933. A topical approach; well written but in parts outdated.

_____, *Byzantine Style and Civilization,* Baltimore, 1975. A fine study of Byzantine art.

• Vasiliev, A. A., *History of the Byzantine Empire,* 2 vols., Madison, Wis., 1928. Supplements Ostrogorsky; valuable for its detail on social and intellectual as well as political history.

Vryonis, S., *Byzantium and Europe,* New York, 1967. Noteworthy for its illustrations.

ISLAMIC CIVILIZATION

Arnold, Thomas, and A. Guillaume, *The Legacy of Islam,* New York, 1931.

Gabrieli, F., *Muhammad and the Conquests of Islam,* New York, 1968.

Gibb, H. A. R., *Arabic Literature: An Introduction,* 2nd ed., Oxford, 1963. An excellent survey.

• _____, *Mohammedanism: An Historical Survey,* 2nd ed., Oxford, 1953. The best brief interpretation of Islamic religion.

• Goitein, S. D., *Jews and Arabs, Their Contacts through the Ages,* New York, 1955.

Grube, E. J., *The World of Islam,* New York, 1966.

• Hodgson, M., *The Venture of Islam,* 3 vols., Chicago, 1974. A masterwork. One of the greatest works of history written by a modern American. Advanced and sometimes difficult, but always rewarding.

Kennedy, Hugh, *The Early Abbasid Caliphate: A Political History,* Totowa, N.J., 1981.

• Lewis, Bernard, *The Arabs in History,* rev. ed., New York, 1966. The best short survey of the conquests and political fortunes of the Arabs.

Lombard, Maurice, *The Golden Age of Islam,* New York, 1975.

Peters, F. E., *Aristotle and the Arabs,* New York, 1968. A well-written and engaging account.

Watt, W. Montgomery, *Islamic Philosophy and Theology,* Edinburgh, 1962.

• _____, *Muhammad: Prophet and Statesman,* Oxford, 1961. A good short biography.

• Watt, W. M., and P. Cachia, *A History of Islamic Spain,* Edinburgh, 1965. Briefly covers an undeservedly neglected subject.

*Rome's Three Heirs: The
Byzantine, Islamic, and Early-
Medieval Western Worlds*

- Barraclough, G., *The Crucible of Europe: The Ninth and Tenth Centuries in European History*, Berkeley, 1976. A controversial and sometimes wrong-headed but clear and stimulating interpretation of political developments.
- Dawson, Christopher, *The Making of Europe*, London, 1932. A brilliant interpretation that emphasizes cultural and religious developments by one of this century's most eminent Catholic historians.
- Duby, G., *The Early Growth of the European Economy*, Ithaca, N.Y., 1974. Emphasizes role of lords and peasants; very sophisticated economic history.
- Fichtenau, H., *The Carolingian Empire*, Oxford, 1957. A highly interpretative account that aims to whittle its subject down to size.

  Ganshof, F. L., *Frankish Institutions under Charlemagne*, Providence, 1958. A straightforward technical exposition.
- Kitzinger, Ernst, *Early Medieval Art*, London, 1940. A very short but masterful introduction.
- Laistner, M. L. W., and King, H. H., *Thought and Letters in Western Europe, A. D. 500–900*, 2nd ed., Ithaca, N.Y., 1966. An old-fashioned but standard account; should be supplemented by Wolff.

  McKitterick, R., *The Frankish Kingdoms under the Carolingians, 751–987*, New York, 1983.
- Pirenne, Henri, *Mohammed and Charlemagne*, New York, 1939. A bold interpretation, now no longer widely accepted but still thought-provoking.

  Stenton, Frank, *Anglo-Saxon England*, 3rd ed., Oxford, 1971. A standard work.
- Sullivan, Richard E., *Heirs of the Roman Empire*, Ithaca, N.Y., 1960. An elementary introduction.
- Wallace-Hadrill, J. M., *The Barbarian West: The Early Middle Ages, A. D. 400–1000*, 2nd ed., London, 1962. A sophisticated short account that emphasizes analysis of the historical sources and questions earlier scholarly assumptions.
- Wemple, S. F., *Women in Frankish Society: Marriage and the Cloister, 500–900*, Philadelphia, 1981. Describes changing attitudes toward marriage among the early Franks.
- Wolff, Philippe, *The Awakening of Europe*, Baltimore, 1968. The "new intellectual history": emphasizes interrelations between the development of thought and material foundations. Masterfully written and organized.

SOURCE MATERIALS

- Arberry, A. J., *The Koran Interpreted*, 2 vols., London, 1955.
- Bede, *A History of the English Church and People*, tr. L. Sherley-Price, Baltimore, 1955.

  Brand, Charles M., ed., *Icon and Minaret: Sources of Byzantine and Islamic Civilization*, Englewood Cliffs, N.J., 1969.
- Brentano, Robert, ed., *The Early Middle Ages: 500–1000*, New York, 1964. The best shorter anthology of the Western Christian sources, enlivened by the editor's subjective commentary.
- Einhard and Notker the Stammerer, *Two Lives of Charlemagne*, tr. L. Thorpe, Baltimore, 1969.
- Gregory Bishop of Tours, *History of the Franks*, tr. E. Brehaut, New York, 1965.

Chapter 13

THE HIGH MIDDLE AGES (1050–1300): ECONOMIC, SOCIAL, AND POLITICAL INSTITUTIONS

I judge those who write at this time to be in a certain measure happy. For, after the turbulence of the past, an unprecedented brightness of peace has dawned again.

—The historian Otto of
Freising, writing around 1158

The period between about 1050 and 1300, termed by historians the High Middle Ages, was the time when western Europe first clearly emerged from backwardness to become one of the greatest powers on the globe. Around 1050 the West was still less developed in most respects than the Byzantine Empire or the Islamic world, but by 1300 it had forged ahead of these two rivals. From a global perspective, only China was its equal in economic, political, and cultural prosperity. Given the sorry state of western Europe around 1050, this startling leap forward was certainly one of the most impressive achievements of human history. Those who think that the entire Middle Ages were times of stagnation could not be more wrong.

Western Europe emerges from backwardness

The reasons for Europe's enormous progress in the High Middle Ages are predictably complex, yet medieval historians agree upon certain broad lines of interpretation. One is that Europe between 900 and 1050 was already poised for growth and could finally begin to live up to its potential once the devastating invasions of Vikings, Hungarians, and Muslims had ceased. Most of these invasions had tapered off by around 1000, but in the eleventh century England was still troubled by the Danes: the year 1066, more famous as the year of the Norman Conquest, was also the year of the last Viking invasion of England.

Reasons for the "great leap forward"

Once foreign invasions were no longer imminent, western Europeans could concentrate on developing their economic life with much less fear of interruption than before. Because of the relative continuity allowed by this change, extraordinarily important technological breakthroughs were made, above all those that contributed to the first great western European "agricultural revolution." The revolution in agriculture made food more bountiful and provided a solid basis for economic development and diversification in other spheres. Population grew rapidly, and towns and cities grew to such a degree that we can speak also of an "urban revolution," even though western Europe remained predominantly agrarian. At the same time political life in the West became more stable. In the course of the High Middle Ages strong new secular governments began to provide more and more internal peace for their subjects and became the foundations of our modern nation-states. In addition to all these advances, there were also striking new religious and intellectual developments, to be treated in the next chapter, which helped give the West a new sense of mission and self-confidence. Although in this chapter we will treat only the economic, social, and political accomplishments of the High Middle Ages, it is well to bear in mind that religion played a pervasive role in all of medieval life, and that all aspects of the high-medieval "great leap forward" were inextricably interrelated.

1. THE FIRST AGRICULTURAL REVOLUTION

The state of agriculture before 1050

The agricultural worker, the "Man with the Hoe," supported European civilization materially by his labors more than anyone else until the industrialization of modern times. Yet, amazing as it seems, until about 1050 he had hardly so much as a hoe. Inventories of farm implements from the Carolingian period reveal that metal tools on the wealthiest rural estates were extremely rare, and even wooden implements were so few in number that many laborers must have had to grapple with nature quite literally with only their bare hands. Between about 1050 and 1250 all that changed. In roughly those two centuries an agricultural revolution took place which entirely altered the nature and vastly increased the output of western European farming.

Prerequisities for the medieval agricultural revolution: (1) shift in area of cultivation

Many of the prerequisites for the medieval agricultural revolution had been present before the middle of the eleventh century. The most important was the shift in the weight of European civilization from the Mediterranean to the North Atlantic regions. Most of northern Europe from southern England to the Urals is a vast, wet, and highly fertile alluvial plain. The Romans had hardly begun to cultivate this area because they only ruled part of it, because it lay too far away from the center of their civilization, and because they did not have the proper tools and systems to work the soil. Starting around the time of the Carolingians much more attention was paid to colonizing and cultivating the great alluvial plain. The Carolingians opened up all of western and central Germany to agricultural settlement and started experimenting with new tools and methods that would be most appropriate for cultivating the newly settled lands. The results helped support other Carolingian achievements, but the Carolingian peace, as we have seen, was too brief to allow for any cumulative development. After the invasions of the tenth century, it was necessary to start again in a systematic attempt to exploit the potential wealth of the north. As long as Western civilization was centered in England, northern France, the Low Countries, and Germany, however, the rich lands remained available for cultivation.

Another prerequisite for agricultural development was improved climate. We know far less about European climatic patterns in past centuries than we would like to, but historians of climate are reasonably certain that there was an "optimum," or period of improved climate for western Europe, lasting from about 700 to 1200. This meant not only that during those centuries the temperature on the average was somewhat warmer than it had been before (at most only a rise of about 1° Centigrade), but also that the weather was somewhat drier. Dryness was of primary advantage to northern Europe, where lands were, if anything, usually too wet for good farming, whereas it was disadvantageous to the Mediterranean south, which was already dry enough. Among other things, the occurrence of this optimum helps explain why there was more agricultural cultivation in northern climes such as Iceland than there has been since then. (Also, with fewer icebergs in the northern seas, Norsemen were able to reach Greenland and Newfoundland, and Greenland then was probably indeed more green than white.) Although the optimum began around 700 and continued through the ninth and tenth centuries, it could not by itself counteract the deleterious effects of the tenth-century invasions. Fortunately the weather stayed propitious when Europeans again were able to take advantage of it.

(2) improved climate

Similar remarks apply to the fact that the Carolingians knew about many of the technological devices to be discussed presently that later helped western Europeans accomplish their first agricultural revolution. Although the most basic new devices were known before 1050, all came into widespread use and were brought to greatest perfection between then and about 1200 because only then was there a conjunction of the most favorable circumstances. Not only did the invasions end and good climate continue, but better government gradually provided the more lasting peace necessary for agricultural expansion. Landlords too became more interested in profit-making than mere consumption. Above all, from about 1050 to 1200 there was a greater consolidation of wealth for further investment as one advance helped support another; quite simply, technological devices could now be afforded.

(3) technology in conjunction with favorable circumstances

One of the first and most important breakthroughs in agriculture

Light Plow and Heavy Plow. Note that the peasant using the light plow had to press his foot on it to give it added weight. The major innovation of the heavy plow (often wheeled, as shown here) was the long moldboard, which turned

Technological innovations: (1) the heavy plow

was the use of the heavy plow. The plow itself, of course, is an ancient tool, but the Romans knew only a light "scratch plow" that broke up the surface of the ground without fully turning it over. This implement was sufficient for the light soil of the Mediterranean regions but was virtually useless with the much heavier, wetter soil of the European north. During the course of the early Middle Ages a much heavier and more efficient plow was developed that could cultivate the northern lands. Not only could this heavier plow deal with heavier soils, but it was fitted with new parts that enabled it to turn over furrows and fully aerate the ground. The benefits were immeasurable. In addition to the fact that the plow allowed for the cultivation of hitherto unworkable lands, the furrows it made provided excellent drainage systems for water-logged territories. It also saved labor: whereas the Roman scratch plow had to be dragged over the fields twice in two different directions, the heavy plow did more thorough work in one operation. In short, the opening up of northern Europe for intensive agriculture and everything that followed would have been inconceivable without the heavy plow.

(2) the three-field system

Closely allied to the use of the heavy plow was the introduction of the three-field system of crop rotation. Before modern times, farmers always let a large part of their arable land lie fallow for a year to avoid exhaustion of the soil because there was not enough fertilizer to support more intensive agriculture, and nitrogen-fixing crops such as clover and alfalfa were almost unknown. But the Romans represented an unproductive extreme in their inability to cultivate any more than half of their arable land in any year. The medieval innovation was to reduce the fallow to one-third by introducing a three-field system. In a given year one third of the land would lie fallow, one third would be

over the ground after the plowshare cut into it. The picture on the right depicts a second crucial medieval invention as well—the padded horse collar which allowed horses to throw their full weight into pulling.

given to cereal that was sown in the fall and harvested in early summer, and one third to a new crop—oats, barley, or legumes—that would be planted in the late spring and harvested in August or September. The fields were then rotated over a three-year cycle. The major innovation was the planting of the new crop which grew over the summer. The Romans could not have supported this system because their lands were poorer and especially because the Mediterranean area is too dry to support much summer growth at all. In this respect the wetter north obviously had a great advantage. The benefits of the new crop were that it did not deplete the soil as much as cereal like wheat and rye (in fact, it restored nitrogen taken from the soil by these crops); that it provided some insurance against loss from natural disasters by diversifying the growth of the fields; and that it produced new types of food. If the third field was planted with oats, the crop could be consumed by both humans and horses; if planted with legumes, it helped to balance the human diet by providing a source of protein to balance the major intake of cereal carbohydrates. Since the new system also helped to diversify labor over the course of the year and raised production from one-half to two-thirds, it was nothing short of an agricultural miracle.

A third major innovation was the use of mills. The Romans had known about water mills but hardly used them, partly because they had enough slaves to be indifferent to labor-saving devices and partly because most Roman territories were not richly endowed with swiftly flowing streams. Starting around 1050, however, there was a veritable craze in northern Europe for building increasingly efficient water mills. One French area saw a growth from 14 water mills in the eleventh century to 60 in the twelfth; in another part of France about 40

(3) use of mills

mills were built between 850 and 1080, 40 more between 1080 and 1125, and 245 between 1125 and 1175. Once Europeans had mastered the complex technology of building water mills, they turned their attention to harnessing the power of wind: around 1170 they constructed the first European windmills. Thereafter, in flat lands like Holland that had no swiftly flowing streams, windmills proliferated as rapidly as water-powered ones had spread elsewhere. Although the major use of mills was to grind grain, they were soon adapted for a variety of other important functions: for example, they were employed to drive saws, process cloth, press oil, brew beer, provide power for iron forges, and crush pulp for manufacturing paper. Paper had been made in China and the Islamic world before this but never with the aid of paper mills, which is evidence of the technological sophistication the West was achieving in comparison to other advanced civilizations.

(4) other technological developments

Other important technological breakthroughs that gathered force around 1050 should be mentioned. Several related to providing the means for using horses as farm animals. Around 800 a padded collar was first introduced into Europe; this allowed the horse to put his full weight into pulling without choking himself. Roughly a century later iron horseshoes were first used to protect hooves, and perhaps around 1050 tandem harnessing was developed to allow horses to pull behind each other. With these advances and the greater abundance of oats due to the three-field system, horses replaced oxen as farm animals in some parts of Europe and brought with them the advantages of working more quickly and working longer hours. Further inventions were the wheelbarrow and the harrow, a tool drawn over the field after the plow to level the earth and mix in the seed. Important for most of these inventions was the greater use of iron in the High Middle Ages to reinforce all sorts of agricultural implements, most crucially the parts of the heavy plow that came into contact with the soil.

So far we have been speaking of technological developments as if they alone account for the high-medieval agricultural revolution. But that is by no means the case. Along with improved technology came a great extension in the amount of land made arable and more intensive cultivation of the land already cleared. Although the Carolingians had begun to open the rich plain of northwestern Europe to tillage, they had only chosen to clear the most easily workable patches: a map of Carolingian agricultural settlements would show numerous tiny islands of cultivated lands surrounded by vast stretches of forests, swamps, and wastes. Starting around 1050, and greatly accelerating in the twelfth century, movements of land-clearing entirely changed the topography of northern Europe. First, greater peace and stability allowed farm workers in northern France and western Germany to begin pushing beyond the islands of settlement, clearing little bits of land at a time. At first they did this surreptitiously because they were poaching on territories that were actually owned by aristocratic lords. In time the aristocratic landowners gave their support to the clearing activities because they demanded their own profits from them. When that happened the work of clearing forests and draining swamps was carried on more swiftly. Thus, as the twelfth century progressed the isolated arable islands of Carolingian times expanded to meet each other. While this was going on, and continuing somewhat later, entirely new areas were colonized and opened to cultivation, for example, in northern England, Holland, and above all the eastern parts of Germany. Finally, in the twelfth and thirteenth centuries, peasants began working all the lands they had cleared more efficiently and intensively in order to gain more income for themselves. They harrowed after plowing, hoed frequently to keep down weeds, and added extra plowings to their yearly cycle, thereby greatly helping to renew the fertility of the soil.

The result of all these changes was an enormous increase in agricultural production. With more land opened for cultivation obviously more crops were raised, but the increase was magnified by the introduction of more efficient farming methods. Thus, average yields from grains of seed sown increased from at best twofold in Carolingian times to three- or fourfold by around 1300. And all the additional grain could be ground far more rapidly than before because a mill could grind grain in the same time that it would have taken forty men to do the same job. Europeans, therefore, could for the first time begin to rely on a regular and stable food supply.

That fact in turn had the profoundest consequences for the further development of European history. To begin with, it meant that more land could be given over to uses other than raising grain. Accordingly, as the High Middle Ages progressed, there was greater agricultural diversification and specialization. Large areas were turned over to sheep-raising, others to viniculture, and others to raising cotton and dyestuffs. Many of the products of these new enterprises were con-

Extension and intense cultivation of arable land

"Dawn." A medieval peasant, up with the roosters, returns from outdoors after attending to some early-morning business. The woman overhead is "dawn" herself.

Consequences of the agricultural revolution

sumed locally, but many were also traded over long distances or used to provide the raw materials for new industries—above all those of cloth-making. The growth of this trade and manufacturing helped initiate and support, as we will see, the growth of towns. The agricultural boom also helped sustain the growth of towns in another way: by supporting a great spurt in population. With more food and a better diet (above all the increase in proteins) life expectancy increased from perhaps as low as an average of thirty years for the poor of Carolingian Europe to between forty and fifty years in the High Middle Ages. Healthier people also increased their birthrate. For these reasons the population of the West grew about threefold between about 1050 and 1300. More people and more labor-saving devices meant that not everybody had to stay on the farm: some could migrate to new towns and cities where they found a new way of life.

Other results

Still other results of the agricultural revolution were that it raised the incomes of lords, thereby underpinning a great increase in the sophistication of aristocratic life, and raised the incomes of monarchs, underpinning the growth of states. European-wide prosperity also helped support the growth of the Church and paid the way for the burgeoning of schools and intellectual enterprises. One final, more intangible, result was that Europeans apparently became more optimistic, more energetic, and more willing to experiment and take risks than any of their rivals on the world scene.

2. LORD AND SERF: SOCIAL CONDITIONS AND QUALITY OF LIFE IN THE MANORIAL REGIME

The meaning of the term manorialism

While agriculture was being transformed, social and economic conditions began to change for both landowners and agricultural laborers. Since for much of the High Middle Ages, however, rural life revolved around the institution of the manor owned by lords and worked by serfs, it is best to describe this manorial regime in its most typical form before describing basic changes. In reading the following it should be understood that the term manorialism is not synonymous with feudalism: manorialism was an economic system in which large agricultural estates were worked by serfs, whereas feudalism, in the sense the word is used by most medieval historians, was a political system in which government was greatly decentralized (see the fourth section of this chapter). It should also be borne in mind that when scholars talk about manorialism based on a "typical manor" they are resorting to a historical approximation: no two manors were ever exactly alike; indeed many differed enormously in size and basic characteristics. Moreover, in those parts of Europe farthest away from the original centers of Carolingian settlement between the Seine and the Rhine, there were few, if any, manors at all. In Italy there was still much agriculture based on slavery, and in central and eastern Germany there were many smaller farms worked by free peasants.

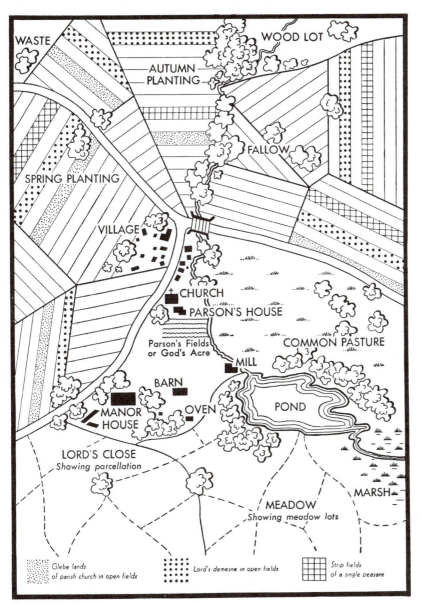

WASTE

WOOD LOT

AUTUMN
PLANTING

FALLOW

SPRING PLANTING

VILLAGE

† CHURCH
PARSON'S HOUSE

Parson's Fields
or God's Acre

MILL

COMMON PASTURE

BARN

OVEN

POND

MANOR
HOUSE

LORD'S CLOSE
Showing parcellation

MARSH

MEADOW
Showing meadow lots

Glebe lands
of parish church in open fields

Lord's demesne in open fields

Strip fields
of a single peasant

Diagram of a Manor

The manor first clearly emerged in Carolingian times and continued
to be the dominant form of agrarian social and economic organization
in most of northwestern Europe until about the thirteenth century. It
descended from the large Roman landed estate, but, unlike the Roman
estate, the manor was worked by serfs (sometimes called villeins) and
not slaves. Serfs were definitely not free in the modern sense: above all,
they could not leave their lands, were forced to work for their lords
regularly without pay, and were subject to numerous humiliating dues
and to the jurisdiction of the lord's court. But they were much better
off than slaves insofar as they were allocated land which they culti-

The manor; serfs

vated to support themselves and which normally could not be taken away from them. Thus, when agricultural improvements took place the serfs themselves could hope to profit at least a little from them. More than that, although the lord theoretically had the right to levy dues at will, in practice obligations tended to remain fixed. Although the lot of the serfs was surely terribly hard, they were seldom entirely at their lord's whim.

The manorial system of agriculture

The lands of the manor, which might run from several hundred to several thousand acres, were divided into those that belonged to the lord and those that were allocated to the serfs. The former, called the lord's *demesne* (pronounced demean), usually comprised between a third and a half of the arable land. It was worked by the serfs on certain days, perhaps three days a week. The demesne did not consist of big parcels but was made up of narrow strips alternating with strips belonging to different peasants (and sometimes also strips set aside for the Church). All these strips were long and narrow because a heavy plow drawn by a yoke of horses or oxen could not be turned around easily. Because all the strips were generally separated only by a narrow band of unplowed turf, the whole regime is sometimes called the *open-field system*. Even when the serfs tilled their own lands they almost always worked together because they usually owned farm animals and implements in common. For the same reason, grazing lands were called "commons" because the commonly owned herds grazed there together. In addition to cultivated fields and pastures, the serfs usually had their own small gardens. Most manors also had forests set aside primarily for the lord's hunting which were also useful for the forag-

Sowing Seed. When the peasant sows his seed broadcast, the crows are not far off to help themselves. Here, one is bold enough to peck at the sack while another is momentarily chased off by a dog.

Medieval Peasants Slaughtering a Pig. Deep in winter, probably around Christmas, it is finally time to slaughter the household pig. But nothing can be wasted, so even the blood is caught in a pan to make blood pudding.

ing of pigs and the gathering of firewood. Insofar as serfs were allowed to take advantage of such opportunities they did that too in common: indeed, the entire manorial system emphasized communal enterprise and solidarity.

Communalism must have helped make a barely endurable life seem slightly more bearable. Even though the lot of the medieval serf was surely far superior to that of the Roman slave, and even though it improved from around 1050 to 1300, it was still primitive and pitiful beyond modern comprehension. Dwellings were usually miserable hovels constructed of wattle—braided twigs—smeared over with mud. As late as the thirteenth century an English peasant was convicted of destroying his neighbor's house simply by sawing apart one central beam. The floors of most huts were usually no more than the bare earth, often cold or damp. For beds there was seldom more than bracken, and beyond that there was hardly any furniture. Not entirely jokingly it may be said that a good meal often consisted of two courses: one a porridge very much like gruel and the other a gruel very much like porridge. Fruit was almost unheard of, and meager vegetables were limited to such fare as onions, leeks, turnips, and cabbages—all boiled to make a thin soup. Meat came at most a few times a year, either on holidays or deep in winter, when all the fodder for a scrawny ox or pig had run out. Cooking utensils were never cleaned, so as to make sure that there was never any waste. In addition, there was always the possibility of crop failures, which affected the serfs far more than their lords, since the lords demanded the same income as

Living conditions of serfs

always. At such times the serfs were forced to surrender whatever grain they had and watched their children die slowly of starvation. It is particularly heart-rending to realize that children might be dying while there was still a bit of grain in the granaries: but that grain could not be touched because it was set aside as next year's seed, and without that there would be no future at all.

*Improvements in the
condition of serfs*

To counterbalance this grim picture we may now turn to patterns of change and improvement. One, as we have already seen, was dietary. In the High Middle Ages famines were actually far rarer than before, and people grew stronger because some protein, mostly in the form of legumes, was added to their fare. There was also a widespread enfranchisement (i.e., freeing) of serfs for many reasons. Once landlords started opening up new lands, they could only attract laborers by guaranteeing their freedom. Such areas of free labor usually attracted runaway serfs and became models of a new system whereby landlords asked for fixed rents rather than demanding services. Then, even on the old manors, lords began to realize that they might be able to raise profits by demanding rents instead of duties. Alternatively, by selling their excess produce at free markets serfs might become sufficiently rich to buy their freedom.

The decline of serfdom

In these different ways serfdom gradually came to an end throughout most of Europe in the course of the thirteenth century. The process, however, moved more or less swiftly in different areas—it was somewhat delayed in England and was seldom so complete that former serfs did not owe some remnant of labor service and dues to powerful local lords. In France some of these obligations continued to exist as nagging indignities right down to the French Revolution in 1789. Serfs who became enfranchised often continued to work communally, but they were now free peasants who produced more for the open market than for their own subsistence.

*Benefits of the agricultural
revolution for lords*

The lords profited even more than their serfs from the agricultural revolution for several reasons. One was that whenever lords enfranchised serfs they obtained large sums of cash, usually about all the wealth that the serfs had hitherto amassed. Afterward the lords lived mainly on their rents. Since some of these were levied on lands that the lords had once owned but had never cultivated, noble income rose greatly. Even more than that, once the lords began to prefer rents to services, they found that rents were easier to increase. In their capacity as rent-collectors the lords did not personally supervise their lands as much as before but traveled more freely, sometimes going off crusading and sometimes living at royal courts. Consequently, added wealth allowed them to live better, and greater mobility gave them new ideas for improving their style of life.

Increased sophistication of the nobility was much enhanced by the fact that in the High Middle Ages there was less tumultuous local warfare than before. Until around 1100 the typical European noble

Jousting in a Tournament

was a crude and brutal warrior who spent most of his time engaging in combat with his neighbors and pillaging the defenseless. Much of this violence decreased in the twelfth century because of ecclesiastical constraints, because emerging states were more effectively enforcing local peace, and because the nobles themselves were beginning to enjoy a more settled existence. Nobles continued to go on crusades and to fight in national wars, but they engaged in petty quarrels with each other less frequently. Apparently as an unconscious surrogate for the old fighting spirit the code of *chivalry* was developed. This channeled martial conduct into relatively benign activities. Chivalry literally means "horsemanship," and the chivalrous noble was expected to be thoroughly adept at the equestrian arts. Chivalry also imposed the obligation of fighting in defense of honorable causes; if none was to be found there were opportunities for combat in tournaments, mock battles that at first were quite savage but later became elaborate ceremonial affairs. Above all, the chivalric lord—typically a "knight" who owned less land than the upper aristocracy—was expected to be not only brave and loyal but generous, truthful, reverent, and disdainful of unfair advantage or sordid gain.

The medieval nobility; the rise of chivalry

By-products of the increase in noble wealth and the rise of chivalry were improvements in the quality of living conditions and the treatment of women. Until around 1100 most noble dwellings were made of wood, and burned down frequently because of primitive heating and cooking methods. With increasing wealth and more advanced

Improvements in the quality of noble life

technology, castles after 1100 were usually built of stone and were thus far less flammable. Moreover, they were now equipped with chimneys and mantled fireplaces, both medieval inventions, which meant that instead of having one large fire in a central great hall, individual rooms could be heated and individuals gained some privacy. Nobles customarily ate fewer vegetables than peasants, but their diet was laden with meat; increased luxury trade also brought costly exotic spices like pepper and saffron to their tables. Although table manners were still atrocious—all used only knives and spoons but no forks and blew their noses on their sleeves—nobles tried to show their superiority to others by dressing elegantly, indeed ostentatiously. During this period snug-fitting clothing also became available because both knitting and the button and buttonhole had just been invented.

Changes in noble attitudes toward women

The history of noble attitudes toward women in the High Middle Ages is somewhat controversial for two reasons. One is that most of our evidence comes from literature, and historians differ as to what degree literature actually reflects life. The other is that according to some scholars women were at best put on a pedestal, itself a position of constraint. Nonetheless, there can be no question that as the material quality of noble life improved it did so for women as well as men. More than that, there definitely was a revolution in some verbalized attitudes toward the female sex. Until the twelfth century, aside from a few female saints, women were virtually ignored in literature: the typical French epic told of bloody warlike deeds that either made no mention of women or portrayed them only in passing as being totally subservient. But within a few decades after 1100 noblewomen were suddenly turned into objects of veneration by lyric poets and writers of romances (see the following chapter). A typical troubadour poet

An Aristocratic Family of the Twelfth Century. Warm family feelings existed among medieval people as they did at any other time. Here a mother is telling her two boys to bid good-bye to their father who is about to depart on the Third Crusade.

Aristocratic Table Manners. There are knives but no forks or napkins on the table. The large stars mark these nobles as members of a chivalric order.

could write of his lady that "all I do that is fitting I infer from her beautiful body," and that "she is the tree and the branch where joy's fruit ripens."

Although the new "courtly" literature was extremely idealistic and somewhat artificial, it surely expressed the values of a gentler culture wherein upper-class women were in practice more respected than before. Moreover, there is no question that certain royal women in the twelfth and thirteenth centuries actually did rule their states on various occasions when their husbands or sons were dead or unable to do so. The indomitable Eleanor of Aquitaine, wife of Henry II, for example, helped rule England even though she was over seventy years old when her son Richard I went on a crusade from 1190 to 1194, and the strong-willed Blanche of Castile ruled France extremely well twice in the thirteenth century, once during the minority of her son Louis IX and again when he was off crusading. No doubt from a modern perspective high-medieval women were still very constrained, but from the point of view of the past the High Middle Ages was a time of progress for the women of the upper classes. The most striking symbol comes from the history of the game of chess: before the twelfth century chess was played in Eastern countries, but there the equivalent of the queen was a male figure, the king's chief minister, who could only move diagonally one square at a time; in twelfth-century western Europe, however, this piece was turned into a queen, and sometime before the end of the Middle Ages she began to move all over the board.

Changes in the status of noblewomen

3. THE REVIVAL OF TRADE AND THE URBAN REVOLUTION

Inseparable from the agricultural revolution, the enfranchisement of serfs, and the growing sophistication of noble life was the revival of

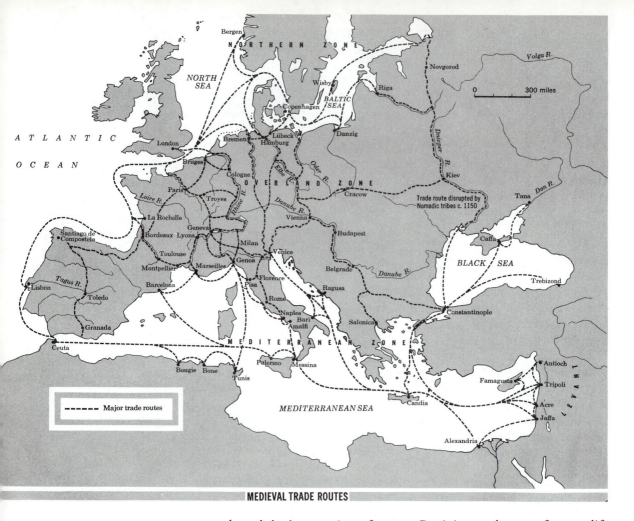

MEDIEVAL TRADE ROUTES

Patterns of trade

trade and the burgeoning of towns. Reviving trade was of many different sorts. Most fundamental was the mundane trade at local markets, where serfs or free peasants sold their excess grain or perhaps a few dozen eggs. But with growing specialization, produce like wine or cotton might be shipped over longer distances. River and sea routes were used wherever possible, but land transport was also necessary, and this was aided by improvements in road-building, the introduction of packhorses and mules, and the building of bridges. Whereas the Romans were really only interested in land *communications,* medieval people, starting in the eleventh century, concentrated on land *transport* to the degree that they were much better able to maintain a vigorous land-based trade. And that is not to say that they ignored Mediterranean communications either. On the contrary, starting again in the eleventh century they began to make the former Roman "lake" the intermediary for an extensive seaborne trade that stretched over shorter and longer distances. Between 1050 and 1300 the Italian city-states of Genoa, Pisa, and Venice freed much of the Mediterranean from Muslim control, started monopolizing trade on formerly

Byzantine waters, and began to establish in eastern Mediterranean outposts a flourishing commerce with the Orient. As a result, luxury goods such as spices, gems, perfumes, and fine cloths began to appear in Western markets and stimulated economic life by inspiring nobles to accelerate the agricultural revolution in order to pay for them.

This revival of trade called for new patterns of payment and the development of new commercial techniques. Most significantly, western Europe returned to a money economy after about four centuries when coined money was hardly used as a medium of exchange. The traditional manor had been almost self-sufficient and the few external items needed could be bartered for. But with the growth of markets coins became indispensable. At first these were coins of only the smallest denominations, but as luxury trade grew in the West the denominations increased apace; by the thirteenth century gold coins were minted by Italian states such as Florence and Venice.

The revival of a money economy

In a similar pattern of development, long-distance trade at first consisted of little more than peddlers crisscrossing over dusty roads with pack-laden mules. But during the course of the twelfth century such peddlers evolved into more prosperous merchants who managed to decrease their year-round traveling and to offer their wares instead at international trade fairs. The most prominent of these fairs, reaching the pinnacle of their prosperity in the thirteenth century, were held in the French region of Champagne, a meeting place between north and south, where Flemish merchants sold cloth to Italians, and Italian merchants sold eastern spices to Flemings. By such means a unified European economy came into being. Thereafter even the trade fairs became outmoded because around 1300 Italian merchants succeeded in replacing costly overland transport over the Alps by means of dispatching shipping fleets via the Straits of Gibraltar and the Atlantic directly to the ports of northern Europe. Now staying at home entirely themselves, such large-scale trading entrepreneurs perfected modern techniques of business partnerships, accounting, and letters of credit. Because they invested in trade intentionally for profit and devised and used sophisticated credit mechanisms, most modern historians agree in calling them the first Western commercial capitalists.

Medieval Tollbooth. Whoever made use of a medieval road for transporting merchandise had to pay tolls to pay for its upkeep.

In addition to the expansion of money and credit, trade was vastly facilitated by the rapid growth of towns. If we could imagine an aerial view of twelfth-century Europe, the mushrooming of towns would be the most strikingly visible phenomenon after the clearing of forests and wastes. Some historians misleadingly include under the heading of towns the numerous new agricultural village communities of peasants that were established in clearings. These, however, were not really urban in any sense. Putting them aside, many urban agglomerations were built from the ground up in the High Middle Ages, and existing towns that had barely survived from the Roman period grew enormously in size. To take some examples, in central and eastern Germany, which had not been part of the old Roman area of settle-

Growth of towns

Causes of the urban revolution

ment, new towns such as Freiburg, Lübeck, Munich, and Berlin were founded in the twelfth century. Farther west, where old Roman towns had become little more than episcopal residences or stockades, formerly insignificant towns like Paris, London, and Cologne roughly doubled in size between 1100 and 1200 and doubled again in the next century. Urban life was above all concentrated in Italy, which encompassed most of Europe's largest cities: Venice, Genoa, Milan, Bologna, Palermo, Florence, and Naples. In the thirteenth century the population of the largest of these—Venice, Genoa, and Milan—was in the range of 100,000. We lack accurate statistics for most Italian cities, but it seems likely that many at least trebled in population between about 1150 and 1300, because we do know that the smaller Italian town of Imola, near Bologna, grew from some 4,200 in 1210 to 11,500 in 1312. Considering that town life had come very close to disappearing in most of Europe between 750 and 1050, it is warranted to speak of a high-medieval urban revolution. Moreover, from the High Middle Ages until now a vigorous urban life has been a major characteristic of western European and subsequently modern world civilization.

It used to be thought that the primary cause of the medieval urban revolution was the revival of long-distance trade. Theoretically, itinerant peddlers, who had no secure place in the dominantly agrarian society of Europe, gradually settled together in towns in order to offer each other much-needed protection and establish markets to sell their wares. In fact, the picture is far more complicated than that. While some towns did receive great stimulus from long-distance trade, and the growth of a major city such as Venice would have been unthinkable without it, most towns relied for their origin and early economic vitality far more on the wealth of their surrounding areas. These brought them surplus agricultural goods, raw materials for manufacture, and an influx of population. In other words, the quickening of economic life in general was the major cause of urban growth: towns

View of Paris. The city looked this way at the end of the Middle Ages, around 1480. Note the prominence of the cathedral of Notre Dame in the center and the large number of other church spires; note, too, how closely all the buildings are packed behind the walls.

A City on Fire. Once a fire began to spread in a medieval city, women, children, and priests were swiftly evacuated and servants of the rich would start carrying out their masters' possessions. Here the Swiss city of Bern is shown in flames: although a "bucket-brigade" tried desperately to extinguish the fire with water taken from the town moat, chronicles report that the city was leveled by flames in less than half an hour.

existed in a symbiotic relationship with the countryside by providing markets and also wares made by artisans, while they lived off the rural food surplus and grew with the migration of surplus serfs or peasants who were seeking a better life. (Escaped serfs were guaranteed their freedom if they stayed in a town a year and a day.) Once towns started to flourish, many of them began to specialize in certain enterprises. Paris and Bologna gained considerable wealth by becoming the homes of leading universities; Venice, Genoa, Cologne, and London became centers of long-distance trade; and Milan, Ghent, and Bruges specialized in manufactures. The most important urban industries were those devoted to cloth-making. Cloth manufacturers sometimes developed techniques of large-scale production and investment that are ancestors of the modern factory system and industrial capitalism. But it must be emphasized that large industrial enterprises were atypical of medieval economic life as a whole.

Medieval cities and towns were not smaller-scale facsimiles of modern ones; to our own eyes they would still have seemed half-rural and uncivilized. Streets were often unpaved, houses had gardens for raising vegetables, and cows and pigs were kept in stables and pigsties. Passing along the streets of a major metropolis one might be stopped by a flock of bleating sheep or a crowd of honking geese. Sanitary conditions were often very poor and the air must often have reeked of excrement—both animal and human. Town-dwellers were cursed by the frequency of fires that swept quickly through closely settled wooden or straw quarters and went unstopped by the lack of fire sta-

Old Houses in Strassburg. In the Middle Ages food was stored in attics, with special openings for ventilation, as insurance against famine. Of course there was still much spoilage.

tions. People were also highly susceptible to contagious diseases bred by unsanitary conditions and crowding. Still another problem was that economic tensions and family rivalries could lead to bloody riots. Yet for all this, urban folk took great pride in their new cities and ways of life. A famous paean to London, for example, written by a twelfth-century denizen of that city, boasted of its prosperity, piety, and perfect climate (!), and claimed that except for frequent fires, London's only nuisance was "the immoderate drinking of fools."

The most distinctive form of economic and social organization in the medieval towns was the guild. This was, roughly speaking, a professional association organized to protect and promote special interests. The main types were merchant guilds and craft guilds. The primary functions of the merchant guild were to maintain a monopoly of the local market for its members and to preserve a stable economic system. To accomplish these ends the merchant guild severely restricted trading by foreigners in the city, guaranteed to its members the right to participate in sales offered by other members, enforced uniform pricing, and did everything possible to ensure that no individual would corner the market for goods produced by its members.

The guild as representative of special interests

The Seal of a Leprosarium. Lepers with their crutches were common sights in medieval cities. This seal of a French leper house dates from 1208.

Craft guilds similarly regulated the affairs of artisans. Usually their only full-fledged voting members were so-called master craftsmen, who were experts at their trades and ran their own shops. Hence if these guilds were anything like modern trade unions, they were unions of bosses. Second-class members of craft guilds were journeymen, who had learned their trades but still worked for the masters (*journeyman* is from the French *journée,* meaning "day," or by extension "day's work"), and apprentices. Terms of apprenticeship were carefully regulated: if an apprentice wished to become a master he often had to produce a "masterpiece" for judging by the masters of the guild. Craft guilds, like merchant guilds, sought to preserve monopolies and to limit competition. Thus they established uniformity of prices and wages, prohibited working after hours, and formulated detailed regulations governing methods of production and quality of materials. In addition to all their economic functions, both kinds of guilds served important social ones. Often they acted in the capacity of religious associations, benevolent societies, and social clubs. Wherever possible guilds tried to minister to the human needs of their members. Thus in some cities they came close to becoming miniature governments.

See color plates facing pages 454 and 518

Town merchants and artisans were particularly concerned to protect themselves because they had no accepted role in the older medieval scheme of things. Usually merchants were disdained by the landed aristocracy because they could claim no ancient lineages and were not versed in the ways of chivalry. Worst of all, they were too obviously concerned with pecuniary gain. Although nobles too were gradually becoming interested in making profits, they displayed this less openly:

Medieval attitudes toward merchants

they paid little attention in their daily lives to accounts and made much of their free-spending largesse. Still another reason why medieval merchants were on the defensive was that the Church, opposed to illicit gain, taught a doctrine of the "just price" that was often at variance with what the merchants thought they deserved. Clergymen too condemned usury—i.e., the lending of money for interest—even though it was often essential for doing business. A decree of the Second Lateran Council of 1139, to take one example, excoriated the "detestable, shameful, and insatiable rapacity of moneylenders." As time went on, however, attitudes slowly changed. In Italy it often became hard to tell merchants from aristocrats because the latter customarily lived in towns and often engaged in trade themselves. In the rest of Europe, the most prosperous town-dwellers, called patricians, developed their own sense of pride verging on that of the nobility. The medieval Church never abandoned its prohibition of usury, but it did come to approve making profits on commercial risks, which was often close to the same thing. Moreover, starting around the thirteenth century leading churchmen came to speak more favorably of merchants. St. Bonaventure, a leading thirteenth-century churchman, argued that God showed special favors to shepherds like David in the time of the Old Testament, to fishers like Peter in the time of the New, and to merchants like St. Francis in the thirteenth century.

All in all, the importance of the high-medieval urban revolution can scarcely be overestimated. The fact that the new towns were the vital pumps of the high-medieval economy has already been sufficiently emphasized: in providing markets and producing wares they kept the entire economic system thriving. In addition, cities and towns made important contributions to the development of government because in many areas they gained their own independence and ruled themselves

Significance of the urban revolution: (1) development of the economy and government

Medieval Walled City of Carcassonne, France. These walls date from 1240 to 1285.

as city-states. Primarily in Italy, where urban life was by far the most advanced, city governments experimented with new systems of tax-collecting, record-keeping, and public participation in decision-making. Italian city-states were particularly advanced in their administrative techniques and thereby helped influence a general European-wide growth in governmental sophistication.

(2) towns as a foundation for intellectual life

Finally, the rise of towns contributed greatly to the quickening of intellectual life in the West. New schools were invariably located in towns because towns afforded domiciles and legal protection for scholars. At first, students and teachers were always clerics, but by the thirteenth century the needs of merchants to be trained in reading and accounting led to the foundation of numerous lay primary schools. Equally momentous for the future was the fact that the stimulating urban environment helped make advanced schools more open to intellectual experimentation than any in the West since those of the Greeks. Not coincidentally, Greek intellectual life too was based on thriving cities. Thus it seems that without commerce in goods there can be little exciting commerce in ideas.

4. FEUDALISM AND THE RISE OF THE NATIONAL MONARCHIES

If any western European city of around 1200 epitomized Europe's greatest new accomplishments it was Paris: that city was not only a bustling commercial center and an important center of learning, it was also the capital of what was becoming Europe's most powerful government. France, like England and the new Christian kingdoms of the Iberian peninsula, was taking shape in the twelfth and thirteenth centuries as a *national monarchy,* a new form of government which was to dominate Europe's political future. Because the developing national monarchies were the most successful and promising European governments we must concentrate on them. But before we do it is well to see what was happening from the political point of view in Germany and Italy.

The political decline of medieval Germany an intriguing historical problem

Around 1050 Germany was unquestionably the most centralized and best-ruled territory in Europe, but by 1300 it had fallen into a congeries of warring petty states. Since most other areas of Europe were gaining stronger rule in the very same period, the political decline of Germany becomes an intriguing historical problem. It is also a problem of fundamental importance because from a political point of view Germany only caught up with the rest of Europe in the nineteenth century and its belated efforts to gain its full place in the European political system created difficulties that have just come to be resolved in our own age.

The major sources of Germany's strength from the reign of Otto the Great in the middle of the tenth century until the latter part of the eleventh century were its succession of strong rulers, its resistance to political fragmentation, and the close alliance of its crown with the Church. By resoundingly defeating the Hungarians and taking the title of emperor, Otto kept the country from falling prey to further invasions and won great prestige for the monarchy. For over a century afterward there was a nearly uninterrupted succession of rulers as able and vigorous as Otto. Their nearest political rivals were the dukes, military leaders of five large German territories (Lorraine, Saxony, Franconia, Swabia, and Bavaria), but throughout most of this period the dukes were overawed by the emperors' greater power. The latter, in order to rule their wide territories—which included Switzerland, eastern France, and most of the Low Countries, as well as claims to northern Italy—relied heavily on cooperation with the Church. The leading royal administrators were archbishops and bishops whom the emperors appointed without interference from the pope and who often came from their own families. The German emperors were so strong that, when they chose to do so, they could come down to Italy and name their own popes. The archbishops and bishops ran the German government fairly well for the times without any elaborate administrative machinery, and they counterbalanced the strength of the dukes. In the course of the eleventh century the emperors were starting tentatively to develop their own secular administration. Had they been allowed to continue this policy, it might have provided a really solid governmental foundation for the future. But just then the whole system shaped by Otto the Great and his successors was dramatically challenged by a revolution within the Church.

The challenge to the German government came in the reign of Henry IV (1056–1106) and was directed by Pope Gregory VII (1073–1085). For reasons that will be discussed in the next chapter, Gregory wished to free the Church from secular control and launched a struggle to achieve this aim against Henry IV. Gregory immediately placed Henry on the defensive by forging an alliance with the dukes and other German princes, who only needed a sufficient pretext to rise up against their ruler. When the princes threatened to depose Henry because of his disobedience to the pope, the hitherto mighty ruler was forced to seek absolution from Gregory VII in one of the most melodramatic scenes of the Middle Ages. In the depths of winter in 1077 Henry hurried over the Alps to abase himself before the pope in the north Italian castle of Canossa. As Gregory described the scene in a letter to the princes: "There on three successive days, standing before the castle gate, laying aside all royal insignia, barefooted and in coarse attire, Henry ceased not with many tears to beseech the apostolic help and comfort." No German ruler had ever been so humiliated. Although the events at Canossa forestalled Henry's deposition, they robbed him of his great prestige. By the time his struggle with the papacy, continued by his son, was over, the princes had won far more practical independence from the crown than they had ever had. More

*The German monarchy in
the tenth and eleventh
centuries*

*The struggle between
Henry IV and Gregory
VII*

Frederick Barbarossa. A stylized contemporary representation.

Frederick's Italian policy

than that, in 1125 they made good their claims to be able to elect a new ruler regardless of hereditary succession—a principle that would thereafter often lead them to choose the weakest successors or to embroil the country in civil war. Meanwhile, the crown had lost much of its control of the Church and thus in effect had its administrative rug pulled out from under it. While France and England were gradually consolidating their centralized governmental apparatuses, Germany was losing its own.

A major attempt to stem the tide running against the German monarchy was made in the twelfth century by Frederick I (1152–1190), who came from the family of Hohenstaufen. Frederick, called "Barbarossa" (meaning "red beard"), tried to reassert his imperial dignity by calling his realm the "Holy Roman Empire," on the theory that it was a universal empire descending from Rome and blessed by God. Laying claim to Roman descent, he promulgated old Roman imperial laws—preserved in the Code of Justinian—that gave him much theoretical power. But he could not hope to enforce such laws unless he had his own material base of support. Therefore the major policy of his reign was to balance the power of the princes by carving out his own geographical domain from which he might draw wealth and strength.

Unfortunately for Frederick, his ancestral lands were located in Swabia, a poorer part of Germany that even today still consists of relatively unproductive hill country and the Black Forest. So Frederick decided to make northern Italy his power base in addition to Swabia. In this he could hardly have made a worse decision. Northern Italy was certainly wealthy, but it was also fiercely independent. Its rich towns and cities, led by Milan, offered stiff resistance. They were further lent helpful moral support by the papacy, which had no wish to see a strong German emperor ruling powerfully in Italy. Frederick came very close to overpowering the urban-papal alliance but ultimately the Alps proved to be too great a barrier to allow him to enforce his will in Italy and hope to rule in Germany as well. Whenever he subdued the towns he would shortly afterward have to leave for home, and the towns, with papal encouragement, would then rise up again. Finally, in 1176, insufficient German imperial forces were resoundingly defeated by the troops of a north Italian urban coalition—the Lombard League—at Legnano, and Barbarossa was forced to concede the area's de facto independence. In the meantime, the princes in Germany were continuing to gather strength, especially by colonizing the rich agricultural lands east of the Elbe where Frederick really should have busied himself, and the emperor's struggle with the popes further alienated elements within the German church. Because Barbarossa was a dashing figure he was well remembered by Germans, but his reign virtually made it certain that the German empire would not rise again during the medieval period.

The reign of Barbarossa's equally famous grandson, Frederick II (1212–1250), was merely a playing out of Germany's fate. In terms of his personality Frederick was probably the most fascinating of all medieval rulers. Because his father, Henry VI, had inherited through marriage the kingdom of southern Italy and Sicily (later called the Kingdom of the Two Sicilies), Frederick grew up in Palermo, where he absorbed elements of Islamic culture. (Arabs had ruled in Sicily for two and a half centuries, from 831 to 1071.) Frederick II spoke five or six languages, was a patron of learning, and wrote his own book on falconry, which takes an honored place in the early history of Western observational science. He also performed bizarre and brutal "experiments," such as disemboweling men to observe the comparative effects of rest and exercise upon digestion. Such practices corresponded to Frederick's overall policy of trying to rule like an Oriental despot. In his autonomous kingdom of southern Italy he introduced Eastern forms of absolutist and bureaucratic government. He established a professional army, levied direct taxation, and promulgated uniform Roman law. Typically, Frederick tried to create a ruler cult and decreed it an act of sacrilege even to discuss his statutes or judgments. For a while these policies seemed successful in ruling southern Italy, but Frederick's power base in Italy led to renewed conflicts with the papacy and the north Italian cities. These dragged on indecisively until his death, but thereafter the papacy was resolved to see no further Hohenstaufens ruling in Italy and proceeded to eliminate the remaining contenders from the line by calling crusades against them. Overtaxed by Frederick's ruthlessness and subsequent wars, southern Italy gradually sank into the backwardness from which it is only barely emerging today. And Frederick's reign was damaging to Germany as well. Bent on pursuing his Italian policies without hindrance, Frederick formally wrote Germany off to the princes by granting them large areas of sovereignty. Although titular "emperors" afterward continued to be elected, the princes were the real rulers of the country. Yet they fought with each other so much that peace was rare, and they subdivided their lands among their heirs to such an extent that the map of Germany began to look like a jig-saw puzzle. As the French writer Voltaire later said, the German "Holy Roman Empire" had become neither holy, nor Roman, nor an empire.

The story of high-medieval Italian politics may be told more quickly. Southern Italy and Sicily had been welded together into a strong monarchical state in the twelfth century by Norman-French descendants of the Vikings. But then, as we have seen, the area went to the Hohenstaufens and was subsequently brought to ruin. Central Italy was largely ruled by the papacy in the High Middle Ages, but the popes were seldom strong enough to create a really well-governed state, partly because they were at constant loggerheads with the German emperors. Farthest north were the rich commercial and manufac-

*Frederick II; his
personality and policies*

The Emperor Frederick II. He is shown holding a *fleur de lis,* as a symbol of rule, with a falcon, his favorite bird, at his side.

*The political situation in
high-medieval Italy*

GERMAN EMPIRE c. 1200 A.D.

turing cities which had successfully fought off Barbarossa. These were usually organized politically in the form of republics or "communes." They offered much participation in governmental life to their more prosperous inhabitants. But because of diverse economic interests and family antagonisms, the Italian cities were usually riven with internal strife. Moreover, although they could unite in leagues against foreign threats such as those represented by Barbarossa or Frederick II, the cities often fought each other when foreign threats were absent. The result was that although economic and cultural life was very far advanced in the Italian cities, and although the cities made important experiments in administrative techniques, political stability was widely lacking in northern Italy throughout most of the high-medieval period.

If one looks for the centers of growing political stability in Europe, then one has to seek them in high-medieval France and England. Ironically, some of the most basic foundations for future political achievement in France were established without any planning just when that area was most politically unstable. These foundations were aspects of a level of political decentralization often referred to by historians as the system of "feudalism." The use of this word is controversial because ever since Marx some historians prefer to use it as a term to describe an agrarian economic and social system wherein large estates are worked by a dependent peasantry. The difficulty with this usage is that it is too imprecise, for such large estates existed in many times and places beyond the European Middle Ages and the medieval agrarian system can best be called manorialism. Some historians on the other extreme argue that even if the word feudalism is used to describe a medieval political system, medieval realities were so diverse that no one definition of feudalism can accurately or even usefully be extended to cover more than a single case. Nonetheless, for convenience we can retain the use of the word here and apply it to a specific point in medieval political development so long as we bear in mind that, like manorialism, it is only meant to serve as an approximation and that other historians may use it as a term for economic or sociological analysis.

Political feudalism was essentially a system of extreme political decentralization wherein what we today would call public power was widely vested in private hands. From a historical perspective it was most fully experienced in France during the tenth century when the Carolingian empire had disintegrated and the area was being buffeted by devastating Viking invasions. The Carolingians had maintained a modicum of public authority, but they proved to be no help whatsoever in warding off the invasions. So local landlords had to fend for themselves. In the end, the landlords turned out to offer the best defense against the Vikings and accordingly were able to acquire practically all the old governmental powers. They raised their own small armies, dispensed their own crude justice, and occasionally issued their own primitive coins. Despite such decentralization, however, it was never forgotten that there once had been higher and larger units of government. Above all, no matter how weak the king was (and he was indeed usually very weak), there always remained a king in France who descended directly or indirectly from the western branch of the Carolingians. There also were scattered remaining dukes or counts, who in theory were supposed to have more power and authority than petty landlords or knights. So, by a complicated and hard-to-trace process of rationalization, a vague theory was worked out in the course of the tenth and eleventh centuries that tried to establish some order within feudalism. According to this, minor feudal lords did not hold their powers outright but only held them as so-called *fiefs* (rhymes with reefs), which could be revoked upon noncompliance with certain obligations. In theory—and much of this theory was ignored in practice for long periods of time—the king or higher lords granted fiefs, that is, governmental rights over various lands, to lesser lords in return for a stipulated amount of military service. In turn, the lesser lords could grant some of those fiefs to still lesser lords for military services until the chain stopped at the lowest level of knights. The holder of a fief was called a *vassal* of the granter, but this term had none of the demeaning connotations that it has gained today. Vassalage—much unlike serfdom—was a purely honorable status and all fief-holders were "noble."

Feudalism as a cause of political progress

Since feudalism was originally a form of decentralization, it once was considered by historians to have been a corrosive or divisive historical force; in common speech today many use the word feudal as a synonym for backward. But scholars more recently have come to the conclusion that feudalism was a force for progress and a fundamental point of departure for the growth of the modern state. They note that in areas such as Germany and Italy, where there was hardly any feudalism, political stabilization and unification came only in later times, whereas in the areas of France and England, which saw full feudalization, stabilization and governmental centralization came rapidly afterward. Scholars now posit several reasons for this. Because feudalism was originally spontaneous and makeshift, it was highly flexible. Local lords, instead of being bound by anachronistic, procrustean principles, could rule as seemed best at the moment, or could bend to the dictates of particular local customs. Thus their governments, however crude, worked the best for their times and could be used for building an even stronger government as time went on. A second reason for the effectiveness of feudalism was that it drew more people into direct contact with the actual workings of political life than had the old Roman or Carolingian systems. Government on the most local level could most easily be seen or experienced; as it became tangible people began to appreciate and identify with it far more than they had appreciated empires. The result was that feudalism inculcated growing governmental loyalty, and once that loyalty was developed it could be drawn upon by still larger units. Third, feudalism helped lead to certain more modern institutions by its emphasis on courts. As the feudal system became more regularized, it became customary for vassals to appear at the court of their overlords at least once a year. There they were expected to "pay court," i.e., show certain ceremonial signs of loyalty, and also to serve on "courts" in the sense of participating in trials and offering counsel. Thus they became more and more accustomed to performing governmental business and began to behave more like courtiers or politicians. As the monarchical states of

Battle of Hastings. A scene from the Bayeux tapestry, embroidered shortly after William the Conqueror's victory. The inscription reads in translation: "Here the English and French have fallen together in battle."

France and England themselves developed, kings saw how useful the feudal court was and made it the administrative kernel of their expanding governmental systems. A final reason why feudalism led to political progress is not really intrinsic to the system itself. Because the theory of larger units was never forgotten, it could be drawn upon by greater lords and kings when the right time came to reacquire their rights.

The greatest possibilities for the use of feudalism were first demonstrated in England after the Norman Conquest of 1066. We have seen that England became unified and enjoyed strong kingship under the Saxon Alfred and his successors in the late ninth and tenth centuries. But then the Saxon kingship began to weaken, primarily as the result of renewed Viking invasions and poor leadership. In 1066 William, the duke of Normandy (in northwestern France), laid claim to the English crown and crossed the Channel to conquer what he had claimed. Fortunately for him the newly installed English king, Harold, had just warded off a Viking attack in the north and thus could not offer resistance at full strength. At the Battle of Hastings Harold and his Saxon troops fought bravely, but ultimately could not withstand the onslaught of the fresher Norman troops. As the day waned Harold fell, mortally wounded by a random arrow, his forces dispersed, and the Normans took the field and with it, England. Duke William now became King William, the Conqueror, and proceeded to rule his new prize as he wished.

The Norman Conquest

With hindsight we can say that the Norman Conquest came at just the right time to preserve and enhance political stability. Before 1066 England was threatened with disintegration under warrior aristocrats called earls, but William destroyed their power entirely. In its place he substituted the feudal system, whereby all the land in England was

The feudal system in Norman England

newly granted in the form of fiefs held directly or indirectly from the king. Fief-holders had most of the governmental rights they had obtained less formally on the Continent, but William retained the prerogatives of coining money, collecting a land tax, and supervising justice in major criminal cases. He also retained the Anglo-Saxon officer of local government, known as the sheriff, to help him administer and enforce these rights. In order to make sure that none of his barons (the English term for major fief-holders) became too powerful, William was careful to scatter the fiefs granted to them throughout various parts of the country. In these ways William used feudal practices to help govern England when there were not yet enough trained administrators to allow any real governmental professionalization. But he also retained much royal power and kept the country thoroughly unified under the crown.

The growth of national monarchy in England; the reign of Henry I

The history of English government in the two centuries after William is primarily a story of kings tightening up the feudal system to their advantage until they superseded it and created a strong national monarchy. The first to take steps in this direction was the Conqueror's energetic son Henry I (1100–1135). One of his most important accomplishments was to start a process of specialization at the royal court whereby certain officials began to take full professional responsibility for supervising financial accounts; these officials became known as clerks of the *Exchequer*. Another accomplishment was to institute a system of traveling circuit-judges to administer justice as direct royal representatives in various parts of the realm.

The struggle between Henry II and Thomas Becket

After an intervening period of civil war Henry I was succeeded by his grandson Henry II (1154–1189), who was very much in his grandfather's activist mold. Henry II's reign was certainly one of the most momentous in all of English history. One reason for this was that it saw a great struggle between the king and the flamboyant archbishop of Canterbury, Thomas Becket, over the status of Church courts and Church law. In Henry's time priests and other clerics were tried for any crimes in Church courts under the rules of canon law. Punishment in these courts was notoriously lax. Even murderers were seldom sentenced to more than penance and loss of their clerical status. Also, decisions handed down in English Church courts could be appealed to the papal *curia* in Rome. Henry, who wished to have royal law prevail as far as possible and maintain judicial standards for all subjects in his realm, tried to limit these practices by the Constitutions of Clarendon of 1164. On the matter of clerics accused of crime he was willing to compromise by allowing them to be judged in Church courts but then have them sentenced in royal ones. Becket, however, resisted all attempts at change with great determination. The quarrel between king and archbishop was made more bitter by the fact that the two had earlier been close friends. It reached a tragic climax when Becket was murdered in Canterbury Cathedral by four of Henry's knights, after

Martyrdom of Thomas Becket. From a thirteenth-century English Psalter. One of the knights has struck Becket so mightily that he has broken his sword.

the king, in an outburst of anger, had rebuked them for doing nothing to rid him of his antagonist. The crime so shocked the English public that Becket was quickly revered as a martyr and became the most famous English saint. More important for the history of government, Henry had to abandon most of his program of bringing the Church courts under royal control, and his aims were only fulfilled in the sixteenth century with the coming of the English Reformation.

Despite this major setback, Henry II made enormous governmental gains in other areas, so much so that some historians maintain that Henry was the greatest king that England has ever known. His most important contributions were judicial. He greatly expanded the use of the itinerant judges instituted by Henry I and began the practice of commanding sheriffs to bring before these judges groups of men who were familiar with local conditions. These were then required to report under oath every case of murder, arson, robbery, or other major crimes known to them to have occurred since the judges' last visit. This was the origin of the grand jury. Henry also for the first time allowed parties in civil disputes to obtain royal justice. In the most prevalent type of case, someone who claimed to have been recently dispossessed of his land could obtain a writ from the crown, which

The judicial reforms of Henry II

would order the sheriff to bring twelve men who were assumed to know the facts before a judge. The twelve were then asked under oath if the plaintiff's claim was true, and the judge rendered his decision in accordance with their answers. Out of such practices grew the institution of the trial jury, although the trial jury was not used in criminal cases until the thirteenth century.

The benefits of Henry's legal work

Henry II's legal innovations benefited both the crown and the country in several ways. Most obviously, they made justice more uniform and equitable throughout the realm. They also thereby made royal justice sought after and popular. Particularly in disputes over land—the most important and frequent disputes of the day—the weaker party was no longer at the mercy of a strong-arming neighbor. Usually the weaker parties were knights, with whom the crown before then had not been in close touch. In helping defend their rights Henry gained valuable allies in his policy of keeping the stronger barons in tow. Finally, the widespread use of juries in Henry's reign brought more and more people into actual participation in royal government. In so doing it got them more interested in government and more loyal to government. Since these people served without pay, Henry brilliantly managed to expand the competence and popularity of his government at very little cost.

Medieval Justice. Medieval sentencing was usually harsh. Here a convicted offender pays for his crime with the loss of his right hand.

The most concrete proof of Henry II's success is that after his death his government worked so well that it more or less ran on its own. Henry's son, the swashbuckling Richard I, the "Lionhearted," ruled for ten years, from 1189 to 1199, but in that time he only stayed in England for six months because he was otherwise engaged in crusading or defending his possessions on the Continent. Throughout the time of Richard's absence governmental administration actually became more efficient, owing to the work of capable ministers. The country also raised two huge sums for Richard by taxation: one to pay for his crusade to the Holy Land and the other to buy his ransom when he was captured by an enemy on his return. But later when a new king needed still more money, most Englishmen were disinclined to pay it.

The reign of John; Magna Carta

The new king was Richard's brother, John (1199–1216), who has the reputation of being a villain but was more a victim of circumstances. Ever since the time of William the Conqueror, English kings had continued to rule in large portions of modern-day France, but by John's reign the kings of France were becoming strong enough to take back much of these territories. John had the great misfortune of facing the able French King Philip Augustus, who won back Normandy and neighboring lands by force of arms in 1204 and reinsured this victory by military successes in 1214. John needed money both to govern England and to fight in France, but his defeats made his subjects disinclined to give it to him. The barons particularly resented John's financial exigencies and in 1215 they made him renounce these in the subsequently famous Magna Carta (Great Charter), a document which was also designed to redress all the other abuses the barons could think of. Most common conceptions of Magna Carta are erroneous. It was not intended to be a bill of rights or a charter of liberties for the common man. On the contrary, it was basically a feudal document in which the king as overlord pledged to respect the traditional rights of his vassals. Nonetheless, it did enunciate in writing the important principles that large sums of money could not be raised by the crown without consent given by the barons in a common council, and that no free man could be punished by the crown without judgment by his equals and by the law of the land. Above all, Magna Carta was important as an expression of the principle of limited government and of the idea that the king is bound by the law.

As the contemporary American medievalist J. R. Strayer has said, "Magna Carta made arbitrary government difficult, but it did not make centralized government impossible." In the century following its issuance, the progress of centralized government continued apace. In the reign of John's son, Henry III (1216–1277), the barons vied with the weak king for control of the government but did so on the assumption that centralized government itself was a good thing. Throughout that period administrators continued to perfect more efficient legal and administrative institutions. Whereas in the reign of Henry I financial administration began to become a specialized bureau of the royal court, in the reign of Henry III this became true of legal administration (the creation of permanent High Courts) and administration of foreign correspondence (the so-called Chancery). English central government was now fully developing a trained officialdom.

The last and most famous branch of the medieval English governmental system was Parliament. This gradually emerged as a separate branch of government in the decades before and after 1300, above all owing to the wishes of Henry III's son, Edward I (1272–1307). Although Parliament later became a check against royal absolutism, nothing could be further from the truth than to think that its first meetings were "demanded by the people." In its origins Parliament actually had little to do with popular representation, but was rather the king's feudal court in its largest gathering. Edward I was a strong king who called Parliaments frequently to raise money as quickly and efficiently as possible in order to help finance his foreign wars. Those present at Parliaments were not only expected to give their consent to taxation—in fact, it was virtually inconceivable for them to refuse—but while they were there they were told why taxes were necessary so that they would pay them less grudgingly. They could also agree upon details of collection and payment. At the same meetings Edward could take advice about pressing concerns, have justice done for exceptional cases, review local administration, and promulgate new laws. Probably the most unusual trait of Edward's Parliaments in comparison to similar assemblies on the Continent was that they

The progress of centralized government in the reign of Henry III

Origins of the English Parliament

began to include representatives from the counties and towns in addition to the higher nobility. These representatives, however, scarcely spoke for "the people" because most of the people of England were unfranchised serfs and peasants—not to mention women, who were never consulted in any way. Most likely, Edward had predominantly financial motives for calling representatives from the "commons." He probably also realized the propaganda value of overawing local representatives with royal grandeur at impressive parliamentary meetings so that they would then spread a favorable impression of the monarchy back home. As time went on, commoners were called to Parliament so often that they became a recognized part of its organization: by the middle of the fourteenth century they sat regularly in their own "house." But they still represented only the prosperous people of countryside and towns and were usually manipulated by the crown or the nobles.

The English monarchy under Edward I

Edward I's reign also saw the culmination of the development of a strong national monarchy in other aspects. By force of arms Edward nearly unified the entire island of Britain, conquering Wales and almost subduing Scotland (which, however, was to rise up again soon after his death). Edward began the practice of regularly issuing statute law, that is, original public legislation designed to apply indefinitely to the entire realm. Because of his role as a lawgiver, Edward is sometimes referred to as the "English Justinian." Most important, Edward also curtailed the feudal powers of his barons by limiting their rights to hold private courts and to grant their own lands as fiefs. Thus, by the end of his reign much of the independent power once consciously vested with the barons by William the Conqueror was being taken away from them. The explanation for this is that in the intervening high-medieval centuries the king was developing his own royal institutions of government to the degree that old-fashioned feudalism was now no longer of any real service. Because Edward pressed his strong government and financial demands somewhat excessively for the spirit of the age, there was an antimonarchical reaction after his death. But it is striking that after Edward's time whenever there were baronial rebellions they were always made on the assumption that England would remain a unified country, governed by the basic high-medieval monarchical institutions. England was unified around the crown in the High Middle Ages and would remain a basically well-governed and unified country right up to modern times.

The process of political centralization in France

While the process of governmental centralization was making impressive strides in England, it developed more slowly in France. But by around 1300 it had come close to reaching the same point of completion. French governmental unification proceeded more slowly because France in the eleventh century was more decentralized than England and faced greater problems. The last of the weak Carolingian monarchs was replaced in 987 by Hugh Capet, the count of Paris, but the

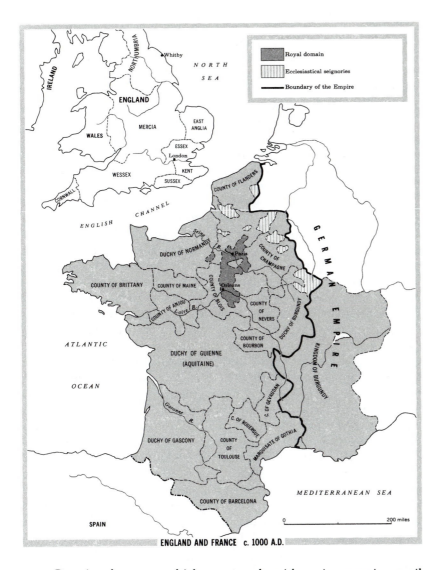

Royal domain

Ecclesiastical seignories

Boundary of the Empire

ENGLAND AND FRANCE c. 1000 A.D.

new Capetian dynasty—which was to rule without interruption until 1328—was at first no stronger than the old Carolingian one. Even through most of the twelfth century the kings of France ruled directly only in a small area around Paris known as the Ile-de-France, roughly the size of Vermont. Beyond that territory the kings had shadowy claims to being the feudal overlords of numerous counts and dukes throughout much of the area of modern France, but for practical purposes those counts and dukes were almost entirely independent. It was said that when the king of France demanded homage from the first duke of Normandy, the duke had one of his warriors pretend to kiss the king's foot but then seize the royal leg and pull the king over backwards, to the mockery of all those present. While the French king-

Factors facilitating the growth of the French monarchy

ship was so weak, the various parts of France were developing their own distinct local traditions and dialects. Thus, whereas William the Conqueror inherited in England a country that had already been unified and was just on the verge of falling apart, the French kings of the High Middle Ages had to unify their country from scratch, with only a vague reminiscence of Carolingian unity to build upon.

In many respects, however, luck was on their side. First of all, they were fortunate for hundreds of years in having direct male heirs to succeed them. Consequently, there were no deadly quarrels over the right of succession. In the second place, most of the French kings lived to an advanced age, the average period of rule being about thirty years. That meant that sons were already mature men when they came to the throne and there were few regencies to squander the royal power during the minority of a prince. More than that, the kings of France were always highly visible, if sometimes not very imposing, when there were power struggles elsewhere, so people in neighboring areas became accustomed to thinking of the kingship as a force for stability in an unstable world. A third favorable circumstance for the French kings was the growth of agricultural prosperity and trade in their home region; this provided them with important sources of revenue. A fourth fortuitous development was that the kings were able to gain the support of the popes because the latter usually needed allies in their incessant struggles with the German emperors. The popes lent the French kings prestige, as they earlier had done for the Carolingians, and they also allowed them much direct power over the local Church, thereby bringing the kings further income and influence from patronage. A fifth factor in the French king's favor was the growth in the twelfth and thirteenth centuries of the University of Paris as the leading European center of studies. As foreigners came flocking to the university, they learned of the French king's growing authority and spread their impressions when they returned home. Finally, and by no means least of all, great credit must be given to the shrewdness and vigor of several of the French kings themselves.

Foundations of the French monarchy; Louis VI and Philip Augustus

The first noteworthy Capetian king was Louis VI, "the Fat" (1108–1137). While accomplishing nothing startling, Louis at least managed to pacify his home base, the Ile-de-France, by driving out or subduing its turbulent "robber barons." Once this was accomplished, agriculture and trade could prosper and the intellectual life of Paris could start to flourish. Thereafter, the French kings had a geographical source of power of exactly the kind that the German ruler Barbarossa sought but never found. The really startling additions to the realm were made by Louis's grandson, Philip Augustus (1180–1223). Philip was wily enough to know how to take advantage of certain feudal rights in order to win large amounts of western French territory from the English King John. He was also decisive enough to know how to defend his gains in battle. Most impressive of all, Philip worked out an excellent formula for governing his new acquisitions. Since these increased his original lands close to fourfold, and since each new area had its own highly distinct local customs, it would have been hopeless to try to enforce strict governmental standardization by means of what was then a very rudimentary administrative system. Instead, Philip allowed his new provinces to maintain most of their indigenous governmental practices but superimposed on them new royal officials known as *baillis*. These officials were entirely loyal to Philip because they never came from the regions in which they served and were paid impressive salaries for the day. They had full judicial, administrative, and military authority in their bailiwicks: on royal orders they tolerated regional diversities but guided them to the king's advantage. Thus there were no revolts in the conquered territories and royal power was enhanced. This pattern of local diversity balanced against bureaucratic centralization was to remain the basic pattern of French government. Thus Philip Augustus can be seen as an important founder of the modern French state.

In the brief reign of Philip's son, Louis VIII (1223–1226), almost all of southern France was added to the crown in the name of intervention against religious heresy. Once incorporated, this territory was governed largely on the same principles laid down by Philip. The next king, Louis IX (1226–1270), was so pious that he was later canonized by the Church and is commonly referred to as St. Louis. He ruled strongly and justly (except for great intolerance of Jews and heretics), decreed a standardized coinage for the country, perfected the judicial system, and brought France a long, golden period of internal peace. Because he was so well-loved, the monarchy lived off his prestige for many years afterward.

That prestige, however, came close to being squandered by St. Louis's more ruthless grandson, Philip IV, "the Fair" (1285–1314). Philip fought many battles at once, seeking to round out French territories in the northeast and southwest and to gain full control over the French Church instead of sharing it with the pope in Rome. All these activities forced him to accelerate the process of governmental centralization, especially with the aim of trying to raise money. Thus his reign saw the quick formulation of many administrative institutions that came close to completing the development of medieval French government, as the contemporary reign of Edward I did in England. Philip's reign also saw the calling of assemblies that were roughly equivalent to the English Parliaments, but these—later called "Estates General"—never played a central role in the French governmental system. Philip the Fair was successful in most of his ventures; above all, as we will later see, in reducing the pope to the level of a virtual French figurehead. After his death there would be an antimonarchical reaction, as there was at the same time in England, but by his reign France was unquestionably the strongest power in Europe. With only a sixteenth-century interruption, it would remain so until the nineteenth century.

While England and France followed certain similar processes of mo-

A Seal Depicting Philip Augustus

St. Louis

King Philip the Fair of France

Comparison of England and France

narchical centralization and nation-building, they were also marked by basic differences that are worth describing because they were to typify differences in development for centuries after. England, a far smaller country than France, was much better unified. Aside from Wales and Scotland, there were no regions in Britain that had such different languages or traditions that they thought of themselves as separate territories. Correspondingly, there were no aristocrats who could move toward separatism by drawing on regional resentments. This meant that England never really had to face the threat of internal division and could develop strong institutions of united national government such as Parliament. It also meant that the English kings, starting primarily with Henry II, could rely on numerous local dignitaries, above all, the knights, to do much work of local government without pay. The obvious advantage was that local government was cheap, but the hidden implication of the system was that government also had to be popular, or else much of the voluntary work would grind to a halt. This doubtless was the main reason why English kings went out of their way to seek formal consent for their actions. When they did not they could barely rule, so wise kings learned the lesson and as time went on England became most clearly a limited monarchy. The French kings, much to the contrary, ruled a richer and larger country, which gave them—at least in times of peace—sufficient wealth to pay for a more bureaucratic, salaried administration at both the central and local levels. French kings therefore could rule more absolutely. But they were continually faced with serious threats of regional separatism. Different regions continued to cherish their own traditions and often supported centrifugalism in league with the upper aristocracy. So French kings often had to struggle with attempts at regional breakaways and take various measures to subdue their aristocrats. Up to around 1700 the monarchy had to fight a steady battle against regionalism, but it had the resources to win consistently and thereby managed to grow from strength to strength.

Medieval Spain

The only continental state that would rival France until the rise of Germany in the nineteenth century was Spain. The foundations of Spain's greatness were also laid in the High Middle Ages on the principle of national monarchy, but in the Middle Ages there was not yet one monarchy that ruled through most of the Iberian peninsula. After the Christians started pushing back the forces of Islam around 1100 there were four Spanish Christian kingdoms: the tiny northern mountain state of Navarre, which would always remain comparatively insignificant; Portugal in the west; Aragon in the northeast; and Castile in the center. The main Spanish occupation in the High Middle Ages was the *Reconquista,* i.e., the reconquest of the peninsula for Christianity. This reached its culmination in the year 1212 in a major victory of a combined Aragonese-Castilian army over the Muslims at Las Navas de Tolosa. The rest was mostly mopping up. By the end of

Bullfighting in a Thirteenth-Century Spanish Arena. Times do not seem to have changed much, although here the spectators are taking a rather unsporting part in the action.

the thirteenth century all that remained of earlier Muslim domination was the small state of Granada in the extreme south, and Granada existed largely because it was willing to pay tribute to the Christians. Because Castile had the largest open frontier, it became by far the largest Spanish kingdom, but it was balanced in wealth by the more urban and trade-oriented Aragon. Both kingdoms developed institutions in the thirteenth century that roughly paralleled those of France. But until the union of Aragon and Castile under King Ferdinand and Queen Isabella in the fifteenth century, the Iberian states individually could not hope to be as strong as the much richer and more populous France.

Before concluding this chapter it is best to assess the general significance of the rise of the national monarchies in high-medieval western Europe. Until their emergence there had been two basic patterns of government in Europe: city-states and empires. City-states had the advantage of drawing heavily upon citizen participation and loyalty and thus were able to make highly efficient use of their human potential. But they were often divided by economic rivalries, and they were not sufficiently large or militarily strong to defend themselves against imperial forces. The empires, on the other hand, could win battles and often had the resources to support an efficient bureaucratic administrative apparatus, but they drew on little voluntary participation and were too far-flung or rapacious to inspire any deep loyalties. The new national monarchies were to prove the "golden mean" between these extremes. They were large enough to have adequate

Historical role of the national monarchies

military strength, and they developed administrative techniques that
would rival and eventually surpass those of the Roman or Byzantine
Empires. More than that, building at first upon the bases of feudalism,
they drew upon sufficient citizen participation and loyalty to help support them in times of stress when empires would have foundered. By
about 1300 the monarchies of England, France, and the Iberian peninsula had gained the primary loyalties of their subjects, superseding
loyalties to communities, regions, or to the government of the
Church. For all these reasons they brought much internal peace and
stability to large parts of Europe where there had been little stability
before. Thus they contributed greatly to making life fruitful. The medieval national monarchies were also the ancestors of the modern nation-states—the most effective and equitable governments of our day.
In short, they were one of the Middle Ages' most beneficial bequests
to modern times.

SELECTED READINGS

• *Items so designated are available in paperback editions.*

GENERAL STUDIES

• Bloch, Marc, *Feudal Society,* Chicago, 1961. A modern classic, first published
   in France in 1940. Full of valuable insights but outdated in some respects.
• Southern, R. W., *The Making of the Middle Ages,* New Haven, 1953. A
   subtle and brilliant reading of eleventh- and twelfth-century develop-
   ments. Difficult but most rewarding.
• Strayer, J. R., *Western Europe in the Middle Ages,* 3rd ed., Glenview, 1982.
   In a class by itself as the best short introduction to medieval political
   and cultural history.
• Wood, Charles T., *The Age of Chivalry* (also published as *The Quest for
   Eternity*), London, 1970. A lively work for the beginner that supplements
   Strayer in its emphasis on economic and social history.

ECONOMIC AND SOCIAL CONDITIONS

Bautier, R. H., *The Economic Development of Medieval Europe,* London, 1971.
• Duby, G., *Rural Economy and Country Life in the Medieval West,* London,
   1968. The best work on agrarian history. Highly recommended as an
   example of recent French historiography at its highest level.
Ennen, E., *The Medieval Town,* New York, 1979. Complements Duby
   on urban development.
• Gies, J. and F., *Life in a Medieval City,* New York, 1973. An engaging
   popular account concentrating on life in thirteenth-century Troyes.

- Herlihy, David, *Medieval Households,* Cambridge, Mass., 1985. Covers family history from late antiquity until the end of the Middle Ages.
- Keen, Maurice, *Chivalry,* New Haven, 1984.

  Labarge, M. W., *A Small Sound of the Trumpet: Women in Medieval Life,* London, 1986. A lively survey.
- Lopez, Robert S., *The Commercial Revolution of the Middle Ages, 950–1350,* Englewood Cliffs, N.J., 1971.
- Pirenne, H., *Economic and Social History of Medieval Europe,* London, 1936. Many of Pirenne's ideas are no longer accepted but this is still an extremely useful brief account.
- Postan, M. M., *The Medieval Economy and Society: An Economic History of Britain, 1100–1500,* Berkeley, 1972.
- Power, Eileen, *Medieval Women,* Cambridge, 1975. Very brief but informative.
- White, Lynn, Jr., *Medieval Technology and Social Change,* Oxford, 1962. Controversial but excellently written and thought-provoking.

POLITICAL DEVELOPMENTS

Baldwin, John W., *The Government of Philip Augustus,* Berkeley, 1986. A landmark of scholarship.
- Barraclough, G., *The Origins of Modern Germany,* 2nd ed., Oxford, 1947. Highly interpretative, should be read in conjunction with Hampe.

Davies, R. G., and J. H. Denton, eds., *The English Parliament in the Middle Ages,* Manchester, England, 1981. Essays communicating the most up-to-date knowledge about the history of Parliament from about 1200 until 1509.

Douglas, David, *The Norman Achievement, 1050–1100,* Berkeley, 1969.

_____, *The Norman Fate, 1100–1154,* Berkeley, 1976.
- Fawtier, R., *The Capetian Kings of France,* London, 1962. The best single volume on medieval French politics.

Hampe, K., *Germany under the Salian and Hohenstaufen Emperors,* Totowa, N.J., 1973. An older, reliable German work.

Hyde, J. K., *Society and Politics in Medieval Italy,* New York, 1973. An excellent survey that integrates political and social history.
- Loyn, H. R., *The Norman Conquest,* London, 1965.

O'Callaghan, Joseph F., *A History of Medieval Spain,* Ithaca, N.Y., 1975.

Petit-Dutaillis, Charles, *The Feudal Monarchy in France and England from the Tenth to the Thirteenth Century,* London, 1936. An excellent essay in comparative history.

Poole, Austin L., *From Domesday Book to Magna Carta, 1087–1216,* 2nd ed., Oxford, 1955. Very detailed yet clear.
- Sayles, G. O., *The King's Parliament of England,* New York, 1974. Emphasizes the role of the crown and downplays the importance of the commons.

_____, *The Medieval Foundations of England,* London, 1952. An excellent interpretation of medieval English political developments.
- Strayer, J. R., *On the Medieval Origins of the Modern State,* Princeton, 1970. A distillation of the ideas of one of America's greatest medievalists.

SOURCE MATERIALS

- Herlihy, David, ed., *The History of Feudalism,* New York, 1970.
- Lopez, Robert S., and I. W. Raymond, eds., *Medieval Trade in the Mediterranean World,* New York, 1955.
- Lyon, Bryce, ed., *The High Middle Ages,* New York, 1964.
- Otto, Bishop of Freising, *The Deeds of Frederick Barbarossa,* tr. C. C. Mierow, New York, 1953. A contemporary chronicle that is interesting enough to read from start to finish.
- Strayer, J. R., ed., *Feudalism,* Princeton, 1965.

Chapter 14

THE HIGH MIDDLE AGES (1050–1300): RELIGIOUS AND INTELLECTUAL DEVELOPMENTS

You would see men and women dragging carts through marshes . . . everywhere miracles daily occurring, jubilant songs rendered to God. . . . You would say that the prophecy was fulfilled, "The Spirit of Life was in the wheels."

—Abbot Robert of Torigni,
on the building of the cathedral
of Chartres, 1145

The religious and intellectual changes that transpired in the West between 1050 and 1300 were as important as the economic, social, and political ones. In the sphere of religion, the most fundamental organizational development was the triumph of the *papal monarchy*. Before the middle of the eleventh century certain popes had laid claim to primacy within the Church, but very few were able to come close to making good on such claims. Indeed, most popes before about 1050 were hardly able to rule effectively as bishops of Rome. But then, most dramatically, the popes emerged as the supreme religious leaders of Western Christendom. They centralized the government of the Church, challenged the sway of emperors and kings, and called forth the crusading movement. By 1300 the temporal success of the papacy had proven to be its own nemesis, but the popes still ruled the Church internally, as they continue to rule the Roman Catholic Church today.

Religious changes

While the papacy was assuming power, a new vitality infused the Christian religion itself, enabling Christianity to capture the human imagination as never before. At the same time too there was a remarkable revival of intellectual and cultural life. In education, thought, and the arts, as in economics and politics, the West before 1050 had been a

Intellectual changes

backwater. Thereafter it emerged swiftly from backwardness to become an intellectual and artistic leader of the globe. Westerners boasted that learning and the arts had moved northwest to them from Egypt, Greece, and Rome—a boast that was largely true. In the High Middle Ages Europeans first started building on ancient intellectual foundations and also contributed major intellectual and artistic innovations of their own.

1. THE CONSOLIDATION OF THE PAPAL MONARCHY

The sorry state of religious life in the tenth and early eleventh centuries

To understand the origins and appreciate the significance of the western European religious revival of the High Middle Ages it is necessary to have some idea of the level to which religion had sunk in the tenth and early eleventh centuries. Around 800 the Emperor Charlemagne had made some valiant attempts to enhance the religious authority of bishops, introduce the parish system into rural regions where there had hardly been any priests before, and provide for the literacy of the clergy. But with the collapse of the Carolingian Empire, religious decentralization and ensuing corruption prevailed throughout most of Europe. Most churches and monasteries became the private property of strong local lords. The latter disposed of Church offices under their control as they wished, often by selling them or by granting them to close relatives. Obviously this was not the best way to find the most worthy candidates, and many priests were quite unqualified for their jobs. They were almost always illiterate, and often they lived openly with concubines. When archbishops or bishops were able to control appointments the results were not much better because such officials were usually close relatives of secular lords who followed their practices of financial or family aggrandizement. As for the popes, they were usually incompetent or corrupt, the sons or tools of powerful families who lived in or around the city of Rome. Some were astonishingly debauched. John XII may have been the worst of them. He was made pope at the age of eighteen in 955 because of the strength of his family. It is certain that he ruled for nine years as a thorough profligate, but there is some uncertainty about the cause of his death: either he was caught *in flagrante delicto* by a jealous husband and murdered on the spot, or else he died in the midst of a carnal act from sheer amorous exertion.

Religious revival: (1) Cluny and monastic reform

Once Europe began to catch its breath from the wave of external invasions that peaked in the tenth century, the wide extent of religious corruption or indifference was bound to call forth some reaction. Bishops could do little to effect change because the work of a bishop was limited to what he could do in his lifetime, and even more because most archbishops and bishops were unable to disentangle themselves from the political affairs of their day. The first successful measures of reform were taken in the monasteries because monasteries could be somewhat more independent and could count more on the support of their reforms by lay lords, insofar as lords feared for the health of their souls if monks did not serve their proper function in saying offices (i.e., prayers). The movement for monastic reform began with the foundation of the monastery of Cluny in Burgundy in 910 by a pious nobleman. Cluny was a Benedictine house but it introduced two constitutional innovations. One was that, in order to remain free from domination by either local secular or ecclesiastical powers, it was made directly subject to the pope. The other was that it undertook the reform or foundation of numerous "daughter monasteries": whereas formerly all Benedictine houses had been independent and equal, Cluny founded a monastic "family," whose members were subordinate to it. Owing to the succession of a few extremely pious, active, and long-lived abbots, the congregation of Cluniac houses grew so rapidly that there were sixty-seven by 1049. In all of them dedicated priors were chosen who followed the dictates of the abbot of Cluny rather than being responsible to local potentates. Cluniac monks accordingly became famous for their industry in the saying of offices. And Cluny was only the most famous of the new congregations. Other similar ones spread just as rapidly in the years around 1000 and succeeded in making the reformed monasteries vital centers of religious life and prayer.

Around the middle of the eleventh century, after so many monasteries had been taken out of the control of secular authorities, the leaders of the monastic reform movement started to lobby for the reform of the clerical hierarchy as well. They centered their attacks upon *simony*—i.e., the buying and selling of positions in the Church— and they also demanded celibacy for all levels of clergy. Their entire program was directed toward depriving secular powers of their ability to dictate appointments of bishops, abbots, and priests, and toward making the clerical estate as "pure" and as distinct from the secular one as possible. Once this reform program was appropriated by the papacy, it would begin to change the face of the entire Church.

*(2) reform of the
secular clergy*

Considering that the reformers were greatly opposed to lay interference, it is ironic that their party was first installed in the papacy by a German emperor, namely Henry III. In 1046 this ruler came to Italy, deposed three rival Italian claimants to the papal title, and named as pope a German reformer from his own retinue. Henry III's act brought in a series of reforming popes, who started to promulgate decrees against simony, clerical marriage, and immorality of all sorts throughout the Church. These popes also insisted upon their own role as primates and universal spiritual leaders in order to give strength to their actions. One of the most important steps they took was the issuance in 1059 of a decree on papal elections. This vested the right of naming a new pope solely with the cardinals, thereby depriving the

*Emperor Henry III and
reform of the papacy*

Roman aristocracy or the German emperor of the chance to interfere in the matter. The decree preserved the independence of papal elections thereafter. In granting the right of election to cardinals the decree also became a milestone in the evolution of a special body within the Church. Ever since the tenth century a number of bishops and clerics, known as cardinals, from sees in and near Rome had taken on an important role as advisors and administrative assistants of the popes, but the election decree of 1059 first gave them their clearest powers. Thereafter the "college of cardinals" took on more and more administrative duties and helped create continuity in papal policy, especially when there was a quick succession of pontiffs. The cardinals still elect the pope today.

The ideals of Pope Gregory VII

A new and most momentous phase in the history of the reform movement was initiated during the pontificate of Gregory VII (1073–1085). Scholars disagree about how much Gregory was indebted to the ideas and policies of his predecessors in the reform movement and how much he departed from them. The answer seems to be that Gregory supported reform as much as others, indeed he explicitly renewed his predecessors' decrees against simony and clerical marriage. Yet he was not only more zealous in trying to enforce these decrees—a contemporary even called him a "Holy Satan"—but he brought with him a basically new conception of the role of the Church in human life. Whereas the older Christian ideal had been that of withdrawal, and the perfect "athlete of Christ" had been a passive contemplative, or ascetic monk, Gregory VII conceived of Christianity as being much more activist and believed that the Church was responsible for creating "right order in the world." To this end he demanded absolute obedience and strenuous chastity from his clergy: some of his clerical opponents complained that he wanted clerics to live like angels. Equally important, he thought of kings and emperors as his inferiors, who would carry out his commands obediently and help him reform and evangelize the world. Gregory allowed that secular princes would continue to rule directly and make their own decisions in purely secular matters, but he expected them to accept ultimate papal overlordship. Put in other terms, in contrast to his predecessors who had sought merely a duality of ecclesiastical and secular authority, Gregory VII wanted to create a papal monarchy over both. When told that his ideas were novel, he and his immediate followers replied: "The Lord did not say 'I am custom'; the Lord said 'I am truth.' " Since no pope had spoken like this before, it is proper to accept the judgment of a modern historian who called Gregory "the great innovator, who stood quite alone."

The investiture struggle

Gregory's actual conduct as pope was nothing short of revolutionary. From the start he was determined to enforce a decree against "lay investiture," the practice whereby secular rulers ceremonially granted clerics the symbols of their office. The German Emperor

Henry IV was bound to resist this because the ceremony was a manifestation of his long-accepted rights to appoint and control churchmen: without these his own authority would be greatly weakened. The ensuing fight is often called "the investiture struggle" because the problem of investitures was a central one, but the struggle was really about the relative obedience and strength of pope and emperor. The larger issue was immediately joined when Henry IV flouted Gregory's injunctions against appointing prelates. Whereas earlier popes might have tried to deal with such insubordination diplomatically, Gregory rapidly took the entirely unprecedented step of excommunicating the emperor and suspending him from all his powers as an earthly ruler. This bold act amazed all who learned of it. Between 955 and 1057 German emperors had deposed five and named twelve out of twenty-five popes; now a pope dared to dismiss an emperor! We have seen in the previous chapter that in 1077 Henry IV abased himself before the pope in order to forestall a formal deposition: that act amazed contemporaries even more. Thereafter Henry was able to rally some support and sympathy for himself and a terrible war of words ensued, while on the actual battlefield the emperor was able to place troops supporting the pope on the defensive. In 1085 Gregory died, seemingly defeated. But Gregory's successors continued the struggle with Henry IV and later with his son, Henry V.

The long and bitter contest on investiture only came to an end with the Concordat of Worms (a city in Germany) of 1122. Under this compromise the German emperor was forbidden to invest prelates with *Results of the conflict* the religious symbols of their office but was allowed to invest them with the symbols of their rights as temporal rulers because the emperor was recognized as their temporal overlord. That settlement was ultimately less significant than the fact that the struggle had lastingly impaired the prestige of the emperors and raised that of the popes. In addition, the dramatic struggle helped rally the Western clergy behind the pope and galvanized the attentions of all onlookers. As one contemporary reported, nothing else was talked about "even in the women's spinning-rooms and the artisans' workshops." This meant that people who had earlier been largely indifferent to or excluded from religious issues became much more absorbed by them.

Gregory VII's successors and most of the popes of the twelfth century were fully committed to the goal of papal monarchy. But they were far less impetuous than Gregory had been and were more inter- *The growth of papal* ested in the everyday administration of the Church. They apparently *monarchy* recognized that there was no point in claiming to rule as papal monarchs unless they could avail themselves of a governmental apparatus to support their claims. To this end they presided over an impressive growth of law and administration. Under papal guidance the twelfth century saw the basic formulation of the canon law of the Church. Canon law claimed ecclesiastical jurisdiction for all sorts of cases per-

Pope Innocent III. A mosaic dating from the thirteenth century.

Innocent's policies in action

taining not only to the clergy but also to problems of marriage, inheritance, and rights of widows and orphans. Most of these cases were supposed to originate in the courts of bishops, but the popes insisted that they alone could issue dispensations from the strict letter of the law and that the papal *consistory*—composed of the pope and cardinals—should serve as a final court of appeals. As the power of the papacy and the prestige of the Church mounted, cases in canon law courts and appeals to Rome rapidly increased; after the middle of the twelfth century legal expertise became so important for exercising the papal office that most popes were trained canon lawyers, whereas previously they had usually been monks. Concurrent with this growth of legalism was the growth of an administrative apparatus to keep records and collect income. As the century wore on, the papacy developed a bureaucratic government that was far in advance of most of the secular governments of the day. This allowed it to become richer, more efficient, and ever stronger. Finally, the popes asserted their powers within the Church by gaining greater control over the election of bishops and by calling general councils in Rome to promulgate laws and demonstrate their leadership.

By common consent the most capable and successful of all high-medieval popes was Innocent III (1198–1216). Innocent, who was elected at the age of thirty-seven, was one of the youngest and most vigorous individuals ever to be raised to the papacy; more than that, he was expertly trained in theology and had also studied canon law. His major goal was to unify all Christendom under papal hegemony and to bring in the "right order in the world" so fervently desired by Gregory VII. He never questioned the right of kings and princes to rule directly in the secular sphere but believed that he could step in and discipline kings whenever they "sinned," a wide opening for interference. Beyond that, he saw himself as the ultimate overlord of all. In his own words he said that "as every knee is bowed to Jesus . . . so all men should obey His Vicar [i.e., the pope]."

Innocent sought to implement his goals in many different ways. In order to give the papacy a solid territorial base of support, like the one drawn upon by the French kings, he tried to initiate strong rule in the papal territories around Rome by consolidating them where possible and providing for efficient and vigilant administration. For this reason Innocent is often considered to be the real founder of the Papal States. But because some urban communities tenaciously sought to maintain their independence, he never came close to dominating the papal lands in Italy so completely as the French kings controlled the Ile-de-France. In other projects he was more completely successful. He intervened in German politics assertively enough to engineer the triumph of his own candidate for the imperial office, the Hohenstaufen Frederick II. He disciplined the French King Philip Augustus for his marital misconduct and forced John of England to accept an unwanted candidate as archbishop of Canterbury. To demonstrate his superiority and also gain income, Innocent forced John to grant England to the papacy as a fief, and he similarly gained the feudal overlordship of Aragon, Sicily, and Hungary. When southern France was threatened by the spread of the Albigensian heresy (to be discussed later) the pope effectively called a crusade that would extinguish it by force. He also levied the first income tax on the clergy to support a crusade to the Holy Land. The crown of Innocent's religious achievement was the calling of the Fourth Lateran Council in Rome in 1215. This defined central dogmas of the faith and made the leadership of the papacy within Christendom more apparent than ever. The pope was now clearly both disciplining kings and ruling over the Church without hindrance.

Innocent's reign was certainly the zenith of the papal monarchy, but it also sowed some of the seeds of future ruin. Innocent himself could administer the Papal States and seek new sources of income without seeming to compromise the spiritual dignity of his office. But future popes who followed his policies had less of his stature and thus began to appear more like ordinary acquisitive rulers. Moreover, because the Papal States bordered on the Kingdom of Sicily, Innocent's successors quickly came into conflict with the neighboring ruler, who was none other than Innocent's protégé Frederick II. Although Innocent had raised up Frederick, he did not suppose that Frederick would later become an inveterate opponent of papal power in Italy.

Problems for Innocent's successors

At first these and other problems were not fully apparent. The popes of the thirteenth century continued to enhance their powers and centralize the government of the Church. They gradually asserted the right to name candidates for ecclesiastical benefices, both high and low, and they asserted control over the curriculum and doctrine taught at the University of Paris. But they also became involved in a protracted political struggle which led to their own demise as temporal powers. This struggle began with the attempt of the popes to destroy Frederick II. To some degree they were acting in self-defense because Frederick threatened their own rule in central Italy. But in combating him they overemployed their spiritual weapons. Instead of merely excommunicating and deposing Frederick, they also called a crusade against him—the first time a crusade was called on a large scale for blatantly political purposes.

After Frederick's death in 1250 a succession of popes made a still worse mistake by renewing and maintaining their crusade against all of the emperor's heirs, whom they called the "viper brood." In order to implement this crusade they became preoccupied with raising funds, and they sought and won as their military champion a younger son from the French royal house, Charles of Anjou. But the latter only helped the popes for the purely political motive of winning the Kingdom of Sicily for himself. Charles in fact won Sicily in 1268 by defeating the last of Frederick II's male heirs. But he then taxed the realm so excessively that the Sicilians revolted in the "Sicilian Vespers" of 1282 and offered their crown to the king of Aragon, who had married Fred-

Charles of Anjou. One of the earliest known medieval statues that may have been done from life.

Pope Boniface VIII. From a portrait by Giotto.

erick II's granddaughter. The king of Aragon accordingly entered the Italian arena and came close to winning Frederick's former kingdom for himself. To prevent this Charles of Anjou and the reigning pope prevailed upon the king of France—then Philip III (1270–1285)—to embark on a crusade against Aragon. This crusade was a terrible failure and Philip III died on it. In the wake of these events Philip's son, Philip IV, resolved to alter the traditional French pro-papal policy. By that time France had become so strong that such a decision was fateful. More than that, by misusing the institution of the crusade and trying to raise increasingly large sums of money to support it, the popes had lost much of their prestige. The denouement would be played out at the very beginning of the next century.

The temporal might of the papacy was toppled almost melodramatically in the reign of Boniface VIII (1294–1303). Many of Boniface's troubles were not of his own making. His greatest obstacle was that the national monarchies had gained more of their subjects' loyalties than the papacy could draw upon because of the steady growth of royal power and erosion of papal prestige. Boniface also had the misfortune to succeed a particularly pious, although inept, pope who resigned his office within a year. Since Boniface was entirely lacking in conventional piety or humility, the contrast turned many Christian observers against him. Some even maintained—incorrectly—that Boniface had convinced his predecessor to resign and had murdered him shortly afterward. Boniface ruled assertively and presided over the first papal "jubilee" in Rome in 1300. This was an apparent, but, as events would show, hollow demonstration of papal might.

Two crucial disputes: (1) the issue of clerical taxation

Two disputes with the kings of England and France proved to be Boniface's undoing. The first concerned the clerical taxation that had been initiated by Innocent III. Although Innocent had levied this tax to support a crusade and had collected it himself, in the course of the thirteenth century the kings of England and France had begun to levy and collect clerical taxes on the pretext that they would use them to help the popes on future crusades to the Holy Land or aid in papal crusades against the Hohenstaufens. Then, at the end of the century, the kings started to levy their own war taxes on the clergy without any pretexts at all. Boniface understandably tried to prohibit this step, but quickly found that he had lost the support of the English and French clergy. Thus when the kings offered resistance he had to back down.

(2) quarrel with the king of France

Boniface's second dispute was with the king of France alone. Specifically it concerned Philip IV's determination to try a French bishop for treason. As in the earlier struggle between Gregory VII and Henry IV of Germany, the real issue was the comparative strength of papal and secular power, but this time the papacy was decisively defeated. As before, there was a bitter propaganda war, but now hardly anyone listened to the pope. The king instead pressed absurd charges of heresy against Boniface and sent his minions to arrest the pope to stand trial. At the papal residence of Anagni in 1303 Boniface, who was in his seventies, was captured and mistreated before he was released by the local citizens. These events exhausted the old man's strength and he died a month later. Immediately thereupon it was said that he had entered the papacy like a fox, reigned like a lion, but died like a dog.

After Boniface VIII's death the papacy became virtually a pawn of French temporal authority for most of the fourteenth century. But the emergence and success of the papal monarchy in the High Middle Ages had several beneficial effects during the course of that period. One was that the international rule of the papacy over the Church enhanced international communications and uniformity of religious practices. Another was that the papal cultivation of canon law aided a growing respect for law of all sorts and often helped protect the causes of otherwise defenseless subjects, like widows and orphans. The popes also managed to achieve some success in their campaigns to eliminate the sale of Church offices and to raise the morals of the clergy. By centralizing appointments they made it easier for worthy candidates who had no locally influential relatives to gain advancement. There was of course corruption in the papal government too, but in an age of entrenched localism the triumph of an international force was mainly beneficial. Finally, as we will see later, the growth of the papal monarchy helped bring vitality to popular religion and helped support the revival of learning.

Beneficial effects of the papal monarchy

2. THE CRUSADES

The rise and fall of the crusading movement was closely related to the fortunes of the high-medieval papal monarchy. The First Crusade was initiated by the papacy, and its success was a great early victory for the papal monarchy. But the later decline of the crusading movement helped undermine the pope's temporal authority. Thus the Crusades can be seen as part of a chapter in papal and religious history. In addition, the Crusades opened the first chapter in the history of Western colonialism.

Two themes of the crusading movement

The immediate cause of the First Crusade was an appeal for aid in 1095 by the Byzantine Emperor Alexius Comnenus. Alexius hoped to reconquer Byzantine territory in Asia Minor which had recently been lost to the Turks. Since he had already become accustomed to using Western mercenaries as auxiliary troops, he asked the pope to help rally some Western military support. But the emperor soon found, no doubt to his great surprise, that he was receiving not just simple aid but a *crusade*. In other words, instead of a band of mercenaries to fight in Asia Minor, the West sent forth an enormous army of volunteers whose goal was to wrest Jerusalem away from Islam. Since the decision to turn Alexius's call for aid into a crusade was made by the pope, it is well to examine the latter's motives.

The direct cause of the First Crusade

The reigning pope in 1095 was Urban II, an extremely competent

THE MAJOR CRUSADES

Legend:
- Population predominantly Christian
- Population predominantly Muslim
- First Crusade
- Second Crusade
- Third Crusade
- Fourth Crusade

Political boundaries are those shown at the time of the First Crusade

0 ___ 300 miles

The Gregorian theory of Christian warfare

disciple of Gregory VII. Without question, Urban called the First Crusade to help further the policies of the Gregorian papacy. Urban's very patronage of Christian warfare was Gregorian. Early Christianity had been pacifistic: St. Martin, for example, a revered Christian saint of the fourth century, gave up his career as a soldier when he converted with the statement "I am Christ's soldier; I cannot fight." The Latin fathers St. Augustine and St. Gregory worked out theories to justify Christian warfare but only in the eleventh century, with the triumph of the Gregorian movement, were these put into practice. Gregory VII engineered papal support for the Norman Conquest even before he became pope, and he, or popes under his influence, blessed Christian campaigns against Muslims in Spain, Greeks in Italy, and Slavs in the German east. All these campaigns were considered by Gregory VII and his followers to be steps toward gaining "right order in the world."

Following in Gregory VII's footsteps, Urban II probably conceived of a great crusade to the Holy Land as a means for achieving at least four ends. One was to bring the Greek Orthodox Church back into the fold. By sending a mighty volunteer army to the East, Urban might overawe the Byzantines with Western strength and convince them to reaccept Roman primacy. If he was successful in that, he would gain a great victory for the Gregorian program of papal monarchy. A second motive was to embarrass the pope's greatest enemy, the German emperor. In 1095 Henry IV had become so militarily strong that Urban had been forced to flee Italy for France. By calling a mighty crusade of all westerners but Germans, Urban might hope to show up the emperor as a narrow-minded, un-Christian persecutor, and demonstrate his own ability to be the spiritual leader of the West. Third, by sending off a large contingent of fighters Urban might help to achieve peace at home. Earlier, the local French Church had supported a "peace movement" which prohibited attacks on noncombatants (the "Peace of God") and then prohibited fighting on certain holy days (the "Truce of God"). Right before he called the First Crusade Urban promulgated the first full papal approval and extension of this peace movement. Clearly the crusade was linked to the call for peace: in effect, Urban told unruly warriors that if they really wished to fight they could do so justly for a Christian cause overseas. Finally, the goal of Jerusalem itself must have genuinely inspired Urban. Jerusalem was thought to be the center of the earth and was the most sacred shrine of the Christian religion. It must have seemed only proper that pilgrimages to Jerusalem should not be impeded and that Christians should rule the city directly. "Right order in the world" could scarcely mean less.

When Urban called his crusade at a Church council in the French town of Clermont in 1095, the response was more enthusiastic than he could possibly have expected. Many in the crowd interrupted the pope's speech with spontaneous cries of "God wills it," and many impetuously rushed off to the East shortly thereafter. All told, there were probably about a hundred thousand men in the main crusading army, an enormous number for the day. Accordingly, the question arises as to why Urban's appeal was so remarkably successful. Certainly there were economic and political reasons. Many of the poorer people who went crusading came from areas that by 1095 were already becoming overpopulated: these Crusaders may have hoped to do better for themselves in the East than they could on their crowded lands. Similarly, some lords were feeling the pressures of growing political stability and a growing acceptance of *primogeniture* (inheritance limited to the eldest male heir). Hitherto younger sons might have hoped to make their own fortune in endemic warfare, or at least inherit a small piece of territory for themselves, but now there were more and longer-lived siblings, warfare was becoming limited, and only the eldest son in-

Religion the dominant motive; crusades as armed pilgrimages

herited his father's lands. Clearly, leaving for the East was an attractive alternative to chafing at home.

But the dominant motive for going on the First Crusade was definitely religious. Nobody could have gone crusading out of purely calculating motives because nobody could have predicted for certain that new lands would be won. Indeed, any rational caculation would have predicted at best an unremunerative return trip, or, more likely, death at the hands of the Muslims. But the journey offered great solace for the Christian soul. For centuries pilgrimages had been the most popular type of Christian penance, and the pilgrimage to Jerusalem was considered to be the most sacred and efficacious one of all. Obviously the greatest of all spiritual rewards would come from going on an armed pilgrimage to Jerusalem in order to win back the holiest of sacred places for Christianity. To make this point explicit, Urban II at Clermont promised that Crusaders would be freed from all other penances imposed by the Church. Immediately afterward some Crusade preachers went even further by promising, without Urban's authorization, what became known as a *plenary indulgence*. This was the promise that all Crusaders would be entirely freed from otherworldly punishments in purgatory and that their souls would go straight to heaven if they died on the Crusade. The plenary indulgence was a truly extraordinary offer and crowds streamed in to take advantage of it. As they flocked together they were further whipped up by preachers into a religious frenzy that approached mass hysteria. They were convinced that they had been chosen to cleanse the world of unbelievers. One terrible consequence was that even before they had fully set out for the East they started slaughtering European Jews in the first really virulent outbreak of Western anti-Semitism.

Burning of Jews. From a late-medieval German manuscript. After the persecutions of the First Crusade, treatment of Jews in western Europe became worse and worse. These Jews were set upon by the populace because they were suspected of poisoning wells.

Armorial Insignia of the Tailors' Guild of Perugia. The rampant griffin is the emblem of Perugia (central Italy) and the scissors denote the city's guild of tailors. A striking example of bourgeois pride expressed in aristocratic terms found in a manuscript dating from the year 1368. (British Library)

THE RISE OF THE MEDIEVAL UNIVERSITY

△ Founded in the 12th century
■ Founded in the 13th century
● Founded in the 14th century   Boundaries ca. 1500 A.D.
△ Founded in the 15th century

King Louis VII of France and His Queen, Eleanor of Aquitaine, Embarking for the Second Crusade. This late-medieval conception is idealized inasmuch as Louis did not travel to the Holy Land by sea but took a land route.

Against great odds the First Crusade was a thorough success. In 1098 the Crusaders captured Antioch and with it most of Syria; in 1099 they took Jerusalem. Their success came mainly from the facts that their Muslim opponents just at that time were internally divided and that the appearance of the strange, uncouth, and terribly savage westerners took the Muslims by surprise. From the start the Crusaders in the Holy Land acted like imperialists. As soon as they conquered new territories they claimed them as property for themselves, carving out their acquisitions into four different principalities. They also exulted in their own ferocity. When they captured Antioch, instead of taking prisoners they killed all the Turks they laid their hands on. Similarly, when they conquered Jerusalem they ignored Christ's own pacifistic precepts, mercilessly slaughtering all the Muslim inhabitants of the city. Some Crusaders actually boasted in a joint letter home that "in Solomon's Porch and in his temple our men rode in the blood of the Saracens up to the knees of their horses." Those Crusaders who stayed on in the Holy Land gradually became more civilized and tolerant, but new waves of armed pilgrims from the West continued to act brutally. Moreover, even the settled Crusaders never became fully integrated with the local population but remained a separate, exploiting foreign element in the heart of the Islamic world.

The brutal conduct of the Crusaders

Given the fact that the Christian states comprised only an underpopulated, narrow strip of colonies along the coastline of Syria and Palestine, it was only a matter of time before they would be won back for Islam. By 1144 the northernmost principality fell. When Christian warriors led by the king of France and emperor of Germany came East in the Second Crusade to recoup the losses, they were too internally

Failure of subsequent crusades; the triumph of Frederick II's diplomacy

divided to win any victories. Not long afterward the Islamic lands of the region were united from the base of Egypt by the Sultan Saladin, who recaptured Jerusalem in 1187. Again a force from the West tried to repair the damages: this was the Third Crusade, led by the German Emperor Frederick Barbarossa, the French King Philip Augustus, and the English King Richard the Lionhearted. Even this glorious host, however, could not triumph, above all because rival leaders again quarreled among themselves. When Innocent III became pope his main ambition was to win back Jerusalem. He called the Fourth Crusade to that end, but that crusade was an unprecedented disaster from the point of view of a united Christendom. The pope could not control its direction and the Crusaders in 1204 wound up seizing Orthodox Christian Constantinople instead of marching on the Holy Land. As we have seen, the ultimate result of this act was to help destroy the Byzantine Empire and open up eastern Europe to the Ottoman Turks. Innocent convened the Fourth Lateran Council in 1215 partially to prepare for yet another crusade that would be more directly under papal guidance. That crusade, the fifth, was launched from the sea against Egypt in order to penetrate Muslim power at its base, but after a promising start it too was a failure. Only the Sixth Crusade, led from 1228 to 1229 by the Emperor Frederick II, was a success; this, however, was not for any military reasons. Frederick, who knew Arabic and could communicate easily with the Egyptian sultan, did not fight but skillfully negotiated a treaty whereby Jerusalem and a narrow access route were restored to the Christians. Thus diplomacy triumphed where warfare had failed. But the Christians could not hold on to their gains and Jerusalem fell again in 1244, never to be recaptured by the West until 1917. The Christian "states" were now only a small enclave around the Palestinian city of Acre.

The papacy's sacrifice of the crusading ideal to political interests

While Frederick II was negotiating for Jerusalem, he was under excommunication by the pope; therefore, when he entered the city, he had to crown himself king of Jerusalem in the Church of the Holy Sepulcher with his own hands. This was indicative of the fact that by then the papacy was becoming more intent on advancing European political aims than on reconquering the Holy Land. The victory of the First Crusade had greatly enhanced the prestige and strength of the papal monarchy, but the subsequent failures were increasingly calling into question the papal ability to unite the West for a great enterprise. The Albigensian Crusade, called by Innocent III in 1208, established the crucial precedent that a believer could receive the same spiritual rewards by crusading within Europe as by going on a much longer and more risky crusade to the East. The Albigensian Crusade did not damage the papacy's religious image, however, because the Albigensian heretics (whose beliefs will be discussed later) were a clear religious threat to the Church. Once the papacy launched its crusade against Frederick II and his heirs, however, it fully sacrificed the crusading ideal to political interests.

Krak des Chevaliers. This Crusader castle in northern Syria is one of the best preserved fortresses of the Middle Ages. The word *krak* comes from the Arabic *karak,* meaning strong fort.

It was then that the decline of the crusading movement and the decline of the papacy became most closely interrelated. In the crusades against Frederick and his successors, and later against the king of Aragon, the popes offered the same plenary indulgence that was by then officially offered to all Crusaders against Islam. Worse, they granted the same indulgence to anyone who simply contributed enough money to arm a Crusader for the enterprise. This created a great inflation in indulgences. By 1291 the last Christian outposts in the Holy Land had fallen without any Western help while the papacy was still trying to salvage its losing crusade against Aragon. Boniface VIII's papal jubilee of 1300, which offered a plenary indulgence to all those who made a pilgrimage to Rome, was a tacit recognition that the Eternal City and not the Holy Land would henceforth have to be the central goal of Christian pilgrimage. Boniface fell from power three years later for many reasons, but one was certainly that the prestige of the papacy had become irreparably damaged by the misuses and failures of crusading.

The decline of the crusading movement and the decline of the papacy interrelated

So, while the crusading idea helped build up the papal monarchy, it also helped destroy it. Other than that, what practical significance did the Crusades have? On the credit side, the almost incredible success of the First Crusade greatly helped raise the self-confidence of the medieval West. For centuries western Europe had been on the defensive against Islam; now a Western army could march into a center of Islamic power and take a coveted prize seemingly at will. This dramatic victory contributed to making the twelfth century an age of extraordinary buoyancy and optimism. To Western Christians it must have seemed as if God was on their side and that they could accomplish almost anything they wished. The Crusades also helped broaden Western horizons. Few westerners in the Holy Land ever bothered to learn

Positive effects of the Crusades

Arabic or profit from specific Islamic institutions or ideas—the most profitable cultural communications between Christians and Muslims took place in Spain and Sicily—but Crusaders who traveled long distances through foreign lands were bound to become somewhat more sophisticated. The Crusades certainly stimulated interest in hitherto unknown luxury goods and presented a wealth of subjects for literature and fable.

From an economic point of view, the success of the First Crusade helped open up the eastern Mediterranean to Western commerce. The Italian cities of Venice and Genoa particularly began to dominate trade in that area, thereby helping to enhance Western prosperity as a whole. The need to transfer money over long distances also stimulated early experiments in banking techniques. Politically, the precedent of taxing the clergy for financing crusades was not only quickly turned to the advantage of the Western monarchies, it also stimulated the development of various forms of national taxation. More than that, the very act of organizing a country to help support a royal crusade by raising funds and provisions was an important stimulus to the development of efficient administrative institutions in the emerging nation-states.

Commerce and taxation

But there was a debit as well as a credit side to the crusading balance sheet. There is no excusing the Crusaders' savage butchery—of Jews at home and of Muslims abroad. As we have seen too in Chapter 12, the Crusades greatly accelerated the deterioration of Western relations with the Byzantine Empire and contributed fundamentally to the destruction of that realm, with all the disastrous consequences that followed. And Western colonialism in the Holy Land was only the beginning of a long history of colonialism that has continued until modern times.

Negative consequences

3. THE OUTBURST OF RELIGIOUS VITALITY

The First Crusade would never have succeeded if westerners had not become enthusiastic about religion. The growth of that enthusiasm itself was a most remarkable development. Had the First Crusade been called about fifty years earlier it is doubtful that many people would have joined it. But the eleventh-century reform movement and the pontificate of Gregory VII awakened interest in religion in all quarters. Thereafter the entire high-medieval period was to be marked by extraordinary religious vitality.

The awakening of religious interest

The reformers and Gregory VII stimulated a European religious revival for two reasons. One was that the campaign to cleanse the Church actually achieved a large measure of success: the laity could now respect the clergy more and increasingly large numbers of people were inspired to join the clergy themselves. According to a reliable estimate, the number of people who joined monastic orders in England increased tenfold between 1066 and 1200, a statistic that does not include the increase in priests. The other reason why the work of Gregory VII in particular helped inspire a revival was that Gregory explicitly called upon the laity to help discipline their priests. In letters of great propagandistic power he denounced the sins of "fornicating priests" (by which he really meant just married ones) and urged the laity to drive them from their pulpits or boycott their services. Not surprisingly, this touched off something close to a vigilante movement in many parts of Europe. This excitement, taken together with the fact that the papal struggle with Henry IV was really the first European event of universal interest, increased religious commitment immensely. Until about 1050 most western Europeans were Christians in name, but religious commitment seems to have been lukewarm and attendance at church services quite rare; after the Gregorian period Christianity was becoming an ideal and practice which really began to direct human lives.

One of the most visible manifestations of the new piety was the spread of the Cistercian movement in the twelfth century. By around 1100 no form of Benedictine monasticism seemed fully satisfactory to aspirants to holiness who sought great asceticism and, above all, intense "interiority"—unrelenting self-examination and meditative striving toward knowledge of God. The result was the founding of new orders to provide for the fullest expression of monastic idealism. One was the Carthusian order, whose monks were required to live in separate cells, abstain from meat, and fast three days each week on bread, water, and salt. The Carthusians never sought to attract great numbers and therefore remained a small group. But the same was by no means true of the Cistercians. The latter were monks who were first organized around 1100 and who sought to follow the Benedictine Rule in the purest and most austere way possible. In order to avoid the worldly temptations to which the Cluniacs had succumbed, they founded new monasteries in forests and wastelands as far away from civilization as possible. They shunned all unnecessary church decoration and ostentatious utensils, abandoned the Cluniac stress on an elaborate liturgy in favor of more contemplation and private prayer, and seriously committed themselves to hard manual labor. Under the charismatic leadership of St. Bernard of Clairvaux (1090–1153), a spellbinding preacher, brilliant writer, and the most influential European religious personality of his age, the Cistercian order grew exponentially. There were only 5 houses in 1115 but no less than 343 on St. Bernard's death in 1153. This growth not only meant that many more men were becoming monks—the older houses did not disappear—but that many pious laymen were donating funds and lands to support the new monasteries.

As more people were entering or patronizing new monasteries, the very nature of religious belief and devotion was changing. One of many examples was a shift away from the cult of saints to emphasis on

The impact of the Gregorian reform movement on religious revival

The new piety: the Carthusian and Cistercian orders; St. Bernard of Clairvaux

St. Bernard of Clairvaux. Here the saint, in the white habit of the Cistercians, has a miraculous vision of Christ during mass. From a manuscript of about 1290.

New forms of religious belief and practice

the worship of Jesus and veneration of the Virgin Mary. Older Benedictine monasteries encouraged the veneration of the relics of local saints that they housed in order to attract pilgrims and donations. But the Cluniac and Cistercian orders were both centralized congregations that allowed only one saintly patron for all their houses: respectively, St. Peter (to honor the founder of the papacy) and the Virgin. Since these monasteries contained few relics (the Virgin was thought to have been taken bodily into heaven, so there were no corporeal relics for her at all) they deemphasized their cult. The veneration of relics was replaced by a concentration on the Eucharist, or the sacrament of the Lord's Supper. Of course celebration of the Eucharist had always been an important part of the Christian faith, but only in the twelfth century was it made really central, for only then did theologians fully work out the doctrine of *transubstantiation*. According to this the priest during mass cooperates with God in the performance of a miracle whereby the bread and wine on the altar are changed or "transubstantiated" into the body and blood of Christ. Popular reverence for the Eucharist became so great in the twelfth century that for the first time the practice of elevating the consecrated host was initiated so that the whole congregation could see it. The new theology of the Eucharist greatly enhanced the dignity of the priest and also encouraged the faithful to meditate on the Passion of Christ. As a result many developed an intense sense of identification with Christ and tried to imitate his life in different ways.

Coming a very close second to the renewed worship of Christ in the twelfth century was veneration of the Virgin Mary. This development was more unprecedented because until then the Virgin had been only negligibly honored in the Western Church. Exactly why veneration of the Virgin became so pronounced in the twelfth century is not fully clear, but, whatever the explanation, there is no doubt that in the twelfth century the cult of Mary blossomed throughout all of western Europe. The Cistercians made her their patron saint, St. Bernard constantly taught about her life and virtues, and practically all the magnificent new cathedrals of the age were dedicated to her: there was Notre Dame ("Our Lady") of Paris, and also a "Notre Dame" of Chartres, Rheims, Amiens, Rouen, Laon, and many other places. Theologically, Mary's role was that of intercessor with her son for the salvation of human souls. It was held that Mary was the mother of all, an infinite repository of mercy who urged the salvation even of sinners so long as they were loving and ultimately contrite. Numerous stories circulated about seeming reprobates who were saved because they venerated Mary and because she then spoke for them at the hour of death.

The significance of the new cult was manifold. For the first time a woman was given a central and honored place in the Christian religion. Theologians still taught that sin had entered the world through the woman, but they now counterbalanced this by explaining how the triumph over sin transpired with the help of Mary. Moreover, this emphasis on Mary gave women a religious figure with whom they could identify, thereby enhancing their own religiosity. A third result

Christ Blessing the Coronation of His Mother, the Virgin Mary. A relief from the cathedral of Notre Dame, Paris.

The Virgin in Majesty. A representation from a stained-glass window in the cathedral of Chartres.

was that artists and writers who portrayed Mary were able to concentrate on femininity and scenes of human tenderness and family life. This contributed greatly to a general softening of artistic and literary style. But perhaps most important of all, the rise of the cult of Mary was closely associated with a general rise of hopefulness and optimism in the twelfth-century West.

Sometimes the great religious enthusiasm of the twelfth century went beyond the bounds approved by the Church. After Gregory VII had called upon the laity to help discipline their clergy it was difficult to control lay enthusiasm. As the twelfth century progressed and the papal monarchy concentrated on strengthening its legal and financial administration, some lay people began to wonder whether the Church, which had once been so inspiring, had not begun to lose sight of its idealistic goals. Another difficulty was that the growing emphasis on the miraculous powers of priests tended to inhibit the religious role of the laity and place it in a distinct position of spiritual inferiority. The result was that in the second half of the twelfth century large-scale movements of popular heresy swept over western Europe for the first time in its history. The two major twelfth-century heresies were Albigensianism and Waldensianism. The former, which had its greatest strength in Italy and southern France, was a recrudescence of Eastern dualism. Like the Zoroastrians before them, the Albigensians believed that all matter was created by an evil principle and that therefore the flesh should be thoroughly mortified. This teaching was completely at variance with Christianity, but it seems that most Albigensians believed themselves to be Christians and subscribed to the heresy mainly because it challenged the authority of insufficiently zealous Catholic priests and provided an outlet for intense lay spirituality. More typical of twelfth-century religious dissent was Waldensianism, a movement that originated in the French city of Lyons and spread to much of southern France, northern Italy, and Germany. Waldensians were laymen who wished to imitate the life of Christ and the Apostles to the fullest. They therefore translated and studied the Gospels, and dedicated themselves to lives of poverty and preaching. Since the earliest Waldensians did not attack any Catholic doctrines, the Church hierarchy did not at first interfere with them. But it was soon recognized that they were becoming too independent and that their voluntary poverty was proving an embarrassing contrast to the luxurious lives of worldly prelates. So the papacy forbade them to preach without authorization and condemned them for heresy when they refused to obey. At that point they became more radical and started to create an alternative church, which they maintained offered the only route to salvation.

When Innocent III became pope in 1198 he was faced with a very serious challenge from growing heresies. His response was characteristically decisive and fateful for the future of the Church. Simply stated it was two-pronged. On the one hand, Innocent resolved to crush all disobedience to papal authority, but on the other, he decided to patronize whatever idealistic religious groups he could find that were willing to acknowledge obedience. Papal monarchy could thus be protected without frustrating all dynamic spirituality within the Church. Innocent not only launched a full-scale crusade against the Albigensians, he also encouraged the use against heresy of judicial procedures that included ruthless techniques of religious "inquisition." In 1252 the papacy first approved the use of torture in inquisitorial trials, and burning at the stake became the prevalent punishment for religious disobedience. Neither the crusade nor the inquisitorial procedures were fully successful in uprooting the Albigensian heresy in Innocent's own lifetime, but the extension of such measures did result in destroying the heresy by fire and sword after about the middle of the thirteenth century. Waldensians, like Albigensians, were hunted down by inquisitors and their numbers reduced, but scattered Waldensian groups did manage to survive until modern times.

Another aspect of Innocent's program was to pronounce formally the new religious doctrines that enhanced the special status of priests and the ecclesiastical hierarchy. Thus at the Fourth Lateran Council of 1215 he reaffirmed the doctrine that the sacraments administered by the Church were the indispensable means of procuring God's grace, and that no one could be saved without them. The decrees of the Lateran Council emphasized two sacraments: the Eucharist and penance. The doctrine of transubstantiation was formally defined and it was made a requirement—as it remains today—that all Catholics confess their sins to a priest and then take Communion at least once a year. The council also promulgated other doctrinal definitions and disciplinary measures which served both to oppose heresy and to assert the unique dignity of the clergy.

As stated above, the other side of Innocent's policy was to support obedient idealistic movements within the Church. The most important of these were the new orders of *friars*—the Dominicans and the Franciscans. Friars resembled monks in vowing to follow a rule, but they differed greatly from monks in their actual conduct. Above all, they did not retreat from society into monasteries. Assuming that the way of life originally followed by Christ and the Apostles was the most holy, they wandered through the countryside and especially the towns, preaching and offering spiritual guidance. They also accepted voluntary poverty and begged for their subsistence. In these respects they resembled the Waldensian heretics, but they professed unquestioning obedience to the pope and sought to fight heresy themselves.

The Dominican order, founded by the Spaniard St. Dominic and approved by Innocent III in 1216, was particularly dedicated to the fight against heresy and also to the conversion of Jews and Muslims. At first the Dominicans hoped to achieve these ends by preaching and public debate. Hence they became intellectually oriented. Many

Innocent III's response to heresy

Innocent III's emphasis on the sacraments

The new orders of friars

The Dominican order

The Earliest Known Portrait of St. Francis. Dating from the year 1228, this fresco shows the saint without the "stigmata," the wounds of Christ's crucifixion he was believed to have received miraculously toward the end of his life.

A Portrait of St. Francis by the Florentine Painter Cimabue. Although this conception, dating from about 1285, may have been modeled on the one shown above, it clearly depicts the stigmata: notice the nail wound in the saint's hand and the lance wound in his side.

members of the order gained teaching positions in the infant European universities and contributed much to the development of philosophy and theology. The most influential thinker of the thirteenth century, St. Thomas Aquinas, was a Dominican who addressed one of his major theological works to converting the "gentiles" (i.e., all non-Christians). The Dominicans always retained their reputation for learning, but they also came to believe that stubborn heretics were best controlled by legal procedures. Accordingly, they became the leading medieval administrators of inquisitorial trials.

In its origins the Franciscan order was quite different from the Dominican, being characterized less by a commitment to doctrine and discipline and more by a sense of emotional fervor. Whereas St. Dominic and his earliest followers had been ordained priests who were licensed to preach by their office, the founder of the Franciscans, the Italian St. Francis of Assisi (1182–1226), was a layman who behaved at first remarkably like a social rebel and a heretic. The son of a rich merchant, he became dissatisfied with the materialistic values of his father and determined to become a servant of the poor. Giving away all his property, he threw off his clothes in public, put on the tattered garb of a beggar, and began without official approval to preach salvation in town squares and minister to outcasts in the darkest corners of Italian cities. He rigorously imitated the life of Christ and displayed indifference to doctrine, form, and ceremony, except for reverencing the sacrament of the Eucharist. But he did wish to gain the support of the pope. One day in 1210 he appeared in Rome with a small ragged band to request that Innocent III approve a primitive "rule" that was little more than a collection of Gospel precepts. Some other pope might have rejected the layman Francis as a hopelessly unworldly religious anarchist. But Francis was thoroughly willing to profess obedience, and Innocent had the genius to approve Francis's rule and grant him permission to preach. With papal support, the Franciscan order spread, and though it gradually became more "civilized," conceding the importance of administrative stability and doctrinal training for all its members, it continued to specialize in revivalistic outdoor preaching and in offering a model for "apostolic living" within an orthodox framework. Thus Innocent managed to harness a vital new force that would help maintain a sense of religious enthusiasm within the Church.

Until the end of the thirteenth century both the Franciscans and Dominicans worked closely together with the papal monarchy in a mutually supportive relationship. The popes helped the friars establish themselves throughout Europe and often allowed them to infringe on the duties of parish priests. On their side, the friars combated heresy, helped preach papal crusades, were active in missionary work, and otherwise undertook special missions for the popes. Above all, by the power of their examples and by their vigorous preaching, the friars helped maintain religious intensity throughout the thirteenth century.

The entire period from 1050 to 1300 was hence unquestionably a great "age of faith." The products of this faith were both tangible and intangible. We will examine the tangible products—works of theology, literature, art, and architecture—presently. Great as these were, the intangible products were equally important. Until the Christian religion became deeply felt in the High Middle Ages hardly any common ideals inspired average men and women. Life in the Middle Ages was extraordinarily hard, and until about 1050 there was not much to give it meaning. Then, when people began to take Christianity more seriously, an impetus was provided for performing hard work of all sorts. As we have seen in the last chapter, Europeans after 1050 literally had better food than before, and now we have seen that they were better fed figuratively as well. With more spiritual as well as material nourishment they accomplished great feats in all forms of human endeavor.

The age of faith

4. THE MEDIEVAL INTELLECTUAL REVIVAL

The major intellectual accomplishments of the High Middle Ages were of four related but different sorts: the spread of primary education and literacy; the origin and spread of universities; the acquisition of classical and Islamic knowledge; and the actual progress in thought made by westerners. Any one of these accomplishments would have earned the High Middle Ages a signal place in the history of Western learning; taken together they began the era of Western intellectual predominance which became a hallmark of modern times.

Four major intellectual accomplishments

Around 800 Charlemagne ordered that primary schools be established in every bishopic and monastery in his realm. Although it is doubtful that this command was carried out to the letter, many schools were certainly founded during the Carolingian period. But their continued existence was later endangered by the Viking invasions. Primary education in some monasteries and cathedral towns managed to survive, but until around 1050 the extent and quality of basic education in the European West were meager. Thereafter, however, there was a blossoming that paralleled the efflorescence we have seen in other human activities. Even contemporaries were struck by the rapidity with which schools sprang up all over Europe. One French monk writing in 1115 stated that when he was growing up around 1075 there was "such a scarcity of teachers that there were almost none in the villages and hardly any in the cities," but that by his maturity there was "a great number of schools," and the study of grammar was "flourishing far and wide." Similarly, a Flemish chronicle referred to an extraordinary new passion for the study and practice of rhetoric around 1120. Clearly, the economic revival, the growth of towns, and the emergence of strong government allowed Europeans to dedicate themselves to basic education as never before.

The spread of primary education

Two Medieval Conceptions of Elementary Education. On the left, an illumination from a fourteenth-century manuscript depicts a master of grammar who simultaneously points to the day's lesson and keeps order with a cudgel. Grammar school education is portrayed more gently on the right, a late-medieval scene in which a woman personifying the alphabet leads a willing boy into a tower of learning wherein the stories ascend from grammar through logic and rhetoric to the heights of theology.

Changes in medieval education: (1) the development of cathedral schools

The high-medieval educational boom was more than merely a growth of schools, for the nature of the schools changed, and as time went on so did the curriculum and the clientele. The first basic mutation was that monasteries in the twelfth century abandoned their practice of educating outsiders. Earlier, monasteries had taught a few privileged nonmonastic students how to read because there were no other schools for such pupils. But by the twelfth century sufficient alternatives existed. The main centers of European education became the cathedral schools located in the growing towns. The papal monarchy energetically supported this development by ordering in 1179 that all cathedrals should set aside income for one schoolteacher, who could then instruct all who wished, rich or poor, without fee. The papacy believed correctly that this measure would enlarge the number of well-trained clerics and potential administrators.

(2) the broadening of the curriculum

At first the cathedral schools existed almost exclusively for the basic training of priests, with a curriculum designed to teach only such literacy necessary for reading the Church offices. But soon after 1100 the curriculum was broadened, for the growth of both ecclesiastical and secular governments created a growing demand for trained officials who had to know more than how to read a few prayers. The revived reliance on law especially made it imperative to improve the quality of primary education in order to train future lawyers. Above all, a thorough knowledge of Latin grammar and composition began to be inculcated, often by studying some of the Roman classics such as the works of Cicero and Virgil. The revived interest in these texts, and attempts to imitate them, have led scholars to refer to a "renaissance of the twelfth century."

Until about 1200 the students in the urban schools remained predominantly clerical. Even those who hoped to become lawyers or administrators rather than mere priests usually found it advantageous to take Church orders. But afterward more pupils entered schools who were not in the clergy and never intended to be. Some were children of the upper classes who began to regard literacy as a badge of status. Others were future notaries (i.e., men who drew up official documents) or merchants who needed some literacy and/or computational skills to advance their own careers. Customarily, the latter groups would not go to cathedral schools but to alternate ones which were more practically oriented. Such schools grew rapidly in the course of the thirteenth century and became completely independent of ecclesiastical control. Not only were their students recruited from the laity, their teachers were usually laymen as well. As time went on instruction ceased being in Latin, as had hitherto been the case, and was offered in the European vernacular languages instead.

(3) the growth of lay education

The rise of lay education was an enormously important development in western European history for two related reasons. The first was that the Church lost its monopoly over education for the first time in almost a millennium. Learning and resultant attitudes could now become more secular, and they did just that increasingly over the course of time. Laymen could not only evaluate and criticize the ideas of priests, they could also pursue entirely secular lines of inquiry. Western culture therefore ultimately became more independent of religion, and much of the traditionalism associated with religion, than any other culture in the world. Second, the growth of lay schools, taken together with the growth of church schools which trained the laity, led to an enormous growth of lay literacy: by 1340 roughly 40 percent of the Florentine population could read; by the later fifteenth century about 40 percent of the total population of England was literate as well. (These figures include women, who were usually taught to read by paid tutors or male family members at home rather than in schools.) When one considers that literacy around 1050 was almost entirely limited to the clergy and that the literate comprised less than 1 percent of the population of western Europe, it can be appreciated that an astonishing revolution had taken place. Without it, many of Europe's other accomplishments would have been inconceivable.

Significance of the rise of lay education

The emergence of universities was part of the same high-medieval

The origins of universities

See color map facing
page 455

*Nature of the medieval
university*

educational boom. Originally, universities were institutions that offered instruction in advanced studies that could not be pursued in
average cathedral schools: advanced liberal arts and the professional
studies of law, medicine, and theology. The earliest Italian university
was that of Bologna, an institution that took shape during the course
of the twelfth century. Although liberal arts were taught at Bologna,
the institution gained its greatest prominence from the time of its
twelfth-century origins until the end of the Middle Ages as Europe's
leading center for the study of law. North of the Alps, the earliest
and most prominent university was that of Paris. The University of
Paris started out as a cathedral school like many others, but in the
twelfth century it began to become a recognized center of northern
intellectual life. One reason for this was that scholars there found
necessary conditions of peace and stability provided by the increasingly
strong French kingship; another was that food was plentiful because
the area was rich in agricultural produce; and another was that the
cathedral school of Paris in the first half of the twelfth century boasted
the most charismatic and controversial teacher of the day, Peter Abelard
(1079–1142). Abelard, whose intellectual accomplishments we will
discuss later, attracted students from all over Europe in droves. According to an apocryphal story that was told at the time, he was such an
exciting teacher that when he was forbidden to teach in French lands,
because of his controversial views, he climbed a tree and students
flocked under it to hear him lecture; when he was then forbidden to
teach from the air he started lecturing from a boat and students massed
to hear him from the banks. As a result of his reputation many other
teachers settled in Paris and began to offer much more varied and
advanced instruction than anything offered in other French cathedral
schools. By 1200 Paris was evolving into a university that specialized
in liberal arts and theology. Around then Innocent III, who had studied
in Paris himself, called the school "the oven that bakes the bread for
the entire world."

It should be emphasized that the institution of the university was really a medieval invention. Of course advanced schools existed in the
ancient world, but they did not have fixed curricula or organized faculties, and they did not award degrees. At first, medieval universities
themselves were not so much places as groups of scholars. The term
university originally meant a corporation or guild. In fact, all of the
medieval universities were corporations, either of teachers or students,
organized like other guilds to protect their interests and rights. But
gradually the word university came to mean an educational institution
with a school of liberal arts and one or more faculties in the professional subjects of law, medicine, and theology. After about 1200
Bologna and Paris were regarded as the prototypic universities. During
the thirteenth century such famous institutions as Oxford, Cambridge,
Montpellier, Salamanca, and Naples were founded or granted formal

recognition. In Germany there were no universities until the fourteenth century—a reflection of the disorganized condition of that area—but in 1385 Heidelberg, the first university on German soil, was founded and many others quickly followed.

Every university in medieval Europe was patterned after one or the other of two different models. Throughout Italy, Spain, and southern France the standard was generally the University of Bologna, in which the students themselves constituted the corporation. They hired the teachers, paid their salaries, and fined or discharged them for neglect of duty or inefficient instruction. The universities of northern Europe were modeled after Paris, which was not a guild of students but of teachers. It included four faculties—arts, theology, law, and medicine—each headed by a dean. In the great majority of the northern universities arts and theology were the leading branches of study. Before the end of the thirteenth century separate colleges came to be established within the University of Paris. The original college was nothing more than an endowed home for poor students, but eventually the colleges become centers of instruction as well as residences. While most of these colleges have disappeared from the Continent, the universities of Oxford and Cambridge still retain the pattern of federal organization copied from Paris. The colleges of which they are composed are semi-independent educational units.

Organization of universities

Most of our modern degrees as well as our modern university organization derive from the medieval system, but actual courses of study have been greatly altered. No curriculum in the Middle Ages included history or anything like the modern social sciences. The medieval student was assumed to know Latin grammar thoroughly before entrance into a university—this he learned in the primary, or "gram-

The courses of study

A Lecture Class in a Medieval University. Some interesting similarities and contrasts may be observed between this scene and a modern classroom.

mar," schools. Upon admission, limited to males, he was required to spend about four years studying the basic liberal arts, which meant doing advanced work in Latin grammar and rhetoric, and mastering the rules of logic. If he passed his examinations he received the preliminary degree of bachelor of arts (the prototype of our B.A.), which conferred no unusual distinction. To assure himself a place in professional life he then usually had to devote additional years to the pursuit of an advanced degree, such as master of arts (M.A.), or doctor of laws, medicine, or theology. For the M.A. degree three or four years had to be given to the study of mathematics, natural science, and philosophy. This was accomplished by reading and commenting on standard ancient works, such as those of Euclid and especially Aristotle. Abstract analysis was emphasized and there was no such thing as laboratory science. The requirements for the doctors' degrees included more specialized training. Those for the doctorate in theology were particularly arduous: by the end of the Middle Ages the course for the doctorate in theology at the University of Paris had been extended to twelve or thirteen years after the roughly eight years taken for the M.A.! Continuous residence was not required, and it was accordingly rare to become a doctor of theology before the age of forty; statutes in fact forbade awarding the degree to anyone under thirty-five. Strictly speaking, doctor's degrees, including even the one in medicine, only conferred the right to teach. But in practice university degrees of all grades were recognized as standards of attainment and became pathways to nonacademic careers.

Student life in medieval universities was often very rowdy. Many students were very immature because it was customary to begin university studies between the ages of twelve and fifteen. Moreover, all university students believed that they comprised an independent and privileged community, set aside from that of the local townspeople. Since the latter tried to reap financial profits from the students and the students were naturally boisterous, there were frequent riots and sometimes pitched battles between "town" and "gown." But actual study was very intense. Because the greatest emphasis was placed on the value of authority and also because books were prohibitively expensive (they were handwritten and made from rare parchment), there was an enormous amount of rote memorization. As students advanced in their disciplines they were also expected to develop their own skills in formal, public disputations. Advanced disputations could become extremely complex and abstract; sometimes they might also last for days. The most important fact pertaining to medieval university students was that, after about 1250, there were so many of them. The University of Paris in the thirteenth century numbered about seven thousand students, and Oxford somewhere around two thousand in any given year. This means that a relatively appreciable proportion of male Europeans who were more than peasants or artisans were gaining at least some education at the higher levels.

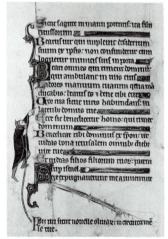

A Scribe with a Sense of Humor. An English scribe of around 1300, having noticed that he left out a whole line in a luxurious prayerbook, devised this ingenious way to rectify the error.

As the numbers of those educated at all levels vastly increased during the High Middle Ages, so did the quality of learning. This was owing first and foremost to the reacquisition of Greek knowledge and to the absorption of intellectual advances made by the Muslims. Since practically no western Europeans knew Greek or Arabic, works in those languages had to be transmitted by means of Latin translations. But there were very few of these before about 1140: of all the many works of Aristotle only a few logical treatises were available in Latin translations before the middle of the twelfth century. But then, suddenly, an enormous burst of translating activity made almost all of ancient Greek and Arabic scientific knowledge accessible to western Europeans. This activity transpired in Spain and Sicily because Christians there lived in close proximity with Arabic speakers, or Jews who knew Latin and Arabic, either of whom could aid them in their tasks. Greek works were first translated into Latin from earlier Arabic translations; then many were retranslated directly from the Greek by a few westerners who had managed to learn that language, usually by traveling in Greek-speaking territories. The result was that by about 1260 almost the entire Aristotelian corpus that is known today was made available in Latin. So also were basic works of such important Greek scientific thinkers as Euclid, Galen, and Ptolemy. Only the milestones of Greek literature and the works of Plato were not yet translated because they had not been made available to the Arabs; they existed only in inaccessible Byzantine manuscripts. But in addition to the thought of the Greeks, Western scholars became familiar with the accomplishments of all the major Islamic philosophers and scientists such as Avicenna and Averroës.

Having acquired the best of Greek and Arabic scientific and speculative thought, the West was able to build on it and make its own advances. This progress transpired in different ways. When it came to natural science, westerners were able to start building on the acquired learning without much difficulty because it seldom conflicted with the principles of Christianity. But when it came to philosophy, the basic question arose as to how thoroughly Greek and Arabic thought was compatible with the Christian faith. The most advanced thirteenth-century scientist was the Englishman Robert Grosseteste (c. 1168–1253), who was not only a great thinker but was also very active in public life as bishop of Lincoln. Grosseteste became so proficient at Greek that he translated all of Aristotle's *Ethics*. More important, he made very significant theoretical advances in mathematics, astronomy, and optics. He formulated a sophisticated scientific explanation of the rainbow, and he posited the use of lenses for magnification. Grosseteste's leading disciple was Roger Bacon (c. 1214–1294), who is today more famous than his teacher because he seems to have predicted automobiles and flying machines. Bacon in fact had no real interest in machinery, but he did follow up on Grosseteste's work in optics, discussing, for example, further properties of lenses, the rapid

Acquisition of Greek and Arabic knowledge

Medicine as Monkey Business. Even after a medieval physician had studied Galen, he was equiped with only two fairly reliable diagnostic methods: taking the pulse and examining urine. A visual parody from a French manuscript of 1316 makes this observation dryly.

The growth of Western scientific and speculative thought; Robert Grosseteste and Roger Bacon

speed of light, and the nature of human vision. Grosseteste, Bacon, and some of their followers at the University of Oxford argued that natural knowledge was more certain when it was based on sensory evidence than when it rested on abstract reason. To this degree they can be seen as early forerunners of modern science. But the important qualification remains that they did not perform any real laboratory experiments.

*The meaning of
Scholasticism*

The story of the high-medieval encounter between Greek and Arabic philosophy and Christian faith is basically the story of the emergence of Scholasticism. This word can be, and has been, defined in many ways. In its root meaning Scholasticism was simply the method of teaching and learning followed in the medieval schools. That meant that it was highly systematic and also that it was highly respectful of authority. Yet Scholasticism was not only a method of study: it was a worldview. As such, it taught that there was a fundamental compatibility between the knowledge humans can obtain naturally, i.e., by experience or reason, and the teachings imparted by Divine Revelation. Since medieval scholars believed that the Greeks were the masters of natural knowledge and that all revelation was in the Bible, Scholasticism consequently was the theory and practice of reconciling classical philosophy with Christian faith.

One of the most important thinkers who paved the way for Scholasticism without yet being fully a Scholastic himself was the stormy petrel Peter Abelard, who was active in and around Paris in the first half of the twelfth century. Probably the first western European who consciously sought to forge a career as an intellectual (rather than being merely a cleric who taught on the side or a schoolteacher who had no goal of adding to knowledge), Abelard was so adept at logic and theology that even as a student he easily outshone the experts of his day who had the misfortune to be his teachers. Others might have been tactful about such superiority, but Abelard gloried in openly humiliating his elders in public debate, thereby making himself many enemies. To complicate matters, in 1118 he seduced a brilliant seventeen-year-old girl, Heloise, who had been taking private lessons with him. When a child was the issue, Abelard married Heloise, but the two decided to keep the marriage secret for the sake of his career. This, however, enraged Heloise's uncle because he thought that Abelard was planning to abandon Heloise; therefore he took revenge for his family's honor by having Abelard castrated. Seeking refuge as a monk, Abelard soon witnessed his enemies engineer his first conviction for heresy. Still restless and cantankerous, he found no spiritual solace in monasticism and after quarreling and breaking with the monks of two different monastic communities he returned to life in the world by setting himself up as a teacher in Paris from about 1132 to 1141. This was the peak of his career. But in 1141 he again was charged with heresy, now by the highly influential St. Bernard, and condemned

The Creator as Architect. An underlying assumption of thirteenth-century philosophy and theology was that God created the universe according to scientific principles. This scene from a late-thirteenth century French Bible shows God working on His Creation with a draftsman's compass.

Peter Abelard

by a Church council. Not long afterward the persecuted thinker abjured, and in 1142 he died in retirement.

Abelard told of many of these trials in a letter called *The Story of My Calamities*, one of the first autobiographical accounts written in the West since St. Augustine's *Confessions*. On first reading, this work appears atypically modern because the author seems to defy the medieval Christian virtue of humility by constantly boasting about himself. But actually Abelard did not write about his calamities in order to boast. Rather, his main intention was to moralize about how he had been justly punished for his "lechery" by the loss of those parts which had "offended" and for his intellectual pride by the burning of his writings after his first condemnation. Since Abelard urged intense self-examination and analysis of human motives in an ethical treatise programmatically entitled *Know Thyself*, it seems wisest to conclude that he never intended to recommend egotism but rather was one of several prominent twelfth-century thinkers (ironically including his mortal enemy St. Bernard) who sought to take stock of the human personality by means of personal introspection.

Abelard. A late-medieval conception.

Abelard's greatest contributions to the development of Scholasticism were made in his *Sic et Non* (Yes and No) and in a number of original theological works. In the *Sic et Non* Abelard prepared the way for the Scholastic method by gathering a collection of statements from the Church fathers that spoke for both sides of 150 theological questions. It used to be thought that the brash Abelard did this in order to embarrass authority, but the contrary is true. What Abelard really hoped to do was begin a process of careful study whereby it could be shown that the highest authority of the Bible was infallible and that the best authorities, despite any appearances to the contrary, really agreed with each other. Later Scholastics would follow his method of studying theology by raising fundamental questions and arraying the answers that had been put forth in authoritative texts. Abelard did not propose any solutions of his own in the *Sic et Non,* but he did start to do this in his original theological writings. In these he proposed to treat theology like a science, by studying it as comprehensively as possible and by applying to it the tools of logic, of which he was a master. He did not even shrink from applying logic to the mystery of the Trinity, one of the excesses for which he was condemned. Thus he was one of the first to try to harmonize religion with rationalism and was in this capacity a herald of the Scholastic outlook.

Sic et Non and the Scholastic method

Immediately after Abelard's death two further steps were taken to prepare for mature Scholasticism. One was the writing of the *Book of Sentences* between 1155 and 1157 by Abelard's student Peter Lombard. This raised all the most fundamental theological questions in rigorously consequential order, adduced answers from the Bible and Christian authorities on both sides of each question, and then proposed

Peter Lombard's Book of Sentences

Peter Lombard

St. Thomas Aquinas

judgments on every case. By the thirteenth century Peter Lombard's work became a standard text. Once formal schools of theology were established in the universities, all aspirants to the doctorate were required to study and comment upon it; not surprisingly, theologians also followed its organizational procedures in their own writings. Thus the full Scholastic method was born.

The other basic step in the development of Scholasticism, as mentioned above, was the reacquisition of classical philosophy that occurred after about 1140. Abelard would probably have been glad to have drawn upon the thought of the Greeks, but he could not because few Greek works were yet available in translation. Later theologians, however, could avail themselves fully of the Greeks' knowledge, above all, the works of Aristotle and his Arabic commentators. By around 1250 Aristotle's authority in purely philosophical matters became so great that he was referred to as "the Philosopher" pure and simple. Scholastics of the mid-thirteenth century accordingly adhered to Peter Lombard's organizational method, but added the consideration of Greek and Arabic philosophical authorities to that of purely Christian theological ones. In doing this they tried to construct systems of understanding the entire universe that most fully harmonized the earlier separate realms of faith and natural knowledge.

By far the greatest accomplishments in this endeavor were made by St. Thomas Aquinas (1225–1274), the leading Scholastic theologian of the University of Paris. As a member of the Dominican order, St. Thomas was committed to the principle that faith could be defended by reason. More important, he believed that natural knowledge and the study of the created universe were legitimate ways of approaching theological wisdom because "nature" complements "grace." By this he meant to say that because God created the natural world He can be approached through its terms even though ultimate certainty about the highest truths can only be obtained through the supernatural revelation of the Bible. Imbued with a deep confidence in the value of human reason and human experience, as well as in his own ability to harmonize Greek philosophy with Christian theology, Thomas was the most serene of saints. In a long career of teaching at the University of Paris and elsewhere he indulged in few controversies and worked quietly on his two great *Summaries* of theology: the *Summa contra Gentiles* and the much larger *Summa Theologica*. In these he hoped to set down all that could be said about the faith on the firmest of foundations.

Most experts think that St. Thomas came extremely close to fulfilling this extraordinarily ambitious goal. His vast *Summaries* are awesome for their rigorous orderliness and intellectual penetration. He admits in them that there are certain "mysteries of the faith," such as the doctrines of the Trinity and the Incarnation, that cannot be approached by the unaided human intellect; otherwise, he subjects all theological questions to philosophical inquiry. In this, St. Thomas relied heavily on the work of Aristotle, but he is by no means merely "Aristotle baptized." Instead, he fully subordinated Aristotelianism to basic Christian principles and thereby created his own original philosophical and theological system. Scholars disagree about how far this system diverges from the earlier Christian thought of St. Augustine, but there seems little doubt that Aquinas placed a higher value on human reason, on human life in this world, and on the abilities of humans to participate in their own salvation. Not long after his death St. Thomas was canonized, for his intellectual accomplishments seemed like miracles. His influence lives on today insofar as he helped to revive confidence in rationalism and human experience. More directly, philosophy in the modern Roman Catholic Church is supposed to be taught according to the Thomistic method, doctrine, and principles.

St. Thomas Aquinas. A fifteenth-century painting by Justus of Ghent, after an earlier copy.

With the achievements of St. Thomas Aquinas in the middle of the thirteenth century, Western medieval thought reached its pinnacle. Not coincidentally, other aspects of medieval civilization were reaching their pinnacles at the same time. France was enjoying its ripest period of peace and prosperity under the rule of St. Louis, the University of Paris was defining its basic organizational forms, and the greatest French Gothic cathedrals were being built. Some ardent admirers of medieval culture have fixed on these accomplishments to call the thirteenth the "greatest of centuries." Such a judgment, of course, is a matter of taste, and many might respond that life was still too harsh and requirements for religious orthodoxy too great to justify this extreme celebration of the lost past. Whatever our individual judgments, it seems wise to end this section by correcting some false impressions about medieval intellectual life.

It is often thought that medieval thinkers were excessively conservative, but in fact the greatest thinkers of the High Middle Ages were astonishingly receptive to new ideas. As committed Christians they could not allow doubts to be cast upon the principles of their faith, but otherwise they were glad to accept whatever they could from the Greeks and Arabs. Considering that Aristotelian thought differed radically from anything accepted earlier in its emphasis on rationalism and the fundamental goodness and purposefulness of nature, its rapid acceptance by the Scholastics was a philosophical revolution. Another false impression is that Scholastic thinkers were greatly constrained by authority. Certainly they revered authority more than we do today, but Scholastics like St. Thomas did not regard the mere citation of texts—except biblical revelation concerning the mysteries of the faith—as being sufficient to clinch an argument. Rather, the authorities were brought forth to outline the possibilities, but reason and experience then demonstrated the truth. Finally, it is often believed that Scholastic thinkers were "antihumanistic," but modern scholars are coming to the opposite conclusion. Scholastics unquestionably gave primacy to the soul over the body and to otherworldly salvation over life in

False impressions concerning Scholastic thinkers

the here and now. But they also exalted the dignity of human nature because they viewed it as a glorious divine creation, and they believed in the possibility of a working alliance between themselves and God. Moreover, they had extraordinary faith in the powers of human reason—probably more than we do today.

5. THE BLOSSOMING OF LITERATURE, ART, AND MUSIC

Medieval Latin literature; the poetry of the Goliards

The literature of the High Middle Ages was as varied, lively, and impressive as that produced in any other period in Western history. The revival of grammatical studies in the cathedral schools and universities led to the production of some excellent Latin poetry. The best examples were secular lyrics, especially those written in the twelfth century by a group of poets known as the Goliards. How these poets got their name is uncertain, but it possibly meant followers of the devil. That would have been appropriate because the Goliards were riotous poets who wrote parodies of the liturgy and burlesques of the Gospels. Their lyrics celebrated the beauties of the changing seasons, the carefree life of the open road, the pleasures of drinking and sporting, and especially the joys of love. The authors of these rollicking and satirical songs were mainly wandering students, although some were men in more advanced years. The names of most are unknown. Their poetry is particularly significant both for its robust vitality and for being the first clear counterstatement to the ascetic ideal of Christianity.

In addition to the use of Latin, the vernacular languages of French, German, Spanish, and Italian became increasingly popular as media of

Charlemagne Weeping for His Knights. A scene from the *Song of Roland.*

literary expression. At first, most of the literature in the vernacular languages was written in the form of the heroic epic. Among the leading examples were the French *Song of Roland,* the Norse eddas and sagas, the German *Song of the Nibelungs,* and the Spanish *Poem of the Cid.* Practically all of these works were originally composed between 1050 and 1150, although some were first set down in writing afterward. These epics portrayed a virile but unpolished warrior society. Blood flowed freely, skulls were cleaved by battle-axes, and heroic warfare, honor, and loyalty were the major themes. If women were mentioned at all, they were subordinate to men. Brides were expected to die for their betrotheds, but husbands were free to beat their wives. In one French epic a queen who tried to influence her husband met with a blow to the nose; even though blood flowed she replied: "Many thanks, when it pleases you, you may do it again." Despite the repugnance we find in such passages, the best of the vernacular epics have much unpretentious literary power. Above all, the *Song of Roland,* though crude, is like an uncut gem.

In comparison to the epics, an enormous change in both subject matter and style was introduced in twelfth-century France by the troubadour poets and the writers of courtly romances. The dramatic nature of this change represents further proof that high-medieval culture was not at all conservative. The troubadours were courtier poets who came from southern France and wrote in a language related to French known as Provençal. The origin of their inspiration is debated, but there can be no doubt that they initiated a movement of profound importance for all subsequent Western literature. Their style was far more finely wrought and sophisticated than that of the epic poets, and the most eloquent of their lyrics, which were meant to be sung to music, originated the theme of romantic love. The troubadours idealized women as marvelous beings who could grant intense spiritual and sensual gratification. Whatever greatness the poets found in themselves they usually attributed to the inspiration they found in love. But they also assumed that their love would lose its magic if it were too easily or frequently gratified. Therefore, they wrote more often of longing than of romantic fulfillment.

In addition to their love lyrics, the troubadours wrote several other kinds of short poems. Some were simply bawdy. In these, love is not mentioned at all, but the poet revels in thoughts of carnality, comparing, for example, the riding of his horse to the "riding" of his mistress. Other troubadour poems treat of feats of arms, others comment on contemporary political events, and a few even meditate on matters of religion. But whatever the subject matter, the best troubadour poems were always cleverly and innovatively expressed. The literary tradition originated by the southern French troubadours was continued by the *trouvères* in northern France and by the *minnesingers* in Germany. Thereafter many of their innovations were developed by later lyric poets in all Western languages. Some of their poetic devices

*The growth of vernacular
literature; the epic*

*The love songs of the
troubadours*

Other troubadour poems

The Arthurian romances; Chrétien de Troyes

"Courtly Love." Although authors of medieval romances did not themselves use the term courtly love, they did propagate the ideal of intense romantic feeling between a knightly lover and his faraway beloved. From a manuscript of the romance *Willehalm* by Wolfram von Eschenbach.

Wolfram von Eschenbach and Gottfried von Strassburg

The fabliaux

were consciously revived in the twentieth century by such "modernists" as Ezra Pound.

An equally important twelfth-century French innovation was the composition of longer narrative poems known as romances. These were the first clear ancestors of the modern novel: they told engaging stories, they often excelled in portraying character, and their subject matter was usually love and adventure. Some romances elaborated on classical Greek themes, but the most famous and best were "Arthurian." These took their material from the legendary exploits of the Celtic hero King Arthur and his many chivalrous knights. The first great writer of Arthurian romances was the northern Frenchman Chrétien de Troyes, who was active between about 1165 and 1190. Chrétien did much to help create and shape the new form, and he also introduced innovations in subject matter and attitudes. Whereas the troubadours exalted unrequited, extramarital love, Chrétien was the first to hold forth the ideal of romantic love within marriage. He also described not only the deeds but the thoughts and emotions of his characters.

A generation later, Chrétien's work was continued by the great German poets Wolfram von Eschenbach and Gottfried von Strassburg. These are recognized as the greatest writers in the German language before the eighteenth century. Wolfram's *Parzival,* a story of love and the search for the Holy Grail, is more subtle, complex, and greater in scope than any other high-medieval literary work except Dante's *Divine Comedy.* Like Chrétien, Wolfram believed that true love could only be fulfilled in marriage, and in *Parzival,* for the first time in Western literature since the Greeks, one can see a full psychological development of the hero. Gottfried von Strassburg's *Tristan* is a more somber work, which tells of the hopeless adulterous love of Tristan and Isolde. Indeed, it might almost be regarded as the prototype of modern tragic romanticism. Gottfried was one of the first to develop fully the idea of individual suffering as a literary theme and to point out the indistinct line which separates pleasure from pain. For him, to love is to yearn, and suffering and unfulfilled gratification are integral chapters of the book of life. Unlike the troubadours, he could only see complete fulfillment of love in death. *Parzival* and *Tristan* have become most famous today in the form of their operatic reconceptions by the nineteenth-century German composer Richard Wagner.

Not all high-medieval narratives were so elevated as the romances in either form or substance. A very different new narrative form was the *fabliau,* or verse fable. Although *fabliaux* derived from the moral animal tales of Aesop, they quickly evolved into short stories that were written less to edify or instruct than to amuse. Often they were very coarse, and sometimes they dealt with sexual relations in a broadly humorous and thoroughly unromantic manner. Many were also strongly anticlerical, making monks and priests the butts of their jokes. Because the *fabliaux* are so "uncourtly" it used to be thought that they were written solely for the new urban classes. But there is now little doubt that they were addressed at least equally to the "refined" aristocracy who liked to have their laughs too. They are significant as expressions of growing worldliness and as the first manifestations of the robust realism which was later to be perfected by Boccaccio and Chaucer.

Completely different in form but similar as an illustration of growing worldliness was the sprawling *Romance of the Rose*. As its title indicates, this was begun as a romance, specifically around 1230 by the courtly Frenchman William of Lorris. But William left his rather flowery, romantic work unfinished, and it was completed around 1270 by another Frenchman, John of Meun. The latter changed its nature greatly. He inserted long, biting digressions in which he skewered religious hypocrisy, and made his major theme the need for procreation. Not love, but the service of "Dame Nature" in sexual fecundity is urged in numerous witty but extremely earthy images and metaphors. At the climax the originally dreamy hero seizes his mistress, who is allegorically depicted as a rose, and rapes her. Since the work became enormously popular, it seems fair to conclude that tastes, then as now, were very diverse.

In a class by itself as the greatest work of medieval literature is Dante's *Divine Comedy*. Not much is known about the life of Dante Alighieri (1265–1321), except that he was active during the early part of his career in the political affairs of his native city of Florence. Despite his engagement in politics and the fact that he was a layman, he managed to acquire an awesome mastery of the religious, philosophic, and literary knowledge of his time. He not only knew the Bible and the church fathers, but—most unusual for a layman—he also absorbed the most recent Scholastic theology. In addition, he was thoroughly familiar with Virgil, Cicero, Boethius, and numerous other classical writers, and was fully conversant with the poems of the troubadours and the Italian poetry of his own day. In 1302 he was expelled from Florence after a political upheaval and was forced to live the rest of his life in exile. The *Divine Comedy*, his major work, was written during this final period.

Dante's *Divine Comedy* is a monumental narrative in powerful rhyming Italian verse, which describes the poet's journey through hell, purgatory, and paradise. At the start Dante tells of how he once found himself in a "dark wood," his metaphor for a deep personal mid-life crisis. He is led out of this forest of despair by the Roman Virgil, who stands for the heights of classical reason and philosophy. Virgil guides Dante on a trip through hell and purgatory, and afterward Dante's deceased beloved, Beatrice, who stands for Christian wisdom and blessedness, takes over and guides him through paradise. In the course of this progress Dante meets both historical beings and the poet's contemporaries, all of whom have already been assigned places in the afterlife, and he is instructed by them and his guides as to why they met

Nature Perpetuates the Species. A miniature from a manuscript of the *Romance of the Rose*.

Dante

Dante and Virgil Journey through Hell. From an Italian manuscript of the late fourteenth century.

The Divine Comedy

See color plates facing page 519

Medieval architecture: (1) the Romanesque style

their several fates. As the poem progresses the poet himself leaves the condition of despair to grow in wisdom and ultimately to reach assurance of his own salvation.

Every reader finds a different combination of wonder and satisfaction in Dante's magnificent work. Some—especially those who know Italian—marvel at the vigor and inventiveness of Dante's language and images. Others are awed by his subtle complexity and poetic symmetry; others by his array of learning; others by the vitality of his characters and individual stories; and still others by his soaring imagination. The historian finds it particularly remarkable that Dante could sum up the best of medieval learning in such an artistically satisfying manner. Dante stressed the precedence of salvation, but he viewed the earth as existing for human benefit. He allowed humans free will to choose good and avoid evil, and accepted Greek philosophy as authoritative in its own sphere; for example, he called Aristotle "the master of them that know." Above all, his sense of hope and his ultimate faith in humanity—remarkable for a defeated exile—most powerfully expresses the dominant mood of the High Middle Ages and makes Dante one of the two or three most stirringly affirmative writers who ever lived.

The closest architectural equivalents of the *Divine Comedy* are the great high-medieval Gothic cathedrals, for they too have qualities of vast scope, balance of intricate detail with careful symmetry, soaring height, and affirmative religious grandeur. But before we approach the Gothic style, it is best to introduce it by means of its high-medieval predecessor, the style of architecture and art known as the Romanesque. This style had its origins in the tenth century, but became fully formed in the eleventh and first half of the twelfth centuries, when the religious reform movement led to the building of many new monasteries and large churches. The Romanesque was primarily a building style: it aimed to manifest the glory of God in ecclesiastical construc-

A Romanesque Vision of Original Sin. One of the masterpieces of Romanesque style, this sculptural relief, dating from about 1100, appears on a bronze door of the cathedral of Hildesheim (West Germany) and depicts the moment of punishment in the Garden of Eden. Anatomical distortion and spare abstraction create a haunting effect of tremulous human vulnerability. Caught in the profoundest act of disobedience the first humans hope to shift the blame for their own actions.

Worms Cathedral, Eleventh-Century Romanesque

tion by rigorously subordinating all architectural details to a uniform system. In this it was very severe: we may think of it as the architectural analogue of the unadorned hymn. Aside from its primary stress on systematic construction, the essential features of the Romanesque style were the rounded arch, massive stone walls, enormous piers, small windows, and the predominance of horizontal lines. The plainness of interiors was sometimes relieved by mosaics or frescoes in bright colors, and, a very important innovation for Christian art, the introduction of sculptural decoration, both within and without. For the first time, full-length human figures appeared on facades. These are usually grave and elongated far beyond natural dimensions, but they have much evocative power and represent the first manifestations of a revived interest in sculpting the human form.

In the course of the twelfth and thirteenth centuries the Romanesque style was supplanted throughout most of Europe by the Gothic. Although trained art historians can see how certain traits of the one style led to the development of the other, the actual appearance of the two styles is enormously different. In fact, the two seem as different as the epic is different from the romance, an appropriate analogy because the Gothic style emerged in France in the mid–twelfth century exactly when the romance did, and because it was far more sophisticated, graceful, and elegant than its predecessor, in the same way that the romance compared with the epic. The rapid development and acceptance of the Gothic shows for a last time—if any more proof be needed—that the twelfth century was experimental and dynamic,

A Romanesque Vision of the Last Judgment. A detail from the reliefs made for the cathedral of Autun (central France) around 1135 shows an angel sounding his trumpet while one of the human elect ascends to heaven. Extreme vertical elongation here creates a sense of dramatic intensity.

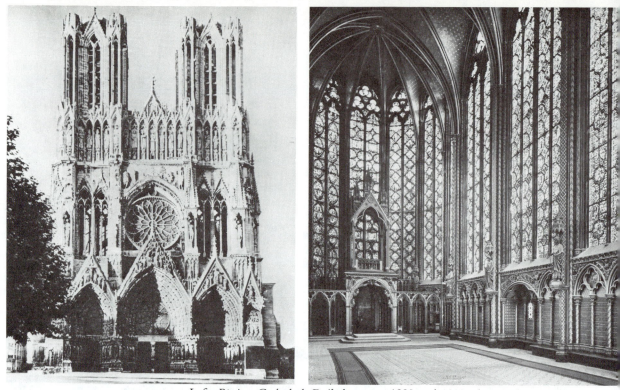

Left: *Rheims Cathedral*. Built between 1220 and 1299, this High Gothic cathedral places great stress on the vertical elements. The gabled portals, the windows above the doorways, the gallery of royal statues, and the multitude of pinnacles all accentuate the height of the structure. Right: *The High Chapel of La Sainte-Chapelle, Paris*. High Gothic is here carried to its logical extreme. Slender columns, tracery, and stained-glass windows take the place of walls.

(2) the development of the Gothic style

arguably at least as much as the twentieth. When the abbey church of St. Denis, venerated as the shrine of the French patron saint and burial place of French kings, was torn down in 1144 in order to make room for a much larger one in the strikingly new Gothic style, it was as if the president of the United States were to tear down the White House and replace it with a Mies van der Rohe or Helmut Jahn edifice. Such an act today would be highly improbable, or at least would create an enormous uproar. But in the twelfth century the equivalent actually happened and was taken in stride.

Elements of the Gothic style

Gothic architecture was one of the most intricate of building styles. Its basic elements were the pointed arch, groined and ribbed vaulting, and the flying buttress. These devices made possible a much lighter and loftier construction than could ever have been achieved with the round arch and the engaged pier of the Romanesque. In fact, the Gothic cathedral could be described as a skeletal framework of stone enclosed by enormous windows. Other features included lofty spires, rose windows, delicate tracery in stone, elaborately sculptured facades, multiple columns, and the use of gargoyles, or representations of mythical monsters, as decorative devices. Ornamentation in the best of the cathedrals was generally concentrated on the exterior. Except for the stained-glass windows and the intricate carving on woodwork and altars, interiors were kept rather simple and occasionally almost severe. But the inside of the Gothic cathedral was never somber or gloomy. The stained-glass windows served not to exclude the light but to glorify it, to catch the rays of sunlight and suffuse them with a richness and warmth of color which nature itself could hardly duplicate even in its happiest moods.

Many people still think of the Gothic cathedral as the expression of purely ascetic otherworldliness, but this estimation is highly inaccurate. Certainly all churches are dedicated to the glory of God and hope for life everlasting, but Gothic ones sometimes included stained-glass scenes of daily life that had no overt religious significance at all. More important, Gothic sculpture of religious figures such as Jesus, the Virgin, and the saints was becoming far more naturalistic than anything hitherto created in the medieval West. So also was the sculptural representation of plant and animal life, for interest in the human person and in the world of natural beauty was no longer considered sinful. Moreover, Gothic architecture was also an expression of the medieval intellectual genius. Each cathedral, with its mass of symbolic figures, was a kind of encyclopedia of medieval knowledge carved in stone for those who could not read. Finally, Gothic cathedrals were manifestations of urban pride. Always located in the growing medieval cities, they were meant to be both centers of community life and expressions

The significance of Gothic architecture

Gothic Scuplture. The three kings bearing gifts, from the thirteenth-century cathedral of Amiens. Note the greater naturalism in comparison to the Romanesque sculptural scenes shown on pages 480 and 481.

of a town's greatness. When a new cathedral went up the people of the entire community participated in erecting it, and rightfully regarded it as almost their own property. Many of the Gothic cathedrals were the products of urban rivalries. Each city or town sought to overawe its neighbor with ever bigger or taller buildings, to the degree that ambitions sometimes got out of bounds and many of the cathedrals were left unfinished. But most of the finished ones are still vast enough. Built to last into eternity, they provide the most striking visual manifestation of the soaring exuberance of their age.

Surveys of high-medieval accomplishments often omit drama and music, but such oversights are unfortunate. Our own modern drama descends at least as much from the medieval form as from the classical one. Throughout the medieval period some Latin classical plays were known in manuscript but were never performed. Instead drama was born all over again within the Church. In the early Middle Ages certain passages in the liturgy began to be acted out. Then, in the twelfth century, primarily in Paris, these were superseded by short religious plays in Latin, performed inside the Church. Rapidly thereafter, and still in twelfth-century Paris, the Latin plays were supplemented or supplanted by ones in the vernacular so that the whole congregation could understand them. Then, around 1200, these started to be performed outside, in front of the Church, so that they would not take time away from the services. As soon as that happened, drama entered the everyday world: nonreligious stories were introduced, character portrayal was expanded, and the way was fully prepared for the Elizabethans and Shakespeare.

The revival of drama

As the drama grew out of developments within the liturgy and then moved far beyond them, so did characteristically Western music. Until the High Middle Ages Western music was *homophonic,* as is most non-Western music even today. That is, it developed only one melody at a time without any harmonic background. The great high-medieval invention was *polyphony,* or the playing of two or more harmonious melodies together. Some experiments along these lines may have been made in the West as early as the tenth century, but the most fundamental breakthrough was achieved in the cathedral of Paris around 1170, when the Mass was first sung by two voices weaving together two different melodies in "counterpoint." Roughly concurrently, systems of musical notation were invented and perfected so that performance no longer had to rely on memory and could become more complex. All the greatness of Western music followed from these first steps.

Medieval music: polyphony

It may have been noticed that many of the same people who made such important contributions to learning, thought, literature, architecture, drama, and music, must have intermingled with each other in the Paris of the High Middle Ages. Some of them no doubt prayed together in the cathedral of Notre Dame. The names of the leading scholars are remembered, but the names of most of the others are

The enduring achievements of the High Middle Ages

forgotten. Yet taken together they did as much for civilization and created as many enduring monuments as their counterparts in ancient Athens. If their names are forgotten, their achievements in many different ways live on still.

SELECTED READINGS

• *Items so designated are available in paperback editions.*

RELIGION AND THE CRUSADES

• Barraclough, G., *The Medieval Papacy,* New York, 1968. A forcefully argued analytical treatment. Noteworthy too for its illustrations.

Daniel-Rops, H., *Cathedral and Crusade,* 2 vols., New York, 1963. The best survey from a Roman Catholic perspective.

Erdmann, Carl, *The Origin of the Idea of Crusade,* Princeton, 1978. A brilliant advanced work on the background to the First Crusade.

Lambert, Malcolm, *Medieval Heresy,* London, 1977. A masterful synthesis.

Leclercq, Jean, *Bernard of Clairvaux and the Cistercian Spirit,* Kalamazoo, Mich., 1976.

• Mayer, Hans Eberhard, *The Crusades,* New York, 1972. The best one-volume survey.

Moorman, J. R. H., *A History of the Franciscan Order from Its Origins to the Year 1517,* Oxford, 1968. Exhaustive.

Runciman, S., *A History of the Crusades,* 3 vols., Cambridge, 1951–54. Colorful and engrossing.

Southern, R. W., *Western Society and the Church in the Middle Ages,* Baltimore, 1970. An extremely insightful and well-written interpretation of the interplay between society and religion.

Tellenbach, G., *Church, State and Christian Society at the Time of the Investiture Contest,* Oxford, 1940. Stresses revolutionary aspects of Gregory VII's thought and career.

THOUGHT, LETTERS, AND THE ARTS

• Baldwin, John W., *The Scholastic Culture of the Middle Ages,* Lexington, Mass., 1971. A fine introduction.

Bergin, T. G., *Dante,* New York, 1965.

Cobban, Alan B., *The Medieval Universities,* London, 1975. The best shorter treatment in English.

• Curtius, E. R., *European Literature and the Latin Middle Ages,* New York, 1953. An exhaustive treatment of medieval Latin literature in terms of its classical background and influence on later times.

Fox, John, *A Literary History of France, I: The Middle Ages,* London, 1974. The best general history.

• Gilson, E., *Reason and Revelation in the Middle Ages,* New York, 1938. A brief but illuminating treatment by the greatest modern student of Scholasticism.

• Haskins, C. H., *The Renaissance of the Twelfth Century,* Cambridge, Mass., 1927. Treats Latin writings in many different genres.

• Henderson, George, *Gothic,* Baltimore, 1967.

Hoppin, Richard H., *Medieval Music,* New York, 1978.
- Knowles, David, *The Evolution of Medieval Thought,* New York, 1962. A very authoritative and well-written but often difficult survey.
- Leclercq, Jean, *The Love of Learning and the Desire for God,* New York, 1961. About monastic culture, with special reference to St. Bernard.

Leff, G., *Paris and Oxford Universities in the Thirteenth and Fourteenth Centuries,* New York, 1968. Covers both thought and institutions of learning.
- Lewis, C. S., *The Discarded Image,* Cambridge, 1964.
- Lindberg, David C., ed., *Science in the Middle Ages,* Chicago, 1978. A collection of introductory essays by leading authorities in their respective fields.
- Mâle, Emile, *The Gothic Image,* New York, 1913.
- Morris, Colin, *The Discovery of the Individual,* London, 1972. A provocative interpretation which sees "individualism" as a twelfth-century discovery.
- Smalley, B., *The Study of the Bible in the Middle Ages,* 3rd ed., Oxford, 1983. A standard work that is also gracefully written and original in its argumentation.

Southern, R. W., *Medieval Humanism,* New York, 1970. A collection of essays, almost all of which are exciting. Most exciting is the title piece.

Ullmann, W., *Medieval Political Thought,* rev. ed., Baltimore, 1976. The best short survey.

Van Steenberghen, F., *Aristotle in the West,* New York, 1970. A short account of the recovery of Aristotelian thought in the High Middle Ages.
- Von Simson, O., *The Gothic Cathedral,* New York, 1956. A controversial argument that Gothic architecture was meant to be "scientific."
- Weisheipl, J. A., *Friar Thomas d'Aquino: His Life, Thought, and Works,* 2nd ed., Washington, D.C., 1983.

SOURCE MATERIALS

- *An Aquinas Reader,* ed. Mary T. Clark, New York, 1972.
- Chrétien de Troyes, *Arthurian Romances,* tr. W. W. Comfort, New York, 1914.
- Dante, *The Divine Comedy,* tr. J. Ciardi, New York, 1977.
- Goldin, F., ed., *Lyrics of the Troubadours and Trouvères,* New York, 1973.
- Gottfried von Strassburg, *Tristan,* tr. A. T. Hatto, Baltimore, 1960.
- Joinville and Villehardouin, *Chronicles of the Crusades,* tr. M. R. B. Shaw, Baltimore, 1963.
- *The Letters of Abelard and Heloise* (includes Abelard's *Story of My Calamities*), tr. B. Radice, Baltimore, 1974.
- Peters, Edward, ed., *The First Crusade: The Chronicle of Fulcher of Chartres and Other Source Materials,* Philadelphia, 1971.
- *The Romance of the Rose,* tr. Harry W. Robbins, New York, 1962.
- *The Song of Roland,* tr. F. Goldin, New York, 1978.
- Thorndike, Lynn, ed., *University Records and Life in the Middle Ages,* New York, 1944.
- Tierney, Brian, ed., *The Crisis of Church and State, 1050–1300,* Englewood Cliffs, N.J., 1964. An excellent anthology of readings introduced and connected by masterful commentary.
- Wolfram von Eschenbach, *Parzival,* tr. H. M. Mustard and C. E. Passage, New York, 1961.

Chapter 15

THE LATER MIDDLE AGES
(1300–1500)

My lot has been to live amidst a storm
Of varying disturbing circumstances.
For you . . . a better age awaits.
Our descendants—the darkness once dispersed—
Can come again to the old radiance.

> —The poet Petrarch,
> writing in the 1340s

If the High Middle Ages were "times of feasts," then the late Middle Ages were "times of famine." From about 1300 until the middle or latter part of the fifteenth century calamities struck throughout western Europe with appalling severity and dismaying persistence. Famine first prevailed because agriculture was impeded by soil exhaustion, colder weather, and torrential rainfalls. Then, on top of those "acts of God," came the most terrible natural disaster of all: the dreadful plague known as the "Black Death," which cut broad swaths of mortality throughout western Europe. As if all that were not enough, incessant warfare continually brought hardship and desolation. Common people suffered most because they were most exposed to raping, stabbing, looting, and burning by soldiers and organized bands of freebooters. After an army passed through a region one might see miles of smoldering ruins littered with putrefying corpses; in many places the desolation was so great that wolves roamed the countryside and even entered the outskirts of the cities. In short, if the serene Virgin symbolized the High Middle Ages, the grinning death's-head symbolized the succeeding period. For these reasons we should not look to the later Middle Ages for the dramatic progress we saw transpiring earlier; but this is not to say that there was no progress at all. In the last two centuries of the Middle Ages Europeans dis-

The later Middle Ages: catastrophe and adaptation

played a tenacious perseverance in the face of adversity. Instead of abandoning themselves to apathy, they resolutely sought to adjust themselves to changed circumstances. Thus there was no collapse of civilization as there was with the fall of the Roman Empire, but rather a period of transition that resulted in preserving and building upon what was most solid in Europe's earlier legacy.

1. ECONOMIC DEPRESSION AND THE EMERGENCE OF A NEW EQUILIBRIUM

Economic crisis

By around 1300 the agricultural expansion of the High Middle Ages had reached its limits. Thereafter yields and areas under cultivation began to decline, causing a decline in the whole European economy that was accelerated by the disruptive effects of war. Accordingly, the first half of the fourteenth century was a time of growing economic depression. The coming of the Black Death in 1347 made this depression particularly acute because it completely disrupted the affairs of daily life. Subsequent recurrences of the plague and protracted warfare continued to depress most of the European economy until deep into the fifteenth century. But between roughly 1350 and 1450 Europeans learned how to adjust to the new economic circumstances and succeeded in placing their economy on a sounder basis. This became most evident after around 1450, when the tapering off of disease and warfare permitted a slow, but steady economic recovery. All told, therefore, despite a prolonged depression of roughly 150 years, Europe emerged in the later fifteenth century with a healthier economy than it had known earlier.

Agricultural adversity

The limits to agricultural expansion reached around 1300 were natural ones. There was a limit to the amount of land that could be cleared and a limit to the amount of crops that could be raised without the introduction of scientific farming. In fact, Europeans had gone further in clearing and cultivating than they should have: in the enthusiasm of the high-medieval colonization movement, marginal lands had been cleared that were not rich enough to sustain intense cultivation. In addition, even the best plots were becoming overworked. To make matters worse, after around 1300 the weather deteriorated. Whereas western Europe had been favored with a drying and warming trend in the eleventh and twelfth centuries, in the fourteenth century the climate became colder and wetter. Although the average decline in temperature over the course of the century was only at most 1° Centigrade, this was sufficient to curtail viticulture in many northern areas such as England. Cereal farming too became increasingly impractical in far northern regions because the growing season became too short: in Greenland and parts of Scandinavia agricultural settlements were abandoned entirely. Increased rainfall also took its toll.

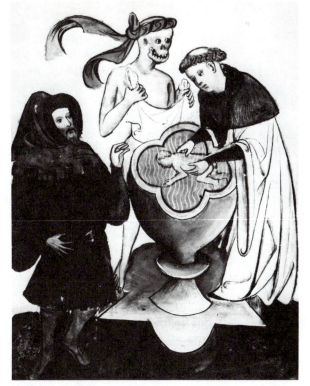

Death at the Baptism. In the later Middle Ages recurrent outbreaks of plague, coupled with other natural and manmade disasters, led to an obsession with the omnipresence of death. This chilling illumination from a fifteenth-century German manuscript shows a friar baptizing a newborn child while death stands ready to "dry him off." The point is that death stands waiting for all of us, even from the first minute of life.

Terrible floods that deluged all of northwestern Europe in 1315 ruined crops and caused a prolonged, deadly famine. For three years peasants were so driven by hunger that they ate their seed grain, ruining their chances for a full recovery in the following season. In desperation they also ate cats, dogs, and rats. Many peasants were so exposed to unsanitary conditions and weakened by malnutrition that they became highly susceptible to disease. Thus there was an appalling death rate. In one Flemish city a tenth of the population was buried within a six-month period of 1316 alone. Relatively settled farming conditions returned after 1318, but in many parts of Europe heavy rains or other climatic disasters came again. In Italy floods swept away Florentine bridges in 1333 and a tidal wave destroyed the port of Amalfi in 1343. With nature so recurrently capricious economic life could only suffer.

Although ruinous wars combined with famine to kill off many, Europe remained overpopulated until the middle of the fourteenth century. The reason for this was that population growth was still outstripping food supply. Since people continued to multiply while cereal production declined, there was just not enough food to go around. Accordingly, grain prices soared and the poor throughout Europe paid the penalty in hunger. And then a disaster struck which was so appalling that it seemed to many to presage the end of the world.

This was the Black Death, a combined onslaught of bubonic and

The pressure of population

Bubonic Plague. This representation from a late-fifteenth-century Dutch manuscript shows a man in the throes of death from the plague. The swelling on his neck is a "bubo," a form of lymphatic swelling that gave the bubonic plague its name.

pneumonic plague which first swept through Europe from 1347 to 1350, and returned at periodic intervals for roughly the next hundred years. This calamity was fully comparable—in terms of the death, dislocation, and horror it wrought—to the two world wars of the twentieth century. The clinical effects of the plague were hideous. Once infected with bubonic plague by a flea-bite, the diseased person would develop enormous swellings in the groin or armpits; black spots might appear on the arms and legs, diarrhea would ensue, and the victim would die between the third and fifth day. If the infection came in the pneumonic form, i.e., caused by inhalation, there would be coughing of blood instead of swellings, and death would follow within three days. Some people went to bed healthy and were dead the next morning after a night of agony; ships with dead crews floated aimlessly on the seas. Although the successive epidemics left a few localities unscathed, the overall demographic effects of the plague were devastating. To take just a few examples: the population of Toulouse declined from roughly 30,000 in 1335, to 26,000 in 1385, to 8,000 in 1430; the total population of eastern Normandy fell by 30 percent between 1347 and 1357, and again by 30 percent before 1380; in the rural area around Pistoia a population depletion of about 60 percent occurred between 1340 and 1404. Altogether, the combined effects of famine, war, and, above all, plague reduced the total population of western Europe by at least one-half and probably more like two-thirds between 1300 and 1450.

At first, the Black Death caused great hardships for most of the survivors. Since panic-stricken people wished to avoid contagion, many fled from their jobs to seek isolation. Town-dwellers fled to the

A Late-Medieval Funeral Scene

ATLANTIC

OCEAN

NORTH SEA

BALTIC SEA

Moscow

Bergen

December 31, 1349

Wisby

June 30, 1350

December 31, 1350

Durham
Drogheda
Dublin   Preston
              York
Kilkenny   Lancaster
Chester   Lincoln
              Nottingham
Leicester
Norwich   Yarmouth
Oxford Cambridge
London
Canterbury
Weymouth
Southampton
Calais
Ghent
Amiens

June 30, 1349

December 31, 1348

Rostock
Lübeck Wismar   Danzig
Hamburg   Thorn
Bremen
Osnabrück
Magdeburg   Frankfurt am Oder

Bruges   Cologne   Erfurt
Liège   Frankfurt
           Würzburg
           Nuremberg

Paris
Strassburg
Colmar
Angers
Bâsel
Lucerne   Zürich
           St. Gall

Vienna

Mühldorf

December 31, 1348

BLACK SE

0   300 miles

Verona Venice
Milan
Bordeaux   Genoa   Bologna Ferrara
Avignon   Sebenico
Toulouse Montpellier Pisa Florence Ancona
Béziers   Perugia
          Narbonne   Marseilles Siena   Ragusa
Huesca Perpignan
Saragossa Lerida   Rome   Constantinople
          Barcelona   Naples
Teruel

Valencia   June 30, 1347

June 30, 1348

Seville
Almeria

MEDITERRANEAN SEA
                              Messina   December 31, 1347
                                         Catania
                          Agrigento   Syracuse

Legend:
- Plague-stricken towns and areas
- - - Progress of plague at certain dates
■ Towns and areas not stricken by the plague

PROGRESS OF THE BLACK DEATH, 14th CENTURY

country and country-dwellers fled from each other. Even the pope retreated to the interior of his palace and allowed no one entrance. With
large numbers dead and others away from their posts, harvests were
left rotting, manufacturing was disrupted, and conveyance systems
were abandoned. Hence basic commodities became scarcer and prices
rose. For these reasons the onslaught of the plague greatly intensified
Europe's economic crisis.

*The Black Death disrupts
society and economy*

But after around 1400 the new demographic realities began to turn
prices around and alter basic economic patterns. Particularly, the
prices of staple foodstuffs began to decline because production gradually returned to normal and there were fewer mouths to feed. Recurrent reappearances of the plague or natural disasters sometimes caused

Economic consequences of the Black Death: (1) agricultural specialization

(2) the growth in importance of urban centers

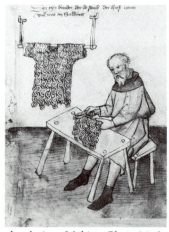

An Artisan Making Chain Mail. One can easily see why late-medieval knightly armor was terribly expensive.

prices to fluctuate greatly in certain years, but overall prices of basic commodities throughout most of the fifteenth century went down or remained stable. This trend led to new agricultural specialization. Since cereals were cheaper, people could afford to spend a greater percentage of their income on comparative luxuries such as dairy products, meat, and wine. Hitherto farmers all over Europe had concentrated on cereals because bread was the staff of life, but now it was wisest, particularly in areas of poorer soil or unpropitious climate, to shift to specialized production. Depending upon whatever seemed most feasible, land might be used for the raising of livestock for milk, grapes for wine, or malt for beer. Specialized regional economies resulted: parts of England were given over to sheep-raising or beer production, parts of France concentrated on wine, and Sweden traded butter for cheap German grain. Most areas of Europe turned to what they could do best, and reciprocal trade of basic commodities over long distances created a sound new commercial equilibrium.

Another economic result of the Black Death was an increase in the relative importance of towns and cities. Urban manufacturers usually could respond more flexibly than landlords to drastically changed economic conditions because their production capabilities were more elastic. When markets shrank, manufacturers could cut back supply more easily to match demand; they could also raise production more easily when circumstances warranted. Thus urban entrepreneurs bounced back from disaster more quickly than landowners. Often they took advantage of their greater strength to attract rural labor by means of higher salaries. Thereby the population balance between countryside and town was shifted slightly in favor of the latter.

Certain urban centers, especially those in northern Germany and northern Italy, profited the most from the new circumstances. In Germany a group of cities and towns under the leadership of Lübeck and Bremen allied in the so-called Hanseatic League to control long-distance trade in the Baltic and North Seas. Their fleets transported German grain to Scandinavia and brought back dairy products, fish, and furs. The enhanced European per capita ability to buy luxury goods brought new wealth to the northern Italian trading cities of Genoa and, especially, Venice because these cities controlled the importation of spices from the East. Greater expenditures on luxury also aided the economies of Florence, Venice, Milan, and other neighboring cities because those cities concentrated on the manufacture of silks and linens, light woolens, and other fine cloths. Milan, in addition, prospered from its armaments industry, which kept the warring European states supplied with armor and weapons. Because of varying local conditions, some cities and towns, above all those of Flanders, became economically depressed, but altogether European urban centers profited remarkably well from the new economic circumstances and emphasis on specialization.

The changed circumstances also helped stimulate the development of sophisticated business, accounting, and banking techniques. Because sharp fluctuations in prices made investments precarious, new forms of partnerships were created to minimize risks. Insurance contracts were also invented to take some of the risk out of shipping. Europe's most useful accounting invention, double-entry bookkeeping, was first put into use in Italy in the mid–fourteenth century and spread rapidly thereafter north of the Alps. This allowed for quick discovery of computational errors and easy overview of profits and losses, credits and debits. Large-scale banking had already become common after the middle of the thirteenth century, but the economic crises of the later Middle Ages encouraged banks to alter some of their ways of doing business. Most important was the development of prudent branch-banking techniques, especially by the Florentine house of the Medici. Earlier banks had built branches, but the Medici bank, which flourished from 1397 to 1494, organized theirs along the lines of a modern holding company. The Medici branches, located in London, Bruges, and Avignon, as well as several Italian cities, were dominated by senior partners from the Medici family who followed common policies. Formally, however, each branch was a separate partnership which did not carry any other branch down with it if it collapsed. Other Italian banks experimented with advanced credit techniques. Some even allowed their clients to transfer funds between each other without any real money changing hands. Such "book transfers" were at first executed only by oral command, but around 1400 they started to be carried out by written orders. These were the earliest ancestors of the modern check.

*The growth of advanced
business and financial
techniques*

In surveying the two centuries of late-medieval economic history, both the role of nature and that of human beings must be emphasized. The premodern history of all parts of the globe tends to show that whenever population becomes excessive natural controls manage to reduce it. Bad weather and disease may come at any time, but when humans are already suffering from hunger and conditions of overcrowding, the results of natural disasters will be particularly devastating. That certainly is what happened in the fourteenth century. Nature intervened cruelly in human affairs, but no matter how cruel the immediate effects, the results were ultimately beneficial. By 1450 a far smaller population had a higher average standard of living than the population of 1300. In this result humans too played their part. Because people were determined to make the best of the new circumstances and avoid a recurrence of economic depression, they managed to reorganize their economic life and place it on a sounder footing. The gross European product of about 1450 was probably smaller than it was in 1300, but this is not surprising given the much smaller population. In fact, per capita output had risen with per capita income, and the European economy was ready to move on to new conquests.

*The interaction of man
and nature in late-
medieval economic history*

2. SOCIAL AND EMOTIONAL DISLOCATION

*Social crisis: lower-class
revolts*

Before the healthy new equilibrium was reached, the economic crises
of the later Middle Ages contributed from about 1300 to 1450 to provoking a rash of lower-class rural and urban insurrections more numerous than Europe had ever known before or has ever known since.
It used to be thought that these were all caused by extreme depriva-
tion, but as we will see, that was often not the case.

*Rural insurrections: the
Jacquerie*

The one large-scale rural uprising that was most clearly caused by
economic hardship was the northern French "Jacquerie" of 1358.
This took its name from the prototypical French peasant, "Jacques
Bonhomme," who had suffered more than he could endure. In 1348
and 1349 the Black Death had brought its terror and wreaked havoc
with the economy. Then a flare-up of war between England and
France had spread great desolation over the countryside. The peasants,
as usual in late-medieval warfare, suffered most from the pillaging
and burning carried out by the rapacious soldiers. To make matters
even less endurable, after the English decisively defeated the French
in 1356 at the Battle of Poitiers the French king, John II, and numerous
aristocrats had to be ransomed. As always in such cases, the peasants
were asked to bear the heaviest share of the burden, but by 1358
they had had enough and rose up with astounding ferocity. Without
any clear program they burned down castles, murdered their lords,
and raped their lords' wives. Undoubtedly their intense economic
resentments were the major cause for the uprising, but two qualifications remain in order. The first is that the peasants who participated
in the Jacquerie were, comparatively speaking, among the richest in
France: apparently those who suffered most abjectly were entirely
unable to organize themselves for revolt. The other qualification is
that political factors surely help account for the Jacquerie as well as
economic ones. While the king was in captivity in England, groups
of townsmen were trying to reform the governmental system by
limiting monarchical powers, and aristocratic factions were plotting
to seize power. Since nobody quite knew which element was going
to rule where, the peasants seem to have sensed an opportunity to
take advantage of France's political confusion. But in fact the opportunity was not as great as they may have thought: within a month the
privileged powers closed ranks, massacred the rebels, and quickly
restored order.

*Background of the English
Peasants' Revolt*

The English Peasants' Revolt of 1381—the most serious lower-
class rebellion in English history—is frequently bracketed with the
Jacquerie, but its causes were very different. Instead of being a revolt
of desperation, it was one of frustrated rising expectations. By 1381
the effects of the Black Death should have been working in favor of
the peasants. Above all, a shortage of labor should have placed their
services in demand. In fact, the incidence of the plague did help to

increase manumissions (i.e., freeings) of serfs and raise salaries or lower rents of free farm laborers. But aristocratic landlords fought back to preserve their own incomes. They succeeded in passing legislation that aimed to keep wages at pre-plague levels and force landless laborers to work at the lower rates. Aristocrats furthermore often tried to exact all their old dues and unpaid services. Because the peasants were unwilling to be pushed down into their previous poverty and subservience, a collision was inevitable.

The spark that ignited the great revolt of 1381 was an attempt to collect a national tax levied equally on every head instead of being made proportional to wealth. This was an unprecedented development in English tax-collecting that the peasants understandably found unfair. Two head-taxes were levied without resistance in 1377 and 1379, but when agents tried to collect a third in 1381 the peasantry rose up to resist and seek redress of all their grievances. First they burned local records and sacked the dwellings of those they considered their exploiters; then they marched on London, where they executed the lord chancellor and treasurer of England. Recognizing the gravity of the situation, the fifteen-year-old king, Richard II, went out to meet the peasants and won their confidence by promising to abolish serfdom and keep rents low; meanwhile, during negotiations, the peasant leader, Wat Tyler, was murdered in a squabble with the king's escort. Lacking leadership, the peasants, who mistakenly thought they had achieved their aims, rapidly dispersed. But once the boy-king was no longer in danger of his life he kept none of his promises. Instead, the scattered peasant forces were quickly hunted down and a few alleged trouble-makers were executed without any mass reprisals. The revolt itself therefore accomplished nothing, but within a few decades the natural play of economic forces caused serfdom to disappear and considerably improved the lot of the rural wage laborer.

Other rural revolts took place in other parts of Europe, but we may now look at some urban ones. Conventionally, the urban revolts of the later Middle Ages are viewed as uprisings of exploited proletarians who were more oppressed than ever because of the effects of economic depression. But this is probably too great a simplification because each case differed and complex forces were always at work. For example, an uprising in the north German town of Brunswick in 1374 was much less a movement of the poor against the rich than a political upheaval in which one political alliance replaced another. A different north German uprising, in Lübeck in 1408, has been aptly described as a "taxpayer's" revolt. This again was less a confrontation of the poor versus the rich than an attempt of a faction that was out of power to initiate less costly government.

The nearest thing to a real proletarian revolt was the uprising in 1378 of the Florentine *Ciompi* (pronounced "cheeompi"). The Ciompi were wool-combers who had the misfortune to be engaged in an industry that had become particularly depressed. Some of them had lost

Tombstone of a Leader of a Fourteenth-Century German Peasant Uprising. In 1336 a petty knight from Franconia (central Germany) marched at the head of impoverished peasants who vented their resentments by robbing and murdering all the Jews they could find in the nearby towns. After several months of leading this rampage the knight was finally apprehended and executed by governing authorities. His tombstone shows him with bound hands at the moment of his beheading, but the inscription calls him "blessed," a sign that some wished to view him as a martyred saint.

their jobs and others were frequently cheated or underpaid by the masters of the woolen industry. The latter wielded great political power in Florence, and thus could pass economic legislation in their own favor. This fact in itself meant that if there were to be economic reforms, they would have to go together with political changes. As events transpired it was a political crisis that called the Ciompi into direct action. In 1378 Florence had become exhausted by three years of war with the papacy. Certain patrician leaders overthrew the old regime to alter the war policy and gain their own political advantage. Circumstances led them to seek the support of the lower classes and, once stirred up, the Ciompi became emboldened after a few months to launch their own far more radical rebellion. This was inspired primarily by economic hardship and grievances, but personal hatreds also played a role. The Ciompi gained power for six weeks, during which they tried to institute tax relief, fuller employment, and representation of themselves and other proletarian groups in the Florentine government. But they could not maintain their hold on power and a new oligarchical government revoked all their reforms.

General observations on the nature of popular uprisings

If we try to draw any general conclusions about these various uprisings, we can certainly say that few if any of them would have occurred had there not been an economic crisis. But political considerations always had some influence, and the rebels in some uprisings were more prosperous than in others. It is noteworthy that all the genuinely lower-class uprisings of economically desperate groups quickly failed. This was certainly because the upper classes were more accustomed to wielding power and giving orders; even more important, they had access to the money and troops necessary to quell revolts. Sometimes elements within the lower classes might fight among themselves, whereas the privileged always managed to rally into a united front when faced by a lower-class threat to their domination. In addition, lower-class rebels were usually more intent on redressing immediate grievances than on developing fully coherent long-term governmental programs; inspiring ideals for cohesive action were generally lacking. The case of the Hussite Revolution in Bohemia—to be treated later—shows that religion in the later Middle Ages was a more effective rallying ground for large numbers of people than political, economic, and social demands.

The crisis of the late-medieval aristocracy

Although the upper classes succeeded in overcoming popular uprisings, they perceived the economic and emotional insecurities of the later Middle Ages and the possibility of revolt as a constant threat, and became obsessed with maintaining their privileged social status. Late-medieval aristocrats were in a precarious economic position because they gained most of their income from land. In times when grain prices and rents were falling and wages rising, landowners were obviously in economic trouble. Some aristocrats probably also felt threatened by the rapid rise of merchants and financiers who could

A Party of Late-Medieval Aristocrats. Notice the pointed shoes and the women's pointed hats, twice as high as their heads.

make quick killings because of sharp market fluctuations. In practice, really wealthy merchants bought land and were absorbed into the aristocracy. Moreover, most landowning aristocrats were able to stave off economic threats by expert estate management; in fact, many of them actually became richer than ever. But most still felt more exposed to social and economic insecurities than before. The result was that they tried to set up artificial barriers behind which they separated themselves from other classes.

Two of the most striking examples of this separation were the aristocratic emphasis on luxury and the formation of exclusive chivalric orders. The late Middle Ages was the period par excellence of aristocratic ostentation. While famine or disease raged, aristocrats regaled themselves with lavish banquets and magnificent pageants. At one feast in Flanders in 1468 a table decoration was forty-six feet high. Aristocratic clothing too was extremely ostentatious: men wore long, pointed shoes, and women ornately festooned headdresses. Throughout history rich people have always enjoyed dressing up, but the aristocrats of the later Middle Ages seem to have done so obsessively to comfort themselves and convey the message that they were entirely different from others. The insistence on maintaining a sharply defined social hierarchy also accounts for the late-medieval proliferation of chivalric orders, such as those of the Knights of the Garter or the Golden Fleece. By joining together in exclusive orders which prescribed special conduct and boasted special insignia of membership,

Duke Philip the Good of Burgundy. The duke proudly wears the emblem of the Order of the Golden Fleece around his neck.

A Late-Medieval Crucifixion Scene. The Virgin has to be held up to keep from swooning, and the angels are weeping.

aristocrats who felt threatened by social pressures again tried to set themselves off from others, in effect, by putting up a sign that read "for members only."

Another explanation for the exorbitant stress on luxury is that it was a form of escapism. Aristocrats who were continually exposed to the sight and smell of death must have found it emotionally comforting to retreat into a dream-world of elegant manners, splendid feasts, and multicolored clothes. In a parallel fashion, nonaristocrats who could not afford such luxuries often sought relief from the vision of death in crude public entertainments: for example, crowds would watch blind beggars try to catch a squealing pig but beat each other with clubs instead, or they would cheer on boys to clamber up greasy poles in order to win prizes of geese.

It must not be thought, however, that late-medieval Europeans gave themselves over to riotous living without interruption. In fact, the same people who sought elegant or boisterous diversions just as often went to the other emotional extreme when faced by the psychic stress caused by the troubles of the age, and abandoned themselves to sorrow. Throughout the period grown men and women shed tears in abundance. The queen mother of France wept in public when she first

Left: *A Dead Man Before His Judge.* A late-medieval reminder of human mortality. Right: *Tomb of François de la Sarra.* This late–fourteenth-century Swiss nobleman is shown with snakes around his arms and toads littering his face.

viewed her grandson; the great preacher Vincent Ferrer had to interrupt his sermons on Christ's Passion and the Last Judgment because he and his audience were sobbing too convulsively; and the English king, Edward II, supposedly wept so much when imprisoned that he gushed forth enough hot water for his own shave. The last story taxes the imagination, but it does illustrate well what contemporaries thought was possible. We know for certain that the Church encouraged crying because of the survival of moving statuettes of weeping St. Johns, which were obviously designed to call forth tears from their viewers.

People also were encouraged by preachers to brood on the Passion of Christ and on their own mortality. Fearsome crucifixes abounded, and the figure of the Virgin Mary was less a smiling madonna than a sorrowing mother: now she was most frequently depicted slumping with grief at the foot of the cross, or holding the dead Christ in her lap. The late-medieval obsession with mortality can also still be seen in sculptures, frescoes, and book illustrations that reminded viewers of the brevity of life and the torments of hell. The characteristic tombs of the High Middle Ages were mounted with sculptures that either showed the deceased in some action that had been typical of his or her accomplishments in life, or else in a state of repose that showed death to be nothing more than peaceful sleep. But in the late fourteenth century, tombs appeared that displayed the physical ravages of death in the most gruesome ways imaginable: emaciated corpses were displayed with protruding intestines or covered with snakes or toads. Some tombs bore inscriptions stating that the viewer would soon be "a fetid cadaver, food for worms"; some warned chillingly: "What you are, I was; what I am, you will be." Omnipresent illustrations displayed figures of grinning Death, with his scythe, carrying off elegant and healthy men and women, or sadistic devils roasting pain-wracked humans in hell. Because people who painted or brooded on such pictures might the next day indulge in excessive revels, late-medieval culture often seems to border on the manic-depressive. But apparently such extreme reactions were necessary to help people cope with their fears.

3. TRIALS FOR THE CHURCH AND HUNGER FOR THE DIVINE

The intense concentration on the meaning of death was also a manifestation of a very deep and pervasive religiosity. The religious enthusiasm of the High Middle Ages by no means flagged after 1300; if anything, it became more intense. But religious enthusiasm took on new forms of expression because of the institutional difficulties of the Church and the turmoils of the age.

After the humiliation and death of Pope Boniface VIII in 1303, the Church experienced a period of institutional crisis that was as severe and prolonged as the contemporary economic crisis. We may distin-

The Prince of the World. A stone figure from the church of St. Sebald, Nuremberg, from about 1330. From the front the man is smiling and master of all he surveys; from the rear he is crawling with vermin.

guish three phases: the so-called Babylonian Captivity of the papacy, 1305–1378; the Great Schism, 1378–1417; and the period of the Italian territorial papacy, 1417–1517. During the Babylonian Captivity the papacy was located in Avignon instead of Rome and was generally subservient to the interests of the French crown. There were several reasons for this: the most obvious was that since the test of strength between Philip the Fair and Boniface VIII had resulted in a clear victory for the French king, subsequent popes were unwilling to risk French royal ire. In fact, once the popes recognized that they could not give orders to the French kings, they found that they could gain certain advantages from currying their favor. One was a safe home in southern France, away from the tumult of Italy. Central Italy and the city of Rome in the fourteenth century had become so politically turbulent and rebellious that the pope could not even count on finding personal safety there, let alone sufficiently peaceful conditions to maintain orderly ecclesiastical administration. But no such danger existed in Avignon. Even though Avignon was not then part of the French kingdom—it was the major city of a small papal territory—French military might was close enough to guarantee the pope his much-needed security. Another advantage of papal subservience to French power was help from the French in pursuing mutually advantageous policies in Germany and southern Italy. Perhaps most important was a working agreement whereby the French king would propose his own candidates to become bishops and the pope would then name them, thereby gaining sizable monetary payments. After 1305 the pro-French system became so entrenched that a majority of cardinals and all the popes until 1378 were themselves French.

At Avignon the popes were more successful than ever in pursuing their policy of centralizing the government of the Church. For the first time they worked out a really sound system of papal finance, based on the systematization of dues collected from the clergy throughout Europe. The papacy also succeeded in appointing more candidates to vacant benefices than before (in practice often naming candidates proposed by the French and English kings), and they proceeded against heresy with great determination, indeed with ruthlessness. But whatever the popes achieved in power they lost in respect and loyalty. The clergy became alienated as a result of being asked to pay so much money, and much of the laity was horrified by the corruption and unbridled luxury displayed at the papal court: there the cardinals lived more splendidly than lords, dining off peacocks, pheasants, grouse, and swans, and drinking from elaborately sculptured fountains that spouted the finest wines. Most of the Avignonese popes themselves were personally upright and abstemious, but one, Clement VI (1342–1352), was worse than his cardinals. Clement was ready to offer any spiritual benefit for money, boasted that he would appoint even a jackass as bishop if political circumstances warranted, and defended

The character of the Avignonese papacy

his incessant sexual transgressions by insisting that he fornicated on doctors' orders.

As time went on the pressures of informed public opinion forced the popes to promise that they would return to Rome. After one abortive attempt by Urban V in 1367, Pope Gregory XI finally did return to the Holy City in 1377. But he died a year later and then disaster struck. The college of cardinals, surrounded in Rome by clamoring Italians, yielded to local sentiment by naming an Italian as pope, who took the title of Urban VI. But most of the cardinals were Frenchmen and quickly regretted their decision, especially because Urban VI immediately began quarreling with them and revealing what were probably paranoid tendencies. Therefore, after only a few months, the French cardinals met again, declared the previous election void, and replaced Urban with one of their own number, who called himself Clement VII.

The return to Rome

Unfortunately, however, Urban VI did not meekly resign. On the contrary, he named an entirely new Italian college of cardinals and remained entrenched in Rome. Clement VII quickly retreated with his own party to Avignon and the so-called Great Schism ensued. France and other countries in the French political orbit—such as Scotland, Castile, and Aragon—recognized Clement, while the rest of Europe recognized Urban as the true pope. For three decades Christians looked on helplessly while the rival pontiffs hurled curses at each other and the international monastic orders became divided into Roman and Avignonese camps. The death of one or the other pope did not end the schism; each camp had its own set of cardinals which promptly named either a French or Italian successor. The desperateness of the situation led a council of prelates from both camps to meet in Pisa in 1409 to depose both popes and name a new one instead. But neither the Italian nor the French pope accepted the council's decision, and both had enough political support to retain some obedience. So after 1409 there were three rival claimants hurling curses instead of two.

The Great Schism

The Great Schism was finally ended in 1417 by the Council of Constance, the largest ecclesiastical gathering in medieval history. This time the assembled prelates made certain to gain the crucial support of secular powers and also to eliminate the prior claimants before naming a new pope. After the council's election of Martin V in 1417, European ecclesiastical unity was thus fully restored. But a struggle over the nature of Church government followed immediately. The members of the Council of Constance challenged the prevailing medieval theory of papal monarchy by calling for balanced, "conciliar," government. In two momentous decrees they stated that a general council of prelates was superior in authority to the pope, and that such councils should meet regularly to govern the Church. Not surprisingly, subsequent popes—who had now returned to Rome—sought to nullify these decrees. When a new council met in Basel in 1431, in accordance with the

*The end of the Schism;
conciliarism*

principles laid down at Constance, the reigning pope did all he could to sabotage its activities. Ultimately he was successful: after a protracted struggle the Council of Basel dissolved in 1449 in abject failure, and the attempt to institute constitutional government in the Church was completely defeated. But the papacy only won this victory over conciliarism by gaining the support of the rulers of the European states. In separate concordats with kings and princes the popes granted the secular rulers much authority over the various local churches. The popes thus became assured of theoretical supremacy at the cost of surrendering much real power. To compensate for this they concentrated on consolidating their own direct rule in central Italy. Most of the fifteenth-century popes ruled very much like any other princes, leading armies, jockeying for alliances, and building magnificent palaces. Hence, although they did succeed for the first time in creating a viable political state, their reputation for disinterested piety remained low.

The decline of clerical prestige

While the papacy was undergoing these vicissitudes, the local clergy throughout Europe was undergoing a loss of prestige for several reasons. One was that the pope's greater financial demands forced the clergy to demand more from the laity, but such demands were bitterly resented, especially during times of prevailing economic crisis. Then too during outbreaks of plague the clergy sometimes fled their posts just like everyone else, but in so doing they lost whatever claim they had for being morally superior. Probably the single greatest reason for growing dissatisfaction with the clergy was the increase in lay literacy. The continued proliferation of schools and the decline in the cost of books—a subject we will treat later—made it possible for large numbers of lay people to learn how to read. Once that happened, the laity could start reading parts of the Bible, or, more frequently, popular religious primers. These made it clear that their local priests were not living according to the standards set by Jesus and the Apostles. In the meantime, the upheavals and horrors of the age drove people to seek religious solace more than ever. Finding the conventional channels of church attendance, confession, and submission to clerical authority insufficient, the laity sought supplementary or alternate routes to piety. These differed greatly from each other, but they all aimed to satisfy an immense hunger for the divine.

The growth of lay piety: (1) devotional practices

The most widely traveled route was that of performing repeated acts of external devotion in the hope that they would gain the devotee divine favor on earth and salvation in the hereafter. People flocked to go on pilgrimages as never before and participated regularly in barefooted religious processions: the latter were often held twice a month and occasionally as often as once a week. Men and women also eagerly paid for thousands of masses to be said by full-time "mass priests" for the souls of their dead relatives and left legacies for the reading of numerous requiem masses to save their own souls after death. Obsession with repeating prayers reached a peak when some pious indi-

A German Flagellant Procession. These penitents hoped they could ward off the Black Death by their mutually inflicted tortures.

viduals tried to compute the number of drops of blood that Christ shed on the cross so that they could say the same number of Our Fathers. The most excessive and repugnant form of religious ritual in the later Middle Ages was flagellation. Some women who lived in communal houses beat themselves with the roughest animal hides, chains, and knotted thongs. A young girl who entered such a community in Poland in 1331 suffered extreme internal injuries and became completely disfigured within eleven months. Flailings were not usually performed in public, but during the first onslaught of the Black Death in 1348 and 1349, whole bands of lay people marched through northern Europe chanting and beating each other with metal-tipped scourges in the hope of appeasing the apparent divine wrath.

An opposite route to godliness was the inward path of mysticism. Throughout the European continent, but particularly in Germany and England, male and female mystics, both clerical and lay, sought union with God by means of "detachment," contemplation, or spiritual exercises. The most original and eloquent late-medieval mystical theorist was the German Dominican, Master Eckhart (c. 1260–1327), who taught that there was a power or "spark" deep within every human soul that was really the dwelling-place of God. By renouncing all sense of selfhood one could retreat into one's innermost recesses and there find divinity. Eckhart did not recommend ceasing attendance at church—he hardly could have because he preached in

(2) mysticism

churches—but he made it clear that outward rituals were of comparatively little importance in reaching God. He also gave the impression to his lay audiences that they might attain godliness largely on their own volition. Thus ecclesiastical authorities charged him with inciting "ignorant and undisciplined people to wild and dangerous excesses." Although Eckhart pleaded his own doctrinal orthodoxy, some of his teachings were condemned by the papacy.

*Heterodox and orthodox
mysticism*

That Eckhart's critics were not entirely mistaken in their worries is shown by the fact that some lay people in Germany who were influenced by him did fall into the heresy of believing that they could become fully united with God on earth without any priestly intermediaries. But these so-called heretics of the Free Spirit were few in number. Much more numerous were later orthodox mystics, sometimes influenced by Eckhart and sometimes not, who placed greater emphasis on the divine initiative in the meeting of the soul with God and made certain to insist that the ministrations of the Church were a necessary contribution to the mystic way. Even they, however, believed that "churches make no man holy, but men make churches holy." Most of the great teachers and practitioners of mysticism in the fourteenth century were clerics, nuns, or hermits, but in the fifteenth century a modified form of mystical belief spread among lay people. This "practical mysticism" did not aim for full ecstatic union with God, but rather for an ongoing sense of some divine presence during the conduct of daily life. The most popular manual that pointed the way to this goal was the Latin *Imitation of Christ,* written around 1427, probably by the north German canon Thomas à Kempis. Because this was written in a simple but forceful style and taught how to be a pious Christian while still living actively in the world, it was particularly attractive to lay readers. Thus it quickly became translated into the leading European vernaculars. From then until today it has been more widely read by Christians than any other religious work outside of the Bible. The *Imitation* urges its readers to participate in one religious ceremony—the sacrament of the Eucharist—but otherwise it emphasizes inward piety. According to its teachings, the individual Christian is best able to become the "partner" of Jesus Christ both by taking communion and also by engaging in biblical meditation and leading a simple, moral life.

*(3) heresy: John Wyclif
and the Lollards*

A third distinct form of late-medieval piety was outright religious protest or heresy. In England and Bohemia especially, heretical movements became serious threats to the Church. The initiator of heresy in late-medieval England was an Oxford theologian named John Wyclif (c. 1330–1384). Wyclif's rigorous adherence to the theology of St. Augustine led him to believe that a certain number of humans were predestined to be saved while the rest were irrevocably damned. He thought the predestined would naturally live simply, according to the standards of the New Testament, but in fact he found most members of the Church hierarchy indulging in splendid extravagances. Hence he concluded that most Church officials were damned. For him the only solution was to have secular rulers appropriate ecclesiastical wealth and reform the Church by replacing corrupt priests and bishops with men who would live according to apostolic standards. This position was obviously attractive to the aristocracy of England, who may have looked forward to enriching themselves with Church spoils and at least saw nothing wrong with using Wyclif as a bulldog to frighten the pope and the local clergy. Thus Wyclif at first received influential aristocratic support. But toward the end of his life he moved from merely calling for reform to attacking some of the most basic institutions of the Church, above all the sacrament of the Eucharist. This radicalism frightened off his influential protectors, and Wyclif probably would have been formally condemned for heresy had he lived longer. His death brought no respite for the Church, however, because he had attracted numerous lay followers—called Lollards— who zealously continued to propagate some of his most radical ideas. Above all, the Lollards taught that pious Christians should shun the corrupt Church and instead study the Bible and rely as far as possible on their individual consciences. Lollardy gained many adherents in the last two decades of the fourteenth century, but after the introduction in England of the death penalty for heresy in 1399 and the failure of a Lollard uprising in 1414 the heretical wave greatly receded. Nonetheless, a few Lollards did continue to survive underground, and their descendants helped contribute to the Protestant Reformation of the sixteenth century.

Much greater was the influence of Wyclifism in Bohemia. Around 1400, Czech students who had studied in Oxford brought back Wyclif's ideas to the Bohemian capital of Prague. There Wyclifism was enthusiastically adopted by an eloquent preacher named John Hus (c. 1373–1415), who had already been inveighing in well-attended sermons against "the world, the flesh, and the devil." Hus employed Wyclifite theories to back up his own calls for the end of ecclesiastical corruption, and rallied many Bohemians to the cause of reform in the years between 1408 and 1415. Never alienating anyone as Wyclif had done by criticizing the doctrine of the Eucharist, Hus gained support from many different directions. The politics of the Great Schism prompted the king of Bohemia to lend Hus his protection, and influential aristocrats supported Hus for motives similar to those of their English counterparts. Above all, Hus gained a mass following because of his eloquence and concern for social justice. Accordingly, most of Bohemia was behind him when Hus in 1415 agreed to travel to the Council of Constance to defend his views and try to convince the assembled prelates that only thoroughgoing reform could save the Church. But although Hus had been guaranteed his personal safety, this assurance was revoked as soon as he arrived at the Council: rather

John Hus

than being given a fair hearing, the betrayed idealist was tried for heresy and burned.

Hus's supporters in Bohemia were justifiably outraged and quickly raised the banner of open revolt. The aristocracy took advantage of the situation to seize Church lands, and poorer priests, artisans, and peasants rallied together in the hope of achieving Hus's goals of religious reform and social justice. Between 1420 and 1424 armies of lower-class Hussites, led by a brilliant blind general, John Zizka, amazingly defeated several invading forces of well-armed "crusading" knights from Germany. In 1434 more conservative, aristocratically dominated Hussites overcame the radicals, thereby ending attempts to initiate a purified new religious and social dispensation. But even the conservatives refused to return to full orthodoxy. Thus Bohemia never came back to the Catholic fold until after the Catholic Reformation in the seventeenth century. The Hussite declaration of religious independence was both a foretaste of what was to come one hundred years later with Protestantism and the most successful late-medieval expression of dissatisfaction with the government of the Church.

4. POLITICAL CRISIS AND RECOVERY

The story of late-medieval politics at first seems very dreary because throughout most of the period there was incessant strife. Almost everywhere neighbors fought neighbors and states fought states. But on closer inspection it becomes clear that despite the turmoil there was ultimate improvement in almost all the governments of Europe. In the course of the fifteenth century peace returned to most of the continent, the national monarchies in particular became stronger, and the period ended on a new note of strength just as it had from the point of view of economics.

Starting our survey with Italy, it must first be explained that the Kingdom of Naples in the extreme south of the Italian peninsula was sunk in endemic warfare or maladministration more or less without interruption throughout the fourteenth and fifteenth centuries. Otherwise, Italy emerged from the prevailing political turmoil of the late Middle Ages earlier than any other part of Europe. The fourteenth century was a time of troubles for the Papal States, comprising most of central Italy, because forces representing the absent or divided papacy were seldom able to overcome the resistance of refractory towns and rival leaders of marauding military bands. But after the end of the Great Schism in 1417 the popes concentrated more on consolidating their own Italian territories and gradually became the strong rulers of most of the middle part of the peninsula. Farther north some of the leading city-states—such as Florence, Venice, Siena, and Genoa—had experienced at least occasional and most often prolonged social warfare in the fourteenth century because of the economic pressures of the age. But sooner or later the most powerful families or interest groups overcame internal resistance. By around 1400 the three leading cities of the north—Venice, Milan, Florence—had fixed definitively upon their own different forms of government: Venice was ruled by a merchant oligarchy, Milan by a dynastic despotism, and Florence by a complex, supposedly republican system that was actually controlled by the rich. (After 1434 the Florentine republic was in practice dominated by the banking family of the Medici.)

Having settled their internal problems, Venice, Milan, and Florence proceeded from about 1400 to 1454 to expand territorially and conquer almost all the other northern Italian cities and towns except Genoa, which remained prosperous and independent but gained no new territory. Thus, by the middle of the fifteenth century Italy was divided into five major parts: the states of Venice, Milan, and Florence in the north; the Papal States in the middle; and the backward Kingdom of Naples in the south. A treaty of 1454 initiated a half-century of peace between these states: whenever one threatened to upset the "balance of power," the others usually allied against it before serious warfare could break out. Accordingly, the last half of the fifteenth century was a fortunate age for Italy. But in 1494 a French invasion initiated a period of renewed warfare in which the French attempt at dominating Italy was successfully countered by Spain.

Peace established in the fifteenth century

North of the Alps political turmoil prevailed throughout the fourteenth century and lasted longer into the fifteenth. Probably the worst instability was experienced in Germany. There the virtually independent princes continually warred with the greatly weakened emperors, or else they warred with each other. Between about 1350 and 1450 near-anarchy prevailed, because while the princes were warring and subdividing their inheritances into smaller states, petty powers such as free cities and knights who owned one or two castles were striving to shake off the rule of the princes. Throughout most of the German west these attempts met with enough success to fragment political authority more than ever, but in the east after about 1450 certain stronger German princes managed to assert their authority over divisive forces. After they did so they started to govern firmly over middle-sized states on the model of the larger national monarchies of England and France. The strongest princes were those who ruled in eastern territories such as Bavaria, Austria, and Brandenburg, because there towns were fewer and smaller and the princes had earlier been able to take advantage of imperial weakness to preside over the colonization of large tracts of land. Especially the Habsburg princes of Austria and the Hohenzollern princes of Brandenburg—a territory joined in the sixteenth century with the easternmost lands of Prussia—would be the most influential powers in Germany's future.

Germany: the triumph of the princes

The great nation-states did not escape unscathed from the late-medieval turmoil either. France was strife-ridden for much of the period, primarily in the form of the Hundred Years' War between France and England. The Hundred Years' War was actually a series of conflicts that lasted for even more than one hundred years—from 1337 to 1453. There were several different causes for this prolonged struggle. The major one was the longstanding problem of French territory held by the English kings. At the beginning of the fourteenth century the English kings still ruled much of the rich southern French lands of Gascony and Aquitaine as vassals of the French crown. The French, who since the reign of Philip Augustus had been expanding and consolidating their rule, obviously hoped to expel the English, making war inevitable. Another cause for strife was that the English economic interests in the woolen trade with Flanders led them to support the frequent attempts of Flemish burghers to rebel against French rule. Finally, the fact that the direct Capetian line of succession to the French throne died out in 1328, to be replaced thereafter by the related Valois dynasty, meant that the English kings, who themselves descended from the Capetians as a result of intermarriage, laid claim to the French crown itself.

France should have had no difficulty in defeating England at the start: it was the richest country in Europe and outnumbered England in population by some fifteen million to fewer than four million. Nonetheless, throughout most of the first three-quarters of the Hundred Years' War the English won most of the pitched battles. One reason for this was that the English had learned superior military tactics, using well-disciplined archers to fend off and scatter the heavily armored mounted French knights. In the three greatest battles of the long conflict—Crécy (1346), Poitiers (1356), and Agincourt (1415)—the outnumbered English relied on tight discipline and effective use of the longbow to inflict crushing defeats on the French. Another reason for English success was that the war was always fought on French soil. That being the case, English soldiers were eager to fight because they could look forward to rich plunder, while their own homeland suffered none of the disasters of war. Worst of all for the French was the fact that they often were badly divided. The French crown had always had to fear provincial attempts to assert autonomy: especially during the long period of warfare, when there were several highly inept kings and the English encouraged internal French dissensions, many aristocratic provincial leaders took advantage of the confusion to ally with the enemy and seek their own advantage. The most dramatic and fateful instance was the breaking away of Burgundy, whose dukes from 1419 to 1435 allied with the English, an act which called the very existence of an independent French crown into question.

It was in this dark period that the heroic figure of Joan of Arc came forth to rally the French. In 1429 Joan, an illiterate but extremely devout peasant girl, sought out the uncrowned French ruler, Charles VII, to announce that she had been divinely commissioned to drive the English out of France. Charles was persuaded to let her take command of his troops, and her piety and sincerity made such a favorable impression on the soldiers that their morale was raised immensely. In a few months Joan had liberated much of central France from English domination and had brought Charles to Rheims, where he was crowned king. But in May 1430 she was captured by the Burgundians and handed over to the English, who accused her of being a witch and tried her for heresy. Condemned in 1431 after a predetermined trial, she was publicly burned to death in the market square at Rouen. Nonetheless, the French, fired by their initial victories, continued to move on the offensive. When Burgundy withdrew from the English alliance in 1435, and the English king, Henry VI, proved to be totally incompetent, there followed an uninterrupted series of triumphs for the French side. In 1453 the capture of Bordeaux, the last of the English strongholds in the southwest, finally brought the long war to an end. The English now held no land in France except for the Channel port of Calais, which they ultimately lost in 1558.

More than merely expelling the English from French territory, the Hundred Years' War resulted in greatly strengthening the powers of the French crown. Although many of the French kings during the long war had been ineffective personalities—one, Charles VI, suffered periodic bouts of insanity—the monarchy demonstrated remarkable staying power because it provided France with the strongest institutions it knew and therefore offered the only realistic hope for lasting stability and peace. Moreover, warfare emergencies allowed the kings to gather new powers, above all, the rights to collect national taxes and maintain a standing army. Hence after Charles VII succeeded in defeating the English, the crown was able to renew the high-medieval royal tradition of ruling the country assertively. In the reigns of Charles's successors, Louis XI (1461–1483) and Louis XII (1498–1515), the monarchy became ever stronger. Its greatest single achievement was the destruction of the power of Burgundy in 1477 when the Burgundian duke, Charles the Bold, fell in the battle of Nancy at the hands of the Swiss, whom Charles had been trying to dominate. Since Charles died without a male heir, Louis XI of France was able to march into Burgundy and reabsorb the breakaway duchy. Later, when Louis XII gained Brittany by marriage, the French kings ruled powerfully over almost all of what is today included in the borders of France.

Louis XI of France. A portrait by Fouquet.

Although the Hundred Years' War was fought on French instead of English soil, England also experienced great turmoil during the later Middle Ages because of internal instability. Indeed, England was a hotbed of insurrection: of the nine English kings who came to the throne between 1307 and 1485, five died violently because of revolts or con-

England: internal turmoil

The Wars of the Roses

The positive aspects of English political developments, 1307–1485

spiracies. Most of these slain kings had proven themselves to be incapable rulers, but there were other reasons for England's political troubles as well. One was that the crown had been too ambitious in trying both to hold on to its territories in France and also to subdue Scotland. This policy often made it necessary to resort to heavy taxation and to grant major political concessions to the aristocracy. When English arms in France were successful, the crown rode the crest of popularity and the aristocracy prospered from military spoils and ransoms; but whenever the tides of battle turned to defeat, the crown became financially embarrassed and thrown on the political defensive. To make matters worse, the English aristocracy was particularly unruly throughout the period, not just because the aristocrats often had reason to distrust the inept kings, but because the economic pressures of the age made them seek to enlarge their agricultural estates at the expense of each other. This led to factionalism, and factionalism often led to civil war.

After the English presence in France was virtually eradicated and the aristocracy could no longer hope to enrich itself on the spoils of foreign warfare, England's political situation became particularly desperate. As bad luck would have it, the reigning king, Henry VI (1422–1461), was one of the most incompetent that England has ever had. According to one recent authority, Henry "paralyzed and confused the whole process of English government with a royal irresponsibility and inanity which had no precedent." Henry's willfulness helped provoke the Wars of the Roses that flared on and off from 1455 to 1485. These wars received their name from the emblems of the two competing factions: the red rose of Henry's family of Lancaster and the white rose of the rival house of York. The Yorkists for a time gained the kingship, under such monarchs as Richard III, but in 1485 they were replaced by a new dynasty, that of the Tudors, who began a new period in English history. The first Tudor king, Henry VII, steadily eliminated rival claimants to the throne, avoided expensive foreign wars, built up a financial surplus, and gradually reasserted royal power over the aristocracy. When he died in 1509 he was therefore able to pass on to his son, Henry VIII (1509–1547), a royal power as great as it had ever been before.

It is tempting to view the entire period of English history between 1307 and the accession of Henry VII in 1485 as one long, dreary interregnum which accomplished nothing positive. But that would not quite be doing justice to the time: in the first place, the fact that England did not entirely fall apart during the recurrent turbulence was an accomplishment in itself. Remarkably, the rebellious aristocrats of the later Middle Ages never tried to proclaim the independence of any of their regions; only once, in 1405, did they seek unsuccessfully to divide the country between them. Discounting that insignificant exception, aristocratic rebels always sought to control the central government rather than destroy or break away from it. Thus when Henry

VII came to the throne, he did not have to win back any English territories as Louis XI of France had had to win back Burgundy. More than that, the antagonisms of the Hundred Years' War had the ultimately beneficial effect of enhancing an English sense of national identity. From the Norman Conquest until deep into the fourteenth century, French was the preferred language of the English crown and aristocracy, but mounting anti-French sentiment contributed to the complete triumph of English by around 1400. The loss of lands in France was also ultimately beneficial because thereafter the crown was freed from the inevitability of war with the French. This freedom gave England more diplomatic maneuverability in sixteenth-century continental politics and later helped strengthen England's ability to invest its energies in overseas expansion in America and elsewhere. Yet another positive development was the steady growth of effective governmental institutions; despite the shifting fortunes of kings, the central governmental administration expanded and became more sophisticated. Parliament too became stronger, largely because both the crown and the aristocracy believed that they could use it for their own ends. In 1307 Parliament had not yet become a regular part of the English governmental system, but by 1485 it definitely had. Later kings who tried to govern without it ran into severe difficulties.

Henry VII. A 1505 portrait by M. Sittow.

While Louis XI of France and Henry VII of England were reasserting royal power in their respective countries, the Spanish monarchs, Ferdinand and Isabella, were doing the same on the Iberian peninsula. In the latter area there had also been incessant strife in the later Middle Ages; Aragon and Castile had often fought each other, and aristocratic factions within those kingdoms had continually fought the crown. But in 1469 Ferdinand, the heir of Aragon, married Isabella, the heiress of Castile, and thereby created a union which laid the basis for modern Spain.

The consolidation of royal power in Spain

Although Spain did not become a fully united nation until 1716 because Aragon and Castile retained their separate institutions, at least warfare between the two previously independent kingdoms ended and the new country was able to embark on united policies. Isabella and Ferdinand, ruling respectively until 1504 and 1516, subdued their aristocracies, and, in the same year (1492), annexed Granada, the last Muslim state in the peninsula, and expelled all of Spain's Jews. Some historians believe that the expulsion of the Jews was motivated by religious bigotry, others that it was a cruel but dispassionate act of state that aimed to keep Spanish "conversos" (Jews who had previously converted to Christianity) from backsliding. Either way, the forced Jewish exodus led Ferdinand and Isabella to suppose that they had eliminated an internal threat to cohesive nationhood and emboldened them to initiate an ambitious foreign policy: not only did they turn to overseas expansion, as most famously in their support of Christopher Columbus, but they also entered decisively into the arena of Italian politics. Enriched by the influx of American gold

Ferdinand and Isabella

and silver after the conquest of Mexico and Peru, and nearly invincible on the battlefields, Spain quickly became Europe's most powerful state in the sixteenth century.

Ultimately the clearest result of political developments throughout Europe in the late Middle Ages was the preservation of basic high-medieval patterns. The areas of Italy and Germany which had been politically divided before 1300 remained politically divided thereafter. The emergence of middle-sized states in both of these areas in the fifteenth century brought more stability than had existed before, but events would show that Italy and Germany would still be the prey of the Western powers. The latter were clearly much stronger because they were consolidated around stronger national monarchies. The trials of the later Middle Ages put the existence of these monarchies to the test, but after 1450 they emerged stronger than ever. The clearest illustration of their superiority is shown by the history of Italy in the years immediately following 1494. Until then the Italian states appeared to be relatively well governed and prosperous. They experimented with advanced techniques of administration and diplomacy. But when France and Spain invaded the peninsula the Italian states fell over like houses of cards. The Western monarchies could simply draw on greater resources and thus inherited the future of Europe.

5. THE FORMATION OF THE EMPIRE OF RUSSIA

Just as the half century after 1450 witnessed the definitive consolidation of the power of the western European nation-states, so it saw the rise to prominence of the state that henceforth was to be the dominant power in the European East—Russia. But Russia was not at all like a Western nation-state; rather, by about 1500 Russia had taken the first decisive steps on its way to becoming Europe's leading Eastern-style empire.

Had it not been for a combination of late-medieval circumstances, one or several Russian states might well have developed along typical Western lines. Indeed, the founders of the first political entity located in the territories of modern-day Russia were themselves westerners—Swedish Vikings who in the tenth century established a principality centered around Kiev for the purposes of protecting their lines of trade between Scandinavia and Constantinople. Within two or three generations these Vikings became linguistically assimilated by their Slavic environment, but the Kievan state they founded remained until about 1200 very much part of the greater European community of nations. Since Kiev lay on the westernmost extremity of the Russian plain (properly speaking, Kiev is not in Russia at all but is the center of a territory known as the Ukraine), it was natural for the Kievan state of the High Middle Ages to maintain close and cordial diplomatic and trading relations with western Europe. For example, in the eleventh

A Swedish Viking. An elk-horn carving showing the sort of Viking warrior who founded the Kievan state.

Kievans Chasing Cumans.
From a fifteenth-century
Russian manuscript.

century King Henry I of France was married to a Kievan princess, Anne, and their son was consequently given the Kievan name of Philip, a christening that marked the introduction of this hitherto foreign first name into the West. Aside from such direct links with Western culture, Kievan government bore some similarity to Western limited monarchy inasmuch as the ruling power of the Kievan princes was limited by the institution of the *veche,* or popular assembly.

The Kievan state's ties to the West

But after 1200 four epoch-making developments conspired to drive a wedge between Russia and western European civilization. The first was the conquest of most of Russia by the Mongols, or Tartars, in the thirteenth century. As early as the mid–twelfth century Kiev had been buffeted by the incursions of an Asiatic tribe known as Cumans, but Kiev and other loosely federated Russian principalities ultimately managed to hold the Cumans at bay. The utterly savage Mongols, who crossed the Urals from Asia into Russia in 1237, however, were quite another matter. Commanded by Batu, a grandson of the dreaded Genghis Khan, the Mongols cut such swaths of devastation as they advanced westward that, according to one contemporary, "no eye remained open to weep for the dead." In 1240 the Mongols overran Kiev, and two years later they created their own state on the lower Volga River—the Khanate of the Golden Horde—that exerted suzerainty over almost all of Russia for roughly the following two centuries. Unwilling or unable to institute governmental arrangements that would permit them to rule the vast expanses of Russia directly, the Mongol Khans instead tolerated the existence of several native Russian states, from whom they demanded obeisance and regular monetary tribute. Under this "Tartar yoke," the normal course of Russian political development was inevitably impeded.

Reasons for retreat from the West: (1) the Mongol conquests in Russia

The native Russian principality which finally emerged to defeat the Mongols and unify much of Russia in the fifteenth century was the

(2) the emergence of Moscow as a unifying force

(3) resentment of Catholic Poland's expansion

(4) impact of the fall of Constantinople

Grand Duchy of Moscow, situated deep in the northeastern Russian interior. Inasmuch as Moscow was located very far away from the Mongol power base on the lower Volga, the Muscovite dukes had greater freedom of initiative to consolidate their strength free from Mongol interference than did some of their rivals, and when the Mongol Khans began to realize what was happening, it was too late to stem the Muscovite tide. But Moscow's remote location also placed it extremely far from western Europe: about 600 miles (often snow covered) farther away from France or Italy than the distance separating those countries from Kiev. This added distance alone would have presented an appreciable obstacle to the establishment of close relations between Moscow and the West, but, to make matters far worse, the rise of Poland-Lithuania after 1386 and the fall of Constantinople in 1453 rendered cordial relations all but impossible.

Throughout most of the Middle Ages the Kingdom of Poland had been a second-rate power, usually on the defensive against German encroachments. But in the fourteenth century that situation changed dramatically, partly because German strength had by then become a ghost of its former self, and above all because the marriage in 1386 of Poland's reigning queen, Jadwiga, to Jagiello, grand duke of Lithuania, more than doubled Poland's size and enabled it to become a major expansionist state. Even before 1386 the Grand Duchy of Lithuania had begun to carve out an extensive territory for itself, not just on the shores of the Baltic where the present territory of Lithuania lies, but in the western Russian regions of Byelorussia and the Ukraine. Obviously, Lithuania's expansionist momentum increased after the union with Poland: in 1410 combined Polish-Lithuanian forces in the battle of Tannenberg inflicted a stunning defeat on the German military order of Teutonic Knights who ruled neighboring Prussia, and Poland-Lithuania extended its borders so far east in the early fifteenth century that the new power seemed on the verge of conquering all of Russia. But Poland-Lithuania subscribed to Roman Catholicism in religion, whereas many of the Russian peoples it had conquered were Eastern Orthodox who accordingly resented the sway of their new rulers. Eastern Orthodox Moscow was the obvious beneficiary of such discontent, becoming a center of religious resistance to Poland. Thus when Moscow was able to move on the offensive against Poland-Lithuania in the late fifteenth century, it appealed to religious as well as national sentiments. Prolonged warfare ensued, greatly exacerbating antagonisms, and since Poland-Lithuania stood in the Muscovites' minds for all the West, Moscow's attitude toward all of Western civilization became ever more etched by hostility.

Finally, interrelated with this trend were the incalculable effects wrought by the fall of Constantinople to the Turks in 1453. We have seen in Chapter 12 that missionaries from the Byzantine Empire had been responsible for converting Russia to the Eastern Orthodox faith in the late tenth century. During the Kievan period Russia's commit-

NORWAY

SWEDEN

*WHITE
SEA*

• Archangel

FINLAND

BALTIC SEA

LIVONIA

TEUTONIC
ORDERS

REP. OF NOVGOROD

• Novgorod

URAL MOUNTAINS

TEUTONIC
ORDER

LITHUANIA

KAZAN

Tannenberg •

BYELORUSSIA

KINGDOM OF POLAND
AND LITHUANIA

Smolensk •

DUCHY OF
MOSCOW

• Moscow

Nizhny
Novgorod •

• Kazan

POLAND

Cracow •

UKRAINE

Kiev •

Dnieper R.

KHANATE OF
THE GOLDEN HORDE

Volga R.

HUNGARY

MOLDAVIA

VALLACHIA

CRIMEA

ASTRAKHAN

CASPIAN

SEA

OTTOMAN

BLACK SEA

Constantinople •

EMPIRE

	Moscow c. 1300
	Expansion to 1389
	Expansion to 1462
	Expansion to 1505
- - -	Kievan Russia
(10-11th centuries)

RUSSIA TO 1505

ment to Eastern Orthodoxy posed no barrier to cordial communications with western Europe because there was as yet no insuperable religious enmity between Orthodox Byzantium and the West. But embittered hatred is the only expression to describe Byzantine attitudes toward Rome after 1204 when the Western Fourth Crusaders sacked Constantinople. Eastern Orthodox Russians came to sympathize with their Byzantine mentors thereafter, and felt all the more that they had extraordinarily good reason to shun the "Roman infection" after the debacle of 1453. This was because in 1438 the Byzantines in Constantinople, sensing correctly that a mighty Turkish onslaught was in the offing, swallowed their pride and agreed to a submissive religious compromise with the papacy in the hope that this might earn them Western military support for their last-ditch stand. But despite this submission, no Western help was forthcoming and Constantinople fell to the Turks in 1453 without any Roman Catholic knight lifting a hand. Meanwhile, however, the Orthodox hierarchy of Moscow had refused to follow Byzantium in its religious submission for the obvious reason that Moscow was in no way threatened by the Turks. Once Constantinople fell, therefore, the Muscovites reached the conclusion that the Turkish victory was a divine chastisement for the Byzantines' religious perfidy, and the Muscovite state became the center of a particularly zealous anti-Roman ideology.

Ivan the Great

It is against this backdrop that we can examine the reign of the man who did the most to turn the Grand Duchy of Moscow into the nascent empire of Russia, Ivan III (1462–1505), customarily known as Ivan the Great. Ivan's immediate predecessor, Vasily II, had already gained the upper hand in Moscow's struggle to overthrow the domination of the Mongols, but Ivan was the one who completed this process by formally renouncing all subservience to the Mongol Khanate in 1480, by which time the Mongols were too awed by Muscovy's strength to offer any resistance. Concurrently, between 1462 and 1485, Ivan annexed one by one all the independent Russian principalities that remained between Moscow and Poland-Lithuania. And finally, as the result of two successive invasions of Lithuania (1492 and 1501), the mighty conqueror wrested away a whole stretch of Byelorussian and Ukranian territory along his western border. Thus when Ivan the Great died in 1505, it had become clear that Muscovy was a power to be reckoned with on the European scene.

Russia's isolation from the West

But it also would have been clear to any observer that Russian culture and government were now very non-Western. Having been divorced from the West for all practical purposes since about 1200, Russia had not kept up with the most basic Western intellectual and cultural developments. For example, there was virtually no secular literature, arithmetic was barely known, Arabic numerals were not used, and merchants made their calculations with the abacus. Nor were manners and customs comparable to those of the West. Women of the upper classes were veiled and secluded, and flowing beards and skirted garments were universal for men.

Perhaps most important, during the reign of Ivan III Russia was evolving in the direction of Eastern-style political autocracy and imperialism. This can be seen most clearly in Ivan's assumption of the title "tsar of all the Russias." The word *tsar* (sometimes spelled czar) is Russian for Caesar, and Ivan's appropriation of it meant that he was claiming to be the successor of the defunct Byzantine emperors, who themselves had been heirs of the Roman Caesars. To reinforce this claim, Ivan married the niece of the last Byzantine ruler, adopted as his insignia the Byzantine double-headed eagle, and rebuilt Moscow's fortified princely residence, the Kremlin, in magnificent style to manifest his imperial splendor. Ivan's appropriation of the Byzantine model was fateful for Russia's future political development because it enabled him and his successors to imitate the Byzantine emperors in behaving like Oriental despots who assumed without discussion that "what pleases the prince has the force of law." Moreover, as "tsar of all the Russias," Ivan conceived of himself as the autocratic potentate not just of the Russians of Moscow but of all Russians, and even of Byelorussians and Ukrainians. As the subsequent course of events would show, this was the beginning of an expansionist policy by which future Russian tsars would incorporate both Russian and a wide variety of non-Russian peoples into Europe's largest empire.

6. TURKISH EXPANSION AND THE OTTOMAN EMPIRE

Advancing into western Asia and eastern Europe, bands of Turks in the later Middle Ages laid the foundations for one of the world's great empires. The Ottoman Empire reached its height in the sixteenth century, when it included all the territories of the defunct Byzantine Empire and most of the lands conquered by the Arabs during the first centuries of Islamic expansion. Bridging the three continents of Europe, Asia, and Africa, the Ottoman Empire thus became a successor state both to Byzantium and to the Arab kingdoms and, while retaining certain features of each, added much that was new and distinctive.

Originally one of the nomadic groups inhabiting the steppes of Central Asia, the Turks forged an empire in the sixth century A.D. by uniting tribal chieftains. This empire, which reached from the Black Sea to the borders of China, quickly disintegrated. The rise of the Turks to a prominent role on the stage of world history began in the eighth century with their conversion to Islam. Introduction to the religion came through contact with Arab warriors, traders, and missionaries who had penetrated into Central Asia. Unlike so many converts, the Turks were never conquered by the Arabs. They embraced Islam voluntarily and enthusiastically, attracted initially by its simple doctrines and its call for heroic action in defense of the faith. Accepted not merely as a personal creed but as the basis for standards of governance, Islam provided a unifying force in a society marked by tribal divisions. Its adoption also brought the Turks into closer association with the mature civilizations of Persia and the Near East. They preserved their own language but abandoned their earlier system of writing for the Arabic script, and they added many Arabic words to their vocabulary.

Military service as a prelude to power

Steeped in the traditions of a hardy nomadic culture and emboldened by the confident belief that it was their mission to spread the true faith, the Turks quickly acquired fame—or notoriety—as intrepid fighters. Over a period of centuries, captured or purchased Turkish slaves were inducted into the armies of established Muslim states, where they became the chief military force and eventually appropriated political power as well. By the mid–eleventh century most Muslim states were ruled by Turks, including the Abbasid Caliphate of Baghdad. Descendants of Turkish military slaves in Egypt finally set themselves up as a ruling dynasty which held the Egyptian throne for three centuries (1250–1517). (These are known as the Mameluke sultans, from the Arabic word *mamluk,* meaning "owned.") Turkish adventurers also strove to win and implant Islam in new regions. Invaders of India in the eleventh century founded Muslim dynasties in Hindustan. Others turned westward and, penetrating the borders of the Byzantine Empire, established bases in Anatolia, which was to become the revered homeland of the Turkish nation.

Court versus camp

The growth of Turkish principalities in Anatolia was accompanied by the tug of two opposing forces. In trying to legitimize authority won on the battlefield, rulers welcomed the help of legal and religious experts from the "classical" Islamic societies of Persia, Iraq, and Arabia. But the winning of new territory was primarily the work of *gazis* (warriors of the faith), hardy frontiersmen who relished the camaraderie of the campaign. A tension between the imperial, hierarchical model of the court and the democratic equalitarian tradition of the camp continued throughout the process of state building in Anatolia.

The Seljuk Dynasty and the sultanate of Rum

In the course of dismembering the Byzantine Empire two successive Turkish dynasties or sultanates, the Seljuk and the Ottoman, rose to prominence. The Seljuks sprang from a family of fighters claiming descent from an ancestor of this name. In 1055 they entered the city of Baghdad and made the caliph their puppet. Sixteen years later, in 1071, the Seljuk sultan Arp Arslan inflicted a crushing blow on the Byzantine emperor by defeating his army in the battle of Manzikert. With a loosely knit empire reaching into Central Asia, the Seljuks created a centralized monarchy in Anatolia with its capital in Konya. The Turks had long referred to Byzantine Anatolia as *Rum* ("Rome"), and their ruler assumed the title "Sultan of Rum." His power was broken in the middle of the thirteenth century by the Mongols, who, after conquering Persia and Iraq, plundered far into central Anatolia.

Building Operations. From a French picture Bible, c. 1250. Note the treadmill, with wheel, ropes, and pulley, by means of which a basket of stones is brought to the construction level. (Morgan Library)

Siege of a City, c. 1470. The use of cannon would soon put an end to traditional medieval fortifications. (Morgan Library)

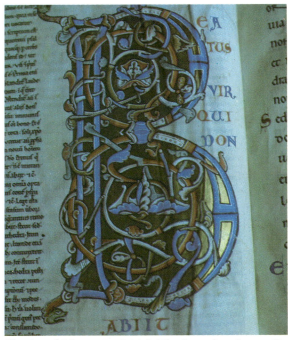

Illuminated Manuscript Initial. The joy taken by medieval monks in splendid ornamentation is nowhere more apparent than in this letter B, opening a book of psalms. From a French manuscript of the later twelfth century. (Teresa Gross-Diaz)

The Virgin and Chancellor Rolin, Jan van Eyck (1390–1444). The early Flemish painters loved to present scenes of piety in the sumptuous surroundings of wealthy burghers. (Louvre)

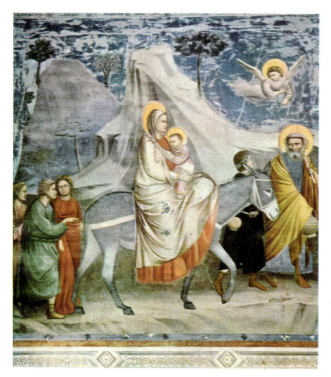

The Flight into Egypt, Giotto (1276–1337). Giotto is regarded as the founder of the modern tradition in painting. A fresco in the Arena Chapel, Padua. (MMA)

The Poet Dante Driven into Exile. On the left Dante is expelled from Florence; on the right he begins work on his great poem, the *Divine Comedy*. From a mid-fifteenth-century Florentine manuscript. (The nearly completed dome of Florence's cathedral can be seen at the far left.) (British Library)

Naval Berths at Alanya, Turkey. Built in 1228 at the behest of the Seljuk sultan, these massive covered docks reveal the profound impact of Byzance on the world view of the highland Turks. This is the only such example of naval architecture from this period known to exist in the Islamic world.

Thereafter the Seljuk state disintegrated.

The dissolution of the Seljuk sultanate only intensified the struggle for Byzantine territories in Asia and Europe. Actually the conquest was carried out less by Seljuk or Ottoman sultans than by independent bands of *gazis,* especially nomadic Turks who had fled ahead of the Mongols and created power bases in western Anatolia. European Crusaders were able to gain a precarious foothold on the Mediterranean coast in the twelfth century because of disunity and conflict among the local Muslim rulers. The famous sultan Saladin, who gained the respect and admiration of Europeans who fought against him, was of Kurdish rather than Turkish extraction. He served as a commander in the Egyptian military and in 1170 founded a new dynasty in Egypt. The European Crusades not only failed to dislodge the Muslims but further weakened the position of the beleaguered emperor in Constantinople, as we saw in Chapter 14.

Failure of the Crusades

The second Turkish dynasty, destined to have more far-reaching historical impact than the Seljuk, arose from modest beginnings. Like the Seljuks, the Ottoman rulers descended from a single family. The title *Osmali*—corrupted by Europeans into "Ottoman"—derives from the name Osman. In the early fourteenth century Osman established a stronghold in the extreme northwestern corner of Anatolia, smaller

Rise of the Ottoman Dynasty

than many of its rivals but strategically located close to the Byzantine capital. From this base the Ottomans managed to absorb and consolidate the scattered principalities of Anatolia. The demoralized Byzantine government offered little resistance and sometimes aided the process. In 1345 one emperor enlisted Ottoman help against a rival claimant to the throne and allowed their troops to occupy the Gallipoli peninsula across the Dardanelles, giving them a vantage point from which to make conquests in the Balkans. Before the end of the century their ruler revived the Seljuk title "Sultan of Rum."

Turkish conquest of Constantinople

Ottoman power was severely but only temporarily shaken in 1402 when Tamerlane invaded eastern Anatolia, crushed a Turkish army, and took the sultan captive. But after a critical decade of rebellion and fratricidal strife the reigning family regained authority and embarked on fresh campaigns. Seeing the Byzantine realm reduced to little more than its heavily fortified capital, Sultan Mehemmed II resolved to take the city that for a thousand years had withstood all such attempts. Even though the large land and naval forces that he assembled for the purpose outnumbered the city's defenders many times over, the siege lasted seven weeks. Finally on May 29, 1453, Turkish troops breached the walls, and Mehemmed "the Conqueror" rode into Constantinople in triumph.

Continued Ottoman expansion

Aside from the intrinsic value of the city, by making Constantinople the capital Ottoman rulers secured a better position from which to unify their realm. The strategically located metropolis served as the connecting link between the Asian and European portions. Anatolia was by this time not only Turkish but fully incorporated into Islamic culture. The Balkans, on the other hand, represented an Islamic frontier, inhabited mainly by a Christian population. The differences between these two regions never entirely disappeared, but they were gradually lessened. The Ottoman domain continued to expand during the century following the fall of Constantinople. Wars against Serbs, Poles, Venetians, the papacy, and Hungarians netted European territory extending to the Danube River. In 1529 Turkish armies laid siege to Vienna, although they never succeeded in taking the city. Paralleling advances in Europe was the conquest of remaining Arab lands, including Syria, Iraq, Egypt, western Arabia, and the North African coast as far west as the border of Morocco.

Rupture with Persia and its consequences

In the opening years of the sixteenth century Turkish relations with Persia underwent a drastic change, occasioned by the accession of the Safavid Dynasty to the Persian throne. The Safavids were Shiite Muslims (claiming descent from Ali, son-in-law of the Prophet) and were regarded as heretics by the Turks, who adhered to the predominant and orthodox Sunni division of Islam. Antipathy between the two Islamic empires led to persecution of minority sects in each of them and in 1514 culminated in war, in which the Turks defeated the shah's armies and occupied his capital of Tabriz. Although the Ottomans did not retain control of Persia, they no longer looked to it as cultural and

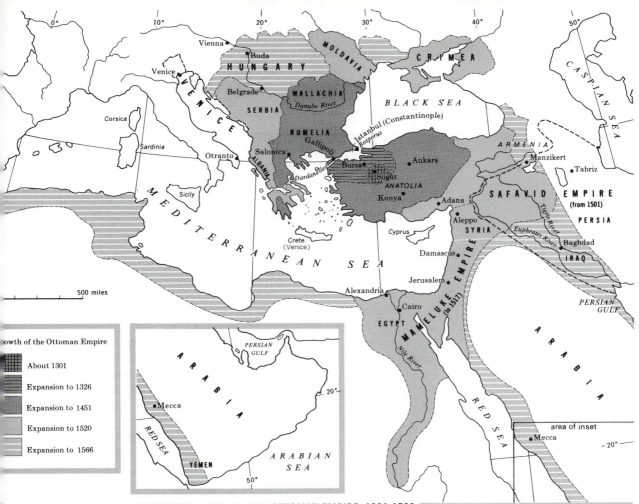

THE RISE OF THE OTTOMAN EMPIRE, 1301-1566

Growth of the Ottoman Empire

- About 1301
- Expansion to 1326
- Expansion to 1451
- Expansion to 1520
- Expansion to 1566

religious mentor. The rupture with Persia also isolated the western Turks from contact with Islamic societies of Central Asia with which they had acknowledged bonds of kinship. They were thus thrown more fully upon their own resources and were impelled toward closer relations with peoples of the West.

For more than a century following the conquest of Constantinople the Ottoman Empire was not only one of the largest and most powerful but also one of the most effectively governed states in the world. The government was a unique blend of Eastern and Western elements, of the traditional and the innovative, the religious and the secular. In theory it rested upon the Holy Law of Islam, and scholars and interpreters of this law—the ulema—played a prominent part in both public and private affairs, especially in the fields of education, charities, and the judiciary. In effect the sultan's rule was absolute, tempered somewhat by religious constraints and by the ancient traditions of an egalitarian nomadic society. The Ottoman state was not a theocracy

The theoretical and practical bases of Ottoman government

as was the Safavid Persian Empire. The sultan considered himself leader of the Islamic world, "Commander of the Faithful," but he deferred to the ulema, headed by a grand mufti (jurist), in matters of faith. The early Ottoman sultans made little display of the title of caliph although they were able to claim it after the conquest of Egypt in 1517. (The Mamelukes had installed a puppet caliph in Cairo after the Mongols ended the Abbasid rule in Baghdad.) Not until the late nineteenth century, when the empire was far into decline, did the sultan formally assume the title of caliph.

The system of "slave government": the devshirme

To govern a large and diverse population, the Ottomans necessarily developed a complex bureaucracy. Numerous departments administered civil and military affairs, subject to the final authority of the sultan but increasingly delegated to his chief minister, the grand vizier. Several features helped make the complicated structure work efficiently. The Turks conceived of rulership as residing in a chosen family but not necessarily passing from eldest son to eldest son. To insure orderly succession to the throne, Ottoman princes were tested by being assigned to provincial administrative posts. The one judged ablest was selected as heir, and his brothers were executed (strangled by a silken cord). The "law of fratricide" was abandoned near the end of the sixteenth century, but despite its ruthlessness it kept sibling rivalry from leading to civil war. Another distinctive aspect of the Ottoman state was its reliance upon "slave government," a device that though not original with them the Ottomans developed most fully. For centuries Turkish slaves had been forced into the service of Islamic rulers. Now the Turks held the other end of the stick. Beginning with prisoners of war, the sultans proceeded systematically to recruit slaves, mainly Christians, by a practice known as *devshirme* ("collecting"), which continued into the seventeenth century. Periodically, Christian boys were carefully picked, converted to Islam, and educated for government employment. The first use of slaves was in the army. A corps of shock infantry troops known as Janissaries, which became internationally famous and ultimately a dangerously powerful hereditary class, started as a group of slaves. The *devshirme* system was used to service the palace and court and to procure talented officials for all departments of government other than religion, not excepting the office of grand vizier. Although a practice of legalized kidnaping shocks the sensibilities and was of dubious justification under Islamic law, it seems to have aroused little protest among the Christian population of the Balkans, where it fell most heavily. Doubtless it was tolerated because it offered opportunity for members of humble families to rise to wealth and prominence. And by staffing the bureaucracy with servants who owed their position solely to his favor, the sultan was insuring himself against rebellion.

Ottoman society, like that of other contemporary states, was stratified. It included a hereditary nobility—the first in Islamic history—originating among military commanders who had been granted fiefs in the form of lands or administrative office. Membership was not based on race nor even religion, and it included some Christian gentry. The Islamic and Ottoman concept of justice was the maintenance of stable relations among existing classes. Merchants, for example, operated under their guild rules; soldiers were subject to the jurisdiction of special military courts. One feature of Ottoman rule that undoubtedly contributed to its success was an enlightened policy toward religious minorities. Monotheistic non-Muslim faiths were not only tolerated but protected by the state, although their adherents were not extended all the privileges of Muslim subjects. The separate religious communities, called *millets*—Greek Orthodox Christians, Armenian Christians, and Jews—were required to conduct their affairs in compliance with their own religious codes under the jurisdiction of their spiritual head, who in turn was responsible to the sultan's officials.

The fall of Constantinople in 1453 did not signify a barbarian conquest. The Anatolian Turks had assimilated Islamic culture and through long association had absorbed much from the Byzantines. They 'had fought with as well as against the Christians; they had intermarried with them. When the Turks fell heir to the region so favored by geography, they did not destroy its civilization but added a brilliant chapter to its annals.

At the time of the conquest Constantinople (known to the Turks as Istanbul although the name was not changed officially until the twentieth century under the Republic) was in a state of disrepair and had only about 50,000 inhabitants. Most of these survivors were sold into slavery, but Mehemmed II immediately undertook to repopulate the capital, offering inducements to Muslims and non-Muslims alike and forcibly resettling some residents. Jews fleeing persecution in Spain and other European countries came in large numbers. The city soon revived as a major commercial center, with trade largely in the hands of non-Muslim subjects and privileged foreigners. Before the close of the sixteenth century its population had grown to more than a million. The sultans launched an ambitious program of restoration and new construction in the capital and other cities of the empire to provide public services and amenities and, especially, religious facilities. Some Christian churches were converted into mosques, notably Santa Sophia, which was reinforced with buttresses and surrounded by four minarets (see above, p. 370). (The priceless mosaics of the interior were covered with a limewash in compliance with the Islamic taboo against images.) The palace and its complex of government buildings—situated on a point overlooking the juncture of three waterways—were constructed largely of wood and so, because of damage from fire and earthquake, had to be rebuilt more than once. (Recent restoration has made them a fascinating museum.) Architecturally, the Ottomans' greatest contribution is seen in their mosques, in which Turkish and Byzantine elements blend to produce an imposing yet graceful style. Instead of the onion-shaped cupola so characteristic of Islamic archi-

The structure of Ottoman society, and the millet *system*

Cultural continuity

The revival of Constantinople and the flowering of Ottoman architecture

tecture in Persia and India, Ottoman-Turkish mosques are crowned by a broad hemispheric dome, inspired by the great dome of Santa Sophia. Frequently the main structure was surrounded by a cluster of smaller buildings that served as schools. A world-renowned architect, Sinan, was active during the mid-sixteenth century, the Ottoman golden age. Of Christian parentage, Sinan entered the royal service through the *devshirme* and rose through military ranks to the position of chief architect of the empire. Among the more than three hundred buildings credited to him, his finest is considered to be the Suleiman *(Süleymaniye)* Mosque, erected for Sultan Suleiman I between 1550 and 1556. Standing on Istanbul's highest hill overlooking the Golden Horn, this magnificent edifice is designed to provide more interior open space than Santa Sophia and it conveys the impression of soaring height achieved seemingly without effort or massive weight.

Suleiman I "the Magnificent"

The reign of Suleiman I (1520–1566) marks the climax of the Ottoman Empire and its civilization. The empire had achieved its greatest territorial extent, a high level of prosperity, and a rich flowering in literature and the fine arts. And although the papacy and sundry European adventurers still talked of driving back the "infidel," it commanded international respect. Suleiman I, a contemporary of Henry VIII of England, Francis I of France, and the Holy Roman emperor Charles V, ranks among the spectacular monarchs of the sixteenth century, of which he was by far the richest. Among his people he acquired the epithet "Lawgiver," but he was called "the Magnificent" by contemporary Europeans.

Süleymaniye Mosque, Istanbul. Built between 1550 and 1556 by the architect Sinan in honor of Sultan Suleiman I, this great domed mosque with its four minarets dominates the Golden Horn.

Interior of the Suley-maniye Mosque. Utilizing the principle of a dome supported by piers as in Santa Sophia, the Süleymaniye Mosque has greater interior open space than its Christian prototype.

Slow but fatal decay set in soon after this brilliant epoch. Suleiman himself foreshadowed the decline when he ended the practice of attending working sessions of the court, leaving the conduct of business to his deputy, the grand vizier. Gradually the sultans abandoned the role of vigorous leadership so necessary for a wide and disparate empire. Reared in the insulated and sensual environment of the harem, they became enervated. Luxurious indulgence in the palace combined with venality and corruption in the bureaucracy sapped the strength of the state. In the nineteenth century the Ottoman Empire, with some justification, was called "the sick man of Europe." But for five centuries it was a power to reckon with, and it bequeathed much of value to its successors.

The decay of the empire

7. THOUGHT, LITERATURE, AND ART

Although it might be guessed that the extreme hardships of the later Middle Ages in western Europe should have led to the decline or stagnation of intellectual and artistic endeavors, in fact the period was an extremely fruitful one in the realms of thought, literature, and art. In this section we will postpone treatment of certain developments most closely related to the early history of the Italian Renaissance, but will discuss some of western Europe's other important late-medieval intellectual and artistic accomplishments.

Theology and philosophy after about 1300 faced a crisis of doubt. This doubt did not concern the existence of God and His supernatural powers, but was rather doubt about human ability to comprehend the supernatural. Whereas St. Thomas Aquinas and other Scholastics in the High Middle Ages had serenely delimited the number of "mysteries of the faith" and believed that everything else, both in heaven and earth, could be thoroughly understood by humans, the floods, frosts, wars, and plagues of the fourteenth century helped undermine such confidence in the powers of human understanding. Once human beings experienced the universe as arbitrary and unpredictable, fourteenth-century thinkers began to wonder whether there was not far more in heaven and earth than could be understood by their philosophies. The result was a thoroughgoing reevaluation of the prior theological and philosophical outlook.

The leading late-medieval abstract thinker was the English Franciscan William of Ockham, who was born around 1285 and died in 1349, apparently from the Black Death. Traditionally, Franciscans had always had greater doubts than Dominicans like St. Thomas concerning the abilities of human reason to comprehend the supernatural; Ockham, convinced by the events of his age, expressed these most formidably. He denied that the existence of God and numerous other theological matters could be demonstrated apart from scriptural revelation, and he emphasized God's freedom and absolute power to do anything He wished. In the realm of human knowledge per se Ockham's searching intellect drove him to look for absolute certainties instead of mere theories. In investigating earthly matters he developed the position, known as *nominalism,* that only individual things, but not collectivities, are real, and that one thing therefore cannot be understood by means of another: to know a chair one has to see and touch it rather than just know what several other chairs are like. Ockham also formulated a logic which was based upon the assumption that words stood only for themselves rather than for real things. Such logic might not say much about the real world, but at least it could not be refuted, since it was as internally valid in its own terms as Euclidean geometry.

Ockham's outlook, which gained widespread adherence in the late-medieval universities, today often seems overly methodological and verging on the arid, but it had several important effects on the development of Western thought. Ockham's concern about what God *might* do led to the raising by his followers of some of the seemingly absurd questions for which medieval theology has been mocked, for example, asking whether God can undo the past, or whether an infinite number of pure spirits can simultaneously inhabit the same place (the nearest medieval thinkers actually came to asking how many angels can dance on the head of a pin). Nonetheless, Ockham's emphasis on preserving God's autonomy led to a stress on divine omnipotence that became one of the basic presuppositions of sixteenth-century Protestantism. Further, Ockham's determination to find certainties in the realm of human knowledge ultimately helped make it possible to discuss human affairs and natural science without reference to supernatural explanations—one of the most important foundations of the modern scientific method. Finally, Ockham's opposition to studying collectivities and his refusal to apply logic to real things helped encourage *empiricism,* or the belief that knowledge of the world should rest on sense experience rather than abstract reason. This too is a presupposition for scientific progress: thus it is probably not coincidental that some of Ockham's fourteenth-century followers made significant advances in the study of physics.

Ockham's search for reliable truths finds certain parallels in the realm of late-medieval literature, although Ockham surely had no direct influence in that field. The major trait of the best late-medieval literature was *naturalism,* or the attempt to describe things the way they really are. This was more a development from high-medieval precedents—such as the explorations of human conduct pursued by Chrétien de Troyes, Wolfram von Eschenbach, and Dante—than a reaction against them. The steady growth of a lay reading public furthermore encouraged authors to avoid theological and philosophical abstractions and seek more to entertain by portraying people realistically with all their strengths and foibles. Another main characteristic of late-medieval literature, the predominance of composition in the European vernaculars instead of Latin, also developed out of high-medieval precedents but gained great momentum in the later Middle Ages for two different reasons. One was that international tensions and hostilities, including the numerous wars of the age and the trials of the universal papacy, led to need for security and a pride of self-identification reflected by the use of vernacular tongues. Probably more important was the fact that continued spread of education for the laity greatly increased a public that could read in a given vernacular language but not in Latin. Hence although much poetry was written during the High Middle Ages in the vernacular, in the later Middle Ages use of the vernacular was widely extended to prose. Moreover, countries such as Italy and England, which had just begun to cultivate their own vernacular literatures around 1300, subsequently began to employ their native tongues to the most impressive literary effect.

The greatest writer of vernacular prose fiction of the later Middle Ages was the Italian Giovanni Boccaccio (1313–1375). Although Boccaccio would have taken an honored place in literary history for some of his lesser works, which included courtly romances, pastoral poems, and learned treatises, by far the most impressive of his writings is the *Decameron,* written between 1348 and 1351. This is a collection of one hundred stories, mostly about love and sex, adventure, and clever trickery, supposedly told by a sophisticated party of seven young ladies and three men who are sojourning in a country villa outside Florence in order to escape the ravages of the Black Death. Boccaccio by no means invented all one hundred plots, but even when he borrowed the outlines of his tales from earlier sources he retold the stories in his own characteristically exuberant, masterful, and ex-

The naturalism of late-medieval literature

Boccaccio

tremely witty fashion. There are many reasons why the *Decameron* must be counted as epoch-making from a historical point of view. The first is that it was the earliest ambitious and successful work of vernacular creative literature ever written in western Europe in narrative prose. Boccaccio's prose is "modern" in the sense that it is brisk, for unlike the medieval authors of flowery romances, Boccaccio purposely wrote in an unaffected, colloquial style. Simply stated, in the *Decameron* he was less interested in being "elevated" or elegant than in being unpretentiously entertaining. From the point of view of content, Boccaccio wished to portray men and women as they really are rather than as they ought to be. Thus when he wrote about the clergy he showed them to be as susceptible to human appetites and failings as other mortals. His women are not pallid playthings, distant goddesses, or steadfast virgins, but flesh-and-blood creatures with intellects, who interact more comfortably and naturally with men and with each other than any women in Western literature had ever done before. Boccaccio's treatment of sexual relations is often graphic, often witty, but never demeaning. In his world the natural desires of both women and men are not meant to be thwarted. For all these reasons the *Decameron* is a robust and delightful appreciation of all that is human.

Chaucer

Similar in many ways to Boccaccio as a creator of robust, naturalistic vernacular literature was the Englishman Geoffrey Chaucer (c. 1340–1400). Chaucer was the first major writer of an English that can still be read today with relatively little effort. Remarkably, he was both a founding father of England's mighty literary tradition and one of the four or five greatest contributors to it: most critics rank him just behind Shakespeare, and in a class with Milton, Wordsworth, and Dickens. Chaucer wrote several highly impressive works, but his masterpiece is unquestionably the *Canterbury Tales,* dating from the end of his career. Like the *Decameron,* this is a collection of stories held together by a frame, in Chaucer's case the device of having a group of people tell stories while on a pilgrimage from London to Canterbury. But there are also differences between the *Decameron* and the *Canterbury Tales.* Chaucer's stories are told in sparkling verse instead of prose, and they are recounted by people of all different classes—from a chivalric knight to a dedicated university student to a thieving miller with a wart on his nose. Lively women are also represented, most memorably the gap-toothed, oft-married "Wife of Bath," who knows all "the remedies of love." Each character tells a story which is particularly illustrative of his or her own occupation and outlook on the world. By this device Chaucer is able to create a highly diverse "human comedy." His range is therefore greater than Boccaccio's, and although he is as witty, frank, and lusty as the Italian, he is sometimes more profound.

As naturalism was a dominant trait of late-medieval literature, so it was of late-medieval art. Already by the thirteenth century Gothic sculptors were paying far more attention than their Romanesque predecessors had done to the way plants, animals, and human beings really looked. Whereas medieval art had previously emphasized abstract design, the stress was now increasingly on realism: thirteenth-century carvings of leaves and flowers must have been done from direct observation and are the first to be clearly recognizable as distinct species. Statues of humans also gradually became more naturally proportioned and realistic in their portrayals of facial expressions. By around 1290 the concern for realism had become so great that a sculptor working on a tomb-portrait of the German Emperor Rudolf of Habsburg allegedly made a hurried return trip to view Rudolf in person, because he had heard that a new wrinkle had appeared on the emperor's face.

In the next two centuries the trend toward naturalism continued in sculpture and was extended to manuscript illumination and painting. The latter was in certain basic respects a new art. Ever since the caveman, painting had been done on walls, but walls of course were not easily movable. The art of wall-painting continued to be cultivated in the Middle Ages and long afterward, especially in the form of *frescoes,* or paintings done on wet plaster. But in addition to frescoes, Italian artists in the thirteenth century first started painting pictures on pieces of wood or canvas. These were first done in tempera (pigments mixed with water and natural gums or eggwhites), but around 1400 painting in oils was introduced in the European north. These new technical developments created new artistic opportunities. Artists were now able to paint religious scenes on altarpieces for churches and for private devotions practiced by the wealthier laity at home. Artists also painted the first Western portraits, which were meant to gratify the self-esteem of monarchs and aristocrats. The earliest surviving example of a naturalistic painted portrait is one of a French king, John the Good, executed around 1360. Others followed quickly, so that within a short time the art of portraiture done from life was highly developed. Visitors to art museums will notice that some of the most realistic and sensitive portraits of all time date from the fifteenth century.

Painting

The most pioneering and important painter of the later Middle Ages was the Florentine Giotto (c. 1267–1337). He did not engage in individual portraiture, but he brought deep humanity to his religious images done on both walls and movable panels. Giotto was preeminently a naturalist, i.e., an imitator of nature. Not only do his human beings and animals look more natural than those of his predecessors, they seem to do more natural things. When Christ enters Jerusalem on Palm Sunday, boys climb trees to get a better view; when St. Francis is laid out in death, one onlooker takes the opportunity to see whether the saint had really received Christ's wounds; and when the Virgin's parents, Joachim and Anna, meet after a long separation, they actually embrace and kiss—perhaps the first deeply tender kiss in Western art. It was certainly not true, as one fanciful storyteller later reported, that an onlooker found a fly Giotto had painted so real that he attempted to brush it away with his hand, but Giotto in fact accomplished some-

The naturalistic style of Giotto

See color plates facing page 518 for The Flight into Egypt by Giotto

The Meeting of Joachim and Anna at the Golden Gate. A fresco by Giotto. Note how the haloes merge: this old and barren couple will soon miraculously have a child, none other than Mary, the mother of Jesus.

thing more. Specifically, he was the first to conceive of the painted space in fully three-dimensional terms: as one art historian has put it, Giotto's frescoes were the first to "knock a hole into the wall." After Giotto's death a reaction in Italian painting set in. This was probably caused by a new reverence for the awesomely supernatural brought about by the horrors of the plague. Whatever the explanation, artists of the mid–fourteenth century briefly moved away from naturalism and painted stern, forbidding religious figures who seemed to float in space. But by around 1400 artists came back down to earth and started to build upon Giotto's influence in ways that led to the great Italian renaissance in painting.

In the north of Europe painting did not advance impressively beyond manuscript illumination until the early fifteenth century, but then it suddenly came very much into its own. The leading northern European painters were Flemish, first and foremost the brothers Hubert and Jan van Eyck (c. 1366–1426; c. 1380–1441), Roger van der Weyden (c. 1400–1464), and Hans Memling (c. 1430–1494). The van Eycks used to be credited with the invention of oil painting; while that is now open to question, they certainly were its greatest early practitioners. The use of oils allowed them and the other fifteenth-century Flemish painters to engage in brilliant coloring and sharp-focused realism. The van Eycks and van der Weyden excelled most at two things: communicating a sense of deep religious piety and portraying minute details of familiar everyday experience. These may at first seem incompatible, but it should be remembered that contemporary manuals

The Flemish painters

See color plates facing page 518 for *The Virgin and Chancellor Rolin* by Jan Van Eyck of practical mysticism such as *The Imitation of Christ* also sought to link deep piety with everyday existence. Thus it was by no means blasphemous when a Flemish painter would portray behind a tender Madonna and Child a vista of contemporary life with people going about their usual business and a man even urinating against a wall. This union between the sacred and profane tended to fall apart in the work of Memling, who excelled in either straightforward religious pictures or secular portraits, but it would return in the work of the greatest painters of the Low Countries, Brueghel and Rembrandt.

8. ADVANCES IN TECHNOLOGY

No account of enduring late-medieval accomplishments would be complete without mention of certain epoch-making technological advances. Sadly, but probably not unexpectedly, treatment of this subject has to begin with reference to the invention of artillery and firearms. The prevalence of warfare stimulated the development of new weaponry. Gunpowder itself was a Chinese invention, but it was first put to particularly devastating uses in the late-medieval West. Heavy cannons, which made terrible noises "as though all the dyvels of hell had been in the way," were first employed around 1330. The earliest cannons were so primitive that it often was more dangerous to stand behind than in front of them, but by the middle of the fifteenth century they were greatly improved and began to revolutionize the nature of warfare. In one year, 1453, heavy artillery played a leading

The Earliest Known Depiction of a Cannon. A fourteenth-century manuscript shows a primitive cannon firing an arrow rather than a cannonball.

Cannons Being Used to Breach the Walls of a Castle. This scene depicts a late engagement of the Hundred Years' War.

Late-medieval technological achievements: (1) the weapons of war

(2) optical and navigational instruments

Devil with Eyeglasses. Once spectacles became common they were even sported by devils in hell.

(3) mechanical clocks

role in determining the outcome of two crucial conflicts: the Ottoman Turks used German and Hungarian cannons to breach the defenses of Constantinople—hitherto the most impregnable in Europe—and the French used heavy artillery to take the city of Bordeaux, thereby ending the Hundred Years' War. Cannons thereafter made it difficult for rebellious aristocrats to hole up in their stone castles, and thus they aided in the consolidation of the national monarchies. Placed aboard ships, cannons enabled European vessels to dominate foreign waters in the subsequent age of overseas expansion. Guns, also invented in the fourteenth century, were gradually perfected afterward. Shortly after 1500 the most effective new variety of gun, the musket, allowed foot-soldiers to end once and for all the earlier military dominance of heavily armored mounted knights. Once lance-bearing cavalries became outmoded and fighting could more easily be carried on by all, the monarchical states that could turn out the largest armies completely subdued internal resistance and dominated the battlefields of Europe.

Other late-medieval technological developments were more life-enhancing. Eyeglasses, first invented in the 1280s, were perfected in the fourteenth century. These allowed older people to keep on reading when nearsightedness would otherwise have stopped them. For example, the great fourteenth-century scholar Petrarch, who boasted excellent sight in his youth, wore spectacles after his sixtieth year and was thus enabled to complete some of his most important works. Around 1300 the use of the magnetic compass helped ships to sail farther away from land and venture out into the Atlantic. One immediate result was the opening of direct sea commerce between Italy and the North. Subsequently, numerous improvements in shipbuilding, map making, and navigational devices contributed to Europe's ability to start expanding overseas. In the early fourteenth century the Azores and Cape Verde Islands were reached; then, after a long pause caused by Europe's plagues and wars, the African Cape of Good Hope was rounded in 1487, the West Indies discovered in 1492, India reached by the sea route in 1498, and Brazil discovered in 1500. Partly as a result of technology the world was thus suddenly made much smaller.

Among the most familiar implements of our modern life that were invented by Europeans in the later Middle Ages were clocks and printed books. Mechanical clocks were invented shortly before 1300 and proliferated in the years immediately thereafter. The earliest clocks were too expensive for private purchase, but towns quickly vied with each other to install the most elaborate clocks in their prominent public buildings. These clocks not only told the time but showed the courses of sun, moon, and planets, and performed mechanical tricks on the striking of the hours. The new invention ultimately had two profound effects. One was the further stimulation of European interest in complex machinery of all sorts. This interest had already been awakened by the high-medieval proliferation of mills, but clocks ultimately became even more omnipresent than mills because after about 1650 they became quite cheap and were brought into practically every European home. Household clocks served as models of marvelous machines. Equally if not more significant was the fact that clocks began to rationalize the course of European daily affairs. Until the advent of clocks in the late Middle Ages time was flexible. Men and women had only a rough idea of how late in the day it was and rose and retired more or less with the sun. Especially people who lived in the country performed different jobs at different rates according to the rhythm of the seasons. Even when hours were counted, they were measured at different lengths according to the amount of light in the different seasons of the year. In the fourteenth century, however, clocks first started relentlessly striking equal hours through the day and night. Thus they began to regulate work with new precision. People were expected to start and end work "on time" and many came to believe that "time is money." This emphasis on time-keeping brought new efficiencies but also new tensions: Lewis Carroll's white rabbit, who is always looking at his pocket watch and muttering, "how late it's getting," is a telling caricature of time-obsessed Western man.

The invention of printing with movable type was equally momentous. The major stimulus for this invention was the replacement of parchment by paper as Europe's primary writing material between 1200 and 1400. Parchment, made from the skins of valuable farm animals, was extremely expensive: since it was possible to get only about four good parchment leaves from one animal, it was necessary to slaughter between two to three hundred sheep or calves to gain enough parchment for a Bible! Paper, made from rags turned into

(4) the invention of printing

Horloge de Sapience. This miniature, from an early–fifteenth-century French manuscript, reflects the growing fascination with machines of all sorts and clocks in particular.

Paper-Making at a Paper Mill

A Printing Press. From a title page of a Parisian printer, 1520.

pulp by mills, brought prices down dramatically. Late-medieval records show that paper sold at one-sixth the price of parchment. Accordingly, it became cheaper to learn how to read and write. With literacy becoming ever more widespread, there was a growing market for still cheaper books, and the invention of printing with movable type around 1450 fully met this demand. By greatly saving labor, the invention made printed books about one-fifth as expensive as handwritten ones within about two decades.

As soon as books became easily accessible, literacy increased even more and book-culture became a basic part of the European way of life. After about 1500 Europeans could afford to read and buy books of all sorts—not just religious tracts, but instructional manuals, light entertainment, and, by the eighteenth century, newspapers. Printing ensured that ideas would spread quickly and reliably; moreover, revolutionary ideas could no longer be easily extinguished once they were set down in hundreds of copies of books. Thus the greatest religious reformer of the sixteenth century, Martin Luther, gained an immediate following throughout Germany by employing the printing press to run off pamphlets: had printing not been available to him, Luther might have died like Hus. The spread of books also helped stimulate the growth of cultural nationalism. Before printing, regional dialects in most European countries were often so diverse that people who supposedly spoke the same language often could barely understand each other. Such a situation hindered governmental centralization because a royal servant might be entirely unable to communicate with inhabitants of the provinces. Shortly after the invention of printing, however, each European country began to develop its own linguistic standards which were disseminated uniformly by books. The "King's English" was what was printed in London and carried to Yorkshire or Wales. Thus communications were enhanced and governments were able to operate ever more efficiently.

In conclusion it may be said that clocks and books as much as guns and ocean-going ships helped Europe to dominate the globe after 1500. The habits inculcated by clocks encouraged Europeans to work efficiently and to plan precisely; the prevalence of books enhanced communications and the flow of progressive ideas. Once accustomed to reading books, Europeans communicated and experimented intellectually as no other peoples in the world. Thus it was not surprising that after 1500 Europeans could start to make the whole world their own.

SELECTED READINGS

• *Items so designated are available in paperback editions.*

Breisach, E., *Renaissance Europe, 1300–1517,* New York, 1973. The best college-level textbook on the period.

Bridbury, A. R., *Economic Growth: England in the Later Middle Ages,* 2nd ed., New York, 1975. A controversial argument against the dominant theory of economic depression.

• Brucker, G., *Renaissance Florence,* New York, 1969. An excellent introduction by one of America's foremost experts.

• Cipolla, C. M., *Clocks and Culture, 1300–1700,* London, 1967. Treats both technological developments and the importance of clocks as items of trade.

• Cole, Bruce, *Giotto and Florentine Painting, 1280–1375,* New York, 1976. A clear and stimulating introduction.

Dollinger, P., *The German Hansa,* Stanford, 1970.

Florinsky, M. T., *Russia: A History and Interpretation,* Vol. I, New York, 1961. The best narrative in English of early Russian developments.

Hanawalt, B., *The Ties That Bound: Peasant Families in Medieval England* New York, 1986. Indispensable for understanding late-medieval English rural society.

Herlihy, David, *Medieval and Renaissance Pistoia: The Social History of an Italian Town,* New Haven, 1967. Important for its use of statistical evidence.

Hilton, R. H., and T. H. Aston, *The English Rising of 1381,* Cambridge, 1984. A collection of articles that includes treatment of the *Jacquerie* and the *Ciompi.* Communicates the results of much recent research without any attempt at synthesis.

• Huizinga, J., *The Waning of the Middle Ages,* London, 1924. An evocatively written classic on forms of thought and art in the Low Countries.

Kaminsky, H., *A History of the Hussite Revolution,* Berkeley, 1967. Detailed and difficult but far and away the best treatment of the subject.

Kaminsky, H., *Simon de Cramaud and the Great Schism,* New Brunswick, N.J., 1983. A brilliant materialist interpretation of the Schism and the activities of one of the foremost ecclesiastical politicians who helped bring it to a close.

• Lerner, R. E., *The Age of Adversity: The Fourteenth Century,* Ithaca, N.Y., 1968.

Lerner, R. E., *The Heresy of the Free Spirit in the Later Middle Ages,* Berkeley, 1972.

Lewis, Bernard, *Istanbul and the Civilization of the Ottoman Empire,* Norman, Okla., 1963. Compact, clear, and informative.

• _____, *The Emergence of Modern Turkey,* 2nd ed., New York, 1968.

Lewis, P. S., *Later Medieval France: The Polity,* London, 1968.

• McFarlane, K. B., *The Nobility of Later Medieval England,* Oxford, 1973. An excellent collection of essays by a late master of the field.

McKisack, M., *The Fourteenth Century: 1307–1399,* Oxford, 1959. A volume in the older "Oxford History of England" series; out of date in some respects, but still the best synthesis available.

• Meiss, M., *Painting in Florence and Siena After the Black Death,* Princeton, 1951. A stimulating attempt to relate art history to the spirit of an age.

• Miskimin, H. A., *The Economy of Early Renaissance Europe, 1300–1460,* Englewood Cliffs, N.J., 1969. The best short work on the subject.

Mollat, G., *The Popes at Avignon, 1305–1378,* London, 1963.

Mollat, M., and P. Wolff, *The Popular Revolts of the Late Middle Ages,* London, 1973.

• Oakley, F., *The Western Church in the Later Middle Ages*, Ithaca, N.Y., 1979.
• Panofsky, E., *Early Netherlandish Painting*, 2 vols., Cambridge, Mass., 1953. A brilliant specialized history by a master art historian.
• Pernoud, R., *Joan of Arc*, New York, 1966. Joan viewed through the eyes of her contemporaries.
  Perroy, E., *The Hundred Years War*, Bloomington, Ind., 1959. The standard account.
• Smart, Alastair, *The Dawn of Italian Painting, 1250–1400*, Ithaca, N.Y., 1978. More detailed than Cole.
  Vaughan, Richard, *Valois Burgundy*, London, 1975.

SOURCE MATERIALS

Allmand, C. T., ed., *Society at War: The Experience of England and France During the Hundred Years War*, Edinburgh, 1973. An outstanding collection of documents.
• Boccaccio, G., *The Decameron*, tr. M. Musa and P. E. Bondanella, New York, 1977.
• Chaucer, G., *The Canterbury Tales*. (Many editions.)
  Colledge, E., ed., *The Medieval Mystics of England*, New York, 1961.
• Froissart, J., *Chronicles*, tr. G. Brereton, Baltimore, 1968. A selection from the most famous contemporary account of the Hundred Years' War.
  The Imitation of Christ, tr. L. Sherley-Price, Baltimore, 1952.
  John Hus at the Council of Constance, tr. M. Spinka, New York, 1965. The translation of a Czech chronicle with an expert introduction and appended collection of documents.
• *Meister Eckhart*, eds. E. Colledge and B. McGinn, 2 vols., New York, 1981–1986. A rich collection of Eckhart's basic works, expertly introduced and annotated.
  Memoirs of a Renaissance Pope: The Commentaries of Pius II (abridged ed.), tr. F. A. Gragg, New York, 1959. A fascinating insight into the Renaissance papacy.
  A Parisian Journal, 1405–1449, tr. J. Shirley, Oxford, 1968. A marvelous panorama of Parisian life recorded by an eyewitness.
• Pitti, B., and G. Dati, *Two Memoirs of Renaissance Florence*, tr. J. Martines, New York, 1967.

Chapter 16

CENTURIES OF TURMOIL AND GRANDEUR IN ASIA

Seldom [have] two civilizations, so vast and so strongly developed, yet so radically dissimilar as the Muhammadan and Hindu, [met and mingled] together. The very contrasts which existed between them, the wide divergences in their culture and their religions, make the history of their impact peculiarly instructive and lend an added interest to the art and above all to the architecture which their united genius called into being.

—Sir John Marshall, in *Cambridge History of India,* Vol. III

The civilizations of India and China had reached a high level of development while the nations of Europe were struggling through an age of semidarkness that followed the decay of the Roman Empire and the impact of barbarian invasions. But when late-medieval western Europe, with a relatively stable and prosperous society, was witnessing a brilliant cultural flowering, both India and China suffered fresh invasions more sweeping than any they had known since the beginning of their recorded history. They were able to survive the shock of these intrusions with essential features of their cultures intact and while adding fresh achievements, but not without permanent effects upon their societies. Japan was unique among the principal Asian states in the fact that it was not subjected to foreign conquest. Tensions and conflicts within Japanese society were nevertheless tremendous, and they gradually produced a pattern of social and political organization remarkably similar to the feudal system of western Europe.

1. THE ESTABLISHMENT OF MUSLIM KINGDOMS IN INDIA
(C. 1000–1500)

At a time when the nations of western Europe were experiencing the economic and intellectual progress that distinguished the later Middle Ages and the Renaissance, India was subjected to a series of invasions that permanently affected its society and culture and implanted the religion of Islam in the subcontinent. Contacts with the Arabs had been chiefly commercial and peaceful, although piratical attacks on shipping provoked the Arab conquest of Sind early in the eighth century. The Islamic impact on India came not from Arabia but from Central Asia and was inflicted by relatively recent converts to the faith. Mahmud, ruler of a Turkish dynasty based at Ghanzi in eastern Afghanistan, between 997 and his death in 1030 conducted seventeen plundering raids through the mountain passes into northwestern India. Hailed as the "Sword of Islam," Mahmud destroyed hundreds of Hindu temples, including one of the greatest centers of Shiva worship in all India, the Somnath temple on the coast of Gujarat. Although he annexed the Punjab to his Afghan kingdom Mahmud's real interest in India was as a rich source of booty, the seizure of which he justified as a crusade to wipe out idolatry. Conquests in India were carried further by a dynasty seated in the Afghan city of Ghur. Muhammad of Ghur captured Delhi in 1193 and within the space of a few years secured control of Bengal, thus bringing all of Hindustan under the rule of Afghan-based Turks.

The seizure of such a large area by relatively small bands of marauders can be attributed partly to the invaders' superior arms and battle techniques. Reared in the nomadic tradition and possessing the world's swiftest steeds, Turkish horsemen could discharge their crossbows at full gallop, making their attacks especially demoralizing when launched against ranks of elephants. Even more decisive for opening the road to conquest was the political fragmentation that had followed the decay of Harsha's empire in the seventh century and prevented the mustering of united efforts for defense. Strong resistance was offered by a martial aristocracy known as the Rajputs, presumably descendants of Huns and other Asian invaders who had become assimilated into Hindu society. Regarded as belonging to the *kshatriya* order (*rajput* means "king's son"), they had formed castes of their own and were grouped into four major dynasties. Skilled swordsmen, proud of their martial traditions, and hypersensitive to insult, the Rajputs were the fiercest and bravest fighters in India, and they made a valiant though unsuccessful stand against the Muslim invaders. Refusing to admit defeat, some of them eventually removed with their retainers into the heart of the Indian desert (Rajasthan) to rebuild their shattered communities.

Jarring as they were, the Turko-Afghan incursions did not disrupt Indian society as deeply as might be expected from a confrontation

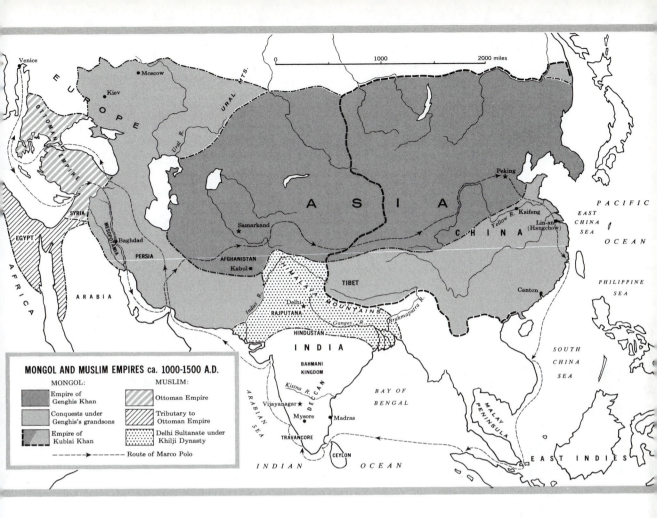

MONGOL AND MUSLIM EMPIRES ca. 1000-1500 A.D.

MONGOL:
- Empire of Genghis Khan
- Conquests under Genghis's grandsons
- Empire of Kublai Khan
- ----→---- Route of Marco Polo

MUSLIM:
- Ottoman Empire
- Tributary to Ottoman Empire
- Delhi Sultanate under Khilji Dynasty

between two apparently irreconcilable cultures. Islam stood at the opposite pole from the religions of India. Strictly monotheistic, it professed a clear-cut and simple but dogmatic creed, regarded graven images as idolatrous, and emphasized the equality of believers. Hinduism was polytheistic in form though open to monotheistic interpretation, lacked any coherent creed, delighted in symbols, pictorial forms, and architectural profusion, and sanctified the concept of human inequality. Most Indians considered it wrong to injure cattle; Muslims butchered and ate them. Indian faiths were for the most part tolerant, acknowledging many equally valid approaches to an understanding of divine being. Muslims considered it their sacred duty to spread the one true faith of Allah and his Prophet. Nevertheless, Hindus and Muslims found it possible to live together and not always as enemies. The sacking and desecration of Hindu temples was a blow that fell most grievously upon the brahmans attached to these foundations. It did not obliterate the religion of the masses, whose worship had always been centered in the home or the village. Lower-class cultivators of the Rajput kingdoms, besides not being equipped to

Contrasts between Islam and Hinduism

Extension of the Muslim
conquests

Kutb Minar, near Delhi. This magnificent "pillar of victory," 238 feet high, was erected in the early thirteenth century by the "Slave King" Kutb-ud-din, the founder of the Muslim sultanate at Delhi.

fight, had little incentive to help the oligarchic masters who had been their exploiters. Replacement of the top command, even by barbarians, was not a new experience for the people of northern India. Actually the Ghaznavids and their Turko-Afghan successors were not utter barbarians. They had learned to covet the refinements of civilization. Mahmud, while robbing northern India of much of its wealth, transformed Ghazni from a frontier fortress into a leading center of Islamic culture.

Some two centuries after its initial impact the Muslim occupation of northern India entered a new phase with the establishment of a fixed seat of government at Delhi. The Delhi Sultanate, which began with the assassination of Muhammad of Ghur in 1206, lasted slightly more than 300 years under five successive Turko-Afghan dynasties. The first of these was named the "Slave Dynasty" because its founder was a slave who had risen through the ranks of military service. His immediate successor began a policy of appeasing his Hindu subjects, leaving them free to practice their religion in exchange for paying a special tax. Neither did he try to depose all the rajas still claiming independence. Remarkably, this dynasty's throne was once occupied by a woman—the capable and energetic Raziyya—India's only female ruler before the twentieth century. Unfortunately she was assassinated after a reign of three years and was succeeded by a ruthless autocrat who aspired to the grandeur of a Persian court.

The history of the Delhi Sultanate during the three centuries of its existence cannot be detailed here. The character of the government depended largely on the personality of the sultan and varied widely from one reign to another. In attempting to administer a realm that included portions of the Deccan as well as Hindustan, the sultans allotted autonomy to subordinate officials who were generally endowed with tax-exempt lands. Under weak rulers they posed a threat to the central authority. Although Hindus were generally excluded from office, existing mechanisms of political control, especially for the collection of taxes, were retained, leading to an Indianization of the Muslim governments.

The Delhi Sultanate reached its highest point during the twenty-year reign of Ala-ud-din of the Khalji Dynasty (1296–1316). A cruel but capable monarch (he gained the throne by murdering his uncle), he required merchants to be licensed and enforced wage and price controls while also collecting the full 50 percent tax on crops. Ala-ud-din's fresh conquests extending to the tip of the Deccan proved impermanent, and he was compelled to raise a large military force to meet the threat of new invasions from Central Asia, that inexhaustible reservoir of nomadic peoples. At this time the chief source of disturbance was the expansion of the Mongols, whose force was felt throughout the breadth of Asia and even in Europe. Early in the thirteenth century the famous Mongol chieftain and empire builder Genghis Khan made a brief foray into the Indus valley. His raid was only an incident, but the danger of a Mongol attack upon India persisted. Gradually groups of Mongols settled in northern India and adopted agricultural or industrial pursuits, most of them embracing the Muslim religion. So numerous were they in Delhi in the late thirteenth century that a section of the city was called "Mongol Town." Mongols were employed by the sultan as mercenary troops, in which capacity they were sometimes victimized by his suspicion of their loyalty, and tens of thousands of them were massacred.

Early in the fourteenth century the Khalji Dynasty was replaced by the Tughlug. The pious, scholarly, and intolerant Muhammad Tughlug (r. 1325–1351) debased the currency by substituting copper tokens for gold and silver—an experiment that disrupted commerce and weakened the economy. Entertaining grandiose dreams of conquering Persia and China, he attempted to tighten his hold in the Deccan by forcing the inhabitants of Delhi to migrate 500 miles to a new capital in the south. He further alienated his subjects by failing to provide relief during a severe and prolonged famine (1335–1342). Although the peaceful and judicious thirty-seven-year rule of Sultan Firuz, Muhammad's successor, helped to restore prosperity, the stability of the Delhi regime was being undermined by the hostility of other Indian states, revolts led by the sultan's viceroys, and mounting restlessness among his Hindu subjects. The province of Bengal broke away from Delhi in 1338 and remained independent for two centuries.

Near the end of the fourteenth century northern India was visited by the most devastating raid in all its history, led by Timur the Lame (Tamerlane). Timur, of Turkish descent, had started his career as the chieftain of a small tribal state in Turkestan. After misfortunes and amazing adventures he had welded together a powerful force of cavalry and embarked on a sensational career of conquest. Although he never assumed the title of Khan, he won recognition as overlord from most of the Mongols who had previously followed Genghis Khan. He overran Afghanistan, Persia, and Mesopotamia; then he invaded India with the avowed intention of converting infidels to Islam and procuring booty. He and his troops spent less than a year in India (1398–1399) but left a ruin behind them. The city of Delhi, sacked in a three-day orgy, was turned into a ghost town, so destitute that—to quote a contemporary—"for two whole months not a bird moved a wing in the city." Any place that offered resistance was destroyed and its inhabitants slaughtered or enslaved. Lord Timur carried off with him inestimable quantities of gold and precious stuffs, slaves for all his soldiers, and thousands of skilled craftsmen, including stonemasons to build a great mosque at his capital city of Samarkand in Turkestan. The Delhi Sultanate never fully recovered from the blow dealt to it and to its helpless Hindu subjects by Timur, the "Earth Shaker."

Peninsular India, although affected by developments in the North, was shielded by distance from the nomadic invasions that shook Hindustan. The Deccan's complex and continually shifting political pattern

The Undermining of the Delhi Sultinate

The Mongol threat to the Khalji Dynasty

The Great Mongol Conqueror Genghis Khan, Grandfather of the Founder of the Mongol (Yüan) Dynasty in China.

Mongol invaders: Timur

Turkish Prisoners before Timur. An Indian painting from the period of Akbar (1556–1605). The use of Arabic script as a decorative device in Indian painting reflects the Muslim influence.

The Hindu peninsular states; the Chola kingdom and the empire of Vijayanagar

was highlighted by the rise of several large and influential states. The Chola kingdom occupying the Coromandel (southeastern) coast, while keeping a navy capable of dominating the Indian Ocean, promoted a flourishing culture, evident in the construction of Hindu temples and in remarkably fine metalwork. A figure of Shiva as Lord of the Dance, cast in the eleventh century, is one of the most exquisite bronze sculptures ever executed. Chola was absorbed by the Hindu state of Vijayanagar, which in the fourteenth century became an empire dominating the whole southern end of the peninsula as far north as the Kistna River. Its strongly fortified capital, also called Vijayanagar ("City of Victory"), had a population of more than one-half million and was, on the testimony of Italian, Portuguese, and Afghan visitors, one of the greatest cities in the world during the fifteenth century. Its oligarchic rulers, enriched by the export of precious stones, kept a sumptuous court and lavishly patronized the arts, endowing temples and encouraging the production of commentaries on the Sanskrit classics. The inhabitants of this imposing Hindu empire apparently inclined to the less ascetic forms of Hinduism. According to reports they practiced animal sacrifice, ate flesh other than beef, and kept prostitutes as "slaves of the god" in some temples.

Eventually eclipsing Vijayanagar and capable of challenging the rulers at Delhi was a Muslim power that gained control of the northern Deccan from the Arabian sea to the Bay of Bengal. This Bahmani kingdom (1347–1489) ended when Bijapur, one of its five provinces, declared itself an independent kingdom under a new dynasty and gradually absorbed adjacent territories. With a solid agricultural base, rich deposits of iron and diamonds, and a profitable commerce, the kingdom of Bijapur held the position of a major power until past the middle of the seventeenth century, winning diplomatic recognition from Persia and the Ottoman Empire as well as from the rulers at Delhi. Governed by an efficient bureaucracy equipped with a fighting force that numbered 80,000 horses and 735 elephants, Bijapur was also a thriving center of Islamic civilization as Vijayanagar was of Hindu. More than their neighboring Hindu sovereigns the sultans of Bijapur welcomed diversity, permitting the growth of an eclectic culture. During the kingdom's most brilliant period in the late sixteenth and early seventeenth centuries it enjoyed the benefits of religious toleration. While splendid Muslim buildings were erected, including the imposing Jami Mosque (1578), the sultan also endowed Hindu temples. Unfortunately a violent and protracted military struggle between Vijayanagar and Bijapur destroyed the Hindu empire in 1565 and weakened Bijapur.

The changes taking place within India's Hindu communities deviated little from patterns already outlined. The caste system became more firmly entrenched than it had been in earlier centuries. Untouchability, assigning the dregs of humanity to a position beneath even the lowest caste, was now a distinctive element in Hinduism. Although the untouchables performed essential services such as disposing of filth, burying corpses, and dressing animal hides, they were excluded from temple worship, forced to live in segregated quarters, and required to warn people of their approach. Even their shadow could be polluting. In some regions of India outcastes became so numerous that they formed castes of their own. A miserable underclass belied the wealth and glitter of every Indian kingdom.

A decline can be noted in the already inferior position of women. The custom of *purdah* (the veiling and seclusion of women) was introduced by the Muslims, but Indian society was already moving toward increasing subjection of the female sex. Child marriage—that is, the arranged marriages of *female* children—became an accepted practice, defended on the theory that because it was sinful for a woman to love anyone other than her husband she must have her allegiance assigned before reaching the age of puberty. Widowhood, a likely

Shiva as Lord of the Dance. This eleventh-century Chola bronze was widely manufactured in its time and continues to be reproduced in southern India in the twentieth century.

The hardening of Hindu institutional patterns: untouchability

Increased subjection of women

*Durga Slaying the Buffalo De-
mon.* This seventh-century relief illustrates a Hindu myth in
which the heavily armed
Durga—"she who is difficult
to go against"—overcomes her
fierce opponent in a bloody
contest.

The bhakti *movement*

destiny for a child bride, did not remove the chains of bondage. A
widow was held blameful in some way for her husband's death and
was forbidden to remarry. It became a point of honor for a widow
to prove her fidelity by burning herself to death on her husband's
funeral pyre. Many fires were required when the death of a polygamous
king widowed all his wives and concubines simultaneously. The widow's rite of self-immolation, called *sati,* (corrupted into the English
"suttee") means literally "virtuous woman." Fortunately these extreme
examples of cruelty were never universal practices in India.

While even learned opinion lent support to male dominance, Indian
attitudes toward women were ambivalent, as they probably are everywhere. India's most ancient cult was that of the Earth Mother, and
worship of the mother goddess has persisted into modern times. Also
each of the Hindu male deities was assumed to have a female consort
who represented not the passive but the active aspect of their shared
divine nature. She was the god's energizing force. Shiva's consort in
her malevolent guise as Kali or the demoness Durga inspired awe
and dread. At the same time a woman was commanded to obey,
even to worship, her husband. To quote a poem of the medieval
period:

> Though he be uncouth and prone to pleasure,
> Though he have no good points at all,
> The virtuous wife should ever
> Worship her lord as a god.

Other writers, however, paid generous tribute to woman's role as
the help and solace of her husband.

Reform movements originating among Dravidian peoples of the
Deccan were molding Hinduism into its essentially permanent form.
As noted in an earlier chapter, during the classical Gupta Age the
bhakti movement had engendered emotional worship of a personal
god endowed with redemptive powers. While addressed to various
deities of the Shaivite and Vaishnavite traditions, *bhakti* cults interpreted the divine nature as universal and held out the promise of
salvation even to the humblest classes. In the Maratha region of the
northwestern Deccan, where most of the population had been pressed
down to the level of *shudras,* the reform movement was readily accepted. It took hold equally in areas under Muslim rule, including
the expanding kingdom of Bijapur. There a Shaivite sect under the
impact of *bhakti* doctrines repudiated Brahmanism and caste distinctions, even while it clung to symbols of the ancient phallic fertility
cult as objects of worship. The *bhakti* movement carried its message
directly to the people by employing vernacular dialects—Marathi,
Kannada, and especially Tamil prevalent in the southeast of the peninsula—and became the medium for an abundant literature with fervent
devotional hymns.

While deepening its popular appeal Hinduism was by no means intellectually stagnant. Sankara, one of India's greatest scholar/theologians, flourished during the first two decades of the ninth century. A South Indian Shaivite, Sankara founded an order of Hindu monks and is said to have traversed all of India engaging in disputations with Buddhists. His major contribution was the definition and interpretation of the Vedanta doctrine—a system of thought derived from the Vedic *Upanishads* (Vedanta means "end of the Vedas"). In his extensive commentaries on the *Upanishads* and other sacred texts, employing brilliant dialectic he attempted the formidable task of reconciling all differences and fusing the various strands of thought into a coherent synthesis. Sankara's commentaries occupy a place in Hindu philosophy comparable to that of St. Thomas Aquinas's *Summa Theologica* in Christian Scholasticism.

Buddhism, which had contributed beyond measure to the shaping of Indian culture, disappeared from the subcontinent during this period although it continued to thrive in other parts of Asia. In India it had been in decline for some time, not only because of opposition from the brahmans but through a blurring of the distinctions separating it from Hinduism, out of which it had originally sprung. The flowering of architecture and the glyptic arts in the classical age had been a joint product of Hindu, Buddhist, and Jain genius. Buddhists often joined Hindu religious processions; deities of the competing faiths intermingled. Vaishnavites accepted the Buddha as one of the avatars of the god Vishnu. The Buddhists were more vulnerable than Hindus to the Turko-Afghan assault because their strength was concentrated in monasteries which could be easily destroyed and their residents dispatched. When the forces of Muhammad of Ghur swept across Bengal at the end of the twelfth century they demolished the great Buddhist university at Nalanda, once one of India's foremost centers of learning. Indisputably the extinction of Buddhism was a loss, but the order had left an indelible mark on Indian civilization. To some extent it had been reabsorbed into Hinduism before disappearing.

Hinduism, too, suffered at the hands of Muslim rulers who destroyed old or forbade the building of new temples, who alternately persecuted and tolerated but consistently imposed discriminatory taxes upon their Hindu subjects. But Hinduism was too broadly based to be extinguished. Surviving in close proximity with a religion in many ways its opposite, it could not fail to be influenced and to exert influence in return. Intermarriage between Hindus and Muslims, which occurred in spite of scruples on both sides, assisted the process of accommodation. Not surprisingly many Hindus converted to Islam, either from conviction or in hope of personal advantage. For whatever reason, conversions continued significantly into modern times, making the Muslim minority of the subcontinent's population as genuinely Indian as its other inhabitants.

Hindu intellectual development: Sankara

The disappearance of Buddhism in India

Hinduism: a survivor through accommodation

The implanting of Islam in India, begun by the sword, was softened somewhat by the zealous but less belligerent endeavor of *sufis* from various parts of the Islamic world. Originating among the Arabs soon after the time of Muhammad, the early *sufi* movement affirmed the immanence of God and the ability of the soul to unite with divine being through a discipline of meditation. This was a concept shared with Christian mystics but hardly consonant with orthodox Islam's doctrine of the transcendence of Allah. In spite of its seeming heterodoxy Sufism took root among both Sunnite and Shiite Muslims and between the ninth and twelfth centuries spread throughout Islamic countries. Several different orders of *sufis* entered India, and the character of the movement changed with the passage of time. Like the Turkish *ghazis* who helped establish the Safavid (Persian) and Ottoman empires, the earliest *sufis* in India were warriors of the faith. They aided the founders of budding Muslim kingdoms, sometimes were rewarded with grants of land and, becoming part of the establishment, grew conservative. From solitary individuals in pursuit of mystic ecstasy the movement evolved into orders with rigidly prescribed rules of discipline and then changed into associations dedicated to the memory of a revered founder.

Although its manifestations varied, Sufism attracted attention and admiration among the common people of India, Hindus as well as Muslims. *Sufi* literati reached a wide audience by writing in the vernacular languages. Mysticism, cultivated by yogis, was a familiar theme in Indian religion and philosophy. And as the *sufi* orders shifted their emphasis to devotional worship they acquired the character of Hindu *bhakti* cults. Imposing tombs, sometimes 20 feet high, erected for *sufi* saints and credited with harboring supernatural forces, proved to be fascinating attractions. Unlike forbidding mosques, these tombs were accessible to Hindus and led some to convert to Islam. While instrumental in winning converts, Sufism contributed significantly to blunting differences between the two faiths, bringing them more nearly into harmony.

2. CHINA UNDER THE SUNG, MONGOL, AND MING DYNASTIES (960–1644)

For about fifty years following the collapse of the great T'ang Dynasty in the early tenth century, China was a divided country with power in the hands of military dictators. After this chaotic but relatively brief interregnum (known to Chinese tradition as the "Five Dynasties"), unity and a strong central government were re-established by an able general who assumed the imperial title and founded the Sung Dynasty. This dynasty, like its predecessor, the T'ang, endured for three centuries (960–1279). The Sung emperors revived the ancient administrative system with its centralized bureaucracy and, to strengthen their grip, commanded the services of provincial landed gentry. For enforcing the laws locally and collecting taxes the emperor conscripted wealthy landowners, imposing heavy and sometimes ruinous responsibilities upon them. In the late eleventh century a scholar-official named Wang An-shih (1021–1086) launched a controversial reform movement. A remarkable man, who was a poet and philosopher as well as statesman, Wang put forward bold proposals to remedy flaws in the administration and relieve the plight of the common people. Though a mystic by temperament with a nostalgia for the supposed golden age of antiquity, he formulated practical and specific measures designed to rationalize the bureaucracy, expand the economy, and correct injustices. Wang promoted the establishment of public schools endowed with state lands, and he advocated revision of the civil-service examinations to encourage a knowledge of practical problems instead of proficiency in classical literary forms. His most determined efforts were directed toward a program of relief for the poor farmers by direct government assistance, by revision of the inequitable tax system and the abolition of forced labor, and by a redistribution of land. He wanted the government to control commerce, fix prices, buy up farm surpluses, and make loans to farmers at a low rate of interest on the security of their growing crops. Wang An-shih's proposals for agrarian relief anticipated some of the measures inaugurated by governments in recent times, and his overall program approximated a kind of state socialism. Although he insisted that he was merely adapting genuine Confucian principles to the needs of the time, his opponents branded him as a dangerous innovator. The contest between the Innovators (Wang's disciples) and the Conservatives continued into the next century, with the emperors favoring sometimes one and sometimes the other group; but the conservative faction ultimately prevailed. Wang's radical proposals, however, have been studied with interest by modern reformers in China and elsewhere.

The Sung empire was not as large as that of the T'ang. Partly because fortifications had not been maintained adequately, territories in the north and the northwest were lost to seminomadic peoples who, while founding independent kingdoms, assimilated many aspects of Chinese culture. One of these northern groups, the Khitan, established a kingdom in southern Manchuria, annexed territory south of the Great Wall in the Peking area, and collected tribute from the Sung emperors. Although the Khitan were entirely separate from the Chinese in origin, a corruption of their name—"Cathay"—came to be a Western designation for China, a circumstance which indicates that the Khitan did not long retain their distinctive traits after coming into close contact with China's mature civilization.

Early in the twelfth century the Khitan state (Liao) was overthrown by a people of similar stock, the Juchên, who not only occupied Manchuria and Mongolia but also conquered the greater part of northern China. Thus, beginning about 1141, the Sung actually controlled only

China under the Sung, Mongol, and Ming Dynasties (960–1644)

The reforms of Wang An-shih (1021–1086)

Territorial losses

The Southern Sung period

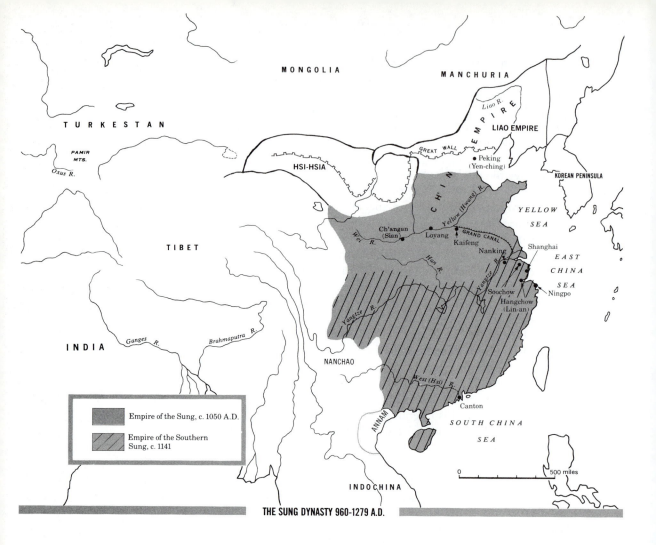

THE SUNG DYNASTY 960-1279 A.D.

the Yangtze valley and regions to the south. The emperors established their capital at Hangchow (then known as Lin-an), a magnificent port but far distant from the traditional centers of imperial administration. The disadvantage of this separation was counterbalanced by the fact that southern China felt the influence of Chinese culture more fully than it had before. The peoples of the south and southwest began to contribute leadership to the state. The center of population was shifting to the south, and there was evidence also that originality and initiative were abundant in this area. During the Southern Sung period (1141–1279) northern China continued to be ruled by the Juchên from the old Sung capital at Kaifeng on the Yellow River. While the loss of so much territory to alien conquerors was humiliating to the Sung emperors, it produced no appreciable permanent changes in the north. The Juchên adapted themselves to Chinese ways as readily as had the Khitan. Both Buddhism and Confucianism obtained a strong hold upon them, and the rulers, following the established convention, adopted a Chinese dynastic title (*Chin* or *Jin,* meaning "Gold").

The unique characteristics of the family as a social unit persisted under the Sung. The family was a tightly organized unit, bent upon preserving the welfare of its members against any outside agency, official or unofficial, and was probably the only safeguard of any consequence against the unlimited exploitation of the lower classes. Typically the Chinese family was large because it embraced several generations. When a son married he customarily brought his bride home to live under the paternal roof or in a closely neighboring house. Theoretically the family also included the departed ancestral spirits, thus extending vertically into time as well as horizontally among contemporary relatives. Authority was vested in the father (or grandfather), and the utmost emphasis was placed upon respect for elders, so that even grown men were bound by their parents' wishes. Such a custom led to extreme conservatism and sometimes inflicted hardships upon youth, but it had the advantage of developing qualities of patience, loyalty, and consideration for the helpless aged.

Women became definitely subordinate to men in the patriarchal family and in Chinese society at large, although their position was not utterly intolerable. Marriages were arranged by the parents of

The family as a social institution

Life Along the River on the Eve of the Ch'ing Ming Festival. This silk handscroll from the Ming Dynasty vividly portrays urban life in the Sung capital of Kaifeng.

The Family Shrine. Traditional Confucian ethics and successive Chinese legal codes have exalted the family and reinforced family loyalties. In this woodblock print from an imperial picture album, a family gives thanks before its family shrine. The mother and daughter watch the proceedings discretely from behind a screen.

Subordination of women

the respective parties, usually with the assistance of a matchmaker or go-between. After the bride was brought to her husband's home she was considered as on probation for a three-month period, after which if she had proved satisfactory she was allowed to participate in the ancestral sacrifice and became an accepted member of the family. In regard to the laxity of conduct permitted and the right of divorce, the woman was also at a disadvantage. Only the husband could have recourse to divorce, and he could obtain it on any one of a number of grounds, including that his wife talked too much. Actually, however, divorces were rare, especially among people of humble circumstance. Undoubtedly the practices of polygamy and concubinage, permitting a man to have more than one consort, added to the hardships and humiliation of women. But these practices were confined to the wealthy classes and were by no means universal among them. In spite of the inferior position of woman in Chinese society, she had definite rights and privileges and on the whole was much better off than in the caste-ridden society of India. It is strange that, in a predominantly agrarian economy such as China's, labor in the fields was not regarded as woman's normal work, although among poor families she often had to assist. The wife's own family did not renounce all interest in her when she left their home for her husband's and might interfere in case she was abused. Children were taught to love and venerate both parents, and as a woman grew older she shared in the honors accorded to age. The domineering position which a grandmother or mother-in-law sometimes assumed became proverbial.

The Chinese family was not only an economic and sociological unit but a religious and political one as well. Throughout the greater part of Chinese history, religion for the ordinary person consisted largely in caring for his family graves and making prayers and offerings to the spirits of his ancestors. As a political unit the family enforced discipline and considered misconduct on the part of one of its members as a collective disgrace. Very commonly the inflicting of punishment for minor offenses was left to the head of a family rather than to a public official. The strong solidarity and sense of collective responsibility of the family had disadvantages as well as advantages. Because the family was answerable for the behavior of its members, one of them might be punished for the misconduct of another if the true offender was not apprehended by the authorities, or a whole family might be wiped out for a crime committed by one person. On the whole, however, the family gave the individual a greater feeling of security and support than has been typical in most societies.

In spite of the many difficulties it had to face, the Sung is generally regarded as the best governed of all Chinese dynasties. In retrospect it seems that the Sung period marked a watershed in the evolution of Chinese civilization. A number of changes, gradual rather than sudden, were bringing about what has been termed a "medieval economic revolution." Its essential features were improvements in agriculture which promoted population growth; advances in science, technology, and mechanics; commercial expansion; and a consequent shift toward a more urbanized society. Taking advantage of the natural riches of the lower Yangtze valley, Southern Sung farmers developed better techniques of soil conservation, seed selection, crop rotation, and irrigation. Domestic and foreign commerce expanded in scope and volume and affected a larger segment of society than heretofore. The number of cities increased; several had populations of 100,000 or more. To facilitate inland transportation, chiefly by waterway, the Sungs installed locks on the Grand Canal which linked the valleys of the Yangtze and the Yellow rivers, allowing the passage of large ships. While overland trade with Central Asia declined, partly because the caravan routes were no longer controlled by the Chinese, business was brisk in port cities on the southeastern coast. Foreign merchants, among whom the Arabs predominated, were granted the right of residence in the trading centers subject to the jurisdiction of an inspector of foreign trade. At the same time, the Chinese themselves were beginning to participate more extensively in oceanic commerce. So great was the demand for seaworthy vessels that a shipbuilding boom threatened to deplete China's southeastern forests.

A lively scientific curiosity and inventiveness paralleled commercial expansion and urban growth. Progress in mathematics, astronomy, and medicine rested on the contributions of a learned few; but a widespread interest in some aspects of science is indicated by published treatises and manuals, one of which bore the title "Mathematics for Daily Use" (1262). Technological advances included the manufacture of a fine translucent porcelain, the use of gunpowder in explosive

The family as a religious and political institution

Material progress and commercial expansion

Scientific and mechanical progress

A State-Owned Iron Foundry. Chinese craftsmen developed sophisticated techniques for iron and steel production, including the principle of blowing air through molten iron to achieve the temperature necessary to produce fine steel that Henry Bessemer used in his nineteenth-century blast furnace.

weapons (bombs and guns), new metalworking processes, and the invention of a spinning machine for producing hemp thread. Taken altogether, scientific and mechanical progress under the Sung suggests that China, with a solid economic base, was on the brink of an industrial revolution such as the West experienced some five hundred years later. If such a revolution had actually come to fruition, the subsequent history of China would undoubtedly have been vastly different. Why China's incipient industrial revolution withered in the bud cannot easily be explained. A partial answer lies in the shock of the Mongol occupation during the thirteenth and fourteenth centuries and the conservative reaction that followed their expulsion.

The Mongol invaders of China: Genghis Kahn and Kublai Khan

An invasion by the Mongols, which brought the final collapse of the Sung Dynasty, subjected all China, for the first time in its history, to the rule of a foreign conqueror. The Mongol Asiatic empire, established with almost incredible swiftness in a series of military campaigns, was for a brief period one of the largest ever known. In the early thirteenth century the great Mongol conqueror Genghis Khan overthrew the kingdoms adjacent to China on the north and then swept westward across all Asia. After making a brief foray into India he subdued Persia and Mesopotamia and occupied large stretches of Russian territory north and west of the Caspian Sea. Although the invasion of China was probably inevitable, the Sung emperor contributed to his own downfall by playing a double game with the Mongols. So eager was he to get rid of the Juchên rulers in north China that he sent troops to help the Mongols against them; then he rashly attacked the Mongol forces and exposed his own dominions to the fury of the ruthless and swift-riding horsemen. The conquest of southern China was completed by Genghis Khan's grandson, Kublai Khan, after many years of hard fighting, during which the Mongols not only had to occupy the coastal cities but also had to accustom themselves to naval warfare. In 1279 the last Chinese army was defeated (the commanding general is said to have jumped into the sea with the infant Sung prince in his arms), and Kublai became the master of China.

The huge Asiatic empire of the Mongols, which reached from the China Sea to eastern Europe, was too large to be administered effectively as a unit and did not long remain intact. Religious differences contributed to its dissolution. Before the end of the thirteenth century most of the western princes (khans) had become Muslims and repudiated the authority of Kublai's family, who favored a Tibetan form of Buddhism. Kublai's descendants, however, from their imperial capital of Peking, governed China for the better part of a century (1279–1368).

The dissolution of Kublai's empire

The accession of the Mongol (or Yüan) Dynasty threatened a serious interruption in the normal course of Chinese civilization. Mongol rule remained essentially a military occupation imposed upon traditional Chinese institutions. The Chinese were subjected to humiliating restrictions. They were forbidden to carry arms or to retaliate if injured by a Mongol. The Mongols were notoriously cruel conquerors, leaving ruined cities and mutilated corpses as monuments to the folly of those who resisted them. The bitterly contested occupation of southern China was accompanied by a decimation of the native population in some areas. Nevertheless, the Mongol rulers were wise enough to recognize the desirability of preserving such a great state as China and the advantage to be gained from taxing its people instead of exterminating them. The nomad warriors could not resist the influence of Chinese culture, and the traditional Chinese administrative system was not completely uprooted. The civil-service examinations were suspended for a time, and Chinese were excluded from most governmental posts, although the Mongol emperors employed foreigners of various nationalities in high positions at court. In the fourteenth century, when the dynasty showed signs of weakening and native unrest became ominous, the emperor reinstituted the examination system and admitted Chinese to office, chiefly at the lower level. Key positions were reserved for Mongols and Central Asians—a mere 3 percent of the population.

The rule of the Mongol emperors

While the Mongol emperors patronized Buddhism, they did not seriously interfere with other native cults and they permitted the introduction of Western religions, although Islam was the only one of these to retain a permanent place. The emperors' lavish endowment of temples and monasteries strained the economy by removing tracts of land from the tax registers and impoverished the peasants, whose holdings had been confiscated. Many peasants lost their lands when conscripted as laborers for the construction of palaces, irrigation works, and an improved transportation system. A notable undertaking was the rebuilding and extension of the Grand Canal linking the capital city of Peking to the Yangtze valley by an inland waterway.

During the Mongol period northern and southern China, separated since the downfall of the Northern Sung, were now reunited, and the area under the jurisdiction of Peking was considerably larger than the empire of the Sung. The emperors attempted to increase it still further by schemes of conquest of dubious value. Kublai Khan made two attempts to invade Japan (in 1274 and 1281), employing both Chinese and Korean vessels, but a typhoon wrecked many of his ships and the Japanese annihilated the landing party. Fortunately, peaceful intercourse was continued with other nations, near and far. Overland commerce was facilitated by imperial highways which the Mongols built deep into Central Asia and even to Persia. That travel was comparatively safe is indicated by the large number of foreign visitors in China during this period. Foreign merchants enjoyed special privileges in the Mongol empire, while Chinese were discriminated against. Russians, Arabs, and Jews entered China for purposes of trade, as did Genoese and Venetians. The effects of this extensive commerce was to impair rather than strengthen the economy because it drained precious metals out of China and led to inflation of the currency.

The Silk Road. The fabled Central Asian route by which the riches of the East made their way to the West and Arab and European merchant-adventurers like Marco Polo were able to pass from the Mediterranean to the Yellow Sea is depicted in this fourteenth-century Catalan map.

Marco Polo, the most famous of many European visitors, who lived and traveled widely in China for seventeen years (1275–1292), astonished his countrymen with his glowing report upon returning home (he described Hangchow, the Southern Sung capital, as "the finest and noblest city in the world"). But Marco Polo moved in privileged circles and failed to notice the condition of the common people. By the fourteenth century starvation was widespread and more Chinese had been reduced to slavery than at any other time in history

In the fourteenth century, Mongol power was undermined by the decadence of the ruling house and by the growing discontent of the Chinese people, who never forgot that they had been subjugated by a barbarian conqueror. Rebellion was brought to a successful conclusion under the leadership of a dynamic, if somewhat grotesque, soldier of fortune, who captured Peking in 1368 and drove the last Mongol emperor into the wastes of Mongolia. This rebel leader was a man of low birth who had been orphaned at an early age and had exchanged the life of a Buddhist monk for that of a bandit. Nevertheless, he was accepted as having won the Mandate of Heaven and became the first emperor of the Ming ("Brilliant" or "Glorious") Dynasty, which lasted from 1368 to 1644. The dynasty gave renewed proof of the potency of Chinese institutions, although it added little that was new. The government adhered to the Sung patterns, or in some ways more closely to the T'ang, particularly in its emphasis upon the forceful expansion of territorial boundaries. Ming China was a large state, with its authority extending into Manchuria, Mongolia, Indochina, Burma, and the southwestern region facing Tibet. While the great Mongol empire of the thirteenth century had fallen to pieces, it gave promise of being resurrected by Timur (Tamerlane), the master of Turkestan and scourge of India. Although the Ming court regarded Timur's emissaries as tribute bearers, the "Earth Shaker" was actually setting forth on an expedition to conquer China when he died prematurely in 1405. In spite of this stroke of fortune, the Ming emperors made little effort to recover either Turkestan or Sinkiang.

The establishment of the Ming Dynasty came at a time when Chinese navigation was rapidly expanding. The mariner's compass had been in use perhaps since the eleventh century, and some large ships had been constructed. Chinese sailing vessels, equipped with as many as four decks and comfortable living quarters, undertook voyages to the East Indies, the Malay Peninsula, Ceylon, India, and Arabia, returning with merchandise, tribute, and valuable geographical information. They may have ventured westward around Africa's Cape of Good Hope. In its heyday the Ming navy was more than equal to that of any contemporary European state, although when stationed in the home waters of the Yangtze region it was exposed to attacks from Japanese pirates. A reversal of China's advantageous position in ocean commerce was the unfortunate result of a restrictive policy imposed by the Ming emperors. In contrast to the Sung, the Ming rulers viewed

China under the Sung, Mongol, and Ming Dynasties (960–1644)

The overthrow of the Mongols and establishment of the Ming Dynasty

Maritime achievements and decline under the Ming Dynasty

Candidates for Scholarly Degrees Await Their Examination Results. The empire relied on the ranks of such scholars for the state bureaucracy.

foreign commerce not as an exchange for mutual benefit but as a device for collecting tribute, and they limited trade to states that acknowledged China's suzerainty. In 1371 the government forbade Chinese to travel overseas, and early in the next century they interdicted coastal shipping as well. This shortsighted and reactionary policy, stemming partly from a fear that rival power centers might develop in coastal cities, entailed a loss of revenue, which led in turn to the issuing of inconvertible paper currency and a consequent inflation which damaged the entire economy. Even worse, it forced China into isolation at a time when the Western peoples were beginning to emerge from their provincialism. Instead of retaining the initiative on the high seas, the later Ming rulers proved ineffectual in defending their own coasts.

Rigidity of the bureaucracy and the examination system

A drift toward rigidity in the state bureaucracy was illustrated—and intensified—by changes in the civil-service examination system. The Ming emperors were the first to pick their officials exclusively from candidates who had passed the examinations. They also opened competition to all classes of the people, but this seemingly democratic reform was of doubtful benefit. To prepare for the examinations entailed much time and expense; the number of successful candidates greatly exceeded the available posts; and, finally, examinations were designed to test the applicant's mastery of literary forms and ideological orthodoxy rather than his practical knowledge or administrative aptitude. By the opening of the sixteenth century the effects of this system had become deadening. Except for palace eunuchs, commanders in charge of border areas, and members of the imperial family, degree holding was the only passport to government service. It also provided entry—even for those never appointed to office—into a privileged class of scholar-gentry whose members considered themselves superior to common folk and kept the management of local affairs in their own hands.

A decline in the vitality of the administration was apparent long before the Ming Dynasty came to a close. Officials became lazy and corrupt; power passed into the hands of court favorites and eunuchs; and exorbitant taxes oppressed the peasants to the point of ruin. While the costs of government mounted dizzily—in 1639 military expenditures alone were ten times greater than the entire revenue of the first Ming emperor—territories were being lost through incompetence and rebellion. Although the dynasty finally succumbed to another foreign invasion, internal dissension was the real cause of its collapse.

Among the cultural developments that took place in China during the Sung, Mongol, and Ming dynasties was a renewal of interest in philosophical speculation, reaching a climax in the latter half of the twelfth century. This revival represented a return to the fountainhead of Chinese thought—the sages of antiquity, particularly Confucius—but it introduced several new ideas and was not a mere repetition of ancient formulas. The most noted Chinese thinker of this period was Chu Hsi (1130–1200), who held a position at the Sung court and was an opponent of the so-called Innovators (disciples of Wang An-shih). Although Chu Hsi claimed to be interpreting Confucius' teachings in accordance with their original and uncorrupted meaning, he and his associates actually founded a Neo-Confucian school, with a metaphysics which incorporated elements of Taoism and Buddhism. They stressed the concept of the "Supreme Ultimate" or Absolute, a Final Cause which underlies the whole material universe and is antecedent to every rational or moral principle. At the same time he upheld the traditional ethical system exemplified by the family and embodied in a paternalistic state administered by a bureaucracy of scholar-officials. The teachings of Chu Hsi, although stoutly contested by rival scholars in his day, eventually came to be regarded as the definitive commentary on the doctrines of the ancient sage and were incorporated in the examination curriculum.

A prodigious output of literature has been characteristic of Chinese civilization during almost every period except the most ancient. Printing was very common from Sung times on. Books were printed from wooden blocks, from metal plates, and from movable type made of earthenware, tin, and wood. Poetry seldom equaled the best of the T'ang age in beauty or spontaneity, but lengthy histories, encyclopedias, dictionaries, geographies, and scientific treatises were produced. The most original literary developments were in the fields of the drama and the novel. The Chinese drama attained the level of a major art form during the Mongol Dynasty, partly because the suspension of the civil-service examinations, by cutting off opportunities for official careers, prompted men of talent to turn their attention to a medium of popular entertainment which they had previously considered unworthy of notice. The dramas of the Mongol period, of which more

The Philosopher Chu Hsi. Chu Hsi's Neo-Confucianism was a powerful synthesis that drew on the collective efforts of generations of thinkers since the late eighth century.

Sung Printed Book. A page from the *Fa-yuan chu-lin* ("Forest of Pearls in the Garden of the Law"). The book was compiled by the Buddhist monk and scholar Tao-Shih in 688. It was printed in 1124, fully three centuries earlier than the Gutenberg Bible.

*Printing and literature:
development of the
Chinese drama*

*Development of the
Chinese novel*

Sung painting

than a hundred have survived, combined lively action with vivid portrayal of character, and they were written in the common idiom of the people rather than in the classical language of scholars. The Chinese theater, like the English theater of Shakespeare's day, was largely devoid of scenery and properties, although the performers made use of elaborate costumes and heavy make-up. Ordinarily all the parts were filled by male actors. The plays were in verse, but, in contrast to the Elizabethan and modern Western drama, the speeches were sung rather than recited and the orchestra (placed directly on the stage) contributed an essential element to the production.

The Chinese novel, originating apparently in the tales of public storytellers, developed contemporaneously with the drama but matured a little later. Its growth was aided indirectly by the sterility of the academic atmosphere that pervaded the court and the bureaucracy of the Ming Dynasty. In the fifteenth century, veneration for Confucian orthodoxy, especially as embodied in the teachings of Chu Hsi, had become such a fetish among the official coterie of scholars that one of them declared: "The truth has been made manifest. . . . No more writing is needed." Some men of letters sought a creative outlet by composing narratives in the plain language of the people. In their hands the novel became a highly successful literary medium, skillfully contrived but purveying robust adventure, humor, warm feeling, and salty realism. Frequently historical themes were chosen for subject matter, but the tales also provided commentary—sometimes satirical—upon contemporary society and government.

A large proportion of the Chinese works of art still extant was produced during the period which is being reviewed here. Sculpture had declined in quality since T'ang times, but painting reached its highest peak of excellence under the Sung. The most beautiful and typical Sung paintings are landscapes, executed in ink monochrome but conveying the impression of an intimate understanding of nature in her various moods. Through economy of line, omission of nonessentials,

Sage under a Pine Tree. Sung Dynasty. The gnarled and twisted tree exemplifies the Chinese interest in nature in both its pleasant and perverse moods.

Spring Morning at the Palace of Han. Sung Dynasty. Chinese painting emphasized landscapes rather than people and the representation of poetic or philosophic ideas rather than facts.

and painstaking treatment of significant detail, the artists sought to bring to light the reality which lies hidden behind the world of appearances. Their dreamy creations were obviously influenced by the mystical teachings of Buddhism and Taoism. Landscape painting was at its ripest during the Southern Sung period, when the leading artists took full advantage of the natural beauty of the Hangchow region. They sometimes painted panoramic scenes on long strips of silk. These were fastened to rollers and could be viewed leisurely by simply holding the rollers in one's hands and winding the painted scroll from one roller to the other.

Architecture attained particular pre-eminence under the Ming, a dynasty which delighted in glorifying and embellishing the visible aspects of Chinese culture. The Ming emperors rebuilt the Great Wall, largely in its present form. Ming architecture was by no means new in conception, but it was prolific and has left many impressive monuments. The popularity of elaborate gardens, summer residences, game preserves, and hunting lodges among the aristocracy provided opportunities for the designing of graceful pavilions and arched bridges. Fully developed by this period was the pagoda style of temple, distinguished by curving roofs which were usually of tile and frequently in brilliant colors.

Ming architecture

China has only rarely been isolated from other parts of the world, and many of her cultural changes were the result of foreign contacts. The Chinese were indebted to the Arabs for contributions in the field of mathematics and probably also in medicine, although the Chinese

"War Spirit." A Ming Dynasty painting.

Achievements in agriculture and in the applied sciences

had themselves accumulated a considerable store of medical data. Inoculation against smallpox seems to have been practiced before the end of the Sung Dynasty. Eyeglasses came into use (from Italy) during the Ming period. New crops of Western origin began to be cultivated in China. Sorghum, introduced in the thirteenth century, and maize in the sixteenth have been raised extensively in northern China ever since. Cotton production, which also began in the thirteenth century, was greatly expanded under the Ming. One innovation which may have been of domestic rather than foreign inspiration was in the technique of warfare. The explosive properties of gunpowder had long been known, but not until the eleventh century were they utilized for the manufacture of lethal weapons. The Mongols, in the thirteenth and fourteenth centuries, employed bombs that perhaps were propelled by primitive cannons, and Ming armorers made further improvements. Although these early artillery pieces were crude, they foreshadowed the increasingly destructive character of modern warfare.

3. THE RISE OF FEUDALISM AND MILITARY DICTATORS IN JAPAN (c. 900–1600)

Contrasts between Japan and China

Even though Chinese culture had been incorporated into the foundations of Japanese civilization and exerted a lasting influence, social and political trends in Japan during the medieval era were very different from those in the great mainland state. While China was frequently harassed by nomadic invaders and was temporarily subjugated by a foreign dynasty, her society and culture departed little from the ancient pattern. By contrast, Japan, enjoying the natural protection of her insular position, was not seriously affected by disturbances from without; yet her institutions were profoundly altered as the result of conflicts taking place within her own society. A theoretical unity and an arbitrary and artificial scheme of government had been imposed upon Japan by the reform of the mid-seventh century, which attempted to introduce the Chinese imperial system in its entirety. How completely the attempt had failed is illustrated by the events of the next thousand years. Only belatedly, and after indecisive and exhausting strife, was the basis discovered for a stable and unified society. And when stability was achieved, it was through improvised institutions which were inadequate to solve the problems certain to arise in the wake of economic and cultural change.

The political history of Japan during this period is characterized mainly by two factors: (1) the persistence of an indirect method of government, with the actual power shifting from one family to another but exercised in the name of an inviolate emperor, whose effective authority rarely extended beyond the environs of Kyoto; (2) the feudalization of society and the growth of extralegal military units which imposed their will upon territories under their control. To the end of the sixteenth century the technique of government was variable and uncertain, although the trend from civilian to military authority was unmistakable. At the opening of the seventeenth century a centralized administration was finally established which ended a long period of civil wars, enforced a coherent national policy, and endured almost unshaken until the middle of the nineteenth century. Even when it was overthrown, the habits which it had instilled in the Japanese people could not easily be uprooted.

*The characteristics of
Japan's political history*

In the ninth century the Fujiwara family, through intermarriage with the imperial family and through possession of the office of regent, had acquired a dominant position in the government, reducing the emperor to a figurehead. The Fujiwara retained their ascendancy until the twelfth century, but their rule over the outlying sections became more and more nominal as new lands were brought into production by reclamation or by conquest of the aborigines, and as aggressive landowners succeeded in withdrawing their estates from the jurisdiction of the imperial tax collectors. The men who possessed estates in these frontier regions were not hampered by the elaborate rules of etiquette or by the mania for classical Chinese studies that absorbed the energies of the courtiers at Kyoto. They formulated their own standards of conduct, largely dictated by the desire to preserve and extend their holdings, and quarreled with one another over conflicting claims. Naturally, many small farmers relinquished their property to powerful neighbors in return for protection and sank to a position of serfdom. Gradually a manorial economy came into existence, showing some points of similarity to the manorial regime in western Europe during the later Middle Ages.

*The decentralization of
power*

By a remarkable coincidence of history Japanese society took on

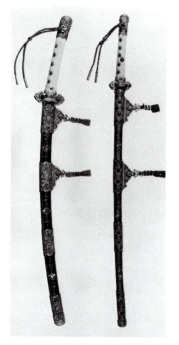

Swords of the Feudal Nobility. This type of curved sword, of fine steel, was worn suspended from the girdle by great daimyo or court nobles during Japan's early feudal age (twelfth to fourteenth centuries). Note the jeweled hilts, the ornately decorated scabbards, and the loops for hanging the swords.

Contrasts between European and Japanese feudalism

The rise of the Shoguns

aspects of feudalism at the very time when feudal institutions were evolving in western Europe. In Japan and western Europe alike, leadership was passing to a class of mounted warriors who owned land, dominated the peasantry, and exercised governmental power as a private right. Members of the landed class established hereditary claims to their holdings and entered into binding agreements with one another, creating a series of dependent relationships equivalent to a system of lords and vassals. As in the case of European feudalism, the system was extended partly through the voluntary surrender of property by small landowners who sought a noble's protection, and partly through the granting of benefices or fiefs by great lords to lesser men in order to secure their services as vassals. Another parallel to the growth of European feudalism is seen in the fact that property belonging to religious foundations was frequently converted into fiefs. Some Buddhist monasteries and temples became formidable military units, but Japanese religious orders never attained an independence like that of the higher clergy in medieval Europe. They remained generally subservient to the aristocracy.

The Japanese warriors, who corresponded in status and in profession to the medieval knights, were known as samurai, or bushi. The samurai developed a fraternal spirit and a code of conduct to which they jealously clung as their special prerogative and which they called "the way of the horse and the bow." (The term *bushido,* not used before the eighteenth century, denoted a romantic and artificial version of the old feudal code.) Like the European code of chivalry it stressed valor, loyalty, and the necessity of preferring death to dishonor. The samurai was bound above all else to protect, defend, or avenge his lord, to this end sacrificing his own life and, if need be, the lives of his family—a remarkable ideal in view of the sacredness of family ties in Japan. So sensitive was the samurai to any taint of dishonor that he was expected to commit suicide (by a ritual of falling on one's sword, known as hara-kiri) if there was no other way to wipe out the stain on his reputation.

In spite of similarities there were significant differences between Japanese feudalism and that of contemporary western Europe. European feudalism arose with the disintegration of centralized government, the decay of cities, and general economic decline. In Japan, by contrast, feudal institutions developed while the economy was expanding and to the accompaniment of strenuous efforts to unify the country and create a strong central authority. Also, when effective government was established, it did not abolish feudalism but incorporated some of its conspicuous features.

Internal conflict in the twelfth century culminated in a struggle between two powerful families, the Taira and the Minamoto. With the victory of the Minamoto, their leader reorganized the government on a basis which frankly recognized the paramount role of the landowning warrior-nobility. To avoid appearing as a usurper, the head of the Minamoto family assumed only a military title, becoming known as Shogun, and pretended to be acting as the agent of the emperor. In reality, for the next six and one-half centuries (1192–1867) Japan had a dual government: the civil authority at Kyoto headed by the emperor and embracing various ranks of court nobility whose functions were ornamental rather than essential, and the Bakufu ("Tent Government") headed by the Shogun and commanding the services of the powerful military leaders who owned most of the land.

Although the Shogunate proved to be a durable institution, it did not remain perpetually in the hands of any one family. On the death of the first Shogun his widow's relatives seized control, with her connivance. This extremely capable woman became known as the "Nun Shogun," because she wielded political influence even after she had nominally retired into holy orders, and with her help the Hojo family came into power. Because the Hojo family had no inherent claim to superiority over other great feudal houses, its ascendancy created jealous dissatisfaction and led inevitably to further conflict. A remarkable incident occurred in 1333 when the Emperor Daigo II attempted to cut through the sham governmental fabric and assert his right to rule as well as reign. He mustered sufficient military forces to capture and burn the Shogun's headquarters at Kamakura and ended the Hojo regency. The sequel to this bold stroke, however, was simply a half century of civil war, with two rival emperors, each bidding for support. The schism in the imperial household was healed and order temporarily restored with the triumph of another great military family, the Ashikaga, who again reduced the emperor to a position of impotence.

The head of the Ashikaga house in 1338 set up a puppet emperor, proclaimed himself Shogun, and established his military base in Kyoto, which was the foremost commercial center as well as the imperial capital. He did not succeed in dissolving the rival imperial court until more than fifty years later—the official dates of the Ashikaga Shogunate are 1392–1573 (known as the Muromachi Period after the name of the section of Kyoto where the Shogun's headquarters was located). Hoping to check disruptive feudal tendencies, the Ashikaga sought to create an autocratic monarchical regime administered by a bureaucracy under their control. Because their own family holdings were relatively small, they entrusted authority throughout the provinces to appointed military officials chosen from among their own vassals. It proved virtually impossible to maintain this system as planned. Rivalry was inevitable between local landed proprietors and the Shogun's representatives, who in turn threatened to challenge the Shogun's supremacy by making their positions hereditary. Many farming villages had developed a solid community structure, and leagues of these villages, formed for mutual protection, resisted attempts to bring them under tight control. During the two centuries of Ashikaga rule a three-legged tussle continued among provincial landlords, peasant leaders,

The Shogunate under the Hojo family; civil war

Failure of attempts to establish a centralized bureaucracy

The Burning of the Sanjo Palace by the Minamoto Forces. Dating from the late thirteenth century, this is an early example of the war-tale category of hand-scrolls that became popular with the onset of military overlordship in Japan

and the Shogun's officials. The clear losers in the struggle were the Shogun's officials, who disappeared as a class, although individuals merged with the nobility of large estate owners, who were becoming the most powerful element throughout the country. Successful proprietors acquired large domains by allowing or forcing smaller holders to become their vassals. To provide a firm revenue base, they made careful surveys of the resources and inhabitants of their domains, which they administered like independent principalities. But in repelling interference by the central authority or local rivals the great proprietors had enlisted the support of peasant leagues and, in return, allowed the peasant villages considerable autonomy in managing their internal affairs. Still more important was the fact that, although not granted legal ownership of the land, the peasants were confirmed in its possession, which in practice amounted to the same thing. Thus another significant difference between European and Japanese feudalism is seen in the condition of the large class of rural laborers: in Europe they began as serfs and only gradually won emancipation; in Japan serfdom had almost disappeared by the time feudal institutions were fully formed.

The decay of the Ashikaga Shogunate inaugurated a century of civil

in the late twelfth century. The work illustrates a critical battle of 1159 in the civil war between the Minamoto and Taira clans.

warfare known as the Sengoku ("Country at War") Period (1500–1600). Robbery and pillage were rampant; almost all vestiges of a central government disappeared; even the private estates which the emperor had owned in various parts of the country were absorbed into the feudal domains. The imperial family as well as the Kyoto courtiers were subjected to humiliation by swaggering soldiers. Reduced to poverty, one emperor eked out a living by selling his autograph. In 1500 an imperial corpse lay unburied for six weeks because there was no money in the treasury. The Ashikaga Shogun was almost as impotent as the emperor and quite unable to stop the brigandage and slaughter carried on wantonly by feudal retainers and robber monks. Conditions in Japan seemed to be fast approaching anarchy when, at the close of the sixteenth century, the Shogunate was drastically and effectively reorganized by the Tokugawa family.

The period of feudal warfare

In spite of all the confusion and turmoil, constructive forces were at work. Feudalism in Japan had assumed a form that would facilitate reunification of the country in the hands of a commanding personality. Leadership was passing from the knightly (samurai) class as a whole to the large estate holders, who were known as daimyo ("Great

Rise of the great daimyo

The Golden Pavilion (Kiukakuji). A residence built by Yoshimitsu, third Ashikaga Shogun in 1397.

Names"). The daimyo absorbed many small estates, developed fairly efficient administrative systems for their domains, and employed samurai to manage them. The ascendancy of the daimyo, while it by no means eliminated feudal dissension, greatly reduced the number of rival units and also ensured a considerable measure of stability within each unit.

Economic progress during the feudal age

That the turbulent sixteenth century had positive aspects is most graphically illustrated by the transformation of Japan's economy during this time. An unprecedented expansion in agricultural productivity was accomplished by large-scale irrigation and land reclamation projects carried out by the daimyo, by improved methods of cultivation, and by the introduction of new varieties of rice. Accompanying the rise in agricultural productivity came an increase in population, initiating a demographic trend that continued through the seventeenth century. A swelling population in turn promoted the growth of cities and enabled a nationwide system of exchange to supplant local markets. Foreign trade, increasing steadily from the twelfth century, led to the substitution of money for rice or cloth as a medium of exchange and promoted diversified economic activity. By the fifteenth century the Japanese were exporting not only raw materials, such as lumber, gold, and pearls, but also manufactured goods. Japanese folding fans and screens were in great demand in China, and steel swords were exported by the thousands to a large Far Eastern market. The curved swords forged by Japanese craftsmen in the thirteenth century are said to have been unsurpassed even by the famous blades of Toledo and Damascus.

Japanese society during the feudal age was aristocratic but not rigidly segregated. City merchants, though of lowly origin like their European counterparts, acquired influence through the profits of trade. Moreover, in contrast to most of western Europe, the feudal classes participated in capitalistic enterprises. In addition to professional merchants, monastic orders, samurai, great nobles, and occasionally even the Shogun invested in trade. Opinions differ as to the condition of the peasants. Recurrent uprisings against the nobles during the fifteenth and sixteenth centuries undoubtedly reflect rural discontent. Nevertheless, there is evidence that the peasants' lot was improving rather than worsening. Labor services due the lords had been largely converted into rents, and the cultivators were well on the road to becoming free tenants. Doubtless they benfited from, as well as contributed to, the increase in economic productivity.

Many cultural changes accompanied the growth of a productive and diversified economy, stimulated by contacts incidental to foreign trade. As in earlier times, various schools of Buddhism contributed to cultural development, largely because they continued to serve as channels for intellectual and aesthetic currents from China. One of the most prominent sects, the Zen (from the Chinese *Ch'an*), was introduced at the close of the twelfth century and spread rapidly among the samurai. Zen Buddhism taught that enlightenment would come to the individual not through study or any intellectual process, but by a sudden flash of insight experienced when one was in tune with nature. Because it stressed physical discipline, self-control, and the practice of meditation in place of formal scholarship, the sect appealed to the warrior class, who felt that Zen teachings gave supernatural sanction to the attitudes which they had already come to regard as essential to their station. Though its doctrines were fundamentally anti-intellectual, its monks fostered both learning and art and injected several refinements into Japanese upper-class society. Among these were an unrivaled type of landscape architecture, the art of flower arrangement, and a delicate social ritual known as the tea ceremony—all of which were Chinese importations but elaborated with great sensitivity in Japan.

Literature flourished during this period, and hand-printed books were produced commercially on a large scale. While sacred writings were being collected and translated in the monasteries, and while courtiers continued to write in the polished but lifeless classical manner, the literary tradition was enriched by the addition of tales of daring and high adventure conceived for the entertainment and edification of men-at-arms. These stories of knightly prowess, composed in a flowing poetical prose and sometimes sung to the accompaniment of a lute, are comparable to the heroic epics of medieval European chivalry. No counterpart of the European poems of romantic love, however, arose in feudal Japan, where women had sunk to a position of abject subordination to male authority. All the arts were influenced by Chinese models, but the Japanese had long since demonstrated their originality

Social classes and the condition of society

The samurai and Zen Buddhism

Literature and the arts

The No *Drama.* This art form is characterized by rhythmical recitation of texts, traditional music, and symbolic movement of players.

Costume for the No *Dance Drama.* (seventeenth century). Lavish and colorful pictorial decoration was characteristic of the costumes worn by *No* actors.

in adapting styles to their own tastes. Particularly impressive were the paintings executed by monks of the Zen sect in the fifteenth and sixteenth centuries. These were chiefly landscapes and similar in style to those of the Chinese artists of the Ming Dynasty, but they possessed an individuality and freshness of their own.

The exacting aesthetic standards of the aristocratic patrons of the Zen sect are also evident in a specialized form of dramatic art, the *No,* which emerged during this period. The *No* "lyric-drama" or "dance-drama" was not a foreign importation but almost purely a native product. Its origins can be traced to ancient folk dances and also to ritualistic dances associated with both Shintoist and Buddhist modes of worship. In its perfected form, it became a unique vehicle of artistic expression and entertainment, which heightened the appeal of rhythm and graceful postures by relating them to dramatic incidents. The themes of the dance-dramas were traditional narratives, but they were presented with great restraint and by suggestive symbolism rather than by literal re-enactment, somewhat in the manner of a series of tableaux. The performers wore masks as well as rich costumes and chanted their lines to the accompaniment of drums and flutes. The *No* drama achieved great popularity among the samurai class and was at its height from the fourteenth to the sixteenth centuries. In spite of its extremely stylized character, it has never entirely disappeared from the artistic heritage of Japan.

• *Items so designated are available in paperback editions.*

INDIA—*See also Readings for Chapters 5 and 11*

Cambridge History of India, Vol. III, Cambridge, 1937.

Eaton, R. M., *Sufis of Bijapur, 1300–1700: The Social Role of Sufis in Medieval India,* Princeton, 1978. Illuminates political as well as social and religious developments.

Ikram, Mohamad, *Muslim Civilization in India,* ed. A. T. Embree, New York, 1964. Scholarly and readable.

Sharma, S. R., *The Crescent in India,* Bombay, 1954.

CHINA—*See also Readings for Chapters 6 and 11*

Bruce, J. P., *Chu Hsi and His Masters,* London, 1923.

Cahill, James, *The Art of Southern Sung China,* Salem, N.H., 1962.

Chan, Albert, *The Glory and Fall of the Ming Dynasty,* Norman, Okla., 1982. A comprehensive study.

• Crump, James, *Chinese Theater in the Days of Kublai Khan,* Tucson, 1980.

————, *The Distant Mountains: Chinese Painting of the Late Ming Dynasty, 1570–1644,* New York, 1982.

• Gernet, Jacques, *Daily Life in China (On the Eve of the Mongol Invasion 1250–1276),* Stanford, 1970.

Hucker, C. O., *The Traditional Chinese State in Ming Times (1368–1644),* Tucson, 1961. Brief but informative on political structure and operation.

————, *The Ming Dynasty: Its Origins and Evolving Institutions,* Ann Arbor, 1978. Readable and reliable.

• Hudson, G. F., *Europe and China: A Survey of Their Relations from the Earliest Times to 1800,* London, 1930. Interestingly presented.

• Langlois, John, ed., *China under Mongol Rule,* Princeton, 1981. An excellent collection of essays.

Liu, James T. C., *Reform in Sung China: Wang An-shih (1021–1086) and His New Policies,* Cambridge, Mass., 1959. A good, brief interpretive study.

Parson, J. B., *The Peasant Rebellions of the Late Ming Dynasty,* Tucson, 1970.

Shih Chung-wen, *The Golden Age of Chinese Drama: Yüan Tsa-chü,* Princeton, 1976.

Waley, Arthur, *An Introduction to the Study of Chinese Painting,* New York, 1958.

Wright, Arthur F., ed., *Studies in Chinese Thought,* Chicago, 1953.

————, ed., *The Confucian Persuasion,* Stanford, 1960.

JAPAN—*See also Readings for Chapter 11*

• Duus, Peter, *Feudalism in Japan,* 2d ed., New York, 1975. Concise account of political developments from the sixth through the nineteenth century.

Grossberg, K. A., *Japan's Renaissance: The Policies of the Muromachi Bakufu,* Cambridge, Mass., 1981. A careful and unconventional analysis of the Ashikaga Shoguns.

Hall, J. W., et al., *Japan before Tokugawa: Political Consolidation and Economic Growth, 1500 to 1650,* Princeton, 1981.

• ———, and T. Takeshi *Japan in the Muromachi Age,* Berkeley, 1977.

Sansom, George B., *A History of Japan, 1334–1615,* Stanford, 1961. A major contribution.

———, *The Western World and Japan,* New York, 1950.

Suzuki, D. T., *Zen and Japanese Culture,* New York, 1959.

• Totman, Conrad, *Japan before Perry: A Short History,* Berkeley, 1981. Brief, clear, interpretive.

• Waley, Arthur, *No Plays of Japan,* New York, 1922.

SOURCE MATERIALS

Boxer, C. R., ed., *South China in the Sixteenth Century* (narratives of Portuguese and Spanish visitors, 1550–1575).

Chinese Novels and Short Stores: Buck, Pearl, tr., *All Men Are Brothers;* Howell, E. B., tr., *Inconstancy of Madam Chuang and Other Stories;* Waley, Arthur, tr., *The Monkey.*

• de Bary, W. T., ed., *Sources of Chinese Tradition,* "The Confucian Revival," New York, 1960.

• ———, ed., *Sources of Indian Tradition,* "Islam in Medieval India," New York, 1950.

• ———, ed., *Sources of Japanese Tradition,* "Medieval Japan," New York, 1958.

• Hall, J. W., and T. Toyoda, eds., *Japan in the Muromachi Age,* New Haven, Conn., 1974.

• Hsiung, S. I., tr., *The Romance of the Western Chamber,* London, 1935.

• Keene, Donald, ed., *Twenty Plays of the No Theatre,* New York, 1970.

Reischauer, E. O., and Y. K. Yamagiwa, *Translations from Early Japanese Literature* (eleventh to thirteenth centuries), Cambridge, Mass., 1951.

Waley, Arthur, tr., *The Travels of an Alchemist, the Journeys of the Taoist Ch'ang Ch'un,* London, 1931.

Yule, Henry, tr., *The Book of Ser Marco Polo,* London, 1903.

Chapter 17

THE AMERICAS AND AFRICA BEFORE THE AGE OF EUROPEAN OVERSEAS EXPANSION

The great war lord has burst from Earth's swollen belly born on his
  shield.
Astride the Snake Hill he triumphs,
between the pyramids,
with his face-paint on and his shield teueuelli.
Not one is so potent as he
And the Earth quivers.

               —Aztec hymn (Brotherston, *Image of the New World*)

R ecent archeological discoveries provide evidence that the process of civilization building began in the Americas at approximately the same time as in the valleys of the Nile, the Tigris-Euphrates, and the Indus. Apparently the earliest successful attempt in this direction occurred along the Pacific coast and western slope of the Andes in what is now Peru. Although this civilization, based on fishing and agricultural economies, lacked a system of writing, its architectural and artistic powers are shown in the remains of great pyramids, temples, and warehouses. Of several cultures that appeared, somewhat later than the Andean, in the central valley of Mexico, Central America, and along the Gulf Coast, that of the Mayas was most distinguished for intellectual progress, which included the invention of writing and a remarkable calendar. While the ancient civilizations of Mesopotamia, Egypt, and China served as foundations for their successors in these respective areas, the early civilizations of the Americas suffered the fate of almost complete extinction with the European conquests of the sixteenth and seventeenth centuries.

Dramatic archeological discoveries in the Americas

572

*The Americas and Africa before
the Age of European Overseas
Expansion*

Nevertheless, they left traces still evident in contemporary Latin American societies.

During these centuries the civilizations of Africa were altered and greatly extended under the influence of trade expansion and the spread of Islam. Great kingdoms and empires encompassing cultures, languages, and religious systems arose, and imposing urban centers reflecting the convergence of Islamic and African cultures flourished. At the same time, slavery and the slave trade became a prominent feature in the societies of northern Africa. Besides being held in African states, slaves were exported to Egypt, Arabia, and India.

1. EARLY CIVILIZATIONS OF THE AMERICAS

A study of skeletal remains indicates that, beginning 15,000 or 20,000 years ago, groups of people from Asia advanced eastward into North America by way of what is now the Bering Strait but was then dry land. As population expanded, the newcomers spread across the continent and southward into Central and South America. These migrants, chiefly of Mongolian stock, were later to become known as "Indians" although they had no connection with the inhabitants of India and some may have come from Polynesia by boat.

A great variety of cultures developed among the numerous Indian communities of both continents. Many North American societies clung to a hunting-fishing-gathering economy. The earliest artifacts thus far discovered in the New World are finely crafted stone knives and spear points—called Clovis after a site in New Mexico—dating from 9000 B.C. Apparently designed by hunters of mammoth, camels, horses, and bison, these weapons have been found widely dispersed over North America. Agriculture, so essential for the maintenance of settled civilized communities, began first in the highlands of Mexico, where corn (maize) was fully domesticated by 5000 B.C. Relatively easy to raise and highly nutritious, corn became a staple crop on both continents. By 1500 B.C. the practice of agriculture had reached the southwest plains of what is now the United States. Indians of that region manufactured pottery (another contribution from Mexico) of high artistry, distinctly original and striking in design. In the Chaco Canyon of New Mexico—now a national park—a society of cliff dwellers sustained a flourishing culture between 900 and 1200 A.D. Its efficiently organized workers operated an elaborate irrigation system employing dams and canals, and exhibited superior engineering and architectural skills. Although for obscure reasons this culture declined after 300 years, the remains of its huge community buildings still inspire admiration. Pueblos, constructed by combining logs with sandstone, reached a height of five stories and provided several hundred rooms.

In the central valley of Mexico and the highlands of Guatemala

GULF OF MEXICO

Tula
Teotihuacán
Tenochtitlán
Uxmal
Chichén Itzá
YUCATÁN PENINSULA
MAYAS
Tikal

AZTEC EMPIRE

MESOAMERICA

ISTHMUS OF PANAMÁ

CARIBBEAN SEA

ATLANTIC OCEAN

Equator

Quito

Tumbes

Chavín de Huantar

ANDES

Amazon River

SOUTH AMERICA

PACIFIC OCEAN

Machu Picchu
Cuzco

Lake Titicaca
Tiahuanaco

INCA EMPIRE

Lake Poopó

MOUNTAINS

80°

60°

20°

0°

0°

20°

40°

60°

100°

40°

80°

0   1000 miles

THE AMERICAS ON THE EVE OF EUROPEAN CONQUEST

Ruins of Pueblo Bonito, Chaco Canyon, New Mexico. This complex, multi-story structure included thirty-two *kivas,* or communal rooms, where the populace gathered to enact rituals.

New archeological discoveries

and the Andes—where the soil is fertile and the climate invigorating—several Indian societies developed cultures sufficiently advanced to qualify as true civilizations. Had they not been conquered, they might well have sustained an indigenous cultural growth equal to that of any other continent. Historical records for America before the European conquests of the sixteenth century are tantalizingly fragmentary. Few writings have survived, and much archeological exploration remains to be done. Sensational discoveries made during the 1980s are forcing a drastic revision of theories that were long unquestioned: that New World civilizations originated much later than those of the Middle East and Asia; that in the Western Hemisphere the greatest advances came first in Mesoamerica (Mexico and Central America). Excavations now in progress in some fifty river valleys draining into the Pacific from the western slopes of the Peruvian Andes have brought to life evidence of a mature civilization roughly contemporary with those of Mesopotamia and the Nile valley 4,000 or 5,000 years ago. Its remains include the ruins of great U-shaped temples and multichambered warehouses with bases as large as a football field. Walls were decorated with brightly colored adobe friezes picturing jaguars, snakes, and spider motifs. Little can yet be determined concerning the social or political structure of this preliterate Andean civilization. Its monuments reflect the work of an efficient labor force with specialized skills, but it is uncertain whether the separate river-valley communities were united under a central authority. A remarkable feature is that, in contrast to the ancient civilizations of Mesopotamia, Egypt, and India, the Andean was not cradled in a river delta but depended primarily upon the sea for sustenance. While the Andeans practiced agriculture with sweet potatoes, peanuts, and beans as chief crops, fishing was their main occupation until, during the second millenium B.C., they shifted their base inland up the mountain slopes and transformed their fishing economy into one of irrigated farming. The move required not only changes in techniques but also adaptation to rough terrain and altitudes as high as 10,000 feet. That the transition was successful is attested by the fact that during the inland agricultural stage even larger structures, both religious and secular, were erected. Two sites currently being excavated are located north of Lima close to the Pan American Highway. One reveals a stepped pyramid, the other a U-shaped temple, each ten stories high and considerably more than 3,000 years old. One archeologist speculates that both the Andean civilization and those of Mesoamerica sprang from a Stone-Age tribal culture indigenous to the Amazon Basin as long as 8,000 years ago. However that may be, the conclusion seems inescapable that the Andean culture provided a base for its successors in northwestern South America, including that of the Incas. Contributions attributable to the Andeans include agriculture, architectural styles, artistic motifs, and religious beliefs and practices (including human sacrifice).

During the 3,000 years between the dawn of a high civilization among the Andeans and its climax under the Incas, several cultures succeeded one another. One that rose to prominence is the Chavín, named after its principal site Chavín de Huantar, north of Lima near where a great Andean pyramid has been uncovered. The Chavín culture flourished during the first half of the first millennium B.C. Little is known about the people who produced it or of the history of the region during the next five or six centuries. A society known as Moche (or Mochital) dominated the western slopes of the Peruvian Andes between 100 and 700 A.D. Named after a principal site at the mouth of the Moche River, this nation of about 50,000 people occupied a 220-mile stretch of the north Peruvian coast. Utilizing the river systems for an extensive irrigation network the Moche turned a searing desert into a productive agricultural area supporting crops of corn, beans, squash, peanuts, peppers, avocados, and other fruits. Although they had no writing, the Moche left a vivid record of their culture through their artifacts, especially their pottery, both sculptured and decorated with fine line drawings. Evidently their society was military and theocratic, with authority in the hands of warrior-priests whose awe-inspiring presence was enhanced by pictorial examples of cruelty and by religious symbols. The warrior-priest played a central role in the elaborate and conspicuous ritual of human sacrifice. At his own death, concubines, servants, and attendants became sacrificial victims to accompany him in the afterlife. For religious and administrative centers

Mortar in the Form of a Jaguar. Chavín Culture. The appearance of massive strength conveyed by this thirteen-inch-long object derives from the Chavín worship of a man-jaguar god.

Portrait Vase with Stirrup Spout. Moche Culture. Moche pottery points to a complex theocratic society in which fighting played a significant role.

The Tiahuanacan culture

The Incas of South America

A confederation under strong centralized control

the Moche raised pyramids with rectangular platforms adjacent, the largest of which stands at the mouth of the Moche River, 350 miles north of Lima. This "Pyramid of the Sun" is 135 feet high and has a base covering 12½ acres. Built of sun-dried brick rather than stone, these monuments have suffered greatly from erosion. Royal tombs were cut into the base of pyramids and sealed. One tomb that escaped detection by robbers and was opened by archeologists in 1987 yielded a store of jewelry, gold objects including figures of animals, warriors, and deities, musical instruments, and a solid gold headdress two feet wide—rivaling treasures from the tomb of the Egyptian pharoah Tutankhamen.

Following the Moche era the Tiahuanacan culture spread throughout the entire northern Andean region. From their center on the shores of Lake Titicaca in western Bolivia the Tiahuanacans dominated surrounding areas for four centuries (600–1000 A.D.). They produced the most massive architecture of the Western Hemisphere, erecting temples and fortifications with gigantic stones that would challenge modern earth-moving machinery, yet put in place without the aid of derrick or pulley. A sunken temple in the ancient capital, Tiahuanaco, has been restored by the Bolivian government. Effective organizers, the Tiahuanacans were the first people to impose their culture over the entire central Andean highlands.

Of the ancient American civilizations, the greatest in territorial extent, and the one with the most tightly knit society, was developed by the Incas of South America. It embraced the ranges and plateaus of the Andes, the mountainous heart of the continent, and at its height included most of the present countries of Peru, Ecuador, Bolivia, and the northern portions of Argentina and Chile. To convert such a rocky terrain into productive cropland and to unify a territory so fragmented by geography was a challenging task, yet it was successfully accomplished. Obviously the Incas were indebted to a long line of predecessors, most immediately to the Tiahuanacans, from whom they borrowed both architectural techniques and patterns of social organization. Inca civilization represents an evolutionary apex and, though destined for destruction, it left an enduring mark upon the area it once occupied.

The ascendancy of the Incas began about 1100 A.D. and reached its peak in the late fifteenth century. Although embracing a wide territory, the Inca dominions never constituted an "empire" as the Spanish conquerors assumed. Basically the nation was a confederation of tribes, which in turn were composed of clans. Each tribe was governed by a council of elders. In spite of this seemingly democratic structure the whole society was effectively centralized under the control of a royal family. The ruler, whose title "Inca" has come to designate the people and their culture, was reputed to be descended from the sun god. In order to maintain the purity of his divine lineage, the Inca sometimes married his sister, as had been the custom with ancient Egyptian phar-

Diorama of Inca Life in the Urubamba Valley near Cuzco (Peru) (mid-fifteenth century). Note the suspension bridge, the terraced cropland, the pack train stopping for refreshment, the village and market in the background, and the temple and fortress above the village.

aohs. He also usually took a number of concubines, whose offspring were counted among the royal family. Thus the "children of the Sun" came to include a large group, a privileged aristocracy. The ruler's far-reaching personal authority rested upon his military and his religious attributes.

Agriculture as practiced by the Incas represents a triumph of will and energy over nature. Cutting through solid rock and leveling steep inclines to terrace the sides of mountains, they brought under cultivation an area larger than is tilled today. Besides corn, their crops included the potato, an indigenous plant, and various others. Domesticated mountain animals—the alpaca and the llama—provided meat, hides, and wool, and the llama made a dependable beast of burden.

Incan agriculture

While displaying artistic talent in superb pottery, textile designs, and metalwork, the Incas, perpetuating the Tiahuanacan tradition, shone particularly as builders on a grand scale. They were the outstanding engineers among Indian peoples, in this respect suggesting a mentality akin to that of the ancient Romans. Their capital at Cuzco in Peru was surrounded by mammoth stone forts. They raised high walls of stone slabs fitted together so perfectly that they stood firmly without any mortar. They laid roadways over the mountains (narrow roads, since they had no wheeled vehicles), constructed bridges, tunnels, and aqueducts, and operated a postal network with human runners stationed close enough together to make rapid communication possible.

Incan accomplishments

Communication among the Inca. Regional and local administrators communicated with the capital by means of runners. The runner carries a *quipu* with the administrator's message and a conch to signal his passage.

AGOSTO
CHACRAIAPVI

The Sowing Season. Note that the digger in front wears a superior tunic and shoes; he is the local inspector of agriculture and works beside his neighbors.

The Incas were the most advanced of their contemporaries in medicine, especially surgery. Their surgeons could perform brain operations by cutting through the top of the skull. In spite of an obviously high mental endowment, they neglected to develop any system of writing. They produced no books nor a single inscription, but kept statistical records by means of rows of knotted strings of different colors. These knotted cords (*quipu*), although seemingly primitive, incorporated the principle of place-value, as in the Mayan vigesimal system[1] and served adequately not only for business but for archival purposes.

Religion included belief in the resurrection of the body and the concept of heaven and hell. The Incas acknowledged several deities but built temples only to the sun god, supposed progenitor of the royal race. In his temple, decorated with sheets of hammered gold, were stored the embalmed bodies of deceased Incas. Sometimes royal attendants and concubines were slaughtered to accompany an Inca to his tomb. In the temple also sacrifices of animals and occasionally of human beings were offered.

Inca society was one of the most rigidly structured ever to be found among human communities. Supreme power, vested in the ruler at the apex of the pyramid, descended through tribe and clan heads to reach the common people, grouped at the bottom in units of ten, each with a squad leader. The result was a social order almost totalitarian in structure but in theory and largely in practice dedicated to promoting the general welfare. To an almost unparalleled degree the Incas exemplified the cooperative ideal, especially in their system of agriculture, which has been described as an agrarian communism. The land, theoretically owned by the Inca, was distributed periodically and equitably and was worked in common under the eye of supervisors. Surplus crops and manufactured articles were stored in public warehouses, as was wool from the herds of llamas and alpacas, which were also sheared cooperatively. The surplus goods were released in times of scarcity. Both private property and freedom of choice were minimal. Occupations were generally hereditary, and all able-bodied persons performed assigned tasks under threat of severe punishment. This coercive social system yielded the benefits of high productivity, full employment, care for the aged and infirm, and an extremely low crime rate. It was a paradise of security but with little freedom. It tended toward uniformity and rigidity, with little scope for individual initiative. The social body was too dependent on the judgment of a single unchallengeable authority. This partly explains why the regime could be toppled by a small band of Spaniards after they had seized the Inca ruler.

Only very recently has it been learned that the civilizations nurtured in Mexico and Central America were far from being the oldest in

[1] See below, p. 582.

the New World. The first identifiable advanced culture to appear in lands bordering the Gulf of Mexico or the Caribbean Sea was that of the Olmecs, who settled on the tropical Gulf Coast of Mexico between 1250 and 1150 B.C. Recently an Olmec site dated at 1200 B.C. has been discovered on the Pacific side of Mexico close to Acapulco. The most striking remains of the Olmec civilization is a group of fourteen gigantic stone heads, each six to nine feet high and weighing ten to forty tons, and displaying faces of African type, distinct from those of any American Indian people. This remarkable characteristic was long dismissed as a puzzling coincidence, but archeological research begun in the late 1930s points to the conclusion that the Olmecs actually came from the continent of Africa.[2] It has been demonstrated that small wooden ships of the type used by Bronze Age navigators could have been carried by prevailing Atlantic Ocean currents from the shores of western Europe or Africa to the northern coast of South America or into the Gulf of Mexico. In addition to the great stone heads, in the coastal regions occupied by the Olmecs dozens of terracotta sculptures with the same facial characteristics and a Negroid hair texture have been discovered. Olmec decorative and ceremonial motifs seem to be linked both to an Egyptian pattern and to that of succeeding early American cultures. The Olmecs erected pyramids with a north-south alignment, made paper out of wood pulp, and used hieroglyphic symbols not found elsewhere in the Western Hemisphere. Other motifs, shared with contemporary or later societies, may represent original contributions: purple as a sacred color, ceremonial feathered fans, a man-jaguar god, perhaps even the cult of the plumed serpent. Examination of a jaguar-headed stone pillar bearing numerical notations suggests that the highly complex calendar of the Mayas may have had its beginning here. Although the Olmecs retained their distinct identity for but a few centuries, they not only made lasting contributions to later cultures but also injected an African strain into America's earliest civilizations.

Olmec Colossal Head 1, San Lorenzo, Veracruz. Dating from about 900 B.C., this nine-foot, four-inch basalt sculpture—believed to portray an Olmec ruler—was fashioned without the aid of metal tools. The nearest basalt deposits were fifty miles away.

For a 600-year period beginning about 100 A.D., a brilliant civilization flourished in the central valley of Mexico. It is known as the Teotihuacán civilization after the name of its sacred city, located close to the present Mexico City, which at its height from the fourth through the sixth century held 200,000 inhabitants. Like contemporary civilizations of Mesopotamia, it was religion-based, governed under a rigid theocracy. As the cultural center of the Indian world for several centuries, Teotihuacán contributed heavily to the Indian religious heritage. Its artisans erected huge stone pyramids, larger than the pyramids of Egypt but formed of smaller stones, covered with stucco, and decorated. Also in contrast to pyramids of the Nile Valley, the Teotihuacán

Teotihuacán civilization

---

[2] This thesis is ably supported by an American anthropologist and linguist: Ivan van Sertima, *They Came Before Columbus: The African Presence in Ancient America,* New York, 1977.

View of Teotihuacán, the Heart of the Earliest High Civilization of Central Mexico.
Laid out on a grid plan, the city covered more than nine square miles. The
"Pyramid of the Sun" was 200 feet high and 700 feet wide. The Teotihuacán
civilization flourished between 100 and 600 A.D.. (Courtesy of René Millon)

structures were temples rather than tombs. The carvings and colored
frescoes that adorned the temples and other stone buildings—portions
of which have been excavated and restored—were magnificent. The
Teotihuacán people worshiped the plumed-serpent god Quetzalcoatl,
whose cult became universal in Mesoamerica.

After Teotihuacán was conquered by invaders from the north about
700 A.D., its culture declined. Two centuries later another warrior folk

Toltec contributions gained control of the valley of Mexico. These were the Toltecs, who
by the year 950 had established a center at Tula (50 miles north of
Mexico City) and also had expanded southward and eastward to occupy
Guatemala and the Yucatán peninsula of Mexico. Inferior in attainments to the Teotihuacán folk, the Toltecs were nevertheless important as transmitters of culture to neighboring peoples. Even after their
power was broken, in the latter half of the twelfth century, they were
long respected as an aristocracy of warriors. The Toltecs absorbed
elements of Teotihuacán civilization, but their art was cruder and their
society was militaristic rather than theocratic. They also practiced human
sacrifice. One of their few original contributions was a game played
on a large court with a rubber ball, which became popular throughout
Mesoamerica. More significant was their embellishment of the Quetzalcoatl cult. An elaborate mythology, based on Toltec tradition,
eventually grew up around the plumed-serpent deity. He was identified as a culture bearer and teacher who had been driven from the

capital, Tula, by a rival warrior god. After much wandering he allegedly burned himself to death, and his flaming heart became the planet Venus. Other legends told how Quetzalcoatl had created mankind out of bones snatched from the Lord of Dead Land.

The Mesoamerican civilization that reached the highest intellectual development was produced by the Mayas, who were probably most indebted to the Olmecs for the foundations of their culture. In their migration southward, the Mayas traversed territory occupied by the Olmecs and settled on the Mexican Gulf coastal plain. By the beginning of the Christian era they had reached the highlands of Guatemala, and here their culture matured. Many living Guatemalans are of Mayan descent, and still speak Mayan dialects. The civilization reached a peak during the period 300–900 A.D., at which time it also spread to the Yucatán peninsula of Mexico. After a century of adversity or obscurity, it rose to another climax in the eleventh and twelfth centuries, when it was fused with Toltec elements. Toltec warriors, already established in the interior of Mexico, entered Yucatán about 950, occupying Chichén Itzá, a chief cult site of the Mayas. Hence the final phase of Mayan civilization is called Maya-Toltec. For several centuries Chichén Itzá in Yucatán remained a brilliant center of worship, ceremonial display, and artistic production, but by the time of the Spaniards' arrival it had lost its vigor.

The Mayas in Mexico and Guatemala

Although their civilization rested on agriculture, like others throughout the world, the Mayas employed primitive methods of cultivation. They had no draft animals, no domesticated animals except dogs and fowls. None of the Indian peoples possessed the wheel. And with the Mayas as with their contemporaries, most individuals lived in miserable homes of mud or reed with thatched roofs. Imposing stone structures, exhibiting a high level of architectural skill, were exclusively for the use of the ruler or for public, especially religious, functions. Remains of the great terraced pyramids that once dotted the landscapes of Mexico and Central America rank among the wonders of the world. But Mayan genius was less evident in technology than in intellectual and artistic fields. Their artistry is shown in wall frescoes, stone sculpture and wood carvings, polychrome pottery, and beautifully dyed textiles. As scientists they excelled in mathematics and astronomy. They kept accurate chronological records, inscribed on stone calendar pillars.

Characteristics of Mayan civilization

The Mayan calendar was a truly remarkable invention. Most of the Indian peoples, in the Northern Hemisphere as well as the Southern, had ingenious methods of recording the passage of time. The Toltecs used a solar calendar, with a 365-day year and provision for an extra day every fourth year. The Mayan device went beyond the solar calendar in complexity, sophistication, and mathematical symmetry. The Mayans were fascinated with the phenomenon of time, and they sought to correlate celestial time—movements of the heavenly bodies—with terrestrial time—historical human events. Thanks to the keenness of

The Mayan calendar

Mural from the Temple of the Warriors at Chichén Itzá, Sacred City of the Maya-Toltec Culture (eleventh to the fourteenth centuries). This mural depicts the arrival of a force of Toltec warriors by sea to reconnoiter a Mayan town on the coast. The plumed serpent deity Quetzalcoatl hovers in the upper right of the painting. Other murals in the Temple of the Warriors tell of battles on land and sea, culminating in the defeat of the Mayas by the Toltecs.

Observatory at Chichén Itzá. The Mayas were skilled astronomers who coordinated their calendar with celestial phenomena.

their astronomers, they largely succeeded. Not only was the Mayan calendar more accurate than any used in Europe before the reform of the Julian calendar by Pope Gregory XIII in 1582, it was also a library of information, combining traditional ritual, mythology, and historical narrative with seasonal and astronomical data. Working from an arbitrary fixed date (identified as August 10, 3113 B.C.), Mayan reckoners were able to determine individual days in any year, counting backward or forward from the immovable base date. Moreover, a single calendrical inscription, while naming the exact day or night of an event, correlated it with planetary phases, the age of the moon, eclipse periods, and other phenomena. The ability to record an enormous amount of precise data in limited space was made possible by a system of place notation. Using the concept of zero (grouping numbers in units of 20 rather than 10, as in the decimal system), the Mayas assigned a particular value to each space on a column of figures. Thus, in a way analogous to the operation of every mechanical counting machine from simple abacus to electronic calculator, by displaying several parallel rows on a chart they could convey exact notions of quantity, duration, or rank without needing a large assortment of symbols.

Knowledge of place-value arithmetic among Indians was not confined to the Mayas, but they were the only people who developed a *notational* system whereby calculations could be recorded and *read*. It was from their calendar and its notational scheme that the Mayas evolved the system of writing that constitutes their crowning achievement. By gradually expanding calendrical statements they learned to depict essential, and even auxiliary, parts of speech. Pictographic in origin, like the Egyptian hieroglyphics, the Mayan script employed some 600 characters, of which about 10 percent represented spoken sounds rather than words or objects. Having grasped the principle of phonetics, the Mayas conceivably might have developed a true alphabet if their culture had endured. In addition to stone inscriptions, they produced illuminated books with characters written on deerskin and paper made from the fiber of the maguey plant. The script has not yet been fully deciphered, and, regrettably, all but fragments of the manuscripts were destroyed after the Spanish conquest.

The Mayan system of writing

To the Mayan people religion must have seemed of overwhelming importance. Their centers of dense population were not cities but the sites of temple-crowned pyramids, where sacred rites were performed. Their chief deities were spirits of the forest and sky (the planet Venus was "Lord Big Eye") and the rain god, vital to the securing of crops. Human sacrifices were sometimes offered to the rain god, typically by throwing a virgin into a well (she might be rescued if the god showed his satisfaction by not drowning her). Highly venerated was the plumed- or feathered-serpent deity, god of the sky and thunder, known to the Toltecs and Aztecs as Quetzalcoatl but as Kukulkan

Mayan religion

Temple I at Tikal (Guatemala), the largest site in the Maya area. This 155-foot-high pyramid temple with stelae in the foreground, located 225 miles southwest of Chichén Itzá, has proven to be a rich source of archaeological evidence. In 1962 a tomb was discovered under the temple which contained jade and shell ornaments, food-filled pottery vessels, and a striking collection of bone tubes and strips with scenes of gods and men incised upon them.

to the Mayas, who regarded him as benevolent. According to their legends, he had once lived on earth as a man, had taught their ancestors the arts of civilization, and would one day come again to save his people.

The latest, but by no means greatest, of the culture complexes indigenous to the Americas was that of the Aztecs, who dominated the central valley of Mexico for a century and a half while Mayan civilization was in decline. Like the Toltecs who had come before them and to whom they were related, the Aztecs migrated southward into Mexico, conquering and merging with the tribes they encountered. About 1325 they established their headquarters on the site of Mexico City. Tenochtitlán, as the Aztecs named it, was created by and was the focal center for twenty federated tribes rather than the capital of a kingdom as the Spanish conquerors supposed. Its high altitude (7,000 feet above sea level), moderate climate, and proximity to rich agricultural land gave it an ideal location. The city was situated on marshy ground, but this was turned to advantage by constructing dikes, causeways, and canals. Its streets, paved with stone, were kept scrupulously clean by an efficient public-works department, and fresh water was supplied by an aqueduct. Under the Aztecs the city attained a population of some 200,000.

Aztec culture was essentially a synthesis of elements derived from others, with a coarsening of certain features. The Aztecs used a crude form of picture writing and produced some written books, few of which have survived. They adopted the Toltec solar calendar which, although inferior to the Mayan, enabled them to record dates accurately. The famous Aztec Calendar Stone (now in the Mexican National Museum), weighing twenty tons, originally stood in front of the Temple

The Aztec Calendar Stone. The priests of Tenochtitlán performed animal and human sacrifices on this disk. These sacrifices were thought to sustain the sun on its course.

The Death God Back-to-Back with Quetzalcoatl, the God of Life. This page from the *Codex Borgia* illustrates the dual aspect of existence.

of the Sun and presumably served as an altar for human sacrifice. It should be noted that, although none went so far as the Mayas in the development of writing, most of the Indian peoples, including the Aztecs, invested their calendars with elaborate symbolic decorations that illustrate aspects of their rituals and traditions. The Aztec Calendar Stone depicts a mythical history of the world, with four cycles of creation and catastrophe. Aztec craftsmen were skillful workers in copper, gold, and silver, and produced delicate mosaics of stone and shell. Their pottery, textiles, and feathered ornaments bear comparison with the Mayan. The Aztecs also continued the prevalent architectural tradition of pyramid building, terracing the sloping sides so cleverly that the structure appeared to soar into the sky. The great pyramid-temple of Tenochtitlán was surrounded by high walls decorated with sculptured serpents. All these, together with the residence of the ruler and his chieftains ("the Halls of Montezuma") have disappeared, but the base of the pyramid serves as the main square of Mexico city.

The derivative character of Aztec culture

Granted that they possessed artistic talent and engineering skill, the Aztecs were basically a society of warriors. Every man was either a soldier or a priest. They fought continually, were cruel to the vanquished, and inflicted harsh punishments upon transgressors within their own society. Aztec religion also reveals an accent on violence. In

A society of warriors

586

*The Americas and Africa before
the Age of European Overseas
Expansion*

their pantheon the benevolent serpent deity Quetzalcoatl was subordinate to the sun god and the war god. And while many Indian tribes resorted to human sacrifice, the Aztecs made the practice almost the basis of their religion. One purpose of their frequent wars was to capture humans for sacrifice, and though the number of victims is not known with certainty, it must have been large.

*Common features of the
early American
civilizations*

Differing as they did in particulars, the early American civilizations shared several common features. There are marked similarities in religious belief, in technique, and in decorative style. None developed the concept of the state to any extent. All were based in principle upon kinship groups—clans, tribes, and confederations. More important was the universal and deeply rooted belief that land belonged to the community as a whole and should therefore be worked for the common benefit. Forms of landholding varied, but in none of the Indian societies was land bought and sold nor was it used to produce crops to be sold for profit. The Spanish and Portuguese conquerors found it hard to uproot this tradition of common as opposed to individual ownership and never entirely succeeded. Taken collectively, the native American civilizations, reaching their height somewhat later than those of the Nile, Tigris-Euphrates, and Indus river valleys, stood not too far below them, at least in potential for future progress. Their extinction under the impact of a totally alien culture must be numbered among the world's losses.

2. EXPANSION AND MATURING OF AFRICAN CIVILIZATIONS

*New patterns of political
economy and social
organization*

Iron technology, the domestication of plants and animals, and new food crops greatly accelerated population growth and mobility in sub-Saharan Africa. Iron Age peoples bearing metal hoes and cutlasses formed compact villages and developed patterns of communally organized agriculture. Where minerals and good soils were limited, societies remained small-scaled and relatively undifferentiated. Other societies became more stratified in areas of fertile soil or abundant iron, copper, or gold. The new political economies, though rooted in pre–Iron Age egalitarian beliefs, were based on an unequal sharing of resources and wealth. Indeed, the management of inequality emerged as a central theme in this period (1000 - 1500).

*Mechanisms for continuity
and social control*

Secret societies and religious cults became key instruments for controlling the new social order and for maintaining a sense of continuity. Exclusive in membership, they served as a powerful acculturative mechanism for their members and their families. The organizations cut across lineages and gradually extended into neighboring communities. They also tended to be gender-exclusive and stratified by age, with the elders commanding greater authority.

This was an era of unprecedented cultural exchange and synthesis.

Iron Age populations fanned out from the river valleys to cultivate higher, drier lands along the watersheds. Patterns of economic interdependence at first emerged from the interaction of densely populated lakeside, riverside, and coastal fishing communities with dry-land farming and herding counterparts. But in many areas, the more mobile pastoralists gradually gained political ascendancy. Interestingly, they concocted largely mythical stories to explain and to justify the process. These fascinating myths of origin, often borrowed in whole or part from conquered peoples, became unwritten charters of governance.

*Increased cultural
exchange and economic
interdependence*

A striking similarity and continuity of fundamental cultural and agricultural traditions eventually prevailed across a vast area of open savanna and woodland, from West Africa through south central Africa. Sharing common themes but exhibiting seemingly infinite ethnic and regional variations, diverse cultures expressed their power, wisdom, and values through panoplies of icons, proverbs, legends, and myths of origin or creation. Inexplicably, one community underwent dramatic transformations while its neighbor seemed frozen in time. A few Stone Age and early Iron Age communities survived into the twentieth century. But most were assimilated or disappeared altogether, leaving only a faint legacy in the vocabulary or physical features of their successors.

*Cultural continuities
punctuated by ethnic and
regional variations*

By 1300, most African languages had acquired their modern form. For example, over 400 language clusters and thousands of dialects evolved from possibly a single original Bantu language. Many of them became mutually unintelligible, but they at least shared a common root and subtle similarities in structure and vocabulary.

*Development of African
languages*

It was during this era that the foundations of the traditional religious systems of modern Africa took shape. Animism, or worship of natural objects, remained all-pervasive. However, many cultures had begun to adopt more elaborate notions of ancestor veneration and of worship of a supreme being whom they perceived as a creative, life-sustaining force. In isolated communities, extremely complex cosmologies, based in part on a remarkably accurate understanding of stellar bodies, were evolved by local priests and priestesses.

Religious developments

In the secular realm, the basic modes of agricultural and industrial production were well established by 1100 A.D., though with substantial regional variations, conditioned by climate, soils, topography, and the dreaded tsetse fly which brought death to cattle and horses. But the social and gender divisions of labor became more pronounced. Men continued to hunt, fish, clear land, and provide security. But women now began to perform most of the agricultural tasks, ranging from planting to harvesting and, in some cultures, to the marketing of produce. Some gained control of local markets, though long-distance trade, a feature in many parts of Africa after 400 A.D., was male-dominated. Men also controlled mining, metallurgy, and, in most cases, cattle. These three elements became vital keys to power in the second

*Division of labor by gender
and specialization*

millennium A.D. With cattle, men acquired more wives and expanded the size of their familial work force. With heavy metals, they obtained imported luxuries. Thus, with few exceptions, most notably agriculture, men generally gained superior access to the sources of power and wealth. Occupational specialization assumed greater importance in numerous skilled fields, especially in iron-working and pottery. For the first time south of the equator, artisans devoted full time to specific trades and passed their secrets on to their own children. There appeared endogamous families of metallurgists, musicians, storytellers, salt-makers, wood-carvers, jewelers, and weavers.

Expansion of mining and trade

Mining and marketing activity expanded significantly in the more densely populated regions. Mineral output greatly increased in the thirteenth century with the shift from alluvial to reef mining. By the fourteenth century, the mining and fabrication of iron, copper, and gold had become firmly established and more proficient in the major mineral zones in the western Sudan, northern Angola, southern Zaire, and Zambia. Cattle also increased the possibility of accumulating wealth and provided a dynamic stimulus to migration and innovation. This output spawned networks of long-distance trade that radiated from isolated communities of market-oriented producers. Mechanisms other than barter evolved for the exchange of goods. These included copper ingots, iron bars, gold dust, and fine cowry and nzimbu shells. Indeed, currency was a concept that spread far beyond the limits of the Muslim and Christian worlds. Copper, especially, became a standard against which everything else could be measured—a currency of exchange as well as an item of barter. In central Africa, copper became central to art as well as to the commercial economy and was used in the fabrication of wire bracelets and bridal rings, objects to enhance power and prestige, and as such much of it was buried with the dead. Until the nineteenth century, only a minority of Africans were directly affected by these transformations, for most societies were not market oriented and existed mainly within closed systems of barter.

The growth of slavery within Africa

The growth of trade encouraged the spread and intensification of voluntary and involuntary forms of dependency. Domestic or household servitude became common in scattered societies, though human bondage remained a marginal feature in most societies until the late eighteenth century. Domestic slaves could become prosperous, powerful, and even acquire servants for themselves. Nevertheless, most slaves were chattel, or property, and enjoyed few rights to their own bodies or to freedom of movement. Moreover, they had no paternity or kin group, and few laws existed through which they could seek protection and succor. In effect, they were outsiders, usually excluded from free societies' rituals and burials. Fortunately, many cultures made provision for their gradual incorporation into the institutions of the host society. This process could take generations, and the social stigma of servile origins often remained. Agricultural slaves, war captives, and kidnap victims fared less well. They were often sold into the international slave trade. Before 1450, the Islamic world was virtually the only external influence in Africa, and Muslims became deeply involved in the slave trade, which greatly accelerated from the twelfth century.

Between 1300 and 1500, slaving and the slave trade became a basic feature of society in North Africa, Ethiopia, along the East African coast, and in the West African savannah. Some North Africans boasted of owning more than 5,000 slaves at one time. Before the era of the Atlantic slave trade, slaves continued to be a major export from the Nile Valley and Ethiopian highlands to Egypt, Arabia, and India. From about 650 A.D. to 1500, approximately 7 million people—the majority of them female—were sold and transported across the Sahara into North Africa to serve in harems and as household servants. Another estimated 2 million were taken from East Africa and sold into Arabian and Indian markets.

*The expansion of the
slave trade*

By 1000 A.D., many positions of authority had become institutionalized and hereditary, and within another half century the line of succession was shifting in some areas from matrilineal to patrilineal, especially in societies affected by Islam. Conflict and competition grew over rights to land and water resources. By 1500 real political power in many parts of sub-Saharan Africa had shifted from kinship-based fertility priests and priestesses to territorially based chiefs. The old cults survived but were grafted onto, or were co-opted by, the new system of authority as chiefs and kings forged alliances with the lead-

Shifts in political power

Slave Market at Zabid in Yemen (thirteenth century). The slave trade from the Horn of Africa to the Arabian peninsula was of great antiquity and involved Arabian as well as African traders.

State formation in the West African Sudan

Ghana's wealth based mainly on gold exports

The Almoravids overrun Ghana

The Almoravid movement

ers of the past. With some major exceptions, the political and economic roles of women in society, perhaps less visible now, and in some ways less powerful, were more subtly articulated in their capacities as queen mothers, market "mammies," senior wives, and priestesses in important cults.

The growth of trade and the increased power of secular chiefs contributed greatly to an accelerated process of state formation in black Africa. Chieftaincies in many areas were consolidated under divine kings. Numerous kingdoms evolved into expansive territorial empires, embracing a rich diversity of cultures, languages, and religious systems. The process of empire-building was most pronounced in the savannah, or Sudanic zone of West Africa.

Trans-Saharan trade expanded at a rapid rate after the eighth century, due in large measure to the initiative of Muslim Arabs and Berbers. Between the eleventh and seventeenth centuries, West Africa played a vital role in the monetarization of the medieval Mediterranean economy and in the maintenance of its trade with South Asia and beyond. Gold exports greatly increased after 1252, when the ore began to replace silver as Europe's main currency. The growing demands from European and North African merchants for gold motivated West Africans to organize themselves on a larger, more efficient scale in order to meet these demands. Ghana's armies, under a black Soninke dynasty, captured the prosperous Berber trading center of Audoghast in the tenth century. Successive Ghanaian monarchs grew immensely rich by tightly controlling the flow of gold across their territory. A production tax was placed on gold exports and nuggets of a certain size were hoarded in order to keep the mineral rare. Ghana's hegemony extended to the upper Niger and Senegal rivers and to the burgeoning commercial centers of Timbuktu, Djenné, and Gao.

Ghana was not a Muslim empire, but its principal customers and those who controlled the strategic desert oases had become Muslims by the tenth century. Rulers in neighboring Takrur accepted Islam about 1000 A.D. and thus became West Africa's first kingdom to do so. Ghana itself had become dangerously dependent on Muslim financial advisers and merchants. Its pagan king was eventually forced to divide the capital city of Kumbi-Saleh into two parts, one for Muslims, the other for pagans.

Islam, the handmaiden of West African commerce, could not be contained. By 1054, large bands of nomadic Muslim Berbers had declared a holy war, or *jihad,* and succeeded in recapturing the vital Audoghast markets. Ghana, on the Saharan fringe, had already been weakened by environmental deterioration brought on by overgrazing of pastures and failure to rotate crops. Its capitulation to these puritanical Berber Muslims, called Almoravids, seemed almost inevitable. But the Almoravids brought insecurity to Ghanaian market places and fear along the caravan routes. This condition upset the delicate trade balance between the forest gold miners, the Ghanaian middlemen, and

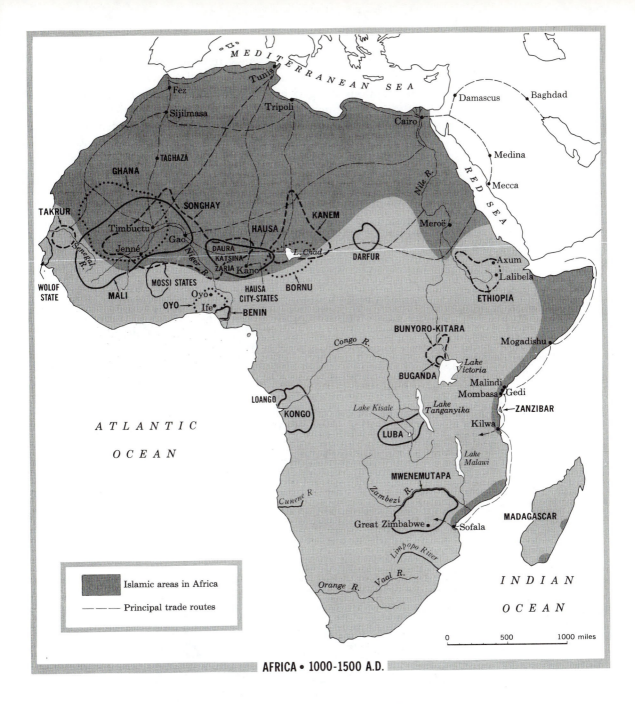

AFRICA • 1000-1500 A.D.

Islamic areas in Africa

Principal trade routes

the North African caravan operators. Indeed, Ghana emerged from the Almoravid movement in such a weakened condition that peripheral chieftaincies were able to secede. One of these vassal chieftaincies sacked the Ghanaian capital in 1224 and enslaved the ruling family. A decade later the victor himself succumbed to the superior magic of a Ghanaian royal hostage, named Sunjata.

Ghana was finished, but a new territorial empire called Mali was forged by the magician Sunjata, who is still regarded in Western Sudanic folk traditions as a god-hero and founding father. By gaining control of the gold-producing regions, Sunjata could attract the caravan traffic formerly monopolized by Ghana. The oral record also reveals that Sunjata expanded agriculture by introducing the cultivation and weaving of cotton.

Mansa Musa

Under Mansa Musa (1312–1337) Mali's authority reached into the middle Niger city-states of Timbuktu, Djenné, and Gao. He put Mali on the European world maps by performing a stunning gold-laden pilgrimage to Mecca, Islam's spiritual capital in the Middle East. Upon returning, Mansa Musa fostered the growth of Islam by constructing magnificent mosques in the major urban centers. With his seemingly inexhaustible supply of gold he commissioned Spanish and Middle Eastern scholars and architects to transform Malian cities into great seats of Islamic learning. Leading intellectuals were sent to Morocco and Egypt for higher studies, and at Timbuktu foundations were laid for a university at the famed Sankoré mosque. For decades after Musa, Mali enjoyed a reputation in the Muslim world for high standards of public morality and scholarship as well as for law, order, and security. People and goods flowed freely, enabling the cosmopolitan cities of Timbuktu, Djenné, and Gao to flower into major market centers. Through the leadership of Sunjata and Mansa Musa Islam became more deeply implanted among the elite and spread widely in the important towns.

Sunni Ali and the formation of Songhay

While Mansa Musa made great advances in establishing an efficient administrative bureaucracy, he neglected to develop a formula for succession. Court intrigue and factional disputes followed the death of each Mansa. Inevitably, central authority weakened. Gao seceded in 1375 and under Sunni Ali (1464–1492) it blossomed into an expansive territorial empire called Songhay.

As in Muslim India, it was not uncommon for slaves in Africa to

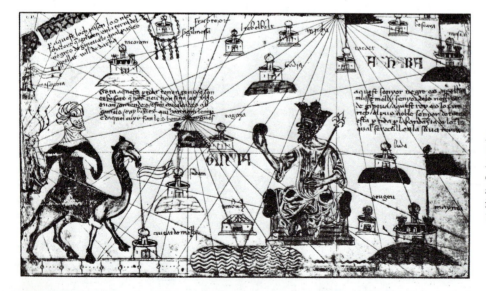

Mansa Musa of Mali Waiting to Receive a Muslim Trader. Detail of the Catalan Atlas, a map drawn on the island of Majorca in 1375.

assume considerable administrative and military responsibilities and on occasion to usurp authority. This happened in Songhay in 1493 when a high-ranking Muslim slave, named Muhammad Touré, staged a brilliant palace coup. Lacking traditional legitimacy rooted in a pagan past, he promoted Islamic practices and found Islam an invaluable instrument for political and cultural control. Using the praise-title of "Askia," Muhammad Touré (1493–1528) extended Songhay's frontiers deep into the strategic Saharan oases, across the middle Niger to include Mali, and eastward to the emporiums of Hausaland. He then created a labyrinthine bureaucracy with ministries for the army, navy, fisheries, forests, and taxation. Songhay itself was decentralized into provinces, each ruled by a governor chosen from among the Askia's family or royal followers. Muhammad Touré also established vast plantations, worked by slaves under conditions sometimes approaching those in the southern United States before the Civil War.

To facilitate commerce, Muhammad Touré introduced a unified system of weights and measures and appointed market inspectors to protect consumers. The Sankoré mosque at Timbuktu was transformed into an institution comparable to the great European universities of the later Middle Ages, with schools of theology, jurisprudence, mathematics, and medicine. On his pilgrimage to Mecca in 1497 he befriended world-famous Muslim scholars. A few of them returned with him to Songhay as advisers on government and religion. And like the earlier Mali empire, Songhay established diplomatic relations with Morocco and Egypt, its major trading partners.

Islamic institutions of law, education, and taxation were deeply rooted in the major urban areas by the close of Askia Muhammad's rule in 1528. However, Islam was but a thin veneer elsewhere. Fully 95 percent of the population, consisting of rural peasants and petty chiefs, continued to follow traditional animistic beliefs and life styles. Nevertheless, in spite of serious internal divisions between Islam and the traditional ways, Songhay continued to prosper, reaching its zenith under Askia Daud (1549–1582). Stretching from the snow-capped Atlas Mountains of North Africa to the tropical Cameroon forests and embracing thousands of different cultures, it was clearly one of the world's most expansive empires.

Songhay had overextended itself; and although its armies numbered more than 35,000, it could not keep the outlying regions in subjection. Its vital eastern markets were lost when several Hausa city-states reasserted their independence. In the northwest, Morocco, after defeating the Portuguese, sought direct control over Songhay's mines. Crack Songhay cavalry and archers were no match for Moroccan cannons and imported European arquebuses. After Songhay's defeat by the Moroccans in 1591, the empire—and indeed western Sudanic civilization—rapidly disintegrated. The Moroccans and their Portuguese mercenaries, unable to locate the gold mines or to maintain security

594

*The Americas and Africa before
the Age of European Overseas
Expansion*

*The emergence of Hausa
kingdoms*

*Islamic penetration and
commercial expansion*

Kanem-Bornu

Gobireau Mosque, Katsina (northern Nigeria). This mosque was built in the fifteenth century, when the Hausa kingdoms shared strong cultural and economic ties with Songhay. It is constructed of mud mixed with a vegetable matter (katse) and oxen blood.

on the roads and in the markets, abandoned Songhay altogether in 1612. Political anarchy filled the vacuum, the great cities declined, and trade and Muslim scholarship drifted eastward to the city-states of Hausaland in what is today northern Nigeria and the Niger Republic.

By the twelfth century, uncoordinated self-governing villages in Hausaland had coalesced into centralized kingdoms under semidivine dynasties. These kingdoms, though politically autonomous, shared a common Hausa language and cultural heritage. Daura, the founding kingdom, exercised a vague spiritual suzerainty over the others.

Islam had begun to penetrate Hausa aristocratic and trading circles in the fourteenth century. After 1452, the rural areas experienced a steady influx of red-skinned Fulani herdsmen, who for centuries had been migrating eastward from the Senegal River. The Fulani, who were fervent Muslims, brought religious books and established new centers of Islamic learning. At this time, Hausaland was experiencing a commercial revolution with the opening of the kola trade with farmers of the southern forests. In Kano, Katsina, and Zaria, huge markets emerged as traders from disintegrating Songhay shifted their operations to the more secure walled towns of Hausaland.

Hausaland was exceptionally secure, thanks to the military protection offered by the wealthy and powerful kingdom of Kanem-Bornu, lying eastward near Lake Chad. Kanem-Bornu's geographical position placed it at the gateway to the West African Sudan. Its stable dynasty gained power in 846 A.D. and embraced Islam in 1087. Under Mai Idris Alooma (1580–1617) Kanem-Bornu reached its peak. Alooma established diplomatic relations with Turkey, which had recently captured Tunis in North Africa from Spain. With Turkish advisers, Alooma bureaucratized his government and set it on firm Islamic foundations. A high court of law was organized and staffed by judges who dispensed only Muslim law. The army was equipped with Turkish muskets. The thirteenth-century hostel in Cairo for Bornuese pilgrims and scholars was greatly expanded. Hausaland, sandwiched between Songhay and Bornu, was commercially exploited by both neighbors, but it received considerable cultural enrichment from pilgrims passing through en route to Mecca.

After Songhay's collapse in 1591, trade shifted not only to Hausaland but also toward the southern forests. Between 1000 and 1500 A.D. the forest people of modern Nigeria experienced new infusions of grasslanders from the Sudanic zone. Leading lineages were transformed into ruling dynasties. They in turn fused scattered villages under priests and elders into small city-states. Ile Ife exercised the same kind of spiritual hegemony for the Yoruba settlers that Daura held for the Hausa in the north. Yoruba warriors from Ile Ife fanned out and established subordinate dynasties at Oyo, Benin, and elsewhere. Under Eware the Great (1440–1473) Benin city expanded into a territorial forest empire. Benin and Ife became centers of high civilization. Their craft guilds produced naturalistic busts and plaques cast in bronze through the lost wax process. Eware encouraged ivory and wood carving and created a national orchestra. All these secular innovations were aimed at glorifying the ruling families. Art was no longer simply for life's adornment. It now upheld authority and graced the hallways of the sprawling Yoruba palaces.

In the hinterlands of modern Ghana, a similar though unrelated political process had begun not long before 1400. Mande traders from old Mali and Songhay pushed southward in a quest for more gold. Stronger demands from North Africa and Europe encouraged them to establish small centers of exchange at the forest's edge. These burgeoning communities represented a curious blend of pagan and Islamic, of forest and Sudanic cultures. The forest people, called the Akan, reacted to this commercial challenge by forging mini-kingdoms at the crossroads of trading activity. Thus, the southward movement of trade stimulated the rise of forest-based states, which in the sixteenth century reached their zenith as new commercial opportunities emanated from Europeans on the coast.

It would be a mistake to assume that the arrival of Europeans on the coast and the emergence of the Atlantic trade put an end to the trans-Saharan traffic in slaves and manufactured goods. On the contrary, the Sudanic economies greatly profited from being couched between two vast trading networks emanating north and south. Sudanic merchants took advantage of the new commercial opportunities and many became wealthy and remarkably cosmopolitan. Hausa cities such as Kano developed huge markets where a vast diversity of goods were sold, including locally manufactured textiles and leather goods.

By the ninth century A.D., Afro-Arabs speaking Swahili, a Bantu-rooted language, had emerged along the northern coast of Kenya and Somalia in East Africa. The term *Swahili* is derived from the Arabic *swahila,* meaning "peoples of the coast." These peoples prospered on a lively trade with Persia and Arabia. They gradually extended their operations southward into Bantu fishing communities. Subsequently, as we saw in Chapter 11, the East African coast from Somalia southward received new arrivals. Some were Bantu from the interior, others were Shirazi Arabs from the Somali coast and Persian Gulf, and a few were from northwestern India. The non-African immigrants were sea-oriented merchants in search of African minerals, ivory, and slaves. The Bantu, with inland connections, were in an excellent position to supply their needs. By the twelfth century the Shirazi had founded a series of coastal Muslim city-states, extending southward to modern Mozambique. They married into local Bantu ruling families and initiated Islamic dynasties. Sofala and Kilwa, founded before the ninth century, became leading Afro-Asian towns and served as major outlets for gold and copper from the Zimbabwean and Katangan plateaus of the interior. Between the eleventh and fifteenth centuries a distinctive Swahili coastal civilization emerged. Swahili civilization grew out of the convergence of Bantu, Arab, and Indian cultures and languages. Swahili mosques, though reminiscent of those gracing the southern Arabian shores, were unique in form and construction.

The Akan forest states

The Griot, Africa's Historian. Daura Emirate. The Praise Singer is the traditional oral historian of African societies. African history has been passed from generation to generation by griots.

The emergence of Swahili civilization

Middleman position of the Swahili city-states

The Mwenemutapa empire and Great Zimbabwe

These mosques reflected a markedly coastal African architecture, based on rectangular lines and utilizing local coral, mangrove, and palm materials. The Swahili language, written in Arabic characters, was soft and melodic.

The Swahili city-states, like their Hausa counterparts, were Muslim, cosmopolitan, socially stratified, culturally homogeneous, yet politically independent of one another. They thrived on their middleman position between producers and consumers. Although Kilwa held commercial sway over Sofala intermittently from 1131 to 1333, it did not exhibit any expansionist tendencies. Rather, the various towns, like Mogadishu and Barawa (in modern Somalia), Gedi, Pate, Malindi, and Mombasa (Kenya), Zanzibar and Kilwa (Tanzania), and Sofala (Mozambique) engaged in vigorous competition with one another. Some towns even minted their own coins and maintained huge treasuries.

Gold and copper had opened south central Africa to the commercial and cultural influence of the Indian Ocean by 1000 A.D. Indian Ocean trade routes from Asia brought Persian pottery, Chinese porcelain, and Indian glassware to Zimbabwean elites. Some goods reached the prosperous fishing communities on Lake Kisale in eastern Zaire. Indian Ocean trade, like that of the trans-Sahara, encouraged African rulers to centralize their societies in order to better meet foreign demands. Indeed, coastal requests for Katangan copper and Zimbabwean gold led to a transition in leadership from ritual-bearing priests to secular kings commanding enormous military and economic power. Great Zimbabwe in the thirteenth century was the first state to consolidate.

Gedi. The ruins of this Afro-Arab town, founded in the early fourteenth century on the Kenya coast. This was the main entrance to the sultan's palace.

Great Zimbabwe. This 34-foot-high conical tower was probably a shrine in the heart of the Mwenemutapa Empire (fifteenth century). The tower and adjacent wall were constructed by placing stone upon stone without mortar.

Within two hundred years, Great Zimbabwe reached its peak of prosperity. Its power rested on control of the markets in cattle and gold. Great Zimbabwe's notions of divine kingship radiated gradually to other societies in the Zambezi valley and on the northern plateau. Great Zimbabwe, like other smaller *zimbabwes,* or "stone enclosures," were fortified with massive elliptical walls of carefully cut stone laid in place without mortar.

In the mid-fourth century A.D. the Axumite king Ezana converted to Christianity and made the faith the state religion in what then came to be called Ethiopia. Ethiopian clerics established churches and monasteries and received large tracts of land as gifts from the nobility and successive monarchs. Coptic Christianity, along with the institution of the monarchy, became powerful unifying forces. The monasteries emerged as centers of learning, and important religious texts were translated into Ge'ez, the language of the church hierarchy.

The Christian kingdoms of Northeast Africa

Shortly after Christianity became the state religion, Ethiopia conquered the neighboring empire of Kush, which was replaced by a number of smaller kingdoms collectively called Nubia. The seventh-century-A.D. Islamic expansion in North Africa led to the collapse of Christian Egypt and to Arab occupation of Persia and of Red Sea ports. In the same century, Beja nomads swept across the Eritrean plateau

Ethiopian expansion

598

*The Americas and Africa before
the Age of European Overseas
Expansion*

and cut Ethiopia off from Mediterranean and Middle Eastern trade and civilization. Ethiopia now expanded into the interior. In about 1100 A.D. its political center shifted southward from Axum to Lalibela in the almost inaccessible northwestern highlands. It became even more isolated from the Greco-Roman world after the conquest of the Nubian kingdoms by Arab rulers of Egypt in the late thirteenth and early fourteenth centuries. The early kingdom of Ethiopia reached its zenith in the fourteenth and fifteenth centuries with the conquest of non-Christian and non-Islamic states to the west. The church became a missionary agent for the monarchy by proselytizing and assimilating these conquered areas.

The Muslim threat

Islamic populations, both internal and foreign, continued to pressure the Christian regime. In the early fifteenth century centrifugal tendencies developed among local nobility. The neighboring state of Adal took advantage of this and proclaimed a jihad in 1529. It achieved a decisive victory over the Ethiopian emperor and brought much of his country under Muslim rule. Christian Ethiopia was saved from complete annihilation when Emperor Lebna Dengel, with the assistance of foreign Portuguese mercenaries, defeated the Muslims in 1541. With mixed success they also halted an invasion of pastoral Kushitic-speaking Galla peoples but were forced over subsequent centuries to share their lands with them. For the next three centuries, Ethiopia **retreated into a sullen xenophobia, marked by civil strife, warlords, economic stagnation, and ultimately the disintegration of central authority.**

Unrelated to these developments was the migration of Nilotic pastoralists into the fertile lands northwest of Lake Victoria in modern Uganda. Between the fourteenth and sixteenth centuries these immigrants, imbued with notions of divine kingship, married Bantu cultivators and established powerful kingdoms. These highly centralized polities, such as Bunyoro, Buganda, and Ankole, were non-Islamic, purely African creations.

SELECTED READINGS

• *Items so designated are available in paperback editions.*

AMERICA

• Coe, Michael D., *The Maya,* 4th ed., New York, 1987.
• Crow, John, *The Epic of Latin America,* 3d ed., Berkeley, 1980. Rich in detail.
 Fagg, J. E., *Latin America, a General History,* 3d ed., New York, 1977.
• Farris, Nancy, *Maya Society under Colonial Rule: The Collective Enterprise of Survival,* Princeton, 1984.
• Miller, Mary Ellen, *The Art of Mesoamerica from Olmec to Aztec,* New York, 1986.

- Morley, S. G., and G. W. Brainerd, *The Ancient Mayas,* 4th ed., Stanford, 1985.

  van Sertima, Ivan. *They Came Before Columbus,* New York, 1977.

  Weaver, Muriel, *The Aztecs, Maya, and Their Predecessors: Archaeology of Mesoamerica,* New York, 1972.

AFRICA

  Ade Ajayi, J. F., and I. Espie, eds., *A Thousand Years of West African History,* Ibadan, 1967.

  Bravmann, Rene A., *Islam and Tribal Art in West Africa,* Cambridge, 1979.

- Connah, Graham, *African Civilizations. Precolonial Cities and States in Tropical Africa: An Archeological Perspective,* Cambridge, 1987.

- Curtin, Philip, Steven Feierman, L. Thompson, and J. Vansina, *African History,* Madison, 1978.

  Davidson, Basil, *et al., The Growth of African Civilization: A History of West Africa 1000–1800,* London, 1966.

  Denyer, Susan, *African Traditional Architecture,* New York, 1978.

- Gillon, Werner, *A Short History of African Art,* New York, 1984.

  Gray, Richard, and David Birmingham, eds., *Pre-Colonial African Trade,* New York, 1970.

  Hountondji, Paulin J., *African Philosophy: Myth and Reality,* Bloomington, 1984.

- Hull, Richard W., *African Cities and Towns before the European Conquest,* New York, 1976.

  ———, *Munyakare: African Civilization before the Batuuree,* New York, 1972.

  Kilson, Martin, and Robert I. Rotberg, eds., *The African Diaspora,* Cambridge, 1977.

  Lewicki, Tadeusz, *West African Food in the Middle Ages,* Cambridge, 1974.

  Mair, Lucy, *African Kingdoms,* Oxford, 1977.

  Maquet, Jacques, *Civilizations of Black Africa,* New York, 1972.

- Mbiti, John S., *Introduction to African Religion,* London, 1975.

  Niane, D. T., ed., *UNESCO General History of Africa, IV: Africa from the Twelfth to the Nineteenth Century,* London, 1984.

- Nketia, J. H. Kwabena, *The Music of Africa,* New York, 1974.

  Ogot, B. A., and J. A. Kieran, eds., *Zamani: A Survey of East African History,* Nairobi, 1968.

  Pouwels, Randall, *Horn and Crescent: Cultural Change and Traditional Islam on the East African Coast, 800–1900,* London, 1986.

  Ranger, T. O., ed., *Aspects of Central African History,* London, 1969.

  Smith, Robert S., *Warfare and Diplomacy in Pre-Colonial West Africa,* London, 1976.

  Swartz, B. K., ed., *West African Culture Dynamics: Archaeological and Historical Perspectives,* The Hague, 1978.

SOURCE MATERIALS

  Brotherston, Gordon, *Image of the New World: The American Continent Portrayed in Native Texts,* London, 1979. Difficult but rewarding.

  Oliver, R., and G. Mathew, eds., *History of East Africa,* Vol. I, Oxford, 1968.

Part Four

THE EARLY-MODERN WORLD

Historians tend to agree that the Middle Ages ended sometime roughly around 1500 and were followed by an "early-modern" period of European history that lasted until the concurrent outbreaks of the French and Industrial Revolutions at the very end of the eighteenth century. As early as about 1350 in Italy representatives of a new cultural movement, usually called the Renaissance, began to challenge certain basic medieval assumptions and offer alternatives to medieval modes of literary and artistic expression. By around 1500 Renaissance ideals had not only triumphed fully in Italy, but they were also spreading to northern Europe where they were reconceived to produce the highly influential movement of Christian humanism. At the same time, in the early sixteenth century western Europe lost much of its medieval appearance by expanding and dividing. Intrepid mariners and conquista-dores *ended Europe's millennium of geographical self-containment by venturing onto the high seas of the Atlantic and Indian oceans and by planting Europe's flag throughout the world. Concurrently, however, Europe lost its religious uniformity as a result of the Protestant Reformation, which divided the Continent up into hostile religious camps. Thereafter, from about 1560 to about 1660 western Europe experienced a period of grave economic, political, and spiritual crisis but emerged from this century of testing with renewed energy and confidence. A commercial revolution spurred the development of overseas colonies and trade, and encouraged agricultural and industrial expansion. Though monarchs continued to meet with opposition from the various estates within their realms, they asserted their power as absolute rulers, stabilizing domestic unrest by continually expanding state bureaucracies.*

Warfare remained the chief instrument of their foreign policies; yet by the end of the period, the mutually recognized goal of those policies was more often the maintenance of a general balance of power than the pursuit of unrestrained aggrandizement. Finally, in the later seventeenth century the scientific revolution, initiated earlier by Copernicus, was completed by Sir Isaac Newton, and was followed during the eighteenth century by the "Enlightenment," or enthronement of a new secular faith in humanity's ability to master nature and better itself by its own efforts.

In Asia, as in Europe, a rise in the level of civilization was accompanied by the establishment of autocratic centralized governments. The Mughal rulers of India and the Manchu Dynasty in China brought a large measure of stability and prosperity to those countries, but extravagance and a series of disastrous wars led the Mughal Dynasty to an early decline. In Japan, although feudalism remained intact, the rise of the Tokugawa Shoguns in 1603 provided the substance if not the form of absolute government. In contrast with western European varieties, both Chinese and Japanese despotism survived into the twentieth century. Meanwhile, the maritime supremacy and commercial initiative of western Europeans enabled them to exploit the riches of Africa. The widespread trade in African slaves, while swelling the coffers of European merchants, not only intensified conflict among and within African states but also hastened the decline of brilliant civilizations on that continent. In the Americas the Mayan, Aztec, and Inca civilizations suffered the same fate as those of Africa under the impact of Spanish and Portuguese conquerors.

The Early-Modern World

POLITICS	PHILOSOPHY AND SCIENCE	
	Civic humanism in Italy, c. 1400–c. 1450	*1400*
	Lorenzo Valla, 1407–1457	
Renaissance popes, 1447–1521	Florentine Neoplatonism, c. 1450–c. 1600	
French invade Italy, 1494	Erasmus, c. 1467–1536	
	Machiavelli, 1469–1527	
	Nicholas Copernicus, 1473–1543	*1500*
Henry VIII of England, 1509–1547	Andreas Vesalius, 1514–1564	
Charles V, Holy Roman Emperor, 1519–1546	More's *Utopia*, 1516	
Troops of Charles V sack Rome, 1527		
Spanish gain supremacy in Italy, 1529	Jean Bodin, 1530–1596	
	Michel de Montaigne, 1533–1592	
Philip II of Spain, 1556–1598		
Elizabeth I of England, 1558–1603	Francis Bacon, 1561–1626	
Revolt of the Netherlands, 1566–1609	Galileo, 1564–1642	
Defeat of Spanish Armada, 1588	Johann Kepler, 1571–1630	
Henry IV of France, 1589–1610	William Harvey, 1578–1657	
	Thomas Hobbes, 1588–1679	
Edict of Nantes, 1598	René Descartes, 1596–1650	*1600*
Thirty Years' War, 1618–1648	Bacon's *Novum Organum*, 1620	
Supremacy of Richelieu in France, 1624–1642	Blaise Pascal, 1623–1662	
	John Locke, 1632–1704	
	Descartes' *Discourse on Method*, 1637	
English Civil War, 1642–1649	Isaac Newton, 1642–1727	
Fronde revolts in France, 1648–1653		
Commonwealth and Protectorate in England, 1649–1660		
Frederick William, Elector of Brandenburg, 1640–1688		
Louis XIV of France, 1643–1715		
Leopold I, Habsburg emperor, 1658–1705		
Restoration of Stuart dynasty in England, 1660		
Charles II of England, 1660–1685		
Peter the Great of Russia, 1682–1725		
Revocation of the Edict of Nantes, 1685		
James II of England, 1685–1688	Newton's *Mathematical Principles of Natural Philosophy*, 1687	
"Glorious" revolution in England, 1688	Montesquieu, 1689–1755	
War of the League of Augsburg, 1688–1697		
John Locke, *Two Treatises of Government*, 1690		
	Voltaire, 1694–1778	*1700*
War of the Spanish Succession, 1702–1714		
Jacques Bossuet, *Politics Drawn from the Very Words of Holy Scripture*, 1708	Linnaeus, 1707–1778	
Treaty of Utrecht, 1713	David Hume, 1711–1776	
Frederick William I of Prussia, 1713–1740	Diderot, 1713–1784	
Louis XV of France, 1715–1774		
Ascendency of Robert Walpole as Britain's "first minister," 1720–1743		
Frederick the Great of Prussia, 1740–1786		
Maria Theresa of Austria, 1740–1780	Condorcet, 1743–1794	
Seven Years' War, 1756–1763	Antoine Lavoisier, 1743–1794	
George III of Britain, 1760–1820	French *Encyclopedia*, 1751–1772	
Catherine the Great of Russia, 1762–1796	Edward Jenner introduces vaccination, 1796	
Louis XVI of France, 1774–1792		
War of American Independence, 1776–1783		
Joseph II of Austria, 1780–1790		
Beginning of the French Revolution, 1789		

The Early-Modern World (continued)

	ECONOMICS	RELIGION	ARTS AND LETTERS
1400	Portugal gains control of East Indian spice trade, 1498–1511	Martin Luther, 1483–1546 Ulrich Zwingli, 1484–1531 Ignatius Loyola, 1491–1556	Francis Petrarch, 1304–1374 Italian Renaissance, c. 1350–c. 1550 Masaccio, 1401–1428 Botticelli, 1444–1510 Leonardo da Vinci, 1452–1519 Erasmus, c. 1467–1536 Albrecht Dürer, 1471–1528 Ariosto, 1474–1533 Raphael, 1483–1520
1500	Spain gains control of Central and South America, c. 1520–c. 1550	John Calvin, 1509–1564 *Letters of Obscure Men,* 1515 Erasmus's Greek New Testament, 1516 Luther attacks indulgences, 1517 Henry VIII of England breaks with Rome, 1527–1534 Anabaptists seize Münster, 1534 Loyola's Society of Jesus approved by Pope Paul III, 1540 Calvin takes over Geneva, 1541 Council of Trent, 1545–1563 Peace of Augsburg divides Germany into Lutheran and Catholic areas, 1555 Elizabethan religious compromise in England, c. 1558–c. 1570	Michelangelo, 1485–1564 Rabelais, c. 1494–1553 Michelangelo's main work on Sistine Chapel, 1508–1512 Peter Brueghel, c. 1525–1569 Palestrina, c. 1525–1594 El Greco, c. 1541–c. 1614 Cervantes, 1547–1616 Shakespeare, 1564–1616 Claudio Monteverdi, 1567–1643 Rubens, 1577–1640 Bernini, 1598–1680 Velásquez, 1599–1660
1600	"Price Revolution" in Europe, c. 1560–c. 1600 Economic decline of Italy, c. 1580–c. 1700 Chartering of English East India Company, 1600 English Poor Law, 1601 Chartering of Dutch East India Company, 1602 Settlement of Jamestown, 1607 Height of mercantilism in Europe, 1650–1750 Colbert's economic reforms in France, 1664–1683 Founding of Bank of England, 1694		Rembrandt, 1606–1669 John Milton, 1608–1674 Molière, 1622–1673 Christopher Wren, 1632–1723
1700	Introduction of maize and potato crops in Europe, c. 1700 Mississippi Bubble, 1715 South Sea Bubble, 1720 Last appearance of bubonic plague in western Europe, 1720 Enclosure movement in England, 1730–1810 General European population increase beginning 1750 Adam Smith, *The Wealth of Nations,* 1776	John Wesley, 1703–1789	Watteau, 1684–1721 J. S. Bach, 1685–1750 G. F. Handel, 1685–1759 Voltaire, 1694–1778 The Enlightenment, c. 1700–c. 1790 Henry Fielding, 1707–1754 Joseph Haydn, 1732–1809 Edward Gibbon, 1737–1794 W. A. Mozart, 1756–1791 Jane Austen, 1775–1817

AFRICA AND THE AMERICAS	INDIA AND EAST ASIA	

Height of West African forest civilizations,
1400–1472

Voyages of discovery and exploration, 1450–1600

| | | **1400** |

Babur, founder of the Mughal Dynasty,
(1483–1530)

European maritime activity along African coasts,
1500–1800
Growth of African slave trade, 1500–1800
Portuguese dominance of East Coast city-states,
1505–1650

| | | **1500** |

Conquest of Mexico, 1522
Conquest of Peru, 1537

Arrival of Portuguese traders in China
and Japan, 1537–1542
Jesuit missionaries active in China and
Japan, 1550–1650
Akbar the Great Mughal, 1556–1605

End of the Ashikaga Shogunate, 1573

Founding of Jamestown, 1607

Landing of Pilgrims, 1620

British East India Co., chartered, 1600
Tokugawa Shogunate, 1603–1867
Shah Jahan, 1627–1658

Taj Mahal, 1632–1647
Japanese isolation, 1637–1854

| | | **1600** |

Downfall of kingdoms of Kongo and Ngola,
1665–1671

Rise of Asante empire, founded on Gold Coast
trade, 1700–1750

Manchu Dynasty in China, 1644–1912
Maratha Confederacy in India, 1650–1760
Aurangzeb, 1658–1707
K'ang Hsi, 1661–1722
British Royal Africa Company, charter, 1672
Decline of Mughal Empire in India, 1700
–1800
Ch'ien Lung 1736–1796

| | | **1700** |

Chapter 18

THE CIVILIZATION
OF THE RENAISSANCE
(c. 1350—c. 1550)

Now may every reflecting spirit thank God he has chosen to live in this
new age, so full of hope and promise, which already exults in a greater
array of nobly-gifted souls than the world has seen in the thousand years
before.

—Matteo Palmieri, *On the Civil Life,* c. 1435

Whatever was done by man with genius and with a certain grace he held
to be almost divine.

—L. B. Alberti, *Self-Portrait,* c. 1460

The prevalent modern notion that a "Renaissance period" followed western Europe's medieval age was first expressed by
numerous Italian writers who lived between 1350 and 1550.
According to them, one thousand years of unrelieved darkness had
intervened between the Roman era and their own times. During these
"dark ages" the Muses of art and literature had fled Europe before the
onslaught of barbarism and ignorance. Almost miraculously, however, in the fourteenth century the Muses suddenly returned and Italians happily collaborated with them to bring forth a glorious
"renaissance of the arts."

"A renaissance of the arts"

Ever since this periodization was advanced historians have taken for
granted the existence of some sort of "Renaissance," intervening
between medieval and modern times. Indeed, in the late nineteenth
and early twentieth centuries many scholars went so far as to argue
that the Renaissance was not just an epoch in the history of learning
and culture but that a unique "Renaissance spirit" transformed all
aspects of life—political, economic, and religious, as well as intellec-

Limits of the term "Renaissance"

tual and artistic. Today, however, most experts no longer accept this characterization because they find it impossible to locate any truly distinctive "Renaissance" politics, economics, or religion. Instead, scholars tend to agree that the term "Renaissance" should be reserved to describe certain exciting trends in thought, literature, and the arts that emerged in Italy from roughly 1350 to 1550 and then spread to northern Europe during the first half of the sixteenth century. That is the approach that will be followed here: accordingly, when we refer to a "Renaissance period" in this chapter we mean to limit ourselves to an epoch in intellectual and cultural history.

Further qualifications

Granted this restriction, some further qualifications are still necessary. Since the word "renaissance" literally means "rebirth," it is sometimes thought that after about 1350 certain Italians who were newly cognizant of Greek and Roman cultural accomplishments initiated a classical cultural rebirth after a long period of "death." In fact, however, the High Middle Ages witnessed no "death" of classical learning. St. Thomas Aquinas, for example, considered Aristotle to be "the Philosopher" and Dante revered Virgil. Similarly, it would be completely false to oppose an imaginary "Renaissance paganism" to a medieval "age of faith" because however much most Renaissance personalities loved the classics, none went so far as to worship classical gods. And finally, all discussions of the post-medieval Renaissance must be qualified by the fact that there was no single Renaissance position on any given subject.

*The continuing
rediscovery and spread of
classical learning*

Nonetheless, in the realms of thought, literature, and the arts important distinguishing traits may certainly be found which make the concept of a "Renaissance" meaningful for intellectual and cultural history. First, regarding knowledge of the classics, there was indubitably a significant quantitative difference between the learning of the Middle Ages and that of the Renaissance. Medieval scholars knew many Roman authors, such as Virgil, Ovid, and Cicero, but in the Renaissance the works of others such as Livy, Tacitus, and Lucretius were rediscovered and made familiar. Equally if not more important was the Renaissance discovery of the literature of classical Greece. In the twelfth and thirteenth centuries Greek scientific and philosophical treatises were made available to westerners in Latin translations, but none of the great Greek literary masterpieces and practically none of the major works of Plato were yet known. Nor could more than a handful of medieval westerners read the Greek language. In the Renaissance, on the other hand, large numbers of Western scholars learned Greek and mastered almost the entire Greek literary heritage that is known today.

*New uses for classical
learning*

Second, Renaissance thinkers not only knew many more classical texts than their medieval counterparts, but they used them in new ways. Whereas medieval writers tended to employ their ancient sources for the purposes of complementing and confirming their own preconceived Christian assumptions, Renaissance writers customarily drew on the classics to reconsider their preconceived notions and alter their modes of expression. Firm determination to learn from classical antiquity, moreover, was even more pronounced in the realms of architecture and art, areas in which classical models contributed most strikingly to the creation of fully distinct "Renaissance" artistic styles.

Third, although Renaissance culture was by no means pagan, it certainly was more secular in its orientation than the culture of the Middle Ages. The evolution of the Italian city-states in the fourteenth and fifteenth centuries created a supportive environment for attitudes that stressed the attainment of success in the urban political arena and living well in this world. Inevitably such secular ideals helped create a culture that was increasingly nonecclesiastical. To be sure, the Church retained its wealth and some of its influence, but it adjusted to the spread of secularity by becoming more secular itself.

A secular Renaissance culture

One word above all comes closest to summing up the most common and basic Renaissance intellectual ideals, namely humanism. This word has two different meanings, one technical and one general, but both apply to the cultural goals and ideals of a large number of Renaissance thinkers. In its technical sense humanism was a program of studies which aimed to replace the medieval Scholastic emphasis on logic and metaphysics with the study of language, literature, history, and ethics. Ancient literature was always preferred: the study of the Latin classics was at the core of the curriculum, and, whenever possible, the student was expected to advance to Greek. Humanist teachers argued that Scholastic logic was too arid and irrelevant to the practical concerns of life; instead, they preferred the "humanities," which were meant to make their students virtuous and prepare them for contributing best to the public functions of the state. (Women, as usual, were generally ignored, but sometimes aristocratic women were given humanist training in order to make them appear more polished.) The broader sense of humanism lies in a stress on the "dignity" of man as the most excellent of all God's creatures below the angels. Some Renaissance thinkers argued that man was excellent because he alone of earthly creatures could obtain knowledge of God; others stressed man's ability to master his fate and live happily in the world. Either way, Renaissance humanists had a firm belief in the nobility and possibilities of the human race.

Humanism

1. THE ITALIAN BACKGROUND

The Renaissance originated in Italy for several reasons. The most fundamental was that Italy in the later Middle Ages encompassed the most advanced urban society in all of Europe. Unlike aristocrats north of the Alps, Italian aristocrats customarily lived in urban centers rather than in rural castles and consequently became fully involved in urban public affairs. Moreover, since the Italian aristocracy built its palaces

The erosion of distinctions between the aristocracy and upper bourgeoisie in Italy

in the cities, the aristocratic class was less sharply set off from the class of rich merchants than in the north. Hence whereas in France or Germany there was never any appreciable variation from the rule that aristocrats lived off the income from their landed estates while rich town dwellers (*bourgeois*) gained their living from trade, in Italy so many town-dwelling aristocrats engaged in banking or mercantile enterprises and so many rich mercantile families imitated the manners of the aristocracy that by the fourteenth and fifteenth centuries the aristocracy and upper bourgeoisie were becoming virtually indistinguishable. The noted Florentine family of the Medici, for example, emerged as a family of physicians (as the name suggests), made its fortune in banking, and rose imperceptibly into the aristocracy in the fifteenth century. The results of these developments for the history of education are obvious: not only was there a great demand for education in the skills of reading and counting necessary to become a successful merchant, but the richest and most prominent families sought above all to find teachers who would impart to their offspring the knowledge and skills necessary to argue well in the public arena. Consequently, Italy produced a large number of secular educators, many of whom not only taught students but demonstrated their learned attainments in the production of political and ethical treatises and works of literature. The schools of these educators, moreover, created the best educated upper-class public in all of Europe and inevitably therewith a considerable number of wealthy patrons who were ready to invest in the cultivation of new ideas and new forms of literary and artistic expression.

*The special appeal of the
classical past*

A second reason why late-medieval Italy was the birthplace of an intellectual and artistic Renaissance lay in the fact that it had a far greater sense of rapport with the classical past than any other territory in western Europe. Given the Italian aristocratic commitment to an educational curriculum which stressed success in urban politics, the best teachers understandably sought inspiration from ancient Latin and Greek texts because politics and political rhetoric were classical rather than medieval arts. Elsewhere, resort to classical knowledge and classical literary style might have seemed intolerably antiquarian and artificial, but in Italy the classical past appeared most "relevant" because ancient Roman monuments were omnipresent throughout the peninsula and ancient Latin literature referred to cities and sites that Renaissance Italians recognized as their own. Moreover, Italians became particularly intent on reappropriating their classical heritage in the fourteenth and fifteenth centuries because Italians then were seeking to establish an independent cultural identity in opposition to a Scholasticism most closely associated with France. Not only did the removal of the papacy to Avignon for most of the fourteenth century, and then the prolonged Great Schism from 1378 to 1415, heighten antagonisms between Italy and France, but during the fourteenth century there was an intellectual reaction against Scholasticism on all fronts which made it natural for Italians to prefer the intellectual alternatives offered by classical literary sources. Naturally too, once Roman literature and learning became particularly favored in Italy, so did Roman art and architecture, for Roman models could help Italians create a splendid artistic alternative to French Gothicism just as Roman learning offered an intellectual alternative to French Scholasticism.

Finally, the Italian Renaissance obviously could not have occurred without the underpinning of Italian wealth. Oddly enough, the Italian economy as a whole was probably more prosperous in the thirteenth century than it was in the fourteenth and fifteenth. But late-medieval Italy was wealthier in comparison to the rest of Europe than it had been before, a fact which meant that Italian writers and artists were more likely to stay at home than seek employment abroad. Moreover, in late-medieval Italy unusually intensive investment in culture arose from an intensification of urban pride and the concentration of per capita wealth. Although these two trends overlapped somewhat, most scholars tend to agree that a phase of predominantly public urban support for culture came first in Italy from roughly 1250 to about 1400 or 1450, depending on place, with the private sector taking over thereafter. In the first phase the richest cities vied with each other in building the most splendid public monuments and in supporting writers whose role was to glorify the urban republics in letters and speeches as full of magniloquent Ciceronian prose as possible. But in the course of the fifteenth century, when most Italian city-states succumbed to the hereditary rule of princely families, patronage was monopolized by the princely aristocracy. It was then that the great princes—the Visconti and Sforza in Milan; the Medici in Florence; the Este in Ferrara; and the Gonzaga in Mantua—patronized art and literature in their courts to glorify themselves, while lesser aristocratic families imitated those princes on a smaller scale. Not least of the great princes in Italy from about 1450 to about 1550 were the popes in Rome, who were dedicated to a policy of basing their strength on temporal control of the Papal States. Hence the most worldly of the Renaissance popes—Alexander VI (1492–1503); Julius II (1503–1513); and Leo X (1513–1521), son of the Florentine ruler Lorenzo de' Medici—obtained the services of the greatest artists of the day and for a few decades made Rome the unrivaled artistic capital of the Western world.

2. THE RENAISSANCE OF THOUGHT AND LITERATURE IN ITALY

In surveying the greatest accomplishments of Italian Renaissance scholars and writers it is natural to begin with the work of Francis Petrarch (1304–1374), the earliest of the humanists in the technical

Pope Julius II. A portrait by Raphael.

*Petrarch, the first
humanist*

sense of the term. Petrarch was a deeply committed Christian who believed that Scholasticism was entirely misguided because it concentrated on abstract speculation rather than teaching people how to behave properly and attain salvation. Petrarch thought that the Christian writer must above all cultivate literary eloquence so that he could inspire people to do good. For him the best models of eloquence were to be found in the ancient literary classics, which he thought repaid study doubly inasmuch as they were filled with ethical wisdom. So Petrarch dedicated himself to searching for undiscovered ancient Latin texts and writing his own moral treatises in which he imitated classical style and quoted classical phrases. Thereby he initiated a program of "humanist" studies that was to be influential for centuries. Petrarch also has a place in purely literary history because of his poetry. Although he prized his own Latin poetry over the poems he wrote in the Italian vernacular, only the latter have proved enduring. Above all, the Italian sonnets—later called Petrarchan sonnets—which he wrote for his beloved Laura in the chivalrous style of the troubadours, were widely imitated in form and content throughout the Renaissance period.

Civic humanism

Because he was a very traditional Christian, Petrarch's ultimate ideal for human conduct was the solitary life of contemplation and asceticism. But in subsequent generations, from about 1400 to 1450, a number of Italian thinkers and scholars, located mainly in Florence, developed the alternative of what is customarily called "civic humanism." Civic humanists like the Florentines Leonardo Bruni (c. 1370–1444) and Leon Battista Alberti (1404–1472) agreed with Petrarch on the need for eloquence and the study of classical literature, but they also taught that man's nature equipped him for action, for usefulness to his family and society, and for serving the state—ideally a republican city-state after the classical or contemporary Florentine model. In their view ambition and the quest for glory were noble impulses which ought to be encouraged. They refused to condemn the striving for material possessions, for they argued that the history of human progress is inseparable from mankind's success in gaining mastery over the earth and its resources. Perhaps the most vivid of the civic humanists' writings is Alberti's *On the Family* (1443), in which he argued that the nuclear family was instituted by nature for the well-being of humanity. Not surprisingly, however, Alberti consigned women to purely domestic roles within this framework, for he believed that "man [is] by nature more energetic and industrious," and that woman was created "to increase and continue generations, and to nourish and preserve those already born."

Leon Battista Alberti. A contemporary medal.

The civic humanists and classical Greek studies

In addition to differing with Petrarch in their preference for the active over the solitary or contemplative life, the civic humanists went far beyond him in their study of the ancient literary heritage. Many of them discovered important new Latin texts, but far more important was their success in opening up the field of classical Greek studies. In this they were greatly aided by the cooperation of several Byzantine scholars who had migrated to Italy in the first half of the fifteenth century. These men gave instruction in the Greek language and taught about the achievements of their ancient forebears. In doing so they inspired Italian scholars to make trips to Constantinople and other cities in the Near East in search of Greek manuscripts. In 1423 one Italian humanist, Giovanni Aurispa, alone brought back 238 manuscript books, including works of Sophocles, Euripides, and Thucydides. In this way most of the Greek classics, particularly the writings of Plato, the dramatists, and the historians, were first made available to western Europe.

Related in his textual interests to the civic humanists, but by no means a full adherent of their movement, was the atypical yet highly influential Renaissance thinker, Lorenzo Valla (1407–1457). Born in Rome and active primarily as a secretary in the service of the king of Naples, Valla had no inclination to espouse the ideas of republican political engagement as the Florentine civic humanists did. Instead, he preferred to advertise his skills as an expert in grammar, rhetoric, and the painstaking analysis of Greek and Latin texts by showing how the thorough study of language could discredit old verities. Most decisive in this regard was Valla's brilliant demonstration that the so-called Donation of Constantine was a medieval forgery. Whereas papal propagandists had argued ever since the early thirteenth century that the papacy possessed rights to temporal rule in western Europe on the grounds of a charter purportedly granted by the Emperor Constantine in the fourth century, Valla proved beyond dispute that the document in question was full of nonclassical Latin usages and anachronistic terms. Hence he concluded that the "Donation" was the work of a medieval forger whose "monstrous impudence" was exposed by the "stupidity of his language." This demonstration not only discredited a prize specimen of "medieval ignorance," but, more importantly, introduced the concept of anachronism into all subsequent textual study and historical thought. Valla also employed his skills in linguistic analysis and rhetorical argumentation to challenge a wide variety of philosophical positions, but his ultimate goals were by no means purely destructive, for he revered the literal teachings of the Pauline Epistles. Accordingly, in his *Notes on the New Testament* he applied his expert knowledge of Greek to elucidating the true meaning of St. Paul's words, which he believed had been obscured by the Latin Vulgate translation. This work was to prove an important link between Italian Renaissance scholarship and the subsequent Christian humanism of the north.

From about 1450 until about 1600 dominance in the world of Italian thought was assumed by a school of Neoplatonists, who sought to blend the thought of Plato, Plotinus, and various strands of ancient mysticism with Christianity. Foremost among these were Marsilio Ficino (1433–1499) and Giovanni Pico della Mirandola (1463–1494),

*Lorenzo Valla and
linguistic analysis*

*Renaissance
Neoplatonism: Ficino and
Pico*

Pico della Mirandola. When the young nobleman Pico arrived in Florence at age nineteen he was said to have been "of beauteous feature and shape." This contemporary portrait may have been done by the great Florentine painter Botticelli.

Niccolò Machiavelli

both of whom were members of the Platonic Academy founded by Cosimo de' Medici in Florence. The academy was a loosely organized society of scholars who met to hear readings and lectures. Their hero was unquestionably Plato: sometimes they celebrated Plato's birthday by holding a banquet in his honor, after which everybody gave speeches as if they were characters in a Platonic dialogue. Ficino's greatest achievement was the translation of Plato's works into Latin, thereby making them widely available to western Europeans for the first time. It is debatable whether Ficino's own philosophy may be called humanist because he moved away from ethics to metaphysics and taught that the individual should look primarily to the other world. In Ficino's opinion, "the immortal soul is always miserable in its mortal body." The same problem holds for Ficino's disciple Giovanni Pico della Mirandola, whose most famous work is the *Oration on the Dignity of Man*. Pico was certainly not a civic humanist since he saw little worth in mundane public affairs. But he did believe that there is "nothing more wonderful than man" because he believed that man is endowed with the capacity to achieve union with God if he so wills.

Hardly any of the Italian thinkers between Petrarch and Pico were really original: their greatness lay mostly in their manner of expression, their accomplishments in technical scholarship, and their popularization of different themes of ancient thought. The same, however, can by no means be said of Renaissance Italy's greatest political philosopher, Niccolò Machiavelli (1469–1527), who belonged to no school and stood in a class by himself. No man did more than Machiavelli to overturn all earlier views of the ethical basis of politics or to pioneer in the dispassionate direct observation of political life. Machiavelli's writings reflect the unhappy condition of Italy in his time. At the end of the fifteenth century Italy had become the cockpit of international struggles. Both France and Spain had invaded the peninsula and were competing with each other for the allegiance of the Italian states. The latter, in many cases, were torn by internal dissension which made them easy prey for foreign conquerors. In 1498 Machiavelli entered the service of the newly founded republic of Florence as second chancellor and secretary. His duties largely involved diplomatic missions to other states. While in Rome he became fascinated with the achievements of Cesare Borgia, son of Pope Alexander VI, in cementing a solidified state out of scattered elements. He noted with approval Cesare's combination of ruthlessness with shrewdness and his complete subordination of morality to political ends. In 1512 the Medici returned to overthrow the republic of Florence, and Machiavelli was deprived of his position. Disappointed and embittered, he spent the remainder of his life in exile, devoting his time primarily to writing. In his *Discourses on Livy* he praised the ancient Roman republic as a model for all time. He lauded constitutionalism, equality, liberty, in the sense of freedom from outside interference, and subordination of religion to the interests of the state. But Machiavelli also wrote *The Prince* in

Madonna of Mercy, Piero della Francesca (c. 1420–1492). This fresco, painted in central Italy in the middle of the fifteenth century, depicts the Virgin Mary protecting her faithful. Piero della Francesca was considered provincial by the Florentines of his day because his severe style lacked the fluidity and charm then fashionable in Florence. Today, however, connoisseurs place his painting in the very highest rank. (Art Resource)

Christ Appears to the Magdalen, Fra Angelico (1387–1455). The Florentine painter Fra Angelico's work is characterized by its grace of line and delicacy of color. (Art Resource)

The Birth of Venus, Sandro Botticelli (1444–1510). Botticelli was a mystic as well as a lover of beauty and the painting is most often interpreted as a neo–Platonic allegory. (Scala)

The Virgin of the Rocks, Leonardo da Vinci (1452–1519). This painting reveals not only Leonardo's interest in human character, but also his absorption in the phenomenon of nature. (Louvre)

Mona Lisa, Leonardo da Vinci. Unlike most other Renaissance painters who sought to convey an understandable message, Leonardo created questions to which he gave no answer. Nowhere is this more evident than in the enigmatic countenance of Mona Lisa. (Louvre)

The Last Supper, Leonardo da Vinci. This great fresco depicts the varying reactions of Jesus' disciples when He announces that one of them will betray Him. (Santa Maria della Grazie, Milan)

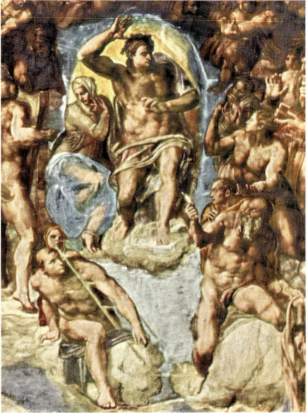

Above: *The Madonna of the Chair*, Raphael (1483–1520). Raphael's art was distinguished by warmth, serenity, and tenderness. (Pitti Palace, Florence) Right: "Christ and Madonna." From *The Last Judgment*, Michelangelo (1475–1564). This painting above the altar in the Sistine Chapel, Rome, shows Christ as judge condemning sinners to perdition. Even the Madonna at His side seems to shrink from His wrath. (Sistine Chapel)

Pope Paul III with His Nephews, Titian (1488–1576). This painting emphasizes action far more than its forebear, Raphael's portrait of Pope Leo X with his nephews. (National Museum, Naples)

The Emperor Charles V, Titian. (Alte Pinakothek)

which he described the policies and practices of government, not in accordance with some lofty ideal, but as they actually were. The supreme obligation of the ruler, he avowed, was to maintain the power and safety of the country over which he ruled. No consideration of justice or mercy or the sanctity of treaties should be allowed to stand in his way. Cynical in his views of human nature, Machiavelli maintained that all men are prompted exclusively by motives of self-interest, particularly by desires for personal power and material prosperity. The head of the state should therefore not take for granted the loyalty or affection of his subjects. The one ideal Machiavelli kept before him in his later years was the unification of Italy. But this he believed could only be achieved through ruthlessness.

Far more congenial to contemporary tastes than the shocking political theories of Machiavelli were the guidelines for proper aristocratic conduct offered in *The Book of the Courtier* (1516) by the diplomat and count Baldesar Castiglione. This cleverly written forerunner of modern handbooks of etiquette stands in sharp contrast to the earlier civic humanist treatises of Bruni and Alberti, for whereas they taught the sober "republican" virtues of strenuous service in behalf of the city-state and family, Castiglione, writing in an Italy dominated by magnificent princely courts, taught how to attain the elegant and seemingly effortless qualities necessary for acting like a "true gentleman." More than anyone else, Castiglione popularized the ideal of the "Renaissance man": one who is accomplished in many different pursuits and is also brave, witty, and "courteous," meaning civilized and learned. By no means ignoring the female sex, Castiglione, much unlike Alberti, was silent about woman's role in "hearth and home," but stressed instead the ways in which court ladies could be "gracious entertainers." Thereby he was one of the first European male writers to offer women an independent role outside of the household, a fact which should not be underrated even though he was offering such a role merely to the richest of the rich and even though his stress on "pleasing affability" today seems demeaning. Widely read throughout Europe for over a century after its publication, Castiglione's *Courtier* spread Italian ideals of "civility" to princely courts north of the Alps, resulted in the ever-greater patronage of art and literature by the European aristocracy, and gave currency to the hitherto novel proposition that all women other than nuns were not fated to be passive vessels of reproduction and nutrition.

*Castiglione's ideal courtier
and court lady*

Had Castiglione's ideal courtier wished to show off his knowledge of contemporary Italian literature, he would have had many works from which to choose, for sixteenth-century Italians were highly accomplished in the creation of imaginative prose and verse. Among the many impressive writers who might be mentioned, Machiavelli himself wrote a delightful short story, "Belfagor," and an engaging bawdy play, *Mandragola;* the great artist Michelangelo wrote many moving sonnets; and the most eminent of sixteenth-century Italian

*Other sixteenth-century
Italian literary
achievements*

epic poets was Ludovico Ariosto (1474–1533), author of a lengthy verse narrative called *Orlando Furioso* (*The Madness of Roland*). Although woven substantially from materials taken from the medieval Charlemagne cycle, this work differed radically from any of the medieval epics because it introduced elements of lyrical fantasy and above all because it was totally devoid of heroic idealism. Ariosto wrote to make readers laugh and to charm them with felicitous descriptions of the quiet splendor of nature and the passions of love. His work represents the disillusionment of the late Renaissance, the loss of hope and faith, and the tendency to seek consolation in the pursuit of pleasure and aesthetic delight.

3. THE ARTISTIC RENAISSANCE IN ITALY

Despite numerous intellectual and literary advances, the most long-lived achievements of the Italian Renaissance were made in the realm of art. Of all the arts, painting was undoubtedly supreme. We have already seen that around 1300 very impressive beginnings were made in the history of Italian painting by the artistic genius of Giotto, but it was not until the fifteenth century that Italian painting began to attain its majority. One reason for this was that in the early fifteenth century the laws of linear perspective were discovered and first employed to give the fullest sense of three dimensions. Fifteenth-century artists also experimented with effects of light and shade (*chiaroscuro*) and for the first time carefully studied the anatomy and proportions of the human body. By the fifteenth century, too, increase in private wealth and the partial triumph of the secular spirit had freed the domain of art to a large extent from the service of religion. As we have noted above, the Church was no longer the only patron of artists. While subject matter from biblical history was still commonly employed, it was frequently infused with nonreligious themes. The painting of portraits for the purpose of revealing the hidden mysteries of the soul now became popular. Paintings intended to appeal primarily to the intellect were paralleled by others whose main purpose was to delight the eye with gorgeous color and beauty of form. The fifteenth century was characterized also by the introduction of painting in oil, probably from Flanders. The use of the new technique doubtless had much to do with the artistic advance of this period. Since oil does not dry so quickly as fresco pigment, the painter could now work more leisurely, taking time with the more difficult parts of the picture and making corrections if necessary as he went along.

The Expulsion of Adam and Eve from the Garden of Eden. Masaccio built on the artistic tradition established by Giotto in stressing emotion and psychological study.

The majority of the painters of the fifteenth century were Florentines. First among them was the precocious Masaccio (1401–1428). Although he died at the age of twenty-seven, Masaccio inspired the work of Italian painters for a hundred years. Masaccio's greatness as a painter is based on his success in "imitating nature," which became a primary value in Renaissance painting. To achieve this effect he employed perspective, perhaps most dramatically in his fresco of the *Trinity;* he also used *chiaroscuro* with originality, leading to a dramatic and moving outcome. In the *Expulsion of Adam and Eve from the Garden,* he records the shame and guilt felt by the individuals in the biblical story.

The best known of the painters who directly followed the tradition begun by Masaccio was the Florentine Sandro Botticelli (1444–1510), who depicted both religious and classical themes. Botticelli's work excels in beautiful and accurate depiction of natural detail; he was a master, for example, at painting the female nude. But his major contribution to Renaissance painting derives from the philosophical basis of much of his work, for he was closely associated with the Florentine Neoplatonists. Two of his most famous paintings are *The Allegory of Spring* and *The Birth of Venus,* which illustrate Neoplatonic concepts regarding the classical goddess of love, Venus or Aphrodite. Later in his life Botticelli became a follower of the evangelical priest Savonarola, who came to Florence from Ferrara to preach fire-and-brimstone sermons against worldliness. Botticelli's *Mystic Nativity* was probably painted as a result of Savonarola's influence; it is a profoundly moving religious painting, in which he anticipates the end of the world. The last years of Botticelli's life are shadowy; his popularity declined, and it is believed he died in poverty.

Perhaps the greatest of the Florentine artists was Leonardo da Vinci (1452–1519), one of the most versatile geniuses who ever lived. Leonardo was practically the personification of the "Renaissance man": he was a painter, architect, musician, mathematician, engineer, and inventor. The illegitimate son of a lawyer and a peasant woman, Leonardo set up an artist's shop in Florence by the time he reached twenty-five and gained the patronage of the Medici ruler of the city, Lorenzo the Magnificent. But if Leonardo had any weakness, it was his slowness in working and difficulty in finishing anything. This naturally displeased Lorenzo and other Florentine patrons, who thought an artist was little more than an artisan, commissioned to produce a certain piece of work of a certain size for a certain price on a certain date. Leonardo, however, strongly objected to this view because he considered himself to be no menial craftsman but an inspired creator. Therefore in 1482 he left Florence for the Sforza court of Milan where he was given freer rein in structuring his time and work. He remained there until the French invaded Milan in 1499; after that he wandered about Italy, finally accepting the patronage of the French king, Francis I, under whose auspices Leonardo lived and worked in France until his death.

The paintings of Leonardo da Vinci began what is known as the High Renaissance in Italy. His approach to painting was that it should be the most accurate possible imitation of nature. Leonardo was like a naturalist, basing his work on his own detailed observations of a blade

Botticelli

See color plates following page 614 for *The Birth of Venus* by Botticelli

Leonardo da Vinci

Lorenzo de' Medici, Known as Lorenzo the Magnificent. A detail from *The Adoration of the Magi* by Benozzo Gozzoli showing the future Florentine ruler and patron of art.

Studies of the Shoulder by **Leonardo da Vinci**

See color plates following page 614 for the *Virgin of the Rocks,* the *Last Supper,* and the *Mona Lisa* by Leonardo da Vinci

The Venetian painters

See color plates facing page 615 for *Pope Paul III and His Nephews* and *Charles V* by Titian

of grass, the wing of a bird, a waterfall. He obtained human corpses for dissection—by which he was breaking the law—and reconstructed in drawing the minutest features of anatomy, which knowledge he carried over to his paintings. Leonardo worshiped nature, and was convinced of the essential divinity in all living things. It is not surprising, therefore, that he was a vegetarian, and that he went to the marketplace to buy caged birds which he released to their native habitat.

It is generally agreed that Leonardo's masterpieces are the *Virgin of the Rocks* (which exists in two versions), the *Last Supper,* and the *Mona Lisa.* The first represents not only his marvelous technical skill but also his passion for science and his belief in the universe as a well-ordered place. The figures are arranged in geometric composition with every rock and plant depicted in accurate detail. The *Last Supper,* painted on the walls of the refectory of Santa Maria delle Grazie in Milan, is a study of psychological reactions. A serene Christ, resigned to his terrible fate, has just announced to his disciples that one of them will betray him. The purpose of the artist is to portray the mingled emotions of surprise, horror, and guilt revealed in the faces of the disciples as they gradually perceive the meaning of their master's statement. The third of Leonardo's major triumphs, the *Mona Lisa,* reflects a similar interest in the varied moods of the human soul. Although it is true that the *Mona Lisa* is a portrait of an actual woman, the wife of Francesco del Giocondo, a Neapolitan, it is more than a mere photographic likeness. The distinguished art critic Bernard Berenson has said of it, "Who like Leonardo has depicted . . . the inexhaustible fascination of the woman in her years of mastery? . . . Leonardo is the one artist of whom it may be said with perfect literalness: 'Nothing that he touched but turned into a thing of eternal beauty.'"

The beginning of the High Renaissance around 1490 also witnessed the rise of the so-called Venetian school, the major members of which were Giovanni Bellini (c. 1426–1516), Giorgione (1478–1510), and Titian (c. 1477–1576). The work of all these men reflected the luxurious life and the pleasure-loving interests of the thriving commercial city of Venice. Most Venetian painters had little of the concern with philosophical and psychological themes that characterized the Florentine school. Their aim was to appeal primarily to the senses rather than to the mind. They delighted in painting idyllic landscapes and gorgeous symphonies of color. For their subject matter they chose not merely the natural beauty of Venetian sunsets and the shimmering silver of lagoons in the moonlight but also the artificial splendor of sparkling jewels, richly colored satins and velvets, and gorgeous palaces. Their portraits were invariably likenesses of the rich and the powerful. In the subordination of form and meaning to color and elegance there were mirrored not only the sumptuous tastes of wealthy merchants, but also definite traces of Eastern influence which had filtered through from Byzantium during the Middle Ages.

The remaining great painters of the High Renaissance all accomplished their most important work in the first half of the sixteenth century. It was in this period that Renaissance Italian art reached its peak. Rome was now the major artistic center of the Italian peninsula, although the traditions of the Florentine school still exerted a potent influence. Among the eminent painters of this period at least two must be given more than passing attention. One was Raphael (1483–1520), a native of Urbino, and perhaps the most beloved artist of the entire Renaissance. The lasting appeal of his style is due primarily to his ennobling humanism, for he portrayed the members of the human species as temperate, wise, and dignified beings. Although Raphael was influenced by Leonardo da Vinci and copied many features of his work, he cultivated a much more symbolical or allegorical approach. His *Disputà* symbolized the dialectical relationship between the Church in heaven and the Church on earth. In a worldly setting against a brilliant sky, theologians debate the meaning of the Eucharist, while in the clouds above, saints and the Trinity repose in the possession of a holy mystery. Raphael's *School of Athens* is an allegorical representation of the conflict between the Platonist and Aristotelian philosophies. Plato (painted as a portrait of Leonardo) is shown pointing upward to emphasize the spiritual basis of his world of Ideas, while Aristotle gestures toward the earth to exemplify his belief that concepts or ideas are inseparably linked with their material embodiments. Raphael is noted also for his portraits and Madonnas. To the latter, especially, he gave a softness and warmth that seemed to endow them with a sweetness and piety quite different from the enigmatic and somewhat distant Madonnas of Leonardo da Vinci.

The last towering figure of the High Renaissance was Michelangelo (1475–1564) of Florence. If Leonardo was a naturalist, Michelangelo was an idealist; where the former sought to recapture and interpret

The painters of the late Renaissance: Raphael

See color plates facing page 615 for the *Madonna of the Chair* by Raphael

Michelangelo

The *School of Athens* by Raphael

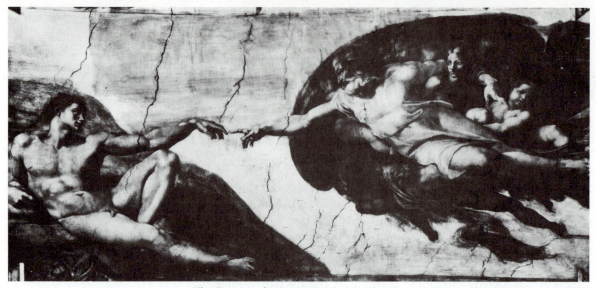

The Creation of Adam by Michelangelo. One of a series of frescoes on the ceiling of the Sistine Chapel in Rome. Suggesting philosophical inquiries into the meaning of life and the universe, it represents Renaissance realism at its height.

fleeting natural phenomena, Michelangelo, who embraced Neoplatonism as a philosophy, was more concerned with expressing enduring, abstract truths. Michelangelo was a painter, sculptor, architect, and poet—and he expressed himself in all these with a similar power and in a similar manner. At the center of all of his paintings is the human figure, which is always powerful, colossal, magnificent. If man, and the potential of the individual, lay at the center of Italian Renaissance culture, then Michelangelo, who depicted the human, and particularly the male, figure without cease, is the supreme Renaissance artist.

The Sistine Chapel Michelangelo's greatest achievements in painting appear in a single location—the Sistine Chapel in Rome—yet they are products of two different periods in the artist's life and consequently exemplify two different artistic styles and outlooks on the human condition. Most famous are the sublime frescoes Michelangelo painted on the ceiling of the Sistine Chapel from 1508 to 1512, depicting scenes from the book of Genesis. All the panels in this series, including *God Dividing the Light from Darkness, The Creation of Adam,* and *The Flood,* exemplify the young artist's commitment to classical Greek aesthetic principles of harmony, solidity, and dignified restraint. Correspondingly, all exude as well a sense of sublime affirmation regarding Creation and the heroic qualities of mankind. (When one considers that Michelangelo executed these magnificent scenes while lying on his back on a scaffold, one can begin to imagine the exalted mood of creativity that must have possessed him.) But a quarter of a century later, when Michelangelo returned to work in the Sistine Chapel, both his style and mood had changed dramatically. In the enormous *Last Judg-*

ment, a fresco done for the Sistine Chapel's altar wall in 1536, Michelangelo repudiated classical restraint and substituted a style that emphasized tension and distortion in order to communicate the older man's pessimistic conception of a humanity wracked by fear and bowed by guilt.

In the realm of sculpture the Italian Renaissance took a great step forward by creating statues that were no longer carved as parts of columns or doorways on church buildings or as effigies on tombs. Instead, Italian sculptors for the first time since antiquity carved freestanding statues "in the round." These freed sculpture from its bondage to architecture and established its status as a separate art frequently devoted to secular purposes.

The first great master of Renaissance sculpture was Donatello (c. 1386?–1466). He emancipated his art from Gothic mannerisms and introduced a new vigorous note of individualism. His bronze statue of David triumphant over the body of the slain Goliath, the first freestanding nude since antiquity, established a precedent of glorifying the life-size nude. Donatello's *David,* moreover, represents a first step in the direction of imitating classical sculpture, not just in the depiction of a nude body but also in the subject's posture of resting his weight on one leg. Yet this David is clearly a lithe adolescent rather than a muscular Greek athlete. Later in his career, Donatello more fully imitated ancient statuary in his commanding portrayal of the proud warrior Gattamelata—the first monumental equestrian statue in bronze executed in the West since the time of the Romans. Here, in addition to drawing very heavily on the legacy of antiquity, the sculptor most clearly expressed his dedication to immortalizing the earthly accomplishments of a contemporary secular hero.

David by Donatello. The first free-standing nude statue executed in the West since antiquity.

Gattamelata by Donatello. Note the debt to the Roman equestrian statue of Marcus Aurelius, shown above, p. 246.

Left: *Moses* by Michelangelo. Far less classical in style than Michelangelo's *David,* this statue stresses a sense of drama. (Moses was depicted with horns in medieval and renaissance art on account of a faulty translation of a passage from the Book of Exodus.) Right: *Descent from the Cross* by Michelangelo. This portrayal of tragedy was made by the sculptor for his own tomb. Note the distortion for effect exemplified by the elongated body and left arm of the figure of Christ. The figure in the rear is Nicodemus, but was probably intended to represent Michelangelo himself. The original is in the cathedral of Florence.

Certainly the greatest sculptor of the Italian Renaissance—indeed, probably the greatest sculptor of all time—was Michelangelo. Believing with Leonardo that the artist was an inspired creator, Michelangelo pursued this conviction to the conclusion that sculpture was the most exalted of the arts because it allowed the artist to imitate God most fully in recreating human forms. Furthermore, in Michelangelo's view the most God-like sculptor disdained slavish naturalism, for anyone could make a plaster cast of a human figure, but only an inspired creative genius could endow his sculpted figures with a sense of life. Accordingly, Michelangelo subordinated naturalism to the force of his imagination and sought restlessly to express his ideals in ever more arresting forms.

As in his painting, Michelangelo's sculpture followed a course from classicism to anticlassicism, that is, from harmonious modeling to dramatic distortion. The sculptor's most noted early work, his *David,* executed in 1501 when he was just twenty-six, is surely his most perfect classical statue in style and inspiration. Choosing, like Donatello, to depict a life-size male nude, Michelangelo nonetheless decided to make his own *David* heroic rather than merely graceful and hence conceived his nude in the purest, well-proportioned Greek terms. The resulting portrait in marble epitomizes for many the Italian Renaissance's facility for employing classical style to express the serenest confidence in human attainments. Deep serenity, however, is no longer prominent in the works of Michelangelo's middle period; rather, in a work such as the *Moses* of about 1515, the sculptor has begun to explore the use of anatomical distortion to create effects of emotional intensity—in this case the biblical prophet's righteous rage. While such statues remain awesomely heroic, as Michelangelo's life drew to a close he experimented ever more with exaggerated stylistic mannerisms for the purpose of communicating moods of brooding pensiveness or outright pathos. The culmination of this trend in Michelangelo's statuary is his moving *Descent from the Cross,* a depiction of the Virgin Mary grieving over the body of the dead Christ, intended for the artist's own tomb.

David by Michelangelo. Over thirteen feet high, this serenely self-confident affirmation of the beauty of the human form was placed prominently by the Florentine government in front of Florence's city hall to proclaim the city's humanistic values.

To a much greater extent than either sculpture or painting, Renaissance architecture had its roots in the past. The new building style was eclectic, a compound of elements derived from the Middle Ages and from antiquity. It was not the Greek or the Gothic, however, but the Roman and the Romanesque which provided the inspiration for the architecture of the Italian Renaissance. Neither the Greek nor the Gothic had ever found a congenial soil in Italy. The Romanesque, by contrast, was able to flourish there, since it was more in keeping with Italian traditions, while the persistence of a strong admiration for Latin culture made possible a revival of the Roman style. Accordingly, the great architects of the Renaissance generally adopted their building plans from the Romanesque churches and monasteries and copied their

St. Peter's, Rome. Built to a square cross plan originally conceived by Bramante and revised by Michelangelo. Completed in 1626, the church rises to a total height of 450 feet.

The Villa Rotonda of Palladio. A highly influential Renaissance private dwelling near Vicenza. Note how Palladio drew for inspiration on the Roman Pantheon, pictured above, p. 248.

decorative devices from the ruins of ancient Rome. The result was an architecture based on the cruciform floor plan of transept and nave and embodying the decorative features of the column and arch, or the column and lintel, the colonnade, and frequently the dome. Horizontal lines predominated; and, though many of the buildings were churches, the ideals they expressed were the secular ones of joy in this life and pride in human achievement. Renaissance architecture also emphasized harmony and proportion because Italian builders, under the influence of Neoplatonism, concluded that perfect proportions in man reflect the harmony of the universe, and that, therefore, the parts of a building should be related to each other and to the whole in the same way as the parts of the human body. A fine example of Renaissance architecture is St. Peter's Basilica in Rome, built under the patronage of Popes Julius II and Leo X and designed by some of the most celebrated architects of the time, including Donato Bramante (c. 1444–1514) and Michelangelo. Equally impressive are the artfully proportioned aristocratic country houses of the northern Italian architect Andrea Palladio (1518–1580), who redesigned ancient temples, such as the Roman Pantheon, to create secular miniatures meant to glorify the aristocrats who dwelled within them.

4. THE WANING OF THE ITALIAN RENAISSANCE

Political factors in the decline of the Italian Renaissance: the French invasion of 1494

Around 1550 the Renaissance in Italy began to decline after some two hundred glorious years. The causes of this decline were varied. Perhaps at the head of the list should be placed the French invasion of 1494 and the incessant warfare that ensued. The French king Charles VIII, who ruled the richest and most powerful kingdom in Europe, viewed Italy as an attractive prey for his grandiose ambitions. Accordingly, in 1494 he led an army of 30,000 well-trained troops across the Alps. The Medici of Florence fled before him, abandoning their city to immediate capture. Halting only long enough to establish peace with a subservient new republican government, the French resumed their advance and conquered Naples. By so doing, however, they aroused the suspicions of the rulers of Spain, who feared an attack on Sicily, which was their possession. An alliance among Spain, the Papal States, the Holy Roman Empire, Milan, and Venice finally forced Charles to withdraw from Italy. Yet upon his death his successor, Louis XII, launched a second invasion, and from 1499 until 1529 warfare in Italy was virtually uninterrupted. Alliances and counteralliances followed each other in bewildering succession, but they only managed to prolong the hostilities. The French won a great victory at Marignano in 1515, but they were decisively defeated by the Spanish at Pavia in 1525. The worst disaster came in 1527 when unruly Spanish and German troops, nominally under the command of the Spanish ruler and Holy Roman Emperor Charles V, but in fact entirely out of control, sacked the city of Rome, causing irreparable destruction. Only in 1529 did Charles finally manage to gain control over most of the Italian peninsula, putting the fighting to an end for a time. Once triumphant, Charles retained two of the largest portions of Italy for Spain—the Duchy of Milan and the Kingdom of Naples—and installed favored princes as the rulers of almost all the other Italian political entities exclusive of Venice and the Papal States. These protégés of the Spanish crown continued to preside over their own courts, to patronize the arts, and to adorn their cities with luxurious buildings, but in fact they were puppets of a foreign power and unable to inspire their retinues with a sense of vigorous cultural independence.

The Entrance of Charles VIII into Florence. A painting by Francesco Granacci.

THE STATES OF ITALY DURING THE RENAISSANCE c. 1494

*The waning of Italian
prosperity*

To the Italian political disasters was added a waning of Italian prosperity. Whereas Italy's virtual monopoly of trade with Asia in the fifteenth century had been one of the chief economic supports for the cultivation of Italian Renaissance culture, the gradual shifting of trade routes from the Mediterranean to the Atlantic region following the overseas discoveries of around 1500 slowly but surely cost Italy its supremacy as the center of world trade. Since the incessant warfare of the sixteenth century also contributed to Italy's economic hardships, as did Spanish financial exactions in Milan and Naples, there was gradually less and less of a surplus to support artistic endeavors.

A final cause of the decline of the Italian Renaissance was the Counter-Reformation. During the sixteenth century the Roman Church sought increasingly to exercise firm control over thought and art as part of a campaign to combat worldliness and the spread of Protestantism. In 1542 the Roman Inquisition was established; in 1564 the Council of Trent issued the first Index of Prohibited Books. The extent of ecclesiastical interference in cultural life was enormous. For example, Michelangelo's great *Last Judgment* in the Sistine Chapel was criticized by some straitlaced fanatics for looking like a bordello because it showed too many naked bodies. Therefore, Pope Paul IV ordered a second-rate artist to paint in clothing wherever possible. (The unfortunate artist was afterward known as "the underwear-maker.") While this incident may appear merely grotesquely humorous, the determination of ecclesiastical censors to enforce doctrinal uniformity could lead to death, as in the case of the unfortunate Neoplatonic philosopher Giordano Bruno, whose insistence on maintaining that there may be more than one world in contravention of the book of Genesis resulted in his being burned at the stake by the Roman Inquisition in 1600.

Giordano Bruno

The most notorious example of inquisitorial censorship of free intellectual speculation was the disciplining of the great scientist Galileo, whose achievements we will discuss in more detail later on. In 1616 the Holy Office in Rome condemned the new astronomical theory that the earth moves around the sun as "foolish, absurd, philosophically false, and formally heretical." Accordingly, the Inquisition proceeded immediately against Galileo when he published a brilliant defense of the heliocentric system in 1632. In short order the Inquisition made Galileo recant his "errors" and sentenced him to house arrest for the duration of his life. Galileo was not willing to face death for his beliefs, but after he publicly retracted his view that the earth revolves around the sun he supposedly whispered, "despite everything, it still moves." Not surprisingly, Galileo was the last great Italian contributor to the development of astronomy and physics until modern times.

In conclusion, it should be emphasized that cultural and artistic achievement was by no means extinguished in Italy after the middle of the sixteenth century. On the contrary, an impressive new artistic style known as Mannerism was cultivated between about 1550 and 1600 by painters who drew on traits found in the later work of Michelangelo, and in the seventeenth century Mannerism was supplanted by the dazzling Baroque style, which was born in Rome under ecclesiastical auspices. Similarly, Italian music registered enormous accomplishments virtually without interruption from the sixteenth to the twentieth century. But whatever seemed threatening to the Church could not be tolerated and the free spirit of Renaissance culture was found no more.

Continued flourishing of Italian art and music

5. THE RENAISSANCE IN THE NORTH

It was inevitable that after about 1500 the Renaissance, which originated in Italy, should have spread to other European countries. Throughout the fifteenth century a continuous procession of northern European students had come down to Italy to study in Italian universities such as Bologna or Padua, and an occasional Italian writer or artist traveled briefly north of the Alps. Such interchanges helped spread ideas, but only after around 1500 did most of northern Europe become sufficiently prosperous and politically stable to provide a truly con-

The diffusion of the Renaissance outside Italy

genial environment for the widespread cultivation of art and literature. Intellectual interchanges, moreover, became much more extensive
after 1494, when France and Spain started fighting on Italian battlefields. The result of this development was that more and more northern Europeans began to learn what the Italians had been accomplishing
(Spain's forces came not just from Spain but also from Germany and
the Low Countries). Then too leading Italian thinkers and artists, like
Leonardo, began to enter the retinues of northern kings or aristocrats.
Accordingly, the Renaissance became an international movement and
continued to be vigorous in the north even as it started to wane on its
native ground.

The Renaissance outside Italy, however, was by no means identical
to the Renaissance within Italy. Above all, the northern European
Renaissance was generally less secular. The main explanation for this
difference lies in the different social and cultural traditions Italy and
northern Europe had inherited from the Middle Ages. As we have
seen, late-medieval Italy's vigorous urban society fostered a secular
educational system which led, in union with a revival of classicism, to
the evolution of new and more secular forms of expression. The north,
on the other hand, had a far less mercantile and urban-oriented economy than did Italy and no northern cities ever attained the political
dominance of their surrounding countrysides as did Florence, Venice,
and Milan. Instead, political power was coalescing around the nation-
states (or in Germany the princedoms), whose rulers were willing until
about 1500 to acknowledge the educational and cultural hegemony of
the clergy. Consequently, northern European universities tended to
specialize in theological studies, and the most prominent buildings in
almost all the leading northern towns were cathedrals.

Simply stated, the northern Renaissance was the product of an
engrafting of certain Italian Renaissance ideals upon preexisting northern traditions. This can be seen very clearly in the case of the most
prominent northern Renaissance intellectual movement, *Christian
humanism*. Agreeing with Italian humanists that medieval Scholasticism was too ensnarled in logical hair-splitting to have any value for
the practical conduct of life, northern Christian humanists nonetheless
looked for practical guidance from purely biblical, religious precepts.
Like their Italian counterparts, they sought wisdom from antiquity,
but the antiquity they had in mind was Christian rather than in any
way pagan—the antiquity, that is, of the New Testament and the early
Christian fathers. Similarly, northern Renaissance artists were moved
by the accomplishments of Italian Renaissance masters to turn their
backs on medieval Gothic artistic styles and became determined instead
to learn how to employ classical techniques. Yet these same artists
depicted classical subject matter far less frequently than did the Italians, and, inhibited by the greater northern European attachment to
Christian asceticism, virtually never dared to portray completely
undressed nudes.

*The religious roots of the
northern Renaissance*

*Northern Christian
humanism*

Any discussion of northern Renaissance accomplishments in the realm of thought and literary expression must begin with the career of Desiderius Erasmus (c. 1467–1536), "the prince of the Christian humanists." The illegitimate son of a priest, Erasmus was born near Rotterdam in Holland, but later, as a result of his wide travels, became in effect a citizen of all northern Europe. Placed as a teenager against his will into a monastery, the young Erasmus found there little religion or formal instruction of any kind but plenty of freedom to read what he liked. He devoured all the classics he could get his hands on and the writings of many of the Church fathers. When he was about thirty years of age, he obtained permission to leave the monastery and enroll in the University of Paris, where he completed the requirements for the degree of bachelor of divinity. But Erasmus subsequently rebelled against what he considered the arid learning of Parisian Scholasticism. In one of his later writings he reported the following exchange: "Q. Where do you come from? A. The College of Montaigu. Q. Ah, then you must be bowed down with learning. A. No, with lice." Erasmus also never entered into the active duties of a priest, choosing rather to make his living by teaching and writing. Ever on the lookout for new patrons, he changed his residence at frequent intervals, traveling often to England, staying once for three years in Italy, and residing in several different cities in the Netherlands before settling finally toward the end of his life in Basel, Switzerland. By means of a voluminous correspondence he kept up with learned friends he made wherever he went, Erasmus became the leader of a northern European humanist coterie. And by means of the popularity of his numerous publications, he became the arbiter of "advanced" northern European cultural tastes during the first quarter of the sixteenth century.

Erasmus

Erasmus's many-sided intellectual activity may best be appraised from two different points of view: the literary and the doctrinal. As a Latin prose stylist, Erasmus was probably without peer since the days of Cicero. Extraordinarily learned and witty, he revelled in tailoring his mode of discourse to fit his subject, creating dazzling verbal effects when appropriate, and coining puns that took on added meaning if one knew Greek as well as Latin. Above all, Erasmus excelled in the deft use of irony, poking fun at all and sundry, including himself. For example, in his *Colloquies* (Latin for *Discussions*) he had a fictional character lament the evil signs of the times thus: "kings make war, priests strive to line their pockets, theologians invent syllogisms, monks roam outside their cloisters, the commons riot, and Erasmus writes colloquies."

Erasmus's literary accomplishments

But although Erasmus's urbane Latin style and wit earned him a wide audience for purely literary reasons, he by no means thought of himself as a mere entertainer. Rather, he intended everything he wrote to propagate in one form or another what he called the "philosophy of Christ." The essence of Erasmus's Christian humanist convictions

His "philosophy of Christ"

Knight, Death, and Devil by Dürer. This engraving of 1513 illustrates the ideal figure of Erasmus's *Handbook of a Christian Knight*. The steadfast knight is able to advance through the world on his charger, his loyal dog at his side, despite intimations of mortality and the snares of the devil.

was his belief that the entire society of his day was caught up in corruption and immorality as a result of having lost sight of the simple teachings of the Gospels. Accordingly, he offered to his contemporaries three different categories of publication: clever satires meant to show people the error of their ways, serious moral treatises meant to offer guidance toward proper Christian behavior, and scholarly editions of basic Christian texts.

The satires and moral treatises

In the first category belong the works of Erasmus that are still most widely read today—the *Praise of Folly* (1509), in which he pilloried Scholastic pedantry and dogmatism as well as the ignorance and superstitious credulity of the masses; and the *Colloquies* (1518), in which he held up contemporary religious practices for examination in a more serious but still pervasively ironic tone. In such works Erasmus let fictional characters do the talking, and hence his own views can only be determined by inference. But in his second mode Erasmus did not hesitate to speak clearly in his own voice. The most prominent treatises in this second genre are the quietly eloquent *Handbook of the Christian Knight* (1501), which urged the laity to pursue lives of serene inward piety, and the *Complaint of Peace* (1517), which pleaded movingly for Christian pacifism.

Despite this highly impressive literary production, however, Erasmus probably considered his textual scholarship his single greatest achievement. Revering the authority of the early Latin Fathers, Augustine, Jerome, and Ambrose, he brought out reliable editions of all their works, and revering the authority of the Bible most of all, he applied his extraordinary skills as a student of Latin and Greek to producing a reliable edition of the New Testament. After reading Lorenzo Valla's *Notes on the New Testament* in 1505, Erasmus became convinced that nothing was more imperative than divesting the text of the entire New Testament of the myriad errors in transcription and translation that had piled up during the Middle Ages, for no one could be a good Christian without being certain of exactly what Christ's message really was. Hence he spent ten years studying and comparing all the best early Greek biblical manuscripts he could find in order to establish an authoritative text. Finally appearing in 1516, Erasmus's Greek New Testament, published together with explanatory notes and his own new Latin translation, was one of the most important landmarks of biblical scholarship of all time.

Erasmus's edition of the New Testament

One of Erasmus's closest friends, and a close second to him in distinction among the ranks of the Christian humanists, was the Englishman Sir Thomas More (1478–1535). Following a successful career as a lawyer and as speaker of the House of Commons, in 1529 More was appointed lord chancellor of England. He was not long in this position, however, before he incurred the wrath of his royal master, King Henry VIII, because More, who was loyal to Catholic universalism, opposed the king's design to establish a national church under subjection to the state. Finally, in 1534, when More refused to take an oath acknowledging Henry as head of the Church of England, he was thrown into the Tower, and a year later met his death on the scaffold as a Catholic martyr. Much earlier, however, in 1516, long before More had any inkling of how his life was to end, he published the one work for which he will ever be best remembered, the *Utopia*. Creating the subsequently popular genre of "utopian fiction," More's *Utopia* expressed an Erasmian critique of contemporary society. Purporting to describe an ideal community on an imaginary island, the book is really an indictment of the glaring abuses of the time—of poverty undeserved and wealth unearned, of drastic punishments, religious persecution, and the senseless slaughter of war. The inhabitants of Utopia hold all their goods in common, work only six hours a day so that all may have leisure for intellectual pursuits, and practice the natural virtues of wisdom, moderation, fortitude, and justice. Iron is the precious metal "because it is useful," war and monasticism are abolished, and toleration is granted to all who recognize the existence of God and the immortality of the soul. Although More advanced no explicit arguments in his *Utopia* in favor of Christianity, he clearly meant to imply that if the "Utopians" could manage their society so

Sir Thomas More and Utopia

A Map of Thomas More's Imaginary Island of Utopia. "Utopia's" fictional discoverer, Hythlodaeus, whose name means "dispenser of nonsense" in Greek, points to the island of Utopia, which means "no place." From an early edition.

well without the benefit of Christian Revelation, Europeans who knew the Gospels ought to be able to do even better.

Whereas Erasmus and More were basically conciliatory in their temperaments and preferred to express themselves by means of wry understatements, a third representative of the Christian humanist movement, Erasmus's German disciple Ulrich von Hutten (1488–1523) was of a much more combative disposition. Dedicated to the cause of German cultural nationalism, von Hutten, in translating the Roman historian Tacitus, employed his command of classical scholarship to demonstrate how "proud and free" Germanic tribes had once triumphed heroically over Roman legions. In other writings he spoke up truculently in his own words to defend the German people against foreigners. But von Hutten's chief claim to fame was his collaboration with another German humanist, Crotus Rubianus, in the authorship of the *Letters of Obscure Men* (1515), one of the most stinging satires in the history of literature. This was written as part of a propaganda war in favor of a scholar named Johann Reuchlin who wished to pursue his study of Hebrew writings, above all, the Talmud. When Scholastic theologians from the University of Cologne and the German inquisitor general tried to have all Hebrew books in Germany destroyed,

Ulrich von Hutten and the Letters of Obscure Men

Reuchlin and his party strongly opposed the move. After a while it became apparent that direct argument was accomplishing nothing, so Reuchlin's supporters resorted to ridicule. Von Hutten and Rubianus published a series of letters, written in intentionally bad Latin, purportedly by some of Reuchlin's Scholastic opponents from the University of Cologne. These were given such ridiculous names as Goatmilker, Baldpate, and Dungspreader, and shown to be learned fools who paraded forth examples of absurd religious literalism or grotesque erudition. Heinrich Sheep's-mouth, for example, the supposed writer of one of the letters, professed to be worried that he had sinned grievously by eating on Friday an egg that contained the yolk of a chick. The author of another boasted of his "brilliant discovery" that Julius Caesar could not have written Latin histories because he was too busy with his military exploits ever to have learned Latin. Although immediately banned by the Church, the letters circulated nonetheless and were widely read, giving ever more currency to the Erasmian proposition that Scholastic theology and Catholic religious ritual had to be set aside in favor of the most earnest dedication to the pursuit of apostolic Christianity.

The decline of Christian humanism

With Erasmus, More, and von Hutten the list of energetic and eloquent Christian humanists is by no means exhausted, for the Englishman John Colet (c. 1467–1519), the Frenchman Jacques Lefèvre d'Étaples (c. 1455–1529), and the Spaniards Cardinal Francisco Ximénez de Cisneros (1436–1517) and Juan Luis Vives (1492–1540), among still many others, all made signal contributions to the collective enterprise of editing biblical and early Christian texts and expounding Gospel morality. But despite a host of achievements, the Christian humanist movement, which possessed such an extraordinary degree of international solidarity and vigor from about 1500 to 1525, was thrown into disarray by the rise of Protestantism and subsequently lost its momentum. The irony here is obvious, for the Christian humanists' emphasis on the literal truth of the Gospels and their devastating criticisms of clerical corruption and excessive religious ceremonialism certainly helped pave the way for the Protestant Reformation initiated by Martin Luther in 1517. But, as will be seen in the following chapter, very few Christian humanists were willing to go the whole route with Luther in rejecting the most fundamental principles on which Catholicism was based, and the few who did became such ardent Protestants that they lost all the sense of quiet irony that earlier had been a hallmark of Christian humanist expression. Most Christian humanists tried to remain within the Catholic fold while still espousing their ideal of nonritualistic inward piety, but as time went on the leaders of Catholicism had less and less tolerance for them because lines were hardening in the war with Protestantism and any suggestion of internal criticism of Catholic religious practices seemed like giving covert aid to "the enemy." Erasmus himself, who remained a Catholic, died early enough to escape opprobrium, but several of his

François Rabelais

His affirmativeness

less fortunate followers lived on to suffer as victims of the Spanish Inquisition.

Yet if Christian humanism faded rapidly after about 1525, the northern Renaissance continued to flourish throughout the sixteenth century in primarily literary and artistic forms. In France, for example, the highly accomplished poets Pierre de Ronsard (c. 1524–1585) and Joachim du Bellay (c. 1525–1560) wrote elegant sonnets in the style of Petrarch, and in England the poets Sir Philip Sidney (1554–1586) and Edmund Spenser (c. 1552–1599) drew impressively on Italian literary innovations as well. Indeed, Spenser's *The Faerie Queene,* a long chivalric romance written in the manner of Ariosto's *Orlando Furioso,* communicates as well as any Italian work the gorgeous sensuousness typical of Italian Renaissance culture.

More intrinsically original than any of the aforementioned poets was the French prose satirist François Rabelais (c. 1494–1553), probably the best loved of all the great European creative writers of the sixteenth century. Like Erasmus, whom he greatly admired, Rabelais was educated as a monk, but soon after taking holy orders he left his monastery to study medicine. Becoming thereafter a practicing physician in Lyons, Rabelais from the start interspersed his professional activities with literary endeavors of one sort or another. He wrote almanacs for the common people, satires against quacks and astrologers, and burlesques of popular superstitions. But by far his most enduring literary legacy consists of his five volumes of "chronicles" published under the collective title of *Gargantua and Pantagruel.*

Rabelais' account of the adventures of Gargantua and Pantagruel, originally the names of legendary medieval giants noted for their fabulous size and gross appetites, served as a vehicle for his lusty humor and his penchant for exuberant narrative as well as for the expression of his philosophy of naturalism. To some degree, Rabelais drew on the precedents of Christian humanism. Thus, like Erasmus, he satirized religious ceremonialism, ridiculed Scholasticism, scoffed at superstitions, and pilloried every form of bigotry. But much unlike Erasmus, who wrote in a highly cultivated classical Latin style comprehensible to only the most learned readers, Rabelais chose to address a far wider audience by writing in an extremely down-to-earth French, often loaded with the crudest vulgarities. Likewise, Rabelais wanted to avoid seeming in any way "preachy" and therefore eschewed all suggestions of moralism in favor of giving the impression that he wished merely to offer his readers some rollicking good fun. Yet, aside from the critical satire in *Gargantua and Pantagruel,* there runs through all five volumes a common theme of glorifying the human and the natural. For Rabelais, whose robust giants were really life-loving human beings writ very large, every instinct of humanity was healthy, provided it was not directed toward tyranny over others. Thus in his ideal community, the utopian "abbey of Thélème," there

Chambord. Built in the early sixteenth century by an Italian architect in the service of King Francis I of France, this magnificent Loire Valley château combines Gothic and Renaissance architectural traits.

was no repressiveness whatsoever, but only a congenial environment for the pursuit of life-affirming, natural human attainments, guided by the single rule of "do what thou wouldst."

Were we to imagine what Rabelais' fictional abbey of Thélème might have looked like, we would do best to picture it as resembling one of the famous sixteenth-century French Renaissance châteaux built along the River Loire, for the northern European Renaissance had its own distinctive architecture that often corresponded in certain essentials to its literature. Thus, just as Rabelais recounted stories of medieval giants in order to express an affirmation of Renaissance values, so French architects who constructed such splendid Loire châteaux as Amboise, Chenonceaux, and Chambord, combined elements of the late-medieval French flamboyant Gothic style with an up-to-date emphasis on classical horizontality to produce some of the most impressively distinctive architectural landmarks ever constructed in France. Yet much closer architectural imitation of Italian models occurred in France as well, for just as Ronsard and du Bellay modeled their poetic style very closely on Petrarch, so Pierre Lescot, the French architect who began work on the new royal palace of the Louvre in Paris in 1546, hewed closely to the classicism of Italian Renaissance masters in constructing a facade that emphasized classical pilasters and pediments.

It only remains to treat the accomplishments of northern Renaissance painting, another realm in which links between thought and art can be discerned. Certainly the most moving visual embodiments of the ideals of Christian humanism were conceived by the foremost of northern Renaissance artists, the German Albrecht Dürer (1471–1528).

*Northern Renaissance
architecture*

Albrecht Dürer

See color plates facing page 710 for *Self-Portrait* by Dürer and *Erasmus* by Hans Holbein the Younger

From the purely technical and stylistic points of view, Dürer's greatest significance lies in the fact that, returning to his native Nuremberg after a trip to Venice in 1494, he became the first northerner to master Italian Renaissance techniques of proportion, perspective, and modeling. Dürer also shared with contemporary Italians a fascination with reproducing the manifold works of nature down to the minutest details and a penchant for displaying various postures of the human nude. But whereas Michelangelo portrayed his naked David or Adam entirely without covering, Dürer's nudes are seldom lacking their fig leaves, in deference to more restrained northern traditions. Moreover, Dürer consistently refrained from abandoning himself to the pure classicism and sumptuousness of much Italian Renaissance art because he was inspired primarily by the more traditionally Christian ideals of Erasmus. Thus Dürer's serenely radiant *St. Jerome* expresses the sense of accomplishment that Erasmus or any other contemporary Christian humanist may have had while working quietly in his study, his *Knight, Death, and Devil* offers a stirring visual depiction of Erasmus's ideal Christian knight, and his *Four Apostles* intones a solemn hymn to the dignity and penetrating insight of Dürer's favorite New Testament authors, Saints Paul, John, Peter, and Mark.

Dürer would have loved nothing more than to have immortalized Erasmus in a major painted portrait, but circumstances prevented him from doing this because the paths of the two men crossed only once, and after Dürer started sketching his hero on that occasion his work was interrupted by Erasmus's press of business. Instead, the accomplishment of capturing Erasmus's pensive spirit in oils was left to the

The West Side of the Square Court of the Louvre by Pierre Lescot. The enlargement of the Louvre, begun by Lescot in 1546, took more than a century to complete. Drawing on the work of Bramante (see above, p. 624), he achieved a synthesis of the traditional château and the Renaissance palace.

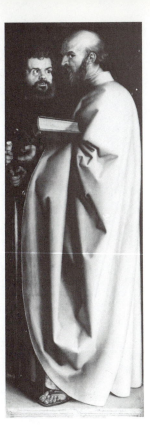

Left: *St. Jerome in his Study* by Dürer. St. Jerome, a hero for both Dürer and Erasmus, represents inspired Christian scholarship. Note how the scene exudes contentment, even down to the sleeping lion which seems rather like an overgrown tabby cat. Right: *The Four Apostles* by Dürer. This painting in two separate panels is a moving statement of the artist's intense religious faith.

second greatest of northern Renaissance artists, the German Hans Holbein the Younger (1497–1543). As good fortune would have it, during a stay in England Holbein also painted an extraordinarily acute portrait of Erasmus's friend and kindred spirit, Sir Thomas More, which enables us to see clearly why a contemporary called More "a man of . . . sad gravity; a man for all seasons." These two portraits in and of themselves point up a major difference between medieval and Renaissance culture because whereas the Middle Ages produced no convincing naturalistic likenesses of any leading intellectual figure, Renaissance culture's greater commitment to recapturing the essence of human individuality created the environment in which Holbein was able to make Erasmus and More come to life.

Sir Thomas More. Portrait by Hans Holbein the Younger.

6. RENAISSANCE DEVELOPMENTS IN MUSIC

Music in western Europe in the fifteenth and sixteenth centuries reached such a high point of development that it constitutes, together with

*The evolution of music as
an independent art*

*Leadership provided by
Italy and France*

painting and sculpture, one of the most brilliant aspects of Renaissance endeavor. While the visual arts were stimulated by the study of ancient models, music flowed naturally from an independent evolution which had been in progress in medieval Christendom. As earlier, leadership came from men trained in the service of the Church, but secular music was now valued as well, and its principles were combined with those of sacred music to bring a decided gain in color and emotional appeal. The distinction between sacred and profane became less sharp; most composers did not restrict their activities to either field. Music was no longer regarded merely as a diversion or an adjunct to worship but came into its own as a serious independent art.

Different sections of Europe vied with one another for musical leadership. As with the other arts, advance was related to the generous patronage afforded by the prosperous cities of Italy and the northern European princely courts. During the fourteenth century a pre- or early Renaissance musical movement called Ars Nova (new art) flourished in Italy and France. Its outstanding composers were Francesco Landini (c. 1325–1397) and Guillaume de Machaut (1300–1377). The madrigals, ballads, and other songs composed by the Ars Nova musicians testify to a rich secular art, but the greatest achievement of the period was a highly complicated yet delicate contrapuntal style adapted for ecclesiastical motets. Machaut, moreover, was the first known composer to provide a polyphonic version for the singing of the Mass.

The fifteenth century was ushered in by a synthesis of French, Flemish, and Italian elements that took place in the ducal court of

Renaissance Trumpeters and Singers. Reliefs by Luca della Robbia.

Burgundy. This music was melodious and gentle, but in the second half of the century it hardened a little as northern Flemish elements gained in importance. As the sixteenth century opened, Franco-Flemish composers appeared in every important court and cathedral all over Europe, gradually establishing regional-national schools, usually in attractive combinations of Flemish with German, Spanish, and Italian musical cultures. The various genres thus created show a close affinity with Renaissance art and poetry. In the second half of the sixteenth century the leaders of the nationalized Franco-Flemish style were the Flemish Roland de Lassus (1532–1594), the most versatile composer of the age, and the Italian Giovanni Pierluigi da Palestrina (c. 1525–1594), who specialized in highly intricate polyphonic choral music written for Catholic church services under the patronage of the popes in Rome. Music also flourished in sixteenth-century England, where the Tudor monarchs Henry VIII and Elizabeth I were active in patronizing the arts. Not only did the Italian madrigal, imported toward the end of the sixteenth century, take on remarkable new life in England, but songs and instrumental music of an original cast anticipated future developments on the Continent. In William Byrd (1543–1623) English music produced a master fully the equal of the great Flemish and Italian composers of the Renaissance period. The general level of musical proficiency seems to have been higher in Queen Elizabeth's day than in ours: the singing of part-songs was a popular pastime in homes and at informal social gatherings, and the ability to read a part at sight was expected of the educated elite.

In conclusion, it may be observed that while accomplishments in counterpoint were already very advanced in the Renaissance period, our modern harmonic system was still in its infancy, and thus there was much room for later experimentation. At the same time one should realize that the music of the Renaissance constitutes not merely a stage in evolution but a magnificent achievement in itself, with masters who rank among the great of all time. The composers Lassus, Palestrina, and Byrd are as truly representative of the artistic triumph of the Renaissance as are the painters Leonardo, Raphael, and Michelangelo. Their heritage, long neglected, has within recent years begun to be appreciated, and is now gaining in popularity as interested groups of musicians devote themselves to its revival.

7. THE SCIENTIFIC ACCOMPLISHMENTS OF THE RENAISSANCE PERIOD

Some extraordinarily important accomplishments were made in the history of science during the sixteenth and early seventeenth centuries, but these were not preeminently the achievements of Renaissance humanism. The educational program of the humanists placed a low value on science because it seemed irrelevant to their aim of making

*Renaissance foundations of
modern science: (1)
Neoplatonism*

A Cannon Foundry by Leonardo da Vinci

*(2) a mechanistic view of
the universe*

*(3) the integration of
theory and practice*

people more eloquent and moral. Science for humanists like Petrarch, Leonardo Bruni, or Erasmus was part and parcel of the "vain speculation" of the Scholastics which they attacked and held up to ridicule. Accordingly, none of the great scientists of the Renaissance age belonged to the humanist movement.

Nonetheless, at least two intellectual trends of the period did prepare the way for great new scientific advances. One was the currency of Neoplatonism. The importance of this philosophical system to science was that it proposed certain ideas, such as the central position of the sun and the supposed divinity of given geometrical shapes, that would help lead to crucial scientific breakthroughs. It is ironic that Neoplatonism seems very "unscientific" from the modern perspective because it emphasizes mysticism and intuition instead of empiricism or strictly rational thought. Yet it helped scientific thinkers to reconsider older notions which had impeded the progress of medieval science; in other words, it helped them to put on a new "thinking cap." Among the most important of the scientists who were influenced by Neoplatonism were Copernicus and Kepler.

A second trend that contributed to the advance of science was very different: the growth in popularity of a *mechanistic* interpretation of the universe. Renaissance mechanism owed its greatest impetus to the publication in 1543 of the works of the great Greek mathematician and physicist Archimedes. Not only were his concrete observations and discoveries among the most advanced and reliable in the entire body of Greek science, but Archimedes taught the view that the universe operates on the basis of mechanical forces, like a great machine. Because his view was diametrically opposed to the occult outlook of the Neoplatonists, who saw the world inhabited by spirits and driven by supernatural forces, it took some time to gather strength. Nonetheless, mechanism did gain some very important late-Renaissance adherents, foremost among whom was the Italian scientist Galileo. Ultimately mechanism played an enormous role in the development of modern science because it insisted upon finding observable and measurable causes and effects in the world of nature.

One other Renaissance development which contributed to the rise of modern science was the breakdown of the medieval separation between the realms of theory and practice. In the Middle Ages Scholastically trained clerics theorized about the natural world but never for a moment thought of tinkering with machines or dissecting corpses because this empirical approach to science lay outside the Scholastic framework. On the other hand, numerous technicians who had little formal education and knew little of abstract theories had much practical expertise in various aspects of mechanical engineering. Theory and practice began to come together in the fifteenth century. One reason for this was that the highly respected Renaissance artists bridged both areas of endeavor: not only were they marvelous craftsmen, but they advanced mathematics and science when they investigated the laws of perspective and optics, worked out geometric methods for supporting the weight of enormous architectural domes, and studied the dimensions and details of the human body. In general, they helped make science more empirical and practically oriented than it had been earlier. Other reasons for the integration were the decline in prestige of the overly theoretical universities and a growing interest in alchemy and astrology among the leisured classes. Here again we can see some irony: alchemy and astrology are today properly dismissed as unscientific superstitions, but in the sixteenth and seventeenth centuries their vogue led some wealthy amateurs to start building laboratories and measuring the courses of the stars. Thereby scientific practice was rendered eminently respectable. When that happened modern science was on the way to some of its greatest triumphs.

The actual scientific accomplishments of the Renaissance period were international in scope. The achievement par excellence in astronomy—the formulation and proof of the heliocentric theory that the earth revolves around the sun—was primarily the work of the Pole Copernicus, the German Kepler, and the Italian Galileo. Until the sixteenth century the Ptolemaic theory that the earth stands still at the center of the universe went virtually unchallenged in western Europe. Nicholas Copernicus (1473–1543), a Polish clergyman who had absorbed Neoplatonism while studying in Italy, was the first to posit an alternative system. Copernicus made few new observations, but he thoroughly reinterpreted the significance of the old astronomical evidence. Inspired by the Neoplatonic assumptions that the sphere is the most perfect shape, that motion is more nearly divine than rest, and that the sun sits "enthroned" in the midst of the universe, "ruling his children the planets which circle around him," Copernicus worked out a new heliocentric theory. Specifically, in his *On the Revolutions of the Heavenly Spheres*—which he completed around 1530 but did not publish until 1543—he argued that the earth and the planets move around the sun in concentric circles. Copernicus's system itself was still highly imperfect: by no means did it account without difficulties for all the known facts of planetary motion. Moreover, it asked people to reject their commonsense assumptions that the sun moves because observation shows it moving across the sky and that the earth stands still because no movement can be felt. More serious, Copernicus contradicted passages in the Bible, such as the one wherein Joshua commands the sun to stand still. As a result of such problems, believers in Copernicus's heliocentric theory remained distinctly in the minority until the early seventeenth century.

It was Kepler and Galileo who ensured the triumph of Copernicus's revolution in astronomy. Johann Kepler (1571–1630), a mystical thinker who was in many ways more like a magician than a modern scientist, studied astronomy in order to probe the hidden secrets of God. His basic conviction was that God had created the universe according to mathematical laws. Relying on the new and impressively accurate

The Ptolemaic System of the Universe

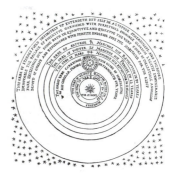

The Copernican System. A diagram devised by Copernicus himself. Note that the planetary orbits are still circular, as they were in the Ptolemaic system. It was Johann Kepler who proved that all the planets move in elliptical orbits.

Galileo. A portrait by Ottavio
Leoni.

astronomical observations of the Dane Tycho Brahe (1546–1601), Kepler was able to recognize that two assumptions about planetary motion that Copernicus had taken for granted were simply not in accord with the observable facts. Specifically, Kepler replaced Copernicus's belief in uniform planetary velocity with his own "First Law" that the speed of planets varies with their distance from the sun, and he replaced Copernicus's view that planetary orbits were circular with his "Second Law" that the earth and the other planets travel in *elliptical* paths around the sun. He also argued that magnetic attractions between the sun and the planets keep the planets in orbital motion. That approach was rejected by most seventeenth-century mechanistic scientists as being far too magical, but in fact it paved the way for the law of universal gravitation formulated by Isaac Newton at the end of the seventeenth century.

As Kepler perfected Copernicus's heliocentric system from the point of view of mathematical theory, so Galileo Galilei (1564–1642) promoted acceptance for it by gathering further astronomical evidence. With a telescope which he manufactured himself and raised to a magnifying power of thirty times, he discovered the moons of Jupiter, the rings of Saturn, and spots on the sun. He was able also to determine that the Milky Way is a collection of celestial bodies independent of our solar system and to form some idea of the enormous distances of the fixed stars. Though many held out against them, these discoveries of Galileo gradually convinced the majority of scientists that the main conclusion of Copernicus was true. The final triumph of this idea is commonly called the Copernican Revolution. Few more significant events have occurred in the intellectual history of the world, for it overturned the medieval worldview and paved the way for modern conceptions of mechanism, skepticism, and the infinity of time and space. Some thinkers believe that it contributed also to the degradation of man, since it swept man out of his majestic position at the center of the universe and reduced him to a mere particle of dust in an endless cosmic machine.

In the front rank among the physicists of the Renaissance were Leonardo da Vinci and Galileo. If Leonardo da Vinci had failed completely as a painter, his contributions to science would still entitle him to considerable fame. Not the least of these were his achievements in physics. Though he actually made few complete discoveries, his conclusion that "every weight tends to fall toward the center by the shortest way" contained the kernel of the law of gravity. In addition, he worked out the principles of an astonishing variety of inventions, including a diving board, a steam engine, an armored tank, and a helicopter. Galileo is especially noted as a physicist for his law of falling bodies. Skeptical of the traditional theory that bodies fall with a speed directly proportional to their weight, he taught that bodies dropped from various heights would fall at a rate of speed which increases with the square of the time involved. Rejecting the Scholastic notions of absolute gravity and absolute levity, he taught that these are purely relative terms, that all bodies have weight, even those which, like the air, are invisible, and that in a vacuum all objects would fall with equal velocity. Galileo seems to have had a broader conception of a universal force of gravitation than Leonardo da Vinci, for he perceived that the power which holds the moon in the vicinity of the earth and causes the satellites of Jupiter to circulate around that planet is essentially the same as the force which enables the earth to draw bodies to its surface. He never formulated this principle as a law, however, nor did he realize all of its implications, as did Newton some fifty years later.

The record of Renaissance achievements in medicine and anatomy is also a most impressive one. Attention must be called above all to the work of the German Theophrastus von Hohenheim, known as Paracelsus (1493–1541), the Spaniard Michael Servetus (1511–1553), and the Belgian Andreas Vesalius (1514–1564). The physician Paracelsus resembled Copernicus and Kepler in believing that spiritual rather than material forces governed the workings of the universe. Hence he was a firm believer in alchemy and astrology. Nevertheless, Paracelsus relied on observation for his knowledge of diseases and their cures. Instead of following the teachings of ancient authorities, he traveled widely, studying cases of illness in different environments and experimenting with many drugs. Above all, his insistence on the close relationship of chemistry and medicine foreshadowed and sometimes directly influenced important modern achievements in pharmacology and healing. Michael Servetus, whose major interest was theology, but who practiced medicine for a living, discovered the lesser or pulmonary circulation of the blood, in an attempt to prove the veracity of the Virgin birth. He described how the blood leaves the right chambers of the heart, is carried to the lungs to be purified, then returns to the heart and is conveyed from that organ to all parts of the body. But Servetus had no idea of the return of the blood to the heart through the veins, a discovery that was made by the Englishman William Harvey in the early seventeenth century.

Michael Servetus

Purely by coincidence the one sixteenth-century scientific treatise that came closest to rivaling in significance Copernicus's work in astronomy, Vesalius's *On the Structure of the Human Body,* was published in 1543, the same year that saw the issuance of Copernicus's *Revolutions of the Heavenly Spheres.* Vesalius, a cosmopolitan who was born in Brussels and studied in Paris but later migrated to Italy where he taught anatomy and surgery at the University of Padua, approached his research from the correct point of view that much of ancient anatomical doctrine was in error. For him the ancient anatomy of Galen (so to speak, the Ptolemy of medicine) could only be corrected on the basis of direct observation. Hence he applied himself to frequent dissections of human corpses to see how various parts of the body actually appear when the skin covering is stripped away. Not content with

Andreas
Vesalius

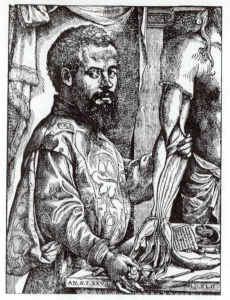

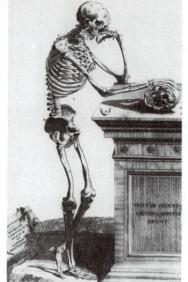

Two Plates from Vesalius's On the Structure of the Human Body. *On the left is a portrait of Vesalius himself displaying the sinews of the forearm. Note the striking similarity to the anatomical drawings of Leonardo, shown above, p. 618. On the right we see "the human skeleton shown from the side." The presence of the sarcophagus with the Latin warning "we live by the spirit, all else will die" shows that scientific illustrations still had to be justified by moralistic sententiousness in the early-modern period.*

merely describing in words what he saw, Vesalius then collaborated with an artist—Jan van Calcar, a fellow Belgian who had come to Italy to study under the Renaissance master Titian—in portraying his observations in detailed engravings. Art historians are uncertain as to whether van Calcar was directly inspired in executing his illustrations for Vesalius by knowledge of earlier anatomical drawings of Leonardo da Vinci, but even if not, he certainly relied on a cumulative tradition of expert anatomical depiction bequeathed to him by Italian Renaissance art. Gathered in Vesalius's *Structure of the Human Body* of 1543, van Calcar's plates offered a new map of the human anatomy just when Copernicus was laying out a new map of the heavens. Since Vesalius in the same work offered basic explanations of how parts of the body move and interact in addition to discussing and illustrating how they look, he is often counted as the father of modern physiology as well as the father of modern anatomy. With his landmark treatise we come to a fitting end to our survey of Renaissance accomplishments inasmuch as his *Structure of the Human Body* represented the fullest degree of fruitful international intellectual exchanges as well as the fullest merger of theory and practice, and art and science.

SELECTED READINGS

• *Items so designated are available in paperback editions.*

Baker, Herschel, *The Image of Man: A Study of the Idea of Human Dignity in Classical Antiquity, the Middle Ages, and the Renaissance,* Cambridge, Mass., 1947. An outstanding and engagingly written survey from the perspective of a modern liberal.

• Baxandall, Michael, *Painting and Experience in Fifteenth Century Italy,* Oxford, 1972.

Benesch, O., *The Art of the Renaissance in Northern Europe*, rev. ed., New York, 1965.

• Boas, Marie, *The Scientific Renaissance: 1450–1630*, New York, 1962. An excellent, straightforward survey.

• Burckhardt, J., *The Civilization of the Renaissance in Italy*, many eds. The nineteenth-century work that formulated the modern view of the Renaissance.

Burke, Peter, *Culture and Society in Renaissance Italy, 1420–1540*, New York, 1972.

• Bush, D., *The Renaissance and English Humanism*, Toronto, 1939.

• Butterfield, H., *The Origins of Modern Science*, London, 1949. Clear and wide ranging. Shows how science developed from major changes in intellectual orientations.

• Chambers, R. W., *Thomas More*, London, 1936. A spirited defense of the view that More was a lifelong committed Catholic.

• Clark, Kenneth M., *Leonardo da Vinci*, 2nd ed., Cambridge, 1952.

• De Tolnay, C., *Michelangelo: Sculptor, Painter, Architect*, Princeton, 1975.

Ferguson, W., ed., *The Renaissance: Six Essays*, rev. ed., New York, 1962.

• Fox, Alistair, *Thomas More: History and Providence*, Oxford, 1982. More reliable in its judgments than Chambers.

• Gilmore, M., *The World of Humanism, 1453–1517*, New York, 1952. A well-written survey.

Gould, Cecil, *An Introduction to Italian Renaissance Painting*, London, 1957.

Hale, J. R., *Machiavelli and Renaissance Italy*, New York, 1960.

• ———, *Renaissance Europe: The Individual and Society, 1480–1520*, London, 1971. A different kind of survey that does not treat the great events but examines the quality of life.

• Hay, D., ed., *The Renaissance Debate*, New York, 1965. A collection of readings on the question of how to define the Renaissance.

Herlihy, D., and C. Klapisch-Zuber, *Tuscans and Their Families*, New Haven, 1985. Best on the social context of Florentine culture.

• Kearney, H., *Science and Change, 1500–1700*, New York, 1971. Supplements Butterfield in arguing that science progressed as the result of contributions made by three different "schools."

• Kristeller, P. O., *Eight Philosophers of the Italian Renaissance*, Stanford, 1964. Admirably clear.

———, *Renaissance Thought: The Classic, Scholastic, and Humanistic Strains*, New York, 1961. Very helpful in defining main trends of Renaissance thought.

• Kuhn, Thomas S., *The Copernican Revolution: Planetary Astronomy in the Development of Western Thought*, Cambridge, Mass., 1957. Admirably clear.

Larner, John, *Culture and Society in Italy, 1290–1420*, New York, 1971.

• Levey, M., *Early Renaissance (Style and Civilization)*, Baltimore, 1967. Art history.

• Martines, L., *Power and Imagination: City-States in Renaissance Italy*, New York, 1979. An expert account of the interrelationships between political and material circumstances and cultural expressions.

• Panofsky, E., *The Life and Art of Albrecht Dürer*, 4th ed., Princeton, 1955.

• ———, *Renaissance and Renascences in Western Art*, Stockholm, 1960. A difficult but rewarding attempt to distinguish the Italian Renaissance from its medieval predecessors.

Phillips, Margaret M., *Erasmus and the Northern Renaissance,* London, 1949.
Pope-Hennessy, J., *The Portrait in the Renaissance,* Princeton, 1966.
• Ralph, Philip L., *The Renaissance in Perspective,* New York, 1973. Both a
    useful summary and a stimulus to thought.
Reese, Gustave, *Music in the Renaissance,* rev. ed., New York, 1959. The
    leading work on the subject.
• Rice, E. F., Jr., *The Foundations of Early Modern Europe, 1460–1559,* New
    York, 1970.
    ———, *Saint Jerome in the Renaissance,* Baltimore, 1985. Employs a fascinat-
    ing strategy for estimating Renaissance values.
Seigel, J., *Rhetoric and Philosophy in Renaissance Humanism,* Princeton, 1968.
    Treats a basic tension in the thought of early Renaissance thinkers.
Stechow, W., *Northern Renaissance Art: 1400–1600,* Englewood Cliffs, N.J.,
    1966.
Tracy, James, *Erasmus: The Growth of a Mind,* Geneva, 1972. The best
    intellectual biography.
• Whitfield, J. H., *A Short History of Italian Literature,* Baltimore, 1960.
• Wittkower, R., *Architectural Principles in the Age of Humanism,* rev. ed.,
    New York, 1965. An art-historical classic.

SOURCE MATERIALS

Alberti, Leon Battista, *The Family in Renaissance Florence,* tr. R. N. Watkins,
    Columbia, S.C., 1969.
• Cassirer, E., et al., eds., *The Renaissance Philosophy of Man,* Chicago, 1948.
    Leading works of Petrarch, Pico, etc.
• Castiglione, B., *The Book of the Courtier,* tr. C. S. Singleton, New York,
    1959.
• Erasmus, D., *The Praise of Folly,* tr. J. Wilson, Ann Arbor, Mich., 1958.
• ———, *Ten Colloquies,* tr. C. R. Thompson, Indianapolis, 1957.
• Kohl, B. G., and R. G. Witt, eds., *The Earthly Republic: Italian Humanists
    on Government and Society,* Philadelphia, 1978. New translations with
    excellent introductions.
• Machiavelli, N., *The Prince,* tr. R. M. Adams, New York, 1976. In addition
    to Machiavelli's text, this edition provides related documents and an
    excellent selection of scholarly interpretations.
• Montaigne, M. de, *Essays,* tr. J. M. Cohen, Baltimore, 1958.
• More, Sir Thomas, *Utopia,* tr. R. M. Adams, New York, 1975. In the
    same series as Adams's translation of Machiavelli's *Prince;* provides back-
    ground materials and selected scholarly interpretations as well as the
    text.
• Rabelais, F., *Gargantua and Pantagruel,* tr. J. M. Cohen, Baltimore, 1955.
    A robust modern translation.

Chapter 19

EUROPE EXPANDS AND DIVIDES: OVERSEAS DISCOVERIES AND PROTESTANT REFORMATION

Formerly we were at the end of the world, and now we are in the middle of it, with an unprecedented change in our fortunes.

> —Hernán Pérez de Oliva, addressing the city fathers
> of Cordova, Spain, 1524

Since then your serene majesty and your lordships seek a simple answer, I will give it in this manner, neither horned nor toothed: unless I am convinced by the testimony of Scripture or by clear reason . . . I am bound by the Scripture I have quoted, and my conscience is captive to the Word of God. I cannot and I will not retract anything, since it is neither safe nor right to violate one's conscience. I cannot do otherwise, here I stand, may God help me. Amen.

> —Martin Luther, addressing the Diet of Worms, 1521

Much as the civilization of the Renaissance made fundamental contributions toward the shaping of the modern world, the two most dramatic developments in the transition from the Middle Ages to the early-modern period of western European history were the overseas ventures of Spain and Portugal, and the Protestant Reformation. More or less overnight, these two developments changed the course of European history forever. Whereas European Christian civilization had been geographically self-contained throughout the thousand years of its prior history (excepting the relatively brief Crusade episode), in just a few decades, from about 1490 to about 1520, Europeans sailed over the open seas to take commanding positions in Southeast Asia and lay claim to the whole Western Hemisphere. Ever since, the course of European history has been inseparable from interactions between events on the landmass of Europe and European engagements in the rest of the world.

Overseas expansion of Spain and Portugal

The Protestant
Reformation

But just when Europe was expanding it was also dividing. Up until the early sixteenth century, despite growing national differences, there remained a distinct European "Community of Christendom," presided over by the pope. Wherever one traveled one could hear the same Latin mass, see infants baptized and couples wed according to the same ecclesiastical formulae, and receive blessings from priests who were all ordained by virtue of the same papal authority. As quickly as Europeans took hold of the world, however, they lost their spiritual unity. The Protestant Reformation initiated by Martin Luther in 1517, as well as the Catholic response to it, were both to have numerous progressive effects, but the most obvious immediate results were that Europe rapidly became divided along several different religious lines and that Europeans quickly started warring with one another in the name of faith.

A common theme of
heroism

Although the overseas discoveries and Protestant Reformation were roughly contemporaneous, it is important to recognize that in their origins they had nothing directly to do with each other. The early explorers sailed prior to or in disregard of European religious dissensions, and the early Protestants gave little thought to the opening up of new trade routes or the discovery of continents. Yet there is warrant for treating the discoveries, the Protestant Reformation, and the Catholic Counter-Reformation all in the same chapter because their effects very quickly became interrelated and also because all these movements were full of incidents of great heroism. As Columbus sailed fearlessly into the unknown and Balboa viewed a new ocean, "silent, upon a peak in Darien," so Luther struggled fearlessly for a new understanding of "the justice of God" and the crippled soldier Ignatius Loyola found inspiration by inward "spiritual exercises," thereby opening up new vistas of their own.

1. THE OVERSEAS DISCOVERIES AND CONQUESTS OF PORTUGAL AND SPAIN

Western Europe seemingly
on the defensive

At first glance the speed with which Europeans in the years around 1500 began to traverse the high seas appears bewildering and almost incomprehensible. With good reason most contemporaries perceived Christian civilization to be on the defensive, not the offensive, in the second half of the fifteenth century. In 1453 Constantinople, a hitherto impregnable barrier to Islamic advance, fell to the Turks, commanded by Sultan Muhammad II "the Conqueror"; Serbia was lost in 1459 and Albania followed in 1470. Most frightening of all to western Europeans was a Turkish landing on the Italian peninsula itself in 1480, which saw the city of Otranto occupied and half the inhabitants slaughtered. Only the death of Sultan Muhammad in 1481 caused the Turks to abandon their Italian foothold, but many feared that the "Infidels" might soon return. In the midst of an unsuccessful attempt to organize united European resistance to the Turks, Pope Pius II (1458–1464) observed: "I see nothing good on the horizon."

Yet Pius II could hardly have been more wrong, for while Christians remained on the defensive against the Turks in eastern Europe until the later sixteenth century, Portuguese and Spanish sailing ships on the Atlantic horizon soon made Christians lords of much of the world. A few facts speak eloquently for themselves: in 1482 the Portuguese built a fortress at Elmina, in modern-day Ghana, which quickly dominated trade on the West African "Gold Coast"; in 1492 Columbus sighted the West Indies; in 1500 the Portuguese established their first trading base on the west coast of India; and in the two years from 1519 to 1521 the Spaniard Cortés seized hold of the Mexican empire of Montezuma.

How did this all happen so quickly? Two different schools of scholarly interpretation offer substantially different responses. Proponents of what may be called the "Renaissance School" point out that the Portuguese and Spanish voyages of discovery occurred at the same time as the spread of Renaissance civilization (Columbus was a direct contemporary of Leonardo da Vinci) and argue that European overseas expansion can only be explained as a manifestation of allegedly new Renaissance principles of curiosity and self-reliance in practical affairs. But this interpretation assumes falsely that medieval people were not curious and self-reliant. Proponents of the Renaissance school also call attention to the fact that many of the mariners who sailed for Portugal and Spain were Italian born, but here they dodge the reality that some Italian voyagers, like Columbus himself, came from Genoa, a city which hardly participated in Italian Renaissance civilization. More important, the Renaissance interpretation seems weak because the leading Italian Renaissance states did not patronize the voyages of discovery at all. Undeniably some bits of classical geographical knowledge acquired in Italy by Renaissance humanists strengthened the resolve of some explorers to pursue certain ocean routes, but otherwise the alternative to the Renaissance explanation, namely the view that the movement of overseas expansion came from medieval preparations, seems far preferable.

Explanations for voyages: "Renaissance School"

Simply stated, the motives, the knowledge, and the wherewithal for the great discoveries were all essentially medieval. Certainly the single most dominant motive for the oceanic voyages was economic— the quest for Asiatic spices and other luxury goods. Pepper, cinnamon, nutmeg, ginger, and cloves could all be grown only in the tropical climates of Southeast Asia, and all were greatly prized throughout the High and late Middle Ages because of their preservative qualities. (Imagine a civilization without refrigeration and one can easily understand why wealthy Europeans hankered after tangy spices to keep their food from putrifying and to relieve the monotony of salt.) In the late Middle Ages, Asiatic spices, as well as luxury cloths and precious gems, reached European households by means of the enterprise of Islamic,

Medieval background to voyages: economic motives

Venetian, and Genoese middlemen, but the costs were exorbitant and a fortune was to be made by anyone who could go directly to the source by sea. (Land routes were out of the question because turbulent conditions in central Asia made them extremely unsafe; moreover, until the invention of railroads it normally was vastly more expensive to transport goods by land than by water.) Complementing the economic motives for overseas exploration were religious ones—hopes for converting unbaptized heathens and of finding imagined "lost Christians" in the East who might serve as allies against Islam. Needless to say, these hopes, like the lust for spices, flourished in the Middle Ages quite independently of the Italian Renaissance.

Then too the most important knowledge that lay behind the great discoveries and also the technological means to execute them were as medieval as the motivations. The popular notion that Europeans before Columbus believed the earth to be flat is simply a mistake: it would have been impossible after the twelfth century to have found an educated person or a mariner who did not accept the fact that the earth is a sphere. Nor did this knowledge remain solely in the realm of theory. As early as 1291 two Genoese, the Vivaldi brothers, sailed out on the Atlantic with the aim of reaching the East Indies by a "westward route." Although the Vivaldis never came back, by the middle of the fourteenth century Portuguese mariners were sailing regularly back and forth on the Atlantic as far west as the Azores Islands. These Portuguese sailings offer proof that by about 1350 European shipbuilding and navigational technology were fully up to the challenge of reaching new continents. Since the Azores are one-third of the distance between Europe and America, from the strictly technological point of view any ship that could sail from Portugal to the Azores could have sailed all the way to the New World.

Why, then, was America not discovered a century before it actually was? Historians are at their greatest disadvantage in trying to explain things that did not happen, but two hypotheses may be offered. One relates to the fact that the fourteenth and fifteenth centuries were times of acute economic depression and political turmoil throughout western Europe. Since the major states of the Atlantic—France, England, and Castile (the dominant kingdom on the Spanish peninsula)—were all weakened by economic contraction and caught up in seemingly interminable wars, it is no wonder that none of them commissioned expensive and risky sailing ventures to the west. The second, less speculative hypothesis pertains to the change in routes pursued by Portugal, the one Atlantic state already deeply involved in ambitious seaward expeditions. After establishing colonies in the second half of the fourteenth century on the Atlantic islands of the Azores and Madeira that yielded a lucrative trade in sugar and wine, the Portuguese in the early fifteenth century quite understandably turned their attention to exploring the coast of West Africa because Africa promised even greater wealth in gold and slaves. Thereafter one Portuguese African

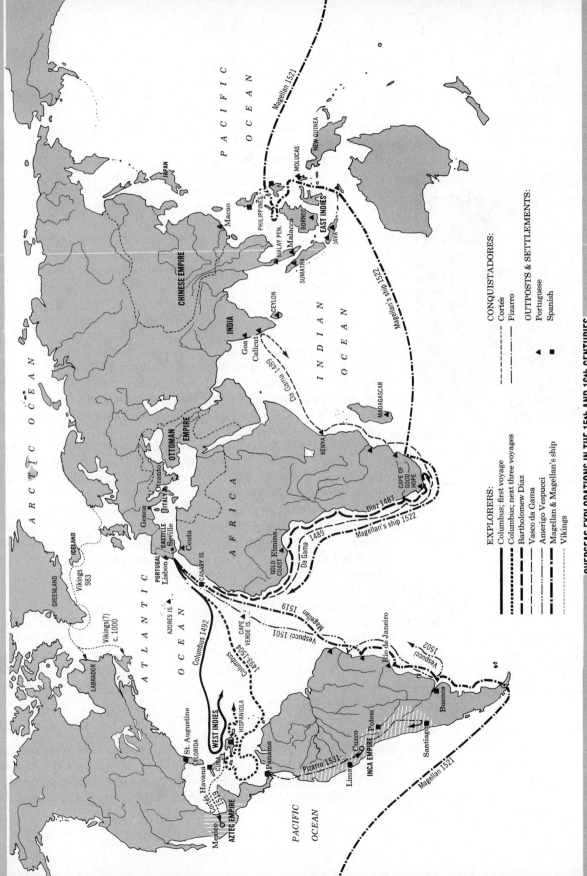

OVERSEAS EXPLORATIONS IN THE 15th AND 16th CENTURIES

EXPLORERS:

— Columbus; first voyage
····· Columbus; next three voyages
━━━ Bartholomew Diaz
— — Vasco da Gama
──── Amerigo Vespucci
—·—·— Magellan & Magellan's ship
········· Vikings

CONQUISTADORES:

—··—··— Cortés
—·—·— Pizarro

OUTPOSTS & SETTLEMENTS:

▲ Portuguese
■ Spanish

ARCTIC OCEAN

PACIFIC OCEAN

GREENLAND

ICELAND
Vikings 983

LABRADOR

Vikings(?)
c. 1000

ATLANTIC OCEAN

AZORES IS.

Columbus 1492

Columbus 1493-1504

CAPE VERDE IS.

Vespucci 1501

Magellan 1519

St. Augustine
FLORIDA

WEST INDIES

Havana
CUBA

Cortés 1519
Mexico
AZTEC EMPIRE

HISPANIOLA

Panama

PACIFIC OCEAN

Pizarro 1531
Lima
Cuzco
Potosi
INCA EMPIRE

Santiago

Buenos Aires

Rio de Janeiro

Vespucci 1502

Magellan 1521

PORTUGAL
Lisbon
CASTILLE
Seville
Genoa
Otranto
ITALY

CANARY IS.

Ceuta

OTTOMAN EMPIRE

AFRICA

GOLD COAST
Elmina

Da Gama 1489

Diaz 1487

Magellan's ship 1522

CAPE OF GOOD HOPE

KENYA

MADAGASCAR

INDIAN OCEAN

Da Gama 1498

Goa
Calicut

INDIA

CEYLON

SUMATRA

MALAY PEN.
Malacca

BORNEO

JAVA

EAST INDIES

PHILIPPINES

Macao

CHINESE EMPIRE

JAPAN

PACIFIC OCEAN

MOLUCAS

NEW GUINEA

Magellan 1521

Magellan's ship 1522

*Prince Henry the Navigator. By
a fifteenth-century Portuguese
painter.*

discovery led to another until the Cape of Good Hope was rounded in 1487 and the race for Asiatic spices that led to the most dramatic of European overseas exploits had begun. Thus seen from the perspective of late-medieval Portuguese sailing and trading history, the great discoveries look much less startlingly revolutionary than they do at first glance.

The fifteenth-century Portuguese voyages that served as the major connecting link to the dramatic achievements of the years around 1500 were commissioned by Portugal's Prince Henry "the Navigator" from 1418 until his death in 1460. Starting from an initial base of Ceuta in North Africa, Portuguese ships advanced steadily southward along the West African coastline, braving the ever-hotter sun and establishing forts and trading posts as they went. The extraordinary heroism of the sailors on these ships can easily be appreciated from a mid–fifteenth-century account, according to which four galleys "were provisioned for several years and were away three years, but only one galley returned and even on that galley most of the crew had died. And those which survived could hardly be recognized as human. They had lost flesh and hair, the nails had gone from hands and feet. Their eyes were sunk deep in their heads and they were as black as Moors. They spoke of heat so incredible that it was a marvel that ships and crews were not burnt. They said also that they found no houses or land and they could sail no farther. The farther they sailed, so the sea became more furious and the heat grew more intense. They thought that the other ships had sailed too far and it was impossible that they should be able to return." But return they did, and despite the terrifying tales that such crews told, new expeditions continually were sent out that ventured still farther.

After Henry the Navigator's death in 1460 some slackening in the Portuguese enterprise ensued, but it regained vigor with the accession of King John II (1481–1495). Inasmuch as the Portuguese had already gained full control of the African Gold Coast and slave trade, they naturally began to set their sights on reaching the wealth of Asia. The

*Discovery of Cape of
Good Hope*

literal as well as figurative turning point in this effort was the accidental rounding of the tip of southernmost Africa by the Portuguese captain Bartholomew Dias in 1487. Since Dias had only accomplished this feat by being caught in a gale, he pessimistically called this promontory the "Cape of Storms," but John II took a more optimistic view of the matter and renamed it the Cape of Good Hope. Furthermore, John resolved to organize a major naval expedition designed to travel beyond the cape all the way to India.

*Vasco da Gama's voyage
to India*

After several delays John's successor, Manuel I (1495–1521), finally sent off a fleet in 1497 captained by Vasco da Gama which accomplished all that was planned. Da Gama's exploits were so heroic that they later became the basis for the Portuguese national epic, *The Lusiad*. After four months beyond sight of land the intrepid captain rounded Africa, sailed up Africa's east coast to Kenya, and then crossed the

Left: *The Tower of Belem.* Right: *A Portuguese Galleon.* The Tower of Belem, a fifteenth-century fort, stands at the beach where Vasco da Gama departed in 1497 to sail beyond the Cape of Good Hope to India. The galleon shown at the right is the sort of ship da Gama might have sailed in.

Indian Ocean to western India, where he loaded his ships with spices. Two years after his departure da Gama returned, having lost half of his fleet and one-third of his men. But his pepper and cinnamon were so valuable that they made his losses seem worthwhile. Now master of the quickest route to riches in the world, King Manuel swiftly capitalized on da Gama's accomplishment. After 1500 Portuguese trading fleets sailed regularly to India; by 1510 Portuguese arms had established full control of the western Indian coastline, and in 1511 Portuguese ships seized Malacca, a center of the spice trade on the Malay peninsula. The Cape of Good Hope thus had lived up to John II's prophetic name and Europeans had arrived in the Far East to stay.

The decision of the Spanish rulers to underwrite Columbus's famous voyage was directly related to the progress of the Portuguese ventures. Specifically, given the strong likelihood that the Portuguese would dominate the sea lanes leading to Asia by the east in the wake of Dias's successful return in 1488, the only alternative for Portugal's Spanish rivals was to finance someone bold enough to try to reach Asia by sailing west. The popular image of Christopher Columbus (1451–1506) as a visionary who struggled to convince hardened ignoramuses that the world was round does not bear up under scrutiny. In fact the sphericity of the earth was never in doubt. Rather the stubborn Genoese seaman who had settled in Spain erred in vastly underestimat-

Reasons for Columbus's westward voyage

ing the distance westward from Europe to Asia. Had Columbus known the actual circumference of the earth, even he would not have dared to set out because he would have realized that the distance to Asia, assuming no barriers lay between, was too great for ships of his day to traverse. America, then, was discovered as the result of a colossal error in reckoning, but when Columbus, with the financial backing of Queen Isabella of Castile, reached what we know today as the Bahamas and the island of Hispaniola in 1492 after only a month's sailing, he felt fully vindicated.

The "discovery" of
America

Strictly speaking, it cannot be said that Columbus "discovered America" for two reasons. In the first place, experts now agree that the earliest Europeans to reach the Western Hemisphere were the Vikings, who touched on present-day Newfoundland, Labrador, and perhaps New England in voyages made around the year 1000. Second, Columbus did not "discover America" because he never knew what he found, dying in the conviction that all the new land he encountered was merely the outer reaches of Asia. Yet neither of these arguments diminishes Columbus's achievement because the Viking landings had been forgotten or ignored throughout Europe for hundreds of years, and if Columbus did not know what he had found, others, following immediately in his path, came to the realization soon thereafter. Although Columbus brought back no Asiatic spices from his voyage of 1492, he did return with some small samples of gold and a few natives who gave promise of entire tribes that might be enslaved. (Columbus and all his contemporaries saw no conflict between converting heathen to Christianity and enslaving them.) This provided sufficient incentive for the Spanish monarchs, Ferdinand and Isabella, to finance three more expeditions by Columbus and many more by others. Soon the mainland was discovered as well as islands, and although Columbus refused until his death to accept the truth, the conclusion quickly became inescapable around 1500 that a new world had indeed been found. Since the recognition that Columbus had really stumbled upon a new world was most widely publicized by the Italian geographer Amerigo Vespucci (one of Vespucci's writings of 1504 was actually called *Mundus novus* or *A New World*), the Western Hemisphere soon became known as "America" after Vespucci's first name.

The search for a
"southwest passage" to
Asia

One might well think that the discovery of a new world around 1500 would have delighted the Spanish rulers who had invested in it, but in fact it came as a disappointment, for with a major landmass standing between Europe and Asia, Spain hardly could hope to beat Portugal in the race for spices. Any remaining doubt that two vast oceans separated Europe from East Asia instead of one was completely removed when Vasco Nuñez de Balboa first viewed the Pacific from the Isthmus of Panama in 1513. Not entirely admitting defeat, Ferdinand and Isabella's grandson King Charles accepted Ferdinand Magellan's offer in 1519 to see whether a feasible route to Asia could be found by sailing around South America. But Magellan's voyage merely

Ferdinand and Isabella Worshiping the Virgin.
A contemporary Spanish painting: the royal
pair are shown with two of their children
in the company of saints from the Dominican order.

demonstrated that the perils of a journey around southern Argentina
were simply too great: of five ships that left Spain, only one returned
three years later, having been forced to circumnavigate the globe.
Nor did Magellan himself live to tell this tale; instead, eighteen survivors out of an original crew of two hundred eighty reported that
most of their comrades had died from scurvy or starvation and that
their captain had been killed in a skirmish with East Indian natives.
After this fiasco, all hope for an easy "southwest passage" came to an
end.

But if it was disappointing that America loomed as a barricade to
the East, it gradually became clear to the Spanish that the New World
had much wealth of its own. From the start Columbus's gold samples,
in themselves rather paltry, had nurtured hopes that somewhere in
America gold might lie piled in ingots, and rumor fed rumor until a
few Spanish adventurers really did strike it rich beyond their most
avaricious imaginings. At first riches were seized by dint of astonishing feats of arms. In two years, from 1519 to 1521, the *conquistador*
(Spanish for conqueror) Hernando Cortés, commanding six hundred
men, subjugated the Aztec empire of Mexico numbering a million,
and carried off all of the Aztecs' fabulous wealth. Then in 1533 another
conquistador, Francisco Pizarro, this time with a mere hundred eighty
men, plundered the fabled gold of the Incas in conquering Peru. Cortés
and Pizarro had the advantage of some cannon and a few horses, but
they achieved their victories primarily by sheer courage, treachery,

The conquistadors
*plunder the New World
for gold*

Left: *An Early Conception of the Encounter between Europeans and American Natives*. This sixteenth-century engraving shows how overseas voyaging was reconceived at home as a mixture of truth and fantasy. Note, for example, the small mermaid to the left of the ship in the foreground. Right: *The Silver Mines of Spanish America*. An engraving of 1602. Some of the miners work naked because of the heat.

and cruelty. Never before or since have so few men won such great realms against such enormous odds, but seldom have men acted in so ruthless and repugnant a manner.

Rapidity of the conquests

Spanish and Portuguese conquests in the Americas were largely the work of individual adventurers, some from the lower strata of society, who were given almost unlimited license by the governments in whose name they acted. As territories were won through the private enterprise of seasoned soldiers or lawless swashbucklers, the home government claimed them as its own domain. The rapidity of the Spanish conquests in Central and South America contrasts sharply with the gradual expansion of English settlements in North America somewhat later. By 1540 Mexico, Central America, and the northern part of South America had been secured. Fierce fighting was needed to subdue Chile and Argentina, where the indigenous population, unlike the Incas of Peru and the Aztecs of Mexico, had never felt the yoke of a strong centralized rule and resisted fiercely. Not before 1580 was the city of Buenos Aires firmly in Spanish hands. Portugal, far inferior to Spain in population and naval power and plagued by British, French, and Dutch attempts to gain footholds on the continent, nevertheless had established a fairly stable colonial government in Brazil by 1549. Thus in considerably less than a century the two Iberian powers had acquired empires with a total area more than twice the size of the United States.

The methods of colonization and colonial administration followed by both Spain and Portugal were of such a character as to influence profoundly the entire history of Latin America. This was particularly true of Spain, which also set the pattern for her neighboring state since both were united under a common sovereign between 1580 and 1640. The cardinal elements in Spanish colonial policy were despotism and paternalism. The highest authorities in the empire were the viceroys, who ruled as the personal representatives of the Spanish king. At first there were two, one in New Spain, including Mexico and Central America, and the other in Peru. In the eighteenth century two additional viceroyalties were created: New Granada (Panama, Colombia, Venezuela, Ecuador) and La Plata, or Buenos Aires. The viceroys were paid magnificent salaries, amounting at one time to the equivalent of $200,000 a year. The purpose behind such generosity was to prevent corruption, an objective by no means universally attained. At the same time their royal master took precautions to prevent the viceroys from becoming too powerful. The authority they exercised was to be that of the Spanish crown, not their own. For this reason they had to tolerate the existence of an advisory council, or *audiencia,* which also served as a court of appeal against their decisions. Members of the *audiencia* had the right to communicate with the king regarding the acts of the viceroy without the latter's knowledge. At the end of his term, and occasionally during it, the viceroy must submit to a searching inquiry or investigation in which a royal judge heard the complaints of all and sundry as to official misconduct.

The Catholic Church, which had contributed to the foundation of absolutism in Spain, served the same function in the New World. The crown reserved the right to appoint church dignitaries, shared in the tithes collected, and allowed no church or convent to be constructed without its permission. Priests taught the population to obey the king and his agents and opposed new ideas and expressions of discontent. In almost any emergency the hierarchy could be counted upon to give loyal support to the government. Deprived of their splendid temples, the Indians accepted the religion of their conquerors, and conversion was rapid in spite of some argument among ecclesiastics as to whether Indians actually possessed souls. Much of the symbolism and imagery of Catholicism appealed to the Indians' imagination, and its teaching offered hope of eventual release from an intolerable life.

The keynote of economic administration in the colonies was paternalism. Nothing else could have been expected, since according to the theory, the land of the Americas was the personal possession of the king. It was his private estate, which he could dispose of as he saw fit. But economic administration in the Spanish colonies was also shaped to a large extent by the theory of mercantilism, which was beginning to dominate the thinking of all Western nations. Mercantilism demanded that colonies should exist for the benefit of the mother country; they should bring bullion into her treasury and contribute in every way possible toward making her rich and powerful. They were expected to supply raw materials—ores from Mexico and Bolivia; sugar from the West Indies, mainland Spanish colonies, and Brazil; forest products, such as the red brazilwood that gave Brazil its name. It followed that the home government had the right to regulate and control the economic activities of the colonies in its own interest. In substance this meant a monopoly of colonial trade for the merchants of the mother country and a prohibition of manufactures.

The encomienda *system*

Gradually it was recognized that the real wealth of the country lay in its land and its labor supply, both of which the conquerors controlled. To promote agriculture the Spaniards introduced the *encomienda* ("trusteeship") system, designed to settle Indians as productive laborers in agricultural units under the supervision of an appointed trustee. In theory it was intended to protect the Indian from exploitation while he was becoming Christianized and "civilized." In practice it bound him to the land, owing labor and tribute to the *encomendero,* who treated the estate as his personal property.

A highly stratified society

Coming from European states that were still semifeudal, the conquerors introduced a highly stratified aristocratic society into the New World. Military commanders, civilian officials appointed by the crown, and ecclesiastical dignitaries made up the highest class. In second place were the Creoles—persons of Iberian descent born in America. This group of landed aristocrats acquired most of the wealth, both agricultural and mercantile. They controlled local government through town councils but were excluded from the higher offices of church and state. Bitterly resentful of their subordination to agents of the crown, the Creoles eventually led the colonial revolutions for independence, and they were the chief beneficiaries of these revolutions. A third class arose from intermingling between the European and Indian races. These mixed-race peoples, known as *mestizos* in the Spanish colonies and as *mamelucos* in Brazil, were looked down upon as inferior and struggled desperately to gain acceptance and minimal justice for themselves, while eagerly joining in the exploitation of those beneath them. At the bottom of the scale were the Indians, regarded primarily as a commodity, the most profitable spoils of conquest. With minor exceptions their condition became one of actual or virtual slavery. Even worse than the fate of the Indians was that of African slaves. These were relatively few in number except in Brazil and the West Indies.

The high human cost

The three centuries between the beginning of the conquests and the emergence of independent states in Latin America witnessed colorful and dramatic events, accompanied by incalculable human suffering. Not only were the rich civilizations of the Mayas, Aztecs, and Incas destroyed, but everywhere indigenous cultures were uprooted. Strong and sustaining communal instincts were extinguished as the Indians were forced to embrace an alien set of values. Colonial rule implanted a tradition of exploitation and hierarchy buttressed by racist doctrines, ranking people according to the alleged purity of their white blood.

A Spaniard Kicking an Indian. As this sixteenth-century drawing makes clear, the Spanish treatment of the indigenous American population was brutal.

The colonial era was not without critics who courageously attacked social and economic injustice. From time to time the royal governments attempted to institute reforms but to little effect, although administrative efficiency improved notably in the Spanish colonies under the Bourbon kings who came to the throne at the opening of the eighteenth century. In spite of the fact that the Church as an institution was a bulwark of authority, the stoutest champions of Indian rights were churchmen. As missions spread and acquired extensive landholdings, they developed their estates with more consideration for the laborers than was typical of the *encomiendas.* In the early sixteenth century a group of monks in Mexico undertook to found missions incorporating the cooperative ideals of Thomas More's *Utopia,* aiming not only to protect the Indians but also to set a moral example for European society. One of these communities, with its own hospital and school, provided homes for 30,000 Indians. Tremendous enterprise and dedication was shown by Jesuit missionaries who worked in the border area between Argentina and Brazil in the seventeenth and eighteenth centuries. These intrepid priests cleared the jungle to build productive and largely self-sufficient communities where Indians shared in the fruits of their labor and were protected from the forays of slavehunters from Brazil. After the Jesuits were expelled from Spain and her colonies by a royal decree of 1767, these settlements, which had played a vital economic as well as humanitarian role, quickly decayed.

Subsequent chapters will pursue the continued development of

Consequences of European
expansion overseas

European overseas expansion and colonization; here it may be said that the overall results of the initial achievements were extremely profound in their implications for at least three reasons. First of all, the emergence of Portugal and Spain as Europe's leading long-distance traders in the sixteenth century permanently moved the center of gravity of European economic power away from Italy and the Mediterranean toward the Atlantic. Deprived of their role as conduits of Oriental trade, Genoa became Spain's banker and Venice gradually a tourist attraction, while Atlantic ports bustled with vessels and shone with wealth. Admittedly the prosperity of Portugal and Spain themselves was fleeting, but the other Atlantic states of England, Holland, and France quickly inherited their mantle as the preeminent economic powers of the world. Second, throughout Europe the increase in the circulation of imported goods and the sudden influx of bullion stimulated entrepreneurial ambitions. Simply stated, the opening of the seas around 1500 provided marvelous opportunities for people with ability and daring to make new fortunes, inspiring a sense that success could only lead to success. Thus not only were many enterprising individuals enriched overnight, but the entire sixteenth century was one of great overall economic growth for western Europe.

The human costs

Unfortunately, however, the enormous riches of America were gained only at an appalling cost in human life. Although exact figures are not available, of an estimated indigenous population of 250,000 on the island of Hispaniola in 1492, only about 500 remained in 1548. The Indian population of Florida fell from an estimated million to 50,000 in the space of fifty years, and the far larger population of Mexico declined by about 90 percent in the first century of Spanish rule. Not all this loss of life was due to conscious ruthlessness; on the contrary, huge numbers of natives died from epidemic diseases unwittingly introduced by the Europeans, for the natives had no biological resistance to such diseases as smallpox and measles. But countless innocent people also died as the result of merciless exploitation— literally worked so hard by their conquerors that they expired from exhaustion and lack of care. Thus, however much Europeans profited from their colonization of the New World, for the original inhabitants the appearance of the white man was an unmitigated disaster.

2. THE LUTHERAN UPHEAVAL

The Lutheran Reformation

While the Portuguese and Spanish were plowing new paths on the seas, a German monk named Martin Luther (1483–1546) was searching for a new path to the understanding of human salvation, and though his discoveries were made in the quiet of a monastic cell rather than in exotic tropical climes, their effects were no less momentous. Indeed, many Europeans felt the impact of Luther's activities much more immediately and directly than they did the results of the overseas discoveries, because once the German monk started attacking the institutions of the contemporary Roman Church he set off a chain reaction which rapidly resulted in the secession of much of northern Europe from the Catholic faith, thereby quickly affecting the religious practices of millions.

In searching for the causes of the Lutheran revolt in Germany, three main questions arise: (1) why Martin Luther instigated a break with Rome; (2) why large numbers of Germans rallied to his cause; and (3) why several ruling German princes decided to put the Lutheran Reformation into effect. Reduced to the barest essentials, the answers to these questions are that Luther broke with Rome because of his doctrine of justification by faith, that the German masses followed him primarily because they were swept away by a surge of religious nationalism, and that the princes were moved to institute Lutheranism above all because of their desire for absolute governmental sovereignty. Within a decade preacher, populace, and princes, so to speak, would all sing the same stirring Lutheran hymn, "A Mighty Fortress Is Our God," in the same church, but they arrived there by rather different paths.

Many people think that Luther rebelled against Rome because he was disgusted with contemporary religious abuses—superstitions, frauds, and the offer of salvation for money—but that is only part of the story. Certainly abuses in Luther's day were grave and intensely upsetting to religious idealists. In a world beset by disease and disaster, frail mortals clutched at supernatural straws to seek health on earth and salvation in the hereafter. Some superstitious men and women, for example, believed that viewing the consecrated host during Mass in the morning would guard them from death throughout the day, and others neglected to swallow the consecrated wafer so that they could use it later either as a charm to ward off evil, an application to cure the sick, or a powder to fertilize their crops. Similarly, belief in the miraculous curative powers of saints was hard to distinguish from belief in magic. Every saint had his or her specialty: "for botches and biles, Cosmas and Damian; St. Clare for the eyes, St. Apolline for teeth, St. Job for pox. And for sore breasts, St. Agatha." Because alleged relics of Christ and the saints were thought to radiate marvelous healing effects, traffic in relics boomed. Even Luther's patron, the Elector Frederick the Wise of Saxony, had a collection in his castle church at Wittenberg of 17,000 relics, including a supposed remnant of Moses's burning bush, pieces of the holy cradle, shreds from Christ's swaddling clothes, and thirty-three fragments of the holy cross. As Mark Twain once sardonically observed, there were indeed enough splinters of the holy cross throughout Europe "to shingle a barn."

Superstitions and gross credulity were offensive enough to religious idealists of Luther's stamp, but worse still were the granting of dispensations and the promises of spiritual benefits for money. If a man wished to marry his first cousin, for example, he could usually receive

Martin Luther. A portrait by Lucas Cranach.

Background to Luther's revolt: superstition

*Background to Luther's
revolt: sale of
dispensations and
indulgences*

an official religious dispensation allowing the marriage for a fee, and annulments of marriage—divorce being prohibited—similarly came for a price. Most malodorous to many, however, was the sale of indulgences. In Catholic theology, an indulgence is a remission by papal authority of all or part of the temporal punishment due for sin— that is, of the punishment in this life and in purgatory—after the guilt of sin itself is absolved by sacramental confession. As we have seen, the practice of granting indulgences began at the end of the eleventh century as an incentive for encouraging men to become Crusaders. Once it became accepted in the course of the High Middle Ages that the pope could dispense grace from a "Treasury of Merits" (that is, a storehouse of surplus good works piled up by Christ and the saints), it soon was taken for granted that the pope could promise people time off in purgatory as well. But indulgences originally granted for extraordinary deeds gradually came to be sold for money; by the fourteenth century, popes started granting indulgences to raise money for any worthy cause whatsoever, such as the building of cathedrals or hospitals; and finally, in 1476 Pope Sixtus IV (the patron of the Sistine Chapel) took the extreme step of declaring that the benefits of indulgences could be extended to the dead already in purgatory as well as to the living. Money, then, could not only save an individual from works of penance but could save his dearest relatives from eons of agonizing torments after death.

Certainly Luther was horrified by the traffic in relics and the sale of indulgences; indeed, the latter provided the immediate grounds for his revolt against Rome. But it was by no means the abuses of the late-medieval Church so much as medieval Catholic theology itself that he came to find thoroughly unacceptable. To this degree the term "Lutheran Reformation" is misleading, for Luther was no mere "reformer" who wanted to cleanse the current religious system of its impurities. Many Christian humanists of Luther's day were reformers in just that sense, but they shrank from breaking with Rome because they had no objections to the basic principles of medieval Catholicism. Luther, on the other hand, by no means would have been satisfied with the mere abolition of abuses because it was the entire Catholic "religion of works" that appalled him.

Simply stated, Luther preferred a rigorously Augustinian system of theology to a medieval Thomistic one. As we have seen, around the year 400 St. Augustine of Hippo had formulated an uncompromising doctrine of predestination which maintained that God alone determined human salvation and that His decisions concerning whom to save and whom to damn were made from eternity, without any regard to merits that given humans might show while sojourning on earth. This extreme view, however, left so little room for human freedom and responsibility that it was modified greatly in the course of the Middle Ages. Above all, during the twelfth and thirteenth centuries theologians such as Peter Lombard and St. Thomas Aquinas (hence the term "Thomistic") set forth an alternative belief system which rested on two assumptions: (1) since God's saving grace is not irresistible, humans can freely reject God's advances and encompass their own doom; and (2) since the sacramental ministrations of the Church communicate ongoing grace, they help human sinners improve their chances of salvation. Except in emergencies, none of the sacraments could be administered by persons other than priests. Having inherited this power from the Apostle Peter, the members of the clergy alone had the authority to cooperate with God in forgiving sins and in performing the miracle of the Eucharist, whereby the bread and wine were transubstantiated into the body and blood of the Saviour. In Luther's opinion, all of this amounted to saying that humans could be saved by the performance of "good works," and it was this theology of works that he became prepared to resist even unto death.

Martin Luther may ultimately have been a source of inspiration for millions, but at first he was a terrible disappointment to his father. The elder Luther, who had risen from Thuringian German peasant stock and gained prosperity by leasing some mines, wanted his son Martin to rise still further. The father thus sent young Luther to the University of Erfurt to study law, but while there in 1505, possibly as the result of unconscious psychological rebellion against parental pressure, Martin shattered his father's ambitions by becoming a monk instead. Afterward, throughout his life Martin Luther was never to "put on airs." Even at the time of his greatest fame he lived simply and always expressed himself in the vigorous and sometimes earthy vernacular of the German peasantry.

Luther's early life

Like many great figures in the history of religion, Luther arrived at what he conceived to be the truth by a dramatic conversion experience. As a monk, young Martin zealously pursued all the traditional medieval means for achieving his own salvation. Not only did he fast and pray continuously, but he confessed so often that his exhausted confessor would sometimes jokingly say that his sins were actually trifling and that if he really wanted to have a rousing confession he should go out and do something dramatic like committing adultery. Yet, try as he might, Luther could find no spiritual peace because he feared that he could never perform enough good deeds to placate an angry God. But then, in 1513 he hit upon an insight that granted him relief and changed the course of his life.

Luther's search for religious solace

Luther's guiding insight pertained to the problem of the justice of God. For years he had worried that God seemed unjust in issuing commandments that He knew men would not observe and then in punishing them with eternal damnation for not observing them. But after becoming a professor of biblical theology at the University of Wittenberg (many members of his monastic order were expected to teach), he was led by the Bible to a new understanding of the problem. Specifically, while meditating on the words in the Psalms "deliver me in thy justice," it suddenly struck him that God's justice had nothing

Luther's "tower experience"

to do with His disciplinary power but rather with His mercy in saving sinful mortals through faith. As Luther later wrote, "At last, by the mercy of God, I began to understand the justice of God as that by which God makes us just in his mercy and through faith . . . and at this I felt as though I had been born again, and had gone through open gates into paradise." Since the fateful moment of truth came to Luther in the tower room of his monastery, it is customarily called his "tower experience."

After that, everything seemed to fall into place. Lecturing on the Pauline Epistles in Wittenberg in the years immediately following 1513, Luther dwelled on the text of St. Paul to the Romans (1:17) "the just shall live by faith" to reach his central doctine of "justification by faith alone." By this he meant that God's justice does not demand endless good works and religious ceremonies, for no one can hope to be saved by his own works. Rather, humans are "justified"—that is, granted salvation—by God's saving grace alone, offered as an utterly unmerited gift to those predestined for salvation. Since this grace is manifested in humans in thoroughly passive faith, men and women are justified from the human perspective by faith alone. In Luther's view those who had faith would do good works anyway, but it was the faith that came first. Although the essence of this doctrine was not original but harked back to the predestinarianism of St. Augustine, it was new for Luther and the early sixteenth century, and if followed to its conclusions could only mean the dismantling of much of the contemporary Catholic religious structure.

Justification by faith

At first Luther remained merely an academic lecturer, teaching within the realm of theory, but in 1517 he was goaded into attacking some of the actual practices of the Church by a provocation that was too much for him to bear. The story of the indulgence campaign of 1517 in Germany is colorful but unsavory. The worldly Albert of Hohenzollern, archbishop of Mainz and youngest brother of the elector of Brandenburg, had sunk himself into enormous debt for several discreditable reasons. In 1513 he had to pay large sums for gaining dispensations from the papacy to hold the bishoprics of Magdeburg and Halberstadt concurrently, and for assuming these offices even though at twenty-three he was not old enough to be a bishop at all. Not satisfied, when the see of Mainz fell vacant in the next year, Albert gained election to that too, even though he knew full well that the costs of becoming archbishop of Mainz meant still larger payments to Rome. Obtaining the necessary funds by loans from the German banking firm of the Fuggers, he then struck a bargain with Pope Leo X (1513–1521). According to this, Leo proclaimed an indulgence in Albert's ecclesiastical territories on the understanding that half of the income raised would go to Rome for the building of St. Peter's Basilica, with the other half going to Albert so that he could repay the Fuggers. Luther did not know the sordid details of Albert's bargain, but he did know that a Dominican friar named Tetzel soon was hawk-

*The scandalous indulgence
campaign*

ing indulgences throughout much of northern Germany with Fugger banking agents in his train, and that Tetzel was deliberately giving people the impression that the purchase of an indulgence regardless of contrition in penance was an immediate ticket to heaven for oneself and one's dear departed in purgatory. For Luther this was more than enough because Tetzel's advertising campaign flagrantly violated his own conviction that people are saved by faith, not works. So on October 31, 1517, the earnest theologian offered to his university colleagues a list of ninety-five theses objecting to Catholic indulgence doctrine, an act by which the Protestant Reformation is conventionally thought to have begun.

In circulating his theses within the University of Wittenberg, Luther by no means intended to bring his criticism of Tetzel to the public. Quite to the contrary, he wrote his objections in Latin, not German, and meant them only for academic dispute. But some unknown person translated and published Luther's theses, an event which immediately gained the hitherto obscure monk wide notoriety. Since Tetzel and his allies outside the university did not mean to let the matter rest, Luther was immediately called upon to withdraw his theses or defend himself. At that point, far from backing down, he became ever bolder in his attacks on the government of the Church. In 1519 in public disputation before throngs in Leipzig, Luther defiantly maintained that the pope and all clerics were merely fallible men and that the highest authority for an individual's conscience was the truth of Scripture. Thereupon Pope Leo X responded by charging the monk with heresy, and after that there was no alternative for Luther but to break with the Catholic faith entirely.

Luther's theses and break with Rome

Pope Leo X. A portrait by the Italian Renaissance master, Raphael.

Luther's year of greatest creative activity came in 1520 when, in the midst of the crisis caused by his defiance, he composed three seminal pamphlets formulating the outlines of what was soon to become the new Lutheran religion. In these writings he put forth his three theological premises: justification by faith, the primacy of Scripture, and "the priesthood of all believers." We have already examined the meaning of the first. By the second he simply meant that the literal meaning of Scripture was always to be preferred to the accretions of tradition, and that all beliefs (such as purgatory) or practices (such as prayers to saints) not explicitly grounded in Scripture were to be rejected. As for "the priesthood of all believers," that meant that the true spiritual estate was the congregation of all the faithful rather than a special club of ordained priests.

From these premises a host of practical consequences followed. Since works themselves had no intrinsic value for salvation, Luther discarded such formalized practices as fasts, pilgrimages, and the veneration of relics. Far more fundamentally, he recognized only baptism and the Eucharist as sacraments (in 1520 he also included penance, but he later changed his mind on this), denying that even these had any supernatural effect in bringing down grace from heaven. For Luther,

Practical implications of the Lutheran faith

Luther and his Wife, Katherine von Bora. Portraits done by Cranach for the couple's wedding in 1525.

Christ was really present in the consecrated elements of the Lord's Supper, but there was no grace in the sacrament as such; rather, faith was essential to render the Eucharist effective as a means for aiding the believer along the road to eternal life. To make the meaning of the ceremony clear to all, Luther proposed the substitution of German for Latin in church services, and, to emphasize that those who presided in churches had no supernatural authority, he insisted on calling them merely ministers or pastors rather than priests. On the same grounds there was to be no ecclesiastical hierarchy since neither the pope nor anyone else was a custodian of the keys to heaven, and monasticism was to be abolished since it served no purpose whatsoever. Finally, firm in the belief that no sacramental distinction existed between clergy and laity, Luther argued that ministers could marry, and in 1525 he took a wife himself.

Widely disseminated by means of the printing press, Luther's pamphlets of 1520 electrified much of Germany, gaining him broad and enthusiastic popular support. Because this response played a crucial role in determining the future success of the Lutheran movement—emboldening Luther to persevere in his defiance of Rome and soon encouraging some ruling princes to convert to Lutheranism themselves—it is appropriate before continuing to inquire into its causes. Of course, different combinations of motives influenced different people to rally behind Luther, but the uproar in Germany on Luther's behalf was above all a national religious revolt against Rome.

Pope Alexander VI: "Appearance and Reality." Even before Luther initiated the German Reformation, anonymous critics of the dissolute Alexander VI surreptitiously spread propaganda showing him to be a devil. By lifting a flap Alexander is transformed into a monster who proclaims "I am the pope."

Left: *Luther with Dove and Halo*. Right: *The Pope as a Donkey Playing Bagpipes*. Two specimens of Lutheran visual propaganda concerning "true" and "false" spiritual insight. While Luther was still a monk (before the end of 1522), the artist Hans Baldung Grien portrayed him as a saint whose insight into Scripture was sent by the Holy Spirit in the form of a dove. At the right is a 1545 woodcut depicting Luther's view that "the pope can interpret Holy Scripture just as well as an ass can play the bagpipes."

Ever since the High Middle Ages many people throughout Europe had resented the centralization of Church government because it meant the interference of a foreign papacy in local ecclesiastical affairs and the siphoning off of large amounts of ecclesiastical fees and commissions to the papal court. But certain concrete circumstances made Germany in the early sixteenth century particularly ripe for religious revolt. Perhaps greatest among these was the fact that the papacy of that time had clearly lost the slightest hint of apostolic calling but was demanding as much, if not more money from German coffers as before. Although great patrons of the arts, successive popes of Luther's day were worldly scoundrels or sybarites. As Luther was growing up, the Borgia pope, Alexander VI (1492–1503), bribed the cardinals to gain the papacy, used the money raised from the jubilee of 1500 to support the military campaigns of his son Cesare, and was so lascivious in office that he was suspected of seeking the sexual favors of his own daughter Lucrezia. Alexander's scandals could hardly have been outdone, but his successor, Julius II (1503–1515), was interested only in

Susceptibility of Germany to religious rebellion

enlarging the papal states by military means (a contemporary remarked that he would have gained the greatest glory had he been a secular prince), and Leo X, the pope obliged to deal with Luther's defiance, was a self-indulgent esthete who, in the words of a modern Catholic historian, "would not have been deemed fit to be a doorkeeper in the house of the Lord had he lived in the days of the apostles." Under such circumstances it was bad enough for Germans to know that fees sent to Rome were being used to finance papal politics and the upkeep of luxurious courts, but worse still to pay money in the realization that Germany had no influence in Italian papal affairs, for Germans, unlike French or Spaniards, were seldom represented in the College of Cardinals and practically never gained employment in the papal bureaucracy.

In this overheated atmosphere, reformist criticisms voiced by both traditional clerical moralists and the new breed of Christian humanists exacerbated resentments. Ever since about 1400 prominent German critics of the papacy had been saying that the entire Church needed to be reformed "in head and members," and as the fifteenth century progressed, anonymous prophecies mounted to the effect, for example, that a future heroic emperor would reform the Church by removing

Left: *The Seven-Headed Papal Beast*. Right: *The Seven-headed Martin Luther*. Around 1530 a Lutheran cartoon was circulated in Germany which turned the papacy into the "seven-headed beast" of the Book of Revelation. The papacy's "seven heads" consist of pope, cardinals, bishops, and priests; the sign on the cross reads "for money, a sack full of indulgences"; and a devil is seen emerging from an indulgence treasure chest below. In response, a German Catholic propagandist showed Luther as Revelation's "beast." In the Catholic conception Luther's seven heads show him by turn to be a hypocrite, a fanatic, and "Barabbas"—the thief who should have been crucified instead of Jesus.

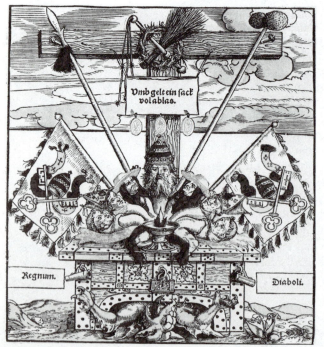

the papacy from Rome to the Rhineland. Then in the early years of the sixteenth century, Christian humanists began to chime in with their own brand of satirical propaganda. Most eloquent of these humanists, of course, was Erasmus, who lampooned the religious abuses of his day with no mercy for Rome. Thus in the *Praise of Folly,* first published in 1511 and frequently reprinted, Erasmus stated that if popes were ever forced to lead Christlike lives, no one would be more disconsolate than themselves, and in his more daring pamphlet called *Julius Excluded,* published anonymously in Basel in 1517, the clever satirist imagined a dialogue held before the pearly gates in which Pope Julius II was locked out of heaven by Saint Peter because of his transgressions.

In addition to the objective reality of a corrupt Rome and the circulation of anti-Roman propaganda, a final factor that made Germany ready for revolt in Luther's time was the belated growth of universities. All revolts need to have some general headquarters; universities were the most natural centers for late-medieval religious revolts because assembled there were groups of enthusiastic, educated young people accustomed to working together, who could formulate doctrinal positions with assurance, and who could turn out militant manifestoes at a moment's notice. There had hardly been any universities on German soil until a spate of new foundations between 1450 and 1517 provided many spawning grounds for cultural nationalism and religious resistance to Rome. Luther's own University of Wittenberg was founded as late as 1502, but soon enough it had become the cradle of the Lutheran Reformation, offering immediate support to its embattled hero.

The role of the German universities

Still, of course, there would have been no Lutheran Reformation without Luther himself, and the daring monk did the most to enflame Germany's dry kindling of resentment in his pamphlets of 1520, above all in one entitled *To the Christian Nobility of the German Nation.* Here, in highly intemperate colloquial German, Luther stated that "if the pope's court were reduced ninety-nine percent it would still be large enough to give decisions on matters of faith"; that "the cardinals have sucked Italy dry and now turn to Germany"; and that, given Rome's corruption, "the reign of Antichrist could not be worse." Needless to say, once this savage indictment was lodged, everyone wanted to read it. Whereas the average press run of a printed book before 1520 had been one thousand copies, the first run of *To the Christian Nobility* was four thousand, and these copies were sold out in a few days with many more thousands following.

Luther's inflammatory pamphlets

Meanwhile, even as Luther's pamphlets were selling so rapidly, his personal drama riveted all onlookers. Late in 1520 the German rebel responded to Pope Leo X's bull ordering his recantation by casting not only the bull but all of Church law as well onto a roaring bonfire in front of a huge crowd. With the lines so drawn, events moved with great swiftness. Since in the eyes of the Church Luther was now

Luther's appearance at the Diet of Worms

The Wartburg. The castle in central Germany where Luther was hidden after the Diet of Worms.

a stubborn heretic, he was formally "released" to his lay overlord, the Elector Frederick the Wise, for proper punishment. Normally this would have meant certain death at the stake, but in this case Frederick was loath to silence the pope's antagonist. Instead, claiming that Luther had not yet received a fair hearing, he brought him early in 1521 to be examined by a "diet" (that is, a formal assembly) of the princes of the Holy Roman Empire convening in the city of Worms.

Luther vs. the Emperor Charles V

At Worms the initiative lay with the presiding officer, the newly elected Holy Roman Emperor, Charles V. Charles was not a German; rather, as a member of the Habsburg family by his paternal descent, he had been born and bred in his ancestral holding of the Netherlands. Since he additionally held Austria, and as grandson of Ferdinand and Isabella by his maternal descent, all of Spain, including extensive Spanish possessions in Italy and America, the emperor had primarily international rather than national interests and surely thought of Catholicism as a sort of glue necessary to hold together all his far-flung territories. Thus from the start Charles had no sympathy for Luther, and since Luther fearlessly refused to back down before the emperor, declaring instead "here I stand," it soon became clear that Luther would be condemned by the power of state as well as by Church. But just then Frederick the Wise once more intervened, this time by arranging a "kidnapping" whereby Luther was spirited off to the elector's castle of the Wartburg and kept out of harm's way for a year.

Thereafter Luther was never again to be in danger of his life. Although the Diet of Worms did issue an edict shortly after his disappearance proclaiming him an outlaw, the Edict of Worms was never properly enforced because, with Luther in hiding, Charles V soon left Germany to conduct a war with France. In 1522 Luther returned in triumph from the Wartburg to Wittenberg to find that all the changes in ecclesiastical government and ceremonial he had called for had spontaneously been put into practice by his university cohorts. Then, in rapid succession, several German princes formally converted to Lutheranism, bringing their territories with them. Thus by around 1530 a considerable part of Germany had been brought over to the new faith.

Lutheranism triumphant

At this point, then, the last of the three major questions regarding the early history of Lutheranism arises: Why did German princes, secure in their own powers, heed Luther's call by establishing Lutheran religious practices within their territories? The importance of this question should by no means be underestimated, because no matter how much intense admiration Luther may have gained from the German populace, his cause surely would have failed had it not been for the decisive intervention and support of constituted political authorities. There had been heretics aplenty in Europe before, but most of them had died at the stake, as Luther would have without the intervention of Frederick the Wise. And even had Luther lived, spontaneous popular expressions of support alone would not have succeeded in instituting Lutheranism because such could easily have been put down by the power of the state. In fact, although in the early years of Luther's revolt he was more or less equally popular throughout Germany, only in those territories where rulers formally established Lutheranism (mostly in the German north) did the new religion prevail, whereas in the others Luther's sympathizers were forced to flee, face death, or conform to Catholicism. In short, the word of the prince in religious matters was simply law.

Importance of German princely support

This distinction between populace and princes, however, should not obscure the fact that the motivations of both for turning to Lutheranism were similar, with the emphasis on the princely side being the search for sovereignty. As little as common people liked the idea of money being pumped off to Rome, princes liked it less: German princes assembled at the Diet of Augsburg in 1500, for example, went so far as to demand the refund of some of the ecclesiastical dues sent to Rome on the grounds that Germany was being drained of its coin. Since such demands fell on deaf ears, many princes were quick to perceive that if Lutheranism were adopted, ecclesiastical dues would not be sent to support ill-loved foreigners and much of the savings would directly or indirectly wind up in their own treasuries.

Economic motives for adoption of Lutheranism

Yet the matter of taxation was only part of the larger issue of the search for absolute governmental sovereignty. Throughout Europe the major political trend in the years around 1500 was toward making the state omnicompetent in all walks of life, religious as well as secu-

Political motives

lar. Hence rulers sought to control the appointments of Church officials in their own realms and to limit or curtail the independent jurisdictions of Church courts. Because the papacy in this period had to fight off the attacks of internal clerical critics who wanted recognition of the "conciliarist" principle that general councils of prelates rather than popes should rule the Church (see Chapter 15), many popes found it advantageous to sign concordats with the most powerful rulers in the West—primarily the kings of France and Spain—whereby they granted the rulers much of the sovereignty they wanted in return for support against conciliarism. Thus in 1482 Sixtus IV conceded to the Spanish monarchs Ferdinand and Isabella the right to name candidates for all major Church offices; in 1487 Innocent VIII consented to the establishment of a Spanish Inquisition controlled by the crown which gave the rulers extraordinary powers in dictating religious policies; and in 1516, by the Concordat of Bologna, Leo X granted the choice of bishops and abbots in France to the French king, Francis I. In Germany, however, primarily because there was no political unity, princes were not strong enough to gain such concessions. Hence what they could not achieve by concordats some decided to wrest by force.

The princes seize their opportunity

In this determination they were fully abetted by Luther. Certainly as early as 1520 the fiery reformer recognized that he could never hope to institute new religious practices without the strong arm of the princes behind him, so he implicitly encouraged them to disappropriate the wealth of the Catholic church as an incentive for creating a new order. At first the princes bided their time, but when they realized that Luther had enormous public support and that Charles V would not act swiftly to defend the Catholic faith, several moved to introduce Lutheranism into their territories. Motives of personal piety cannot be discounted from case to case, but the common aim of gaining sovereignty by naming pastors, cutting off fees to Rome, and curtailing the jurisdiction of Catholic church courts ultimately must have been the most decisive consideration. Given the added fact that under Lutheranism monasteries could be shut down and their wealth simply pocketed by the princes, the temptation to ordain the new faith regardless of any deeply felt religious convictions must have been simply overwhelming.

Luther's growing political and social conservatism

Once safely ensconced in Wittenberg as the protégé of princes, Luther began to express ever more vehemently his own profound conservatism in political and social matters. In a treatise of 1523, *On Temporal Authority,* he insisted that "godly" rulers must always be obeyed in all things and that even ungodly ones should never be actively resisted since tyranny "is not to be resisted but endured." Then, in 1525, when peasants throughout Germany rose up in economic revolt against their landlords—in some places encouraged by the religious radical Thomas Müntzer (c. 1490–1525), who urged the use of fire and sword against "ungodly" powers—Luther responded with intense hostility. In his vituperative pamphlet of 1525, *Against the Thievish,*

Murderous Hordes of Peasants, he went so far as to urge all who could to hunt the rebels down like mad dogs, to "strike, strangle, stab secretly or in public, and remember that nothing can be more poisonous than a man in rebellion." Once the princes had ruthlessly put down the Peasants' Revolt of 1525, the firm alliance of Lutheranism with the powers of the state helped ensure social peace. In fact, after the bloody punishment of the peasant rebels there was never again to be a mass lower-class uprising in Germany.

As for Luther himself, he concentrated in his last years on debating with younger, more radical, religious reformers, and on offering spiritual counsel to all who sought it. Never tiring in his amazingly prolific literary activity, he wrote an average of one treatise every two weeks for twenty-five years. To the end Luther was unswerving in his faith: on his deathbed in 1546 he responded to the question "Will you stand firm in Christ and the doctrine which you have preached?" with a resolute "Yes."

Luther's last years

3. THE SPREAD OF PROTESTANTISM

Originating as a term applied to Lutherans who "protested" an action of a German Imperial Diet of 1529, the word "Protestant" has come to mean any non-Catholic, non–Eastern Orthodox Christian. In fact it was soon applied to non-Lutherans after 1529 because the particular form of Protestantism developed by Luther did not prove to be popular much beyond its native environment of Germany. To be sure, Lutheranism was instituted as the state religion of Denmark, Norway, and Sweden by official decrees of rulers made during the 1520s, and remains the religion of most Scandinavians today. But elsewhere early Protestantism spread in different forms. In England a break with Rome was introduced from above, just as in Germany and Scandinavia, but since Lutheranism appeared too radical for the reigning English monarch, a compromise variety of religious belief and practice, subsequently known as Anglicanism (in America, Episcopalianism), was worked out. On the other extreme, Protestantism spread more spontaneously in several cities of Switzerland and there soon took on forms that were more radical than Lutheranism.

Other forms of Protestantism

Although the original blow against the Roman Church in England was struck by the head of the government, King Henry VIII (1509–1547), in breaking with Rome the English monarch had the support of most of his subjects. For this there were at least three reasons. First, in England, as in Germany, many people in the early sixteenth century had come to resent Rome's corruption and the siphoning off of the country's wealth to pay for the worldly pursuits of foreign popes. Second, England had already been the scene of protests against religious abuses voiced by John Wyclif's heretical followers known as Lollards. The Lollards had indeed been driven underground in the course of

Henry VIII. Portrait by Hans Holbein.

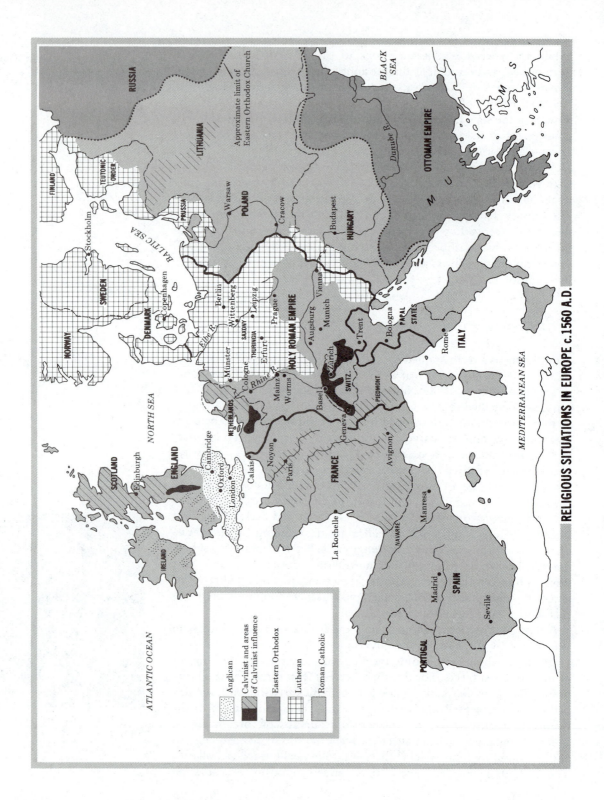

RELIGIOUS SITUATIONS IN EUROPE c.1560 A.D.

ATLANTIC OCEAN

NORTH SEA

BALTIC SEA

MEDITERRANEAN SEA

BLACK SEA

RUSSIA

FINLAND

TEUTONIC ORDER

PRUSSIA

LITHUANIA

POLAND

Warsaw

Cracow

HUNGARY

Budapest

OTTOMAN EMPIRE

Danube R.

M U S

NORWAY

SWEDEN

Stockholm

DENMARK

Copenhagen

Berlin

Wittenberg

Leipzig

SAXONY

Prague

THURINGIA

Erfurt

Elbe R.

Münster

Cologne

Rhine R.

Mainz

Worms

Basel

Zürich

SWITZ.

Geneva

HOLY ROMAN EMPIRE

Augsburg

Munich

Vienna

Trent

PIEDMONT

Bologna

PAPAL STATES

Rome

ITALY

Approximate limit of
Eastern Orthodox Church

SCOTLAND

Edinburgh

ENGLAND

Cambridge

Oxford

London

NETHERLANDS

Calais

Noyon

Paris

FRANCE

Avignon

La Rochelle

NAVARRE

Manresa

SPAIN

Madrid

Seville

PORTUGAL

IRELAND

Anglican

Calvinist and areas
of Calvinist influence

Eastern Orthodox

Lutheran

Roman Catholic

the fifteenth century, but numbers of them survived in pockets throughout England, where they promulgated their anticlerical ideas whenever they could and enthusiastically welcomed Henry VIII's revolt from Rome when it occurred. Finally, soon after the outbreak of the Reformation in Germany, Lutheran ideas were brought into England by travelers and by the circulation of printed tracts. As early as 1520 a Lutheran group was meeting at the University of Cambridge, and Lutheranism began to gain more and more clandestine strength as the decade progressed.

Despite all this, England would never have broken with Rome had Henry VIII not issued the command because of his marital difficulties. In 1527 the imperious Henry had been married for eighteen years to Ferdinand and Isabella's daughter, Catherine of Aragon, yet all the offspring of this union had died in infancy, save only the Princess Mary. Since Henry needed a male heir to preserve the succession of his Tudor dynasty, and since Catherine was now past childbearing age, Henry had good reasons of state to rid himself of her, and in 1527 an immediate incentive arose when he became infatuated with the dark-eyed lady-in-waiting, Anne Boleyn, who would not give in to his advances out of wedlock. The king hence appealed to Rome to allow the severance of his marriage to Catherine so that he could make Anne his queen. Although the law of the Church did not sanction divorce, it did provide that a marriage might be annulled if proof could be given that conditions existing at the time of the wedding had made it unlawful. Accordingly, the king's representatives, recalling that Queen Catherine had previously been married to Henry's older brother, who had died shortly after the ceremony was performed, rested their case on a passage from the Bible which pronounced it "an unclean thing" for a man to take his brother's wife and cursed such a marriage with childlessness (Leviticus 20:31).

King Henry VIII's divorce suit

Henry's suit put the reigning pope, Clement VII (1523–1534), in a quandary. If he rejected the king's appeal, England would probably be lost to Catholicism, for Henry was indeed firmly convinced that the Scriptural curse had blighted his chances of perpetuating his dynasty. On the other hand, if the pope granted the annulment he would provoke the wrath of the Emperor Charles V, Catherine of Aragon's nephew, for Charles was then on a military campaign in Italy and threatening the pope with a loss of his temporal power. There seemed nothing for Clement to do but to procrastinate. At first he made a pretense of having the question settled in England, empowering his officials to hold a court of inquiry to determine whether the marriage to Catherine had been legal. Then, after a long delay, he suddenly transferred the case to Rome. But meanwhile Henry had lost patience and resolved to take matters into his own hands. In 1531 the king obliged an assembly of English clergy to recognize him as "the supreme head" of the English Church. Next he induced Parliament to

Henry's break with Rome

The Burning of Archbishop Cranmer. In this Protestant conception an ugly Catholic, "Friar John," directs the proceedings, while the martyred Cranmer repeats Christ's words, "Lord, receive my spirit." John Foxe's *Book of Martyrs* (1563), in which this engraving first appeared, was an extraordinarily successful piece of English Protestant propaganda.

enact a series of laws abolishing all payments to Rome and proclaiming the English Church an independent, national unit, subject alone to royal authority. With the passage of the parliamentary Act of Supremacy (1534), declaring "the King's highness to be supreme head of the Church of England [having] the authority to redress all errors, heresies, and abuses," the last bonds uniting the English Church to Rome had been cut.

The conservative nature of the Henrician Reformation

Yet these enactments did not yet make England a Protestant country. Quite to the contrary, although the break with Rome was followed by the dissolution of all England's monasteries, with their lands and wealth being sold to many of the king's loyal supporters, the system of Church government by bishops (episcopalianism) was retained, and the English Church remained Catholic in doctrine. The Six Articles, promulgated by Parliament in 1539 at Henry VIII's behest, left no room for doubt as to official orthodoxy: oral confession to priests, masses for the dead, and clerical celibacy were all confirmed; moreover, the Catholic doctrine of the Eucharist was not only confirmed but its denial made punishable by death.

Nonetheless, the influence of Protestantism in the country at large at this time was growing, and during the reign of Henry's son, Edward VI (1547–1553), Protestantism gained the ascendancy. Since the new king (born from Henry's union with his third wife, Jane Seymour) was only nine years old when he inherited the crown, it was inevitable that the policies of the government should be dictated by powers behind the throne. The men most active in this regard were Thomas Cranmer, archbishop of Canterbury, and the dukes of Somerset and Northumberland, who successfully dominated the regency. Inasmuch as all three had strong Protestant leanings, the creeds and ceremonies of the Church of England were soon drastically altered. Priests were permitted to marry; English was substituted for Latin in the services; the veneration of images was abolished; and new articles of belief were drawn up repudiating all sacraments except baptism and communion and affirming the Lutheran doctrine of justification by faith alone. Thus when the youthful Edward died in 1553 it seemed as if England had definitely entered the Protestant camp.

The consolidation of English Protestantism

But Edward's pious Catholic successor, Mary (1553–1558), Henry VIII's daughter by Catherine of Aragon, thought otherwise. Because Mary associated the revolt against Rome with her mother's humiliations and her own removal from direct succession, upon coming to the throne she attempted to turn the clock back. Not only did she restore the celebration of the Mass and the rule of clerical celibacy, but she prevailed upon Parliament to vote the unconditional return of England to papal allegiance. Yet her policies ended in failure for several reasons. First of all, not only had Protestantism by then already sunk in deeply among the English masses, but many of the leading families which had profited from Henry VIII's dissolution of the monasteries had become particularly committed to Protestantism because a restoration of Catholic monasticism would have meant the loss of their newly acquired wealth. Then too, although Mary ordered the burning of Cranmer and a few hundred Protestant extremists, these

Popular resistance to Queen Mary's Catholicism

Philip of Spain and Mary Tudor. This double portrait was done on the occasion of the royal marriage.

executions were insufficient to wipe out religious resistance—indeed, Protestant propaganda about "Bloody Mary" and the "fires of Smithfield" soon actually hardened resistance to Mary's rule, making her seem like a vengeful persecutor. But perhaps the most serious cause of Mary's failure was her marriage to Philip, Charles V's son and heir to the Spanish throne. Although the marriage treaty stipulated that in the event of Mary's death Philip could not succeed her, patriotic Englishmen never trusted him. Hence when the queen allowed herself to be drawn by Philip into a war with France on Spain's behalf, in which England lost Calais, its last foothold on the European continent, the nation became highly disaffected. No one knows what might have happened next because death soon after ended Mary's troubled reign.

*The Elizabethan religious
settlement*

The question of whether England was to be Catholic or Protestant was thereupon settled definitively in favor of Protestantism by Elizabeth I (1558–1603). Daughter of Anne Boleyn and one of the most capable and popular monarchs ever to sit on the English throne, Elizabeth was predisposed in favor of Protestantism by the circumstances of her father's marriage as well as by her upbringing. But Elizabeth was no zealot, and wisely recognized that ordaining radical Protestantism in England posed the danger of provoking bitter sectarian strife because some English people were still Catholic and others resisted extremism. Accordingly, she presided over what is customarily known as "the Elizabethan compromise." By a new Act of Supremacy (1559), Elizabeth repealed all of Mary's Catholic legislation, prohibited the exercise of any authority by foreign religious powers, and made herself "supreme governor" of the English Church—a more Protestant title than Henry VIII's "supreme headship" insofar as most Protestants believed that Christ alone was the head of the Church. At the same time she accepted most of the Protestant ceremonial reforms instituted in the reign of her brother Edward. On the other hand, she retained Church government by bishops and left the definitions of some controversial articles of the faith, especially the meaning of the Eucharist, vague enough so that all but the most extreme Catholics and Protestants could accept them. Long after Elizabeth's death this settlement remained in effect. Indeed, as a result of the Elizabethan compromise, the Church of England today is broad enough to include such diverse elements as the "Anglo-Catholics," who differ from Roman Catholics only in rejecting papal supremacy, and the "low-church" Anglicans, who are as thoroughgoing in their Protestant practices as members of most other modern Protestant denominations.

*Protestantism in
Switzerland*

If the English compromise came about through royal decision-making, in Switzerland more spontaneous movements to establish Protestantism resulted in the victory of greater radicalism. In the early sixteenth century Switzerland was neither ruled by kings nor dominated by all-powerful territorial princes; instead, prosperous cities there were either independent or on the verge of becoming so. Hence when the leading citizens of a Swiss municipality decided to adopt Protestant reforms no one could stop them, and Protestantism in Switzerland could usually take its own course. Although religious arrangements tended at first to vary in detail from city to city, the three main forms of Protestantism that emerged in Switzerland from about 1520 to 1550 were Zwinglianism, Anabaptism, and, most fateful for Europe's future, Calvinism.

Zwinglianism, founded by Ulrich Zwingli (1484–1531) in Zürich, was the most moderate form of the three. At first a somewhat indifferent Catholic priest, around 1516 Zwingli was led by close study of the Bible, as Luther was, to conclude that contemporary Catholic theology and religious observances conflicted with the Gospel. But he did not speak out until Luther set the precedent. Then, in 1522, Zwingli started attacking the authority of the Catholic church in Zürich, and soon all Zürich and much of northern Switzerland had accepted his leadership in instituting reforms that closely resembled those of the Lutherans in Germany. Yet Zwingli did differ from Luther concerning the theology of the Eucharist: whereas Luther believed in the real presence of Christ's body, for Zwingli Christ was present merely in spirit. Thus for him the sacrament conferred no grace at all and was to be retained merely as a memorial service. This disagreement may seem trifling to many of us today, but then it sufficed to prevent Lutherans and Zwinglians from uniting in a common Protestant front. Going his way, Zwingli fell in battle against Catholic forces in 1531, whereupon his successors in Zürich lost their leadership over Swiss Protestantism, and the Zwinglian movement was soon after absorbed by the far more radical Protestantism of John Calvin.

Before that happened, however, the phenomenon of Anabaptism briefly flared up in Switzerland and also Germany. The first Anabaptists were members of Zwingli's circle in Zürich, but they quickly broke with him around 1525 on the issues of infant baptism and their conception of an exclusive Church of true believers. The name Anabaptism means "rebaptism," and stemmed from the Anabaptists' conviction that baptism should only be administered to adults because infants have no understanding of the meaning of the service. Yet this was only one manifestation of the Anabaptists' main belief that men and women were not born into any church. Although Luther and Zwingli alike taught the "priesthood of all believers," they still insisted that everyone, believer or not, should attend services and be part of one and the same officially instituted religious community. But the Anabaptists were sectarians or separatists, firm in the conviction that joining the true Church should be the product of an individual's inspired decision. For them, one had to follow the guidance of one's own "inner light" in opting for Church membership, and the rest of the world could go its own way. Since this was a hopelessly apolitical doctrine in an age when almost everyone assumed that Church and

Zwinglianism

Anabaptism

The turning point at
Münster

state were inextricably connected, Anabaptism was bound to be anathema to the established powers, both Protestant and Catholic. Yet in its first few years the movement did gain numerous adherents in Switzerland and Germany, above all because it appealed to sincere religious piety in calling for extreme simplicity of worship, pacifism, and strict biblical morality.

Unhappily for the fortunes of Anabaptism, an unrepresentative group of Anabaptist extremists managed to gain control of the German city of Münster in 1534. These zealots combined sectarianism with millenarianism, or the belief that God wished to institute a sweepingly new order of justice and spirituality throughout the world before the end of time. Determined to help God bring about this goal, the extremists attempted to turn Münster into a new Jerusalem. A former tailor named John of Leyden assumed the title of "King of the New Temple," proclaiming himself the successor of David. Under his leadership Anabaptist religious practices were made obligatory, private property was abolished, the sharing of goods was introduced, and even polygamy was instituted on the grounds of Old Testament precedents. Nonetheless, Münster succumbed to a siege by Catholic forces little more than a year after the Anabaptist takeover, and the new David, together with two of his lieutenants, was put to death by

The Anabaptists' Cages, Then and Now. After the three Anabaptist leaders who had reigned in Münster for a year were executed in 1535, their corpses were prominently displayed in cages hung from a tower of the marketplace church. As can be seen from the photo on the right, the bones are now gone but the iron cages remain to this very day as a grisly reminder of the horrors of sixteenth-century religious strife.

excruciating tortures. Given that Anabaptism had already been proscribed by many governments, this episode thoroughly discredited
the movement, and all of its adherents were subjected to ruthless
persecution throughout Germany, Switzerland, and wherever else they
could be found. Among the few who survived were some who banded
together in the Mennonite sect, named for its founder, the Dutchman
Menno Simons (1492–1559). This sect, dedicated to the pacifism
and simple "religion of the heart" of original Anabaptism, has continued to exist until the present. Various Anabaptist tenets were also
revived later by religious groups such as the Quakers and different
Baptist and Pentecostal sects.

A year after events in Münster sealed the fate of Anabaptism, a
twenty-six-year-old French Protestant named John Calvin (1509–1564),
who had fled to the Swiss city of Basel to escape religious persecution,
published the first version of his *Institutes of the Christian Religion,* a
work which was soon to prove the single most influential systematic
formulation of Protestant theology ever written. Born in Noyon in
northern France, Calvin originally had been trained for the law and
around 1533 was studying the Greek and Latin classics while living
off the income from a Church benefice. But then, as he later wrote,
while he was "obstinately devoted to the superstitions of Popery," a
stroke of light made him feel that God was extricating him from "an
abyss of filth," and he thereupon opted for becoming a Protestant
propagandist. Though some of these details resemble the early career
of Luther, there was one essential difference: namely, whereas Luther
was always a highly volatile personality, Calvin remained a cool French
legalist through and through. Thus, whereas Luther never wrote systematic theology but only responded to given problems as they arose
or as the mood struck him, Calvin resolved in his *Institutes* to set forth
all the principles of Protestantism comprehensively, logically, and consistently. Accordingly, after several revisions and enlargements (the
definitive edition appeared in 1559), Calvin's *Institutes of the Christian
Religion* became the most theologically authoritative statement of basic
Protestant beliefs and the nearest Protestant equivalent of St. Thomas
Aquinas's *Summa Theologica.*

The hallmark of Calvin's rigorous theology in the *Institutes* is that
he started with the omnipotence of God and worked downward. For
Calvin the entire universe is utterly dependent on the will of the
Almighty, who created all things for his greater glory. Because of the
original fall from grace, all human beings are sinners by nature, bound
hand and foot to an evil inheritance they cannot escape. Nevertheless,
the Lord for reasons of His own has predestined some for eternal salvation and damned all the rest to the torments of hell. Nothing that
human beings may do can alter their fate; their souls are stamped with
God's blessing or curse before they are born. But this does not mean,
in Calvin's opinion, that Christians should be indifferent to their conduct on earth. If they are among the elect, God will implant in them

John Calvin

John Calvin. A recently discovered anonymous portrait.

Calvin's theology

the desire to live right. Upright conduct is a sign, though not an infallible one, that whoever practices it has been chosen to sit at the throne of glory. Public profession of faith and participation in the sacrament of the Lord's Supper are also presumptive signs of election to be saved. But most of all, Calvin required an active life of piety and morality as a solemn obligation resting upon members of the Christian commonwealth. For him, good Christians should conceive of themselves as chosen instruments of God with a mission to help in the fulfillment of His purposes on earth, not striving for their souls' salvation but for the glory of God. In other words, Calvin clearly did not encourage his readers to sit with folded hands, serene in the knowledge that their fate was sealed.

Calvinism and
Lutheranism compared

Although Calvin always acknowledged a great theological debt to Luther, his religious teachings differed from those of the Wittenberg reformer in several essentials. First of all, Luther's attitude toward proper Christian conduct in the world was much more passive than Calvin's: for the former, the good Christian should merely endure the trials of this life in suffering, whereas for the latter the world was to be mastered in unceasing labor for God's sake. Second, Calvin's religion was more legalistic and more nearly an Old Testament faith than Luther's. This can be illustrated in the attitude of the two men toward Sabbath observance. Luther's conception of Sunday was similar to that which prevails among most Christians today. He insisted, of course, that his followers attend church, but he did not demand that during the remainder of the day they refrain from all pleasure or work. Calvin, on the other hand, revived the Jewish Sabbath with its strict taboos against anything faintly resembling worldliness. Finally, the two men differed explicitly on basic matters of Church government and ritual. Although Luther broke with the Catholic system of a gradated ecclesiastical hierarchy, Lutheran district superintendents were not unlike bishops, and Luther also retained a good many features of Roman worship such as altars and vestments (special clothing for the clergy). On the other hand, Calvin utterly rejected everything that smacked to him of "popery." Thus he argued for the elimination of all traces of the hierarchical system, instead having congregational election of ministers and assemblies of ministers and "elders" (laymen responsible for maintaining proper religious conduct among the faithful) governing the entire Church. Further, he insisted on the barest simplicity in church services, prohibiting all ritual, vestments, instrumental music, images, and stained-glass windows. When these teachings were put into practice, Calvinist services became little more than "four bare walls and a sermon."

Calvinist theocracy in
Geneva

Not content with mere theory, Calvin was intent upon putting his teachings into practice. Sensing an opportunity to influence the course of events in the French-speaking Swiss city of Geneva, then in the throes of combined political and religious upheaval, he moved there late in 1536 and began preaching and organizing immediately. In 1538 his activities caused him to be expelled, but in 1541 he returned to Geneva, and this time had both the government and the religion of the city completely under his sway. Under Calvin's guidance Geneva's government became theocratic. Supreme authority in the city was vested in a "Consistory," made up of twelve lay elders and five ministers. (Although Calvin himself was seldom the presiding officer, he usually dominated the Consistory's decisions until his death in 1564.) In addition to passing on legislation submitted to it by a congregation of ministers, the Consistory had as its main function the supervision of morals. This activity was carried out not merely by the punishment of antisocial conduct but by a persistent snooping into the private life of every individual. Geneva was divided into districts, and a committee of the Consistory visited every household without warning to check on the habits of its members. Even the mildest forms of self-indulgence were strictly prohibited. Dancing, card-playing, attending the theater, working or playing on the Sabbath—all were outlawed as works of the devil. Innkeepers were forbidden to allow anyone to consume food or drink without first saying grace, or to permit any patron to stay up after nine o'clock. Needless to say, penalties were severe. Not only were murder and treason classified as capital crimes, but also adultery, "witchcraft," blasphemy, and heresy. During the first four years after Calvin gained control in Geneva, there were no fewer than 58 executions out of a total population of only 16,000.

As reprehensible as such interference in the private sphere may seem today, in the middle of the sixteenth century Calvin's Geneva appeared as a beacon-light of thoroughgoing Protestantism to thousands throughout Europe. Calvin's disciple John Knox, for example, who brought Calvinism to Scotland, declared that Geneva under Calvin was "the most perfect school of Christ that ever was on earth since the days of the Apostles." Accordingly, many foreigners flocked to the "perfect school" for refuge or instruction, and usually returned home to become ardent proselytizers of Calvinism. Moreover, since Calvin himself thought of Geneva as merely a way station for bringing Calvinism to France and the rest of the world, he encouraged the dispatching of missionaries and propaganda into hostile territories, with the result that from about the middle of the sixteenth century Geneva became the center of a concerted and militant attempt to spread the new faith far and wide. Soon Calvinists became a majority in Scotland, where they were known as Presbyterians; a majority in Holland, where they founded the Dutch Reformed Church; a substantial minority in France, where they were called Huguenots; and a substantial minority in England, where they were called Puritans. In addition, Calvinist preachers zealously tried to make converts in most other parts of Europe. But just as the Calvinists were fanning out through Europe, the forces of Catholicism were hardening in their determination to head off any further Protestant advances. The result, as we

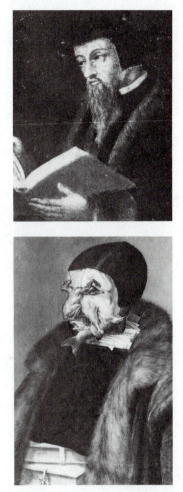

Calvin as Seen by His Friends and His Enemies. Above, an idealized contemporary portrait of Calvin as a pensive scholar. Below, a Catholic caricature in which Calvin's face is a composite made from fish, a fledgling bird, and a chicken drumstick.

will see in the next chapter, was that many parts of a hitherto united Christendom became mired in bloody religious wars for decades after.

4. THE PROTESTANT HERITAGE

Inasmuch as Luther's revolt from Rome and the spread of Protestantism occurred after the height of the civilization of the Renaissance and before some particularly fundamental advances in modern European political, economic, and social development, it is tempting to think of historical events unfolding in an inevitably cumulative way: Renaissance, Reformation, "Triumphs of the Modern World." But history is seldom as neat as that. Although scholars will continue to disagree on points of detail, most agree that the Protestant Reformation inherited little from the civilization of the Renaissance, that indeed in certain basic respects Protestant principles were completely at odds with major assumptions of Renaissance humanists. As for the relationship between "Protestantism and Progress," the most apt formulation appears to be a statement from a book of that title by the great German religious historian Ernst Troeltsch, according to which "Protestantism has furthered the rise of the modern world . . . [but nowhere] does it appear as its actual creator."

*Renaissance and
Reformation*

In considering the relationship between the Renaissance and the origins of the Protestant Reformation, it would admittedly be false to say that the one had absolutely nothing to do with the other. Certainly, criticisms of religious abuses by Christian humanists helped prepare Germany for the Lutheran revolt. Furthermore, close humanistic textual study of the Bible led to the publication of new, reliable biblical editions used by the Protestant reformers. In this regard a direct line ran from the Italian humanist Lorenzo Valla to Erasmus to Luther insofar as Valla's *Notes on the New Testament* inspired Erasmus to produce his own Greek edition and accompanying Latin translation of the New Testament in 1516, and that in turn enabled Luther in 1518 to reach some crucial conclusions concerning the literal biblical meaning of penance. For these and related reasons, Luther addressed Erasmus in 1519 as "our ornament and our hope."

*The Christian humanists'
opposition to Protestantism*

But in fact Eramus quickly showed that he had no sympathy whatsoever with Luther's first principles, and most other Christian humanists shunned Protestantism as soon as it became clear to them what Luther and other Protestant reformers actually were teaching. The reasons for this were that most humanists believed in free will while Protestants believed in predestination, that humanists tended to think of human nature as basically good while Protestants found it unspeakably corrupt, and that most humanists favored urbanity and tolerance while the followers of Luther and Calvin emphasized faith and conformity. Thus when Erasmus, for example, defended *The Freedom of the Will* in a treatise of 1524, Luther attacked it vehemently in his

Bondage of the Will of the following year, insisting that original sin makes all humans "bound, wretched, captive, sick, and dead." And when Henry VIII introduced the Reformation into England, England's foremost Christian humanist, Sir Thomas More, resisted the break with Rome even unto martyrdom, mounting the scaffold with some stirring words about the primacy of the individual conscience.

If the Protestant Reformation, then, was by no means the natural outgrowth of the civilization of the Renaissance, it very definitely contributed to certain traits most characteristic of modern European historical development. Foremost among these was the rise of the untrammeled powers of the sovereign state. As we have seen, those German princes who converted to Protestantism were moved to do so primarily by the search for sovereignty, and the kings of Denmark, Sweden, and England followed suit for the same reasons. Not at all accidentally, the earliest act of the English Parliament announcing Henry VIII's break with Rome, the Act in Restraint of Appeals of 1533, put forth the earliest official statement that England is a completely independent country, "governed by one supreme head and king," possessed of "plenary, whole, and entire power. . . . to render and yield justice and final determination to all manner of folk." Since Protestant leaders—Calvin as well as Luther—preached absolute obedience to "godly" rulers, and since the state in Protestant countries assumed direct control of the Church, the spread of Protestantism definitely resulted in the growth of state power. But, as we have also seen, the power of the state was growing anyway, and it continued to grow in Catholic countries like France and Spain where kings were granted most of the same rights over the Church that were forcibly seized by Lutheran German princes or Henry VIII.

As for the growth of nationalism, a sense of national pride was already present in sixteenth-century Germany that Luther played upon in his appeals of 1520. But Luther himself then did the most to foster German cultural nationalism by translating the entire Bible into a vigorous German idiom. Up until then Germans from some regions spoke a language so different from that of Germans from other areas that they could not understand each other, but the form of German given currency by Luther's Bible soon became the linguistic standard for the entire nation. Religion did not help to unite the German nation politically because the non-German Charles V opposed Lutheranism and as a result Germany soon became politically divided into Protestant and Catholic camps. But elsewhere, as in Scotland and Holland, where Protestants fought successfully against Catholic overlords, Protestantism enhanced a sense of national identity. And perhaps the most familiar case of all is that of England, where a sense of nationhood had existed before the advent of Protestantism even more markedly than it had in Germany, Scotland, or Holland, but where the new faith, as we shall see, helped underpin the greatest accomplishments of the Elizabethan age.

685

The Protestant Heritage

Catholic and Protestant Views of a Cardinal. A genuine papal medal (shown above) depicted a cardinal (right-side up) merged with a bishop (upside down). In response, a Protestant replica (shown below), probably struck in the Netherlands, depicted a cardinal merged with a grinning fool.

Protestantism and the rise of the modern state

Protestantism and modern
economic development

The problem of Protestantism's relationship to modern commercial and industrial economic development is more controversial. Around 1900 the great German sociologist Max Weber, noticing that the economically advanced territories of England, Holland, and North America had all been Protestant, argued that Protestantism, particularly in its Calvinist forms, was especially conducive to acquisitive economic enterprise. According to Weber, this was because Calvinistic theology, as opposed to Catholicism, sanctified the ventures of profit-oriented traders and moneylenders, and gave an exalted place in its ethical system to the business virtues of thrift and diligence. But historians have found shortcomings in Weber's thesis. Although Calvin did indeed praise diligence and acknowledge that merchants could be "sanctified in their calling," he no more approved of exorbitant interest rates than Catholics did. Moreover Calvin argued vehemently that people should put their excess wealth at the service of the poor rather than piling up capital for the sake of gain or subsequent investments. Thus it appears that the "work ethic" necessary for economic success in commercial ventures did have some Calvinistic roots, but that Calvin's ideal merchant would by no means have been a great speculator or maker of fortunes. Bearing in mind that the European economy had already made great strides forward in the High Middle Ages and was advancing again in the early-modern period, not least because of the overseas ventures initiated by the Catholic powers of Portugal and Spain, Calvinism thus was at most just one of many contributory factors to the triumph of modern capitalism and the Industrial Revolution.

Protestantism's effects on
relations between the sexes

Finally, there arises the subject of Protestantism's effects on social relationships, specifically those between the sexes. As opposed to the question of Protestantism and economic development, this topic is still relatively unstudied. What is certain is that Protestant men as individuals could be just as ambivalent about women as Catholics, heathens, or Turks. John Knox, for example, inveighed against the Catholic regent of Scotland, Mary Stuart, in a treatise called *The First Blast of the Trumpet Against the Monstrous Regiment of Women,* yet maintained deeply respectful relationships with women of his own faith. But if one asks how Protestantism as a belief system rising above individual vagaries affected women's lot, the answer appears to be that it enabled women to become just a shade more equal to men, albeit still clearly within a subject status. Above all, since Protestantism, with its stress on the primacy of Scripture and the priesthood of all believers, called on women as well as men to undertake serious Bible study, it sponsored primary schooling for both sexes and thus enhanced female as well as male literacy. But Protestant male leaders never hesitated to insist that women were naturally inferior to men and thus should always defer to men in case of arguments. As Calvin himself said, "let the woman be satisfied with her state of subjection and not take it ill that she is made inferior to the more distinguished sex." Both Luther and Calvin appear to have been happily married, but that clearly meant being happily married on their own terms.

5. CATHOLIC REFORM

The historical novelty of Protestantism in the sixteenth century inevitably tends to cast the spotlight on such religious reformers as Luther and Calvin, but it must be emphasized that a powerful internal reform movement within the Catholic church exercised just as profound an effect on the course of European history as Protestantism did. Historians differ about whether to call this movement the "Catholic Reformation" or the "Counter-Reformation." Some prefer the former term because they wish to show that significant efforts to reform the Catholic church from within antedated the posting of Luther's theses and that therefore Catholic reform in the sixteenth century was no mere counterattack to check the growth of Protestantism. Others, however, insist quite properly that for the main part sixteenth-century Catholic reformers were indeed inspired primarily by the urgency of resisting what they regarded as heresy and schism. Fortunately the two interpretations are by no means irreconcilable, for they allude to two complementary phases: a Catholic Reformation that came before Luther and a Counter-Reformation that followed.

The Catholic Reformation beginning around 1490 was primarily a movement for moral and institutional reform inspired by the principles of Christian humanism and carried on with practically no help from the dissolute Renaissance papacy. In Spain around the turn of the fifteenth century, reform activities directed by Cardinal Francisco Ximénes de Cisneros (1436–1517) with the cooperation of the monarchy led to the imposition of strict rules of behavior for Franciscan friars and the elimination of abuses prevalent among the diocesan clergy. Although Ximénes aimed primarily at strengthening the Church in its rivalry with Jews and Muslims, his work had considerable effect in regenerating the spiritual life of the nation. In Italy there was no similarly centralized reform movement, but a number of earnest clerics in the early sixteenth century labored on their own to make the Italian Church more worthy of its calling. The task was a difficult one on account of the entrenchment of abuses and the example of profligacy set by the papal court, but despite these obstacles, the Italian reformers did manage to establish some new religious orders dedicated to high ideals of piety and social service. Finally, it cannot be forgotten that such leading Christian humanists as Erasmus and Thomas More were in their own way Catholic reformers, for in criticizing abuses and editing sacred texts, men like these certainly helped to enhance spirituality.

Once Protestantism began threatening to sweep over Europe, however, Catholic reform of the earlier variety clearly became inadequate to defend the Church, let alone turn the tide of revolt. Thus a second,

Catholic reform before and after Luther

The Catholic Reformation

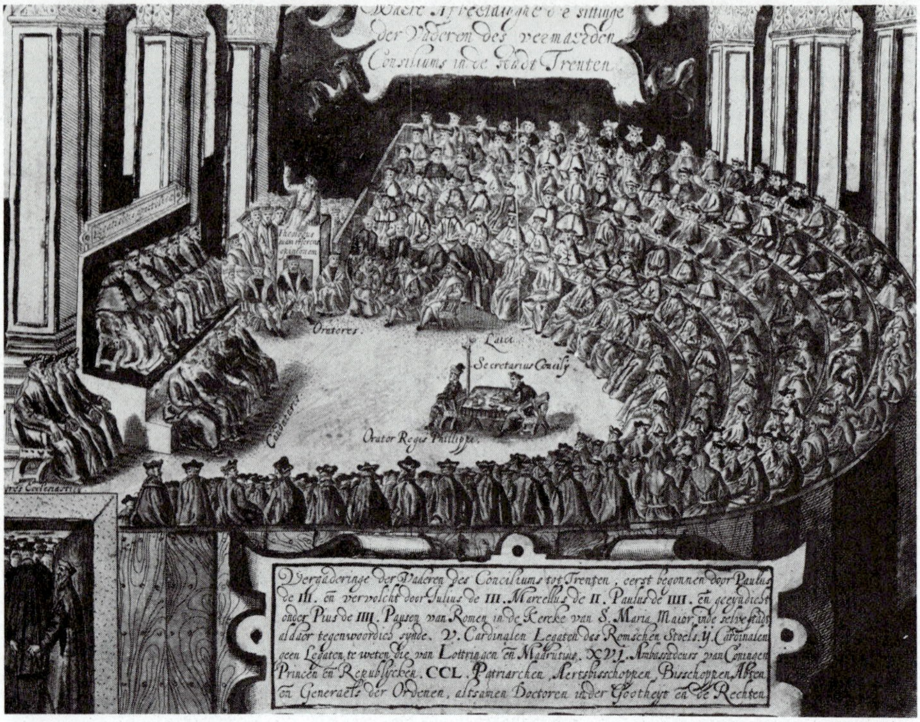

A Session of the Council of Trent. The pope is not present, but the cardinals who represent him are enthroned, facing the semicircle of bishops. The orator with a raised right hand is a theologian advancing an opinion.

The Counter-Reformation popes

more aggressive, phase of reform under a new style of vigorous papal leadership gained momentum during the middle and latter half of the sixteenth century. The leading Counter-Reformation popes—Paul III (1534–1549), Paul IV (1555–1559), St. Pius V (1566–1572), and Sixtus V (1585–1590)—were collectively the most zealous crusaders for reform who had presided over the papacy since the High Middle Ages. All led upright personal lives. Indeed, some were so grimly ascetic that contemporaries were unsure whether they were not too holy: as a Spanish councillor wrote in 1567, "We should like it even better if the present Holy Father were no longer with us, however great, inexpressible, unparalleled, and extraordinary his holiness may be." But in the circumstances of the Protestant onslaught, a pope's reputation for excessive asceticism was vastly preferable to a reputation for profligacy. More than that, becoming fully dedicated to activist revitalization of the Church, the Counter-Reformation popes reorganized their finances and filled ecclesiastical offices with bishops and abbots as renowned for austerity as themselves, and these appointees in turn set high standards for their own priests and monks.

The Council of Trent: doctrinal matters

These papal activities were supplemented by the actions of the Council of Trent, convoked by Paul III in 1545 and meeting at intervals thereafter until 1563. This general council was one of the most important in the history of the Church. Concerning basic matters of doctrine, the Council of Trent without exception reaffirmed all the tenets challenged by the Protestant Reformers. Good works were held to be as necessary for salvation as faith. The theory of the sacraments as indispensable means of grace was upheld. Likewise, transubstantiation, the apostolic succession of the priesthood, the belief in purgatory, the invocation of saints, and the rule of celibacy for the clergy were all confirmed as essential elements in the Catholic system. On the question as to the proper source of Christian belief, the Bible and the traditions of apostolic teaching were held to be of equal authority. Not only was papal supremacy over every bishop and priest expressly maintained, but the supremacy of the pope over the Church council itself was taken for granted in a way that left the monarchical government of the Church undisturbed. The Council of Trent also reaffirmed the doctrine of indulgences which had touched off the Lutheran revolt, although it did condemn the worst scandals connected with the selling of indulgences.

The Council of Trent: practical reform and discipline

The legislation of Trent was not confined to matters of doctrine, but also included provisions for the elimination of abuses and for reinforcing the discipline of the Church over its members. Bishops and priests were forbidden to hold more than one benefice, so that absentees could not grow rich from a plurality of incomes. To eliminate the evil of an ignorant priesthood, it was provided that a theological seminary must be established in every diocese. Toward the end of its deliberations the council decided upon a censorship of books to prevent heretical ideas from corrupting those who still remained in the faith. A commission was appointed to draw up an index or list of writings which ought not to be read. The publication of this list in 1564 resulted in the formal establishment of the Index of Prohibited Books as a part of the machinery of the Church. Later, a permanent agency known as the Congregation of the Index was set up to revise the list from time to time. Altogether more than forty such revisions have been made. The majority of the books condemned have been theological treatises, and probably the effect in retarding the progress of learning has been slight. Nonetheless, the establishment of the Index must be viewed as a symptom of the intolerance which had come to infect both Catholics and Protestants.

St. Ignatius Loyola

In addition to the independent activities of popes and the legislation of the Council of Trent, a third main force propelling the Counter-Reformation was the foundation of the Society of Jesus, commonly known as the Jesuit order, by St. Ignatius Loyola (1491–1556). In the midst of a youthful career as a worldly soldier, the Spanish nobleman Loyola was wounded in battle in 1521 (the same year in which Luther defied Charles V at Worms), and while recuperating, decided to change his ways and become a spiritual soldier of Christ. Shortly afterward he lived as a hermit in a cave near the Spanish town of Manresa for ten months, during which, instead of reading the Bible as a Luther or a Calvin might have done, he experienced ecstatic visions and worked out the principles of his subsequent meditational guide, *The Spiritual Exercises*. This manual, completed in 1535 and first published in 1541, offered practical advice on how to master one's will and serve God by

The Inspiration of St. Jerome by Guido Reni. In 1546 the Council of Trent declared St. Jerome's Latin translation of the Bible, known as the Vulgate, to be the official version of the Catholic Church; then, in 1592, Pope Clement VIII chose one edition of the Vulgate to be authoritative above all others. Since Biblical scholars had known since the early sixteenth century that St. Jerome's translation contained numerous mistakes, Counter-Reformation defenders of the Vulgate insisted that even his mistakes had been divinely inspired and thus were somehow preferable to the original meaning of Scripture. The point is made visually in Guido Reni's painting of 1635.

a systematic program of meditations on sin and the life of Christ. Soon made a basic handbook for all Jesuits, and widely studied by numerous Catholic lay people as well, Loyola's *Spiritual Exercises* had an influence second only to Calvin's *Institutes* of all the religious writings of the sixteenth century.

Nonetheless, St. Ignatius's foundation of the Jesuit order itself was certainly his greatest single accomplishment. Originating as a small group of six disciples who gathered around Loyola in Paris in 1534 to serve God in poverty, chastity, and missionary work, Ignatius's Society of Jesus was formally constituted as an order of the Church by Pope Paul III in 1540, and by the time of Loyola's death already numbered fifteen hundred members. The Society of Jesus was by far the most militant of the religious orders fostered by the Catholic reform movements of the sixteenth century. It was not merely a monastic society but a company of soldiers sworn to defend the faith. Their weapons were not to be bullets and spears but eloquence, persuasion, instruction in the right doctrines, and, if necessary, more worldly methods of exerting influence. The organization was patterned after that of a military company, with a general as commander-in-chief and iron discipline enforced on all members. Individuality was suppressed, and a soldierlike obedience to the general was exacted of the rank and file. The Jesuit general, sometimes known as "the black pope" (from the color of the order's habit), was elected for life and was not bound to

Jesuit militancy; educational accomplishments

take advice offered by any other member. But he did have one clear superior, namely the Roman pope himself, for in addition to the three monastic vows of poverty, chastity, and obedience, all senior Jesuits took a "fourth vow" of strict obedience to the Vicar of Christ and were held to be at the pope's disposal at all times.

The activities of the Jesuits consisted primarily of proselytizing not just heathens but Christians, and establishing schools. Originally founded with the major aim of engaging in missionary work abroad, the early Jesuits by no means abandoned this goal, preaching to the heathen reached by the voyages of discovery in India, China, and Spanish America. For example, one of St. Ignatius's closest early associates, St. Francis Xavier (1506–1552), baptized thousands of natives and covered thousands of miles missionizing in the Indies. Yet, although Loyola had not at first conceived of his society as comprising shock-troops against Protestantism, that is what primarily became of it as the Counter-Reformation mounted in intensity. Working by means of preaching and diplomacy—sometimes at the risk of their lives—Jesuits in the second half of the sixteenth century fanned out through Europe in direct confrontation with Calvinists. In many places the Jesuits succeeded in keeping rulers and their subjects loyal to Catholicism, in others they met martyrdom, and in some others— notably Poland and parts of Germany and France—they actually succeeded in regaining territory temporarily lost to the Protestant faith. And wherever they were allowed to settle, the Jesuits set up schools and colleges, for they firmly believed that a vigorous Catholicism could rest only on widespread literacy and education. Indeed their schools were often so efficient that, after the fires of religious hatred began to subside, upper-class Protestants would sometimes send their children to receive a Jesuit education.

The society of Jesus as defenders of the faith

From the foregoing it should be self-evident that there is a "Counter-Reformation Heritage" every bit as much as there is a Protestant one. Needless to say, for committed Catholics, the greatest achievement of sixteenth-century Catholic reform was the defense and revitalization of the faith. Without any question, Catholicism would not have swept over the globe and reemerged in Europe as the vigorous spiritual force it remains today had it not been for the heroic efforts of the sixteenth-century reformers. But there were more practical results stemming from the Counter-Reformation as well. One was the spread of literacy in Catholic countries due to the educational activities of the Jesuits, and another was the growth of intense concern for acts of charity. Since Counter-Reformation Catholicism continued to emphasize good works as well as faith, charitable activities took on an extremely important role in the revived religion: hence spiritual leaders of the Counter-Reformation such as St. Francis de Sales (1567–1622) and St. Vincent de Paul (1576–1660) urged alms-giving in their sermons and writings, and a wave of founding orphanages and houses for the poor swept over Catholic Europe.

Results of the Counter-Reformation

Two other areas in which the Counter-Reformation had less dramatic but still noteworthy effects were in the realm of women's history and intellectual developments. Whereas Protestantism encouraged female literacy for the purpose of making women just a little bit more like men in the ability to read the Bible, reinvigorated Catholicism pursued a different course. Most Catholic women were kept in a more subordinate position in the life of the faith than women under Protestantism, but Catholicism fostered a distinctive role for a female religious elite—countenancing the mysticism of a St. Teresa of Avila (1515–1582), or allowing the foundation of new orders of nuns such as the Ursulines and the Sisters of Charity. Under both Protestantism and Catholicism women remained subordinate, but in the latter model they were able to pursue their religious impulses more independently.

Finally, it unfortunately cannot be said that the Counter-Reformation perpetuated the tolerant Christianity of Erasmus, for Christian humanists lost favor with Counter-Reformation popes and all of Erasmus's writings were immediately placed on the Index. But sixteenth-century Protestantism was just as intolerant as sixteenth-century Catholicism, and far more hostile to the cause of rationalism. Indeed, because Counter-Reformation theologians returned for guidance to the Scholasticism of St. Thomas Aquinas, they were much more committed to acknowledging the dignity of human reason than their Protestant counterparts who emphasized pure Scriptural authority and blind faith. Thus although a hallmark of the subsequent seventeenth-century scientific revolution was the divorce between spirituality of any variety and strict scientific work, it does not seem entirely coincidental that René Descartes, one of the founders of the scientific revolution who coined the famous phrase "I think, therefore I am," was trained as a youth by the Jesuits.

SELECTED READINGS

• *Items so designated are available in paperback editions.*

Boxer, C. R., *The Portuguese Seaborne Empire, 1415–1825,* New York, 1969. The standard work on the subject.

• Elliott, J. H., *The Old World and the New, 1492–1650,* Cambridge, 1970. A superb short analysis of the many ways in which the discovery of the New World affected life in the Old.

• Hale, J. R., *Renaissance Exploration,* New York, 1968. A scintillating brief introduction. Highly recommended as a point of departure.

• Morison, S. E., *Christopher Columbus, Mariner,* New York, 1955. A convenient abridgment of the master storyteller's definitive biography of Columbus, *Admiral of the Ocean Sea* (1942).

• Newitt, M., ed., *The First Portuguese Colonial Empire,* Exeter, 1986.

• Parry, J. H., *The Age of Reconnaissance,* London, 1963. Probably the best one-volume survey of the entire subject of early-modern European expansion; particularly strong on details of shipbuilding and navigation.

_____, *The Spanish Seaborne Empire*, London, 1966. The counterpart to Boxer for the early Spanish colonial experience.

• Penrose, B., *Travel and Discovery in the Renaissance, 1420–1620*, Cambridge, Mass., 1960. Engrossing narratives of the major voyages.

PROTESTANT REFORMATION

• Bainton, R. H., *Here I Stand: A Life of Martin Luther*, Nashville, Tenn., 1950. The best introductory biography in English: absorbing and authoritative, though clearly partisan in Luther's favor.

_____, *Women of the Reformation*, 3 vols., Minneapolis, 1970–1977. Full of interesting narrative, but little analysis.

• Brandi, K., *The Emperor Charles V*, New York, 1939. The standard narrative biography of the emperor who faced Luther and ruled much of Europe as well.

• Davis, Natalie Z., *Society and Culture in Early Modern France*, Stanford, 1975. A collection of pioneering essays in historical anthropology, including a brilliant piece on the role of women in sixteenth-century religious movements.

• Dickens, A. G., *The English Reformation*, New York, 1964. The best introduction.

• _____, *Reformation and Society in Sixteenth-Century Europe*, London, 1966. A highly stimulating introductory survey, with the added advantage of being profusely illustrated.

• Erikson, E. H., *Young Man Luther*, New York, 1958. A classic psychobiography that analyzes the young Luther's "identity crisis."

Grimm, Harold J., *The Reformation Era: 1500–1650*, 2nd ed., New York, 1973. The best college-level text; consistently informative, balanced, and reliable.

Harbison, E. H., *The Age of Reformation*, Ithaca, N.Y., 1955. A magnificent elementary introduction by a master of the field.

_____, *The Christian Scholar in the Age of the Reformation*, New York, 1956. Discusses the relationship between Christian humanism and early Protestantism.

• Hillerbrand, H., *The World of the Reformation*, London, 1975. A stimulating overview.

• Hurstfield, Joel, ed., *The Reformation Crisis*, London, 1965. Lively essays on all major aspects of Reformation history.

• McNeill, John T., *The History and Character of Calvinism*, New York, 1945. A basic, reliable, older work.

Monter, E. William, *Calvin's Geneva*, New York, 1967. Standard on the history of Calvin's Geneva.

Mullett, M., *Radical Religious Movements in Early Modern Europe*, London, 1980. Thematic analysis of some of the major effects of Protestantism, with as much attention given to the seventeenth as to the sixteenth century. Contains a particularly valuable annotated bibliography.

Oberman, H. A., *Masters of the Reformation*, Cambridge, 1981. A challenging study of the emergence of Protestantism as seen from the perspective of activities at the University of Tübingen. For more advanced readers.

Samuelsson, K., *Religion and Economic Action*, New York, 1961. The standard critical evaluation of Max Weber's thesis that Calvinism fostered the modern "spirit of capitalism."

• Skinner, Q., *The Foundations of Modern Political Thought: 2. The Age of Reformation,* Cambridge, 1978. In a class by itself as the best analysis of Reformation and Counter-Reformation trends in political theory.

• Smith, Lacey B., *Henry VIII: The Mask of Royalty,* Boston, 1971. A breathtaking interpretation of the last years of Henry VIII and the age in which he lived.

• Spitz, Lewis W., ed. *The Reformation: Basic Interpretations,* 2nd ed., Lexington, Mass., 1972. A collection of readings on points of scholarly dispute.

Tawney, R. H., *Religion and the Rise of Capitalism,* New York, 1926. The most sophisticated and elegantly written defense of the "Weber thesis."

• Troeltsch, E., *Protestantism and Progress,* New York, 1931. An enduring classic.

Wendel, F., *Calvin,* London, 1963. A standard biography.

Williams, George H., *The Radical Reformation,* Philadelphia, 1962. Detailed account of Anabaptism and the "left wing" of the Protestant Reformation.

CATHOLIC REFORM

Broderick, James, *The Origin of the Jesuits,* London, 1940. An older work, but still unsurpassed.

Delumeau, J., *Catholicism between Luther and Voltaire: A New View of the Counter-Reformation,* Philadelphia, 1977. A sympathetic account stressing the positive aspects of Reformed Catholicism.

• Dickens, A. G., *The Counter-Reformation,* London, 1968. A splendid counterpart to Dickens's *Reformation and Society;* like its companion, profusely illustrated.

Janelle, P., *The Catholic Reformation,* Milwaukee, 1949. A reliable brief introduction.

Jedin, H., *A History of the Council of Trent,* 2 vols., London, 1957–1961. Authoritative and exhaustive.

Knowles, D., *From Pachomius to Ignatius: A Study in the Constitutional History of the Religious Orders,* Oxford, 1966. In less than one hundred masterful pages Knowles places the organizational principles of the Jesuits in historical perspective.

SOURCE MATERIALS

• Dillenberger, J., ed., *John Calvin: Selections from His Writings,* Garden City, N.Y., 1971.

• _____, *Martin Luther: Selections from His Writings,* Garden City, N.Y., 1961.

• Hillerbrand, H. J., ed., *The Protestant Reformation,* New York, 1967.

St. Ignatius Loyola, *The Spiritual Exercises,* tr. R. W. Gleason, Garden City, N.Y., 1964.

Ziegler, D. J., *Great Debates of the Reformation,* New York, 1969.

Chapter 20

A CENTURY OF CRISIS FOR EARLY-MODERN EUROPE
(c. 1560—c. 1660)

I do not wish to say much about the customs of the age in which we live. I can only state that this age is not one of the best, being a century of iron.

—R. Mentet de Salmonet, *History of the Troubles in Great Britain* (1649)

>   What in me is dark
> Illumine, what is low raise and support.

—John Milton, *Paradise Lost*

O n the night before St. Bartholomew's Day in August of 1572 the Catholic queen mother of France, Catherine de Medici, authorized the ambush of French Protestant leaders who had come to Paris to attend a wedding. Thereupon, during the hours after midnight, unsuspecting people found themselves awakened to be stabbed in bed or thrown out of windows. Soon all the targeted Protestants were eliminated, but the killing did not stop because roving bands of Parisian Catholics seized the opportunity of licensed carnage to slaughter at will any enemies they happened upon, Protestant or otherwise. By morning the River Seine was clogged with corpses and scores of bodies hung from gibbets in witness to an event known ever since as the Massacre of St. Bartholomew's Day.

A massacre in Paris

Had this lamentable incident been an isolated event it hardly would be worth mentioning, but in fact throughout the hundred years from roughly 1560 to roughly 1660 outbreaks of religious mayhem—with Protestants the ruthless killers in certain cases as Catholics were in others—recurred in many parts of Europe. Moreover, to make matters far worse, economic hardships and prolonged wars accompanied religious riots to result in a century of pronounced crisis for European civilization.

A century of crisis

The St. Bartholomew's Day Massacre. A contemporary painting depicts the merciless slaughter of Huguenots in Paris. At the top left (in front of the large gate next to the Seine) the Queen Mother Catherine looks over a pile of naked dead bodies; to the right a Huguenot leader is being pushed out of a window.

Lack of uniformity in causes and effects

In many respects Europe's early-modern period of crisis resembled the terrible times of the late Middle Ages, but the early-modern crisis was much less uniform in its nature and extent. From the economic point of view, there were two different major difficulties—first a dramatic price inflation lasting from about 1560 to 1600 that hurt the poor far worse than it did the rich, and then a period of overall economic stagnation which was marked, however, by significant exceptions from place to place. Similarly, although the main theme of political history during the entire era was intense warfare, the causes of war differed greatly according to place and time, with some areas occasionally even managing to bask in intervals of peace. Nonetheless, seen from the broadest perspective the period from 1560 to 1660 was western Europe's "iron century"—an age of enormous turbulence and severe trials.

1. ECONOMIC, RELIGIOUS, AND POLITICAL TESTS

Impending crisis

Europe's time of troubles crept up on contemporaries unawares. For almost a century before 1560 most of the West had enjoyed steady economic growth, and the discovery of the New World seemed to harbinger even greater prosperity to come. Political trends too seemed auspicious, since most western European governments were becoming ever more efficient and providing more internal peace for their subjects. Yet around 1560 thunderclouds were gathering in the skies that would soon burst into terrible storms.

Although the causes of these storms were interrelated, each may be examined separately, starting with the great price inflation. Nothing like the upward price trend which affected western Europe in the second half of the sixteenth century had ever happened before. The cost of a measure of wheat in Flanders, for example, tripled from 1550 to 1600, grain prices in Paris quadrupled, and the overall cost of living in England advanced well over 100 percent during the same period. Certainly the twentieth century has seen even more dizzying inflations than this, but since the skyrocketing of prices in the later sixteenth century was a novelty, most historians agree on calling it the "price revolution."

Soaring prices

If experts agree on the terminology, however, very few of them agree on the exact combination of circumstances that caused the price revolution, for early-modern statistics are patchy and many areas of economic theory remain under dispute. Nonetheless, for present purposes two widely accepted dominant explanations for the great inflation may be offered with confidence. The first is demographic. Starting in the later fifteenth century, Europe's population began to mount again after the plague-induced fall off: roughly estimated, there were about 50 million people in Europe around 1450 and 90 million around 1600. Since Europe's food supply remained more or less constant owing to the lack of any noteworthy breakthrough in agricultural technology, food prices inevitably were driven sharply higher by greater demand. In contrast, the prices of manufactured goods did not rise as steeply because there was a greater match between supply and demand. Yet prices of manufactured items did rise nonetheless, especially in cases where the supply of agricultural raw materials crucial to the manufacturing process remained relatively inelastic.

*Causes of inflation: (1)
population increase*

Population trends therefore explain much, but since Europe's population did not grow nearly as rapidly in the second half of the sixteenth century as prices, complementary explanations for the great inflation are still necessary, and foremost among these is the enormous influx of bullion from Spanish America. Around 1560 a new technique of extracting silver from silver ore made the working of newly discovered mines in Mexico and Bolivia highly practical, soon transforming the previous trickle of silver entering the European economy into a flood. Whereas in the five years between 1556 and 1560 roughly 10 million ducats worth of silver passed through the Spanish entry point of Seville, between 1576 and 1580 that figure had doubled, and between 1591 and 1595 it had more than quadrupled. Inasmuch as most of this silver was used by the Spanish crown to pay its foreign creditors and its armies abroad or by private individuals to pay for

(2) influx of silver

imports from other countries, Spanish bullion quickly circulated throughout Europe, where much of it was minted into coins. This dramatic increase in the volume of money in circulation further fueled the spiral of rising prices. "I learned a proverb here," said a French traveler in Spain in 1603, "everything costs much here except silver."

Effects of inflation on the laboring poor

Aggressive entrepreneurs and landlords profited most from the changed economic circumstances, while the masses of laboring people were hurt the worst. Obviously, merchants in possession of sought-after goods were able to raise prices at will, and landlords either could profit directly from the rising prices of agricultural produce or, if they did not farm their own lands, could always raise rents. But laborers in country and town were caught in a squeeze because wages rose far more slowly than prices, owing to the presence of a more than adequate labor supply. Moreover, because the cost of food staples rose at a sharper rate proportionately than the cost of most other items of consumption, poor people had to spend an ever-greater percentage of their paltry income on necessities. In normal years they barely managed to survive, but when disasters such as wars or poor harvests drove grain prices out of reach, some of the poor literally starved to death. The picture that thus emerges is one of the rich getting richer and the poor getting poorer—splendid feasts enjoyed amid the most appalling suffering.

Political results

In addition to these direct economic effects, the price inflation of the later sixteenth century had significant political effects as well because higher prices placed new pressures on the sovereign states of Europe. The reasons for this were simple. Since the inflation depressed the real value of money, fixed incomes from taxes and dues in effect yielded less and less. Thus merely to keep their incomes constant governments would have been forced to raise taxes. But to compound this problem, most states needed much more real income than previously because they were undertaking more wars, and warfare, as always, was becoming increasingly expensive. The only recourse, then, was to raise taxes precipitously, but such draconian measures incurred great resentments on the part of subject populations—especially the very poor who were already strapped more than enough by the effects of the inflation. Hence governments faced continuous threats of defiance and potential armed resistance.

Economic stagnation after 1600

Less need be said about the economic stagnation that followed the price revolution because it interfered little with most of the trends just discussed. When population growth began to ease and the flood of silver from America began to abate around 1600, prices soon leveled off. Yet because the most lucrative economic exploitation of the New World only began in the late seventeenth century and Europe experienced little new industrial development, the period from about 1600 to 1660 was at best one of very limited overall economic growth, even though a few areas—notably Holland—bucked the trend. Within this context the rich were usually able to hold their own, but the poor as a group made no advances since the relationship of prices to wages remained fixed to their disadvantage. Indeed, if anything, the lot of the poor in many places deteriorated because the mid–seventeenth century saw some particularly expensive and destructive wars, causing helpless civilians to be plundered either by rapacious tax collectors, looting soldiers, or sometimes by both.

It goes without saying that most people would have been far better off had there been fewer wars during Europe's iron century, but given prevalent attitudes, newly arisen religious rivalries made wars inevitable. Simply stated, until religious passions began to cool toward the end of the period, most Catholics and Protestants viewed each other as minions of Satan who could not be allowed to live. Worse, sovereign states attempted to enforce religious uniformity on the grounds that "crown and altar" offered each other mutual support and in the belief that governments would totter where diversity of faith prevailed. Rulers on both sides felt certain that religious minorities, if allowed to survive in their realms, would inevitably engage in sedition; nor were they far wrong since militant Calvinists and Jesuits were indeed dedicated to subverting constituted powers in areas where they had not yet triumphed. Thus states tried to extirpate all potential religious resistance, but in the process sometimes provoked civil wars in which both sides tended to assume there could be no victory until the other was exterminated. And of course civil wars might become international in scope when one or more foreign powers resolved to aid embattled religious allies elsewhere.

Religious wars

Compounding the foregoing problems were more strictly political ones: namely, while strapped by price trends and racked by religious wars, governments brought certain provincial and constitutional grievances down upon themselves. Regarding the provincial issue, most of the major states of early-modern Europe had been built up by conquests or dynastic marital accretions, with the result that many smaller territories had been subjected to absentee rule. At first some degree of provincial autonomy was usually preserved and hence the inhabitants of such territories did not object too much to their annexation. But in the iron century, when governments were making ever-greater financial claims on all their subjects or trying to enforce religious uniformity, rulers customarily moved to destroy all semblances of provincial autonomy in order to implement their financial or religious policies. Naturally the province-dwellers were usually not inclined to accept total subjugation without a fight, so rebellions might break out on combined patriotic and economic or religious grounds. Nor was that all, since most governments seeking money and/or religious uniformity tried to rule their subjects with a firmer hand than before, and thus sometimes provoked armed resistance in the name of traditional constitutional liberties. Given this bewildering variety of

Governmental crises

motives for revolt, it is by no means surprising that the century between 1560 and 1660 was one of the most turbulent in all European history.

2. A HALF CENTURY OF RELIGIOUS WARS

Despite the multiplicity of overlapping causes for instability, the greatest single cause of warfare in the first half of Europe's iron century was religious rivalry. Indeed, wars between Catholics and Protestants began as early as the 1540s when the Catholic Holy Roman Emperor Charles V tried to reestablish Catholic unity in Germany by launching a military campaign against several German princes who had instituted Lutheran worship in their principalities. At times thereafter it appeared as if Charles was going to succeed in reducing his German Protestant opponents to complete submission, but since he was also involved in fighting against France, he seldom was able to devote concerted attention to affairs in Germany. Accordingly, religious warfare sputtered on and off until a compromise settlement was reached in the Religious Peace of Augsburg (1555). This rested on the principle of *"cuius regio, eius religio"* ("as the ruler, so the religion"), which meant that in those principalities where Lutheran princes ruled, Lutheranism would be the sole state religion, and the same for those with Catholic princes. Although the Peace of Augsburg was a historical milestone inasmuch as Catholic rulers for the first time acknowledged the legality of Protestantism, it boded ill for the future in assuming that no sovereign state larger than a free city (for which it made exceptions) could tolerate religious diversity. Moreover, in excluding Calvinism it ensured that Calvinists would become aggressive opponents of the *status quo*.

Even though wars in the name of religion were fought in Europe before 1560, those that raged afterward were far more brutal, partly because the combatants had become more fanatical (intransigent Calvinists and Jesuits customarily took the lead on their respective sides), and partly because the later religious wars were aggravated by political and economic resentments. Since Geneva bordered on France, since Calvin himself was a Frenchman who longed to convert his mother country, and since Calvinists had no wish to displace German Lutherans, the next act in the tragedy of Europe's confessional warfare was played out on French soil. Calvinist missionaries had already made much headway in France in the years between Calvin's rise to power in Geneva in 1541 and the outbreak of religious warfare in 1562. Of the greatest aid to the Calvinist (Huguenot) cause was the conversion to Calvinism of many aristocratic French women because such women often won over their husbands, who in turn maintained large private armies. The foremost example is that of Jeanne d'Albret, queen of the tiny Pyrenean kingdom of Navarre, who brought over to Calvinism

Jeanne D'Albret

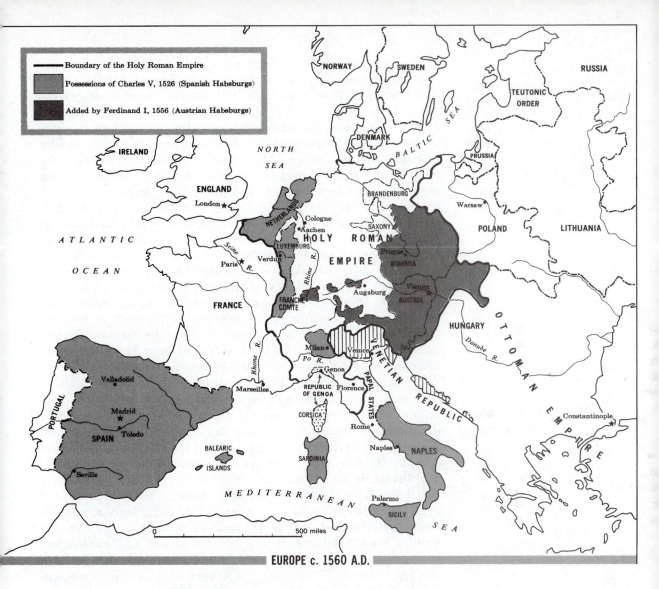

EUROPE c. 1560 A.D.

her husband, the prominent French aristocrat Antoine de Bourbon, and her brother-in-law, the prince de Condé. Not only did Condé take command of the French Huguenot party when civil war broke out in 1562, but he later was succeeded in this capacity by Jeanne's son, Henry of Navarre, who came to rule all of France at the end of the century as King Henry IV. In addition to aristocrats, many people from all walks of life became Huguenots for a variety of motives, with Huguenot strength greatest in areas of the south which had long resented the dominance of northern rule from Paris. In short, by 1562 Calvinists comprised between 10 and 20 percent of France's population of roughly 16 million, and their numbers were swelling every day.

Since both Catholics and Protestants assumed that France could have

Background of the French wars of religion

French warfare: The St. Bartholomew's Day Massacre

only a single *roi, foi,* and *loi* (king, faith, and law), civil war was inevitable, and no one was surprised when a struggle between the Huguenot Condé and the ultra-Catholic duke of Guise for control of the government during a royal minority led in 1562 to a show of arms. Soon all France was aflame. Churches were ransacked and local scores were settled by rampaging mobs who often were incited on both sides by members of their clergy. After a while it became clear that the Huguenots were not strong or numerous enough to gain victory, but they were also too strong to be defeated. Hence, despite intermittent truces, warfare dragged on at great cost of life until 1572. Then, during an interval of peace, the cultivated queen mother Catherine de Medici, normally a woman who favored compromise, plotted with members of the Catholic Guise faction to kill all the Huguenot leaders while they were assembled in Paris for the wedding of Henry of Navarre. In the early morning of St. Bartholomew's Day (August 24) most of the Huguenot chiefs were murdered in bed and two to three thousand other Protestants were slaughtered in the streets or drowned in the Seine by Catholic mobs. When word of the Parisian massacre spread to the provinces, some ten thousand more Huguenots were killed in a frenzy of blood lust that swept through France.

The St. Bartholomew's Day episode effectively broke the back of Huguenot resistance, but even then warfare did not cease because the neurotic King Henry III (1574–1589) tried to play off Huguenots against the dominant Catholic Guise family and because die-hard Huguenots sometimes were able to ally with Catholics revolting against overburdensome taxes or inequities in tax assessments. Only when the politically astute Henry of Navarre succeeded to the French throne as Henry IV[1] (1589–1610), initiating the Bourbon dynasty that would rule until 1792, did civil war finally come to an end. In 1593 Henry abjured his Protestantism in order to placate France's Catholic majority ("Paris is worth a mass") and then, in 1598, offered limited religious freedom to the Huguenots by the Edict of Nantes. According to the terms of this proclamation, Catholicism was recognized as the official religion, but Huguenot nobles were allowed to hold Protestant services privately in their castles, other Huguenots were allowed to worship at specified places (excluding Paris and all cities where bishops and archbishops resided), and the Huguenot party was permitted to fortify some towns, especially in the south, for military defense if the need arose. Thus, although the Edict of Nantes certainly did not countenance absolute freedom of worship, it nevertheless represented a major stride in the direction of toleration. With religious peace established, France quickly began to recover from decades of devastation, but Henry IV himself was cut down by the dagger of a Catholic fanatic in 1610.

Henry IV establishes French religious peace

---

[1]Here, as elsewhere, dates following a ruler's name refer to dates of reign.

The Assassination of Henry IV. This contemporary engraving shows Henry seated in an open carriage without any concern for his personal danger while his assassin climbs on the spoke of the carriage wheel to attack him. The entire composition conveys a vivid impression of early-modern Paris.

Contemporaneous with the religious warfare in France was equally bitter religious strife between Catholics and Protestants in the neighboring Netherlands, where national resentments gravely compounded religious hatreds. For almost a century the Netherlands (or Low Countries), comprising modern-day Holland in the north and Belgium in the south, had been ruled by the Habsburg family. Particularly the southern part of the Netherlands prospered greatly from trade and manufacture: southern Netherlanders had the greatest per capita wealth of all Europe and their metropolis of Antwerp was northern Europe's leading commercial and financial center. Moreover, the half-century-long rule of the Habsburg Charles V (1506–1556) had been popular because Charles, who had been born in the Belgian city of Ghent, felt a sense of rapport with his subjects and allowed them a large degree of local self-government.

Habsburg rule in the Netherlands

But around 1560 the good fortune of the Netherlands began to ebb. When Charles V retired to a monastery in 1556 (dying two years later) he ceded all his vast territories outside of the Holy Roman Empire and Hungary—not only the Netherlands, but Spain, Spanish America, and close to half of Italy—to his son Philip II (1556–1598). Unlike Charles, Philip had been born in Spain, and thinking of himself as a Spaniard, made Spain his residence and the focus of his policy. Thus he viewed the Netherlands primarily as a potentially rich source of income necessary for pursuing Spanish affairs. (Around 1560 silver was only beginning to flood through Seville.) But in order to tap the wealth of the Netherlands Philip had to rule it more directly than his father had, and such attempts were naturally resented by the local magnates who until then had dominated the government. To make matters worse, a religious storm also was brewing, for after a treaty of 1559 ended a

Philip II and the impending crisis

The Emperor Charles V. This portrait by the Venetian painter Titian depicts the emperor in a grandiloquent equestrian pose. (Another depiction of Charles V by Titian appears in the section of color plates following p. 614.)

Philip II of Spain. Titian's portrait shows Philip's resemblance to his father, Charles V, particularly in the protruding lower jaw of the Habsburgs.

long war between France and Spain, French Calvinists had begun to stream over the Netherlandish border, making converts wherever they went. Soon there were more Calvinists in Antwerp than in Geneva, a situation that Philip II could not tolerate because he was an ardent Catholic who subscribed wholeheartedly to the goals of the Counter-Reformation. Indeed, as he wrote to Rome on the eve of conflict: "rather than suffer the slightest harm to the true religion and service of God, I would lose all my states and even my life a hundred times over because I am not and will not be the ruler of heretics."

Evidence of the complexity of the Netherlandish situation is found in the facts that the leader of resistance to Philip, William the Silent, was at first not a Calvinist and that the territories which ultimately succeeded in breaking away from Spanish rule were at first the most Catholic ones in the Low Countries. William "the Silent," a prominent nobleman with large landholdings in the Netherlands, was in fact very talkative, receiving his nickname rather from his ability to hide his true religious and political feelings when the need arose. In 1566, when still a nominal Catholic, he and other local nobles not formally committed to Protestantism appealed to Philip to allow toleration for Calvinists. But while Philip momentarily temporized, radical Protestant mobs proved to be their own worst enemy—ransacking Catholic churches throughout the country, methodically desecrating hosts, smashing statuary, and shattering stained-glass windows. Though local troops soon had the situation under control, Philip II nonetheless decided to dispatch an army of ten thousand commanded by the steely

Spanish duke of Alva to wipe out Protestantism in the Low Countries forever. Alva's tribunal, the "Council of Blood," soon examined some twelve thousand persons on charges of heresy or sedition, of whom nine thousand were convicted and one thousand executed. William the Silent fled the country, and all hope for a free Netherlands seemed lost.

But the tide turned quickly for two related reasons. First, instead of giving up, William the Silent converted to Protestantism, sought help from Protestants in France, Germany, and England, and organized bands of sea rovers to harass Spanish shipping on the Netherlands coast. And second, Alva's tyranny helped William's cause, especially when the hated Spanish governor attempted to levy a repressive 10 percent sales tax. With internal disaffection growing, in 1572 William, for tactical military reasons, was able to seize the northern Netherlands even though the north until then had been predominantly Catholic. Thereafter geography played a major role in determining the outcome of the conflict. Spanish armies repeatedly attempted to win back the north, but they were stopped by a combination of impassable rivers and dikes which could be opened to flood out the invaders. Although William the Silent was assassinated by a Catholic in 1584, his son continued to lead the resistance until the Spanish crown finally agreed by a truce in 1609 to stop fighting and thus implicitly recognized the independence of the northern Dutch Republic. Meanwhile, the pressures of war and persecution had made the whole north Calvinistic, whereas the south—which remained Spanish—returned to uniform Catholicism.

Predictably, religious strife which could take the form of civil war, as in France, or war for national liberation, as in the Netherlands, could also take the form of warfare between sovereign states, as in the

The Duke of Alva. The gaunt Spanish general who attempted in vain to extirpate Calvinism in the Netherlands.

Protestants Ransacking a Catholic Church in the Netherlands. The "Protestant fury" of 1566 was responsible for the large-scale destruction of religious art and statuary in the Low Countries, provoking the stern repression of Philip II.

*Antagonism between
England and Spain*

case of the late-sixteenth-century struggle between England and Spain. After narrowly escaping domination by the Catholic Queen Mary and her Spanish husband Philip II, English Protestants rejoiced in the rule of Queen Elizabeth I (1558–1603) and naturally harbored great antipathy for Philip II and the Counter-Reformation. Furthermore, English economic interests were directly opposed to those of the Spanish. A seafaring and trading people, the English in the later sixteenth century were steadily making inroads into Spanish naval and commercial domination, and were also determined to resist any Spanish attempt to block England's lucrative trade with the Low Countries. But the greatest source of antagonism lay in naval contests in the Atlantic, where English privateers, with the tacit consent of Queen Elizabeth, could not resist raiding silver-laden Spanish treasure ships. Beginning around 1570, and taking as an excuse Spanish oppression of Protestants in the Netherlands, English admirals or pirates (the terms were really interchangeable) such as Sir Francis Drake and Sir John Hawkins began plundering Spanish vessels on the high seas. In a particularly dramatic sailing exploit lasting from 1577 to 1580, lust for booty and prevailing winds propelled Drake all the way around the world, to return with stolen Spanish treasure worth twice as much as Queen Elizabeth's annual revenue.

All this would have been sufficient provocation for Philip II to have

Left: *The Defeat of the Spanish Armada.* Right: *Queen Elizabeth I.* The contemporary English oil painting of the great sea battle gives only a schematic idea of its turbulence. Note, however, the prominence of the papal insignia (tiara over crossed keys of St. Peter) on the ship in the middle foreground. Englishmen were convinced that had they not defeated the Spanish Armada in 1588 the pope would have planted his banner on their shores. At the right is a typically overblown portrait of Queen Elizabeth, known to her admiring subjects as "Gloriana," standing on a map of England.

retaliated against England, but because he had his hands full in the Netherlands he resolved to invade the island only after the English openly allied with the Dutch rebels in 1585. And even then Philip did not act without extensive planning and a sense of assurance that nothing could go wrong. Finally, in 1588 he dispatched an enormous fleet, confidently called the "Invincible Armada," to punish insolent Britannia. After an initial standoff in the English Channel, however, English fireships outmaneuvered the Spanish fleet, setting some Spanish galleons ablaze and forcing the rest to break formation. "Protestant gales" did the rest and a battered flotilla soon limped home with almost half its ships lost.

The defeat of the Spanish Armada

The defeat of the Spanish Armada was one of the most decisive battles of Western history. Had Spain conquered England it is quite likely that the Spanish would have gone on to crush Holland and perhaps even to destroy Protestantism everywhere. But, as it was, the Protestant day was saved, and not long afterward Spanish power began to decline, with English and Dutch ships taking ever-greater command of the seas. Moreover, in England itself patriotic fervor became intense. Popular even before then, "Good Queen Bess" was virtually revered by her subjects until her death in 1603, and England embarked on its golden "Elizabethan Age" of literary endeavor. War with Spain dragged on inconclusively until 1604, but the fighting never brought England any serious harm and was just lively enough to keep the English people deeply committed to the cause of their queen, their country, and the Protestant religion.

The salvation of Protestantism

3. YEARS OF TREMBLING

With the promulgation of the Edict of Nantes in 1598, the peace between England and Spain of 1604, and the truce between Spain and Holland of 1609, religious warfare tapered off and came to an end in the early seventeenth century. But in 1618 a major new war broke out, this time in Germany. Since this struggle raged more or less unceasingly until 1648 it bears the name of the Thirty Years' War. Meanwhile, far from returning to enduring peace, Spain and France became engaged in the Thirty Years' War and war with each other, and internal resentments in Spain, France, and England flared up in the decade of the 1640s in concurrent outbreaks of uprisings and civil turmoil. As an English preacher said in 1643, "these are days of shaking, and this shaking is universal." He might have added that while in some instances religion remained one of the contested issues, secular disputes about powers of government were now becoming predominant.

A new phase of turmoil

The clearest example is that of the Thirty Years' War, which began in a welter of religious passions as a war between Catholics and Prot-

Two Artistic Broadsides from the Thirty Years' War. On the left the German peasantry is ridden by the soldiery; on the right is an allegorical representation of "the monstrous beast of war."

The Thirty Years' War

estants but immediately raised basic German constitutional issues and ended as an international struggle in which the initial religious dimension was almost entirely forgotten. Between the Peace of Augsburg in 1555 and the outbreak of war in 1618, Calvinists had replaced Lutherans in a few German territories, but the overall balance between Protestants and Catholics within the Holy Roman Empire had remained undisturbed. In 1618, however, when a Protestant uprising against Habsburg Catholic rule in Bohemia (not a German territory, but nonetheless part of the Holy Roman Empire) threatened to upset the balance, German Catholic forces ruthlessly counterattacked, first in Bohemia and then in Germany proper. Led by Charles V's Habsburg descendant Ferdinand II, who was archduke of Austria, king of Hungary, and from 1619 to his death in 1637, Holy Roman Emperor, a German Catholic league seized the military initiative and within a decade seemed close to extirpating Protestantism throughout Germany. But Ferdinand, who was intent on pursuing political goals as well, imposed firm direct rule in Bohemia in order to build up the strength of his own Austro-Hungarian state, and attempted to revive the faded authority of the Holy Roman Empire in whatever ways he could.

See color map facing page 711

Thus when the Lutheran king of Sweden, Gustavus Adolphus, marched into Germany in 1630 to champion the nearly lost cause of Protestantism, he was welcomed by several German Catholic princes who preferred to see the former religious balance restored rather than stand the chance of surrendering their sovereignty to Ferdinand II. To make matters still more ironic, Gustavus's Protestant army was secretly subsidized by Catholic France, then governed by a cardinal of the

The involvement of Sweden and France

Church, because Habsburg Spain had been fighting in Germany on the side of Habsburg Austria and France's Cardinal Richelieu was determined to resist any possibility of being surrounded by a strong Habsburg alliance on the north, east, and south. In the event, the military genius Gustavus Adolphus started routing the Habsburgs, but when the Swedish king fell in battle in 1632, Cardinal Richelieu had little choice but to send ever-greater support to the remaining Swedish troops in Germany, until in 1639 French armies entered the war directly on Sweden's side. From then until 1648 the struggle was really one of France and Sweden against Austria and Spain, with most of Germany a helpless battleground.

The result was that Germany suffered more from warfare in the terrible years between 1618 and 1648 than it ever did before or after until the twentieth century. Several German cities were besieged and sacked nine or ten times over, and soldiers from all nations, who often had to sustain themselves by plunder, gave no quarter to defenseless civilians. With plague and disease adding to the toll of outright butchery, some parts of Germany lost more than half their populations, although it is true that others went relatively unscathed. Most horrifying was the loss of life in the last four years, when the carnage continued unabated even while peace negotiators had already arrived at broad areas of agreement and were dickering over subsidiary clauses.

The toll of warfare in Germany

Nor did the Peace of Westphalia, which finally ended the Thirty Years' War in 1648, do much to vindicate anyone's death, even though it did establish some abiding landmarks in European history. Above all, from the international perspective the Peace of Westphalia marked the reemergence of France as the predominant power on the continental European scene, replacing Spain—a position France was to hold

The Peace of Westphalia

A Swearing of Oaths at the Peace of Westphalia, 1648

for two centuries more. In particular, France moved its eastern frontier directly into German territory by taking over large parts of Alsace. As for strictly internal German matters, the greatest losers were the Austrian Habsburgs, who were forced to surrender all the territory they had gained in Germany and to abandon their hopes of using the office of Holy Roman Emperor to dominate central Europe. Otherwise, something very close to the German *status quo* of 1618 was reestablished, with Protestant principalities in the north balancing Catholic ones in the south, and Germany so hopelessly divided that it could play no united role in European history until the nineteenth century.

The decline of Spain

Still greater losers from the Thirty Years' War than the Austrian Habsburgs were their Spanish cousins, for Spain had invested vast sums in the struggle it could not afford and ceased being a great power forever after. The story of Spain's swift fall from grandeur is almost like a Greek tragedy in its relentless unfolding. Even after the defeat of the "Invincible Armada," around 1600 the Spanish empire—comprising all of the Iberian peninsula (including Portugal, which had been annexed by Philip II in 1580), half of Italy, half of the Netherlands, all of Central and South America, and even the Philippine Islands—was the mightiest power not just in Europe but in the world. Yet a bare half century later this empire on which the sun never set had come close to falling apart.

Economic causes of Spain's decline

Spain's greatest underlying weakness was economic. At first this may seem like a very odd statement considering that in 1600, as in the three or four previous decades, huge amounts of American silver were being unloaded on the docks of Seville. Yet as contemporaries themselves recognized, "the new world that Spain had conquered was conquering Spain in turn." Lacking either rich agricultural or mineral resources, Spain desperately needed to develop industries and a balanced trading pattern as its rivals England and France were doing. But since the dominant Spanish nobility had prized ideals of chivalry over practical business ever since the medieval days when it was engaged in winning back Spanish territory from the Muslims, the Spanish governing class was only too glad to use American silver to buy manufactured goods from other parts of Europe in order to live in splendor and dedicate itself to military exploits. Thus bullion left the country as soon as it entered, virtually no industry was established, and when the influx of silver began to decline after 1600 the Spanish economy remained with nothing except increasing debts.

Spain's continued aggressiveness

Nonetheless, the crown, dedicated to supporting the Counter-Reformation and maintaining Spain's international dominance, would not cease fighting abroad. Indeed, the entire Spanish budget remained on such a warlike footing that even in the relatively peaceful year of 1608 four million out of a total revenue of seven million ducats were paid for military expenditures. Thus when Spain became engaged in fighting France during the Thirty Years' War it fully overextended itself. The clearest visible sign of this was that in 1643 outnumbered French

Self-Portrait, Albrecht Dürer (1471–1528). Dürer was the first major artist to paint self-portraits at different phases of his life. Here, aged twenty-eight, he makes himself seem almost Christlike. Note also the prominent initials "A.D." under the date of the painting at the upper left. (Alte Pinakothek)

Erasmus, Hans Holbein the Younger (1497–1543). This portrait is generally regarded as the most telling visual characterization of "the prince of the Christian humanists." (Louvre)

The Harvesters, Peter Brueghel (c. 1525–1569). Brueghel chose to depict both the hard work and recreation of the peasantry. (MMA)

The Crucifixion, Tintoretto (1518–1594). This Venetian master of Mannerism combined typically Venetian richness of color with an innovative concern for movement and emotion. (Scala)

Saint Andrew and St. Francis, El Greco (c. 1541–1614). A striking exemplification of the artist's penchant for elongation as well as his profound psychological penetration. (The Prado)

View of Toledo, El Greco. One of the most awesomely mysterious paintings in the entire Western tradition. (MMA)

The Maids of Honor, Diego Velásquez (1599–1660). The artist himself is at work on an idealized double portrait of the king and queen of Spain (who may be seen in the rear mirror), but reality is more obvious in the foreground in the persons of the delicately impish princess, her two maids, and a misshapen dwarf. The twentieth-century Spanish artist Picasso gained great inspiration from this work. (The Prado)

Pope Innocent X, Velásquez. A trenchant portrait of a decisive man of affairs. (Doria-Pamphili Collection)

England and Scotland Crowning Charles I, Peter Paul Rubens (1577–1640). A typical piece of Baroque propaganda, in this case painted to glorify the English monarch of the Stuart family in the years before his ill-fated demise. (Minneapolis Institute of Art)

The Horrors of War, Rubens. The war god Mars here casts aside his mistress Venus and threatens humanity with death and destruction. In his old age Rubens took a far more critical view of war than he did for most of his earlier career. (Gall. Palatina)

Aristotle Contemplating the Bust of Homer, Rembrandt van Rijn (1606–1669). One of the greatest painters' view of one of the greatest of philosophers caught up by the aura of one of the greatest poets. (MMA)

The Calling of St. Matthew, Caravaggio (1565–1609). Among the earliest of the great Baroque painters, Caravaggio specialized in contrasts of light and shade *(chiaroscuro),* and preferred to conceive of religious scenes in terms of everyday life. Here Christ (extreme right), whose halo is the only supernatural detail in the composition, enters a tavern to call St. Matthew (pointing doubtfully at himself) to his service. (Art Resource)

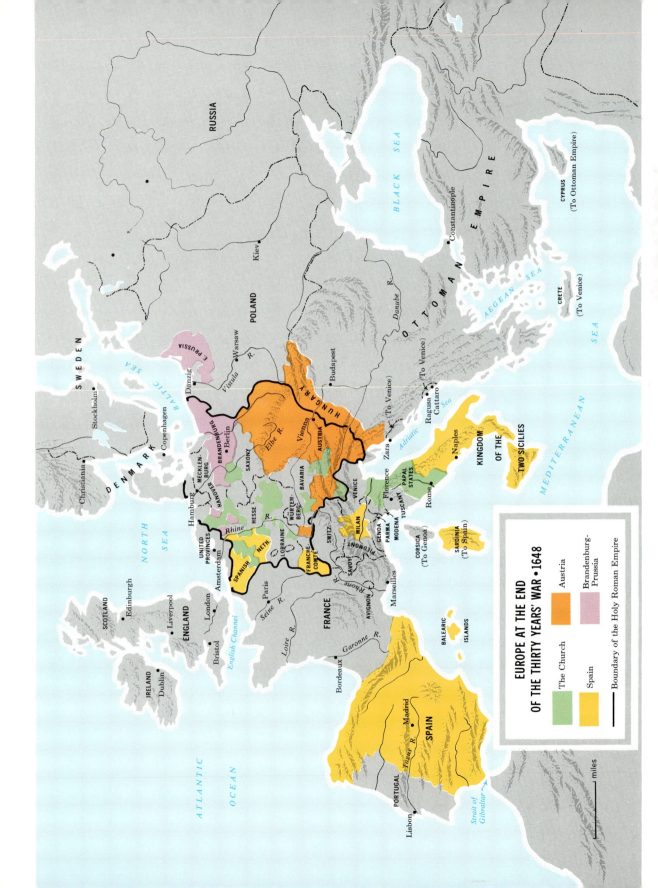

RUSSIA

SWEDEN

POLAND

BLACK SEA

OTTOMAN EMPIRE

CYPRUS
(To Ottoman Empire)

AEGEAN SEA

Constantinople

CRETE
(To Venice)

Kiev

Warsaw

Vistula R.

Danube R.

Budapest

HUNGARY

Vienna

AUSTRIA

Zara
(To Venice)

Adriatic Sea

Ragusa
Cattaro
(To Venice)

MEDITERRANEAN SEA

E. PRUSSIA

Danzig

BRANDENBURG

Berlin

SAXONY

Elbe R.

BAVARIA

MILAN

VENICE

Florence

TUSCANY

PAPAL STATES

Rome

Naples

KINGDOM
OF THE
TWO SICILIES

Stockholm

Christiania

Copenhagen

DENMARK

BALTIC SEA

MECKLEN-
BURG

HANOVER

Hamburg

HESSE

WÜRTEM-
BERG

R.

Rhine

UNITED
PROVINCES

Amsterdam

NETH.

LORRAINE

SWITZ.

SPANISH

FRANCHE
COMTÉ

SAVOY

PIEDMONT

GENOA

PARMA

MODENA

CORSICA
(To Genoa)

SARDINIA
(To Spain)

*NORTH
SEA*

SCOTLAND

Edinburgh

Liverpool

ENGLAND

London

Bristol

IRELAND

Dublin

English Channel

Paris

Seine R.

FRANCE

Loire R.

Garonne R.

Bordeaux

Rhône R.

Marseilles

Avignon

*ATLANTIC
OCEAN*

BALEARIC
ISLANDS

SPAIN

Madrid

Tagus R.

PORTUGAL

Lisbon

*Strait of
Gibraltar*

EUROPE AT THE END
OF THE THIRTY YEARS' WAR · 1648

The Church	Austria
Spain	Brandenburg-Prussia
	Boundary of the Holy Roman Empire

miles

troops at Rocroi inflicted a stunning defeat on the famed Spanish infantry, the first time that a Spanish army had been overcome in battle since the reign of Ferdinand and Isabella. Yet worse still was the fact that by then two territories belonging to Spain's European empire were in open revolt.

In order to understand the causes of these revolts one must recognize that in the seventeenth century the real "nation of Spain" was Castile—all else was acquired territory. After the marriage of Isabella of Castile and Ferdinand of Aragon in 1469, geographically central Castile emerged as the dominant partner in the Spanish union, becoming even more dominant when Castile conquered the Muslim kingdom of Granada in southern Spain in 1492 and annexed Portugal in 1580. In the absence of any great financial hardships, semi-autonomous Catalonia (the most fiercely independent part of Aragon) endured Castilian hegemony. But in 1640, when the strains of warfare induced Castile to limit Catalonian liberties in order to raise more money and men for combat, Catalonia revolted. Immediately afterward the Portuguese learned of the Catalonian uprising and revolted as well, followed by southern Italians who revolted against Castilian viceroys in Naples and Sicily in 1647. At that point only the momentary inability of Spain's greatest external enemies, France and England, to take advantage of its plight saved the Spanish empire from utter collapse. Nothing if not determined, the Castilian government quickly put down the Italian revolts and by 1652 also brought Catalonia to heel. But Portugal retained its independence forever, and by the Peace of the Pyrenees, signed with France in 1659, Spain in effect conceded that it would entirely abandon its ambitions of dominating Europe.

A comparison between the fortunes of Spain and France in the first half of the seventeenth century is highly instructive because some

Internal revolts against the Castilian government

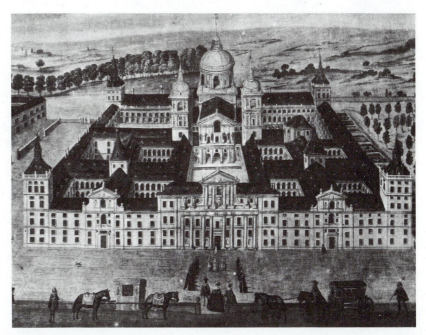

The Escorial. Philip II of Spain ordered the building between 1563 and 1584 of this somber retreat—part royal residence, part monastery—on an isolated spot, well removed from Madrid. Conceived on a grid-iron plan to honor the grid-iron martyrdom of St. Lawrence (on whose feast day Philip had won a decisive victory against the French), the Escorial symbolizes for many the Spanish crown's dedication to the ideals of the Counter-Reformation as well as its attempt to impose rationalized central government on the refractory outlying provinces of the Spanish Empire.

striking similarities existed between the two countries, but in the end differences turned out to be most decisive. Spain and France were of almost identical territorial extent, and both countries had been created by the same process of accretion. Just as the Castilian crown had gained Aragon in the north, Granada in the south, and then Portugal, so the kingdom of France had grown by adding on such diverse territories as Languedoc, Dauphiné, Provence, Burgundy, and Brittany. Since the inhabitants of all these territories cherished traditions of local independence as much as the Catalans or Portuguese, and since the rulers of France, like those of Spain, were determined to govern their provinces ever more firmly—especially when the financial stringencies of the Thirty Years' War made ruthless tax-collecting urgently necessary—a direct confrontation between the central government and the provinces in France became inevitable, just as in Spain. But France weathered the storm whereas Spain did not, a result largely attributable to France's greater wealth and the greater prestige of the French crown.

In good times most French people, including those from the outlying provinces, tended to revere their king. Certainly they had excellent reason to do so during the reign of Henry IV. Having established religious peace in 1598 by the Edict of Nantes, the affable Henry, who declared that there should be a chicken in every French family's pot each Sunday, set about to restore the prosperity of a country devastated by four decades of civil war. Fortunately France had enormous economic resiliency, owing primarily to its extremely rich and varied agricultural resources. Unlike Spain, which had to import food, France normally had been able to export it, and Henry's finance minister, the duke of Sully, quickly saw to it that France became a food exporter once more. Among other things, Sully distributed throughout the country free copies of a guide to recommended farming techniques and financed the rebuilding or new construction of roads, bridges, and canals to help expedite the flow of goods. In addition, Henry IV was not content to see France rest its economic development on agricultural wealth alone; instead he ordered the construction of royal factories to manufacture luxury goods such as crystal glass and tapestries, and he also supported the growth of silk, linen, and woolen cloth industries in many different parts of the country. Moreover, Henry's patronage allowed the explorer Champlain to claim parts of Canada as France's first foothold in the New World. Thus Henry IV's reign certainly must be counted as one of the most benevolent and progressive in all French history.

Cardinal Richelieu. A contemporary portrait emphasizing the cardinal's awesome bearing.

Far less benevolent was Henry's *de facto* successor as ruler of France, Cardinal Richelieu (1585–1642), yet Richelieu fully managed to maintain France's forward momentum. The cardinal, of course, was never the real king of France—the actual title was held from 1610 to 1643 by Henry IV's ineffectual son Louis XIII. But as first minister from 1624 to his death in 1642 Richelieu governed as he wished, and what he wished most of all was to enhance centralized royal power at home and expand French influence in the larger theater of Europe. Accordingly, when Huguenots rebelled against restrictions placed on them by the Edict of Nantes, Richelieu put them down with an iron fist and emended the Edict in 1629 by depriving them of all their military rights. Since his armed campaigns against the Huguenots had been very costly, the cardinal then moved to gain more income for the crown by abolishing the semi-autonomy of Burgundy, Dauphiné, and Provence so that he could introduce direct royal taxation in all three areas. Later, to make sure all taxes levied were efficiently collected, Richelieu instituted a new system of local government by royal officials known as *intendants* who were expressly commissioned to run roughshod over any provincial obstructionism. By these and related methods Richelieu made French government more centralized than ever and managed to double the crown's income during his rule. But since he also engaged in an ambitious foreign policy directed against the Habsburgs of Austria and Spain, resulting in France's costly involvement in the Thirty Years' War, internal pressures mounted in the years after Richelieu's death.

A reaction against French governmental centralization manifested itself in a series of revolts between 1648 and 1653 collectively known as "the slingshot tumults," or in French, the *Fronde.* By this time Louis XIII had been succeeded by his son Louis XIV, but because the latter was still a boy, France was governed by a regency consisting of Louis's mother Anne of Austria and her paramour Cardinal Mazarin. Considering that both were foreigners (Anne was a Habsburg and Mazarin originally an Italian adventurer named Giulio Mazarini), it is not surprising that many of their subjects, including some extremely powerful nobles, hated them. Moreover, nationwide resentments were greater still because the costs of war and several consecutive years of bad harvests had brought France temporarily into a grave economic plight. Thus when cliques of nobles expressed their disgust with Mazarin for primarily petty and self-interested reasons, they found much support throughout the country, and uncoordinated revolts against the regency flared on and off for several years.

France, however, was not Spain, and thus did not come close to falling apart. Above all, the French crown itself, which retained great reservoirs of prestige owing to a well-established national tradition and the undoubted achievements of Henry IV and Richelieu, was by no means under attack. On the contrary, neither the aristocratic leaders of the *Fronde* nor the commoners from all ranks who joined them in revolt claimed to be resisting the young king but only the alleged corruption and mismanagement of Mazarin. Some of the rebels, it is true, insisted that part of Mazarin's fault lay in his pursuance of Richelieu's centralizing, antiprovincial policy. But since most of the aristocrats who led the *Fronde* were merely "outs" who wanted to be "in," they often squabbled among themselves—sometimes even arranging

Cardinal Richelieu

The Fronde

French absolutism triumphant

agreements of convenience with the regency or striking alliances with France's enemy, Spain, for momentary gain—and proved completely unable to rally any unified support behind a common program. Thus when Louis XIV began to rule in his own name in 1651 and pretexts for revolting against "corrupt ministers" no longer existed, all opposition was soon silenced. As so often happens, the idealists and poor people paid the greatest price for revolt: in 1653 a defeated leader of popular resistance in Bordeaux was broken on a wheel, and not long afterward a massive new round of taxation was proclaimed. Remembering the turbulence of the *Fronde* for the rest of his life, Louis XIV resolved never to let his aristocracy or his provinces get out of hand again and ruled as the most effective royal absolutist in all of French history.

The case of England

Compared to the civil disturbances of the 1640s in Spain and France, those in England proved the most momentous in their results for the history of limited government. Whereas all that the revolts against Castile accomplished was the achievement of Portuguese independence and the crippling of an empire that was already in decline, and all that happened in France was a momentary interruption of the steady advance of royal power, in England a king was executed and barriers were erected against royal absolutism for all time.

Henry VIII and Elizabeth I increase royal power

England around 1600 was caught up in a trend toward the growth of centralized royal authority characteristic of all western Europe. Not only had Henry VIII and Elizabeth I brought the English Church fully under royal control, but both monarchs employed so-called prerogative courts wherein they could proceed against subjects in disregard of traditional English legal safeguards for the rights of the accused. Furthermore, although Parliament met regularly during both reigns, members of Parliament were far less independent than they had been in the fifteenth century: any parliamentary representative who might have stood up to Henry VIII would have lost his head, and almost all parliamentarians felt sufficiently in rapport with Elizabeth that they were willing to abide by her policies. Thus when the Stuart dynasty succeeded Elizabeth, the last of the Tudors, it was only natural that the Stuarts would try to increase royal power still more. And indeed they might have succeeded had it not been for their ineptness and an extraordinary combination of forces ranged against them.

James I. "The wisest fool in Christendom."

Lines of contention were drawn immediately at the accession of Elizabeth's nearest relative, her cousin James VI of Scotland, who in 1603 retained his Scottish crown but also became king of England as James I (1603–1625). Homely but vain, addled but erudite, James fittingly was called by Henry IV of France "the wisest fool in Christendom," and presented the starkest contrast to his predecessor. Whereas Elizabeth knew how to gain her way with Parliament without making a fuss about it, the schoolmasterish foreigner insisted on lecturing parliamentarians that he was semi-divine and would brook no resistance: "As it is atheism and blasphemy to dispute what God can do, so it is presumption and high contempt in a subject to dispute what a king can do." Carrying these sentiments further, in a speech to Parliament of 1609 he proclaimed that "kings are not only God's lieutenants on earth . . . but even by God Himself they are called gods."

That such extreme pretensions to divine authority would arouse strong opposition was a result even James should have been able to foresee, for the English were still intensely committed to the theory of parliamentary controls on the crown. Yet not just theory was at stake since the specific policies of the new king antagonized large numbers of his subjects. For one, James insisted upon supplementing his income by modes of money-raising which had never been sanctioned by Parliament; and when the leaders of that body remonstrated, he angrily tore up their protests and dissolved their sessions. Worse, he interfered with the freedom of business by granting monopolies and lucrative privileges to favored companies. And, worst of all in the eyes of most patriotic Englishmen, James quickly put an end to the long war with Spain and refused thereafter to become involved in any foreign military entanglements. Today many of us might think that James's commitment to peace was his greatest virtue; certainly his pacifism was well advised financially since it spared the crown enormous debts. But in his own age James was hated particularly for his peace policy because it made him seem far too friendly with England's traditional enemy, Spain, and because "appeasement" meant leaving seemingly heroic Protestants in Holland and Germany in the lurch.

Causes of antagonism to James I

Although almost all English people (except for a small minority of clandestine Catholics) objected to James I's pacific foreign policy, those who hated it most were a group destined to play the greatest role in overthrowing the Stuarts, namely, the Puritans. Extremist Calvinistic Protestants, the Puritans believed that Elizabeth I's religious compromises had not broken fully enough with the forms and doctrines of Roman Catholicism. Called Puritans from their desire to "purify" the English Church of all traces of Catholic ritual and observance, they most vehemently opposed the English "episcopal system" of church government by bishops. But James I was as committed to retaining episcopalianism as the Puritans were intent on abolishing it because he viewed royally appointed bishops as one of the pillars of a strong monarchy: "No bishop, no king." Since the Puritans were the dominant party in the House of Commons and many Puritans were also prosperous businessmen who opposed James's monopolistic policies and money-raising expediencies, throughout his reign James remained at loggerheads with an extremely powerful group of his subjects for a combination of religious, constitutional, and economic reasons.

The Puritans

Nonetheless, James survived to die peacefully in bed in 1625, and had it not been for mistakes made by his son Charles I (1625–1649), England might have gone the way of absolutistic France. Charles held the same inflated notions of royal power and consequently was quickly at odds with the Puritan leaders of Parliament. Soon after his accession

Charles I

Charles I. This portrait by Van Dyck vividly captures the ill-fated monarch's arrogance.

to the throne Charles became involved in a war with France and needed revenue desperately. When Parliament refused to make more than the customary grants, he resorted to forced loans from his subjects, punishing those who failed to comply by quartering soldiers in their homes or throwing them into prison without a trial. In reaction to this, Parliament forced the Petition of Right on the king in 1628. This document declared all taxes not voted by Parliament illegal, condemned the quartering of soldiers in private houses, and prohibited arbitrary imprisonment and the establishment of martial law in time of peace.

Angered rather than chastened by the Petition of Right, Charles I soon resolved to rule entirely without Parliament—and nearly succeeded. From 1629 to 1640 no Parliaments were called. During this "eleven-years' tyranny," Charles's government lived off a variety of makeshift dues and levies. For example, the crown sold monopolies at exorbitant rates, revived highly antiquated medieval financial claims, and admonished judges to collect the stiffest of fines. Though technically not illegal, all of these expedients were deeply resented. Most controversial was the collection of "ship money," a levy taken on the pretext of a medieval obligation of English seaboard towns to provide ships (or their worth in money) for the royal navy. Extending the payment of ship money from coastal towns to the whole country, Charles threatened to make it a regular tax in contravention of the Petition of Right, and was upheld in a legal challenge of 1637 brought against him on these grounds by the Puritan squire John Hampden.

By such means the king managed to make ends meet without the aid of taxes granted by Parliament. But he became ever more hated by most of his subjects, and above all the Puritans, not just because of his constitutional and financial policies but also because he seemed to be pursuing a course in religion that came much closer to Catholicism than to Calvinism. Whether the English Puritans would have risen up in revolt on their own is a moot question, but they were ultimately emboldened to do so by a chain of events beginning with a revolt in Scotland. The uprising in Scotland of 1640 against the policy of an English king was not unlike those in Catalonia and Portugal of the same year against the Spanish crown except that the Scottish rising was not just nationalistic but also explicitly religious in nature. Like his father, Charles believed in the adage "no bishop, no king" and hence foolhardily decided to introduce episcopalian church government into staunchly Presbyterian Scotland. The result was armed resistance by Charles's northern subjects and the first step toward civil war in England.

The Scottish uprising

In order to obtain the funds necessary to punish the Scots, Charles had no other choice but to summon Parliament and soon found himself the target of pent-up resentments. Knowing full well that the king was helpless without money, the Puritan leaders of the House of Commons determined to take England's government into their own

The convening of Parliament

hands. Accordingly, they not only executed the king's first minister, the earl of Strafford, but they abolished ship money and the prerogative courts which ever since the reign of Henry VIII had served as instruments of arbitrary rule. Most significantly, they enacted a law forbidding the crown to dissolve Parliament and requiring the convening of sessions at least once every three years. After some indecision, early in 1642 Charles replied to these acts with a show of force. He marched with his guard into the House of Commons and attempted to arrest five of its leaders. All of them escaped, but an open conflict between crown and Parliament could no longer be avoided. Both parties collected troops and prepared for an appeal to the sword.

These events initiated the English Civil War, a conflict at once political and religious, which lasted from 1642 to 1649. Arrayed on the royal side were most of England's most prominent aristocrats and largest landowners, who were almost all "high-church" Anglicans. Opposed to them, the followers of Parliament included smaller landholders, tradesmen, and manufacturers, the majority of whom were Puritans. The members of the king's party were commonly known by the aristocratic name of Cavaliers. Their opponents, who cut their hair short in contempt for the fashionable custom of wearing curls, were derisively called Roundheads. At first the royalists, having obvious advantages of military experience, won most of the victories. In 1644, however, the parliamentary army was reorganized, and soon afterward the fortunes of battle shifted. The Cavalier forces were badly beaten, and in 1646 the king was compelled to surrender.

Civil war: the Cavaliers vs. the Roundheads

The struggle would now have ended had not a quarrel developed within the parliamentary party. The majority of its members, who had allied with the Presbyterian Scots, were ready to restore Charles to the throne as a limited monarch under an arrangement whereby a uniform Calvinistic Presbyterian faith would be imposed on both Scotland and England as the state religion. But a radical minority of Puritans, commonly known as Independents, distrusted Charles and insisted upon religious toleration for themselves and all other non-Presbyterian Protestants. Their leader was Oliver Cromwell (1599–1658), who had risen to command the Roundhead army. Taking advantage of the dissension within the ranks of his opponents, Charles renewed the war in 1648, but after a brief campaign was forced to surrender. Cromwell now resolved to end the life of "that man of blood," and, ejecting all the Presbyterians from Parliament by force of arms, obliged the remaining so-called Rump Parliament to vote an end to the monarchy. On 30 January 1649 Charles I was beheaded; a short time later the hereditary House of Lords was abolished, and England became a republic.

Oliver Cromwell

But founding a republic was far easier than maintaining one, and the new form of government, officially called a Commonwealth, did not last long. Technically the Rump Parliament continued as the leg-

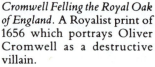

Cromwell Felling the Royal Oak of England. A Royalist print of 1656 which portrays Oliver Cromwell as a destructive villain.

From republic to dictatorship

islative body, but Cromwell, with the army at his command, possessed the real power and soon became exasperated by the attempts of the legislators to perpetuate themselves in office and to profit from confiscating the wealth of their opponents. Accordingly, in 1653 he marched a detachment of troops into the Rump, and, saying "Come, I will put an end to your prating," ordered the members to disperse. Thereby the Commonwealth ceased to exist and was soon followed by the "Protectorate" or virtual dictatorship established under a constitution drafted by officers of the army. Called the Instrument of Government, this text was the nearest approximation of a written constitution England has ever had. Extensive powers were given to Cromwell as Lord Protector for life, and his office was made hereditary. At first a Parliament exercised limited authority in making laws and levying taxes, but in 1655 its members were abruptly dismissed by the Lord Protector. Thereafter the government became a thinly disguised autocracy, with Cromwell now wielding a sovereignty even more absolute then any the Stuart monarchs would have dared to claim.

The Stuart Restoration

Given the choice between a Puritan military dictatorship and the old royalist regime, when the occasion arose England unhesitatingly opted for the latter. Above all, years of Calvinistic austerities such as the prohibition of any public recreation on Sundays—then the workingperson's only holiday—had discredited the Puritans, making most people long for the milder Anglicanism of the original Elizabethan settlement. Thus not long after Cromwell's death in 1658, one of the deceased Protector's generals seized power and called for elections for a new Parliament which met in the spring of 1660 and proclaimed as king Charles I's exiled son, Charles II. With the reign of Charles II

(1660–1685) Anglicanism was immediately restored, but by no means the same was true for untrammeled monarchical power. Rather, stating with characteristic good humor that he did not wish to "resume his travels," Charles agreed to respect Parliament and observe the Petition of Right. Of greatest constitutional significance was the fact that all the legislation passed by Parliament immediately before the outbreak of the Civil War, including the requirement to hold Parliaments at least once every three years, remained as law. Thus in striking contrast to absolutistic France, England became a limited monarchy. Putting its constitutional struggles behind it after one brief further test in the late seventeenth century, the realm of England would soon live up to the poet Milton's prediction of "a noble and puissant nation rousing herself like a strong man after sleep."

4. QUESTS FOR LIGHT OUT OF DARKNESS

Caught up in economic uncertainty, religious rivalries, and political turmoil, many Europeans between 1560 and 1660 understandably cast about for emotional or intellectual resolutions of their most pressing problems. Sometimes, as in the case of the great witchcraft delusion, this quest led merely to an intensification of hysteria. But in the case of more dispassionate reflections, the search for ways of resolving Europe's crises led to some of the most enduring statements of moral and political philosophy of all time.

Witchcraft and philosophy

Although no one simple explanation can be offered for the outbreak of western Europe's fearful witchcraft hysteria that reached its peak between 1580 and 1660, it is certain that persecutions of witches in those years were fiercest during times of greatest disaster and that people who burned witches genuinely thought they were fighting the powers of darkness. Looking for the origins of the great early-modern witchcraft delusion, historians recognize that peasant culture throughout the Middle Ages included belief in the possibilities of sorcery. In other words, most simple rural people assumed that certain unusual individuals could practice good, or "white," magic in the form of healing, divination for lost objects, and fortune-telling, or perhaps also evil, "black" magic that might, for example, call up tempests or ravage crops. Yet only in the later Middle Ages did learned authorities begin to insist on theological grounds that black magic could be practiced only as a result of pacts with the devil. Naturally, once this belief became accepted, judicial officers soon found it urgent to prosecute all "witches" who practiced black magic because warfare against the devil was paramount to Christian society and "the evil one" could not be allowed to hold any sway. Accordingly, as early as 1484 Pope Innocent VIII ordered papal inquisitors to root out alleged witchcraft with all the means at their disposal, and the pace of witch hunts gained momentum in the following decades. Nor were witch trials curtailed

The origins of the witchcraft delusion

in areas that broke with Rome, for Protestant reformers believed in the insidious powers of Satan just as much as Catholics did. Indeed, Luther himself once threw an inkpot at a supposed apparition of the devil, and Calvin saw Satan's evil workings wherever he looked. Thus both urged that alleged witches be tried more peremptorily and sentenced with less leniency than ordinary criminals, and persecutions of innocent people continued apace in Protestant as well as Catholic lands.

Yet the outbreak of a real mania for catching and killing "witches" did not begin until about 1580. Therefore it can only be supposed that the witchcraft hysteria was connected in some way with Europe's general crisis—all the more since it continued for about as long as the age of crisis itself and was most severe in just those localities where warfare or economic dislocation was most intense. In such places, whenever crops failed or cattle sickened people assumed that a "witch"—usually a defenseless old woman—was responsible, and rushed to put her to death. If not always old, the victims were most frequently women, no doubt in part because preachers had encouraged their flocks to believe that evil had first come into the world with Eve and in part because men in authority felt psychologically most ambivalent about members of the opposite sex. Pure sadism certainly cannot have been the original motive for such proceedings, but once trials began, horrendous sadism very often was unleashed. Thus old women, young girls, and sometimes even mere children might be brutally tortured by having needles driven under their nails, fires placed at their heels, or their legs crushed under weights until marrow spurted

Supposed Witches Worshiping the Devil in the Form of a Billy-Goat. In the background other "witches" ride bareback on flying demons. This is one of the earliest visual conceptions of witchcraft, dating from around 1460.

Burning of Witches at Dernberg in 1555. From a sixteenth-century German pamphlet denouncing witchcraft.

from their bones, in order to make them confess to having had filthy orgies with demons. The final death toll will never be known, but in the 1620s there was an average of one hundred burnings a year in the German cities of Würzburg and Bamberg, and around the same time it was said the town square of Wolfenbüttel "looked like a little forest, so crowded were the stakes."

Why persecution quickly ended in the years immediately after 1660 will remain a matter for scholarly speculation. Aside from the fact that better times returned to most of Europe around then, probably the best explanation is that shortly after 1660 educated magistrates began to adhere to a mechanistic view of the universe. In other words, once the leaders of society came to believe that storms and epidemics arose from natural rather than supernatural causes, they ceased to countenance witch hunts.

The end of the witch hunts

Fortunately, other attempts of Europeans between 1560 and 1660 to master the darkness around them were not in themselves so dark. Indeed, one of the most "enlightened" of all European moral philosophers was the Frenchman Michel de Montaigne (1533–1592), who wrote during the height of the French wars of religion. The son of a Catholic father and a Huguenot mother of Jewish ancestry, the well-to-do Montaigne retired from a legal career at the age of thirty-eight to devote himself to a life of leisured reflection. The *Essays* which resulted were a new literary form originally conceived as "experiments" in writing (French *essai* simply means "trial"). Because they are extraordinarily well written as well as being searchingly reflective, Montaigne's *Essays* ever since have ranked securely among the most enduring classics of French literature and thought.

Although the range of subjects of the *Essays* runs a wide gamut from "The Resemblance of Children to Their Fathers" to "The Art of Conversing," two main themes are dominant. One is a pervasive skepticism. Making his motto "Que sais-je?" (What do I know?),

Michel de Montaigne

A *"Camel-Leopard."* In the sixteenth century burgeoning overseas travel led to proliferating rumors of strange sights. This "camel-leopard" is obviously a crude conception of what was really a giraffe. Uncertain of absolute truth and falsity, Montaigne concluded that what seemed true one day might be cast into doubt tomorrow.

Jean Bodin

Montaigne decided that he knew very little for certain. According to him, "it is folly to measure truth and error by our own capacities" because our capacities are severely limited. Thus, as he maintained in one of his most famous essays, "On Cannibals," what may seem indisputably true and proper to one nation may seem absolutely false to another because "everyone gives the title of barbarism to everything that is not of his usage." From this Montaigne's second main principle followed—the need for tolerance. Since all people think they know the perfect religion and the perfect government, no religion or government is really perfect and consequently no belief worth fighting for to the death.

If the foregoing description makes Montaigne sound surprisingly modern, it must be emphasized that he was by no means a rationalist. On the contrary, he believed that "reason does nothing but go astray in everything," and that intellectual curiosity "which prompts us to thrust our noses into everything" is a "scourge of the soul." Moreover, concerning practical affairs Montaigne was a fatalist who thought that in a world governed by unpredictable "fortune" the best human strategy is to face the good and the bad with steadfastness and dignity. Lest people begin to think too highly of their own abilities, he reminded them that "sit we upon the highest throne in the world, yet we do sit upon our own behinds." Nonetheless, despite his passive belief that "fortune, not wisdom, rules the life of mankind," the wide circulation of Montaigne's *Essays* did help combat fanaticism and religious intolerance in his own and subsequent ages.

If Montaigne sought refuge from the trials of his age in skepticism, tolerance, and resigned dignity, his contemporary, the French lawyer Jean Bodin (1530–1596), looked for more light to come out of darkness from the powers of the state. Like Montaigne, Bodin was particularly troubled by the upheavals caused by the religious wars in France—he had even witnessed the frightful St. Bartholomew's Day Massacre of 1572 in Paris. But instead of shrugging his shoulders about the bloodshed, he resolved to offer a political plan to make sure turbulence would cease. This he did in his monumental *Six Books on the Commonwealth* (1576), the earliest fully developed statement of governmental absolutism in Western political thought. According to Bodin, the state arises from the needs of collections of families, but once constituted should brook no opposition, for the maintenance of order is paramount. Whereas writers on law and politics before him had groped toward a theory of governmental sovereignty, Bodin was the first to offer a succinct definition; for him, sovereignty was "the most high, absolute, and perpetual power over all subjects," consisting principally in the power "to give laws to subjects without their consent." Although Bodin acknowledged the theoretical possibility of government by aristocracy or democracy, he assumed that the nation-states of his day would be ruled by monarchs and insisted that such monarchs could in no way be limited, either by legislative or judicial bodies, or even by laws made by their predecessors or themselves. Expressing the sharpest opposition to contemporary Huguenots who were saying (in contravention of the original teachings of Luther and Calvin) that subjects had a right to resist "ungodly princes," Bodin maintained that a subject must trust in his ruler's "mere and frank good will." Even if the ruler proved a tyrant, Bodin insisted that the subject had no warrant to resist, for any resistance would open the door "to a licentious anarchy which is worse than the harshest tyranny in the world." Since in his own day Bodin knew much "licentious anarchy" but had hardly any notion of how harsh the "harshest tyranny" could be, his position is somewhat understandable. Yet in the next century his *Commonwealth* would become the point of departure for justifications of an increasingly oppressive French royal absolutism.

Quite understandably, just as the French civil wars of the sixteenth century provoked a variety of responses, so did the English Civil War of the seventeenth. Drawing on a tradition of resistance to untrammeled state power expressed by French Huguenots and earlier English parliamentarians and Puritans, the great English Puritan poet John Milton enunciated a stirring defense of freedom of the press in his *Areopagitica* (1644). Similarly bold upholders of libertarianism were a party of Milton's Puritan contemporaries known as Levellers, the first exponents of democracy since Greek times. Organizing themselves as a pressure group within Cromwell's army in the later 1640s when Charles I's monarchy seemed clearly doomed, the Levellers—who derived their name from their advocacy of equal political rights for all classes—agitated in favor of a parliamentary republic based on nearly universal manhood suffrage. For them, servants and other wage-laborers had no right to vote because they formed part of their employer's "family" and allegedly were represented by the family head. Moreover, the Levellers did not even deign to argue about women's rights. Otherwise, however, in the immortal words of one of their spokesmen, they argued that "the poorest He that is in England hath a life to live as the greatest He, and therefore . . . every man that is to live under a government ought first by his own consent to put himself under that government." But since Oliver Cromwell, who believed that the only grounds for suffrage was sufficient property, would have none of this, once Cromwell assumed virtually dictatorial powers the Leveller party disintegrated. More radical still were the communistic Diggers, so called from their attempts to cultivate common lands in 1649. Claiming to be "true Levellers," the Diggers argued that true freedom lies not in votes, but "where a man receives his nourishment," and hence argued for the redistribution of property. Cromwell, however, dispersed them quickly and thus the Diggers have merely historical interest as vanguards of movements to come.

Far to the other extreme of the libertarian Puritans was the political philosopher Thomas Hobbes (1588–1679), whose reactions to the

John Milton and the Levellers

English Civil War led him to become the most forceful advocate of unrestrained state power of all time. Like Bodin, who was moved by the events of St. Bartholomew's Day to formulate a doctrine of political absolutism, Hobbes was moved by the turmoil of the English Civil War to do the same in his classic of political theory entitled *Leviathan* (1651). Yet Hobbes differed from Bodin in several respects. For one, whereas Bodin assumed that the absolute sovereign power would be a royal monarch, the more radical Hobbes, writing without any respect for tradition in Cromwell's England two years after the beheading of a king, thought the sovereign could be any ruthless dictator whatsoever. Then too, whereas Bodin defined his state as "the lawful government of families" and hence did not believe that the state could abridge private property rights because families could not exist without property, Hobbes's state existed to rule over atomistic individuals and thus was licensed to trample over both liberty and property.

The Title Page of Hobbes's Le-viathan

But the most fundamental difference between Bodin and Hobbes lay in the latter's uncompromisingly pessimistic view of human nature. Whereas Bodin was pessimistic about mankind only by implication, Hobbes posited that the "state of nature" which existed before civil government came into being was a condition of "war of all against all." For Hobbes, since man naturally behaves as "a wolf" toward man and hence increasing fear of violent death in the state of nature makes human life "solitary, poor, nasty, brutish, and short," people for their own good at some purely theoretical point in time surrender their liberties to a sovereign ruler in exchange for his agreement to keep the peace. Having thus granted away their liberties, subjects have no right whatsoever to seek them back, and the sovereign can tyrannize as he likes—free to oppress his charges in any way other than to kill them, an act which would negate the very purpose of his rule. It is a measure of the relentless logic and clarity of Hobbes's abstract exposition that his *Leviathan* is widely regarded as one of the four or five greatest political treatises ever written, for practically nobody really likes what he says. Indeed, even in his own age Hobbes's views were vastly unpopular—libertarians detested them for obvious reasons, and royalists hated them as much because Hobbes was contemptuous of dynastic claims based on blood lineage and rationalized absolutistic rule not on the grounds of powers granted from God, as most royalists did, but on powers surrendered by society. Yet because many important thinkers felt compelled to argue against Hobbes, he had enormous influence, if only in provoking the responses of others.

Hobbes's pessimism

Perhaps fittingly, the most moving and in certain ways most modern attempt to bring light out of pervasive darkness was that of the seventeenth-century French moral and religious philosopher Blaise Pascal (1623–1662). In certain superficial ways Pascal's most enduring legacy, his *Pensées* (*Thoughts*), resemble Montaigne's *Essays* because both are highly introspective collections of informal short pieces written with great literary power. But Pascal, who turned away in a conversion experience from scientific rationalism to become a firm adherent of Jansenism (the most puritanical wing of French Catholicism), was as ardent a religious believer as Montaigne was a cool skeptic. Thus while Pascal agreed with Montaigne that human life on earth was fraught with peril—he defined man as "a thinking reed"—he had no doubt that a just Providence ruled the world, and he believed as firmly as did Luther or Calvin that faith alone could show the way to salvation. Yet, recognizing that skeptics or secular rationalists could never be brought to the true faith by dogmatic authority, he hoped to convert doubters by appealing simultaneously to their intellects and their emotions in a major defense of Christianity. Unfortunately, premature death prevented him from accomplishing this ambitious goal, but the *Pensées* survive as previews of his approach. In these he conceded his own sense of terror and anguish in the face of evil and eternity, but made the awe itself a sign of the existence of God. Individuals today will be moved by Pascal's *Pensées* in varying degrees according to their own convictions, but few people of any persuasion will dispute Pascal's famous paradox that "man knows he is wretched; he is therefore wretched because he is so; but he is very great because he knows it."

Blaise Pascal

5. LITERATURE AND THE ARTS

The combined wretchedness and greatness of humanity may be taken as the theme for the extraordinary profusion of towering works of literature and art produced during western Europe's period of crisis from 1560 to 1660. Of course not every single writing or painting of the era expressed the same message. During a hundred years of extraordinary literary and artistic creativity, works of all genres and sentiments were produced, ranging from the frothiest farces to the darkest tragedies, the serenest still lifes to the most grotesque scenes of religious martyrdom. Nonetheless, the greatest writers and painters of the period all were moved by a realization of the ambiguities and ironies of human existence not unlike that expressed in different ways by Montaigne and Pascal. They all were fully aware of the horrors of war and human suffering so rampant in their day, and all were directly or indirectly aware of the Protestant conviction that men are "vessels of iniquity"; but they also inherited a large degree of Renaissance affirmativeness, and most of them accordingly preferred to view life on earth as a great dare.

Major statements concerning the human condition

From the host of remarkable writers who flourished during what was probably the most extraordinary century in the entire history of western European poetry and drama, we may take the very greatest: Cervantes, the Elizabethan dramatists—Shakespeare to the fore—and John Milton. Although Miguel de Cervantes (1547–1616) was not

Miguel de Cervantes

Miguel de Cervantes

Elizabethan drama

strictly speaking either a poet or a dramatist, his masterpiece, the satirical romance *Don Quixote,* exudes great lyricism and drama. The plot recounts the adventures of a Spanish gentleman, Don Quixote of La Mancha, who has become slightly unbalanced by constant reading of chivalric epics. His mind filled with all kinds of fantastic adventures, he sets out at the age of fifty upon the slippery road of knight-errantry, imagining windmills to be glowering giants and flocks of sheep to be armies of infidels whom it is his duty to rout with his spear. In his distorted fancy he mistakes inns for castles and serving girls for courtly ladies on fire with love. Set off in contrast to the "knight-errant" is the figure of his faithful squire, Sancho Panza. The latter represents the ideal of the practical man, with his feet on the ground and content with the modest but substantial pleasures of eating, drinking, and sleeping. Yet Cervantes clearly does not wish to say that the realism of a Sancho Panza is categorically preferable to the "quixotic" idealism of his master. Rather, the two men represent different facets of human nature. Without any doubt, *Don Quixote* is a devastating satire on the anachronistic chivalric mentality that would soon help hasten Spain's decline. But for all that, the reader's sympathies remain with the protagonist, the man from La Mancha who dares to "dream the impossible dream."

Directly contemporaneous with Cervantes were the English Elizabethan dramatists who collectively produced the most glorious age of theater known in the Western world. Writing after England's victory over the Spanish Armada, when national pride was at a peak, all exhibited great exuberance but none was by any means a facile optimist. In fact a strain of reflective seriousness pervades all their best works, and a few, like the tragedian John Webster (c. 1580–c. 1625), who "saw the skull beneath the skin," were if anything morbid pessimists. Literary critics tend to agree that of a bevy of great Elizabethan playwrights the most outstanding were Christopher Marlowe (1564–1593), Ben Jonson (c. 1573–1637), and, of course, William Shakespeare (1564–1616). Of the three, the fiery Marlowe, whose life was cut short in a tavern brawl before he reached the age of thirty, was the most youthfully energetic. In plays such as *Tamburlaine* and *Doctor Faustus* Marlowe created larger-than-life heroes who seek and come close to conquering everything in their path and feeling every possible sensation. But they meet unhappy ends because, for all his vitality, Marlowe knew that there are limits on human striving, and that wretchedness as well as greatness lies in the human lot. Thus though Faustus asks a reincarnated Helen of Troy, conjured up by Satan, to make him "immortal with a kiss," he dies and is damned in the end because immortality is not awarded by the devil or found in earthly kisses. In contrast to the heroic tragedian Marlowe, Ben Jonson wrote corrosive comedies which expose human vices and foibles. In the particularly bleak *Volpone* Jonson shows people behaving like deceitful and lustful animals, but in the later *Alchemist* he balances an attack on quackery and gullibility with admiration for resourceful lower-class characters who cleverly take advantage of their supposed betters.

Incomparably the greatest of the Elizabethan dramatists, William Shakespeare, was born into the family of a tradesman in the provincial town of Stratford-on-Avon. His life is enshrouded in more mists of obscurity than the careers of most other great people. It is known that he left his native village, having gained little formal education, when he was about twenty, and that he drifted to London to find employment in the theater. How he eventually became an actor and still later a writer of plays is uncertain, but by the age of twenty-eight he had definitely acquired a reputation as an author sufficient to excite the jealousy of his rivals. Before he retired to his native Stratford about 1610 to spend the rest of his days in ease, he had written or collaborated in writing nearly forty plays, over and above 150 sonnets and two long narrative poems.

William Shakespeare. Portrait made for the First Folio edition of his works, 1623.

As everyone knows, Shakespeare's plays rank as a kind of secular Bible wherever the English language is spoken. The reasons lie not only in the author's unrivaled gift of expression, and in his scintillating wit, but most of all in his profound analysis of human character seized by passion and tried by fate. Shakespeare's dramas fall rather naturally into three groups. Those written during the playwright's earlier years are characterized by a sense of confidence. They include a number of history plays, which recount England's struggles and glories leading up to the triumph of the Tudor dynasty; the lyrical romantic tragedy *Romeo and Juliet;* and a wide variety of comedies including the magical *Midsummer Night's Dream* and Shakespeare's greatest creations in the comic vein—*Twelfth Night, As You Like It,* and *Much Ado about Nothing.* Despite the last-named title, few even of the plays of Shakespeare's early, lightest period are "much ado about nothing." Rather, most explore with wisdom as well as wit fundamental problems of psychological identity, honor and ambition, love and friendship. Occasionally they also contain touches of deep seriousness, as in *As You Like It,* when Shakespeare has a character pause to reflect that "all the world's a stage, and all the men and women merely players" who pass through seven "acts" or stages of life.

Shakespeare's three periods: (1) confidence

Such touches, however, never obscure the restrained optimism of Shakespeare's first period, whereas the plays from his second period are far darker in mood. Apparently around 1601 Shakespeare underwent a crisis during which he began to distrust human nature profoundly and to indict the whole scheme of the universe. The result was a group of dramas characterized by bitterness, frequent pathos, and a troubled searching into the mysteries of things. The series begins with the tragedy of indecisive idealism represented by *Hamlet,* goes on to the cynicism of *Measure for Measure* and *All's Well That Ends Well,* and culminates in the cosmic tragedies of *Macbeth* and *King Lear,* wherein characters assert that "life's but a walking shadow . . .

(2) crisis

a tale told by an idiot, full of sound and fury signifying nothing," and that "as flies to wanton boys are we to the gods; they kill us for their sport." Despite all this gloom, however, the plays of Shakespeare's second period generally contain the dramatist's greatest flights of poetic grandeur.

(3) reconciliation

Although *Macbeth* and *Lear* suggest an author in the throes of deep depression, Shakespeare managed to resolve his personal crisis and end his dramatic career with a third period characterized by a profound spirit of reconciliation. Of the three plays (all idyllic romances) written during this final period, the last, *The Tempest,* is the greatest. Here ancient animosities are buried and wrongs are righted by a combination of natural and supernatural means, and a wide-eyed, youthful heroine rejoices on first seeing men with the words "O brave new world, that has such people in it!" Here, then, Shakespeare seems to be saying that for all humanity's trials life is not so unrelentingly bitter after all, and the divine plan of the universe is somehow benevolent and just.

John Milton. From the First Edition of his poems, 1645.

Though less versatile than Shakespeare, not far behind him in eloquent grandeur stands the Puritan poet John Milton (1608–1674). The leading publicist of Oliver Cromwell's regime, Milton wrote the official defense of the beheading of Charles I as well as a number of treatises justifying Puritan positions in contemporary affairs. But he was also a man full of contradictions who loved the Greek and Latin classics at least as much as the Bible. Hence he could write a perfect pastoral elegy, *Lycidas,* mourning the loss of a dear friend in purely classical terms. Later, when forced into retirement by the accession of Charles II, Milton, though now blind, embarked on writing a classical epic, *Paradise Lost,* out of material found in Genesis concerning the creation of the world and the fall of man. This magnificent poem, which links the classical tradition to Christianity more successfully than any literary work written before or since, is surely one of the greatest epics of all time. Setting out to "justify the ways of God to man," Milton in *Paradise Lost* first plays "devil's advocate" by creating the compelling character of Satan, who defies God with boldness and subtlety. But Satan is more than counterbalanced in the end by the real "epic hero" of *Paradise Lost,* Adam, who learns to accept the human lot of moral responsibility and suffering, and is last seen leaving Paradise with Eve, the world "all before them."

Italian and Spanish Mannerism

The ironies and tensions inherent in human existence also were portrayed with extraordinary eloquence and profundity by several immortal masters of the visual arts who flourished between 1560 and 1660. The dominant style in painting in Italy and Spain in the second half of the sixteenth century was Mannerism. Originally a term of opprobrium for alleged imitators—supposedly second-rate artists who painted in the "manner" of Michelangelo's late phase—the term *Mannerism* in current analysis has come to mean much more than that; indeed art historians now rank some Mannerist painters among the

West's greatest masters. Unquestionably Mannerism did take as its point of departure Michelangelo's tendency toward anticlassicism and distortion of nature for emotional effects, but Mannerist painters went so much further in emphasizing restlessness, imbalance, and distortion that they left Michelangelo far behind. Admittedly many of them lacked skill and depth of vision, contenting themselves with portraying brawn instead of muscle, melodrama instead of drama. But some others fully succeeded in balancing great artistic virtuosity with the communication of radiant inner light.

Of the latter, the two most outstanding are the Venetian Tintoretto (1518–1594) and the Spaniard El Greco (c. 1541–1614). Combining Manneristic distortion and restlessness with a traditionally Venetian taste for rich color, Tintoretto produced an enormous number of monumentally large canvases devoted to religious themes that still inspire awe with their broodingly shimmering light and gripping theatricality. More emotional still is the work of Tintoretto's disciple, El Greco. Born Domenikos Theotokopoulos on the Greek island of Crete, this extraordinary painter absorbed some of the stylized elongation characteristic of Greco-Byzantine icon painting before traveling to Italy to learn from great contemporary Mannerist painters such as Tintoretto and then finally settling in Spain, where he was nicknamed "El Greco"—Spanish for "the Greek." El Greco's paintings were too bizarre to be greatly appreciated in his own age, and even now they often appear so unbalanced as to seem the work of one almost deranged. Yet such a view slights El Greco's deeply mystical Catholic fervor as well as his technical achievements. Best known today is his transfigured landscape, the *View of Toledo,* with its somber but awe-

Fray Felix Hortensio Paravicino, by El Greco. More restrained in composition than most of the artist's other work, this portrait nonetheless communicates a sense of deep spiritual intensity.

See color plates following page 710 for the *Crucifixion* by Tintoretto and the *View of Toledo* by El Greco

The Laocoön, by El Greco. An extreme example of Manneristic stress on restlessness and distortion. Note that the Spanish painter here drew for inspiration on the famous Hellenistic sculpture group shown on p. 219.

Left: *David,* by Bernini. Whereas the earlier conceptions of David by the Renaissance sculptors Donatello and Michelangelo were reposeful (see pp. 621 and 623), the Baroque sculptor Bernini chose to portray his young hero at the peak of physical exertion. Right: *St. Theresa in Ecstasy,* by Bernini. As David is seen at the peak of bodily exertion, St. Theresa is shown at the peak of spiritual transport.

some light breaking where no sun shines, but equally inspiring are his swirling religious allegories such as *The Burial of the Count of Orgaz* (thought by the painter to be his masterpiece), and his myriad stunning portraits in which gaunt, dignified Spaniards radiate a rare blend of austerity and spiritual insight.

The dominant artistic school of southern Europe succeeding Mannerism was that of the Baroque, a school not just of painting but of sculpture and architecture lasting from about 1600 until the early 1700s. The term *Baroque* is derived from a Portuguese word for an irregular, rough pearl, and this reveals much about its meaning. Picking up where Mannerism left off, the Baroque style emphasized the emotional and the swirling as much as Mannerism, but Baroque works of art characteristically were less shrouded by somber mystery and were far more affirmative than Manneristic paintings. One major explanation for this is that Baroque art in all genres was usually semi-propagandistic. Originating in Rome as an expression of the ideals of the Counter-Reformation papacy and the Jesuit order, Baroque architecture in particular aimed to gain adherence for a specific worldview. Similarly, Baroque painting often was done in the service of the Counter-Reformation Church, which at its high tide around 1620 seemed everywhere to be on the offensive, and when Baroque painters were not celebrating Counter-Reformation ideals, most of them worked in the service of monarchs who sought their own glorification.

Indubitably the most imaginative and influential figure of the original Roman Baroque was the architect and sculptor Gianlorenzo Bernini (1598–1680), a frequent employee of the papacy who created one of the most magnificent celebrations of papal grandeur in the sweeping colonnades leading up to St. Peter's basilica. Breaking with the serene Renaissance classicism of Palladio, Bernini's architecture retained the use of classical elements such as columns and domes, but combined them in ways meant to express both aggresssive restlessness and great power. In addition Bernini was one of the first to experiment with church facades built "in depth"—building frontages, that is, not conceived as continuous surfaces but which jutted out at odd angles and seemingly invaded the open space in front of them. If the purpose of these innovations was to stir the viewer and draw him emotionally into the ambit of the work of art, the same may be said for Bernini's aims in sculpture. Harking back to the restless motion of Hellenistic statuary—particularly the Laocoön group—and building on tendencies already present in the later sculpture of Michelangelo, Bernini's statuary emphasizes drama and incites the viewer to respond to it rather than serenely observe.

Since most Italian Baroque painters lacked Bernini's artistic genius, to view the very greatest masterpieces of southern European Baroque painting one must look to Spain and the work of Diego Velásquez (1599–1660). Unlike Bernini, Velásquez, a court painter in Madrid just when Spain hung on the brink of ruin, was not an entirely typical

The Church of S. Carlo alle Quattro Fontane, Rome. Built by Bernini's contemporary Francesco Borromini in 1665, the facade of S. Carlo well exemplifies the frontage "in depth" characteristic of Baroque architecture.

The Surrender of Breda, by Velásquez. Celebrating a Spanish victory over the Dutch in an early phase of the Thirty Years' War, the Spanish lances point proudly skyward in contrast to the desolate Dutch smoke, but the Spanish commander displays magnanimity for the defeated enemy.

A Dwarf, by Velásquez. The great Spanish artist had an enduring fascination with the less favored of the earth.

See color plates following page 710 for *Maids of Honor* and *Pope Innocent X* by Velásquez and *Harvesters* by Breughel

exponent of the Baroque style. Certainly many of his canvases display a characteristically Baroque delight in motion, drama, and power, but Velásquez's best work is characterized by a more restrained thoughtfulness than usually found in the Baroque. Thus his famous *Surrender at Breda* shows muscular horses and splendid Spanish grandees on the one hand, but un-Baroque humane and deep sympathy for defeated, disarrayed troops on the other. Moreover, Velásquez's single greatest painting, *The Maids of Honor,* done around 1656 after Spain's collapse, radiates thoughtfulness rather than drama and is one of the most probing artistic examinations of illusion and reality ever executed.

Southern Europe's main northern rival for artistic laurels in the "iron century" was the Netherlands, where three extremely dissimilar painters all explored the theme of the greatness and wretchedness of man to the fullest. The earliest, Peter Brueghel (rhymes with frugal) (c. 1525–1569), worked in a vein related to earlier Netherlandish realism. But unlike his predecessors, who favored quiet urban scenes, Brueghel exulted in portraying the busy, elemental life of the peasantry. Most famous in this respect are his rollicking *Peasant Wedding* and *Peasant Wedding Dance,* and his spacious *Harvesters,* in which guzzling and snoring fieldhands are taking a well-deserved break from their heavy labors under the noon sun. Such vistas give the impression of uninterrupted rhythms of life, but late in his career Brueghel became appalled by the intolerance and bloodshed he witnessed during the time of the Calvinist riots and the Spanish repression in the Netherlands and expressed his criticism in an understated yet searing manner. In *The Blind Leading the Blind,* for example, we see what happens when ignorant fanatics start showing the way to each other. More powerful still is Brueghel's *Massacre of the Innocents,* which from a distance looks like a snug scene of a Flemish village buried in snow. In fact, however, heartless soldiers are methodically breaking into homes and slaughter-

The Massacre of the Innocents. This painting by Brueghel shows how effectively art can be used as a means of social commentary. Many art historians believe that Brueghel was tacitly depicting the suffering of the Netherlands at the hands of the Spanish in his own day.

The Triumph of the Eucharist, by Rubens. A typical Baroque work, this painting proclaims the victory of the Cross and the Eucharistic Chalice, symbols of Counter-Reformation Catholicism.

ing babies, the simple peasant folk are fully at their mercy, and the artist—alluding to a Gospel forgotten by warring Catholics and Protestants alike—seems to be saying "as it happened in the time of Christ, so it happens now."

Vastly different from Brueghel was the Netherlandish Baroque painter Peter Paul Rubens (1577–1640). Since the Baroque, unlike Mannerism, was an international movement closely linked to the spread of the Counter-Reformation, it should offer no surprise that Baroque style was extremely well represented in just that part of the Netherlands which, after long warfare, had been retained by Spain. In fact, Rubens of Antwerp was a far more typical Baroque artist than Velásquez of Madrid, painting literally thousands of robust canvases that glorified resurgent Catholicism or exalted second-rate aristocrats by portraying them as epic heroes dressed in bearskins. Even when Rubens's intent was not overtly propagandistic he customarily revelled in the sumptuous extravagance of the Baroque manner, being perhaps most famous today for the pink and rounded flesh of his well-nourished nudes. But unlike a host of lesser Baroque artists, Rubens was not entirely lacking in subtlety and was a man of many moods. His gentle portrait of his son Nicholas catches unaffected childhood in a moment of repose, and though throughout most of his career Rubens had celebrated martial valor, his late *Horrors of War* movingly portrays what he himself called "the grief of unfortunate Europe, which, for so many years now, has suffered plunder, outrage, and misery."

In some ways a blend of Brueghel and Rubens, the greatest of all Netherlandish painters, Rembrandt van Rijn (1606–1669), defies all attempts at facile characterization. Living across the border from the Spanish Netherlands in staunchly Calvinistic Holland, Rembrandt

See color plates following page 710 for the *Horrors of War* and *England and Scotland Crowning Charles I* by Rubens

Rubens's Portrait of his Son Nicholas.

The Polish Rider, by Rembrandt. Unlike Titian's equestrian Charles V (above, p. 704), Rembrandt's rider is self-reflective and hence more humane.

See color plates following page 710 for *Aristotle Contemplating the Bust of Homer* by Rembrandt

belonged to a society which was too austere to tolerate the unbuckled realism of a Brueghel or the fleshy Baroque pomposity of a Rubens. Yet Rembrandt managed to put both realistic and Baroque traits to new uses. In his early career he gained fame and fortune as the painter of biblical scenes which lacked the Baroque's fleshiness but retained its grandeur in their swirling forms and stunning experiments with light. In this early period too Rembrandt was active as a realistic portrait painter who knew how to flatter his self-satisfied subjects by emphasizing their Calvinistic steadfastness, to the great advantage of his purse. But gradually his prosperity faded, apparently in part because he grew tired of flattering and definitely because he made some bad investments. Since personal tragedies also mounted in the painter's middle and declining years his art inevitably became far more pensive and sombre, but it gained in dignity, subtle lyricism, and awesome mystery. Thus his later portraits, including those of himself, are imbued with introspective qualities and a suggestion that only the half is being told. Equally moving are explicitly philosophical paintings such as *Aristotle Contemplating the Bust of Homer,* in which the supposedly earthbound philosopher seems spellbound by the otherworldy luminous radiance of the epic poet, and the *The Polish Rider,* in which realistic and Baroque elements merge into a higher synthesis portraying a pensive young man setting out fearlessly into a perilous world. Like Shakespeare, Rembrandt knew that life's journey is full of perils, but his most mature paintings suggest that these can be mastered with poetry and courage.

SELECTED READINGS

• *Items so designated are available in paperback editions.*

• Aston, T., ed., *Crisis in Europe: 1560–1660*, London, 1965. A collection of highly valuable essays.
• Braudel, F., *The Mediterranean and the Mediterranean World in the Age of Philip II*, 2 vols., New York, 1972. One of the most brilliant history books of our age. Treats life in the Mediterranean regions in the second half of the sixteenth century with particular emphasis on how geography determines the course of human history.
• Chute, M., *Shakespeare of London*, New York, 1949. The best popular biography.
• Dean, Leonard F., ed., *Shakespeare: Modern Essays in Criticism*, New York, 1958. A variety of scholarly appraisals.
• Dunn, Richard S., *The Age of Religious Wars, 1559–1715*, 2nd ed., New York, 1979. The best college-level text on this period. Extremely well written.
• Elliott, J. H., *Imperial Spain, 1469–1716*, London, 1963. A masterpiece of sophisticated synthesis.
• _____, *Europe Divided: 1559–1598*, London, 1968. An extremely lucid narrative of complex events.
• Elton, G. R., *England under the Tudors*, 2nd ed., London, 1977. Engagingly written and authoritative.
• Ford, Boris, ed., *The Age of Shakespeare*, Baltimore, 1955. A good shorter handbook.
• Frame, D., *Montaigne: A Biography*, New York, 1965. By far the best study in English.
• Fraser, Lady Antonia, *Cromwell: The Lord Protector*, London, 1973. A popular biography.
  Held, J. S., and D. Posner, *17th and 18th Century Art: Baroque Painting, Sculpture, Architecture*, New York, 1979. The most complete introductory review of the subject in English.
• Hibbard, Howard, *Bernini*, Baltimore, 1965. The basic study in English of this central figure of Baroque artistic activity.
• Hill, Christopher, *A Century of Revolution: 1603–1714*, 2nd ed., New York, 1982. A valuable survey of English developments that holds narrative to a minimum and stresses economic and social trends.
  Hirst, Derek, *Authority and Conflict: England, 1603–1658*, London, 1986. Integrates recent interpretations. The best survey out of several available.
• Kahr, M. M., *Velázquez: The Art of Painting*, New York, 1976.
  Kamen, Henry, *The Iron Century: Social Change in Europe, 1559–1660*, New York, 1971. One of the most detailed and persuasive statements of the view that there was a "general crisis" in many different aspects of European life.
  Le Roy Ladurie, Emmanuel, *Carnival in Romans*, New York, 1979. A closeup view of social turmoil in France in 1580.
• Mattingly, Garrett, *The Armada*, Boston, 1959. Fascinating narrative; thoroughly reliable but reads like a novel.
• Monter, E. W., ed., *European Witchcraft*, New York, 1969. Selected readings with fine introductions by one of the world's leading experts.

Parker, Geoffrey, *The Dutch Revolt,* Ithaca, N.Y., 1977. Now the standard survey in English on the revolt of the Netherlands.

• ———, *Europe in Crisis: 1598–1648,* Brighton, Sussex, 1980. A primarily political narrative of war and revolution in Europe exclusive of England.

• Pennington, D. H., *Seventeenth-Century Europe,* London, 1970. An extremely thorough and reliable survey that follows the conventional periodization of treating a century bounded by the round numbers 1600 and 1700.

Pierson, Peter, *Philip II of Spain,* London, 1975. An absorbing attempt to study Philip's personality and actions in terms of the dominant assumptions of his age.

• Rabb, T. K., *The Struggle for Stability in Early Modern Europe,* New York, 1975. A stimulating essay arguing for a shift from crisis to stability around 1660.

Roots, Ivan, ed., *Cromwell, A Profile,* New York, 1973. A collection of readings on problems in interpretation; complements Fraser.

• Rosenberg, Jakob, *Rembrandt: Life and Work,* London, 1964.

• Russell, Conrad, *The Crisis of Parliaments: English History, 1509–1660,* New York, 1971. The best survey covering this broad range of time.

• Shearman, John, *Mannerism,* Baltimore, 1967. Treats trends in late-sixteenth-century architecture and sculpture as well as Manneristic painting.

• Steinberg, S. H., *The Thirty Years' War and the Conflict for European Hegemony, 1600–1660,* New York, 1966. The best scholarly account.

• Stone, Lawrence, *The Causes of the English Revolution, 1529–1642,* New York, 1972. A judicious analysis by one of the foremost social historians of our age.

• Thomas, Keith, *Religion and the Decline of Magic,* London, 1971. A marvelously insightful study of popular belief in England.

• Trevor-Roper, H. R., *The European Witch-Craze of the Sixteenth and Seventeenth Centuries and Other Essays,* New York, 1968. A collection of path-breaking essays.

• Walzer, Michael, *The Revolution of the Saints: A Study in the Origins of Radical Politics,* Cambridge, Mass., 1965. An attempt by a political scientist to demonstrate that English Puritanism was the earliest form of modern political radicalism.

• Wedgwood, C. V., *William the Silent,* London, 1944. A laudatory and urbanely written biography.

SOURCE MATERIALS

• Cervantes, Miguel de, *Don Quixote,* tr. Walter Starkie, New York, 1957.

Hobbes, Thomas, *Leviathan,* abridged by F. B. Randall, New York, 1964.

• Montaigne, Michel de, *Essays,* tr. J. M. Cohen, Baltimore, 1958.

Pascal, Blaise, *Pensées,* French-English ed., H. F. Stewart, London, 1950.

Sprenger, Jakob, and H. Kramer, *The Malleus Maleficarum,* tr. M. Summers, 2nd ed., London, 1948. A frightful yet fascinating work, the *Malleus* ("The Hammer of Witches") was the most frequently used handbook of early-modern witchcraft prosecutors.

Chapter 21

INDIA, EAST ASIA, AND AFRICA DURING THE EARLY-MODERN ERA (c. 1500–1800)

Fuji-ichi was a clever man, and his substantial fortune was amassed in his own lifetime. . . . He noted down the market ratio of copper and gold; he inquired about the current quotations of the rice brokers; he sought information from druggists' and haberdashers' assistants on the state of the market at Nagasaki; for the latest news on the prices of ginned cotton, salt, and saké, he noted the various days on which the Kyoto dealers received dispatches from the Edo branch shops. Every day a thousand things were entered in his book, and people came to Fuji-ichi if they were ever in doubt. He became a valuable asset to the citizens of Kyoto.

—I. Saikaku, *The Tycoon of All Tenants* (1688)

Between the sixteenth and the nineteenth centuries a reinvigorated Indian empire headed by a new dynasty attained the rank of a major power; China, under the last of a long series of imperial dynasties, waxed even stronger, becoming the largest and most populous country in the world; and Japan adapted her feudal institutions to the requirements of a despotic government. In both India and China, and to a lesser degree in Japan, splendor and magnificence reflected the tastes of wealthy societies and mighty rulers, as was also true in much of Europe during this same period. In the long run, however, the great Asian states found themselves at a disadvantage because they played a passive rather than an active role in the Commercial Revolution. As western European nations turned to empire building and expanded their naval forces, they established direct contacts with the coastal regions of Asia, took over the bulk of the trade between East and West, and frequently threatened the independence of non-European peoples. For several centuries the principal Eastern states were strong enough to protect themselves against the threat of aggression from the West. Faced with rigid trade restrictions in China and almost totally excluded from Japan, the seafaring Europeans

Impact of the West upon the East

turned to other quarters. In the 1570s the Spanish occupied the Philippines, subduing the native tribes and the communities of Chinese colonists in the Islands. A few years later the Dutch, through their East India Company, laid the foundations of a rich empire in Indonesia, dislodging the Portuguese who had preceded them by almost a century. The British and French somewhat belatedly turned their attention to the mainland of India, where they secured valuable trading posts in the course of the seventeenth century. During this same period the Portuguese, the British, and the Dutch established commercial enclaves on the coast of Africa.

1. INDIA UNDER THE MUGHAL DYNASTY

By the end of the fifteenth century the Delhi Sultanate, which under successive Turko-Afghan dynasties had endured for three hundred years, was in a weakened condition. Early in the sixteenth century northern India fell by conquest to a new dynasty that provided more effective rule than any India had known since the reign of Harsha in the seventh century and inaugurated one of the more productive periods of Indian civilization. This dynasty, which reached its height in the seventeenth century, is known as the Mughal from the Persian term for "Mongol" (corrupted into the English "Mogul"), although it was not of Mongol origin. Its founder, Babur (1483–1530), was descended from two of the world's most renowned conquerors—the Turk Timur on his father's side and the Mongol Genghis Khan on his mother's. His own son and heir was born of a Persian mother, and later descendants mingled their blood with that of Hindu royal families.

Babur was a man of tremendous energy, intelligence, and sensitivity as shown by his remarkable autobiography, but he earned the epithet "The Tiger" through his dazzling military exploits. Beginning as ruler of a tiny principality in Turkestan, Babur crossed the mountains into Afghanistan to seize Kabul. Failing in attempts to expand his kingdom in Central Asia, he turned his attention southward to the demoralized and divided Delhi Sultanate. Conveniently the viceroy of the Punjab invited Babur to help "save" him from his overlord the sultan. After defeating the sultan's army near Delhi in April 1526, Babur determined to make himself master of Hindustan. The small size of his forces relative to those opposing him was compensated for by their intense loyalty and by the fact that they possessed primitive but destructive artillery and match-fired muskets of European manufacture. The conqueror's closest brush with disaster came in 1527 when he faced the armies of a Rajput confederacy far outnumbering his own and led by a prince who had never submitted to Muslim rule. But clever strategem and reckless courage prevailed against a host divided in its loyalties. After exhorting his men to valor and vowing to abstain from wine henceforth if Allah gave him victory, Babur carried the

The rise of the Mughal Dynasty

Babur "the Tiger"

*The Court of the Emperor Babur "the Tiger,"
Founder of the Mogul Dynasty*

day. Bengal fell to him in 1529, leaving him master of most of northern India.

The twenty-five years following Babur's death in 1530 were critical for the fate of the dynasty. His son Humayun, able but too often indolent, was driven out of India by Afghan generals and fled to the court of Persia, his mother's homeland. With the help of a Persian army Humayun recovered the Delhi throne in 1555 but he died following an accident the next year, leaving his fragile kingdom in the hands of a thirteen-year-old son, Akbar. Fortunately for the Mughals the lad had the protection of an able and loyal general, Bayran Khan, who served as regent, crowned the young prince, and fought off rival claimants until through palace intrigue he was expelled and stabbed to death in 1561 while on pilgrimage to Mecca. The next year, at the age of twenty, Akbar surprised the court and schemers of the harem by taking personal command of the government.

Humayun and the regency

Akbar, justifiably remembered as the "Great Mughal," was an outstanding world figure in a century that boasted several "magnificent monarchs." By a coincidence his long reign (1556–1605) coincided almost exactly with that of England's Elizabeth I, whose unique talents for governance were parallel to his own. By military force Akbar consolidated his position in northern and central India, holding Kabul

Akbar "the great Mughal"

The administration of Akbar

in the northwest and securing Gujarat on the Kathiawar peninsula, essential for commercial exports via the Arabian Sea. He extended his rule by taking Orissa on the Bay of Bengal in 1592 and Baluchistan, west of the Indus River, three years later. His forays into the Deccan won victories but few permanent conquests.

Although Akbar's reign was occupied with warfare and marked with occasional acts of cruelty, he established an effective and on the whole judicious administration. To break the opposition of the Rajput clans he coaxed one into a marriage alliance and punished any that threatened, once massacring 30,000 defenders of a captured fortress. For the separate provinces into which he divided the empire he appointed military governors with extensive powers but, unlike his predecessors, he paid them regular salaries instead of endowing them with land grants or letting them assess the people under their jurisdiction. Taxes were collected by nonmilitary officials, the revenue transmitted to the capital and thence disbursed by the central government. Provincial governors were periodically transferred from one district to another to prevent them from developing a local following that might challenge imperial authority. Akbar kept his subordinates under close observation, held them to strict accountability, and punished them for misconduct. As with most Indian regimes ancient or modern, the principal source of state revenue under the Mughals was the land tax. Akbar's assessment was comparatively light, amounting to one-third of the annual crop value of the lands actually under cultivation, and based on the average yield over a ten-year period. He had the lands surveyed to determine the value of holdings and he reduced or waived the tax in areas troubled by famine. The emperor's annual income is estimated as the equivalent of $200,000,000 and his higher officials were rewarded with very generous salaries. This was an age of autocratic rule in Europe as in Asia, with extreme disparities between the upper and lower classes. While Indian cities expanded and a substantial middle class of traders and artisans flourished, common laborers were far from prosperous and some were slaves. Rural villagers, comprising an overwhelming majority of the population, could expect only a low standard of living—but they were probably better off than they have been in modern times. Akbar's revenue system enriched the governing class but it was honestly administered and permitted the growth of a vigorous economy.

Akbar's rule as an Indian sovereign

The most innovative of Akbar's policies and the key to his success was his determination to rule as an Indian sovereign rather than as a foreign conqueror. His criminal code was harsh, although not more barbarous than that of many contemporary European states. Civil law for Muslim subjects was based upon Islamic tradition and the Koran, but he permitted Hindus to settle disputes among themselves according to their own laws by the decision of village councils or Brahmanical opinion. Surpassing all of his predecessors in his efforts to conciliate his Indian subjects, Akbar abolished the special taxes

THE MUGHAL EMPIRE IN INDIA

Map labels:
CHINA
(AFGHANISTAN)
SIKHS
Lahore
PUNJAB
(PAKISTAN)
HIMALAYA
Indus R.
Delhi ★
RAJPUTS
MOUNTAINS
Agra ★
Ganges R.
Brahmaputra R.
BALUCHISTAN
INDIA
HINDUSTAN
(BANGLA DESH)
GUJARAT
VINDHYA MTS.
BENGAL
Calcutta
Surat
Damão (Daman)
Diu
ORISSA
Bombay
Poona
Golconda
ARABIAN
MARATHAS
DECCAN
BAY OF
SEA
BIJAPUR
BENGAL
Goa
Madras
0   500 miles
Under Akbar, 1556-1605
Expansion under Shah Jahan, 1627-1658
and Aurangzeb, 1658-1707
INDIAN   OCEAN

that had been laid on non-Muslims, granted freedom of worship, and encouraged the building of Hindu temples. With an eye to political expediency he chose women of different nationalities for his harem (said to number over 5,000). His favorite wife and the mother of his successor to the throne was a Rajput princess. He employed Hindus in the military and administrative services, placing a raja in the key post of minister of finance.

Akbar's complex personality and rare combination of interests left their mark upon all aspects of his reign. He apparently suffered from epileptic attacks and occasional spells of depression, but usually displayed buoyant spirits. Endowed with a superb physique, he loved

Akbar's personality and his cultural interests

Akbar, a Contemporary Portrait.
The genius of the "Great Mughal" lay in his ability to consolidate his wide-ranging
conquests through his atten-
tiveness to Indian sensibilities
and the creation of an administrative framework that sustained the empire for about one
hundred and fifty years.

Shah Jahan

feats of strength and dangerous exploits, sometimes risking his life
in the most reckless fashion by attacking a lion singlehandedly or by
riding wild elephants. In a fit of temper he could be pitilessly cruel,
but he was generally fair in judgment and frequently generous to a
defeated opponent. This high-strung emperor was endowed with lively
intellectual curiosity and a capacious mind. He is credited with several
inventions, chiefly in connection with the improvement of artillery.
Although he stubbornly refused to learn to read or write, he was
fond of literature and collected a huge library. A gifted musician, he
not only acquired skill as a performer (especially on a type of kettle
drum) but also became versed in the highly intricate theory of Hindu
vocalization.

Akbar's innovative boldness led him not only to tolerate Hinduism
but finally to abandon the religion of his own people. A strain of
mysticism in his psyche attracted him toward Islamic Sufism, but
his restless intellect kept him from finding satisfaction in any established
dogma. Because he enjoyed philosophical argument he instituted a
series of weekly debates among spokesmen for various religions from
within and without India, and he enlivened the discussions by sharply
questioning the participants. Midway through his reign, in 1581,
Akbar inaugurated a religion of his own devising which he called
the "Divine Faith." A synthetic monotheism affirming the virtues of
wisdom, courage, chastity, and justice, it incorporated the Hindu
prohibition of cow slaughter, a Parsee ceremony of fire worship,
and a Christian baptismal rite. Adherents were required to perform
the traditional Muslim prostration before the prophet, namely Akbar
himself—whom the less sophisticated probably worshiped as God.
The Divine Faith did not spread far beyond the circle of the court
and disappeared soon after Akbar's lifetime. Meanwhile it alienated
many orthodox Muslims who regarded the emperor as a traitor to
Islam.

The most illustrious period of the dynasty was the century and a
half embracing four generations of "Great Mughals." These rulers
did not lack heirs, but each reign was marred by quarrels over the
succession, with princes revolting against their father and joining in
fratricidal strife against one another. Jahangir (1605–1627), Akbar's
son and successor, probably poisoned his father. Talented, crafty,
self-indulgent, and dissipated, Jahangir let the power slip into the
hands of his Persian wife. The reign of her son, Shah Jahan, provided
three decades of splendor (1627–1658) but at a staggering cost. Extravagant spending to adorn two capitals—Delhi and Agra—together with
continuous wars in the Deccan and military expeditions into Central
Asia and against Persia so drained the treasury that the land tax was
raised to one-half the annual crop value, laying a crushing burden
upon poor cultivators. Shah Jahan ended his days a prisoner of his
rebellious son, Aurangzeb, who during a long reign missed an opportunity to restore the state to sound health.

Aurangzeb, perhaps innately the ablest of Akbar's descendants, ruled for the same number of years as his great-grandfather (1658–1707). Ambitious and energetic, he had demonstrated his capacity and gained experience in statecraft before succeeding to (and while plotting to obtain) the throne. As viceroy of the still unconquered Deccan he skillfully enticed some *sufis* and nobles in Bijapur away from their loyalty to the sultan of that rival Muslim kingdom. During the first half of his reign Aurangzeb governed prudently, adhering to the pattern established by Akbar. During the second half he depleted his resources in attempting to crush every independent state in India, whether Hindu or Muslim, and he alienated his Hindu subjects by reverting to a policy of religious persecution. Seemingly obsessed with a desire to enforce Islamic orthodoxy, he reinstituted special taxes on non-Muslims, forbade the construction of temples, and had some demolished. A man of sincere but fanatical piety, he frowned upon art as idolatrous and disparaged literature on the ground that it exalted human vanity. The royal "prayer-monger" banished music from his court and replaced the Persian solar calendar with the clumsier lunar calendar because the latter had been used by Muhammad.

Warring simultaneously against "idolators" within the kingdom and political adversaries without, Aurangzeb resorted to shortsighted policies that weakened the administration and jeopardized the economy. To avoid paying salaries to territorial governors as Akbar had done, he gave them grants of land, enabling unscrupulous officials to evade their responsibilities to the state and to squeeze the peasants beneath them. Aurangzeb (whose imperial name was Alamgir, "World Conqueror") spent the last twenty-six years of his life in the Deccan directing military campaigns. In 1686 his forces overthrew the long-buffeted kingdom of Bijapur and the following year absorbed the small neighboring state of Golconda. These victories were of dubious benefit because they destroyed a precarious balance of power in the Deccan, encouraging the outbreak of fresh hostilities. Although Aurangzeb's conquests extended farther into the peninsula than those of his predecessors, they could not be secured, and at the end of his reign he left the Mughals with more enemies than they had faced at the beginning.

Aurangzeb, the Last of the Great Mughals. In stark contrast to his illustrious great-grandfather, Aurangzeb sought to transform the empire into an orthodox Islamic state, and his conquests only heralded its precipitous decline.

Most intractable of the emperor's foes were the Marathas, a confederacy of Hindu tribes occupying hilly terrain in the northwestern Deccan. Some of their leaders had served with the Mughals or with Bijapur—the two rival Muslim powers between which they were wedged—but by 1662 the Marathas had established an independent kingdom of their own, dominating the western quarter of Bijapur and with Poona as its capital. Under their intrepid king Shivaji, a master of guerilla tactics, they frustrated all attempts to crush them, even when their strongholds were taken and the "mountain rat" himself was held captive for a time. The Marathas operated as a de facto state over a large section of the Deccan until late in the eighteenth century

The Sikhs

when the confederacy broke into several independent principalities.

Whereas Akbar had tried to placate the Rajputs, Aurangzeb provoked them into open rebellion. Similarly he made enemies of the Sikhs of the Punjab, thus creating challenges to imperial authority in the very heart of his domain. In origin the Sikhs were a religious group with progressive and humane convictions. The sect had been founded in the fifteenth century by Nanak, a philanthropic and spiritually minded preacher whose teachings and influence have been the subject of conflicting interpretation. Recent scholars question the claim of some admirers that Nanak sought to establish a common bond between Hindus and Muslims by combining the best elements of each of the two faiths. Undoubtedly he drew much of his inspiration from contemporary Hindu beliefs and traditions, but he was a genuinely original thinker. The essence of his teaching was the brotherhood of man, the oneness of God, and the duty of acts of charity:

Make love thy mosque; sincerity thy prayer-carpet; justice thy Koran;
Modesty thy circumcision; courtesy thy Kaaba; truth thy Guru; charity thy
    creed and prayer;
The will of God thy rosary, and God will preserve thine honor, O Nanak.

The evolution of the sect

Nanak rejected formal scriptures and mechanical rites, and because he repudiated caste he gained many adherents from among the depressed classes of Hindus. Although his religion contained doctrines common to Islam and Hinduism (and Christianity), the Sikhs ("disciples") became a distinctive community rather than a branch of Hinduism. Nanak was succeeded by a line of spiritual leaders or gurus, to the fourth of whom Akbar granted a site in Amritsar. Here they erected the Golden Temple, a holy of holies to the Sikhs and repository of their scriptures. While Akbar had treated the Sikhs kindly, his successor, Jahangir, executed the fifth guru for supporting the emperor's rebellious son, and Aurangzeb, unable to coerce the Sikh leader into accepting Islam, had him killed. Not surprisingly the belligerent hostility of the later Mughals goaded the Sikhs to fury. The sect which had begun as a peaceful reformist movement was gradually transformed into a military order. Its members were initiated by a rite called "Baptism of the Sword," and many of them adopted the surname Singh, meaning "Lion." While they retained an antipathy toward caste and subscribed to a strict code of personal discipline, they lost much of the generous idealism of their early leaders. Appearing sometimes as no better than brigands, they showed particular relish for slaughtering Muslims. Thus at the opening of the eighteenth century the Mughal power was menaced not only by the usual court intrigues but also by the spirited defiance of powerful Indian groups—Rajputs, Marathas, and Sikhs.

Thirty-two years after the exhausting reign of Aurangzeb the kingdom was stricken by a disaster from without. In 1739 a usurper to the throne of Persia, Nadir Shah, invaded India and sacked Delhi savagely, leaving much of the city in ruins. The empire never fully recovered from this blow, although it remained a force to reckon with and the Mughals were accorded the formal dignity of ruling sovereigns until long after the British had entrenched themselves in India.

The three centuries of Mughal rule were constructive in many respects. The Mughal administrative system proved useful to the British as they extended their jurisdiction over sections of the subcontinent. More important was the continuing evolution of cultural patterns, enriched by the addition of Persian and other Islamic strains to the Indian amalgam. The emperors were generally cosmopolitan in outlook and welcomed both commercial and cultural intercourse with foreign states. A fusion of Indian, Turkish, Arabic, and Persian was manifest in literature, the arts, and the tone of society. Literature was stimulated by royal patronage and also by the fact that several languages could be drawn upon. Both Turkish and Persian were spoken in court circles; familiarity with Arabic, the language of the Koran, was a necessity for educated Muslims, and a knowledge of the native dialects of northern India was essential for administrators. A permanent result of the intermingling between Turko-Persian and Indian cultures was the rise of a variety of speech known as Urdu ("the camp language"). While Urdu in its vocabulary includes many Persian and Arabic words and is written in Arabic script, its grammatical structure is basically the same as that of Hindi, the most prevalent Aryan vernacular of northern India. Both Urdu and Hindi came to be standard mediums of communication throughout northern India. (Urdu is now confined chiefly to Pakistan.)

While many Persian scholars and poets were attracted to the cosmopolitan Mughal court, the literary works of most enduring value were produced by Hindus, especially during the tolerant regime of Akbar. This emperor showed great interest in India's literary treasures as well as in her art and music, and he appointed a poet laureate for Hindi. He had Persian translations made from the *Vedas* and the Epics. Tulsi Das, one of India's greatest poets, lived during Akbar's reign. His principal work was an idealized and highly spiritual version of the ancient epic the *Ramayana*. This poem, which combines fine craftsmanship with a warm and fervent moral earnestness, was written in Hindi rather than in Sanskrit, although its author was a brahman.

Architecture illustrates most perfectly the interaction of Hindu and Islamic motifs. Muslim builders introduced the minaret or spire, the pointed arch, and the bulbous dome; Hindu and Jain traditions emphasized horizontal lines and elaborate ornamentation. Because Indian stonemasons and architects were frequently employed even on Muslim religious edifices, there was bound to be a fruitful interchange of ideas, and this culminated in the sixteenth and seventeenth centuries in the production of a distinctive Indo-Muslim architectural style. Some of Akbar's constructions at Agra, of durable red sandstone,

The Mughal legacy

Languages and the foundations of literature

Hindu literature

Mughal architecture

The Builders of the Mughal Empire. Left: *Akbar Inspecting the Progress of the Construction of Fatehpur Sikri in 1584.* This new city, only 26 miles from Agra, was built in honor of a Sufi saint whose promise of a male heir for Akbar had come to fruition. Described by a contemporary English traveler as larger than London, Fatehpur Sikri was abandoned five years after its completion, possibly due to the failure of its water supply. Right: *The Great Mosque at Lahore.* Built during the reign of Aurangzeb, this mosque of red sandstone with marble-covered domes shows Persian influence.

are still standing; and so is most of an entire city which he conceived and had completed at a site a few miles west of Agra and then abandoned only five years later. But Akbar's forts and government halls lacked the choice materials, the refinement, and the sensuous beauty of the buildings executed for Shah Jahan a half-century later. In place of sandstone, these employed the finest marbles, agate, turquoise, and other semiprecious stones, and were frequently decorated with inlays of gold and silver. Shah Jahan's dazzling structures, contrasting markedly with the robustness of Akbar's work, betray an excessive elegance bordering on decadence.

The public works of Shah Jahan

Shah Jahan established his chief royal residence at Delhi, where he laid out a new city and named it after himself. Both Delhi and Agra in the seventeenth century were among the world's greatest cities in respect to number of inhabitants and impressive public buildings. Agra, with a population of 600,000, was divided into separate sections for the different types of merchants and artisans and contained 70 great mosques and 800 public baths. The new Delhi was protected by walls rising 60 feet above the river. Here was constructed a huge royal palace that beggars description. It housed the famous Peacock Throne, inlaid with precious metals and jewels, the value of which has been estimated as in excess of $5,000,000. (It was seized in Nadir

Shah's raid in 1739 and carried off to Persia.) Shah Jahan's most celebrated monument is the Taj Mahal, located at Agra and designed as a mausoleum and memorial to his favorite wife (who died while bearing her fourteenth child to the emperor and while the Deccan was ravaged by famine). The Taj engaged the labor of 20,000 workmen and was some twenty years in construction. The building is a unique blend of Persian and Indian architectural elements, executed with meticulous craftsmanship. Its charm is enhanced by its setting, amid shaded walks, lakes, and gardens.

The Islamic taboos against pictorial representation were almost totally disregarded by the Mughal rulers, who were enthusiastic collectors and connoisseurs of painting. Reflecting the influence of contemporary Persian art, the most typical examples were miniatures, including landscapes and especially portraits, executed with realism and meticulous detail. Calligraphy also enjoyed the status of a fine art; many manuscripts were illuminated with pictures as in medieval Europe. Texts from the Koran were employed as decorative devices on screens and the façades of buildings in keeping with a general practice in Muslim countries. In many parts of India exacting craftsmanship and artistic standards were carried on much as they had been before the Muslim invasions. Particularly notable was the Rajput school of painting, fostered at the courts of native princes in Rajputana, more vigorous and less sensuous than the Mughal school.

In South India as in the North, reciprocal interaction between Muslim and Hindu elements stimulated creative activity. The reign of Sultan Ibrahim II of Bijapur (1580–1627) resembled that of his more famous contemporary Akbar in its encouragement of free expression and eclecticism in the arts as well as in religion. Architectural monuments from the era of this "Teacher of the World"—as the sultan's admirers

Top: *Mumtaz Mahal ("Ornament of the Palace")*. The favorite wife of Shah Jahan, who died in childbirth in 1631 at the age of 39. Bottom: *Shah Jahan (1627–1658)*. The Mughal emperor was famous for his luxurious court and his magnificent buildings.

The Taj Mahal at Agra. Built by Shah Jahan in memory of Mumtaz Mahal, it is considered one of the finest examples of Indian Muslim architecture.

The coming of the Europeans

A European Traveler in the Late Sixteenth Century. This Mughal painting shows the subject leaving his world behind for a distinctly Indian setting.

Sir Thomas Roe: "War and traffic are incompatible"

called him—are embellished with lotus stems and budding shoots, reflecting an exuberance more typically Indian than Arabic or Persian.

One aspect of the Mughal period bound to have tremendous consequences for the future of India was the impact of European traders and adventurers. Although the footholds they secured at various points on the coast were small and seemingly insignificant, they denoted the awakening of Europeans to the commercial possibilities of South and Southeast Asia. The maritime enterprise shown by Indian states in earlier times was no longer evident, and even the Mughal empire for all its splendor and formidable armies did not maintain a navy. During most of the sixteenth century the Portuguese dominated the Indian Ocean, giving them a profitable position not only in commerce but also as providers of transport for the annual Muslim pilgrimage to Mecca. The Dutch and English—budding rivals of the great Catholic powers Spain and Portugal—cooperated for several years in ousting the Portuguese from the East Indies Spice Islands, but after the Dutch demonstrated forcefully their unwillingness to share the lucrative spice trade the British were compelled to turn their attention to the Indian mainland. Here they were impeded by the Portuguese, who held several fortified ports on the Indian coast and in Ceylon. Portuguese Jesuit missionaries at the Mughal court also discouraged any cordial reception of Protestant intruders. The British East India Company, chartered by Queen Elizabeth I in 1600, failed during the first two decades of its existence to obtain trading privileges. A swashbuckling captain, William Hawkins, representing the Company, was royally entertained by the convivial emperor Jahangir, but after two frustrating years Hawkins left Agra without a treaty. The company's bargaining position improved after the British shattered a Portuguese navy and began to dominate the Arabian Sea and the Persian Gulf. Sir Thomas Roe, dispatched to Agra as ambassador by King James I, in 1619 obtained Jahangir's permission for the English to build a factory at Surat, the Mughal's principal port. Notwithstanding an increasing British presence in India, Portugal retained Goa, Damão (Daman), and Diu on the west coast until forcibly dispossessed by the government of independent India in 1961.

Sir Thomas Roe warned his countrymen to shun the Portuguese policy of seizing territory and attempting to found colonies in India. He advised them instead to seek profit "at sea and in quiet trade," remembering that "war and traffic are incompatible." For some time the British were hard pressed to keep their trade channels open, let alone found colonies. The British East India Company languished under the early Stuart monarchs, especially when King Charles I licensed a rival association to engage in the eastern trade. But the Company recovered its monopoly under the Protectorate of Oliver Cromwell—who invigorated British commerce by defeating the Dutch and negotiating a favorable treaty with the Portuguese—and after the Restoration, King Charles II issued a new charter granting the

Portuguese Goa. A map from Pedro Barreto de Resende's revised edition of Antinio Bocarto's *Curo do Estado da India Oriental,* 1646. Wrested from the Deccan state of Bijapur in 1510, Goa remained under Portuguese control for 451 years.

East India Company the right to coin money, exercise jurisdiction over Englishmen residing in its factories, and make war or peace with "non-Christian powers." During the next several decades the Company reaped profits averaging 25 percent annually. Before the close of the century it had secured three locations of strategic as well as commercial importance in widely separated regions of India: the island of Bombay off the western coast (given by Portugal in 1661 when the English King Charles II married a Portuguese princess), Madras on the southeastern coast, and Port William (Calcutta) at the mouth of the Ganges. The French, who organized their own East India Company in 1664, acquired stations in India paralleling those of the British and able to compete successfully with them. In the mid-eighteenth century it seemed that France might surpass Britain in the race for empire when the able François Dupleix, with the backing of a French fleet, captured Madras and made himself virtual ruler of the whole southeastern quarter of the peninsula. But British victories in the Seven Years War (1756–1763), fought in Europe, America, India, and on the high seas, while not immediately dispossessing the French insured England's position as the dominant European power on the subcontinent.

Sir Thomas Roe. The British royal envoy to the court of the Mughal Emperor Jahangir set the tone for the British East India Company's role on the subcontinent for more than one hundred years.

2. CHINA UNDER THE MANCHU (CH'ING) DYNASTY

With the disintegration of the Ming Dynasty it was China's fate to succumb once more to the rule of foreign invaders. The conquerors, who occupied Manchuria on China's northern border and from which they derived the name Manchu, were essentially the same people as the Juchên, who had divided China with the Sung emperor 500 years before. Although of nomadic origin and differing from the Chinese in language and culture, the Manchus had long admired, and, to their lasting benefit, adopted important aspects of the Ming imperial system. While sparsely inhabited northern Manchuria was still a region of hunting and herding, by the sixteenth century settled agricultural communities had been established in the south along the Liao River. Early in the seventeenth century a minor chieftain named Nurhachi (died 1636) brought several tribes under his jurisdiction, established his

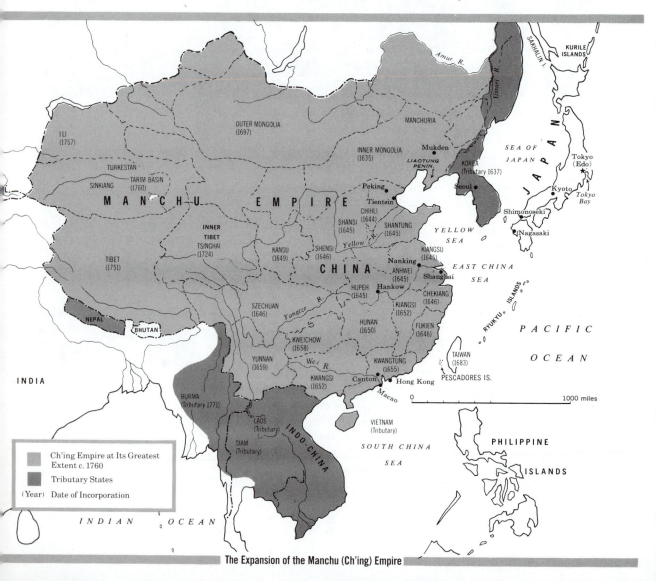

The Expansion of the Manchu (Ch'ing) Empire

capital at Mukden, and assumed a dynastic name, Ch'ing (meaning "Clear" or "Pure"). Before embarking on the conquest of China the Manchus had not only proclaimed a new dynastic rule for East Asia but had also created a political structure with ministries fashioned after those of the Ming, thus marking a transition from a tribal society to a territorial state. To conquer China the Manchus had, to a significant degree, Sinicized their own institutions.

Originating in military conquest, the Ch'ing Dynasty lasted nearly 300 years, until the institution of monarchy was overthrown by revolution in 1911. Although the dynasty is dated from 1644 when Peking was taken by the Manchus, their rule was not firmly secured until nearly 40 years later because of resistance offered by Chinese loyal to the Ming. In their conquest the Manchus were heavily indebted to Chinese generals whose allegiance they had won. Pacification of the southern and southwestern regions was left to Chinese commanders who were given such broad powers that they threatened to become independent. One general set himself up as ruler of a new dynasty, but Peking's authority was assured in 1681 by victory in the "War of the Three Feudatories." Eventually the state's frontiers were extended farther than ever before in China's history. Manchuria of course was an essential part of the empire, and the peripheral regions of Korea, Burma, Nepal, and sections of Indochina were linked as tributary dependencies. Imperial forces defeated nomadic tribes in Outer Mongolia (1696) and in 1720 invaded Tibet and installed at Lhasa a Dalai Lama friendly to the Ch'ing. The island of Taiwan, which had been occupied by Dutch traders and later by an enterprising Chinese merchant family with an extensive maritime network, was in 1683 annexed as part of the mainland province of Fukien.

While attempting to conciliate the Chinese, the Manchu rulers were careful to preserve their own people's ethnic identity. They closed Manchuria to Chinese immigration, forbade intermarriage between Chinese and Manchu, and required Chinese males to shave their foreheads and braid their hair in a queue after the Manchu fashion as a token of submission. To guard against rebellion Manchu garrisons were stationed in the principal cities, while Chinese troops were used as auxiliaries or as a police force. Repressive measures notwithstanding, the Ch'ing emperors were determined to be accepted as legitimate rulers rather than be resented as usurpers to the throne. In the face of domestic turmoil, prolonged armed resistance, and Chinese antipathy toward invading "barbarians," they succeeded to a remarkable degree not merely in retaining authority but in revitalizing the state as well. The Ch'ing's success is explained partly by its good fortune in having nearly half of the dynasty's entire history encompassed within the administrations of two able and energetic rulers. K'ang Hsi, who reigned for sixty-one years (1661–1722) and was thus a contemporary of King Louis XIV, though less celebrated in Western annals was an abler statesman than France's famous "Sun King." While still a youth

The conquest of China

The Emperor K'ang Hsi Engaged in Study. His devotion to the Confucian classics and the pursuit of science contributed to K'ang Hsi's image as an enlightened monarch.

The success of Manchu administrative policies in the reign of K'ang Hsi

*Ch'ien Lung (1736–1796). The
great Manchu emperor under
whom the Ch'ing Dynasty
reached its climax. (Painting
on silk by a nineteenth-century
artist.)*

*Growth and prosperity in
the age of Ch'ien Lung*

he crushed the rebellion of the Three Feudatories in southwest China. He not only promptly reinstated the civil service examinations but also schooled himself in the Chinese classics upon which they were based. As the Ch'ing administration developed, more than 80 percent of the lower offices came to be filled by Chinese, although they obtained a much smaller share of the higher posts. The system whereby educated Chinese were recruited for government service through the competitive state examinations resembled somewhat the Indian Civil Service developed by the British East India Company, which in the eighteenth and nineteenth centuries enlisted native talents in the service of foreign masters. Finding that some scholars, through loyalty to the Ming, refused to sit for the triennial state examinations, K'ang Hsi sought to attract them by creating new degrees to be earned through special examinations. But although his rule was vigorous and on the whole judicious, he failed to win the unquestioned allegiance of well-to-do landholding families, particularly those of the Yangtze region where China's wealth was concentrated. Routine local affairs such as the supervision of markets, charities, and waterworks were left in the hands of the local gentry, an elite group which, under the direction of an official appointed for each county, provided the central government with an able and locally respected staff of administrators. The emperor's reluctance to antagonize this influential class kept him from making a comprehensive land survey on which a realistic tax structure could have been based. Poor peasants and tenants—and also the state's revenue—suffered from the rapacity and corruption of landlords and local officials. The examination system in effect strengthened the dominance of the landed gentry in Chinese society. Although the system was theoretically based upon merit rather than birth, only candidates who had had the benefit of an education could compete successfully, and poor families could not give their sons such an education.

Under the sixty-three-year reign of K'ang Hsi's grandson Ch'ien Lung (1736–1799)—the longest reign in Chinese history—the empire's physical boundaries and its prestige reached new dimensions. A vast nomadic area in the northwest, incorporated as the "New Dominion" (Sinkiang), doubled the state's area. Although Ch'ien Lung, lacking his grandfather's acuity, was inclined to accept purely theoretical solutions to problems and although in his later years he indulged undeserving favorites, he was conscientious and diligent, and his long reign compares favorably with those of contemporary sovereigns. During the eighteenth century China was not only the largest and most populous but also one of the best-governed states in the world. The inequalities and suffering known to earlier periods were still present, but a generally high level of prosperity is evidenced by a rapid increase in China's population. Estimated at below 80 million in 1390, it grew to more than 300 million during the eighteenth century. Unevenly distributed, population was densest in the Yangtze valley and along the southeast coast, the most prosperous regions of China and those where loyalty to the Manchu regime was weakest. While agriculture remained the primary source of private wealth and of the government's tax revenues, China's southern ports had become centers of a brisk maritime commerce, bringing profits to Chinese merchants but little revenue to the government because of the absence of a central agency to regulate trade and collect customs duties. The Manchu shared the Ming prejudice against overseas voyages and forbade the building of ships large enough to engage in them. Unfortunately for the dynasty this policy placed it at an increasing disadvantage as European traders, backed by armored fleets, sought entrance into China's ports.

The growth of population, which by mid-nineteenth century had risen to about 450 million, brought severe internal problems. The lack of sufficient arable land to support such a large number of people led to the clearing and cropping of upper river valleys that had hitherto been left to nature. Soil erosion increased the danger of floods and droughts, aggravating China's agrarian problems in the modern era. The Chinese custom of dividing land equally among male heirs tended to reduce farm plots below the size necessary to support a family. At the same time the more comfortably situated landed gentry found opportunities for state employment narrowing because the government neglected to enlarge the examination system or create new posts to keep pace with population growth. When the foundations of the dynasty were being laid, the great emperor K'ang Hsi, to allay fears that private holdings might be confiscated, had decreed that tax quotas assigned to various districts should remain fixed at their existing levels. Consequently, as population increased and the country's prosperity rose the central government was denied access to an adequate share of the nation's income, while the profits of powerful provincial families expanded. The failure of the Ch'ing to develop a sound tax structure was an important cause of the dynasty's eventual decline.

Chinese society, rooted in the closely united patriarchal family, was not significantly altered under Manchu rule. Woman's position remained far inferior to man's, and her oppression may actually have become heavier. Widows were expected not to remarry and some proved their fidelity to a departed husband by committing suicide. The cruel and crippling custom of female foot-binding, which dated from the Sung Dynasty and was supposed to make a woman more attractive to a man and effectively ensure her remaining dependent upon him, became more prevalent in spite of the efforts of Ch'ing emperors to stamp it out. Not until the twentieth century was the practice completely abandoned.

The Manchu emperors, whose own religious background was one of shamanism, cultivated and exalted the Chinese state cult of Confucius, requiring temples to be maintained in every district and elevating the spirit of the ancient sage to the highest rank of official deities. Tolerant in religion, the early Ch'ing emperors were generally cordial to Christian missionaries, especially the French Jesuits, whom they

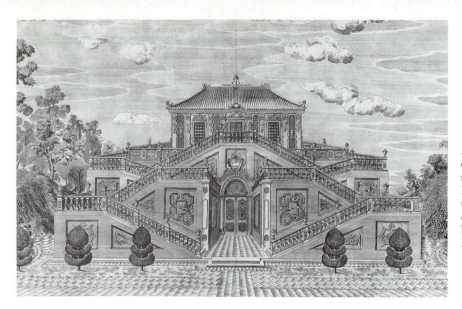

The Summer Palace of the Emperor Ch'ien Lung. This exquisite European-style summer palace just outside Peking was designed for the emperor by Jesuit architects. The palace was burned to the ground by British troops in 1860.

Intellectual activity in the Manchu era

Father Adam Schall with His Astronomical Instruments. Director of the Imperial Board of Astronomy, he wears the "mandarin square" of a Manchu civilian official.

employed at court as instructors in science, mathematics, and cartography. The emperor Ch'ien Lung patronized Jesuit painters and hired Jesuit architects to build a beautiful European-style summer palace for the imperial family.

Chinese culture of the Manchu era was characterized by refinement and fulfillment—to some extent overripeness and decadence—rather than innovation. Although the classical curriculum basic to the civil service examinations had become rigid and sterile, lively intellectual activity was displayed both by scholars and by individuals without the benefit of formal education. A thorough reexamination of the classical canon produced limited but iconoclastic textual criticism. To repair an alleged distortion of Confucian dogma under the Ming, the Neo-Confucianism of the Sung philosopher Chu Hsi was revived. "Han Learning" scholars sought to recover the unsullied wisdom of more remote antiquity. Other thinkers, disenchanted with the metaphysical idealism of Neo-Confucianism, rejected abstract speculation in favor of the study of such factual subjects as mathematics, astronomy, geography, and linguistics. Criticism was also voiced against the state examinations for their neglect of the practical and immediate.

If philosophical speculation was somewhat lacking in spontaneity, the age was one of tremendous literary productivity. Scholars who shunned the state examinations were recruited by the court to write dictionaries and encyclopedias and to compile anthologies of prose and poetry. A compilation of Chinese history and literature prepared for Ch'ien Lung filled 36,000 manuscript volumes. This emperor at the same time imposed a literary inquisition, searching libraries and private collections to remove and destroy works considered antidynastic or dangerous to authority. Creative imagination was most evident in the novel, which reached an even higher state of development than under the Ming. The best Chinese novels of this period readily bear comparison with major prose works of other nations. Satire was employed to expose social follies and political corruption; some authors dared to attack the subjection of women. *Dream of the Red Chamber,* generally regarded as China's greatest novel, was composed about the middle of Ch'ien Lung's reign. With a tragic love story as its central plot, the novel provides an exposé of the life of the rich while also probing into the nature of reality and the meaning of human existence. Some painters, bred in the Ming tradition and averse to dynastic change, portrayed a bleak and disharmonious world. One famous artist splashed the word "Dumb" on the closed door of his studio. Nevertheless, the visual arts survived and flourished under the Ch'ing. A perceptive aesthete celebrated the true painter as one who is able "to participate in the metamorphoses of the universe" and through his art evoke a mood of exaltation.

During the Manchu period Chinese civilization created a more distinct impression upon nations of the West than had ever been true before. In the eighteenth century Chinese-style gardens, pagodas, and pavilions became fashionable among the wealthy classes of western Europe. Other items borrowed from China included sedan chairs, lacquer, and incense, while the craze for Chinese porcelain reached such proportions that it had the unfortunate effect of lowering the quality of the product. In addition, largely through translations and commentaries prepared by the Jesuits, European intellectuals were introduced to Chinese thought and literature. European acquaintance with these subjects was, of course, limited and superficial, but it was sufficient to arouse admiration. Spokesmen of the Enlightenment cited fragments of Confucian texts in support of Deism and as evidence that human society could be guided by reason. Voltaire praised the emperor Ch'ien Lung as exemplifying the ideal of philosopher king.

European appraisals of the Ch'ing regime became less generous as Western maritime adventurers encountered obstacles in their efforts to open China to commercial intercourse. The overseas expansion of the Western nations during the Commercial Revolution affected China as well as India and other Eastern lands. By the early sixteenth century the Portuguese had occupied Malacca, and one of their trading vessels reached Canton in 1516. The Chinese authorities, long accustomed to peaceful commercial intercourse with Arabs and other foreigners, at first had been disposed to grant the normal privileges to the newcomers. Portuguese adventurers, however, pillaged Chinese ships engaged in trade with the Indies and raided coastal cities, looting and massacring the inhabitants. Such actions convinced the Chinese that Europeans were no better than pirates; nor was their opinion favorably revised with the arrival, a little later, of the Dutch and the English. The wanton depredations perpetrated by these early Western seafarers were responsible for the unflattering name which the Chinese came to apply to Europeans—"Ocean Devils." The government finally determined to exclude Europeans from the coastal cities but allowed the Portuguese to maintain a trading center and settlement at Macao

A Painted Scene from The Dream of the Red Chamber. *The novel reveals much about the life of mid-Ch'ing upper-class life, its underside as well as its grandeur.*

The influx of the "Ocean Devils"

Chinoiserie. Even as the Jesuits designed Ch'ien Lung's summer palace, eighteenth-century Europeans were developing a taste for the exotic designs and benign autocracy of China. This French tapestry dating from the 1720s shows the emperor receiving tributaries in a fanciful setting.

in the far south. Established in 1557, this post has been retained by the Portuguese to the present day. As a security measure, the local officials constructed a wall blocking off the Portuguese settlement on the island of Macao and imposed rigid restrictions upon the activities of the foreigners. The trade was too profitable for the Chinese to want to abolish it altogether, and the Portuguese were soon extended the privilege of docking at Canton at prescribed times and under strict supervision.

Imperial resistance to foreign intrusion

The imperial government was inclined to resist attempts to draw it into close relationship with societies and cultures alien to Chinese traditions. In 1759 an English captain, sailing under orders of the British East India Company, was arrested and imprisoned for violating a prohibition against entering China's northern ports. The government's hostility toward any foreign intrusion into its affairs is illustrated by one item in the charges against the offending trader: He had learned the Chinese language! The military strength of the Celestial Empire during the early phase of European overseas expansion is shown in its relations with a rival land-based power. While Portuguese, Spanish, French, and British were knocking at the ports of East Asia, Tsarist Russia was pushing its eastern frontiers overland toward the Pacific and by the late seventeenth century was encroaching on the Manchurian border. Defeated by Manchu forces, the Russians signed a treaty in 1689 acknowledging China's sovereignty and fixing its northern border approximately as it has remained to the present. The day of humiliation in confrontation with Western imperialist powers was still in the distance.

The long reign of Ch'ien Lung, which marked the apex of Ch'ing grandeur, also witnessed the beginning of the dynasty's decline. In the late eighteenth century troubles, for which the government was partly to blame, multiplied. Intrigue among rival court factions sapped the administration's efficiency; the bureaucracy had grown corrupt and rapacious. Bungled military campaigns in Burma and Vietnam wasted resources and intensified popular discontent, evident in the emergence of secret societies hostile to the Ch'ing. The White Lotus, an underground organization dating from Sung times, became active in central China and in the large western province of Szechwan. Miao tribesmen staged rebellions in the southwest as did Muslims in the northwest. And the latent disaffection of the Chinese populace for Manchu rule threatened the state's vigor when it was most needed to oppose the inroads of profit-hungry Westerners.

The seeds of Ch'ing decline

3. JAPAN UNDER THE TOKUGAWA SHOGUNATE

The most turbulent period of Japanese feudalism was ended rather abruptly at the close of the sixteenth century when a series of military campaigns forced the daimyo (great lords) to acknowledge the authority of a single ruler. The rise of the daimyo[1] had led to the establishment of fairly effective government within their individual domains, some of which were large enough to include several of the ancient provinces. Hence, when the great lords were brought under a common central authority, the way was open for a genuine unification of the country, and Japan entered upon an era of comparative peace and stability extending to the threshold of modern times.

The rise of the daimyo

The establishment of a stable central government after the century of civil warfare was achieved in the space of one generation by three military heroes whose careers were marked with bloodshed, treachery, and pitiless cruelty, but whose work endured. Nobunaga, a small provincial lord who dared to challenge the great daimyo fought his way to control of the imperial city of Kyoto, where he rebuilt palaces and took the Shogun under his protection. When this official proved troublesome, Nobunaga expelled him, thus ending the Ashikaga Shogunate (1573). He moved swiftly to break the power of the great Buddhist monasteries, storming their strongholds and massacring thousands of monks, women, and children. Before his death in battle (1582) he had conquered about half of Japan's provinces.

The work of consolidation was carried forward by Nobunaga's

Nobunaga

[1] See above, pp. 565–66.

Hideyoshi

Tokugawa Ieyasu

*Centralization of
authority*

*Persistence of dual
government*

ablest general, Hideyoshi, who is commonly regarded as the greatest man in Japanese history. Hideyoshi was a brilliant commander, highly intelligent, and usually sound in judgment, but his fame rests equally on the fact that he is the only figure in Japan's history to rise from the lowest rank (he was a peasant's son) to ruler of the nation. By 1590 he had broken all resistance in Japan and nourished still larger ambitions. He sent an army into Korea, insulted envoys from the Ming imperial court, and launched a second ill-fated expedition with the avowed intention of conquering China.

The third member of the triumvirate of heroes was Tokugawa Ieyasu. Once a vassal of Nobunaga, he had become the most powerful of the daimyo by the time of Hideyoshi's death in 1598. Following a decisive military victory over rebellious rivals, Ieyasu had himself appointed Shogun in 1603 (the title had been in abeyance for thirty years) and took steps to ensure that this office would remain henceforth in his family, the Tokugawa. Reaping the fruits of the labors of his two predecessors, Tokugawa Ieyasu made the Shogunate a much more efficient instrument of government than it had ever been before.

Under the Tokugawa Shogunate (1603–1867), Japan's feudal institutions remained intact, but they were systematized and made to serve the interests of a strong central government. Ieyasu founded his capital at Edo (now Tokyo), where he built a great castle surrounded with moats and an elaborate series of outer defenses. The great domains of central and eastern Japan were held by members of the Tokugawa or by men who had helped Ieyasu in his campaigns. These trusted supporters of the regime were known as "hereditary daimyo," while the lords who had acknowledged Ieyasu's supremacy only when forced to do so were called "outer daimyo." The members of both groups were hereditary vassals of the Shogun and were kept under careful surveillance lest they should try to assert their independence. The Shogun employed a corps of secret police to report any signs of disaffection throughout the country. As a special precaution he required all daimyo to maintain residences in Edo and reside there every other year, and also to leave their wives and children as hostages when they returned to their own estates. The system Ieyasu devised was so well organized and thorough that it did not depend on the personal ability of the Shogun for its operation. For the first time Japan had a durable political framework, which remained undisturbed in the hands of the Tokugawa for two and a half centuries. While the Shogunate was essentially a feudal power structure, it developed for administrative purposes a large bureaucracy of carefully recruited and competent officials.

It should be noted that the Japanese government was still dual in form. The imperial family and a decorative court nobility continued to reside at Kyoto, while the real power was lodged in the Bakufu, the military hierarchy headed by the Shogun at Edo. The Tokugawa Shoguns cultivated the fiction that they were carrying out the will of

Left: *A Feudal Stronghold*. Hirosaki Castle, in northern Japan, was the residence of one of the "outer daimyo" during the Tokugawa Shogunate. The castle grounds are now a popular resort for cherry-blossom viewing. Right: *Five-storied Pagoda at Nikko, in Central Japan*. It was built in 1636 and dedicated to Tokugawa Ieyasu, founder of the Tokugawa Shogunate. The structure (about 100 feet high) is ornately carved, painted, and lacquered, but is given a magnificent natural setting by the surrounding forest.

a divine emperor. By emphasizing the emperor's sanctity they added an aura of invulnerability to their own position, and by keeping him in seclusion they rendered him harmless. The shadow government at Kyoto was now entirely dependent upon the Shogun even for its financial support, but it was carefully and respectfully preserved as a link with Japan's hallowed past.

The most serious problem of the early Tokugawa period concerned relations with Europeans. Before the close of the sixteenth century both the Portuguese and the Spanish were carrying on considerable trade in Japan, and the Dutch and the British secured trading posts early in the following century. Europeans had been accorded a favorable reception by the Japanese, who seemed eager to learn from them. Firearms, acquired from the Portuguese, came into use for the first time in Japan and played a part in the feudal battles of the late sixteenth century. The introduction of gunpowder had the effect temporarily of stimulating the construction of heavy stone castles by the daimyo, a practice which was carefully regulated by the Tokugawa after they had seized the Shogunate.

Along with the Western traders came missionaries, who at first

Relations with Europeans

The European Presence in Japan. Jesuit missionaries arrive with a Portuguese merchant fleet in this early seventeenth-century Japanese screen. The merchants came for profits; the Jesuits wanted souls.

The growth and suppression of Christianity

encountered little hostility. Vigorous proselyting by Portuguese Jesuits and Spanish Franciscans met with remarkable success in winning converts to the Catholic faith among all classes of the population, including some of the feudal nobles. By the early seventeenth century there were close to 300,000 Christian converts in Japan, chiefly in the south and west where the European trading centers were located. Eventually, however, the Shoguns decided that Christianity should be proscribed, not because they objected to the religion as such but because they were afraid it would divide the country and weaken their authority. They were annoyed by the bickering between rival European groups and also feared that their subjects were being enticed into allegiance to a foreign potentate, the pope. The first persecutions were mild and were directed against Japanese Christians rather than against the Europeans; but when the missionaries refused to halt their work they were severely dealt with, and many were executed. Finally, in 1637, when a peasant revolt against oppressive taxation developed into a Christian rebellion, the Shogun's forces conducted a real war against the Christian strongholds in southwestern Japan and, in spite of the most heroic resistance, wiped out the Christian communities and exterminated the religion almost completely.

Following this bloody purge, the Shoguns adopted a policy of excluding all Europeans from Japanese settlement. That they were able to enforce it shows how strong their government had become. Reluctant to cut off Western trade entirely, they made a slight exception in the case of the Dutch, who seemed to be the least dangerous politically. The Dutch were permitted to unload one ship each year at the port of Nagasaki in the extreme western corner of Japan, but only under the strictest supervision. Going even further along the line of reaction, the Shogun next forbade his Japanese subjects to visit foreign lands on pain of forfeiting all their rights and commanded that no ship should be built large enough to travel beyond the coastal waters of the island empire. But in spite of the exclusion of most Westerners, Japan was not a completely isolated nation during the Tokugawa era. The Shoguns utilized foreign policy as a means of strengthening their regime internally, and they maintained both trade and diplomatic relations with China, Korea, and the Ryukyu Islands (then an independent kingdom).

The Tokugawa era gave Japan a long period of peace and orderly government and promoted the ideal of a perpetually hierarchical society. Theoretically, the social structure was arranged in accordance with the classes of China, which ranked, in order of importance: (1) scholar-officials, (2) farmers, (3) artisans, (4) merchants, and (5) soldiers, bandits, and beggars. In Japan, however, the realities of a feudalized society produced a peculiar distortion of the ideal arrangement, which was somewhat fanciful even in China. The warrior (*samurai*), who had enjoyed a position of leadership for centuries, was elevated from the lowest category to the highest. In return for the place of honor assigned to him he was expected to exhibit the qualities of the scholar also, and to a considerable extent he did. The daimyo and the samurai were no longer the uncouth, lawless ruffians of early feudal days but refined aristocrats, who cultivated literature and the arts and took pride in the rigorous discipline to which they were bred. Still, their pre-eminence had been won in the first instance by force, and their position was regarded as a hereditary right, not to be challenged by men of superior ability who had been born to a lower class. It was only in the late stage of feudalism under the Tokugawa Shogunate that separation became complete between the warrior and the laboring classes. Peasants had frequently fought in the battles of the turbulent Ashikaga period; now they were forbidden to own weapons, a right that became the prerogative of the samurai. But while the peasants were confined to their fields and paddies, their erstwhile masters, the samurai, were being removed from the land. In early feudal days the typical samurai had lived on and supervised the cultivation of his fief. Now he became a retainer, supported by revenues assigned to him by his daimyo overlord, with whom he usually resided.

The artificiality and formal rigidity of the Tokugawa regime did not stifle economic progress. By the early eighteenth century Japan's population had reached a total of 30 million; thenceforth it increased but slightly for a century and a half. This slow rate of population growth apparently was more the result of voluntary family planning than of a scarcity of resources, although occasional famines did occur. The country as a whole was prosperous; industry and internal trade

Social stress: the samurai and the merchants

Changing views of the Japanese peasantry

Expansion of agricultural productivity

continually expanded even though foreign commerce had been curtailed. Communication was relatively easy through all parts of Japan, both by waterways and by improved highways. A brisk exchange of agricultural and manufactured goods promoted the growth of a capitalist economy. Rice merchants occupied a strategic position in the world of finance and their establishments, offering commercial credit and daily price quotations, bore some resemblance to a modern stock exchange. Cities grew in size, especially in the central area of the country. By the late eighteenth century Edo had attained a population of one million and was probably the largest city in the world at that time.

Economic progress, coupled with a rigid and inherently authoritarian political regime, produced severe strains within society. The position of the samurai became more and more anomalous. While they possessed a monopoly of the profession of arms, they found little opportunity to practice it because the Shogun discouraged feudal quarrels, and there were no foreign wars. Thus the samurai became, by and large, a group of respectable parasites, although many of them displayed both talent and energy. They were often employed in administrative functions by the daimyo, and sometimes took over the management of a great domain so completely that the daimyo was reduced to little more than a figurehead. On the other hand the merchants, who were ranked at the bottom of the social pyramid, steadily accumulated wealth, formed their own trade associations to replace the older and more restrictive guilds, and exerted a potent influence over the whole national economy. Inevitably they imparted a bourgeois tone to society in the bustling cities.

Until recently historians commonly assumed that the peasants' lot under the Tokugawa was a miserable one, but research in Japanese sources has discredited this assumption. It is true that peasant labor supported the upper classes of daimyo and samurai as well as the Shogun and his bureaucracy. It is also true that peasants endured privation and sometimes cruel treatment at the hands of their social superiors, who dismissed them contemptuously as seeds to be pressed or cattle to be driven. The outbreak of riots and actual local rebellions—in a society as disciplined as the Tokugawa—indicates the reality and the depth of popular discontent. But the evidence is undeniable that Japanese farmers and tenants shared in the country's rising prosperity. Forbidden to bear arms, they were relieved from the burden of military service, and they benefited from the two and a half centuries of almost uninterrupted peace that followed the accession of Tokugawa Ieyasu.

Japanese agriculture continued to progress. The amount of land under cultivation doubled, new crops were introduced, intensive fertilization and better tools, including a mechanical thresher, came into use, and irrigation was extended through the cooperative efforts of farm villages. A steady expansion in productivity, together with regional specialization keyed to market demands, enabled the majority of peasants to sustain a rising standard of living in spite of tax increases during the eighteenth century. But while agriculture enjoyed a flourishing condition, its rewards were not evenly distributed. A trend away from large family combinations to smaller units that could be run more efficiently widened the spread between prosperous and indigent peasants, and there was an increase in tenantry as opposed to individual farm ownership. At the same time the emergence of a mobile class of wage earners stimulated growth of village industries—processing silk, cotton, salt, tobacco, saké, and sugar cane—and provided a reserve labor force which eventually contributed to the rapid industrialization of Japan in the post-Tokugawa period.

During the Tokugawa era Japanese culture, being largely cut off from outside contacts, acquired a distinctive national character. This is not negated by the fact that intellectual circles manifested a heightened interest in Chinese philosophy. A number of Chinese scholars had fled to Japan when the Ming Dynasty was overthrown by the Manchus and, more importantly, the Shoguns encouraged study of the Confucian classics, particularly among the aristocracy, because they thought it would help to inculcate habits of discipline in their subjects. These writings, of course, had long been honored in Japan, but now they were diligently examined for the purpose of developing a native school of philosophers who, through their example and through their position as administrators, could inculcate the principles of virtue—especially obedience—among all classes of the population.

The most significant social and cultural changes were those related to the growth of large cities, such as Edo, Osaka, and Kyoto, where men of wealth were creating an atmosphere of comfort and gaiety in contrast to the restrained decorum of the feudal nobility. In these populous commercial and industrial centers the trend in art and literature and especially in the field of entertainment was toward a distinctly middle-class culture, which was sometimes gaudy but appealing in its exuberance and spontaneity. In the pleasure quarters of the cities an important figure was the geisha girl, who combined the qualities of a modern beauty queen with the talents of a nightclub entertainer. Trained in the art of conversation as well as in song and dance, she provided the sparkling companionship which men too often missed in their own homes because of the habits of docility and self-effacement that they instilled into their wives and daughters. Prostitution, also, was prevalent on a large scale in the towns, in spite of attempts by the authorities to curtail the evil. Inherently sordid as was the practice, it took on a specious refinement under the patronage of the well-do-do, and some courtesans acquired an enviable standing in the loose but highly sophisticated society which flouted established conventions. Not only merchants and businessmen but even samurai and daimyo were attracted by the gay diversions of city life, and surreptitiously exchanged the boredom of their routine existence for the delights of

The Art of Tile Making. A wood block by Hokusai (1760–1849), an artist famous for landscapes.

Woman Playing the Flute. The flutist is by Harunobu (1724–1770), earliest master of the multicolored-print technique.

a "floating world" of pleasure and uninhibited self-expression.

The dissolute society of the Tokugawa cities was by no means utterly degenerate. Some of the best creative talents in Japan catered to bourgeois appetites, just as they did in Italy during the Renaissance. Racy novels, satirizing contemporary figures and piquant with gossip, innuendo, and scandal, came into vogue. Previously art had been chiefly aristocratic and religious except for the exquisitely designed articles of ordinary household use produced by the various handicrafts. Now a type of folk art was appearing that mirrored society realistically and also was enlivened with humor and caricature. Its chief medium was the wood-block color print, which could be produced cheaply enough to reach a wide public and which has ever since been a popular art form. Another proof of the influence that urban tastes were exerting in the aesthetic sphere is seen in the evolution of the Kabuki drama. In contrast to the No, the highly stylized and austere dance-drama that had been perfected a few centuries earlier under the patronage of the aristocracy, the Kabuki offered entertainment appealing to the middle and lower classes of the towns. Although it owed something to traditional dance forms, the Kabuki drama was derived more immediately from the puppet theater and, unlike the No, it was almost entirely secular in spirit. As developed in the seventeenth and eighteenth centuries, the Kabuki drama attained a high degree of realism, with exciting plots, lively action, and effective stage devices. In the opinion of some theatrical experts, it deserves to rank as the greatest drama any civilization has ever produced.

Various forces at work in Japan tended to undermine the foundations of Tokugawa institutions in spite of their apparent durability. The partial transformation of Japan's economy from an agrarian to a mercantile basis enhanced the importance of men engaged in manufacture, trade, and transport. As a result feudalism was rendered obsolete, and the feudal classes began to feel the pinch of adversity. Although money had been in circulation for many centuries, the incomes of daimyo and of their samurai retainers were still computed in measures of rice, the chief agricultural staple. The merchants who provisioned such great cities as Edo and Osaka controlled the marketing of a large proportion of the rice crop; hence they were able to foresee fluctuations in price and sometimes even to induce fluctuations for their own benefit. Naturally, the daimyo and samurai were at a disadvantage in a period of unstable prices, because their incomes were from land rents, and because their necessities were increasingly supplied by articles that had to be purchased in the cities. Often the price of rice was considerably below the general price level; and even when it was high, the middleman appropriated most of the profit. The landed aristocrats found their real incomes diminishing while low-born traders and brokers grew richer and richer.

Inevitably, class lines began to break down, just as they did in west-

Economic changes

Kabuki Theater. Left: Famous actor Mitsugoro Bando portraying the aged warrior Ikyu in the play *Sukeroku*. Right: Kabuki actor (Matsumoto Koshiro) portrayed here as a fishmonger by Sharaku, a wood-block artist noted for his caricatures of actors (1794 or 1795).

The disruption of classes

*Cultural trends generate
unrest*

*Contributions of the
Tokugawa period*

ern Europe under similar conditions during the period of the Commercial Revolution. Wealthy Japanese merchants purchased samurai rank and title, while nobles adopted children of bourgeois families or contracted marriage alliances with this class in an effort to recoup their fortunes. Feeling honor-bound to maintain their accustomed style of living—at least in appearances—the aristocrats borrowed recklessly. As early as 1700 the indebtedness of the daimyo class was reputed to have reached a figure one hundred times greater than the total amount of money in Japan. Impoverished samurai pawned their ceremonial robes and even the swords which were their badge of rank. While townspeople in large numbers were entering the lower grades of samurai, samurai and farmers were flocking to the towns, where the more successful ones merged into the bourgeois class.

The unrest generated by economic dislocation was further augmented by cultural trends in the later Tokugawa period. As a national spirit developed, it was accompanied by a renewal of interest in Japan's past. Shintoism, the ancient cult over which the imperial family presided, had been largely eclipsed by Buddhism. Gradually its popularity revived, and several new Shinto sects obtained an enthusiastic following. The study of ancient records (historical and mythological) stimulated reflection on the unique character of Japan—"founded by a heavenly ancestry, country of the gods"—and on the alleged origins of the imperial office. It directed attention to the fact that the Shogunate was a comparatively recent innovation or actually a usurpation, not an authentic part of the ancient political structure. At the same time, familiarity with China's political heritage—fostered by the vogue of Confucian scholarship which the Shoguns themselves had promoted—raised doubts among Japanese intellectuals as to the merits of a dual administrative system and of feudal institutions. Moreover, Western books and ideas were seeping into Japan through the port of Nagasaki where the Dutch were permitted a very limited trade. Even before Japan was "opened" in the nineteenth century, considerable interest had been aroused in Western guns, ships, watches, glassware, and scientific instruments. Thus Japan's insulation from the outside world was beginning to develop cracks at the same time that internal discontent had reached a dangerous point. By the opening of the nineteenth century the Shogun's position was precarious, unlikely to withstand the shock of a severe crisis, especially since other powerful families were eagerly watching for any sign of weakness on the part of the Tokugawa.

The sweeping and revolutionary changes in Japan since the abolition of the Shogunate in 1867 have made it difficult to view the Tokugawa period with an undistorted perspective. Inward-looking, conservative, and devoted to hierarchy as it was, the Tokugawa regime went far toward unifying the nation, instilled habits of discipline, and provided a long period of security. Class structure was not so rigid as to prevent the realization of a fairly homogeneous society, especially as urban centers grew and communication improved. Education advanced significantly; by the end of the Tokugawa period about 45 percent of the male population was literate (only 15 percent of the female), a record unmatched in the rest of Asia and better than that of many countries today. Although Japan was still a predominantly agrarian society, capital techniques had been developed and applied to agriculture as well as to commerce and manufacture. Seemingly, although certainly unintentionally, the Tokugawa Shoguns had laid the foundation for Japan's transformation into a modern state.

Recently a group of Japanese historians—disillusioned with the effects of modernization and proponents of what they call "people's history"—have depicted the Tokugawa period as a kind of golden age. They claim that it contained the seeds of a freer society and even of democracy, evidenced by the growth of village cooperatives which stimulated social initiative and active participation among the peasants. They indict the imperial restoration as a "failed vision," a regretable step toward state worship, and they argue that the Tokugawa era could have provided the base for a structure different from and better than a duplication of Western industrialized society.[2]

4. AFRICA UNDER DIVINE RULERS AND RITUAL CHIEFS

The period 1500 to 1800 marked the beginning of Africa's incorporation into the capitalist world economy. From about 1500, western Europe transformed Africa into a satellite of its own burgeoning capitalistic system. The network of international trade established by the Arabs by the thirteenth century was seized and extended by the Europeans from the opening of the sixteenth century. This maritime contact ended Africa's long isolation from the West and brought all coasts of the continent into the European commercial orbit.

This period also witnessed the arrival of European traders and adventurers on Africa's sub-Saharan shores. A revolution in maritime and military technology enabled Europeans to navigate beyond sight of land and to conduct an efficient ocean-borne trade with swift, well-armed ships. For West Africans this provided an opportunity to expand their trade from their ancient North African markets across the Sahara to western Europe and the Americas via the Atlantic. A voluminous and highly profitable Atlantic traffic ensued with explosive force and required a concentration of territorial power in the hands of a few rulers. Instability generated by the introduction of arms trafficking and slave raiding forced weaker communities either to coalesce in self-defense or to seek the protection of larger, better organized societies

An unconventional interpretation

Africa as Europe's economic satellite

European presence on the coast forces a reorientation of trade

[2] Carol Gluck, "The People in History: Recent Trends in Japanese Historiography," *Journal of Asian Studies,* November 1978, pp. 25–50.

Long-standing trade networks

in neighboring areas. First coastal kingdoms, then empires, emerged in the tall forests after the 1650s in response to increasing opportunities for trade in guns, gunpowder, and exotic luxury items.

Long-distance trading networks across the Sahara, along the coasts, and through major river valleys flourished long before European contact. Canoemen traveled between the Niger Delta and the Ivory Coast and between the Gold Coast and Central Africa's Congo estuary. Small, independent fishing communities had dotted the palm-studded West and Central African coasts at least since 1300 and much earlier in East

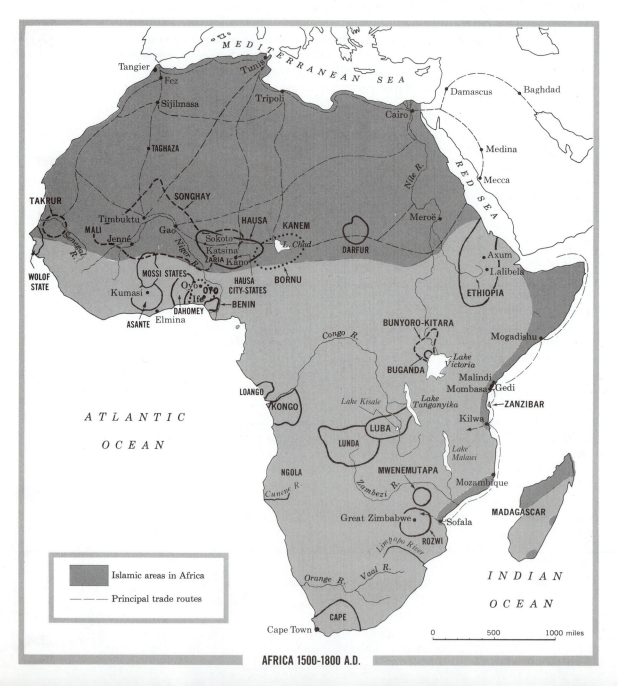

AFRICA 1500-1800 A.D.

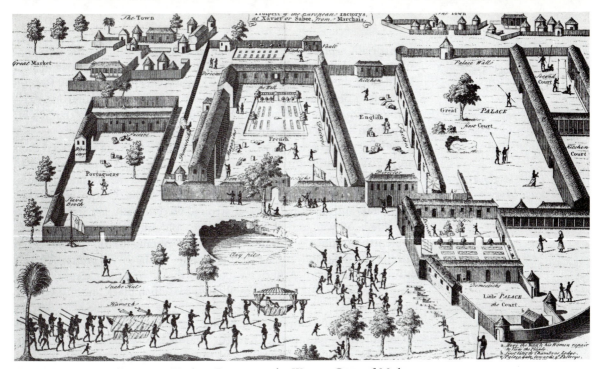

An Early Seventeenth-Century Trading Outpost on the Western Coast of Modern Nigeria. African rulers as well as Europeans actively participated in slaving and other commercial operations. They usually tried to restrict European trading activities in order to limit the European influence and to monopolize the trading relationship. Moving from left to right, note the presence of Portuguese, French, and English compounds abutting the grounds of the royal palace.

Africa. Fisherfolk exchanged ocean salt and dried fish with forest farmers for yams, goats, and cattle. For centuries, peoples of the Loango coast between the Congo river estuary and the Gabon forests produced for export fine raffia textiles, salt, and copper. By the twelfth century, cotton textiles produced in West Africa in the Hausa city-state of Kano found ready markets in Italy.

After 1500, some local industries like fishing and brewing were weakened when communities turned to less expensive European substitutes. Ultimately, European traders fostered economic rivalries and precipitated civil wars between African communities to prevent indigenous traders and chiefs from uniting. Such unity could inflate prices and weaken the European trade advantage. Nevertheless, on an individual basis, African traders sometimes proved superior to Europeans in the art of bargaining.

Impact of the European presence on trade networks

Between about 1730 and 1800 the less accessible interior states sought to extend their authority to the sea in order to trade directly with the Europeans. Seldom, however, were foreign traders permitted to operate beyond the coast. In Benin, Dahomey, and Oyo they were restricted to designated seaports and could only lease the land upon which they constructed their warehouses, fortresses, and slave markets. Some states, like Lunda, Luba, Oyo, Benin, and Asante, prospered and became

European traders restricted to the coast

Royal Dignitary. Bronze plaque
fragment. Bini tribe, Benin.

territorial empires. Others, particularly Kongo, Ngola, and Mwene-mutapa, failed to keep the Europeans at arm's length or to comprehend fully their true motives. Their history was punctuated by foreign intrigue, political instability, and eventual collapse. Numerous African governments became so dependent on European trade that a shift in pattern spelled economic doom.

During this era, kings, claiming divine attributes, aggrandized their authority through military force. Often, neighbors were reduced to tributary status. Royal subordinates, dispatched to the conquered areas, guarded against conspiracies and assimilated the vanquished. Folkways and authority patterns, if strong, were usually left intact, while prisoners of war and dissidents were sold into slavery in order to replenish supplies of gunpowder and to obtain luxury imports that might enhance the prestige and grandeur of the royal court. Africa's human losses were America's gains in this vicious circle initiated by amoral white traffickers and facilitated by selfish black and mixed-race collaborators.

Like the divine emperors of Japan, the Obas of Benin, Asantehenes of Asante, Manikongos of Kongo, Alafins of Oyo, and other African monarchs shrouded themselves in mystery and appeared only on ceremonial occasions. Much of their time was devoted to state rituals and sacrifices to ancestral heroes. They evolved rigid codes of court etiquette and communicated with commoners only through intermediaries. Some wore finely crafted, oversized sandals to shield their feet from direct contact with the sacred earth. All of them fostered a hieratic art, aimed as exalting the sanctity of the state. To achieve this, guild artists were supported by the monarchy and forced to remain within the palace confines so that their talents would not pass to others.

These kings, their paramount chiefs, and lesser titled hereditary officials devised ingenious systems of checks and balances to prevent a concentration of power in any single office. In the Oyo empire (in western Nigeria) the Alafin served as hereditary secular leader. Yet his power had to be shared with a royally appointed nobility, which organized itself into a kind of electoral college and administrative watchdog called the Oyo *Mesi*. Its leading member, the *Bashorun*, acted as prime minister and as spokesman for most of the powerful national cults or religious orders. As a counterforce to the Oyo *Mesi*, the Alafin appointed trusted slaves, called *Ilari*. They were responsible for collecting tribute and overseeing local government. At the same time, every important town was headed by a hereditary mayor or *Oba*. Though the *Oba*'s authority derived from ancestral mandate and tradition, his powers were limited by the Ogboni Society. This organization of influential and prosperous townsfolk linked the masses of peasants, traders, and artisans to royal authority. Everyone in the Oyo empire, from the Alafin down to the poorest peasant, swore allegiance to the Oni of Ifé. Ifé was the founding city-state of the Oyo empire, the fount of Yoruba civilization; and the ancient office of Oni served as the supreme authority over spiritual matters. Power was therefore diffused throughout society. From at least the fifteenth to the late eighteenth century, the Yoruba peoples of Oyo were well served by their unwritten constitution.

In the 1790s, the authority and prestige of the Alafin's office, so vital to national solidarity, was severely diminished when its holder challenged the spiritual supremacy of the Oni of Ifé. The time-honored rules of the game eroded further when the *Bashorun,* or prime minister, tested his own strength against the Alafin's. Preoccupation with such power struggles weakened central authority and enabled the tributary states to secede. Civil war erupted, and in the mid-nineteenth century the crumbling empire fell prey to European intrigue from the south and Muslim Fulani challenges from the north.

*Weakening of the central
authority*

Even though the Oyo empire disintegrated, its artistic and musical traditions continued to thrive. In both Oyo and neighboring Benin, guilds of Yoruba craftsmen turned out a rich variety of sculpture in brass, bronze, ivory, and wood. Metal commemorative busts and plaques, some antedating European contact by centuries, were delicate, strikingly naturalistic, and secular in intent. Companies of professional acrobats, dancers, and musicians traveled about the countryside giving performances which were sometimes critical of government practices, royal behavior, and social convention. In many ways, their programs were like an editorial column of a modern newspaper.

Belt Mask. Ivory. Bini Tribe. Benin.

Many forest states could boast of magnificent capital cities, holding sprawling palaces and temples with sunken atriums surrounded by columns. Benin City was one of the world's few urban centers to be laid out on a gridiron pattern, with broad tree-lined avenues intersecting streets at near right angles. Kumasi, the capital of Asante, was described by foreigners as Africa's garden city because of its lush flowering undergrowth set against tidy compounds with multicolored stylized façades. Slave populations tended to be concentrated around the capital cities. By 1800, slave-worked estates ringed many capitals and provided cheap food for the armies and for the urban dwellers. It was an ethnic and social apartheid, with some workers suffering varying degrees of bondage.

Capital cities

Islam experienced a revival after 1725 in the open, fertile grasslands of West Africa. Jihads, or holy wars, were declared by Muslim intellectuals and led to the establishment of numerous, mainly Fulani-led theocratic states. Islam continued to be both a factor of religious and social division and an engine of political and cultural change. The revival culminated in 1804–1810 with the Fulani conquest and consolidation of northern Nigeria's walled Hausa city-states into the sprawling caliphates of Sokoto and Gwandu. Hausa culture endured, and the Hausa language became a trade lingua franca in the major interior market towns of West Africa.

Islamic revival

It is significant that most West African forest civilizations had emerged, and in some cases reached their zenith, before European involvement. The Obaship in Benin was well established before Portuguese explorers arrived at Benin's major seaport of Gwato in 1472. Likewise, the Manikongo of Kongo ruled over an expansive domain with almost unchallenged authority before Portuguese contact a decade later. And Ifé was already recognized by the Yoruba as their major religious and cultural center.

Many African leaders received the Portuguese initially with great enthusiasm, hoping to taste the fruits of new techniques in agriculture, industry, and warfare. Before 1505 Benin and Kongo dispatched ambassadors and young intellectuals to Lisbon and the Vatican. But when America's vast resources were discovered by European explorers, it became obvious that the wealth could best be exploited by cheap labor in massive quantities. Only nearby Africa seemed to possess that necessary commodity. Thus, after about 1505, traders, missionaries, and other European visitors to Africa had different intentions from their predecessors. They came not as skilled technicians but as "advisers" who would gradually infiltrate African governments in order to better organize them for the slave trade. Thus, even though the political unification of Portugal and Spain in 1580 sacrificed African involvement to other interests, it in no way spelled an end to the Atlantic trade in humans.

Afro-European relations poisoned by the demands of the slave trade

Portuguese initiative in nautical science had already passed to the English, Dutch, and French—all of whom had begun to establish their own colonies of exploitation and settlement in the New World. Between 1637 and 1642 the Portuguese lost almost all their enclaves in West Africa to the Dutch. The Hollanders, unable to buy enough slaves on the West African coast, soon looked to the Ngola kingdom farther south. Only there did the Portuguese mount a successful resistance.

Demoralizing effects of the slave and arms trade

In the course of the seventeenth century, royally chartered companies from many European states formed monopoly enterprises and constructed warehouses and strings of stone fortresses along the West African coast. In 1672 the Royal African Company received a charter from the English crown and soon became the most active buyer of West African gold and slaves. Still, fierce competition with the Dutch in arms and munitions sales to Africans quickly led to a proliferation of deadly weapons among certain forest societies. To many African chiefs, slave raiding and trading became a painful necessity. If they refused to engage in it, the Europeans would supply arms to rivals who might in turn use them to sell their people into captivity. Dahomey and the Kongo, initially opposed to the slave trade, soon found it necessary either to play the European game or face possible economic and political ruin. Benin was one of the few African states that successfully controlled slave trading. It remained an independent political entity until the British invasion of 1897.

A number of small states were born in the seventeenth century in the Akan forest behind the Gold Coast. They were known to have supplied by that time more than 20 percent of Europe's gold reserves. Under the stimulus of the Royal African Company, this trade increased and led in the late seventeenth century to the rise of the Asante empire. The Akan peoples of Asante grew extremely powerful and wealthy by taxing trade passing through their territory en route to the coast. Between 1721 and 1750 Asante civilization reached its zenith. Asante artisans crafted earrings, anklets, pendants, and armbands from gold and bronze. On horizontal looms they wove polychromed togas of varied designs. Each pattern had a name and conveyed a symbolic meaning.

Asante civilization

The slave trade reached monumental proportions. If the relative paucity of thorough ships' records promises to keep historians from ever knowing exactly how many Africans were sold into slavery and shipped overseas, the evidence does permit educated estimates. Most scholars agree that between 1500 and 1800 nearly 11 million Africans were involuntarily exported: 7.8 million embarked on the Atlantic passage destined mainly for Brazil and the Caribbean. Another 3 million left Africa on routes across the Sahara, Red Sea, and Indian Ocean. But this was only a fraction of the total enslaved. Many served in African states, and others died defending themselves or en route to markets.

Dimensions of the slave trade

The Atlantic slave trade received a great boost after 1713 when England secured the Spanish *Asiento,* or license, to supply slaves to Spanish New World possessions. In response, the Yoruba state of Oyo expanded into a territorial empire, serving as middleman in the slave trade between the Hausaland interior and the coast. Other states exhibited a similar pattern. Immediately west of Oyo appeared the highly centralized kingdom of Dahomey. Between 1724 and 1729 Dahomey swept into the coastal Aja states and assimilated them. Unable to foster other sorts of trade with the Europeans, the Dahomeans became both suppliers and brokers in the slave trade. Oyo, fearful of this competition, diverted traffic to its own ports in 1750. To survive the consequent economic dislocation, the Dahomean government developed a state-controlled totalitarian economic and political system unparalleled in the eighteenth century. All state officials were appointed by the king, who ruled as a dictator, and a secret police was established to enforce his will. No system of checks and balances existed; only precedent and ancestral sanction guided his rule. Acting as high priest, the king dominated the major cults. He also controlled the craft guilds which produced pictorial tapestries and graceful statues to glorify royal power. A national military draft of men and women was instituted as well as a census bureau to administer it. Slave-worked plantations were established and placed under the close supervision of a minister of agriculture. Dahomey's economy was tightly regulated with central control over taxation and currency. Prices and wages, on the other hand, were set by producers' organizations. Culturally, westernization was actively discouraged by recourse to an aggressive policy of

Dahomey: example of extreme centralization

conquest and enforced assimilation into the traditional Fon way of life. Dahomey outlived the destructive effects of the slave trade and was able to safeguard its dynamic cultural institutions until French guns disrupted them in 1894.

*Kongo and Ngola become
major sources for slaves
and fail to survive
European intrusions*

Kongo and Ngola, in the savannah zone of west Central Africa, did not fare as well. After 1482 the Kongolese monarch, anxious to learn the secrets of European technology, assumed a Christian name and converted to Catholicism. But within two decades, Catholic missionaries had driven a wedge between the king and the nobility, who wished to follow the time-honored indigenous traditions. In 1556 rivalries among Portuguese advisers in the Kongo and Ngola dragged these two kingdoms into a destructive war against each other. Ngola won, but the real beneficiaries were European and mulatto slavers who reaped huge profits selling the war prisoners and refugees. Escalating demands for miners in Portuguese Brazil finally led to the total destruction of Kongo and Ngola (called Angola by the Portuguese) in 1665 and 1671 respectively. Their governments collapsed, although the Kongolese tradition of fine raffia cloth weaving remained vigorous.

*New kingdoms deeper in
the heart of central Africa*

Queen Nzinga, the former Angolan monarch, laid the foundations for a new kingdom, called Matamba, deeper in the interior. From the 1660s, Matamba became an important commercial state in Central Africa and a major broker in the growing international slave trade. Slave trading persisted and resulted in a further moral and ethical deterioration among certain segments of the population. Other African kingdoms, Lunda and Luba, arose deep in the interior, safely beyond direct Portuguese interference. Some of these highly centralized kingdoms survived into the twentieth century, but only to lose their independence to a new wave of Europeans, in search not of slaves but of copper.

*The Portuguese reaction to
Swahili civilization*

Portuguese involvement on the East African coast was equally destructive, even though it had little to do with the slave trade. In 1498 Vasco Da Gama rounded the Cape and sailed northward along the Swahili coast in search of the East Indies. He was astounded to discover a series of prosperous and highly civilized city-states with strong commercial and cultural links to Arabia, the Persian Gulf, and India. But it was distressing to him that their Sultans were fervent practitioners of Islam. It is no wonder that Da Gama had battles in three of the four city-states he visited. At Malindi his reception was cordial, only because Da Gama had sacked Malindi's commercial rival, Mombasa.

*Swahili city-states as
Portuguese tributaries*

The Portuguese were impressed by the gold and copper flowing out of Central Africa and by the extensive Indian Ocean trading network which carried the ore to distant ports. They hoped to use the Swahili city-states as a springboard to the Indies and as a source of gold for financing commercial operations in India and the Spice Islands. By 1505, after several Portuguese voyages of plunder and bombardment, the city-states were reduced to tributary status.

Portuguese in East Africa. Fort Jesus was built in 1593 at Mombasa by the Portuguese. It served as their major foothold in East Africa until 1728, when they were driven out under a combined Afro-Arab siege.

The Portuguese did not intend to govern the Swahili city-states. Rather, they attempted, with only limited success, to monopolize the Indian Ocean trade through their Viceroy at Goa on the western coast of India. After troubles with Turkish pirates and pillaging Zimba tribesmen, the Portuguese in 1593 constructed a massive stone citadel, called Fort Jesus, at Mombasa, and the malleable Sultan of Malindi was appointed to govern on their behalf. In 1622 the Portuguese were driven out of Ormuz, their strategic stronghold in the Persian Gulf, by a powerful Persian fleet. The fragility of Portuguese rule soon became evident to others. From the 1630s they had to suppress costly revolts in numerous Swahili towns. After Muscat, the gateway to the Persian Gulf, fell in 1650, the Omani Arabs emerged as a formidable naval power. In 1698 they drove the Portuguese out of Mombasa, their major port of call en route to India, and the Portuguese supremacy north of Mozambique crumbled like a house of cards. In its wake lay the ruins of a once magnificent Swahili civilization. The Omani came to East Africa as liberators, but stayed on as conquerors, practicing a kind of benign neglect which led to further cultural and economic deterioration.

Fragility of Portuguese rule

The Portuguese also failed in their attempts to control the gold and copper mines of the Zimbabwean and Katangan plateaus. After one hundred eighty years of interference in the political and religious institutions of the Mwenemutapa empire, they were forced to retreat to the Mozambique coast. Their traders and soldiers were simply no match against the more determined and better organized Shona armies. African resistance was clearly stronger than the Portuguese will to conquer. In 1798 the Portuguese attempted to link their colony in Angola with Mozambique in the hope of forging a transcontinental African empire. But malaria and the unwillingness of the crown to administer such a vast area were responsible for its failure.

Portuguese repelled

Islam in East Africa. Mombasa Mosque with minaret. Sixteenth century.

Segregation and domination in the Cape colony

History took another, more tragic, course in the extreme southwest corner of Africa. In 1652, the Netherlands East India Company established a replenishment station at the Cape's Table Bay for ships passing between western Europe and the Orient. It rapidly grew into a company-governed colony of white settlement, centered on the fort in Cape Town harbor. Almost from the start the company, anxious to avoid interracial clashes, passed decrees segregating the whites from the indigenous Khoikhoi herders. Over the next half century, the European settlers displaced and subjugated the Khoikhoi and the San, an indigenous population of Stone Age hunters and gatherers. The Khoikhoi were gradually reduced from independent cattlemen to indigent clients of the ever-expanding white stock farmers. This source of cheap labor helped to alleviate the colony's chronic shortage of manpower. By 1715, the once-proud Khoikhoi had lost nearly all their cattle and lands and had been decimated by European diseases like smallpox for which they had no natural immunity. The more primitive San were hunted down like wild game and driven into the arid north, but only after fierce guerrilla wars of resistance. By 1750 the San had been dispersed, and the Khoikhoi, literally "men of men," and their civilization had disintegrated. Khoikhoi remnants merged with Bantu-speaking slaves imported from other regions of Africa and poor whites to form a new, mixed-race population called Cape Coloreds. Though emulating European ways and adopting the evolving Afrikaans language, they were brutally discriminated against. At the same time, they refused to become part of indigenous black society, perceiving it as too primitive.

From the beginning, slave-owning became a widespread and deeply entrenched feature of Cape society. By 1800, the approximately 20,000 white settlers were outnumbered by their slaves, whom they tried to keep in tow through laws limiting their movement, employment, and ability to organize.

The company failed to control the white diaspora, and the frontier moved steadily eastward. In about 1770, the rigidly Calvinistic trek-boers, isolated from the European Enlightenment's liberal and humanitarian traditions, came up against a far more formidable competitor—the Iron-Age Bantu speakers. They, too, valued cattle and sought new pastures. But, unlike the Khoi and San, they were more socially cohesive, better organized governmentally, and greatly outnumbered the whites.

Almost immediately, Bantu-Boer relations were marked by mutual suspicion and distrust, which quickly evolved into bitterness, fear, and hate as acts of violence escalated over the struggle for land and cattle. As in the past, company efforts at racial segregation in hopes of limiting costly frontier wars failed. Some forms of frontier interracial cooperation evolved, based on mutual interests. But conflict was more common and pervasive.

Cosmopolitan Cape Town had become an internationally strategic harbor in the southern Atlantic, and in 1795 the British occupied it for fear of the French in the Napoleonic Wars. The near-bankrupt company, weakened by rebellious and independent-minded colonists, did not resist. Between 1806 and 1833 the British sought, with only limited success, to impose an Anglo-Saxon inspired color-blind legal and

Slavery in Cape society

Boer expansion and Bantu speakers

Bantu-Boer relations

British occupation of Cape Town

The Dutch Colony of Cape Town on the Cape of Good Hope as It Appeared in a 1762 Drawing by J. Rach

social system on a predominantly Dutch Cape society that saw race as a key indicator of social and political status.

Viewing the collective sub-Saharan experience, African trade with the Europeans was a mixed blessing. The exchange of guns, powder, cheap manufactured textiles, and nondurable consumer goods such as alcoholic beverages for gold, ivory, pepper, and palm oil accelerated the trend in some areas toward centralization of authority and the growth of territorially based states. Certain families monopolized the trade and enriched themselves at the expense of the broad masses. Lineage structures in the areas subjected to slave raids were severely weakened socially, economically, and materially. Yet the south Atlantic trade system also led to the introduction into Africa of new food crops, including plantain from Asia, cassava from Brazil, sweet potatoes, pineapples, peanuts, and guava from other areas of the Americas, and corn from Brazil via Spain and Egypt. Increased long-distance trade also led to the wider dispersion of existing crops, such as East African coconut trees into West Africa. Thus, African diets improved, and the crops enabled societies blessed with fertile soils and reliable water supplies to sustain much higher population densities. This in turn contributed to the tendency to state creation and expansion. However, it also accelerated the process of deforestation and soil erosion. The Great Drought of 1738–1756 caused a massive decline in food output, malnutrition, and in some areas self-enslavement to avoid death from starvation.

Unlike Japan, Africa's real economic growth was slowed by the exploitative, nonproductive nature of the European trade. Europeans exported items which could not be used in the production of other goods. In West Africa, guns and gunpowder by the eighteenth century had become the most important foreign trade commodity. In the two centuries after 1600, at least 20 million guns were exported to sub-Saharan Africa. Between 1796 and 1805 more than 1.6 million guns were sent to West Africa from England alone. A strong connection developed between firearms and the acquisition of slaves. The weapons were used mainly for interethnic raids and wars connected with the gathering of people for the slave markets. Wars which created many slaves for the Atlantic markets were particularly stimulated by competition among Africans for control of trade routes to the coast. Some African ethnic groups sold slaves to obtain guns to ensure their own political survival against internal rivals. In other words, slave exports were sometimes the result of politically motivated warfare rather than of pure economic incentive.

African contact with the Euro-American capitalist system contributed to the evolution of state formation. However, in the long run it generated political instability, bred by struggles for power and status between the old elites and the emerging military and commercial entrepreneurs. The existing bases of political and social differentiation were challenged. Greater popular involvement in warfare and in the trade in gold, slaves, and forest agricultural products enabled clever and ambitious commoners to generate independent wealth. It bred a new "bourgeoisie" of African brokers, merchants, interpreters, and caravan operators. In Asante, Oyo, Dahomey, and elsewhere the traditional royal lineages were forced to alter the hereditary political structures by incorporating ability and meritocracy into them. The rulers who failed to accommodate themselves to the changing order were faced with destructive civil wars and chronic political instability which ultimately rendered them more susceptible to European imperialist conquest in the late nineteenth century.

Yet, in spite of these disruptive influences, these three centuries witnessed an explosion in artistic endeavor and output. New, more sophisticated aesthetic standards evolved in communities exposed to international trade. There was a richer diversity in styles and an improvement in techniques. European and Islamic trade injected new designs and motifs as well as greater quantities of material, particularly metals for castings and yarns for weaving. Social and religious cults and guild associations grew in number and membership and became powerful agencies for the maintenance of traditions and for the adaptation and institutionalization of social and artistic change. Slave raiding and warfare triggered massive population migrations. This led to greater intercultural contact between refugees and indigenes and to the creation of a social climate in which people became more responsive to change and innovation.

Growth of artistic activity

This era saw the professionalization of craftspersons. In the past, most art was expressed through rock and body painting, stoneworking, and ceramics. But from the 1500s, there was dramatic growth in textile design and manufacturing, metal-casting, and mask and figurine wood sculpting. Nearly every large village could boast of guilds of weavers, cloth-dyers, spinners, and tailors. Increasing numbers of societies shifted from woven grass or bark-cloth waistbands to elaborate garments covering much more of the body. Also, greater use was made of cosmetics and scarification. Dress became a form of communication and a symbol of status and wealth.

*The professionalization of
the crafts*

In this period, males began to exert greater social and political control through their secret societies. They also played a preponderant role in the sculptural arts, even though art was employed by both sexes in their masked festivals. Women often dictated the forms, but most of the actual carving or casting was performed by men. Pottery-making, in most cultures, remained in women's hands, though weaving was done by both sexes. However, certain types of looms were reserved for men only.

Gender roles in the arts

Royal families in the centralized states became wealthy and commissioned artisans to fashion rings, pendants, bracelets, and hairpins from gold, copper, ivory, and exotic woods. Impressive mud or reed palaces were constructed with galleries and courtyards adorned with polychromed woven, batik, or tied-and-dyed tapestries. Basic ideals

Artistic advances

Stool with Caryatid. Wood.
Luba, Congo.

of beauty were expressed through distinct symbols stamped onto cloth, molded in high relief on the façades of buildings, or shaped into fine wood or metal sculpture. Forms such as the circle, rectangle, oval, and square were brilliantly translated into artistic symbols and given deep philosophical and religious meaning. And complex notions of God and the universe were expressed in the verbal symbolism of proverbs and epic poems or in the intricate designs of royal thrones, scepters, swords, and craftsmen's tools. Over the course of these three centuries, the forest civilizations, with their unlimited supplies of timber, used a wide variety of wood as the primary art medium for sculpturing. They achieved a brilliant artistic synthesis of surrealist and expressionist, abstract and naturalistic elements. The cubist tradition itself was born not in western Europe in the early twentieth century but among artistic circles in the West African forest societies centuries before. Although Europeans robbed Africans of much of their physical and human resources, they did not succeed in weakening their artistic vitality. Indeed, the trauma of European contact seemed to propel Africans toward even greater cultural achievements.

Patterns of traditional African religion and thought also proved to be remarkably durable. Although Africans were intensely spiritual and thoughtful, no single "African" religion or philosophy evolved on a continental scale, such as we found with "Chinese" philosophy or in Hindu religion on the Indian subcontinent. Beyond Coptic Christian Ethiopia, there were no texts or written discourses of speculative and/or conceptual thought. Nevertheless, each culture possessed a collective wisdom, a set of principles or beliefs, with varying degrees of coherence, that governed human behavior. There was a considerable divergence in notions of good and evil, and in perceptions of physical and natural beauty. Different societies held to distinct moral and ethical

Reconstruction of a Kabaka's Reed Palace in Kampala, Uganda. These structures, once common to Buganda royalty, have disappeared.

African Craftsmen. Dye pits in Kano (northern Nigeria) were and still are owned by traditional craft guilds.

systems operating within their own ethos. For example, one culture might regard the birth of twins an evil omen, and the infants would be cast out. A few hundred miles away, another culture would see such an event as blessed and worthy of celebration.

Nearly all African cultures, however, shared a fundamental base for their belief systems. Over their panoplies of spirits and divinities presided a Supreme Being, a God that was viewed not as aloof but acting as an integral member of society. Africans saw the universe as a hierarchical and dialectic system of forces, each related to the other. God was the almighty creative force, the primordial artist. He was omnipresent, omnipotent, and omniscient, the ultimate judge and the great provider. Different cultures had different names for God: in Dahomey it was "Mawu," in Asante "Nyame." The Igbo called Him "Chuku." Most Africans believed that a person is born free of sin and with a benign soul that resides in the body. African societies, especially the Yoruba, placed enormous importance on achieving a dynamic harmony with God and the spirits. This was attempted through constant sacrifice, prayer, and divination. Diviners were mediums concerned with the moral order and with relations between man and the spiritual realms. Diviners were also in charge of oracles, and families consulted them on a child's birth to learn of the infant's destiny.

Everyone was believed to be in possession of a spiritual guardian who, if well served, would preserve and enhance one's life. By the sixteenth century, many African societies had assigned names to individuals. They were loaded with meaning and symbolism. For example, a common Yoruba name for boys was Olugunna, meaning "God straightens the path." The Yoruba shared the Asante belief that every-

The dominance of a Supreme Being in African religions

Belief in the individual's direct access to God

Life-size Ancestor Statues Guarding the Carved Entrance to an Important Chief's Audience Chamber in Cameroun. Ancestor veneration gave continuity to societies and enhanced the legitimacy of ruling dynasties.

one has a direct access to God, and this is expressed in the Asante maxim "No man's path crosses another's."

The veneration of ancestors

Most African cultures venerated their ancestors and looked to them for philosophical and spiritual guidance. The ancestors "owned" the land, shaped the behavioral patterns of their descendants, and provided a vital sense of continuity. To be cut off from the ancestors was, in essence, to be cut off from life itself. Some anthropologists believe that ancestor veneration stifled innovation and reform by placing taboos on thoughts or actions not attributable to societies' leading forebearers.

"Vital force"

"Essence" or "vital force" was a concept shared by many Bantu-speaking cultures. It presumed a hierarchy of forces, ranging downward from *muntu* (man, ancestors, God), *kintu* (things such as plants, animals, rocks); *hantu* (time, space), and *kuntu* (manner or modality). Every object, it was believed, possesses a certain amount of vital force. The problem is to release and then control it to one's benefit. For the Bantu and others, the earth was especially sacred. It was generally associated with the female dimension and was not to be touched by secular authorities. Thus, in many societies divine kings wore over-sized sandals so as to avoid direct contact with the earth.

Clearly, between 1500 and 1800, Islam and Christianity had made significant inroads on the continent. But in very few cultures did they succeed in destroying the fundamental tenets of traditional beliefs and rituals. By 1550, classical Christianity in North Africa, Nubia, and Egypt had practically disappeared as a result of internal theological discord and the commercial challenge of Islam. In Ethiopia it remained the almost exclusive preserve of royalty and the monastic clergy. European-inspired Christianity, mainly Catholicism, was associated with post-fifteenth-century trade in slaves and arms—not education and technology—and thus failed to become deeply rooted or African-ized in the Kongo, Angola, Benin, and Mwenemutapa. Islam, on the other hand, also failed to captivate the broad masses. It remained essentially an urban-based, market-oriented faith, practiced by mal-lams (Islamic scholars), merchants, and princes. Hinduism had even less success and seldom radiated beyond the Swahili city-states of the East African coast.

The limited appeal of Christianity, Islam, and Hinduism

SELECTED READINGS

- *Items so designated are available in paperback editions.*
- Binyon, Laurence, *The Spirit of Man in Asian Art*, New York, 1935.
- Nakamura, Hajime, *Ways of Thinking of Eastern Peoples: India, China, Tibet, Japan*, Honolulu, 1964.

INDIA: *See also Readings for Chapters 5, 11, and 16*

Archer, J. C., *The Sikhs*, Princeton, 1946.
- Cole, W. O., and P. S. Sambhi, *The Sihks: Their Religious Beliefs and Practices*, Boston, 1978. Based on recent scholarship.
Garratt, G. T., ed., *The Legacy of India*, Oxford, 1937.
Ikram, Mohamad, *Muslim Civilization in India*, ed. A. T. Embree, New York, 1964.
Kabir, Humayun, *The Indian Heritage*, New York, 1955.
Kulke, H., and D. Rothermund, *A History of India*, Totowa, N.J., 1986.
Moreland, W. H., and A. C. Chatterjee, *A Short History of India*, 4th ed., New York, 1957.
Prawdin, Michael, *The Builders of the Mogul Empire*, New York, 1965.
Rawlinson, H. G., *A Concise History of the Indian People*, 2d ed., New York, 1950.
- ———, *India, a Short Cultural History*, New York, 1952. An excellent interpretive study.
Smith, V. A., *Akbar the Great Mogul*, Oxford, 1917.
Spear, Percival, *India: A Modern History*, 2d ed., Ann Arbor, 1972. An excellent survey.
- ———, *The Oxford History of India, 1740–1975*, 2d ed., New York, 1979.
- Wolpert, Stanley, *A New History of India*, New York, 1977. An admirable survey, informative and well written.

CHINA: *See also Readings for Chapters 6, 11, and 16*

Blunden, C., and M. Elvin, *Cultural Atlas of China,* New York, 1983. One of the most valuable works on China available.

• Eberhard, Wolfram, *A History of China,* 4th ed., Berkeley, 1977.

• Elvin, Mark, *The Pattern of the Chinese Past,* Stanford, 1975.

• Fairbank, J. K., *The United States and China,* 4th ed., Cambridge, Mass., 1983.

Fairbank, J. K., E. O. Reischauer, and A. M. Craig, *East Asia: Tradition and Transformation,* rev. ed., Boston, 1978. A shortened edition of a major text.

• Fitzgerald, C. P., *China, a Short Cultural History,* 3d ed., New York, 1961. Unconventional in viewpoint.

Hucker, C. O., *China's Imperial Past: An Introduction to Chinese History and Culture,* Stanford, 1975. Remarkably clear, comprehensive, and readable.

• Hudson, G. F., *Europe and China: A Survey of Their Relations from the Earliest Times to 1800,* London, 1930.

• Moore, C. A., ed., *The Chinese Mina: Essentials of Chinese Philosophy and Culture,* Honolulu, 1967.

Ronan, C. A., ed., *The Shorter Science and Civilization in China,* I, New York, 1978, II, 1981. Abridgement of the first four volumes of a monumental study by Joseph Needham.

Rowbotham, A. H., *Missionary and Mandarin: The Jesuits at the Court of China,* Berkeley, 1942.

Scott, A. C., *The Classical Theater of China,* New York, 1957.

Shryock, J. K., *The Origin and Development of the State Cult of Confucius,* New York, 1932.

Sickman, L., and A. Soper, *The Art and Architecture of China,* Baltimore, 1956. Reliable, richly illustrated.

• Spence, Jonathan D., *Emperor of China: Self-Portrait of K'ang Hsi,* New York, 1975.

• _____, *The Memory Palace of Matteo Ricci,* New York, 1984. An elegant and evocative portrait of the late sixteenth and early seventeenth centuries.

_____, *The Search for Modern China,* New York, 1990.

• Sullivan, Michael, *A Short History of Chinese Art,* rev. ed., Berkeley, 1970.

Tuan Yi-fu, *China,* Chicago, 1970. An excellent cultural geography.

JAPAN: *See also Readings for Chapters 11 and 16*

Berry, Mary, *Hideyoshi,* Cambridge, Mass., 1982. A vivid and informative account.

• Brandon, J. R., W. P. Malm, and D. H. Shively, *Studies in Kabuki: Its Acting, Music, and Historical Context,* Honolulu, 1978.

Cole, Wendell, *Kyoto in the Momoyama Period,* Norman, Okla., 1967.

Dore, R. P., *Education in Tokugawa, Japan,* Berkeley, 1965.

• Duus, Peter, *Feudalism in Japan,* 2d ed. New York, 1975. A concise account of political developments through the nineteenth century.

Eliot, Charles, *Japanese Buddhism,* New York, 1959. A standard text.

Embree, J. F., *The Japanese Nation,* New York, 1945. A brilliant and well-balanced study by an anthropologist.

• Hall, J. W., *Japan: From Prehistory to Modern Times,* New York, 1971.

————, et al., *Japan before Tokugawa: Political Consolidation and Economic Growth, 1500–1650*, Princeton, 1981.

• Keene, Donald, *Japanese Literature: An Introduction for Western Readers*, New York, 1955.

• Moore, C. A., ed., *The Japanese Mind: Essentials of Japanese Philosophy and Culture*, Honolulu, 1967.

• Munsterberg, Hugo, *The Arts of Japan: An Illustrated History*, Rutland, Vt., 1957.

• Reischauer, E. O., *Japan: The Story of a Nation*, 5th ed., New York, 1974. Lucid and well organized.

Sadler, A. L., *The Maker of Modern Japan: The Life of Tokugawa Ieyasu*, London, 1937.

Sansom, G. B., *Japan, a Short Cultural History*, rev. ed., New York, 1952. A substantial but highly readable work by an eminent British scholar.

————, *The Western World and Japan*, New York, 1950.

• Smith, T. C., *The Agrarian Origins of Modern Japan*, Stanford, 1959

Toby, Ronald, *State and Diplomacy in Early Modern Japan: Asia in the Development of Tokugawa Bakufu*, Princeton, 1984.

• Warner, Langdon, *The Enduring Art of Japan*, Cambridge, Mass., 1952.

Yukio, Y., *Two Thousand Years of Japanese Art*, New York, 1958.

AFRICA: *See also Readings for Chapters 11 and 16*

Beach, David N., *The Shona and Zimbabwe 900–1850*, London, 1980.

Birmingham, David, and Phyllis M. Martin, eds., *History of Central Africa*, vol. 1, New York, 1983.

Blusse, L., and F. Gaastra, eds., *Companies and Trade: Essays on Overseas Trading Companies During the Ancien Régime*, Leiden, 1981. Examines the crucial role played by the great trading companies in opening new markets in the Asian and Atlantic worlds and as instruments of European expansion in the seventeenth and eighteenth centuries.

Curtin, Philip D., ed., *Horizon History of Africa*, New York, 1972.

• Davidson, Basil, *The African Genius*, Boston, 1969.

Egharevba, Jacob, *A Short History of Benin*, Ibadan, 1960.

Eltis, David, and James Walvin, eds., *The Abolition of the Atlantic Slave Trade: Origins and Effects in Europe, Africa and the Americas*, Madison, 1981.

Gailey, H. A., *History of Africa: From Earliest Times to 1800*, New York, 1970.

Gray, Richard, ed., *The Cambridge History of Africa*, Vol. 4: *c. 1600 to c. 1790*, Cambridge, 1975.

Hallett, Robin, *Africa to 1875*, Ann Arbor, 1970.

Hilton, Anne, *The Kingdom of Kongo*, Oxford, 1985.

Hull, Richard W., *Munyakare: African Civilization before the Batuuree*, New York, 1972.

Lovejoy, Paul E., *Transformations in Slavery*, Cambridge, 1983.

McLeod, M. D., *The Asante*, London, 1981.

Oliver, Roland, and Anthony Atmore, *The Middle Age in African History: 1400–1800*, New York, 1981.

Rawley, James A., *The Transatlantic Slave Trade*, New York, 1981.

Roberts, A., ed., *Tanzania before 1900*, Nairobi, 1968.

Smith, Robert S., *Kingdoms of the Yoruba*, London, 1969.

Vansina, Jan, *Kingdoms of the Savanna*, Madison, Wis., 1968.

India, East Asia, and Africa
During the Early-Modern Era
(c. 1500–1800)

Ade Ajayi, J. F., and Michael Crowder, eds., *Historical Atlas of Africa*, Cambridge, 1985

Davenport, T. R. H., and K. S. Hunt, eds., *The Right to the Land: Documents on Southern African History*, Capetown, 1974.

• de Bary, W. T., ed., *Sources of Chinese Tradition*, Chaps. XXII, XXIII, New York, 1960.

• ———, ed., *Sources of Indian Tradition*, "Islam in Medieval India"; "Sikhism," New York, 1958.

• ———, ed., *Sources of Japanese Tradition*, "The Tokugawa Period," New York, 1958.

Freeman-Grenville, G. S. P., ed., *The East African Coast: Select Documents from the First to the Early Nineteenth Century*, 2nd ed., London, 1975.

Gallagher, L. J. tr., *China in the Sixteenth Century. The Journals of Matthew Ricci: 1583–1610*, Milwaukee, 1942.

• Hibbett, Howard, *The Floating World in Japanese Fiction*, New York, 1959.

• Keene, Donald ed., *Anthology of Japanese Literature*, New York, 1960.

Lu, David, ed., *Sources of Japanese History*, Vol. 1, New York, 1973.

Markham, C. R., ed., *The Hawkins' Voyages*, London, 1878.

Oliver, Roland, ed., *The Middle Age of African History*, New York, 1967.

Smith, V. A., ed., *F. Bernier: Travels in the Mogul Empire* A.D. *1656–1668*, London, 1914.

Vansina, Jan, *Kingdoms of the Savanna*, Madison, Wis., 1966.

Wang, C. C., tr., *Dream of the Red Chamber*, New York, 1929.

Whiteley, W. H., compiler, *A Selection of African Prose: Traditional Oral Texts*, Oxford, 1964.

RULERS OF PRINCIPAL STATES SINCE 700 A.D.

The Carolingian Dynasty

Pepin, Mayor of the Palace, 714
Charles Martel, Mayor of the Palace, 715–741
Pepin I, Mayor of the Palace, 741; King, 751–768
Charlemagne, King, 768–814; Emperor, 800–814
Louis the Pious, Emperor, 814–840

West Francia

Charles the Bald, King, 840–877; Emperor, 875
Louis II, King, 877–879
Louis III, King, 879–882
Carloman, King, 879–884

Middle Kingdoms

Lothair, Emperor, 840–855
Louis (Italy), Emperor, 855–875
Charles (Provence), King, 855–863
Lothair II (Lorraine), King, 855–869

East Francia

Ludwig, King, 840–876
Carloman, King, 876–880
Ludwig, King, 876–882
Charles the Fat, Emperor, 876–887

Holy Roman Emperors

Saxon Dynasty

Otto I, 962–973
Otto II, 973–983
Otto III, 983–1002
Henry II, 1002–1024

Franconian Dynasty

Conrad II, 1024–1039
Henry III, 1039–1056
Henry IV, 1056–1106
Henry V, 1106–1125
Lothair II (of Saxony), King, 1125–1133; Emperor,
  1133–1137

Hohenstaufen Dynasty

Conrad III, 1138–1152
Frederick I (Barbarossa), 1152–1190
Henry VI, 1190–1197
Philip of Swabia, 1198–1208 ⎫
Otto IV (Welf), 1198–1215 ⎬ Rivals
Frederick II, 1220–1250
Conrad IV, 1250–1254

Interregnum, 1254–1273

Emperors from Various Dynasties
Rudolf I (Hapsburg), 1273–1291

Adolf (Nassau), 1292–1298
Albert I (Hapsburg), 1298–1308
Henry VII (Luxemburg), 1308–1313
Ludwig IV (Wittelsbach), 1314–1347
Charles IV (Luxemburg), 1347–1378
Wenceslas (Luxemburg), 1378–1400
Rupert (Wittelsbach), 1400–1410
Sigismund (Luxemburg), 1410–1437

Hapsburg Dynasty

Albert II, 1438–1439
Frederick III, 1440–1493
Maximilian I, 1493–1519
Charles V, 1519–1556
Ferdinand I, 1556–1564
Maximilian II, 1564–1576
Rudolf II, 1576–1612
Matthias, 1612–1619
Ferdinand II, 1619–1637
Ferdinand III, 1637–1657
Leopold I, 1658–1705
Joseph I, 1705–1711
Charles VI, 1711–1740
Charles VII (not a Hapsburg), 1742–1745
Francis I, 1745–1765
Joseph II, 1765–1790
Leopold II, 1790–1792
Francis II, 1792–1806

Rulers of France from Hugh Capet

Capetian Kings

Hugh Capet, 987–996
Robert II, 996–1031
Henry I, 1031–1060
Philip I, 1060–1108
Louis VI, 1108–1137
Louis VII, 1137–1180
Philip II (Augustus), 1180–1223
Louis VIII, 1223–1226
Louis IX, 1226–1270
Philip III, 1270–1285
Philip IV, 1285–1314
Louis X, 1314–1316
Philip V, 1316–1322
Charles IV, 1322–1328

House of Valois

Philip VI, 1328–1350
John, 1350–1364
Charles V, 1364–1380
Charles VI, 1380–1422
Charles VII, 1422–1461
Louis XI, 1461–1483
Charles VIII, 1483–1498
Louis XII, 1498–1515
Francis I, 1515–1547

Bourbon Dynasty

Henry IV, 1589–1610
Henry II, 1547–1559
Francis II, 1559–1560
Charles IX, 1560–1574
Henry III, 1574–1589

Louis XIII, 1610–1643
Louis XIV, 1643–1715
Louis XV, 1715–1774
Louis XVI, 1774–1792

After 1792

First Republic, 1792–1799
Napoleon Bonaparte, First Consul, 1799–1804
Napoleon I, Emperor, 1804–1814
Louis XVIII (Bourbon dynasty), 1814–1824
Charles X (Bourbon dynasty), 1824–1830
Louis Philippe, 1830–1848
Second Republic, 1848–1852
Napoleon III, Emperor, 1852–1870
Third Republic, 1870–1940
Pétain regime, 1940–1944
Provisional government, 1944–1946
Fourth Republic, 1946–1958
Fifth Republic, 1958–

Rulers of England

Anglo-Savon Kings

Egbert, 802–839
Ethelwulf, 839–858
Ethelbald, 858–860
Ethelbert, 860–866
Ethelred, 866–871
Alfred the Great, 871–900
Edward the Elder, 900–924
Ethelstan, 924–940
Edmund I, 940–946
Edred, 946–955
Edwy, 955–959
Edgar, 959–975
Edward the Martyr, 975–978
Ethelred the Unready, 978–1016
Canute, 1016–1035 (Danish Nationality)
Harold I, 1035–1040

Hardicanute, 1040–1042
Edward the Confessor, 1042–1066
Harold II, 1066

Anglo-Norman Kings

William I (the Conqueror), 1066–1087
William II, 1087–1100
Henry I, 1100–1135
Stephen, 1135–1154

Angevin Kings

Henry II, 1154–1189
Richard I, 1189–1199
John, 1199–1216
Henry III, 1216–1272
Edward I, 1272–1307
Edward II, 1307–1327

Edward III, 1327–1377
Richard II, 1377–1399

House of Lancaster

Henry IV, 1399–1413
Henry V, 1413–1422
Henry VI, 1422–1461

House of York

Edward IV, 1461–1483
Edward V, 1483
Richard III, 1483–1485

Tudor Sovereigns

Henry VII, 1485–1509
Henry VIII, 1509–1547
Edward VI, 1547–1553
Mary, 1553–1558
Elizabeth I, 1558–1603

Stuart Kings

James I, 1603–1625
Charles I, 1625–1649

Commonwealth and Protectorate, 1649–1659

Later Stuart Monarchs

Charles II, 1660–1685
James II, 1685–1688
William III and Mary II, 1689–1694
William III alone, 1694–1702
Anne, 1702–1714

House of Hanover

George I, 1714–1727
George II, 1727–1760
George III, 1760–1820
George IV, 1820–1830
William IV, 1830–1837
Victoria, 1837–1901

House of Saxe-Coburg-Gotha

Edward VII, 1901–1910
George V, 1910–1917

House of Windsor

George V, 1917–1936
Edward VIII, 1936
George VI, 1936–1952
Elizabeth II, 1952–

Prominent Popes

Silvester I, 314–335
Leo I, 440–461
Gelasius I, 492–496
Gregory I, 590–604
Nicholas I, 858–867
Silvester II, 999–1003
Leo IX, 1049–1054
Nicholas II, 1058–1061
Gregory VII, 1073–1085
Urban II, 1088–1099
Paschal II, 1099–1118
Alexander III, 1159–1181
Innocent III, 1198–1216
Gregory IX, 1227–1241
Boniface VIII, 1294–1303
John XXII, 1316–1334
Nicholas V, 1447–1455
Pius II, 1458–1464
Alexander VI, 1492–1503

Julius II, 1503–1513
Leo X, 1513–1521
Adrian VI, 1522–1523
Clement VII, 1523–1534
Paul III, 1534–1549
Paul IV, 1555–1559
Gregory XIII, 1572–1585
Gregory XVI, 1831–1846
Pius IX, 1846–1878
Leo XIII, 1878–1903
Pius X, 1903–1914
Benedict XV, 1914–1922
Pius XI, 1922–1939
Pius XII, 1939–1958
John XXIII, 1958–1963
Paul VI, 1963–1978
John Paul I, 1978
John Paul II, 1978–

Rulers of Austria and Austria-Hungary

*Maximilian I (Archduke), 1493–1519
*Charles I (Charles V in the Holy Roman Empire), 1519–1556
*Ferdinand I, 1556–1564
*Maximilian II, 1564–1576
*Rudolph II, 1576–1612
*Matthias, 1612–1619
*Ferdinand II, 1619–1637
*Ferdinand III, 1637–1657
*Leopold I, 1658–1705
*Joseph I, 1705–1711
*Charles VI, 1711–1740
Maria Theresa, 1740–1780

*Joseph II, 1780–1790
*Leopold II, 1790–1792
*Francis II, 1792–1835 (Emperor of Austria as Francis I after 1804)
Ferdinand I, 1835–1848
Francis Joseph, 1848–1916 (after 1867 Emperor of Austria and King of Hungary)
Charles I, 1916–1918 (Emperor of Austria and King of Hungary)
Republic of Austria, 1918–1938 (dictatorship after 1934)
Republic restored, under Allied occupation, 1945–1956
Free Republic, 1956–

* Also bore title of Holy Roman Emperor.

Rulers of Prussia and Germany

*Frederick I, 1701–1713
*Frederick William I, 1713–1740
*Frederick II (the Great), 1740–1786
*Frederick William II, 1786–1797
*Frederick William III, 1797–1840
*Frederick William IV, 1840–1861
*William I, 1861–1888 (German Emperor after 1871)
Frederick III, 1888
William II, 1888–1918

Weimar Republic, 1918–1933
Third Reich (Nazi Dictatorship), 1933–1945
Allied occupation, 1945–1952
Division into Federal Republic of Germany in west and German Democratic Republic in east, 1949–1990
Reunification of Federal Republic of Germany and German Democratic Republic as Federal Republic of Germany, 1990–

*Kings of Prussia.

Rulers of Russia

Ivan III, 1462–1505
Basil III, 1505–1533
Ivan IV, 1533–1584
Theodore I, 1584–1598
Boris Godunov, 1598–1605
Theodore II, 1605
Basil IV, 1606–1610
Michael, 1613–1645
Alexius, 1645 1676
Theodore III, 1676–1682
Ivan V and Peter I, 1682–1689
Peter I (the Great), 1689–1725
Catherine I, 1725–1727

Peter II, 1727–1730
Anna, 1730–1740
Ivan VI, 1740–1741
Elizabeth, 1741–1762
Peter III, 1762
Catherine II (the Great), 1762–1796
Paul, 1796–1801
Alexander I, 1801–1825
Nicholas I, 1825–1855
Alexander II, 1855–1881
Alexander III, 1881–1894
Nicholas II, 1894–1917
Soviet Republic, 1917–

Rulers of Italy

Victor Emmanuel II, 1861–1878
Humbert I, 1878–1900
Victor Emmanuel III, 1900–1946
Fascist Dictatorship, 1922–1943
  (maintained in northern Italy until 1945)

Humbert II, May 9–June 13, 1946
Republic, 1946–

Rulers of Spain

Ferdinand { and Isabella, 1479–1504
          and Philip I, 1504–1506
          and Charles I, 1506–1516

Charles I (Holy Roman Emperor Charles V),
  1516–1556
Philip II, 1556–1598
Philip III, 1598–1621
Philip IV, 1621–1665
Charles II, 1665–1700
Philip V, 1700–1746
Ferdinand VI, 1746–1759
Charles III, 1759–1788

Charles IV, 1788–1808
Ferdinand VII, 1808
Joseph Bonaparte, 1808–1813
Ferdinand VII (restored), 1814–1833
Isabella II, 1833–1868
Republic, 1868–1870
Amadeo, 1870–1873
Republic, 1873–1874
Alfonso XII, 1874–1885
Alfonso XIII, 1886–1931
Republic, 1931–1939
Fascist Dictatorship, 1939–1975
Juan Carlos I, 1975–

Principal Rulers of India

Chandragupta (Maurya Dynasty), c. 332–298 B.C.
Asoka (Maurya Dynasty), c. 273–232 B.C.
Vikramaditya (Gupta Dynasty), 375–413 A.D.
Harsha (Vardhana Dynasty), 606–648
Babur (Mogul Dynasty), 1526–1530
Akbar (Mogul Dynasty), 1556–1605
Jahangir (Mogul Dynasty), 1605–1627
Shah Jahan (Mogul Dynasty), 1627–1658

Aurangzeb (Mogul Dynasty), 1658–1707
Regime of British East India Company, 1757–1858
British *raj*, 1858–1947
Division into self-governing dominions of India and
  Pakistan, 1947
Republic of India, 1950–
Republic of Pakistan, 1956–
Republic of Bangladesh, 1971–

Dynasties of China

Hsia, c. 2205–1766 B.C. (?)
Shang (Yin), c. 1766 (?)–1100 B.C.
Chou, c. 1100–256 B.C.
Ch'in, 221–207 B.C.
Han (Former), 206 B.C.–8 A.D.
Interregnum (Wang Mang, usurper), 8–23 A.D.
Han (Later), 25–220
Wei, 220–265
Tsin (Chin), 265–420
Southern Dynasties: Sung (Liu Sung), Ch'i, Liang,
  Ch'eñ, 420–589

Northern Dynasties: Northern Wei, Western Wei,
  Eastern Wei, Northern Ch'i, Northern Chou, 386–
  581
Sui, 589–618
T'ang, 618–907
Five Dynasties: Later Liang, Later T'ang, Later Tsin,
  Later Han, Later Chou, 907–960
Sung, 960–1279
Yüan (Mongol), 1279–1368
Ming, 1368–1644
Ch'ing (Manchu) Dynasty, 1644–1912

Periods of Chinese Rule

Chinese Republic, 1912–1949

Communist Regime, 1949–

Periods of Japanese Rule

Legendary Period, c. 660 B.C. –530 A.D.
Foundation Period, 530–709 A.D.
Taika (Great Reform) Period, 645–654
Nara Period, 710–793
Heian Period, 794–1192
Kamakura Period, 1192–1333
Namboku-cho ("Northern and Southern Dynasties") Period, 1336–1392

Muromachi (Ashikaga) Period, 1392–1568
Sengoku ("Country at War") Period, c. 1500–1600
Sengoku Period, c. 1500–1600
Edo (Tokugawa) Period, 1603–1867
Meiji Period (Mutsuhito), 1868–1912
Taisho Period (Yoshihito), 1912–1926
Showa Period (Hirohito), 1926–1989
Heisei Period (Akihito), 1989–

Rulers of Principal African States

Ewuare the Great, Oba of Benin, 1440–1473
Muhammad Runfa, King of Kano, 1463–1499
Afonso I, King of Kongo, 1506–1543
Ibrahim Maje, King of Katsina, 1549–1567
Idris Alooma, Mai of Bornu, 1569–ca. 1619
Osei Tutu, King of Asante, ca. 1670–1717
Agaja, King of Dahomey, 1708–1740
Sayyid Said, ruler of Zanzibar and Muscat, 1804–1856
Shaka, King of the Zulu, 1818–1828
Moshesh, King of Basutoland, 1824–1868
Menelik, King of Shoa, 1865–1889; Emperor of Ethiopia, 1889–1913
Haile Selassie, Emperor of Ethiopia, 1930–1974
H. F. Verwoerd, Prime Minister of South Africa, 1958–1966
Gamal Abdul Nasser, President of Egypt, 1956–1970

Leopold Sedar Senghor, President of Senegal, 1960–1980
Felix Houphouet-Boigny, President of the Ivory Coast, 1960–
Kwame Nkrumah, President of Ghana, 1960–1966
Julius K. Nyerere, President of Tanzania, 1962–1985
Kenneth D. Kaunda, President of Zambia, 1964
Jomo Kenyatta, President of Kenya, 1964–1978
Sese Seko Mobutu, President of Zaire, 1965–
Houari Boumedienne, head of Algeria, 1965–1978
Anwar el Sadat, President of Egypt, 1970–1981
Agostinho Neto, President of Angola, 1975–1979
Olusegun Obasanjo, head of Nigeria, 1975–1979
P. W. Botha, Prime Minister of South Africa, 1978–1984
Robert Mugabe, Prime Minister of Zimbabwe, 1980–
Hosni Mubarak, President of Egypt, 1981–
P. W. Botha, President of South Africa, 1984–1989
F. W. de Klerk, President of South Africa, 1989–

Index

Guide to Pronunciation

The sounds represented by the diacritical marks used in this Index are illustrated by the following common words:

āle	ēve	īce	ōld	ūse	bōōt
ăt	ĕnd	ĭll	ŏf	ŭs	fŏŏt
fâtality	ĕvent		ȯbey	u̇ite	
câre			fôrm	ûrn	
ärm					
ȧsk					

Vowels that have no diacritical marks are to be pronounced "neutral," for example: Aegean = ē-je′an, Basel = bäz′el, Basil = bă′zil, common = kŏm′on, Alcaeus = ăl-sē′us. The combinations ou and oi are pronounced as in "out" and "oil."